TOTAL QUALITY MANAGEMENT

TEXT AND CASES

Prof. K. SHRIDHARA BHAT

B.E. (Mech), PG DIM, M.B.A. F.I.I.M.M.

Managing Director

Akshaya Management Consultancy Services

Bangalore - 560 085

Karnataka, India

Assisted By

NAVYA K.S.

B.Com., PGDM

Himalaya Publishing House

ISO 9001:2015 CERTIFIED

First Edition : 2002
Reprint : 2005, 2007, 2009
Second Revised Edition : 2016
Reprint : 2018
Reprint : 2019
Reprint : 2020
Reprint : 2025

Published by : Mrs. Meena Pandey
for **HIMALAYA PUBLISHING HOUSE PVT. LTD.,**
"Ramdoot", Dr. Bhalerao Marg, Girgaon, Mumbai - 400 004.
Phone: 022-23860170, 23863863; **Fax:** 022-23877178
E-mail: himpub@bharatmail.co.in; **Website:** www.himpub.com

Branch Offices :

New Delhi : "Pooja Apartments", 4-B, Murari Lal Street, Ansari Road, Darya Ganj, New Delhi - 110 002. Phone: 011-23270392, 23278631; Fax: 011-23256286

Nagpur : Kundanlal Chandak Industrial Estate, Ghat Road, Nagpur - 440 018. Mobile: 09325409992, 09325908881

Bengaluru : Plot No. 91-33, 2nd Main Road, Seshadripuram, Behind Nataraja Theatre, Bengaluru - 560 020. Phone: 080-41138821; Mobile: 09379847017, 09379847005

Hyderabad : No. 3-4-184, Lingampally, Besides Raghavendra Swamy Matham, Kachiguda, Hyderabad - 500 027. Phone: 040-27560041, 27550139

Chennai : No. 34/44, Motilal Street, T. Nagar, Chennai - 600 017. Mobile: 09380460419

Pune : "Laksha" Apartment, First Floor, No. 527, Mehunpura, Shaniwarpeth (Near Prabhat Theatre), Pune - 411 030. Phone: 020-24496323, 24496333; Mobile: 09370579333

Cuttack : Plot No. 5F-755/4, Sector-9, CDA Markat Nagar, Cuttack - 753 014, Odisha. Mobile: 09338746007

Kolkata : 3, S.M. Bose Road, Near Gate No. 5, Agarpara Railway Station, North 24 Parganas, West Bengal - 700 109. Mobile: 09674536325

Printed at : Geetanjali Press Pvt. Ltd., Nagpur. On behalf of HPH (P).

PREFACE TO THE SECOND REVISED EDITION

In today's global business environment, quality can not be under estimated or overlooked by any firm, whether it is a manufacturing firm or a service firm, regardless of its size or assets. The challenge for business today is to produce quality products or services efficiently and in a cost effective manner. Quality has become the most important factor in the long-term profitability and success of any business organisation.

Managing quality and offering value to the customer is still a major concern for many firms all over the world. Quality management involves the understanding of the principles of total quality that allows the organisation to become more effective and competitive in its performance characteristics viz. cost efficiency, quality, dependability and flexibility.

Quality management has moved beyond the emphasis on management of quality to a focus on the quality of managing all the areas of operation through out the organisation's "quality value chain" in order to have a favourable impact on overall effectiveness of the organisation. The total quality approach to quality management is now widely practiced. This approach attempts to maximize the competitiveness of an organisation through the continual improvement of the quality of products, services, people, processes and environment.

Customer support, customer orientation and customer satisfaction are the major objectives for the quality-oriented organisation. Total quality management (TQM) is essentially about the development of an ideology, a philosophy, methods and actions that are designed to satisfy customers completely, through continuous improvement. The total quality approach focuses all the resources of an organisation on the continued and simultaneous improvement of both quality and productivity and the continuous improvement of the organisation's performance and inturn competitiveness.

The term "total quality management" is used to describe the process of transformation by which all parts of an organisation have a focus on quality with the ultimate objective of customer satisfaction and delight. The concept of total quality management has been in application in most of the modern organisations for quite some time. Many organisations have moved on to newer concepts, for example, business excellence, benchmarking, business process reengineering, "six-sigma" quality, customer focus, world-class manufacturing and lean management etc. However, irrespective of what an organisation terms an important initiative, quality as a competitive reality in the global market place remains as powerful as it was ever. The challenge is not just to produce great quality, but to provide the best quality of products and services in the most efficient and cost-effective manner.

The tools and techniques, along with management practices and the organizational infrastructure are fundamental components of total quality management. The tools and techniques are powerful and effective in helping organisations to design their products and processes and to identify and solve quality problems that will ultimately lead to better customer value and operational performance.

Quality management has a great burden placed on it. The first is to satisfy customers continuously, the second is to provide a learning environment within the organisation and the third is to ensure the survival of the organisation. These can all be accomplished through using TQM and this challenge will remain as competitors take this challenge into the future.

About this book: The subject of TQM is vast. There are many issues and interfaces to be considered; and there are many principles and practices to be understood. Also there are many tools, techniques an organisation can use to assist the introduction and development of the TQM concept. An attempt has been made in this book to cover the main aspects and functions of TQM, from the "quality system" concepts, through management issues and technical issues in quality management, to the management of total quality which includes the tools and techniques of total quality management.

This book is organized into 21 chapters, the first three chapters concerned with the concepts and principles of TQM, the next seven chapters (Chapter 4 to 10) concerned with management issues in quality, chapter 11 to chapter 14 concerned with technical issues in quality and the remaining 7 chapters (chapter 15 to chapter 21) concerned with management of total quality. The Learning Objectives, Box Illustrations, Exhibits, Tables, Summary, Key Words Used, Objective Questions, Discussion Questions, Assignments and Chapter Cases are value additions to the text in each chapter.

ACKNOWLEDGEMENTS

I have immense pleasure to express my sincere gratitude to Sri Niraj Pandey and Sri Anuj Pandey of Himalaya Publishing House, Pvt. Ltd., for their keen interest and effort to publish this book. I am also grateful to Sri Vijay Pandey for his interest and effort in printing and promoting this book.

I thank Sri B.S.Madhu and Smt. Divya of M/S Page Designers for their excellent DTP work. I also thank Smt. Nimisha and staff of HPH production unit for their effort in designing the cover page and printing this book

I thank my daughter Smt. Navya. K.S. for assisting me in thoroughly revising the first edition of this book published in the year 2002 and bringing the revised version.

I also thank my family members, friends and well-wishers for their constant support and encouragement for this endeavor.

I invite readers to offer their valuable suggestions as feedback to me to enable me to improve the book in its future editions.

K. SHRIDHARA BHAT
No.680, 'Akshaya', 1 'C' Main,
Kempegowda Layout, 3rd Block,
3rd Phase, Banashankari III Stage
Bangalore - 560 085.
Phone : (080) 26694761
Email : sbhat680@yahoo.com

PREFACE TO THE FIRST EDITION

In a competitive business environment, growth of any business organisation would entirely depend upon customer appreciation and loyalty it can command. These can be ensured only by offering products and services of high quality on a durable basis. Therefore, continuous enhancement of quality on a sustaining basis has become essential for the prosperity of any business organisation at present and in the future as well.

Management of quality is important both for manufacturing and service organisations. For most business organisations today, superior quality is at the core of their business strategy. Attaining near-perfect quality of products/services is seen as a principal means of capturing market shares and profitability in global competition. Achieving superior product/ service quality within a business requires a long-term process of changing the fundamental culture of the organisation.

Today, managers of many manufacturing and service organisations have overhauled the structure of their organisation, changed their organisation climates and redirected their product/service quality programs toward becoming global quality leaders, through an effort that is known as "Total Quality Management".

The growing importance of quality management has emphasised the need for the study of principles and techniques of total quality management both by students of management programs in universities and management institutions and also by practising managers in the manufacturing and service industries.

This book is divided into four parts. Part 1 deals with the introduction to the quality system; Part 2 deals with management issues in quality; Part 3 deals with technical issues in quality; and Part 4 deals with topics connected with management of total quality in the management scenario at present in our country.

Running through 21 chapters, the text has a fairly comprehensive coverage of all aspects of quality, quality management, quality systems, quality assurance and reliability and total quality management. The text has been reinforced with exhibits, box illustrations, quality snap shots, case study illustrations and case study exercises. Also, at the end of each chapter, summary of key points and review questions are given for the benefits of the students. Last, but not of the least importance is the subject index given for quick reference of topics of interest by the readers.

I sincerely thank Shri D. P. Pandey and Shri Niraj Pandey of Himalaya Publishing House who are the main initiators and monitors of this project. I express my sincere gratitude to both of them.

I also thank M/s Page Designers for their excellent D.T.P. work and Cover Design.

I sincerely thank my wife Mrs. Vijaya and my daughters Soumya and Navya for their constant encouragement for writing this book.

I invite readers to offer their valuable comments on the book for continuous improvement in my venture as an author.

K. SHRIDHARA BHAT

CONTENTS

CHAPTER 1

Introduction to Quality Management

LEARNING OBJECTIVES

After reading this chapter, you should be able to:

- Understand the meaning and importance of quality.
- Know the various definitions of quality.
- Discuss the dimensions of product quality and service quality.
- Discuss the types and levels of quality.
- Know the five views of quality.
- Discuss the various determinants of quality.
- Discuss 'quality' in production systems.
- Discuss the evolution of quality management.
- Discuss the concept and principles of total quality.
- Discuss the principles of total quality control.

1.0 INTRODUCTION

Nowadays, we are all victims of quality failures or poor quality, such as late trains and aeroplanes, delayed mail deliveries, leaking car-door seals and prematurely expiring light bulbs. The consumer is invariably the loser as the real cost of a quality failure may be much more than the value of a defective good or service.

Consumers are becoming increasingly intolerant of poor service, late deliveries, unreliable goods, shoddy workmanship and the like. They are exerting control over the suppliers by preferring to buy from alternative sources.

In today's global competitive market place, the demands of customers are for ever increasing as they require improved quality of products and services. Also, in some markets there is an increasing supply of competitively priced products and services from low labour cost countries. Continuous improvement in total business activities with a focus on the customer throughout the entire organisation and an emphasis on flexibility and quality is one of the main means by which companies face up to these competitive threats. This is why quality and its management and the associated continuous improvement are looked upon by many organisations as the means by which they can survive in increasingly aggressive markets and maintain a competitive edge over their rivals. The companies that do not respond to this change will fail. As a result of the efforts made by organisations to respond to these market place demands, the quality of products, services and process has increased considerably during the last three decades.

Meeting or better still exceeding, customer's expectations is an essential task for a business. The growing awareness of the importance of the dimension of quality performance was stimulated in the 1970s and 80s by the improvements made and sustained in Japanese companies and the impact that the resulting improvements had in terms of their increased sales and market share. The quality movement that followed accelerated the introduction of a range of philosophies, approaches, tools and techniques.

1.1 WHAT IS QUALITY

"Quality" is often used to signify excellence of a product or service.

In order to understand total quality, one must first understand ***quality***. Quality is now a familiar word. However it has a variety of interpretations and uses, and there are many definitions. Many people say they know what is meant by quality, they typically claim that they know it when they see it (*i.e.,* by sensing and/or instinct).

In a linguistic sense, quality originates from the Latin word **'qualis'** which means **"such as the thing really is"**. There is an international definition of quality, the "degree to which a set of inherent characteristics fulfils requirements" (BSEN ISO 9000-2000). However in today's business world, there is no single accepted definition of quality. Irrespective of the context in which it is used, it is usually meant to distinguish one organisation, event, product, service, process, person, result, action or communication from another.

Quality is often used to signify **'excellence'** of a product or service - we talk about 'Rolls-Royce quality' and 'top quality'. If we are to define quality in a way which is useful in its management, then we must recognise the need to include in the assessment of quality, the true requirements of the 'customer'.

***Quality* then is simply *meeting the requirements* and this has been expressed in many ways :**

(i) 'fitness for purpose or use' (Juran)

(ii) 'the totality of features and characteristics of a product or service that bear on its ability to satisfy stated or implied needs - BS 4778, 1987 (ISO 8402, 1986)

(iii) 'the total composite product and service characteristics of marketing, engineering, manufacture, and maintenance through which the product and service in use will meet the expectation by the customer' (Feigenbaum).

Although no universally accepted definition of quality exists, enough similarity does exist among the definitions that common elements can be extracted. **These common elements are :**

Quality is "meeting the customer requirements"

(i) Quality involves meeting or exceeding customer expectations.

(ii) Quality applies to products, services, people, processes and environments.

(iii) Quality is an ever-changing state (*i.e.,* what is considered quality today may not be good enough to be considered quality tomorrow).

With these common elements extracted, 'quality' can be defined as :

"Quality is a dynamic state associated with products, services, people, processes, and environments that meets or exceeds customer expectations".

There is another word that is used synonymously with quality - *i.e.,* ***"reliability"***. The acceptability of a product or service will partly depend on its ability to function satisfactorily over a period of time and it is this aspect of performance which is referred to as "reliability". It is the ability of the product or service to continue to meet the customer requirements.

If quality is meeting the customer requirements, then this has wide implications. The requirements may include availability, delivery, reliability, maintainability and cost effectiveness, amongst many other features.

***Box 1.1* illustrates "What is quality?"**

Box 1.1 : What is Quality?

Traditional thinking would say that quality is ***conformance to specifications;*** that is, does the product do what it was designed to do? Some feel that this definition is the only meaningful definition of quality; because conformance is something that can be measured.

According to Philip Crosby :

That is precisely the reason we must define quality as ***"conformance to requirements"*** if we are to manage it. Thus, those who want to talk about **quality of life** must talk about that life in specific terms, such as desirable income, health, pollution control, political programs and other items that can be measured. Crosby makes a good point. By defining quality in terms of conformance, we avoid making unreasonable comparison. Is a Rolls-Royce a better quality product than a Toyota Corolla? Not necessarily. The Toyota may be a higher quality product relative to ***what it was designed to do.***

This does not tell the entire story, however. Just as beauty is in the eye of the beholder, so is quality in the mind of the customer. If the customer is not happy with the product, it is not high quality. Viewed in this way, **quality is a measure of the conformance of the product to the *customer's needs*.**

Why is this different? **Conformance to specifications** assumes a given design and the specifications resulting from that design. **Conformance to customer needs** means that the design of the product is part of the evaluation. Given two washing machines with comparable repair records, what determines which one the customer will buy? The answer is a combination of ***aesthetics, features and design***. Viewing quality in this broader way is both good and bad. It is good that it gets to the heart of the issue : ***quality is what the customer thinks it is***. It is bad in that it makes it difficult to measure quality and then difficult to improve it.

1.2 DEFINITIONS OF QUALITY

"Quality" is defined as:

(i) "The ability of a product or service to meet customer needs".

(ii) "The **totality of features and characteristics** of a product or service that bears on its ability to satisfy stated or implied needs" – definition adopted by the American Society for Quality.

(iii) "Meeting or exceeding customer requirements now and in the future". This means that the product or service is ***fit for customer's use. Fitness for use*** is related to benefits received by the customer and to ensure customer satisfaction.

(iv) "The integrity in delivering what a customer has a legitimate right to expect in view of what was promised at the time of the agreement or purchase".

Other definitions of quality are:

(i) "The quality of a product or service is a ***customer's perception*** of the degree to which the product or service meets his or her expectation".

(ii) "Quality is meeting or exceeding customer's expectations".

(iii) Quality requires continuous improvement.

(iv) Quality is the single most important force leading to organisational success and company growth in national and international markets.

(v) Quality is a measure of how closely a good or service conforms to specified standards or specifications.

(vi) "Quality is every one's concern, it is job one".

(vii) "Quality can be described as doing the right thing, doing it the right way, doing it on time, doing it right the first time and doing it right every time".

(viii) Quality is a critical factor in strategic performance.

(ix) Quality is what is in the eye of the customer.

(x) Quality is the basic customer's decision factor for an explosively growing number of products and services today.

There are many ways or senses in which quality may be defined. All definitions can be boiled down to either meeting requirements and specifications and delighting the customer.

(xi) Quality is in its essence a way of managing the organisation.

(xii) Quality is what the customers say it is-not what the company says.

(xiii) Quality has become the most powerful corporate change agent of our time and perhaps the single most important managerial demand facing many companies today.

(xiv) Quality means meeting customer's (agreed) requirements, formal and informal, at the lowest cost, first time and every time.

(xv) Quality is a means to an end.

(xvi) **A study that asked managers of 86 firms in the eastern United States to define quality produced the following different responses:**

- perfection
- eliminating waste
- compliance with policies and procedures
- doing it right the first time
- total customer service and satisfaction
- consistency
- speed of delivery
- providing a good, usable product
- delighting or pleasing customers

(xvii) **Service Quality is determined by:**

- Reliability
- Courtesy
- Understanding and
- Responsiveness
- Communication
- Tangibles
- Competence
- Credibility
- Access
- Security

(xviii) W. Edward Deming, a leading quality guru called quality as ***"continuous improvement".*** Another expert, Joseph M. Juran, speaks of quality as ***"fit for use"*** while Philip Crosby uses the phrase ***"conformance to requirements".*** Americans speak of ***"value received for dollars spent",*** while Europeans emphasize ***quality engineered into their goods.*** Kaoru Ishikawa, another quality guru, thought in terms of products ***"most economical, most useful and always satisfactory to the consumer"***

(xix) **New thinking about 'quality':**

Old quality is		***New quality is***
About products	⟷	About organizations
Technical	⟷	Strategic
For inspectors	⟷	For every one

Led by experts	⟷	Led by Management
High grade	⟷	The appropriate grade
About control	⟷	About improvement
Little 'q' / Small 'q'	⟷	"Big 'Q'"

(xx) Quality may be defined as the customer's expectations and requirements, it is determined by the customer and the market place and includes all products and service attributes. Quality addresses defects, errors and complaints, but goes well beyond such traditional values : quality includes anything the customer expects and requires and it is everchanging.

1.2.1 Old Quality Versus New Quality

Small "q" (old quality) denotes the management of quality in a limited capacity – traditionally only in manufactured products and manufacturing processes.

Big 'Q' (new quality) is a term used to describe the process of managing quality in all business processes and products.

Old quality is referred to as little 'q' or small 'q' whereas new quality is referred to as big 'Q'

The small 'q' approach to quality focuses on inspection to segregate the good from the bad rather than eliminating the defects. In cases where defects exist in products, an attempt is made to rework and salvage rather than try to prevent the defects recurring in the future.

The big 'Q' approach to quality is the closest to total quality management. To start with, customer needs are converted into product features (specification) which are then optimised to maximise customer satisfaction by providing highest quality at the lowest cost. The emphasis in the manufacturing process is to prevent defects (*i.e.,* zero defects) rather than detection of defects and correction or rework.

***Box 1.2* gives the differences between small 'q' and big 'Q'.**

Box 1.2 : Small 'q' and the Big 'Q'

Small 'q' – The symbol for a product focus on quality.

A small 'q' is a symbol for a firm's approach to quality where emphasis is just on product quality.

Features of the small 'q' approach to quality are :

- Emphasis on the product alone to make sure that the goods produced are fit to be sent to the customers.
- Whether there is a method to prevent the recurrence of defects, is not considered.
- The focus is on segregating the good from the bad and not on eliminating the defects.
- This approach exists in situations where demand exceeds supply and competition is negligible.
- If defects occur in products, attempt is made to rework them and salvage rather than attempting to prevent the defects recurring in the future.
- Total absence of a system of learning based on feedback information on quality of product being produced.

Big Q – The symbol for product, process and customer focus.

The big 'Q' is a symbol to denote.

- Focus that goes beyond the product and includes the processes and the customers also.

Features of the big 'Q' approach to quality are :

- Approach closest to total quality management.
- Starting point consists of the customers and their needs.
- Customers' needs are converted into product features, which are then optimised to maximise customer satisfaction by providing maximum quality at the least cost.
- Products are produced just as desired by the customers, right the first time, every time.
- Focus is on "zero defects", prevention of defects rather than correction of defects or rework.
- Mechanism that provides feedback information on product quality provides a high degree of learning that will prevent recurrence of the errors in the process.
- People are considered as a major source of variability in any process and efforts are made to enable them to perform tasks without error.
- Conscious effort is exerted to provide the employees with the training, the tools and the authority (empowerment) to do the job right the first time.
- Reliance on feedback from customers, feedback from those assessing the conformity of the output to the requirements of customers.
- Existence of a proper system that enables the utilisation of the feedback information which in turn enables the organisation to learn from its past mistakes.

1.2.2 Customer-Driven Definitions of Quality

Quality has multiple dimensions in the mind of the customer.

Quality has multiple dimensions in the mind of the customer and one or more of the following may apply at any one time :

(i) ***Conformance to specifications or requirements.***

(ii) ***Value for price paid*** : Quality is defined in terms of the utility of the product or service for the price paid.

(iii) ***Fitness for use :*** How well the product or service performs the intended purpose? Aspects of fitness for use include the mechanical features of a product or the convenience of a service, appearance, style, durability, reliability and serviceability.

(iv) ***Support :*** Often the product or service support provided by the firm is as important to customers as the quality of the product or service itself.

(v) ***Psychological Criteria :*** A way of defining quality that focuses on judgemental evaluation of what constitutes product or service excellence.

Box 1.3 **lists customer's conditions to be satisfied by quality.**

Box 1.3 : Customer's Conditions to be Satisfied by Quality

1. Specification of dimensions and operating characteristics
2. Life and reliability objectives
3. Safety requirements
4. Relevant standards
5. Engineering, manufacturing and quality costs
6. Production conditions
7. Field installation, maintenance and service objectives
8. Energy utilisation and material conservation factors
9. Environmental and side effects considerations
10. Costs of customer operation and use and productive service.

Two important customer driven definitions of quality are : ***(i) Perceived quality and (ii) Customer-driven quality.***

Perceived quality is defined as "an assessment of quality based on the reputation of the firm". Customers do not always have complete information about the overall quality of a good or service. Such customers must base their assessments of quality on factors such as advertisements, media reports, reputations and past experience to indicate perceived quality.

Customer-driven quality states ***"Quality is meeting or exceeding customer expectations".*** The customer who is the ultimate purchaser of a product or service is referred to as ***consumer.*** But before a product reaches the consumers, it may flow through a chain of many firms, each of which adds some value to the product. These customers are called ***external customers.***

Every employee in the company also has ***internal customers*** who receive goods or services from suppliers within the company. *For example,* an assembly department is an internal customer of the machining department. The machining department is an internal customer of the stores department which in turn is an internal customer of purchase department. Most businesses consist of many such ***"chain of customers".***

Understanding who are one's customers and what their expectations are is fundamental to achieving customer satisfaction.

1.3 THE CONCEPT OF QUALITY

People define quality in many ways : Quality is thought of as excellence or lack of manufacturing or service defects or as related to product features or price. **A study that asked managers of 86 firms in the US to define quality produced several different responses including the following :**

(i) Perfection, *(ii)* Consistency, *(iii)* Eliminating waste, *(iv)* Speed of delivery, *(v)* Compliance with policies and procedures, *(vi)* Providing a good, usable product, *(vii)* Doing it right the first time, *(viii)* Delighting or pleasing customers and *(ix)* Total customer service and satisfaction.

Today, most managers agree that the main reason to pursue quality is to satisfy customers. The American National Standards Institute (ANSI) and the American Society for Quality (ASQ) define quality as ***"the totality of features and characteristics of a product or service that bears on its ability to satisfy given needs"***. The view of quality as the satisfaction of customers needs is often called "fitness for use". In highly competitive markets, merely satisfying customer needs will not achieve success. To beat competition, organisations often must exceed customer expectations. **Thus, one of the most popular definitions of quality is *meeting or exceeding customer expectations.***

One of the most popular definitions of quality is meeting or exceeding customer expectations.

Customer-driven quality is fundamental to high-performing organisations. Organisations now play a lot of attention to quality of their products in order to meet or exceed their customers' expectations and achieve maximum customer satisfaction. Ford uses the slogan, ***"Quality is Job One"***; IBM says "We will deliver defect free competitive products and services on time to our customers"; Vauxhall says that **"Quality is a right, not a privilege"**. A large number of organisations advertise that they are ISO 9000 certified for quality; and the main objective of many of them is to make "products of highest quality".

1.4 IMPORTANCE OF QUALITY

The challenge for business today is to produce products and services efficiently. Quality is one of the four key objectives in operations management along with ***cost, flexibility and delivery*** of goods and services.

Three issues that are critical to managers of manufacturing service organisations are : *productivity, cost and quality.*

Productivity, the cost of operation and the quality of the goods and services that create customer satisfaction - all contribute to ***profitability***. Of these three determinants of profitability *viz.*, productivity, cost and quality, the most significant factor in determining the long-term success or failure of any organisation is quality.

Good quality goods and services can provide an organisation with ***competitive edge*** over competitors. Good quality reduces costs due to product returns, rework and scrap. Good quality increases productivity, profits and other measures of success such as brand image. Good quality generates satisfied customers, who reward the organisation with continued patronage and favourable word-of-mouth advertising. The importance of consistently meeting the service or product specification is that it will influence whether customers repurchase in the future and in-turn customer retention levels significantly affect the growth and success of an enterprise. The importance of quality can be stated in the following sentences – **"No quality, no sales, No salest, no profit.... No profit, no jobs"**.

To understand the importance of quality, the following points may be noted :

(i) Quality and service improvements can be directly and logically linked to enhanced revenue within one's own company.

(ii) Higher quality allows companies to obtain higher margins.

(iii) Problems decrease customer loyalty by 15 percent to 30 percent.

(iv) 50 percent of individual consumers and 25 percent of business customers who have problems never complain to any one at the company.

(v) "If the call centre can resolve a customer's problem using quality service, thus changing a dissatisfied customer to a satisfied one, the company usually gets an increase in loyalty of 50 percentage points.

(vi) One potential customer will be lost for every 50 who hear someone complain about a product or service.

(vii) Market leaders can charge between 5 percent and 10 percent premiums for outstanding quality and service.

1.5 BENEFITS OF QUALITY

Producing superior quality products or providing a quality service is vital to the continued growth and success of a firm. ***Box 1.4* indicates the benefits of quality to a firm.**

Box 1.4 : Benefits of Quality to a Firm

1. It gives a positive company image.
2. It improves competitive ability both nationally and internationally.
3. It increases market share, which translates into improved profits.
4. Overall, it reduces costs, which also translates into improved profits.
5. It reduces or eliminates product liability problems, avoiding unnecessary costs.
6. It creates an atmosphere for high employee morale, which improves productivity.

1.6 DIMENSIONS OF QUALITY

Quality is a multidimensional construct. Various dimensions have been developed that define the quality of a product and/or service.

1.6.1 Dimensions of Product Quality

Quality is a multi-dimensional construct.

Garvin's eight dimensions of product quality are :

1. **Performance :** How well a product performs the customers' intended use? *For example*, the speed of an automobile which indicates its primary operating characteristics.
2. **Features :** The special characteristics that appeal to customers. *For example,* power steering and central locking system of an automobile.
3. **Reliability :** The likelihood of a product's breakdown, malfunction or the need for repairs.
4. **Conformance :** The degree to which a product's design and operating characteristics meet established standards.
5. **Durability :** The expected product life - the length of time or amount of use before a product needs to be repaired or replaced.
6. **Serviceability :** The speed, cost and convenience or ease of repair and maintenance.
7. **Aesthetics :** The effect on the human sense - the look, feel, taste, smell or sound.
8. **Perceived quality :** Reputation and other indirect measures of quality.

1.6.2 Dimensions of Service Quality

1. **Reliability :** Ability to perform the promised service with dependable and accurate results.
2. **Assurance :** Knowledge and courtesy of employees and their ability to inspire trust and confidence.
3. **Tangibles :** Physical facilities, equipment and appearance of personnel.
4. **Empathy :** Caring, individualised attention provided by the firm to its customers.
5. **Responsiveness :** Willingness to help customers and provide prompt service.

1.6.3 Criteria Used To Judge Quality of Products And Services

(A) Criteria Used to Judge Product Quality

(i) Innate excellence, *(ii)* Fitness for intended use, *(iii)* Performance, *(iv)* Reliability, *(v)* Durability, *(vi)* Specific features for safety or convenience, *(vii)* Technology used, *(viii)* Conformance to design specifications, *(ix)* Uniformity, with small variability, *(x)* Perception of high quality by customers, *(xi)* Convenience of use, *(xii)* Attractive appearance and style, *(xiii)* Ratio of performance to cost, *(xiv)* Customer service before and during sales, *(xv)* On-time deliveries, *(xvi)* After-sales service.

(B) Criteria Used to Judge Service Quality

(i) Reliability, *(ii)* Availability, *(iii)* Credibility, *(iv)* Security, *(v)* Competence of staff, *(vi)* Understanding of customer needs, *(vii)* Responsiveness to customers, *(viii)* Courtesy of staff, *(ix)* Comfort of surroundings, *(xi)* Communication between participants, *(xi)* Associated goods provided with the service.

1.7 TYPES OF QUALITY

Kano breaks down quality into four categories to understand its relationship to competition. These types or categories of quality are *(i)* Indifferent quality, *(ii)* Expected quality, *(iii)* One-dimensional quality and *(iv)* Exciting quality.

Major types or categories of quality are:
1. Indifferent quality
2. Expected quality
3. One-dimensional quality
and
4. Exciting quality

Indifferent quality is the quality that the customer does not notice or appreciate.

Indifferent quality evokes a response like, "That is fine, but who cares?" *For example,* a garnish on a dinner plate or finger bowl, while nice, would probably not seem very important.

Expected quality is the quality that the customer expects and demands. *For example,* people expect cars to be safe and reliable, hotel rooms to be clean and quiet and coffee to be hot. People notice expected quality only when it is missing.

One-dimensional quality is the quality that the customer expects, but that does not necessarily result in lots of order or displeased customer, when lacking. *For example,* a restaurant server who is rude and slow may not cause customers to leave, though they might leave smaller tips. However, customers would leave if they found an insect in the food served to them. The restaurant's **slow service** is an **one-dimensional quality**.

Exciting quality is the quality that exceeds the customer's expectations, attracting favourable attention of customers. It is the quality that pleasantly surprises customers, perhaps creating an order winner. *For example,* quality experienced by owners of Mercedes-Benz and BMW cars while driving these cars. It has to a great extent surpassed their expectations.

1.8 FIVE VIEWS OF QUALITY

Garvin's review of literature identifies five different definitions or views of quality. They are: *(i)* Transcendental view, *(ii)* Product-based view, *(iii)* User-based view, *(iv)* Manufacturing-based view and *(v)* Value-based view.

According to the ***transcendental view,*** quality is synonymous with ***"innate excellence"***. This approach claims that quality cannot be defined precisely, we learn to recognise quality only through experience. *For example,* Mercedes Benz and Rolls-Royce as products of the automobile industry that have achieved this level of excellence.

Product-based definitions view quality as a precise and measurable variable. Differences in quality reflect differences in the quality of some ingredient or attribute possessed by a product. *For example,* high quality icecream has a high butter fat content. However, the limitations of this approach are:

According to Garvin the five views of quality are:

1. Transcendental view
2. Product-based view
3. User-based view
4. Manufacturing-based view

and

5. Value-based view

(i) A one-to-one correspondence between product attribute and quality does not always exist and

(ii) When quality is a matter of aesthetics, this approach fails to accommodate differences in tastes.

In the ***user-based approach***, the goods or services that ***best satisfy*** individual consumer's different wants or needs are regarded as having the ***highest quality.*** This view of quality is personal *i.e.* ***perceived quality***. It is highly subjective and focuses on issues of ***"fitness for use"*** by the individual consumer.

Manufacturing-based definitions focus on producers of goods and services and identity quality as ***"conformance to requirements"***. Once designs or specifications have been established, any deviation implies a reduction in quality.

A value-based approach defines quality in terms of ***costs*** **and** ***prices***. A quality product is one that provides performance or conformance at an acceptable price or cost. An inexpensive product is expected to be of lower quality than a similar and more expensive product.

1.9 LEVELS OF QUALITY

Quality has to be examined from three levels:

1. Organisational level
2. Process level and
3. Performer/job level.

An organisation that is committed to quality must examine quality at three levels: ***(i)*** **the organisational level,** ***(ii)*** **the process level and** ***(iii)*** **the performer/job level.**

At the ***organisational level,*** quality concerns centre on meeting external customer requirements. An organisation must seek customer input on a regular basis. **Questions such as the following help to define quality at the organisational level:**

(i) Which products and services meet your expectations?

(ii) Which do not?

(iii) What products or services do you need that you are not receiving?

(iv) Are you receiving products or services that you do not need?

Customer-driven performance standards should be used as the basis for goal setting, problem solving, performance appraisal, incentive compensation, non-financial rewards and resources allocation.

At the ***process level***, organisational units are classified as functions or departments, such as marketing, design, product development, operations, finance, purchasing, billing and so on. Since most processes are cross-functional, the managers of particular organisational units may try to optimise the activities under their control, which can sub-optimise activities for the organisation on the whole. **At this level, managers must ask questions such as:**

(i) What products or services are most important to the external customer?

(ii) What processes produce those products and services?

(iii) What are the key inputs to the process?

(iv) Which processes have the most significant effect on the organisation's customer-driven performance standards?

(v) Who are our internal customers and what are their needs?

At the ***performer level*** (sometimes called the ***job level*** or the ***task-design level***), standards for output must be based on quality and customer-service requirements that originate at the organisational and process level. These standards include requirements for accuracy, completeness, innovation, timeliness and cost. For each output of an individual's job, one must ask questions such as:

(i) What is required by the customer, both internal and external?

(ii) How can the requirements be measured? and

(iii) What is the specific standard for each measure?

Viewing an organisation from this perspective clarifies the roles and responsibilities of all employees in pursuit of quality. Top managers must focus attention at the ***organisational level,*** middle managers and supervisors at the ***process level*** and all employees must understand quality at the ***performer level.***

1.10 DETERMINANTS OF QUALITY

Several activities or accomplishments are necessary to achieve quality. They are: *(i)* Quality of design, *(ii)* Quality capability of production processes, *(iii)* Quality of conformance, *(iv)* Quality of customer service and *(v)* Organisation quality culture.

The various determinants of quality are:
(a) Quality of design
(b) Quality capability of production processes
(c) Quality of conformance
(d) Quality of customer service
and
(e) Organisation quality culture

Quality of design is determined before the product is produced. After identifying who its customers are, a company must determine what its customers want from its products and services. Then products and services are designed to exhibit the attributes necessary to meet its customers' expectations.

Quality of design is determined by a cross functional product design team including members from marketing, engineering, operations and other functions. Quality of design is determined by market research, design concept and specifications. Market research is aimed at assessing customer needs. A particular design concept is developed to meet the customer needs. The design concept then results in a set of specifications for the product.

Quality capability of production processes: Production processes must be designed and built that have the ***capability*** of producing products with the attributes wanted by customers.

Quality of conformance means producing a product to meet the specifications. Production facilities and processes are used to produce products and services that meet design and performance specifications, aimed at quality expectations of customers. When the product conforms to specifications, it is considered as a quality product regardless of the quality of the design specifications.

Quality of customer service: All contacts between customers and companies must be managed so that customers perceive that they have been treated fairly and courteously with their needs attended to promptly and with care and concern.

Organisation quality culture: The entire organisation must become energised to doing what is necessary to design products and services that meet customers' expectations. Mechanisms must be in place to continuously improve every facet of the organisation towards the objective of building ever-increasing levels of customer satisfaction.

Other Aspects of Quality

Another aspect of quality involves the so called abilities *viz.*, ***availability, reliability*** **and *maintainability.***

Availability, maintainability, and field service are other dimensions or determinants of quality

Availability defines continuity of service to the customer. A product is available if it is in an operational state and not down for repairs or maintenance.

Availability can be measured as follows:

$$\text{Availability} = \frac{\text{Uptime}}{\text{Uptime} + \text{Down time}}$$

Reliability refers to the length of time that a product can be used before it fails. In other words, reliability is the probability that a product will function for a specified period of time without failure. *For example,* the reliability of a light bulb for a specified period of time, say 1000 hours might be 80 per cent. This means, if many light bulbs are tested (lighted} for 1000 hours, 80 per cent of them will remain lighted for the entire period of time (*i.e.* 1000 hours) and 20 per cent will fail within 1000 hours.

The reliability of the product is also related to ***meantime between failures*** **(MTBF)** which is just the average time that the product functions from one failure to the next. The longer the MTBF, the more reliable the product.

Maintainability refers to the restoration of a product or service once it has failed. Since all customers consider maintenance or repairs as a nuisance, a high degree of maintainability is desired so that the product can be restored to be used quickly. Maintainability can be measured by the ***mean time to repair*** **(MTTR)** the product.

Availability is a combination of reliability and maintainability.

***Availability*, then is a combination of *reliability* and *maintainability*.** If a product is high in both reliability and maintainability, it will also be high in availability. Availability, then can be expressed as follows:

$$\text{Availability} = \frac{\text{MTBF}}{\text{MTBF} + \text{MTTR}}$$

For example, if a product has an MTBF of 8 hours and a MTTR of 2 hours each time it fails, then its availability is calculated as follows:

$$\text{Availability} = \frac{\text{MTBF}}{\text{MTBF} + \text{MTTR}} = \frac{8}{8+2} = 0.8 \text{ or } 80\%.$$

Field Service is another dimension or determinant of quality which represents ***warranty*** and repair or replacement of the product after it has been sold. Field service is also called as ***customer service, sales service*** or just ***service***. Field service is intangible, since it is related to variables such as ***promptness, competence*** and ***integrity***. The customer expects that any problem will be corrected quickly, in a satisfactory manner, and with a high degree of honesty and courtesy.

***Exhibit 1.1* summarises the dimensions of quality**. It is evident from this that quality is more than just good product design, it extends to quality control of production, quality over the service life of the product and quality of field service after the sale.

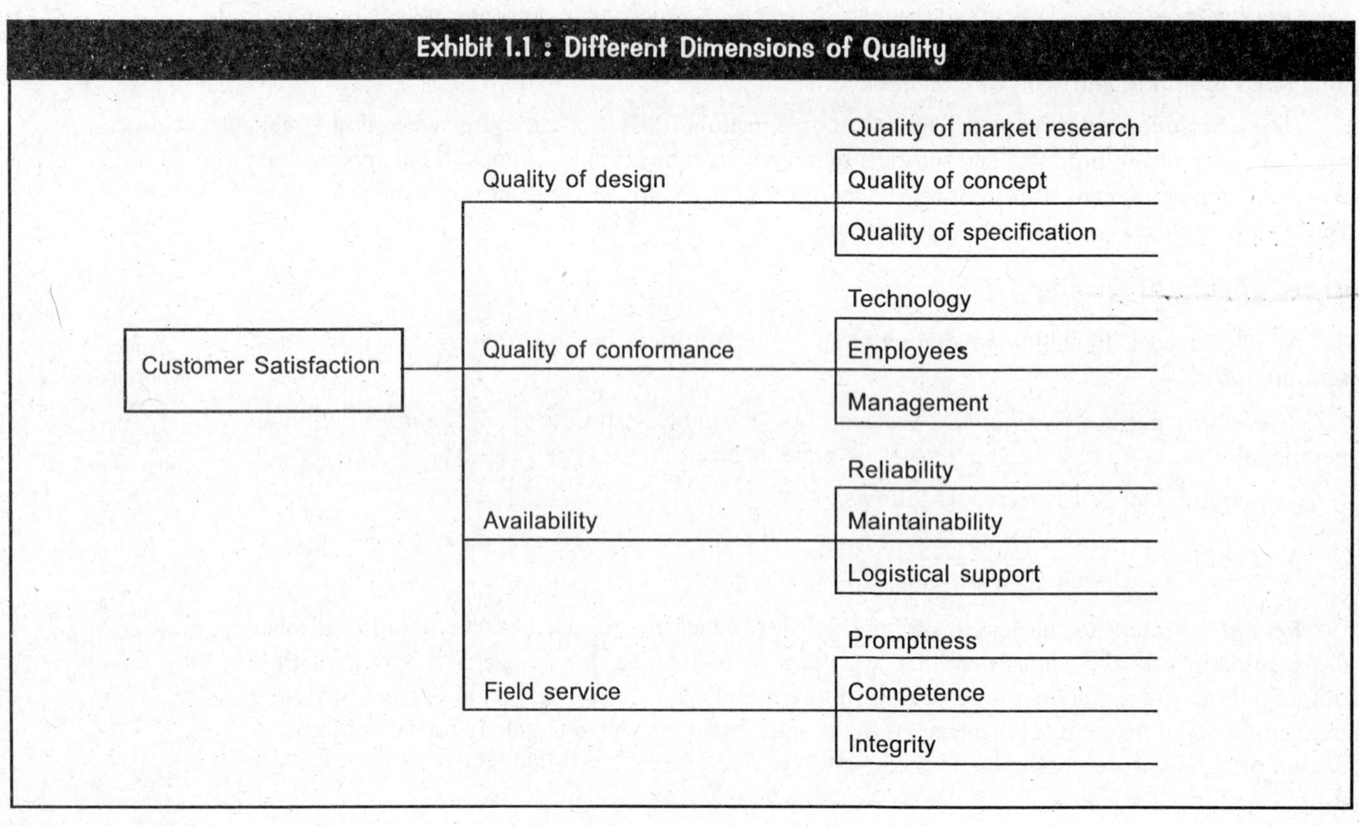

1.11 QUALITY IN PRODUCTION SYSTEMS

Production is the process of converting the resources available to an organisation into products (goods and services). The collection of activities and operations involved in producing an organisation's goods and services is referred to as a ***production system***. Production systems include both the manufacturing systems producing tangible goods and the service organisations offering service to the customers.

A production system has three major components: *(i)* Inputs *(ii)* Outputs and *(iii)* Processes.

Three major components of a production system are:

(i) ***Inputs:*** Physical facilities, materials, capital, equipment, people and energy.

(ii) ***Outputs:*** The products and services produced by the system.

(iii) ***Processes:*** The means by which inputs are transformed into outputs.

Earlier, the businesses viewed production systems as ***closed systems***, their views were focussed internally on the above three components of the system and excluded consideration of customers or suppliers. Japanese built their production systems from a different view point. W. Edwards **Deming illustrated his view of a production system to a group of Japanese industrialists which is shown in *Exhibit 1.2.***

Exhibit 1.2 : Quality in Production System – Deming's View

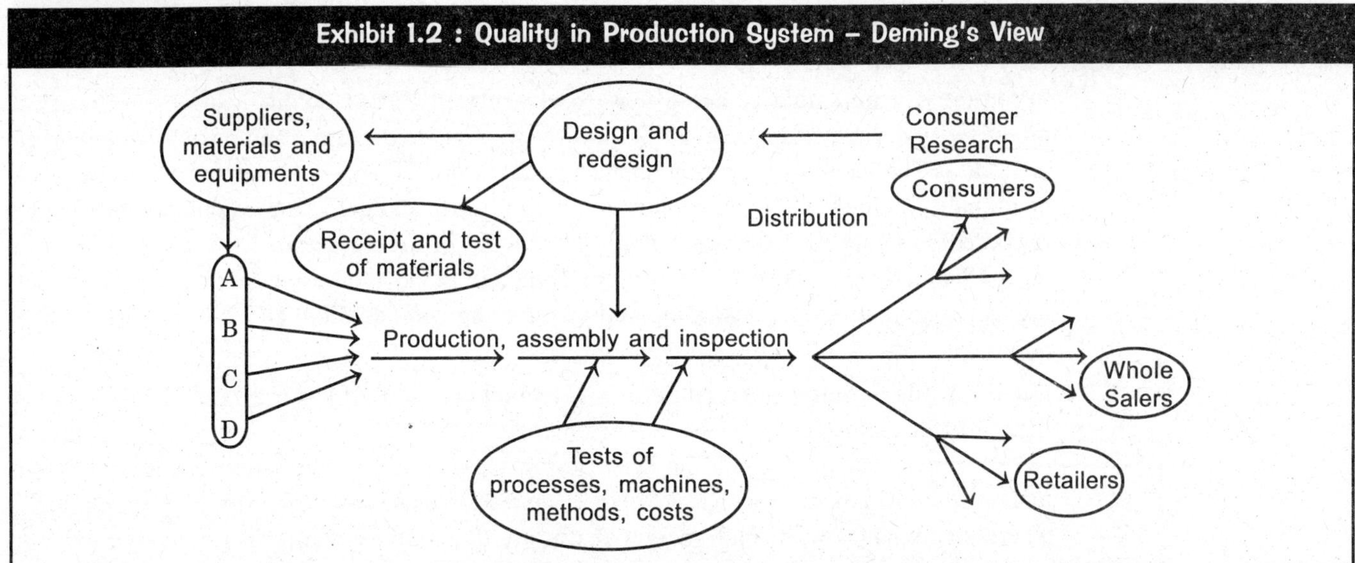

This figure depicts not only the relationships among inputs, processes and outputs, but also the roles of consumers and suppliers, the interdependency of organisational processes, the usefulness of consumer research and the importance of continuous improvement of all elements of the production system.

According to Deming, understanding customers and suppliers was crucial to planning for quality. He advocated continuous improvement of both products and production processes through better understanding of customer requirements which is the key to capturing world markets. ***Box 1.5* illustrates the meaning of 99.9 per cent quality.**

Box 1.5 : What does 99.9% Quality Mean?

Total quality aims at 100% improvement. See what you get when you have only 99.9% quality.

- Your heart fails to beat 32000 times each year.
- 500 incorrect surgical operations performed each week.
- Two unsafe landings at Indira Gandhi Airport every month.
- 19000 new born babies dropped at birth by doctors each year.
- 16000 lost pieces of mail per hour.
- 22000 cheques deducted from the wrong account every day.
- 20000 incorrect drug prescriptions each year.

1.12 SOME ASPECTS OF QUALITY

1. **Quality is not negotiable :** An order, contract or customer which is lost on the grounds of non-conforming product and/or service is much harder to regain than one lost on price or delivery terms.

2. **Quality is all pervasive :** Total quality management is a much broader concept than previous initiatives, encompassing not only product, service and process improvements but those relating to costs and productivity and to people involvement and development.

Productivity and quality are often closely related.

3. **Quality increases productivity :** The traditional view of quality control was that it costs more to get higher product quality. But this is no longer the prevalent view. Japanese manufacturers are credited with popularising the notion that ***quality drives the productivity machine***. This means that if production does it right the first time, and produces products and services that are defect free, waste is eliminated and costs are reduced. In this new way of thinking, when operations managers work to eliminate defects, the quality of products and services is improved and at the same time productivity also improves. Costs are reduced as product quality improves because there are few products returned for warranty work, fewer reworks and scrap. Quality management programs today are therefore viewed by many companies as productivity improvement programs.

   "Productivity and quality are often closely related". Poor quality can adversely affect productivity during the manufacturing process if parts are defective and have to be reworked or if an assembler has to try a number of parts before finding one that fits properly. Also, poor quality in tools and equipment can lead to injuries and defective output, which must be reworked or scrapped, thereby reducing the amount of usable output for a given amount of input. *Similarly,* poor service can mean having to re-do the service and reduced service productivity. Conversely, improving and maintaining good quality can have a positive effect on productivity.

4. **Quality leads to better performance in the market place :** It has been established that the factors having most leverage on return on investment are : *(i)* relative perceived quality (RPQ) which is the product and service offering as perceived by the customer and *(ii)* relative market share. Companies with large market shares are those whose quality is relatively high, whereas companies with small market shares are those whose quality is relatively low.

Quality means improved business performance

5. **Quality means improved business performance :** Companies that invest in quality management efforts experience outstanding returns and improvements in performance. Winners of the Malcolm Baldrige National Quality Award, which represent companies having the highest level of commitment to quality management, have achieved outstanding operational and financial results. These companies achieved better employee relations, higher productivity, greater customer satisfaction, increased market share and improved profitability.

Quality is an important source of competitive advantage

6. **Quality improves competitive advantage :** ***Competitive advantage*** denotes a firm's ability to achieve market superiority. In the long run, a sustainable competitive advantage provides above-average performance. **Six characteristics of a strong competitive advantage identified by S.C. Wheelwright are:**

   (i) It is driven by customer needs and wants. A company provides value to its customers that competitors do not.

   (ii) It makes a significant contribution to the success of the business.

   (iii) It matches the organisation's unique resources with opportunities in the environment.

(iv) It is durable and lasting and difficult for the competitor to copy. A superior research and development department can consistently develop new products or processes that enable the firm to remain ahead of competitors.

(v) It provides a basis for further improvement.

(vi) It provides direction and motivation to the entire organisation.

Each of these characteristics relates to quality, suggesting that quality is an important source of competitive advantage.

Attaining quality in all areas of business is a difficult task. To make things even worse, consumers change their perceptions about quality because of changes in lifestyles and economic conditions.

In general, the success of a business depends on the accuracy of its perceptions of consumer expectations and its ability to bridge the gap between those expectations and operating capabilities. Consumers are much more quality minded now than in the past. Perceptions play as important role as performance. A product or service that is perceived to be of higher quality stands a much better chance of gaining market share than does one perceived to be of low quality, even if the actual levels of quality are the same.

7. **Quality improves profitability :** Good quality can also pay off in higher profits. High-quality products and services can be priced higher than comparable low quality ones and yield a greater return for the same sales rupees. Poor quality erodes the firm's ability to compete in the market place and increases the cost of producing the product or service. *For example,* by improving quality (*i.e.* conformance to specifications), a firm can increase its market share and reduce the cost of its products or services which in turn increases profits.

Good quality results in higher profitability for the firm.

The importance of quality in achieving competitive advantage through higher profitability was demonstrated by several research studies undertaken by PIMS Associates Inc.

PIMS researchers have found that:

- Product quality is an important determinant of business profitability.
- Businesses that offer premium-quality products and services usually have large market shares and were early entrants into their markets.
- Quality is positively and significantly related to a higher return on investment for all kinds of products and market situations.
- Instituting a strategy of quality improvement usually leads to increased market share, but at the cost of reduced short-run profitability.
- High quality producers can usually charge premium price.

A product's value in the market place is influenced by the quality of design. Improvements in such aspects as performance, features, and reliability will differentiate the product from its competitors, improve a firm's quality reputation, and improve the perceived value of the product. This allows the company to command higher prices as well as to achieve a greater market share. This in turn leads to increased revenues, which offset the costs of improving the design.

Improved conformance in production leads to lower manufacturing and service costs through savings in rework, scrap and warranty expenses. The net effect of improved quality of design and quality of conformance is increased profits.

8. **Quality is a source of value :** Many customers regard quality as an important source of value. Quality was recognised for its significant impact on the development and maintenance of a sustainable ***competitive advantage.*** **The experiences of quality-oriented companies such as Hewlett-Packard, Xerox, Motorola and IBM have shown several effects on value of improvements in quality. They are:**

Quality has a significant impact on the development and maintenance of a sustainable competitive advantage.

   ***(i) Improved Reputation*:** Competing on quality has a positive impact on the reputation of a company. People buy from a company such as Motorola because they know of its reputation for quality as a winner of the Malcolm Baldrige National Quality Award.

   ***(ii) Easier Selling*:** Increasingly companies that compete on quality want to buy products from quality oriented suppliers. *For example,* Motorola's quality-based six sigma program demands a level of quality consistent with 6 sigma or 6 standard deviations. Six sigma seeks to ensure that the firm produces fewer than three defective parts per million. Motorola recognises that quality of its products depends on the quality of its inputs from suppliers. As a result, Motorola has informed suppliers that they must implement their own versions of the six sigma program to keep Motorola's business.

   ***(iii) Legal Implication*:** By emphasising quality, the firm benefits from demonstrating its concern about the effects of its goods and services and its actions to make them work well.

   ***(iv) Reduced Lead Times*:** Lead times increase for any inspection and for correction of quality-related problems in the products. By improving quality, the firm can eliminate the time consuming activities such as inspection and rework and thereby reduce lead times.

   ***(v) Enhanced Flexibility*:** Emphasis on quality also enhances flexibility as it reduces lead times.

   ***(vi) Improved Productivity*:** The improved quality results in reduced wastages and reduced costs (due to elimination of inspection, rework, scrap etc.) and thereby improved productivity.

   ***(vii) Reduced Cost*:** Competing on quality introduces a paradox. In the short-term, improving quality does increase costs since time and resources are needed to identifying and eliminating quality problems. However, in the long term, eliminating quality related problems reduces costs because it eliminates inspection and rework.

   ***(viii) Employee Pride*:** Employees including workers and managers want to be associated with a good company that has an image of a provider of high quality products and services. Employees are motivated by knowledge that they produce some of the best products in the industry.

   Clearly, lead time, flexibility and quality are interdependent. To reduce lead time, a firm must emphasise quality, to become flexible, it must manage lead time. These three components of value also have a positive impact on costs, as careful evaluation of lead time, flexibility and costs will drive costs downward.

Employees must embrace quality as their personal value at the individual level.

9. **Quality must begin at a personal level :** Today, companies are asking employees to take more responsibility for acting as the point of contact between the organisation and the customer, to be team players and to provide more effective and efficient customer service. Rath & Strang, a US-based consulting firm conducted a survey of 200 executives of Fortune 500 companies which revealed that ***personal initiative***, when combined with ***customer orientation*** has a positive impact on business success and sales growth rate.

Unless quality is internalised at the personal level, it will never become rooted in the culture of an organisation. **Quality must begin at a personal level (*i.e.* individual level).** Employees who embrace quality as a personal value often go beyond what they are asked or normally expected to do in order to reach a difficult goal or provide extraordinary service to a customer.

'Personal quality" may be thought of as **personal empowerment**, it is implemented by systematically keeping personal checklists for quality improvement. Personal quality is an essential ingredient to make quality happen in the workplace.

"Personal quality" may be thought of as personal empowerment.

10. **The cost of non-quality is high :** Based on a variety of companies, industries and situations, the cost of quality (*i.e.,* cost of not getting it right the first time) ranges from 5 to 25 percent of an organisation's annual sales turnover in manufacturing or annual operating costs in service-type situations.
11. **Quality is a way of life :** Quality is a way of organisational and everyday life. It is a way of doing business, living and conducting one's personal affairs. In whatever each person does and in whatever situation, the tasks must be undertaken in a quality conscious way. Quality is driven by a person's own internal mechanism - 'heart and soul', personal beliefs. Companies like Toyota emphasise strongly the need for the commitment of all employees to managing and improving quality.

An organisation committed to quality needs quality of working life of its people in terms of participation, involvement and development and quality of systems, processes and products.

1.13 THE EVOLUTION OF QUALITY MANAGEMENT

Systems for improving and managing quality have evolved rapidly in recent years. During the last two decades or so, simple inspection activities have been replaced or supplemented by ***quality control, quality assurance*** has been developed and refined, and now many companies, using a process of ***continuous and companywide improvement,*** are working towards ***total quality management*** (TQM). In this progression, four fairly discrete stages can be identified : 1. **Inspection,** 2. **Quality control,** 3. **Quality assurance** and 4. **Total quality management.**

1.13.1 Inspection (Conformity evaluation by observation and judgement accompanied as appropriate by measurement, testing or gauging)

Under a simple inspection - based system, one or more characteristics of a product, or service or activity are examined, measured, tested or assessed and compared with specified requirements to assess conformity with a specification or performance standard. In a manufacturing environment the system is applied to incoming goods and materials, manufactured components and assemblies at appropriate points in the process and before finished goods are passed into the warehouse.

The inspection system is an after-the-event screening process.

The inspection system is an after-the-event screening process with no prevention content other than identifying suppliers, operations or workers who are producing non-conforming products/services. There is an emphasis on reactive quick-fix corrective actions.

1.13.2 Quality Control (Part of quality management focused on fulfilling quality requirements)

Quality control refers to all those functions or activities that must be performed to fulfil the company's quality objectives. Quality control begins long before products and services are delivered to the customers. Quality begins with the design of a product in accordance with the customer's specification. Early in the production system, raw materials, parts and supplies must be of acceptable quality before they are allowed to be used in production. Materials must meet the appropriate specifications as stipulated in the product design. As the inputs of the production system proceed through production processes, the quality of the semi-finished parts and sub-units is monitored to

Quality control involves:
1. Assesing actual quality performance
2. Comparing performance with goals and
3. Acting on differences between performance and goals

determine whether the system is operating as intended. This monitoring of quality alerts the operations managers to take corrective action needed before poor quality products are produced. Then finished products are examined to determine their acceptability.

Quality control involves the establishment of ***quality standards***, the use of proper materials, the selection of appropriate manufacturing processes and the necessary tooling to make the product, the performance of the necessary manufacturing operations and the inspection of the product to check on conformance with the specifications.

Quality control is an effective system of principles and methods for prevention of defects and control of variability in materials, bought-out items, manufactured parts and sub units, by taking timely preventive measures.

Quality control starts with product design and includes materials, bought-out items, manufacturing processes and finished products in the hands of the customers.

Quality control is a staff function concerned with the prevention of defects in manufacturing so that the items may be manufactured **right at the first time** and not have to be reworked or rejected. In order to achieve this, there must be inspection and control of incoming raw materials to ensure that they meet the specifications, in-process inspection of manufacturing processes and final inspection and testing of the finished product to ensure satisfactory performance.

Box 1.6 **describes what is meant by "Quality Control".**

Box 1.6 : What is Quality Control (Q.C)?

Quality Control denotes all those activities which are directed to maintaining and improving quality. Quality control involves,

(a) Setting of Quality Targets
(b) Appraisal of Conformance
(c) Taking corrective action where any deviation is noticed.
(d) Planning for improvements in quality.

What is Statistical Quality Control (SQC)?

SQC is a powerful tool to reduce the variations observed in the quality of different items of the manufactured product..

SQC offers a practical way for detecting and eliminating variations due to extraneous or assignable causes encountered in the production process.

Two techniques of SQC are: *(i)* Statistical Process Control (SPC) used for controlling the quality of on-going processes and *(ii)* Acceptance Sampling used for accepting or rejecting a lot based on the quality of samples chosen from the lots.

1.13.3 Quality Assurance (Part of quality management focused on providing confidence that quality requirements will be fulfilled)

Quality assurance refers to any action directed towards providing consumers with products of appropriate quality.

In a broad sense, ***quality assurance*** refers to any action directed towards providing consumers with products of appropriate quality.

The term ***"quality assurance"*** is intended to include all of the activities that are performed to ensure that the product performs to the customer's satisfaction and many departments are involved in this effort. **Some of the activities involved in quality assurance are:**

(i) ***Reliability engineering,*** to ensure that the design will have an adequate useful life.

(ii) ***Value engineering,*** to ensure that the product will perform the necessary function at the minimum cost.

(iii) ***Evaluation of usability*** to see that the product will be convenient and safe in the hands of the user.

(iv) ***Process control,*** to ensure that the materials, processes and other inputs to the transformation process are adequate for the intended product.

(v) ***Product screening*** and appraisal, to see that the output that is sold to the customer is of adequate quality.

(vi) ***Service assurance***, to see that the customer is adequately trained to use and maintain the product and that service parts (spare parts) and manuals are made available.

(vii) ***Quality feedback*** to provide corrective action when field use indicates inadequate quality.

The activities mentioned above include those aimed at ***quality of design, quality of conformance and quality of performance or service.*** They are not always performed within the quality assurance department of a company. Every department of a company plays a role in achieving quality. The responsibility for quality extends even beyond the company, through the purchasing department to the suppliers and on to their suppliers. (*i.e.*, suppliers of suppliers).

1.13.4 Quality Improvement

Quality improvement means finding ways to do better than standard and breaking through to ***unprecedented levels of performance.*** The desired end results are quality levels that are even higher than the planned performance levels. According to Joseph M. Juran, proper quality planning and quality control leads to quality improvement. Proper quality planning results in processes capable of meeting quality goals under certain operating conditions. Quality control consists of ***measuring*** actual quality performance, ***comparing*** it with the standard and ***acting*** on any differences or ***variances.*** Then quality improvement is imposed on quality control.

Quality improvement involves actions taken throughout the organisation to increase the effectiveness and efficiency of activities and processes in order to provide added benefits to both the organisation and its customers.

Quality improvement-at the source : The primary responsibility for quality rests with the front-line producers or servers. Their responsibility extends from participating in teams for product and service design all the way through the conversion process. Quality improvement is the responsibility of those who produce the products (workers) and not that of inspectors.

1.13.5 Total Quality Management (Involves the application of quality management principles to all aspects of the organisation, including customers and suppliers and their integration with the key business processes)

Total quality is an approach to doing business that attempts to maximise the competitiveness of an organisation through the continual improvement of the quality of products, services, people, processes and environments.

Total Quality Management (TQM) is a systems approach to management that aims to continuously increase value to customers by designing and continuously improving organisational processes and systems. TQM involves all employees and extends backward and forward to include the supply chain and the customer chain. As the word ***total*** implies, TQM is concerned with managing the entire system and not only subsystems or functional departments.

TQM consists of continuous improvement activities involving everyone in the organisation - managers and workers - in a totally integrated effort toward improving performance at every level.

TQM requires that the principles of quality management should be applied in every branch and at every level in the organisation with an emphasis on integration into business practices and a balance between technical, managerial and people issues. It is a company-wide approach to quality, with improvement undertaken on a continuous basis by everyone in the organisation.

TQM is the mutual cooperation of everyone in an organisation and associated business processes to produce value-for-money products and services which meet and hopefully exceed the needs and expectations of customers.

TQM is both a philosophy and a set of guiding principles for managing an organisation to the benefit of all stakeholders.

1.14 PRINCIPLES OF QUALITY MANAGEMENT

A quality management principle is a comprehensive and fundamental rule/belief, for leading and operating an organisation, aimed at continually improving performance over the long term by focusing on customers while addressing the needs of all other stakeholders.

The eight quality management principles are defined in ISO 9000 : 2000 standards. These principles are discussed below :

1. **Customer focus :** Organisations depend on their customers and therefore should understand current and future customer needs, meet customer requirements and strive to exceed customer expectations.
2. **Leadership :** Leaders establish unity of purpose and directions of the organisation. They should create and maintain the internal environment in which people can become fully involved in achieving the organisation's objectives.
3. **Involvement of people :** People at all levels are the essence of an organisation and their full involvement enables their abilities to be used for the organisation's benefit.
4. **Process approach :** A desired result is achieved more efficiently when activities and related resources are managed as a process.
5. **Systems approach to management :** Identifying, understanding and managing interrelated processes as a system contributes to the organisation's effectiveness and efficiency in achieving its objective.
6. **Continual improvement :** Continual improvement of the organisation's overall performance should be a permanent objective of the organisation.
7. **Factual approach to decision making :** Effective decisions are based on the analysis of data and information.
8. **Mutually beneficial supplier relationships :** An organisation and its suppliers are interdependent and a mutually beneficial relationship enhances the ability of both to create value.

1.15 THE CONCEPT OF TOTAL QUALITY

Total quality consists of continuous improvement activities involving every one in the organisation in a totally integrated effort toward improving performance at every level.

In the 1970s, a General Electric task force studied consumer perceptions of the quality of various GE product lines. Lines with relatively poor reputations for quality were found to de-emphasize the customer's viewpoint, regard quality as synonymous with tight tolerance and conformance to specifications, tie quality objectives to manufacturing flow, express quality objectives as the number of defects per unit, and use formal quality control system only in manufacturing. In contrast, product lines that received customer praise were found to emphasize satisfying customer expectations, determine customer needs through market research, use customer-based quality performance measures and have formalised quality control systems in place for all business functions, not solely for manufacturing. The task force concluded that ***"Quality must not be viewed solely as a technical discipline, but rather as a managerial discipline"***. That is, quality issues permeate all aspects of business enterprise: design, marketing, manufacturing, human resources management, supplier relations and financial management, to name just a few.

As companies came to recognise the broad concept of quality, the concept of ***total quality*** emerged.

Total Quality (TQ) : Total quality is a people focused management system that aims at continued increase in customer satisfaction at continually lower real cost. TQ is a ***"total systems approach"*** and an integral part of high-level strategy. It works ***horizontally*** across functions and departments, involves ***all employees, top to bottom*** and extends ***backward*** and ***forward*** to include the ***supply chain*** and the ***customer chain***. TQ stresses ***learning*** and ***adaptation*** to continual change as keys to organisational success.

Total quality includes systems, methods and tools. The systems permit change but the philosophy remains the same. TQ is anchored in values that stress the dignity of the individual and the power of community action. The concise definition of TQ used by Procter & Gamble is: ***"Total quality is the unyielding and continually improving effort by everyone in an organisation to understand, meet and exceed the expectations of customers."***

Total quality management (TQM) is a management approach to long-term success through customer satisfaction

The term ***"total quality management" (or TQM)*** has been commonly used to denote the system of managing for total quality. TQM is a total, company-wide effort-through full involvement of the entire workforce and a focus on continuous improvement that companies use to achieve customer satisfaction. TQM is both a comprehensive managerial philosophy and a collection of tools and approach for its implementation.

While the concept of TQM has been around for some time, A.V. Feigenbaum recognised the importance of a comprehensive approach to quality in the 1950s and coined the term ***"total quality control."***

Feigenbaum observed that the quality of products and services is directly influenced by what he terms the 9M's: ***"markets, money, management, men and women, motivation, materials, machines and mechanisation, modern information methods and mounting product requirements".***

According to Feigenbaum, total quality control is defined as:

"An effective system for ***integrating*** **the** ***quality development, quality maintenance*** and ***quality improvement*** efforts of the various groups in an organisation so as to enable marketing, engineering, production and service at the most economical levels which allow for ***full customer satisfaction***".

The Japanese adopted Feigenbaum's concept and renamed it ***"company-wide quality control"*** (CWQC). **Wayne S. Reiker listed the following five aspects of total quality control practiced in Japan:**

(i) Quality emphasis extends through market analysis, design and customer service rather than only the production stages of making a product.

(ii) Quality emphasis is directed towards operations in every department from executives to the clerical level.

(iii) Quality is the responsibility of the individual and the workgroup, not some other group such as inspection.

(iv) There are two types of quality characteristics as viewed by customers: those that ***satisfy*** and those that ***motivate***. Only the latter are strongly related to repeat sales and a "quality" image.

(v) The first customer for a part or piece of information is usually the next department in the production process (*i.e.,* the internal customer).

1.16 PRINCIPLES OF TOTAL QUALITY

The core principles of total quality are:
1. A focus on customer
2. Participation and team work
3. Employee involvement and empowerment and
4. Continuous improvement and learning

The core principles of total quality are:

(i) A focus on the customer, *(ii)* Participation and team work, *(iii)* Employee involvement and empowerment, *(iv)* Continuous improvement and learning.

These principles are briefly discussed in the following paragraphs:

1. Customer Focus

The modern definition of quality centres on meeting or exceeding customer expectations. Thus, the customer is the principal judge of quality. Perceptions of ***value*** and ***satisfaction*** are influenced by many factors throughout the customer's overall purchase, ownership and service experiences. Companies must focus on all product and service attributes that contribute to perceived value to the customer and lead to customer satisfaction. To accomplish this task, a company's efforts need to extend well beyond merely meeting specifications, reducing defects and errors and eliminating complaints. They must include both designing new products that truly delight the customers and responding rapidly to changing consumer and market demands.

From a total quality perspective, all strategic decisions a company makes are ***"customer-driven"***. A customer-driven company knows what the customer wants, how the customer uses its products and anticipates needs that the customer may not even be able to express. It also continually develops new techniques to obtain ***customer feedback***.

A firm also must recognise that ***internal customers*** are as important in assuring quality as are ***external customers***. Employees who view themselves as both customers of and suppliers to other employees understand how their work links to the final product.

Customer focus extends beyond the consumers and internal relationships to the society which represents an important customer of business. Business ethics, public health and safety, environment and the sharing of quality-related information in the company's business and geographic communities are necessary activities of a world-class company.

2. Participation and Team Work

Employees' participation in management can be encouraged by implementing suggestion systems and quality circles.

Japanese managers made full use of the knowledge and creativity of the entire workforce for their rapid quality achievements. When managers give employees the ***tools*** to make good decisions and the ***freedom*** and ***encouragement*** to make contributions individually or in teams, they virtually guarantee that better quality products and production processes will result. In any organisation, the person who performs a job is the person who best understands the job and how to improve both the product and the process. By training employees to think creatively and rewarding good suggestions, managers can develop employee loyalty and trust. Managers must formulate systems and procedures and put them in places to ensure that ***participation*** becomes a part of the ***work culture***. Participation of employees can be encouraged by implementing suggestion systems or schemes that act quickly, provide feedback and reward good suggestions. **These systems should also facilitate the following:**

(i) recognise team and individual accomplishment.

(ii) share success stories throughout the organisation.

(iii) encourage risk taking by removing the fear of failure.

(iv) promote the formation of employee involvement teams and

(v) provide financial and technical support to develop their ideas.

Team work is a fundamental element of total quality. Team work can be viewed as : *(i)* Vertical *(ii)* Horizontal and *(iii)* Inter-organisational partnership.

Team Work: Team work can be viewed in three ways: *(i)* ***Vertical*** - team work between top management and lower-level employees, *(ii)* ***Horizontal*** - team work within groups and across functional lines (often called cross-functional teams) and *(iii)* ***Inter-organisational-partnership*** with suppliers and customers.

3. Employee Involvement and Empowerment

Employee involvement involves changing organisational culture, fostering individual development through training, establishing awards and incentives and encouraging team work.

Employee empowerment means involving employees in every step of the production process. It means enlarging employee jobs so that the added responsibility and authority is moved to the lowest level possible in the organisation.

Techniques for building employee empowerment include:

(i) building communication networks that include employees.

(ii) developing open, supportive supervisors.

(iii) moving responsibility from managers to production employees.

(iv) building high employee morale in the organisations and

(v) creating such formal organisation structures as ***teams*** and ***quality circles***.

A ***"quality circle"*** is a small group of employees who meet regularly with a ***facilitator*** to solve work-related problems in their work area. The group may have 6 to 8 members with a leader and they usually meet once a week after their working hours.

Team work*:** Team work is another important element of total quality attention on ***customer-supplier relationships among the employees and encourages the involvement of the total work force in attacking ***systemic*** problems, particularly those that cross functional boundaries. Success of team work needs managers' acceptance of workers' suggestions. The "quality circles" implemented in Japan in 1962 achieved dramatic results. Today, the use of ***self-directed*** or ***self-managed*** teams is growing. These teams combine ***team work*** and ***empowerment*** into a powerful method of **"employee involvement"**.

Quality circle is an example of team work.

An important type of team is the ***cross-functional team***. This type of team facilitates ***horizontal co-ordination*** between organisational units which is essential for achieving total quality. ***Partnerships*** are an additional way of promoting team work. Partnerships between a company and organised labour and between customers and suppliers are useful for practicing total quality.

Cross-functional team is an important type of team.

General Motors (GM), *for example,* tries to eliminate the practice of competing internally and instead promotes team work. To counter internal competition, GM developed a system called ***"Quality Network"*** made up of a joint union-management, **Quality Councils** at the corporate, division and plant levels. The heart of the Quality Network is a customer-satisfaction model that encourages team work and co-operation (*Exhibit 1.3*). *For example,* the plants hold periodic corporate analysis meetings during which entire plants shutdown operations briefly for thorough audits of the quality system. The plant-level work team and workers focus on ways to improve quality and productivity.

***Exhibit 1.3* illustrates the Quality Network Process Model.**

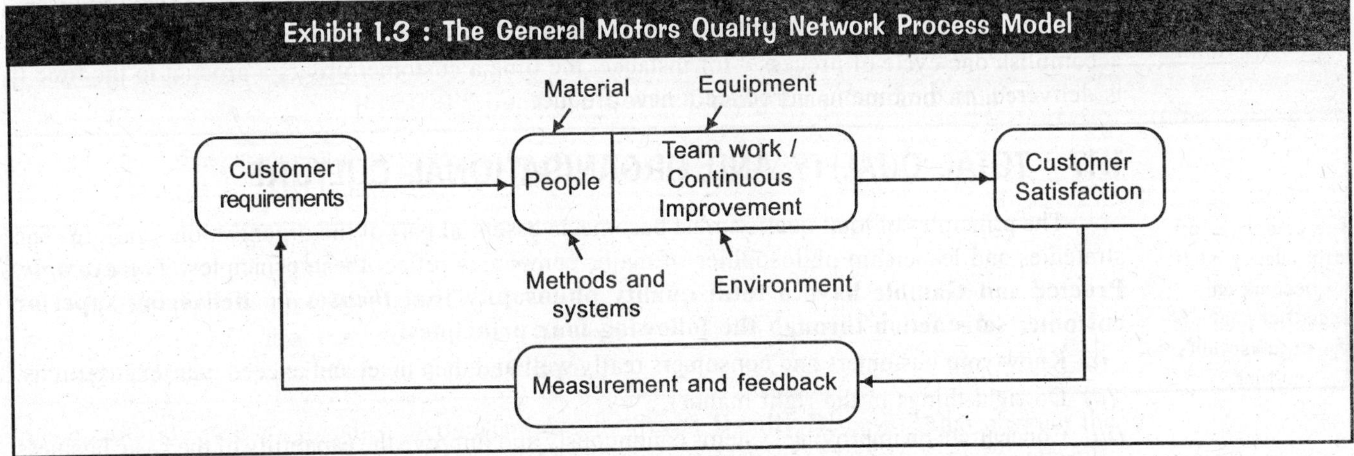

4. Continuous Improvement and Learning

Continuous improvement and learning should be an integral part of the management of all systems and processes. Continuous improvement refers to both ***incremental*** (*i.e.* small and gradual) and ***breakthrough*** (*i.e.* large and rapid) improvement.

Improvements may take any one of several forms:

(i) Enhancing ***value*** to the customer through new and improved products and services.

(ii) Reducing ***errors, defects, waste*** and ***related*** **costs.**

(iii) Improving ***productivity*** and ***effectiveness*** in the use of all resources.

(iv) Improving ***responsiveness*** and ***cycle time*** performance.

Learning refers to adapting to change, leading to new goals and approaches. Learning takes place via feedback between practices and results. Four stages of a ***learning cycle*** are: *(i)* planning, *(ii)* execution of plans, *(iii)* assessment of progress and *(iv)* revision of plans based upon assessment findings.

Continuous improvement includes a philosophy and actions for repeatedly improving an organisation's capabilities and processes with the objective of customer satisfaction

Peter Senge, a professor at the Massachusetts Institute of Technology (MIT) USA, defines the **learning organisation** as "an organisation that is continually expanding its capacity to create its future. For such an organisation, it is not enough merely to survive. ***"Survival learning"***, or what is more often termed ***"adaptive learning"***, is important-indeed it is necessary. But for a learning organisation, "adaptive learning" must be joined by ***"generative learning"***, learning that enhances our capacity to create. Senge often points out, ***"over the long run, superior performances depend on superior learning"***.

Learning refers to adapting to change leading to new goals and approaches Learning can be categorised as:

1. Adaptive learning
2. Generative learning and
3. Survival learning

Continuous improvement is part of the management of all systems and processes. To achieve the highest levels of performance it is necessary to have a well-designed and well-executed approach to continuous improvement and learning. Improvement and learning need to be embedded in the way an organisation operates. Management should provide the leadership for continual improvement and innovation in processes and systems, products and services.

Improving products and services involves determining needs of customer and designing products and services to reflect those needs. **According to a Japanese professor, Noriaki Kano, there are three classes of customer needs:**

(i) ***Dissatisfiers*** – those needs that are expected in a product or service and not stated by customers but are assumed as given. If they are not present, customers are dissatisfied.

(ii) ***Satisfiers*** – needs that customers ask for and fulfilling these needs creates satisfaction.

(iii) ***Delighters/exciters*** – new and innovative features that customers do not expect but if present, delight or excite them. The presence of unexpected features, if valued by customers, leads to high perceptions of quality.

Improving work processes and administrative systems may lead to major reduction in defects and scrap and hence reduction in costs and improvement in quality. Continuous improvement also involves improving flexibility, responsiveness and cycle time. Flexibility refers to the ability to adapt quickly and effectively to changing requirements, (*for example,* rapid changeover from one product to another, rapid response to changing demands). Cycle time refers to the time it takes to accomplish one cycle of process - for instance, the time a customer orders a product to the time it is delivered, or the time to introduce a new product.

1.17 TOTAL QUALITY AND ORGANISATIONAL CULTURE

The principles of total quality must become an essential part of the organisation's culture.

The principles of total quality must become an essential part of the organisation's culture. The strategies and leadership philosophies of major companies reflect these principles. ***For example,*** **Procter and Gamble have a total quality philosophy that focuses on delivering superior customer satisfaction through the following four principles:**

(i) Know your customers and consumers really well and then meet and exceed their expectations.

(ii) Do right things in the right manner.

(iii) Concentrate on improving systems continuously and improve the capability of the basic business systems and sub systems.

(iv) Empower people by removing barriers and providing a climate in which every employee of the organisation is encouraged and trained to make his or her maximum contribution to business objectives.

In the previous paragraphs, we discussed the importance of the concept of total quality and the principles of total quality. We now discuss the evolution of total quality control and concepts of Total Quality Control and Total Quality Management.

1.18 THE EVOLUTION OF TOTAL QUALITY CONTROL

The first step in the development of the quality field was ***operator quality control*** in the manufacturing job upto the end of the 19th century. According to this, each worker could totally control the quality of personal work.

In the early 1900s, the focus was on ***foreman quality control*** in which many individuals performing a similar task were grouped and directed by a foreman, who then assumed responsibility for the quality of the work of the group.

During the period 1920-1930, focus was on ***inspection quality control*** in which a group of inspectors were assigned the responsibility of controlling the quality of the output of the workers.

The fourth step of quality control *viz.*, ***statistical quality control*** came into practice in factories after World War II. Inspectors were provided with few ***statistical tools*** such as ***sampling*** and ***control charts***. The ***total quality control approach*** came into practice since 1960s. As total quality control has come to have a major impact on management and engineering practices, it has provided the foundation for the evolution of ***company wide quality control*** (CWQC) or ***total quality management*** in the decade of 1980s and beyond.

1.19 PRINCIPLES OF TOTAL QUALITY CONTROL

Principles of TQC comprise:
(i) Top management policies
(ii) Q.C training for every one
(iii) Product or service design
(iv) Quality materials from suppliers
(v) Control in production and
(vi) Distribution, installation and use.

(i) **Top management policies :** These are statements regarding how the quality of products and services fits into the business strategies of the organisation. Support of the top management is crucial to the total commitment of the organisation and to the production of superior products and services. The philosophy of ***defect-free production (zero defects)***, ***"Do it right the first time"*** and ***"Continuous Improvement (Kaizen in Japan)*** are fundamental to TQC.

(ii) **Quality control training for everyone :** Comprehensive training programmes involving participation of every employee from the shop floor to the board room, both staff and line, as well as suppliers and major customers are essential for implementing the TQC philosophy.

(iii) **Product or service design :** Product design should ensure product quality. The degree of ***product standardisation*** can have important specifications for product quality. *For example,* standarised product designs facilitate implementation of ***"Just-in-Time production"*** which leads to superior product quality. Also, engineering designs determine how well the product functions, its level of reliability and the customers' perception of quality. The materials specified in the product design and the part tolerances affect the ease of manufacturing and consistency of production.

(iv) **Quality materials from suppliers :** Suppliers' involvement in the company's quality control programs ensures supply of materials of the highest quality from them. *For example,* Ford Motor Company has about 300 suppliers whose personnel attend Ford's training program in quality control. Ford has long-term supply contracts with its suppliers in order to achieve highest quality at competitive costs.

(v) **Control in production :** Total commitment to producing products and services of perfect quality, a commitment to strive relentlessly for improvement in product quality and the constant diligence applied to improving every detail of manufacturing brought the Japanese manufacturers to where they are now as far as product quality and productivity are concerned. The idea of ***perfect quality*** should be all pervasive, right from the raw material suppliers to every worker on production and assembly lines and to every warehouse worker. The responsibility for producing products of high quality rests with the workers who produce the products rather than with quality control personnel. In this sense, quality control is viewed as a line function rather than a staff function. Even though inspection and quality control techniques can assist in identifying the quality problems, ***quality cannot be inspected into products and high quality products must be produced.***

(vi) **Distribution, installation and use :** TQC must include packaging, shipping methods and installation of the products at the customer's premises. If the product gets damaged during shipment or if it is not properly installed, the product performance will be affected and customers equate this poor performance with poor quality.

1.20 QUALITY IN PRACTICE

Box 1.7 : Managing Quality Provides a Competitive Advantage at Motorola

Motorola decided some years ago to become a world leader in quality. Soon, it became the first winner of the Malcolm Baldrige National Quality Award. Motorola believes in total quality management commitment that permeates this entire global organisation.

To make the quality focus work, Motorola did a number of things:

- Aggressively began a worldwide education program to ensure that employees understood quality and statistical process control.
- Established goals namely its Six-Sigma program. Motorola's Six Sigma program means that it can expect to have a defect rate no more than a few parts per million. (3.4 parts/million)
- Established extensive employee participation and employee teams. (More than 4000 Total Customer Satisfaction Teams from throughout the world compete for awards based on team performance).

Other salient features of Motorola's quality management are :

(i) Motorola's divisions can expect a ***quality service review*** every two years. Five member teams are selected from various parts of the company to perform the review. After the review, the general manager and staff have a session with the teams and go over the review. The strengths and weaknesses are discussed and recommendations are given to the local management about improvements that must be made.

(ii) ***Corporate goals*** receive commitment throughout the organisation and that is a powerful quality tool. The quality effort has allowed Motorola to move from 6000 defects per million just five years ago to only 40 defects per million in the year 1999. Motorola believes that it has saved $700 million in manufacturing costs over five years.

1.21 SUMMARY

Nowadays customers are becoming increasingly intolerant of poor service, late deliveries, unreliable goods, shoddy workmanship and the like. Organisations everywhere are growing increasingly conscious of competitive potential of quality, which has now become a new competitive weapon.

The role of quality needs no emphasis for a firm because it is the key to success in business in addition to price, flexibility and delivery speed to achieve maximum customer satisfaction. Today "quality" is a watchword for the survival and growth of any organisation in the global business environment. Good quality increases productivity and profits in addition to improving product image, brand image and company image.

"Quality" can be defined in so many ways, but the simplest definition of quality is "the ability of a product or service to meet customer needs" or "fitness for use" of a product or service for the intended customer.

The small 'q' (or old quality) approach to quality focuses on inspection to seggregate the good from the bad rather than eliminating the defects. **The big 'Q'** (or new quality) approach to quality is the closest to total quality management.

Customer-driven definitions of quality include multiple dimensions such as conformance to specifications, value, fitness for use, customer support/service, psychological impressions, perceived quality and the like. From the customer's view point quality is that which meets or exceeds customer expectations.

"Quality" is important for any kind of business-either manufacturing or service, because it is one of the key objectives of operations management along with cost, flexibility and delivery of goods and services. Good quality goods and services can provide an organisation with competitive edge over competitors. Good quality reduces costs due to product returns, rework and scrap, increases productivity, profits and brand image.

Benefits gained by quality to a firm are : *(i)* Positive company image, *(ii)* Better competitive ability, *(iii)* Increased market share, *(iv)* Reduced overall costs, *(v)* Reduced product/service liability costs, *(vi)* High employee morale, *(vii)* Higher productivity and *(viii)* Higher profits.

Product quality has eight dimensions. They are : *(i)* Performance, *(ii)* Features, *(iii)* Reliability, *(iv)* Serviceability, *(v)* Durability, *(vi)* Appearance (aesthetics), *(vii)* Conformance and *(viii)* Perceived quality. The five dimensions of **service quality** are : *(i)* Reliability, *(ii)* Assurance, *(iii)* Tangibles, *(iv)* Empathy and *(v)* Responsiveness.

Quality can be categorised as : *(i)* Indifferent quality, *(ii)* Expected quality, *(iii)* One-dimensional quality and *(iv)* Exciting quality.

Quality can be viewed in five ways according to Garvin. These five views are : *(i)* Transcendental view, *(ii)* Product-based view, *(iii)* User-based view, *(iv)* Manufacturing-based view and *(v)* Value-based view.

An organisation committed to quality must examine quality at three levels namely, *(i)* the organisation level, *(ii)* the process level and *(iii)* the performer/job level.

The five determinants of quality are : *(i)* Quality of design, *(ii)* Quality capability of production processes (process capability), *(iii)* Quality of conformance, *(iv)* Quality of customer service and *(v)* Organisation quality culture. Quality also comprises availability, maintainability and reliability.

According to Deming, understanding customers and suppliers was crucial to planning for quality in production systems.

Some aspects of quality are : *(i)* Quality is not negotiable, *(ii)* Quality is all pervasive, *(iii)* Quality increases productivity, *(iv)* Quality leads to better performance in the market place, *(v)* Quality means improved business performance, *(vi)* Quality improves competitive advantage, *(vii)* Quality improves profitability, *(viii)* Quality is a source of value, *(ix)* Quality must begin at a personal level, *(x)* The cost of non-quality (or lack of quality) is high and *(xi)* Quality is a way of life.

Quality management has evolved progressively through four discrete stages which are identified as *(i)* Inspection, *(ii)* Quality control, *(iii)* Quality assurance and *(iv)* Total quality management.

The inspection system is an after-the-event screening process involving detection of defects rather than prevention.

Quality control refers to all those functions or activities that must be performed to fulfil the company's quality objectives. **Quality at source** is an important concept in quality control which puts the production worker in the driver's seat in controlling product quality, thereby completely eliminating the need for inspectors to control the quality of the output of workers.

Quality assurance includes all activities that are performed to ensure that the product performs to the customer's satisfaction. Some of the activities included in quality assurance are : *(i)* Reliability engineering, *(ii)* Value engineering, *(iii)* Evaluation of usability of products, *(iv)* Process control, *(v)* Product screening, *(vi)* Service assurance and *(vii)* Quality feed-back.

Quality improvement means finding ways to do better than quality standards and breaking through to unprecedental levels of performance.

Total quality management (TQM) is a systems approach to management that aims to continuously increase value to customers by designing and continuously improving organisational processes and systems.

The eight quality management principles as defined in ISO 9000 : 2000 standards are : *(i)* Customer focus, *(ii)* Leadership, *(iii)* Involvement of people, *(vi)* Process approach, *(v)* Systems approach to management, *(vi)* Continual improvement, *(vii)* Factual approach to decision making, *(viii)* Mutually beneficial supplier relationships.

The **concept of total quality** evolved in US in the 1970s and consists of a people focused management system that aims at continued increase in customer satisfaction. It involves all employees, executives and top management personnel and extend backward and forward to include the supply chain and the customer chain.

The **core principles of total quality are :** *(i)* A focus on the customer, *(ii)* Participation and team work, *(iii)* Employee involvement and empowerment and *(iv)* Continuous improvement and learning.

Total quality control which is the previous step to total quality management is an effective system for integrating the quality development, quality maintenance and quality improvement efforts of the various groups in an organisation to achieve highest productivity and customer satisfaction.

Principles of total quality control comprise : *(i)* Top management policies, *(ii)* Quality control training for everyone, *(iii)* Product or service design, *(iv)* Quality material from suppliers, *(v)* Control in production, *(vi)* Distribution, installation and use.

1.22 KEY WORDS USED

Quality, Old Quality, New Quality, Indifferent Quality, Expected Quality, One-dimensional Quality, Exciting Quality, Levels of Quality, Perceived Quality, Customer-driven Quality, Quality of Design, Quality of Conformance, Quality of Customer Service, Organisation Quality Culture, Availability,

Reliability, Maintainability, Field Service, Inspection, Quality Control, Quality Assurance, Quality Improvement, Quality-at-the-source, Total Quality, Total Quality Control, Total Quality Management, Customer Focus, Leadership, Continual Improvement, Participation, Team Work, Employee Involvement, Employee Empowerment.

1.23 OBJECTIVE QUESTIONS

(A) Match the following :

Column A	Column B
1. Responsiveness	1. Quality assurance
2. Performance	2. Right at the first time
3. Fitness for use	3. Product quality
4. Conformance to requirements	4. Service quality
5. Continuous improvement	5. Philip Crosby
6. Value engineering	6. Edward Deming
7. Quality control	7. Joseph M. Juran

(B) State whether the following statements are True or False :

1. A value-based approach defines quality in terms of costs and prices. (T / F)
2. Dimensions of product quality are the same as that of service quality. (T / F)
3. Higher quality means greater costs and lesser profits. (T / F)
4. Quality control involves the establishment of quality standards. (T / F)
5. The internal customers are more important than the external customers in assuring quality. (T / F)

(C) Multiple choice Questions :

1. The view of quality that focuses on "fitness for use" and "user perception" is known as:
   (a) transcendental view (b) product based view
   (c) user-based view (d) manufacturing based view
   (e) value-based view.
2. "Quality is meeting or exceeding customer expectations" - This definition of quality is known as:
   (a) Perceived quality (b) Customer-driven quality
   (c) Indifferent quality (d) One-dimensional quality
   (e) Expected quality.
3. ___________ means producing a product to meet the specifications :
   (a) Quality of design (b) Quality of performance
   (c) Quality of conformance (d) Quality of customer service
4. Reliability engineering is one of the activities involved in :
   (a) Quality control (b) Quality assurance
   (c) Quality improvement (d) Total quality management
   (e) Total quality control
5. Availability can be measured as follows :

   (a) $\dfrac{\text{Up time} + \text{Down time}}{\text{Up time}}$ (b) $\dfrac{\text{Down time}}{\text{Up time} + \text{Down time}}$

   (c) $\dfrac{\text{Up time}}{\text{Up time} + \text{Down time}}$ (d) $\dfrac{\text{Up time}}{\text{Up time} - \text{Down time}}$

1.24 REVIEW QUESTIONS

1. "Quality is a new competitive weapon". Justify the statement.
2. Distinguish between small 'q' and big 'Q'.
3. Discuss the concept of quality.
4. Why quality is important to any kind of business organisation?
5. List the benefits of quality.
6. Discuss the dimensions of product quality and service quality.
7. Discuss the criteria used to judge quality of products and services.
8. Discuss the four categories of quality according to Kano.
9. Explain the five views of quality according to Garvin.
10. Discuss the various levels of quality.
11. Explain briefly various determinants of quality.
12. Define the terms "reliability", "maintainability" and "availability".
13. Define the terms : *(i)* Inspection, *(ii)* Quality control, *(iii)* Quality assurance, *(iv)* Total quality management.
14. Examine quality as :
    (i) a competitive advantage
    (ii) a source of value
    (iii) a means of increasing productivity
    (iv) a means to improve business performance.
15. Discuss the principles of quality management.
16. Discuss the concept of total quality.
17. Discuss the principles of total quality and total quality control.

1.25 DISCUSSION QUESTIONS

1. Discuss how either good or poor quality affects you personally as a consumer. Give some examples based on your experience.
2. Discuss the importance of quality to the national interest of any country in the world.
3. Describe your experiences in which your expectations were met, exceeded or not met when you purchased goods or services.
4. Think of a product or service that you are planning to purchase and develop the 'fitness-for-use' criteria that you expect the product or service to fulfil.
5. Illustrate how several definitions of quality can apply simultaneously for a product (say an automobile for your personal use) or a hospital in which you would like to be admitted in case of your illness.

1.26 ASSIGNMENTS

1. Give example of a high quality consumer durable product you have used and discuss its various quality dimensions.
2. Choose any two services which you have availed and compare them based on their quality dimensions.

1.27 CHAPTER CASE

THE CASE OF QUALITY AT ABC COMPANY

ABC company recently discovered that the costs due to shipment of defective items had risen to an alarming level. To correct the situation, they decided to implement a quality assurance program. Previously, all inspection was done by workers on their own work. Because of the lack of formal education in quality assurance for the present employees and managers, it was decided to form a team of recent college graduates for quality assurance programs. (QAP)

The team which was formed was given the responsibility of reducing the percentage of defective items being produced to half of the present level in one month.

Problems, however, began to crop up immediately. Conflicts arose between the inspectors of the QAP and the workers. Some of the older employees felt they were being insulted whenever a quality problem was traced to their work. This resentment often resulted in their work deteriorating further instead of improving. Other workers believed they were being wrongly accused of shoddy workmanship. Some even accused the inspectors of actually making defects in their work so that they could claim they had found a problem spot (defect) and hence, look good in the eyes of the QAP manager.

Monitoring reports after the first month showed that the quality level had actually worsened. Management felt that perhaps they had introduced the quality assurance program improperly.

Discussion Questions :

(a) What errors do you feel the ABC company made in the implementation of QAP?

(b) What remedial actions would you take to improve the present situation?

CHAPTER 2

TOTAL QUALITY IN ORGANISATIONS

LEARNING OBJECTIVES

After reading this chapter, you should be able to:

- Discuss quality in manufacturing and service systems
- Distinguish between traditional versus modern quality management
- Discuss the terms: 'quality planning', 'quality control' and 'quality improvement'
- Discuss the concept of "cost of quality"
- Discuss the concept of total quality management (TQM)
- Discuss the principles of total quality management
- Discuss the scope of TQM
- Discuss the major elements of a total quality infrastructure
- Distinguish between total quality management and traditional management practices
- Know the benefits of TQM
- Discuss the elements of total quality management concept

2.0 INTRODUCTION

For all types of organisations, whether manufacturing goods or offering services, or both, quality is absolutely vital to retain customers, sustain profitability and gain market share. Eventhough the concept of quality has its roots in manufacturing, today it has moved far beyond. As consumer expectations have risen, a focus on quality has permeated other key sectors of the economy such as health care, education, not-for-profits and government. This chapter explores the role of quality in manufacturing and service organisations, large and small, including education, health care, not-for-profit and government. All organisations are viewed as **systems** and the role that each component of an organisation plays in achieving high quality is examined.

Quality and Systems Thinking

A **'system'** is a set of functions or activities within an organisation that work together for achieving the objectives or goals of the organisation.

Quality is crucial for all types of organisations to retain customers, sustain profitability and gain market share.

A **production system** is composed of many smaller, interacting subsystems. *For example,* a manufacturing plant is viewed as a production system which has various subsystems such as the procurement sub-system, conversion sub-system, distribution sub-system, transportation sub-system, communication sub-system, control sub-system etc. Eventhough every organisation is composed of many individual functions which are often seen as separate units or departments, (*for example,* marketing, production, finance, accounting, human resources, etc.), managers need to view the organisation as a whole and focus on the important organisational linkage among these functions. *For example,* the total quality system has the infrastructure elements such as customer relationship management, leadership and strategic planning, human resources management, process management and information and knowledge management. The top management executives need to focus on strategic directions and on customers, strategies need to be linked to human resource plans and key processes in order to effectively align resources, training and work system design must support manufacturing and service processes and information and knowledge management provide the means for obtaining useful feedback to evaluate the strategy implementation and a means for improvement. Successful management relies on a ***system perspective*** which is one of the most important elements of total quality.

2.1 QUALITY IN MANUFACTURING AND SERVICE SYSTEMS

Quality in Manufacturing

Well developed quality assurance systems have existed in manufacturing for sometime. However, these systems focused primarily on technical issues such as equipment reliability, measurement of defects and statistical quality control techniques. Nowadays, manufacturing organisations are transformed into customer-driven organisations and are adopting changes particularly in the areas of product design, human resource management and supplier relations. *For example.* product design activities now closely integrate marketing, engineering (Research & Development) and manufacturing operations. Human resource practices concentrate on empowering workers to collect and analyse data, make critical operations decisions and take responsibility for continuous improvement. This has shifted the responsibility for quality from the quality control department to the shop floor of the factory. Suppliers are treated as partners in product design and manufacturing efforts.

Manufacturing systems: *Exhibit 2.1* illustrates a typical manufacturing system and the key relationships among its functions.

The relationship between quality and various departments of the manufacturing system is discussed in the following paragraphs.

Exhibit 2.1 : Functional Relationships in a Typical Manufacturing System

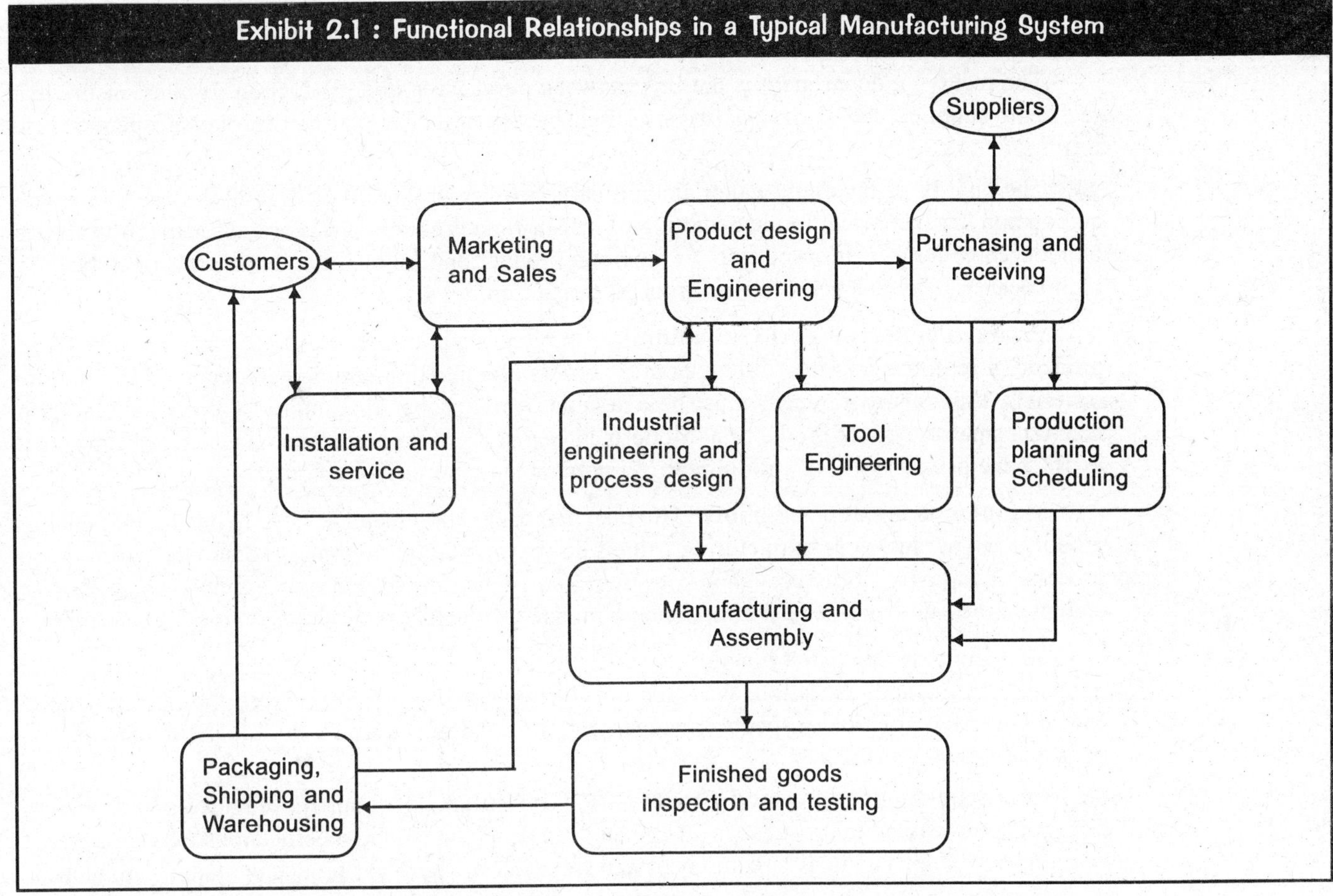

Marketing and Sales: Marketing and sales personnel have important responsibilities for quality. They are responsible for determining the needs and expectations of consumers. This includes gaining knowledge regarding the products and products' features desired by the consumers and also knowing the prices that consumers are williing to pay for them. This information enables a firm to define products that are ***fit for use*** and capable of being manufactured within the technological and budgetery constraints of the firm. Effective market research and active solicitation of customer feedback are necessary for developing quality products. Sales people can help to obtain feedback on product performance from customers and convey this information to product designers and engineers. They should also help to ensure that customers receive adequate assistance and are completely satisfied.

Product Design and Engineering: The product design and engineering functions develop technical specifications for products and production processes to determine the requirements determined by the marketing function. Under-designed products will fail in the market place because they will not meet customer needs. Products that are overdesigned may not find a profitable market. Poorly designed manufacturing processes result in poor quality or higher costs.

Motorola has been a role model for improving manufacturing quality through its product and process design activities. It set an ambitious goal of ***six-sigma quality*** (a level of quality representing no more than 3.4 defects per million parts) for every process in the company.

Purchasing and Receiving: The ***quality*** of purchased parts and services and the ***timeliness of their delivery*** are critical. **The purchasing department can help a firm achieve quality by:**

(i) selecting quality-conscious suppliers.

(ii) ensuring that purchase orders clearly define the quality requirements specified by product design.

(iii) establishing long-term supplier relationships based on trust.

(iv) providing quality-improvement training to suppliers.

The receiving department is the link between purchasing and production. It must ensure that the items supplied are of the quality specified by the purchase contract through inspection and testing.

The quality of incoming materials and parts has become more critical as the use of flexible automation has increased. Implementation of just-in-time production (JIT) requires that inventories be reduced to the barest minimum. To maintain production, the quality of materials must be very high because there are no buffer inventories to take up the slack.

Production Planning and Scheduling: A production plan specifies long-term and short-term production requirements for filling customer orders and meeting anticipated demand. The correct materials, tools and equipment must be available at the proper time and in the proper places to maintain smooth flow of production. Modern concepts of production planning and scheduling such as JIT have been shown to lead to quality improvement and cost savings.

Manufacturing and Assembly: The manufacturing and assembly have to ensure that quality products are produced. Manufacturing cannot do its job without a good product design and good process technology. No defects should be accepted in manufacturing and assembly operations. If and when they do occur, every effort must be made to identify their causes and eliminate them.

Tool Engineering: This function is responsible for designing and maintaining the tools used in manufacturing and inspection. Worn manufacturing tools (cutting tools) result in defective parts and improperly calibrated inspection gauges give misleading information. Tool problems lead to poor quality and inefficiency.

Industrial Engineering and Process Design: The job of industrial engineers and process designers is to work with product design engineers to develop realistic specifications. Also, they must select appropriate technologies, equipment and work-out methods for producing quality products.

Finished Goods Inspection and Testing: Final product inspection is required to judge the quality of manufacturing, to discover and help to resolve production problems that may arise and to ensure that no defective items reach the customer.

Packaging, Shipping and Warehousing: Packing, shipping and warehousing-often termed logistics activities are the functions that protect quality after goods are produced and prevent damages in transit.

Installation and Service: Users must understand a product and have adequate instructions for proper installation and operation. Good after-sales-service ensures customer satisfaction. Service after the sales is one of the most important factors in establishing customer perception of quality and customer loyalty.

Quality in Services

Quality in service includes both the quality of core services and facilitating services.

Service has been defined as "a social act which ***takes place in direct contact between the customer and representatives of the service company***". The service sector has grown rapidly in the last few decades and began to recognise the importance of quality.

Service quality includes both the quality of ***core services*** and ***facilitating services***. *For example,* all banks provide checking account services. A checking account is a core service product. In addition, many banks provide services such as automated teller services, rapid clearing of cheques deposits and 24 hour telephone access to account information. These represent facilitating services which enhance the value of core service to the customers.

The service must respond to the needs of the customer, *i.e.,* the services must ***"meet or exceed customer expectations"***. Because employee's performance and behaviour and service transaction are the strongest determinants of perceived service quality, the two key components of service system quality are ***employees*** and ***information technology***.

Employees : Customers evaluate a service primarily by the quality of human contact. When service employee's job satisfaction is high, customer satisfaction is high and when job satisfaction is low, customer satisfaction is also low.

Two key components of service system quality are : *(i)* Employees and *(ii)* Information technology.

Information Technology : This incorporates computing, communication, data processing and various other means of converting data into usedful information. Intelligent use of information technology not only leads to ***improved quality*** and ***productivity*** but also to ***competitive advantage***. Every service industry is exploiting information technology to improve customer services. *For example,* computerised booking of railway and air tickets.

Information technology is reducing the labour intensity of many service operations. Automated teller machines, *for example.* have eliminated some banking-industry jobs. While information technology reduces labour intensity and increases the speed of service, it can have adverse effect on the other dimensions of quality. It may be argued that customer satisfaction is decreased when there is less personal interaction. Thus, service providers must balance conflicting quality concerns.

Quality in Healthcare : Health care industry is a service industry which faces continuing pressure to improve quality. Quality has been a focus for the industry for quite sometime. *For example,* under the **"end result system for hospital standardisation"** proposed by Ernest Codman in 1910, a hospital would be able to track every patient it treated long enough to determine whether the treatment was effective. If the treatment was not effective, the hospital would then attempt to determine the reason and take necessary action to successfully treat similar patients in the future. In the US, the Joint Commission on Accreditation of Health Care Organisations and National Committee for Quality Assurance, facilitated continuous quality improvement in the health care organisations. Although many health care organisations have turned toward quality as a means of achieving better performance and customer satisfaction, the industry faces considerable challenges because of several types of quality problems in health-care.

Quality in Education : Education represents one of the most interesting and challenging areas for quality improvement. Total quality principles used to improve education include:

(i) **active involvement** – of school administration, sponsors, parents and students working together on teams that are empowered to make decisions and implement change.

(ii) **a system for continuous improvement** – establishing consistent standards of excellence, setting and communicating clear expectations, looking at a work task as a process, involving all who have a stake in the outcome of the improvement process, measuring results and recognising and rewarding success - for bringing about a change for improvement

(iii) **environment that celebrates success** – focus on celebrating student successes and

(iv) **committed leadership** of school administrators to bring about change and improvement by inspiring the faculty, students, parents, sponsors and other administrators to work with them.

Business organisations play an important role in fostering quality improvement efforts in higher education by transferring knowledge and expertise on quality processes and implementation practices.

Quality in Small Business and Not-for-Profits Organisations

Small businesses and not-for-profits organisations have usually been slow to adopt quality initiatives because they lack understanding and knowledge of what need to be done and how to do it. Managers or owners of small business enterprises are busy in entrepreneurial activities which focus on sales strategies and market growth, day-to-day cash flow problems, and routine fire fighting. In addition, small firms and not-for-profit organisations often lack the resources needed to establish and maintain more formal quality systems. Three total quality principles relevant to small business executives are: *(i)* **focus on customers,** *(ii)* **team work and participation** and *(iii)* **process focus and continuous improvement.**

Small business executives, especially in family-owned enterprises, have an attitude of **'command and control'** while making decisions and rarely empowering their employees.

Eventhough small business firms have many characteristics that adversely affect the implementation of total quality principles, many successful small businesses have shown that quality initiatives can be successfully accomplished. In case of not-for-profits organisations, the managers often lack business acumen and technical expertise needed. Among the key challenges that not-for-profits organisations face are: *(i)* overcoming the fear of change, *(ii)* changing the mind-set that not-for-profits organisations are different and cannot apply quality principles, *(iii)* identifying a vision and customers, *(iv)* understanding work processes, *(v)* dealing with limited resources and *(vi)* understanding relationships with government and large corporations.

However, many not-for-profits organisations are adopting TQ principles because of their impact on the public and society who are their major customers and stake holders.

Quality in the Public Sector

Quality in the public sector – central, state and municipal government organisations has not achieved growth as rapidly as in the private sector. However many public sector entities have made remarkable strides to incorporate the principles of quality in their operations.

To promote quality initiatives in Federal Government organisations in the US, the Federal Quality Institute (FQI) was established in the 1980s as the primary source of leadership, information and consulting services on quality management in the Federal Government. In 1990, the FQI was given responsibility for administering the President's Quality Award and the Quality Improvement Award which are the equivalent of Malcolm Baldrige National Award given to private organisations. The criteria for the President's Quality Award were raised in the year 2000. The award criteria now focuses on recognising accomplishments that further the administration's objectives as noted in the President's Management Agenda. In 2002, the program was redesigned to recognise organisations for their performance and results in any or all of the five following categories: *(i)* Budget and Performance Integration, *(ii)* Strategic Management of Human Capital, *(iii)* Competition Sourcing, *(iv)* Improved Financial Performance and *(v)* Expanded Electronic Government.

To summarise, we may say that **quality concepts and principles are universal** and can be applied in all types of organisations. However the difficulty lies in developing an infrastructure to make it happen and the discipline to sustain efforts over time.

2.2 QUALITY MANAGEMENT

Quality management function determines the quality policy, objectives, and responsibilities and implements them by means of quality planning, quality control, quality assurance and quality improvement within the quality system.

Quality management is cross-functional in nature and involves the entire organisation. Operations in an organisation have a special responsibility to produce a quality product for the customer. This requires the cooperation of the entire organisation and careful attention to the management and control of quality.

Quality management has had many different meanings over the years. In the early 1900s, quality meant ***inspection*** which was the primary method to ensure quality of products. In the 1940s, quality took on a ***statistical connotation*** as ***statistical methods*** were first used to control quality within the natural variation of the process. Statistical control charts were developed to maintain a process within a ***state of statistical control*** and thus reduce the amount of inspection required. In the 1960s, the meaning of the term ***'quality management'*** was expanded to include the entire organisation as all functions helped in designing and producing quality products and services.

Quality was not viewed as just an act of production; rather it was something the entire organisation should strive to provide for the customer. Nowadays, quality is assuming a broader meaning, including ***continuous improvement, competitive advantage*** and ***consumer focus*** (*i.e.* customer satisfaction). ***Exhibit 2.2*** **illustrates the ever expanding influence of quality.**

Exhibit 2.2 : Ever-expanding Influence of Quality

2.3 TRADITIONAL VS MODERN QUALITY MANAGEMENT

Traditional Quality Management

In this view, the way to ensure that customers receive quality products and services is to have a rigorous system of inspection. The idea is that if there is enough inspection, the defective product will be identified and discarded, leaving only good products to be shipped to customers. In this approach, the main decision is how many products to inspect so that the total quality control costs are minimised by an optimal trade-off between the cost of scrap, rework and detecting defects and the cost of defective products to customers.

Traditional quality management implies that quality can be inspected into products.

What is fundamentally wrong in this approach is that it implies quality can be inspected into products. But what is true is that superior product quality is not attained through mere inspection. The manufacturers must have a look at the production and make fundamental changes in the way they design and produce products and ***do it right the first time.*** This will shift the inspection's job from discarding bad products to preventing defects and providing feedback on how production can continue to improve product quality.

Modern Quality Management

The modern approach to quality is reflected by the idea that ***quality drives the productivity machine.*** The modern era of quality management was heralded by a few new thinkers known as ***Quality Gurus.*** Among them **Deming, Crosby, Feigenbaum, Ishikawa, Juran** and **Taguchi** are noteworthy.

Modern quality management promotes the idea that quality drives the productivity machine.

W. Edwards Deming was a statistician and consultant. He was known as the father of quality control in Japan. He taught the Japanese that ***higher quality means lower cost.*** He was well known for his fourteen management principles for a business to remain competitive in providing goods and services that will have a market. He emphasised the role that the management should take in quality improvement and defined quality as ***continuous improvement*** of a stable system.

Philip B. Crosby who wrote the book titled ***"Quality is Free"*** in 1979, contended that any level of defects is too high and companies should work continuously towards the goal of **zero defects.**

Armand V. Feigenbaum developed the concept of ***total quality control*** **(TQC)**. He contended that the responsibility for quality must rest with the person who does the work. This concept is known as ***quality at the source*** and means that every employee must be responsible for performing his or her work with perfect quality. In TQC, where product quality is more important than production rate, workers are given the authority to stop production whenever quality problems occur.

Kaoru Ishikawa is credited with the concept of ***quality circles***. He also suggested the use of fishbone diagrams (also known as **Ishikawa diagrams**) which are used to trace back customer complaints about quality problems to the responsible production operations.

Joseph M. Juran played an important and early role in teaching Japanese manufacturers how to improve product quality. He advocated ***top management commitment*** to improve product quality, quality planning, statistics to identify discrepancies and continuous improvement of every aspect of product quality. He originated the idea of the **quality trilogy**: ***planning, control*** and ***improvement of quality***.

Genichi Taguchi was consultant for US companies such as Ford and IBM to assist them in developing improved statistical control of their production processes. He contended that products should be designed so that they are ***robust*** enough to function satisfactorily, despite variations on the production line or in the field.

2.4 QUALITY PLANNING, CONTROL AND IMPROVEMENT

Quality management includes:
1. Quality Planning
2. Quality Control and
3. Quality Improvement

Quality Planning begins with identifying customers, both external and internal, determining their needs and developing product features that respond to customer needs.

Quality Control involves determining what to control, establishing units of measurement so that data may be objectively evaluated, establishing standards of performance, measuring actual performance, interpreting the difference between actual performance and the standard and taking corrective action on the difference.

Quality Improvement is best achieved by identifying specific projects for improvement, getting the right people involved, diagnosing causes of poor performance, developing remedies for the causes, proving that the remedies will be effective and providing control to hold improvements.

The process of quality planning, control and improvement requires a continuous interaction between the customer, operations and other parts of the organisation. ***Exhibit 2.3* illustrates how these interactions occur through a *quality cycle*.** The customer needs are determined usually through the marketing function. The engineering department designs a product to meet those needs or works with the customer on design specifications that fit within production capabilities. ***Box 2.1* lists the basic activities of quality planning.**

Box 2.1 : The Quality Planning 'Road Map'

Quality planning comprises the following basic activities

- Identify the customer and their needs.
- Develop a product that responds to those needs.
- Develop a process able to produce that product.

A road map for quality planning has the following sequence of steps :

- Identify who are the customers.
- Determine the needs of those customers.
- Translate those needs into your language.
- Develop a product that can respond to those needs.
- Optimise the product features so as to meet your needs as well as customer's needs.
- Develop a process which is able to produce the product.
- Optimise the process.
- Prove that the process can produce the product under operating conditions.
- Transfer the process to the operating forces.

Exhibit 2.3 : The Quality Cycle

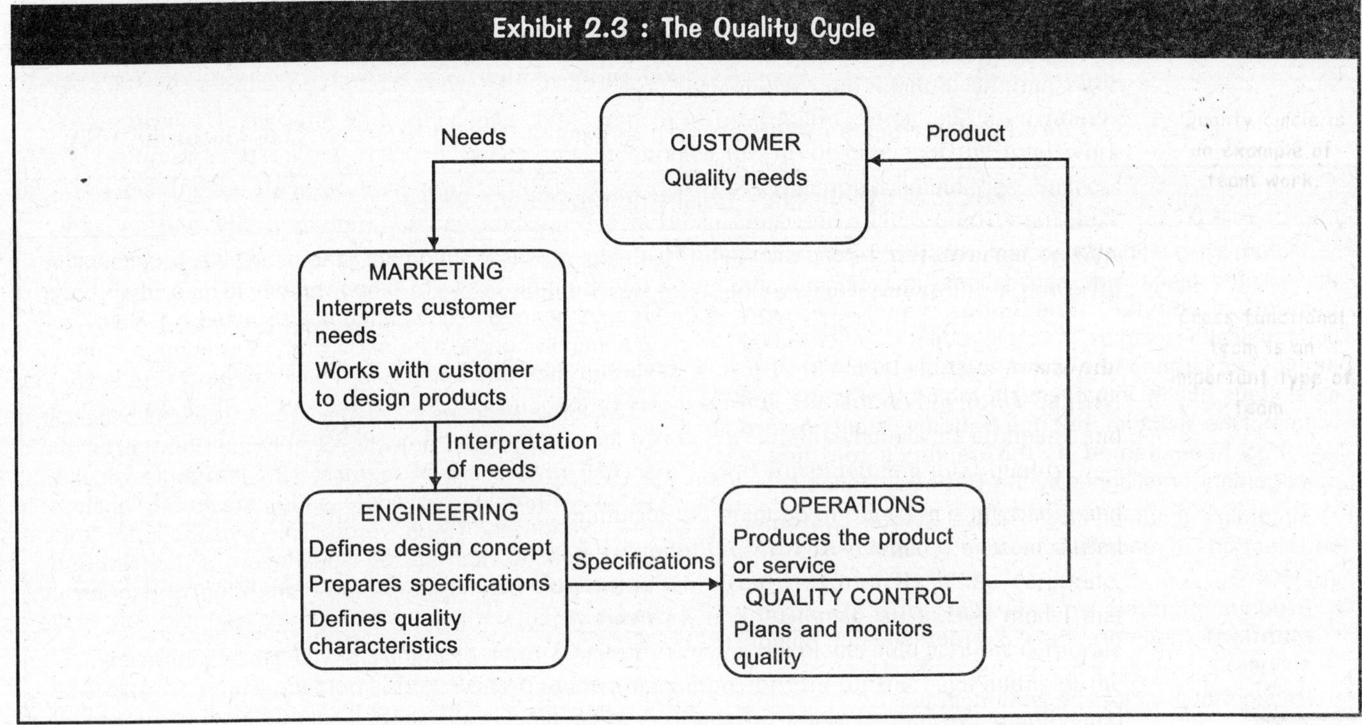

Once the design concept and specifications have been completed, the ***quality of design*** has been established, operations must continually ensure that the product is produced as specified by insisting on ***quality of conformance.*** This is usually done through proper training, supervision, machine maintenance and operator inspections. Also, operations should strive to reduce the variances of its processes and products over time to achieve ***continuous improvement. Box 2.2*** **lists the various opportunities for quality improvement.**

Box 2.2 : The Long List of Opportunities for Quality Improvement

The long list of opportunities for quality improvement

- The list of customers is not fully known.
- The list of products is not fully identified.
- The vital few customers have not been identified.
- The needs of customers are not fully known or understood.
- Customer's needs are judged by inadequate criteria.
- Customer's needs are not being met.
- Reactions of non-customers are not known.
- Products are not competitive.
- The relationship of product value compared to cost is not known.
- The relationship of product value is inadequate.
- Products do not serve a useful purpose.
- Much work must be done over again because of deficiencies in the processes.

The implementation of planning, control and improvement of quality through the quality cycle requires the following sequence of steps:

(i) Define quality attributes on the basis of customer needs.

(ii) Define how to measure each attribute.

(iii) Set quality standards.

(iv) Establish appropriate tests for each standard.

(v) Find and correct causes of poor quality.

(vi) Continue to make improvements.

Box 2.3 describes how this six-step approach is used in practice at Motorola, USA.

Box 2.3 : Motorola's Quality Improvement Process

Motorola is a leading manufacturer of semi-conductors and related electronics applications, including paging systems, cellular telephones and two-way communications radios. It employs more than 130,000 employees around the world who are committed to continuous quality improvement. Motorola was the first winner of the **Malcolm Baldrige National Quality Award** and has been named as the country's top quality management practitioner by the Business Roundtable.

Motorola's fundamental objective is **total customer satisfaction**. To reach this objective, it has five initiatives in place:

- Produce products and services to a **six-sigma standard** (no more than 3.4 defects per million actions).
- Reduce total cycle time in all activities.
- Lead in the area of products, manufacturing and the environment.
- Improve profitability.
- Provide a creative, cooperative workplace in which employees are empowered.

These initiatives for customer satisfaction are led by all levels of management from the bottom to the top.

Motorola is a strong believer in the value of education for all employees. To empower employees, they have found the need for continuous education. Employees continually renew their skills and knowledge in quality, design, manufacturing and their own specializations.

Motorola believes that it has been successful because of its management process. Simply put, the process is to (1) have a set of metrics, (2) determine results, (3) pick a problem, (4) address the problem, (5) analyze the solution and (6) move on. This process is far from earthshaking, it's just an application of **continuous improvement** and the **quality planning and control cycle**.

Motorola's stretch goals are 10 times improvement in two years in whatever is being measured. If cycle time for an activity is 100 days, it would be cut to 10 days. If defects were 100 parts per million (ppm), they would be cut to 10 ppm.

At Motorola, all employees take responsibility for quality. Quality is not an assignable task. It must be rooted and institutionalized in every process. Motorola believes that it is everyone's responsibility to improve the system for total customer satisfaction.

Planning for quality must always start with the ***product attributes***. The quality planner determines which attributes are important to customer satisfaction and which are not. *For example, (i)* **an attractive appearance** and *(ii)* **a long service life**. A method must then be devised to test and measure ***quality*** for each of the product attributes. *For example,* visual inspection.

After deciding on the measurement techniques to use, the quality planner should set ***standards*** that describe the amount of quality required on each attribute. Usually, these standards are stated as ***tolerances*** or minimum and maximum acceptable limits.

After standards have been set, a ***testing program*** should be established. It is not enough simply to inspect the products for defects. As the saying goes, ***"you cannot inspect quality into a product, you must build it in"***. Upon discovering the defects, the quality personnel and workers should find the ***underlying causes*** and correct them. Causes for poor quality could include defective raw materials, lack of training, unclear procedures, a faulty machine and so on. When causes of poor quality are regularly found and corrected, the production system will be under constant control and improvement will be possible.

An even better approach is to ***prevent error*** from occurring in the first place. This requires designing products and internal procedures that are foolproof, working with suppliers to prevent errors, training employees before problems occur and performing preventive maintenance of machines and equipments. However, when errors do occur, they need to be quickly corrected and the system itself changed to prevent errors of the same type from recurring.

The concept of ***fool proofing*** was first developed in the 1960s by ***Shigeo Shingo*** who worked for Toyota Motors in Japan. It was called ***Poka-Yoke*** which means ***"mistake proofing"*** in Japanese.

The idea of **Poka-Yoke** is to design the product and processes so that it is impossible to make mistakes or they are easily detected when mistakes do occur. *For example.* your microwave won't start if the door is open and your car beeps when the key is in ignition. **The Poka-Yoke approach has the following concepts:**

(i) Parts should be designed so that they cannot be put on backward or left off the product by mistake.

(ii) Services should be designed so that the customer gets exactly what he or she ordered.

(iii) If the error cannot be prevented from occurring, it should be made easy to detect.

2.5 QUALITY AND FINANCIAL PERFORMANCE

Quality has a significant impact on financial performance of a firm

Quality and financial performances are intimately related. To understand this relationship better, first we must consider the relationship between quality and cost. A powerful idea in the area of quality is to calculate the ***cost of quality*** which includes ***prevention, appraisal, external failure*** and ***internal failure*** cost categories related to quality. All these except the prevention cost are **costs of *not doing things right the first time*.** By assigning cost to poor quality, it can be managed and controlled like any other cost. Since cost is the most important concern of managers, putting quality in terms of cost offers a powerful means of communication and control. Generally, it was found that most companies were spending 20 to 40 percent of sales revenue to manage quality (*i.e.* cost of quality). Since these figures were three to four times greater than the profit margins, a reduction in the cost of quality can lead to a significant improvement in profit. Today, the best managed companies have been able to reduce their costs of quality from 30 percent of sales to as little as 3 percent over a period of several years. This has been done while improving the quality of the product.

2.5.1 The Cost of Quality

Four major categories of costs associated with quality management are : *(i)* Prevention costs, *(ii)* Appraisal costs, *(iii)* Costs of internal failure and *(iv)* Costs of external failure.

These are certain costs which are associated with product and service quality. Some costs are associated with ***preventing poor quality*** and some costs occur after poor quality occurs. Most experts on the costs of poor quality estimate losses in the range of 20 to 30 percent of gross sales for defective or unsatisfactory products. Four major categories of costs associated with quality management are: *(i)* Prevention costs, *(ii)* Appraisal costs, *(iii)* Costs of internal failure and *(iv)* Costs of external failure.

Prevention costs are associated with ***preventing defects*** before they happen. They include the costs of redesigning the product to make it simpler to produce, redesigning the process to remove causes of poor quality, training employees in the methods of continuous improvement, working with suppliers to increase the quality of purchased items or contracted services, charting of quality performance to study trends and so on.

Appraisal costs are incurred in assessing the level of quality attained by the operating system. They include the cost of ***detecting defects*** *i.e.* the cost of all activities aimed at finding products and services that do not conform to specifications before they are shipped to customers (this includes cost of inspection, testing and other quality control activities). As preventive measures improve quality, appraisal costs decrease, because fewer resources are needed for quality inspections and the subsequent search for the causes of any problems that are detected.

Internal failure costs result from defects that are discovered during the production of a product or service. When products are found to be defective while in production, they must either be scrapped or repaired. The costs include the cost of producing the items that are scrapped, the cost of repairing, reworking and retesting defective products and all the costs of delays, paperwork, rescheduling and other hassles caused by defective products. Internal failure costs fall into two major cost categories: *(i)* ***yield losses*** which are incurred if a defective item must be scrapped and *(ii)* ***rework costs*** which are incurred if the item is re-routed to correct the defects or if the service must be performed again.

External failure costs arise when a defect is discovered after the customer has received the product or service. These costs include warranty costs, product liability suits or settlements, the cost of product returns or recalls and lost business and customer goodwill.

Encountering defects and correcting them after the product is in the customer's hands is costly. Dissatisfied customers talk about bad product or service to their friends who in turn tell others (word-of-mouth communication). External failure costs erode market share and profits. Defective products can injure and even kill consumers who purchase and use them. Strict product liability laws force companies to pay damages to the affected customers.

A more complete listing of all the above costs is shown in *Box 2.4.*

Box 2.4 : Costs of Quality

Prevention Costs

Quality planning: Costs of preparing an overall plan, numerous specialized plans, quality manuals, procedures.

New- product review: Review or preparation of quality specifications for new products, evaluation of new designs, preparation of tests and experimental programs, evaluation of vendors, marketing studies to determine customers' quality requirements.

Training: Developing and conducting training programs for employees.

Process planning: Design and develop process control devices.

Quality data: Collecting data, analysing data and reporting.

Improvement projects: Planned failure investigations aimed at chronic quality problems.

Appraisal Costs

Incoming materials inspection: The cost of determining quality of incoming raw materials.

Process inspection: All tests, sampling procedures and inspections done while the product is being produced.

Final goods inspection: All inspections or tests conducted on the finished product in the plant or the field.

Quality laboratories: The cost of operating laboratories to inspect materials at all stages of production, cost of calibrating inspection gages and testing instruments.

Internal Failure Costs

Scrap: The cost of labour and material for product which cannot be used or sold.

Rework: The cost of redoing a product which can be made to conform.

Downgrading: Product which must be sold at less than full value due to quality problems.

Retest: Cost of inspection and tests after rework.

Downtime: Idle facilities and people due to quality failures.

External Failure Costs

Warranty: The cost of refunds, repairing or replacing products on warranty.

Returned merchandise: Merchandise which is returned to the seller because of defects.

Complaints: The cost of settling customer complaints due to poor quality.

Allowances: Cost of concessions made to customers due to substandard quality.

Illustration of Computation of Costs of Quality

Given the following cost elements, determine the total percentage in each of the four major quality cost categories for ABC company.

Cost element	Costs (₹)
(i) Incoming materials inspection	₹ 8,000
(ii) Scrap	₹ 30,000
(iii) Quality training	₹ 10,000
(iv) Process inspection	₹ 20,000
(v) Product testing	₹ 5,000

(vi) Customer complaints	₹ 15,000
(vii) Quality audits	₹ 5,000
(viii) Maintenance of tools and gages	₹ 10,000
(ix) Laboratory testing	₹ 2,000
(x) Rework/repair	₹ 50,000
(xi) Quality improvement projects	₹ 20,000
(xii) Calibration of test equipments	₹ 10,000
(xiii) Equipment downtime	₹ 5,000
(xiv) Product returns and replacements	₹ 25,000
(xv) Writing procedures and instructions	₹ 10,000
Total cost	**₹ 2,25,000**

Cost of quality implies the total costs incurred related to the quality of a product or service.

Four categories of quality costs are:

1. Internal failure costs
2. External failure costs
3. Appraisal costs

and

4. Prevention costs.

Solution:

Computations of costs of quality under the categories: *(a)* Prevention costs, *(b)* Appraisal costs, *(c)* Internal failure costs and *(d)* External failure costs are shown below.

(a) Prevention costs

Cost element	Costs (₹)
(i) Quality training	₹ 10,000
(ii) Quality improvement projects	₹ 20,000
(iii) Writing procedures and instructions	₹ 10,000
Total	₹ **40,000**

(b) Appraisal costs

Cost element	Costs (₹)
(i) Incoming materials inspection	₹ 8,000
(ii) Process inspection	₹ 20,000
(iii) Product testing	₹ 5,000
(iv) Quality audits	₹ 5,000
(v) Maintenance of tools and gages	₹ 10,000
(vi) Laboratory testing	₹ 2,000
(vii) Calibration of test equipments	₹ 10,000
Total	₹ **60,000**

(c) Internal failure costs

Cost element	Costs (₹)
(i) Scrap	₹ 30,000
(ii) Rework/repair	₹ 50,000
(iii) Equipment downtime	₹ 5,000
Total	₹ **85,000**

(d) ***External failure costs***

	Cost element	Costs (₹)
(i)	Product returns and replacements	₹ 25,000
(ii)	Customer complaints	₹ 15,000
	Total	₹ **40,000**

Computation of cost of quality as a percentage of total costs

(i) Prevention cost (% ge) $= \frac{40,000}{2,25,000} \times 100 = \mathbf{17.8\%}$

(ii) Appraisal cost (% ge) $= \frac{60,000}{2,25,000} \times 100 = \mathbf{26.7\%}$

(iii) Internal failure cost (% ge) $= \frac{85,000}{2,25,000} \times 100 = \mathbf{37.7\%}$

(iv) External failure cost (% ge) $= \frac{40,000}{2,25,000} \times 100 = \mathbf{17.8\%}$

2.5.2 How To Reduce The Cost Of Quality?

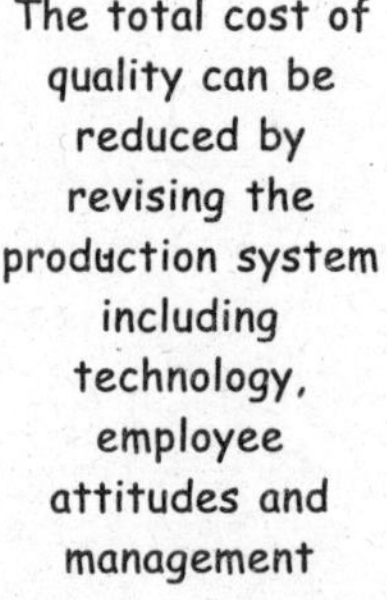

The total cost of quality can be minimised by observing the relationship between cost of quality and the degree of conformance to customer requirements. When the degree of conformance is very high (low defects), the costs of failures are low but the costs of control are quite high. When the degree of conformance is low (high defects), the opposite situation exists. **Thus there is, between the two extremes, an optimal level of conformance where total quality costs are minimised. (*See Exhibit 2.4*)**

It is being recognised now, however, that the optimal point is close to zero defects in many cases. What is in stake is not simply finding the minimum cost point for quality and operating there but constantly reducing the cost of quality. This can be done by revising the production system, including technology, employee attitudes and management. **As a result, the cost of failures and the cost of control are both reduced. This is shown in *Exhibit 2.5.***

Exhibit 2.4 : Costs of Quality

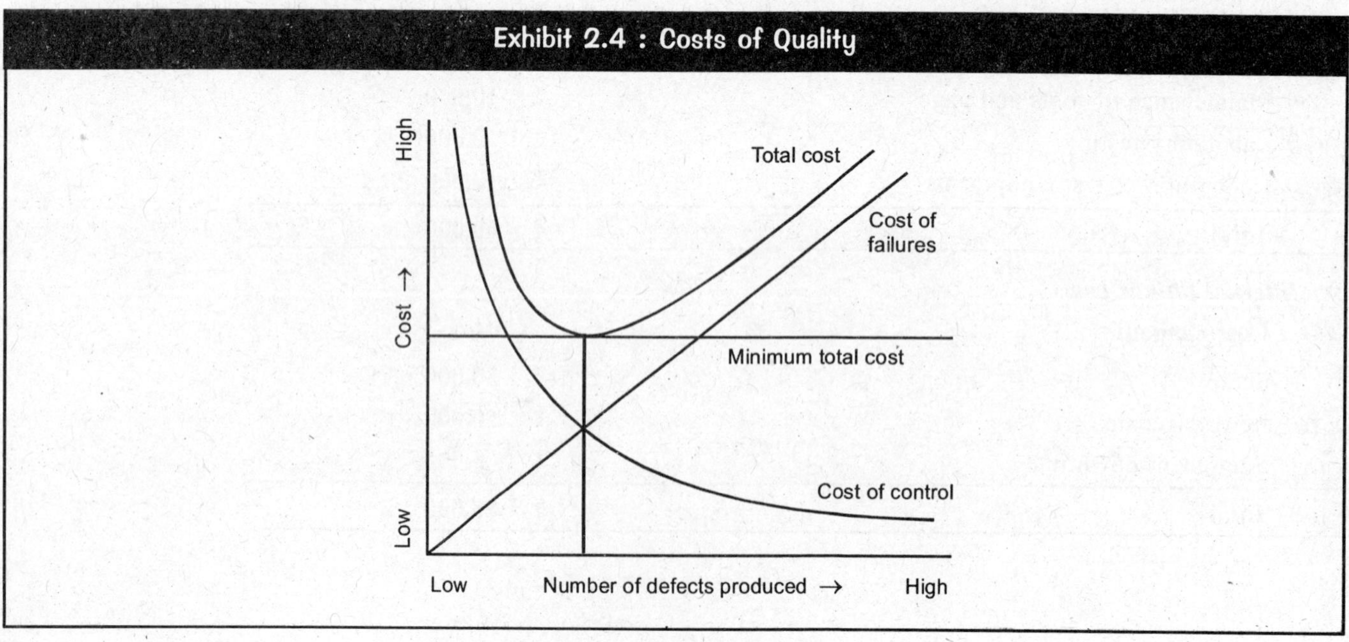

Exhibit 2.5 : Reducing the Cost of Quality

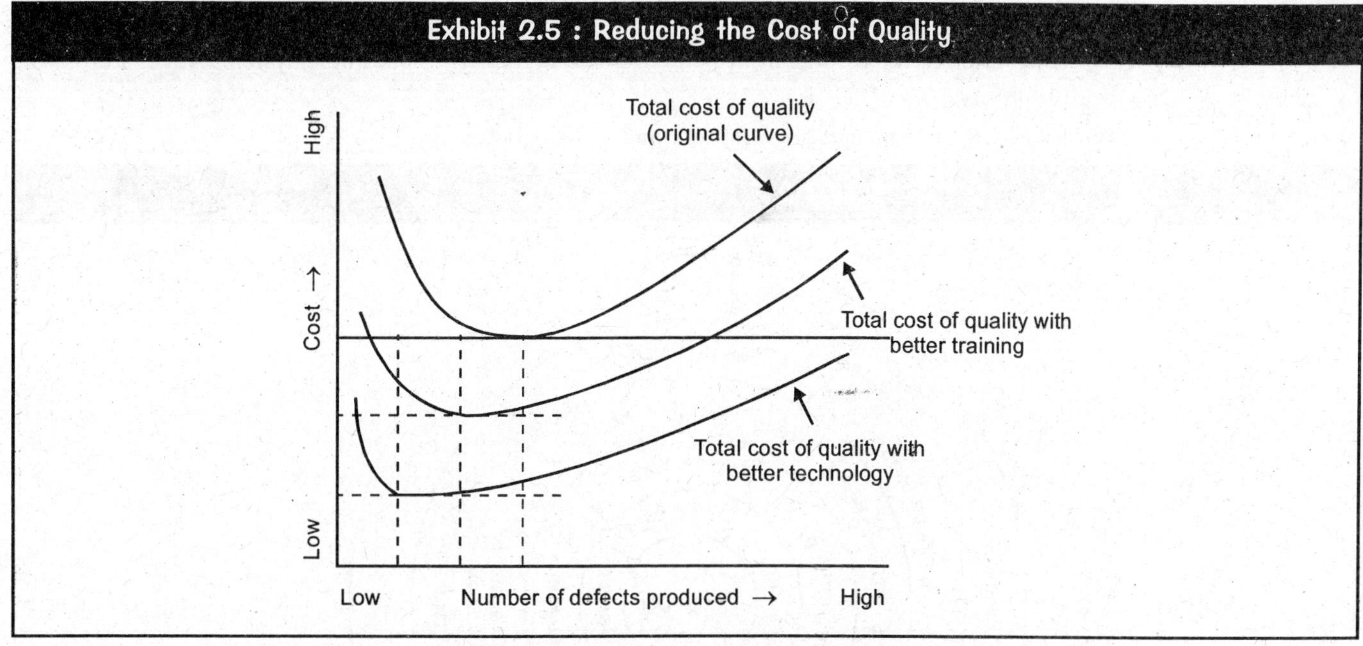

The cost of quality can be a powerful tool for quality improvement if properly used. It focuses management attention on waste due to excess failure or high control costs.

Quality improvement programs can also dramatically increase revenues either through a more consistent product or new products or services that better meet customer needs. Improving customer satisfaction can be a powerful driver of revenue and market share when customers receive a product or service that they really like.

2.6 WHAT IS TOTAL QUALITY MANAGEMENT?

A primary role of management is to lead an organisation in its day-to-day operations as well as to maintain it as a viable entity into the future. Quality has become an important factor to success in this latter strategic responsibility.

In the late 1980s, providing ***customer satisfaction in customer terms*** became a specific goal of business organisation. Providing high quality was recognised as a key element for success. At the end of the twentieth century, business organisations were involved in what has become a quality revolution. It began in Japan and has spread to other parts of the world. It involves an entirely new way of thinking about and dealing with quality that encompasses the entire organisation. This new approach has been given a variety of names *viz.*, ***"Six Sigma"*** at Motorola, ***"Leadership through quality"*** at Xerox, ***"Perfect Design Quality"*** at Intel and ***"Total Quality Control"*** at Hewlett-Packard, but more often referred to as ***"Total Quality Management"***.

"***Total Quality Management*** **(TQM)** is a philosophy that involves everyone in an organisation in a continual effort to improve quality and achieve customer satisfaction." There are two key philosophies in TQM. One is a never-ending push to improve (*i.e.* ***continuous improvement*** or Kaizen in Japanese) and the other is a goal of ***customer satisfaction*** which involves meeting or exceeding customer expectations. ***Exhibit 2.6*** **illustrates the overview of TQM and** ***Box 2.5*** **lists the six basic steps of TQM.**

The salient features of TQM approach are:

(i) Find out what the customers want. Customers include both the ***internal customer*** (the next person in the process) as well as the ***external customer*** (the final customer).

(ii) Design a product or service that will meet or exceed what customers want.

(iii) Design a production process that facilitates ***doing the job right the first time.***

(iv) Keep track of the results and use them to guide improvement in the system. Never stop trying to improve.

(v) Extend these concepts to suppliers and to distributors.

Exhibit 2.6 : Over View of TQM

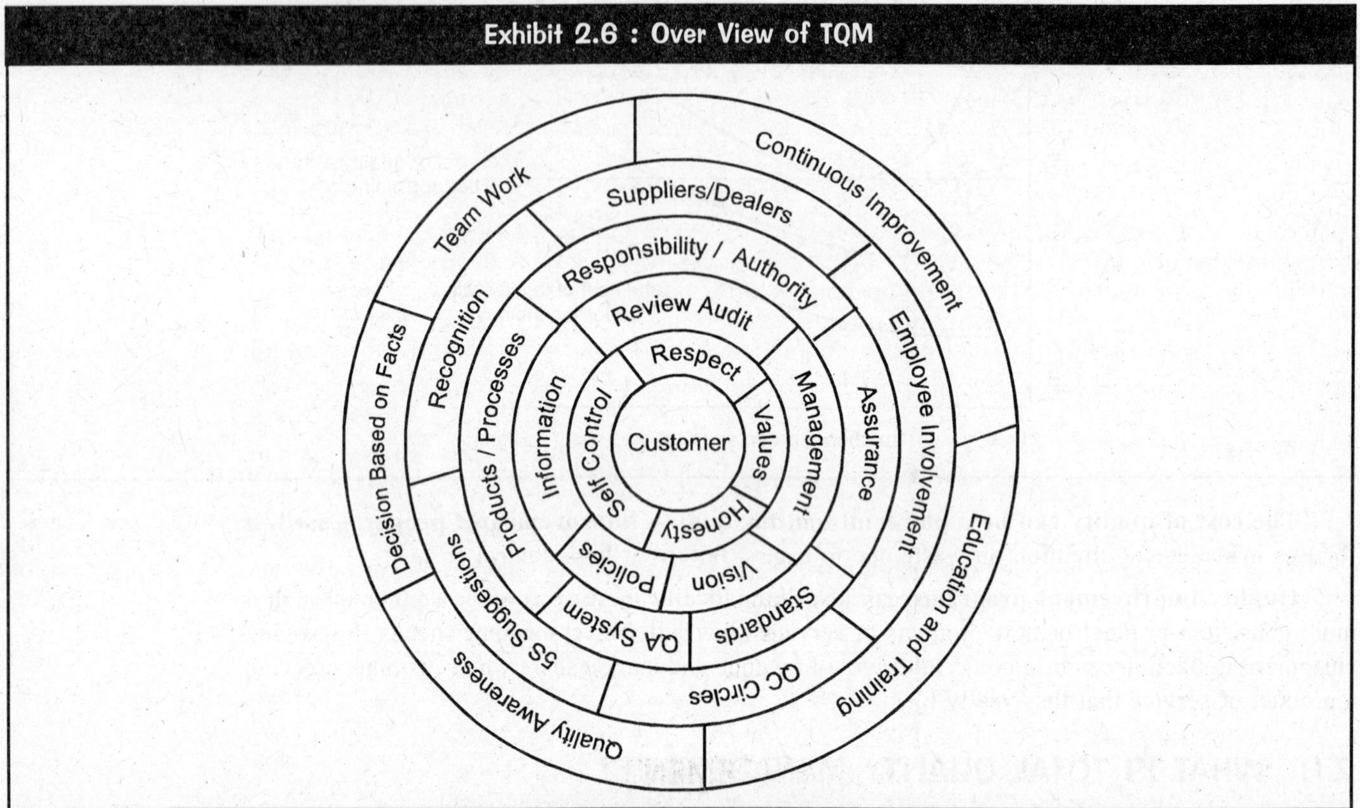

Box 2.5 : Six Basic Concepts of TQM

(i) A committed and involved management to provide long-term top-to-bottom organisational support (Top Management Commitment).

(ii) An unwavering focus on the customer, both internally and externally (Customer focus).

(iii) Effective involvement and utilisation of the entire workforce (Employee involvement).

(iv) Continuous improvement of the business and production process (Continuous improvement).

(v) Treating suppliers as partners (Supplier partnership).

(vi) Establishing performance measures for the processes (Performance measurement).

Box 2.6 **describes what is meant by Total Quality Management.**

Box 2.6 : What is Total Quality Management?

- Intense focus on the customer - both external and internal customers.
- Concern for continuous improvement – quality can always be improved.
- Improvement in the quality of everything the organisation does – not only related to final product, but also to services, response to complaints and the like.
- Accurate measurement of every critical performance variable in the company's operations.
- Empowerment of employees – TQM involves the people on the line in the improvement process. Teams are empowered for finding and solving problems.

2.7 PRINCIPLES OF TQM

***Exhibit 2.7* illustrates the TQM wheel showing three important principles of TQM.**

Exhibit 2.10 : TQM Wheel

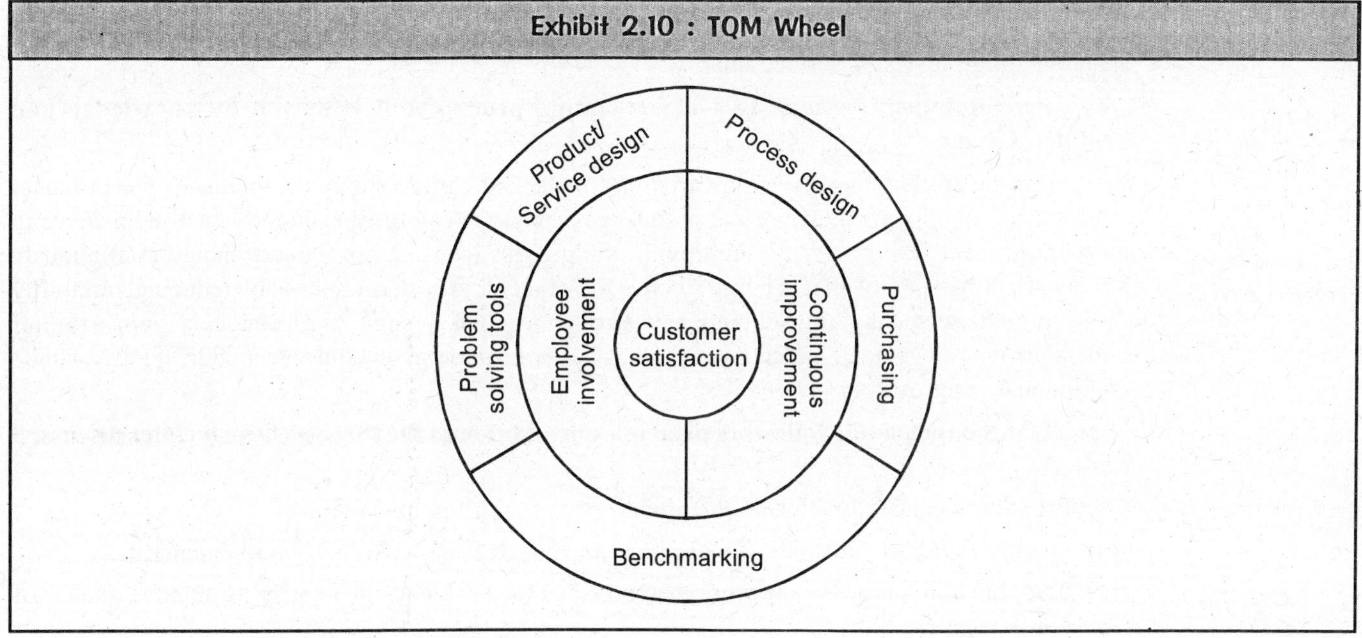

Total quality management stresses on three principles:

(i) Customer satisfaction.

(ii) Employee involvement.

(iii) Continuous improvements in quality.

Three important principles of TQM are : (i) Customer satisfaction (ii) Employee involvement and (iii) Continuous improvement of quality.

Customer satisfaction is a relative concept that varies from one customer to another. Also, a customer may be satisfied with today's products but not satisfied in the future. *For example,* while one customer may consider a Ford automobile perfectly satisfactory, another may not. Each person defines quality in relation to his or her own needs and means at a particular point of time. ***Box 2.7* lists 8 essentials of TQM focus and *Box 2.8* lists the dimension of customer satisfaction.**

Box 2.7 : 8 Essentials of TQM Focus

- Customer satisfaction
- Decision based on facts
- Employee involvement
- Supplier selection and development
- Leadership
- Continuous improvement
- Process approach
- Recognition and reward

Box 2.8 : Dimensions of Customer Satisfaction

- Fitness for use
- After-sales-service and support
- Packaging
- Maintainability
- Customer confidence in the organisation
- Reliability and life of product
- Value for money
- Customer information
- Speed of service (delivery)
- Company image.

Employee involvement in quality management is crucial in achieving and sustaining high levels of quality. Employees may have to be empowered to take preventive and if necessary corrective actions without management approval. Employees must be involved in quality management by encouraging them to use quality control tools and techniques to track performance and identify areas needing improvement. Employee training and motivation are essential for achieving and sustaining high levels of service quality.

Continuous improvement is a never ending process and is driven by knowledge and problem solving

Continuous improvement **is a never ending process and is driven by knowledge and problem solving.**

From the producer's viewpoint, variation from specifications cannot be tolerated. The producer must specify quality attributes of the product or service as carefully as possible and then strive to meet those specifications. While improving the process overtime, producers should continuously strive to improve quality, that is doing a better job of meeting customer needs by reducing variability in all processes and by introducing new products when needed. As producers gain a better understanding of customer expectations and as better technology becomes available, quality can be continuously improved.

TQM is based on the following principles in addition to the three basic principles discussed earlier:

(i) Primary responsibility for product quality rests with top management.

(ii) Quality should be customer-focused and evaluated using customer-based standards.

(iii) The production process and work methods must be designed consciously to achieve quality of conformance.

(iv) Quality cannot be inspected into a product. So make it right the first time.

(v) Quality must be monitored to identify problems quickly and correct quality problems immediately.

(vi) Companies must work with and extend TQM programs to their suppliers to ensure quality inputs.

Box 2.9 **lists seven underlying principles of TQM.**

Box 2.9 : Seven Underlying Principles of TQM

- Strive for quality in all things.
- The customer is the criterion of quality.
- Improve the process or system by which products are produced.
- Quality improvement is continuous, never ending activity.
- Worker involvement is essential.
- Ground decisions and actions on knowledge.
- Encourage team work and cooperation.

Necessity for Total Quality Management

(i) TQM adds value to the services offered to the customers.

(ii) All personnel are involved, which improves motivation and commitment.

(iii) TQM provides assurance that performance and processes are well understood.

(iv) TQM is economic in the long term to both the company and its customers.

Why TQM Programs Fail?

The most common causes for TQM program failures appear to be the following:

(i) Lack of commitment from the top management.

(ii) Focusing on specific techniques rather than on the system.

(iii) Not obtaining employee buy-in and participation.

(iv) Program stops with training.

(v) Expecting immediate results, not a long term pay-off.

(vi) Forcing the organisation to adopt methods that are not productive or compatible with its production system and personnel.

2.8 THE SCOPE OF TOTAL QUALITY MANAGEMENT

The three core principles of total quality namely *(a)* focus on the customer, *(b)* participation and team work and *(c)* continuous improvement and learning are supported and implemented by:

(i) an integrated organisational infrastructure *(ii)* a set of management practice and

(iii) a wide variety of tools and techniques

which all must work together and support each other. **This concept is illustrated in *Exhibit 2.8.***

Exhibit 2.8 : The Scope of Total Quality Management

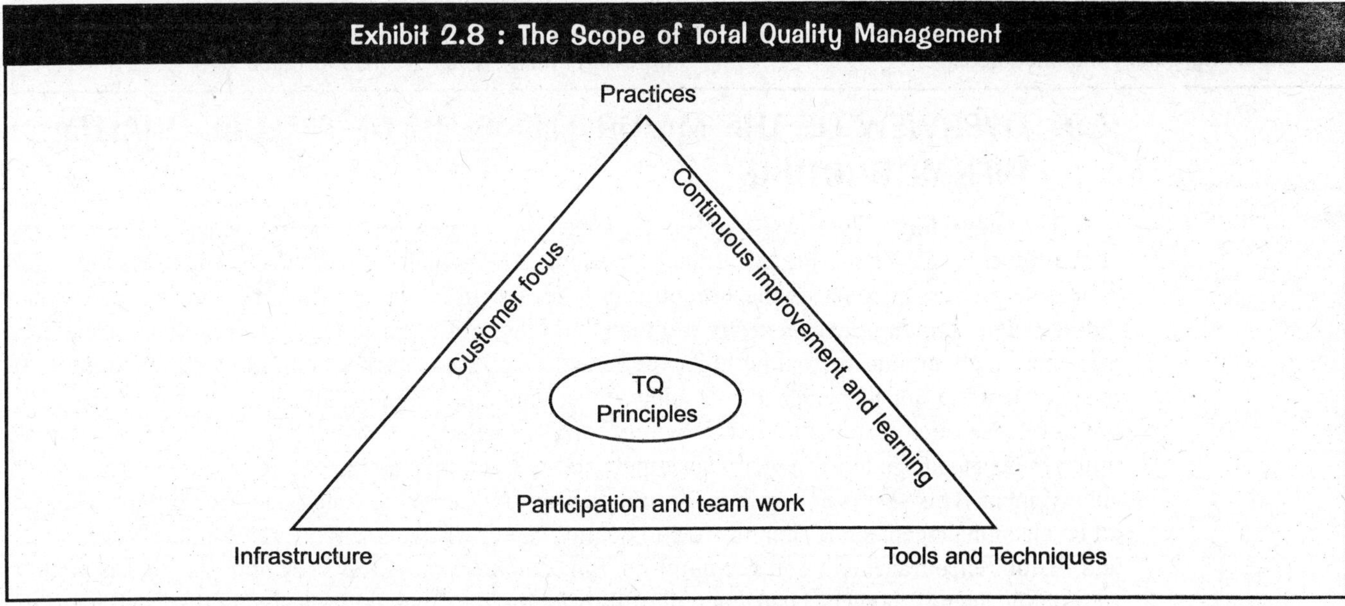

Infrastructure: Infrastructure refers to the basic systems of management that are necessary to function as a high-performing organisation. **The elements of an infrastructure that support the core principles of total quality are:**

(i) leadership *(ii)* strategic planning

(iii) human resource management *(iv)* process management

(v) data and information management

These elements will be discussed in depth in the later chapters.

Successful implementation of TQM requires :
(i) An integrated organisational infrastructure
(ii) A set of management practice and
(iii) A wide variety of tools and techniques.

Practices: Practices are those activities that occur within a management system to achieve high performance objectives. **Examples of activities and the corresponding practices are listed below.**

Activities	Practices
Reviewing company performance	Leadership
Determining employee satisfaction	Human resource management
Co-ordinating design and production/delivery processes to ensure trouble-free introduction and delivery of products and services	Process management

Tools include various graphical and statistical methods to plan work activities, collect data, analyse results, monitor progress and solve problems. *For example,* a chart showing trends in defects in manufacturing as workers progress through a training program is a simple tool to monitor the effectiveness of the training program. ***Box 2.10*** **distinguishes between quality control and total quality management.**

Box 2.10 : Quality Control Versus Total Quality Management

Quality Control	Total Quality Management
• Inspection after production	• Design quality into the product and production system
• Focus on consequences of poor quality	• Focus on identifying and eliminating causes of poor quality
• Customer is purchaser	• Customer is user
• Some number of defects is normal	• Goal is zero defects
• Responsibility for quality control in assigned to individuals or departments	• Quality is the responsibility of everyone
• Improving quality increases cost	• Improving quality typically pays for itself

2.9 OVERVIEW OF THE MAJOR ELEMENTS OF A TOTAL QUALITY INFRASTRUCTURE

Leadership is an essential part of a quality improvement effort

1. Leadership : The success of any organisation depends on the performance of the workers at the lower levels of the organisational structure. All managers, ideally starting with the chief executive officer must act as the organisation's leaders for quality. Their task is to create clear ***quality values*** and ***high expectations*** and then build these into the company's operations strategies. Systems and methods for achieving excellence are created through initiation and support of management. Senior management personnel must personally and regularly involve themselves in the activities such as planning, reviewing company quality performance, serving on quality improvement teams, interacting with customers and recognising and rewarding employees for quality achievement. This serves as a role model for reinforcing the values and encouraging leadership at all levels of management. By committing to quality, senior management provides broad perspectives and vision, encouragement and recognition. *For example,* the CEO of Motorola, placed quality first on the agenda at every board meeting followed by the financial issues and other matters to be discussed. In most TQ-focused companies, the middle level management personnel serve as a quality council to set quality policy, guide the deployment of quality initiatives and review performances whereas the top-management personnel act as leaders to encourage exemplary ethical conduct and good community citizenship.

Strategic business planning drives the quality improvement effort throughout the organisation

2. Strategic Planning : Achieving quality and market leadership is a long-term objective of any company which requires strategic planning to have a long-range view of the future. Some of the basic strategic questions that must be addressed are: *(i)* Who are our customers? *(ii)* What is our mission? *(iii)* What principles do we value? *(iv)* What are our long-range and short-range goals? *(v)* How do we achieve these goals?

Strategic business planning drives the quality improvement throughout the organisation. Strategic planning helps to anticipate many changes, such as customer's expectations, new business opportunities, technological developments, new customer segments, community/societal expectations, evolving regulatory requirements and thrusts by competitors. The plans, strategies and resource allocations need to reflect these commitments and changes.

3. Human Resource Management : Meeting the company's quality and performance goals requires a fully committed, well-trained workforce which is also fully involved. First-line workers need the skill to listen to customers, production workers need specific skills in developing technologies and all employees need to understand how to use data and information to achieve continuous improvement. **To achieve these, the following are essential:**

(i) Appropriate education and training of employees.

(ii) Reward and recognition systems to provide reinforcement and motivation for achieving company objectives.

(iii) Safety, health, well being and high morale of employees to motivate them for continuous improvement.

Human resource management is critical to implementing TQM because of the need to have a fully committed, well trained workforce

Major challenges in the area of employee development include:

(i) The integration of human resource practices such as selection, performance, recognition, training and career advancement.

(ii) The alignment of human resource management with business directions and strategic change processes.

Addressing these challenges requires the use of employee-related data on knowledge, skills, satisfaction, motivation, safety and well-being. Such data need to be tied to indicators of company or work unit performance, such as customer satisfaction, customer retention and productivity.

4. Process Management: A ***process*** is how work creates value for customers. Process management involves the design of processes to develop and deliver products and services that meet the needs of customers and control so that they perform as required and their continued improvement. Well-designed processes lead to better quality products and services and less waste and rework.

Process management involves practices used to implement and improve process effectiveness

Process management activities strongly emphasise on prevention of defects which is best achieved by designing quality into products and services and also into the processes that produce them. Obviously, costs of preventing defects (or problems) at the design stage are much lower than costs of correcting defects (or problems) at the "downstream" stages.

An important aspect of process management is working with suppliers who provide goods and services and the other internal and external partners. By having a partnership with suppliers, an organisation can improve its ability to satisfy customers and boost productivity and quality.

Internal partnerships might include labour-management co-operation, such as agreements with labour unions, or networking relationships among company units to improve flexibility, responsibility and sharing of knowledge and so on. External partnerships might be with customers, educational institutions or research and development organisations. Strategic alliances that blend a company's core competencies with complementary strength and capabilities of partners represent an increasingly important type of external partnership. Managing such partnerships requires an understanding of key requirements for success, regular communication, approaches to evaluating progress and means for adapting to changing conditions-the elements of effective process management.

5. Data and Information Management: Measurement and analysis of performances is necessary to support a variety of activities of modern businesses such as planning, reviewing company performance, improving operations and comparing company quality performance with competitor's performance. Statistical analysis and interpretation of factual data provide the basis for problem solving and continuous improvement. Many types of data and information needed for quality assessment and quality improvement are: *(i)* customer needs, *(ii)* product and service performance, *(iii)* operations performance, *(iv)* market assessments, *(v)* competitive comparisons, *(vi)* supplier performance, *(vii)* employee performance, *(viii)* cost and financial performance.

Many types of data and information are needed for quality assessment and quality improvement

The measures and indicators used should best represent the factors that lead to improved customer, operational and financial performance. The data and information must be analysed to support evaluation and decision making at all levels of management within the company.

Exhibit 2.9 **illustrates the elements of Total Quality Management.**

2.10 TOTAL QUALITY MANAGEMENT VS TRADITIONAL MANAGEMENT PRACTICES

TQM practice differs from traditional management practices in several ways. The key differences are described in *Box 2.11*.

Exhibit 2.9 : Elements of Total Quality Management

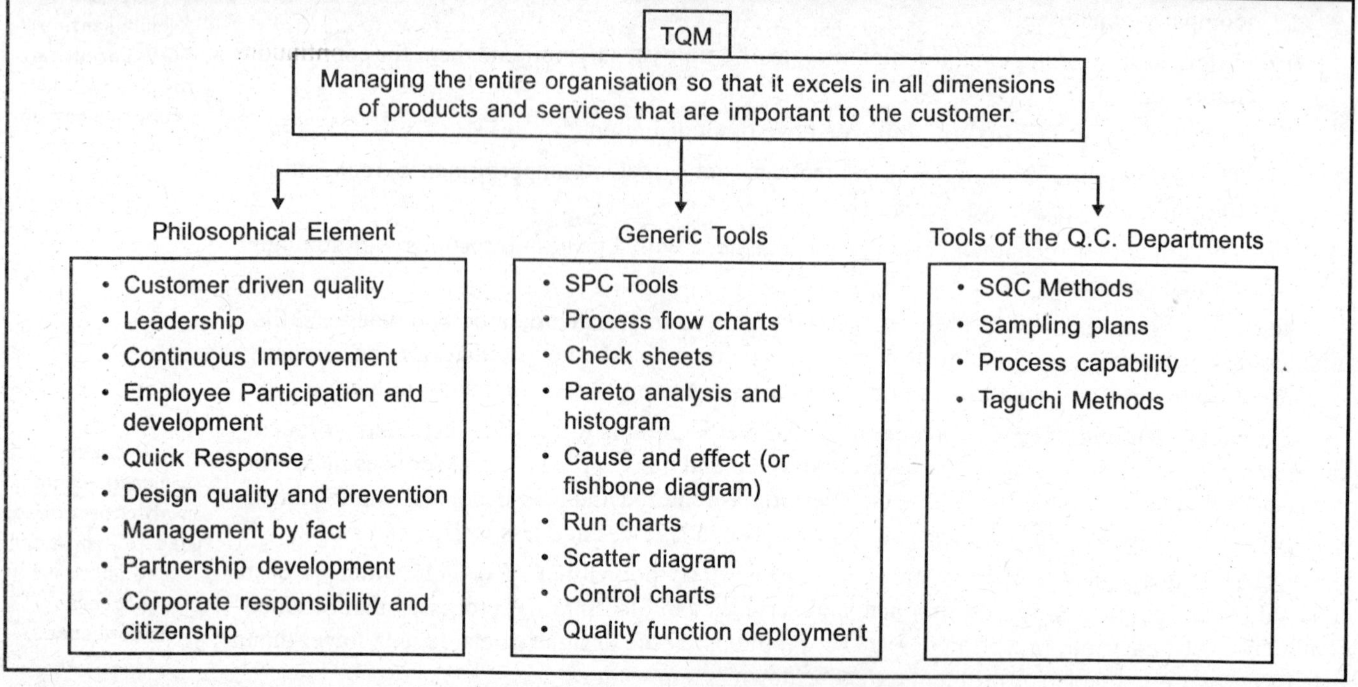

TQM

Managing the entire organisation so that it excels in all dimensions of products and services that are important to the customer.

Philosophical Element

- Customer driven quality
- Leadership
- Continuous Improvement
- Employee Participation and development
- Quick Response
- Design quality and prevention
- Management by fact
- Partnership development
- Corporate responsibility and citizenship

Generic Tools

- SPC Tools
- Process flow charts
- Check sheets
- Pareto analysis and histogram
- Cause and effect (or fishbone diagram)
- Run charts
- Scatter diagram
- Control charts
- Quality function deployment

Tools of the Q.C. Departments

- SQC Methods
- Sampling plans
- Process capability
- Taguchi Methods

Box 2.11 : Differences between Traditional Management and TQM Practice

Criteria	*Traditional management practice*	*TQ management practice*
1. Organisational structures	Views an enterprise as a group of separate, highly specialised individual performers and units, linked within a functional hierarchy	Views the enterprise as a *system* of interdependent processes, linked laterally, over time, through a network of collaborating (internal and external) suppliers and customers
2. Role of people	Views people as a commodity, virtually interchangeable and to be developed based on the perceived need of the organisation. People are passive contributors with little autonomy.	Views people as the organisation's true competitive edge. Leadership provides people with opportunities for personal growth and development. People are active contributors, valued for their creativity and intelligence.
3. Definition of quality\	Quality is the adherence to internal specifications and standards (*i.e.* absence of defects). Inspection is required to control defects. Innovation is not required.	Quality is defined as products and services that go beyond the present needs and expectations of customers. Innovation is required.
4. Goals and objectives	People do not co-operate unless it serves their own or their unit's best interests. They compete among themselves.	Self-interest and the greater good are served simultaneously by serving one's customers. Cooperation takes the place of competition.
5. Knowledge	Quality embodies knowledge applicable only to manufacturing and engineering.	Quality embodies knowledge applicable to all the disciplines of the organisation.
6. Management systems	Managers oversee departments or functions and groups of individuals. Quality problems occur when individual people or departments do not do their best.	Managers oversee interdependent systems and processes and exercise managerial leadership through participative management. Quality results from the organi-sation's systems and individuals working together.
7. Management's role	Management is reluctant to change its success formula. Maintains status-quo by preventing change.	Environment in which the organi-sation interacts constantly changes. Management provides leadership for continual improvement and innovation in processes and systems, products and services.

8. Union management relations	Adverse relationship between union and management is inevitable. Traditional issues such as wages, health and safety are negotiated and not issues such as quality, cost and productivity.	Union becomes a partner and a stake holder in the success of the organisation. Unlimited potential for partnership in the areas of employee education, training and meaningful involvement of employees in process improvement.
9. Teamwork	Hierarchical organisation structures promote identification with functions and tend to create competition, conflict and adverse relation between functions.	Formal and informal mechanisms encourage and facilitate team work and team development across the entire organisation.
10. Supplier relationships	Suppliers are pilted against each other to obtain the lowest price. Customer company encourages competition among its suppliers.	Suppliers are partners with their customers. Partnership aims to encourage innovation, lower costs and improves quality. Reducing the number of suppliers and establishing long-term relationships helps to achieve this aim.
11. Control	Control is achieved by preestablished inflexible responsive patterns laid down as per rules and procedures. Behaviour of employees is prescribed by the rule "book".	Control results from shared values and beliefs, as well as knowledge of mission, purpose and customer requirements.
12. Customers	Customers are always outsiders to the organisation and are within the domain of marketing and sales.	Every one inside the organisation is a customer of an internal or external supplier.
13. Responsibility	The manager's job is to do the subordinates' planning and inspect the work to make sure the plans are executed. Manager is a director.	The manager's job is to manage his or her own process and relationships with others and give subordinates the capability to manage their own processes through empowerment. Manager is a facilitator rather than a director.
14. Motivation	Motivation is achieved by aversive control. People are motivated to work to avoid failure and punishment.	Managers provide leadership rather than intervening in the processes of their subordinates. Subordinates are viewed as process managers rather than functional specialists.
15. Competition	Competition is inevitable and inherent in human nature.	Competitive behaviour seeks to improve the methods of pleasing the customer, eliminating waste of resources and the like.

Total Quality demands new styles of managing and an entirely new set of skills. These new styles include the following characteristics:

Total Quality demands new styles of managing and an entirely new set of skills

- Thinking in terms of systems
- Defining customer requirements
- Planning for quality improvement with each customer
- Dealing with customer dissatisfaction
- Ensuring ongoing quality efforts
- Developing a life-long learning style
- Team building
- Encouraging openness
- Creating climates of trust and eliminating fear
- Listening and providing feedback
- Leading and participating in group meetings
- Solving problems with data
- Clarifying goals and resolving conflicts
- Delegating and coaching
- Implementing change
- Making continuous improvement a way of life

2.11 BENEFITS OF TQM

TQM refers to total quality in fulfilling the needs of the customers, the quality of the products and the qualify of life both at the work place and at home. These focuses lead to better business results and also benefit businesses in many ways. **Some of the major benefits of TQM are :**

1. **Creates a good corporate culture :** Total quality management approach has the customer at the focal point of the business rather than the department. Quality has become a strategic business entity to meet global competition. The TQM philosophy revolves around developing a corporate culture that advocates total commitment to customer satisfaction through continuous improvement.
2. **Better reviews from customers :** TQM establishes quality assurance procedures to ensure that products and services of the company will consistently meet the requirements of the customers. As a result, the customers will develop long-term relationship with the company, show less price sensitivity to the company's products and services and recommend the same to others. Customer satisfaction and high performance results lead to high reviews in the media which further enhances the company image and performance.
3. **Better performance from employees :** TQM approach views employees as internal and strives to meet their needs also. Employee training programs can boost employee morale at the workplace and motivate them to work harder to achieve the company goals.

Benefits of TQM are listed in *Box 2.12.*

Box 2.12 : Benefits of TQM

Tangible benefits	Intangible benefits
• Better product quality	• Effective team work
• Productivity improvement	• Enhancement of job interest
• Reduced quality costs	• Improvement in human relation and work area morale
• Increased market	• Participation culture
• Increased profitability	• Customer satisfaction
• Reduced employee grievances	• Enhanced problem solving capacity
	• Improved corporate health and character of the company
	• Better company image.

TQM Increases Competitiveness

TQM efforts make an organisation more competitive. Two pathways through which improved quality enhances a company's profitability are *(i)* market-route benefits and *(ii)* cost-route benefits. This is illustrated in *Exhibit 2.10.*

Exhibit 2.10 : Competitive benefits of TQM

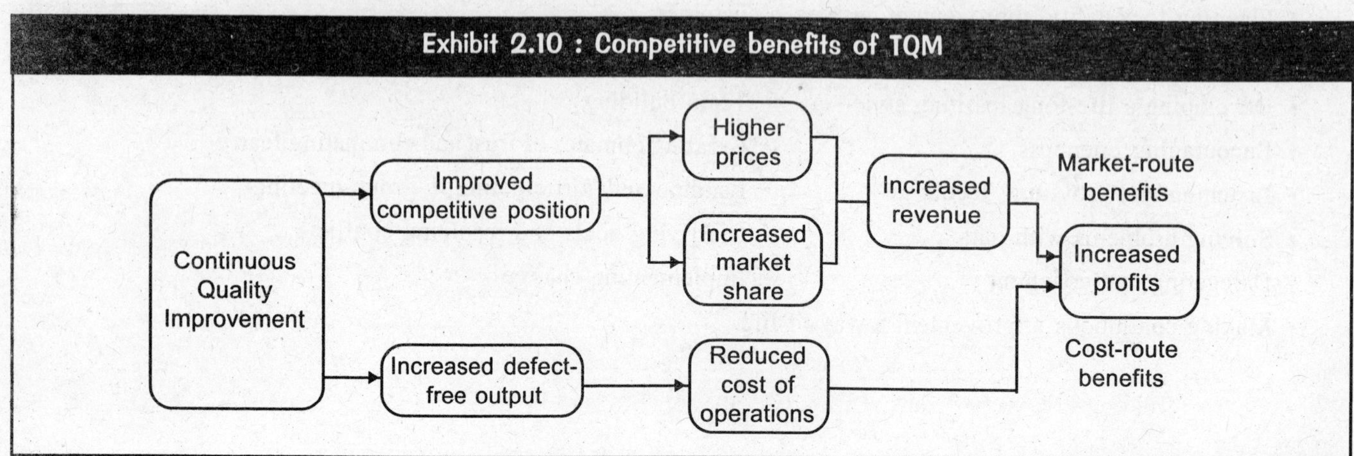

Market-route benefits begin when improved quality increases the products' value in the eyes of customers. The provider (manufacturer or seller) may raise prices or by holding prices steady, realise a gain in market share and revenue increases in either case. Cost-route benefits accrue because increased defect-free output cuts operating costs per unit and lower costs also enhance profits.

TQM efforts make an organisation more competitive.

TQM Imporves Profitability

Improvement in quality helps firms increase market share and reduce costs both of which can increase profitability. Increase in market share often occurs as firms speed response, lower selling prices as a result of economies of scale and improve their reputation for quality products. *Similarly,* improved quality allows costs to drop as firms increase productivity and lower costs of rework, scrap and warranty.

***Exhibit 2.11* shows the ways quality improves profitability.**

Exhibit 2.11 : Ways Quality Improves Profitability

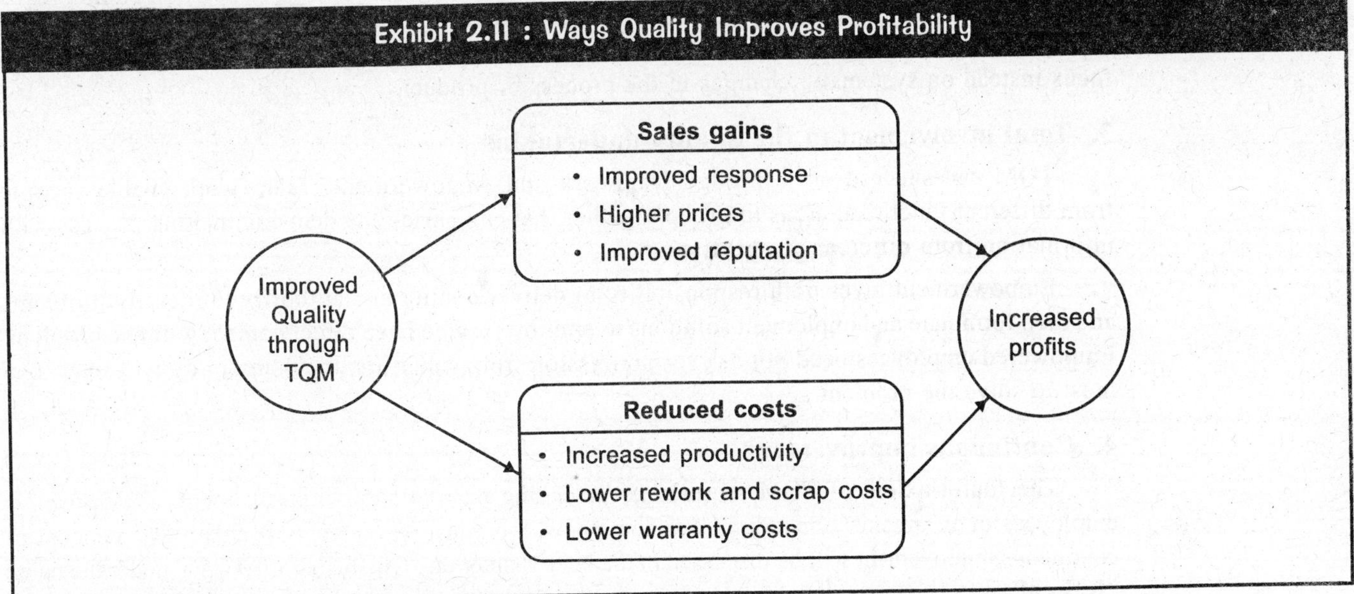

2.12 MAJOR AXIOMS OF TQM

TQM is described by Logothetis as "a culture, inherent in this culture is a total commitment to quality and attitude expressed by everybody's involvement in the process of continuous improvements of products and services, through the use of innovative scientific methods". **This definition highlights four major TQM axioms illustrated in *Exhibit 2.12*.**

Exhibit 2.12 : Major Axioms of TQM

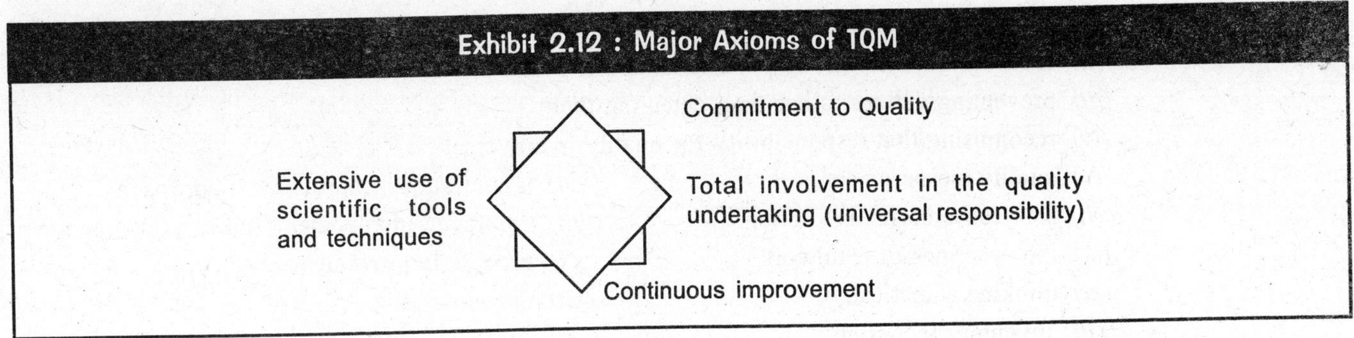

Four axioms of TQM are:
1. Commitment to quality
2. Extensive use of scientific tools and technologies
3. Total involvement in the quality undertaking and
4. Continuous improvement.

These axioms are briefly discussed below:

1. Commitment to Quality

Successful TQM requires:

(i) everyone in the organisation must make a ***commitment to producing quality products.***

(ii) organisation members must make a ***commitment to customers*** (both internal and external customers).

(iii) ***a commitment by top management*** to support the organisation's move towards TQM and allocate resources to that move.

(iv) ***a commitment of the firm as a whole.*** For TQM to work, everyone who contributes to a firm's product, including employees, managers and suppliers must accept quality as a critical component.

2. Extensive use of Scientific tools, Technologies and Methods

Total quality management requires an organisation to replace subjective procedures and rules with powerful statistical tools. These tools can help to identify and ignore random variations to focus instead on systematic changes in the process or product.

3. Total involvement in the quality undertaking

TQM can succeed only through teamwork and empowerment. Team work enables people from different functional areas to group together that can enrich the decision making process with information from different perspectives.

Empowerment gives both responsibility to deliver quality and authority to identify problems and then formulate and implement solutions to employees who have direct contact with the problem. Empowered employees need not ask for permission from superiors, they simply do whatever they must to solve the problem.

4. Continuous improvement

The fourth axiom of TQM requires never ending or continuous improvement. TQM inspires employees of an organisation to improve something everyday, no matter how small. The concept of continuous improvement will be discussed in the later chapter on "Organising for TQM" under the name **"Kaizen"**.

2.13 ELEMENTS OF TOTAL QUALITY MANAGEMENT CONCEPT

The TQM concept supports the philosophies of ***customer focus, continuous improvement, defect prevention and a recognition that responsibility for quality is shared by all employees of an organisation.***

The basic elements of TQM concept are:

(i) sustained management commitment to quality

(ii) focusing on customer requirements and expectations

(iii) preventing defects rather than detecting them

(iv) recognising that responsibility for quality is universal

(v) quality measurement

(vi) a continuous improvement approach

(vii) root cause corrective action

(viii) employee involvement and empowerment

(ix) the synergies of teamwork

(x) process improvement

(xi) thinking statistically

(xii) benchmarking

(xiii) inventory reduction

(xiv) value improvement

(xv) supplier teaming

(xvi) employee training

Exhibit 2.13 **shows the basic elements of TQM concept.**

Exhibit 2.13 : Elements of TQM Concept

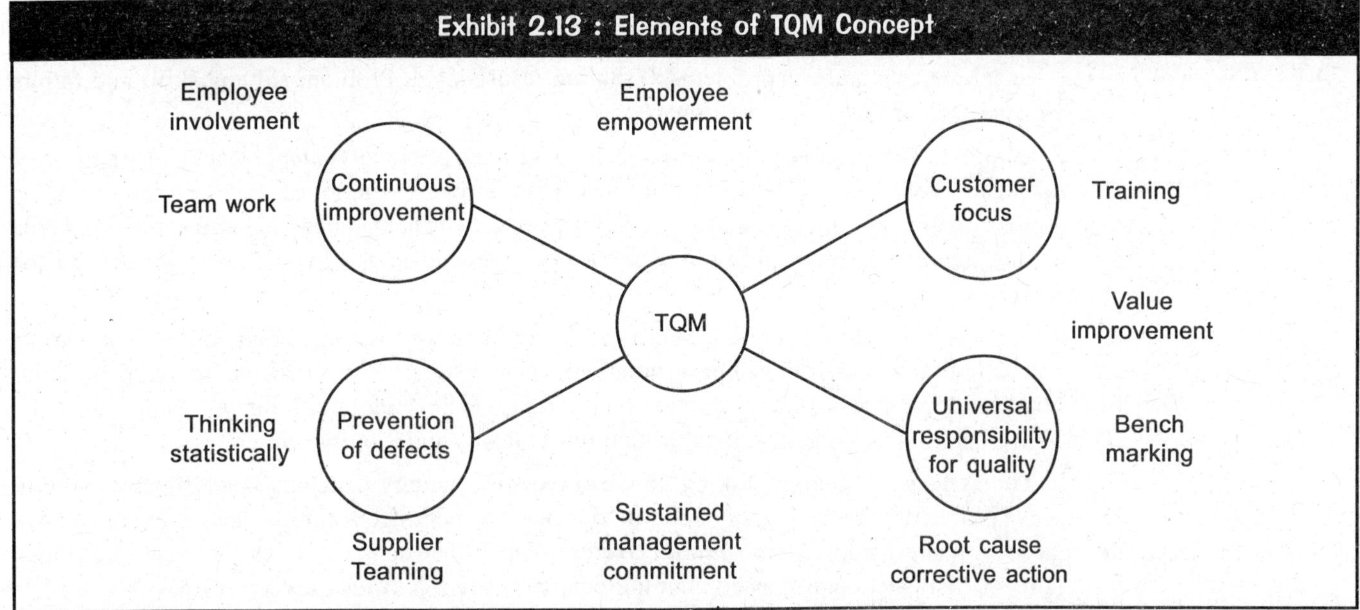

A brief overview of the key TQM concepts is given in the following paragraphs:

1. Sustained management commitment to quality: If an organisation is serious about implementing TQM, the commitment to do so has to start at the top management level. Top management commitment and involvement in implementing TQM is very crucial for the success. Top management gets involved in setting business strategies based on using product quality as a competitive weapon to capture the global market share and rewarding employees for achieving excellence in product quality.

The major basic elements of TQM concept are:

1. Top management commitment to quality
2. Focusing on customer
3. Prevention of defects
4. Universal responsibility
5. Quality measurement
6. Continuous improvement
7. Employee involvement and empowerment
8. Team work
9. Process improvement and
10. Benchmarking

2. Focusing on the customer: Customer's needs and expectations drive the TQM system. The characteristics that customers value more are built into products from design to after-sales service.

3. Preventing rather than detecting defects: TQM prevents poor quality products or services rather than simply to detect and sort out defects. ***"Prevention rather than detection"*** is a very strong single characteristic of TQM. Some of the techniques of TQM which aim at defect prevention rather than defect detection are: statistical process control, continuous process improvement, **Taguchi design of experiments**, problem solving and system failure analysis, which will be discussed in later chapters.

4. Universal responsibility for quality: Another basic TQM precept is that the responsibility for quality is not restricted to only the quality assurance department, but is the guiding philosophy started by every one in the organisation. The traditional thinking was that inspection (or detection rather than prevention) is necessary to ensure quality of products, thereby installing a deep belief in people who actually manufacture the products that they are no longer responsible for the quality of their output. In TQM approach, everyone takes responsibility for quality. As quality improves, the inspection activity reduces and the quality assurance department gets smaller and ultimately may disappear.

5. Quality measurement: The quality measurement aspect of TQM asks the questions: Where are we and where are we going? Quality is a measurable entity and we need to know what the current quality levels are (Where are we?) and what quality levels we aspire to (Where we are going?).

6. Continuous improvement: TQM involves a never-ending process of continuous improvement that covers people, equipment, suppliers, materials and procedures. The basis of the philosophy is that every aspect of an operation can be improved. The Japanese use the word **"Kaizen"** to describe the **ongoing process of unending improvement**-the setting and achieving of ever-higher goals. In US, TQM, **zero defects** and **six-sigma** are used to describe such efforts.

7. Root cause corrective action: TQM seeks to prevent repetition of problems which were thought to have been corrected by identifying the root causes of problems and by implementing corrective actions that address problems at the root cause level. Problem-solving skills and failure analysis approach are useful in this regard.

8. Employee involvement and empowerment: Employee involvement means every employee is involved in every step of the production process and every employee plays an active role in helping the organisation meet its goals. Employee empowerment means enlarging the employee jobs so that the added responsibility and authority is moved to the lowest level possible in the organisation.

Techniques for building employee empowerment include *(i)* building communication networks that include employees, *(ii)* developing open, supportive supervisors, *(iii)* moving responsibility from both managers and staff to production employees, *(iv)* building high-morale organisations and *(v)* creating such formal organisational structures as teams and quality circles.

9. The synergy of teams: Taking advantage of the synergy of teams is an effective way to address the problems and challenges of continuous improvement. Dr. Kaoru Ishikawa first developed the concept of teams by developing ***quality circles*** in Japan. The concept of quality circles developed into more sophisticated and focused teaming concept known as ***focus teams*** in USA.

10. Thinking statistically: Statistical methods or techniques are useful for reducing process or product design variations for improving quality. Statistical process control (SPC) using charts for control of ongoing processes and Taguchi concepts for variability reduction are used for achieving continuous improvement. These will be discussed in later chapters.

11. Benchmarking: Benchmarking involves selecting a demonstrated standard of performance that represents the very best performance for a process or activity.

The steps for developing benchmarks are:

(i) Determine what to benchmark

(ii) Form a benchmark team

(iii) Identify benchmarking partners

(iv) Collect and analyse benchmarking information and

(v) Take action to match or exceed the benchmark.

Benchmarking will be discussed in detail in a later chapter.

The philosophy behind JIT is one of continuous improvement and enforced problem solving.

12. Inventory reduction through Just-in-time production and procurement: The philosophy behind JIT is one of continuous improvement and enforced problem solving. JIT systems are designed to produce or deliver goods just as they are needed. JIT reduces the amount of inventory that a firm has on hand by establishing quality and purchasing controls that bring inventory to the firm just-in-time for use. **JIT is related to quality in three ways:**

(i) JIT cuts the cost of quality by cutting the cost of scrap, rework, inventory carrying cost and damage costs.

(ii) JIT improves quality. It creates an early warning system for quality problems both within the firm and with vendors.

(iii) Better quality means less inventory and a better, easier to employ JIT system. If consistent quality exists, JIT allows firms to reduce all the costs associated with inventory.

JIT production will be discussed in detail in a later chapter.

13. Value improvement: The essence of value improvement is the ability to meet or exceed customer expectations while removing unnecessary costs. TQM removes unnecessary costs while simultaneously customer expectations and requirements are satisfied. However, simply cutting cost without satisfying the customers will not result in value improvement.

14. Supplier teaming: TQM aims at developing long-term relationships with a few high quality suppliers rather than simply selecting those suppliers who supply at lowest cost.

15. Training: People have to be trained to use the TQM concepts and technologies. Employees are empowered by providing the tools necessary for continuous improvement Training is the most basic tool for this. ***Exhibit 2.14* illustrates a model for total quality.**

Exhibit 2.14 : A Model for Total Quality

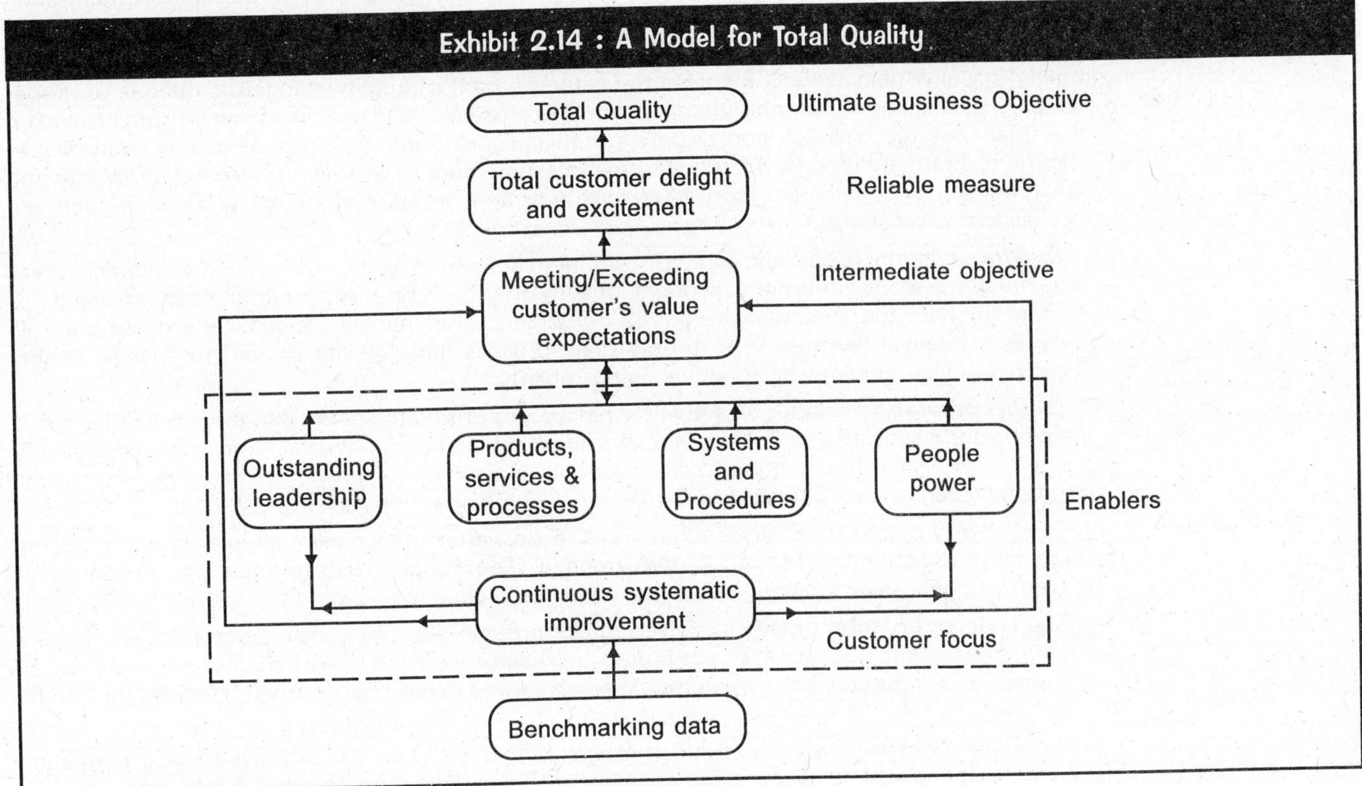

2.14 QUALITY IN PRACTICE

Box 2.13 : Robust Quality at Mazda

Ford Motor Company which controlled the Japanese-based Mazda Company, asked Mazda to build transmissions for one of Ford's models sold in the United States. Although the transmission built by Mazda were identical in specification to those built by Ford, the Ford transmissions produced higher rates of malfunction and customer complaints. Consequently Ford incurred increased levels of warranty costs.

To correct the situation, Ford carried out investigation by comparing samples of transmissions from both companies. Ford found that although its own transmissions fell within a preset range of acceptability on a zero defect standard, the Mazda samples were more exact, with little, if any variation from the design specification. In some Ford transmission, many components fell near the outer limits of tolerance from the target. When randomly assembled together, a series of deviations tended to "stack up". Otherwise, trivial variation in one point compounded variations in others. Because of deviations, parts interacted with greater friction than they could withstand individually or with greater vibration than customers were prepared to tolerate.

Further investigations also indicated that *creative management* played a part in Mazda's more reliable transmissions. Mazda management aimed at manufacturing products that consistently met target values. Mazda became the first Japanese automaker to receive ISO 9002 certification.

2.15 SUMMARY

Quality management in production systems focus primarily on technical issues such as equipment reliability, measurement of defects and statistical quality control techniques (process control). But today quality management has penetrated into other areas such as product design, research and development, human resources practices (employee empowerment) team work and organisational culture and the like. Quality management pervades through the entire organisation (company wide quality control).

Quality control refers to all those functions or activities that must be performed to fulfil the company's quality objectives. It involves the establishment of quality standards, the use of proper materials, the selection of appropriate manufacturing processes and necessary tooling and inspection of the final product to check conformance with specifications. Benefits of quality control are: *(i)* minimum scrap and rework, *(ii)* reduced material and labour costs, *(iii)* uniformity of quality and reliability of products, *(iv)* increased sales turn over and profits, *(iv)* higher productivity and *(vi)* higher customer satisfaction.

Quality at source is an important concept in quality control which puts the production worker in the driver's seat in controlling product quality, thereby completely eliminating the need for inspectors to check the quality of the output of workers. This involves "statistical process control" techniques to control the quality of the on-going process and "quality circles" to analyse quality problems and ensure teamwork to solve such problems.

Quality assurance includes all activities that are performed to ensure that the product performs to the customer's satisfaction. Some of the activities included in quality assurance are: *(i)* Reliability Engineering, *(ii)* Value Engineering, *(iii)* Evaluation of usability of products, *(iv)* Process control, *(v)* Product screening, *(vi)* Service assurance and *(vii)* Quality feed-back.

Quality improvement means finding ways to do better than quality standards and breaking through to unprecedented levels of performance. The "quality action cycle" or the cycle of improvement consists of "design - discover - improve" sequence.

The concept of **"total quality"** evolved in US in the 1970s and consists of a people focussed management system that aims at continued increase in customer satisfaction. It involves all employees, executives and top management personnel and extend backward and forward to include the supply chain and the customer chain.

Total quality control which is the previous step to TQM is an effective system for integrating the quality development, quality maintenance and quality improvement efforts of the various groups in an organisation to achieve highest productivity and customer satisfaction. The core principles of total quality are: *(i)* A focus on the customer, *(ii)* Participation and team work and *(iii)* Continuous improvement and learning.

Total quality management (TQM) denotes the system of managing for total quality. TQM is a total, companywide effort through full involvement of the entire workforce with a focus on continuous improvement to achieve maximum possible customer satisfaction.

These principles of total quality need to become an essential part of the organisation's culture and the strategies and leadership philosophies of the organisation must reflect these principles: *(i)* customer orientation (both internal and external customer), *(ii)* Product or service design that will meet or exceed what customers want, *(iii)* Doing the job right the first time, *(iv)* Use feed-back information to takeup improvement projects, *(v)* Never stop trying to improve (continuous improvement) and *(vi)* Extension of TQM concepts to suppliers and distributors.

2.16 KEY WORDS USED

Quality Planning, Quality Control, Quality Improvement, Quality Cycle, Poka-Yoke, Cost of Quality, Reliability, Quality-at-Source, Company-Wide Quality Control (CWQC), Quality Assurance, Quality Action Cycle, Total Quality, Customer Focus, Participation and Team Work, Employee Involvement and Empowerment, Quality Circle, Team Work, Quality Network, Continuous Improvement, Total Quality Control, Total Quality Management, Customer Satisfaction, Leadership, Strategic Planning, Human Resource Management, Process Management, Data and Information Management, Quality Measurement, Benchmarking, Value Improvement, Supplier Teaming.

2.17 OBJECTIVE QUESTIONS

(A) Match the following:

Column A	Column B
1. W. Edward Deming	1. Quality circles
2. Philip. B. Crosby	2. Quality trilogy
3. Kaoru Ishikawa	3. Zero defects
4. Joseph. M. Juran	4. Robust design
5. Genichi Taguchi	5. Continuous improvement

(B) State whether the following statements are True or False:

1. 'Poka-Yoke' or mistake proofing was developed by Shigeo Shingo. (T / F)
2. "Total quality control" and "company-wide quality control" are totally different approaches in TQM. (T / F)
3. "Quality action cycle" is also referred to as "cycle of improvement". (T / F)
4. "Total quality control" and "Total quality management" are one and the same. (T / F)
5. Continuous improvement is known as "kaizen" in Japanese language. (T / F)

(C) Multiple choice Questions: Choose the correct answer from the alternatives given under each question:

1. Process inspection is associated with _____ costs:
   (a) Prevention costs (b) Appraisal costs
   (c) Internal failure costs and (d) External failure costs.
2. Quality manual of a TQ organisation covers the following areas
   (a) Quality planning (b) Training of personnel
   (c) Quality appraisal methodology (d) All of these areas
   (e) None of these areas.
3. The core principles of total quality are:
   (a) Customer focus (b) Participation and teamwork
   (c) Employee involvement and empowerment
   (d) Continuous improvement (e) All of these mentioned at (a), (b) and (c)
4. Quality control involves:
   (a) Setting quality targets (b) Appraisal of conformance
   (c) Correcting the defects (d) Planning for quality improvement
   (e) All of these activities.

2.18 REVIEW QUESTIONS

1. What is meant by "quality management"?
2. Discuss the differences between traditional quality management and modern quality management.
3. Distinguish between "quality of design" and "quality of conformance".
4. Briefly explain the activities involved in
   (a) Quality planning, *(b)* Quality control and *(c)* Quality improvement.
5. "Quality and financial performance are intimately related." Elaborate.
6. Describe the four major categories of costs associated with quality management.
7. Explain how "costs of quality" can be reduced.
8. Why some quality improvement efforts fail? Give reasons.
9. Explain the difference between quality in manufacturing and quality in services with reference to the quality systems existing in manufacturing and service organisations.

10. What is meant by "quality improvement"?
11. Define the term "Total quality management".
12. State the principles of TQM.
13. Discuss the salient features of TQM approach.
14. What is "TQM wheel"? Explain.
15. Why TQM is necessary? Why TQM programs fail? Give reasons.
16. Discuss the scope of Total Quality Management practices.
17. Explain briefly the benefits an organisation can achieve by implementing TQM.
18. What is meant by "major axioms of TQM"? Explain.
19. Explain briefly the basic elements of TQM concept.
20. Describe the major elements of a total quality infrastructure.

2.19 DISCUSSION QUESTIONS

1. Why is customer focus a critical element of total quality?
2. Give examples of a product or service which you did not purchase because it lacked "dissatisfiers". Also give an example of a product or service in which you received some "exciters/ delighters" that you did not expect.
3. Discuss how lack of top management leadership in a quality effort hinder or destroy it.
4. Discuss some possible ways in which vertical, horizontal and interorganisational team work can be applied at a college or university.
5. Describe the various areas within an organisation in which continuous improvement and learning may take place.

2.20 ASSIGNMENTS

1. Visit a medium or large scale private or public sector industry and prepare a report about the implementation of TQM in that organisation.
2. Visit a service organisation such as a multispeciality hospital or an educational institution and examine the various costs of quality incurred by that organisation and submit a report.

2.21 CHAPTER CASE

CHRYSLER'S TRANSMISSION PROBLEM

Chrysler pioneered its immensely popular mini van in 1984, which quickly became the best selling product the company had ever built. Within five years, Chrysler held more than 50 percent of the market share for mini vans. In 1989 Chrysler offered a new automatic transmission as an option in some of its top models of mini vans and luxury automobiles. The new transmission immediately ran into trouble when many customers reported serious problems.

Claiming that it had made improvement to reduce the initial problem, Chrysler continued to use the transmission. Mean while the Centre for Auto Safety, a consumer group that monitors the auto industry charged that Chrysler had not tested the transmission before introducing it. The group's claim was supported by data on owner complaints and frequency of repairs. During the first years of ownership itself, about 20 percent of the owners were reporting problems with the new transmission

For the 1991 model, Chrysler extensively modified the design of the vehicle but continued to use the same problematic transmission as standard equipment, with most of the larger engines in high demand.

As a result, the Chrysler which was placed at the top in the magazine "Consumer Reports" for many years, dropped to the bottom of the list in 1991, citing the transmission in particular as well as other signs of deteriorating quality. A new Toyota model captured the top spot that year.

Discussion Questions :

1. To what factors might you attribute Chrysler's failure to maintain market leadership.
2. What might Chrysler have done differently? How might a stronger focus on quality have helped?

CHAPTER 3

QUALITY MANAGEMENT PHILOSOPHIES

LEARNING OBJECTIVES

After reading this chapter, you should be able to:

- Discuss Deming's philosophy and his contribution to quality
- Discuss 'Demings triangle, Theory of variance and Seven deadly diseases and sins'
- Describe the P-D-C-A cycle or Deming cycle
- Discuss Juran's philosophy and quality trilogy
- Discuss Crosby's philosophy and his "Absolutes of Quality"
- Briefly discuss Crosby's 14 steps for quality improvement
- Discuss the contributions of Masaaki Imai, Kaoru Ishikawa, Genichi Taguchi, Shigeo Shingo and Dr. Walter Shewhart to total quality management
- Briefly explain the significant characteristics of quality circles.

3.0 INTRODUCTION

Although many individuals have made substantial contributions to the theory and practice of quality management, three individuals—Dr. W. Edwards Deming, Dr. Joseph Juran and Phillip B. Crosby—are regarded as the "management gurus" in the quality revolution. These three "quality gurus" together with Masaaki Imai led the development of the current set of management tools within total quality management.

- Dr. W. Edwards Deming articulated his 14 points for management, five deadly sins and diseases, the theory of variance and the role of management in TQM.
- Dr. Joseph Juran outlined the habit of quality, quality trilogy and universal break-through sequence. His "Quality Control Handbook" is often called the "bible" of quality.
- Philip B. Crosby enumerated absolutes for quality management and 14 steps for quality improvement. He promoted the concept of **"zero defects"** and authored the book ***"Quality is free"***.

Other individuals who have helped to shape current thinking in quality management include Masaaki Imai, Armand V. Feigenbaum, Kaoru Ishikawa, Genichi Taguchi, Shigeo Shingo and Walter A. Shewhart. ***Box 3.1*** **lists key contributors to quality management.**

Box 3.1 : Key Contributors to Quality Management

Contributor	Key Contributions
Deming	14 points, special versus common causes of variation
Juran	Quality is fitness-for-use, quality trilogy.
Feigenbaum	Quality is a total field, the customer defines quality
Crosby	Quality is free, zero defects
Ishikawa	Cause-and-effect diagrams, quality circles
Taguchi	Taguchi loss function

3.1 THE DEMING PHILOSOPHY

No individual has had more influence on quality management than Dr. W. E. Deming. To many, the name of W. E. Deming is synonymous with quality and total quality management. Deming exposed Japanese managers to the fundamental concepts of quality production. He first envisioned quality management as an organisation-wide activity rather than a technical task for inspectors or a specialised quality-assurance group. He identified quality as a management responsibility, observing that managers must create the systems and processes that generate quality.

Thousands of Japanese managers attended Deming's courses on statistical process control which began in 1950 when Deming visited Japan in response to an invitation from the Union of Japanese Scientists and Engineers (JUSE). Deming was awarded Japan's highest decoration, the second order Medal of Sacred Treasure in 1960.

Deming made the initial insight that a firm could never inspect quality into a product. A quality product combines a good design with effective production methods. Only by meeting both these conditions could a firm assure quality.

Deming advocated a never-ending cycle of product design, manufacture, test and sales, followed by market surveys and then redesign and so forth. He claimed that higher quality leads to higher productivity, which in turn leads to long term competitive strength. **The Deming "chain reaction" theory summarises this view. (*See Exhibit 3.1*).**

Exhibit 3.1 : The Deming Chain Reaction

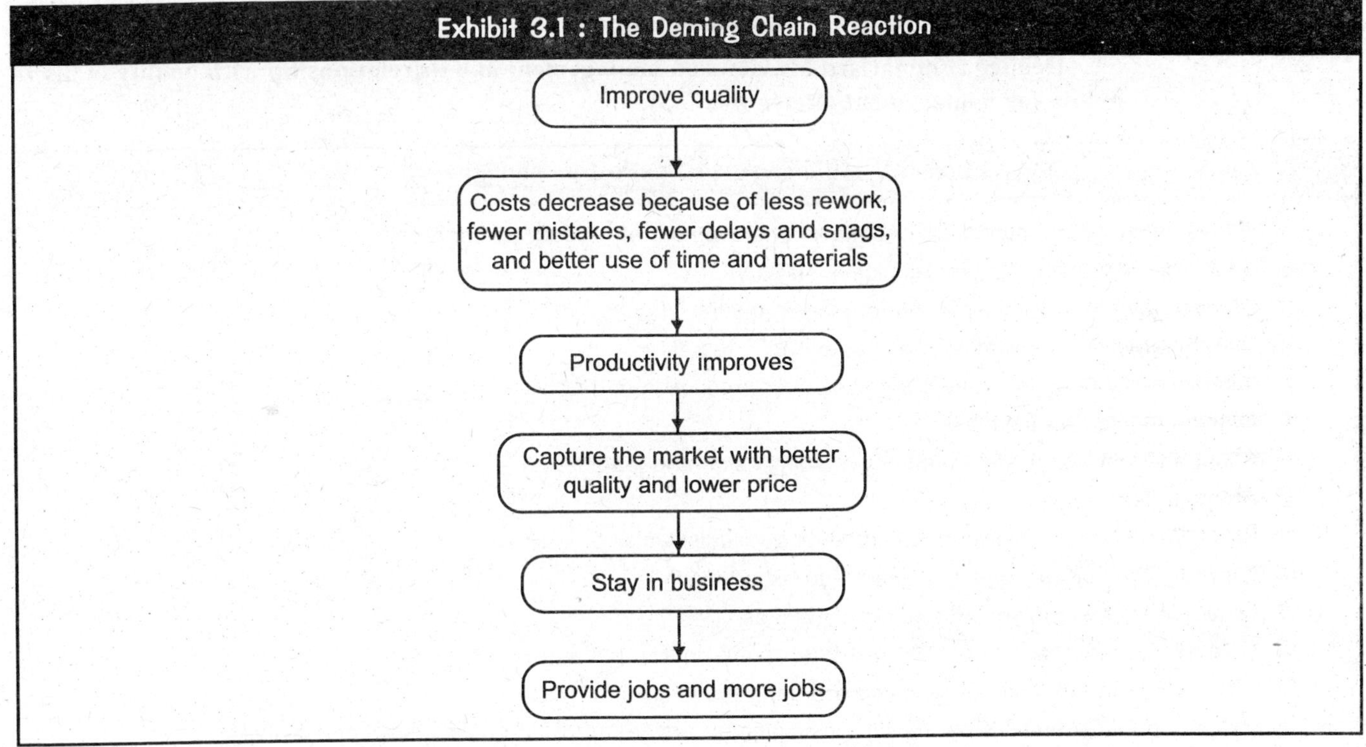

The theory states that "improvements in quality lead to lower costs because they result in less rework, fewer mistakes, fewer delays and snags, and better use of time and materials. Lower costs, in turn, lead to productivity improvements. With better quality and lower prices, a firm can achieve a higher market share and thus stay in business, providing more and more jobs."

Deming stressed that the top management has higher responsibility for quality improvement than middle and junior level management personnel.

Box 3.2 : Deming and Quality

- Advanced use of statistical analysis to gain control over variability in manufacturing processes (*i.e.,* statistical quality control using control charts for process control).
- Extended statistical quality control to cover the systematic approach to problem solving in any sector – manufacturing or not.
- Viewed the control chart as the ideal tool for assigning the responsibilities for quality improvement, according to the ratio 15 : 85 for workforce : management, which he later on revised to 6 : 94.
- First visited Japan in 1946 and conducted courses on statistical process control in the 1950s, when he visited Japan again on invitation from the Union of Japan Scientists and Engineers (JUSE).
- Each year since 1951, the Japanese industry started awarding **"Deming Prize"** to a company or individual that or who has actively contributed to the spread and development of statistical techniques for quality improvement.
- In 1960, Deming was decorated with the second order Medal of Sacred Treasure, awarded by the Emperor of Japan for the development of quality in Japan.
- Major contributions to quality management:
  - His ***fourteen*** points for management.
  - His ***seven deadly*** diseases and sins.
  - His ***cycle*** or *action plan* : Plan-Do-Check-Action.
  - His ***triangle***.
  - His ***chain reaction***.

Deming's 14 Points for Management

Deming summarised his views on management and its relationship with quality in his 14 points for management (Refer *Box 3.3*).

Box 3.3 : Deming's 14 Points for Management

1. Create constancy of purpose for continual improvement of product and service.
2. Adopt the new philosophy for economic stability.
3. Cease dependency on inspection to achieve quality.
4. End the practice of awarding business on price tag alone.
5. Improve constantly and forever the system of production and service.
6. Institute training on the job.
7. Adopt and institute modern methods of supervision and leadership.
8. Drive out fear.
9. Break down barriers between departments and individuals.
10. Eliminate the use of slogans, posters and exhortations.
11. Eliminate work standards and numerical quotas.
12. Remove barriers that rob the hourly worker of the right to pride in workmanship.
13. Institute a vigorous program of education and retraining.
14. Define top management's permanent commitment to ever-improving quality and productivity.

Altogether, these guidelines describe a fundamental basis for an organisation's culture. They define a process by which managers seek out bad practices and habits and replace them with better, more effective practices.

Deming's 14 points stated above in *Box 3.3* are explained in the following paragraphs:

- **Create constancy of purpose for continual improvement of product and service :** An organisation must define its values, mission and vision of the future to provide long-term direction for its management and employees.

Deming believed that businesses are social entities whose basic purpose is to serve their customers and employees. To do this, they must take a long-term view and invest in innovation, training and research.

- **Adopt the new philosophy for economic stability :** Old methods of management built on F.W. Taylor's principles, such as quota driven production, work-measurement and adversarial work relationships will not work in today's global environment. Production and service processes often contain considerable waste and inefficiencies. Companies cannot survive if products of poor quality of conformance or poor fitness for use leave their customers dissatisfied. Instead, companies must take a customer-driven approach based on mutual co-operation between labour and management and a never-ending cycle of improvement. Everyone, from the CEO to the lowest level employee of the organisation must recognise the need for a new philosophy to keep the firm and its functions alive and growing in today's competitive environment and must learn the new philosophy.

- **Cease dependency on inspection to achieve quality :** "Routine inspection acknowledges that defects are present, but does not add value to the product. Defects are inherent to any product or process, and we can hope to prevent those defects from reaching customers only by inspecting them". This is the traditional view of operation's managers.

Deming contradicted the above view, since inspections increase costs rather than reduce them and create more problems than they solve. The rework of defective products decreases productivity and in service industries, rework cannot be performed. **The reasons for ceasing dependency on inspection to achieve quality are:**

(i) Inspections are no more perfect than other activities, so they allow defective products to pass.

(ii) Inspections correct symptoms in the form of defects, leaving the causes of defects intact to create more symptoms.

(iii) Inspections rarely increase value for customers.

(iv) Inspections often form bottlenecks that restrict the flow of products through the operating system.

(v) Inspections create complacency, divide responsibility for quality between opcrators and inspectors and reduce overall concern for quality.

Workers must take responsibility for their work rather than leave the problems for the inspectors. Managers need to understand the concept of ***variance*** and how it affects their processes and seek to reduce the common cause of variation. Statistical tools can be used to help control processes and eliminate mass inspection as the principal activity in controlling quality.

- **End the practice of awarding business on price tag alone :** Purchase departments have long been driven by cost minimisation, without regard to quality. There is a need for a total cost assessment of any purchase. Low prices are often associated with low quality, which can actually raise overall costs through increased expenses for inspection, scrap and rework, inventory to replace defective items and employee frustration. Managers must identify and assess all of the effects and costs created by every purchase and buy from the supplier that offers the lowest total cost.

Deming urged businesses to establish long-term relationships with a few suppliers, leading to loyalty and opportunities for mutual improvement. Constantly changing suppliers solely on the basis of price, increases the variation in the material supplied to production, since each supplier's process is different.

- **Improve constantly and forever the system of production and service :** Whereas western management has viewed improvement in the context of large, expensive technological innovations such as robotics and computer-integrated manufacturing, Japanese manufacturer's success is primarily due to incremental improvements.

Improvements are necessary in both design and production. Improved design comes from understanding customer needs through continual market surveys and other sources of feedback. Also, understanding the manufacturing process and developing designs having ***producibility*** (economic manufacture) are essential to achieve improved design. Improved production is achieved by reducing the ***causes of variation*** and establishing stable, predictable processes.

Improvement means reducing variation by eliminating ***special causes*** and reducing the effects of ***common causes***. This improves quality which in turn improves productivity and decreases costs. The special causes can be reduced by the efforts of workers, using statistical methods. Common causes of variation are due to the system that the management designs. Deming estimated that 85 to 95 percent of variation results from the system.

To build a system that can consistently produce a quality product, managers must identify and eliminate waste and variability throughout the system. Statistical methods can be used by managers to understand common causes and lead to their reduction.

- **Institute training on the job :** For continuous improvement, employees-both management and workers-require the proper tools and knowledge. People are an organisation's most valuable resource and the management must take the responsibility of training them on their jobs so that they do a good job.

However, most firms view training as a requirement of newly hired employees only. Later, they implicitly and wrongly assume that the employees no longer need any training. The critical need to learn never ends. All employees should be trained in statistical tools for solving quality problems. Not only does training result in improvement in quality and productivity, but it adds to worker's morale. In addition, training removes barriers between workers and supervisors, giving both more incentives to improve further.

- **Adopt and institute modern methods of supervision and leadership :** The job of managers is leadership, not supervision. Supervision is simply overseeing and directing work, whereas leadership means providing guidance to help employees do their job better with less effort. Supervisors and managers must see themselves as teachers, coaches and facilitators who support the activities of workers in immediate contact with process problems. They must encourage and promote team work and reward innovation and initiative. Leadership qualities in supervisors and managers can help to eliminate the element of fear from the job and encourage team work.
- **Drive out fear :** Deming identified fear as a major obstacle to improve efficiency and effectiveness and a major barrier to change and survival. Fear is manifested in many ways: ***fear of reprisal, fear of failure, fear of the unknown, fear of losing control*** and ***fear of change***. Fear affects an operating system in many ways. Some people are afraid to ask questions and reveal weaknesses in their knowledge, other people fear co-operating because it may leave them vulnerable to opportunistic threat from others. Fear of the perceived cost of failure, such as poor performance reviews or even termination, prevents some people from challenging current practices or trying new techniques. Many people simply fear change because it forces them to deal with new and unfamiliar methods in place of known and familiar, though inefficient, methods. Workers are often afraid to report quality problems because they might not meet their quotas, their incentive earnings might be reduced, or they might be blamed for the problems in the system.

To drive out fear, managers must create an environment that encourages people to ask questions, report problems and try new ideas. Employees must know that the firm will not punish them if their new ideas fail. Managers must demonstrate the importance of trying something new that offers a chance for a major leap in effectiveness rather than sticking with safe methods that offer only stable or declining benefits.

- **Breakdown barriers between departments and individuals :** Many organisations tolerate weaknesses because they look at problems within strict functional limits and ignore insights and concerns raised by related functional areas. As a result, firms often optimise activities within a function but fail to exploit potential gains from organisation wide changes.

Interdisciplinary teams can enhance quality and effectiveness of efforts to design and build products as compared with a strictly functionally oriented process. ***Team work*** helps to break down barriers between departments and individuals. In Japan, firms emphasise that the next department or individual in the production process is actually the customer (internal customer) and train those workers to manage such customer relationships. To overcome the barriers between individuals, managers must encourage team work by making changes such as moving work stations closer together, assigning people to teams and changing the performance measurement system to reward group performance rather than individual results.

- **Eliminate the use of slogans, posters and exhortations :** Posters, slogans and motivational programs calling for ***'zero defects', "Do it right the First Time", "Improve Productivity and Quality"*** and so on are directed at the wrong people. These slick messages assume that all quality problems are due to human behaviour and workers can improve simply through such motivational methods.

Motivational methods overlook the source of many problems—the system rather than individual workers. Quality problems usually come from limits in the current system. Rather than using promotional messages designed to urge workers to work harder, managers should give them the tools and training they need to work smarter. The statistical thinking and training are the best route to improve quality. Motivation can be better achieved from trust and leadership than from slogans and goals.

- **Eliminate work standards and numerical quotas :** Standards and quotas are born in short-term perspectives and create fear of punitive action for not achieving them. They do not encourage improvement, particularly if rewards or performance appraisals are tied to meeting quotas. Workers may short-cut quality to reach the numerical quotas. Attempts to meet reasonable quotas lead to complacency over time since workers achieve their goal and need do no more. Excessively demanding quotas discourage workers who can never meet them, or induce them to compromise quality standards. Unreasonable quotas cause fear and frustration and ***leave room*** for improvement. TQM sets one ultimate task for any employee: ***to produce quality products***.

- **Remove barriers that rob the hourly worker of the right to pride in workmanship :** People on the factory floor and even in management have become, in Deming's words, a "commodity" which can be used as per the whims and fancies of the employers. Employees are not recognised as valuable human resources of the organisations in which they work. Workers are given monotonous tasks, provided with inferior machines, tools or materials, asked to work at odd hours and on holidays too to make up for the production delays and so on. Under these circumstances, many individuals cannot take pride in their work. Further, many cannot be certain about their job tenure, they have the fear of losing their jobs any time.

Deming used his fourteen points for management to emphasise the critical role of managers in TQM.

Deming believed that one of the highest barriers to pride in workmanship is ***performance appraisal***. Performance appraisal destroys team work by promoting competition for limited resources, focusses on short term and discourages risk taking.

Deming sorted performance into three categories: *(a)* the majority of performances that are within the system, *(b)* performance outside the system on the superior side and *(c)* performance outside the system on the inferior side. Statistical methods provide the basis for these classifications. Superior performance should be compensated specially and inferior performers need extra training or replacement.

- **Institute a vigorous program of education and retraining :** Continual training keeps the work force up-to-date with information about new developments, changes in product designs and machinery, new tools and procedures and innovative techniques. Organisations must invest in their people at all levels to ensure success in the long term. Investment in training represents the firm's ongoing commitment to its employees. Also developing the worth of the individual employee is a powerful motivation method.
- **Define top management's permanent commitment to ever-improving quality and productivity :** Top manager's actions communicate the true importance of quality and TQM throughout the firm. The commitment of top managers to quality encourages many managers and employees to follow top managers towards personal and organisational success. For TQM to succeed, a firm's top managers must publicly demonstrate their vigorous commitments to ensure continuous quality improvement and innovation and they must openly practice what they preach.

Deming used his 14 points for the management to emphasise the critical role of managers in TQM. He saw managers rather than workers or equipments as the real obstacle to TQM. In his opinion, 85 percent of quality problems could be traced to the management while workers are responsible for the remaining 15 percent.

Exhibit 3.2 : Deming's Triangle

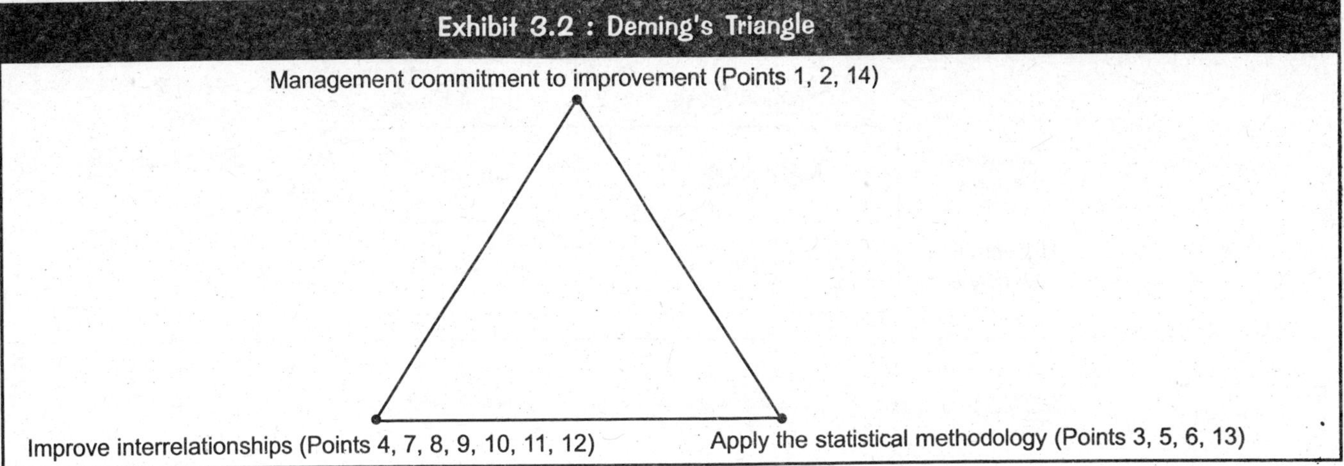

Box 3.4 : Deming on Management

- The prevailing system of management has smothered the individual and has completely dampened innovation, applied science and joy in learning, joy in work.
- The wealth of a nation depends on its people, management and government, more than its natural resources.
- The workers are handicapped by the system and the system belongs to the management .
- The big problem for management may be the difficulty in making any kind of change.
- When will the management learn that they have a moral obligation to protect investment and safeguard jobs.
- Management needs training to learn about their company.
- The job of management is not supervision but leadership.
- Absenteeism is a function of poor management. If people feel important to a job, they will come to work.
- A company can do well with poor management – for a while!
- Management too often supposes that they have solved their problems of quality by establishing a Quality Control Department and forgetting about it.
- The management is at fault for terms of reference that are outmoded.

Deming's Theory of Variance

Most of Deming's work revolves around his ***theory of variance***. This theory views variations from standard activities as a major source of problems for all processes and most firms. Variance causes unpredictability which increases uncertainty and reduces control over processes. TQM assigns managers the task of finding the sources of their variance and eliminating it so that the process can be improved significantly.

All variances can be categorised into two categories: ***controlled variance*** and ***uncontrolled variance***. A controlled variance is a variation from standard process that a worker can correct or manage. An uncontrolled variance is a variation from the standard process due to the impact of some factor outside the control of the employee.

Variances can be corrected by workers or managers by either changing its common causes or removing its special causes. ***Common causes*** reflect systematic problems in an operating process. These include weaknesses in product design, equipment malfunctions, poor maintenance of equipment and incomplete or inaccurate routing documents and bills of materials. ***Special causes*** reflect short-term sources of variation in an operating process that workers could correct. These include lack of knowledge or skill, worker negligence, or a batch of incoming materials having bad quality.

***Exhibit 3.3* defines the matrix of responsibility for correcting the variances.**

Exhibit 3.3 : Category of Variances

	Common cause	Special cause
Controlled variance	Management	Employee
Uncontrolled variance	Management	Management

Box 3.5 : Deming on Quality

- The right ***quality*** and uniformity are the foundations of commerce, prosperity and peace.
- ***Defects*** are not free, somebody makes them and gets paid to make them.
- A ***quality*** program launched by ceremonies, speeches, raising of flags, beating of drums, badges and heavy applause, is a delusion and a snare!
- ***Specification limits*** are not action limits.
- A work standard is a fortress against improvement of ***quality*** and productivity. It is a manifestation of inability to understand and provide adequate supervision.
- Focusing on outcome is not an effective way to ***improve a process*** or an activity.
- Abolish distinction between ***major*** and ***minor*** defects. A defect will be a defect.
- ***Quality*** and innovation are inseparable, necessary ingredients for achievement of quality are innovation and profound knowledge of variation.
- ***Quality*** is generated in the board room; limitations on quality are also made in the board room.
- Good operations on the factory floor are necessary, but good operations don't ensure *quality*. ***Best efforts*** will not ensure ***quality***. ***Hardwork*** will not ensure ***quality***. Experience will not ensure quality.
- There is no ***process***, no ***capability*** and no meaningful ***specification***, except in ***statistical control***.
- A usual stumbling block in most places is management's supposition that ***quality*** is something you install, like a Dean or a new carpet!
- The price tag is easy to read, but ***understanding quality*** requires education.
- People get rewarded for ***"conforming"***. No wonder we are on the decline!
- We have learnt to live in a world of ***mistakes*** and ***defective*** products as if they were necessary to life.
- Putting out fires is not ***improvement***.
- ***Problems*** are different, but the principles that will help to solve them are universal.

Deming's Deadly Diseases and Sins

Box 3.6 : Deming's Seven Deadly Diseases and Sins

(i) Lack of constancy of purpose.
(ii) Emphasis on short-term profits.
(iii) Over reliance on performance appraisals.
(iv) Mobility of management.
(v) Overemphasis on visible figures.
(vi) Excessive medical costs for employee health care.
(vii) Excessive costs of warranty and legal costs.

In addition to the 14 points, Deming proposed **"Seven Deadly Diseases"** that obstruct the quest for quality. For successful implementation of Deming's guidelines (14 points for management), managers must first eliminate the bad practices known as seven deadly diseases and sins. These are:

Deming proposed "seven deadly diseases" that obstruct the quest for quality.

(i) **Lack of constancy of purpose :** Many companies have only short-term quality programs. They do not look towards the long term, nor do they ingrain the philosophy of quality into the corporate culture. *For example*, at one small plant, the plant manager stated vehemently that no one should ever compromise on quality. After sometime, a customer called for a rush order to meet his urgent needs and willing to take any product that the plant could ship irrespective of quality. The plant manager could not offer a batch of acceptable quality and decided to ship parts of inferior quality which the customer would accept. The schedule requests took precedence over quality, destroying the quality programme in practice.

(ii) **Emphasis on short-term profits :** A process that focusses on short-term profits encourages short-term thinking and short-term actions. Firms seeking only to increase the quarterly dividend undermine quality. Managers may cut costs in the short-term while sacrificing the long-term planning that TQM demands and raising costs overall.

(iii) **Over reliance on performance appraisals :** A performance appraisal system can hinder the implementation of TQM by encouraging rivalry, fear and short term thinking. It can also undermine teamwork and mutual respect.

(iv) **Mobility of management (Job hopping) :** Managers who continually job-hop fail to understand the companies for which they work, focus on the short-term and are unable to implement the long-term changes necessary for lasting quality improvement. Even though it may be argued that job hopping exposes managers to a beneficial diversity of experiences, excessive job hopping encourages short-term thinking and inhibits the ability of the manager to understand the long-term implications of actions.

(v) **Overemphasis on visible figures :** Managers tend to evaluate performance by looking only at measures that they can easily capture. But most important figures may be unknown or often unknowable, such as the effect of a satisfied customer. TQM requires the managers to evaluate the total effect of any action by reviewing both quantitative information like the number of defects and qualitative data like expressions of customer satisfaction or employee perception about the firm.

(vi) **Excessive medical costs for employee health care that increases the final cost of goods and services :** Health care costs and rate of absenteeism due to illness have increased at a phenomenal rate over the years. The long-term effect has been a deterioration in competitiveness.

(vii) **Excessive costs of warranty and legal costs :** Due to proliferation of law suits and multi-million-dollar judgements concerned with compensation to be paid to the patients, the medical professionals in US spend lot of money for paying insurance premium to cover the risk in practising their medical profession. This may lead to excessive professional charges by doctors or even some doctors abandoning their practices.

The Deming Prize

Recognising Deming's important effect on the performance of Japanese firms, the Japanese government instituted the Deming Prize in 1951. This annual award recognises a company or individual for active contributions to the development of quality management tools or to the spread and implementation of quality improvement programs. The Union of Japanese Scientists and Engineers (JUSE) awards Deming Prize to a company or its division based on the distinctive

Box 3.7 : The Deming Application Prize Checklist

Item	Checking Points
1. Policies	1. Management, quality and quality control/management policies 2. Methods for establishing policies 3. Appropriateness and consistency of policies 4. Utilisation of statistical methods 5. Communication and dissemination of policies 6. Checks on policies and status of their achievement 7. Their relationship to long and short-term plan
2. The organization and its operations	1. Clarity of authority and responsibility 2. Appropriateness of the delegation of authority 3. Inter-departmental coordination 4. Committee activities 5. Utilisation of staff 6. Utilisation of QC Circle activities 7. Quality control/management diagnosis

3. Education and dissemination	1. Educational plan and results 2. Consciousness of quality and how it is managed and understanding of quality control/management 3. Education on statistical concepts and methods and the degree to which they are disseminated 4. Grasp of effects 5. Education of associated companies (especially, group companies, vendors, contractors and distributors) 6. QC Circle activities 7. The system of improvement suggestions and its status
4. Information gathering, communication and its utilisation	1. Collection of external information 2. Inter-departmental communication 3. Utilisation of statistical methods 4. Information processing, (statistical) analysis and utilisation of information
5. Analysis	1. Selection of important issues and improvement themes 2. Appropriateness of analytical methods 3. Utilisation of statistical methods 4. Linkage with industry intrinsic technology 5. Quality analysis and process analysis 6. Utilisation of analysis results 7. Action taken on improvement suggestions
6. Standardisation	1. System of standards 2. Methods of establishing, revising and abolishing standards 3. Actual performance in establishing, revising and abolishing standards 4. Contents of the standards 5. Utilisation of statistical methods 6. Accumulation of technology 7. Utilisation of standards
7. Control/management	1. Management systems for quality and other related elements, such as cost and delivery (quantity) 2. Control points and control items 3. Utilisation of statistical methods and concepts, such as control charts 4. Contributions of QC Circle activities 5. Status of control/management activities 6. In-control situations
8. Quality assurance	1. New product and service development methods (quality deployment and analysis, reliability testing and design review) 2. Preventive activities for safety and product liability 3. Degree of customer satisfaction 4. Process design, process analysis and process control and improvement 5. Process capabilities 6. Instrumentation and inspection 7. Management of facilities, vendors, procurement and services 8. Quality assurance system and its diagnosis 9. Utilisation of statistical methods 10. Quality evaluation and audit 11. Status of quality assurance
9. Effects	1. Measurements of effects 2. Tangible effects such as quality, service, delivery, cost, profit, safety and environment 3. Intangible effects 4. Conformity of actual performance to planned effects
10. Future plans	1. Concrete understanding of current situation 2. Measures for solving defect problems 3. Future promotion plans 4. Relationship between future plans and long-term plans

performance improvements achieved by it through the application of ***Company Wide Quality Control*** (CWQC). ***Box 3.7* shows the Deming application prize check list**

The judging criteria consists of a check list of 10 major categories: policies, the organisation and its operations, education and dissemination, information gathering communication and its utilisation, analysis, standardisation, control/management, quality assurance, effects and future plans.

Deming Wheel

To successfully practice total quality management in a firm, top managers must take the first step: accepting and committing themselves to the guidelines and points that form the basis of TQM. The firm can then begin to implement TQM using the **Deming Wheel illustrated in *Exhibit 3.4.***

Exhibit 3.4 : Deming Wheel (or Deming cycle) (or P-D-C-A Cycle)

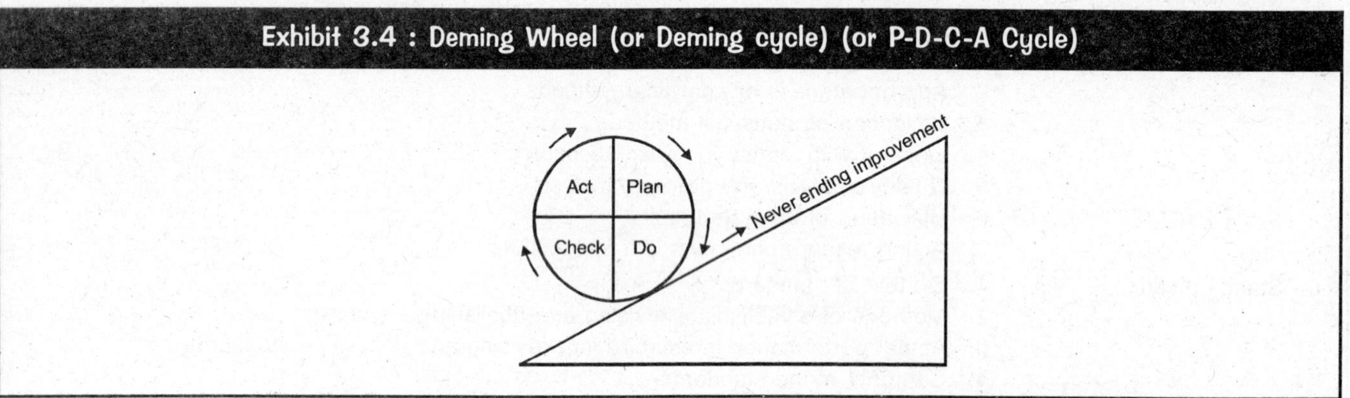

The **'Deming wheel'** or **'Deming cycle'** which is also known as the **PDCA Cycle (Plan-Do-Check-Act)** or **PDSA cycle (Plan-Do-Study-Act)** is a problem-solving process adopted by firms engaged in continuous improvement (CI).

The cycle consists of the following steps:

(i) **Plan :** The team selects a process that needs improvement, documents the selected process, sets qualitative goals for improvement and discusses various ways to achieve the goals. After assessing the benefits and costs of the alternatives, the team develops a plan with quantifiable measures for improvement.

Deming wheel or Deming cycle is a problem-solving process.

(ii) **Do:** The team implements the plan and monitors progress. Data are collected continuously to measure improvements in the process. Changes if any, in the process, are documented and further revisions are made as needed.

(iii) **Check/Study:** The team analyses the data collected during the 'do' step to find out how closely the results correspond to the goals in the 'plan' step. If major shortcomings exist, the team may have to re-evaluate the plan or stop the project.

(iv) **Act:** If the results are successful, the team documents the revised process so that it becomes the standard procedure for all who may use it.

The Deming Triangle

TQM needs the establishment of the following three fundamental characteristics :

1. **Commitment** (to never ending quality improvement and innovation).
2. **Scientific knowledge** (of the proper tools and techniques for the technical change).
3. **Involvement** (all in one team, for the social change).

The above characteristics are considered as the axioms of the TQM culture, which are of equal significance and hence expressed as the three corners of an equilateral triangle as shown in ***Exhibit 3.5***.

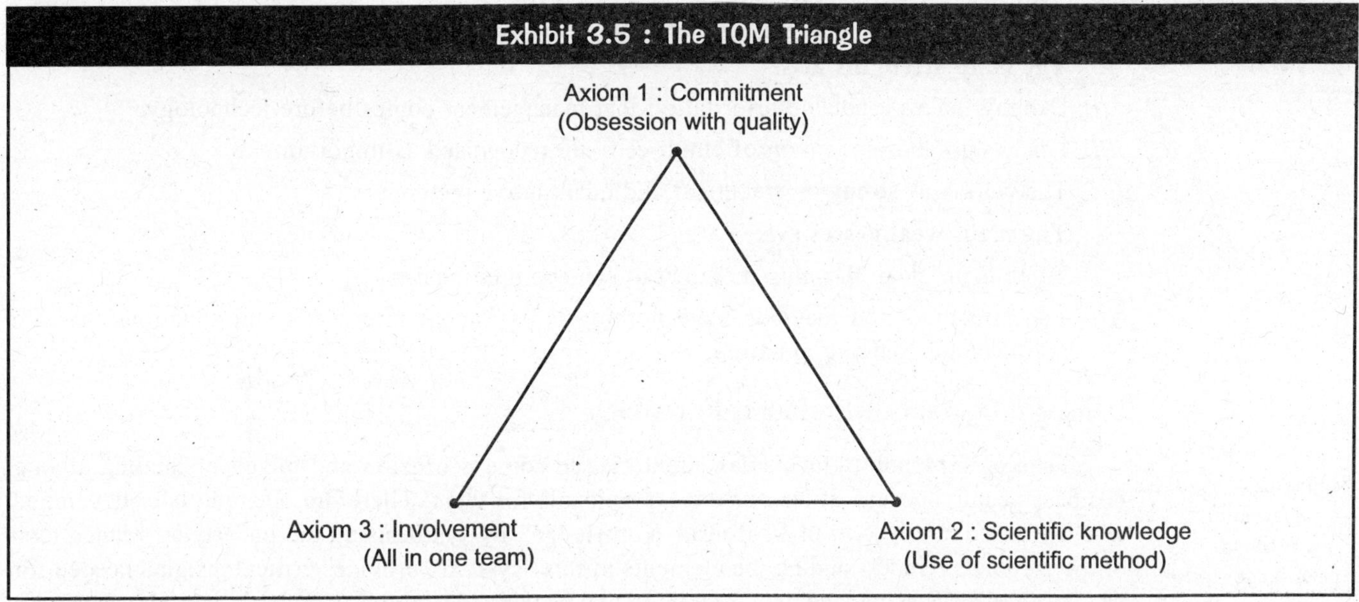

This is also known as the **TQM triangle** (or **Deming triangle**, **Juran triangle** or **Crosby triangle** since all these "quality gurus" emphasised these three axioms in their quality philosophies).

Deming's Chain Reaction

Deming's Chain Reaction was first presented in 1950 in Japan after World War II. ***Exhibit 3.6*** illustrates Deming's chain reaction based on Shewart's concept that productivity and quality improved as variations reduced.

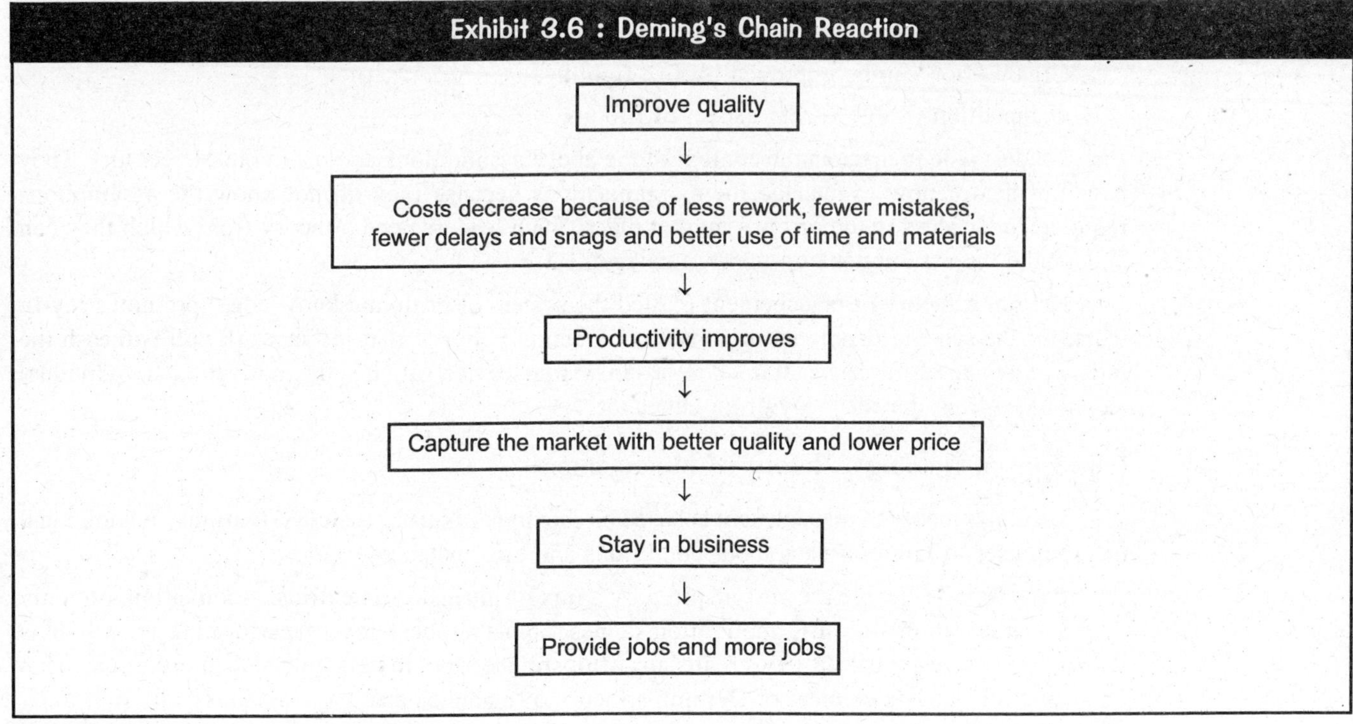

Strength and Weaknesses of Deming's Philosophy

The main strengths are:

(i) Deming makes a notable prioritation-that management comes before technology.

(ii) Leadership and motivation of employees are recognised as important.

(iii) The work was strong on statistical and quantitative methods.

The main weaknesses are:

(i) There is no clear "Deming method" to achieve total quality.

(ii) The principles and methods have nothing to say about intervention in situations that are political and coercive in nature.

Deming's System of Profound Knowledge

Deming developed 'a system of profound knowledge' by synthesising his 14 points for management.

Deming's 14 points for management caused some confusion and misunderstanding among business people because of lack of a clear rationale for them. Therefore, Deming later developed what he called **"A system of Profound Knowledge"** by synthesising the underlying foundations of the 14 points. Understanding the elements of this **"system"** provides critical insights needed for designing effective management practices and making decisions in today's complex business environment.

The **system of profound knowledge** is appropriate for leadership in any culture. However, applying this theory in a particular culture requires a focus on issues that are unique to that culture. ***For example,*** **in the Western world, managers have frequently operated using the following assumptions.**

- Rewards and punishments are the most effective motivators of people.
- Optimisation in every area of an organisation leads to optimisation of the entire organisation.
- Results are achieved by setting objectives.
- Quality is inversely related to quantity.
- Rational decisions can be made on the basis of guesswork and opinion.
- Organisation can be improved by fire fighting.
- Competition is a necessary aspect of life.

Leaders who manage in the context of the above assumptions are lost in the 21st century. They have no idea of how to manage their organisations because they do not know the assumptions required for success in tomorrow's market place. Such leaders need a theory from which they can understand the assumptions of quality management.

Deming's theory of management (called the system of profound knowledge) promotes **joy in work** for the stakeholders in an organisation. Deming believed that joy in work will "unleash the power of human resource constrained in **intrinsic motivation** which is the motivation an individual experiences from the sheer joy of an endeaour".

Paradigm of Deming's Theory of Management

Deming's theory of management is based on four **paradigms** or **belief systems** that an individual or group uses to interpret data about conditions and circumstances.

Paradigm 1: People are best inspired by a mix of intrinsic and extrinsic motivation, not only extrinsic motivation. Intrinsic motivation comes from the sheer joy of performing an act. It is management's responsibility to create an **atmosphere** that fosters intrinsic motivation. This atmosphere is a basic element of Deming's theory of management.

Paradigm 2: Manage using both a **process** and a **results orientation** ; not only a results orientation. Management's job is to improve and innovate the processes that create results, not just to manage results. This paradigm shift allows management to define the capabilities of processes and consequently predict and plan the future of a system to achieve organisational optimisation which requires that managers make decisions based on facts, not on guesswork or opinion.

Paradigm 3: Management's function is to **optimise the entire system** so that everyone wins, not to maximise only its components of the system. Optimisation of one component may cause suboptimisation of another component. In order to optimise the entire system towards its objective or goal, it may be necessary to knowingly suboptimise one or more components of the system.

Paradigm 4: Co-operation works better than competition. In a co-operative environment, everybody wins whereas in a competitive environment most people lose. Costs resulting from competition are huge. They include the costs of rework, waste and redundancy, as well as the costs of warranty, retesting, reinspection, customer dissatisfaction, schedule disruptions and destruction of individual joy in work.

According to Deming, if leaders practice these four paradigms, they will reap enormous benefits.

Components of Deming's Theory of Management or the System of Profound Knowledge

Deming's profound knowledge system consists of four components:

(i) Appreciation for a system. *(ii)* Theory of variation or understanding a variation.
(iii) Theory of knowledge and
(iv) Psychology.

Four components of Deming's theory of management or the system of profound knowledge are :
(i) Appreciation of the system
(ii) Theory of variation
(iii) Theory of knowledge and
(iv) Psychology.

All these components or parts are interrelated or inter-dependent. Each component is explained in the following paragraphs:

1. Appreciation for a System: A system is a collection of components or parts that interact and have a common purpose or aim. The components of any system must work together if the system is to be effective. Managers can not manage the system well by simply managing the components or parts (sub systems) in isolation. They must understand the process that cross functional boundaries, align these processes toward a common vision or goal and optimise their interactions. The aim of any system should be for all stake holders – share holders, employees, customers, suppliers, communities and the environment - to benefit over the long term. While the top management is responsible to optimise the entire system, the managers of individual components or sub-systems of the system are responsible to promote the aim of the entire system even it means sub-optimising serve components.

2. Theory of Variation: Variation is inherent in all processes. The same kind of variation exists in any production and service process, generally due to factors inherent in the design of the system, which can not easily be controlled. There are two types of variation, ***special*** and ***common***. Special causes of variation are external to the system, whereas common causes of variation are due to the inherent design and structure of the system, while modern technology of today has improved our ability to produce the parts or products with very little variation, the variation that occurs due to human behaviour and performance continues to hamper quality efforts. Deming suggested that management must first understand the variation and then work to reduce the same through improvements in technology, process design, and employee training. With less variation, both producer and consumer are benefitted and higher productivity and customer satisfaction will result. Deming advocated that statistical methods are used to identify and quantify variation and every employee in the firm be familiar with statistical techniques and other problem solving tools.

3. Theory of Knowledge: Information is not knowledge. Knowledge is indicated by the ability to predict future events with a quantifiable risk of being wrong and the ability to explain past events without fail.

Deming emphasised that ***knowledge*** can not be developed without theory and ***experience*** alone does not establish a theory. Therefore Deming never gave managers any **"solutions"** or prescriptions for achieving quality. He wanted them to learn and discover what works and what is appropriate for their individual organisations. The modern concept of **organisational learning** reflects the theory of knowledge. *For example,* performance reviews conducted after completion of projects allow managers to understand what went wrong and what went right, helping them to develop a knowledge base and provide concrete information to improve in the future. Objective data and a systematic problem-solving process provide a rational basis for making decisions.

4. Psychology: Psychology helps us to understand people, the interactions between people and the interactions between the people and the system of which they are part. It is critical to designing a work environment that promotes employee satisfaction and well-being. Much of Deming's philosophy is based on **understanding human behaviour and treating people fairly.** Managers or leaders must be aware of the individual differences among people (employees) and work towards optimising everybody's abilities and preferences. Management must understand the difference between **intrinsic motivation** and **extrinsic motivation.** All people require different amounts of intrinsic and extrinsic motivation and managers should know the proper mix of these two motivations for each person. If people can not enjoy their work, they will not be productive and focused on quality principles. Psychology helps managers to understand what motivates the employees and then to nurture and preserve the positive innate attributes of people (employees). Deming strongly believed that financial reward alone is not a motivator whereas the joy of working-an intrinsic motivator results in higher motivation and productivity.

Impacts of Profound Knowledge: Peter Scholtes, a reputed consultant makes some observations about the failure to understand the components of profound knowledge. They are:

1. ***When people don't understand systems?***
   - They see events as individual incidents rather than the net result of many interactions and interdependent forces.
   - They see the symptoms but not the root causes of problems.
   - They don't understand how an intervention in one part of an organisation can cause havoc in another place or at another time.
   - They blame individuals for problems even when those individuals have little or no ability to control the events around them.
2. ***When people don't understand variation***
   - They don't see trends which are occurring.
   - They see trends where there are none.
   - They don't know when expectations are realistic.
   - They don't understand past performance so they can't predict future performance.
   - They don't know the difference between prediction, forecasting and guesswork.
   - They are less likely to distinguish between fact and opinion.
3. ***When people don't understand psychology***
   - They don't understand motivation and why people do what they do.
   - They resort to carrots and sticks and other forms of motivation which offer no positive effect.
   - They don't understand the process of change and the resistance to it.
   - They revert to coercive approaches when dealing with people.
4. ***When people don't understand the theory of knowledge***
   - They don't know how to plan and accomplish learning and improvement.
   - They don't understand the difference between improvement and change.
   - Problems remain unsolved, despite their best efforts.

Revised Version of Deming's 14 Points

The original version of Deming's 14 points listed in *Box 3.3* were developed by Deming in 1981. Deming's philosophy underwent many changes and the 14 points were revised in the

due course of time. These revised 14 points of Deming are listed below:

1. Create a Vision and Demonstrate Management Commitment
2. Learn the New Philosophy (top management and everyone in the organisation)
3. Understand the Purpose of Inspection
4. Stop Making Decisions Purely on the Basis of Costs
5. Improve Constantly and Forever
6. Institute Training
7. Institute Leadership
8. Drive Out Fear, Create Trust and a Climate for Innovation
9. Optimise the Efforts of Teams Towards the Aims and Purposes of the Organisation
10. Eliminate Exhortations for the Workforce
11. Eliminate Numerical Quotas and Management By Objectives (MBO)
12. Remove Barriers to Pride in Workmanship
13. Encourage Education and Self-Improvement for Everyone
14. Take Action to Accomplish the Transformation.

3.2 THE JURAN PHILOSOPHY

After Deming, Dr. Joseph Juran has had the greatest impact on the theory and practice of quality management. Besides writing 12 books on the subject (he is well known for his book titled "Quality Control HandBook"), Juran has pioneered training manuals for managers and spoken across the world on quality.

Like Deming, Juran taught quality principles to Japanese in the 1950s and was a principal force in their quality reorganisation. He has also been awarded the Second Order of the Sacred Treasure by the Emperor of Japan.

Juran's contribution to TQM centres on four themes :

- Compelling definitions of ***quality*** and the cost of quality (COQ)
- Quality habit
- Quality trilogy
- Universal breakthrough sequence

Juran's concepts promoted the development of the theory and practice of TQM beginning on the shop floor and working upto the level of the top management.

Box 3.8 : Juran and Quality

- **Books Published**
  - Quality Control Hand Book (1981)
  - Upper Management and Quality
  - The Corporate Director
  - Juran on Planing for Quality (1988)
- Invited to Japan by the Union of Japanese Scientists and Engineers in the early 1950s to conduct seminars for top and middle level executives.
- Recipient of over thirty honourary medals, including the highest Japanese decoration, "the Second Order of the Sacred Treasure" awarded to him by the Emperor of Japan for the development of quality control in Japan.
- Major contributions to quality management:
  - Developing a quality habit
  - Quality trilogy: Quality Planning, Quality Control and Quality improvement
  - The universal breakthrough sequence

Box 3.9 : Juran's 10 Steps for Quality Improvement

1. Build awareness for the need and opportunity for improvement.
2. Set goals for improvement.
3. Organise people to reach the goals
4. Provide training throughout the organisation
5. Carryout projects to solve problems
6. Report progress
7. Give recognition
8. Communicate results
9. Keep score
10. Maintain momentum by making annual improvement part of the regular system and processes of the company.

Quality Defined

Juran defined quality as *(i)* product performance that results in customer satisfaction, *(ii)* freedom from product deficiencies, which avoids customer dissatisfaction, simply summarised as ***"fitness for use"***.

Fitness for use results from five major product traits:

(i) ***Quality of design***, *(ii)* ***Quality of conformance***, *(iii)* ***Availability***, *(iv)* ***Safety*** and *(v)* ***Field use***.

Quality of design reflects the suitability of a product's design concept and specifications for the intended use. It concentrates on market research, the product concept and design specifications. The design strengths differentiate the products of a firm from those of its competitors.

Quality of conformance reflects how well an actual product achieves the intentions of its design determined by the choice of process, employee capabilities (or skills), equipment condition and the feasibility of the design (*i.e.*, producibility).

Availability reflects an absence of problems that could affect the product's use. It focusses on reliability, maintainability and logistical support. Reliability or the probability of a breakdown affects availability, as does the case of maintenance and repair.

Safety reflects the threat of harm to the user of the product.

Field service represents the condition of the product once it reaches the customer's hands, which depends on such characteristics as packaging, storage, field support and maintenance. Field service quality comprises promptness, competence and integrity.

The pursuit of quality is viewed on two levels: *(i)* The mission of the firm as a whole is to achieve high product quality and *(ii)* The mission of each department in the firm is to achieve high production quality.

Concept of Cost of Quality

Juran also developed the concept of the ***cost of quality***. The costs associated with defective products include cost of making, finding, repairing and avoiding defects.

Juran categorised the cost of quality into four categories:

(i) Internal failure costs, *(ii)* External failure costs, *(iii)* Appraisal costs and *(iv)* Prevention costs.

The concept of cost of quality and the four categories were already discussed in detail in Module No. 1.

Quality habit emphasises objective results and lessons that those results teach rather than slogans and exhortations.

Quality habit : According to Juran, the ultimate goal for a TQM programme for the firm as a whole has to be set on a process of continuous improvement. Rather than slogans and exhortations, TQM requires an unwavering focus on the need for better quality. This focus should develop into a ***habit of quality*** that emphasises objective results and the lessons that those results teach. Juran advocated a four stage process to develop the quality habit for any firm. **These stages are:**

(i) Establish specific goals that identify what organisation members should do and why.

(ii) Establish plans for reaching those goals with enough detail to guide people's actions from beginning to end.

(iii) Assign clear responsibilities for meeting the goals and

(iv) Base rewards on results.

Juran advocated management action as the key to success in developing the quality habit.

Quality trilogy : Juran broke down the requirements for successful TQM into three major activities, the ***quality trilogy***: quality planning, quality control and quality improvement. The three stages of the quality trilogy define a sequence of events similar to the Deming Wheel or Deming Cycle. ***Exhibit 3.7* illustrates the quality trilogy.**

Exhibit 3.7 : Quality Trilogy

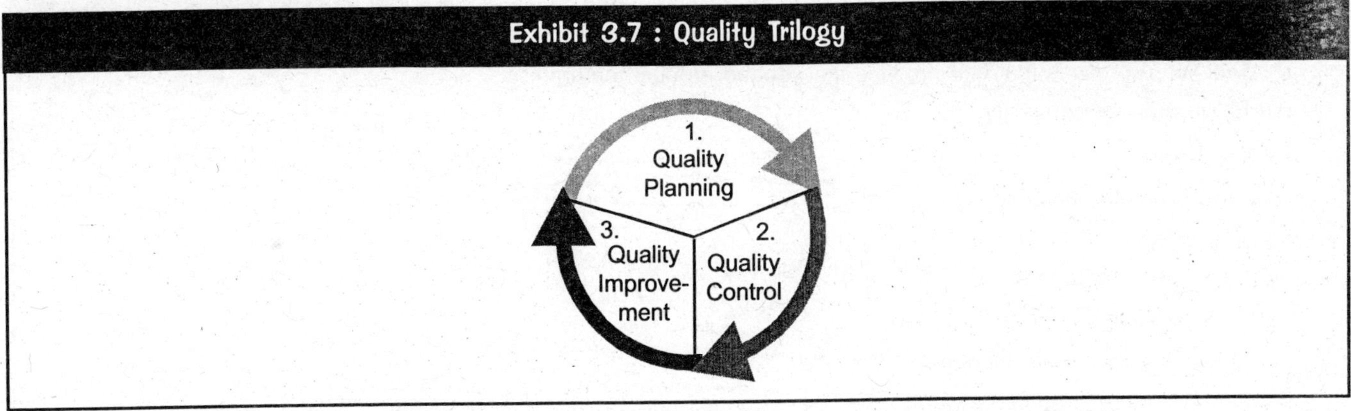

Quality trilogy comprises *(i)* Quality planning, *(ii)* Quality control and *(iii)* Quality improvement.

Quality planning : Quality does not happen by accident, rather it results directly from good planning. Quality planning begins with identifying customers, both external and internal, determining their needs and developing product features that respond to those needs. Juran wanted employees to know who uses their products, whether in the next department or in another organisation. Quality goals based on meeting the needs of customers and suppliers alike at a minimum combined cost are then established. Next, the process that can produce the product to satisfy the customers' needs and meet quality goals under operating conditions must be designed.

Quality control : Juran stated that quality control involves determining what to control, establishing units of measurement to evaluate data objectively, establishing standards of performance, measuring actual performance, interpreting the differences between actual performance and the standard and taking corrective action on the difference.

Quality improvement : While quality control pursues the goal of maintaining an existing level of quality, the quality habit pushes the firm onward to the next, higher level of quality. Quality improvement focusses on this goal seeking to achieve quality break-throughs that move the firm to a new level of performance. These breakthroughs reflect long-term thinking and planning by managers as part of the universal breakthrough sequence.

Box 3.10 : Juran's Quality Trilogy Process

Quality trilogy has a sequence of events namely ***"quality planning", "quality control"*** and ***"quality improvement"*** which fits all functions, levels of management and product lines.

Quality triology process starts with quality planning at various levels of the organisation (*for example,* strategic quality planning at top management level, tactical quality planning at middle management level and operational quality planning at junior management level).

The second phase is quality control which has a goal to run the process effectively such that the plans are successfully implemented. The third phase of the trilogy process is quality improvement which deals with the continuous improvement of the product and the process. (This phase is also called as quality breakthrough sequence).

Quality Planning

Steps involved in the quality planning process are:

(*i*) *Identify the customer – both external and internal*

(*ii*) Determine customer needs

(*iii*) Develop product features that respond to customer needs

(*iv*) Establish quality goals that meet the needs of customers and suppliers alike and do so at a minimum combined cost.

(*v*) Develop a process that can produce the needed product features.

(*vi*) Prove process capability.

Quality Control

(*i*) Choose control subjects

(*ii*) Choose units of measurement

(*iii*) Establish measurement

(*iv*) Establish standards of performance

(*v*) Measure actual performance

(*vi*) Interpret the difference between actual performance and standard performance

(*vii*) Take action on the difference.

Quality Improvement

(*i*) Prove the need for improvement

(*ii*) Identify the specific projects for improvement

(*iii*) Organise to guide the projects

(*iv*) Organise for diagnosis for discovery of causes

(*v*) Find the causes

(*vi*) Provide remedies

(*vii*) Prove that the remedies are effective under operating conditions.

(*viii*) Provide control mechanisms to hold the gains.

Strength and Weaknesses of Juran Philosophy

The main strengths are:

(*i*) New understanding of the customer, referring to both internal and external customer.

(*ii*) Management involvement and commitment is stressed.

The main weaknesses are:

(*i*) The emphasis on management's responsibility for quality fails to get the grips with the literature on motivation and leadership.

(ii) The contribution that the worker can make is undervalued.

(iii) The methods advocated are traditional and old fashioned, getting at the basic control systems and failing to deal adequately with the human dimensions of organisations.

Comparison of Deming Philosophy with-Juran Philosophy

Similarities

(i) Both agreed on the importance of top managers in TQM.

(ii) Both agreed on the importance of both internal and external customers, the importance of continuous improvement and the need for effective training and tools.

(iii) Both recognised a crisis of quality in manufacturing.

Differences

(i) Deming is more process oriented while Juran is more concerned about the output.

(ii) Deming believed that everyone in the firm must contribute to the successful implementation of TQM. Juran emphasised on middle managers as key players in this change.

(iii) Deming set a goal of project quality. Juran advocated accepting lower quality if the benefits of achieving perfection would not justify the costs.

(iv) Juran focussed on quantitative costs more than Deming who emphasised more subtle indicators of quality.

(v) Deming identified variance as the target of TQM initiative, while Juran tolerated variances more willingly.

(vi) Juran continued and extended traditional ways of thinking about quality, while Deming advocated a break with tradition and a new approach to quality management.

3.3 THE CROSBY PHILOSOPHY

Philip B. Crosby, the third major influence on the management tools of TQM, was a management consultant and the director of Crosby's Quality College. He also authored several popular books; his first book ***"Quality is Free"*** was the most popular one and sold about one million copies.

Crosby contributed three major ideas to TQM:

- Absolutes of quality management
- 14 steps for quality improvement and
- Quality vaccine.

Box 3.11 : Crosby's 6 'C's

(i) Comprehension (Understanding)
(ii) Commitment (By all)
(iii) Competence (Improvement)
(iv) Correction (Elimination of errors)
(v) Communication (Support of all people, customers and suppliers)
(vi) Continuance (Improvement)

The other aspects of Crosby's quality philosophy are:

(i) He addressed his message to the top management.

(ii) He saw a viable strategy for corporate survival and growth.

(iii) He derived that a firm must invest large sums to improve quality: rather such investments save money (ultimately quality becomes free).

(iv) He advocated a more ambitious goal than simply eliminating problems through improved inspection: rather managers should strive for a goal of zero defects.

(v) Managers should design and build products with the objective of producing products without defects.

(vi) He urged managers to set a corporate tone that denies the inevitability which contrasts his position with Juran.

Absolutes of Quality Management

Box 3.12 : Crosby's "Four Absolutes of Quality"

(i) Quality is ***defined*** as conformance to requirements, not "goodness".

(ii) The ***system*** for achieving quality is prevention, not appraisal.

(iii) The performance ***standard*** is zero defects, not "that is" close enough..

(iv) The ***measurement*** of quality is the price of non-conformances, not indexes.

Crosby's absolutes of quality management includes the following points:

(i) **Quality means conformance to requirements, not elegance :** Crosby recognised only one sensible definition of quality based on exactly what the customer wants. According to him, a firm produces quality only when its good or service meets or exceeds customer's expectations. Managers must ensure that everyone within the firm understands these requirements and must provide the necessary tools to achieve those requirements.

(ii) **There is no such thing as a quality problem :** Problems must be identified by those individuals or departments that cause them. The firm may experience accounting problems, manufacturing problems, design problems and so on. Quality originates in functional departments, not in the quality department.

(iii) **There is no such thing as the economics of quality, doing the job right the first time is always cheaper :** Crosby supports the premise that "economics of quality" has no meaning. Quality is free. What costs money are all actions that involve not doing the job right the first time.

(iv) **The only performance measurement is the cost of quality, which is the expense of non-conformance :** According to Crosby, most companies spend 15 to 20 percent of their sales revenue on quality costs. A company with a well-run quality management program can achieve a cost of quality that is less than 2.5 percent of the sales.

(v) **Quality systems amount to prevention :** The path to successful quality management must begin with a thorough study and evaluation of current processes in which managers identify every opportunity for quality problems to disrupt a process and eliminate those opportunities.

(vi) **The only performance standard is "Zero Defects" (ZD) :** Crosby feels that the **"Zero Defect"** concept is widely misunderstood and resisted. According to Crosby, any effective TQM system sets a goal of zero defects. More than a slogan, the call for zero defects promotes a comprehensive method for defining, producing and delivering a good or service that tries to eliminate any possibility for defects. It also advocates a corporate environment that accepts no possibility of errors.

Box 3.13 : Five Symptoms of a Company that Always has Problem with Quality (Crosby's Diagnosis of a Troubled Company)

(i) The company has an extensive field service for reworking and corrective actions.

(ii) The outgoing product normally deviates from the customer's requirements.

(iii) Management does not provide a clear performance standard, so that employees develop their own.

(iv) Management denies that it is the cause of the problem. Managers tend to blame the workers in order to hide their inability to improve the system.

(v) Management does not recognise the price of the non-conformance.

Crosby's 14 Steps for Quality Improvement

Before managers begin improving quality by implementing Crosby's 14 steps for quality improvement, they should have determined their firm's position on the ***"management maturity grid"*** to assess their firm's current quality culture.

The Management Maturity Grid (or Quality Maturity Grid)

The five states of quality awareness and quality culture are:

(i) **Uncertainty:** The firm remains unaware of the importance of quality as a strong imperative.

(ii) **Awakening:** Managers understand the importance of quality, but they have not yet acted to improve it.

(iii) **Enlightenment:** Managers openly acknowledge the importance of quality and the corporate need for improvement and they have to begin to take concrete action to improve overall quality by establishing a formal program.

(iv) **Wisdom:** Managers have established a quality management program that is working well, identifying problems early and routinely pursuing corrective actions. The program emphasises prevention rather than appraisal.

(v) **Certainty:** Quality has become an unavoidable component of the current management culture. The entire system is designed to ensure that the system can attain its goal of zero defects.

Crosby's 14 steps for quality improvement begin with an echo from Deming's work:

(i) ***Establish management commitment:*** Managers must believe in the importance of quality and demonstrate a real commitment to improvement throughout the organisation by aligning their actions, policies and procedures with the principles of TQM.

(ii) ***Form a quality improvement team:*** With representatives from each department, the team should play a role in establishing all educational and quality oriented policy activities, leading to larger work co-ordinating and supervising the change in corporate culture.

(iii) ***Establish quality measures*** for each activity throughout the company. *For example*, a measure of the operations management function might state the percentage of production time lost due to inadequate operator training or poor equipment maintenance.

(iv) ***Evaluate the cost of quality*** by providing an indication of where corrective action will be profitable for a company.

(v) ***Establish quality awareness*** of employees by training supervisors and communicating through booklets, films and posters.

(vi) ***Instigate corrective action by*** encouraging working people to identify and set right the defects or pass on defects to the next supervisory level who have authority to deal with them.

(vii) ***Zero defect planning:*** Establish an adhoc committee for the "Zero Defect" program to investigate the ZD concept and ways to implement the program.

(viii) ***Employee education:*** Undertake supervisor and employee training so that all managers understand and can explain each step in the quality improvement program.

(ix) ***Hold a zero-defect day*** to establish the new attitude. This day signals to every one that their work must meet a new, higher standard of performance and that expectations have risen significantly.

(x) ***Employee goal setting*** should take place, usually on a 30, 60, 90 day basis. These goals guide performance measurement and evaluation and they keep quality in its necessary place at the forefront of organisational priorities.

(xi) ***Error cause removal*** should follow the identification of problems that prevent error-free work from being achieved. All employees should accept responsibility for identifying problems, correcting them and preventing them from occurring.

(xii) ***Establish recognition*** for those who meet goals or perform outstandingly by the non-financial award program. This recognition motivates others in the firm and sets example for all to imitate.

(xiii) ***Establish and hold*** regular meetings of ***quality councils*** composed of quality professionals and team chair persons, to communicate with each other and to determine action necessary to improve the quality program.

(xiv) ***Do it all over again:*** Because the march towards quality is a never-ending journey, the final step returns the program to the beginning to repeat the entire process. This action reviews everyone's commitment to quality and identifies a new round of opportunities for improvements.

Box 3.14 : Crosby's 14 Points for Quality

(i) Management commitment	*(ii)* Quality improvement team
(iii) Quality measurement	*(iv)* Cost of quality
(v) Quality awareness	*(vi)* Corrective action
(vii) Zero defect planning	*(viii)* Supervisor training
(ix) Zero defects day	*(x)* Goal setting
(xi) Error cause removal	*(xii)* Recognition
(xiii) Quality councils	*(xiv)* Do it all over again

Quality vaccine: Crosby advocated making TQM an integral part of an organisation's activities through his concept of ***quality vaccine.*** The quality vaccine describes a corporate quality management regimen that improves the overall health of the firm and corrects many of its pressing problems. **The major components of Crosby's quality vaccine are illustrated in *Exhibit 3.8.***

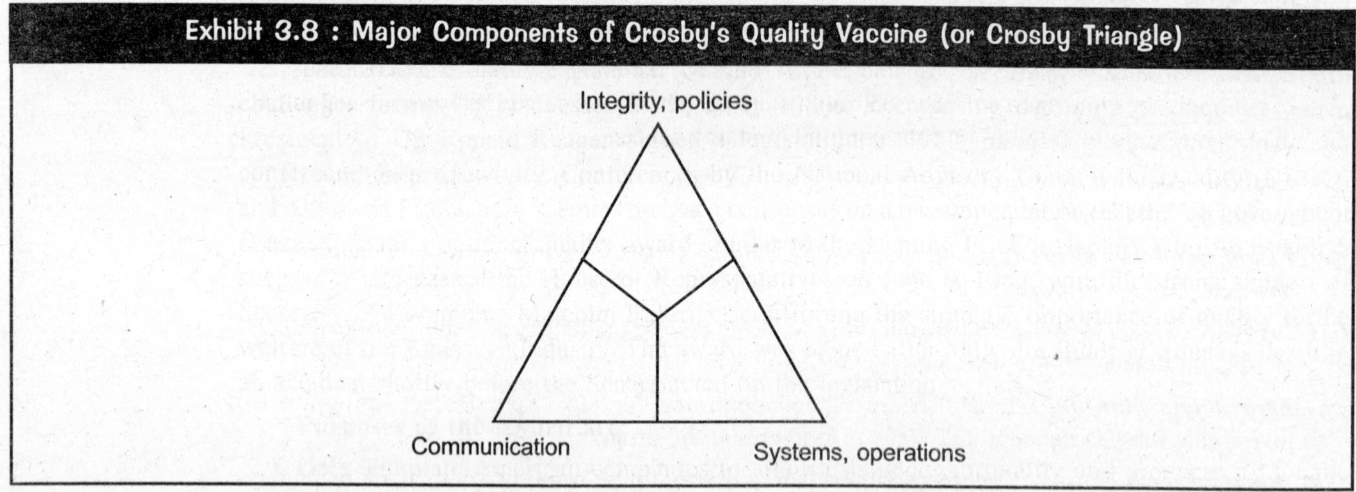

Exhibit 3.8 : Major Components of Crosby's Quality Vaccine (or Crosby Triangle)

Quality vaccine describes a corporate management regimen that improves the overall health of the firm and corrects many other pressing problems.

The three major components of Crosby's quality vaccine are:

- ***Integrity*** **:** Integrity represents an honest attempt by the management to eliminate bureaucracy, improve performance and satisfy customers in the most effective manner possible. It reflects the importance of the firm's commitment to offer products that are right the first time, every time.
- ***Communication*** **:** Communication represents the flow of information, both between functional departments (internal communication) and between the firm and its customers and suppliers (external communication). The vaccine requires regular exchange of information about quality problems, performance on quality characteristics, progress towards quality goals and opportunities for quality improvement.

- ***Systems and operations*** : Systems and operations designed to maintain the firm's new quality environment are the elements of the third component of quality vaccine.

  Top managers use quality vaccine to reorient their firm's culture towards TQM.

  The quality vaccine is administered through:

- Determination—action is the only way forward.
- Education—developing a common language, understanding other's role and acquiring quality knowledge.
- Implementation—guiding the flow of improvement.

Crosby provided a number of tools to help implement his 14 steps for quality improvement in addition to the "Management Maturity Grid" (or Quality Maturity Grid) and "Quality Vaccine" that were discussed earlier under Crosby's philosophy. **These tools are:**

- "Make Certain Programme" and
- Management Style Evaluation which are discussed in the following paragraphs.

"Make Certain Programme" instigates an ongoing examination of procedures and methods by the personnel involved to help them contribute to defect prevention activities regularly. It asks people in groups guided by a facilitator, what their biggest problem is and points out that in most cases, the problems selected are caused for them by others, not themselves.

The group members are asked to find out a solution to tackle these problems and a feedback is obtained. More problems including the self-created ones are then identified. Group members are encouraged to join their supervisors to set up a defect programme to tackle them and make the "Make Certain Programme" a success.

***Management Style Evaluation* encourages managers to evaluate themselves as either ordinary, super or spectacular regarding the following:**

- Listening—taking time to understand people.
- Co-operating—being part of a team.
- Helping—letting someone lean on you without leaning back.
- Transmitting—in writing, prepared speaking and conversation.
- Creating—developing original concepts or expanding on the ideas of others.
- Implementing—figuring out how to do it and doing it right.
- Learning—Pursuing personal development programs.
- Leading—stating objectives clearly, getting commitment of others to those objectives, defining methods of measurement and providing the inspectors to get things done.
- Following—achieving the intent of superior's requests.
- Pretending—acting, a dangerous method of management.

This valuation helps managers to evaluate what assets they have and is the basis for learning about them and subsequently making use of their assets.

Strengths and Weaknesses of Crosby's Philosophy

(i) Crosby's approach is clearer than those of Deming and Juran and is supported by a number of tools.

(ii) Work participation is recognised as having value.

(iii) The idea of 'quality problem' is rejected.

Weaknesses

(i) The philosophy implies that workers are to be blamed for quality problems and

(ii) 'Zero defect' is often misunderstood to mean avoidance of risk and hence may have a negative effect on creativity.

Comparison of the Three Major Quality Philosophies

Crosby's Basic Elements of Improvement include ***determination, education*** and ***implementation***. Determination means that the top management must take quality improvement seriously. Everyone should understand the "Absolutes of Quality Management" which can be accomplished only through education. Finally, every member of the management team must understand the implementation process.

Unlike Deming & Juran, Crosby's program is primarily behavioural. He emphasises using management and organisational processes rather than statistical techniques to change corporate culture and attitudes. Like Juran and unlike Deming, his approach fits well within the existing organisational structures.

Crosby's approach, however, provides relatively few details about how firms should address the finer points of quality management.

Even though Deming, Juran and Crosby, view quality as imperative in the future competitiveness of Western Industry, they have significantly different approaches to implementing organisational change. In each philosophy, quality clearly requires a total commitment from everyone in an organisation. Many managers view quality as a set of tasks to be performed by specialists in quality control. Other managers view quality as a process in which many people at the operating level from a number of functional areas of the organisation are involved. Still, some other managers view quality as an idealogy or philosophy that pervades the entire organisation.

Inspite of the differences in their perspectives, the philosophies of Deming, Juran and Crosby are more alike than different. Each views top management commitment as an absolute necessity, demonstrates that quality management practices will save money, not cost money, places responsibility for quality on management, not the workers, stress the need for continuous, never-ending improvement, acknowledges the importance of the customer and strong management-worker partnerships and recognises the need for and difficulties associated with changing the organisational culture.

3.4 GENICHI TAGUCHI AND TQM

Is it sufficient to control process, inspect output, identify and remove defects and rely on customer feedback? Genichi Taguchi says no. To improve quality, he argues, one must look upstream at the design stage because that is where quality begins. Quality must be designed in, it cannot be inspected later. One fact of obtaining better design is experimentation on variables that contribute to a product's performance. Taguchi's strong belief in this approach has brought ***Design of Experiments*** (DoE) into wider use by quality experts, designers and other members of design-building teams.

Taguchi also believes that teams should aim for ***robust designs*-designs** that can withstand the hard-to-eliminate variabilities that occur in transformation processes or later in customer use.

Taguchi originated ***quality engineering*** which is an approach that involves combining engineering and statistical methods to reduce costs and improve quality by optimising product design and manufacturing processes. ***Taguchi methods*** help product designers estimate the true cost of quality and then cost-effectively improve quality. This is done by improving the design of the product as well as the process by which it is made.

Taguchi's quality loss function: Taguchi asserts that the quality of a product is a function of key product characteristics referred to as performance characteristics. The ideal value (or state) of a performance characteristic is its target value. A high-quality product performs near these target values consistently throughout its life span and under all operating conditions. Taguchi's quality loss function estimates the loss to society from the failure of a product to meet its target value for a particular performance characteristic. This loss can be incurred by the consumers (*e.g.*, short product life, increased maintenance and repair costs), by the company (*e.g.*, increased scrap, rework and warranty costs, damage to the company's reputation, loss of market share) or by society in general (*e.g.*, pollution, safety).

Taguchi's **quality loss function** is a statement that any deviation from the target value of a quality characteristic results in extra costs to some segment of the society. Taguchi defines quality in terms of the social loss - loss to producers and consumers from the time a product is conceived. The smaller the value of this social loss, the more desirable is the product.

***Exhibit 3.9* illustrates Taguchi's Quality Loss Function.**

Exhibit 3.9 : Taguchi's Quality Loss Function

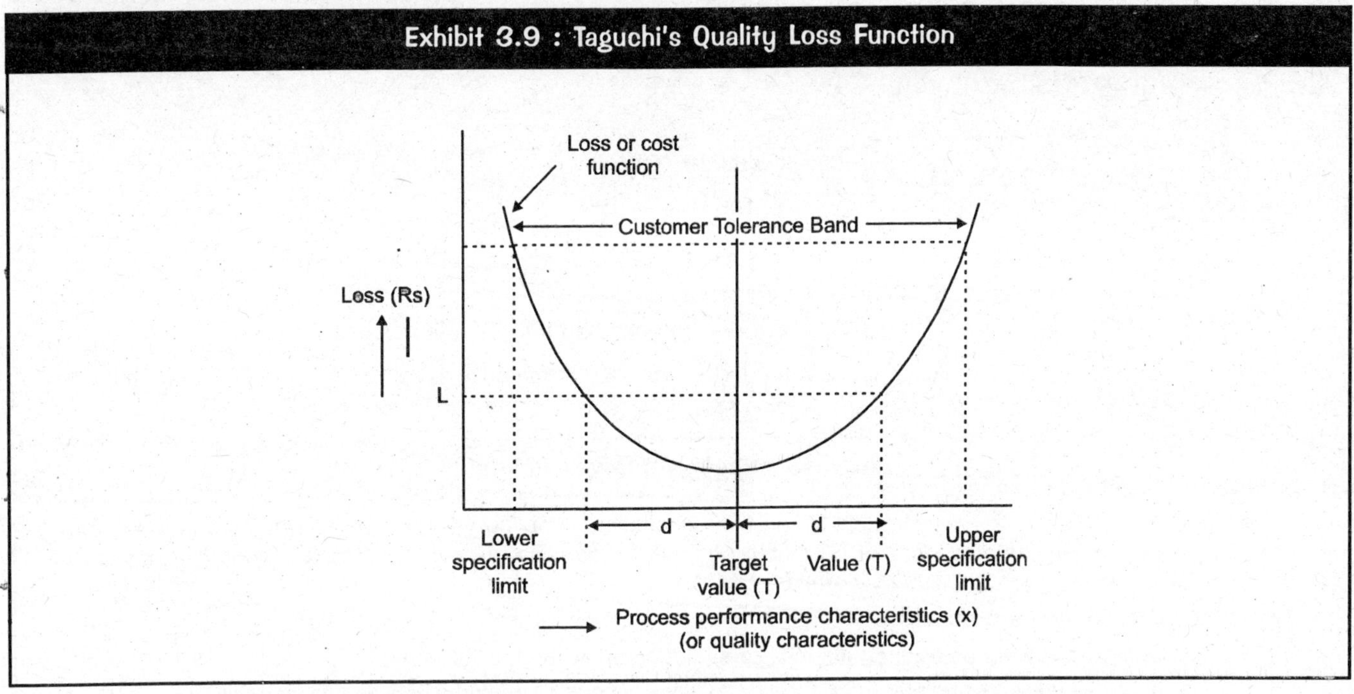

Quality loss function is expressed as

$$L = C (X - T)^2$$

Where L = Total loss

C = a cost constant

X = actual average value of quality characteristic and

T = target value of quality characteristic.

Taguchi holds that the unwelcome costs are associated with any deviation of process performance (or quality characteristic) from the quality characteristic's target value. The loss from performance variation (L) is directly related to the square of the deviation (d) of the performance characteristic (X) from its target value (T).

i.e. $$L = C d^2 = C (X - T)^2$$

Where L = Total loss

C = a cost constant

X = actual average value of quality characteristic and

T = target value of quality characteristic.

According to Taguchi, social loss must affect quality cost management decisions.

Taguchi intends that the loss function remains valid at all times during a product's life. In theory, when process output performance reaches the specification limit (upper or lower specification limit), the customer's ***economic*** interest in the item is neutral, that is, the losses will exactly offset any gain from having the item.

For Taguchi, social loss must affect quality cost management decisions, that is, investments in quality improvement should be compared with savings to society rather than to the firm alone. Ultimately, the society will reward or penalise the firm for its record of societal savings or loss respectively. Taguchi's view is meant to be sound for business.

Example: Estimating the Taguchi Loss function

A certain quality characteristic has a specification of 1.00 ± 0.020. An analysis of company records reveals that if the value of the quality characteristic exceeds the target of 1.00 by the tolerance of 0.020 on either side (*i.e.*, ± 0.020), the product is likely to fail during the warranty period and costs Rs. 100/- for repair. Determine the total loss using Taguchi's loss function for a deviation of ± 0.010.

Solution:

$$100 = C\,(0.020)^2$$

$$C = \frac{100}{(0.020)^2} = \frac{100}{0.0004} = 250{,}000$$

The loss function is

$$L(X) = C\,(X - T)^2 = 2{,}50{,}000\,(X - T)^2$$

If the deviation is only ± 0.010, then the estimated loss is

$$L\,(0.010) = 250{,}000\,(0.010)^2 = \text{Rs. } 25/\text{-}$$

Box 3.15 : Taguchi's Seven Points

Conventionally, quality control activities centre on final inspection sampling or on control charts and process control. This is known as ***"on-line quality control"***. Taguchi pushed the process upstream to focus on product and process design. This is known as ***"off-line quality control"***.

Taguchi's *seven points* are stated as:

(i) Product quality is measured by the total loss to society created by that product.

(ii) Continuous quality improvement and cost reduction are necessary to survive in world competition.

(iii) Quality improvement requires continual and repeated reduction of variation in the product/process performance around the standard nominal values.

(iv) Quality loss is frequently proportional to the square of the deviation of the performance from the nominal value.

(v) Product and process design can have an important impact on a product's quality and cost.

(vi) Performance variation can be reduced by suitable adjustment of the product's parameters and/or the process parameters.

(vii) The appropriate parameter settings that reduce variation can be identified with the appropriate statistically designed experiments.

Strength and Weaknesses of Taguchi's Ideas

The main strengths are:

(i) Taguchi's method pulls quality right back into the design stage rather than relying on adjustments to the process online or inspection of the final product.

(ii) The philosophy identifies quality as a societal issue and not just an organisational one.

The main weaknesses are:

(i) There are no directives about how to manage a quality-oriented organisation, particularly the people.

(ii) Taguchi has nothing to say about humans as social, cultural or political beings and therefore makes no contribution to managing employees.

3.5 KAORU ISHIKAWA AND TQM

Kaoru Ishikawa was a Japanese quality authority until his death in 1989. He acknowledged Deming's and Juran's influence in his thinking. However, Dr. Ishikawa must be recognised for his own contribution to TQM. He was instrumental in the development of the broad outlines by Japanese quality strategy, the concept of CWQC, the audit process used for determining whether a company will be selected to receive the Deming Prize, team-based problem solving and a variety of problem solving tools that he thought any worker could use. He was responsible for the initial deployment of ***Quality Control Circles***—small groups of employees that meet regularly to plan and carry out process changes to improve quality, productivity and the work environment.

He also developed Ishikawa cause and effect charts or fish-bone diagrams: Like Deming, Juran and Feigenbaum, Ishikawa also emphasised on quality as a way of management. He influenced the development of participative, bottom-up view of quality, which became the trademark of the Japanese approach to quality management. **Some key elements of his philosophy are:**

(i) Quality begins with education and ends with education.
(ii) The first step in quality is to know the requirements of customers.
(iii) The ideal state of quality control occurs when inspection is no longer necessary.
(iv) Remove the root cause, not the symptoms.
(v) Quality control is the responsibility of all workers and all divisions.
(vi) Do not confuse means with the objectives.
(vii) Put quality first and set your sights on long-term profits.
(viii) Market is the entrance and exit of quality.
(ix) Top management must not show anger when facts are presented by subordinates.
(x) Ninety-five percent of problems in a company can be solved with simple tools for analysis and problem solving.
(xi) Data without dispersion information (variability) are false data.

3.6 MASAAKI IMAI AND TOTAL QUALITY MANAGEMENT

Masaaki Imai, the chairman of the Cambridge Corporation, an international management consultancy firm, based in Tokyo, brought together the management philosophies, theories and tools as a single concept—"Kaizen", which he says, has been responsible for Japan's economic success.

***"Kaizen"* is a Japanese name for a formal system to promote continuous improvement.**

Understanding Kaizen

Kaizen begins with the notion that an organisation can assure its long-term survival and success only when every member in the operating system and throughout the firm, actively pursues opportunities to identify and implement improvements everyday. *Kaizen* sets no conditions for the magnitudes of improvement. Infact, it often favours small, incremental improvements by understanding the functions of the current system and its weaknesses or relative inefficiencies. Furthermore, small improvements gain returns for the firm without the need for large, initial investments to fund major innovations like a new, automated assembly line. The quality improvement perspective of *Kaizen* is best described by an old saying, ***"Every day and in every way, we are getting better and better."***

"Kaizen" is a Japanese term that means gradual unending improvement by doing little things better and setting and achieving increasingly higher standards. It is also referred to as "continuous improvement".

***"Kaizen"* refines its emphasis on daily, incremental improvement for three guiding principles:**

(i) **Process view of the system :** The process analysis could affect a process for making a product or a process for designing a product among other processes.
(ii) **Stress comes from people :** *Kaizen* program relies heavily on people's knowledge of their firm's processes and their insights and intuition to conceive improvements. Success requires discipline, employee participation, skill development and effective communication.

(iii) **Constant sense of urgency :** A successful Kaizen program depends on unceasing awareness of the need for change. Everyone must feel that they can improve their performances and never accept a current process, however, good as sufficient. Complacency and overconfidence weaken *Kaizen.* More about Kaizen will be discussed in later chapters.

3.7 A.V. FEIGENBAUM AND TQM

Armand V. Feigenbaum is best known for originating the concept of total quality control (TQC). His book 'Total Quality Control' was first published in 1951 under the title "Quality Control, Principles, Practice and Administration". He viewed quality as a strategic business tool that requires involvement from everyone in the organisation and promoted the use of quality costs as a measurement and evaluation tool. Feigenbaum's philosophy is summarised in his ***"Three Steps To Quality"***.

(i) **Quality Leadership :** A continuous management emphasis is based on sound planning rather than reaction to failures. Management must maintain a constant focus and lead the quality effort.

(ii) **Modern Quality Technology :** The traditional quality development cannot resolve 80 to 90 per cent of quality problems. This task requires the integration of office staff, engineers as well as shop-floor workers in the process who continually evaluate and implement new techniques to satisfy customers in the future.

"Poka-Yoke" is a Japanese term for "mistake proofing" and "fool proofing". It is a technique to help avoid human error.

(iii) **Organisational Commitment :** Continuous training and motivation of the entire workforce as well as an integration of quality in business planning indicate the importance of quality and provide the means for including it in all respects of the firm's activities.

The concept of **'total quality control'** was used as the foundation by Japanese for their practice called Company-Wide Quality Control (CWQC) which began in 1960s. Feigenbaum's ideas also have become important elements of the Malcolm Baldrige National Quality Award Criteria.

Box 3.16 : Key Elements of Feigenbaum's Philosophy of Quality Control

1. Total quality control is a system for integrating quality development, maintenance and improvement efforts in an organisation that will enable engineering, marketing, production and service to function at optimal economic levels while achieving customer satisfaction.
2. The "control" aspect of quality control should involve setting quality standards, appraising performance relative to these standards, taking corrective action when the standards are not met and planning for improvement in the standards.
3. Factors that affect quality can be divided into two major categories: technological and human. The human factor is the more important one.
4. Operating quality costs can be divided into four categories: prevention costs, appraisal costs, internal failures costs and external failure costs.
5. It is important to control quality at the source.

3.8 SHIGEO SHINGO AND TQM

Shigeo Shingo had interest in scientific management very early in his career. Later on he took interest in the application of statistical quality control. His contribution to quality management, however, arose from a personal realisation that statistical methods detect errors too late in the manufacturing process. What is needed is to identify errors as they happen and to correct or deal with them right away.

To this end, Shingo proposed his own version of **"zero defects"**. This is called **"Poka-yoke"** in Japanese which means **"fool proofing"**. The idea is to handle errors as they occur. Initially, potential error sources in the manufacturing process are identified. All potential points of error must be located and at each point, monitoring for error is undertaken.

To produce perfect quality the first time every time, operations managers must identify all the opportunities for error and eliminate them. They must design parts and processes that make the desired results inevitable. This goal guides "Poka-Yoke" or fool proofing.

Opportunities for error arise for many reasons. An incomplete process may leave workers to supply missing pieces. Poor markings may allow confusion about how to combine parts. Poor communication about the exact sequence of activities may lead to variance when workers follow conflicting procedures.

Poka-Yoke tries to change either the process or its resources to eliminate the need to rely on human experience and accumulated knowledge.

Business Process Reengineering which will be discussed in a later chapter can be viewed as a form of "Poka-Yoke".

Strength and Weaknesses

The main strengths are :

(i) The method provides online, real-time measures for immediate use.

(ii) Poka-Yoke emphasises dealing with technological issues with a relevant technical feedback and control system.

The main weaknesses are :

(i) The emphasis on source inspection by non-human instruments can only effectively be employed in manufacturing.

(ii) Shingo's ideas have nothing to say about human beings in terms of them as social, cultural or political beings.

3.9 DR. WALTER SHEWHART AND TQM

Dr. Walter Shewhart, a mathematician at Bell Laboratories, specialising in statistics, recognised that the variability associated with manufactured component dimensions followed a **"normal distribution"**. He reasoned that one could track component dimensions to determine whether they were starting to drift out of normal range. He recognised that as long as the dimensions remained in the normal range, their variability was under control. If they start to drift out of normal range, some assignable cause was occurring in the process leading to production of parts which fall outside their limits of allowed variation (*i.e.,* tolerance on dimensions or any other quality characteristic). Shewhart identified the difference between common (or chance) causes and special (or assignable) causes of variation in the manufacturing process. He developed a simple but powerful tool, *i.e.,* the control chart to separate the chance causes and assignable causes of variation. This tool is also known as **"statistical process control"** which is defined as a process used to monitor standards, making measurements and taking corrective action as a product or service being produced.

The statistical process control is used to measure performances of a process. A process is said to be operating in the ***state of statistical control*** when the only source of variation pertains to common (or chance or natural) causes which are inherent in the process and do not cause any major variation in the quality characteristic of the product or service produced by the process. The process must first be brought into statistical control by detecting and eliminating special (or assignable) causes of variation. The objective of a process control system such as **"Statistical Process Control"** (SPC) is to provide a *statistical signal* when assignable causes of variation are present in the process. Such a signal can quicken appropriate action to eliminate assignable causes of variation in the process. More about statistical process control and construction of control charts will be discussed in the later chapters.

Even though the methods of statistical quality control were introduced by Dr. Walter Shewhart in 1924 itself, in the following years, Dr. W. Shewhart, Dodge and Romig did early work on the concept of acceptance sampling. Much of Shewhart's thinking on these techniques was published in 1931 in his book *"Economic Control of Quality of Manufactured Product"*, in which he introduced the basic concepts of Statistical Quality Control (SQC), including the control chart. Dr. W. Shewhart is rightly known as the father of "SQC".

Thinking statistically is a basic part of the TQM philosophy. Much of the challenge in implementing continuous improvement is centred on controlling the ongoing processes by statistical methods, by detecting the assignable causes of variation and eliminating them by the use of control charts.

Advantages of statistical process control are :

(i) It places the responsibility for quality in the hands of the operator (or worker).

(ii) It allows operators (or workers) to determine whether the process is drifting out of control before defective component is produced from the process and in doing so, allows the prevention of defects (rather than detection).

3.10 OVERVIEW AND CRITICISM OF QUALITY PHILOSOPHIES

Each quality guru whose contributions to TQM were discussed in this chapter has his own knowledge base and interests. Each has worked in different situations and several have contributed in contrasting eras. This naturally has influenced the way their ideas have developed. Hence, we find a great diversity in their philosophies, principles and methods.

There are two main areas of focus of the various philosophies discussed earlier.

They are: *(i)* the technical needs of quality control and *(ii)* the human dimension of quality management.

Technical needs of prediction and control are met largely by statistical and quantitative methods. The philosophies of some quality gurus cover technical needs from design right through to inspection of the final product.

Management of the human dimensions of organisation is not clearly provided for in these quality philosophies. The gurus mention their interest in managing people, but offer a few tangible principles and virtually no applicable methods. Quality Control Circles (QCC) provide the clearest exposition to generate motivation, autonomy and creativity through an approach that is clearly defined. While QCCs target groups of people (*i.e.*, employees), individuals have been targeted by the management method like ***"quality of work life"*** (QWL) which is not a part of the quality philosophies of quality gurus. "Quality of work life" shifts the key perspective to the individual worker as regards his/her potential and skills and feeling about the job. It promotes meaningful recognition for workers and members of organisations as individuals. "Employee suggestion schemes" and "job-enrichment programs" are other management methods to complement the quality philosophies discussed.

3.11 QUALITY IN PRACTICE

Box 3.17 : Ford becomes a "Deming Company"

Ford Company has been one of the leaders in adopting the Deming philosophy. Dr. Deming visited Ford in 1981. He met the President and other company officials who were stimulated by NBC's program, "If Japan can... why can't we?" Deming gave several seminars for top executives of Ford Company and had meetings with various employees, suggesting changes corresponding to his 14 points. Ford managers visited Nashua Corporation to learn how statistical methods were used. Chief executives from many of Ford's major suppliers visited Japan. Deming's 14 points became the basis for a transformation of Ford's philosophy.

Company Mission, Values and Guiding Principles of Ford Motor Company

Mission: Ford Company is a world-wide leader in automotive and automotive related products and services as well as in newer industries such as aerospace, communication and financial services. Its mission is stated as "Our mission is to improve continually our products and services to meet our customer's needs, allowing us to prosper as a business and to provide a reasonable return for our stockholder, the owners of our business."

Values: How we accomplish our mission is as important as the mission itself. Fundamental to success for the company are these basic values.

People: Our people are the source of our strength. They provide our corporate intelligence and determine our reputation and vitality. Involvement and teamwork are our core human values.

Products: Our products are the end result of our efforts; and that should be best in serving customers world-wide. As our products are viewed, so are we viewed.

Profits: Profits are the ultimate measure of how efficiently we provide customers with best products for their needs. Profits are required to survive and grow.

GUIDING PRINCIPLES

- **Quality** comes first.
- **Customers** are the focus of everything we do.
- **Continuous improvement** is essential to our success.
- **Employee involvement** is our way of life.
- Dealers and suppliers are our **partners**.
- **Integrity** is never compromised.

Ford has developed a policy of ***"Total Quality Excellence"*** that emphasises the importance of quality in every action, operation and product associated with Ford Motor Company. The fundamental precepts of this policy are:

- Quality is defined by the customer.
- Quality excellence can best be achieved by preventing problems rather than by detecting and correcting them after they occur.
- The company employees, suppliers and dealers can influence some part of the process and affect the quality of the output and the ultimate customer satisfaction.
- Sustained quality excellence requires continuous process improvement.
- People provide the intelligence and generate the actions that are necessary to realise these improvements.
- Each employee is a customer for work done by other employees or suppliers, with a right to expect good work from others and an obligation to contribute work of high calibre to those who, in turn, are his or her customers.
- The goal of Ford Total Quality Excellence is to achieve superior external and internal customer satisfaction level.

3.12 SUMMARY

Three eminent persons of the US – Dr. W. Edward Deming, Dr. Joseph Juran and Phillip B. Crosby, who are known as **"quality gurus"** together with Masaki Imai of Japan led the development of quality management tools and philosophies that created a **"quality revolution"** in the 20th century and laid the foundation for total quality management practices of today.

Dr. Deming is known for his "14 points for management", 7 deadly sins and diseases", "the theory of variance" and "the role of management in TQM".

Dr. Juran outlined "habit of quality", "quality trilogy" and "universal break-through sequence". His "Quality Control Hand Book" is called the Bible of quality. Philip B. Crosby enumerated absolutes of quality management and 14 steps for quality improvement. He is well known for his concept of "zero defects" and his book titled "Quality is free".

Masaki Imai is known for his concept of "Kaizen" meaning "Continuous Improvement".

In addition to the above pioneers in quality management, the other contributors are: *(i)* A.V. Feigenbaum, *(ii)* Kaoru Ishikawa, *(iii)* Genichi Taguchi, *(iv)* Dr. Walter Shewhart and *(v)* Shigeo Shingo.

All these made significent contribution to quality leadership and total quality management.

Deming's philosophy is based on improving products and services by reducing uncertainty and variations. Systems thinking, statistical understanding of variation, the theory of knowledge and psychology are the foundations of his philosophy. His 14 points advocate radical cultural change in organisations.

Deming's ***chain reaction*** states that quality improvement reduces costs, increases productivity, increases market share and allows firms to stay in business and provide jobs.

Joseph Juran's philosophy seeks to provide change in the management system. Quality is defined as fitness for use. The **quality trilogy** – planning, control and improvement provides a direction for quality assurance in organisations.

Philip Crosby's approach to quality is summarised in his **"Absolutes of Quality Management"**. He emphasises more on behavioural change than the use of statistical techniques.

Masaki Imai's concept of **"Kaizen"** has been largely responsible for Japan's economic success. Three guiding principles of "Kaizen" are: *(i)* Process view of the system, *(ii)* Stress comes from people and *(iii)* Constant sense of urgency.

A.V. Feigenbaum views quality as a strategic business tool and coined the phrase **"total quality control"**. He promoted the importance of shifting quality responsibility to everyone in the organisation and developing cost of quality approach.

Kaoru Ishikawa was instrumental in the Japanese quality movement, particularly in advocating a **companywide quality control** approach, the use of employee teams and the use of problem solving tools for quality improvement.

Genichi Taguchi advocated that to improve quality one must look upstream at the design stage because that is where quality begins. Taguchi's strong belief in this approach has brought **"design of experiments"** into wider use by quality experts and designers. He believed that design teams should aim for robust designs. He also originated "quality engineering" which is an approach to combine engineering and statistical methods to reduce costs and improve quality. Taguchi is well known for his ***"quality loss function"*** called **"Taguchi's quality loss function"**, which estimates the loss to society from the failure of a product to meet its target value for a particular performance characteristic.

Dr. Walter Shewhart recognised that the variability associated with manufactured component dimensions followed a ***"normal distribution"***. He advocated the use of statistical process control (control charts) to monitor the on-going process and to ensure that the process is operating in the ***"state of statistical control"***. He also did some early work on acceptance sampling technique along with Dodge and Romig.

Shigeo Shingo proposed his own version of "zero defects" called ***"poka-yoke"*** in Japanese meaning **"fail safing"**. The idea is to avoid making errors and handle errors as they occur.

3.13 KEY WORDS USED

Deming Chain Reaction, Deming Prize, Seven Deadly Diseases and Sins, Deming Wheel, Deming Cycle, P-D-C-A Cycle, Deming Triangle, Quality Trilogy, Quality Habit, Quality Planning, Quality Control, Quality Improvement, Quality Vaccine, Crosby's Triangle, Kaizen, Continuous Improvement, Quality Control Circle, Ishikawa Diagram, Fish-bone Diagram, Quality Engineering, Design of Experiments, Taguchi Methods, Robust Design, Taguchi's Quality Loss Function, Poka-Yoke, Fool-Proofing, Statistical Process Control, Quality of Work Life.

3.14 OBJECTIVE QUESTIONS

(A) Match the following :

Column A	Column B
1. Deming	1. Quality vaccine
2. Juran	2. Total Quality control
3. Feigenbaum	3. Seven Deadly Diseases
4. Crosby	4. Quality Trilogy
5. Ishikawa	5. Poka-Yoke
6. Taguchi	6. Kaizen
7. Shigeo shingo	7. Quality control circle
8. Masaaki Imai	8. Quality Loss Function
9. W. Shewhart	9. Statistical Quality control

(B) State whether following statements are True or False :

1. Most of Deming's work revolves around his "Theory of variance". (T / F)
2. 'Deming cycle' and "PDCA cycle" are not one and the same. (T / F)
3. Philip Crosby developed the concept of "cost of quality". (T / F)
4. Juran authored the book titled "Quality is Free". (T / F)
5. Crosby advocated the concept of "Quality vaccine". (T / F)
6. Quality circle is a large group of employees from different work areas. (T / F)
7. Feigenbaum is known as the "Father of Statistical Quality control". (T / F)
8. Poka-yoke is Shigeo Shingo's version of 'zero defects'. (T / F)
9. "Cause-and-Effect Diagram" is also known as "Fish-bone Diagram" or Ishikawa Diagram. (T / F)
10. Taguchi advocated robust designs. (T / F)

(C) Multiple choice Questions : Choose the correct answer from the alternatives given under each question :

1. Which quality guru's work is based on "theory of variance" :
   (a) Juran (b) Crosby
   (c) Deming (d) W. Shewhart
   (e) Taguchi
2. The book titled "Quality Control Hand Book" was authorised by :
   (a) Deming (b) Juran
   (c) Crosby (d) Feigenbaum
   (e) Masaaki Imai
3. Who developed the concept of the "Cost of Quality" :
   (a) Crosby (b) Deming
   (c) Shigeo Shingo (d) Juran
   (e) W. Shewhart.
4. Dodge and Romig are known for their work on the concept of _______
   (a) Statistical process control (b) Quality loss function
   (c) Acceptance sampling (d) Design of experiments
   (e) Quality vaccine.
5. Genichi Taguchi's quality loss function is expressed as:
   (a) $L = \frac{C}{(X-T)^2}$ (b) $L = \frac{C}{(X+T)^2}$
   (c) $L = C(X - T)^2$ (d) $L = \frac{(X-T)^2}{C}$
   (e) $L = C(X + T)^2$

3.15 REVIEW QUESTIONS

1. What is meant by "Deming Chain Reaction"? Explain.
2. State Deming's 14 points for quality management. Explain the interrelationships among them. How do they support each other? Why must they be reviewed as a whole rather than individually?
3. What are "Deming's Deadly Diseases"? How do they relate to his 14 points.
4. Explain Deming's "Theory of variance".
5. Discuss the strengths and weaknesses of Deming's philosophy.
6. Explain Juran's "Quality Trilogy".
7. Define the terms quality of design, quality of conformance and quality habit.
8. Discuss the strengths and weaknesses of Juran's philosophy.
9. Briefly describe Crosby's "Absolutes of Quality Management ".
10. Define the terms "quality vaccine" and quality habit.
11. Explain the 14 steps involved in Crossby's quality management.
12. Discuss the strengths and weaknesses of Crossby's philosophy.
13. Discuss the concept of "total quality control" originated by A.V. Feigenbaum.
14. Discuss the contribution of Kaoru Ishikawa to quality management.
15. Discuss the strengths and weaknesses of Taguchi's ideas of quality management.
16. Discuss the contributions of Shigeo Shingo and Dr. Walter Shewhart to quality management.
17. Explain how is Juran's philosophy similar or different from Deming's.
18. Explain Taguchi's "Quality Loss Function" with an illustration for estimating the same.

3.16 DISCUSSION QUESTIONS

1. Discuss the interrelationships among Deming's 14 points. How do they support each other? Why must they be viewed as a whole rather than separately?
2. What is Juran's Quality Trilogy? How is it different from management approches in other functional areas of business, such as finance?
3. Which quality philosophy - Deming, Juran or Crosby - do you personally feel more comfortable with? Why?
4. Summarise Juran's philosophy. How is it similar to and different from Deming's?
5. Discuss how Deming's 14 points can be applied to an academic environment. How can learning and class room performance be improved by applying Deming's philosophy.

3.17 ASSIGNMENTS

1. Study the annual reports of any medium or large scale company of your choice over a period of five years. Prepare a report about the evidence of implementation of the quality philosophies of the quality gurus discussed in this chapter.
2. Discuss the quality of the service experienced by you while using the services of *(i)* Bank *(ii)* Post office *(iii)* Public transport and *(iv)* Hospital
   Suggest some TQM approaches that might help these organisations to improve their services.

3.18 CHAPTER CASE

HOW JAPAN CAUGHT UP WITH UNITED STATES AND HOW UNITED STATES CAUGHT BACK UP WITH JAPAN

Immediately following World War II, the quality of products produced by Japanese companies was not good enough to compete in the international market place. The only advantage Japanese companies had was price. Japanese goods were cheaper than that of Western manufacturers. The manufacturing companies in the US considered the Japanese threat as being rooted in cost rather than quality.

Reading the future more realistically, Japanese companies saw quality as the key to success and in 1950, began doing something seriously about it. By the late 1940s, key industrial leaders in Japan realised that the key to competing in the international market place is quality. Some industrial leaders in Japan invited Deming to visit Japan and share his views on quality. Unlike their counterparts in the US, the Japanese industrialists accepted Deming's views, learnt his techniques and adopted his philosophy. While Japanese companies were slowly but patiently and persistently creating a quality based infrastructure (people, processes and facilities), American companies were still focusing on cost, shifting the manufacture of labour-intensive products off-shore and and at the same time, neglecting infrastructure improvements.

By the mid 1970s the quality of Japanese manufactured goods in such key areas as automobiles and consumer electronics products was better than that of competing American firms. As a result, Japanese exports increased exponentially while those of Western countries experienced corresponding decreases.

This explains how Japan rose up out of the ashes of World War II to become a world leading industrial nation. But the story did not end there. After losing market share to the Japanese for more than two decades, companies in the United States began to embrace the principles of quality management. As a result, by the mid 1990s companies in the US had reasserted themselves in the global market place.

Now the two countries are like well-matched heavy-weight boxers who slug it out everyday in the world of global business. On any given day either can win the global business battle. There are no longer any automatic winners. Regardless of whether they are Japanese or American, those companies that adhere to the principles of quality management and continually improve are the ones that will win in today's market place.

Questions :

1. Why do you think that companies in the United States were slow to adopt the quality management principles Japanese had used to gain market share world-wide?
2. What were Deming's contributions to the quality revolution in Japan?

CHAPTER 4

FRAMEWORKS FOR ORGANISATIONAL QUALITY

LEARNING OBJECTIVES

After reading this chapter, you should be able to:

- Understand the models of achieving total quality management.
- Discuss Malcolm Baldrige National Quality Award and the criteria for performance excellence.
- Discuss the various international quality award programs.
- Briefly describe the features of TQMEX model.
- Understand the meaning of "Kite-Marks" and how to achieve TQM kitemarks.
- Discuss CII-EXIM Bank Award for excellence.
- Discuss RGNQ Award, GPNQ Award and IMCRBNQ Award and their features.

4.0 INTRODUCTION

The philosophies of Deming, Juran, Crosby and others provide much guidance and wisdom in the form of **"best practices"** to managers around the world, leading to the development of numerous awards and certifications for recognising effective application of total quality principles. Although awards justifiably recognise only a select few, the award or certification criteria provide **frameworks for managing** from which every organisation can benefit. The two frameworks that have had the most impact on quality management practices worldwide are the US Malcolm Baldrige National Quality Award (MBNQA) and international ISO 9000 certification process. Recently, the concept of Six Sigma has evolved into unique framework for managing quality.

4.1 MODELS OF ACHIEVING TQM

Effective quality management programs focus on prevention of defects rather than detection of defects through inspection.

In the previous chapter, we discussed the quality management philosophies of the ***quality gurus*** and their contribution to the development of total quality management.

Essentially, quality is a strategic goal that an organisation must achieve to survive and grow. This is true because of the high costs created by poor quality. Because of the importance of quality, it is essential for an organisation to extend responsibility for quality beyond any single functional unit such as the quality control department or quality assurance department to every member of the organisation since every employee in an organisation affects the quality of the product or service delivered to customers.

Effective quality management programs focus on prevention of defects rather than detection of defects through inspection. To reliably improve quality, an organisation must ensure that it understands and improves the process that generates quality. Continuous improvement helps in achieving success for an organisation to deliver a little better quality on a continuous basis. Effective quality management requires support and commitment of managers, from the top down, to inspire and direct the actions of employees who must ultimately deliver quality. **Total employee involvement and an organisation culture for total quality are as equally important as top management initiative and support to total quality**. Quality improves when an organisation focusses its corporate culture on the goal of building quality into its most essential structures.

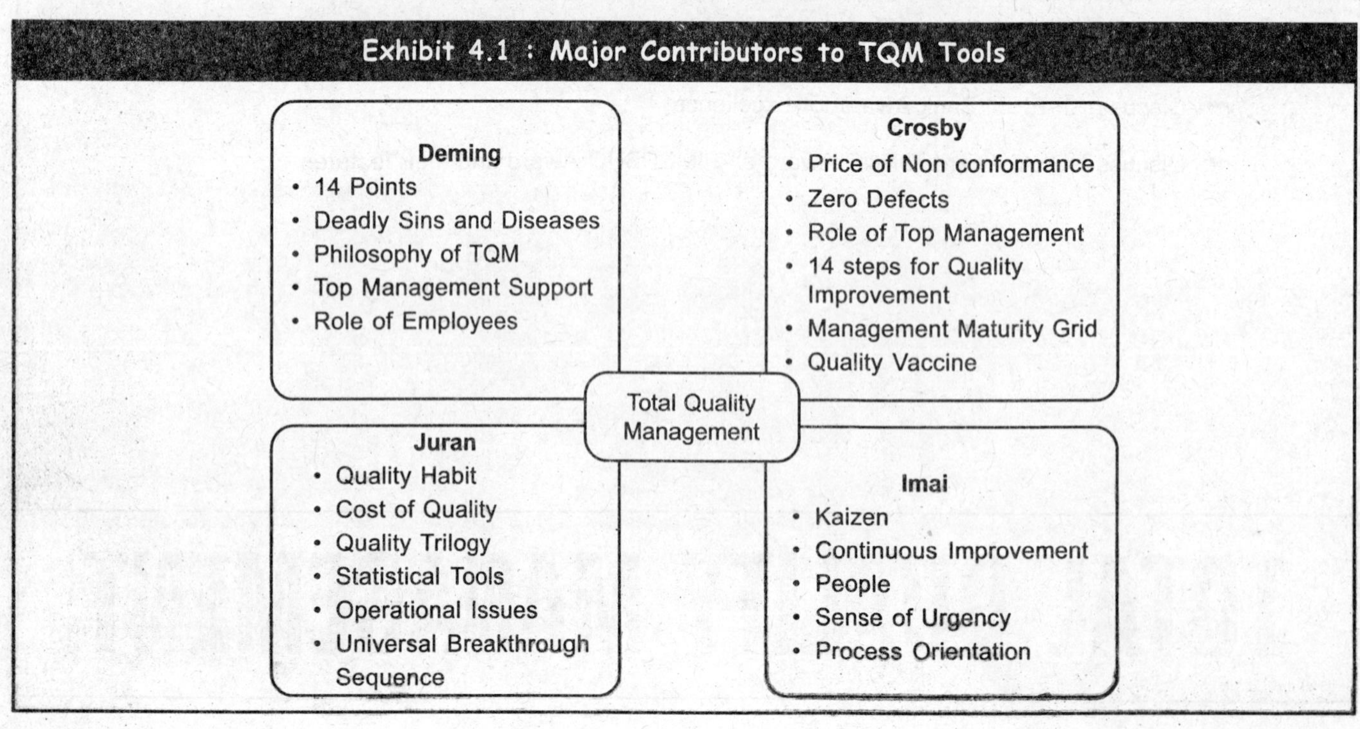

Workers can deliver quality only if their managers provide them appropriate tools and adequate education and training in the use of these tools.

***Exhibit 4.1* illustrates the contributions of Deming, Juran, Crosby and Imai to the current practice of total quality management in a summarised form.**

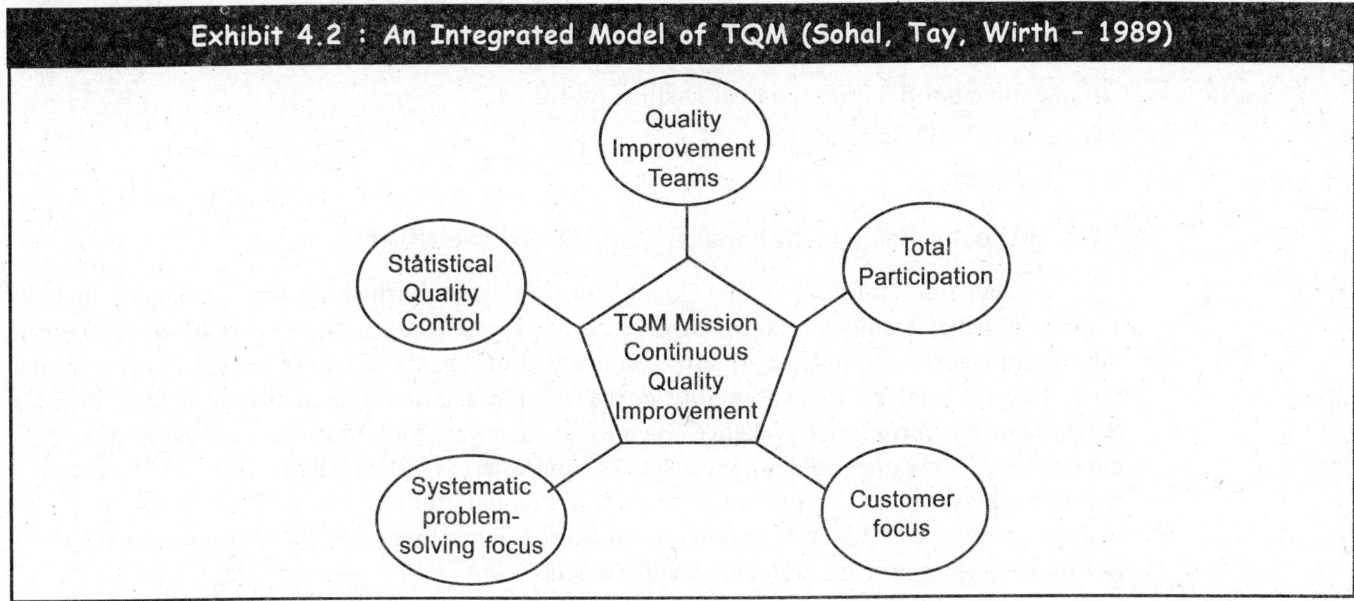

Exhibit 4.2 : An Integrated Model of TQM (Sohal, Tay, Wirth - 1989)

The mission of continuous quality improvement can be achieved to deliver satisfying service to the customer (internal and external) by :

- involving people at the grass-root level
- improving their morale, sense of belonging and responsibility
- using statistical techniques to analyse collected data and adopting plan-do-check-action (PDCA) cycle.

***Exhibit 4.2* illustrates an integrated model of TQM and *Exhibit 4.3* illustrates the building blocks of Zaire model for achieving total quality.**

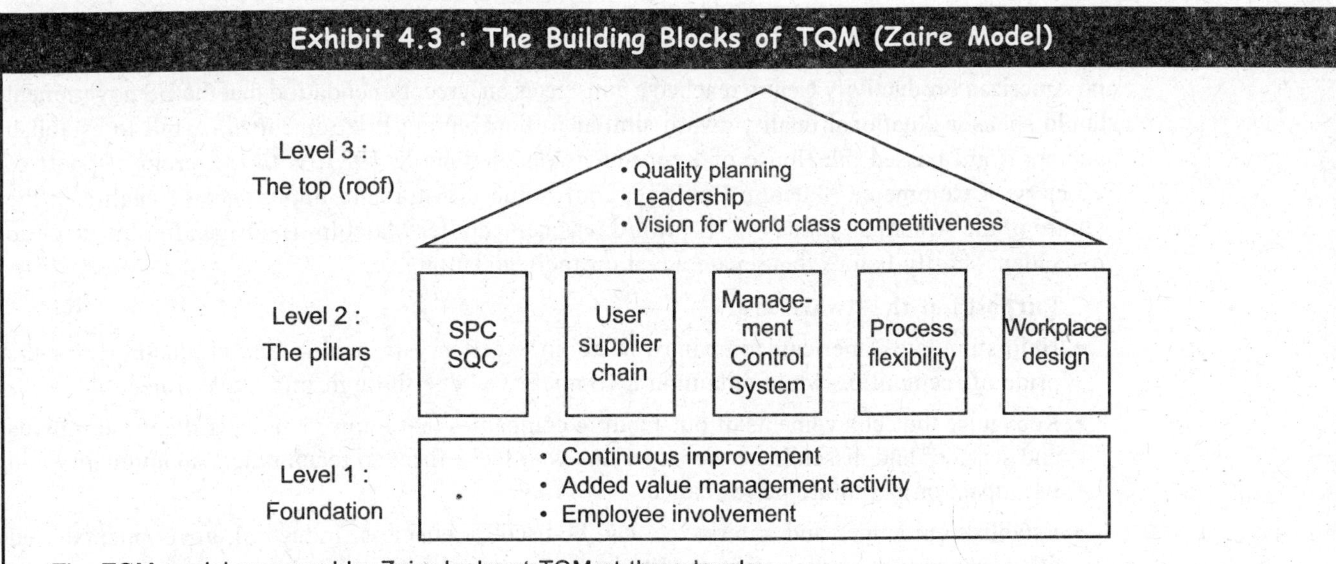

Exhibit 4.3 : The Building Blocks of TQM (Zaire Model)

The TQM model proposed by Zaire looks at TQM at three levels:

1. The ***foundation*** is formed by the continuous improvement, added value management and employee involvement.
2. The ***pillars*** of the model constitute statistical process control, statistical quality control, user-supplier chain, management control systems, advanced manufacturing systems and work place design.
3. The ***top level (roof)*** of the model is formed by quality planning, leadership and vision for the world class competitiveness.

"TQM depends on these building blocks which together determine the strength and safety of the organisation."

4.2 EMERGING QUALITY STANDARDS

Quality standards specify commonly accepted global standards or specifications for quality

Quality management is a continuous process. Its essential importance requires vigilant protection from compromises driven by short-term considerations or actions. The interest in quality of products and services has created a need for commonly accepted global standards or specifications for quality, as standards for routine activities and as a basis for competition. **Three developments are contributing towards this phenomenon. They are:**

(i) the Malcolm Baldrige National Quality Award

(ii) the ISO 9000 Standards and

(iii) Six Sigma.

4.2.1 Malcolm Baldrige National Quality Award (MBNQA)

The Malcolm Baldrige National Quality Award was established by the US Congress in 1987 to promote better quality management practices and improved quality results by the American industry. In many ways, it is the American equivalent of Japan's **"Deming Prize"**. It is one of the most powerful catalysts of total quality in the US and also throughout the world. The award's **"Criteria for Performance Excellence"** establish a framework for integrating total quality principles and practices in any organisation. The award is administered by the National Institute of Standards and Technology and only US-based companies are eligible for the award. The Malcolm Baldrige National Quality Award Web Page at ***www.quality.nist.gov.*** provides current information about the award, the performance criteria and award winners.

Each year, the ***Baldrige Award*** is given to almost two US companies in each of **three categories**: **manufacturing, service** and **small business**, that best represent the successful **implementation of quality in the design, production and delivery of the products** for the market place. The award recognises companies that represent the most effective pursuit and attainment of total quality. **See *Box 4.1* which lists the past winners from 1988 to 2003.**

The Malcolm Baldrige National Quality Award emerged as a response to the competitive challenges facing US businesses in the early 1980s. Recognising declining productivity , then President of US Ronald Reagan signed a legislation in 1982 mandating a national study and conference on productivity. Conferences by the National Advisory Council for Quality (NACQ) and American Productivity Centre reached a consensus on a recommendation that the US government should sponsor a national quality award similar to the Deming Prize in Japan. A bill to establish such an award passed the House of Representatives on June 8, 1987, with the strong support of Secretary of Commerce Malcolm Baldrige, confirming the strategic importance of quality to the welfare of the American Industry. The award was named after Malcolm Baldrige after his death in an accident shortly before the Senate acted on the legislation.

Purposes of the Award are:

- Help stimulate American companies to attain excellence in quality and productivity for the pride of recognition while obtaining a competitive edge through improved projects.
- Recognise the achievements of outstanding companies that improve the quality of their goods and services and disseminate the experiences of these firms to teach others about quality and its impact on corporate performance.
- Establish guidelines and criteria that can be used by business, industrial, governmental, and other enterprises in evaluating quality improvement efforts.
- Gather detailed information from award winners about how to manage for superior quality by changing corporate cultures and practices and provide specific guidance for other American enterprises.

Box 4.1 : The Malcolm Baldrige National Quality Award Winners

Year	Manufacturing	Small Business	Service
1988	(i) Motorola Inc, Schaumburg IL.	Globe Metallurgical Inc. – Beverly, OH.	None awarded
	(ii) Commercial Nuclear Fuel division of Westing house Electric Corp., Pittsburg. PA.	None awarded	None awarded
1989	(i) Milliken & Co., Spartanburg, S.C		
	(ii) Xerox Corp. Business Products and Systems, Rochester. NY.	None awarded	None awarded
1990	(i) Cadillac Motor Car Divison of General Motors, Detroit, MI	Wallace Co. Inc. Houston TX.	Federal Express Corp., Memphis TN
	(ii) IBM – Rochester, Rochester, Mn		
1991	(i) Solectron corp, Milpitas, CA. (ii) Zytec corp, Eden Prairie, Mn	Marlow Industries, Dallas, TX	None awarded
1992	(i) AT&T Network Systems Group/ Transmission systems Business unit, Morristown, NJ (ii) Texas Instruments Inc, Defence systems & Electronics Group, Dallas.	Granite Rock Co. Watsonville, CA	(i) AT & T Universal Card Services, Jackson ville, FL. (ii) The Ritz Carlton Hotel Co. Atlanta, GA
1993	Eastman Chemical Co., Kingsport, TN	None awarded	None awarded
1994	None awarded	Wain wright Industries Inc. St. Peters, MO	(i) AT&T consumer Communications Services, Basking Ridge, NJ. (ii) GTE Directories Corp Dallas/ Fortworth TX
1995	(i) Armstrong World Industries, Building Products Operations, Lancaster, PA (ii) Corming Tele -Communications Products Division, Corning, NY	None awarded	None awarded
1996	ADAC Laboratories Milpitas, CA	(i) Custom Research Inc. Minneapolis, (ii) Trident Precision Manufacturing Inc. Webster, NY	Dana Commercial Credit Corp., Toledo, OH.
1997	(i) 3M Dental Products Division, St Paul, MN (ii) Solectron Corp., Milpita, CA	None awarded	(i) Merryl Lynch Credit Corp., Jackson ville, FL (ii) Xerox Business Services, Rochester, NY

1998	(i) Boeing Airlift and Tanker Programs, Long Beach, CA (ii) Solar Turbines Inc SanDiego. CA.	Texas Nameplate Company Inc., Dallas, TX.	None awarded
1999	ST Microelectronics, Inc., Region Americas, Carrolton, TX	Sunny Fresh Foods Monticello, MN	(i) The Ritz Carlton Hotel Company, LLC, Atlanta GA (ii) BI Performance Services, Minneapolis, MN
2000	(i) Dana Corp. – Spicer Driveshaft Division, Toledo OH (ii) KARLEE Company Inc., Garland, TX	Los Alamos National Bank, Los Alamos, NM	Operations Management Internationals, Greenwood Village, CO.
2001	Clarke American Checks, incorporated San Antonio, TX	Pal's Sudden Service, Kingsport TN	**Education** (i) Chugach School District, Archorage, AK (ii) Pearl River School District Pearl River, NY (iii) University of Wisconsin, Stout, Menomonie, WI
2002	Motorola Inc, Commercial, Government and Industrial Sector, Schaumburg, IL	Branch – Smith Printing Division Fortworth. TX	**Health care** SSM Health Care, St. Louis, MO
2003	Medrad Inc, Indianola, PA	Stoner Inc. Quarry Ville, PA	**Service** (i) Boeing Aerospace Support, St. Louis, MO. (ii) Caterpillar Financial Services Corp, Nashville, TN **Education** Community Consolidated School District Palatine, IL **Health care** *(i)* Baptist Hospital Inc Pensacola, FL *(ii)* Sait lukes Hospital of Kansas City, Kansas city, MO.
2004	The Bama Companies Tulsa, OK	Texas Nameplate Company, Inc. Dallas, TX	**Education** Kenneth.W, Monfort College of Business, Greeley, CO. **Health care** Robert Wood Johnson University Hospital, Hamilton, N.J
2005	Sunny Fresh Foods Inc, Monticello, MN	None awarded	**Service** DynMcDermott Petroleum Operations, New orleams, LA, **Education** (i) Richland college, Dallas, TX (ii) Jenks Public School Jenks, OK. **Health care** Bronson Methodist Hospital, Kalamazoa, MI

2006	None awarded	MESA Products Inc., Tulsa, OK.	**Service** Premier Inc. San Diego, CA **Health care** North Missisipi Medical Centre Tupelo, MS
2007	None awarded	PRO-TEC Coating Co, Leipsic, OH.	**Health care** (i) Mercy Health System Janesville, WI (iii) Sharp Healthcare San Diego. CA **Non profit** (i) City of Coral Springs, Coral Springs, FL (ii) US Army Armament Research Development and Engineering Centre. Picatinny Arsenal, NJ
2008	Cargill Corn Milling, North America, Wayzata, MN	None awarded	**Health care** Poudre Valley Health system Fort Collins CO. **Education** Irdell-States Ville Schools, States-ville, NC
2009	Honeywell Federal Manufacturing and Technologies, Kansas city, MO	Midway USA, Columbia, MO	**Health care** (i) Atlantic Care, Egg Harbor Township, NJ (iii) Heartland Health, St. Joseph, MO **Non profit** VA Cooperative Studies Program Clinical Research Pharmacy Co-ordinating Centre, Albuquerque, NM
2010	(i) MEDRAD, Warrandale, PA (ii) Nestle Purina Pet Care Co. St. Louis, MO.	(i) Freese and Nichols Inc. Fort worth, TX (ii) K & N Management, Austin, TX. (iii) Studer Group, Gulf Breeze, FL.	**Health care** Advocate Good Samaritan Hospital, Downers Grove, IL.

The above objectives are designed to support two result-oriented goals: delivery of ever improving value to customers and improvement of overall corporate performance. The **Baldrige Award recognises quality efforts that have senior management leadership, business results, employer involvement, control of internal processes and strong customer satisfaction.**

Box 4.2 **describes the criteria for selection for the Malcolm Baldrige National Quality Award.**

Box 4.2 : The Malcolm Baldrige National Quality Award

The Malcolm Baldrige National Quality Award was established in 1987 and named after a former secretary of commerce. Its purpose is to recognise US companies that attain pre-eminent quality leadership, encourage other US companies to improve their quality programs, develop and publish award criteria that serve as quality improvement guidelines, and disseminate non-proprietary information about the quality strategies of the award recipients. Upto two awards may be issued annually in three categories: large manufacturers, large services, and small businesses. To be eligible, a company must be incorporated and located in the United States, and it must submit a 75-page application package. A board of examiners reviews and evaluates the applications. High-scoring applications receive site examinations. Criteria for selection are:

1. **Leadership** : The company's leadership system, values, expectations and public responsibilities.
2. **Strategic planning** : The effectiveness of strategic and business planning and deployment of plans, with a strong focus on customer and operational performance requirements.
3. **Customer and market focus** : How the company determines customer and market requirements and expectations, enhances relationships with customers and determines their satisfaction.
4. **Measurement, analysis and knowledge management** : Selection, collection, analysis, management and improvement of data, information and knowledge assets.
5. **Human resource focus** : The success of efforts to realise the full potential of the workforce to create a high performance organisation.
6. **Process management** : The effectiveness of systems and processes for assuring the quality of products and services.
7. **Business results** : Performance results, trends and comparison to competitors in key business areas—customer satisfaction, financial and marketplace, human resources, suppliers and partners and operations.

4.2.2 The Criteria for Performance Excellence

The criteria for performance excellence as a measure for award of MBNQ Award consists of
1. Leadership
2. Strategic planning
3. Customer and market focus.
4. Measurement Analysis and Knowledge Management.
5. Human Resource Focus
6. Process Management and
7. Business Results.

The award examination is based upon a rigorous set of criteria called the ***Criteria for Performance Excellence,*** **designed to encourage companies to enhance their competitiveness through an aligned approach to organisational performance management that results in :**

(i) Delivery of ever-improving value to customers, resulting in improved market-place success.

(ii) Improvement of overall company performance and capabilities.

(iii) Organisational and personal learning.

The criteria consists of a hierarchical set of *categories, items* and *areas to address.* The seven categories are:

(i) **Leadership :** Examines senior executives' personal leadership and involvement in creating and sustaining values, company direction, performances, expectations, customer focus and a leadership system that promotes performance excellence.

(ii) **Strategic Planning :** Examines how the company sets strategic goals and how it determines key action plans and how plans are translated into an effective performance management system.

(iii) **Customer and Market Focus :** Examines how the company determines the requirements and expectations of customers and markets and also how the company enhances relationships with customers and determines their satisfaction.

(iv) **Measurement, Analysis and Knowledge Management :** This category examines how an organisation selects, gathers, analyses, manages and improves its data, information and knowledge assets.

(v) **Human Resource Focus :** Examines how the work force is enabled to develop and utilise its full potential, aligned with company objectives. The company's efforts to build and maintain an environment conducive to performance excellence, full participation and personal and organisational growth are also examined.

(vi) **Process Management:** Examines the key aspects of process management which includes customer focussed design, product and service delivery processes, support processes and supplier and partnering processes involving all work units. Also examines how key processes are designed, effectively managed and improved to achieve better performance.

(vii) **Business Results :** Examines the company's performance and improvement in key business areas—customer satisfaction, financial and market performance and also operational performance. Also examined are performance levels relative to competitors.

***Box 4.3* provides details of Malcolm Baldrige National Quality Award criteria, 1998, indicating point values for various categories/items.**

Box 4.3 : Malcolm Baldrige National Quality Award Criteria- 2010

Categories / Items	Point Values
1. Leadership	**120**
1.1 Senior Leadership	70
1.2 Governance and social responsibilities	50
2. Strategic Planning	**85**
2.2 Strategy development	40
2.3 Strategy deployment	45
3. Customer and market focus	**85**
3.1 Customer and market knowledge	40
3.2 Customer relationships and satisfaction	45
4. Measurement, analysis and knowledge management	**90**
4.1 Measurement, analysis and improvement of organisational performance	45
4.2 Measurement of Information, Information Technology and Knowledge Management	45
5. Workforce Focus	**85**
5.1 workforce engagement	45
5.2 workforce environment	40
6. Process Management	**85**
6.1 worksystems design	35
6.2 workprocess management and improvement	50
7. Business results	**450**
7.1 Product-focused outcomes	100
7.2 Customer-focused outcomes	70
7.3 Financial and market outcomes	70
7.4 Workforce-focused outcomes	70
7.5 Process effectiveness outcomes	70
7.6 Leadership outcomes	70
Total points	**1000**

The seven Baldrige categories shown in *Box 4.3* are judged by a self-evaluation report prepared by each applicant for the award and a site visit by Baldrige examiners for those applicants who pass an initial screening of their key-evaluation report.

The Baldrige criteria have a total of 1000 points allocated among the seven categories shown in *Box 4.3*.

The seven categories form an integrated management system as illustrated in the *Exhibit 4.4*.

Exhibit 4.4 : Baldrige Award Criteria Framework (A Systems Perspective)

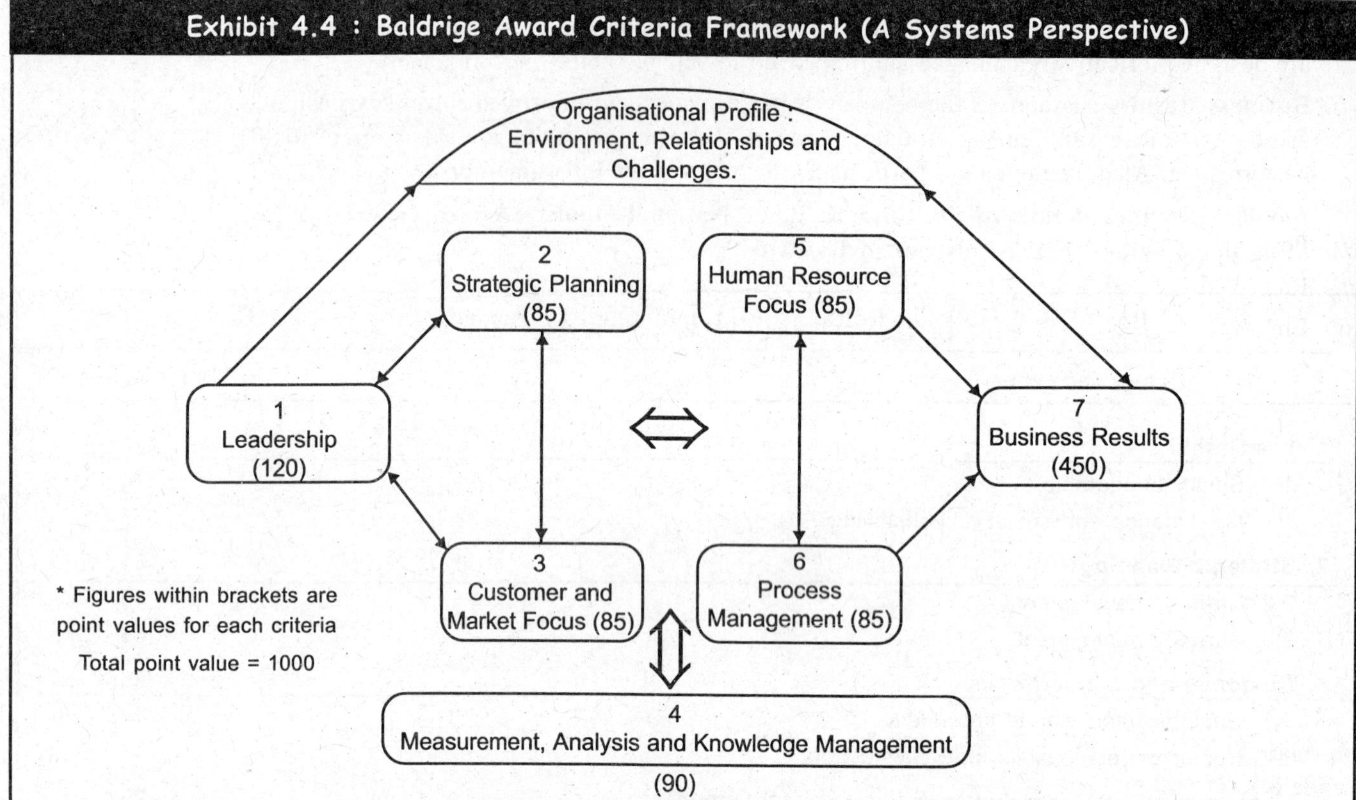

Leadership, strategic planning and customer and market focus represent the 'leadership triad' and suggest the importance of integrating these three functions. Human Resource Focus and Process Management represent how the work in an organisation is accomplished and leads to Business Results. These functions are linked to the leadership triad. Finally, measurement, analysis and knowledge management support the entire framework by providing the foundation for a fact-based system for improvement.

4.2.3 The Baldrige Award Evaluation Process

The Baldrige evaluation process is rigorous. In the first stage, each application is thoroughly reviewed by upto 15 examiners chosen from among leading quality professionals in business, academia, health care and government. Examiners evaluate the applicant's response to each criteria, listing major strengths and areas of improvement relative to the criteria. Based on the strengths, a percentage score from 0 to 100, in increments of 10 is given to each item. Each examination item is evaluated on ***approach/deployment*** **or** ***results***.

Approach refers to the methods the company uses to achieve the requirements addressed in each category. **The factors used to evaluate approaches include :**

(i) The appropriateness of the methods to the requirements.

(ii) The effectiveness of methods, namely the degree to which the approach is systematic, integrated and constantly applied, the degree to which the approach embodies effective evaluation/ improvement cycles, and the degree to which the approach is based upon reliable information and data.

(iii) Alignment with organisational needs

(iv) Evidence of innovation.

Deployment refers to the extent to which the approaches are applied to all relevant areas and activities addressed and implied in each category. The factors used to evaluate deployment include:

(i) Use of the approach in addressing item requirements relevant to the organisation and

(ii) Use of the approach by all appropriate work units.

Results refer to the outcomes and effects in achieving the purposes addressed and implied in the criteria. **The factors used to evaluate results include :**

(i) Current performance levels.

(ii) Performance relative to appropriate comparisons and/or benchmarks.

(iii) Rate, breadth and importance of performance improvements and

(iv) Linkage of results measures to important customer, market, process and action plan performance requirements identified in the approach/deployment items and the organisational profile.

Scores for each examination item are computed by multiplying the examiner's score by the maximum point value that can be earned, with a total possible score of 1000. The scores are reviewed by a panal of nine judges without knowledge of the specific companies. The higher scoring applications (companies who are competing for the award) enter a ***consensus stage*** in which a selected group of examiners discuss variations in individual scores and arrive at ***consensus scores*** for each item. The panel of judges then reviews the scores and selects the highest-scoring applicants for site visits.

At this point, six or seven examiners visit the companies selected for site visits for upto a week for each company, to verify information contained in the written application and resolve issues that are not clear. The judges use the ***site visit reports*** to recommend award recipients. All information is kept strictly confidential, and examiners are bound by conflict-of-interest rules and a code of conduct.

All applicants receive a feed back that critically evaluates the company's strengths and areas for improvement relative to the award criteria. The feed back report, frequently 30 or more pages in length, contains the evaluation team's response to the written application. It includes a distribution of numerical scores of all applicants and a scoring summary of the individual applicant. The typical score for winners is in the range of 650-750 out of a total score of 1000. This indicates that although their practices and results are indeed outstanding, they still have opportunities for improvement because **"quality is a race without a finish line"**.

The entire review and evaluation process is driven by the following fundamental beliefs about TQM:

- Customers define quality.
- Senior corporate leaders must create clear quality values and build them into company operations.
- Excellent quality evolves from well-designed and well executed systems and processes.
- Firms must integrate continuous improvement into the management of all systems and processes.
- Companies must develop detailed goals and strategic and operational plans to achieve quality leadership.
- Quality-improvement efforts must include initiatives to reduce response times for all operations.
- Operations and decisions of the company must be based on fact.
- All employees must be appropriately trained, developed and involved in quality-improvement activities.
- Quality systems must emphasise design quality and error prevention as key elements.
- Companies must communicate quality requirements to suppliers and work to elevate their performance.

4.2.4 Benefits of the Malcolm Baldrige National Quality Award Program

The firms that apply for the Baldrige Award have the following benefits:

- **Self Assessment Tool :** As they apply the award's categories to company processes, both managers and employees learn much about their own operations and their success in serving their customers. This self-assessment can yield dramatic and important insights.
- **Baldrige effect :** Many firms never really intend to apply for the award, their managers use its categories and evaluation process as guidelines for improving their processes.
- **Sharing information :** All winners of the Baldrige Award agree to work actively, teaching others about quality and about their firm's experiences with quality. This leads to beneficial exchanges of information through formal education and training programs.

4.2.5 Using The Baldrige Criteria

The Baldrige Award Criteria form a model for business excellence in any organisation – manufacturing or service, large or small. Many small businesses feel that the Baldrige Criteria are too difficult to apply to their organisations because they can not afford to implement the same types of practices as large companies.

However, there is no need for an organisation's practices to be formal or complex. *For example,* the ability to obtain customer and market knowledge through independent third-party surveys, extensive interviews and focus groups which are common practices among large companies, may be limited by the resources of a small company. What is important, however, is whether the company is using appropriate mechanisms to gather information and use the same to improve customer focus and satisfaction.

Many organisations are using the award criteria to evaluate their own quality programs, set up and implement quality initiatives, communicate better with suppliers and partners and for education and training, even if they have no intention to apply for the award.

4.2.6 The Baldrige Criteria and the Deming Philosophy

Even though Deming was not an advocate of the Baldrige Award, many of his principles are reflected directly or in spirit within the criteria. Specific portions of the Baldrige Criteria that support each of Deming's 14 points are summarised below:

(i) **Statement of Purpose :** Strategy development requires a mission and a vision. Commitment to aims and purpose by senior leaders is specifically addressed in the "Leadership Category" and in enhancing customer satisfaction and relationships.

(ii) **Learn the New Philosophy :** Communication of values, expectations, customer focus and learning is the key area of the organisational leadership item.

(iii) **Understand Inspection :** The process management category addresses the development of appropriate measurement plans. The criteria also seek evidence of how a company aims to minimise costs associated with inspection.

(iv) **End Price Tag Decisions :** The process management category addresses this in the form of emphasis on overall performances and linkages among processes and results.

(v) **Improve Constantly :** Baldrige criteria has "continuous improvement and learning" as its core value. The criteria specifically asks how the company evaluates and improves its processes.

(vi) **Institute Training :** The importance of employee education, training and development in meeting performance objectives is very well recognised in Baldrige Criteria (The Human Resource Category).

(vii) **Teach and Institute Leadership :** Leadership is recognised as the principal driver of the management system in Baldrige Criteria.

(viii) **Drive out Fear and Innovate :** The Human Resource Focus, Customers and Market Focus and Strategic Planning categories of Baldrige Criteria focus on work design, employee empowerment and implementation issues.

(ix) **Optimise the Efforts of Team and Staff :** Baldrige Criteria focusses significantly on team work and customer knowledge in product/process design and process management, as well as in the Human Resource Focus Category.

(x) **Eliminate Exhortations :** The focus on work and job design as the driver of high performance supports this point.

(xi) **Eliminate Quotas and MBO, Institute improvement and Understand Processes :** The Organisational Leadership and Strategy Deployment items, as well as the Measurement, Analysis and Knowledge Management and Process Management Categories deal with the fact- based management and understanding processes.

(xii) **Remove Barriers :** The Leadership and Human Resource Focus Categories as well as Customer Satisfaction, and Relationship Building support this goal.

(xiii) **Encourage Education :** The items of Baldrige Criteria *viz.* Human Resource Focus Category addresses this point.

(xiv) **Take Action :** This is the role of leadership, addressed directly in the Leadership Category.

4.3 INTERNATIONAL QUALITY AWARD PROGRAMS

There are many other award programs which followed the Deming Prize and which are similar in nature to the Baldrige Criteria. They are:

European Quality Award : In October 1991, The European Foundation for Quality Management in partnership with the European Commission and the European Organisation for Quality announced the creation of the European Quality Award. The award was designed to increase awareness throughout the European Community and businesses, of the growing importance of quality to their competitiveness in the global market and also to improve their standard of life. Two parts of the ***European Quality Award*** are: The **European Quality Prize,** given to the companies that demonstrate excellence in quality management practice by meeting the award criteria and the **European Quality Award,** awarded to the most successful applicant. In 1992, four prizes and one award were granted for the first time.

Applicants must demonstrate that their TQM approach has contributed significantly to satisfying the expectations of customers, employees and other constituencies. The assessment is based on customer satisfaction, business results, processes, leadership, people satisfaction, resources, people management, policy and strategy and impact on society.

4.3.1 European Quality Award

Exhibit 4.5 **shows the integrated management framework for European Quality Award now known as the Business Excellence Model.**

Results including customer satisfaction, people (employee) satisfaction and impact on society, constitute a high percentage of the total score. These are driven by ***"leadership"***, the means by which an organisation approaches its business responsibilities. The results criteria consists of people results, customer results, and society results and these are somewhat different than those in Baldrige. The impact on society results category focuses on the perceptions of the company by the community at large and the company's approach to the quality of life, the environment and the preservation of global business.

Exhibit 4.5 : European Quality Award Framework

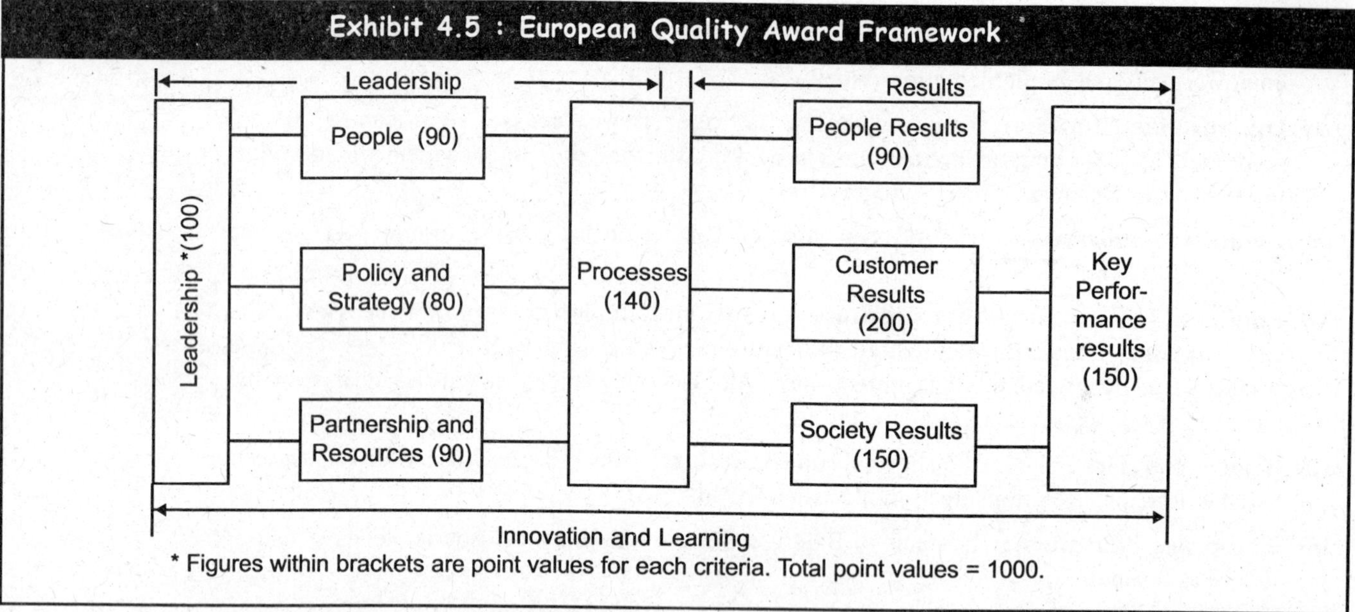

* Figures within brackets are point values for each criteria. Total point values = 1000.

4.3.2 Canadian Awards for Business Excellence

The Canadian Awards for Excellence instituted by Canada's National Quality Institute (NQI) stimulate and support quality-driven innovation within all Canadian enterprises and institutions including business, government, education and healthcare. **The major categories and items within each category are:**

(i) **Leadership :** Strategic direction, leadership involvement and outcomes.

(ii) **Customer focus :** Customer's voice, management of customer's relationships, measurement and subsequent outcomes.

(iii) **Planning for improvement :** Development and content of improvement plan, assessment and outcomes.

(iv) **People focus :** Human resources planning, participatory environment, continuous learning environment, employee satisfaction and outcomes.

(v) **Process optimisation :** Process definition, process control, process improvement and outcomes.

(vi) **Supplier focus :** Partnering and outcomes.

4.3.3 Australian Business Excellence Awards

The Australian Business Excellence Awards were developed independently from the Baldrige Awards in 1988 and are administrated by the Australian Quality Awards Foundation, a subsidiary of the Australian Quality Council.

Four levels of the awards are :

(i) **The Business Improvement Level :** Encouragement, recognition for "Progress Toward Business Excellence" or "Foundation in Business Excellence".

(ii) **The Award Level :** Representing Australian best practices, recognition as a winner or finalist.

(iii) **The Award Gold Level :** Open only to former award winners, represents revalidation and on-going improvement.

(iv) **The Australians Business Excellence Prize :** Open only to former award winners, represents international best practices evident throughout the organisation.

The assessment criteria address leadership, strategy and planning, information and knowledge, people, customer focus, processes, products and services and business results. Leadership and customer focus drive the management system and enable performance. Strategy, policy and planning, information and analysis and people are the key internal components of the management system. Quality of process, product and service is focused on how work is done to achieve the required results and achieve improvement. Business results are the outcome of the management system - a results category.

As with Baldrige, the Australian Business Excellence Award framework emphasises the holistic and inter-connected nature of the management process. The criteria are benchmarked with the criteria of Baldrige Award and the European Business Excellence Model. ***Exhibit 4.6* shows Australian Business Excellence Award Framework.**

Exhibit 4.6 : Australian Business Excellence Award Framework

4.3.4 Criticism and Debate

Much criticism has arisen regarding TQM and the Baldrige Award, especially during the early 1990s as quality became a business buzzword. In reference to Douglas Aircraft, a subsidiary of McDonnel Douglas Corporation, ***News Week*** stated, "The aircraft maker three years ago embraced "Total Quality Management", Japanese import that had become the American business cult of the 1980s. At Douglas, TQM appeared to be just one more hothouse Japanese flower never meant to grow on rocky ground." Other articles in ***Wall Street Journal*** and ***New York Times*** suggested that total quality approachers were passing fads and inherently flawed. These opinions were supported by critics. *For example,* a 1992 Rath & Strong survey found that only 20 percent of Fortune 500 companies were satisfied with the results of their TQM initiatives. Applications for the Malcolm Baldrige National Quality Award declined from 106 in 1991 to 30 in 1992. A survey of 300 electronics companies by the American Electronic Association found that among the 73 percent of the companies that had quality programs in place, more than half noted that quality had not improved by even 10 percent.

Despite the critics, a study by the Conference Board indicated that total quality was alive and well. Many companies achieved astounding success through a total quality emphasis. The world has become more quality conscious and companies that resist implementing total quality principles may not be in business for long. The Conference Board study, based on more than five years research on hundreds of US companies, found that companies need at least four years to persuade employees to buy into the quality philosophy and eight to ten years to fully establish a quality culture. When any company begins to think of how to improve quality, it will find itself using the core principles of Total Quality.

To conclude, we can say that reasons for failures of TQ usually are rooted in organisational approaches and management systems. ***"TQM is not dead. TQM failures just prove that bad management is still alive and kicking."***

4.4 THE TQMEX MODEL (TOTAL QUALITY MANAGEMENT FOR EXCELLENCE)

The various practices involved in TQMEX model are:

1. Japanese 5 's' practice
2. Business Process Reengineering.
3. Quality circles
4. ISO 9000:2000 Quality Management System Requirements
5. Total Productive Maintenance and
6. Six-sigma concept.

With the creation of the global market, the need for international orientation of management that sweeps national boundaries, introduction of new technologies and shift towards customer focussed strategies gained momentum and made competition stronger than ever. **The criteria for success in this global, internationally oriented market have been changing rapidly. In order to expand business, enter new markets and set realistic competitive long-term objectives, *excellence* became an imperative. Management's effort has been directed towards discovering what makes a** company excellent.

To achieve excellence companies must develop a corporate culture of treating people as their most important asset and provide a consistent level of high quality products and services in every market in which they operate. The emphasis is on the importance of relation with customers and the role of quality in the search for excellence.

Such an environment has supported the wide acceptance of TQM which involves three spheres of changes in an organisation – ***people, technology* and *structure.*** The role of top management in implementation of total quality is crucial and its input on people far reaching. TQM, therefore should be understood as management of the system through system thinking, which means understanding all the elements in the company and putting them to work together towards the common goal.

The TQMEX (TQM and Excellence) model advocates an integrated approach in order to support the transition to system management which is an ongoing process of continuous improvement that begins when the company commits itself, to the managing by quality. ***Exhibit 4.7* shows the "TQMEX" model.**

Exhibit 4.7 : The TQMEX Model

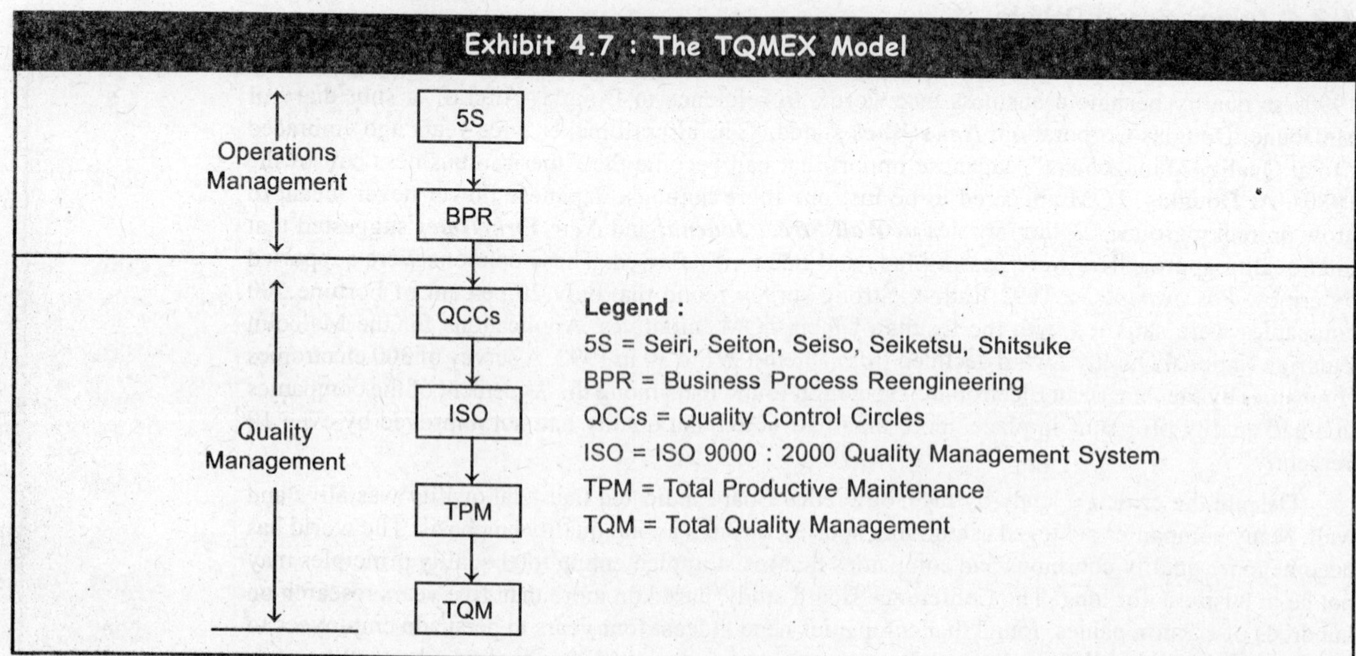

In order to have a systematic approach to TQM, it is necessary to develop a conceptual model. A model is a sequence of steps arranged logically to serve as guideline for implementation of a process in order to achieve the ultimate goal. The TQMEX model which is made up of TQM and

Excellence, indicates that high standards and outstanding successes are the goals. TQMEX is a sequential model which is easy to remember and to implement.

Companies starting to implement TQM should follow TQMEX step-by-step. **Some of the challenges that everyone within each unit of a company should aim at using TQMEX are :**

(i) To be profitable
(ii) To be recession proof
(iii) To enjoy the results
(iv) To reinforce personal quality standards
(v) To maintain customer confidence
(vi) To build customer loyalty
(vii) To improve customer satisfaction
(viii) To maintain corporate vitality
(ix) To use employee's creative energies
(x) To develop a good reputation
(xi) To promote human dignity
(xii) To lower costs
(xiii) To retain employees
(xiv) To increase productivity
*(xv)*To contribute to society
(xvi) To erect a clear vision of the organisation
(xvii) To improve technology
(xviii) To solve problems effectively
(xix) To increase competitiveness and
(xx) To develop internal cooperation.

As a guideline, the 'TQMEX' model will facilitate the company's effort to achieve the standards required by TQM Kitemarks world-wide.

The various practices involved in 'TQMEX' model are briefly discussed in the following paragraphs and the same will be discussed in greater detail in the later chapters.

Japanese 5-S Practice (5-S)

The 5 'S' practice is a technique used to establish and maintain quality environment in an organisation. 5 'S' stands for five Japanese words – ***Seiri, Seiton, Seiso, Seiketsu*** **and** ***Shitsuke***. **Their English equivalent, their meaning and typical examples are shown below in** ***Box 4.4.***

Box 4.4 : Japanese 5 'S' Practice

Japanese Word	English Word	Meaning	Typical Example
Seiri	Structurise	Organisation	Throw away rubbish
Seiton	Systematise	Neatness	30 second retrieval of a document
Seiso	Sanitise	Cleaning	Individual cleaning responsibility
Seiketsu	Standardise	Standardisation	Transparency of storage
Shitsuke	Self-discipline	Discipline	Do 5-S daily

This technique has been widely practised in Japan. It is thought by Japanese as useful both for improving their physical environment and for improving their thinking processes also. Many of the daily problems could be solved through the adoption of this practice.

Business Process-Reengineering (BPR)

BPR is a management process used to re-define a mission statement, analyse the critical success factors, redesign the organisational structure and reengineer the critical processes in order to improve customer satisfaction. BPR challenges managers to rethink their traditional methods of doing work and commit themselves to a customer – focussed process. Many outstanding organisations have achieved and maintained their leadership by BPR.

Quality Control Circles (QCC) : A QCC is a small group of staff working together to contribute to the improvement of the enterprise, to respect humanity and to build a cheerful work group through the development of the staff's infinite potential. The members of the Q.C. Circle team usually come from the same area and voluntarily meet on a regular basis to identify, investigate, analyse and solve their work-related problems.

The ISO 9000 : 2000 Quality Management System : ISO 9000 : 2000 is the Quality System Model for quality assurance in design, development, production, installation and servicing. The requirements specified are aimed primarily at achieving customer satisfaction by preventing non-conformity at all stages from design through to servicing.

Total Productive Maintenance (TPM) : TPM is defined as a system of maintenance covering the entire life of the equipment in every division including planning, manufacturing and maintenance. TPM aims at increasing productivity.

Prerequisities for Implementing TQMEX

The three requisites are :

(i) The ten 'commandments' of TQM

(ii) The four pillars of TQM

(iii) The 4 'C's of TQM.

These are discussed as under :

The Ten Commandments of TQM : The ten commandments (guiding principles to ensure that no important steps have been neglected in formulating corporate strategies). are :

(i)	Approach	–	Management Led
(ii)	Method	–	Prevention not Detection (of defects)
(iii)	Objective	–	Total Customer Satisfaction
(iv)	Measure	–	The Costs of Quality
(v)	Standard	–	Right First Time
(vi)	Scope	–	Ownership and Commitment
(vii)	Theme	–	Continuous Improvement
(viii)	Ability	–	Training and Education
(ix)	Communication	–	Cooperation and Teamwork
(x)	Reward	–	Recognition and Pride

The Four Pillars of TQM: Refer to *Exhibit 4.8* shown below.

Exhibit 4.8 : Four Pillars of TQM

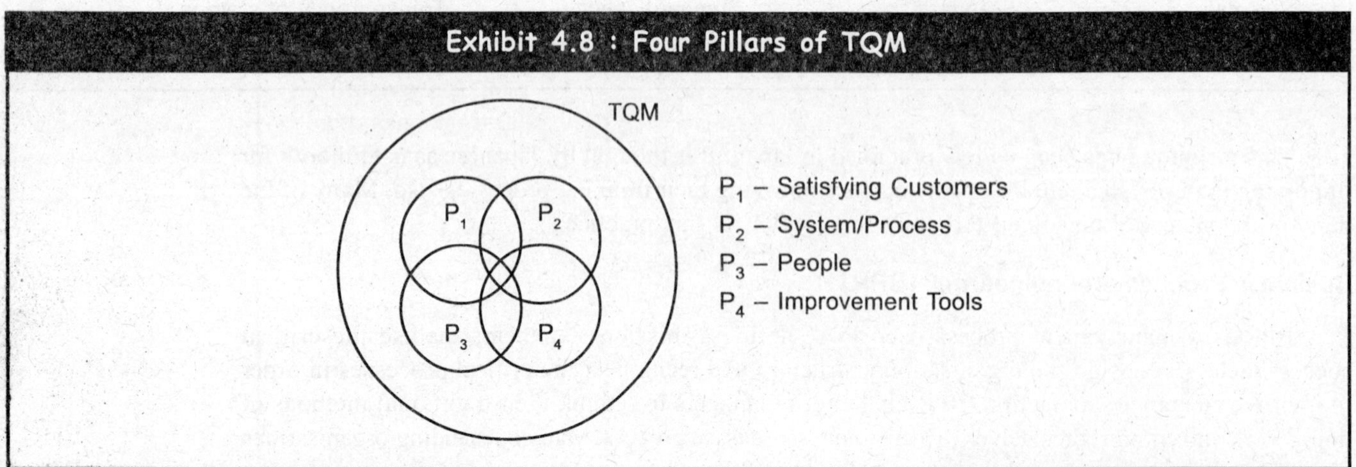

P_1 – Satisfying Customers – TQM aims not just to meet customer requirements (expressed needs) but also to achieve customer satisfaction (satisfying implied needs).

P_2 – System/Process : Establishing a system such as ISO 9000 is the initial building block. TQM relies on an effective quality management system which ensures that preventive measures are in place and the culture of continuous improvement exists to enable the process to deliver quality products and services.

P_3 – People : Management commitment, training, teamwork, leadership, motivation, empowerment etc. would have a vital and complementary role to play in establishing a total quality environment.

P_4 – Improvement Tools : TQM recognises the need for continuous improvement and uses a set of QC tools.

The 4 'C's of TQM : The 4 'C's are ***Commitment, Competence, Communication*** **and** ***Continuous Improvement.***

(i) **Commitment :** Commitment to quality at work is defined as ***a decisive personal or organisational choice to follow on an agreed-upon plan of action.*** Workers will be committed to quality to the extent that management is committed.

(ii) **Competence :** Along with commitment, quality goals require actions and attitudes based on competence, which in turn is based on knowledge. Competence includes certain specific measurable skills, sound education, good intuitive judgement, an ability to apply related knowledge to solve problems and a responsible attitude. Competence and quality of work go hand in hand.

(iii) **Communication :** The purpose of communication is to achieve mutual understanding. ***Box 4.5*** **shows the Quality Communication Model.**

Box 4.5 : Quality Communication Model

Sender	Message	Receiver	Feedback
• Strategy	• Standards	• Interpretation	• Ideas
• Direction	• Requirement	• Implementation	• Suggestions
• Goals	• Expectations	• Participation	• Problems
	• Training		• Challenge

(iv) **Continuous Improvement :** Continuous improvement is a programme, a philosophy and a strategy to improve the quality of goods and services of an organisation. ***Team Work (QCCs)*** and competence in ***problem solving*** are the foundation for ***Kaizen***. More about *Kaizen* will be discussed in later chapters.

4.5 TQM KITEMARKS

What are TQM Kitemarks?

TQM Kitemarks are quality standards that provide discipline, external assessment and a clear process for implementing TQM.

Going through all the five steps of the TQMEX model makes an organisation to have been built on a strong basis and a proactive environment for the final stage – TQM. There are clear business objectives and effective processes installed, with empowered employees committed to quality, ISO 9000 quality management system is in place to demonstrate the disciplined approach to quality improvement and all equipment and facilities are in good condition and utilisation consistently. This is the right time for the management of an organisation to consider obtaining a nationally or internationally recognised quality standard registration.

TQM kitemarks are nationally or internationally recognised quality standards that provide discipline, external assessment and a clear process for switching to TQM. They also have tremendous potential publicity value within the organisation and with the general public. The best known TQM kitemarks are the ISO 9004 – 4, (revised as ISO 9004 : 2000), Japan's Deming Prize, USA's Malcolm Baldrige National Quality Award and the European and UK Quality Awards.

ISO 9004 – 4 : 1993 (Revised as ISO 9004 : 2000)

In 1992, the British Standard Institution developed the BS 7850 guideline on TQM. It is a guideline for quality improvement, with emphasis on management commitment and company-wide involvement. BS 7850 is not a standard and it is not envisaged to have a system of third-party assessment like ISO 9000. It is a guide to the type of approach and methodology which an organisation pursuing TQM might adopt.

In 1993, the International Organisation for Standardisation published a similar guide as a part of the ISO 9000 series called ISO 9004-4 – "Quality management and quality system elements – Part 4, Guidelines for quality improvement". In 1994, the BSI revised its BS7850 : 1992 in accordance with the ISO 9004-4 : 1993.

The ISO 9004 – 4 emphasises the participation and cooperation of all employees in the production of goods or services. The purpose is to ensure that customers are satisfied with the goods and services and that society as a whole benefits.

The ISO 9000 series of standards was revised in the year 2000 as ISO 9000:2000 series of standards, ISO 9004 – 4 was revised as ISO 9004:2000 – Quality Management systems (QMS) – **guidelines for performance improvement** which provides guidelines that an organisation can use to establish a QMS focused on improving performance.

Japan's Deming Prize

The Japanese Deming Prize is awarded by the Japanese Union of Scientists and Engineers (JUSE) to companies with outstanding TQM. This prize is given for the overall performance of the company. Five years after a company has received the Deming Prize, it is eligible to compete for the Japan Quality Control Prize.

USA's Malcolm Baldrige National Quality Award (MBNQA)

The MBNQA is the American response to the prestigious Japanese Deming Prize. The Award is designed to recognise US companies that excel in quality achievement and quality management. **The award is designed to promote:**

- an awareness of quality
- understanding the requirements of quality,
- sharing of information on successful strategies and the benefits derived from implementation.

The Baldrige criteria fit well with the Deming philosophy of quality. There is a strong emphasis on the non-procedural aspects of quality (unlike ISO 9000) such as leadership, human resources management including employee well-being, their morale and customer satisfaction.

The European Quality Award (EQA) : The EQA was launched during the 1991 European Foundation for Quality Management (EFQM) meeting in Paris. The aim of the EFQM Award is specially geared to encourage the development of TQM. The award aims to recognise organisations who are paying exceptional attention to total quality and to encourage others to follow their example. The EQA is not a standard but a competitive award like the Japanese Deming Prize and the US Malcolm Baldrige Award. ***Exhibit 4.9* illustrates the European/UK Quality Award Framework.**

The UK Quality Award : In UK, the British Quality Foundation started the British Quality Award in 1990, with its own criterion check list. In view of the popularity and conformity to the European Quality Award, the British Quality Foundation decided to start a new award called the UK Quality Award in 1994.

Exhibit 4.9 : The European/UK Quality Award Framework

<table>
<tr><td colspan="3">1. Leadership (100)</td></tr>
<tr><td>2. Policy and strategy
(80)</td><td>3. People Management
(90)</td><td>4. Partnership and Resources
(90)</td></tr>
<tr><td colspan="3">5. Processes (140)</td></tr>
<tr><td>6. People results
(90)</td><td>7. Customer results
(200)</td><td>8. Society results
(60)</td></tr>
<tr><td colspan="3">9. Key performance results (150)</td></tr>
<tr><td colspan="3">1 to 5 are Leadership Factors, 6-9 are Result Factors</td></tr>
</table>

Why are TQM Kitemarks useful?

TQM is being adopted by companies around the world. It is a key element to the competitiveness of a company that intends to win in the market place. The main reason that award processes such as the Deming Award, MBNQA and EQA are gaining acceptance is that their underlying core quality values and principles are commonly perceived as being beneficial and relevant to the development of most organisations in today's competitive global markets, fast paced technological innovation and rapidly changing working practices.

How to Achieve TQM Kitemarks

Each of the awards has criteria do be met and evaluations and visits to be conducted before the final selection of winners. On the other hand, ISO 9004-4 can be used as a guideline for quality improvement, an essential part of all TQM Kitemarks.

Implementation of TQM Kitemarks consist of two stages :

Stage 1 : To decide on the most appropriate kitemark to achieve and

Stage 2 : To implement TQM according to the requirements effectively.

The first stage requires the study and evaluation of the requirements for the kitemarks. A key task is then to select a framework for self-assessment. Deming Prizes are almost exclusively won by Japanese firms. The EQA and MBNQA are both excellent and robust models. Organisations which are not linked to Japan, USA or Europe can still choose one of these kitemarks as their TQM framework or can use their own national quality award (if exists).

Most likely the choice of TQM kitemark is driven by the location or the parentage of the firm. If the firm is based in USA or has a strong USA parent organisation, then the MBNQA will probably be the most appropriate choice. If the firm is based in Europe, the EQA or UK Quality Award will be the most appropriate model.

After deciding on which of the kitemarks to adopt, the next stage is to implement the kitemark requirements effectively. The procedures for implementing TQM kitemarks are similar to that of ISO 9000. Apart from the ***quality assurance system,*** TQM kitemarks implementation should focus on quality improvement (as expressed in ISO 9004 : 2000) and ***customer care*** as well.

4.6 ISO 9000 : 2000 STANDARDS

In order to best fulfill customer needs, requirements and expectations, effective organisations create and utilise quality systems. Within a quality management system the necessary ingredients exist to enable the organisation's employees to identify, design, develop, produce, deliver and support products or services that the customer wants. Effective quality management systems are dynamic, able to adapt and change to meet the needs, requirements and expectations of their customers. Effective organisations use standards such as ISO 9000 and QS 9000, programs such as six sigma and awards such as the Malcolm Baldrige National Quality Award to provide guidance for establishing quality management system's structure, maintaining records and using quality techniques to improve processes and systems.

What is ISO 9000?

ISO 9000 series standards comprise a set of individual but related international standards and guidelines on quality management developed to help companies effectively document the quality system elements to be implemented to maintain an efficient quality system.

With the continued growth in international trade, there was a need for a set of quality standards to facilitate the relationship between suppliers and purchasers across the world. When the European Community moved toward the European free trade agreement, which went into effect at the end of 1992, quality management became a key strategic objective. To standardise quality requirements for European countries within the common market and those wishing to do business with those countries, a specialised agency for standardisation, the International Organisation for Standardisation, (IOS) founded in 1946 and composed of representations from the national standards bodies of 91 nations, adopted a series of written quality standards in 1987 referred to as ISO 9000 series standards. These standards were later revised in 1994 and again in 2000 to a very significant level. The most recent version is called the ISO 9000 : 2000 family of standards.

ISO 9000 defines quality system standards, based on the assumption that certain general characteristics of management practices can be standardised and that a well-designed, well-implemented, and carefully managed quality system provides confidence that the outputs will meet customer expectations and requirements.

ISO 9000 : 2000 is composed of three areas :

(i) **ISO 9000 - 2000** – Quality Management Systems and Vocabulary.

(ii) **ISO 9001 : 2000** – Quality Management Systems : Requirements and

(iii) **ISO 9004 : 2000** – Quality Management Systems : Guidelines for Performance Improvement.

Detailed discussion of ISO 9000 family of standards will be done in a later chapter.

QS 9000 Certification

Three major automotive manufacturers of US – General Motors, Ford and Chryster - as well as several truck manufacturers developed QS 9000, an interpretation and extension of ISO 9000 for automotive manufacturers in 1994, to overcome the deficiencies of old ISO 9000 standards. QS 9000 is based on ISO 9000 and includes all ISO requirements. It has two major components. ISO 9001 and customer-specific requirements. Automotive suppliers must be ISO 9001 certified. Customer-specific requirements include additional requirements such as continuous improvement, manufacturing capability and production part approval processes.

4.7 SIX SIGMA CONCEPT

"Six Sigma" is a quality philosophy, a collection of techniques and tools for use in reducing variation and improving quality.

The Six Sigma concept was conceived by Bill Smith, a reliability engineer for Motorola corporation. 'Six Sigma' can be described as a **business improvement approach** that seeks to find and eliminate causes of defects and errors in manufacturing and service processes by focusing on outputs that are critical to customers and a clear financial return to the organisation. The term *Six Sigma* is based on a statistical measure that equates to 3.4 or fewer errors or defects per million opportunities. An ultimate **"stretch"** goal of all organisations that adopt **'Six-Sigma'** philosophy is to have all critical processes, regardless of functional area, at a six sigma level of capability.

More about six-sigma philosophy would be discussed in a later chapter.

4.8 QUALITY AWARDS PROGRAMS IN INDIA

We are aware that there are many Quality Awards in India and each one of them is uniquely positioned as the milestone in the journey to excellence. The awards are also coveted as symbols of recognition for organisations which have achieved certain level in their pursuit of excellence.

In today's super competitive world market, there is a race to achieve the best. In pursuit of excellence the countries and the regions have started to provide a bench mark in the form of quality awards for enterprises to strive to reach the mark. **In the quest for quality, three trophies stand out:**

(i) Japan's Deming Award, *(ii)* The Malcolm Baldrige National Quality Award of US and *(iii)* The European Quality Award created by the European Foundation for Quality Management (EFQM).

The Japanese started the Deming Award in 1951 to demonstrate that their companies have reached world-class quality. In 1987, The US Federal government instituted Malcolm Baldrige National Quality Award open to US companies. The European countries started the unified approach to accelerate quality as a strategy for global competitive advantage and stimulate and assist the development of quality improvement activities, set their own collective bench mark for quality and started European Quality Award in 1991.

In India, the Government sensed a need for a national commitment to quality after Prime Minister Rajiv Gandhi's visit to Japan. So, in pursuit of excellence in its goods and services following liberalization of Indian economy and facing the challenges of global competition, there was a need for institution of a National Quality Award as a bench mark for enterprises striving to achieve and excel in world market. Therefore, the Rajiv Gandhi National Quality Award was instituted in 1991 in line with similar awards in other developed countries, like MBNQ Award in US, Deming Prize in Japan and European Quality Award. The Golden Peacock National Quality Award was instituted in 1991 to encourage total quality improvements in both manufacturing as well as service sectors. This award was based on the European Quality Award Model. Further, the Indian Merchant's chamber instituted the 'IMC Ramakrishna Bajaj National Quality Award" in 1997 and the Confederation of Indian Industries (CII) and EXIM Bank of India jointly instituted CII-EXIM Bank Award for Business Excellence in 1994.

To accelerate and facilitate implementation of TQM in the industry, a number of quality awards are given in India, periodically, generally annual awards. Certification under ISO 9000 is not considered as a quality award, but a quality certification which has become necessary especially for companies doing international business. Any number of organisations meeting the ISO 9000 standards requirements can receive the ISO 9000 certification by the certifying agency. On the contrary, quality awards, both national and international are limited in number. These awards are given to a few successful organisations implementing TQM principles and practices. The award criteria provide guidelines for organisations to evolve and practice TQM in their organisation and compete for the quality awards. Any organisation which receives any of the national or international quality award will indicate that it is practicing TQM and has achieved significant success in implementing the same. Some of the popular International Awards are *(i)* The Deming Prize in Japan, *(ii)* Malcolm Baldrige National Quality Award (MBNQA) in USA, *(iii)* The European Quality Award (EQA), *(iv)* The Canadian Award instituted by Canada's National Quality Institute, *(v)* The Australian Business Excellence Quality Award in Australia.

The awards instituted in India for Indian companies are:

(i) CII-EXIM Bank Award, *(ii)* Rajiv Gandhi National Quality Award,

(iii) The Golden Peacock National Quality Award, and

(iv) IMC Ramakrishna Bajaj National Quality Award

Earlier we discussed the various awards instituted in countries like US, Japan, UK and Australia for their own industries. We will discuss the awards instituted in India for Indian industries in the following paragraphs.

4.9 THE BUSINESS EXCELLENCE MODEL

Besides ISO 9000:2000 standards, there are other approaches to the management of quality which, though perhaps not carrying the same global authority, have delivered significant value to the firms which have adopted them.

The Business Excellence Model (BEM) was sponsored by the European Foundation for Quality Management (EFQM) The European Foundation for Quality Mangement (EFQM) was established in 1988 by 14 leading Western European companies, as a non profit organisation with the aim of creating a culture of common values on quality and stake holder satisfaction in an attempt to meet the tough competition offered by Japanese and American companies. The European Quality Award was introduced in 1992 for organisational excellence and is based on what is known as the EFQM Excellence Model or Business Excellence Model (after revising the criteria in the year 2000). This model is developed from the belief that contented customers, satisfied staff and positive societal impact can be achieved only through **effective leadership**.

Leadership in turn steers both organisational policy and strategy in relation to organisational processes and human resource actions. Taken together, this integrated approach is considered to drive the organisation towards excellence in business.

Using the 'Business Excellence Model' (BEM) the organisaton assesses itself (self assessment) against **nine performance criteria (Refer *Box 4.6*)** divided into two sets: *(i)* 'Enablers' – those aspects of the organisation which provide the foundation for excellent performance and *(ii)* 'Results' – the impact of those enablers on staff, customers, society at large, and ultimately on business performance.

Box 4.6 : The Business Excellence Model: Criteria

(i) Leadership,	*(ii)* Policy and strategy,	*(iii)* People,
(iv) Partnerships and Resources,	*(v)* Processes,	*(vi)* Customer Results,
(vii) People results,	*(viii)* Society Results,	*(ix)* Key performance Results.

'Leadership' considers how effectively those who manage the organisation act in relation to the drive for excellence.

'Policy and strategy' examines how these aspects of the organisation are oriented toward the achievement of total quality and how it goes about delivering them.

'People management' in concert with the revised requirements of ISO 9001:2000 explicitly recognizes that quality is ultimately delivered ***by people, to people, through people***. 'People management' considers how the organisation works to realise the capabilities of its employees in driving improvement.

'Resources' (or resource management) is focused on the effective use and maintenance of the organisation's physical assets such as buildings, finance, technology, information, suppliers and materials.

'Processes' is concerned with the design, development, production, delivery and service processes which add the value to the organisation.

'Results' criteria focus on people, customer and societal satisfaction with the organisations and on the business results. This criterion attempts to compare the organisation's actual achievements with the internal standards, with its competitor's performance and with those organisations considered to be the best in the organisation's market.

'People satisfaction' attempts to determine the degree of satisfaction of staff in terms of how the employees feel about the organisation in relation to the issues such as ***morale, terms and conditions of employment, management behaviours, development, the work environment*** and ***participation*** in the quality program. Objective measures of people satisfaction include issues such as employee turnover, development activity, absenteeism and number of employees involved in suggestion schemes and improvement programs.

'Customer satisfaction' considers the response of customers to the goods and services provided. The results are split between **customer perceptions of performance** on delivery, reliability, service levels, complaints, warranty and accessibility of service staff and **objective measures** based on error and rejection rates, actual delivery performance, numbers of complaints and warranty claims and significantly, numbers of repeat customers. (customer loyalty and customer retention).

'The impact on society' examines many of the issues which would be considered under ISO 14000 such as environmental impact, impact on quality of life, preservation of resources and internal measures of resource utilization efficiency. The model looks at both **external perceptions** – how well the organisation represents itself to its community and **objective internal measures** of employment, recycling, waste reduction, pollution and complaints.

"Business results" is concerned with the success or otherwise of the organisation in meeting the expectations of its financial stakeholders and in meeting business objectives. The objective aspects of business performance include statutory, accounting information (profit loss, margins, sales, net worth), cash flows, share price and ratings, dividends productivity and returns on investments. Other aspects include market share, performance of suppliers, error rates, process performance and cycle times.

The 'Business Excellence Model, (BEM) is suitable for companies which have already made significant progress towards excellence in all aspects of their operations. While the basic process of using the BEM is primarily an internal matter, companies can pursue the "European Quality Award" (EQA). The process leading to the award engages external assessors in evaluating the performance of the company against the award criteria – and in competition with other organisations also pursuing the programme. EQA can be thought of as a target to work towards for organisations which have already achieved the ISO standard.

Limitations of Business Excellence Model

(i) The key limitation of the BEM is that it relies rather heavily on ***perceptions*** rather than on ongoing ***objective measures***.

(ii) It has been observed by some organisations to be cumbersome and bureaucratic in use.

(iii) Its reliance on self-assessment leaves creative managers free to evaluate their performance at a lower level than is actually being achieved, enabling them to show improvement at their next evaluation – without changing anything.

(iv) The model lacks real dynamism. The BEM framework has the potential to represent a network of interrelated enablers and results and could be used, with appropriately objective performance measurement, to drive a dynamic business model in which the impacts of change on other areas could be usefully assessed before being made, rather than reflected upon after the event.

4.10 CII–EXIM BANK AWARD FOR EXCELLENCE

The CII-EXIM Bank Award for Excellence was established jointly by Confederation of Indian Industry (CII) and Export-Import (EXIM) Bank of India in 1994 to enhance the competitiveness of Indian companies.

4.10.1 The Basic Concepts of Excellence Model

The Excellence Model is a non-prescriptive framework which recognises multiple approaches to achieving sustainable excellence. With-in this non-prescriptive approach, **there are some basic (or fundamental) concepts which are listed below.**

(i) **Results orientation**: *Excellence is achieving results that delight all the stake holders of the organisation.*

(ii) **Customer Focus:** *Excellence means creating sustainable customer value.*

(iii) **Leadership and Constancy of Purpose:** *Excellence is visionary and inspirational leadership coupled with constancy of purpose.*

(iv) **Management by Processes and Facts:** *Excellence is managing the organisation through a set of interdependent and interrelated systems, processes and facts.*

(v) **People Developments and Involvement:** *Excellence is maximising the contribution of employees through their development and involvement.*

(vi) **Continuous Learning, Innovation and Improvement:** *Excellence is challenging the status – quo and effecting change by using learning to create innovation and improvement opportunities.*

(vii) **Partnership Development:** *Excellence is developing and maintaining value-adding relationship.*

(viii) **Corporate Social Responsibility:** *Excellence is exceeding the minimum regulatory frame work in which the organisation operates and to strive to understood and respond to the expectations of their stakeholders in society.*

The Excellence Model: The Excellence Model is a non-prescriptive framework based on nine criteria of which five are "**Enablers**" and four are "**Results**". The 'Enabler' criteria cover what an organisation ***does*** and the '***Results***' criteria cover what an organisation ***achieves***. Enablers cause results. ***Exhibit 4.10*** **shows the Excellence Model framework.**

Exhibit 4.10 : The Excellence Model Framework

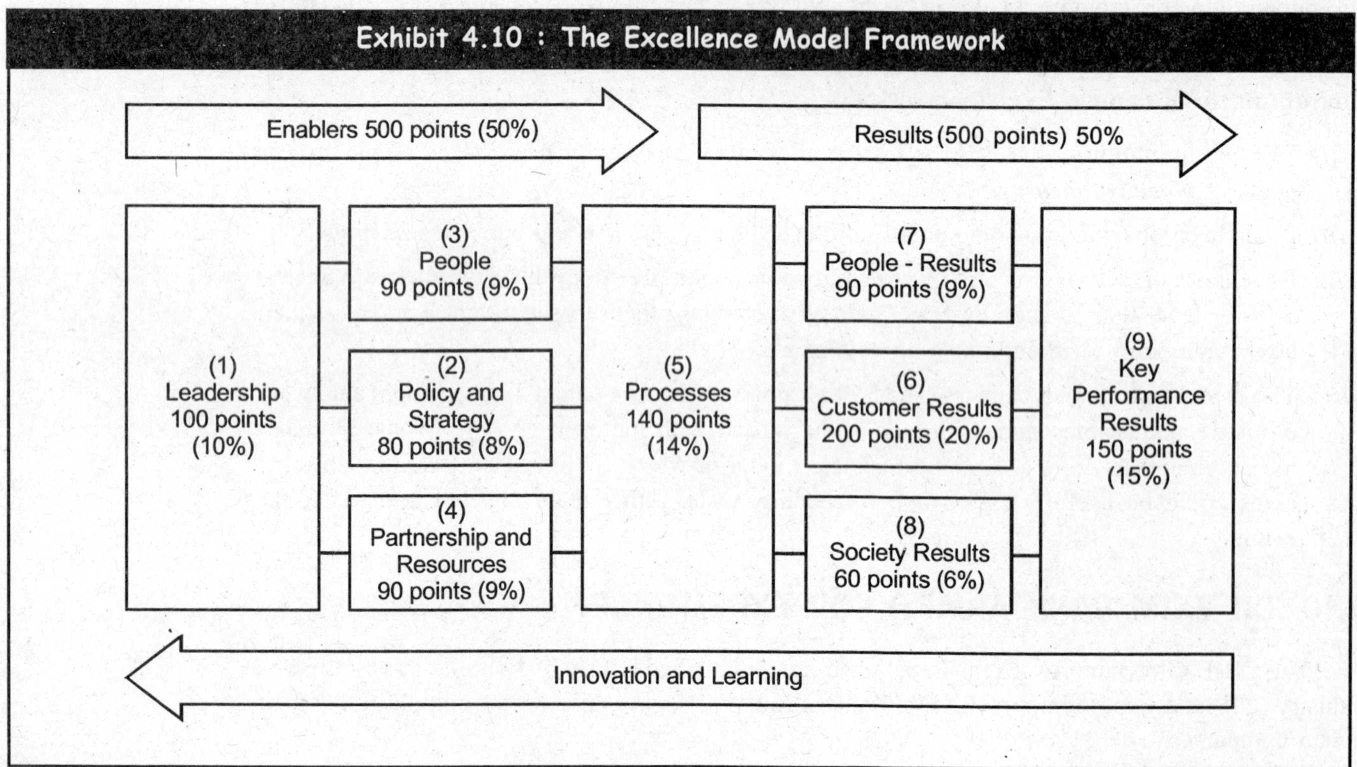

The Model recognises that there are many approaches to achieving sustainable excellence in all aspects of performance. It is based on the premise that:

"Excellent results with respect to Performance, Customers, People and Society are achieved through Leadership driving Policy and Strategy, People, Partnerships & Resources and Processes'.

4.10.2 Model Content and Structure

In the *Exhibit 4.10* showing the excellence model, the nine boxes represent the criteria against which an organisation's progress towards excellence is assessed.

To develop the meaning of each criteria, a number of sub-criteria are developed to support each of the nine criteria. Each sub criteria pose a number of questions that should be considered in the course of an assessment.

Any organisation has a logic consisting of the following four elements: *(i)* Results, *(ii)* Approach, *(iii)* Development and, *(iv)* Assessment and Review.

These are briefly discussed below:

(i) **Results :** The organisation needs to determine the ***results*** it is aiming to achieve as part of its ***policy*** and ***strategy*** making process. These results encompass the performance of the organisation both financially and operationally and also the perceptions of its stake holders.

(ii) **Approach :** The organisation needs to ***plan*** and ***develop*** an integrated set of sound approaches to deliver the required ***results***, both for the present as well as in the future.

(iii) **Deployment :** The organisation needs to ***deploy*** the approaches in a systematic manner to ensure full implementation of the same.

(iv) **Assessment and Review :** The organisation needs to ***assess*** and ***review*** the approaches followed based on monitoring and analysis of the ***results*** achieved and on going learning activities. Finally, the organisation must identify, prioritise, plan and implement improvements where needed.

Exhibit 4.11 **illustrates the logic which lies at the heart of the Excellence Model.**

Exhibit 4.11 : Logic of Excellence Model

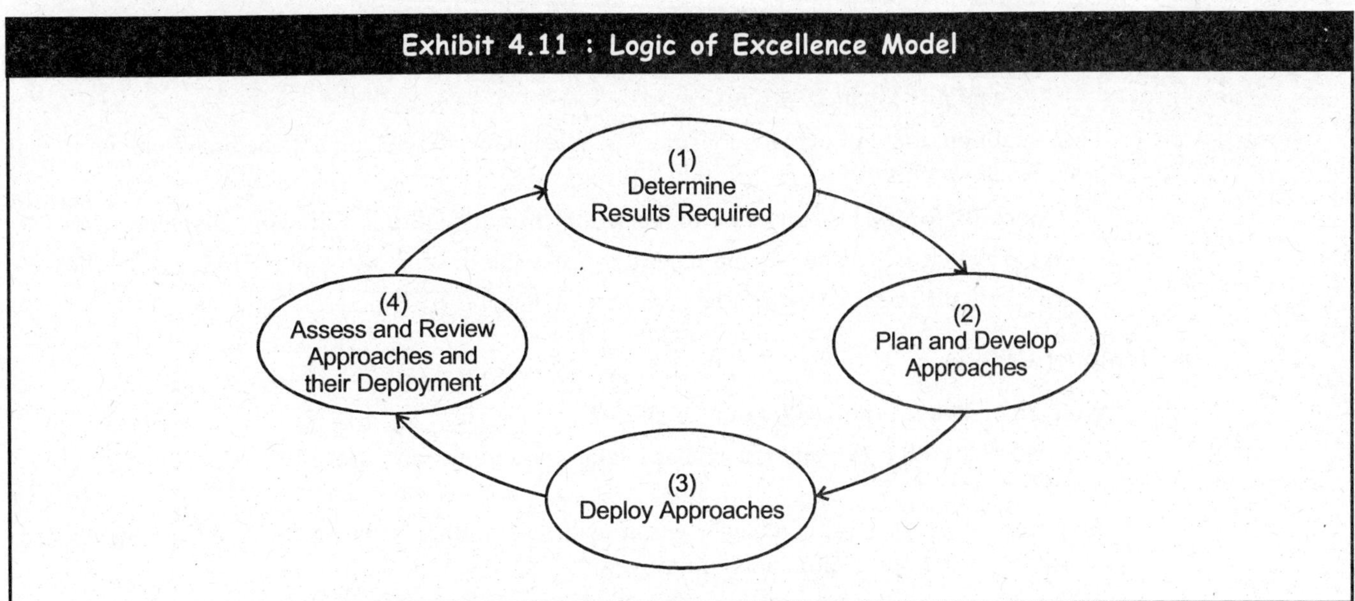

When using The Excellence Model within an organisation; for example for the purpose of Self-Assessment, the 'Approach', 'Deployment' 'Assessment & Review' elements of the organisation's logic should be addressed for each 'Enabler' sub criterion and the 'Results' element should be addressed for each 'Results' sub criterion.

The four elements of the Excellence Model namely 'Results', 'Approach', 'Deployment' and "Assessment and Review" are briefly discussed below:

(i) **Results:** This covers what an organisation is achieving. In an excellent organisation, the results show ***positive trends*** and/or sustained good performance. **Targets** are set at the appropriate level and met or exceeded. **Performance** is **compared** externally, particularly against the **best-in-class** and/or **world class** performance.

(ii) **Approach:** This covers **what** an organisation plans to do and the reasons for it. A **sound approach** has a clear rationale which focuses on the organisation's current and future needs. It is delivered through a well defined and developed process or processes and also has a clear **focus on the needs of the stakeholders.**

(iii) **Deployment:** This covers **what** an organisation does to **deploy** the **approach**. In an excellent organisation, the **approach** will be **implemented** in relevant areas **in a systematic** manner.

(iv) **Assessment and Review:** This covers **what** an organisation does to **review** and **improve** both the approach and the deployment of the approach. In an excellent organisation, the approach and its deployment will be subject to regular measurement. Learning activities will be undertaken and the output from both will be used to identify, prioritise, plan and implement improvement.

Eligibility Criteria

All organisations operating in India and overseas units of the Indian Companies are eligible to apply for the award. The applicant must be actively in business at least for the past three years. Two categories of "For - Profit Business Organisations" are *(i)* Business units and, *(ii)* Operating units.

Business units are whole companies or part of companies run as business units satisfying all the following characteristics:

(a) Run as an independent profit centre with a full set of accounts (publicly published balance sheet)

(b) More than 50% of turnover are external to itself and the parent company where on exists.

(c) The unit has a broad range of support functions/policies, which it has autonomy over (e.g. HR, Finance, IT etc).

In addition, the unit may demonstrate its independence by using a name/brand unique to that of the parent organisation.

Operating units are part of an organisation (parent) with the following characteristics:

(a) The unit is dependent on a parent organisation in some areas (e.g. HR, Finance, IT etc).

(b) Self-sufficient enough to be assessed on all nine criteria.

Model Criteria

Criterion 1: Leadership (100 points/10%)

(a) Leaders develop the mission, vision, values and ethics and are role models of a culture of excellence.

(b) Leaders are personally involved in ensuring the organisation's management system is developed, implemented and continuously improved.

(c) Leaders interact with customers, partners and representatives of society.

(d) Leaders reinforce a culture of excellence with the organisation's people.

(e) Leaders identify and champion organisational change.

Criterion 2: Policy and Strategy (80 points/8%)

(*a*) Policy and strategy are based on the present and future needs and expectations of stakeholders.

(*b*) Policy and strategy are based on information from performance measurement, research, learning and external related activities.

(*c*) Policy and strategy are developed, reviewed and updated.

(*d*) Policy and strategy are communicated and deployed through a framework of key processes.

Criterion 3: People: (90 points/9%)

(*a*) People resources are planned, managed and improved.

(*b*) People's knowledge and competencies are identified, developed and sustained.

(*c*) People are involved and empowered.

(*d*) People and the organisation have a dialogue.

(*e*) People are rewarded, recognized and cared for.

Criterion 4: Partnerships & Resources (90 points/9%)

(*a*) External partnerships are managed.

(*b*) Finances are managed.

(*c*) Building, equipment and materials are managed.

(*d*) Technology is managed.

(*e*) Information and knowledge are managed.

Criterion 5: Processes (140 points/14%)

(*a*) Processes are systematically designed and managed.

(*b*) Processes are improved, as needed, using innovation in order to fully satisfy and generate increasing value for customers and other stakeholders.

(*c*) Products and services are designed and developed based on customer needs and expectations.

(*d*) Products and services are produced, delivered and serviced.

(*e*) Customer relationships are managed and enhanced.

Criterion 6: Customer Results (200 points/20%)

(a) **Perception measures** – customer's perceptions of the organisation, for example, image, products and services, sales and after-sales support, loyalty etc.

(b) **Performance Indicators** – internal measures used by the organisation to monitor, understand, predict and improve the performance of the organisation and to predict perceptions of external customers.

Criterion 7: People Results (90 points/9%)

(a) **Perception Measures** – People's perception of the organisation. Depending on the purpose of the organisation, examples of measures may include *(i)* motivation and, *(ii)* satisfaction.

(b) **Performance Indicators** – internal measures used by the organisation to monitor, understand, predict and improve the performance of the organisation's people and to predict their perceptions. Examples of measures may include *(i)*achievements, *(ii)* motivation and involvement, *(iii)* satisfaction and, *(iv)* services provided to the organisation's people.

Criterion 8: Society Results (60 points/6%)

(a) **Perception measures** – those measures are of society's perception of the organisation. Examples of measures may include *(i)* image, *(ii)* performance as a responsible citizen (corporate citizenship), *(iii)* involvement in the communities where it operates, *(iv)* reduction and prevention of nuisance and harm from its operations and/or throughout the life cycle of its products and services, *(v)* reporting on activities to assist in the preservation and sustainability of resources.

(b) **Performance Indicators** – internal measures used by the organisation in order to monitor, understand, predict and improve the performance of the organisation and to predict perceptions of society. For example, the measures may include

(i) Handling changes in employment levels.

(ii) Dealing with authorities on issues such as certification, clearances, import/export, planning, product release etc.

(iii) Aecolades and awards received.

Criterion 9: Key performance Results (150points/15%)

(a) **Key performance outcomes** – These measures are key results defined by the organisation and agreed in their policy and strategies. Examples are *(i)* financial outcomes, *(ii)* non – financial outcomes.

(b) **Key performance Indicators** – these measures are the operational ones used in order to monitor and understand the processes and predict and improve the organisation's likely key performance outcomes.

Examples of measure may include: *(i)* Financial and, *(ii)* Non financial.

4.10.3 Characteristics of Excellent Organisations

1. **Leadership :** Excellent leaders develop and facilitate the achievement of the mission and vision. They develop organisational values and systems required for sustainable success and implement these via their actions and behaviours. During period of change, they retain a constancy of purpose. Where required such leaders are able to change the direction of the organisation and inspire others to follow.
2. **Policy and strategy :** Excellent organisations implement their mission and vision by developing a stakeholder focused strategy and that takes account of the market and sector in which it operates. Policies, plans, objectives and processes are developed and deployed to deliver the strategy.
3. **People :** Excellent organisations manage, develop and release the full potential of their people at an individual, team-based and organisational level. They promote fairress and equality and involve and empower their people. They care for, communicate, reward and recognise, in a way that motivates staff and builds commitment to using their skills and knowledge for the benefit of the organisation.
4. **Partnerships & Resources :** Excellent organisations plan and manage external partnerships, suppliers and internal resources in order to support policy and strategy and the effective operation of processes. During planning and while managing partnerships and resources, they balance the current and future needs of the organisation, the community and the environment.
5. **Processes :** Excellent organisations design, manage and improve processes in order to fully satisfy and generate increasing value for customers and other stakeholders.
6. **Customer Results :** Excellent organisations comprehensively measure and achieve outstanding results with respect to their customers.
7. **People Results :** Excellent organisations comprehensively measure and achieve outstanding results with respect to their people (employees).
8. **Society Results :** Excellent organisations comprehensively measure and achieve outstanding results with respect to society.
9. **Key performance Results :** Excellent organisations comprehensively measure and achieve outstanding results with respect to the key elements of their policy and strategy.

How the Organisation is Assessed

A team of assessors, all of whom have undergone training, to ensure a high level of consistency in scoring will examine the application document.

Assessors are drawn from the ranks of experienced practicing managers from Indian organisations. The application document will be assessed and scored on a scale of 0 to 1000 points, using the Excellence Model, based on EFQM Excellence Model.

Essentially, the model conveys that:

(i) Excellent results with respect to performance, customers, people and society are achieved through leadership, driving policy and strategy, people, partnership and resources and processes.

(ii) The 'results' criteria are concerned with what the organisation has achieved and is achieving.

(iii) The 'enablers' criteria are concerned with how results are being achieved.

(iv) 'Enablers' and 'results' are valued at 500 points each.

4.10.4 Award Assessment Process

Step 1: Companies order application brochure: Potential applicants check the eligibility criteria for entry and requirements of the Award Secretariat.

Step 2: Selection of Assessors: Senior managers from industry are selected as Assessors. They go through four day training programme or understanding the award criteria and assessment process.

Step 3: Applicant submits documents: Applicants send 75 page (maximum) application document to CII.

Step 4: Assessment and consensus scoring: Assessor team is appointed for each applicant. Assessors individually list strengths/opportunities for improvement and award scores. Team meets to reach consensus.

Step 5: Screening for site visits: On the basis of consensus report, the applicants are short listed for site visits.

Step 6: Site visits: Assessor Teams are appointed to make site visits. Assessors to plan site visits. Site visits (4 to 6 days typically) are made to check validity of application and clarify issues. Applications are rescored and reports are finalised.

Step 7: Jury meeting: Distinguished individuals (about 9) from business and academic appointed as jurors. Jurors are trained on the award model and the process. Based on reports from site-visit teams, jurors decide on the winners of the award, prizes and commendation certificates.

Step 8: Award presentation: The CII-Exim Bank Excellence Award, Prizes and Commendations are presented to the winning applicants.

Step 9: Feed back report: Senior assessors (leaders of the assessment team) write feedback reports to all applicants identifying the strengths/opportunities for improvement. Score ranges are also given for each criterion. On request, senior assessor visits applicant to discuss feed back report.

Levels of Recognition

There are four levels of recognition, starting from the commendation certificate for strong commitment and going upto the Award. These levels signify the various milestones which the organisations can aim for as they progress on their journey towards excellence.

Award criteria used for assessing the applications is based on the European Foundation for Quality Management (EFQM) Excellence Model and hence provides a mechanism to benchmark against world class organisations which are using TQM to drive excellence.

The levels of recognition are:

(i) Commendation for strong commitment to excel

(ii) Commendation for significant achievement

(iii) Prize

(iv) Award.

CII-EXIM Bank Award for Excellence is presented to organisations judged to be "Role Models" Prizes are awarded to organisations that demonstrate excellence in the management of quality as their fundamental process for continuous improvement.

Organisations which have made good progress on their journey towards excellence but fall short of the level set for prize winners are given commendation certificates. There are two levels for communication: *(i)* significant achievement on the journey towards excellence and, *(ii)* strong commitment to excel on the journey towards excellence.

(The second level is lower than the first level)

Apart from getting an opportunity for peer recognition, each company gets an external perspective on their practices and performance. A team of trained assessors with diverse and extensive experience assesses each applicant company. The assessors spend around 1000 man hours to identify strengths and opportunities for improvement. A detailed feed back report is sent to all the applicant companies that gives an objective and comprehensive assessment of the current status of the organisations and forms a sound basis for developing organisation wide consensus on strategy for reaching higher level of competitiveness. ***Box 4.7* lists Winners of CII - EXIM Bank Award for Business Excellence.**

Box 4.7 : Winners of CII-EXIM Bank Award for Business Excellence

Year	Category	Company Name
2010	Manufacturing	*(i)* Crompton Greaves Limited (Award)
		(ii) The Tinplate company of India Ltd. (Prize)
	Services	Indelox services pvt ltd
2009	Manufacturing	Bosch-Diesel Systems Bangalore (Award)
	Services	Indelox Services Pvt Ltd
2008	Manufacturing	The Tin plate company of India Ltd. (Prize)
	Manufacturing	Aditya Auto (Award)
2007	Manufacturing	Eastman Industries Ltd. (Award)
2006	Services	Tata Consultancy Services Ltd. (Award)
	Manufacturing	BHEL, Haridwar (Prize)
2005	Manufacturing	Tata Motors Ltd. Commercial Vehicle Business unit (Award)
2004	Manufacturing	Larsen & Toubro Ltd. (Award)
2002	Services	Infosys Technologies Ltd. Bangalore (Award)
2000	Manufacturing	Tata Iron and Steel Ltd. (Award)
1998	Manufacturing	Maruthi Udyog Ltd. (Award)
1997	Services	Hewlett Packard (India) (Award)

4.11 RAJIV GANDHI NATIONAL QUALITY AWARD

Rajiv Gandhi National Quality Award (RGNQA) was instituted by the Bureau of Indian standards in 1991, with a view to encouraging Indian Manufacturing and Service organisations to strive for excellence and giving special recognition to those who are considered to be the leaders of quality movement in India. This award is intended to generate interest and involvement of Indian Industry in quality programs, drive our products and services to higher levels of quality and equip our industry to meet the challenges of domestic and international markets.

RGNQ Award would help Indian Industry to improve quality by:

(i) Encouraging Indian Industry to make significant improvements in quality for maximising consumer satisfaction and for successfully facing competition in the global market as well.

(ii) Recognising the achievement of those organisations which have improved the quality of their products and services and thereby set an example to others.

(iii) Establishing guidelines and criteria that can be used by industry in evaluating their own quality improvement efforts and

(iv) Providing specific guidance to other organisations that wish to learn how to achieve excellence in quality, by making available detailed information on the "Quality Management Approach" adopted by award winning organisations to change their culture and achieve eminence.

The award has been designed in line with similar awards in other developed countries, like MBNQA in USA, Deming Prize in Japan, and European Quality Award.

The RGNQ Award is an annual feature on the basis of financial year i.e. from 1st April to 31st March of the next year. (For example the 2008 award will be considered for results achieved from 1st April 2007 to 31st March 2008)

Benefits to the Award Winners

Award Winners will be reckoned as champions of quality movement in India. They may have good quality image and may have leverage in business on being recognised as the best in their field. Apart from these intangible benefits, there are some financial incentives – organisations winning the "Best of All" Award would be given cash award of Rs 5 lakhs. Organisations winning the other awards would be given award of Rs 1 lakh. Organisations receiving the commendation certificate would be given cash award of Rs 50,000.

There are five awards consisting of one for large scale manufacturing organisations, one for small scale manufacturing organisations, one for large scale service sector organisations, one for small scale service sector organisations and one for "Best of All". In addition there are eight commendation certificates, each for large scale and small scale manufacturing organisations as per industrial sectors given below:

(i) Biotechnology, *(ii)* Chemical industry, *(iii)* Electrical and electronic industry, *(iv)* Food and drug Industry, *(v)* Gems, jewellery and allied Industry, *(vi)* Metallurgical Industry, *(vii)* Textile Industry, and *(viii)* Engineering industry and others.

Further there are six commendation certificates each for large and small-scale service organisations in the following areas:

(i) Education, *(ii)* Finance, *(iii)* Healthcare, *(iv)* Information Technology, *(v)* Utilities and *(vi)* Others.

Assessment Criteria

The assessment for large scale organisation will be made on the basis of nine parameters namely *(i)* Leadership (100 points), *(ii)* Policies, objectives and strategies (100 points), *(iii)* Human

Resource Management (50 points), *(iv)* Resources (100points), *(v)* Processes (150 points), *(vi)* Customer focused Results (200 points), *(vii)* Employee satisfaction (50 points), *(viii)* Impact on environment and society (100 points) and *(ix)* Business Results (150 Points).

The assessment of small scale organisations will be made on the basis of six parameters namely:

(i) Leadership, *(ii)* Human Resource Management, *(iii)* Processes, *(iv)* Customer -focused Results, *(v)* Impact on environment and society and *(vi)* Business Results.

Assessment Process

All the applications received shall be screened as per the criteria laid down on the basis of information provided by the applicant organisation. Applicants selected in the preliminary screening will become eligible for fact finding and evaluation visits. A team of experts appointed for this purpose would visit the applicant organisation for on-the-spot study and evaluation.

RGNQ Award Winners

Rajiv Gandhi National Quality Awards for the year 2009 were presented to the winners on January 12, 2011.

The "Best of All" Award was given to Tata Motors Limited. Lucknow. The other category award winners include: Glaxosmithkline Consumer Health Care Ltd., Sonepat, Haryana (Large Scale Manufacturing Industry), Karnataka State Road Transport Corporation, Bangalore (Large Scale Service Industry), Elin Appliances Pvt. Ltd., Solan, Himachal Pradesh (Small Scale Manufacturing Industry) and Quality Evaluation and Systems Team Pvt. Ltd., Bangalore (Small Scale Service Industry). In addition to these awards, thirteen organisations were honoured with commendation certificates under various categories. ***Box 4.8* list RGNQ Award Winners since 1991-92**

Box 4.8 : RGNQ Award Winners since 1991-92

Year	Category of Award	Winner
1992	"Best of All"	Kirloskar Cummins Ltd. Pune
1992	Large Scale Manufacturing Engineering Industry	Widia (India) Ltd. Bangalore.
1993	"Best of All"	Steel Authority of India Ltd. Bhilai Steel plant – Bailai
1993	Large scale Manufacturing Industry	Indian Aluminium Company Ltd. Electronics Division. Mysore Bharath Heavy Electricals Ltd., Chennai.
1994	"Best of All"	ITC Ltd. ILTD Division, Chirala A.P.
	Large Scale Manufacturing Industry	Mathura Refinery of IOC Ltd. Madhurai
	Small Scale Manufacturing Industry	Laxmi Hydraulic Pvt. Ltd., Solapur (Maharashtra)
1995	"Best of All"	ITC Ltd. ILTD Division, Anaparti. (A.P)
	Large Scale Manufacturing Industry	Lakshmi Machine Tools, Coimbatore.
	Small Scale Manufacturing Industry	John's Umbrella Mart, Alappuza Kerala
1996	"Best of All"	Tata Bearings, Kharagpur, West Bengal.
	Large Scale Manufacturing Industry	C.G. Newage Electral Ltd., Ahmed Nagar, Maharashtra.
	Service Sector	Tamilnadu Medical Services Corporation Ltd., Chennai. TN.
	Small Scale Manufacturing Industry	Sharp Industries, Coimbatore. TN

1997	"Best of All"	Larsen & Toubro Ltd, Bangalore Works Bangalore. Karnataka
	Large Scale Manufacturing	SAIL – Bhilai Plant – Bihialai (MP) Vikram Cement, Mandsaur (MP).
	Service Sector	Wipro Ltd. - Infotech Group, Bangalore.
	Small Scale Manufacturing Industry	Auto Shell Moulders Ltd., Coimbatore – TN
1998	"Best of All"	Mathura Refinery of IOC Ltd., Mathura.
	Large Scale Manufacturing Industry	Gujarat Refinery of IOC, Vadodara.
	Service Sector (Joint winners)	Larsen & Toubro Ltd. EPC Projects Group, Mumbai and Cummins Diesel Sales and Service (India) Ltd., Pune.
	Small Scale Manufacturing Industry	Wings Automobile Products Pvt. Ltd., Faridabad.
1999	"Best of All"	Gujarat Cooperative Milk Marketing Federation Ltd. Anand. and Tata Cummins Ltd, Jamshedpur.
	Service Sector	Honey well India Software Operation Pvt. Ltd., Bangalore.
	Small Scale Manufacturing Industry (Joint Winners)	John's Umbrella Mart, Alleppey and Popy Umbrella Mart, Alappuza.
2000	"Best of All"	Tata International Ltd. – Dewas.
	Large Scale Manufacturing Industry	CG – Newage Electrical Ltd., Ahmednagar.
	Small Scale Manufacturing Industry	Polytrusions Pvt Ltd., Ponneri Taluk.
	Service Sector	Bharat Heavy Electricals Ltd. Power Sector Northern Region, Noida.
2001	"Best of All"	Birla Cellulosic, Bharuch. Gujarat.
	Large Scale Manufacturing Industry (Joint winners)	JK Tyre, Kankroli and Reliance Industries Ltd. (Hazira Manufacturing Division) Surat
	Small Scale Industry	Chola Pumps (Pvt) Ltd., Coimbatore.
	Service Sector	Indian Oil Corporation Ltd. Kandla, Bhatinda (Pipe line, Panipat).
2003	"Best of All" (Joint winners)	Indian Oil Corporation Ltd. (Gujarat Refinery) Vadodara and Grasim Industries Ltd. (Chemical Division) Nagda.
	Large Scale Manufacturing (Joint winners)	Hindal Co. Industries Ltd, Renukoot and VIP Industries Ltd., Nasik.
	Service Sector	Tata Consultancy Services Ltd. SEEPZ, Mumbai
	Small Scale Manufacturing Industry	Auto Print Machinery Manufacturers Pvt. Ltd., Coimbatore.
2005	"Best of All"	Moser Baer India Ltd., Greater Noida.
	Large Scale Manufacturing Industry	Panipat Refinery, IOC Ltd, Panipat
	Large Scale Service Industry	Tata Consultancy Services Ltd, Deccan Park, Hyderabad.
	Small Scale Manufacturing Industry	Sakthi Masala (Pvt) Ltd., Erode.
2006	"Best of All"	Steel Authority of India Ltd. Bhilai Steel Plant Bhilai
	Large Scale Manufacturing Industry	Lucas – TVS Ltd. Chennai.
	Large Scale Service Industry	"Nipuna" Services Ltd., Hyderabad.
	Small Scale Manufacturing Industry	Himedia Laboratories – Pvt Ltd., Nasik.
2007	"Best of All"	Steel Authority of India Ltd., Bokaro "Steel Plant, Bakaro.
	Large Scale Manufacturing Industry	Tata Motors Ltd. Commercial Vehicles Business unit. Pune.
	Large Scale Service Industry	Tata Ryerson Ltd., Jamshedpur
	Small Scale Manufacturing Industry	TV Super Filter Industries, Jammu.
	Small Scale Service Industry	Wealthmax Enterprises Management Pvt Ltd. Bangalore.

2008	Best of All	Satluj Jal Vidyut, Nigam Ltd, Shimla, Himachal Pradesh.
	Large Scale Manufacturing Industry	GAIL (India) Ltd., Gas Processing Unit, Vijaipur, Guna, (MP).
	Large Scale Service	IOC Ltd, Haldia – Barauni Crude Oil Pipeline. Purba Midinpur West Bengal.
	Small Scale Manufacturing Industry	Jet Knit Wears Pvt Ltd., Kanpur (U.P)
	Small Scale Service Industry	Logistics Park (India) Pvt. Ltd. Nagpur, Maharashtra.
2009	Best of All	Tata Motors Ltd. Luck now (UP)
	Large Scale Manufacturing Industry	Glaxosmith kline Consumer Health Care Ltd. Sonepat. Haryana
	Large Scale Service Industry	Karnataka State Road Transport Corporation. Bangalore Karnataka.
	Small Scale Manufacturing Industry	Elin Appliances Pvt Ltd., Solan. (H.P)
	Small Scale Service Industry	Quality Evaluation and Systems Team Pvt. Ltd. Bangalore. Karnataka.

4.12 GOLDEN PEACOCK NATIONAL QUALITY AWARD (GPNQA)

The Golden Peacock National Quality Award was instituted by the Golden Peacock Awards Secretariate in February 1991 to encourage total quality improvements in both manufacturing as well as service organisations in India including

- Public and private undertakings.
- All sectors of industry and commerce.
- Government and semi government departments.
- Trade and professional associations.
- Educational, Service and Research establishments.

The GPNQ Awards are normally presented at the world congress on Total Quality in January/ February each year to organisations in different sectors adjudged to have made the most significant achievements in the field of total quality.

The GPNQ Award stimulates and helps organisations to rapidly accelerate the pace of customer – oriented improvement process. It is a powerful self – assessment process and a way to build organisation's brand equity on "Quality".

The Golden Peacock National Quality Award is named after India's national bird the "Peacock". The award winners may use the Golden Peacock National Quality Award logo in their printed and promotional material for the next three years. **The GPNQ Award will be given separately for manufacturing and service organisations in different sectors under the following categories.**

(i) **Large Enterprises** – Annual turnover of Rs 300 crores and above.

(ii) **Medium and Small Enterprises** – Annual Turnover less than Rs 300 crores.

(iii) **Special Categories** – *(a)* Education, Training, Research and Development, Testing and Inspection. *(b)* Service Sector covering Tourism, Transport, Couriers, Hotels and Hospitality, Health care, Telecommunication, Professional consultancies, Financial institutions. *(c)* Government organisations, undertakings and services.

How companies are assessed for the GPNQA Award?

The application submitted by the companies to be considered for the award will be assessed and scored on a scale of zero to thousand points using the GPNQA Model for Total Quality **Management which is illustrated in the *Exhibit 4.12* below.**

Exhibit 4.12 : The Golden Peacock National Quality Award Model

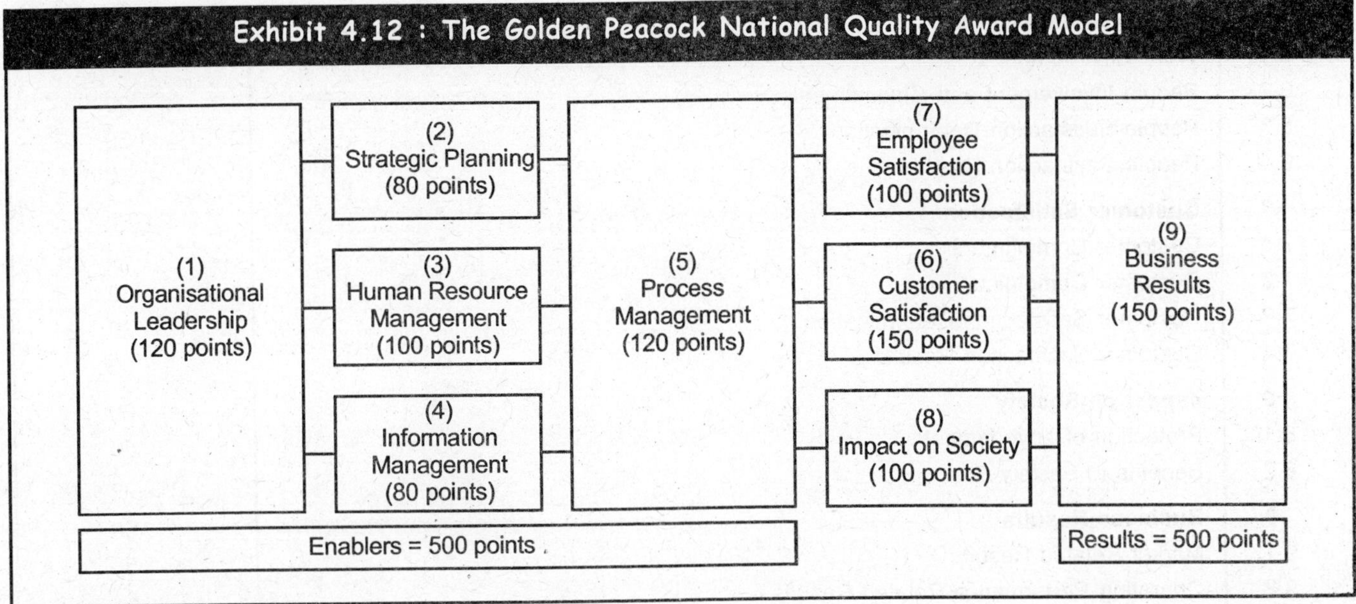

Box 4.9 **gives the breakup of points against each criteria for self assessment by the company intending to apply for the award.**

Box 4.9 : GPNAQ Management Model - GPNQ Award Criteria

Sl No.	Categories/Items	Point Values
1	**Organisational Leadership**	120
1.1	Senior Leadership – commitment and Involvement	50
1.2	Total Quality Culture	40
1.3	Responsibilities Towards Society	30
2	**Strategic Planning**	80
2.1	Strategic Planning Process	20
2.2	Customer and Market Focus	20
2.3	Innovation and Growth	20
2.4	Strategy Deployment	20
3	**Human Resource Management**	100
3.1	HR policies and strategies	25
3.2	Skills and Competency enhancement	25
3.3	Organisation Design and Self-directed Responsibilities	25
3.4	Reward, Recognition and Encouragement	25
4	**Information Management**	80
4.1	Performance Measures and Data Integration	20
4.2	Selection and Use of Comparative Information including Competitive Data	20
4.3	Information Analysis and Use	40
5	**Process Management**	120
5.1	Process design and Management	20
5.2	Development of Products/Services	20
5.3	Supplier Selection and Management	20
5.4	Development of Processes	20
5.5	Delivery of Products/Services,	20
	Feedback and Improvement	20
5.6	Handling Complaints and Customer Relationship Mangement	20

6	**Employee Satisfaction**	100
6.1	Work Environment	20
6.2	People Involvement and Commitment	20
6.3	People Satisfaction Determination	20
6.4	People Satisfaction Results	40
7	**Customer Satisfaction**	150
7.1	Customer Commitment	30
7.2	Customer Complaints	30
7.3	Customer Satisfaction Determination	30
7.4	Customer Satisfaction Results	60
8	**Impact on Society**	100
8.1	Protection of environment	50
8.2	Benefits to Society	50
9	**Business Results**	150
9.1	Market Related Results	50
9.2	Operating Performance-Related Results	50
9.3	Financial Results	50

4.13 IMC RAMAKRISHNA BAJAJ NATIONAL QUALITY AWARD

In the early 1960 s, the Indian business community realised that it needed to progress beyond the ISO 9000 standard. As a result, the Indian Merchant's Chamber (IMC) and the Confederation of Indian Industries (CII) each carried out research on the prevailing world-class management models: Malcolm Baldrige National Quality Award, European Quality Award and the Deming Prize. Subsequently the IMC and CII independently announced quality management models to help the Indian Industry turn globally competitive.

To match the stature of international awards, the IMC Ramakrishna Bajaj National Quality Award criteria are set as the same as the Malcolm Baldrige criteria of US and follow a similar rigorous process of training and evaluation.

The IMC Ramakrishna Bajaj National Quality Award (IMC RBNQA) was instituted in 1996 by IMC to give special recognition to performance excellence by Indian companies. The IMC RBNQA criteria for assessment have been developed by the IMC to enable organisations to achieve business excellence. Consistent with the principles of continuous improvement, the award criteria have been revised and approved every year.

Box 4.10 **lists the names of the past winners of IMCRBNQA.**

Since 1996 The IMC Ramakrishna Bajaj National Quality Award Criteria have been used by many Indian organisations to stay abreast of ever-increasing competition and to improve performance.

Core values and concepts

The criteria are built upon the following set of interrelated corevalues and concepts :

(i) visionary leadership, *(ii)* customer-driven excellence, *(iii)* organisational and personal learning, *(iv)* valuing employees and partners, *(v)* ability, *(vi)* focus on the future, *(vii)* managing innovation, *(viii)* management by fact, *(ix)* social responsibility, *(x)* focus on results and creating value and *(xi)* systems perspective.

Criteria for Performance Excellence Framework :

The criteria are built on the set of interrelated core values and concepts mentioned earlier. ***Exhibit 4.13*** **illustrates the criteria for performance excellence framework.**

Box 4.10 : Winners of IMC Ramakrishna Bajaj National Quality Award

Year	Category	Awardee
2010	Manufacturing	LANXESS India Pvt Ltd. Nagda
	Service	• Information Systems Resource Centre Pvt Ltd
	Education	• Global Indian International School, Queens town, Singapore
	Health care	• Apollo speciality Hospitals, Madurai.
2009	Manufacturing	• Larsen and Toubro Ltd, Electrical Standard Products, Powai & Ahmednagar.
	Service	• Dahanu Thermal Power Station, Reliance Infrastructure Ltd, Dahanu.
	Education	• Mepco Schlenk Engineering College, Sivakasi.
2008	Manufacturing	• Marico Ltd, Edible Oil Business, Jalgaon and Goa sites.
	Service	• Hindalco Industries Ltd, Sonebadra.
	Small Business	• Venture Infotek Global Pvt Ltd. Mumbai.
	Overseas	• P. T. Indo-Bharat Rayon, Purwakarta, Indonesia.
	Education	• SIES college of Management Studies, Nerul, Navi Mumbai.
	Healthcare	• Dr. L.H. Hiranandani Hospital, Mumbai.
2007	Manufacturing	• Bihar Caustic & Chemicals Ltd. Palamau, Jharkand.
	Service	• Ma-Foi Management Consultants Ltd. Chennai.
	Small Business	• Prima Automation (India) Pvt. Ltd. Rakanpur, Gandhinagar.
	Education	• Manipal university, Manipal.
	Healthcare	• P. D. Hinduja National Hospital and Medical Research Centre, Mumbai.
2006	Service	• Datamatics Technologies, Mumbai.
	Education	• National Education Society, Mumbai.
	Overseas	• P.T. Indo Liberty Textiles, West Java, Indonesia.
2004	Manufacturing	• Tata Chemicals Ltd., Chemicals Division, Mithapur
		• Bharat Heavy Electricals Ltd. Ranipet
	Service	• I-flex Solutions Ltd, Mumbai.
2003	Manufacturing	• Birla Cellulosic, Kharach unit,
		• Grasim Industries (Aditya Birla Group)
2002	Manufacturing	• Reliance Industries Ltd., Hazira.
	Service	• University of Mumbai, Institute of Chemical Technology.
2001	Manufacturing	• Indo-Gulf Corporation. Ltd., Lucknow.
	Service	• Satyam Computers Services Ltd., Secunderabad.
2000	Manufacturing	• Thai Acrylic Fibre co. Thailand, (Aditya Birla Group)
	Service	• Infosys Technologies Ltd, Bangalore.

Features of the Award

There are six applicant categories for the IMC RBNQ Award. They are : *(i)* Manufacturing organisations *(ii)* Service organisations *(iii)* Small businesses *(iv)* Indian overseas organisation *(v)* Education *(vi)* Healthcare.

The types of awards in the order of merit are *(i)* IMC RBNQ Award *(ii)* Certificate of merit and *(iii)* Commendation certificate.

Exhibit 4.13 : Criteria for Performance Excellence Fromework for IMC-RBNQ Award

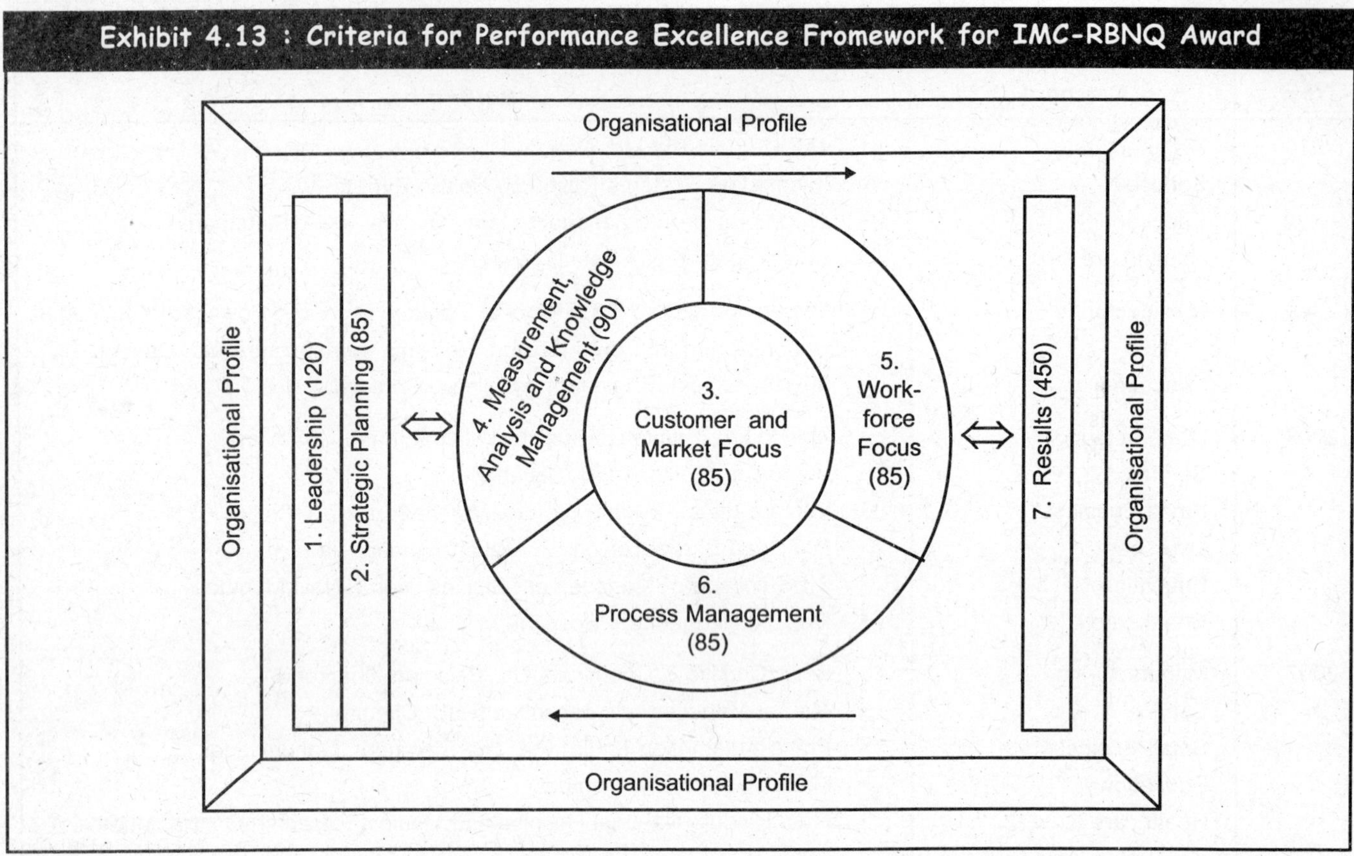

Ideally, only one Award is presented in each of the six categories. If the standards of the Awards are not met, no Award is announced. An organisation receiving an Award is not eligible to apply for another Award in the same category for a period of five years. A special trust for the IMC RBNQ Award was created to foster the success of the program. The trust has the objective of raising funds to permanently endow the Award programs. The IMC Quality Awards committee has evolved from the IMC Technology and Quality Improvement Committee. The committee advertises and selects the Board of Examiners. In addition, the committee screens the applicant scores and feedback reports submitted by the Certified Examiners. Finally, it shortlists organisations to be reviewed by the Panel of Judges.

The Board of Examiners evaluate Award applications and prepares feedback reports. The board consists of quality experts and senior managers from industry, academics, healthcare and consulting organisations.

Board members are assigned to applications taking into account the nature of the applicant's businesses and the expertise of the examiners. **Applications are reviewed and evaluated by members of the board in a four-stage process.**

Stage 1: Independent reviews and evaluation by at least five members of the Board.

Stage 2: Consensus review and evaluation by the above examiners.

Stage 3: Site visits to applicants that score well at the end of stage 2, by the relevant examiners.

Stage 4: Revision of scores and finalisation of the feedback report by the examiners.

The feedback reports are reviewed by the IMC Quality Awards Committee. The Awards Committe shortlists organisations for review by the Panel of Judges.

All applicants will recieve feedback reports commenting on their strengths and opportunities for improvement.

4.14 QUALITY IN PRACTICE

Box 4.11 : Baldrige Pays Off for Texas Instruments

Texas Instruments (TI) Defense Systems and Electronics Group faced a critical issue that many businesses struggle with. What is the payoff of greater competitive advantage worth the effort of achieving total quality, specifically competing for the Baldrige Award? Their answer is a definitely "yes".

TI understands that the real benefit of applying for the Baldrige Award lies in adopting its quality criteria. The application itself is the single most powerful catalyst for the kinds of organisational and cultural changes that companies must make to compete.

TI's commitment to quality and productivity improvement started in the 1950s. But most of its efforts were aimed at improving manufacturing and product quality. In the 1980s, a total quality initiative was formalised across the entire corporation. Some business units made tremendous progress, the semiconductor operation in Japan won the Deming Prize in 1985.

When the Baldrige Award criteria appeared, TI used them to provide focus and coherence to the activities across the corporation. Using the criteria, they were able to tackle a part of total quality that previously had been unreachable, implementing quality efforts in staff, support and non-manufacturing areas. In 1989, TI asked every business unit to prepare a mock award application as a way of measuring its progress. This task represented a radical change for some operations because, until that time, most staff functions were not required to measure their processes or these results.

The Defense Systems and Electronics Group's self-assessment revealed that they were a long way from applying for and winning the Baldrige Award. But the group aggressively adopted the criteria for improving its business.

Many executives did not believe that the criteria could be applied to defense contractors and small businesses. TI discovered that all companies have one thing in common : customers. Focusing on customers to make the company more competitive gives meaning to the award.

The Baldrige Award application process changed almost everything within the Defense Systems and Electronics Group. Before applying, the group had no way of systematically measuring how well it understood its customers' concerns. Eventhough large amount of data were being collected, but most of the data measured internal criteria, not customer satisfaction. The structured, hierarchical management environment made it difficult to adopt ideas from outside sources.

The Baldrige Award process provided a way to make the customer the centre place of daily activities. It led to much better communication with customers and employees and accelerated progress toward less hierarchical, more functional work teams. It changed the management process from an individual activity to a team effort, leading to better decisions. Finally, it introduced two radical new ideas : benchmarking and stretch goals. Changing the culture was not easy and did not happen quickly. It took team work, consensus building, and buy-in. At TI, it took about five years of dedicated pulling in the same direction to begin seeing measurable results.

4.15 SUMMARY

For managing quality and high performance, an organisation needs to embody the ***core principles of total quality*** in its strategies and leadership philosophies. These core principles are : *(i)* A focus on the customer, *(ii)* Participation and teamwork and *(iii)* Continuous improvement and learning. The various element of total quality management are : *(i)* Top management commitment and involvement, *(ii)* Customer involvement, *(iii)* Designing products for quality and reliability, *(iv)* Designing and controlling production processes, *(v)* Developing supplier partnerships, *(vi)* Employee training programs, *(vii)* Work teams and empowerment and *(viii)* Benchmarking and continuous improvements.

Further, the contributions of Deming, Juran, Crosby and Imai have laid the foundation for the current practice of TQM. The need for commonly accepted global standards or specifications for quality led to the development of quality standards such as *(i)* The Malcolm Baldrige National Quality Award (MBNQA), *(ii)* The Deming Prize and *(iii)* The ISO 9000 standards. The purpose of MBNQA to stimulate U.S. companies to attain excellence is quality and productivity and compete for the award for the pride of recognition. Criteria for selection include : *(i)* Leadership, *(ii)* Strategic Planning, *(iii)* Customer and Market Focus, *(iv)* Information and Analysis, *(v)* Human Resource Focus, *(vi)* Process Management and *(vii)* Business Results.

The Baldrige evaluation process employs 15 examiners chosen from among leading quality professionals to evaluate each applicant's response to each evaluation criteria. Based on the strength's of each applicant, scores are allotted for each examination item evaluated on approach, deployment and results.

The other international quality award programs include : *(i)* European Quality Award, *(ii)* Canadian Award for Business Excellence and *(iii)* Australian Quality Award.

Effective implementation of total quality depends on : *(i)* infrastructure, *(ii)* practices and tools and *(iii)* development of a supportive corporate culture. Eventhough TQM had been criticised in the media as a passing fad and a flawed philosophy, a number of objective studies have shown that total quality principles are alive and well and that the benefits of TQ far outweigh its weaknesses.

The Total Quality Management for Excellence (TQMEX) Model advocates an integrated approach in order to support the transition to system management which is ongoing process of continuous improvement that begins when the company commits itself to the managing by quality.

The various practices involved in TQMEX model are : *(i)* Japanese 5S practice, *(ii)* Business process reengineering, *(iii)* ISO 9000:2000 quality management system requirements, *(iv)* Quality circles, *(v)* Total productive maintenance and *(vi)* Six-sigma concept.

The Japanese 5 'S' practice is a technique used to establish and maintain quality environment in an organisation.

Business Process-Reengineering (BPR) is a management process used to redefine a mission statement, analyse the critical success factors, redesign the organisational structure and reengineer the critical processes in order to improve customer satisfaction.

Quality control circles comprise a small group of staff working together to contribute to the improvement of the enterprise. The ISO 9000:2000 is the quality management system model for quality assurance in design, development, production, installation and servicing.

Total productive maintenance (TPM) is a system of maintenance covering the entire life of the equipment in every division including planning, manufacturing and maintenance.

TQM kitemarks are quality standards that provide discipline, external assessment and a clear process for implementing TQM. The best known TQM kitemarks are the ISO 9004 : 2000, Japan's Deming Prize, USA's Malcolm Baldrige National Quality Award and the European and UK Quality Awards.

Six-sigma Concept is a quality philosophy, a collection of techniques and tools for use in reducing variation and improving quality. The business excellence model is used to assess an organisation by itself against nine performance characteristics : *(i)* Leadership, *(ii)* Policy and strategy, *(iii)* People, *(iv)* Partnerships and resources, *(v)* Processes, *(vi)* Customer results, *(vii)* People results, *(viii)* Society results and *(ix)* Key performance results.

CII-EXIM Bank Award for Excellence Model recognises multiple approach to achieving sustainable excellence.

The Rajiv Gandhi National Quality Award was instituted by Bureau of Indian Standards in 1991 to generate interest and involvement of Indian Industry in quality programs and equip the industry to meet the challenges of domestic and international markets.

The Golden Peacock National Quality Award was instituted in 1991 to encourage total quality improvements in both manufacturing as well as service organisations in India.

The IMC Ramakrishna Bajaj National Quality Award was instituted in 1996 by Indian Merchant's Chamber (IMC) and the Confederation of Indian Industries (CII) to help the Indian Industry turn globally competitive.

4.16 KEY WORDS USED

Zaire Model, Malcolm Baldrige National Quality Award, European Quality Award, The TQMEX Model, TQM Kite Marks, Six-Sigma Concept, The Business Excellence Model, Rajiv Gandhi National Quality Award, Golden Peacock National Quality Award, IMC Ramkrishna Bajaj National Quality Award.

4.17 OBJECTIVE QUESTIONS

(A) Match the following :

Column A	Column B
1. TQMX model	1. Established by BIS in 1991.
2. Dr Kaoru Ishikawa	2. Business Excellence Model.
3. MBNQA	3. Japanese 5S practice
4. European Quality Award	4. Established by the US congress in 1987.
5. RGNQA	5. Quality circles.

(B) Fill in the blanks :

1. The TQM model proposed by _______ looks at TQM at three levels.
2. The six-sigma concept was conceived by __________
3. The _______ is a technique used to establish and maintain quality environment in an organisation.
4. The Golden Peacock National Quality Award was instituted by the _____ in February 1991.
5. _______ Award criteria are the same as the Malcolm Baldrige criteria of the USA.

(C) Multiple choice Questions : Choose the correct answer from the alternatives given under each question :

1. A quality circle is a small group of employees made up of _______ members.
   (a) 4 to 6 (b) 6 to 8
   (c) 8 to 10 (d) 20 to 25
   (e) 25 to 30
2. Which Japanese word means "neatness" in English?
   (a) Seiri (b) Seiso
   (c) Seiton (d) Seiketsu
   (e) Shitsuke
3. The TQM model which looks at TQM at three levels - foundation, pillars and roof is known as:
   (a) TQMEX model (b) Zaire model
   (c) Integrated model of Sohal, Tay, Wirth(d) Business EXcellence model
   (e) Deming model.
4. _______ is a national quality award similar to Deming prize in Japan :
   (a) RGNQA (b) GPNQA
   (c) MBNQA (d) IMCRBNQA
   (e) EQA.

4.18 REVIEW QUESTIONS

1. State the purposes of Malcolm Baldrige National Quality Award. Explain the Baldrige Award framework and discuss why each element is important in any quality system.
2. Discuss the seven criteria for "Performance Excellence" to evaluate any organisation for Malcolm Baldrige National Quality Award.
3. Explain the Baldrige Award Evaluation Process".
4. State the benefits of MBNQA program.
5. Compare Baldrige Criteria and the Deming's philosophy.
6. Briefly discuss the international quality award programs other than MBNQA and state the differences among them.
7. Describes the Baldrige Award Scoring System. What do you mean by "approach" and "deployment".
8. How are the Baldrige Award criteria commonly used by a company that do not apply for the award.
9. What is TQMEX model?
10. What is Japanese 5 's' practice?
11. What are the ten commandments of TQM?
12. What are four pillars of TQM?
13. What are 4 'C's of TQM?
14. What are the TQM kite marks? How are they achieved?
15. Discuss "The Business Excellence Model" criteria what are the limitations of Business Excellence Model?

16. Discuss the salient features of CII-EXIM Bank Excellence Model.
17. Discuss the assessment criteria used in Rajiv Gandhi National Quality Award.
18. Discuss the features of Golden Peacock National Quality Award and IMC Ramakrishna Bajaj National Quality Award.

4.19 DISCUSSION QUESTIONS

1. "TQM begins with top management commitment and involvement" Discuss.
2. "Total employee involvement and an organisation culture for total quality are equally important as top management initiative and support to total quality" - Discuss.
3. "TQM is not dead. TQM failures just prove that bad management is still alive and kicking" - Comment.
4. Discuss the role of various national and international quality awards in promoting world-class quality management.

4.20 ASSIGNMENTS

1. Visit any organisation that has been awarded with CII-EXIM award or RGNQ award or IMC RBNQ award and prepare a report on the quality initiatives undertaken by the organisation in order to win the award.
2. Visit the website www. baldrige. org and prepare a report based on the information available on the website.

4.21 CHAPTER CASE

QUALITY AT THE RITZ-CARLTON HOTEL COMPANY

"Ritz Carlton" was the first hotel company to win the Malcolm Baldrige National Quality Award. The name alone evokes images of luxury and quality. Ritz treats quality as if it is the heartbeat of the company. This means a daily commitment to meeting customer expectations and making sure that each hotel is free of any deficiency.

In the hotel industry, guests buy an experience when they stay at the hotel and not products. Hence, quality is difficult to quantify. Thus, creating the right combination of the elements to make the experience stand out is the challenge and goal of every employee, from maintenance to management.

Before applying for the Baldrige Award, company management undertook a rigorous self-examination of its operations in an attempt to measure and quantify quality. Nineteen processes are studied, including room-service delivery, guest reservation and registration, message delivery and break fast service. This period of study included statistical measurement of process work flows and cycle times for areas ranging from room service delivery times and reservations to valet parking and house keeping efficiency. The results were used to develop performance benchmarks against which future activity could be measured.

With specific, quantifiable targets in place, Ritz Carlton managers and employees now focus on continuous improvement. The goal is 100% customer satisfaction. If a guest's experience does not meet expectations, the Ritz-Carlton risks losing that guest to competition.

One way the company has put more meaning behind its quality efforts is to organise its employees into "self directed" work teams. Employee teams determine work scheduling, what work needs to be done and what to do about quality problems in their own areas. Employees are also given the opportunity to take additional training in hotel operations so that they can underst and the relationship of their specific area to the overall goals. Ritz-Carlton believe that a more educated and informed employee is in a better position to make decisions in the best interest of the organisation.

Disucssion Questions :

(i) In what ways could the Ritz-Carlton monitor its success in achieving quality?

(ii) Why might it cost the Ritz-Carlton less to "do things right" the first time?

(iii) What are the non-financial measures of customer satisfaction that might be used by the Ritz-Carlton.

CHAPTER 5

FOCUSSING ON CUSTOMERS

LEARNING OBJECTIVES

After reading this chapter, you should be able to:

- Understand the importance of focusing on customers- both internal and external, in TQM.
- Discuss the importance of customer perception of quality and driver of customer satisfaction
- Discuss the importance of customer satisfaction in business.
- Describe 'Kano' model of customer satisfaction.
- Understand the meaning of "voice of the customer".
- Describe the concept of "customer-driven quality cycle", know what is meant by "delighting the customers" and "customer relationship management".
- Discuss the process of measuring customer satisfaction.
- Discuss the characteristics of companies that have successfully established a customer focus.

5.0 INTRODUCTION

World-class organisations are obsessed with meeting and exceeding customer expectations. Many companies such as Disney and Nissan Motor Company's Infinity division were built on the notion of satisfying the customer. Home Depot, the best retail organisation in the US has a service philosophy which states *"Every customer has to be treated like your mother, your father, your sister and your brother"*.

World-class organisations are obsessed with meeting and exceeding customer expectations.

It is necessary that the firms have to learn to be customer-focussed, often in response to competitive crisis. Motorola, for example created new markets by essentially telling customers what they wanted. When the customers became more sophisticated and competition increased, customers told Motorola that the company needed to improve. Hence, Motorola changed its focus from product to the customer. In 1979, Motorola set ***"total customer satisfaction"*** as its fundamental goal, and it went on to win the Malcolm Baldrige National Quality Award within 10 years. A quality conscious company plans its products and the system that makes or delivers those products with a focus on fulfilling the needs and expectations of customers. **The organisation performs the following functions to achieve customer satisfaction:**

(i) identifies customer needs.

(ii) designs the production and service systems to meet these needs.

(iii) measures the results as the basis for improvement.

(iv) integrates customers into the strategic planning activities of all managers.

***Box 5.1* describes the importance of customers in business.**

Box 5.1 : Customers Mean Business

It is obvious that businesses cannot survive without satisfied customers. Yet in many companies, only a small proportion of managerial effort is spent on customers. Those who have prospered by aligning the business around customer needs plan to spend even more this way. For attracting customers today is very tough, losing them is disastrous. Even satisfying our customers may not be enough, the competitive edge may only come from customer delight.

5.1 WHO IS THE CUSTOMER?

A customer can be defined as ***"one who purchases a product or service"*. This traditional concept of customer/supplier is shown in *Exhibit 5.1.***

Exhibit 5.1 : Traditional Customer/Supplier Concept

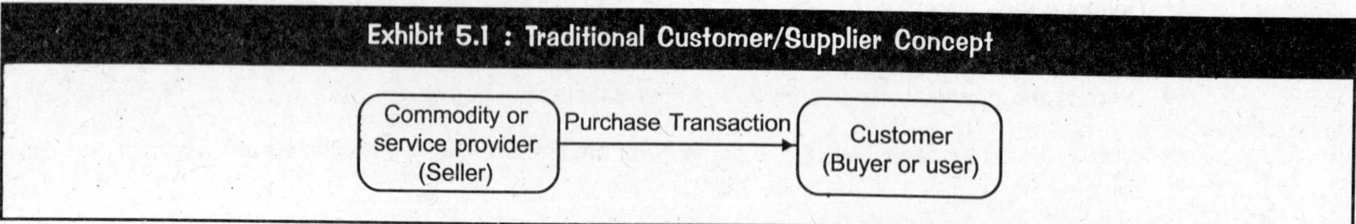

In a total quality set up, customers define quality and employees produce it.

However, the above definition of the customer is not complete from a TQM perspective. This definition is of one type of customer known as the ***external customer*** who exists outside the organisation and buys the organisation's products or services. Every employee in the organisation must understand how his or her job enhances the total satisfaction of the external customer. Performance must be continually improved in order to retain existing customers and gain new ones. ***Box 5.2* describes the customers from the sellers view point and *Box 5.3* gives Deming's views on customer and competition.**

Box 5.2 : Who are the Customers? (Seller's View Point)

- Customers are the most important people in any business.
- Customers are not dependent on us, we are dependent on them.
- Customers are not interruption of our work.
- They are the purpose of it
- Customers are doing a favour in doing business with us. We are not doing customers a favour by waiting on them.
- Customers are part of our business-not outsiders. Customers are not just money in cash register.
- Customers are human beings with feelings and they deserve to be treated with respect.
- Customers are people who come to us with needs and wants. It is our job to fill them.
- Customers deserve the most courteous attention we can give them.
- Customers are the lifeblood of each and every business. Customers pay our salary. Without customers, we would have to close our doors.
- Don't ever forget it.

Box 5.3 : Deming on Customer and Competition

- Customer? What does he know about it? If you wait until the customer knows what he wants, you will lose the customer!
- The consumer is no longer willing to subsidise the waste.
- Who would buy a tyre for their automobile at lowest price?
- It will not suffice to meet the competition, he who hopes only to meet the competition is already licked!
- Charles Darwin's theory of survival of the fittest holds in free enterprise as well as in natural selection.
- You do not have to compete, survival is not compulsory!

However, another important category of the customer is the ***"internal customer"***. Every function in an organisation, whether it is marketing, engineering, production or purchasing has an internal customer - each receives a product or service and in exchange provides a product or service. Every person in a process is considered a customer of the preceding operation. Each worker's goal is to ensure that the quality of his operation meets the expectations of the next worker in the process chain.

Two categories of customers that need to be focused are: *(i)* external customers and *(ii)* Internal customers.

All processes have outputs, which are used by internal or external customers and inputs, which are provided by internal and external suppliers. Each performs work that produces some service or product that is used by another. Each forms a link in the customer/supplier chain where every chain ends with an external customer and starts with an external supplier. Every employee throughout the organisation is part of the chain of internal customers and suppliers. ***Box 5.4* lists six basic requirements of internal and external customers.**

***Exhibit 5.2* shows the customer/supplier chain.**

Exhibit 5.2 : Customer/Supplier Chain

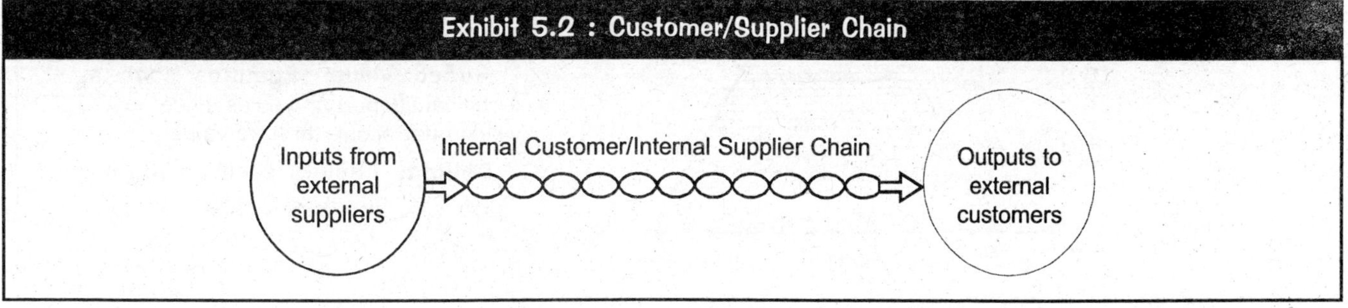

Box 5.4 : Six Basic Requirements of Internal and External Customers

(i) **High levels of quality:** From the customers' standpoint, quality has multiple dimensions.

(ii) **A high degree of flexibility:** Customers admire providers' ability to react easily to shifting requirements and irregular arrival patterns.

(iii) **High levels of service:** Subjective measures of customer service include humanity in service delivery and objective measures can include having a required item in stock.

(iv) **Low costs:** External customers are price conscious; internal customers are concerned when they see costly wastes.

(v) **Quick response (speed):** Customers want delay-free service and quick response to changing requirements. The provider aims to satisfy by shortening cycle times and quickly introducing attractive new goods and services.

(vi) **Little or no variability:** Customers expect consistency; the ideal is zero deviation from targeted or expected results.

General customer requirements

High ↑	Low ↓
Quality	Costs
Flexibility	Response times
Service	Variability

Customers do not view the above requirements as potential trade-offs. They do not want to settle for just high quality or just low costs or for just increased flexibility or just quick response. They require all these needs to be met. From the provider's standpoint, excelling in all six basic needs of customers is a considerable challenge.

One basic concept of TQM is unwavering customer focus or orientation - both external and internal.

One basic concept of TQM is ***unwavering customer orientation*** or ***focus on customers***, both internal and external.

In an ideal organisation, every employee would have direct contact with customers and be effective in meeting their needs. But, in reality, it is not so and most employees are shielded from customers by various layers existing in the organisation.

For successful internal customer/supplier relationship, three basic questions to be asked to internal customers are: *(i)* What do you need from me? *(ii)* What do you do with my output? *(iii)* Are there any gaps between what you need and what you get?

Each department must determine what activities are important to both external and internal customers and manage quality at each and every step of the customer/supplier chain. Both requirements of external customers and what each internal customer expects must be documented. ***Exhibit 5.3*** **illustrates the hierarchy of customer requirements.**

Exhibit 5.3 : Hierarchy of Customer Requirements

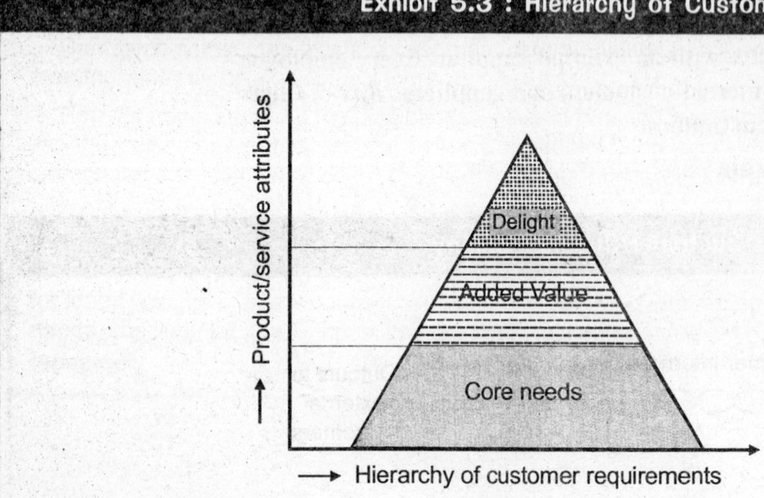

Core needs: Product consistency, on-time delivery etc. which have to be met first to give satisfaction.

Added Value: Features such as technical support and sales office access which offer scope for 'true value".

Delight: Factors such as product innovation and research findings.

Customer orientation or focus on customers: Being customer oriented implies that an organisation is clear about who its customers are at every level and stage of the process and armed with this information, strives to provide more value to them. The process of adding value involves tasks performed by every member of the organisation. Being customer oriented does not mean being oriented towards the end-users alone. It includes focussing on the needs of the internal customers also in the value-adding chain. Conflicts frequently arise between the need of internal and external customers. In many cases, processes are designed to meet the needs of internal customers. *For example,* in a hospital, the registration process is designed to meet the needs of the admitting departments, business office or medical records rather than to meet the needs of external customers that is, the patient.

The key to establishing a customer focus is putting employees in touch with customers and empowering those employees to act as necessary to satisfy the customers.

5.2 CUSTOMER PERCEPTION OF QUALITY

To have customer focus, it is essential to understand the customers' perception of quality. Since the customers' needs, values and expectations are constantly changing and becoming more demanding, there is no acceptable quality level for the customers. This means there is a need for continuous improvement of quality to meet customers' expectations.

An American Society for Quality (ASQ) survey on end user perceptions of important factors that influenced purchase showed the following ranking: *(i)* **performance** *(ii)* **features** *(iii)* **service** *(iv)* **warranty** *(v)* **price** and *(vi)* **reputation (brand image)**. This implies that product quality and service are more important than price.

Product performance involves ***fitness for use*** for the customer. Other considerations are ***availability, reliability*** **and** ***maintainability***. Identifiable features or attributes of a product or service are psychological, time oriented, contractual, ethical and technological. Features are secondary to performance, service is an intangible characteristic contributing to customer satisfaction. Organisations that emphasise on service never stop looking for and finding ways to serve their customer better, even if their customers are not complaining. Product warranty represents an organisation's public promise of quality product backed up by a guarantee of customer satisfaction. It also represents public commitment to guarantee a level of service sufficient to satisfy the customer. A warranty also provides feedback by providing information on the product and service quality. It also gives a feed back to the organisation to develop a system for corrective action and improvement. Price is an indicator of value of a product or service to the customer and the customer's willingness to spend his/her money for the benefits he/she gets from the product or service. Nowadays, customers are willing to pay a higher price to obtain value for money. However, the customer's perception of value in relation to each product or service varies from customer to customer. Total customer satisfaction is based on the entire experience with the organisation, not just the product alone. Often, customers spread their bad experience with product or service much faster than their good experiences. Again, today's customers are willing to pay a premium for a well known or trusted brand name and often become loyal customers of such brands.

To have customer focus, it is essential to understand the customers' perception of quality.

Since it costs five times as much to win a new customer as it does to retain an existing one, customer orientation is a vital strategy for any organisation. An increase in the customer retention rate indicates satisfaction for existing customers by the product or service offered.

5.3 THE DRIVER OF CUSTOMER SATISFACTION

The issues in building customer satisfaction are to acquire satisfied customers, know when you have them and keep them. Organisations identify the key excellence indicators for customer satisfaction before conducting customer surveys to collect data regarding customer satisfaction. *Box 5.5* lists the reasons why customers quit the relationship with particular suppliers.

Box 5.5 : Customer Satisfaction and Retention

Le Boeuf (1987) cited a study on the reasons why customers quit the relationship with particular suppliers:

- 3% move away giving no reasons.
- 5% develop other supplier – relationship.
- 9% leave for competitive reasons.
- 15% are dissatisfied with the product
- 68% quit because of an attitude of indifference towards the customer by the owner, manager or some employees.

Le Boeuf claimed that businesses spend ***six times more*** to get new customers than to retain old customers.

Box 5.6 **shows some of the key excellence indicators for customer satisfaction.**

Box 5.6 : Key Excellence Indicators for Customer Satisfaction

- Service standards derived from customer requirements.
- Understanding customer requirements
  - Thoroughness/Objectivity
  - Customer types
  - Product/service features
- Front-line empowerment
- Strategic infrastructure support for frontline employees
- Attention to hiring, training, attitude, morale for front-line employees
- High levels of satisfaction – customer awards
- Proactive customer service systems
- Proactive management of relationships with customer
- Use of all listening posts
  - Surveys
  - Product/service follow-ups
  - Complaints
  - Turnover of customer
  - Employees
- Quality requirement of market segments (surveys go beyond current customers)
- Commitment to customer (trust/confidence/making good on word)

5.4 THE IMPORTANCE OF CUSTOMER SATISFACTION

Satisfying customers and creating customer enthusiasm and loyalty thourgh understanding thier currrent needs and future needs is the crux of TQM.

Four goals of any business are:

(i) To satisfy its customers, *(ii)* To achieve higher customer satisfaction than its competitors, *(iii)* To retain customers in the long run and *(iv)* To gain market share.

The above goals can be achieved by a business that can deliver ever-improving ***value*** to its customers. Value is quality related to price. Consumers do not buy products or services solely on the basis of price. They compare the **total package of products and services that a business offers (also known as *consumer benefit package*) with the price and with competitive offerings.** The consumer benefit package influences the perception of quality and includes the tangible product along with its quality dimensions such as pre-sales support, (ease of ordering, rapid, on-time and accurate delivery) and post-sales support (such as field service, warranties and technical support). If competitors offer better choices for a similar price, consumers are more likely to select the package with a higher perceived quality. Thus, understanding what exactly the consumers want is absolutely crucial to competitive success. To be competitive, a firm must be able to offer to the customer the same package of goods and services offered by competitors, but at a lower price. Since lower prices require lower costs, to maintain the profits, firms focus on quality improvement in operations to reduce costs. Therefore, business must focus on both continually improving the consumer benefit package and reducing costs.

Customer satisfaction can be achieved only when the products and services meet or exceed customer expectations. Customer satisfaction results in increased profits. Satisfied customers purchase more and are willing to pay higher prices. Studies have revealed that it costs about five times more to attract new customers than to keep old ones. On the other hand, poor quality products and services lead to customer dissatisfaction which results in complaints, return of goods and unfavourable word-of-mouth publicity.

Customer retention is a key factor for competitive success, and is closely tied to quality

Strong competitive advantage is driven by customer needs and wants. Satisfying customers through superior products and service excellence is a principal means of achieving competitive advantage. Customer retention is a key factor for competitive success, and is closely tied to quality and customer satisfaction. Product features have a great influence on the first sale to a customer. At this time, customers are not aware of what quality problems may result. However, product quality and the services rendered during the product's life determine the volume of subsequent sales. Growth in the market share of a company is strongly correlated with customer satisfaction. ***Box 5.7* discusses the approach to satisfy the customer.**

Box 5.7 : Satisfying the Customer

The first test of the effectiveness of a firm's operating system is the ability of the firm to supply customers with products and services they actually want, leaving enough of a margin to enable the firm to prosper in the long term. *This means supplying the products and services needed in the quantities desired and at the time required.* This practice is called ***total product quality***. If a firm is not prepared to do this, another firm will oblige its customers.

Although the 'who', 'what' and 'how much' questions asked by the firm in trying to develop the ability to satisfy customers are inter-related, the 'who' and 'how many' questions are usually asked first in the traditional model of ***demand management***. In the traditional model, the focus is on the firm's operating system and the emphasis is on figuring out how to move enough products to the final customers to keep the operations running at a profitable capacity. But this approach of managing demand 'outward' does not involve listening to the customers. Managing demand 'inward' however, places customers at the centre of the process and fast-response organisation (or TQ organisation) must do this.

Demand is a reflection of the ability of products to provide *value* to customers. To stimulate the greatest demand, therefore, it is necessary to determine exactly *what* the customers require and not merely producing something and then finding a market-clearing price. Instead, it involves understanding what customers' needs and expectations are and meeting those needs and expectations profitably.

Customer Satisfaction Index: American Society for Quality Control released the first American Customer Satisfaction Index (ACSI), a new economic indicator that measures customer satisfaction at the national level. The ACSI is based on customer evaluations of the quality of goods and services purchased in the US and produced by both domestic and foreign firms with a substantial US market share. ***Exhibit 5.4* shows the ACSI Model.**

Exhibit 5.4 : ACSI Model

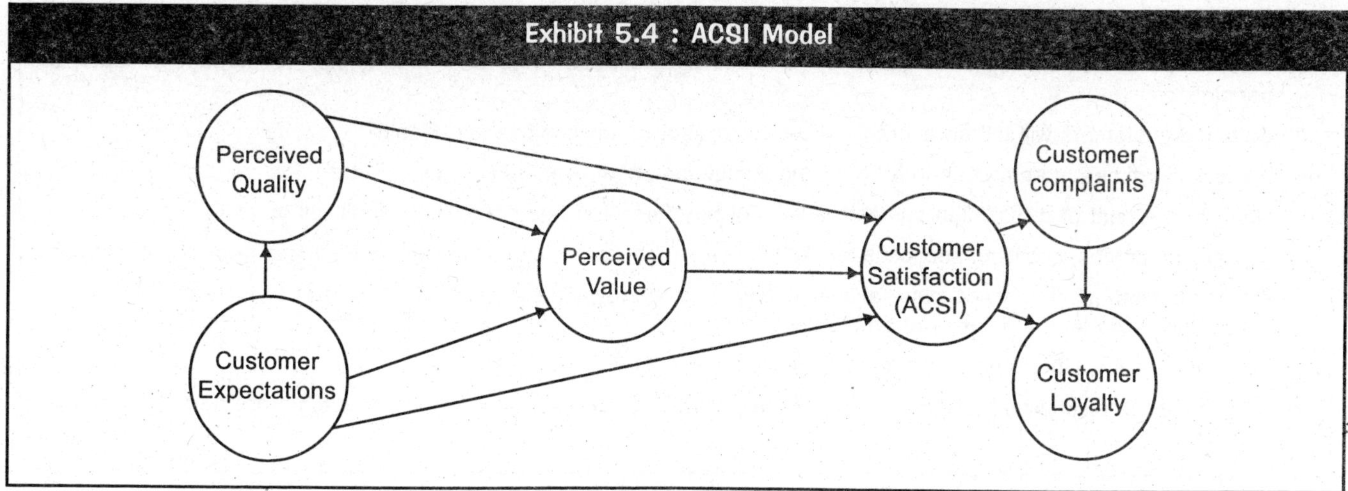

Satisfying Customer Expectations and Understanding their Needs and Future Requirements

The attributes of a product and/or service which, as perceived by the customer, makes the product/service attractive to them and gives them satisfaction.

Satisfying customers and creating customer enthusiasm through understanding their needs and future requirements is the crux of TQM and all organisations are dependent on having satisfied customers. TQM is all about **customer orientation** and many company missions are based entirely on satisfying customer perceptions. The customer is the major reason for an organisation's existence and ***customer loyalty*** and ***retention*** is perhaps the only measure of organisational success.

The superior performing organisations go beyond satisfying their customers, they emphasise the need to delight them by giving them more than what is required by them or expected by them. A **customer-focused** organisation also puts considerable effort into anticipating the future expectations of its customers, and by working with them in long-term relationships, helps them to define their future needs and expectations. They listen very closely to their customers and 'actual' users of the product or service, in order to gain a clearer perspective on customer experiences. They aim to build quality into the product, service, system and/or process as upstream as is practicable.

A customer-focused organisation puts considerable effort into anticipating the future expectations of its customers.

Those companies intent on satisfying customer needs and expectations will have in place a mechanism for facilitating a continuous two-way flow of information between themselves and their customers. **Companies need to assess customer issues such as:**

- How well they are meeting customer expectations?
- How well the brand is respected by customers?
- What customer's chief causes of concern are?
- What the main complaints of customers are?
- What suggestions for improvements customers might have?
- What they might add value to the product and/or service?
- How will they act on what the customer says?
- The best means differentiating themselves in the market place.

Box 5.8 **lists customer service facts which emphasise the importance of customer acquisition and retention.**

Box 5.8 : Customer Service Facts

Do your know that:

(i) If 20 customers are dissatisfied with your service, 19 won't tell you. 14 of the 20 will take their business elsewhere.

(ii) Dissatisfied customers tell an average of 10 other people about their bad experience. 12 percent tell upto 20 people.

(iii) Satisfied customers will tell an average of 5 people about their positive experience.

(iv) It costs five times more money to attract a new customer than to keep an existing one.

(v) Upto 90 pre cent of dissatisfied customers will not buy from you again and they won't tell you why?

(vi) In many industries, quality of service is one of the few variables that can distinguish a business from its competition.

(vii) Providing high-quality service can save your business money. The same skills that lead to increased customer satisfaction also lead to increased employee productivity.

(viii) Customers are willing to pay more to receive better service.

(ix) 95 per cent of dissatisfied customers will become loyal customers again if their complaints are handled well and quickly.

5.5 MODEL OF CUSTOMER SATISFACTION

Product features can be classified into: *(i)* basic features *(ii)* performance features and *(iii)* excitement features.

Basic features include features which customers expect to have and providing basic features will not result in customer satisfaction.

Performance features include those features which are typically spoken by customers. Customer satisfaction is directly related to the degree of achievement. Satisfaction level is enhanced when product performance is better than expected.

Excitement features include those product features that customers do not normally expect such as the extra functions and convenience features. Excitement features make the product pleasantly unique to the customers. This represents added value to the customers with little or no extra perceived cost.

Kano Model shown in *Exhibit 5.5* is a representation of customer satisfaction relative to the various types of product features discussed above.

Exhibit 5.5 : Kano Model

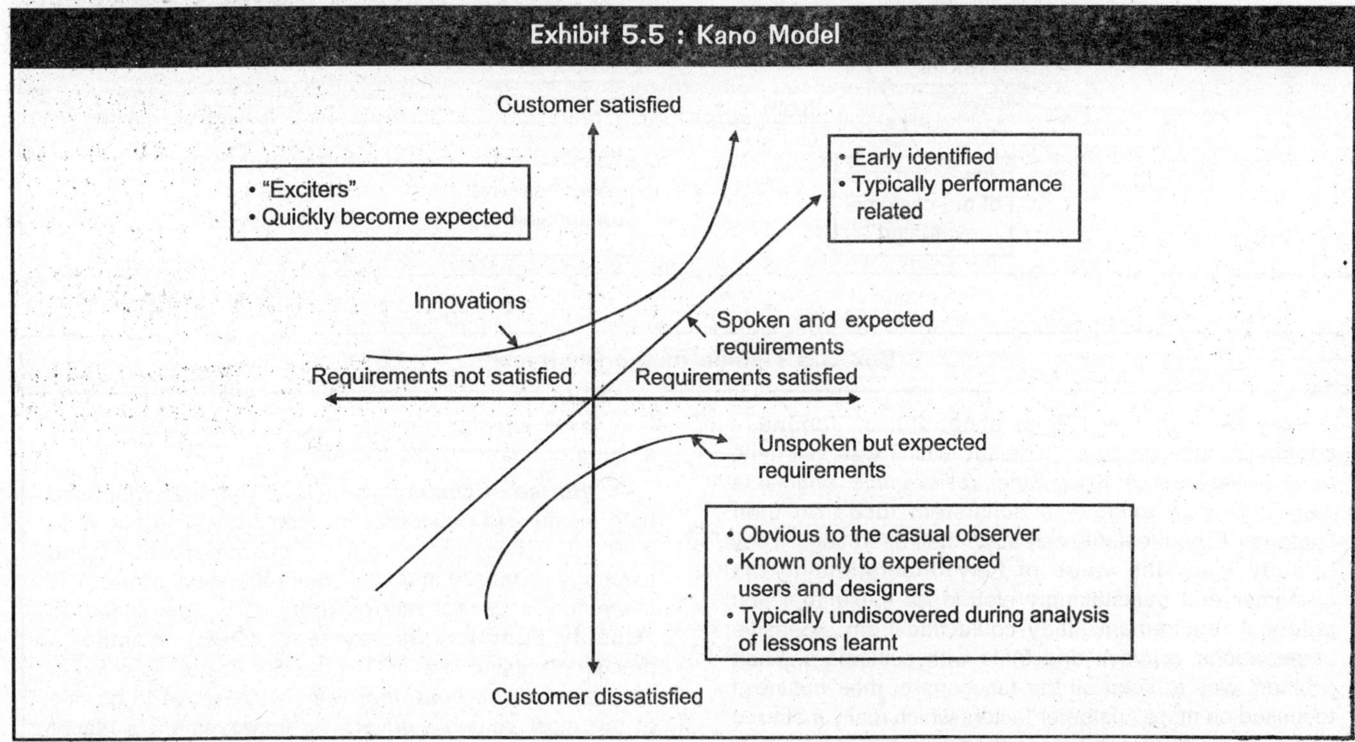

The model represents three areas of customer satisfaction. The first area of customer satisfaction depicted by the diagonal line represents **explicit requirements**. These include written or verbal requirements and are easily identified, expected to be met and typically performance related. Satisfying customers would be rather simple if these were the only requirements.

Kano model represents three areas of customer satisfaction: *(i)* Explicit requirements *(ii)* Innovation and *(iii)* Unstated or unspoken requirements.

The second area of customer satisfaction represents **innovation**, shown by the curved line. A customer's written instructions are often purposefully vague to avoid stifling new ideas during conceptualisation and product definition. Because they are unexpected, these creative ideas often excite and delight the customer. However, these ideas quickly become expected.

The third and most significant area of customer satisfaction represents **unstated or unspoken requirements** as shown by the lower curve. The customers may be unaware of them or may assume that such requirements will be automatically provided.

Just meeting a customer's needs is not enough, the organisation must exceed the customer's needs.

***Exhibit 5.6* shows the "Voice of the Customers" diagram which summarises topics discussed earlier in this chapter. *Box 5.9* describes what is meant by "Voice of the customer" and *Box 5.10* describes what is meant by "Listening to the customer".**

Exhibit 5.6 : Voice of the Customer

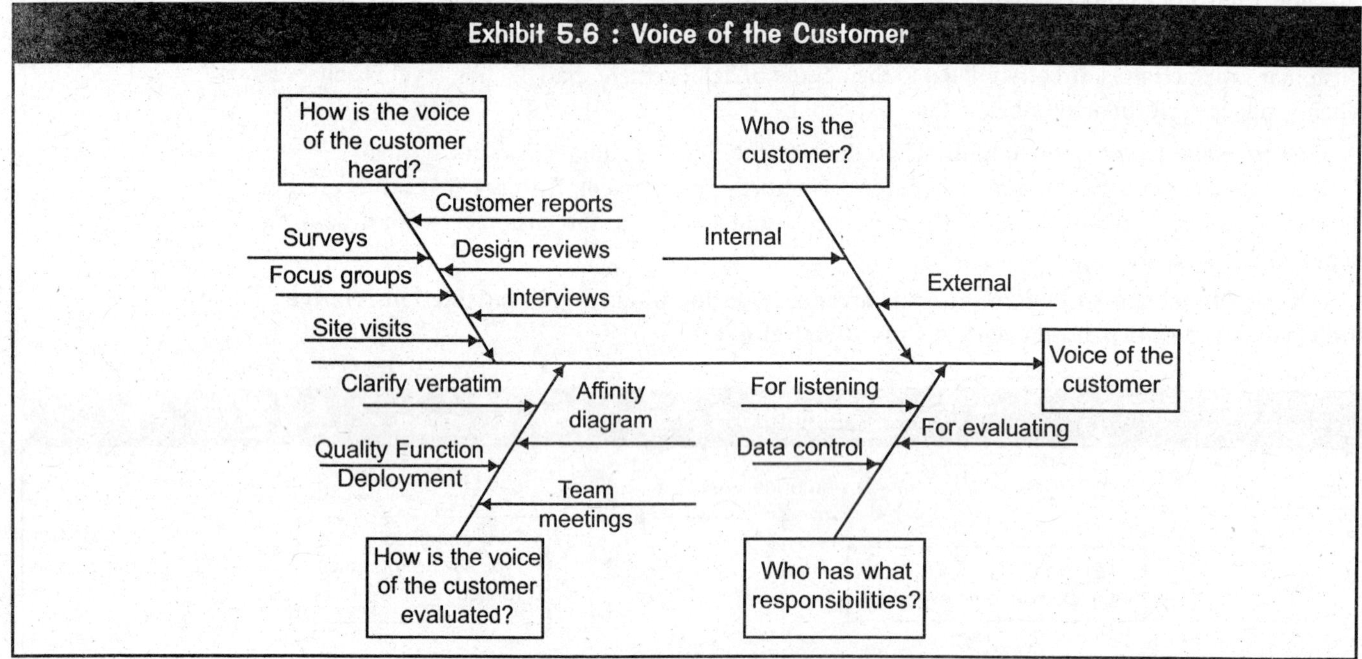

Box 5.9 : Voice of the Customer

Way back in the 1950s, a handful of Japanese companies developed a technique which was still quite novel in the west. At Kobe Steel, *for example*, engineers were trying to achieve a consistent focus on their customer's requirements across all their operations. They already knew the value of fully understanding the customer and painstakingly plotted all the actual and potential requirements they could find from extensive observations, surveys and trials with customers. Their problem was to keep all the functions of their business focussed on those customer factors which really mattered and to avoid everyone having their own (different) ideas of what was important or necessary. At the same time, they were looking for the maximum involvement and sharing of ideas across the functions.

A ***"House of Quality"*** is built up from data gathered both inside and outside of the company. The aim is to match the two dimensions of customer needs and company capability in a vital comprehensive format. The technique is deceptively powerful. It is now called as **"Quality Function Deployment" (QFD)**. Whether a precise discipline like QFD is needed or not, listening to the ***voice of the customer*** will always prove to be one of the most valuable drivers for improvement a leader can have.

Creating Satisfied Customers: Customer satisfaction results from providing goods and services that meet or exceed customer's needs. *Exhibit 5.7* provides a view of the process in which customer needs and expectations are translated into outputs during the design, production and delivery processes. **True customer needs and expectations are called *expected quality*.** Expected quality is what the customer assumes will be received from the product. The producer identifies these needs and expectations and translates them into specifications for products and services. ***Actual quality* is the outcome of the production. Actual quality may differ considerably from expected quality due to the following reasons:**

- When information gets lost or is misinterpreted from one step to the next. For instance, ineffective market research efforts may not correctly assess the true customer needs and expectations.

Box 5.10 : Listening to the Customer

An important aspect of designing quality products is ***giving people what they want.*** A perfectly designed and built coffee maker sold in a place where no one drinks coffee, is by definition, a failure. Hence, part of the process of delivering quality to the customer is knowing what the customer wants.

While listening to the customer is an important part of the manufacturing/design cycle link, it is generally more closely associated with marketing than with operations. Still, manufacturing can not operate in a vacuum. It must be part of the link with the customer.

Finding out what the customer wants and incorporating those wants into product design and manufacture is a multi-step process. These steps are:

- Obtaining the data
- Characterising customer needs
- Prioritising customer needs and
- Linking needs to design.

Traditionally, customer opinion is solicited through interviews and surveys. Focus groups are another popular technique for soliciting the ***voice of the customer.***

Once the data base is developed, the customer needs and desires must be prioritised and grouped. One method adopted for this is ***conjoint analysis*** which is a statistically based technique to estimate utilities for product attributes based on customer preference data.

Once attributes are determined and grouped, one needs to link those attributes to the design and manufacturing processes. This can be done with ***quality function deployment (QFD)*** in which customer needs are related to the product attributes and/or aspects of the production process through a matrix. QFD is used in conjunction with traditional methods such as survey and focus groups. The strength of the correlations between customer needs and product attributes or design characteristics shows where the emphasis should be placed when considering design of new products or design changes in existing products.

However, one must be careful not to put too much emphasis on the voice of the customer. Real innovations do not come from the customer but from visionaries. By letting the customer be king, innovation could be stifled.

- Designers of products and services may develop specifications that may not adequately reflect the customer needs.
- Manufacturing operations may not produce the product according to the specifications.
- The perceived quality (quality of the product as seen by the customer) may be different from the actual quality.

Exhibit 5.7 : Customer-Driven Quality Cycle

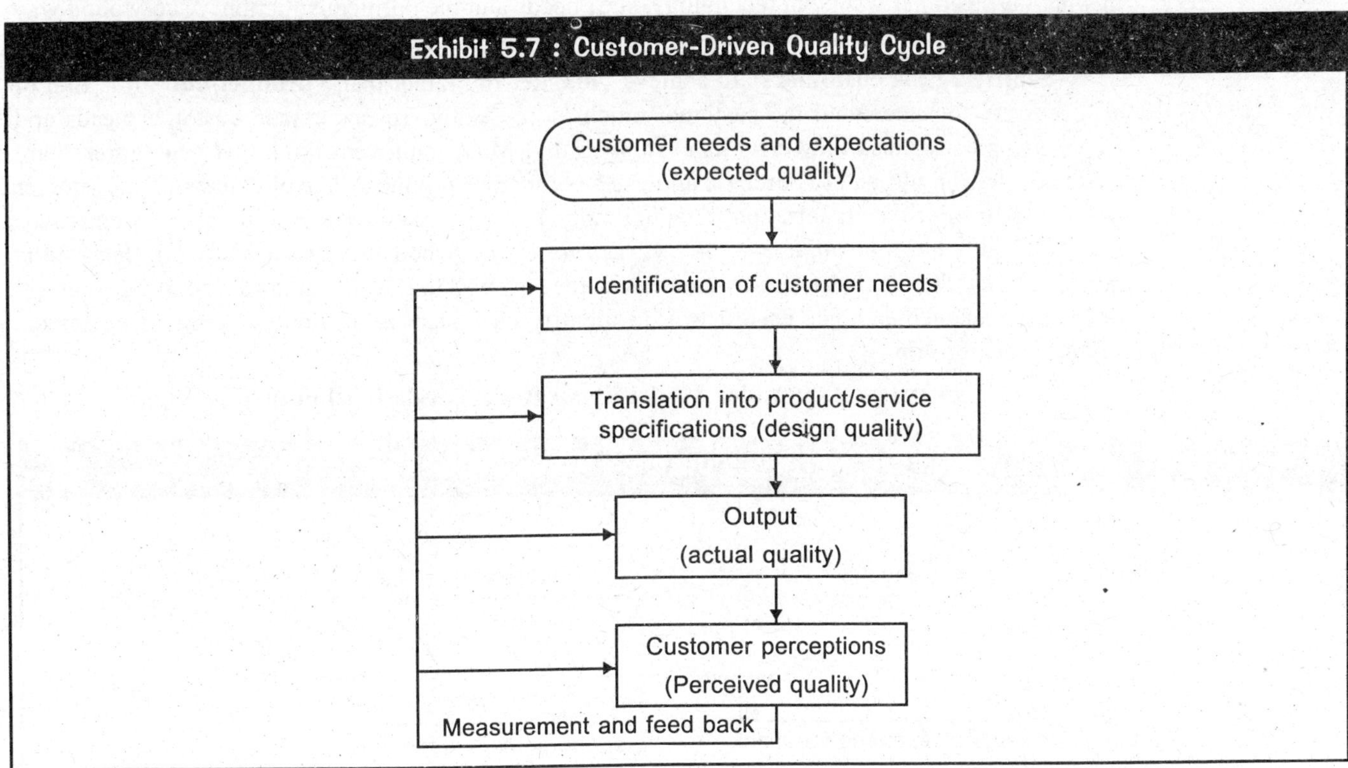

The different levels of quality can be summarised as:

Perceived quality = Actual quality – Expected quality

Any differences between the expected quality and actual quality can cause either unexpected satisfaction (actual quality is higher than expected quality) or dissatisfaction (actual quality is lower than expected quality). A system of measuring customer satisfaction and the feedback from customer helps in understanding these relationships and improving quality.

The various levels of quality are *(i)* customer expected quality *(ii)* Design quality *(iii)* Actual quality and *(iv)* Perceived quality

Customer-oriented practices that lead to profitability and market share, engaged by successful companies are given below:

(i) Understanding both short-term and long-term customer needs and expectations (the voice of the customer) and using systematic processes for gathering information regarding customer needs and managing such information.

(ii) Understanding the linkages between the voice of the customer and design, production and delivery processes.

(iii) Making commitment to customers that promote trust and confidence in those products and services.

(iv) Having effective customer relationship management processes by which customers can easily seek assistance, complain and receive prompt resolution of their concerns.

(v) Measuring customer satisfaction, comparing the results relative to competitors and using the information to evaluate and improve internal processes.

"Focus on market-in rather than product-out" is a strategic statement of a company which listens well to the market place and puts efforts to satisfying that market place rather than producing what it feels the market should want and then to try to ***"re-educate"*** the market. Under the "product-out" framework, the workers specialise in following efficient standard routines, while managers work for improvement. But under the "market-in" frame work, the force of constantly changing customer needs makes such specialisation inefficient. Every one in the company must do both routine daily work and also contribute to improvement. Rapid changes take place everywhere — in what the customer wants, in technology, staff needs and the political situation. A very good way to think of TQM is as ***"management in the face of rapid change"***.

Identifying the customers: To achieve **"market-in"** rather than **"product-out"**, it is first of all necessary to understand the customer much more deeply. To understand customer needs and wants, a company must know ***who its customers are***. Most employees think that **"customers"** are those people who ultimately purchase and use a company's products. The old view of the customer as someone outside the organisation is not unifying. The newer view, however is that every employee in the company has a ***customer — "the next process"*** *i.e.* whoever receives the work that I do is my customer. **"The next-process-as-customer"** idea is owed to Kaoru Ishikawa, one of the pioneers of quality management. The easiest way to identify customers is to think in terms of customer-supplier relationship.

AT & T's Customer-Supplier Model illustrates this relationship in *Exhibit 5.8.*

Exhibit 5.8 : AT & T's Customer - Supplier Model

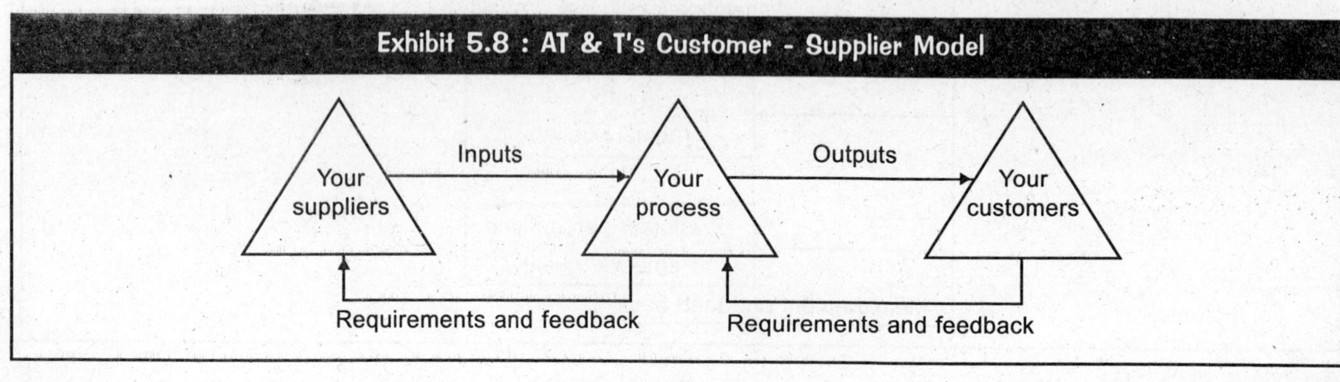

Every process receives inputs from suppliers and creates outputs for customers. The feedback loops suggest that suppliers must also be considered as customers.

This model of customer-supplier relationship can be applied at three levels—the organisation level, the process level and the performer level. At the ***organisation level***, a business has various ***external customers*** that may exist between the organisation and the consumer or end user. *For example,* the wholesalers and retailers are the external customers between the manufacturer and the consumer. The manufacturers are customers of the suppliers of raw materials and components to them.

Customer-supplier relationship can be applied at three levels:

1. organisation level
2. process level and
3. performer level.

At the ***process level***, the individual departments have ***internal customers***. *For example,* the manufacturing department is an internal customer to the purchasing department and the inspection department is an internal customer to the manufacturing department.

At the ***performer level***, each employee receives inputs from others and produces some output to the internal customers. A customer may be the assembly line worker at the next station. **Some fundamental questions to be asked to identify the customers are:**

- What products or services are produced?
- Who uses these products and services?
- Who do employees call, write to or answer questions for?
- Who supplies the inputs to the process?

As individuals, departments and functions develop their customer–supplier models, natural linkages become evident. These linkages build up the ***"chain of customers"*** throughout the company that connect every individual and function to the external customers and consumers. As a result, every one can better understand their role in satisfying not only their internal customers, but also the external customers.

If an organisation remembers that its customers include its employees and the public, then it consciously maintains the work environment conducive to the well-being and growth of all employees. In addition to expected training and job-related education, quality improvement activities should include health, safety and ergonomics (the study of physical capabilities of people in the design of workplaces, tools, instruments and so on). To satisfy the internal customers, many firms offer special service such as counselling, recreational and cultural activities, non-work related education, day care, flexible work hours and the like to their employees.

The public is also an important customer of business. A firm must look ahead to anticipate public concerns and assess possible impacts on the society of its products, service and operations. Business ethics, environmental concerns and safety are important societal issues.

Customer Segmentation

Customers generally have different requirements and expectations. A firm cannot satisfy all customers with the same products or services, especially if the firm targets a global market. Therefore, firms segment customers into natural groups and customise the products or services so that they are better able to respond to customers' needs. Juran suggests classifying customers into two groups: ***the vital few*** and ***the useful many***. *For example,* organisers of conventions and meetings book large blocks of hotel rooms and have large catering needs. They represent the ***vital few*** and deserve special attention on an individual basis.

According to Juran, customers can be classified into two groups or segments:

1. vital few and
2. useful many

Individual travellers and families are the ***useful many*** and need only standardised attention as a group. Customer segmentation might be based on geography, demographic factors, ways in which products are used and volumes or expected levels of service. Such segmentation allows a firm to prioritise customer groups. One way to prioritise segments is to consider, for each group, the benefits of satisfying their requirements and the consequences of failing to satisfy their requirements.

5.6 UNDERSTANDING CUSTOMER NEEDS AND WANTS

The provider of goods or services has one notion about what the customer wants and the customer may have quite another. **The real requirements of a customer comprises of three components:**

(i) A statement of recognised need.

(ii) The expected manner in which it must be met and

(iii) Some idea of the benefits of having the need met.

Basic requirements of both internal and external customers are: (i) High level of quality (ii) High degree of flexibility (iii) Low costs (iv) High service level (v) Quick response and (vi) Little or no variability

This is the customer's view. The provider or supplier's view of the requirement is called a ***specification***. The specification is the supplier's target which should be rated as closely as possible, to the customer's actual needs.

The personal requirements of costomers constantly change. The same is true of consumers of business products. Regardless of the type of business, internal and external customers generally have these basic requirements:

(i) ***High levels of quality.***

(ii) ***A high degree of flexibility*** (ability of the supplier to respond to changing requirements of customers).

(iii) ***High levels of service.***

(iv) ***Low costs.***

(v) ***Quick response (speed of delivery)*** and

(vi) ***Little or no variability.***

Companies need to focus on the key drivers of customer satisfaction that leads to business success. Considerable marketing efforts go into correctly identifying customer needs. Ford, *for example,* has identified about 90 features that customers want in sales and service. **Five key dimensions of service quality that contribute to customer perceptions are:**

(i) ***Reliability:*** The ability to provide what was promised, dependably and accurately.

(ii) ***Assurance:*** The knowledge and courtesy of employees and their ability to convey trust and confidence.

(iii) ***Tangibles:*** The physical facilities and equipment and the appearance of the personnel rendering service.

(iv) ***Empathy:*** The degree of caring and individual attention provided to customers.

(v) ***Responsiveness:*** The willingness to help customers and provide prompt service.

According to Noriaki Kano, a Japanese professor, three classes of customer requirements are:

(i) **Dissatisfiers:** Requirements that are expected in a product or service, which if not provided, the customer is dissatisfied.

(ii) **Satisfiers:** Requirements that customers say they want, and fulfilling them creates satisfaction.

(iii) **Exciters/delighters:** New or innovative features that customers do not expect, the presence of which leads to high perceptions of quality. *For example,* emerging satellite navigational systems for automobiles.

Meeting customer expectations (*i.e.* providing ***satisfiers***) is often considered the minimum required to remain in business. To be competitive, in the real sense, companies must surprise and delight customers by providing ***exciters*** or ***delighters***.

As customers become familiar with the exciters/delighters, these exciters/delighters become satisfiers over time. Eventually the satisfiers become dissatisfiers.

Understanding the needs of internal customers is as important as understanding those of external customers. ***Exhibit 5.9*** **illustrates the "Pyramid of Needs".**

Exhibit 5.9 : The Pyramid of Needs

- Customers commonly state their needs as seen from their viewpoint and in their language.
- Customers may state their needs in terms of goods and/or services they wish to buy.
- Understanding the needs of clients requires answer to questions such as
  "Why are you buying this product?"
  "What service do you expect from it?"
- Customers understandably state their needs based on their perceptions that are product based or based on culture.

The pyramid of needs for the automobile is illustrated below:

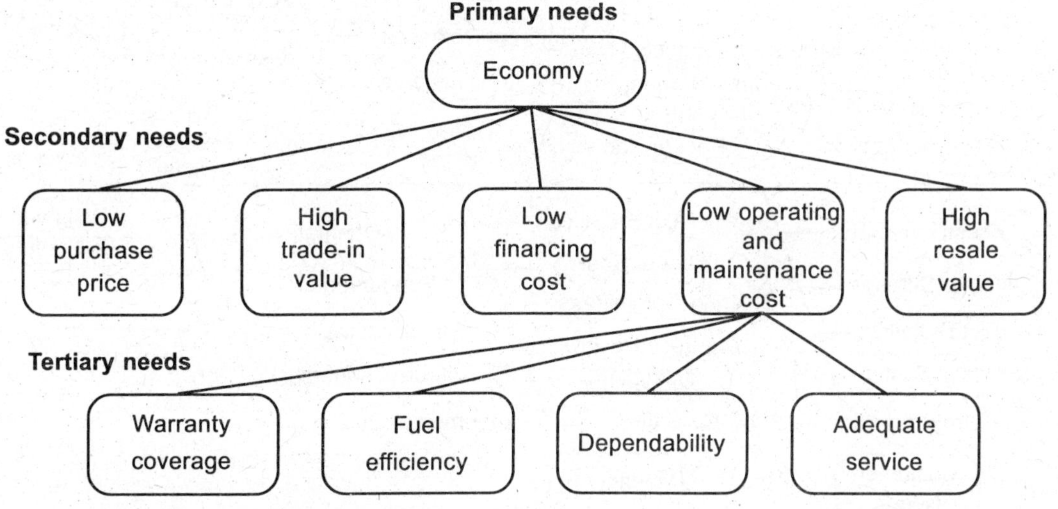

5.7 DELIGHTING THE CUSTOMERS

Delighting the customer means doing something special to the customer – exceeding his/her expectations. This does not mean surprising the customers. Customers who receive special attention and service spread the good news to others. The service provider and his team feel happy about their good work being appreciated by their customers. But the problem is that customers can't be thrilled every time. Once the service providers have raised the expectations of customers, they have no chance but to set their sights higher and do something better and better. This is the true power of customer orientation. Thus, to please the customers, continuous improvement is mandatory.

Delighting the customer means exceeding the expectations of customers interms of quality of products or services.

For example, some automobile manufacturers (Toyota and Suzuki) have offered their services to all of their customers to collect their vehicles and carry out the repairs free of cost when some manufacturing defects were detected in some models of cars sold by them. This act of the service providers delighted the customers. ***Exhibit 5.10* illustrates the factors that lead to customer satisfaction.**

5.8 CUSTOMER RELATIONSHIP MANAGEMENT

A company builds its customer loyalty by developing trust and effectively managing the interactions and inter-relationships with customers through customer-contact employees. They are people whose main responsibilities bring them into regular contact with customers-in person, by telephone or through other means. These employees must be carefully selected, extensively trained and empowered to meet and exceed customer expectations.

Excellent customer relationship management depends on four aspects:

(i) Commitment to customers.

(ii) Customer-focussed service standards.

(iii) Training and empowerment and
(iv) Effective complaint management.

Exhibit 5.10 : Factors that Lead to Customer Satisfaction

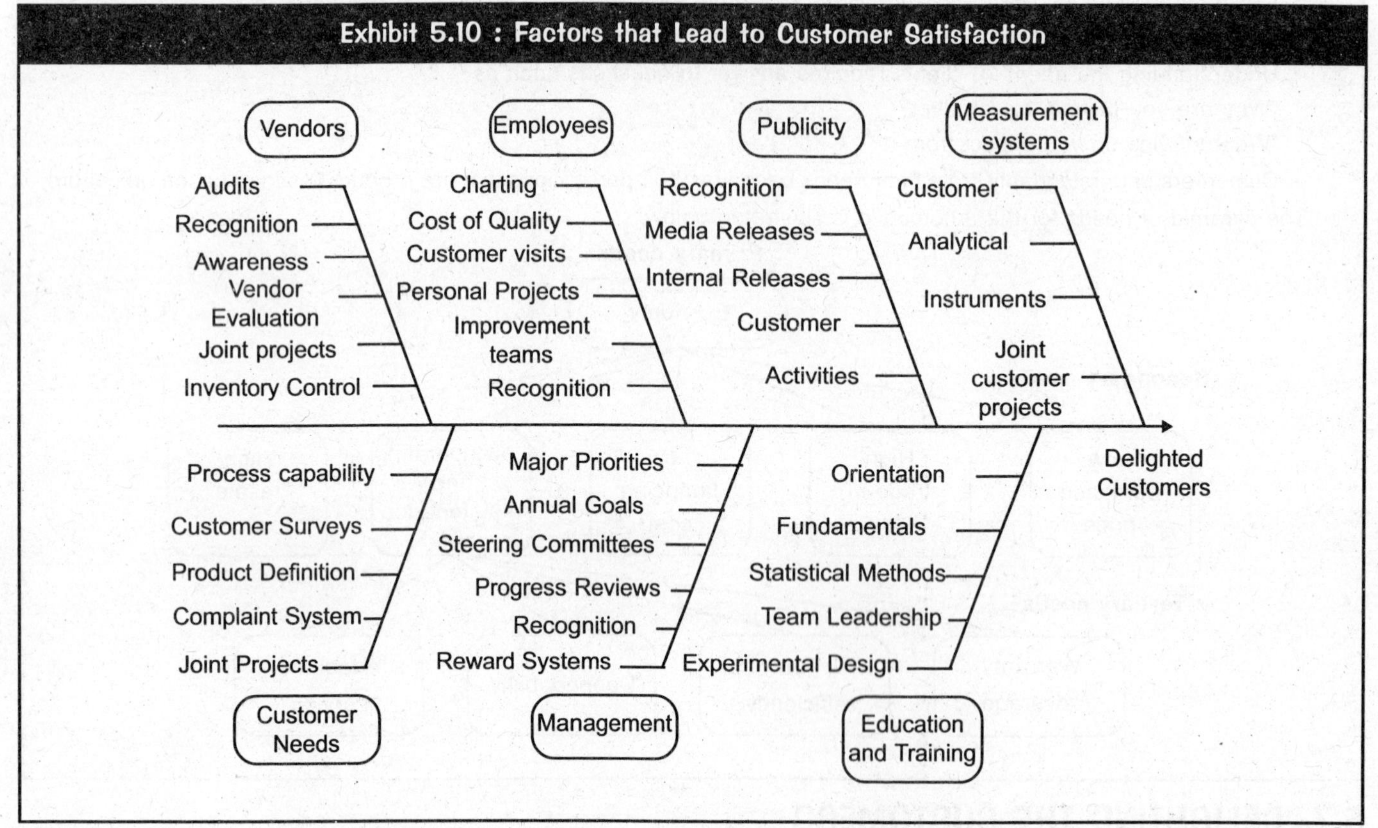

> Customer relationship management (CRM) refers to an organisation's knowledge of its customer's unique requirements and expectations and using that knowledge to develop a closer and more profitable link to business processes and strategies.

Commitment to customer: Companies that believe in the quality of their product, make strong commitments to their customers. Commitments address the principal concerns of customers and are communicated clearly and simply to customers. Many commitments take the form of **explicit guarantees** and **warranties**.

Customer focussed service standards: Service standards are measurable performance levels or expectations that define the quality of customer contact. They may include **technical standards** such as **response time** or **behavioural standards**. Customer needs and expectations form the basis of measurable service standards.

Companies need to communicate service standards to all customer-contact employees. This communication often initially takes place during new employee orientations.

Training and Empowerment: Good customer relationship management depends on the quality of training of customer-contact personnel. Companies, committed to customer relationship management, ensure that customer contact employees understand the products and services well enough to answer any questions of customers, develop good listening skills and problem recovery skills and feel able to handle problems.

Customer-contact employees also need access to a variety of company information to do their jobs which require support from the information technology component of the organisation. Also, they are empowered to make decisions on their own to satisfy the customers. TQ focussed companies empower their front-line people to do whatever necessary to satisfy the customer.

Effective Complaint Management: Despite all efforts to satisfy customers, every business experiences unhappy customers. Complaints can adversely affect business, if not dealt with effectively. Effective resolution of complaints increases customer loyalty and retention.

Companies involved in customer relationship management train customer-contact personnel to deal effectively with angry customers and to resolve the problems quickly.

Complaints provide a source of product and process improvement ideas. Companies need a systematic process for collecting and analysing the complaint data and then using that information for improvements.

Strategic Partnerships and Alliances

Today's suppliers are being asked to take on greater responsibilities to help their customers. Customer-supplier relationships represent an important strategic alliance in achieving excellence and business success.

Many companies work closely with suppliers that share common values. This close relationship improves supplier capabilities by teaching them quality related tools and approaches.

Measuring Customer Satisfaction

Customer feedback is vital to a business. Through feedback, a company learns how satisfied its customers are with its products and services and sometimes about the competitor's products and services.

Measures of customer satisfaction allow a business to:

- discover customer perceptions of how well the business is performing in meeting customer needs.
- compare the company's performance relative to competitors.
- discover areas for improvement, both in the design and delivery of products and services and
- track trends to determine if changes actually result in improvements.

An effective customer satisfaction measurement system results in the following:

(i) reliable information about customer ratings of specific product and service features.

(ii) reliable information about the relationship between those ratings and the customer's likely future market behaviour.

Customer satisfaction measures may include the following:

(i) product attributes such as product quality, product performance, usability and maintainability.

(ii) service attributes such as attitude, lead time, on-time delivery, exception handling, accountability and technical support.

(iii) image attributes such as reliability and price and overall satisfaction measures.

Customer satisfaction measures may include: *(i)* Product attributes *(ii)* Service attributes and *(iii)* image attributes

The most helpful customer data include comparisons with key competitors. Companies often rely on third parties to conduct blind surveys to determine who key competitors are and how their products and services compare. Competitive comparisons often clarify how improvements in quality can translate into better customer satisfaction or whether key quality characteristics are being overlooked.

Designing Satisfaction Surveys

The first step in developing a customer satisfaction survey is to determine its purpose. Surveys should be designed to clearly provide the users of the survey results with the information they need to make decisions. A critical question to consider is "Who is the customer?" Managers, purchasing agents and users and others all may be affected by a company's products and services. Customer satisfaction measurement should not be confined to external customers. Information from internal customers also contributes to the assessment of the organisation's strength and weaknesses. Often the problems that cause employee dissatisfaction are same issues that cause dissatisfaction in external customers. Many companies use employee opinion surveys to seek employee feedback on the work environment, benefits, compensation, management, team activities, rewards and recognition, and company plans and values. However, other indicators of employee satisfaction are absenteeism, turnover, grievances and strikes, which can often supply better information than surveys that many employees may not take seriously.

The next question to address is who should conduct the survey. Independent third party organisations often have more credibility to respondents and can ensure objectivity in the results. Then the ***sample frame*** is defined. (The sample frame is the target group from which a sample is chosen). The entire customer base or a specific segment may be chosen depending on the purpose of the survey.

The next step is to select the appropriate instrument to conduct the survey and collect the necessary data. The various techniques used for measuring customer satisfaction are formal written surveys (using questionnaires) face-to-face interviews, telephone interviews, and focus groups. Written surveys have low data collection costs and the advantages of self-administration and ease of analysis. Also they can probe deeply into the issues. The disadvantages are: high non-response bias and need for large sample sizes. Written surveys measure predetermined perceptions of what is important to customers, thereby reducing the scope of qualitative information that can be obtained. Face-to-face interviews and focus groups on the other hand require much smaller sample sizes and can generate a significant amount of qualitative information. However, the disadvantages are high costs and participant time commitments. Telephone interviews fall somewhere in between these extremes. Telephone interviews are preferred for companies with a limited number of business customers and mail-based surveys are used to track routine transactions, where key attributes are stable over time.

The types of questions to ask must be properly worded to achieve ***actionable*** results. By actionable, we mean that responses are tied directly to key business processes so that what needs to be improved is clear and responses are translated into cost/revenue applications to support the setting of improvement priorities. Leading questions, ambiguous questions, acronyms and jargons must be avoided.

Most customer satisfaction measures evaluate service characteristics. Developing measurable service characteristics can be difficult and therefore, such quality characteristics are translated into specific statements that clearly describe the concept.

A **"Likert" scale** is used to measure the response. ***Box 5.11*** **illustrates the examples of Likert scales used for customer satisfaction measurement.**

Box 5.11 : Likert Scales used for Customer Satisfaction Measurement

(i)	Very poor	Poor	Neither Poor nor Good	Good	Very Good
	(1)	(2)	(3)	(4)	(5)
(ii)	Strongly Disagree	Disagree	Neither Agree nor Disagree	Agree	Strongly Agree
	(1)	(2)	(3)	(4)	(5)
(iii)	Very Dissatisfied	Dissatisfied	Neither Satisfied nor Dissatisfied	Satisfied	Very Satisfied
	(1)	(2)	(3)	(4)	(5)

Responses in the range of '5' tell a company that it is doing very well. Responses in the range of '4' suggest that customer expectations are being met, but that the company may be vulnerable to competitors. Responses in the range of '3' means that the product or service barely meets customer expectations and that much room for improvement exists. Responses in the range of "2" and "1" indicate serious problems for the company.

The final task is to design the reporting format and the data entry methods. Modern technology such as computer database in conjunction with a variety of statistical analysis tools assists in tracking customer satisfaction and provides information for continuous improvement.

Analysing and Using Customer Feedback

By examining trends in customer satisfaction measures and linking satisfaction data to its internal processes, a business can see its progress and areas for improvement. Then the company should assign the responsibility and accountability for developing improvement plans based on customer satisfaction results to an employee or to a group of employees.

Appropriate customer satisfaction measurement distinguishes between processes that have high impact on satisfaction and low performance and those that are performing well. One way to ensure that measurement is appropriate is to collect information on both the importance and the performance of key characteristics. A firm ideally wants high performance on important characteristics and not to waste resources on characteristics of low importance. Many companies have integrated customer feedback into their continuous improvement activities. ***Exhibit 5.11*** **describes the "Quality Review Process" which enables a company to achieve customer commitment – a step beyond customer satisfaction.**

Exhibit 5.11 : Beyond Customer Satisfaction

Competitive advantage is achieved when the partnership and commitment between a business and its customers is so close that competitor products and services have to be significantly better in terms of quality and value if they are to have any chance of winning business from you.

To gain such an advantage managers have to understand in depth and in detail their customers' requirements, expectations and needs and be able to track continually and measure the performance perceived by the customers.

Customer commitment is the highly influential step beyond customer satisfaction. It will require determination and ability to use appropriate, practical techniques and systems to ensure the voice of the customer is heard loudly and clearly throughout the organisation.

One technique currently gaining worldwide acceptance for practicality and result-based effectiveness is QRP, which links together your employees and customer/supplier objectives in a true partnership of continuous improvement.

QRP by definition provides a framework necessary to involve employees, customers and suppliers in a continuous process of quality improvement.

The system of review is based predominantly on involvement. Every employee has a potential role to play in determining internal and external customer requirements. Progress over time means the process can be used as a measurement and documentation system to determine the effectiveness of the quality initiatives to gain improvement.

Steps in the process

There are five key steps in managing QRP.:

- Create a structured interview guide to fit the business's unique requirements.
- Interview customers, internal and external, using teams of employees to determine how effectively customers' needs are being met.
- Implement actions developed by the employee teams to respond to the needs identified.
- Review outside suppliers' performance using employee teams.
- Repeat periodically the customer interview process using an appropriate sample of suppliers, internal and external customers.

The information gathering stages will reveal the detail of customer requirements and how well the company is satisfying the expectation. Responses will determine what improvements need to be made and help to identify customers' expectancy in the future.

Information pointers about improving customer commitment and maintaining a long term relationship are frequently uncovered in this process to identify areas for change.

Workgroup selects review team and develops quality improvement plans
What quality improvements do we need to make?

Requirements
Reviews
Reviews
Requirements

Quality review team conducts internal and external customer reviews
What are our customers' requirements? Are we meeting or exceeding those requirements?

Quality review team conducts external supplier reviews
Do suppliers know our requirements? What quality improvements do they need to make?

Requirements, expectations and needs

Confusion sometimes exists between an understanding of requirements, expectations and needs. Does quality mean meeting all three or exceeding them?

Requirements are often the tangible aspects of a product or service and the main reason a customer buys. Expectations are the customers' perceptions of how the product or service should be delivered. Looking for ways to exceed these expectations is clearly important. So, requirements and expectations are clearly not the same thing.

Needs can be expressed as the tangibles of a product or service not currently available to customers; it is only when somebody actions the need and produces the product or service that it becomes a requirement. It is hard, if not possible to determine needs effectively without developing good relationships in which customers provide information as a basis for ideas which can freely be discussed and exchanged. When an organisation has shown that it can anticipate customer needs consistently, it will have demonstrated also the value of having committed customers willing to do business repeatedly.

Customer Focus in the Baldrige Award Criteria

Category 3 of the 1998 Malcolm Baldrige National Quality Award Criteria for Performance Excellence is titled ***Customer and Market Focus***.. This category examines how it enhances relationships with customers and determines their satisfaction. The basic premises of this criteria category are:

(i) **relationship enhancement is an important part of an overall listening and learning strategy and**

(ii) **customer satisfaction results provide vital information for understanding the *voice of customers.***

The criteria suggests that in a rapidly changing competitive environment, many factors may affect customer preference and customer loyalty, making it necessary to listen and learn on a continuous basis. Such listening and learning must be closely connected with a company's overall business strategy. Strategies often need to be tailored to specific customer groups and market segments to understand their specific product and service requirements and relative importance on value. This should be supported by good data and information, such as complaints and gains/ losses of customers.

Customers need access to seek assistance, conduct business and voice complaints. Prompt and effective resolution of complaints is critical, but so is the elimination of causes of complaints. Systematic follow-up with customers, along with more formal approaches, is important in understanding customer satisfaction. Customer satisfaction measurements should reflect those factors that best reflect customers' market behaviour – repurchase, new business and positive referral – and be supported by competitive comparisons to better understand the factors that drive markets.

Finally, relationship building provides an important means for companies to understand and manage customer expectations by obtaining actionable information such as feedback and complaints from customers. Front-line employees may provide vital information to build partnerships and other long-term relationships with customers.

Customer Retention

Customer retention is more powerful and effective than customer satisfaction.

Customer defection is a problem and ***customer retention*** an opportunity in both manufacturing and service firms. Customer retention is more powerful and effective than customer satisfaction. Customer retention represents the activities that produce the necessary customer satisfaction that creates customer loyalty, which actually improves the bottom line. Customer satisfaction surveys, focus groups, interviews and observations can help determine what customers think of a service or a product.

Customer retention moves customer satisfaction to the next level by determining what is truly important to the customers and making sure that the customer satisfaction system focusses valuable resources on things that really matter to the customer. Customer retention is the nexus between customer satisfaction and the bottom line. High employee retention has a significant impact on high retention of customers.

Service Quality and Customer Retention

Nowadays, service industries are playing an increasingly important role in a nation's economy. Management of customer satisfaction and retention of customers is critical for the growth of service industries because of the growing importance of service as a means of strategically competing in the marketplace. Management of services is one of the most important problems managers and executives are facing today.

Management of customer satisfaction and retention is critical for the growth of service industries.

Because many services are intangible, the interaction between employees and the customer is critical. The one-to-one or face-to-face contact between the customer and the deliverer of the service is extremely important. Customer defections because of poor service have a substantial impact on cost and profits, economies of scale, market share and unit cost.

Customer Retention and Profitability

What is the ultimate desired outcome of customer focus and satisfaction? Is it achieving profit in the private sector or productivity in the public or non-profit sectors? The answer must be yes. However, an accurate cause-and-effect relationship has yet to be established between profit and customer satisfaction. This is due to the difficulty in measuring satisfaction and relating it to profit. However, there is a proven relationship between customer satisfaction and profit.

One way to put a value on customer retention is to assign or estimate a ***"life time retention value"***, the additional sales would result if the customer were retained. An American credit card company has found that a 5-percent improvement in customer defections increases its average customer value by 125 percent. An US automobile dealer believes that the life time value of retaining a customer is US $3 lakhs in sales. **The system for improving customer retention and profit is illustrated in *Exhibit 5.12.***

Exhibit 5.12 : Profitability and Customer Retention

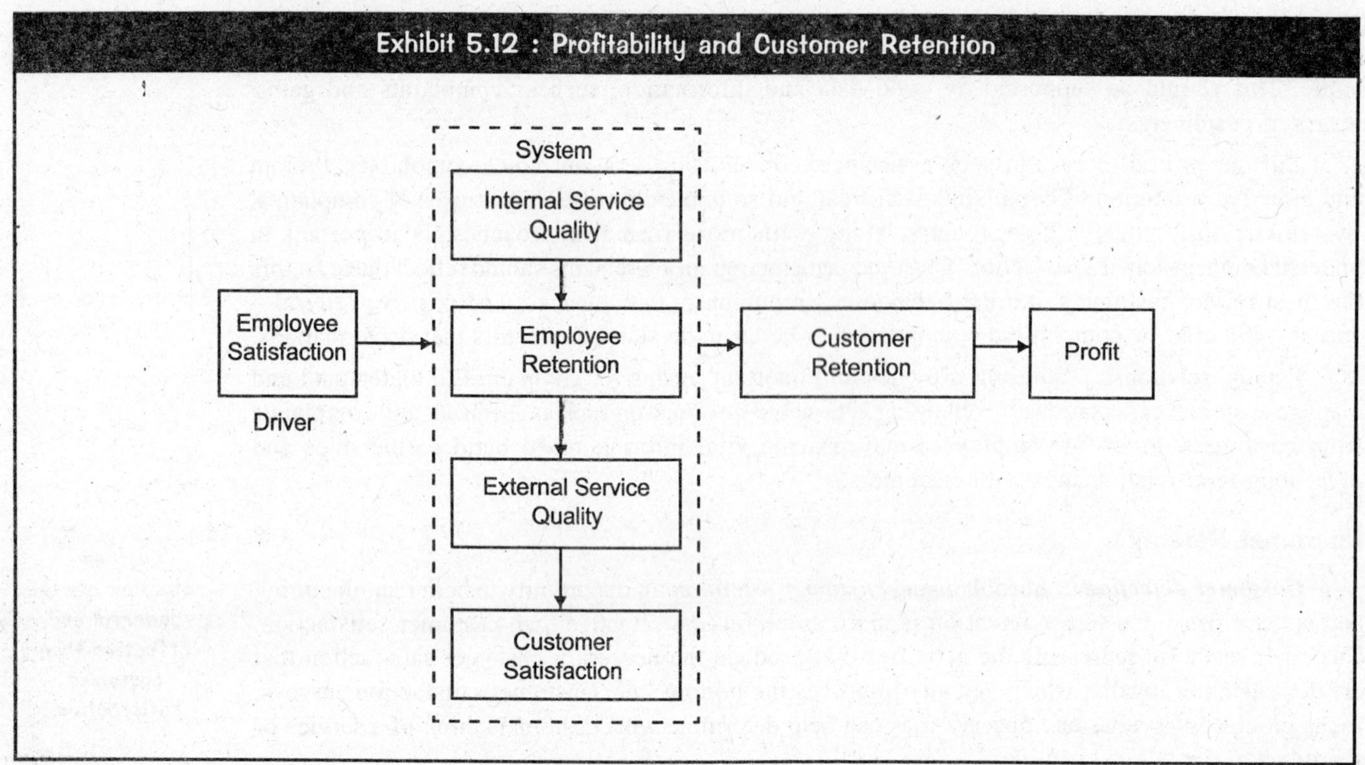

Employee satisfaction and employee retention leads to consumer retention and increased profits to the service provider

The *drivers* are employee satisfaction and employee retention. The system components are:

- ***Internal service quality,*** which establishes and reinforces a climate and organisation culture directed towards quality.
- ***Employee retention,*** which is achieved through good human resources management practices and organisation development methods such as teams, job development and empowerment. Employee retention depends on employee satisfaction, which in turn can be related to external service and customer satisfaction.
- ***External service quality,*** which is delivered through the organisation's quality infrastructure.
- ***Customer satisfaction and follow up,*** in order to reduce customer defections and improve retention.

Box 5.12 **describes what is meant by "Think Customer, Act Customer".**

Box 5.12 : Think Customer; Act Customer

- **Who is your customer?** Identify your markets and focus on the people you deliver to, both inside and outside your organisation. Aim to concentrate on one person – the customer – at a time.
- **Have you allocated time for your customer?** Believe that your customers are your business and therefore divide your time so that you see them.
- **Do you understand their needs?** Observe and listen. Immerse yourself in their environment.
- **Have you pinned down their immediate requirements and agreed to them?** Don't make assumptions, test that your interpretation is correct by asking them to confirm.
- **Have you built feedback mechanisms?** Enable the customer to tell you easily how you are doing. Run surveys, open and blind check the occurrence of this channel.
- **Are you smoothing the interface?** Continually make it easy for the customer to do business with you.
- **Have you built-in flexibility?** Expect the customer to have needs way outside the agreed parameters and be prepared to help by having the capacity to adjust.
- **Are you serving, not selling?** Be attentive and courteous, indifference or arrogance is heavily penalised. He is your partner, don't short-change him.
- **Are you looking for trends and anticipating emerging needs?** Accumulate data on the customer and look for patterns. Look around all the influence on the customer – competitors (yours and his), regulatory bodies, community, consumer taste – and imagine how any potential changes would affect the customer and his needs. Be just ahead of the game, don't raise expectations you cannot sustain.
- **Can you do something special?** Periodically, get out of your way to do something extra for your customer. *A delighted customer is your best sales person.*

5.9 ESTABLISHING A CUSTOMER FOCUS

Companies that have successfully established a customer focus share the following common characteristics:

1. ***Vision, Commitment and Climate:*** A customer-driven company is totally committed to satisfying customer needs. Management demonstrates by words and deeds that the customer is important to them, that the company is committed to customer satisfaction and customer needs are given a higher priority over internal needs.
2. ***Alignment with Customers:*** Customer-driven companies align themselves with their customers. **This alignment is reflected in many ways:**
   (a) Customers play a consultative role in selling.
   (b) Customers are never promised more than what can be delivered.
   (c) Employees understand what product/service attributes customers value most and
   (d) Customer feed back and input are incorporated into the product/service development process.
3. ***Willingness to find and eliminate customers' problems:*** Customer-driven companies work hard to continually identify and eliminate problems for customers. This willingness is manifested in the following ways: *(a)* Customer complaints are monitored and analysed, *(b)* Customer feed back is sought continually and *(c)* Internal processes, procedures and systems that create no value for customers are identified and eliminated.
4. ***Use of customer information:*** Customer-driven companies not only collect customer feed back but also use it and communicate it to those who need to make improvements. The use of customer information manifests itself in the following ways: *(a)* all employees know how the

The characteristics of companies having customer focus are:
(i) Vision, commitment and climate.
(ii) Alignment with customers.
(iii) Willingness to find and eliminate, customer's problems.
(iv). Use of customer information
(v) Reaching out to customers
(vi) Competence, capability and enpowerment of people and
(vii) Continuous improvement of products and processes.

customer defines quality, *(b)* employees at different levels are given opportunities to meet with customers, *(c)* employees know who the 'real' customer is, *(d)* customers are given information that helps them develop realistic expectations and *(e)* employees and managers understand what customers want and expect.

5. ***Reaching out to customers:*** Customer-driven companies reach out to their customers in a total quality setting. It is not enough for a company to wait for customers to give evaluative feed back. A more assertive or proactive approach is required in a competitive global market place. Reaching out to customers means doing the following: *(a)* making it easy for customers to do business, *(b)* encouraging employees to go beyond the normal call of duty to please customers, *(c)* attempting to resolve all customer complaints, *(d)* making it convenient and easy for customers to make their complaints known.
6. ***Competence, capability and empowerment of people:*** Employees are treated as competent, capable professionals and are empowered to use their judgement in doing what is necessary to satisfy customer needs. This means that all employees have a through understanding of the products they provide and the customer needs relating to those products. It also means that employees are given the resources and support needed to meet the customer's needs.
7. ***Continuous improvement of products and processes:*** Customer-driven companies do what is necessary to continually improve their products and the processes that produce them. This approach to doing business manifests itself in the following ways: *(a)* internal functional groups co-operate to reach shared goals, *(b)* best practices in the business are studied and implemented wherever they will result in improvements, *(c)* research and development cycle time is continually reduced, *(d)* problems are solved immediately and *(e)* investments are made in the development of innovative ideas.

The above seven clusters of characteristics can be used as a guide in establishing a customer focus. First a self-analysis is made to determine which of these characteristics are present in the organisation and which are missing. Characteristics which are missing form the basis for an organisation-wide implementation effort.

5.10 QUALITY IN PRACTICE

Box 5.13 : Motorola's Commitment to Customer Satisfaction

Motorola is a world-class leader in the manufacture of consumer electronics products. As a corporation, its fundamental objective is total customer satisfaction and achieving this objective is every employee's responsibility. Motorola sets the tone for its customer focus by stating its key beliefs, key goals and key initiatives as below.

Key Beliefs - How We Will Always Act

- Constant Respect for People
- Uncompromising Integrity.

Key Goals - What We Must Accomplish

- Increase Global Market Share
- Best in class
- People
- Marketing
- Technology
- Product
- Manufacturing
- Service
- Superior Financial Results

Key Initiatives - How We Will Do It

- Six-sigma Quality.
- Total Cycle Time Reduction
- Product and Manufacturing Leadership
- Profit Improvement
- Participative Management within and Cooperation between organisations.

Box 5.14 : Quality at Sea Ray Boats

"To help us to meet the challenges of continual quality improvement Sea Ray Boats has put together a program called P.A.C.E – People Achieving Customer Expectations.

In a very real sense, quality is a closed loop, beginning and ending with the customer. The quality process starts when we seek to understand what is takes to satisfy customers in our market place

Quality then goes full circle. We define specifications to meet the customer requirements. We manufacture products and develop the services necessary to satisfy those requirements. Then we go back to the customer and get feedback.

In a pace-setting company, quality must mean more than just a product characteristic. Rather it is an attitude that "the customer is king" That belief must permeate the entire company, driving every decision and involving every employee. When quality improvement becomes truly ingrained in the corporate culture, error rates and defects plummet. Productivity and customer satisfaction improves.

The goal of the P.A.C.E program is to continually improve the quality of our products and services and to enhance our ability to satisfy the customer".

5.11 SUMMARY

Achieving customer satisfaction is perhaps the most important competitive goal of any business. This will in turn help to retain customers in the long run and also gain substantial market share. To achieve customer satisfaction, an organisation identifies customers' needs, designs the production and service systems to meet those needs and measures the results as a basis for improvement.

The concept of "focussing on customers" includes both ***'internal'*** and ***external*** customers in the customer/supplier chain. This forms the basic concept of TQM because of the importance of ***customer perception of quality*** of goods and services offered by the organisation.

Key excellence indicators of customer satisfaction are: *(i)* Service standards derived from customer requirements, *(ii)* Understanding customer requirements, *(iii)* Front-line empowerment, *(iv)* Attention to hiring, *(v)* training and motivation of front-line employees, *(vi)* Pro-active customer-service systems and customer-relationship management, *(vii)* Quality requirement of market segments and *(viii)* Commitment to customers.

The American Customer Satisfaction Index is a national measure of customer satisfaction, linking customer expectations, perceived quality and perceived value to customer satisfaction, which in turn is linked to customer loyalty and profitability.

Customer satisfaction occurs when products or services meet or exceed customer expectations. Customers form perceptions of the quality of service by comparing their expectations with actual outcomes. The following practices help in achieving customer satisfaction: *(i)* Identifying customer needs and expectations, *(ii)* Understanding the linkage between customer needs and design / production/ delivery processes, *(iii)* Making extra-ordinary commitments, *(iv)* Managing the customer relationship process effectively and *(v)* Measuring customer satisfaction and acting on the results.

Customer needs differ. Kano's model of customer satisfaction relates customer satisfaction to various types of product features such as ***basic*** features, ***performance*** features and ***excitement*** features. This model segments customer requirements into dissatisfiers, satisfiers and exciters/delighters. Successful companies aim at understanding the exciters/delighters and develop products and services that truly delight customers. The concept of ***"voice of the customer"*** helps in this direction.

Customer information may be gathered by various methods, including comment cards and formal surveys, focus group interviews, direct customer contact, field intelligence, complaint analysis and Internet monitoring. Customer relationship management includes establishing commitments, developing customer focussed service standards, training and empowering customer contact employees, effectively dealing with complaints and forming strategic partnerships and alliances with customers.

A scientifically designed, good customer – satisfaction measurement process includes performance and importance measures, provides actionable information to improve a company's operations and products to further satisfy its customers.

5.12 KEY WORDS USED

Internal Customer, External Customer, Customer/Supplier Chain, Customer Satisfaction, Customer Retention, Customer Satisfaction Index, Kano Model, Voice of the Customer, House of Quality, Quality Function Deployment, Customer Segmentation, The Pyramid of Needs, Customer Relationship Management, Customer Defection.

5.13 OBJECTIVE QUESTIONS

(A) Match the following :

Column A	Column B
1. A C S I	1. Statistically based technique.
2. Kano Model	2. Used for measuring customer satisfaction.
3. Conjoint Analysis	3. Enables achievement of customer commitment.
4. Likert scale	4. Economic indicator to measure customer satisfaction.
5. Quality Review Process	5. Representation of customer satisfaction relative to various types of product features.

(B) Fill in the blanks :

1. The total package of products or services that a business offers with the price and with competitive offerings is known as ______.
2. Strong competitive advantage is driven by customer ______ and ______.
3. True customer needs and expectations are called ______ quality.
4. Customer ______ is a problem and customer ______ is an opportunity.
5. ______ results provide vital information for understanding the voice of customers.

(C) Multiple choice Questions : Choose the correct answer from the alternatives given under each question :

1. Basic requirements of internal and external customers are :
   (a) High levels of quality and service (b) High degree of flexibility and quick response
   (c) Low costs and little or no variability (d) (a) and (b) only
   (e) (a), (b) and (c)
2. Important factors that influence purchase are :
   (a) Performance (b) Features
   (c) Price (d) (a) and (c) only
   (e) (a), (b) and (c) (f) (b) and (c) only
3. Important dimensions of service quality are:
   (a) Reliability and Assurance (b) Tangibles, Empathy and Responsiveness
   (c) Satisfiers and dissatisfies, Exciters/Delighters
   (d) (a), (b) and (c) (e) (b) and (c) only.
4. Factors that lead to customer satisfaction are :
   (a) Commitment to customer and customer focussed service standards
   (b) Training and empowerment (c) Effective complaint management
   (d) (a) and (c) only (e) (a), (b) and (c).
5. The "pyramid of needs" comprises
   (a) Primary and secondary needs only (b) Secondary and tertiary needs only
   (c) Primary, secondary and tertiary needs (d) None of the above.

5.14 REVIEW QUESTIONS

1. What are the four key customer related goals of any business?
2. Define the terms *(a)* Internal customer, *(b)* External customer, *(c)* Customer satisfaction index and *(d)* Voice of the customer.
3. Explain the customer-driven quality cycle.
4. Define the terms – expected quality, actual quality and perceived quality.
5. What is "customer relationship management"? Explain.
6. Describe Kano's model of customer satisfaction.
7. What is meant by delighting the customers?
8. What is customer retention. Discuss its relationship with service quality and profitability.
9. Discuss the steps involved in designing customer-satisfaction surveys.
10. What specific issues of customer focus are addressed in the Baldrige Award Criteria?

5.15 DISCUSSION QUESTIONS

1. Why do you think that many firms fail to recognise the importance of customers until they are faced with a crisis?
2. Give several examples of dissatisfiers, satisfiers and exciters/ delighters in product or services that you recently purchased. Why did you classify them into these categories?
3. "One basic concept of TQM is unwavering customer orientation or focus on customers, both internal and external" - Explain.
4. "Customer satisfaction can be achieved only when the products and services meet or exceed customer expectations" - Discuss.
5. "Delighting the customer means doing something special to the customer – exceeding his/her expectations". - Elaborate.
6. Discuss the seven clusters of characteristics that can be used as a guide in establishing a customer focus.

5.16 ASSIGNMENTS

1. Visit any small scale industry or business in your neighbourhood and interview the manager to understand how they respond to complaints and use complaint information to improve the quality of their product or services.
2. Using focus groups of students in your class or the colleagues in the organisation in which you are employed, conduct an interview to determine what factors are important in selecting a restaurant or pizza delivery.

5.17 CHAPTER CASE

THE CASE OF MISSING RESERVATION

Ramesh, Ramya and their children, along with another family traditionally attended New Year Party at a prestigious hotel. This year as in the past, Ramya called and made a reservation about two weeks prior to New Year Day. Because majority of the party consisted of small children, they arrived 30 minutes prior to the 11:30 PM reservation to ensure being seated early. When they arrived however, the party hall supervisor said that they did not have a reservation. He explained that guests sometimes failed to show and hence the seats were not reserved. However, he promised that he would make available a table for them as early as possible. Ramesh and Ramya were quite upset and insisted that they had made a reservation and expected to be seated promptly. The supervisor told them "I believe that you made the reservation, but I can't seat you until all the people who have come earlier and are waiting for seat are accommodated. You are welcome to go to the lounge and have complementary coffee and relax while you wait".

When Ramesh asked to see the manager, the supervisor replied "I am the manager" and turned to other duties. Ramesh and his party members were eventually seated at 11.45 P.M. but they were not at all happy with the experience.

The next day, Ramesh wrote a letter to the hotel manager explaining the entire incident. Ramesh was in the executive MBA program of a prestigious Business School and taking a course on Total Quality Management. In his class, they had just studied issues of customer focus and some of the approaches used at Ritz-Carlton Hotel, a 1992 Baldrige Award winner. Ramesh concluded his letter with the statement, "I doubt that we would have experienced this situation at a hotel that truly believes in quality."

About a week later, Ramesh received the following reply :

"We enjoy hearing from our valued guests, but wish you had experienced the type of service and accommodations that we aim to achieve here at our hotel. Our restaurant manager received your letter and asked me to respond as Total Quality Lead."

Looking back at our records, we did not show a reservation on the books for your family. I have discussed your comments with the appropriate department head so that others will not have to experience the same inconveniences that you did.

Thank you once again for sharing your thoughts with us. We believe in a philosophy of

"Continuous Improvement" and it is through feedback such as yours that we can continue to improve the service to our customers.

Discussion Questions :

1. Were the party hall supervisor's actions consistent with a customer focussed quality philosophy? Comment. What might he have done differently?
2. How would you have reacted to the letter Ramesh received? Could the Total Quality Lead have responded differently?
3. What does the fact that the hotel manager did not personally respond to the customer indicate to you?

CHAPTER 6

LEADERSHIP AND STRATEGIC PLANNING FOR TQM

LEARNING OBJECTIVES

After reading this chapter, you should be able to:

- Understand the importance of 'Leadership' and "Strategic Planning" in total quality management.
- Know the requirements of effective leadership.
- Briefly discuss the various leadership theories and their implications on quality management.
- Discuss the concept of "Strategic Quality Planning".
- Discuss the steps involved in "Strategic Quality Planning Process".
- Describe the various management and planning tools used for implementing policy deployment.
- Discuss the relevance of organisational culture to the development of total quality.
- Discuss the steps involved in creating "TQM culture".
- Discuss the role of organisational culture and ethics in TQM.
- Discuss the steps involved in establishing quality culture.
- Discuss the factors that influence ethical behaviour.

6.0 INTRODUCTION

Most quality experts agree that strong leadership from the senior management of the organisation is absolutely necessary to develop and sustain a quality based organisational culture.

Leadership is the ability of a person to positively influence people and systems to achieve important results.

Leadership is the ability to positively influence people and systems under one's authority to have a meaningful impact and achieve important results. Leaders may seek to motivate employees and develop enthusiasm for quality with rhetoric, but actions speak louder than words. *For example*, the former CEO of Motorola, Robert Galvin, made a habit of making quality as the first item on the agenda of executive staff meetings. His leadership guided Motorola to become one of the first winners of the Malcolm Baldrige National Quality Award.

Leaders create clear and visible quality values, and integrate these values into the organisation's strategy. ***Strategic planning*** involves the process of envisioning the organisation's future and developing the necessary procedures and operations to achieve that future. It involves formulating ***strategies*** which are the patterns of decisions that determine a company's goals; policies and plans to meet the needs of its stakeholders. A business can create a sustainable ***competitive advantage*** through an effective strategy. In today's business environment, **quality is a key element of strategic planning.**

The role of leadership and strategic planning for quality and performance excellence is discussed in this chapter. The emphasis is on the application of leadership concepts in a total quality environment and the process of formulating and implementing TQ-based strategies.

Leadership for quality

Even though many leadership theories have been developed, no single approach adequately captures the essence of the concept of leadership. In practice, both the concepts of leadership and quality are equally elusive. Hence, it is necessary to have a clear understanding of the principal concepts of leadership and the prominent leadership practices in quality management.

Leadership is an essential part of a quality improvement effort.

Executive leadership is a kind of leadership which focusses the role of senior managers in guiding an organisation to fulfil its mission and achieve its goals.

Some of the important roles of senior executives are :

- Defining and communicating business directions.
- Ensuring that goals and expectations are met.
- Reviewing business performance and taking appropriate action.
- Creating a work environment that promotes creativity, innovation and continuous improvement.
- Soliciting input and feedback from customers
- Ensuring that employees contribute effectively to the organisation.
- Motivating, inspiring and energising the employees.
- Recognising employee contributions and
- Providing reliable feedback.

Other kinds of leadership are *individual leadership, team leadership* and *organisational leadership.*

***Individual leadership* is revealed through :**

- Maintaining the focus and discipline to consistently complete jobs.
- Being proactive in identifying and solving problems.
- Working for win-win agreement and
- Making continuous learning a personal habit.

***Team leadership* is seen by :**

- making those around you successful
- removing barriers to team performance
- establishing good lines of communication and
- resolving problems.

Organisational leadership is manifest in :

- Clear values
- Creating a competitive advantage, customer and market focus and
- Continual learning.

***Box 6.1* lists six new skills for newage managers.**

Box 6.1 : Six New Skills for Newage Managers

The Six Newage Skills are :

(i) **Creative insight :** Asking right questions and framing right answers for them.

(ii) **Sensitivity :** Being sensitive to a culture created by people in an organisation.

(iii) **Vision :** Leaders who have vision can create the future for the organisations.

(iv) **Versatility :** Adapt to change comfortably, pursue difficult skills to be versatile.

(v) **Focus :** Focus enables leaders to invest available resources towards implementing successful and long lasting change.

(vi) **Patience :** Means living in the long term.

6.1 REQUIREMENT OF EFFECTIVE LEADERSHI

Effective leadership comprises
(i) Vision
(ii) Empowerment
(iii) Intuition
(iv) Self - understanding and
(v) Value congruence.

Five core leadership skills required for effective leadership are : *(i)* **vision,** *(ii)* **empowerment** *(iii)* **intuition,** *(iv)* **self-understanding** and *(v)* **value congruence.**

These skills are briefly descussed below:

(i) **Vision :** ***Vision*** is crucial for leaders during times of change. Leaders recognise the radical organisational changes taking place today as opportunities to achieve total quality.

(ii) **Empowerment :** Leaders ***empower*** employees to assume ownership of problems or opportunities and to be proactive in implementing improvements and making decisions in the best interests of the organisation.

(iii) **Intuition :** Leaders usually follow their ***intuition***. They must be prepared to make difficult decisions even in the face of uncertainty and change and anticipate the future.

(iv) **Self-understanding :** ***Self-understanding*** requires the ability to look at one's self and then identify relationships with employees and within the organisation. It requires an examination of one's weaknesses as well as strengths.

(v) **Value congruence :** ***Value congruence*** occurs when leaders integrate their values into the company's system. Values are basic assumptions and beliefs about the nature of the business, mission, people and relationships of an organisation. Values include trust and respect of individuals, openness, teamwork, integrity and commitment to quality.

***Box 6.2* lists the guidelines for effective leadership.**

Box 6.2 : 12 Guidelines for Effective Leadership

(i) Give priority attention to external and internal customers and their needs.

(ii) Empower rather than control the subordinates.

(iii) Emphasise improvement rather than maintenance.

(iv) Emphasise prevention rather than cure.

(v) Encourage collaboration rather than competition.

(vi) Train and coach rather than direct and supervise.

(vii) Learn from problems.

(viii) Continually try to improve communications.

(ix) Continually demonstrate commitment to quality.

(x) Choose suppliers on the basis of quality, not price.

(xi) Encourage and recognise team effort.

(xii) Establish organisational systems to support the quality effort.

Box 6.3 **lists Demings view on learning, training, leadership and innovation.**

Box 6.3 : Deming on Learning, Training, Leadership and Innovation

- ***Learn*** the theory, then improve it.
- Management needs ***training*** to learn about their company.
- ***Experience*** without theory teaches nothing about quality and competitive positions. *Experience* will answer a question, but the question comes from theory.
- The job of management is not supervision but ***leadership***.
- The big problem in ***leadership*** and ***training*** arises from a standard of what is acceptable work and what is not.
- Requirement for ***innovation***; faith that there will be future.

Box 6.4 **describes the seven habits of highly effective people according to Stephen R Covey.**

Box 6.4 : The Seven Habits of Highly Effective People (Stephen R Covey)

Stephen R. Covey has based his foundation for success on ***character ethic*** – things like ***integrity, humility, fidelity, temperance, courage, justice, patience, industry, simplicity*** and ***modesty.*** The ***personality ethic – personality growth, communication skill, training*** and ***education in the field of influence strategies*** and ***positive thinking*** – is secondary to *character ethics.* What we *are* communicates far more eloquently than what we *say* or *do*.

A **habit** is the intersection of ***knowledge, skill and desire.*** **Knowledge** is the ***what to do*** and the ***why, skill*** **is the *how to do it* and desire is the motivation or *want to do.*** The *seven habits* are a highly integrated approach that moves from dependency to independence to interdependence. The first three habits deal with independence – the essence of character growth, habits 4, 5 and 6 deal with interdependence – teamwork, cooperation and communication. Habit 7 is the habit of renewal.

Habit 1 : Be Proactive: Being proactive means having the ability to choose the response to a situation. Proactive behaviour is a product of conscious choice based on values rather than reactive behaviour which is based on feelings.

Habit 2 : Begin with the End in Mind : Begin each day with an image, picture or paradigm of the end of your life as your frame of reference. If you want to have a successful organisation, you begin with a plan that will produce the appropriate end. Leadership is the first creation and management is the second. Leadership is doing the right things, management is doing things right.

Habit 3 : Put First Things First : It is the day to day, moment to moment management of your time. The ***time management matrix*** **is** shown below :

	Urgent	Not urgent
Important	1. Crisis, fire-fighting, pressing problems, deadline driven projects	2. Prevention, relationship building, recognising new opportunities, planning, recreation
Not Important	3. Interruptions, pressing matters, some mail, calls, reports, some meetings, proximate popular activities	4. Trivial busy work, time wasters, pleasant activities

Habit 4 : Think Win-Win : Win-Win is a frame of mind and heart that constantly seeks mutual benefits in all human interactions. Win-Win embraces five interdependent dimensions of life – ***character, relationship, agreements, systems*** **and *processes.*** In order to obtain win-win, a four step process is needed : *(i)* See the problem from the other viewpoint *(ii)* identify the key issues and concerns *(iii)* determine acceptable results and *(iv)* seek possible new options to achieve those results.

Habit 5 : Seek First to Understand, Then to be Understood : We usually try to be understood first instead of understanding others. **Empathic listening** is the key to effective communication and to understand the other person emotionally as well as intellectually. To be understood, use ethos (your personal credibility), pathos (empathy you have with the other person's communication) and logos (logic or reasoning part of your presentation).

Habit 6 : Synergy : Synergy means the whole is greater than the sum of the parts. The first 5 habits build towards habit 6. It focusses on the concept of win-win and the skills of empathic communication on tough challenges that bring about new alternatives that did not exist before. Synergy occurs when people abandon their humdrum presentations and win/lose mentality and open themselves upto creative cooperation.

Habit 7 : Sharpen the Saw (Renewal) : Habit 7 is taking time to sharpen the saw so it will cut faster. It is preserving and enhancing the greatest asset which you have. It is renewing the four dimensions of your nature – physical, spiritual, mental and social/emotional.

Leading Practices

In firms committed to total quality, various leadership practices share common elements. Quality and business performance excellence is promoted by true leaders in several ways:

- Readers create a strategic vision and clear quality values that serve as a basis for business decisions at all levels of the organisation.
- Leaders create and sustain a leadership system and environment for quality excellence.
- Leaders set high expectations.
- Leaders demonstrate substantial personal commitment and involvement in quality, often with a missionary like enthusiasm.
- Leaders integrate quality values into daily leadership and management.
- Leaders integrate societal responsibilities and community involvement into their business practices.

True leaders are able to promote quality and business performance excellence.

Leadership is the *"driver"* of the entire quality system. Without leadership, a total quality initiative simply becomes the flavour of the mouth; which is why total quality efforts fail in many organisations.

6.2 LEADERSHIP THEORIES

Leadership theories can be studied from at least five perspectives.:

(i) trait approach
(ii) behavioural approach
(iii) situational or contingency approach
(iv) the role approach and
(v) emerging theories.

The various approaches to the study of leadership theories are:
(i) Trait approach
(ii) Behavioural approach
(iii) Situational/ contingency approach
(iv) Role approach and
(v) Emerging theories

The ***trait approach*** involves discovering how to be a leader by examining the characteristics and methods of recognised leaders. This approach is the earliest approach to leadership theory and has been discredited later due to the finding that leaders do not necessarily share a common set of traits.

The ***behavioural approach*** attempts to determine the type of leadership behaviours that lead to successful task performance and employee satisfaction. Extensive series of leadership studies showed that effective leadership depends on a proper blending of an employee relationship centred approach to employee's needs with a task centred approach to getting work done. **A recent study by Zenger-Miller, an international consulting and training firm, developed a list of 17 leadership competencies that people most often associate with leadership. They are :**

(i) Setting or sharing a vision.
(ii) Managing a change
(iii) Focussing on the customer
(iv) Dealing with individuals
(v) Supporting teams and groups
(vi) Sharing information
(vii) Solving problems, making decisions
(viii) Managing business processes
(ix) Managing projects
(x) Displaying technical skills
(xi) Managing time and resources
(xii) Taking responsibility
(xiii) Taking initiative beyond job requirements
(xiv) Handling emotions
(xv) Displaying professional ethics
(xvi) Showing compassion and
(xvii) Making credible presentations.

The ***contingency or situational approach*** holds that there is no universal approach to leadership, rather effective leadership behaviour depends on situational factors that may change over time. This approach to leadership is very much relevant to today's business which has to perform in the rapidly and continuously changing environment. According to this approach, effective leadership depends on three variables : the ***leader,*** the ***led*** and the ***situation.***

The role approach suggests that leaders perform certain roles to be effective. This approach is similar to trait approach and behavioural approach, but also takes into account situational factors which have an impact on the leadership roles played by the leaders. According to Henry Mintzberg, leaders at the higher levels of the organisation may have to play the role of a figurehead, a liaison person between the firm and the outside environment. At lower levels of management, leaders have to play motivational, co-ordination or disturbance handling roles to be effective.

Emerging theories of leadership enhance or enlarge the current theory by attempting to answer questions raised, but not answered by contingency approaches.

Two such emerging theories are :

(i) ***Attributional theory*** which states that leaders' judgement on how to deal with subordinates in a specific situation is based on their attributions of the internal or external causes of the behaviours of their followers.

(ii) ***Transactional or charismatic theory*** assumes that certain leaders may develop the ability to inspire their subordinates to exert extraordinary efforts to achieve organisational goals owing to the leader's vision and understanding of how to tap into the developmental needs of the subordinates.

An emerging leadership theory that falls within the transactional category shows potential for dealing with the leadership needs of organisations that want to develop a ***total quality management*** process. This approach, called ***Transformational Leadership Theory,*** explains the impact of leadership in a TQ environment. According to this model, leaders adopt many of the behaviours discussed earlier in this chapter. They take a long-term perspective, focus on customers, promote a shared vision and values, work to stimulate their organisations intellectually, invest in training, take some risks and treat employees as individuals. Transformational leadership is strongly correlated with lower employee turnover, higher productivity and quality and higher employee satisfaction than other approaches.

6.3 QUALITY IMPLICATIONS OF LEADERSHIP THEORIES

Today's leaders are including many TQ principles in their routine leadership activities. ***Box 6.5*** **compares** ***traditional management*** **practice with the true** ***quality leadership.***

Box 6.5 : TQ Leadership Contrasts

Managers	**Leaders**
Plan projects	**Practice**
* Make *plans* for the *future.*	* *Envision* the future
* *Organise* materials and methods	* *Optimise* materials and methods
* *Preach* management by objectives	* Use *participative* management
Push products	**Produce**
* Give "lip-service" to quality	* Exemplary quality
* Sell to customers	* Services to the customers
* Cut costs	* Less waste through better processes
* Perform R & D	* Innovative products and services
Control people	**Motivate people**
* Control people and things through systems	* Develop people's talents, control things with systems
* Reward conformance, punish deviation	* Reward effort, skill development and innovation, empower employees.
* Maintain status quo.	* Look to the future through continuous improvement.

Traditional management relies on mechanistic planning and organising, reacting to events, pushing products and controlling people. McGregor's theory X-Y model has two types of managers – "Theory X" manager who assumes that subordinates must be coerced and controlled in order to prevent quality problems in their work and to obtain high productivity. "Theory Y" manager on the other hand assumes that work is a natural activity and people who are led well can be expected to be self-motivated to perform their best work if given the opportunity. Much of Deming's philosophy follows the principle of Theory Y.

According to the various contingency leadership theories, quality can be enhanced with the correct blend of the leader's style of management, the characteristics of the followers, (who are led) and the situation. It was found that when the leader (supervisor) emphasised *daily **performance measures*** and used ***positive reinforcement,*** quality benefits result within that organisation. However, the same approach may not work in a different situation such as Research & Development (R & D). The R & D leader would probably be more effective by using a ***participative approach,*** taking into consideration the situation of the high technical skills and professional expertise of the employees.

In the present situation, the appropriate role for managers also depend on situational factors. The managers take a TQ approach to reorganising and their roles may move away from the highly structuring roles of decision maker, disturbance handler and entrepreneur towards the more "facilitating" roles that assist subordinates such as motivator, liaison and spokesperson.

Senior managers need to champion the transformation to a ***TQ culture.*** The transformation depends on changing the view of the organisation from a ***vertical perspective*** based on an organisation chart to a ***horizontal*** one based on a ***system*** and ***process perspective.*** Transformational leadership may be the key ingredient in making the change to a TQ culture a lasting one. The charismatic transformation leader is rare and most effective at the top. An organisation pursuing TQ needs both those who establish visions and those who are effective at the day-to-day tasks needed to achieve them. These transactional leaders play a critical role in promoting total quality.

Exhibit 6.1 **dercribes American quality guru Tom Peter's model of leadership (Management by Wandering Around).**

Exhibit 6.1 : Peter's Model (Management By Wandering Around)

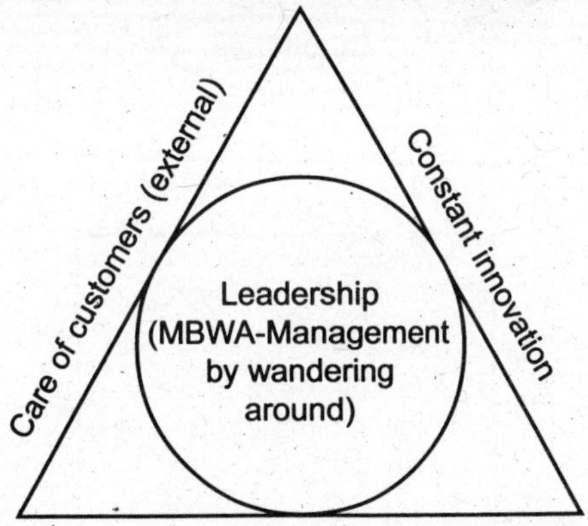

According to Tom Peters, one of the youngest American quality gurus, **constant innovation** is one of the two pre-requisites for achieving and sustaining superior company performance. The second pre-requisite is **exceptional care for the customer,** through superior service and quality for the external customer and through proper leadership for the internal customer.

Leadership is the element which connects all other elements in the model.

By **management by wandering around (MBWA)**, that is by walking around and listening, a manager would be able to lead, to teach and to help the internal customers. Contact through MBWA can help in appreciating better everyone's performance and in discovering what is happening, what goes wrong so as to lead and convey values effectively.

6.3.1 Creating the Leadership System

The ***leadership system*** refers to how leadership is exercised throughout a company. This includes how key decisions are made, communicated and carried out at all levels. It includes the formal and informal mechanisms for leadership development used to select leaders and managers, to develop their leadership skills and to provide guidance and examples regarding behaviours and practices.

***Exhibit 6.2* shows the leadership system at Custom Research Inc. USA.**

An effective leadership system does the following :

- Creates clear values that reflect the requirements of company stakeholders.
- Sets high expectations for performance and performance improvements.
- Builds loyalties and teamwork based upon the shared values.
- Encourages initiative and risk taking.
- Subordinates organisation to purpose and function.
- Includes mechanisms for leaders' self examination and improvement.

Exhibit 6.2 : Custom Research Inc. (CRI) Leadership System

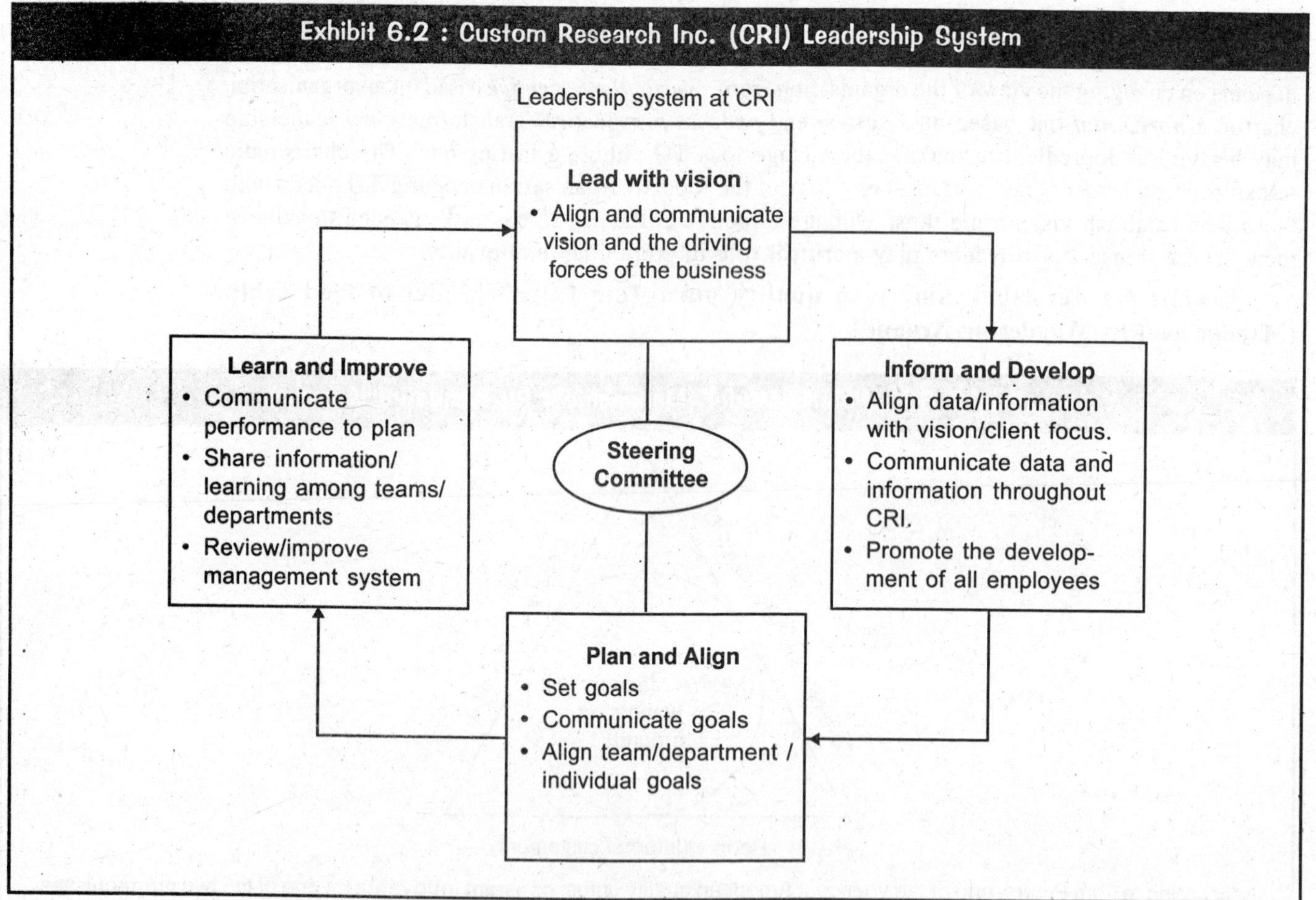

A four person steering committee is the centre of the leadership system. The company's vision is developed by the senior leaders. This is exemplified by "The Star" which designs the five driving forces of the business.

***Exhibit 6.3* shows the "CRI star".**

The star defines the five driving forces of the business :

(i) Driving competent and empowered ***people.***

(ii) Managing work through technology-driven ***processes.***

(iii) Meeting or exceeding unique client ***requirements*** and expectations.

(iv) Building partnering ***relationships*** with major clients and suppliers.

(v) Producing ***growth*** and ***profit results.***

Exhibit 6.3 : CRI Star

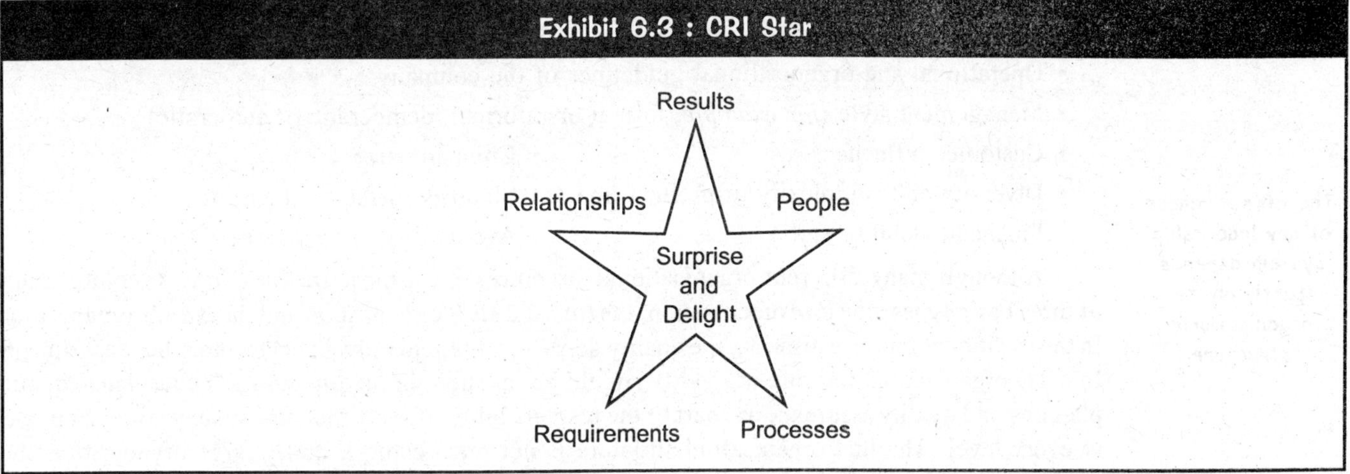

The Steering Committee does the following :

- Sets the directions for the company
- Promotes the development of all employees
- Reviews overall company performance and
- Integrates performance excellence goals
- Interacts with associates
- Identifies area of improvement.

The use of steering teams of senior managers (quality councils) is prevalent in total quality organisations. A leadership system may have quality councils at various levels of management, *for example*, an executive quality council, manager quality council, vice president quality council, director quality council and the like. All these councils are networked together. Responsibilities of quality councils include incorporating total quality principles into the company's strategic planning process and coordinating the overall efforts.

Box 6.6 **lists the six 'E's of outstanding leadership.**

Box 6.6 : The 6 'E's of Outstanding Leadership

Leadership of high calibre is essential to bring into sharp focus of all those desirable forces that can transform an organisation into a world-class producer of goods and services that can continuously delight its customers.

The six elements of outstanding leadership are :

- ***Exposing*** the possibility of moving away from the way things currently exist.
- ***Envisioning*** what sort of a future is to be created ahead in time.
- ***Enlisting*** the support of all the others in the organisation.
- ***Empowering*** all those who are willing to work to reach the final goal.
- ***Exemplifying*** the right actions and behaviours for others to emulate.
- ***Encouraging*** the actions of others that support the movement forward.

6.3.2 Quality and Organisational Structure

The effectiveness of any leadership system depends partly on its organisational structure which embodies the classification of authority, responsibility, reporting lines (chain of command) and performance standards among individuals at each level of the organisation. Traditional organisations tend to develop structures that help them to maintain stability. They tend to be highly structured, both in terms of rules and regulations as well as the height of the "corporate ladder" with seven or more levels of hierarchy between the CEO and the first-line-worker.

On the contrary, modern organisations have to build flexibility into the organisational structures. They tend to have fewer written rules and regulations and flatter organisational structures.

The factors having to do with the context of the organisations that have an impact on how work is organised are :

- Operational and organisational guidelines of the company.
- Management style (*for example*, formal or informal, democratic or autocratic)
- Customer influences
- Company size
- Diversity and complexity of product line
- Stability of the product line
- Financial stability and
- Availability of personnel.

The effectiveness of any leadership system depends partly on its organisational structure

Although many different organisational structures exist, most are variations or combinations of three basic types : the ***line*** organisation, the ***line*** and ***staff*** organisation and the ***matrix*** organisation. In the traditional line organisation, the quality department is generally distinct from other departments. In a TQ organisation, the role of quality should be invisible in the organisation chart since quality planning and quality assurance are part of the responsibility of each operating manager and employee at every level. The line organisation structure is not practicable in fairly large organisations but generally used in small firms.

The line and staff organisation is the most prevalent type of structure for medium to large firms. In such structures, quality department does the staff function, assisting the line managers and workers of the production department in attaining quality.

In the matrix type of organisation, a quality assurance technician might be assigned to a quality assurance department for technical and administrative activities, but would be attached to a project manager for day to day assignments. The major drawback of this type of organisation structure is that the project manager who is under pressure to complete a project by a certain deadline may try to influence the QA personnel to relax inspection so that the project can be completed within the deadline.

As more and more companies accept the process view of organisation, they are structuring the quality organisation around functional or cross-functional teams. **The organisational structures of many organisations are built around high performance, cross functional teams as shown in *Exhibit 6.4*.**

Exhibit 6.4 : Team based Organisational Chart

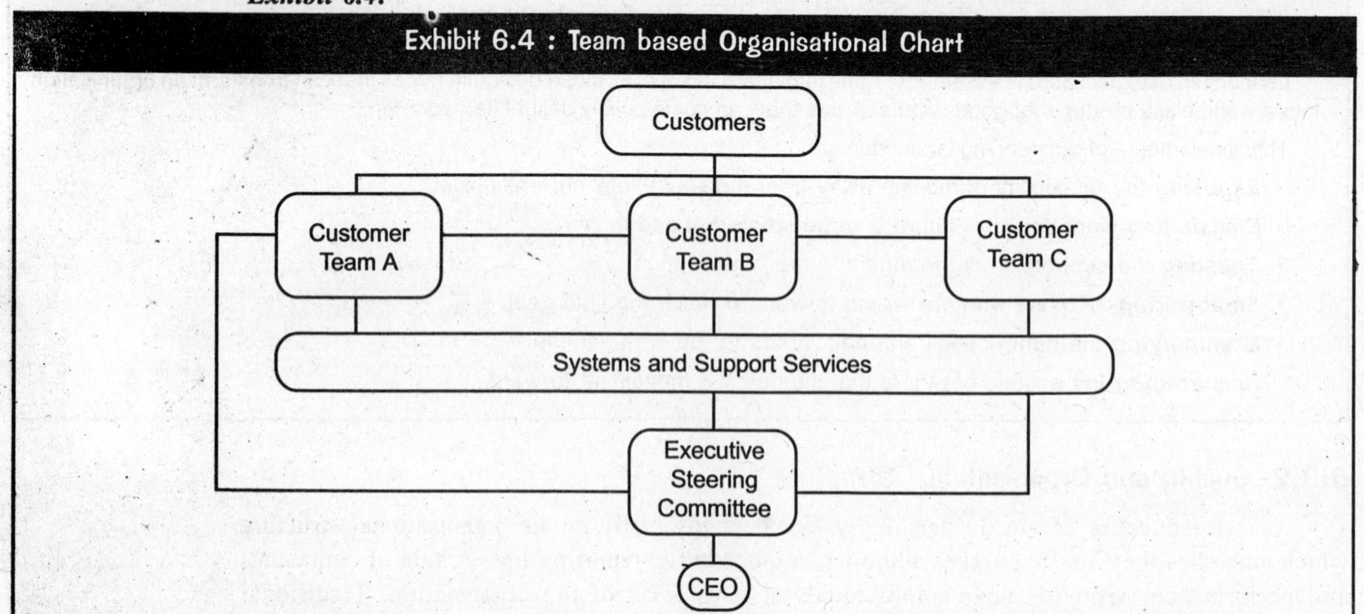

In a typical TQ organisational structure, the management board leads the quality effort. Quality is implemented through various teams: core business process team, cross-functional co-ordinating committee, regional management councils, major business process management teams (PMTs), Malcolm

Baldrige National Quality Award (MBNQA) teams and quality improvement teams. The "quality department" serves as an internal consulting group, providing advice, training and organisational development to the team. ***Exhibit 6.5* shows a typical TQ organisational structure.**

Exhibit 6.5 : TQ Organisational Structure

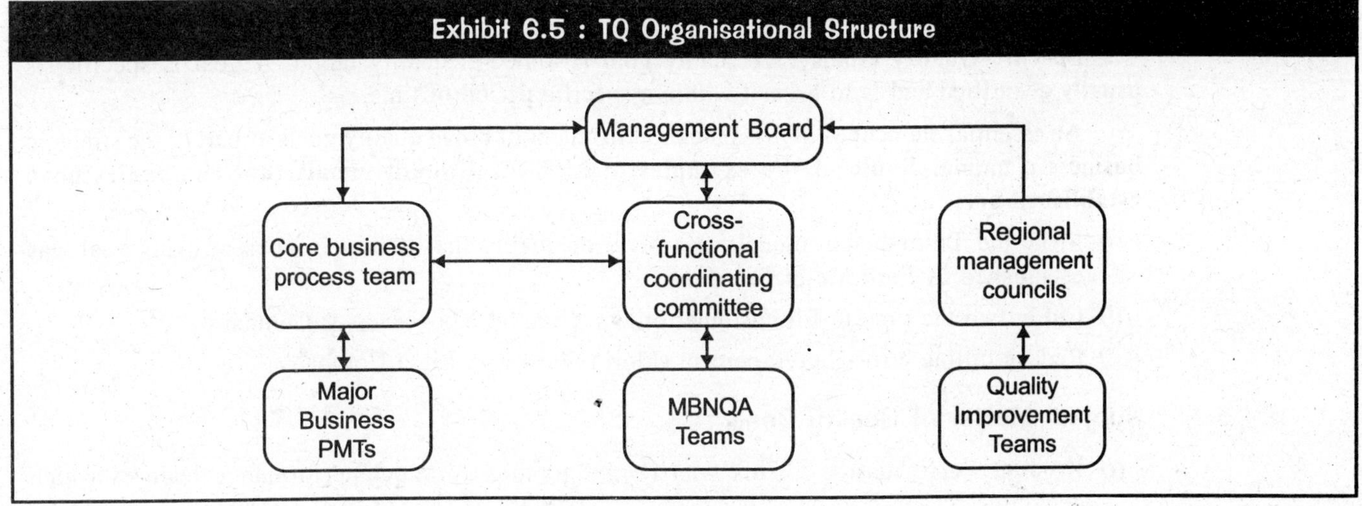

6.4 STRATEGIC QUALITY MANAGEMENT (SQM)

Strategic Quality Management (also known as ***Strategic Quality Planning)*** is a structured process for establishing long range quality goals, at the highest levels of the organisation and defining the means to be used to reach these goals.

Strategic Quality Management **(SQM)** includes ***quality planning, quality control*** **and quality improvement** (processes of the Juran trilogy).

Strategic quality management includes:
(i) Quality planning
(ii) Quality control and
(iii) Quality improvement.

The Concept of Strategic Quality Planning

Strategic business planning is essentially a structured process for defining the broad mission and strategic goals for the company and then determining the means to be used to reach these goals. These strategic business goals include financial goals as sales, net income and return-on-investment.

Until the 1980s, strategic business planning seldom included planning for quality. Planning for quality did exist on the **"little 'q' level"**. The 1980s then witnessed a significant trend towards the adoption of the **"Big Q" concept** and an associated trend towards the adoption of the concept of strategic quality planning

Establishing SQM : The Quality Council

A fundamental step in establishing SQM is the creation of the ***Quality Council*** (or Quality Committee). The Quality Council membership properly consists of the senior managers and senior executive staff. In large organisations, quality councils may be formed at multiple levels of organisation. The Quality Council is responsible to define and incorporate the elements of SQM into the company's strategic business planning. It also has the responsibility to ensure that any needed infrastructure is created at subordinate levels of organisation.

Quality Policies : The purposes of SQM include establishing guidelines for the action to be taken is order to reach the quality goals. A major tool for establishing such guide lines is ***"Quality Policies"***. "Policy" means a guide to managerial action. Published policy statements are the result of a good deal of deliberation in high places, followed by approval at the highest level. The Quality Council plays a major role in the formulation of quality policies.

Quality policy reflects an organisation's formally stated beliefs about quality, how it will occur and the expected result.

All published quality policies declare the intention to ***meet the needs of customers.*** *For example,* the policy states ***"the company's products should provide customer satisfaction"*** **or**

"the company's product shall equal or exceed competitive quality". Also, the quality policy statements may declare the intention to ***conduct improvements in quality annually*** or include specific reference to internal customers, *e.g.*, ***quality should extend to all phases of the business.*** The quality council should make sure that the prevailing quality policies correctly reflect the company's intention with respect to quality.

Specific Quality Goals : A quality goal is aimed-at quality target. A goal is specific, is usually quantified and is to be met within a specific period of time.

An essential element of SQM is the establishment of broad quality goals as part of the strategic business planning. **Some of the examples of high-level quality goals that companies have established are:**

(i) Make the Taurus/Sable models at a level of quality that is best in chosen. (This goal was established by Ford Motor Company).

(ii) Cut in two the time to fill customer orders. (Becton, Dickenson & Company).

(iii) Reduce billing errors by 90 percent (Florida Power & Light Company)

Subject Matter of Quality Goals

(i) **Product Performance :** This goal relates to those product performance features which determine response to customer needs, promptness of service, fuel consumption, meantime between failure and so on. Such features directly influence product stability.

(ii) **Quality Competitiveness :** This has always been a goal in market-based economies, but seldom part of the strategic business plan. The trend to bring quality competitiveness into the business plan is recent but irreversible.

(iii) **Quality Improvement :** This goal may be aimed at improving product salability and/or reducing the cost of poor quality. Either way, the end result after deployment is a formal list of quality improvement projects with the associated assignment of responsibilities.

(iv) **Reduction of the cost of poor quality :** The goal of quality improvement usually includes a goal of reducing the costs due to poor quality.

Deployment of Quality Goals : A list of strategic quality goals is a **"wish list"**. To convert this list into potential realities requires getting deep into specifics. What action needs to be taken in order to meet the goals, who is to take those actions and so forth. The process of identifying these specifics are called ***"deployment of quality goals".***

Deployment means subdividing the goals and allocating the subgoals to lower levels. The purposes of deployment of goals are :

(i) The subdivision of goals continues until it identifies the specific actions to be taken.

(ii) The allocation continues until it assigns clear responsibility for taking the actions.

(iii) Those who are assigned to take the actions then respond by determining the resources needed and communicating this back to higher levels.

Allocate to Subordinate Levels : The subdivided goals are allocated to appropriate organisation units; following a hierarchical pattern; corporate to division, division to functional department etc. But if meeting of goals requires tackling quality improvement projects, then such goals are assigned to ***teams.***

Identify the Needed Actions and Resources

The allocations establish responsibility but do not make clear what actions are to be taken. Each organisation unit or project team examines its mission and assigns responsibility and defines the actions to be taken.

Provide Resources : The proposals from the action level flow upward to the Quality Council along with requests for resources. After discussing the proposals, negotiating and revising, agreements emerge regarding actions to be taken, resources to be provided and results to be achieved.

The Infrastructure for Control : Strategic business management includes provisions for control – for evaluating the results of operations, comparing the results with goals and taking action on the difference. The same process is applicable to strategic quality management, but only if the necessary infrastructure has been built by the Quality Council.

Performance Evaluation : The means for evaluating performance relative to the strategic goals is established first. This requires agreement on just what is to be evaluated, the units of measure, the methods of measurement and so on.

Performance Review: SQM requires that the top level managers regularly review performance against strategic quality goals. The emerging practice is one of regarding review of performance in quality as an extension of the traditional corporate reviews of performance relative to other matters of strategic importance.

Quality Audits : A quality audit is an independent review of quality performance. The purpose of audit is to provide independent, unbiased information not only to the operating heads but also to others who have a need to know. **Subject matter of quality audits expands to provide answers to such questions.**

Quality audit involves independent review of quality performance against pre determined quality goals.

(i) Does our quality provide product satisfaction to our clients?

(ii) Is our quality competitive with the moving target to the market place?

(iii) Are we meeting our responsibility to society?

(iv) Are we making progress in reducing the cost of poor quality?

(v) Are our quality policies and quality goals appropriate to our company's mission?

6.5 LEADERSHIP AND STRATEGIC PLANNING

One of the critical aspects of leadership is strategic planning. Strategic planning enables leaders to manage change by focussing on an ideal vision of what the organisation should and could be five to ten years in the future.

A strategy is a plan that integrates an organisation's major goals, policies and action sequences into a cohesive whole.

Formal strategies contain three elements :

(i) Goals to be achieved

(ii) Policies that guide or limit action and

(iii) Action sequences or programs that accomplish the goals.

Strategic planning is a process to set an organisation's long - range goals and identify the actions needed to reach the goals.

Effective strategies revolve around the key concepts or thrust areas such as customer satisfaction – which provide focus. Strategic planning helps to build a strong posture to enable the organisation achieve its goals despite unforeseeable external forces. ***Exhibit 6.6*** **describes the strategic planning process.**

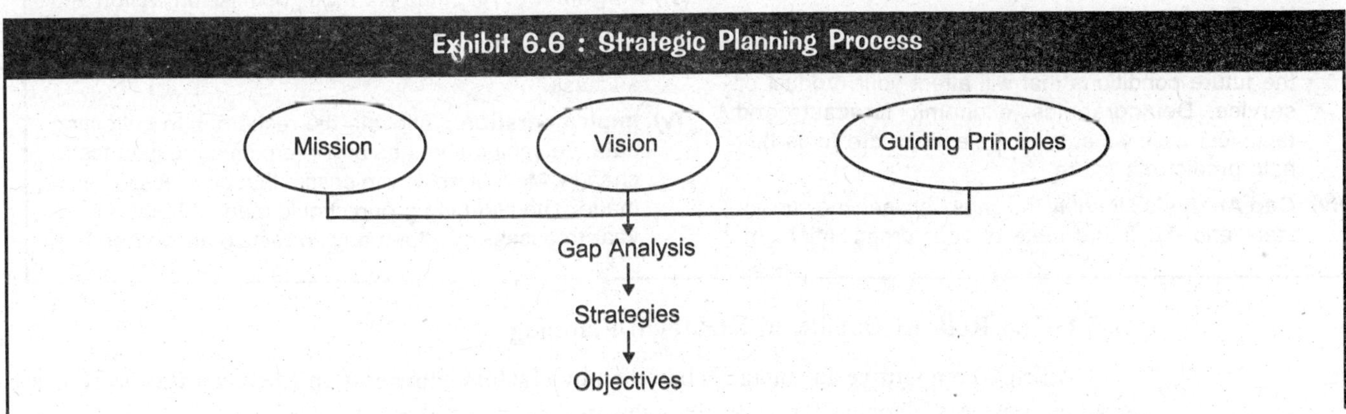

The Vision/Mission Values Are Real to Everyone.

Vision

Our products are the love of users and the envy of competitors.

Mission

We value people who create value for customers and shareholders by deploying, producing, selling and supporting state-of-the art products for our customers.

Values

- Continue Growing • Be Proud • Be Honest • Help Others • Build Trust.

Foundation for Strategic Planning

Mission : The ***mission*** of a firm defines its reason for existence, it asks the question "why are we in business?"

Mission might include :

- A definition of products and services the organisation provides
- Technologies used to provide these products and services
- Types of markets
- Important customer needs and
- Distinctive competencies.

Vision : ***Vision*** describes where the organisation is headed and what it intends to be, it is a statement of the future that would not happen by itself. It articulates the basic characteristics that shape organisations strategy.

Values : ***Values*** or ***guiding principles*** guide the journey to the vision by defining attitudes and policies for all employees, which are reinforced through conscious and subconscious behaviour at all levels of the organisation.

Goals, Strategies and Objectives

Goals are broad statements that set the direction for the organisation to take in realising its mission and closing the gap between where it is and where it wants to be.

Strategies are key actions towards achieving the goals.

Objectives are specific, measurable actions that support the strategies.

Box 6.7 **lists the seven steps to strategic planning.**

Box 6.7 : Seven Steps to Strategic Planning

(i) **Customer Needs :** Discover the future needs of the customers. Who will they be? Will your customer base change? What will they want? How will your organisation meet and exceed expectations?

(ii) **Customer Positioning :** Determine where your organisation is to be in relation to the customers. Do you want to retain, reduce or expand the customer base?

(iii) **Predict the Future :** Look into the future to predict the future conditions that will affect your product or service. Demographics, economic forecasts and technical assessments or projections are tools that help predict the future.

(iv) **Gap Analysis :** Identify the gaps between the current state and the future state of your organisation. An analysis of the core values and concepts is an excellent technique for pinpointing the gaps.

(v) **Closing the gap :** Develop the plan to close the gap by establishing goals and responsibilities. All stakeholders should be included in the development of the plan.

(vi) **Alignment :** Align the plan with the mission, vision and core values and concept of your organisation. Without this alignment, the plan will have little chance of success.

(v) **Implementation :** Allocate the resources to collecting data, designing changes and overcoming resistance to change. Monitor activity to ensure that progress is being made. The planning group should meet at least once a year to assess and take any corrective action needed.

6.5.1 The Role of Quality in Strategic Planning

A firm's competitive advantage is based on two factors – **low cost** and **differentiation.** Hence, strategic business planning typically revolves around financial and marketing goals.

(A) Strategic quality planning – a systematic approach to setting quality goals has been viewed as separate and distinct from strategic business planning.

The role of quality in business strategy has taken two significant steps since 1980. First, many firms recognised that a strategy driven by quality can lead to significant market advantages. Second, the difference between a quality strategy and business strategy has become very narrow. Customer driven quality and operational performance excellence are key strategic business issues and an integral part of overall business planning. Quality improvement objectives such as increasing customer satisfaction, reducing defects and reducing process cycle times are treated as important as financial and marketing objectives. Quality planning is integrated within normal business planning because quality drives financial and marketing success. Thus, ***strategic quality planning* is synonymous with *strategic business planning.***

In companies that aspire to become world-class companies, quality has become an integral part of the overall strategic plan as a central operating strategy. ***For example,* quality strategy of Xerox Corporation has three elements :**

Quality Principles

- Quality as the basic business principle for Xerox Corporation in its leadership position.
- An understanding of the customer's existing and latent requirements.
- Employee involvement in improving quality (through participative problem solving)
- Error-free work as the most cost effective way to improve quality.

Management Action and Behaviour

- Assure strategic clarity and consistency.
- Provide visible supportive management practice, commitment and leadership.
- Set quality objective and measurement standards.
- Establish and reinforce a management style of openness, respect, patience and discipline.
- Develop an environment in which each person can be responsible for quality.

Quality Tool

- The Xerox quality policy.
- Competitive benchmarking and goal setting.
- Systematic defect-detection and error-prevention processes.
- Training for leadership through quality.
- Communication and recognition programs that reinforce leadership through quality.
- A measure for the cost of quality. (or its lack)

Leading Practices

***Exhibit 6.7* shows the strategic quality planning process at a typical company.**

Effective organisations share several common approaches in their strategic planning efforts :

(i) Top management and employees all actively participate in the planning process.

(ii) They use customer wants and needs to drive the strategy.

(iii) They involve suppliers in the strategic planning process and

(iv) They have well-established planning systems for strategy development and deployment including measurement, feedback and review.

(B) Strategy development : Strategy development needs to take into account customer and market requirements and expectations, the competitive environment, financial market, technological and societal risks, company capabilities such as human resources, technology and business processes and supplier and/or partner capabilities. This information is gathered and maintained as input to the planning process.

Exhibit 6.7 : Strategic Quality Planning Process

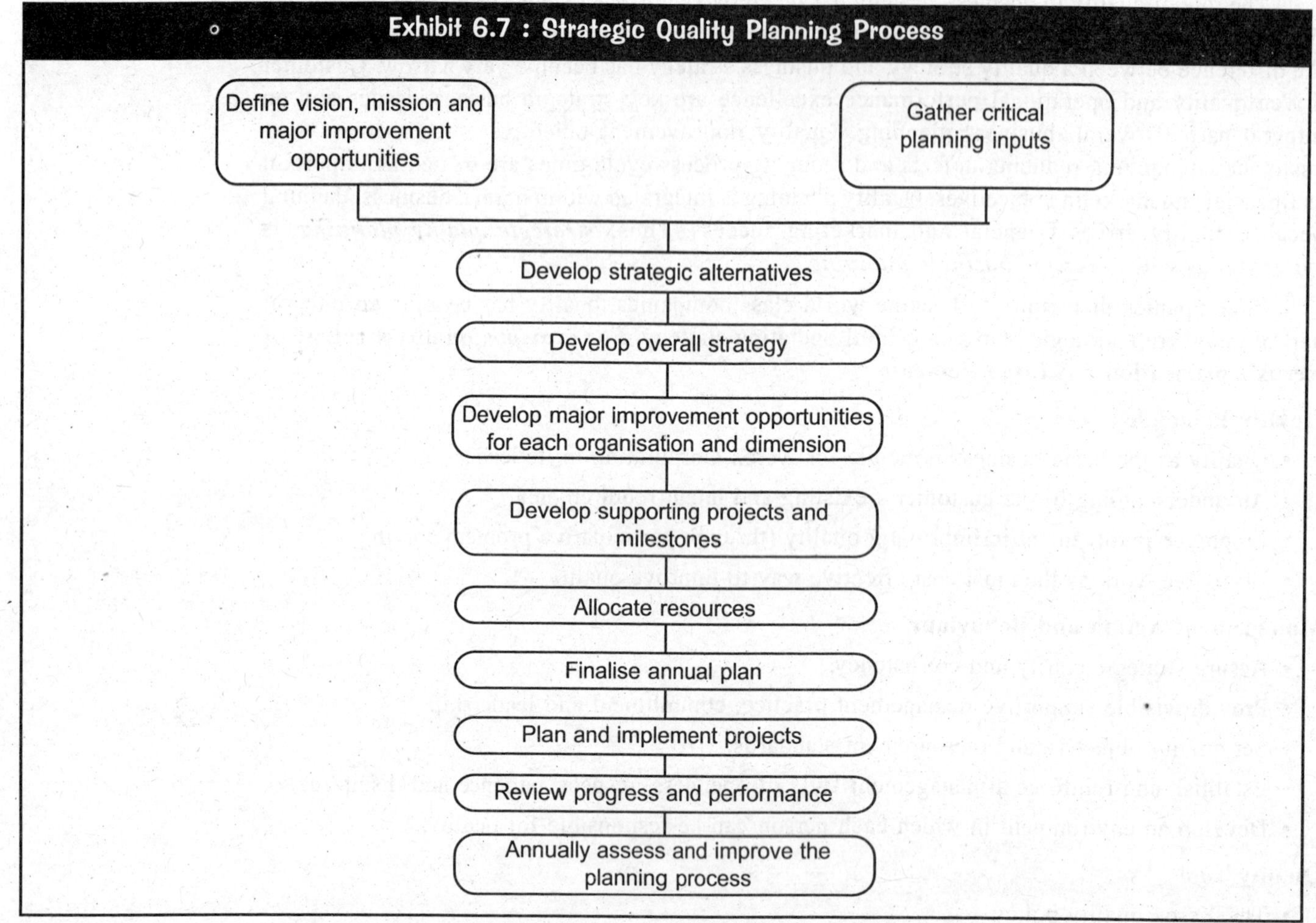

Strategy deployment ensures that the plans and strategies are executed successfully within the organisation.

(C) Strategy Deployment : Strategy deployment is the method to ensure that the plans and strategies are executed successfully within the organisation. Managers determine specific responsibility for meeting objectives at lower levels of the organisation and provide the rewards which are necessary. **Policy deployment** emphasises organisation wide planning and setting of priorities, provides resources to meet objectives and measures performance as a basis for improving performance. It is essentially a TQ – based approach for executing a strategy by ensuring that all employees understand the business direction and are working according to plan to make the vision a reality.

The Japanese deploy strategies through a process known as ***hoshin kanri***, or ***hoshin planning.*** In the US, this process is often referred to as ***policy deployment*** or ***management by planning.*** The meaning of ***hoshin kanri*** (Japanese word) is ***"pointing direction"*** which means to point or align the entire organisation in a common direction.

The various definitions of *policy deployment* are :

(i) The executive deployment of selected policy driven priorities and the necessary resources to achieve performance breakthroughs.

(ii) A process of annual planning and implementation which focusses on areas needing significant improvement.

(iii) An organisation wide and customer focussed management approach aimed at planning and executing breakthrough improvements in business performance.

6.6 MANAGEMENT AND PLANNING TOOLS FOR IMPLEMENTING POLICY DEPLOYMENT

Managers use a variety of tools and techniques known as ***the seven management and planning tools*** to implement policy deployment. These tools are useful in structuring unstructured ideas, making strategic plans and organising and controlling large, complex projects. **These tools are:**

(i) Affinity Diagrams
(ii) Inter-relationship Digraph
(iii) Tree Diagrams
(iv) Matrix Diagrams
(v) Matrix Data Analysis
(vi) Process Decision Program Charts and
(vii) Arrow Diagrams

1. Affinity Diagrams

Affinity diagram is a management and planning tool used to organise ideas into natural groupings in a way to stimulate new, creative ideas.

The affinity diagram is a tool for organising a large number of ideas, opinions and facts relating to a broad problem or subject area. In developing a vision statement, the top management might conduct a brainstorming session to develop a lot of ideas to incorporate into the vision. The list might include ideas such as low product maintenance, low production costs, satisfied employees, innovative product features, low price, high returns on investment, technology innovation, quick delivery, high quality, growth in shareholder values, motivated employees, teamwork, responsive technical support, unique products, personal employee growth, small light weight designs etc.

The large number of ideas generated can be grouped according to their "affinity" or relationship to each other. ***Exhibit 6.8* shows the affinity diagram for Micro Tech Company.**

Exhibit 6.8 : Affinity Diagram for Micro Tech Company

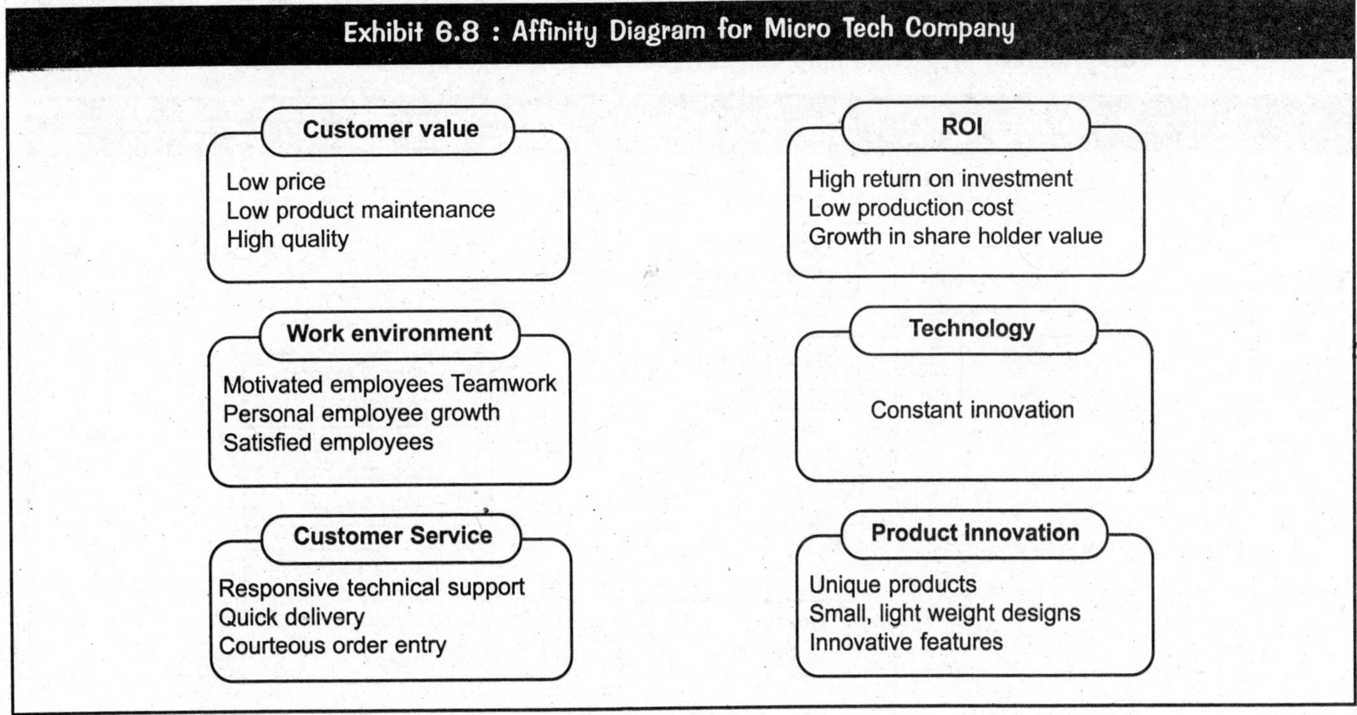

2. Inter-relationship Digraph

An inter-relationship digraph identifies and explores causal relationships among related concepts or ideas. It shows that every idea can be logically linked with more than one other idea at a time and allows for **"lateral thinking"** rather than "linear thinking". This technique is often used after the affinity diagram had clarified issues and problems. ***Exhibit 6.9* shows the inter-relationship diagraph of MicroTech's strategic factors.**

Exhibit 6.9 : Inter-relationship Digraph of Micro-Tech's Strategic Factors

Customer value
ROI
Customer service
Product innovation
Work environment
Technology

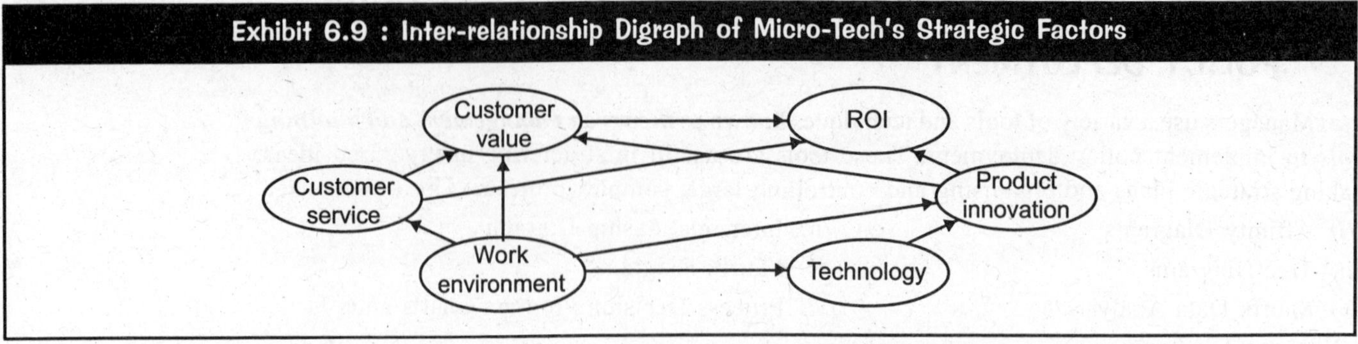

The elements having the most net outward – pointing arrows (number of arrows out minus number of arrows in) which represent the primary drivers of the company's vision and in this case, work environment and customer service.

3. Tree Diagrams

A "tree diagram" shows the complete range of sub tasks required to achieve an objective.

A tree diagram maps out the paths and tasks necessary to complete a specific project or reach a specific goal. This technique is used to seek answers to such questions as "what sequence of tasks will address this issue?" or "what factors contribute to the existence of the key problem?"

A tree diagram brings the issues and problems revealed by the affinity diagram and the inter-relationship digraph down to the operational planning stage. A clear statement specifies problem or process. From this statement, a team can be established to recommend steps to solve the problem or to implement the plan. The 'product' produced by this team would be a tree diagram with activities and perhaps recommendations for timing the activities. ***Exhibit 6.10*** **shows how a tree diagram can be used to map out key goals and strategies for MicroTech.**

Exhibit 6.10 : Tree diagram of MicroTech – Goals and Strategies

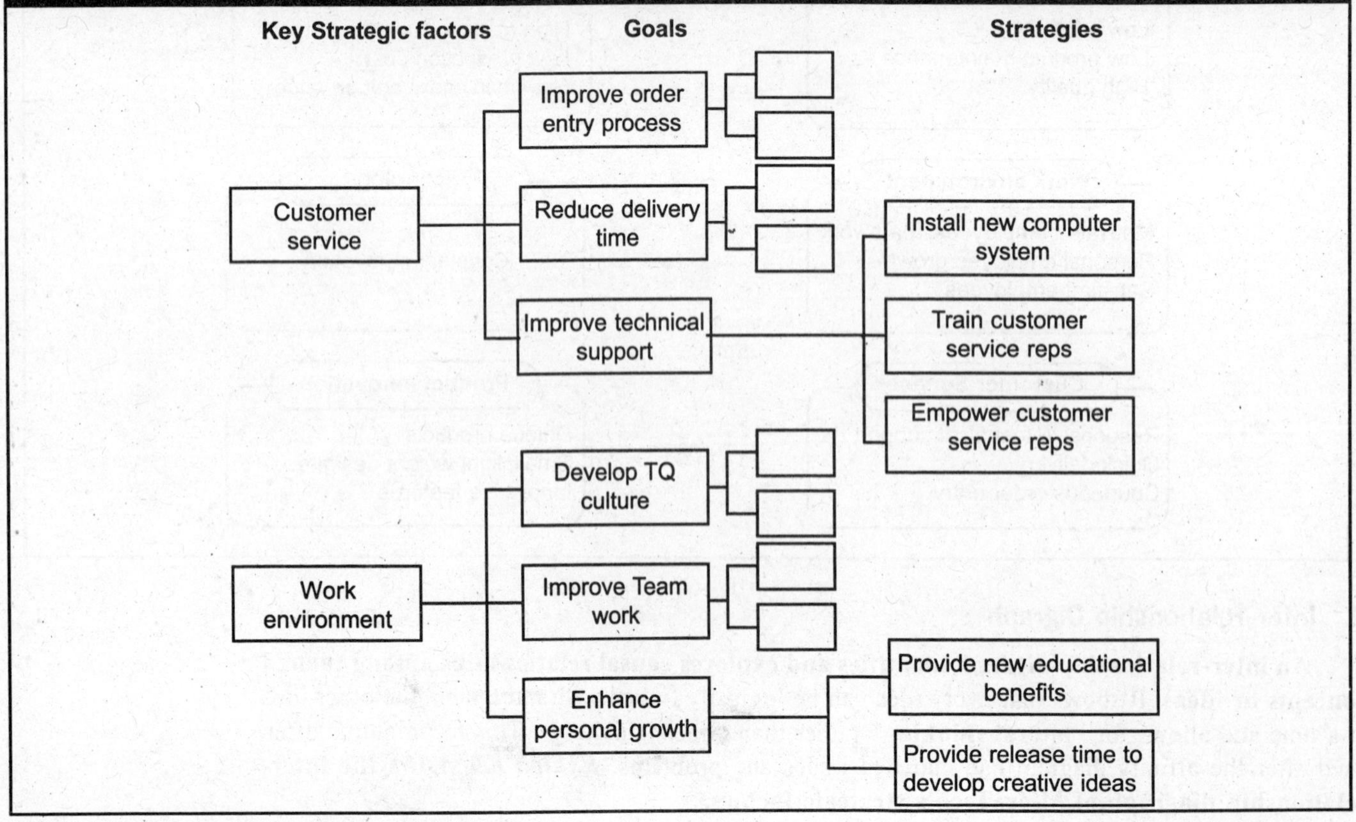

Key Strategic factors
Goals
Strategies
Customer service
Improve order entry process
Reduce delivery time
Improve technical support
Install new computer system
Train customer service reps
Empower customer service reps
Work environment
Develop TQ culture
Improve Team work
Enhance personal growth
Provide new educational benefits
Provide release time to develop creative ideas

4. Matrix Diagrams

Matrix diagrams are "spreadsheets" that graphically display relationships between ideas and activities in such a way as to provide logical connecting points between each item. It is one of the most versatile tools in quality planning. ***Exhibit 6.11* shows the matrix diagram for MicroTech's goals and strategies.**

Exhibit 6.11 : Matrix Diagram

Goals \ Actions	Improve Work Environment	Improve Manufacturing Technology	Develop New Products
Cost Effectiveness	●	○	
High quality	●	●	
Shareholder value		Δ	●

● = strong relationship ○ = medium relationship Δ = weak relationship

Matrix diagram provides a picture of how well two sets of objects or issues are related and can identify missing pieces in the thought process. These visual depictions can help managers set priorities on plans and actions.

5. Matrix Data Analysis

Matrix data analysis takes data and arranges them to display qualitaive relationship among variables to make them more easily understood and analysed. It is a rigorous, statistically based "factor analysis" technique.

***Exhibit 6.12* shows an example of matrix data analysis.**

Exhibit 6.12 : Matrix Data Analysis of Customer Requirement for Micro Tech.

Requirement	Importance Weight	Best Competition Evaluation	Micro Tech Evaluation	Difference
Price	0.2	6	8	+2
Reliability	0.4	7	8	+1
Delivery	0.1	8	5	-3
Technical Support	0.3	7	5	-2

Micro-Tech market researchers determined that the four most important consumer requirements are price, reliability, delivery and technical support. Through market research, importance weighting was determined for each of the customer requirements. The researchers also determined numerical ratings for the company and their best competitor. Such an analysis provides information as to which actions the company should deploy to better meet key customer requirements. ***For example*, in *Exhibit 6.12* reliability is the highest in importance (weight of 0.4) and MicroTech has a**

narrow lead over its competitor, thus they should continue to strive for improving product reliability. Next to reliability, technical support has high importance, but MicroTech is perceived to be inferior to its best competitor in this category. Hence, improving the quality of support services should be a major objective for MicroTech.

A process decision program chart identifies all events that can go wrong and the appropriate counter - measures for those events.

6. Process Decision Program Charts

A process decision program chart (PDPC) is a method for mapping out every conceivable event and contingency that can occur when moving from a problem statement to possible solutions. A PDPC takes each branch of a tree diagram, anticipates possible problems and provides counter measures that will *(i)* prevent the deviation from occurring or *(ii)* be in place if the deviation does occur.

Exhibit 6.13 **shows one example for implementing a strategy to educate and train all employees to use a new computer system.**

Exhibit 6.13 : A Process Decision Program Chart

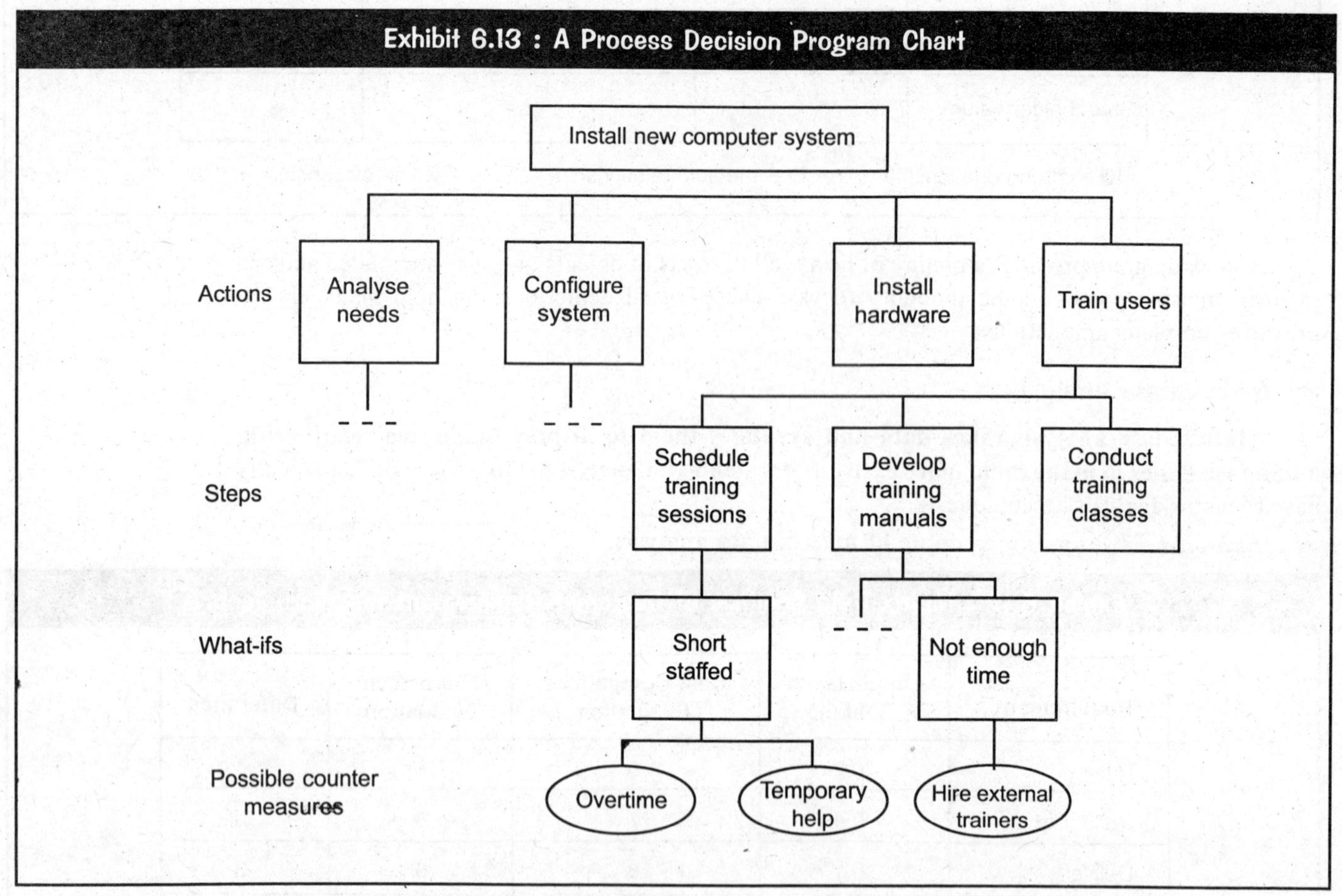

7. Arrow Diagrams

An arrow diagram is used to develop the best possible schedule and appropriate controls to accomplish the schedule.

Arrow diagrams are usually used in the form of CPM and PERT project planning techniques. Even though arrow diagrams are used by technical experts in project management, they can be used as quality tools also. ***Exhibit 6.14*** **shows an example.**

Time estimates can be added to each activity in order to schedule and control the project.

The seven tools discussed above provide managers with improved capability to make better decisions and facilitate the implementation process. With proper planning, managers can use their time more effectively to continuously improve and innovate.

Exhibit 6.14 : An Arrow Diagram for Project Planning

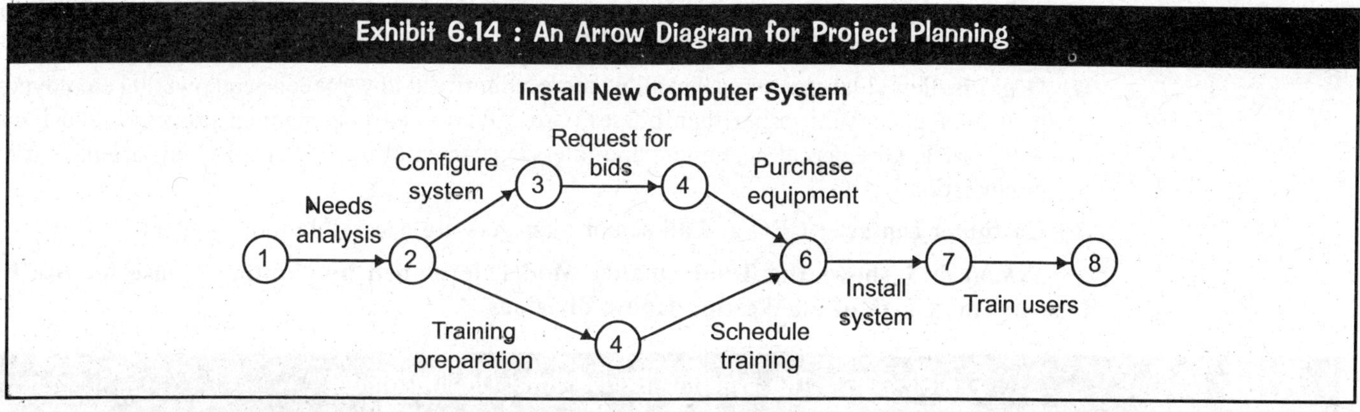

6.7 LEADERSHIP AND STRATEGIC PLANNING IN THE BALDRIGE CRITERIA

Category 1 of the 2009 Malcolm Baldrige National Quality Award Criteria for Performance Excellence is Leadership. It is the first of the seven categories, signifying the critical importance of leadership to business success. The criteria seek the following :

(i) Information about the company's senior leadership management style.

(ii) Information regarding how seniors build and sustain effective leadership system, set directions and guide the company and

(iii) Information regarding how the senior leaders project a strong customer focus, communicate values and expectations and review performance.

Reviewing company performance is a crucial aspect of leadership. Reviews help to build consistency behind goals and allocation of resources. Through their roles in developing strategy and reviewing performance, senior leaders develop leadership and create an organisation capable of adopting to changing opportunities and requirements.

Strategic planning is the focus of category 2. Customer-driven quality and operational performance excellence are key strategic business issues that need to be an integral part of overall company planning. Specifically, a strategic view of quality focusses on drivers of customer satisfaction, customer retention, new markets and market share – all key factors in competitiveness, profitability and business success. Operational performance improvement contributes to productivity growth and cost/price competitiveness.

Dr. Curt Reimann, who was the Director of the Malcolm Baldrige National Quality Award, summarised the characteristics of excellent leadership as follows :

(i) **Visible, committed and knowledgeable :** Leaders promote the emphasis on quality and know the details and how well the company is doing. They personally involve in education, training and recognition of employees. They are accessible to employees and have routine contact with employees, customers and suppliers.

(ii) **A missionary zeal :** The leaders are trying to effect as much change as possible through their suppliers, through the government and through any other vehicle that promotes quality. They are active in promotion of quality outside the company also.

(iii) **Aggressive targets :** Going beyond incremental improvement and looking at the possibility of long gains, getting the whole workforce and thinking about different processes – not just improving existing processes.

(iv) **Strong drivers :** Cycle time, zero defects, six-sigma or other targets to drive improvements, clearly defined customer satisfaction and quality improvement objectives.

(v) **Communication of values :** Effecting ***cultural change*** related to quality. Written policy, mission, guidelines and other documented statements of quality values or other bases for clear

and consistent communications. Developing a quality based organisational culture is a major task of managers who are excellent leaders.

(vi) **Organisation :** Flat structures that allow more authority at lower levels, empowering employees, managers as coaches rather than bosses. Cross-functional management processes and focus on internal and external customers and inter-departmental improvement teams are part of an organisation.

(vii) **Customer contact :** CEO and all senior managers are accessible to customers.

Exhibit 6.15 **shows the Total Quality Model developed by Westing House for use by divisional managers of all Westing House divisions.**

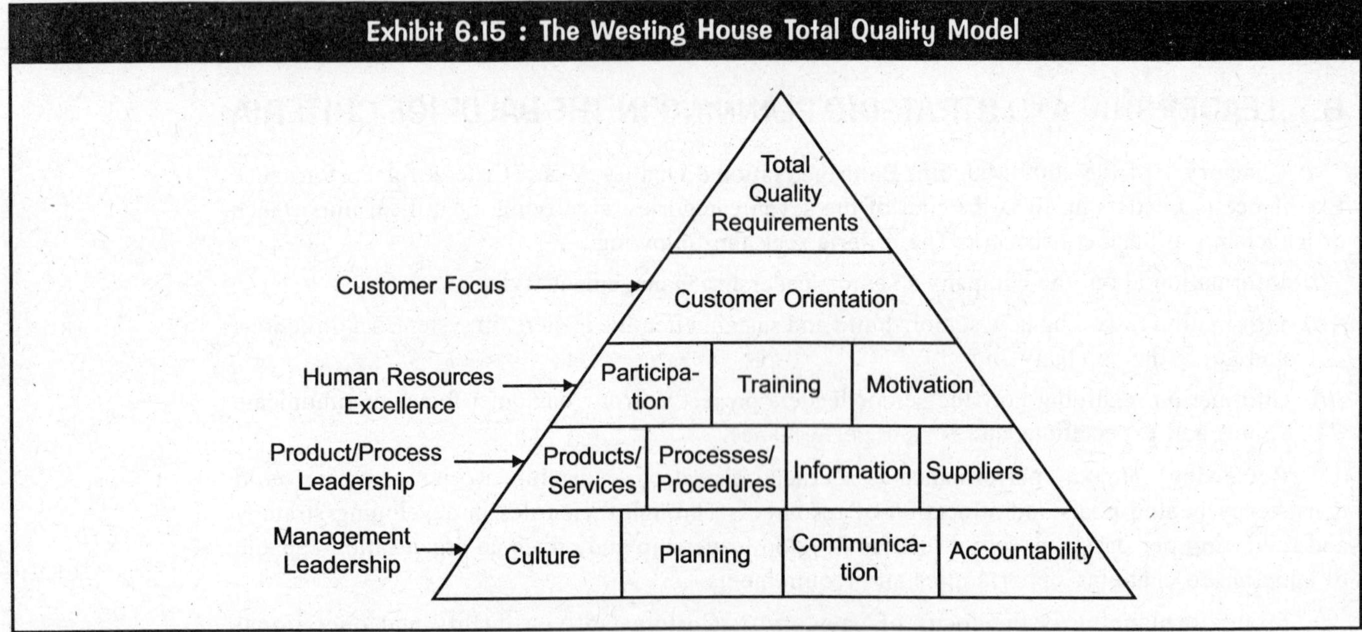

6.8 DEPLOYING A QUALITY CULTURE

"Culture" refers to the collection of beliefs, values, attitudes, manners, customs, behaviours and artifacts unique to the members of an organisation.

Culture is the pattern of shared belief and values that provides the members of an organisation rules of behaviour or accepted norms for conducting operations. It is the philosophies, ideologies, values, assumptions, beliefs, expectations, attitudes and norms that knit an organisation together and are shared by employees.

For example, **the basic beliefs of IBM are :**

(i) respect for the individual

(ii) best customer service and

(iii) pursuit of excellence.

In turn, these beliefs are operationalised in terms of strategy and customer values. Culture provides a framework to explain ***"the way things are done around here".***

Other examples of basic beliefs include :

Ford	→	Quality is job one
Delta	→	A family feeling
3M	→	Product innovation
Lincoln Electric	→	Wage proportion to productivity
McDonalds	→	Fast service, consistent quality.

Institutionalising strategy requires a culture that supports the strategy. For most organisations, a strategy based on TQM requires a significant change in the way people think. According to Jack Welch, the CEO of General Electric, "cultural change must be sweeping – not incremental change but quantum". **The quality experts or gurus agree on the need for a cultural or value system transformation, *for example,***

- Deming's calls for a transformation of the American Management style.
- Fiegenbaum's suggestion for a pervasive improvement throughout the organisation.
- Crosby's statement – Quality is the result of a carefully constructed culture; it has to be the fabric of the organisation".

In a survey of 615 business executives, 43 percent rated a ***change in corporate culture*** as an integrated part of improving quality. The needed change may be called by different names in different companies. *For example,* it is called ***"an innovative environment"*** in American Airlines, ***"the way people think"*** at Dupont and ***"Leadership through Quality"*** at Xerox.

Successful organisations have a central core culture around which the rest of the company revolves. An organisation must have a sound basis of ***core values*** into which management and other employees will be drawn. Without this central core, the members of the organisation will not have a fundamental criteria of relevance to guide them as they develop plans, make decisions, communicate and carry out operations, especially related to quality. Research has shown that quality means different things to different people and levels in the organisation. Employees tend to think like their peers and think differently from those at other levels. This suggests that organisations will have considerable difficulty in improving quality unless core values are embedded into the organisation.

Embedding a Culture of Quality

It is one thing for the top management to state a ***commitment to quality*** but quite another for this commitment to be accepted or embedded in the company. The basic vehicle for embedding on organisational culture is a teaching process in which desired behaviours and activities are learnt through experiences, symbols and explicit behaviour. The component of the total quality system provides the vehicles for change. ***Box 6.8* shows these components as well as other mechanisms of cultural change.**

Box 6.8 : Cultural Change Mechanisms

Focus	From traditional	To quality
Plan	Short-range budgets	Future strategic issues
Organise	Hierarchy chain of command	Participation/empowerment
Control	Variance reporting	Quality measures and information for self-control
Communication	Top down	Top down and bottom up
Decisions	Adhoc/crisis management	Planned change
Functional management	Parochial, competitive	Cross-functional, integrative
Quality management	Fixing/one-shot manufacturing	Preventive/continuous, all functions and processes

Above all, demonstration of commitment by the top management is essential. This commitment is demonstrated by the behaviours that are exhibited throughout the company. **Categories of behaviours include :**

(i) **Signalling :** Making statements or taking actions that support the vision of quality such as mission statements, creeds or charters directed towards customer satisfaction.

(ii) **Focus :** Every employee must know the mission, his or her part in it and what has to be done to achieve it. What management pays attention to and how they react to crisis is indicative of

this focus. When all functions and systems are aligned and when practice supports the culture, everyone is more likely to support the vision.

(iii) **Employee policies :** These may be the clearest expression of culture, at least from the viewpoint of the employees. A culture of quality can be demonstrated in such policies as the reward and promotion systems, status symbols and other human resources actions.

Exhibit 6.16 **illustrates the transition to a Quality Culture at Xerox.**

Exhibit 6.16 : Total Quality Transition

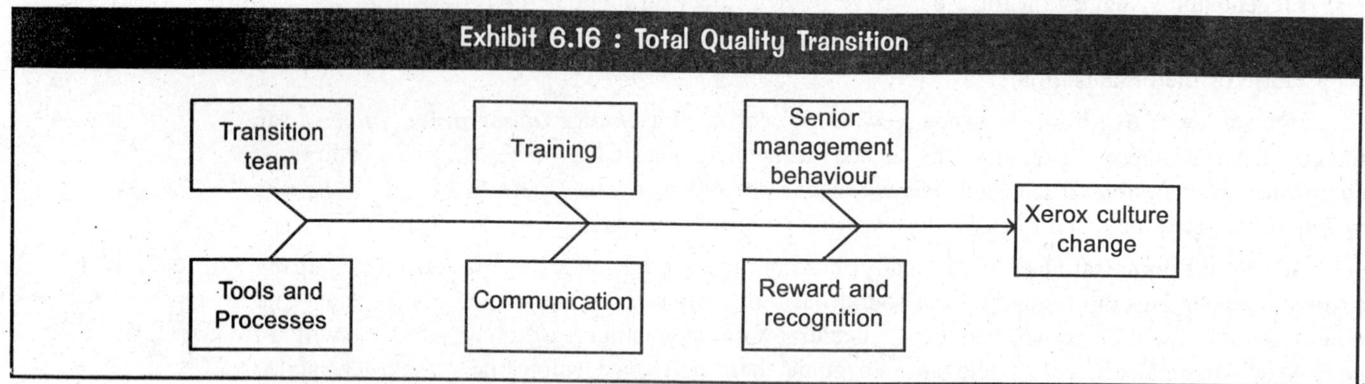

David T. Kearns, Chairman and CEO of Xerox Corporation wrote in an article for the academic journal *"Academy of Management Executive"*, describing the change at Xerox. "At the time ***Leadership-through-quality*** was introduced, I told our employees that ***customer satisfaction*** would be our top priority and that it would change the culture of the company. We redefined quality as meeting the requirements of our customers. It may have been the most significant strategy Xerox ever embarked on".

The management style and the role of the first-line management changed by cultural change at Xerox. The role of the first-line management was changed from that of the traditional dictatorial foreman to that of a supervisor functioning primarily as a coach or expeditor.

Technology and Culture

To become superior in quality, an organisation must pursue two courses of action :

(i) Developing technologies to create products and processes which meet customer needs, and

(ii) Stimulating a "culture" throughout the organisation that continually views quality as a primary goal. Since culture is not a technical issue, there are no techniques available for creating quality culture.

Quality culture can be "positive quality culture" or negative quality culture".

However, there are approaches that provide a path towards a quality culture.

Quality culture is defined as the pattern of human habits, beliefs and behaviour concerning quality. ***"While technology touches the head, culture touches the heart".***

Quality problems are mostly controllable by the management. Hence, cultural issues apply to all levels of management – top, middle and junior level and also the supervisors, technical specialists, business specialists and the work force.

A discussion on culture quickly moves into an examination of the actions necessary for change. Kinmann (1989) suggests that there are five tracks necessary for change *viz.,* ***culture, management skills, team building, strategy-structure*** **and the** ***reward system.*** **Peters and Waterman (1982) believe that seven factors are essential for change,** ***viz., shared values, strategy, systems, staffing, style, structure and skills*** **(the 7 'S' model) which is shown in** ***Exhibit 6.17.***

The three S's – **strategy, structure and systems** are called as **3 hard Ss** while the **remaining 4 Ss – staff, skills, styles and shared values** are called as **4 soft Ss.**

The 4 soft Ss supplement the 3 hard Ss. Organisations which blend the hard Ss with the soft Ss make TQM a dominant force within their culture. The three hard Ss alone will not be sufficient to establish success in the long run. Since TQM comes from the people, it is not possible to gain the benefits of TQM without the use of 4 soft Ss namely staff, skills, styles and shared values. Creativity, flexibility, teamwork, participation, continuous improvement and leadership are critical to the success of TQM.

Exhibit 6.17 : The 7 'S' Approach to TQM Culture

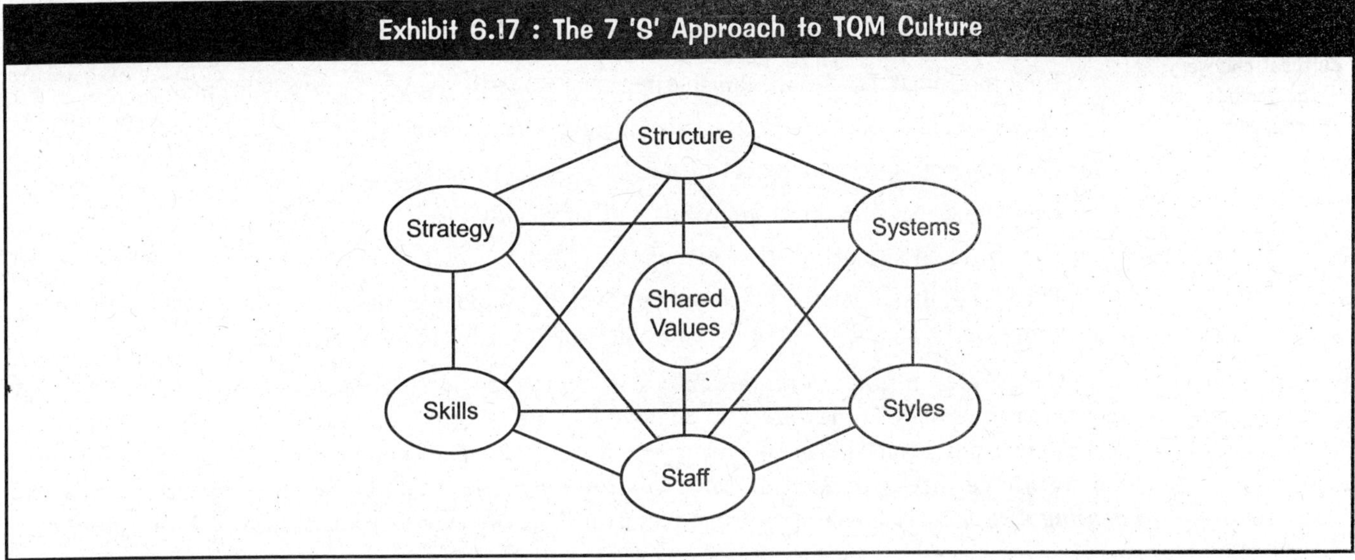

Quality culture can be ***"negative quality culture"*** or ***positive quality culture.*** While negative quality culture is characterised by "hide the scrap" – scenario, positive quality culture is characterised by "climb the ladders to delight the customer" – scenario.

Culture can be changed. We need to provide awareness of quality, evidence of top management leadership, self-development and empowerment, participation and recognition and rewards. These paths must be integrated with the methodologies and structure for quality. ***(See Exhibit 6.18).***

Exhibit 6.18 : Technology and Culture

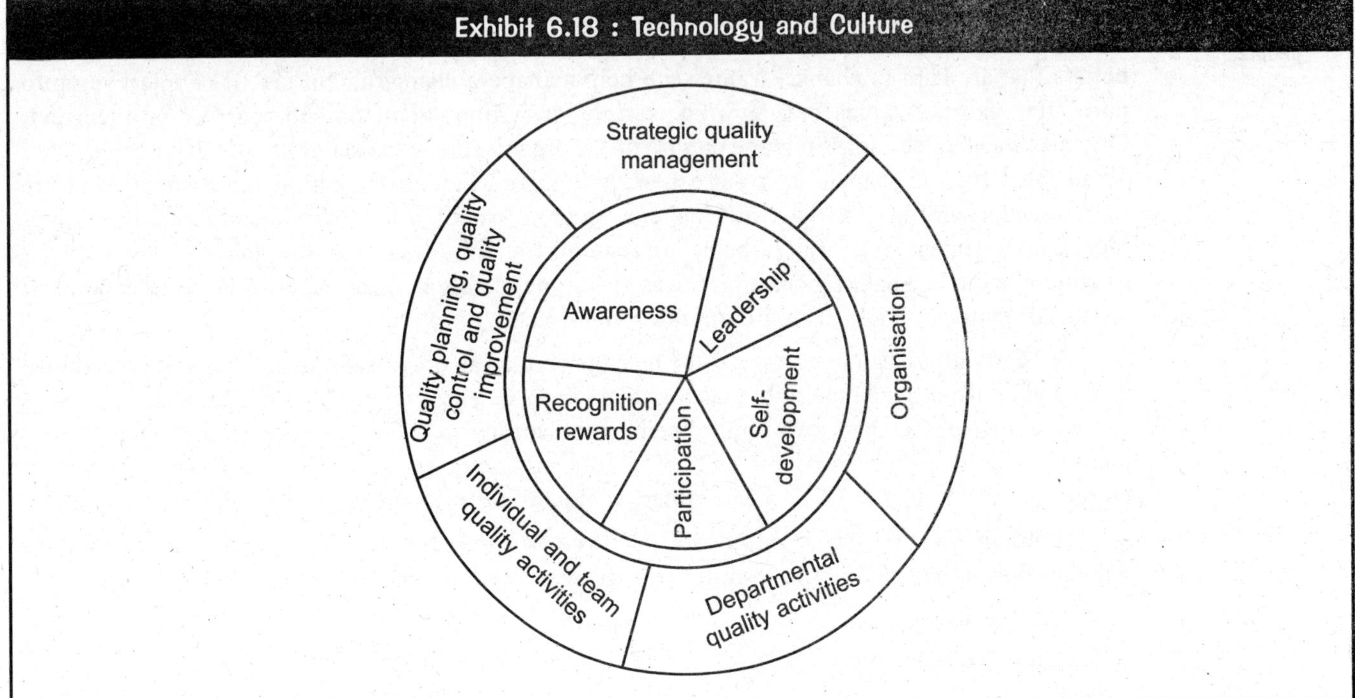

Resistance to cultural change. **People resist change for a number of reasons. Some reasons to resist culture changes are :**

People resist cultural change for various reasons.

- People fear that the change will affect their usual way of working.
- They perceive that they will lose control over things.
- They feel uncertain about their ability to live upto the expectations of others.
- They feel that change may mean more work for them.
- They resist change because of their past resentments against the management.
- They think that TQM will vanish after some time like several other concepts.
- They have an attitude – "TQM will fade away if ignored".
- They are not willing to accept ownership and feel committed.
- They think that it is the responsibility of somebody else.
- They have an attitude – "first you change, then I will."
- They think that others will find out that what they (people) have been doing over the years is wrong and hence they (people) could be penalised for their misdeeds.

Corporate Culture : Corporate culture is represented by a set of values that guide the decisions of a company's staff as they work to achieve its objectives. Corporate cultures develop from the basic philosophies embedded in the management of the company coupled with managerial behaviour. **Corporate culture is defined as *"the way the majority of employees in a company act when dealing with their customers and suppliers as well as the way they behave towards one another."***

6.9 DEVELOPING CULTURE FOR TQM

A "TQM culture" can be created if the management of an organisation starts learning the values of its people.

Many traditional Indian companies portray the old culture which is not exactly geared up for TQM. This is indicated by symptoms such as poor lay-out design, untidy manufacturing areas, uncared for service facilities, poor lighting and environmental conditions. In addition, the managerial behaviour may be erratic with focus on achieving short-term results. To managers, ends are more important than means. The negative and out-moded cultures need to be changed for effective implementation of TQM.

Values and Culture : Values are the building blocks of a culture. Values are stable long-term beliefs that are hard to change. Values can help manage a change in culture, if people live up to particular values. Values define what is right or wrong, good or bad, correct or incorrect. Organisational values constitute the culture of the organisations, the set of beliefs that people share about what sort of behaviour is correct or wrong. The factors indicating pre-dominant culture within a company may include atmsophere, ethos, spirit of teamwork, warmth and friendship, ideals, management style, way of behaving with others, attitudes towards employees, involvement of employees, telephone response, promises kept, type of communication, criteria for selection and appraisal, motivation and shared corporate values etc.

A TQM culture can be created if the management of an organisation starts learning the values of its people. To promote the right value system which is sensitive to TQM, managers have to learn to treat employees as their own family members. Learning to value the workers as human beings, learning to value people as people and not merely paid workers is a major step towards creating a culture for TQM. ***Box 6.9*** **lists the requisite changes to implement quality culture.**

Building a TQM culture requires a solid and well executed strategy. TQM implementation depends upon organisation's philosophy, will and size. 12 dimensions of TQM culture identified are:

(i) Striving for excellence
(ii) Customer focus
(iii) Employee orientation
(iv) Sense of direction
(v) Fact-based decision making
(vi) Continuous improvement

(vii) Collaboration
(viii) Open communication
(ix) Empowerment of employees
(x) Rewards and recognition
(xi) Training and development and
(xii) Corporate citizenship.

Box 6.9 : Requisite Changes to Implement Quality Culture

From traditional culture	To TQM culture
• Hierarchical style	• Participation style
• Top down information flow	• Top down, lateral and upward information flow
• Inward quality focus	• Customer defined quality focus
• Functional focus	• Process focus
• Short-term planning	• A vision for the future
• Episodic improvements	• Comprehensive/continuous improvements
• Top down initiatives	• All staff involved and engaged
• Manage and delegate	• Lead and coach
• Direct	• Empower
• Counsel	• Ownership and participation
• Functional and narrow scope of jobs	• Integrated functions
• Enforcement	• Promoting mutual trust
• Fire fighting with few individuals/group	• Team initiatives for group focussing on continuous improvement.

Steps involved in creating TQM culture

Step 1 : Instituting Management accountability and a deep sense of responsibility towards employees : Management should provide a forum to employees to employ their brainpower for creative thinking and to present their ideas openly without any inhibition or fear. Management should develop systems and procedures that demonstrate to employees that the management values their contributions.

Step 2 : Instituting Management's thought and actions towards delighting its customers : Companies should strive to provide products and services to customers beyond expected quality. A quality culture must be evolved where complaints and warranty claims are treated as opportunities for improvement, a culture that excites or delights customers by doing things beyond what is expected by them. The management should begin to demonstrate a customer-oriented philosophy.

Step 3 : Removing organisational boundaries and internal competition : No department, section or division of a company has exclusive rights over the customer. Management should encourage and reward cooperative efforts among departments and individuals.

Step 4 : Using fact-based decision making : Practice of ***"management by fact"*** is important in a TQM culture. Everyone should be encouraged to use ***seven simple problem solving tools*** for decision making.

Step 5 : Use of Kaizen – continuous improvement must be encouraged : Gradual, small and ***continuous improvements*** are advocated in TQM culture rather than ***"great leap forward"*** or ***"breakthrough improvements"*** **or** ***innovations.***

Step 6 : Do not use specially designed organisation structure for TQM : The organisations may sometimes create a ***quality assurance department,*** steering committees, quality councils, advising groups, facilitators etc. TQM may cause a change in the structure of a management, but the change should occur as a result of an examination of the change process, not as a result of adopting TQM.

It was discussed earlier in this section that we need to provide **awareness of quality, evidence of top management leadership, self-development and empowerment, participation and recognition and rewards,** which are the paths that must be integrated with the methodologies and structure for quality. These paths are discussed in detail in the following paragraphs.

(i) Create and Maintain Awareness of Quality

To ensure development of a quality culture and action on quality, the starting point is to create and disseminate information on the current state of quality. Often this information provides dramatic evidence of a serious quality problem, provides ***"proof of the need"*** and prepares the way for presenting a program of action. Two important issues in presenting this evidence are the language used and the content of the information.

To create awareness, we need to present information in different languages for different people in the organisation. ***Exhibit 6.19*** **depicts the people and different languages to be used to present information to them.**

Exhibit 6.19 : Common Languages in the Company

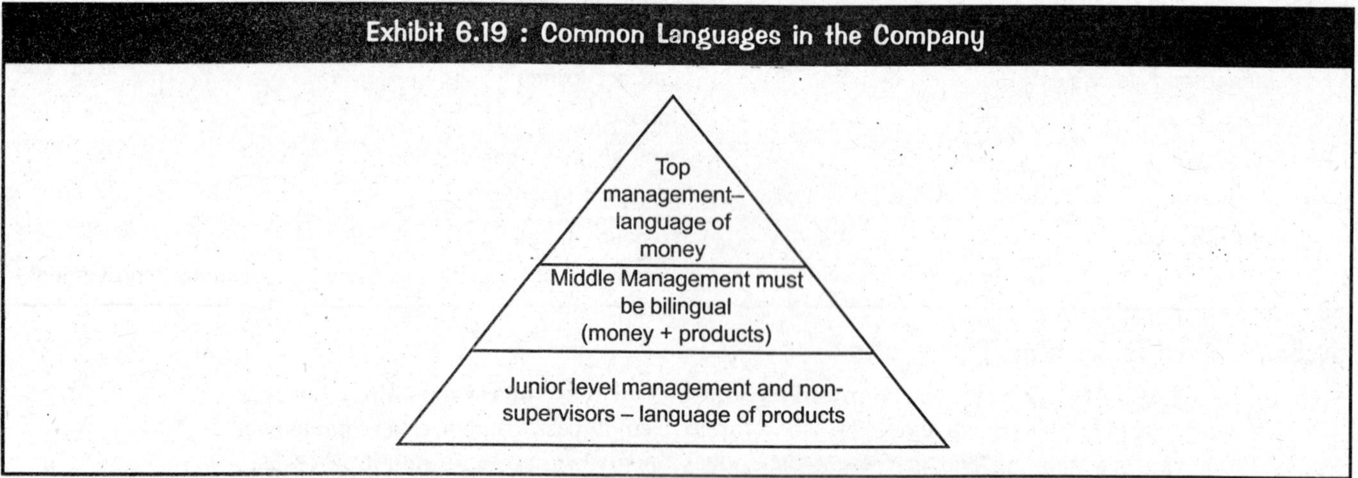

Language of money means highlighting threats to sales income or opportunities for cost reduction and quality is related to these factors. At middle management and junior management levels, the impact of quality is directly into the language of job security.

(ii) Providing Evidence of Management Leadership

Commitment to total quality by the top management is not enough. To inspire the employees, it is crucial that the top management exhibit **leadership on quality** and show evidence to prove the same.

Eight key tasks identified under role of top management are :

(i) Establishing and serving in a Quality Council *(ii)* Establishing quality policies

(iii) Establishing and deploying quality goals *(iv)* Providing the necessary resources

(v) Providing problem-oriented training.

(vi) Serving on top management quality improvement teams

(vii) Simulating improvement and *(viii)* Providing for reward and recognition.

The above activities take about 10 percent of the time of top management personnel. Establishing **"proof of the need"** is necessary to convince the top management to devote 10 percent of their precious time on these tasks. When top management spends time on these activities, it provides the evidence of leadership that inspires others to follow. In some organisations, top management personnel visibly participate as leaders in quality training programs and also in quality improvement teams.

(iii) Provide for Self-development and Empowerment

Inspiring people to take positive steps on quality is greatly influenced by the nature of the work performed by those people. The activities in any organisation can be viewed as a set of inter-dependent functions that produce goods or services. The three roles played by people in an organisation are : supplier, processor and customer. These roles are executed by individuals at each stage of a process. Each stage is a supplier to the subsequent stage and also a customer of previous stage.

Self-control and job design : People must be provided with knowledge of what they are supposed to do, feedback on their performance and the means of regulating their work in the event that they are failing to meet the goals. The lack of one or more of these three elements means that quality problems are management controllable (generally 80 percent of quality problems are management controllable). Workers should be placed in a **state of self-control** before using behavioural approaches to motivate them.

Job design helps in providing jobs that are more meaningful and satisfying to workers. ***Box 6.10*** **shows job characteristics and actions needed to enrich the jobs.**

Approaches to ***redesign*** of jobs take several forms of job enlargement. In ***horizontal job enlargement,*** the scope of a job is increased by having workers be responsible for tasks previously performed by others vertically higher in the organisation (*e.g.* a supervisor).

Empowerment : ***Empowerment*** is the process of delegating decision-making authority to lower levels within the organisation. Empowering workers means encouraging them to take initiative and broaden their scope by delegating authority and providing additional training to them.

Box 6.10 : Job Enrichment Characteristics and Management Actions

Characteristics	Definitions	Action
Skill variety	Degree to which the job has a sufficient variety of activities to require diversified employee skills and talents	Combine sequential tasks to produce larger work modules (horizontal job enlargement)
Task identity	Extent to which work requires doing a job from beginning to end and results in completed visible unit of output	Arrange work into meaningful groups *e.g.* by customer, by product
Task significance	Extent to which the job impacts internal and external customers contact with customer	Provide means of direct communication and personal
Autonomy	Amount of employee self-control in planning and doing the work (vertical enlargement)	Provide employee greater self-control for decision making
Feedback	Degree to which direct knowledge of results is provided to the employee	Create feedback systems to provide employees information directly from doing the job

When employees are empowered in their work, they have the feeling of ownership and responsibility. The act of empowerment provides evidence of management's trust in employees. In addition to empowering the employees, management may also share confidential business information with employees which is clearly a change in the culture.

The concept of empowerment is applicable to both individuals and to groups of workers. ***"Self-managed teams"*** provide an example of empowerment for a group of employees.

Establishing company quality goals and deploying them as subgoals and activities throughout the organisation is part of strategic quality management. Clear quality goals for individuals are important stimuli for inspiring superiority in quality.

Selection and training of personnel have an important influence on people's development. The Japanese have invested extensively in selection and training. Interviews and testing prior to employment assure compatibility of the candidate and the job.

(iv) Provide Participation as a Means of Inspiring Action

By personally participating in quality activities, people acquire new knowledge, see the benefits of the quality disciplines and obtain a sense of accomplishment by solving problems. The participation leads to lasting changes in behaviour. **The various kinds of participation are listed in the *Table 6.1.***

Participation at all levels is decisive in inspiring action on quality.

Table 6.1 : Forms of Participation of Employees

Form	Description	Level			
		Top Management	Middle Management	Specialist	First-line Supervisors/ workers
Quality Council	Serve on the council	✓	✗	✗	✗
Quality improvement teams	Serve as a leader or member of a cross-functional improvement team	✓	✓	✓	✓
Quality Circles	Serve as a leader or member of a circle within the department	✗	✓	✓	✓
Quality task forces	Serve on quality task forces appointed by the Quality Council	✓	✓	✓	✓
Process owner	Serve as owner of a business process	✓	✓	✗	✗
Design review	Participate in design review meetings	✗	✓	✓	✗
Process review	Participate in process review meetings	✗	✓	✓	✓
Provide planning	Identify obstacles of self-control	✗	✓	✓	✓
Set quality goals	Provide input or set goals	✓	✓	✓	✓
Plan own work	Handle all aspects of planning	✓	✓	✓	✓
Customer visits	Hold discussions on quality with customers	✓	✓	✓	✓
Supplier visits	Hold discussions on quality with suppliers	✓	✓	✓	✓
Meeting with management	Make presentations on quality activities	✗	✓	✓	✓
Visit other companies	Learn about quality activities	✓	✓	✓	✓
Job rotation	Work in the Quality Department or other departments	✓	✓	✓	✓
Conferences	Make presentations or chair sessions	✓	✓	✓	✗

(v) Provide Recognition and Rewards

"Recognition" is defined as public acknowledgement of superior performance of specific activities. **"Rewards"** are benefits (such as salary increases, bonuses and promotions) which are conferred for generally superior performance against goals. Recognition and rewards play an important role in inspiring people on quality. People develop positive feeling internally when their job has been designed to focus on self-development and also when they are given opportunities to participate in planning and decision making. This tells employees that their skills, their judgement and their integrity are trusted by the management. For instance, workers feel happy when independent inspection is changed to self-inspection. Recognition through public acknowledgement of superior performance can be provided at individuals, teams or business units levels.

Forms of recognition : Forms of recognition may vary from a simple verbal message of appreciation for a job well done to modest or token awards. Awards may be tangible (*e.g.*, a savings bond, time off, a dinner) or intangible (a letter of appreciation, sending an employee to attend a seminar or conference). In deciding on forms of recognition, managers should invite suggestions from respected work force employees. Not only will their ideas fit the culture better, but also the act of asking for suggestion shows recognition of their judgement.

6.10 ORGANISATIONAL CULTURE AND ETHICS

One of the greatest obstacles faced by organisations attempting to implement total quality is the cultural barrier. In many organisations inspite of doing an excellent job of committing to total quality, involving employees in all aspects of quality planning and implementation and providing the training needed to ensure that employees have the necessary skills, their efforts to implement total quality fall flat because of ***organisational inertia.*** No effort has been made to overcome the comfort employees at all levels feel in doing things the way they have always been done. No effort has been made to change the ***organisation's culture.***

What is Quality Culture?

To understand what a quality culture is, one must first understand the concept of organisational culture. An organisation's culture is the everyday manifestation of its underlying values and traditions. It shows up in how employees behave on the job, their expectations of the organisation and each other and how employees approach their jobs. **The elements of an organisation's culture are: *(i)* Business environment, *(ii)* Organisation values, *(iii)* Cultural role models, *(iv)* Organisational rites, rituals and customs and *(v)* Cultural transmitters.** The business environment in which an organisation must operate is a critical determinant of its culture. In a highly competitive business environment that changes rapidly and continually, organisations are likely to develop a ***change oriented culture.***

A quality culture is an organisational value system that results in an environmental and continual improvement of quality It consists of values, traditions, procedures and expectations that promote quality.

Organisational values describe what the organisation thinks is important. Adherence to these values in synonymous with success. Consequently, an organisation's values are the heart and soul of its culture.

Cultural role models are employees at any level who represent the organisation's values. They serve as living examples of what the organisation wants its employees to be.

Organisational rites, rituals and customs express the organisation's unwritten rules about how things are done. How employees dress, interact with each other and approach their work are all part of this element of an organisation's culture.

Cultural transmitters are the vehicles by which an organisation's culture is passed down through successive generations of employees. Examples of cultural transmitters are: grapevine, organisation's symbol, slogans and recognition ceremonies.

What an organisation truly values will show up in the behaviour of employees. An organisation's culture is its value system as manifested in organisational behaviour.

A quality culture is an organisational value system that results in an environment and continual improvement of quality. It consists of values, traditions, procedures and expectations that promote quality.

***Box 6.11* lists the characteristics shared by organisations with a quality culture.**

Box 6.11 : Characteristics Shared by Organisations with a Quality Culture

1. Behaviour matches slogans.
2. Customer input is actively sought and used to continually improve quality.
3. Employees are both involved and empowered.
4. Work is done in teams.
5. Responsibility for quality is not delegated.
6. Sufficient resources are made available where and when they are needed to ensure the continuous improvement of quality.
7. Education and training are provided to ensure that employees at all levels have the knowledge and skills needed to continually improve quality.
8. Reward and promotion systems are based on contributions to the continuous improvement of quality.
9. Fellow employees are viewed as internal customers and
10. Suppliers are treated as partners in business.

Activating Cultural Change

It is impossible to implement total quality without creating a quality culture. Successful total quality requires cultural change.

Organisations in which the prevailing culture is based on traditional management practices are not likely to succeed in the implementation of total quality. **It is impossible to implement total quality without creating a quality culture.** Successful total quality requires ***cultural change.*** Reasons for cultural change to precede or occur simultaneously with the implementation of total quality are:

(i) ***Change cannot occur in a hostile environment:*** The total quality approach to doing business may be radically different from what management and employees are used to. Managers may not feel comfortable with the concept of employee involvement and empowerment. Employees who are used to compete against their colleagues for promotions and wage increases may not be open to mutually supportive internal partnerships and teamwork. Such situations can create an environment which is hostile toward change, even if the change is highly desirable. Even if people want change, it will be difficult in a hostile environment to implement change.

(ii) ***Moving to total quality takes time:*** In a conversion to total quality, positive results are rarely achieved in the short run. Therefore non believers and people who are averse to change have an opportunity to demonstrate their opposition to implementing total quality.

(iii) ***It can be difficult to overcome the past:*** If the organisation culture is such that employees are not serious about management's change and improvement initiatives in the past and then let them die, then, they will remember their past attitudes and extend the same approach to the implementation of total quality also. Therefore such an attitude of employees can be most difficult to change or overcome.

Leadership has a major responsibility in initiating/activating organisational change to establish a quality culture. Sometimes it may become necessary to change the leadership inorder to change the organisational culture. As the senior managers are most likely to have resistance to change, the CEO of the organisation must be the key player in changing the organisational culture. **The following are the requirements to be met by the senior executives of an organisation in order to bring about organisational change to implement total quality:**

(i) Current leaders must be fully knowledgeable of the need to change and the ramification of not changing.

(ii) Current leaders must be able to articulate a vision for the new organisation.

(iii) Current leaders must set the tone for change and establish an organisation-wide sense of urgency.

(iv) Current leaders must be willing to remove all obstacles to cultural change.

(vi) Current leaders must be willing to empower employees at all levels in the organisation to make cultural change.

Understanding the "laws of organisational change" is the foundation for quality culture.

Laying the Groundwork for a Quality Culture

According to Peter Schotles, laying the ground work for quality culture should begin by developing an understanding of the "laws of organisational change". These laws are:

(i) ***Understand the history behind the current culture:*** Policies, traditions and other aspects of the existing culture that now seem questionable may have been put in place for good reason in the past and under different circumstances. Therefore it is necessary to understand the reasons for the existing culture before trying to change it.

(ii) ***Don't tamper with systems - improve them:*** Tampering with existing systems is not the same as improving them. Tampering occurs when changes are made without understanding why a given system works the way it does and without understanding what needs to be changed and why.

(iii) ***Be prepared to listen and observe:*** It is quite natural for people to resist change in any organisation. Therefore it is important to pay attention to both people and systems rather than trying to change the system alone. Managers must be prepared to listen and observe, try to hear what is being said and observe what is not being said. Employees who are listened to are more likely to participate in changes than those who are not.

(iv) ***Involve everyone affected by change in making it:*** Resisting change is normal behaviour of people. People don't like being changed. It is impossible to implement change when people feel that changes are being imposed on them. Therefore the most effective way to ensure that employees will go along with changes is to involve them in planning and implementing the changes. They must be given opportunities to express their concerns and fears.

Knowing the laws of organisational change and understanding the characteristics of organisations that have strong quality cultures is important to any executive team that hopes to change the culture of its organisation. ***Box 6.12*** **lists the characteristics of organisations having strong quality cultures.**

Box 6.12 : Characteristics of Organisations Having Strong Quality Cultures

(i) Widely shared philosophy of management.

(ii) Emphasis on the importance of human resources to the organisation.

(iii) Ceremonics to celebrate organisational events/achievements.

(iv) Recognition and rewards for successful employees.

(v) Effective internal network for communicating the culture.

(vi) Informal rules of behaviour.

(vii) Strong value system.

(viii) High standards for performance.

(ix) Definite organisational character.

Overcoming Resistance to Change

Change is resisted in any organisation because resistance to change is a normal inherent organisational behaviour. But continuous improvement requires continuous change. Therefore,

Resistant to change is a normal inherent organisational behaviour.

managers should be effective change agents or catalysts for change. However to be an effective change agent, one must understand why change is resisted. Any organisation has two separate cultures relating to change: ***the advocates and the resisters.***

Exhibit 6.20 **shows these two separate cultures.**

Exhibit 6.20 : A Classic Confrontation: Irrestible versus Immovable Object

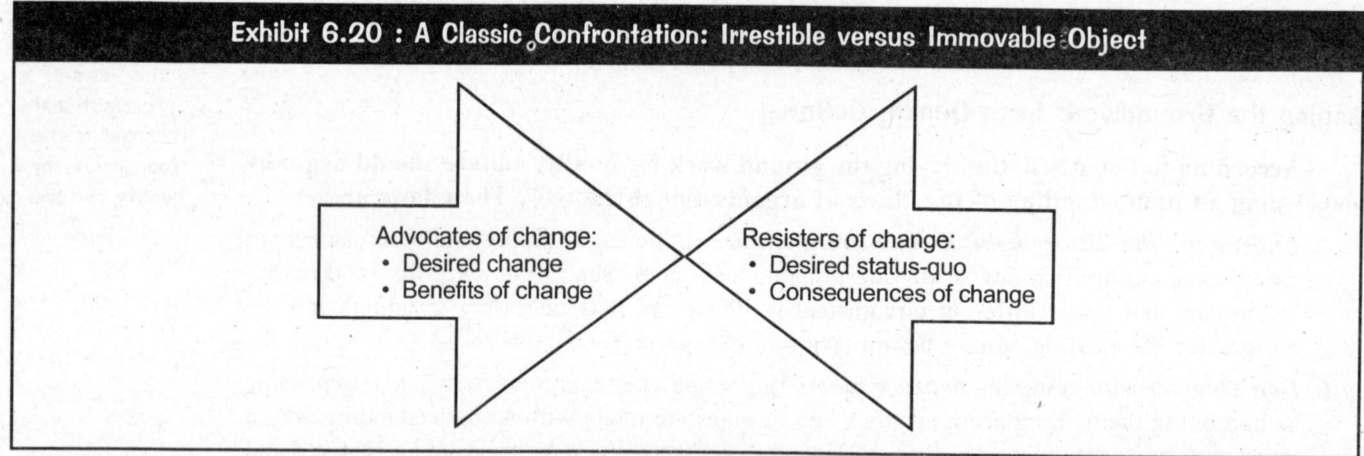

Two separate cultures relating to changes are *(i)* advocates and *(ii)* resisters.

Advocates focus on the anticipated benefits of the change while the resisters focus on perceived threats to their status, beliefs, habits and security. Advocates and resisters can have different perceptions of the same proposed change, *for example,* a proposed change to automate production processes may be viewed as a means of improving productivity by advocates, but as a threat to job security by resisters.

The responsibility for facilitating change necessarily falls to its advocates. Three broad steps in facilitating change are:

Step 1. Begin with a new advocacy paradigm.

Step 2. Understand the concerns of potential resisters and

Step 3. Implement change promoting strategies.

These steps are briefly discussed in the following paragraphs:

Three broad steps in facilitating change are: *(i)* Beginning with a new advocacy paradigm. *(ii)* Understanding the concerns of potential resisters and *(iii)* Implementing change promoting strategies.

Step 1. Begin with a New Advocacy Paradigm: The first step in facilitating change is to adopt a facilitating paradigm. **If change is to take place, advocates must ask such questions as the following:**

(i) Who will be affected by this change and how?

(ii) How will the change be perceived by those it affects?

(iii) How can the conoerns of those affected be alleviated?

Step 2. Understand Concerns of Potential Resisters: The second step is to understand the concerns of potential resisters and be empathetic towards them. **People resist change for the following reasons:**

(i) ***Fear:*** People fear the unknown. They assume worst consequences of change which are further compounded by rumours.

(ii) ***Loss of control:*** Change can threaten the sense of security which people have over 'their life'. Change can cause people to feel as if they are losing control of their lives, jobs, areas of responsibility etc.

(iii) ***Uncertainty:*** People like to know where they stand and they don't like uncertainty about what will happen after change.

(iv) ***More work:*** Change sometimes means more work, at least in the beginning. Also this concern include work in the form of learning new skills, knowing more information, working for longer hours and the like.

Step 3. Implement change-promoting strategies: There are strategies that require an advocacy paradigm and take into account the concerns people have when confronted with change. Some of the strategies recommended by Juran for handling and overcoming resistance to change are:

(i) ***Involve potential resisters*** in planning for change and help them to develop a sense of ownership in the change.

(ii) ***Avoid surprises*** – Even though change is by and large unpredictable, it is better to bring potential resisters into the process from the outset rather than surprising them.

(iii) ***Move slowly at first*** – To gain the support of potential resisters, it is necessary to let them evaluate the proposed change, express their concerns, weigh the expected results and find ways to alleviate problems, even if it takes time.

(iv) ***Start small and be flexible*** – Change will be more readily accepted if advocates start in a low key and are flexible enough to revise strategies that are not working as planned.

(v) ***Create a positive environment*** – The environment in which change takes place is determined by reward and recognition systems and examples set by managers. Well-thought-out, sincere attempts to make improvements should be recognised and rewarded even when they fail. This approach will create a positive environment that is conducive to change.

(vi) ***Incorporate the change*** – Change will be more readily accepted if it can be incorporated into the existing organisational culture.

(v) ***Respond quickly and positively:*** When potential resisters raise questions or express concerns, advocates should respond quickly and positively. A quick response can often eliminate the concern before it becomes a problem and it will show employees that their concerns are considered important.

(vi) ***Work with established leaders:*** Change requires the support of people who are regarded as leaders - those in leadership positions or informal leaders by virtue of their experience or superior knowledge and skills. The best way to get their support is to involve them in planning for change from the outset.

(ix) ***Treat people with dignity and respect:*** All aspects of total quality require this strategy. It requires behaviour that acknowledges the human resource as the organisation's most valuable resource.

(x) ***Be constructive:*** Change is not made simply for the sake of change. It is made for the sake of continuous improvement. It should be broached constructively from the perspective of how it will bring about improvements.

6.11 ESTABLISHING A QUALITY CULTURE

Establishing a quality culture involves specific planning and activities in every business or department. Steps involved are:

Establishing a quality culture involves specific planning and activities in every business or department.

1. **Identify the Changes Needed:** An organisations culture dictates how people in it behave, respond to problems and interact with each other. If the existing culture is a quality culture, it will have the following characteristics:
   - Open, continual communication
   - Mutually supportive internal partnerships
   - Teamwork approach to problems and processes
   - Obsession with continual improvement
   - Broad-based employee improvement and empowerment
   - Sincere desire for customer input and feedback.

   It is required to assess whether the organisation's culture have these characteristics. The best way is to prepare a questionnaire and involve the entire workforce from bottom to top in a systematic assessment that is stratified by level (*i.e.,* executive management, middle management, first-line employee, etc.).

2. **Put the Planned Change in Writing:** A comprehensive assessment of an organisation's existing culture will usually identify improvements that need to be made. These improvements will require changes in the status-quo.

3. **Develop a Plan for Making the Changes:** The plan for effecting change is developed according to the who-what-when-where-how model. Each of these elements represents a major section of the plan, as follows:

   - **Who** will be affected by the change? **Who** will be involved in order for the change to succeed? **Who** is likely to challenge the change?
   - **What** tasks must be accomplished? **What** are the most likely barriers? **What** are the related processes and procedures that will be affected by the change?
   - **When** should the change be implemented? When should progress be measured? **When** should the various tasks associated with the change be accomplished? **When** should implementation be completed?
   - **Where** will the change be implemented? **Where** are the people and processes that will be affected?
   - **How** should the change be made? **How** will it affect existing people and processes? **How** will it improve quality, productivity and competitiveness?

   The plan should contain all five elements and each element should be comprehensively dealt with.

4. **Understand the Emotional Transition Process:** Advocates of the change will play key roles in its implementation. The success of the implementation will depend to a large extent on how well advocates play their roles. It is essential that they understand the emotional transition people go through when forced to deal with change, particularly unwanted change.

   The transition consists of seven steps: ***shock, denial, realisation, acceptance, rebuilding, understanding*** **and** ***recovery.*** People who confront a change they don't want to make may have to go through all seven steps in the transition. Advocates should understand this and proceed accordingly.

5. **Identify Key People and Make them Advocates:** Key people are those who can facilitate and those who can inhibit implementation of the change. These people should be identified, brought together, and given the plan. Advocates and inhibitors should be given opportunities to state their cases: All concerns should be recorded and dealt with. Executive managers must use their judgement in applying the right amount of the carrot, the stick and peer pressure (from advocates) to turn inhibitors into advocates.

6. **Take a "Hearts and Minds" Approach:** Advocates should be conscious of human nature as they work to implement change. On an intellectual level, people may understand and even agree with the reasons behind a change. But understanding intellectually is not enough. People tend to react to change more on an emotional (hearts) level than on an intellectual (minds) level, at least initially. Therefore, it is important to take time to deal with the inevitable emotional response that occurs in the early stage of implementation.

   Frequent, open communication-preferably face-to-face is the best strategy. Advocates should allow even the most negative opponents to voice their concerns and objections in open forums. Then these concerns should be answered in an objective, patient, non-defensive manner. When the majority of employees accept the change, critical mass will set in and peer pressure will begin to work on the side of the advocates.

7. **Apply Courtship Strategies:** Courtship is a phase in a relationship that moves slowly but deliberately toward a desired end. During the courtship, the partner hoping to move the

relationship forward listens carefully to the other partner and patiently responds to any concerns expressed. This partner is on his or her best behaviour. If advocates think of their relationship with potential resisters as a courtship, they will be better able to bring them along and eventually win them over.

8. **Support, Support and Support:** This final strategy is critical. It means that the material, moral, and emotional support needed by the people undergoing change should be provided. Undergoing change is a lot like walking a tight-rope for the first time. Planning is important. Communication is critical. But support is essential.

Quality Management and Ethics

It is universally agreed that all business practices in the modern workplace should be above reproach with regard to **ethical behaviour**. Few people are willing to defend unethical behaviour. Business and industry operate within the scope of acceptable legal and ethical standards. Ethical behaviour is particularly important in a total quality setting in which trust, integrity, and values figure prominently in everyday human interactions.

Ethics is a an individual or an organisation's adherence to a belief or documented code of conduct that is based on moral principles and tries to balance what is fair for individuals with what is right for society.

Managing ethical behaviour is one of the most pervasive and complex problems facing business organisations today. Employee's decisions to behave ethically or unethically are influenced by a myriad of individual and situational factors. Background, personality, decision history, managerial philosophy, and reinforcement are but a few of the factors which have been identified by researchers as determinants of employee behaviour when faced with ethical dilemmas.

Ethics is a body of principles or standards of human conduct that govern the behaviour of individuals and organisations. It is knowing what is right thing to do and is learnt when a person is growing up or at a later date during an organisation's ***ethics training program.***

Quality and ethics have a common premise, which is **"to do right things right"**. Ethics can mean something different to different people especially given an organisation's multinational workforce and the varying cultural norms. Because individuals have different concepts of what is right and what is wrong, the organisation will have to develop the ethical standards or code of ethics for the organisation and its employees to follow and practice.

The terms ***conscience, morality, loyalty, trust, values, responsibility*** **and** ***integrity*** are often associated with the term **"ethics"**. Ethics can be viewed as the study of **'morality'**. Morality refers to the **values** that are subscribed to and fostered by society in general and by individuals within society. **Ethical behaviour** is that which falls within the limits prescribed by morality. The concepts of trust, responsibility and integrity are part of the value system of total quality.

The terms conscience, morality, trust, values, responsibility and integrity are often associated with the term "ethics".

Ethical Behaviour: The concepts of legal and ethical are not the same. Just because a choice made is legal, does not necessarily mean it is ethical. A person's behaviour can be well within the prescribed limits of the law and still be unethical.

A person's ethics are influenced by his or her morality – core values and belief that act as a guide when formulating courses of action. Ethics can be more clearly understood when compared with behaviours governed by laws and by free choice. Human behaviour falls into three categories: *(i)* Domain codified by law (legal standard), *(ii)* Domain of ethics (social standard), and *(iii)* Domain of free choice (personal standard).

The area of ethics lies between the domain of codified law and the domain of free choice. In the domain of codified law, obedience is to laws prescribed by the legal system. In the domain of free choice, obedience is strictly to one-self. In the domain of ethics, there are no specific laws, yet it does have standards of conduct based on shared principles and values about moral conduct that guide an individual or company.

Ethical Dilemma: Because ethical standards are not codified, disagreements and dilemmas about proper behaviour often occur. Ethics might be defined as ***doing the right thing right the first***

time. If there were no agreements on what is the "right thing", then the issue of ethical behaviour of managers would be far less controversial. It is difficult to define what is the right thing because there are so many different bases of ethics. A decision involving ethics usually is made in the context that some one will be hurt and harmed is some way by the decision. *For example,* is it ethical to fire some one who has worked for a company for many years and is near retirement?

An **ethical dilemma** arises in a situation when each alternative choice or behaviour is undesirable because of potentially harmful ethical consequences. Right or wrong cannot be clearly identified. Most ethical dilemmas involve a conflict between the needs of the part and the whole- the individual versus the organisation or the organisation versus society as a whole.

Factors that Influence Ethical Behaviour

Three personality measures that can influence a person's ethical behaviour are:
(i) ego strength
(ii) machiavellianism and
(iii) locus of control.

Managers in a total quality setting need to understand the factors that can influence a person's behaviour. Research indicates that ethical behaviour in organisations is influenced by both individual and social factors. Three personality measures that can influence a person's ethical behaviour are: *(i)* ***ego strength,*** *(ii)* ***machiavelliansim*** and *(iii)* ***locus of control.***

A person's ***ego strength*** is his or her ability to undertake self-directed tasks and to cope with tense situations.

Machiavellianism is the extent to which a person will attempt to deceive and confuse others.

Locus of control is the perspective of people concerning who or what controls their behaviour. People with an ***internal locus of control*** feel they control their own behaviour. People with an ***external locus of control*** feel their behaviour is controlled by external factors (rules, regulations, their supervisors, etc.).

Certain social factors can also influence ethical behaviour in organisations, including gender, role differences, religion, age, work experience, nationality and the influence of other people who are significant in an individual's life. People learn appropriate behaviour by observing the behaviour of significant role models (parents, teachers, public officials, etc.). Because managers are role models in organisations, it is critical that they exhibit ethical behaviour that is beyond reproach in all situations.

Trust and Total Quality: The total quality approach cannot be successfully implemented in an organisation that does not subscribe to high standards of ethical behaviour. This is because ethical behaviour builds trust, and trust is an essential ingredient in total quality. The various elements of total quality that depend on trust are: *(a)* communication, *(b)* interpersonal relations, *(c)* conflict management, *(d)* problem solving, *(e)* teamwork, *(f)* employee involvement and empowerment and *(g)* customer focus.

Ethics plays a critical role in a successful application of total quality.

Ethics plays a critical role in a successful application of total quality. Ethical behaviour on the part of the organisation is just as important as the behaviour of managers and employees. Managers must be able to establish themselves as trust-worthy and must also be able to build trust in the organisation and among its employees.

Keeping promises is a way managers can build trust. Dependability builds trust. Motivating employees and continually developing their job skills are important responsibility of managers in a total quality setting. Managers who are not trusted will not be effective at fulfilling these responsibilities.

Values and Total Quality: Values are those deeply held beliefs that form the very core of who we are. A person's *conscience* is based on his or her values. Our values guide our behaviour. An organisation will not produce a quality product or provide a quality service unless the organisation values quality. Having knowledge and skills by themselves do not guarantee results. This is because individual employees and organisations as a whole will most willingly apply their knowledge and skills to what they value, what they believe in, what they feel is important.

Ethical behaviour begins with values. Values that lead to ethical behaviour include ***fairness, dependability, integrity, honesty*** **and** ***truthfulness.*** Values that lead to peak performance and excellence include ***achievement, contribution, self-development, creativity, synergy, quality*** and ***opportunity.*** These different sets of values tend to support and supplement each other in a work environment that involves, empowers, values, and nurtures people, one that holds employees responsible but also gives them the support, leeway and resources needed to fulfil their responsibilities.

Ethical behaviour builds trust which is an essential ingredient of total quality.

Integrity and Total Quality: ***Integrity,*** as a personal and organisational characteristic, combines honesty and dependability. When an individual or an organisation has integrity, ethical behaviour automatically follows. People with integrity can be counted on to do the right thing, do things right, accomplish tasks thoroughly and completely, complete work on time and keep promises. The same is true of organisations.

Responsibility and Total Quality: Part of ethical behaviour is accepting responsibility. In a total quality setting, people are responsible for their actions and accountable for their performance.

Accepting responsibility helps build trust, integrity and all the other elements of ethics that are so important in a total quality environment.

Manager's Role in Ethics: Managers are expected to make ethical decisions. Deciding what is ethical is much easier than actually doing what is ethical. Managers have three main responsibilities. *(a)* they are responsible for setting an example of ethical behaviour, *(b)* they are responsible for helping employees make ethical choices, and *(c)* they are responsible for helping employees follow through and exhibit ethical behaviour after the appropriate choice has been made.

Organisations and managers have a critical role to play in promoting ethical behaviour among their employees.

Organisations Role in Ethics: Organisations have a critical role to play in promoting ethical behaviour among their employees. Managers cannot establish ethical standards without support from all levels above them in the organisation. An organisation's tasks in ethics are: *(i)* creating an internal environment that promotes, expects and rewards ethical behaviour and *(ii)* setting an example of ethical behaviour in all external dealings.

An organisation creates an ethical environment by establishing policies and practices that ensure that all employees are treated ethically and, then by enforcing those policies.

One effective way to create an ethical environment is to develop an ethics philosophy, with specific guidelines for putting the philosophy into operation, to put it in writing and to share it with all employees.

Organisations that take the "Do as I say, not as I do" approach to ethics will not succeed. Employees must be able to trust their employers to conduct all external and internal dealings in an ethical manner.

Finally, in addition to creating an ethical internal environment and handling external dealings in an ethical manner, organisations must support managers who make ethically correct decisions - not just when such decisions are profitable but in all cases.

Handling Ethical Dilemmas: Every manager eventually confronts an ethical dilemma. When this happens, the manager's response is very important. **The guidelines managers can use in such situations are listed in *Box 6.13.***

Box 6.13 : Guidelines for Handling Ethical Dilemmas

Before taking any action in stituations involving ethical dilemmas, answer the following questions.

(i) What solution is most likely to build trust among those involved?

(ii) What solution fits best into the company's value system?

(iii) What solution is most likely to enhance the organisation's integrity?

(iv) What solution is the most respoinsible option?

6.12 QUALITY IN PRACTICE

Box 6.14 : Leadership for Quality at ABC Electric Compay

ABC Electric company in karnataka, India, manufactures arc welding equipment. ABC has the highest paid workers in this extremely competitive market and it is protected neither by patents nor price supports. Inspite of this, ABC Electric Company controls 40 % of the arc welding market. How is this possible? ABC Electric out performs its competitors in both quality and productivity. By way of comparison, ABC Electric has sales in excess of Rs 20 lakhs per employee while the industry average is Rs 7 lakhs per employee.

This is accomplished by applying, in the age of high technology, the following leadership principles set forth by the CEO of the company.

- Viewing people as the company's most valuable asset
- Practicing ethics
- Observing simplicity in all things
- Focusing on the customer.
- Making decisions based on principles
- Competing and

6.13 SUMMARY

Leadership is the ability to positively influence people and systems under one's authority to have a meaningful impact and achieve important results. Leaders may seek to motivate employees and develop enthusiasm for quality. They create clear and visible quality values and integrate these into the organisation's strategy.

Strategic planning involves the process of envisioning the organisation's future and developing the necessary procedures and operations to achieve that future. It involves formulation of ***strategies*** for creating a sustainable ***competitive advantage*** for a business organisation.

In today's business environment, quality is a key element of strategic planning. Leadership for quality and strategic planning for quality are essential in a total quality environment. Some of the kinds of leadership are : *(i)* Executive leadership, *(ii)* Individual leadership, *(iii)* Team leadership and *(iv)* Organisational leadership.

Five core leadership skills required for effective leadership are : *(i)* vision, *(ii)* empowerment, *(iii)* intuition, *(iv)* self-understanding and *(v)* value congruence. These skills help true leaders to promote and practice total quality by creating customer-driven vision, setting high expectations, demonstrating personal involvement, integrating quality into daily management and sustaining an environment for quality excellence.

The ***leadership system*** refers to how leadership is exercised throughout a company, including how key decisions are made, communicated and carried out at all levels, mechanisms for leadership development and guidance regarding behaviours and practices. Effective leadership systems include quality steering teams of senior managers who head the quality efforts.

The effectiveness of any leadership system depends partly on its organisational structure. Organisational structures for quality must reflect individual company differences and provide the flexibility and ability to change. Processes rather than hierarchical reporting relationships drive quality in the organisation.

Strategic management is one of the critical role of leadership. ***Strategic quality planning*** include understanding key customer requirements, optimisng the use of resources, ensuring that quality initiatives will be understood at all levels in the organisation and ensuring that the organisation will plan for breakthrough and continuous improvements. Effective strategic planning includes active participation by both top management and lower-level employees, a strong customer focus, supplier involvement and well-established measurement and feedback systems.

Strategy formulation includes determination of the organisation's mission, vision and guiding principles. These lead to goals and strategies that set the direction for achieving the mission. Strategic planning involves ***strategy development*** and ***strategy deployment***. Strategy development gathers information regarding customer and market requirements and expectations, the business environment, competitive environment, company's strengths and supplier capabilities and provides the same as input to the strategic planning process.

Strategy deployment is done through a process called *Hoshin Kanri* or policy deployment which emphasises organisation- wide planning and setting of priorities, providing resources to meet objectives and measuring performance as a basis for improving it. It is a total quality approach to executing a strategy.

Managers use a variety of tools and techniques, known as the *seven management and planning tools* to implement policy deployment. These tools are the affinity diagram, inter-relationship digraph, tree diagram, matrix diagram, matrix data analysis, process decision program chart and arrow diagram.

Leadership has a major responsibility in initiating/activating organisational change to establish a quality culture. Managers must act as change agents and catalysts for overcoming resistance to change, which is normally inherent in organisational behaviour. Advocates of change must facilitate change by focusing on resisters of change and changing their perceptions of change from negative to positive. The steps involved in facilitating change include: *(i)* beginning with a new advocacy paradigm, *(ii)* understanding the concerns of potential resisters, and *(iii)* implementing change-promoting strategies.

Steps involved in establishing a quality culture are: *(i)* Identify the change needed, *(ii)* Put the planned change in writing, *(iii)* Develop a plan for making the change, *(iv)* Understand the emotional transition process, *(v)* Identify key people and make them advocates, *(vi)* Take a 'heart and minds' approach, *(vii)* Apply courtship strategies and *(viii)* Support, support and support.

Ethics and ethical behaviour has a major role to play in the implementation of total quality in organisations. Quality and ethics have a common premise which is "to do right things right". Eventhough an organisation establishes ethical standards to be adhered to by its executives and employees often managers and executives are confronted with situations that create an ethical dilemma. In such situations right or wrong cannot be clearly identified.

Factors that influence ethical behaviour are: *(i)* ego strength, *(ii)* machiavellianism, and *(iii)* locus of control.

In addition to ethical behaviour, the other factors that affect successful implementation of total quality are: *(i)* trust, *(ii)* values, *(iii)* integrity, and *(iv)* responsibility.

Managers are expected to make ethical decisions which have a major role in implementing total quality. Also organisations have a critical role to play in promoting ethical behaviour among their employees. Ethical dilemmas need to be handled carefully and appropriately without affecting trust, value, integrity and responsibility aspects of organisational behaviour.

6.14 KEY WORDS USED

Leadership, Strategic Planning, Executive Leadership, Individual Leadership, Team Leadership, Organisational Leadership, Effective Leadership, Vision, Empowerment, Value congruence, Leadership Theories, Attribution Theory, Transcational or Charismatic Theory, Peter's Model, Leadership System, Strategic Quality Management, Strategic Quality Planning, Quality Policies, Quality Audits, Seven Management and Planning Tools, Affinity Diagrams, Inter-relationship Digraph, Tree Diagrams, Matrix Diagrams, Matrix Data Analysis, Process Decision Program charts, Arrow Diagrams. Quality Culture, Corporate culture, Job design, Employee empowerment, Self – managed Teams.

6.15 OBJECTIVE QUESTIONS

(A) Match the following :

Column A	Column B
1. Stephen Covey	1. Management by walking around.
2. Douglas Mc Gregor	2. Lateral thinking.
3. Tom Peter's model	3. Pointing direction.
4. Hoshin kanri	4. Seven habits of highly effective people.
5. Inter-relationship Diagraph	5. Theory X and Theory - Y.

(B) State whether the following statements are True or False :

1. Quality is a key element of strategic planning. (T / F)
2. Leaders usually do not follow their intuition. (T / F)
3. 'Leadership' is the driver of the entire quality system. (T / F)
4. Leaders control people whereas managers motivate people. (T / F)
5. "Management By Wandering About" helps managers to become good leaders. (T / F)

(C) Multiple choice Questions : Choose the correct answer from the alternatives given under each question :

1. New age managers require the following skills
   (a) Creative insight and sensitivity (b) vision and versatility
   (c) Focus and patience (d) (a) and (b) only
   (e) (a), (b) and (c)
2. Effective leadership requires :
   (a) Vision and empowerment (b) Intuition and self-understanding
   (c) Value congruence (d) (a) and (c) only
   (e) (a), (b) and (c)
3. Outstanding leadership has the following elements :
   (a) Exposing and Envisioning (b) Enlisting and Empowering
   (c) Exemplifying and Encouraging (d) (a), (b) and (c)
   (e) (b) and (c) only
4. Policy deployment requires the following management and planning tools :
   (a) Affinity diagrams and Tree diagrams (b) Arrow diagrams and Matrix diagrams
   (c) Interrelationship diagraph and Matrix data analysis
   (d) Process Decision Program Charts (e) (b), (c) and (d) only
   (f) (a), (b), (c) and (d)
5. Top management committment can be demonstrated by the following behaviours :
   (a) Signalling (b) Focus
   (c) Employee policies (d) (a) and (b) only
   (e) (a), (b) and (c) (f) (b) and (c) only

6.16 REVIEW QUESTIONS

1. Discuss the necessity of leadership for successful quality management.
2. How does leadership relate to strategic planning?
3. Discuss the five core leadership skills required for effective leadership.
4. Briefly discuss the various leadership theories and their implications in quality management.
5. What is strategic planning for TQM? Explain the role of quality in strategic planning.
6. Explain the terms : *(i)* Strategy Development and *(ii)* Strategy Deployment.
7. Define the terms – mission, vision and guiding principles. State the purpose of each.
8. What is "hoshin kanri"? Is it same as policy deployment?
9. List and explain the uses for the seven management and planning tools for improvement of policy deployment.
10. Discuss the leadership and strategic planning in the Baldrige criteria.
11. List the 12 dimensions of TQM culture
12. Discuss the steps involved in creating TQM culture.
13. What is meant by organisational culture?
14. What is meant by quality culture?

15. Discuss the characteristics shared by organisations with a quality culture.
16. What is meant by "activating cultural change"?
17. Discuss the characteristics of organisations having strong quality culture.
18. How resistance to change can be overcome? – Explain.
19. Explain how a quality culture can be established in an organisation.
20. Discuss the importance of ethics and ethical behaviour in quality management.
21. What is meant be "ethical dilemma"?
22. Discuss the factors that influence ethical behaviour.
23. Discuss the relationship between: *(a)* trust and total quality, *(b)* values and total quality, *(c)* integrity and total quality, *(d)* responsibility and total quality
24. Discuss the role of managers and organisations in ethics.
25. How ethical dilemmas are handled?

6.17 DISCUSSION QUESTIONS

1. "Leadership is the 'driver' of a total quality system" What does this statement imply and what implications does it have for future top management, middle management and junior management level executives?
2. Discuss the "Seven Habits of Highly Effective People" as advocated by Stephen Covey.
3. "Leadership is the driver of the entire quality system" - Discuss
4. Discuss the six elements of outstanding leadership.
5. "One of the critical aspects of leadership is strategic planning" – Discuss.
6. "Strategic quality planning is synonymous with strategic business planning". Do you agree or disagree? Give reasons for your view.
7. "Building a TQM culture requires a solid and well executed strategy" – Explain.
8. Discuss Tom Peter's model of leadership.

6.18 ASSIGNMENTS

1. Design a questionnaire to be used to conduct a survey of employees (of an organisation to which you have access) to understand the leadership effectiveness in that organisation.
2. Visit any business organisation in the vicinity and discuss with the chief executive officer to determine whether the organisation has well-defined mission, vision and guiding principles.

6.19 CHAPTER CASES

1. QUALITY AT QUALITY FOUNDRY

Quality Foundry was established in the mid 1960s in a 300 square metre building with 10 people as a small family business to produce castings. In the 1980s as business grew, the company expanded its facilities and its capability to develop its own tooling patterns and eventually moved into a 4000 square metre building. Over this time period from 1960s to 1980s, the foundry industry declined from more than 1200 companies to about 400.

With such a shrinking market, Quality Foundry began to listen more to its customers. They discovered that customers were not happy with the quality of the products supplied by them. In 1990, Quality Foundry made a commitment to quality by hiring a quality assurance manager Ravikumar. Ravikumar felt that the top management was committed to quality and saw an opportunity to change the company's culture. He also firmly believed in Deming's philosophy. The first thing he did was to work with top management to develop a mission statement which reads as below : Our mission at Quality Foundry is to improve the return on investment. We can achieve this by changing attitudes and incorporating a quality/team environment. This will improve the quality of our products, enhance our productivity and elevate our service and response level to our customers.

As we are in a low-growth, mature market and the standards for competitive levels of quality and service are becoming more demanding, we must develop a strategy to improve quality and responsiveness in all areas of the company in order to improve our return on investment. We need to have all employees recognise the importance of product quality and service and move toward more favourable pricing. We need to change thinking throughout the organisation to get employees involved, to encourage team work, to develop a more flexible workforce and adaptable organisation. We need to instill pride in the work place and the product.

Under Ravikumar's direction, Quality Foundry made some substantial improvements in the quality of castings, particularly reducing scrap and reject rates. Ravikumar worked closely with the factory workers directly responsible for the products, asking them what they needed to get the job done and ensuring management commitment to provide the necessary resources. Quality Foundry invested in new control equipments for furnaces to control temperatures with digital read out. This helped the workers to adjust the process as needed. The success of this project led the company to empower employees to control many other aspects of the system.

Five years later, the chief executive officer (CEO) of Quality Foundry retired and the General Manager of a manufacturing company was appointed as the new CEO. The new CEO felt that the mission statement did not provide a clear direction. Consequently he set up a new task for senior management (including Ravikumar) to develop a new strategic vision.

Discussion Questions :

1. Comment on the current mission statement. Does it provide a strategic direction necessary for success for Quality Foundry?
2. How can the mission statement be improved? Suggest a better statement of mission, vision and guiding principles.

2. AN ETHICAL DILEMMA

Vinay kumar is the manager of the phenolics department of Plasti Tech, a manufacturer of industrial plastics and composite materials. He is facing a dilemma. There is an opening in his department and his brother has applied for it. Because his brother has been unemployed for several months, he is having a great deal of trouble supporting his wife and two children. The family pressure on Vinay to hire his brother is intense. But there is a problem. Although Vinay has no doubt that his brother could do the job well, two other applicants are better qualified. Further, Vinay, his brother and two better qualified applicants are all minorities, so his company's equal employment opportunity policies will not help in making the decision, nor will the company's other employment policies, which allow the hiring of familiy members. Vinay feels a strong sense of responsibility for the productivity of his department. He also wants to help is brother. This is the first real ethical dilemma he has ever faced.

If Vinay doesn't help his brother, he might be ostracised by his family and his brother's already precarious financial condition might get even worse. On the other hand he is responsible for hiring the best new team member he can identify. This type of ethical dilemma is not uncommon in the modern work place.

Discussion Questions :

1. If you found yourself facing a similar dilemma, what would you do? Why?
2. Suggest some ethical guidelines that could be established by the top management of the organisation to help managers to handle ethical dilemmas.

CHAPTER 7

HUMAN RESOURCE PRACTICES FOR TQM

LEARNING OBJECTIVES

After reading this chapter, you should be able to:

- Discuss the scope of human resource management in TQM.
- Discuss how human resource plans are linked to business strategy.
- Discuss how the high performance work teams are designed.
- Discuss the process of developing successful teams.
- Discuss how the human resources are managed in a total quality environment.
- Discuss the application of motivation theories to total quality.
- Describe how employee satisfaction and effectiveness of human resource management can be measured in a TQ environment.

7.0 INTRODUCTION

The role of human beings at work has changed as business and technology have changed over the years. Prior to the industrial revolution, skilled people had a major stake in the quality of the products produced and they were motivated by pride in their work as well as the need for survival. Later, in the era of scientific management, F.W. Taylor's system improved productivity by focussing on work methods design, the establishment of standards for daily work, selection and training of workers and piece work incentives.

In the context of TQM, Human Resource Management focuses on design and management of high - performance work systems and maintenance of an environment for quality excellence.

Taylor's system philosophy assumes that *(i)* people are part of the process, *(ii)* the process needs to be controlled externally to be productive and *(iii)* managers have to control carefully what people do. Recently, managers have begun to realise that these human resources practices no longer work very well. **The new thinking is that *(i)* people design and improve the process, *(ii)* workers who run the process must control it and managers must obtain the commitment of people to design, control and improve processes so that they can remain productive.** Studies have shown that this new thinking results in higher quality, lower costs, less waste, better utilisation, increased capacity, reduced employee turnover and absenteeism, faster implementation of change, greater human skills development and better individual self-esteem.

Nowadays, the total quality movement has caused business to look more closely at the **human side of work.** The focus on customer satisfaction and flexibility to meet ever-changing customer demands has brought new approaches to **work design** and **employee development.** In this chapter, human resources management is addressed within a total quality environment, focussing on the design and management of high-performance work systems. **In this context, it is worth mentioning the following statements:**

- Deming emphasised that no organisation can survive without good people, people who are improving.
- Businesses are beginning to learn that to satisfy customers, they must first satisfy employees.
- Secret of Toyota Quality is the workforce – the team members in the production line, the suppliers, the engineers – everybody who has a hand in production – having an attitude that they are making world-class vehicles.
- The human resource is only one that competitors cannot copy and the only one that can synergise.

7.1 THE SCOPE OF HUMAN RESOURCE MANAGEMENT

Human Resource Management (HRM) involves those activities defined to provide for and coordinate the people of an organisation. These include:

(i) determining the organisation's human resource needs
(ii) assisting in the design of work systems
(iii) recruiting, selecting, training and developing, counselling, motivating and rewarding employees
(iv) acting as a liaison with trade unions and government organisations and
(v) handling other issues related to the welfare of employees.

HRM seeks to build and maintain an ***environment for quality excellence*** to better enable the workforce to achieve the company's quality and operational performance objectives.

In addition to the traditional tasks of personnel managers, human resource managers now take on a **strategic leadership role** in their organisations. They must consider and plan for the development of the organisation's **corporate culture,** at the same time overseeing day-to-day operations involved with maintenance of the HRM system of their companies.

Just as all managers are responsible for quality even though their organisation may have quality professionals, all managers are responsible for human resources, even if the organisation has HR managers. Developing skills through training and coaching, promoting teamwork and participation, motivating and recognising employees, and providing meaningful communication are important human resources skills that all managers embrace for total quality to succeed. **Understanding HRM practices is essential for a total quality environment and a critical task for all managers.**

Understanding HRM practices is essential for a total quality environment and a critical task for all managers.

Leading companies have revolutionised all (or nearly all) of their major human resource policies and procedures.

***Box 7.1* contrasts traditional HRM policies with those supporting the total quality perspective.**

In traditional organisations, HRM functions identify, prepare, direct and reward employees for following rather narrow objectives. In TQ organisations, HRM units develop policies and procedures to ensure that employees can perform multiple roles, improvise when necessary and direct themselves towards **continuous improvement of both product quality and customer service.** The new HRM paradigm has been successfully used to develop a more cooperative, productive, flexible and innovative work environment that recognises the value of the human resources in meeting customer needs and achieving strategic business objectives.

Box 7.1 : Traditional Versus Total Quality Human Resource Paradigms

Corporate Context Dimension	Traditional Paradigm	Total Quality Paradigm
Corporate Culture	Individualism, Differentiation Autocratic leadership, Profits Productivity	Collective effort, Cross functional work Coaching/enabling, Customer satisfaction Quality
Human Resource Characteristics	**Traditional Paradigm**	**Total Quality Paradigm**
Communications	Top down	Top down, Horizontal, lateral, Multidirectional
Voice and involvement	Employment-at-will	Due process, Quality circles, Attitude surveys
Job design	Efficiency Productivity Standard procedures Narrow span of control Specific job descriptions	Quality Customization Innovation Wide span of control Autonomous work teams, Empowerment
Training	Job related skills Functional, technical Productivity	Broad range of skills Cross functional Diagnostic, problem solving Productive and quality
Performance measurement and evaluation	Individual goals Supervisory review Emphasise financial performance	Team goals Customer, peer and supervisory review Emphasize quality and service
Rewards	Competition for individual merit increases and benefits	Team/group - based rewards, Financial rewards, financial and non-financial recognition
Health and safety	Treat problems	Prevent problems, Safety programs Wellness programs, Employee assistance
Selection/promotion Career development	Selected by manager Narrow job skills Promotion based on individual accomplishment Linear career path	Selected by peers Problem-solving skills Promotion based on group facilitation Horizontal career path

Leading Practices

TQ – based HRM practices work to accomplish the following tasks:

(i) **Communicate** the importance of each employee's contribution to total quality

(ii) **Stress** quality related synergies available through teamwork.

(iii) **Empower** employees to "make a difference" and

(iv) **Reinforce** individual and team commitment to quality with a wide range of rewards and reinforcements.

The practices adopted by leading companies to achieve the above goals are:

(i) **Integrate** human resource plans with overall quality and operational performance plans to fully address the need and development of the entire workforce.

(ii) **Involve** all employees at all levels and in all functions.

(iii) **Use** suggestions and recognition systems to promote involvement and motivate employees.

(iv) **Emphasise** and support teamwork throughout the organisation.

(v) **Empower** individuals and teams to make decisions that affect quality and customer satisfaction.

(vi) **Make** extensive investment in training and education.

(vii) **Maintain** a work environment conducive to the well-being and growth of all employees.

(viii) **Monitor** the extent and effectiveness of human resource practices and measure employee satisfaction as a means of continuous improvement.

7.2 LINKING HUMAN RESOURCE PLANS AND BUSINESS STRATEGY

Human Resource Management plays a key role in developing a viable competitive strategy.

Until recently, HRM was considered as a support function, neglecting its strategic aspects by most organisations. Today, most progressive firms recognise that **HRM plays a key role in developing a viable competitive strategy.**

Because work is accomplished by people, human resource plans should be aligned with business plans derived from company strategy. *For example*, Motorola aligns its training plans to business goals. If a company goal is to reduce cycle time, then it creates a training course on how to achieve this. ***Exhibit 7.1* illustrates linking human resource plans and business strategy at Cadillac.**

Exhibit 7.1 : Linking Human Resource Plans and Business Strategy at Cadillac

Today, most progressive firms recognise that HRM plays a key role in developing a viable competitive strategy. Cadillac, for instance, recognised the need to integrate human resource plans with its quality processes in 1987. *Exhibit* shows Cadillac's people strategy structure.

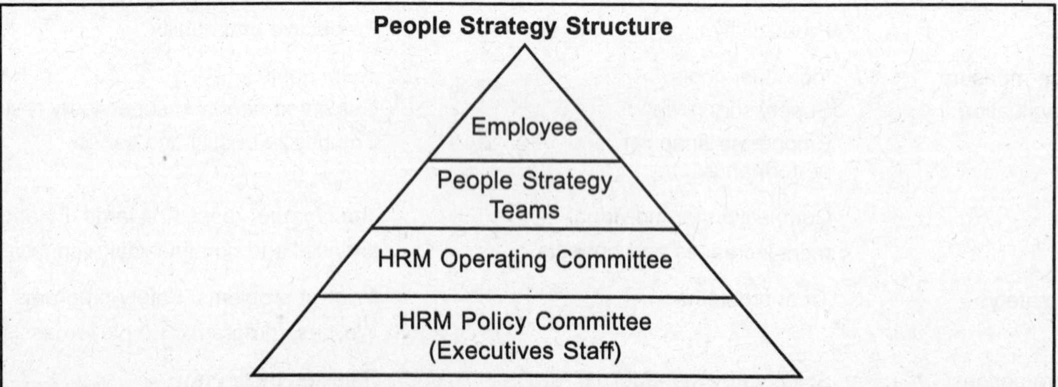

Employee is the centre of the process and the reason for existence of the company. The employee is supported by seven People Strategy Teams with cross-functional, salaried and hourly membership. The teams conduct research and design and recommend, implement and evaluate the company's people process. The People Strategy Teams receive policy leadership and coaching from the human resource management committee, which provides direction and support.

Prudential Insurance Company identified five critical success factors that must be consistently implemented well in order to widen its lead over competitors. One of these factors is superior service to its customers and field force. **Prudential considered eight areas as key performance areas for becoming a customer-driven and market-driven company. These eight areas are:**

- People recruitment and retention
- Continuing education
- Accessibility to customers
- Recognition for superior performance and
- Training
- Creative use of information technology
- Performance measuring and monitoring
- Customer satisfaction monitoring.

All eight areas are related to quality issues of excellence in selection and retention, internal performance, customer service and continuous improvement. However, five of these involve HRM issues. Thus, to achieve the company's goal of superior service, Prudential needs to ensure that HRM strategies support this goal.

HRM focuses on issues such as employee development, reward, recognition, benefits and compensation and recruitment.

The focus of human resource plans is on issues such as employee development, reward, recognition, benefits and compensation and recruitment. They also include one or more of the following:

(i) Mechanisms for promoting co-operation (internal customer/supplier relationship)
(ii) Initiative to promote labour-management co-operation (partnerships with trade unions)
(iii) Creation and/or modification of recognition systems and compensation systems.
(iv) Creating opportunities for employees to learn and use skills that go beyond current job assignments through re-designing processes and
(v) Education and training initiatives.

In most organisations, one of the three **competitive strategies** dominate: *(i)* **Cost reduction,** *(ii)* **Quality enhancement** and *(iii)* **Innovation.** Each of these strategies requires different employee role behaviours and HRM practices.

In aligning human resource plans with company strategy, managers must make choice in five areas of the HRM system: **planning, staffing, appraising, compensating and training and development.**

Each of these five areas has dimensions that can be viewed as a continuum from a structured environment with rigid practices to an unstructured environment with flexible practices as shown in *Box 7.2*.

7.3 DESIGNING HIGH PERFORMANCE WORK TEAMS

Work design and Job design are the most important elements in designing high - performance work systems.

The most important elements in designing high performance work systems that support a total quality focus are discussed in this section.

Work design refers to how employees are organised in formal and informal work groups or units such as departments and teams. ***Job design*** refers to responsibilities and tasks assigned to individuals. Both work and job designs are vital to organisational effectiveness and personal job satisfaction.

The design of the high performance work system can be addressed viewing the organisation at three levels: the ***individual level,*** the ***process level*** and the ***organisational level.*** At the individual level, work systems should promote flexibility and individual initiative in managing and improving work processes. This requires extensive ***employee involvement, empowerment*** **and** ***training and education.***

At the process level, co-operation and teamwork are key ingredients. At the organisational level, compensation and recognition and attention to employee well-being through health, safety and support services are major factors for outstanding performance. The entire work system must be managed effectively through sound motivational principles and practices such as recruitment and career development, performance appraisal and continuous evaluation and improvement of HRM practices.

Box 7.2 : Human Resource Management Practice Continuums

1. Planning Choices	
Informal	Formal
Short term	Long term
Explicit job analysis	Implicit job analysis
Job simplification	Job enrichment
Low Employee involvement	High employee involvement
2. Staffing choices	
Internal sources	External sources
Narrow paths	Broad paths
Single ladder	Multiple ladders
Explicit criteria	Implicit criteria
Limited Socialisation	Exclusive socialisation
Closed procedures	Open procedures
3. Appraising Choices	
Behavioural criteria	Results' criteria
Purposes : Development, Remedial, Maintenance	
Low employee participation	High employee participation
Short-term criteria	Long-term criteria
Individual criteria	Group criteria
4. Compensating Choices	
Low base salaries	High base salaries
Internal equity	External equity
Few perks	Many perks
Standard, fixed package	Flexible package
Low participation	High participation
No incentives	Many incentives
Short-term incentives	Long term incentives
No employment security	High employment security
Hierarchical	High participation
5. Training and Development Choices	
Short term	Long term
Narrow application	Broad application
Productivity emphasis	Quality of work-life emphasis
Spontaneous, unplanned	Planned, systematic
Individual orientation	Group orientation
Low participation	High participation

The design of work should provide individuals with both intrinsic and extrinsic motivation to achieve quality and operational performance objectives. Managers should have a proper understanding of the **top five needs of employees in the work place** namely *(i)* **Interesting work,** *(ii)* **Recognition,** *(iii)* **Feeling "in" on things** *(iv)* **Security** and *(v)* **Pay.** Some of the common approaches to work design are **job enlargement, job rotation** and **job enrichment.**

***Exhibit** 7.2* **describes Hackman and Oldham Work design model**

Exhibit 7.2 : Hackman and Oldham Work Design Model

An interesting theory that helps us understand how job design impacts motivation, satisfaction and organisational effectiveness was proposed by Hackman and Oldham.

The model contains four segments :

(i) Critical psychological states
(ii) Core job characteristics
(iii) Moderating variations and
(iv) Outcomes.

Three ***critical psychological states*** which drive the model are :

(i) ***Experienced meaningfulness*** which is the psychological need of workers to have the feeling that their work is a significant contribution to the organisation and society.

(ii) ***Experienced responsibility*** which indicates the need of workers to be accountable for the quality and quantity of work produced and

(iii) ***Knowledge of results*** which implies that all workers feel the need to know how their work is evaluated and what the results of the evaluation are :

Five core job characteristics that have been identified as having an impact on the critical psychological states are:

(i) ***Task significance :*** The degree to which the job gives the participant the feeling that it has a substantial impact on the organisation or the world.

(ii) ***Task identity :*** The degree to which the worker can perceive the task as a whole, identifiable piece of work from start to finish.

(iii) ***Skill variety :*** the degree to which the job requires the worker to use a variety of skills and talents.

(iv) ***Autonomy :*** the degree to which the task permits freedom, independence and personal control to be exercised over the work.

(v) ***Feedback from the job :*** the degree to which clear, timely information about the effectiveness of performance of the individual is available.

Quality is related in a primary or secondary sense to all five of the core job characteristics mentioned above. Quality of a product or service is increased by a worker's dedicated application of skills, which is enhanced by task identity and a feeling of task significance. More directly, quality of work is enhanced by a job design that incorporates autonomy and feedback relating to quality characteristics. The key outcome of high general job satisfaction and high work-effectiveness can then be seen as results that define and reinforce excellent quality.

Hackman and Oldham Work Design Model

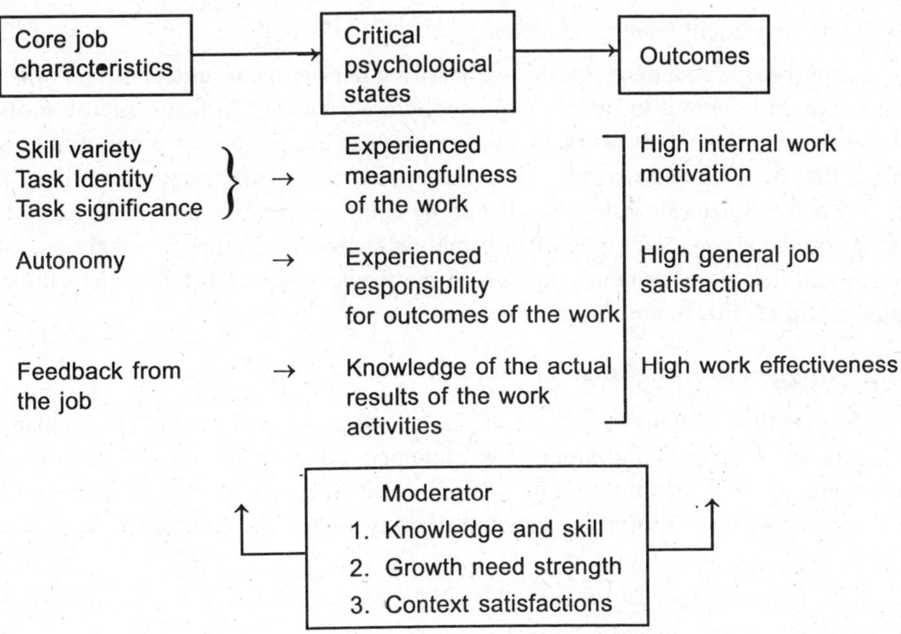

In ***job enlargement***, the worker's job is expanded to include several tasks rather than one single low-level task. This leads to reduced fragmentation of jobs and lower production costs, greater work satisfaction and higher quality.

Job rotation is a technique by which individual workers learn several tasks by rotating from one job to another job. The purpose is to renew interest or motivation of the individual and to increase his or her complement of skills. The main benefit of job rotation is to increase worker's skills.

Job enrichment entails "vertical job loading" in which workers are given more authority, responsibility and autonomy rather than simply more or different works to do.

7.3.1 Employee Involvement

Employee involvement (EI) refers to any activity by which employees participate in work-related decisions and improvement activities with the objectives of tapping the creative energies of all employees and improving their motivation.

Employee involvement is a practice within an organisation where-by employees regularly participate in making decisions on how their work areas operate, including making suggestions for improvement, planning, objective setting, and monitoring performance.

The range of activities involved in EI approaches are: *(i)* sharing of information *(ii)* providing input on work related issues, *(iii)* making suggestions and *(iv)* self-directed responsibilities such as setting goals, making business decisions and solving problems, often in cross-functional teams. Total quality management needs higher levels of employee involvement.

Some of the EI approaches include **"quality of work life (QWL) teams", productivity action teams (PATs), quality circles and self-managed or self-directed teams.**

EI offers many advantages over traditional management practices:

- Replacing the adversarial mentality with trust and co-operation.
- Developing the skills and leadership capability of individuals, creating a sense of mission and fostering trust.
- Increasing employee morale and commitment to the organisation.
- Fostering creativity and innovation, the source of competitive advantage.
- Helping people understand quality principles and instilling these principles into the corporate culture.
- Allowing employees to solve problems at the source immediately and
- Improving quality and productivity.

Employee involvement should begin with a personal commitment to quality. The employees who accept and commit to quality philosophy are more apt to learn quality tools and techniques and use them in their daily work. As the employees begin to see the benefits of a commitment to quality, they will be more willing to working in teams. This team interaction, in turn reinforces personal commitment, driving a never ending cycle of improvement. Employee involvement also depends on the amount and type of information shared with employee training, compensation and rewards and the empowerment practices of the firms. Thus, **HRM practices must be designed to support and facilitate employee involvement.**

7.3.2 Suggestion Systems

"Suggestion systems" is one of the easiest ways to involve employees on an individual basis. An employee suggestion system is a management tool for the submission, evaluation and implementation of an employee's idea to save cost, increase quality or improve other elements of work such as safety. **Companies reward employees for implemented suggestions.**

Suggestion systems though originated in the West, were refined in Japan. In Japan, they are designed to create small, gradual but continuous improvements. The overall participation rate in Japan exceeds 65 percent and Japanese workers submit dozens of suggestions each year.

Participation in suggestion systems is relatively poor in the US due to the following reasons:

- Most US suggestion systems emphasise cost savings or favour significant, innovative ideas rather than small, but useful improvements.
- Many employees may feel they are unable to generate ideas that will save significant sums of money.
- Many managers typically take a passive approach, waiting for suggestions to be submitted.
- Many companies do not provide time for employees to develop suggestions during the regular working time and employees are often unable to find time outside their regular work schedules to develop ideas.

In contrast, the suggestion process in Japan is included in formal training sessions and involves continual guidance from supervisors with strong management support. The group-based culture in Japan facilitates co-operation rather than individual competition.

***Box 7.3* summarises strategies that can foster the success of suggestion systems.**

Box 7.3 : Success Factors for Suggestion Systems

1. Ensure that management, first and foremost, is involved in the program. Involvement should begin at the top and filter down through all levels until all employees participate.
2. Push decision making regarding suggestion evaluation to lower levels.
3. Gain union support by pledging no lay-offs due to productivity gains from adopted suggestions.
4. Train everyone in all facets of the suggestion system. Improve problem-solving capability by promoting creative problem solving through the use of the seven basic statistical tools.
5. Resolve all suggestions within one month.
6. Encourage all suggestors to personally describe their idea to a supervisor, engineer or manager.
7. Promote pride in work and quality and productivity gain from suggestions rather than the big cash award possible.
8. Remove ceilings on intangible suggestion awards. Revise evaluation of intangible suggestions to value them more on par with tangible suggestions.
9. Estimate restrictions prohibiting suggestions regarding a worker's immediate work area.
10. Continuously promote the suggestion program, especially through supervisor support.
11. Trust employees enough to make allowances for generation, discussion and submittal of suggestions during work hours.
12. Keep the program simple.

7.3.3 Empowerment

Empowerment means giving people authority to make decisions based on what they feel is right, have control over their work, take risks and learn from mistakes. Empowerment requires a sincere belief and trust in people. At Motorola, *for example,* sales representatives have the authority to replace defective products upto six years after purchase, a decision that used to require top management approval.

Empowerment is a condition whereby employees have the authority to make decisions and take actions in their work areas, within stated bounds, without prior approval of their superiors.

The need to empower the entire work force in order for quality to succeed has long been recognised, even if only recently put into practice. According to Juran, "ideally, quality control should be delegated to the workforce to the maximum extent possible." Five of Deming's 14 points relate directly to the notion of empowerment and suggest involving employees more directly in decision making processes, giving them security and confidence to make decisions and providing them with the necessary tools and training.

Empowered employees must have the wisdom to know ***what to do*** and ***when to do it***, the ***motivation to do it*** and the ***right tools*** *to* accomplish the task. **This requires significant changes in work systems specially, that**

- Employees be provided education, resources and encouragement.
- Policies and procedures be examined for needless restrictions on the ability of employees to serve customers.

- An atmosphere of trust be fostered rather than resentment and punishment for failure.
- Information be shared freely rather than closely guarded as a source of control of power.
- Workers feel their efforts are desired and needed for the success of the organisation.
- Managers be given the required support and training to adopt a "hands-off" leadership style.
- Employees be trained in the amount of latitude they are allowed to take. Formulating decision rules and providing role-playing scenarios are excellent ways of teaching employees.

Empowerment also means that leaders and managers must relinquish some of their powers and shift the same to the workers. This power shift often creates management fears that workers will abuse this privilege. However, experience shows that front-line workers are more conservative than managers in using the powers given to them. In some companies, empowered employees are required to report decisions they make or discuss them with their supervisors in a learning context.

Empowerment gives managers new responsibilities. They must hire and develop people capable of handling empowerment, encourage risk taking and recognise achievement. Giving employees information about company finances and financial implications of empowered decisions is also important.

Empowerment can be viewed as *vertical teamwork* between managerial and non-managerial personnel. Benefits of empowerment are:

(i) It builds confidence in workers by showing them that the company has confidence in their ability to make decisions on their own.

(ii) It generates commitment and pride among employees.

(iii) It gives employees better experience and opportunity to advance their careers.

John Akers, former chairman of IBM, said, "Empowering our employees and inculcating a sense that everyone owns his or her piece of the business not only unleashes the talent and energy of our people, but also flattens the organisation and reduces stifling bureaucracy." More about empowerment in the context of TQM will discussed in the next chapter.

7.3.4 Training and Education

Training refers to the skills that employees need to learn in order to perform or improve the performances of their current job or tasks, or the process of providing those skills.

Companies committed to TQ invest heavily in training and education. **Training is one of the largest initial costs in a total quality initiative.** Not surprisingly, it is one in which many companies are reluctant to invest. Training and education have become an essential responsibility of the HRM department in TQ organisations, particularly as empowered employees require new knowledge and skills, which should not have to be cost-justified.

The leaders in quality, Deming, Juran and Crosby actively promoted quality training and education. Training generally includes **quality awareness, leadership, project management, communications, team work, problem solving, interpreting and using data, meeting customer requirements, process analysis, process simplification, waste reduction, cycle time reduction, error-proofing and other issues that affect employee effectiveness, efficiency and safety.**

In a total quality environment, employees need to understand the goal of customer satisfaction, to be given the training and responsibilities to achieve this goal and to feel that they do indeed make a difference. Training plans should be based upon job skill requirements and strategic initiatives of the company. Customer needs should always drive training strategies.

Leading companies have formal training departments, whose systems and approaches evolved along with their overall quality systems. Smaller companies often use external training consultants. The content of training programs should be customised to the company's needs.

Continuous reinforcement of lessons learnt in training programs is essential. On the job coaching may be used to reinforce training. Finally, companies need an approach for evaluating training effectiveness. Many measure behaviour and attitude changes. However, the true test of training effectiveness is results. By establishing a linkage between training and results, companies can show the impact on customer satisfaction and also identify gaps in training.

7.4 TEAM WORK AND CO-OPERATION

Traditionally, human resources management has focussed on individuals. Practices such as management by objectives, individual performance evaluation, professional status and privileges and individual promotion indicate the mind-set built into the management system. The disadvantages of focussing on individuals are rivalries, competition between individuals, favouritism and self-centredness which collectively work against accomplishing the true mission of an organisation serving customers. Research has shown that the effectiveness of supervisors and subordinates alike is positively related to co-operation and negatively related to competitiveness.

Team work refers to work performed by teams such as determining customer needs, brainstorming to discover opportunities for improvement, selecting improvement projects, recommending corrective actions and tracking effectiveness of solutions.

Any formal competition that may develop has to be discouraged by the management. Management should go out of the way to design co-operative workgroups and incentive systems.

Since a single person rarely has enough knowledge or experience to understand all aspects of the most important work processes, team approaches are essential for process improvement. Team-work breaks down barriers between individuals, departments and line and staff functions.

A ***team*** is a small number of people with complementary skills, who are committed to a common purpose, set of performance goals and an approach for which they hold themselves mutually accountable. In a TQ environment, teamwork has taken on a new meaning. Teams may perform a variety of problem solving activities, such as determining customer needs, brainstorming to discover opportunities for improvement, selecting projects, recommending corrective actions and tracking effectiveness of solutions.

Effective teams are goal-oriented, independent, open, supportive and empowered. Employees who participate in team activities or who work in organisations that have formal quality improvement initiatives feel more empowered and are more satisfied with the rate of improvement in quality in their companies. Also, these employees are far more likely to have received training on both job-related and problem solving/team building skills.

The types of teams existing in different companies and industries are:

(i) **Quality Circles:** Teams of workers and supervisors that meet regularly to address work place problems involving quality and productivity.

(ii) **Problem-Solving Teams:** Teams whose members gather to solve a specific problem and then disband.

(iii) **Management Teams:** Teams consisting mainly of managers from various functions like sales and production that co-ordinate work among teams.

(iv) **Work Teams:** Teams which are organised to perform entire jobs rather than specialised, assembly line type works. When work teams are empowered, they are called ***self-managed teams.***

(v) **Project Teams:** Teams with a specific mission to develop something new or to accomplish a complex task.

(vi) **Virtual Teams:** Relatively new, these team members communicate by computers, take turns as leaders and jump in and out as necessary.

Teams may be ***intra-orgnisational teams*** or ***cross-functional teams.*** Work teams and quality circles are ***intra organisational*** whereas management teams, problem-solving teams, project teams and virtual teams are **cross functional teams.** Intra-functional teams have members who usually come from the same department or function whereas cross functional teams work on specific tasks or processes that cut across boundaries of several different departments. Self-managed teams are the most advanced concept in teamwork. They are complex and vary a great deal in how they are structured and how they function.

Functions of Teams: Problem solving drives the team concept. *Exhibit 7.3* illustrates the process by which teams usually operate. The three basic functions are to identify, analyse and solve quality and productivity problems.

Exhibit 7.3 : Functions of Teams

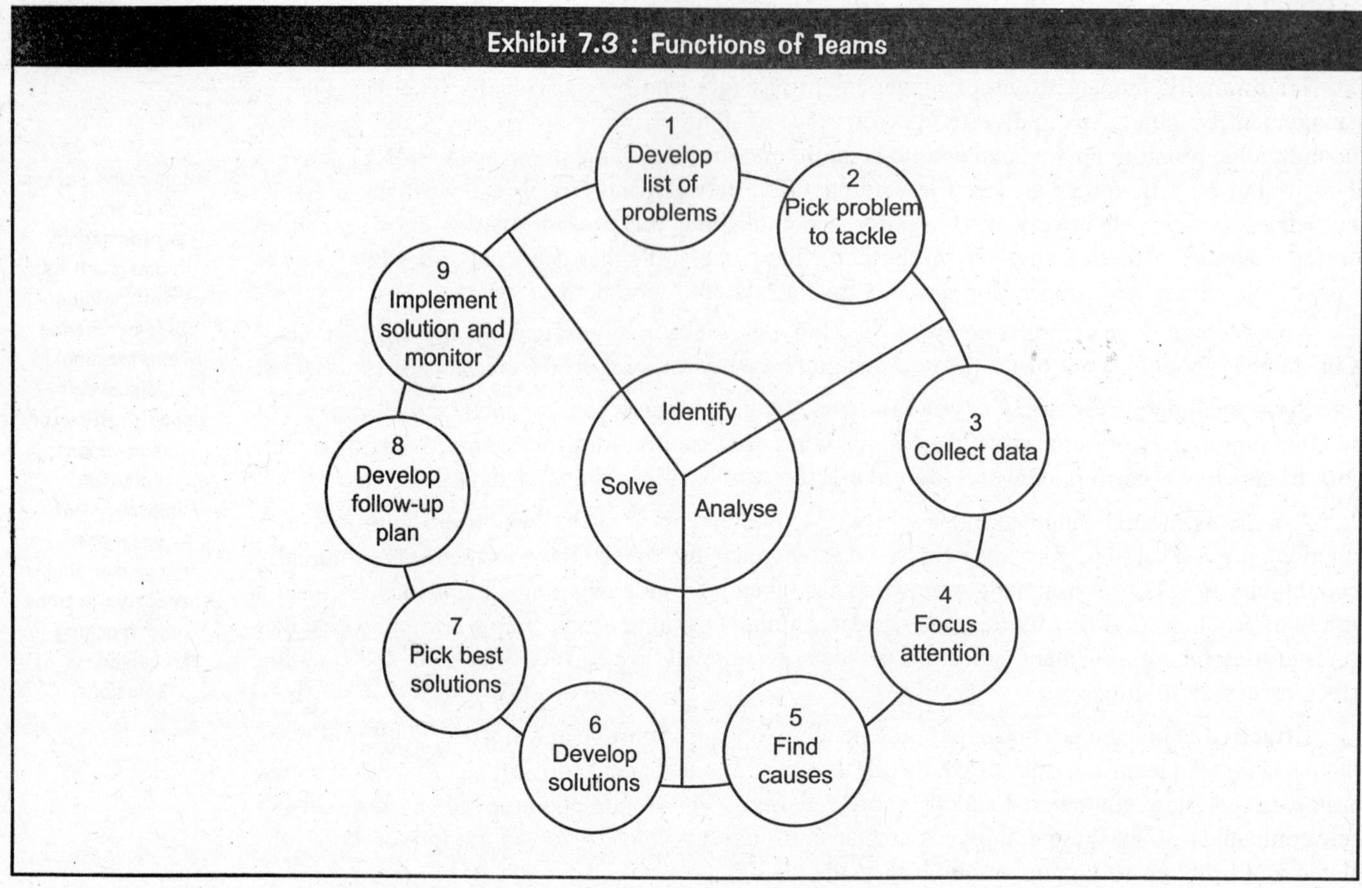

7.5 DEVELOPING SUCCESSFUL TEAMS

Team building or development is the process of transforming a group of people into a team and developing the team to achieve its goals.

Team approaches need adequate planning. A certain period of investigation, reflection and soul searching is necessary before plunging into any team initiatives. Some companies may form the wrong kind of teams for a specific job in a hurry. Managers should examine their organisation's goals, objectives and culture to evaluate its readiness to develop and support team-based initiatives.

Most organisations benefit by establishing a **steering committee** made up of a group of interested, committed line and staff managers together with a union representative if a union exists. The steering committee establishes initial policies and procedures and choose a person or persons to be the **facilitators.** If employees choose to join the team, they are given 8 to 16 hours of initial or concurrent training before or during the first few group meetings. Usually, the facilitator or group leader will conduct the training. Teams are taught to use brainstorming and problem solving tools as well as skills in presentation techniques, group leadership and motivation. **Ten ingredients for a successful team for quality improvement are:**

(i) Clarity in team goals
(ii) An improvement plan
(iii) Clearly defined roles
(iv) Clear communication
(v) Beneficial team behaviours
(vi) Well-defined decision procedures
(vii) Balanced participation
(viii) Established ground rules
(ix) Awareness of group process and
(x) Use of the scientific approach.

Self-managed teams (SMTs) represent the greatest challenge because the teams are empowered:

(i) Creating a work unit responsible for an entire task
(ii) Establishing specific measures of the work units' output

(iii) Designing multi-skilled jobs

(iv) Creating internal management and co-ordination tasks

(v) Creating boundary management tasks

(vi) Establishing access to information and

(vii) Establishing support systems.

More about teams and team work in the context of a TQM organisation will be discussed in the next chapter.

7.5.1 Overcoming Resistance to Change

Many individuals resist change to teamwork and cooperative efforts. Managers may be reluctant to share power with employees. Workers may resist because of past management credibility problems.

Resistance to change is the unwillingness of people to change their beliefs, habits and ways of doing things.

Keys to overcoming resistance to change are early involvement of all parties, open and honest dialogue and good planning. Managers, as organisational leaders must believe in workers and their ability to contribute. Managers must also show commitment and support by providing the right training, rewards and recognitions.

Some specific suggestions to overcome resistance to change are:

(i) Design the change process to include significant management involvement in its implementation.

(ii) Create significant dissatisfaction with status quo, stimulating a need for change.

(iii) Provide support to raise comfort levels with the new concepts.

(iv) Be consistent in the pursuit of participative management, continuously involving the desired behaviour and

(v) Be intolerant of subordination and deal immediately and decisively with flagrant resisters.

7.5.2 Compensation and Recognition

Total quality requires willing, sustained individual effort and coordinated teamwork. When the organisations ask employees to assume new challenges and responsibilities, the question "What is in it for me?" arises in the minds of employees. Extrinsic and intrinsic rewards are the key to sustained individual efforts. ***Compensation and recognition*** **refer to all aspects of pay and reward, including promotions, bonuses and recognition, either monetary or non-monetary and individual or group.**

Compensation is closely tied to the subject of motivation and employee satisfaction. Money is the strongest motivator for people who are at the bottom of Maslow's hierarchy of needs. Pay for performance can diminish intrinsic motivation and may cause employees to believe they are being treated unfairly. The objectives of a good compensation system should be to attract, retain and not demotivate employees. The other objectives are reducing unexplainable variation in pay and encouraging internal co-operation rather than competition. Traditional financial measures such as revenue growth, profitability and cost management are used as basis for compensation.

Compensation is closely tied to the subject of motivation and employee satisfaction.

More progressive organisations use quality measures such as customer satisfaction, defect prevention and cycle time reduction to make compensation decisions.

Many TQ-based companies now base competition on the market rate for an individual with proven abilities, and then make adjustments as capabilities are increased, along with enhanced responsibilities, seniority and business results. Many companies link compensation to company track records, unit performance, team success or individual achievement. Another method is ***gain sharing*** which is an approach in which all employees share savings equally. Another method is to tie pay to the acquisition of new skills, often within the context of a continuous improvement program in which all employees are given opportunities to broaden their work related competencies.

For an organisation to move from a traditional control approach to a TQ-based approach, Richard E. Walton suggests that managers should modify the assumptions and structure of compensation systems. Pay policies must shift from an individual focus to a group focus, using gain sharing and profit sharing systems. Such programs reinforce the importance of group contributions instead of concentrating only on individual contributions. Individual pay should be tied to the development and mastery of skills instead of job evaluation.

Special Recognition and Rewards: Special recognition and rewards could be in the form of monetary or non-monetary, formal or informal, individual or group recognition or rewards. Awards provide a visible means of promoting quality efforts and telling employees that the organisation values their efforts, which stimulates their motivation to improve. It is important that rewards should lead to behaviour that increase customer satisfaction.

Certain key practices leading to effective employee recognition and rewards are:

(i) Giving both individual and team awards
(ii) Involving everyone.
(iii) Tying rewards to quality based on measurable objectives.
(iv) Allowing peers and customers to nominate and recognise superior performance and
(v) Publicising extensively.

7.6 HEALTH, SAFETY AND EMPLOYEE WELL-BEING

Since all employee are key stakeholders of any organisation, their health, safety and well-being are important factors in the work environment.

Most companies have many opportunities to contribute to the quality of working life. They can provide personal and career counselling, career development and employability services, recreational and cultural activities, special leave for non work- related responsibility or community services, flexible work hours and extended health care for retired employees.

Labour Relations Issues: In a rapidly changing business environment, both managers and union leaders experience varying degrees of difficulty with sharing power with workers at every level. However, in a TQ environment, co-operation between unions and the management in new and innovative ways is essential for the survival of both. Traditionally, both union leaders and industrial relations managers emphasised collective bargaining, work rules, grievance procedures etc.

To move towards TQ culture, labour and management must first agree that a new paradigm is desirable and then work co-operatively. This will require union members and leaders to:

(i) take new approach towards resolution of disputes
(ii) develop flexible work rules
(iii) initiate peer performance feedback methods designed to improve work operations and
(iv) establish new contract terms and conditions and ongoing labour – management negotiation.

The actions required on the part of management are as below:

(i) Work with union representatives on how or whether new work systems will be adopted.
(ii) Examine values within a joint framework and adopt new ones to guide the transformed organisation.
(iii) Include labour representation at every level at which process and job transformations are taking place.
(iv) Fill key training and employee involvement (EI) facilitator's positions with both union and management representatives and
(v) Recognise union strengths, such as the ability to take the pulse of its membership on various issues.

7.7 MANAGING HUMAN RESOURCES IN A TOTAL QUALITY ENVIRONMENT

The way human resources are managed include:

(i) how employees are selected and developed *(ii)* how they are motivated at work and *(iii)* how their performance is appraised.

All the above can have a major impact on the success or failure of total quality efforts in an organisation.

7.7.1 Recruitment and Career Development

Meeting and exceeding customer expectations begins with hiring the right people whose skills and attitudes will support and enhance the organisation's objectives. Motorola ties recruitment and selection activities to results in order to gauge the quality of its recruiting efforts as it strives for TQ at every level. The recruiting department is measured by a **new quality oriented criterion: success of recruits on the job.** In recruiting activities, Motorola plans and sets objectives for recruiting, charts progress over time in order to reduce 'defects' in the hiring process and determines whether the "output" of the process is under control rather than simply measuring inputs (dollars per recruit).

The characteristics that must be exhibited by customer focussed employees are as follows:

- The ability to remain calm under stressful conditions.
- Optimism, initiative and a 'people-orientation'.
- The ability to listen well.
- An orientation towards analysis and prevention.
- The ability to solve problems.

To ensure that job candidates have the requisite skills, new approaches, such as psychological testing and situational role playing are now being used in the hiring process.

Cisco systems, one of the most successful Silicon Valley companies, provides a good example of how far recruiting processes have recently evolved.

Career development is also changing because of TQ. As managerial roles shift from directing and controlling to coaching and facilitating, managers who must deal with cross-functional problems, benefit more from horizontal movement than from upward movement in narrow functional areas. Flatter organisations limit promotion opportunities. Thus, career development expands learning opportunities and creates more challenging assignments rather than increasing spans of managerial control.

Motivation: Motivation and human behaviour are major elements in human resources development and management. There is no such thing as an unmotivated employee. The system within which employees work can seriously affect motivation. The concept of motivation, inspite of a number of studies and researches, still remains an extremely complex phenomenon that is not yet fully understood.

Motivation and human behaviour are major elements in human resources development and management.

In the TQ environment, managers need to take on new roles as coaches and facilitators and their skills in motivating employees become even more crucial. Managers and workers need to apply some appropriate motivational tools to aid them in job design and organisational processes.

Motivation is defined as "the art of creating conditions that allow everyone of us to get our work done at our peak level of efficiency". Motivation is also defined as an individual's response to a felt need. Some stimulus or activating event, must spur the need to respond to that stimulus, generating the responses itself.

Researches have proposed many theories and models to describe how and why people are motivated. The motivation theories are often classified as ***content, process*** and ***environmentally based*** theories. These theories are studied under the subject "organisational behaviour" subject. ***Box 7.4* summarises the motivational theories.**

Box 7.4 : Classification of Motivation Theories

Motivation Theory	Pioneer/Developer	Type of Theory
Content Theories		
Hierarchy of needs	Abraham Maslow	Need
Motivation and hygiene (maintenance)	Frederick Herzberg	Need/satisfaction
Theory X, Theory Y	Douglas McGregor	Managerial expectations
Three factor theory (n-Ach, n-Aff, n-Pow)	David McClelland	Acquired need
Process Theories		
Preference-Expectancy	Victor H. Vroom	Expectancy
Contingency	Porter and Lalwer	Expectancy/reward
Goal setting	Edward Locke	Goal
Path-goal theory of leadership	Robert J. House	Goal
Environmentally Based Theories:		
Operant conditioning	B.F. Skinner	Reinforcement
Equity	J. Stacy Adams	Equity
Social Learning/ Self-efficacy	A. Bandura , Snyder and Williams	Social Learning/ Self-Efficacy

7.8 APPLYING MOTIVATIONAL THEORIES TO TQ

All the motivational theories mentioned in *Box 7.5* can be applied to support TQ in an organisation. Motivating factors such as achievement recognition and responsibility lead to personal satisfaction and sustained motivation for continuous improvement. Applying motivation theories to management practices in TQ environment has both advantages and drawbacks. On one hand, efforts to empower employees may appeal to individuals who have a high need for power, since they are likely to feel that management is correcting a long standing problem of not giving most employees sufficient power to influence conditions on the job. On the other hand, empowerment may be dangerous if not carried out properly. *For example*, Herzberg's two factor theory suggests that ignoring hygiene (maintenance) factors such as supervision, working conditions, salary, peer relations, status and security will produce dissatisfaction

Hence to implement TQ, it is necessary to address the hygiene factors before thinking of motivating factors.

Box 7.5 : Applying Motivation Theories to TQ

Situation	TQ example	Applicable Motivation Theories
Choice of employees	Decisions to join employee Involvement groups	Expectancy
Prediction of choices	Management desires employee "buy-in" for reengineering	Equity; goal setting
Effort exerted on a task	Group members' responses in performing a process improvement project	Reinforcement, equity
Work satisfaction	Responses to a survey on how well employees are responding to empowerment initiatives encouraged by management	Need, equity
On-the-job performance	Reduction of customer complaints in a hospital billing department, due to reduction of errors	Reinforcement, equity, goal setting
Withdrawal from the job.	Absenteeism, turnover	Reinforcement, equity or expectancy

Box 7.5 **illustrates a set of common management situations with examples relating to TQ and gives suggestions for the type of motivation theory that could be applied to understand individual motivation and to shape it to meet individual and organisational goals.**

More about motivation in the context of TQM will be discussed in the next chapter.

Performance Appraisal: Performance appraisal is an exceedingly difficult HRM activity. It is used by organisations for a number of reasons:

(i) To provide feedback to employees who can recognise and build on their strengths and overcome their weaknesses.

(ii) To determine salary increases (iii) To identify people for promotion and

(iv) To deal with human resource legalities.

Performance appraisal/ evaluation is a formal method of measuring employees' progress against performance standards and providing feed back to them.

Conventionally, appraisal processes involve setting objectives for a certain period of time. (usually for one year ahead), either unilaterally or jointly by the manager with his or her subordinate. The supervisor reviews the accomplishments, strengths and weaknesses and/or personal characteristics of the subordinate related to the job at the end of the review period.

Dissatisfaction with conventional performance appraisal systems is common among both managers, who are the appraisers and workers who are appraised. **Some of the problems and pitfalls of performance appraisals are as below:**

- They tend to foster mediocrity and discourage risk taking.
- They focus on short-term measurable results, thereby discouraging long-term planning or thinking and ignoring important behaviours that are more difficult to measure.
- They focus on the individuals and therefore tend to discourage or destroy teamwork within and between departments.
- The process is detection-oriented rather than prevention-oriented.
- They are often unfair, since managers frequently do not possess observational accuracy.
- They fail to distinguish between factors that are within the employees' control and system-determined factors that are beyond their control.

Performance appraisals are most effective when they are based on the objectives of the work teams that support the organisation. They act as a diagnostic tool and review process for individual, team and organisational development and achievement. Performance appraisal can be a motivator when it is developed and used by the work team itself.

In a TQ culture, ***quality improvement*** is one of the major dimensions on which employees are evaluated. The employees are evaluated on the basis of problem solving and team contributions in addition to quality improvement. Many firms use peer review, customer evaluations and self-assessment as part of the appraisal process.

One approach that has been gaining increasing acceptance is called ***"360 degree feedback"***. In this approach, a group of individuals who interact with the employees or team on a frequent basis, participate in both the goal-setting process and the performance appraisal process. This group might include suppliers, clients, peers, internal customers, managers and subordinates. The process involves two-way communication in which both parties discuss such needs as service levels, response times, accuracy of work and so on which are often expressed as written service contracts. At the end of the performance period, selected representatives who participated in the goal setting evaluate how well the goals of the service contracts have been met and provide feedback.

In a TQ culture, many companies replaced their traditional performance reviews with personnel development planning process in which managers meet with employees to set future expectations, identify training needs, provide coaching and reward continuous improvement. A TQ organisation requires a closely monitored performance appraisal process that is oriented towards "best practices" and continuous improvement of quality.

7.9 MEASURING EMPLOYEE SATISFACTION AND HRM EFFECTIVENESS

Measuring employee satisfaction and effectiveness of HR practices is crucial to assess the linkages with company strategy and to provide a basis for improvement.

Measurement of employee satisfaction and HRM effectiveness is necessary to assess the linkages with company strategy and to provide a basis for improvement. Both outcome and process measures provide data by which HRM effectiveness can be assessed. Outcome measures include cost savings, productivity improvements, defect rate reduction, customer-satisfaction improvements, cycle time reductions and employee turnover.

Typical process measures of success are the number of suggestions that employees make for productivity and quality improvements and the number of participants in project teams and educational programs. Team process effectiveness can be assessed by tracking the average time it takes to complete a process improvement project and determining whether the teams are getting better, smarter and faster at performing improvements.

Facilitators and program coordinators should also look for other indicators of success, such as improvements in team selection and planning processes, frequency of use of quality improvement tools by employees, employee understanding of problem-solving approaches and senior management involvement. Employee surveys can also help in providing this information.

Team effectiveness surveys address important team and individual behaviours such as unit for a common purpose, listening effectively and acknowledging other's contribution, obtaining the participation of all members of the team, gathering and analysing relevant data and information, sharing responsibility, using problem-solving processes and tools and meeting company objectives for quality improvement.

Employee surveys also help organisations better understand the ***"voice of the employee"*** particularly with regard to employee satisfaction, management policies and their internal customers and suppliers. Such a feedback helps organisations improve their human resources management practices.

In evaluating results, trends and long term results should be emphasised and communicated to employees. A good system should report results on a regular basis (monthly or quarterly) with a summary year-end report, using graphical aids wherever possible. Detailed reports should be sent to lower-level managers, showing results at their levels. Summary reports should go to higher management levels. Specific action such as training, changes in reward or recognition or improvements to support employee well-being should be taken based on results.

7.10 HUMAN RESOURCE FOCUS IN THE BALDRIGE CRITERIA, ISO 9000 AND SIX SIGMA

Category 5 of the 2009 Malcolm Baldrige National Quality Award Criteria for Performance Excellence is **Human Resource Focus.** This category examines how an organisation's work systems and human resource practices lead to performance excellence and align with strategic objectives and action plans.

Item 5.1 – Work Systems focuses on how work and jobs are organized to promote cooperation, initiative, empowerment, innovation and organizational culture, how they capitalise on diversity within the organisation and how high performance work is reinforced. It also addresses hiring and career development approaches, including effective succession planning for senior leadership.

Item 5.2 – Employee Education Training and Development: Focuses on how employee education, training and career development support the achievement of organizational objectives and build employee knowledge, skills and capabilities. It examines how education and training addresses issues such as key organizational needs such as performance measurement and improvement, technological change, ethical business practices, leadership development and safety. It examines how education and training are delivered and reinforced on the job, and how the effectiveness of education and training are evaluated It also addresses how an organisation motivates employees to develop and utilise their full potential and attain objectives related to job and career related development and learning.

Item 5.3 – Employee well-being and satisfaction: examines how an organisation ensures a safe and healthy work environment and support climate that contributes to the well-being, satisfaction and motivation of all employees. It includes identifying appropriate measures and targets for key workplace factors so that status and progress can be tracked and how preparation for emergencies or disasters is addressed. The criteria also asks how the organisation determines the key factors that affect employee well-being, satisfaction and motivation, how services, benefits and policies support employees, how well-being, satisfaction and motivation are assumed and measured and how assessment findings are used to identify priorities for improving the work environment and employee support climate.

The focus of human resources in ISO 9000: 2000 revoked primarily around training and the work environment, but does not address the subject as comprehensively as Baldrige criteria does, As per the standard, it is necessary that **"Personnel performing work affecting product quality shall be competent on the basis of appropriate education, training, skills and experience"**. The standard further requires that organisations determine the level of competence that employees need, provide training or other means to ensure competency, evaluate the effectiveness of training or other actions taken, ensure that employees are aware of how their work contributes to quality objectives and maintain appropriate records of education, training and experience. The standards also address the work environment in terms of provision of buildings, work space, utilities, equipment and supporting services needed to achieve conformity to product requirements as well as determining and managing the work environment including safety, ergonomics and environmental factors

Six sigma approach also requires human resource focus. Six-Sigma owes its success to all the quality efforts that have come before it, and teams are an integral part of Six Sigma implementation. In addition to teams, selecting the right people to serve on teams, training and skill development and reward and recognition approaches to drive employee behaviour are vital to Six-Sigma efforts. Six Sigma efforts often result in significant change recommendations to the organisations, work processes change and employees need to do things differently. Understanding how changes affect people is a necessary issue that organisations must address after the completion of six sigma projects.

***Box 7.6* discribes the recruiting process in Cisco Systems.**

7.11 QUALITY IN PRACTICE

Box 7.6 : Recruiting Process in Cisco Systems

Cisco Systems employs over 10,000 people, they hired over 1000 new employees in each quarter in 1996 alone. "Cisco has an overall goal of getting the top 10 percent to 15 percent of people in our industry", said CEO John Chambers. This has proven to be a major challenge for recruiters for Cisco, as the job market for technically trained people was tight in U.S. Cisco has developed several recruiting innovations to help cope with the challenge. The company has targetted what it terms "passive job seekers". These are excellent employees who have survived lay-offs in their current firms and who are not seeking opportunities to change jobs. To get them to come to Cisco, the firm found that it had to analyse the characteristics of its target job seekers, as well as reengineer its own recruiting procedures.

The company has also assembled focus groups of typical recruiting targets such as experienced engineers and marketing personnel. They determined what they did in their spare time, which web sites they visited most frequently and how they felt about job hunting. A significant finding was that the target population hated job hunting. Cisco then began to develop a non-traditional recruiting strategy to make prospects aware of opportunities at the firm and also make hiring them a more comfortable process.

Recruiters went to locations where job prospects might be found such as local festivals and home shows. They took newspaper ads that listed general job categories rather than specific jobs, and asked prospects to apply directly from Cisco's home page on the web (http/www.cisco.com). They also developed a 'Friends at Cisco' program, whereby volunteer Cisco employees make themselves available to talk to prospects who want to know what it is like to work at Cisco and even advertised this program at area movie houses, a favourite hang-out for relaxing "techies".

As a last resort, Cisco has also gained new talented employees by acquiring firms. It acquired 12 firms in 1996 and kept almost all of those firm's employees.

7.12 SUMMARY

Human resource management (HRM) consists of activities designed to provide for and co-ordinate all the people of an organisation. In traditional organisations, HRM includes determining the organisation's human resource needs, recruiting, selecting, training, developing and rewarding employees and handling labour-relations and industrial relations matters in addition to handling matters concerning employee welfare. In a TQ environment, HR managers strategically support the organisation's TQ approaches and deployment.

In a TQ environment, HR practices include integrating HR plans with overall business plans, involving employees at all levels and in all functions, using suggestions and recognition systems effectively, emphasising and supporting team work, empowering individual employee's and teams, investing in training and education, maintaining the well-being and growth of all employees, monitoring the effectiveness of the practices and measuring customer – employee satisfaction.

To align HR plans with business plans, it is necessary to make strategic choices in planning, staffing, appraising, compensating and training and development. Designing high-performance work teams involves work design, job design, job-enlargement, job rotation and job enrichment to support TQ principles.

Employee involvement (EI) refers to the activity by which employees participate in work-related decisions and improvement activities. EI approaches support TQ principles by developing trust, encouraging cooperation and developing leadership abilities.

High performance work systems are enhanced by well-designed suggestion systems, empowerment, training and education, team work, compensation and recognition and attention to safety, health and welfare of employees.

Various types of teams include quality circles, problem-solving teams, management teams, work teams, project teams, virtual teams and self-managed teams. Good planning is necessary for developing successful teams.

Motivation and human behaviour are major elements in HR development and management. Compensation and recognition (pay and reward, promotion, bonus, monetary and non-monetary forms of recognition), extrinsic and intrinsic rewards are important to sustaining employee motivation.

Effective TQM requires cooperation between union and management. Managing human resources in a TQ environment requires increased attention to recruitment and career development for customer-contact employees, motivation and performance appraisal.

In a TQ environment, performance appraisal should be based on quality related issues, problem identification, coaching and continuous improvement rather than being tied to compensation and merit rating systems. ***"360 degree feedback"*** is an appraisal system which focusses on two-way communication between employees and customers, suppliers, managers, subordinates and peers. Performance appraisal systems are being replaced by planning and development systems in many modern organisations.

Employee satisfaction and HRM effectiveness have to be measured to assess the linkages with strategy and to provide a foundation for improvement. Some of the measures are productivity improvement, defect reduction, employee turn over and process measures such as suggestion rates and problem-solving effectiveness.

7.13 KEY WORDS USED

Human Resource Management, High Performance Work Teams, Work Design, Job Design, Task significance, Task Identity, Skill Variety, Autonomy, Job enlargement, Job enrichment, Job Rotation, Quality of Work Life Teams, Productivity Action Teams, Self Managed Teams, Self Directed Teams, Employee Involvement, Suggestion Systems, Employee empowerment, Vertical Team Work, Problem Solving Teams, Management Teams, Work Teams, Project Teams, Virtual Teams, Quality Circles, Steering Committee, Resistance to change, Compensation, Gain Sharing, Career Development, Motivation, Performance Appraisal, Quality Improvement, 360 Degree Feedback, Employee satisfaction, Team Effectiveness Surveys, Employee Surveys, Human Resource Focus.

7.14 OBJECTIVE QUESTIONS

(A) Match the following :

Column A	Column B
1. Work design	1. Employee involvement on individual basis.
2. Job design	2. Responsibilities and tasks assigned to individuals.
3. Quality circles	3. Vertical teamwork.
4. Suggestion systems	4. How employees are organised.
5. Empowerment	5. Employee involvement as teams.

(B) State whether the following statements are True or False :

1. Human resource managers now take on a strategic leadership role in their organisations. (T / F)
2. Understanding human resource practices has no relevance to a total quality environment. (T / F)
3. HRM has no role in developing a viable competitive strategy for an organisation. (T / F)
4. Employee involvement should begin with a personal commitment to quality. (T / F)
5. Project teams and virtual teams are cross-functional teams. (T / F)

(C) Multiple choice Questions : Choose the correct answer from the alternatives given under each question :

1. Top needs of employees in the work place are :
   (a) Interesting work (b) Job security and pay
   (c) Feeling "in" on things and recognition.
   (d) (a), (b) and (c) (e) (b) and (c) only.
2. Employee involvement approaches include :
   (a) Quality of work-life teams (b) Productivity action teams
   (c) Quality circles and self-managed teams
   (d) (b) and (c) only (e) (a), (b) and (c)
3. Process theories include :
   (a) Expectancy theory only (b) Three factor theory
   (c) Goal setting theory and path-goal theory.
   (d) (a) and (b) only. (e) (a) and (c) only.
4. The Equity Theory was developed by :
   (a) B. F. Skinner (b) Victor H. Vroom (c) J. Stacy Adams
   (d) Frederick Herzberg (e) David McClelland
5. The design of the high-performance work system can be addressed viewing the organisation at :
   (a) Individual level (b) Process level (c) Organisational level
   (d) (a),(b) and (c) (e) (b) and (c) only

7.15 REVIEW QUESTIONS

1. Discuss the role of human resource development and management in quality management.
2. Contrast traditional HRM approaches with those required in a TQM environment.
3. Summarise the leading HRM practices encountered in TQ organisations.
4. Discuss the linkage between human resource plans and business strategy with an example.
5. Define the terms work design, job design, job enlargement, job rotation and job enrichment.
6. What is *employee involvement?* Discuss some of the early developments in EI approaches. What are the advantages of EI over traditional management practices.

7. What is a *suggestion system?* Discuss the various success factors for suggestion systems.
8. Discuss the role of training and education in quality management.
9. What is *employee empowerment?* Discuss the changes that empowerment brings to organisations.
10. What is a *team?* What are its various types? Discuss the role of *teamwork* and *cooperation* in quality management.
11. Briefly describe the various functions of teams.
12. Explain how managers can develop successful teams.
13. Explain how human resources can be managed in a total quality environment.
14. Discuss the differences between quality circles and self managed teams.
15. Define the term *motivation*. Why is motivation critical in a TQ environment?
16. Outline the difference between process, content and environmentally based theories of motivation. Which type is essential to quality managers?
17. Explain how motivational theories can be applied to total quality management.
18. What is performance appraisal? How it is done in a total quality environment?
19. What is 360-degree feedback? How it is different from traditional performance appraisal approaches? How does it support TQ efforts?
20. Why is it important to measure employee satisfaction and HRM effectiveness? Mention some common approaches.

7.16 DISCUSSION QUESTIONS

1. "Nowadays, the total quality movement has caused business to look more closely at the human side of work" – Explain.
2. "Today, most progressive firms recognise that HRM plays a key role in developing a viable competitive strategy" – Discuss.
3. "Employee involvement should begin with a personal commitment to quality" – Elaborate.
4. "Training is one of the largest initial costs in total quality initiative" – Comment
5. "Performance appraisal is an exceedingly difficult HRM activity" – Do you agree or disagree? Give reasons for your answer.

7.17 ASSIGNMENTS

1. Select a nearby organisation and discuss with the HR manager about their HRM practices with a focus on work design and job design.
2. Select a local company and study the extent of team participation, the kinds of teams existing in the company and the effectiveness of teams.

7.18 CHAPTER CASE : HEAVY TRUCK (HT) CORPORATION

HT Corporation, a manufacturer of heavy trucks had a long, sad and bitter history of employee relations. The company openly practiced *"management through terrorism"*. Engineers and technicians dominated the culture. One of the company's assembly plants devoted major resources to statistical process control. An entire department staffed with engineers justified its existence by keeping control charts. The engineers collected and stored data on a computer and posted the charts in every production department once each week. They also posted lists of problems and defects attributable to each department. Another department kept itself busy with *"work redesign"* and *"assembly line balancing"*. The plant was highly product focused. Material moved smoothly from one operation to next. Subassemblies flowed into assemblies like the tributaries of a river, all moving toward the final assembly line.

Despite this effort, quality was mediocre at best. HT corporation devoted more factory space to rework and repair operations than to the original assembly. The individual and social aspects of the system were largely ignored. People lacked interpersonal skills, common goals and trust and they could not hope to attain these qualities under the existing power structure and reward system.

Discussion Questions :

1. Comment on the human resource management of HT corporation.
2. If you take over as the chief executive officer of HT corporation, what changes would you make? How would you begin?

CHAPTER 8

TOTAL QUALITY AND ORGANISATIONAL BEHAVIOUR

LEARNING OBJECTIVES

After reading this chapter, you should be able to:

- ➟ Understand the role of quality teams in continuous improvement.
- ➟ Discuss the types of quality teams.
- ➟ Discuss the criteria for team effectiveness.
- ➟ Discuss the characteristics of various team members.
- ➟ Discuss the processes used in teams.
- ➟ Discuss the relationship between empowerment and motivation and the role of empowerment in quality improvement.
- ➟ Discuss the principles of empowerment.

8.0 INTRODUCTION

Effective organisations follow good human resource practices. The involvement of leadership, through supportive actions, provide employees with the knowledge and skills they need to do their jobs and provide value for the customer. Effective organisations engage in a continuous cycle of learning and training. To support this cycle of continuous improvement, effective organisations design recognition and reward systems that motivate their employees. Effective organisations utilise teams to solve problems and enhance processes. Participants on these teams can expect their talents, skills and personality types to be appreciated and used to their best advantage. Leadership, motivation and teamwork are all elements of organisational behaviour. We have earlier discussed the role of leadership and human resource practices in total quality management in the previous two chapters. In this chapter we will discuss concepts of organisational behaviour such as teamwork, empowerment and motivation, and organisational culture and ethics and their role in total quality organisations.

8.1 QUALITY TEAM WORK

Teamwork is a key element of any TQM approach.

The development of people and their involvement in improvement activities both individually and through teamwork is a key feature in a company's approach to total quality management. A key aspect of this is to make full use of the skills and knowledge of all employees to the benefit of individuals and the organisation and to create a **good culture**. There are a number of different types of teams with different operating characteristics, all of which can act as a vehicle for getting people involved in improvement activities and improving organisational performance.

Teams are everywhere in total quality organisations at all levels - top, middle and bottom, and in every function and department. The TQ philosophy recognises the interdependence of various parts of the organisation and uses teams as a way to co-ordinate work. Teamwork enables various parts of the organisations to work together in meeting customer needs that can seldom be fulfilled by employees limited to one area of specialisation. Teams promote equality among individuals, encouraging a positive altitude and trust among team members. Teams develop a greater sense of responsibility for achieving goals and performing tasks. The diversity inherent in teams often provide unique perspectives on work, spontaneous thought and creativity.

Some teams have a narrow focus, with members coming from one functional area, whereas some others are wider and cross-functional, dealing with the deep-rooted problems between internal customers and suppliers. Various types of teams are: *(i)* quality circles, *(ii)* yield improvement teams, *(iii)* quality improvement teams, *(iv)* continuous improvement teams, *(v)* cost reduction teams, *(vi)* problem elimination teams, *(vii)* self-directed workteams, *(viii)* self-managed teams, *(ix)* process improvement teams or groups, *(x)* Kaizen teams, *(xi)* statistical process control teams, *(xii)* error-cause removal teams, *(xiii)* corrective action teams and *(xiv)* cross-functional teams in areas such as design, quality assurance, costs, standardisation, delivery and supply.

8.1.1 The Role of Teams in Continuous Improvement

Teams have a number of roles to play as a component in a process of continuous improvement. Teams can:

Teams have a major role in a process of continuous improvement.

(i) Aid the commitment of people to the principles of TQM.

(ii) Provide an additional means of communication between individuals, management and their direct reports, across functions and with customers and suppliers.

(iii) Provide the means and opportunity for people to participate in decision-making.

(iv) Improve inter-personal relationships, and knowledge, develop trust, facilitate cooperative activity and adjust to change.

(v) Help to develop people and encourage leadership traits.

(vi) Build collective responsibility and develop a sense of ownership.

(vii) Aid personal development and build confidence.

(viii) Develop problem-solving skills.

(ix) Facilitate awareness of quality improvement potential, leading to behaviour and attitude change.

(x) Help facilitate a change in management style and culture.

(xi) Improve morale.

(xii) Imbue a sense of accomplishment.

(xiii) Improve operating effectiveness as people work in a common direction and through this generate interaction and synergy.

8.2 TYPES OF TOTAL QUALITY TEAMS

TQ uses many different types of teams with differing characteristics in terms of membership, mode of participation, autonomy, problem selection, scope of activity, decision making authority, access to information, problem solving potential, resources and permanency which can be used in the improvement process. It is important that the right kind of team is formed for the project, problem or activity under consideration.

There are a variety of teams with different operating characteristics which can be used in TQM.

Some common types of teams include:

1. ***Steering committees or quality councils :*** Management teams that lead an organisation and provide direction and focus.
2. ***Quality circles :*** A quality circle is a voluntary group of 6 to 8 employees from the same work area. They meet usually in company time, for one hour every week or fortnight, under the leadership of their work supervisor, to solve problems relating to improving their work activities and environment.
3. ***Problem-solving teams :*** Teams of workers and supervisors that meet to address workplace problems involving quality and productivity, or ad-hoc teams with a specific mission such as organisational design teams that act as architects of change.
4. ***Natural workteams :*** People who work together everyday to perform a complete unit of work.
5. ***Self-managed teams :*** Workteams that are empowered to make and control their own decisions. Also known as ***self-directed workteams***, self-managed teams consist of highly trained group of employees, from 6 to 18, on average, fully responsible for turning out a well-defined segment of finished work. The segment could be a final product or a service or a sub-unit of a final product.
6. ***Virtual teams :*** Teams whose members communicate by computer, take turns as leaders, and jump in or out as needed. Virtual teams are becoming more and more relevant because of the Internet and electronic communication.
7. ***Quality improvement teams :*** Teams which comprise members of a single department, or which can be cross-functional and include representatives of either or both customers and suppliers. The objective of such teams could be: *(a)* improving quality, *(b)* eliminating waste and non-value added activity and *(c)* improving productivity.
8. ***Department improvement team :*** Most common type of team, composed of the personnel who make up a specific unit, department or function within the organisation and are sometimes called a ***quality circle.***
9. ***Process improvement teams :*** Type of teams which have the objective of improving an entire process. Consequently such teams are made of people from each individual phase of the process.

10. *Task force:* Sometimes called ***project teams***, these are temporary teams formed for a specific, well-defined mission. Special project and problem-solving teams fall into this category. Task forces are composed of the people who are most likely to be able to accomplish their specific missions and are disbanded once the mission has been accomplished.

8.2.1 Rationale for Teams

Teamwork is a fundamental element of total quality.

Teamwork is a fundamental element of total quality. In an organisation, some individual may be great in his or her job, but what counts at work is the success of the organisation rather than that of the individual. Performance of athletic teams (*e.g.*, relay race), basket ball, foot-ball or volley ball games are best examples of teamwork of players of the team. **The rationale for teams are:**

(i) Two or more heads are better than one.

(ii) The whole (the team) is greater than the sum of its parts (individual members) or in otherwords, teams promote ***synergy.***

(iii) People in teams get to know each other, build trust, and as a result, want to help each other.

(iv) Teamwork promotes better communication.

It is well established that teams can out-perform individuals, provided they are properly handled.

8.3 EFFECTIVE TEAM WORK

Effective teamwork is critical to a successful TR effort.

Teams are the main structure of many TQ organisations. Therefore, effective teamwork is critical to a successful TQ effort. If teams are not effective, total quality processes will suffer. *For example,* if steering committees choose poor directions and policies for the organisation, departmental and cross-functional problem-solving teams choose in-appropriate problems or won't be able to solve the problems they identify, and if self-managed teams are not able to fulfill the promise of an empowered, creative workforce, the TQ efforts of the organisation will fail to accomplish the objectives.

8.3.1 Criteria for Team Effectiveness

The various criteria for team effectiveness are:

(i) the team must achieve its goals of quality improvement,

(ii) teams that improve quality performance quickly, are more effective than those that take a long period of time to do so

(iii) teams should have the potential for rapid adaptation to changing conditions

(iv) the team must maintain or increase its strength as a unit, and

(v) the team must preserve or strengthen its relationship with the rest of the organisation.

An effective quality team will be able to improve quality performance quickly and achieve its quality improvement goals.

Peter Scholtes, a leading authority on teams for quality improvement, has suggested 10 ingredients for a successful team:

1. ***Clarity in team goals :*** A team agrees on a mission, purpose and goals.
2. ***An improvement plan :*** A plan guides the team in determining schedules and milestones by helping the team decide what advice, assistance, training, materials and other resources may be needed.
3. ***Clearly defined roles :*** All members must understand their duties and know who is responsible for what issues and tasks.
4. ***Clear communication :*** Team members should be able to speak with clarity, listen actively and share information with other team members.
5. ***Beneficial team behaviours :*** Teams should encourage members to use effective skills and practices to facilitate meetings and discussions.
6. ***Well-defined decision procedures :*** Teams should be able to use data as the basis for decisions and learn to reach consensus on important issues.

7. ***Balanced participation :*** Every team member should participate, contribute their talents and share commitment to the team's success.
8. ***Established ground rules :*** The team outlines the acceptable and unacceptable behaviour of its members.
9. ***Awareness of group process :*** Team members should express sensitivity to non-verbal communication, understand group dynamics and work on group process issues.
10. ***Use of scientific approach :*** With structural problem-solving processes, teams can find root causes of problems with considerable ease.

8.3.2 Team Excellence and Performance

Poorly run teams can do more harm to an organisation's performance and corresponding competitiveness than having no teams at all. Therefore, it is critical that excellence in team performance be an overriding goal of the organisation.

The ten team commandments recommended by Dennis King, personnel manager for Proctor & Gamble are:

1. ***Interdependence :*** Team members should be mutually dependent on each other for information, resources, task accomplishment and support.
2. ***Stretching tasks :*** Teams needs to be challenged. Responding to a challenge as a team builds *esprit de corps* and instills pride and unity.
3. ***Alignment :*** An aligned team is one in which all team members not only share a common mission but are willing to put aside individualism to accomplish it.
4. ***Common language :*** Teams often consist of members from different departments (*i.e.,* cross-functional teams). These different departments typically have their own languages that may not be understood by team members from other departments. Therefore it is important that team leaders ensure that the team members have a common language which is understood by all team members.

Excellence in team performance can be an overriding goal of the organisation.

5. ***Trust/respect :*** For team members to work well together, there must be trust and respect. Time and effort spent building trust and respect among team members is time invested well.
6. ***Shared leadership/followership :*** If team leaders are allowed to dominate, the group will not achieve its full potential. A better approach is to draw out the special talent of each individual team member so that leadership and followership are shared.
7. ***Problem-solving skills :*** Time invested in helping group members become better problem solvers is time well spent. Much of the business of teams is problem solving.
8. ***Confrontation/conflict handling skills :*** Human conflict is inevitable in a high pressure, competitive workplace. Learning to disagree without being disagreeable and to air disagreement openly and frankly - attacking ideas, issues and proposed solutions without attacking people proposing them - are critical skills required in a total quality environment.
9. ***Assessment/action :*** Assessment is a matter of asking and answering the question "How are we doing?" The yardsticks for answering this question are the team's mission statement and corresponding action plan, which contains goals, objectives, schedules and assignments of responsibility. By monitoring these continuously the team members can assess how the team is doing.
10. ***Celebration :*** An effective team reinforces its success by celebrating them. Recognition of a job well done can motivate team members to work even harder and smarter to achieve its next goal.

8.4 TEAM MEMBERSHIP AND ROLES

Teams, like any system cannot function effectively without high quality inputs. Team members are the most important elements of team processes. Managers need to know why people do and do not join teams.

To be effective, team members must be representative of the departments or functions related to the problem being addressed. Team members assume a variety of roles in performing their duties. Some are ***task oriented,*** *for example,* initiating projects, collecting information, analysing data, using QC tools, creating action plans, writing reports, etc. Others are ***relationship oriented,*** such as encouraging other team members, listening carefully, and respecting others' opinions. Both types of roles are necessary for teams to function effectively and proper selection and training of team members is important to ensure that they possess both technical and interpersonal skills to perform these roles.

Team members assume a variety of roles in performing their duties which may be task - oriented or relationship - oriented.

Team members must possess the necessary technical knowledge to solve the problem at hand. All members need not share the same knowledge and infact team members are often selected on the basis of specialised knowledge, but all of the appropriate technical bases must be covered for the team to be effective.

Interpersonal skills of team members is of critical importance for a team to be effective. People with good interpersonal skills are good listeners, have appropriate attitude, do not ignore or downgrade someone else's ideas in order to promote their own. They try to understand other people's positions, even when they do not agree with them. They are willing and able to communicate their opinions, ideas and any information that needs to be shared. They can deal with conflict effectively. Finally, they are willing to share credit for accomplishments with other members of the group.

Another important attribute of team membership is ***diversity.*** Many organisations have found that the best decisions stem from cross-fertilisation of ideas from individuals with diverse backgrounds, experiences and interests.

8.4.1 Team Sponsor

The characteristics of a team sponsor are:

(i) member of quality steering committee and a senior manager

(ii) actively support the team in its task

(iii) helps resolve priority conflicts

(iv) mentor to the team leader

(v) ensures that the team leader has the required skills and training to lead the team

(vi) acts as a link for communication between the team and the quality steering committee

(vii) agrees a charter with the team which includes: objectives, deliversable/outcomes, resources, boundaries and time frame

(viii) holds regular meetings with the team's facilitators.

8.4.2 Team Facilitator

The characteristics of the team facilitator are:

(i) helps the team mentor and team leader in establishing the team

(ii) ensures that the right balance of skills is on the team

(iii) acts as a coach to the team leader and assists with tasks as requested by the leader

(iv) responsible for team progress and direction

(v) ensures that all team members contribute

(vi) responsible for communication from the team to the world outside the team
(vii) communicates team road-blocks and help remove them
(viii) identifies training needs of the team and provides and implements the training programs
(ix) celebrates success of the team.

8.4.3 Team Leader

A team leader can be either chosen by management or be appointed by the team. The responsibilities of team leader include:

(i) organising and sending out agenda
(ii) ensures that the team members are familiar with the protocol of team meetings
(iii) ensures that the team has a convenient place to meet
(iv) consults with line managers on suitable times for team meetings
(v) serves as the official contact between the team and the rest of the organisation
(vi) serves as the official record keeper, for the team. Records include minutes of the meeting, correspondence, agendas and reports
(vii) communicates minutes and follow-up actions
(viii) needs to be an active contributor and listener
(ix) ensures that members know what is expected of them
(x) responsible for team progress and direction
(xi) serves of full-fledged team member, but with care to avoid dominating team discussions
(xii) implements team recommendations that fall within the team leader's realm of authority and work with higher management to implement those that fall outside it.

8.4.4 Team Member

Characteristics of a team member are:

(i) is clear on why he/she wishes to become a member of a team
(ii) enthusiastic about the project of the team or the goal to be achieved
(iii) is a willing team member, not coerced to join the team
(iv) should contribute relevant experience
(v) takes responsibility, as requested, for follow-up actions
(vi) respects the role of team leader
(vii) is an active listener
(viii) needs to be able to follow through actions
(ix) should respect the ideas and views of other members
(x) takes minutes of the meeting as and when requested by the team leader.

The team leader is responsible for the team's day - to - day success.

8.5 TEAM PROCESSES

The various processes undertaken within total quality teams are: *(i)* ***quality planning,*** *(ii)* ***problem selection and diagnosis,*** *(iii)* ***work allocation,*** *(iv)* ***communication,*** *(v)* ***data collection,*** and *(vi)* ***implementation of solutions.***

Some of the processes used in teams are discussed in the following section:

1. **Problem Selection :** One of the processes undertaken by most teams and especially problem-solving teams is the ***choice of problems*** or issues on which to work. New teams are generally not skilled enough to solve major problems. Therefore it makes sense for a team initially to select a problem of moderate importance and difficulty and to move on to more complex and

difficult problems when the team is better established.

Another problem among new teams is that they select problems that are not associated with important business or quality issues. The selection of 'trivial' problems by teams may indicate that management has not done an effective job of sharing information about the business with team members.

The various processes undertaken within total quality teams are:
(i) Problem selection
(ii) Problem diagnosis
(iii) Work allocation
(iv) Communciation
*(v)*Co - ordination and
(vi) Organisational support.

2. **Problem Diagnosis :** After problems to be addressed are identified, their causes must be ascertained. Problem diagnosis is the process by which the team investigates potential causes of problems to identify potential solutions. **The diagnostic journey consists of three parts:**

   (i) understanding the symptoms (*for example,* a process out of control),

   (ii) theorizing as to causes and

   (iii) testing the theories.

   Teams that spend more time diagnosing problems have been shown to be much more effective than those that proceed immediately to solutions.

3. **Work Allocation :** Assigning tasks is one of the key to team effectiveness and should not be taken lightly. Each team member has certain skills and will perform well on tasks that use those skills and not so well on tasks that use other skills. The team needs to assign people tasks that will utilise their skills to the greatest extent possible.

4. **Communication: Communication is a key process for any team attempting to improve quality :** Steering committee communicates priorities to employees. Members of problem-solving teams communicate among themselves and to their internal and external customers. The communication process can be improved by carefully assigning people to key communication tasks and by training people in communication. Listening and asking questions are vital to effective communication. Communication within and across teams also can be enhanced by using a variety of media.

5. **Coordination :** Coordinating the team's work with other teams and departments in the organisation is another key element in team processes. Teams cannot work in isolation and maintaining good relationships outside the team is one criterion of team effectiveness. Coordination often involves resolving issues of interdependent schedules but may also include some negotiation regarding sharing of information, resources and support services. Good communication should also help to coordinate work with other teams and departments.

6. **Organisational Support :** However skillful the team, they will find it hard to be successful unless their efforts are supported by the organisation in general and by management in particular. **Organisational support is the foundation for effective team work.**

   Organisational support is the foundation for effective teamwork

   For a total quality to be successful, management must provide the following:

   (i) Management must issue a clear charge to the group, *i.e.,* a description of what the group is and is not expected to do. This is often called a ***"team charter"*.**

   (ii) Human resource management systems often must be adjusted. Conventional HRM systems may be barriers to effective teamwork that will undermine total quality if not changed. The need to enhance training is particularly acute as team members must be trained to improve their skills necessary for effective teamwork.

   Performance appraisal and reward systems are also a concern. Many of these systems are designed to reward individual effort or the attainment of functional goals rather than teamwork. Selection process may also be changed in conjuction with TQ implementation. TQ organisations want their new employees to think in terms of creating quality and value for consumers, to understand their customers and their needs and to work toward results despite obstacles.

(iii) Management must provide the team with the resources necessary to be successful. These include a place and time to meet and the tools to get the job done. Management should avoid moving people on and off teams frequently as this can disrupt teamwork.

(iv) When teams make a proposed, management must respond swiftly and constructively. However, it is not realistic to expect that every quality improvement proposal made by a team will be implemented. However, self-managed teams generally have broad authority to implement their own solutions.

8.5.1 Guidelines for Developing Effective Teams

To ensure that teams work effectively and efficiently the following factors should be taken into account:

(i) Management must commit themselves to nurturing and supporting teams.

(ii) It must be ensured that the appropriate awareness training and education with regard to TQM have been undertaken before launching team creativity.

(iii) Each team member must be clear about the aims and objectives of the team, the work to be accomplished by the team and its potential contribution to day-to-day operations.

(iv) Team members must be trained in appropriate data collection, problem solving, experimental and decision-making methods and the team must ensure that it uses the target skills and methods effectively.

(v) Special coaching and counselling should be provided to the team leaders since they are critical to a team's success.

(vi) The team mentors must actively support and contribute to the team.

(vii) The team should be disciplined and should have and utilise a set method of problem-solving based on fact and not opinion.

(viii) There should be a set of rules and operating procedures that guide the meetings of the team.

(ix) Teams should meet on a regular basis and work to an agenda.

(x) Periodic reports to management and the mentor on team activities must be prepared.

(xi) People who are likely to be affected by the results of the project should be involved in the team activity.

(xii) The team should receive appropriate recognition and celebration for successful improvements.

(xiii) The performance of the team on completion of a project should be evaluated and reviewed to see what worked and what did not and what could be done better, including identification of training needs and pinpointing of barriers.

8.6 EMPOWERMENT AND MOTIVATION

Involving people in decision-making relating to their work is a fundamental principle of total quality management. Employees are involved not only in decision-making but also in the creative thought processes that precede decision-making. Not only are employees involved, they are empowered.

Employee involvement and empowerment are closely related concepts, but they are not the same.

Employee involvement and empowerment are closely related concepts, but they are not the same. In a total quality setting, employees should be empowered. **Empowerment** means giving someone power-granting the authority to do whatever necessary to satisfy customers and trusting employees to make the right choices without waiting for management approval. The objective of empowerment is "to tap the creative and intellectual energy of everybody in the company, not just those in the executive suite..... to provide everyone with the responsibility and the resources to display real leadership within their own individual spheres of competence. **By empowering employees, organisations drive decision-making down to its lowest possible level.**

One of the core components of quality leadership is that of having everyone in the organisation involved in managing and improving quality of the processes for which they are responsible. This might be done as part of day-to-day operations as a member of a natural work team or a self-directed team, or in becoming part of a group that is going to take on a special process design or improvement project. Regardless of the way it occurs, it involves giving employees greater responsibility and authority and is commonly referred to as ***empowerment.***

Empowerment is based on the belief that employees have the ability to take on more responsibility and authority to take on more responsibility and authority than has traditionally been given them, and that heightened productivity and a better quality of work life will result. Juran defined empowerment as "conferring the right to make decisions and take action".

By empowering employees organisations drive decision making down to its lowest possible level.

Empowerment is a natural extension of employee involvement concepts such as worker participation in decision-making. It represents high degree of involvement in which employees make decisions themselves and are responsible for their outcomes. **For empowerment to occur, managers must undertake two major initiatives:**

(i) Identify and change organisational conditions that make people powerless and

(ii) increase people's confidence that their efforts to accomplish something important will be successful.

Empowerment is an application of the teamwork principle of total quality, embodying "vertical" teamwork between managerial and non-managerial personnel. Employees are given important responsibilities and the authority that goes along with them.

Empowerment is based on the concepts of ***job enlargement*** and ***job enrichment.*** Job enlargement means changing the scope of the job to include a greater portion of the horizontal process. Job enrichment means increasing the depth of the job to include responsibilities that have been traditionally carried out at higher levels of the organisation.

Empowerment of employees will require the following:

(i) A work environment and managing style that supports empowerment.

(ii) Training in the skills necessary in order to carryout the additional responsibilities.

(iii) Access to information upon which decisions can be made, and

(iv) Willingness and confidence on the part of the employee to take on greater responsibility.

Empowerment is based on the concepts of job enlargement and job enrichment.

Empowerment also means management giving up some of the power traditionally held by it, which means management must take on new roles and responsibilities and gain new knowledge. It does not mean that management relinquishes all authority, totally delegates decision-making, and allows operating without accountability. It requires a significant investment of time and effort to develop mutual trust, assess and add to individual's competencies as well as develop clear agreement about roles, responsibilities, risk taking and boundaries.

Empowerment is difficult to implement because it is often a major change from past ways of working. It involves behavioural changes in all members of the organisation: management, operation personnel and support staff. To start, an organisation should develop an operational definition of empowerment and communicate a strong commitment to it, starting from top management. It should develop a time-phased implementation plan and build or modify the necessary organisational systems to support empowerment.

8.6.1 Role of Empowerment in Quality Improvement

Empowerment improves organisational performance.

Empowerment is important primarily because it improves organisational performance. Empowerment results in four employee attitudes which correlate strongly with higher profits. These are: *(i)* workers feel they are given the opportunity to do what they do best every day, *(ii)* they believe their opinions count, *(iii)* they sense their fellow workers are committed to quality and *(iv)* they have made a direct connection between their work and the company's mission.

Giving employees responsibility for their own work has led not only to improvements in motivation, customer service and morale, but also to improvements in quality, productivity and the speed of decision-making.

Although empowerment is relevant for all aspects of organisational performance, it plays a special role in quality improvement. Total quality requires people to make real changes in the way work is done and relies on in-depth understanding of the current system. Only employees involved in the system day to day possess such an understanding. Therefore employee involvement and empowerment are seen as integral parts of total quality. **The relationship between empowerment and quality is illustrated in *Exhibit 8.1.***

Exhibit 8.1 : How Empowerment Leads to Quality

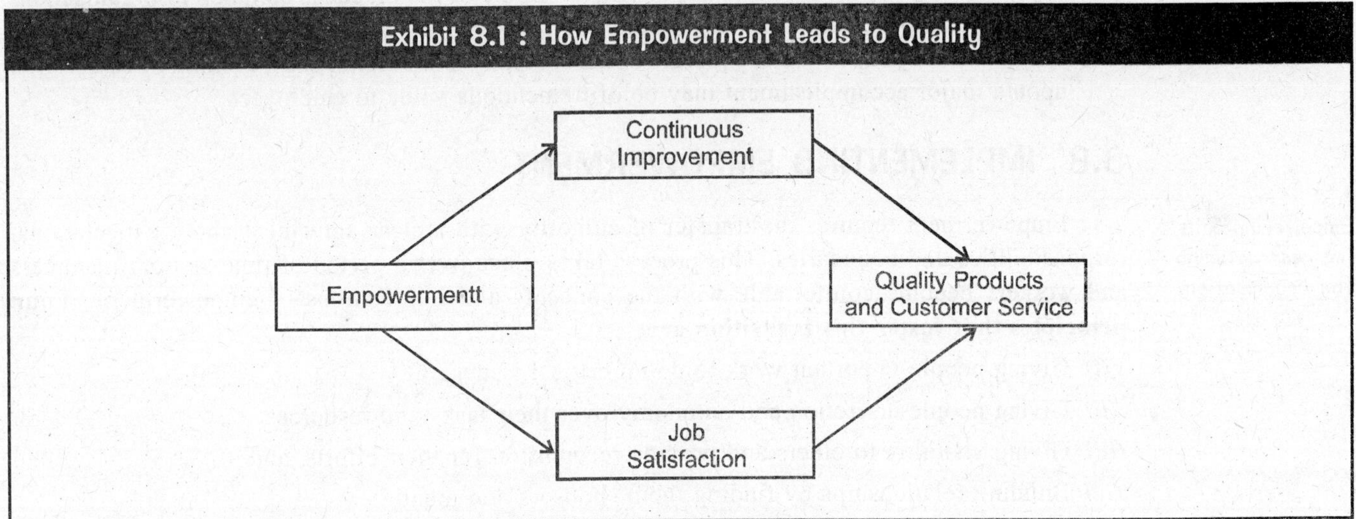

8.7 PRINCIPLES OF EMPOWERMENT

A number of principles are involved in successfully giving power to employees. They are:

(i) ***Empower sincerely and completely :*** Empowerment should be done sincerely and not superficially. Managers must think long and hard before making commitment to empowerment - once done, it can't be done half-way. Semi-empowerment just doesn't work. Managers must be clear on exactly what responsibility and authority rests with employees.

(ii) ***Establish mutual trust :*** The managers must trust the workforce enough to be willing to make the delegation and the workforce must have confidence in the managers to be willing to accept the responsibility. Employee empowerment boosts morale of employees and motivates them to improve productivity. However, management must assure employees that they will not take advantage of productivity increases to cut the workforce. The ultimate issue for many employees is job security and management must make explicit commitments to this effect to employees.

(iii) ***Provide employees with business information :*** For empowerment to succeed, it must focus on making the organisation more competitive. Empowerment can contribute organisational performance only if employees have access to the necessary information about the business and its performance such as their resources (quality improvement budgets). Sharing business information with employees relates directly to quality, customer service and competitiveness. In the absence of appropriate information, empowered employees may use their power on problems that are not very important.

(iv) ***Ensure that employees are capable :*** To operate in an empowered TQ environment, employees must possess not only technical skills but also interpersonal and problem-solving skills.

Employee capability can be ensured through selection and training processes. Unless the human resource processes are adapted to provide capable employees, empowerment cannot succeed. Empowerment also requires that employees understand their appropriate limits of discretion.

(v) ***Dont ignore middle management :*** Managers must consider how empowering lower-level employees will affect middle managers. If the needs and expectations of middle managers are ignored, empowerment will be confusing at best and disastrous at worst. Middle management people in an empowered TQ environment must be trained to think differently and manage their departments by acting as teachers and coaches or facilitators.

(vi) ***Change the reward system :*** When organisations ask employees to assume new challenges and responsibilities, substantial organisational change cannot be created without changing the reward system for the employees. It is difficult to specify exactly what kind of reward system will be needed to complement empowerment. Some of the practices common to organisations utilising employee empowerment include ***pay-for-skills*** and ***profit sharing***. In addition, sincere appreciation by supervisors, a picture in the company's newsletter or an evening of celebration upon a major accomplishment may be of tremendous value to employees.

8.8 IMPLEMENTING EMPOWERMENT

Empowering calls for restructuring the organisation.

Empowerment requires the transfer of authority with a clear agreement about expectations, responsibilities and boundaries. This process takes place over a period of time as both managers and workers become comfortable with the concepts and implications of empowerment. **Four principles that foster this transition are:**

(i) Giving people important work to do on critical issues.

(ii) Giving people discretion and autonomy over their tasks and resources.

(iii) Giving visibility to others and provide recognition for their efforts, and

(iv) Building relationships by finding them sponsors and mentors.

Often, empowerment calls for restructuring the organisation to reduce levels of hierarchy or to provide a more customer and process-focussed organisation. Empowerment is often viewed as an inverted triangle of organisational power. ***Exhibit 8.2*** **illustrates traditional versus empowered organisation.**

Exhibit 8.2 : Traditional versus Empowered Organisation

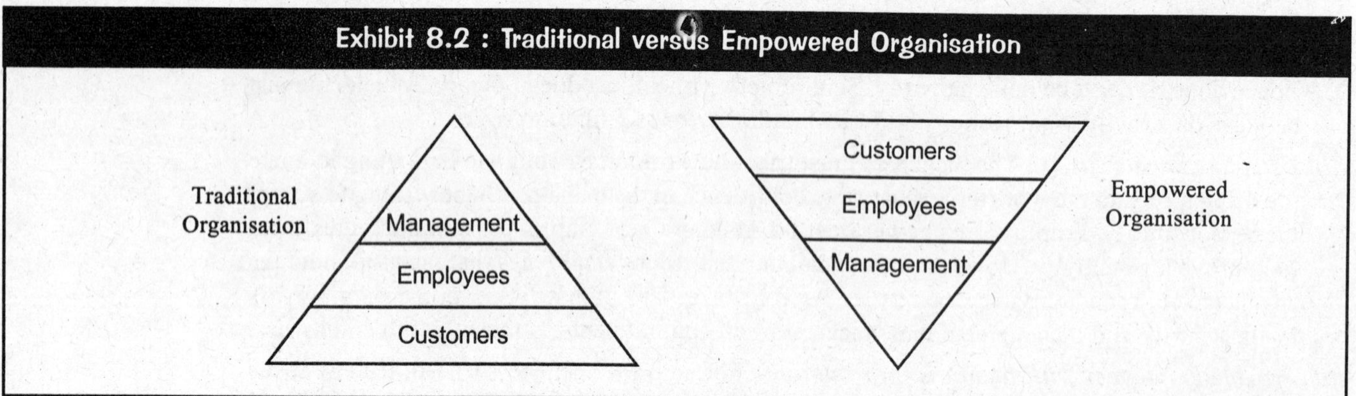

For empowerment to be successfully implemented, the leader's role must shift from that of a traditional ***manager*** to that of an ***enabler***. Leaders must balance their need of personal control with the ability to provide freedom to others to act on their own authority. This is a mindset as well as a negotiated agreement between leaders and their followers (subordinates). Leaders who empower others create an environment in which this balance can take place. They involve their subordinates in planning, delegate responsibility, clarify the scope of authority, delineate boundaries, encourage, provide a motivational environment and reward accomplishments.

The process also needs to occur from top to bottom. Frontline managers need to understand how to implement the process and how to transition from a traditional role to that of an empowering leader. Middle management needs to work to remove barriers to empowerment and to help frontline managers in their new roles. Changes in performance review and compensation systems are usually required to align these systems with the new responsibilities.

People who are well-matched with their current jobs don't require force or coercion to work hard and produce quality work. They are internally motivated.

Although ***work design*** is the most visible change in empowerment, the relationships of managers and employees is perhaps the most significant and difficult aspect of that change.

Table 8.1 **below summarises these changes, emphasising the inherent difficulty in trying to change from a traditional to an empowered organisation.**

Table 8.1 : Relationship Changes in an Empowered Organisation

Issue for Comparison	Traditional Organisation	Empowered Organisation
Employee's primary focus is on:	Management	Customers
Management's role is:	Monitoring and controlling	Facilitating and coaching
Management-employee relationship is:	Boss to subordinate	Peer-to-peer

8.8.1 Barriers to Empowerment

1. ***A lack of clear commitment :*** To succeed, top management must clearly communicate its support to the implementation of empowerment.
2. ***Failure to define empowerment :*** Failing to develop an operational definition of empowerment results in confusion and inconsistent implementation.
3. ***Failure to establish the boundaries within which employees can be empowered.***
4. ***Failure to provide appropriate training to management and the performers.***
5. ***Failure to implement appropriate incentives :*** People who have been rewarded for behaviour that serves a traditional hierarchical system will resist transitioning to a new role unless incentives to encourage change are in place.
6. ***Lack of an implementation plan :*** Empowerment takes time, resources and up-front costs for training and organisational support systems. Therefore an implementation plan is essential to prepare the groundwork.
7. ***Inability to modify organisational culture :*** In many traditional organisations, empowerment is hindered by the hierarchical structures, reward processes and cultural values. Unless appropriate changes are made, empowerment will fail.
8. ***Some people will resent a shift to empowerment :*** They often don't want to assume the responsibility involved upon empowerment. Others may feel that management is trying to pass down their responsibility in order to save money or whatever.
9. ***Not everyone will buy in at first :*** Some will wait and see if this is just another passing scheme of management.
10. ***Middle and first-level management resent giving up their authority :*** Learning and practicing new behaviour is tough on those who grew up in the "old school" ways.
11. If top management is not visibly and continually seen using empowerment techniques, the effort will likely to fail.

Managers should overcome barriers to empowerment in order to obtain the benefits from empowerment.

12. Changing the culture from a traditional hierarchieal mode to one where empowerment is practiced takes a long time and costs money.
13. The organisation structure and reporting relationships will need to be changed.
14. Major systems and processes will require modification or replacement; *for example,* strategic planning process, compensation system, employee recognition and reward process, customer service processes, expense reimbursement procedure etc.

8.8.2 Benefits from Empowerment

A survey administered in several companies to evaluate the perceived benefits of employees' involvement and empowerment revealed the following benefits:

(i) Significant improvements in attitudes and behaviour of employees.
(ii) Increase in individual self-respect.
(iii) Increased respect for employees by supervisors.
(iv) Increased employee understanding of management.
(v) Reduced conflict between employees and managers.
(vi) Increased employee awareness of why problems are not solved quickly.
(vii) Increase in employee productivity.
(viii) Improved customer satisfaction.

8.8.3 Empowerment and Motivation

Empowerment is the key to motivation and productivity

Empowerment is the key to motivation and productivity. An employee who feels he or she is valued and can contribute is ready to help and grow in the job. Empowerment enables a person to develop personally so that his or her contributions in the workplace is maximised. Empowerment is not the same as participatory management. Empowerment is getting employees to help themselves, each other and the company whereas participatory management is about manager and supervisors asking for their employees help. This is why empowerment can be so effective in helping to maintain a high level of motivation among employees. It helps employees develop a sense of ownership of their jobs and in the company. This in turn, leads to a greater willingness on the part of employees to make decisions, take risks in an effort to make improvements and speakout when they disagree.

8.8.4 Management's Role in Empowerment

Management's role in empowerment is best described by commitment, leadership and facilitation.

Management must do everything necessary to ensure successful implementation of the concept of empowerment. The three words that best describe management's role in empowerment are ***commitment, leadership*** **and** ***facilitation.*** All these three functions are required to break down the barriers of empowerment and overcome the inherent resistance often associated with implementation of empowerment or with any other major change in the corporate culture.

Manager's role in empowerment is demonstrated by the following support behaviour: *(i)* Exhibiting a supportive attitude, *(ii)* Being a role model, *(iii)* Being a trainer, *(iv)* Being a facilitator, *(v)* Practicing management by walking around (MBWA), *(vi)* Taking quick action on recommendations and *(vii)* Recognising the accomplishments of employees.

8.9 MOTIVATION

For total quality to succeed, it is necessary to have willing, sustained, individual effort and co-ordinated teamwork focused on meeting organisational goals. However, when organisations ask employees to assume new challenges and responsibilities, the employees expect some personal benefits. Understanding human behaviour and motivation are major elements which affect total quality management approach in organisations. Both intrinsic and extrinsic rewards are vital to sustained individual efforts. In a TQ environment, managers take on the roles of coaches and facilitators and their skills in motivating employees become more crucial. The system in which people work can either seriously impede motivation or enhance it. Compensation, recognition/reward systems and the work environment must be carefully designed to motivate employees to achieve organisational as well as personal objectives.

The TQ approach to the management of employees in general and empowerment in particular, is quite consistent with organisational behaviour theory. Organisational psychologist Chris Argyris proposed the idea that quality problems are usually attributable to management created systems rather than employee motivation. Renis Likert described an organisational system which featured empowered work groups and cross-functional teams. Douglas McGregor's well known 'Theory Y' approach to managing employees is based on the assumption that people wish to do a good job and emphasises that people in organisations should make decisions for themselves (*i.e.*, empowerment). These are fundamental principles of the TQ approach to managing people.

The TQ approach to empowerment is consistent with organisational behaviour theories such as Douglas Mc Gregor's "Theory Y" and more recent theories of work motivation such as

(i) job characteristics theory

(ii) acquired needs theory and

(iii) goal setting theory.

The TQ philosophy is also consistent with several more recent theories of work motivation such as: *(a)* ***job characteristics theory,*** *(b)* ***acquired needs theory*** *and (c)* ***goal setting theory.***

"Job Characteristics Theory" states that people will be more motivated to work and more satisfied with their jobs to the extent that their jobs possess certain core characteristics such as ***skill variety, task identity, task significance, autonomy*** **and *feedback.***

TQ approach increases the motivating potentials of jobs through increases in the foregoing task characteristics. Employee involvement in problem solving should increase both the variety of skills they use in their jobs and their perception of doing a meaningful unit of work. Employee empowerment should increase the degree of autonomy people feel they have in doing their work.

'Acquired Needs Theory' states that people are motivated by work that fulfills their needs (specially the need for achievement, the need for affiliation and the need for power). The need most likely to be fulfilled by participation in TQ is the need for affiliation. Obviously, this would occur through the formation of self-managed or cross-functional teams. TQ promotes close relationships between people in the same or different subunits or even in different organisations in the customer-supplier chain. TQ and empowerment are likely to be motivating for employees with a high need for power. Effective utilisation of TQ should allow organisations to achieve higher levels of performance in such areas as quality and customer satisfaction but such achievements are more likely to come through team rather than individual efforts. Therefore, people with high achievement motivation can be motivated only if they align their own work with the team performance and feel a sense of achievement as a member of the team and not as an individual.

'Goal Setting Theory' states that people whose goal are clear will work more quickly, perform better and generally are more motivated than people who lack clear goals. According to this theory, goals will be motivating to people when they are specific and difficult, and people accept them as their own. However, goals should also be attainable, specific. Challenging goals that seem impossible are demotivating.

People who set their own goals (as in empowerment) are likely to be more motivated by them than are people whose goals are set by their superiors (managers) as in traditional organisations.

8.10 QUALITY IN PRACTICE

Box 8.1 Union Resistance to Empowerment

Florida Power and Light Company (FP & L) is well known for its commitment to employee empowerment. FP & L's Quality Improvement Program (QIP) is one of the best in the country. However what works well was not universally popular at first. In fact, the idea was originally rejected by the union leadership of FP & L. This resistance on the part of the union resulted in a difficult beginning for FP & L's Quality Improvement Program. Why did the union resist at first? Because union leaders were not involved in the development and implementation of the program. What overcame this resistance? Getting them involved.

8.11 SUMMARY

Concepts of organisational behaviour such as teamwork, empowerment and motivation, and organisational culture and ethics have an important role in total quality organisations.

A major characteristic of a total quality organisation is the existence of teams and teamwork at all levels - top, middle and bottom and in every function and department. TQ philosophy uses teamwork as a way to coordinate work and achieve synergy in operations. Teams encourage positive attitude and trust among team members and diversity inherent in teams provide unique perspectives on work and creativity.

Major types of total quality teams include: *(i)* steering committees or quality councils, *(ii)* quality circles, *(iii)* problem-solving teams, *(iv)* natural work teams, *(v)* self-managed teams, *(vi)* virtual teams, *(vii)* quality improvement teams, *(viii)* department improvement team, *(ix)* process improvement team and *(x)* task force.

Teamwork is a fundamental element of total quality and teams have a number of roles to play as a component in a process of continuous improvement in total quality organisations. Effective teamwork is critical to a successful total quality effort.

According Peter Scholtes, ten ingredients for a successful team are: *(i)* clarity in team goals, *(ii)* an improvement plan, *(iii)* clearly defined goals, *(iv)* clear communication, *(v)* beneficial team behaviours, *(vi)* well-defined decision procedures, *(vii)* balanced participation, *(viii)* establish ground rules, *(ix)* awareness of group process, and *(x)* use of scientific approach.

The ten commandments recommended by Dennis King for team excellence and performance are: *(i)* interdependence, *(ii)* stretching tasks, *(iii)* alignment, *(iv)* common language, *(v)* trust/respect, *(vi)* shared leadership/followership, *(vii)* problem-solving skills, *(viii)* confrontation/conflict handling skills, *(ix)* assessment/action, and *(x)* celebration.

Team members are the most important elements of team processes. Team members must be representative of the departments or functions related to the problem being addressed. Their roles may be ***task-oriented*** or ***relationship-oriented***. Both types of roles are necessary for teams to function effectively and proper selection and training of team members is important to ensure that they possess both ***technical*** and ***interpersonal skills*** to perform these roles. Another important attribute of team membership is ***diversity***.

The various types of team membership and roles include: *(i)* team sponsor, *(ii)* team facilitator, *(iii)* team leader and *(iv)* team member.

Team processes are the various processes undertaken within total quality teams. They include: *(i)* quality planning, *(ii)* problem selection and diagnosis, *(iii)* work allocation, *(iv)* communication, *(v)* data collection, and *(v)* implementation of solutions.

Empowerment and motivation is another major organisational behaviour aspect that impacts total quality approach in organisations.

Employee involvement and empowerment are closely related concepts. In a total quality setting employees must be not only involved in their activities but also must be empowered to take decisions relating to their work responsibilities. To successfully implement employee empowerment, they must be adequately trained to handle their responsibilities and to take appropriate decisions. Also they must be well motivated to accept authority to carryout their responsibilities.

The principles of empowerment are: *(i)* empower sincerely and completely, *(ii)* establish mutual trust, *(iii)* provide employees with business information, *(iv)* ensure that employees are capable, *(v)* don't ignore middle management, *(vi)* change the reward system.

To implement empowerment, authority is required to be transferred to employees with a clear agreement about expectations, responsibilities and boundaries.

Often, empowerment calls for restructuring the organisation to reduce levels of hierarchy or to provide a more customer and process focused organisation. For empowerment to be successfully implemented, the leader's role must change from that of a manager to that of an enabler.

The barriers to empowerment include: *(i)* a lack of clear commitment, *(ii)* failure to define empowerment, *(iii)* failure to establish the boundaries within which employees can be empowered, *(iv)* failure to provide appropriate training to management and the performers, *(v)* failure to implement appropriate incentives, *(vi)* lack of an implementation plan, *(vii)* inability to modify organisational culture, *(viii)* not everyone will buy it first, *(ix)* some people will resent a shift to empowerment, *(x)* middle and first level management resent giving up their authority, *(xi)* failure of top management to use empowerment techniques, *(xii)* long time taken to change the organisational culture, *(xiii)* failure to change the reporting relationships and *(xiv)* need to make modifications in major systems and processes or to replace them.

Empowerment has several benefits and is the key to motivation and productivity. For total quality to succeed, it is necessary to have willing, sustained, individual effort and coordinated teamwork focused on meeting organisational goals. For this to happen, employees need to assume new challenges and responsibilities for which they must be motivated both intrinsically and extrinsically.

The total quality philosophy is consistent with the classical motivational theories (*for example,* Douglas McGregor's "Theory Y") as well as modern theories of work motivation such as: *(i)* job characteristics theory, *(ii)* acquired needs theory, and *(iii)* goal-setting theory.

8.12 KEY WORDS USED

Quality Teamwork, Quality Teams, Steering Committee, Quality Council, Quality Circles, Problem-Solving Teams, Natural Work Teams, Self-managed Teams, Self-directed Teams, Virtual Teams, Quality Improvement Teams, Department Improvement Teams, Process Improvement Teams, Task Force, Effective Teamwork, Team Effectiveness, Team Membership, Team Sponsor, Team Facilitator, Team Leader, Team Member, Team Processes, Empowerment, Motivation, Job Enlargement, Job Enrichment, Principles of Empowerment, Douglas McGregor's 'Theory Y', Job Characteristics Theory, Acquired Needs Theory, Goal-setting Theory.

8.13 OBJECTIVE QUESTIONS

(A) Match the following :

Column A	Column B
1. Task force	1. Sometimes called "project teams".
2. Principle of empowerment	2. Lack of clear commitment.
3. Barrier to empowerment	3. Establish mutual trust
4. Team process	4. Clear communication.
5. Team effectiveness	5. Data collection.

(B) State whether the following statements are True or False :

1. Self-managed teams are also known as self-directed teams. (T / F)
2. Task force and project teams are not the same. (T / F)
3. Team work is not an important element of total quality. (T / F)
4. A team leader can be either chosen by management or be appointed by the team. (T / F)
5. Organisational support is the foundation of team work. (T / F)

(C) Multiple choice Questions : Choose the correct answer from the alternatives given under each question :

1. Department improvement team is also referred to as :
   (a) Task force (b) Quality circle (c) Virtual team
   (d) Problem-solving team (e) Self-managed team.
2. According to Peter Scholtes, successful team has the following ingredients :
   (a) Clearly defined team goals and roles.
   (b) Clear communication and balanced participation.
   (c) Beneficial team behaviour (d) (a), (b) and (c)
   (e) (b) and (c) only.
3. Recent theories of work motivation include :
   (a) Job characteristics theory (b) Acquired needs theory
   (c) Goal setting theory (d) (a), (b) and (c)
   (e) (a) and (b) only.
4. People resist change for the following reasons :
   (a) Fear (b) Loss of control (c) Uncertainty
   (d) More work (e) (a), (b), (c) and (d) (f) (a) and (b) only
   (g) (c) and (d) only.
5. Organisation culture includes the following elements :
   (a) Business environment and organisational values
   (b) Cultural role models and organisational rites, rituals and customs.
   (c) Cultural transmitters. (d) (a) and (b) only (e) (a), (b) and (c)

8.14 REVIEW QUESTIONS

1. Explain why teamwork is essential for total quality management.
2. Discuss the role of teams in continuous improvement.
3. What are the various types of teams used in total quality approach? Discuss briefly.
4. Discuss the rationale for teams in TQ.
5. What is an "effective team"? List the criteria for team effectiveness.
6. Discuss the 10 ingredients for a successful team according to Peter Scholtes.
7. What is meant by team excellence and performance. Discuss the 10 commandments recommended by Dennis King for team performance.
8. Discuss the characteristics of team sponsor, team facilitator, team leader and team member in teams for total quality.
9. Discuss the various team processes undertaken within TQ teams.
10. Discuss the guidelines for developing effective teams.
11. Discuss the role of empowerment in total quality management.
12. What is empowerment? What are its objectives?
13. Briefly discuss the principles of empowerment.
14. How empowerment is implemented?
15. Discuss the barriers to empowerment.
16. State the benefits of empowerment.
17. Discuss the relationship between empowerment and motivation.
18. Discuss the role of management in empowerment.
19. Discuss the role of employee motivation in total quality.
20. Discuss the motivational theories which are relevant to TQ approach.
21. What is meant by organisational culture?

22. What is meant by quality culture?
23. Discuss the characteristics shared by organisations with a quality culture.
24. What is meant by "activating cultural change"?
25. Discuss the characteristics of organisations having strong quality culture.
26. How resistance to change can be overcome? – Explain.
27. Explain how a quality culture can be established in an organisation.
28. Discuss the importance of ethics and ethical behaviour in quality management.
29. What is meant be "ethical dilemma"?
30. Discuss the factors that influence ethical behaviour.
31. Discuss the relationship between: *(a)* trust and total quality, *(b)* values and total quality, *(c)* integrity and total quality, *(d)* responsibility and total quality
32. Discuss the role of managers and organisations in ethics.
33. How ethical dilemmas are handled?

8.15 DISCUSSION QUESTIONS

1. "No matter what you are trying to do, teams are the most effective way to get the job done". Do you agree? Why or why not?
2. Discuss the similarities and differences among the various types of teams used in TQ.
3. Are teams absolutely necessary for total quality to successful? Explain.
4. Discuss the circumstances in which employee empowerment would hurt rather than improve quality. Why would this occur?
5. What can managers do to mitigate the risks of failure associated with empowerment? Explain.
6. Which theory of motivation do you see as most consistent with empowerment? Why? Give reasons.
7. How does empowerment differ from such approaches as job enrichment and employee participation? Explain.

8.16 ASSIGNMENTS

1. Visit one or two companies in your city and conduct a survey of several managers on the topic of motivation for quality.
2. Visit some local companies and conduct a survey to determine if and how they use suggestion systems and quality circles in improving their quality management.

8.17 CHAPTER CASE

GAPBUSTER TEAMS AND CUSTOMERS AT NORTHWEST BANK

Follow the process. Refer to the credit manual. Do it by the look. Yes; controls are important. Managing risk is essential. But, what does the customer want? Are we exceeding customer's expectations? How do we know? You need a team problem-solving process to get at the heart of the problem. At Northwest Bank, it is called "Gapbusters", employees coming together as teams to identify and bridge "gaps" between customer expectations and service reality. Last year more than 600 Northwest employees worked together in teams to change existing procedures in order to put customers first, save money, improve operating efficiency, and improve communications.

For example, streaming the approval process so that certificates of deposit can be released immediately. Developing a training course to help customer-contact employees remember customer names early in a relationship. Or giving every customer-contact employee on the bank floor a recipe box with index cards containing productivity tips suggested by employees of that bank location.

"Gapbusters say a team can accomplish a lot more than one person" says Marketing Vice President Chethan Kumar. The process smooths the way so that customers can receive the very best service when they come to Northwest. We have made progress but we still have a long way to go, especially across business lines. Gapbuster never ends. There will always be room for improvement. The process is working. Annually, Northwest asks customers at each of its 410 banking locations how they think Northwest bankers are doing in service delivery, solving problems, proactive service and communication. Bank presidents and their staff team review the results and suggest ways to close any service gaps which customers perceive.

Discussion Questions :

1. Compare the advantages and disadvantages of proximity to customers of a service firm.
2. Describe the advantages and disadvantages of empowered teams in a service firm.

CHAPTER 9

ORGANISING FOR TQM

LEARNING OBJECTIVES

After reading this chapter, you should be able to:

- Understand the need for organising for quality.
- Discuss transition from traditional organisation to TQM organisation.
- Discuss the roles of top management, middle management, work force and teams in organisational transition to TQM.
- Discuss the concept and philosophy of quality circles.
- Discuss the role of self-managing teams in TQM.
- Describe the process of building a change oriented organisation.
- Discuss the steps involved in change process.
- Define 'Kaizen' and discuss the steps involved in the continuous improvement strategy.
- Discuss 5 's' Kaizen movement.
- Discuss the principles of "gemba kaizen".
- Describe the concept of "Theory of Constraints" and discuss the steps involved in its application.

9.0 INTRODUCTION

Quality or lack of quality impacts the entire organisation from supplier to customer and from product design to maintenance. However, most importantly, building an organisation that can achieve quality also affects the entire organisation and it is a demanding task.

Exhibit 9.1 **lays out the flow of activities that are necessary for an organisation to achieve total quality management.**

Exhibit 9.1 : The Flow of Activities that are Necessary to Achieve Total Quality Management

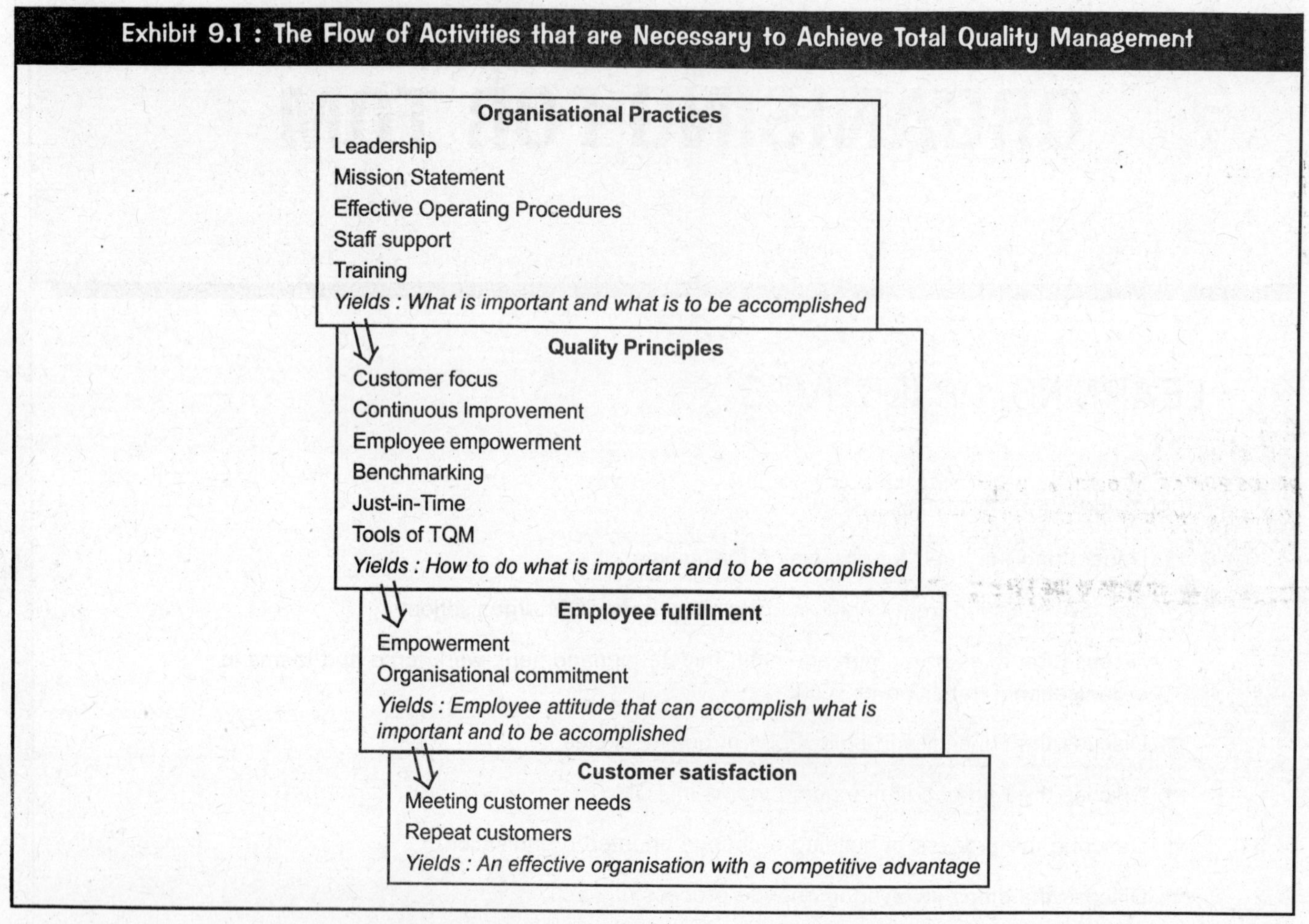

Organising process recognises a structural as well as a behavioural or people oriented dimension.

A successful set of activities begins with an organisational environment that fosters quality, followed by an understanding of the principles of quality and then an effort to engage employees in the necessary activities to implement quality. When things are done well, the organisation typically satisfies its customers and obtains a competitive advantage. The ultimate goal is to win customers.

9.1 NEED FOR ORGANISING FOR QUALITY

Synthesising quality values and policies to every person's job and every operation is a complex task that must be supported by an appropriate organisational infrastructure. Organising is defined as ***"the process of creating a structure for the organisation that will enable its people to work together effectively toward its objectives."*** Thus, the organising process recognises a ***structural*** as well as a ***behavioural*** or people-oriented dimension.

Organising for total quality management has two dimensions: the *macro dimension* concerned with the overall approach the company might take to establish a quality infrastructure and the *micro dimension* concerned with organising the quality department and designing the duties and responsibilities of the "top quality manager."

9.2 EVOLUTION OF ORGANISATION FOR QUALITY

Historically, organisations have tended to focus on the classical principles of ***specialisation of labour, delegation of authority, span of control* and *unity of command.*** The result in many cases was the traditional pyramid organisation chart, accompanied by budgets, rules, procedures and chain of command hierarchy.

Prior to the emergence of total quality management in the early 1980s, responsibility for quality was vague and confusing. Executive management was detached from the idea of managing to achieve quality. The general workforce had no stake in increasing the quality of products and services. Quality had become the task of specialists – product specification or design engineers and process control statisticians who determined acceptable levels of product variability and performed ***quality control inspection*** on the shop floor of manufacturing departments.

Quality management emerged in the early 1980s.

Many organisations particularly in manufacturing industries, have focussed quality-related activities to a **"Quality Department"**. Over the decades, the names and scope of activities have changed – inspection, statistical quality control, quality control, reliability engineering, quality assurance, total quality control and at present "total quality management". **During the 1980s, in the United States, four major trends in organising for quality emerged. They are:**

(i) Quality management tasks were assigned to functional line departments rather than quality control departments. *For example,* **process capability studies were transferred from 'Quality Department' to "Process Engineering Department".**

(ii) The scope of quality management was broadened from **operations only (little 'q') to all activities (big 'Q')** and from **external customers to internal customers.**

(iii) A major expansion occurred in the use of **quality teams** (*eg.,* **Quality Circles, Company Wide Quality Control**) and

(iv) Authority to make decisions was delegated to lower levels **(Total Employee Involvement, Employee Empowerment** and **Self-Managing Teams).**

9.3 TODAY'S REQUIREMENTS FOR ORGANISING FOR QUALITY

Today, it is generally recognised that there are two pre-requisities for a TQM organisation:

(i) **A *quality attitude*** that pervades the entire organisation. Quality is not just a special activity supervised by a high ranking quality director. Developing ***a quality attitude***, a ***quality vision*** and ***a quality culture*** is largely a challenge for the top management.

(ii) An ***organisational structure*** to support the pervasive attitude. Companies must have the ***means*** and the ***structure*** to set goals, assign them to appropriate people and convert them to action plans. People must be aware of the importance of quality and trained to accomplish the necessary tasks and objectives/goals.

Two perrequisities for a TQM organisation are:
(i) a quality altitude and
(ii) an organisational structure.

9.3.1 Co-ordination of quality activities

In today's organisations, the approach used to coordinate quality activities throughout the organisation (company wide or organisation wide quality control) takes two major forms:

(i) **Coordination** for control is achieved by the ***line*** and ***staff*** departments through the use of formal procedures and feedback information. *For example,* sampling inspections to evaluate process and product quality, control charts, reports on quality etc.

(ii) **Coordination** for creating change (quality improvement on a continuous basis) is achieved through the use of ***quality control circles, quality project teams*** etc.

9.3.2 Organising for creating change

"All organisations are engaged in creating beneficial change as well as preventing adverse change." Much of the work of creating change consists of processing small, similar changes. (*for* *example, **Kaizen*** **or continuous improvement**) Coordination for this level of change can often be handled by carefully prepared procedures.

Box 9.1 **discusses what is meant by "Organising for quality"**

Box 9.1 : Organising for Quality

TQM requires total commitment on the part of the management and workers. The organisation must be structured to enhance product quality, not detract from it. Workers must be secure in their positions and have a stake in the success of the organisation if quality programs are going to be successful.

According to Feigenbaum :

(i) The quality function within a company should not be a single function housed within a single department. Quality should be recognised as a systematic group of disciplines to be applied on a coordinated basis by all functions throughout the company and the plant.

(ii) The quality function must have direct and ongoing contract with the buyers and customers of the company's products and services.

(iii) The quality function must be organised to transcend individual functional organisational boundaries.

(iv) The overall quality function must be overseen from a high level of the firm as new products are developed, to be sure that quality issues are adequately dealt with, that "early warnings" of impending problems are easily recognised and corrected and that management can properly manage quality.

What are the root causes of quality problems and what can be done to address these causes? A survey of executives of 30 Fortune 500 firms to determine their opinion as to the cause of quality problems in the United States revealed workmanship and workforce as the major cause of quality problems. But a similar survey of workers if conducted, would reveal management as the cause. Management's policies determine worker's job security and working conditions. Reward structures determine incentives for behaviour. For TQM to be successful, the entire organisation must line-up behind a quality imperative. To make this happen, the management must be responsible for creating an organisational structure in which workers are empowered and in which workers have incentives to do their best, not one that stifles excellence.

For non-motive, unusual programs of change, it is necessary to create new forms of organisations called **"parallel organisations"** which exist in addition to and simultaneously with the regular ***"line"*** organisations.

Use of *"parallel organisations"* is important for innovation in quality. Regular organisations for quality do the ***"maintenance activity"*** (refers to activities to achieve conformance to specifications or procedures) whereas the ***"parallel organisations"*** are responsible for improvement activities to change the ***"level of quality."***

Regular organisations for quality do the "maintenance activity" whereas the parallel organisations improve levels of quality.

Examples of "parallel" organisation for achieving change in quality (innovations in quality or major improvements in quality) are ***quality circles, quality councils, quality improvement project teams*** **and *business process reengineering teams.*** Parallel organisations may be permanent or ad-hoc and may be mandatory or voluntary.

9.4 ORGANISING FOR TQM – THE SYSTEMS APPROACH

Since the total quality control guides and coordinates the actions of people, machines, and information across the whole range of key company activities, it is essential that quality be organised effectively and economically company wide.

The development and operation of this total quality organisation include three considerations:

(i) Identification and confirmation of the specific quality work and teamwork – including the responsibility, authority, accountability and relationships for quality – of each of the key individuals and groups in the organisation.

(ii) Identification and confirmation of these same areas for quality control function itself so that it may help the company achieve its quality objectives.

(iii) Leadership of company and plant management itself in the establishment and ongoing maintenance of the quality organisation.

The basic managerial and technological foundation for the work and inter-relationships of this organisation is provided by the ***total quality system*** of the organisation. Without the strong quality system, there cannot be a strong organisation for quality.

9.4.1 The Systems Approach

A *system* can be defined as an entity composed of interdependent components that are integrated for achievement of an objective. The organisation is a social system comprised of a number of components such as marketing, production, finance, research and so on. These organisational components are activities that may or may not be integrated and they do not necessarily have objectives or operate towards achievement of an objective. Thus ***synergism,*** a necessary attribute of a well-organised system, may be lacking as each activity takes a parochial view or operates independently of the others. This lack of synergism is removed under the TQM approach to strategic management because interdependency across functions and departments is a necessary precondition. **The concepts of an organisational system is shown in *Exhibit 9.2.***

A "system" is a network of interdependent processes that work together to accomplish a common mission.

The activities of the organisation are ***subsystems*** of the whole system, but are also individual systems with inputs and outputs that provide input to other systems such as customers and other internal activities. **This chain of input/output operations is shown in *Exhibit 9.3.***

Exhibit 9.2 : The Organisational System

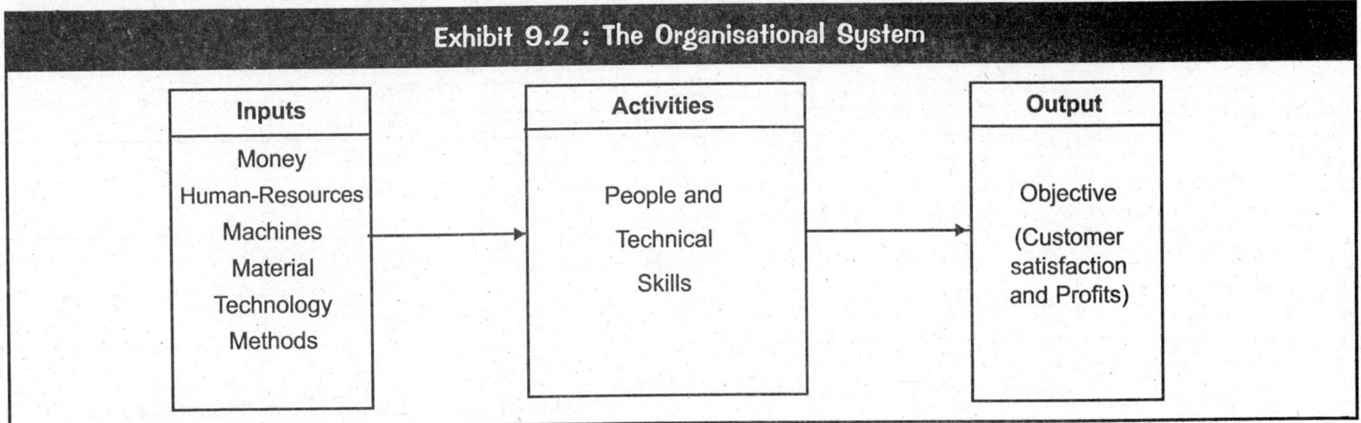

Despite the simplicity of the concept, it most often fails in practice. Individuals carrying out activities do not understand the objectives or results of their **"subsystems"** nor can they define their output in measurable terms. Quality output is stated in such vague terms as ***"do a good job"*** or ***"keep the customer happy".*** People can describe what they do (activity) but not what they are supposed to get done (objective or result). They may be very efficient at ***"doing things right"*** but ineffective in ***"doing the right things."***

Exhibit 9.3 : Chain of Subsystems

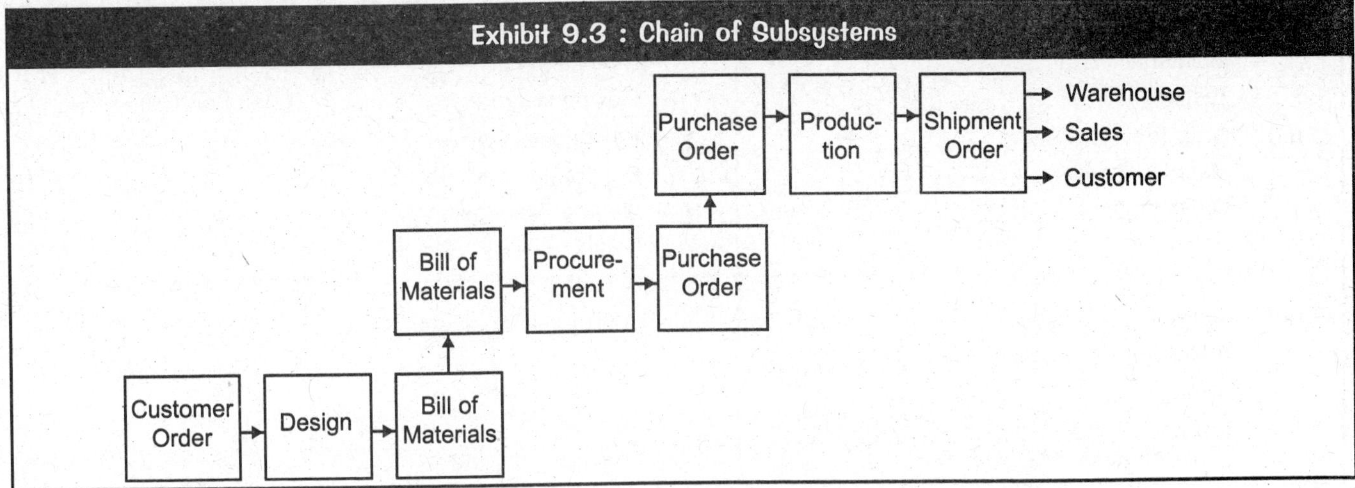

Concepts of Generic Value Chain: Michael Porter in his book **"Competitive Advantage"** has taken the systems theory a major practical step forward with his concept of the ***value chain.*** He suggests that ***"competitive advantage"*** (in this case quality) cannot be understood by looking at a firm as a whole. It stems from many discrete activities a firm performs in designing, producing, marketing, delivering and supporting its product.

The discrete activities of an organisation can be represented using the *generic value chain* shown in *Exhibit 9.4.*

Exhibit 9.4 : Subdividing a Generic Value Chain

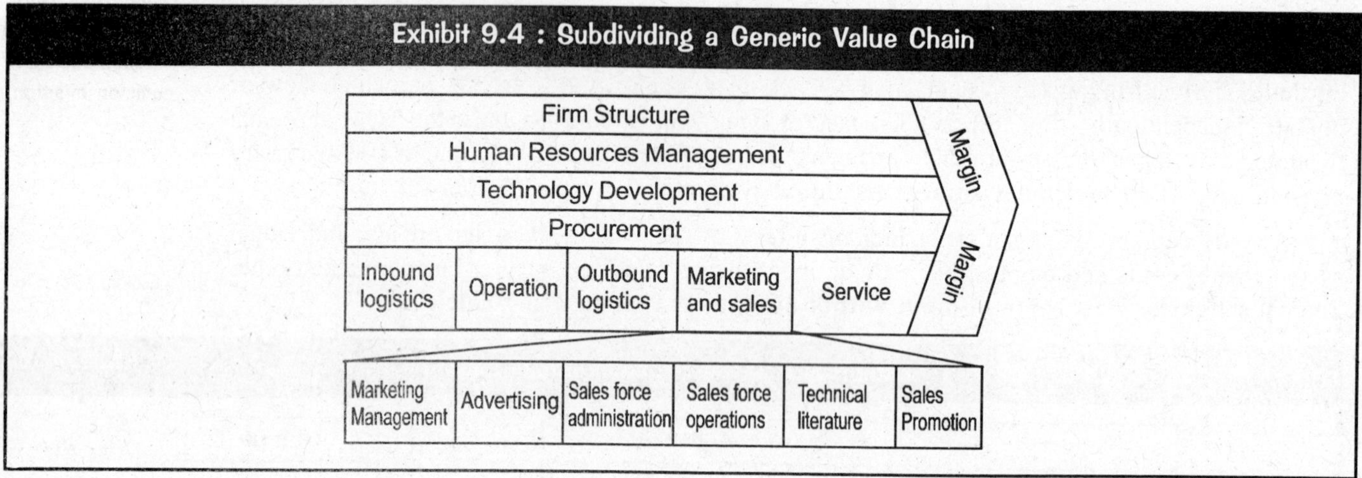

Box 9.2 **shows the chain activities in the generic value chain.**

Box 9.2 : Chain Activities

Primary activities	Support activities
(i) **Inbound logistics** Material handling Warehousing Inventory control Vehicle scheduling Returns to suppliers *(ii)* **Operations** Machining and processing Packaging, Assembly Maintenance Testing *(iii)* **Outbound logistics** Material handling Order processing Scheduling Finished goods warehouse *(iv)* **Marketing and sales** Advertising, promotion, sales force, Pricing. **Service** Installation, repair, training of customers, spare parts supply.	*(i)* **Procurement** Dispersion of procurement function throughout the firm *(ii)* **Technology Development** Efforts to improve products and processes **Human Resource Management** Recruiting Hiring Training Development Compensation *(iii)* **Firm Infrastructure** Supports entire chain General Management Planning Accounting Quality management

Customers, channels and suppliers also have value chains and the firm's output of product or service becomes an input to the customer's value chain. The firm's differentiation and its competitive advantage depend on how the activities in its value chain relate to the needs of the customer, channel or supplier. If quality has been chosen as a competitive advantage, it now remains to determine the customer's value chain and how the product or service can add value to the customer's system. Following this determination, the value chain should be organised into the required discrete activities, each one of which can improve quality of the output for the purpose of meeting the customer's expectations. Before asking what you can do for the customer, ask what the customer expects to accomplish. The answer to this question forms the basis for a quality organisation.

9.5 ORGANISING FOR QUALITY IMPLEMENTATION

The traditional approach to organisation views the process as a set of activities or functions which are grouped together without a great deal of attention to strategy or desired results. The process takes the product as given and groups the necessary skills and activities into homogeneous functions and departments. This approach to building an organisation structure has been criticised by Peter Drucker. According to him, it is necessary to build the structure of the organisation on the ***key activities.*** Key activities will differ depending on the nature of the organisation, its products and its strategy. *For example,* advertising may be a key activity of Coca-Cola and Pepsi, whereas designing may be the key activity for Boeing Aircraft in the value chain.

The value chain concept provides a systematic way to identify the key activities necessary for quality differentiation and a way to group them into homogeneous departments and functions. Indeed, an organisation structure that corresponds to the value chain is the most economic and effective way to deliver quality and thereby achieve a competitive advantage.

It should be noted that the Quality Assurance Department is generally not the key activity when organising for TQM. Any activity or function is a potential source of quality differentiation. Not only those functions normally classified as "line" but a variety of "staff" function as well can be the source of quality in the organisation structure. **Consider the simple activities in *Box 9.3.***

Box 9.3 : Activity and Value to Customer

Activity		Value to Customer
Purchasing	→	Improved cost and quality of product
Engineering and design characteristics	→	Unique product
Manufacturing	→	Product reliability
Order processing	→	Response time
Service	→	Customer installation
Scheduling	→	Response time
Inspection	→	Defect free product
Spare parts	→	Maintenance
Human Resources	→	Customer training

Delivery of quality products or services depends on how well the various activities of the company are organised and integrated. **The measurement of effectiveness is fundamental to the TQM process.** It is also necessary to organise for customer feedback, another key activity that impacts other functions and activities throughout the organisation.

***Box 9.4* lists the ten core values for everyone in TQ Organisations.**

Box 9.4 : 10 Core Values for Everyone in TQ Organisations

1. Make it right for the customer at any cost.
2. Internal customers are as important as external customers.
3. Respond to every customer inquiry or complaint by the end of the day.
4. Answer the phone within two rings.
5. The customer is always right.
6. Not only meet customer's expectations, but delight the customers in the process.
7. Teamwork and cooperation are more important than individual action and game-manship.
8. Everyone is involved in the quality effort, no exceptions or bench sitting is allowed.
9. Respond to every employee suggestion for quality improvement within one week.
10. Never be satisfied with the level of quality, always strive for continuous improvement.

9.5.1 Transition from a Traditional to a TQM organisation

Several modern market places, technological and economic factors have established major new requirements upon organising for quality. Four important factors are:

(i) Traditional quality programs were, in the past, thought of as a single function in the company. Today, they must be recognised as a systematic group of quality discipline, to be applied on a coordinated basis by all functions throughout the company.

(ii) Traditional quality programs were, in the past, several organisational layers, separated from satisfactory direct, ongoing contact with buyers and customers of the company's products and services.

Today, instead, they must be continuously coupled with the buyer and customer on both a ***feedforward*** and ***feedback*** **basis.**

In a TQM organisation quality is the responsibility of every one and not just the quality assurance department.

(iii) Quality problems transcend and do not respect individual functional organisational boundaries within companies. Today, the quality program must be organised accordingly if it is to be realistic.

(iv) Quality-related operations have become so extended, intricate and involved today that the need for integrated, high-level control is of primary importance. This is necessary to assure orientation to the real facts of the quality of new products under development, to receive "early warning" of impending production quality problems.

Exhibit 9.5 **shows a typical traditional organisation which operates with a vertical, functional structure based on reporting relationships, budgeting procedures and specific and detailed job classifications.**

Departmentation is by function and communications, rewards and loyalties are functionally oriented. Processes flow vertically from the top down, creating costly barriers to process flow.

The systems approach to organising suggests three significant changes, one conceptual and two requiring organisational realignment. They are:

(i) The concept of the inverted organisational chart.

(ii) A system of intra-company internal quality and

(iii) Horizontal and vertical integration of functions and activities.

To make the transition from traditional to TQ management, it may be desirable to conceptualise a new organisational chart which is obtained by inverting the existing one and putting the customer on the top followed by employees and front line supervisors. These are the deliverers of quality to customers. **Quality is now the responsibility of every one and not just the quality assurance department.**

Exhibit 9.5 : Transition from Traditional to TQM Organisation

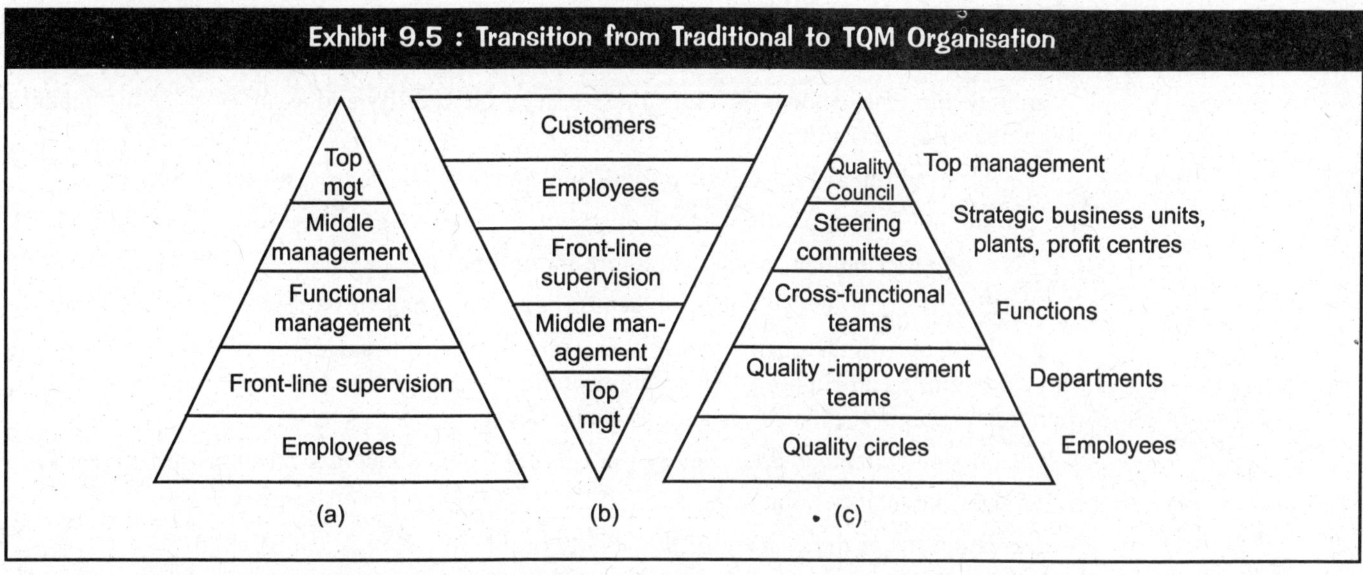

The systems approach requires the integration of organisational activities for achievement of a common goal. This goal is the satisfaction of customer requirements, but the customers are now considered to be both external and internal customers.

***Exhibit 9.6* illustrates comparison of traditional organisational structure with TQM view of organisational structure.**

Exhibit 9.6 : Traditional Organisational Structure versus TQM View of the Organisational Structure

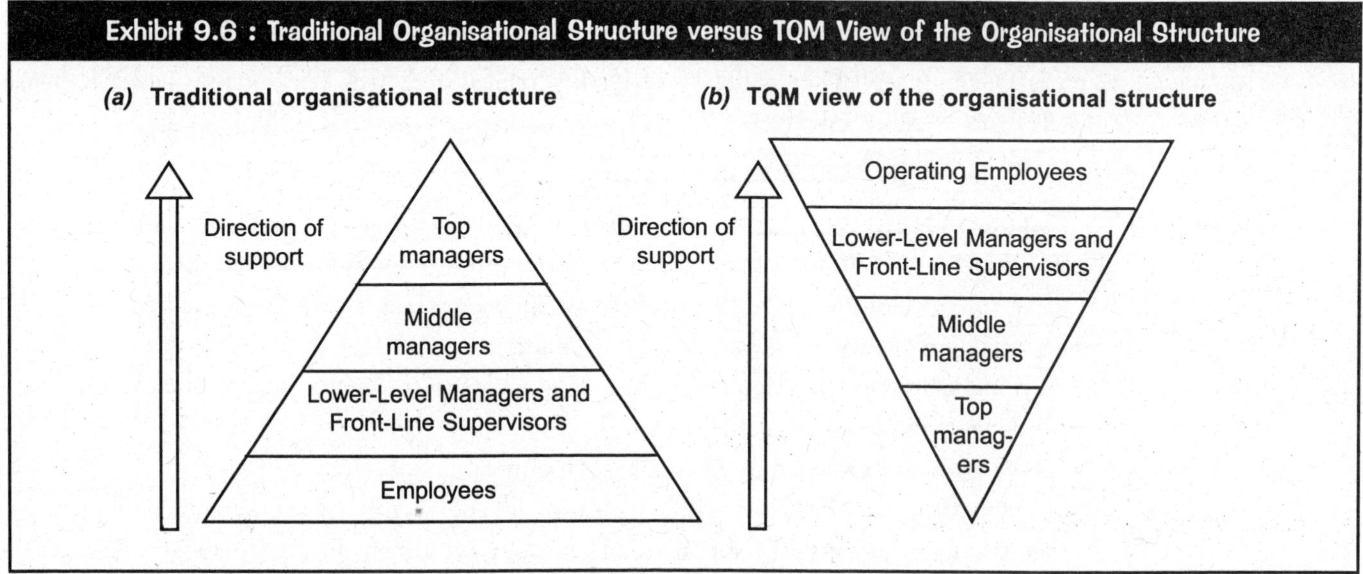

9.6 ROLES IN ORGANISATIONAL TRANSITION TO TQM

Members of a successful organisation need a sound understanding of their roles during the transition to a TQM program. People at all levels require orientation on how they will be impacted under the new philosophy of ***employee involvement.*** Each level has a role to play in the improvement process.

Role of top management: The role of the top management is critical. Some of the roles identified are:

(i) Establishing and serving in a ***quality council.***
(ii) Establishing ***quality policies.***
(iii) Establishing and deploying ***quality goals.***
(iv) Providing the **resources.**

(v) Providing **problem oriented training.** *(vi)* Stimulating **improvements.**

(vii) Providing the **reward** and **recognition.**

In brief, top management develops the **strategy for quality** and assumes its implementation through **personal leadership.**

The **three "natural phases" of a quality effort** as identified by Waite (1989) are:

(i) **"Euphoria"** (initial problems are being solved).

(ii) **"Slow down"** (tougher problems require more time) and

(iii) **"Settling in"** (making the improvement process a permanent part of the company).

Quality Council: A quality council is a group of top managers who develop the quality strategy and guide and support their implementation. Quality councils may be established at the corporate level, unit or plant level and divisional level.

Every member of the organisation top management, middle management and the work force all have to understand their specific roles in organisational transformation to TQM.

The mission statement prepared by the Quality Council includes responsibilities such as:

- Formulating quality policy
- Estimating major dimensions of the quality problems
- Assignment of roles and responsibilities
- Planning for training at all levels
- Establishing support for teams
- Providing for coordination
- Establishing new measures for progress review
- Revising the merit rating approach
- Designing a plan for recognition and
- Establishing a plan for publicity of quality related activities. (*e.g.* quality news, in-house quality journals etc.)

9.6.1 Role of the Middle Management

Middle managers, executives, supervisors, functional specialists and the work force are the people who execute the quality strategy developed by the top management.

The role of middle managers, executives, specialists and supervisors include:

- Nominating quality problems for finding solutions
- Serving as leaders of various types of quality teams (*for example,* quality circles).
- Serving as members of quality teams
- Serving on task forces to assist the Quality Councils in developing quality strategies.
- Leading the quality activities within their own area of work by enecouraging their employees.
- Identifying customers and suppliers and meeting with them to discover and address their needs.

Role of the work force: Work force include all types of employees excluding those people belonging to the management and those who are professional experts (quality specialists).

It may be noted that most quality problems are management or system controllable.

This means that management must:

(i) direct the steps necessary to identify and remove the causes of quality problems and

(ii) provide the system that places workers in the state of self-control.

The role of the workforce includes:

- Nominating quality problems for finding solutions.
- Serving as members of various types of quality teams, *for example,* quality circles.

- Identifying elements of their own jobs that do not meet the criteria of self control.
- Becoming knowledgeable as to the needs of their customers (both internal as well as external customers).

Managers must tap the potential of the workforce by using its experience, training and knowledge. **"No one knows the workplace better than the worker". Quality goals cannot be achieved without using the hands and heads of the work force.**

Role of teams: The "organisation of the future" will be viewed as a **"socio-technical system"** consisting of a technical system (equipment, processes, technology etc.) and the social system (people, roles etc.). The organisation is influenced by the interaction of these two systems.

Research on socio-technical systems has concentrated on designing new ways of organising work, particularly at the workforce level. **"Team"** concepts play an important role in these new approaches. ***Box 9.5* gives the summary of the most common types of quality teams.**

Box 9.5 : Summary of the Most Common Types of Quality Teams

Name of the team	Purpose	Membership	Basis of and size of membership	Continuity	Other names
Quality project team	Solve cross functional quality problems	Combination of managers, professionals and workforce from multiple departments	Mandatory, 4 to 8 members	Team disbands after project is completed	Quality improvement team
Quality circles	Solve problems within a department	Primarily work force from one department	Voluntary, 6 to 12 members	Team remains intact, project after project	Employee involvement group
Business process quality team	Plan, control and implement the quality of a key functional process	Primarily managers and professionals from multiple departments	Mandatory, 4 to 6 members	Permanent	Business process management team, process team
Self managing team	Plan, execute and control work to achieve a defined output.	Primary workforce from one work area	Mandatory, all members in the work area, 6 to 18 members	Permanent	Self-supervising team, semi-autonomous team.

9.7 TEAMS FOR TOTAL QUALITY MANAGEMENT

In organising for total quality, the most critical factor is ***"employee involvement"*** around which the management system of TQM should be based. In an organisational chart, only 10 percent is top management and functional management which is visible while the 90 percent which is not visible in the organisation chart and where the true potential for quality exists, comprises of front-line supervisors and non-managerial employees. This is analogous to the iceberg in which about 10 percent is visible on its top while 90 percent is hidden from view. Hence it makes good sense to tap into the 90 percent which represents a reservoir of ideas for quality and productivity improvement by means of teams. The various kinds of teams are discussed in the following paragraphs.

Quality circle is the most widespread form of an employee involvement team.

9.7.1 Quality circles

The most widespread form of an employee involvement team is the quality circle which is defined as below:

"Quality circle is a small group of employees in the same work area or doing similar type of work who voluntarily meet regularly for about an hour every week to identify, analyse and resolve work-related problems, leading to improvement in their total performance and enrichment of their work life."

A quality circle is also referred to as "quality control circle" (Q.C.C)

Although the concept has had some success in white collar operations, the major impact has been among **"direct labour"** employees in manufacturing where concerns are primarily with quality, cost, specifications, productivity and schedules. By their very nature, quality circles were limited to concerns of the small group of members and few cross-sectional problems were considered.

The major growth of quality circles occurred in the late 1970s and early 1980s, as thousands of companies adopted the concept. However, the concept never met expectations and widespread abandonment resulted by the late 1980s. **The major reason for failure was a general lack of commitment to the concept of participation and the lack of interest and participation by the management.** From a TQM perspective, quality circles lack the prerequisities of integration with strategy, company goals and management systems. Organisations can go beyond using quality circles by creating task forces, work teams and cross-functional teams.

***Exhibit 9.7* illustrates the function of Q.C. circle.**

Exhibit 9.7 : How QC Circle Works

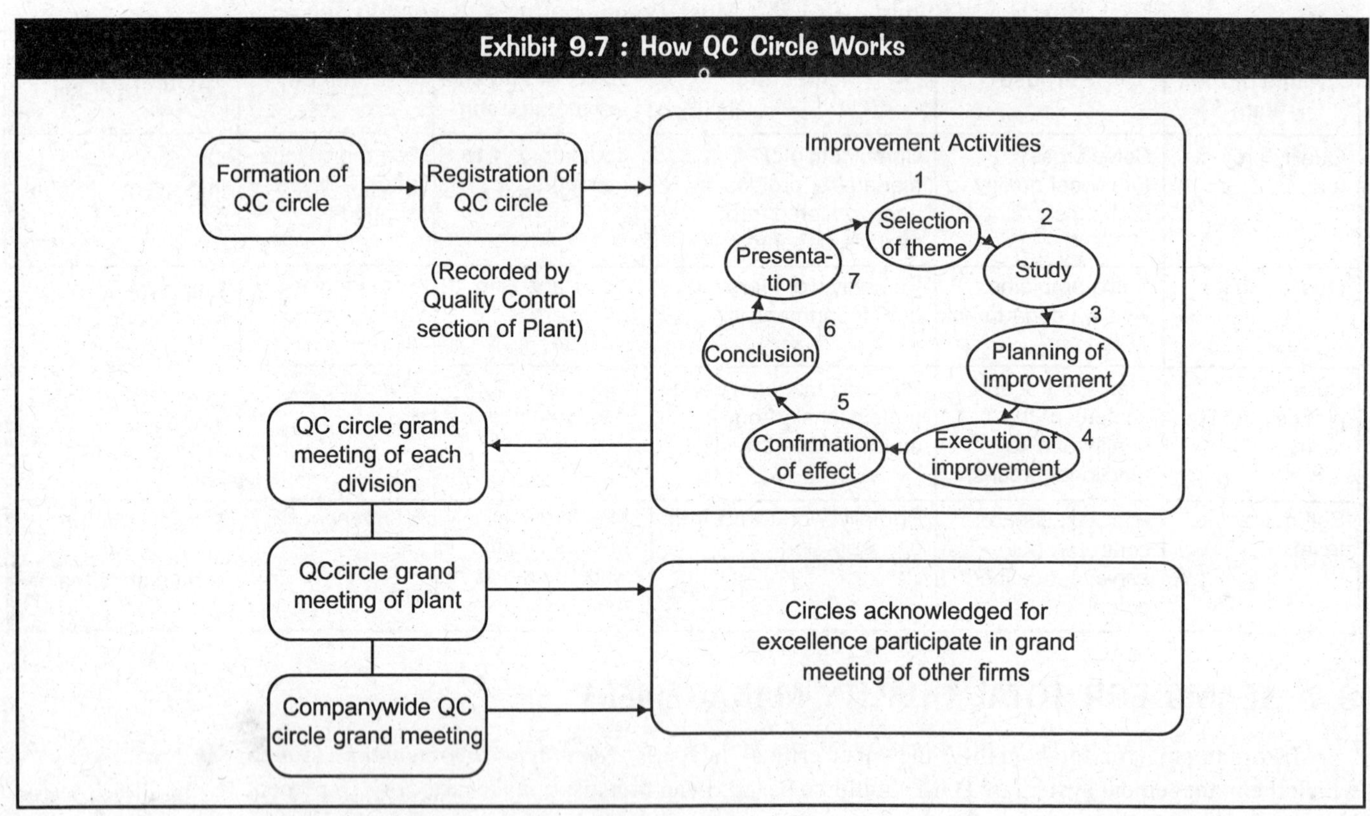

9.7.2 Significant Characteristics of Quality Circles

(i) **Small group of employees:** It has been learnt by experience that the optimum number of members in any quality circle is about 8 to 10. The minimum and maximum number of members recommended are 5 and 15 respectively to avoid a circle becoming inactive (if members are less than 5) or resulting in deprivation of opportunity for active participation by every member (if members are more than 15).

(ii) **Members are from the same work area or doing similar type of work:** A quality circle is a homogeneous group and not an inter-departmental or interdisciplinary group (*for example,* in an assembly area, welding section, stores department etc.).

(iii) **Membership of the quality circle is voluntary:** Employees decide to join the quality circles voluntarily. No coercion or pressure is to be exerted on them to join or not to join. Nor can

any one be barred from joining quality circles by virtue of his being a union leader or for lack of qualification.

(iv) **Members meet regularly for about an hour every week:** The members of quality circles should meet regularly once in a week for an hour after their working hours or during working hours to discuss the problems related to their work and find solutions to the problems.

(v) **Members meet to identify, analyse and resolve work–related problems:** Employees who work in a work place, know best what problems are hindering achievement of good quality, productivity and optimum performance and also how those problems could be solved. It should be noted that only work-related problems come under the purview of the quality circles and not other issues such as personal grievances or demands.

(vi) **Members resolve work related problems leading to improvement in their total performance:** As a result of quality circles resolving work related problems relating to quality, productivity, cost reduction, safety etc., the total performance of the work-unit improves, resulting in both tangible and intangible gains to the whole organisation.

(vii) **Quality circles enrich the work life of the employees:** Quality circles help in enriching the work life of the employees apart from attitudinal changes, cohesive team culture etc. This is because of avoidance of rework, greater job satisfaction, improved working environment and better human relationships among employees. The quality of work life (QWL) of any individual is said to be good only if he/she is enjoying the work that he/she is doing and is happy in the work-environment and finds his/her work meaningful.

9.8 THE CONCEPT AND PHILOSOPHY OF QUALITY CIRCLES

In organisations lacking the culture of *participative management,* it would be difficult for employees to understand the role of quality circles. At the time when quality circles were first organised in Japan, there were three basic aims which determined their activities. They are:

The three basic functions of quality circles and problem-solving teams are to identify, analyse, and solve quality and productivity problems.

(i) To contribute to the improvement and development of the enterprise.

(ii) To respect humanity and build a happy work place. In the quality circle philosophy, workers are not treated as a part of the machinery or equipment, but are afforded opportunities to explore their full potential and display their true capability. The quality circle concept enables employees to utilise their intrinsic wisdom and creativity in the work that they are engaged in.

(iii) To satisfy the higher human needs of recognition and self-development.

9.8.1 The Impact of Quality Circles

- Improvement of human relations and work-place morale
- Promotion of participative culture
- Enhancement of job interest
- More effective teamwork
- Reducing defects and improving quality
- Improving housekeeping, cost-effectiveness, safety etc.
- Improvement of productivity
- Enhancing problem-solving capability
- Encouraging an attitude of problem prevention
- Improving communication and interaction
- Promotion of personal and leadership development and
- Catalysing attitudinal changes.

***Box 9.6* lists the tangible and intangible gains of quality circles.**

Box 9.6 : Gains of Quality Circles

Tangible gains	Intangible gains
• Better quality	• Enriched quality of work life
• Productivity improvement	• Attitudinal changes
• Higher safety (Reduced number of accidents)	• Harmony, mutual trust
• Greater cost-effectiveness	• Effective team-working
• Better housekeeping	• Better human relations
• Increased profitability	• Participative culture
• Waste reduction	• Human Resource Development
• Reduced absenteeism	• Promotion of job knowledge
• Reduced grievances	• Greater sense of belonging.

Quality circles pursue problems concerned with
(i) personal well-being of the worker
and
(ii) well being of the company.

Quality circles pursue two types of problems: those concerned with the personal well being of the worker and those concerned with the well-being of the company. Worker's problems are concerned with the work itself, the manufacturing operations or processes, machines, tools and equipments handled, working conditions, safety in the work place, health hazards, working environment and the like. **The potential benefits of quality circles may be examined under three categories:**

(i) Effect of quality circles on individual employee's characteristics.

(ii) Effect of quality circles on individual employee's relationship with other employees and managerial personnel and

(iii) Effect of quality circles on the employees and their attitudes towards the company.

These benefits are listed in *Box 9.7*.

Box 9.7 : Potential Benefits of Quality Circles

1. Effect on individual's characteristics
- Enable the individual to improve personal capabilities.
- Improve the individual's self-respect.
- Help employees change certain personality characteristics.

2. Effect on individual's relations with others
- Increase the respect of the supervisor for employees.
- Increase employee's understanding of the difficulties faced by supervisors.
- Increase management's respect for employees.

3. Effect on employees and their attitudes towards the company
- Change some employees' negative attitude.
- Reduce conflict stemming from the working environment.
- Help employees to understand better the reasons why many problems cannot be solved quickly.
- Instill in the employees a better understanding of the importance of quality.

9.8.2 What Management Should Do To Support And Sustain Quality Circles?

Baker (1988) provided some recommendations for the management to support and sustain quality circles. These are:

(i) Recognising and rewarding the efforts of employees even if their suggestions/recommendations are not implemented.

(ii) Giving employees increased discretion and self-control to act on their own recommendation.

(iii) Offering monetary rewards through the suggestion schemes.

(iv) Providing sufficient training to expand employee skills to take up more complex projects or tasks.

(v) Providing scope and a system for quality circles to expand into cross-functional teams when needed.

(vi) Training middle managers in the use of quality circle tools and techniques.

(vii) Addressing resistance of the middle management when diagnosed.

(viii) Measuring effectiveness by focussing on the quality of the process such as the training, group discussion, inter-relationship, supervisory leadership – rather than outcomes (such as reduction of scrap and costs). The outcome of the right process will reinforce the ***employee involvement*** and ***management commitment***.

***Box 9.8* lists seven principles for activating teamwork in QC circles.**

Box 9.8 : Seven Principles for Activating Teamwork in QC Circles

(i) ***Create symbols or norms :*** The team needs an identity through a team's name, flag, banner and logo. Behavioural norms facilitate teamwork.

(ii) ***Universal team members :*** The four basic elements in this effort are :

- Motives are highly complex
- Lower level needs must be satisfied before higher level needs.
- There are always higher level needs to be satisfied.
- There are more ways to satisfy higher needs than lower level needs.

(iii) ***Walk, then run :*** Teams need early success. Start each team on a problem that is worthwhile but can be solved easily. Choose a problem theme that is slightly beyond the team's current knowledge and ability. Provide support for analysis and solution.

(iv) ***Delegation is only for daily work :*** Do not delegate downward — team members must do the work themselves. Neither should you delegate upward – team members are responsible for finding the solution. The job of improvement cannot be delegated. Every one is equal in the team. The team members themselves have to gather supplies, take meeting notes and participate in problem-solving processes of the team.

(v) ***Active listening speaks louder than words :*** Creative problem-solving capacity exists in every individual. The following principles are to be followed for active listening :

- Listen with empathy, understanding both feeling and content.
- Clarify by restating, paraphrasing or summarising.
- Question and explore.

Active listening reduces defensiveness, enhances self-esteem, encourages co-operation and identifies problems and solutions.

(vi) ***Create an environment for team learning :*** Creating an environment conducive to team learning involves attending to three elements :

- the set up of meeting
- the physical arrangement of people at meetings and
- the psychological rhythm of meetings.

The most difficult part of teamwork activities is getting people to reliably come to meeting. It is important to prepare adequately for meetings. Schedule them at fixed times well in advance. Do not postpone meetings, start and finish meetings on time.

(vii) ***Structure group and individual work :*** Finally, it is important to structure both group and individual work. In group work, consensus is sought on tasks to be done and the methods of accomplishing the tasks. The tasks are then allocated to individuals or combinations of individuals for execution.

9.9 SELF MANAGING TEAMS/SELF-MANAGED TEAMS (SMT)

Self-managing teams or self-managing work teams are an extension of quality circles. They are also known as self-managed teams or self-directed teams.

A **self-managed team** is defined as "a highly trained group of employees, from 6 to 18 on an average, fully responsible for turning out a well-designed segment of finished work. The segment could be a final product/service, or a complete but intermediate product/service."

A **self-managing team** is also defined as "a group of people who work together continuously and who plan, execute the control their work to achieve a defined output."

Self managed teams are **empowered** to take corrective action and resolve day-to-day problems. They also have **direct access to information** that allows them to plan, control and improve their operations. In short, employees in SMTs manage themselves. SMTs offer a way to put the **concepts of *job enrichment* and *job enlargement* into active operation.**

A self-managed team is a team that requires little supervision and manages itself and the day-to-day work it does.

Two examples of SMTs are given below:

(i) In an electronic plant, an assembly team handles all aspects of a customer order *viz.*, receiving the order, preparing the components, assembling and soldering the circuit boards, testing the boards, packing and shipping the boards, monitoring the inventory levels and processing all paperwork.

(ii) At an insurance company, work was originally organised into three areas *viz.* life insurance, health insurance and support services such as billing. Under the new organisational design, teams of 20 to 30 employees (in SMTs) perform all the 167 tasks that formerly were split among the three functional sections.

Now field agents deal solely with one team (SMT). The result is a shorter processing time for processing the customer's claims.

SMTs have the following characteristics:

Self-directed teams are responsible for whole work processes with each team member performing multiple tasks.

- Empowerment to share various management and leadership functions.
- Plan, control and improve their work.
- Set their own goals and inspect their own work.
- Often create their own schedule and review their performance as a group.
- May prepare their own budgets and coordinate their work with other departments.
- Usually order materials, keep inventories and deal with suppliers.
- Frequently are responsible for acquiring any new training needed.
- May hire their own replacements or assume responsibility for disciplining their own members and
- Take responsibility for the quality of their products and services.

Benefits of Self-Managed Teams: SMTs have many benefits which are given below:

(i) They facilitate continuous improvement in work methods.

(ii) They provide greater flexibility and faster response.

(iii) They offer employees higher level of involvement and job satisfaction.

(iv) They increase organisational commitment and help attract and retain the best people.

(v) They are 30 to 50 percent more productive than conventional teams.

(vi) They facilitate improvement in quality of products and services.

(vii) They help in improving productivity.

(viii) They reduce supervision.

(ix) They help in improved decision making and

(x) They decrease the levels of grievances, absenteeism and employee turnover.

Problems of SMTs

(i) Salary and wages may go up

(ii) Higher training costs

(iii) Personnel needed for training

(iv) Unmet expectations may occur.

(v) Resistance by staff groups and middle management.
(vi) Time lost in team meetings and
(vii) Conflict between participants and non-participants.

9.10 COMPARISON OF ORGANISATIONAL FORMS

***Box 9.9* shows the contrasting features of the traditional organisation of the workforce and self managing teams.**

Box 9.9 : Comparison of Organisational Forms

Feature	Traditional organisation	Self-managed team
Scope of work	Individual's responsibility is limited	Team is responsible for a broad scope
Job categories of personnel	Many narrow categories	A few broad categories
Organising, scheduling and assigning work	Primarily by supervisor or staff	Primarily by team.
Measuring and taking corrective action	______do_____	______do_____
Training provided	Training for task assigned to an individual	Extensive training for multiple tasks, plus interpersonal skill training
Opportunity for job rotation	Minimum	High because of extensive training.
Reward system	Related to job, individual performance and seniority	Related to team performance and scope of skills acquired by individual.
Handling of personnel issues	Primarily by supervisory personnel or staff	Many issues handled by team
Sharing of business information.	Limited to non-confidential information.	Open sharing of all information.

Task Teams: Task teams are modification of quality circles. The major differences are that task teams can exist at any level and the goal or topic for discussion is given, whereas in quality circles, members are generally free to choose the problems they will solve.

Cross-Functional Teams: Traditionally, organisations were integrated vertically by linking all the levels of management in hierarchical fashion. Total quality requires horizontal coordination between organisational units. Poor quality often results from breakdown in responsibility that occur when an organisation focusses solely on vertical structure and fails to recognise horizontal interactions. Vertical structures lead to internal competition rather than promoting the good of the whole organisation.

Linking business process improvement (billing, procurement, recruiting, record keeping, design, sales etc.) to the key business objectives of the organisation is necessary if quality is to become real and relevant. **There is widespread agreement that *cross functional teams* provide the best vehicle for linking these activities and processes. The concept of linkage is shown in *Exhibit 9.8*.**

It may be noted that a cross-functional approach achieves the objectives of:

- Customers
- Functions
- Processes and
- The organisation.

***Box 9.10* illustrates the trends that will shape the structure and process of employee involvement efforts in the future according to Michael Donovan.**

Exhibit 9.8 : Cross-functional Linkages

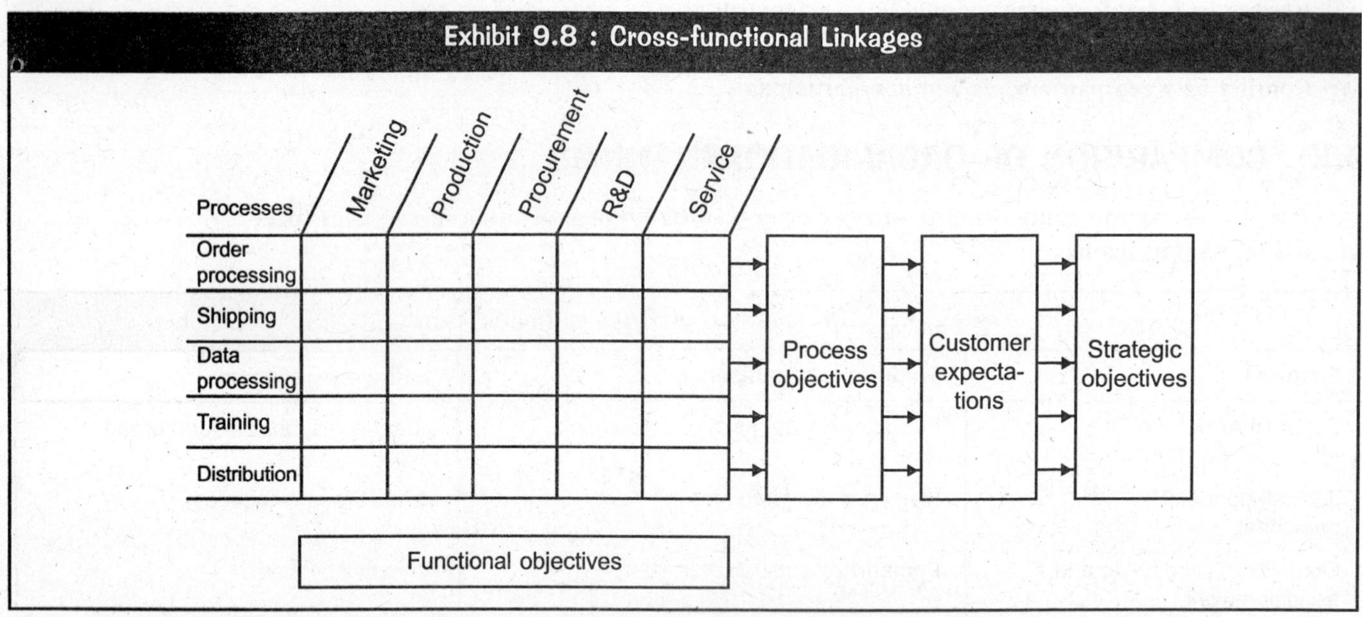

Box 9.10 : Trends in Employee Involvement Efforts

From	To
• Perception of employee involvement as a program	• Perception as an ongoing process
• Voluntary participation	• Participation by all members as natural work team
• Quality circles	• Several types of teams at many levels
• Project focus	• Goal focus
• Limited management involvement	• Active management involvement
• Functional management skills	• Building participative leadership and facilitative leader ship and facilitation skills into management roles
• Employee participation in operating problems	• Employee participation in broader issues

9.11 FUTURE ORGANISATION FOR TQM

The organisation for TQM (The Quality Department) in the future will be headed by a Quality Director whose two primary roles will be – administering the Quality Department and assisting top management with ***Strategic Quality Management.***

The major activities of the quality department of the future are listed in *Box 9.11.*

Box 9.11 : Function of the quality department of the future

(i) Company wide quality planning
(ii) Producing executive reports on quality
(iii) Auditing outgoing quality
(iv) Auditing quality practices
(v) Coordinating and assisting with improvement projects
(vi) Training for quality
(vii) Consulting for quality
(viii) Developing new quality methodologies
(ix) Transferring activities to line department.

Some of the examples of transferring activities from Quality Departments to line departments are:

- Shifting the sorting type of inspection activity from a Quality Department to the workforce itself (*e.g.* counting the quantity of an item received by the inwards goods store by the storekeeper instead of the inspector).
- Transfer of reliability engineering work from the Quality Department to the Design Engineering Department.
- Transfer of supplier quality activities from the Quality Department to the Purchasing Department.

Further, the Quality Director of the Quality Department of the future will have a role to assist the top management with Strategic Quality Management (SQM). ***Box 9.12*** **lists the activities that will be carried by the Quality Director.**

Box 9.12 : Assisting Upper Management with Strategic Quality Management

- Assessing quality
- Formulating goals
- Formulating policies
- Developing strategies for selecting and implementing new directions for the three quality processes.
- Delegating organisational responsibilities
- Carrying out reward and recognition
- Reviewing progress
- Determining personal roles for upper management
- Strategic business planning cycle.

The Quality Director of the future could act as right hand of the top management in the same way as that of the finance director.

Box 9.13 **focusses on the ingredients for success as a Quality Director.**

Box 9.13 : Ingredient for Success as a Quality Director

- Emphasis on business, not technology.
- Focus on customer needs, not just conformance to specifications.
- Attitude of services to the top management and line departments.
- Emphasis on company quality goals, not goals of Quality Department.
- Role as a catalyst/facilitator.
- Being a proponent for resources for other departments.

9.12 PROVIDING FOR SELF-DEVELOPMENT AND EMPOWERMENT

Inspiring people to take positive steps on quality is greatly influenced by the nature of the work performed by those people. Some of the issues to be addressed are ***job content, empowerment, personal commitment and selection*** **and** ***training.***

Job content: Every person doing whatever job in an organisation has three roles: ***supplier, processor*** **and** ***customer.*** These roles are executed by individuals in each state of a process. Each stage is a supplier to subsequent stages and also a customer of previous stages. The design of individual jobs is often based on functional specialisation.

Self control and job design are two important aspects of any job.

Self control and job design are two important aspects of any job. People must be provided with knowledge of what they are supposed to do, feedback on their performance and the means of regulating their work in the event that they are failing to meet the goals. The lack of one or more of these elements means that quality problems are management – controllable. Placing workers in a state of self-control is a prerequisite to using behavioural approaches to motivate employees.

Job design is a task of managers which includes assigning specific tasks and company resources to particular workers to create a system that effectively accomplishes the mission of the firm through daily contributions of individuals. Job design decides ***who*** will perform each task, ***how*** each employee will complete his or her work and ***where*** each job will take place. Managers must provide more meaningful and satisfying jobs for workers.

Job enlargement involves expanding the variety of tasks performed by an employee.

Job enrichment involves increasing the worker's responsibilities and authority in work to be done.

Firms try to enhance job design to provide a more demanding and less monotonous work place. This effort can seek to enhance either the duties of individual jobs or the settings in which workers perform those jobs. ***Job enlargement*** enhances a job by stretching its limits horizontally to include more tasks. *For example,* job enlargement might assign a worker on an assembly line to complete a number of assembly operations rather than one or two more repetitive tasks. ***Job enrichment,*** also called ***vertical job enlargement,*** expands the scope of a worker's activities to include tasks that require different skill levels. *For example,* a machine operator may set up the machine accessories and tools, carry out the machining operations, lubricate and maintain the machine and also check the quality of the output. This requires an individual worker to be trained in learning multiple skills and perform a variety of tasks.

Empowerment: Empowerment is the process of delegating decision-making authority to the lower levels within the organisation. Empowerment gives both responsibility for delivering quality and authority to identify problems and then formulate and implement solutions to employees who have direct contact with a problem. Employers free employees from the need to ask for permission from a manager. Employees simply do whatever they must to solve the problem.

As employees become more empowered in their work, the feeling of ownership and responsibility becomes more meaningful. Further, the act of empowering employees provides evidence of the management's trust in the employees.

The concept of empowerment applies to both individuals and to groups of workers. Self-managed teams provide an example of empowerment for groups of workers. With empowerment, there arises a need to redefine the basic roles of top, middle and junior managerial personnel and that of the workforce.

Personnel commitment: Successful total quality management requires a fundamental belief in and commitment to quality at four different levels:

(i) Every one in the organisation must make a ***commitment to producing quality products.***

(ii) Organisational members must make a ***commitment to customers*** (both internal and external customers)

(iii) TQM demands ***commitment by top managers.***

(iv) TQM requires a ***commitment of the firm as a whole.***

For TQM to work, everyone who contributes to the firm's product, including employees, managers and suppliers must accept quality as a critical component of both the survival of the firm and its ability to satisfy its customers.

Selection and Training: Selection and training of personnel have an important influence on people's development in an organisation. The Japanese have invested extensively in selection and training. Interviews and testing prior to employment assure compatibility of the job candidate and the job. Rotational assignments (job rotation) help to develop a broad base of technical skills, thus facilitating cooperation across departments.

9.13 PROVIDING PARTICIPATION AS A MEANS OF INSPIRING ACTION

It is a common belief that, to inspire action on quality, we must start by changing people's attitudes. A change in attitude then should lead to a change in behaviour. But in reality, the opposite is true. If we first change people's behaviour, then that will change their attitude.

The concept of participation helps to change behaviour. By personally participating in quality activities, people acquire new knowledge, see the benefits of quality disciplines and develop a sense of accomplishment by solving problems. This pariticipation leads to enduring changes in behaviour for the better.

A change in attitude leading to a change in behaviour is necessary to inspire action on quality.

Providing recognition and rewards: 'Recognition' is public acknowledgement of superior performance of specific activities. **Rewards** are benefits (such as salary increase, bonuses and promotions) which are conferred for generally superior performance against goals.

Recognition and rewards play an essential role in inspiring people on quality. People have positive feelings when *(i)* their job has been designed to focus on self-development and *(ii)* they are given opportunities to participate in planning and decision making. This tells employees that their skills, their judgement and their integrity are trusted by the management. For instance, employees feel happy when independent inspection is changed to self inspection.

Forms of recognition range from appreciating words for a job well done to modest or token awards which may be tangible (a savings bond, time off or a dinner) or intangible (a letter of praise, sending an employee to a seminar or conference). In deciding the forms of recognition, managers should ask for suggestion from respected workforce employees so that they fit their culture better.

Forms of rewards for improvement activities relating to quality improvement could be financial incentives, annual bonus, gain sharing and so on.

9.14 BUILDING A CHANGE ORIENTED ORGANISATION

The importance of this activity changes with variations in the turbulence of a firm's business environment. A staid business with few competitive threats and a stable workforce may not need to focus acutely on building systems that can respond to change. Any business with respectable sales growth and profit margins will attract competition, however, and unforeseen threats often blind-side those who make the smug assumption that everything will remain constant.

The best way to deal with change is to predict it and prepare a response.

A healthy sense of vulnerability can help a firm to fight smugness. The leader of a successful firm can benefit from a keen sense of wariness. Bill Gates, the CEO of Microsoft sends memos to his employees warning them that unseen new competitors are sowing the seeds of their highly successful firm's destruction.

The best way to deal with change is to predict it and prepare a response. This requires close relationship with customers, suppliers, employees and relevant technologies.

An appreciation of the thrill of discovery contributes to this work, helping the firm to track what its customers want along with the need and preferences of competitor's customers. The firm must also try to anticipate technical and social changes that will affect its operations.

A ***change-accepting culture*** stimulates and reinforces this awareness of new developments by encouraging experimentation without recrimination. An organisational culture should support individuals when they constructively challenge conventional wisdom and protect them from jeopardising their positions within the organisations.

The following section on "Change Management" includes discussions on "Total Quality Culture" and also on "How organisation culture is changed". It also includes topics on **continuous improvement (Kaizen)** and **"universal break-through sequence".**

9.15 CONTINUOUS IMPROVEMENT (KAIZEN)

***Continuous improvement*, based on a Japanese concept called *Kaizen*, is the philosophy of continually seeking ways to improve operations.** In this regard, it is not unique to quality, but applies also to **process improvement.** Continuous improvement involves identifying benchmarks of excellent practice and instilling a sense of employee ownership in the process. The focus can be on reducing the length of time required to carry out a process, reducing the amount of scrap generated in a manufacturing process or the number of accidents in the work place and the like. Continuous improvement also can focus on problems with customers or suppliers. The bases of the continuous improvement philosophy are the beliefs that virtually any aspect of an operation or process can be improved and that the people most closely associated with an operation or process are in the best position to identify the changes that should be made.

Continuous improvement is an inherent part of the total quality management process

***Continuous improvement* is an inherent part of the total quality management process.** It transforms the drive towards quality into a never-ending journey. Every day, the firm must try to be better than it was a day before. Once benchmarks have been set and a plan has been developed to move companies towards best practices, the need for continuous improvement arises. This concept allows companies to accept modest beginning and make small incremental improvements towards excellence. **The advantages of such an approach are:**

(i) Because early results are likely to be modest at best, frustration and abandonment are avoided.

(ii) Gradual and continuous progress through incremental improvements means that companies can never accept that where they are is the best that will ever be.

(iii) Results in companies, even world-class companies struggling for even higher levels of performance. This result is essential to compete globally.

Continuous improvement consists of measuring key quality and other process indices in all areas and taking action to improve them. Effective continuous improvement needs the support of performance measurement methods. Performance measurement systems help people to identify and measure, in quantitative terms, the sizes of improvements. This effort also keeps attention focussed on quality. Reliable performance measurement must accurately assess progress towards intended objectives and behaviour.

Getting started with continuous improvement

Several steps are essential to the eventual success of the philosophy of continuous improvement. They are:

(i) Train employees in the methods of statistical process control (SPC) and other tools for improving quality and performance.(7 QC Tools)

(ii) Make SPC methods a normal aspect of daily operations.

(iii) Build work teams and employee involvement.

(iv) Utilise problem solving tools within the work teams.

(v) Develop a sense of operator ownership in the process.

9.16 THE CONTINUOUS IMPROVEMENT STRATEGY

***Exhibit 9.9* shows a strategy for implementing continuous improvement in an organisation.**

Step 1: Defining the Current Strategies

The continuous improvement approach begins by defining an organisation's current ***quality status.*** This can be addressed from any of several perspectives *viz.* number of defects, the cost of defects, customer satisfaction indices and the like.

Step 2: Defining Continuous Improvement Objectives

Once the organisation's current quality is known, the objectives of continuous improvement are selected. While the first step asks the question **"where are we?"** (*i.e.* the current status) the second step asks the question, **"where are we going?"** (*i.e.* what we want to achieve?). The organisation's quality improvement objectives based on a realistic appraisal of what the organisation, with its available resources, is capable of achieving. If the established objectives of continuous improvement are unrealistic, it may result in failure which can have a demotivating effect on the organisation. Hence it is better to set modest improvement goals or objectives at first to realise few initial successes, which will help to motivate other employees of the organisation to accept the continuous improvement philosophy.

Exhibit 9.9 : Steps in Continuous Improvement Strategy

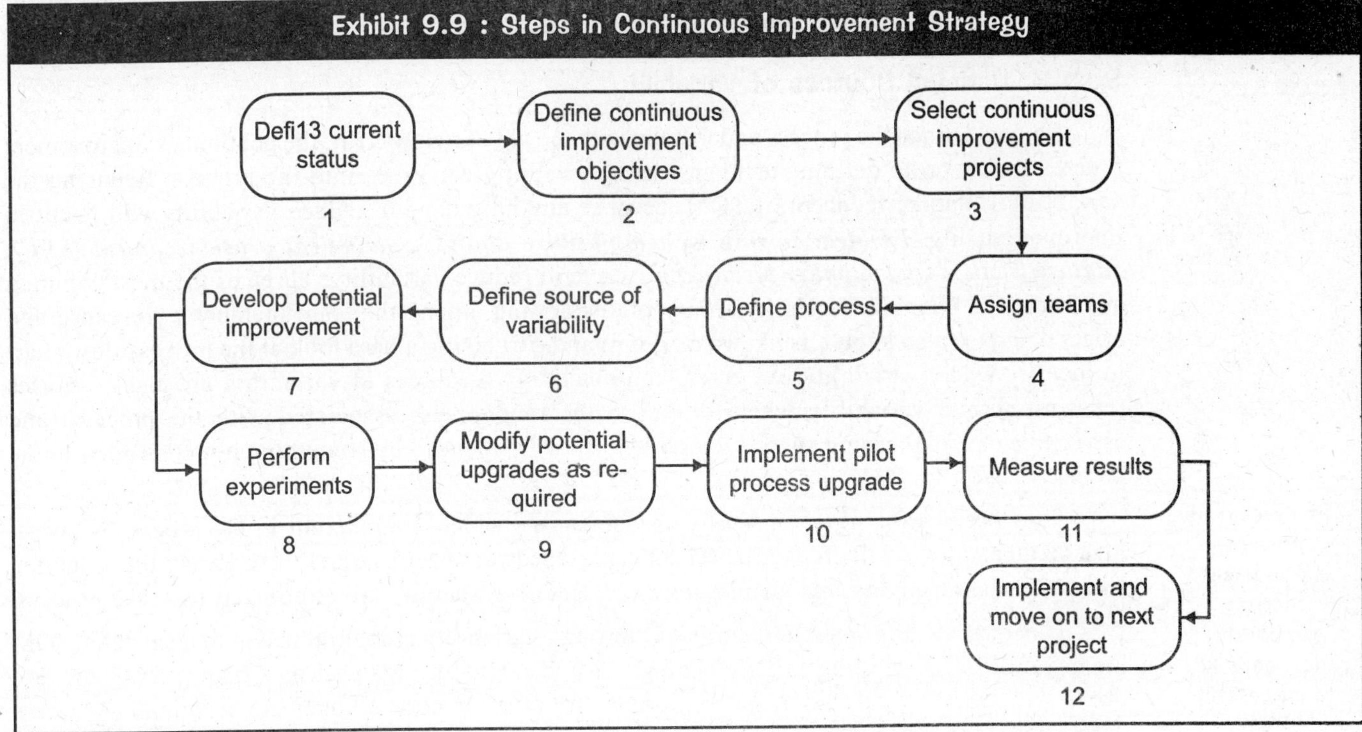

Step 3: Converting Objectives into Action

This step involve selecting continuous improvement projects in order to convert the continuous improvement objectives into action. These are the specific areas in which an organisation desires to seek improvement. Some of the examples of improvement projects are *(i)* a product fails too often during acceptance testing and the objective is to reduce test failures by 50 percent, *(ii)* the finance department is habitually late in paying account payable and the goal is to assure all payments are made in less than 30 days and *(iii)* the work instructions contain too many errors and the goal is to reduce work instruction errors to less than one-tenth the current values. Each of these projects provide the framework of an action plan for the organisation to realise continuous improvement.

Step 4: People Make it Happen (Assign teams)

After selecting the areas in which to focus continuous improvement efforts, the organisation has to design people to work on these projects and empower them to attain the continuous improvement objectives set. The concept of ***employee involvement, empowerment and teamwork*** are extremely important to achieve ***continuous improvement,*** as they allow an organisation to attain significant synergies and fully utilise its human resources.

Step 5: Defining the Process

Once the team has been assigned to a continuous improvement project, the first task of the team is to define the process it is assigned to improve. This is done by preparing flow charts for the process involved in the improvement projects. Flow charts provide the visibility of the entire process to all those who work in the process. Flow charting also often reveals many problem areas and inefficiencies. The human inputs in the process should be identified. Wherever a human input is required, potential sources of ***variability*** can enter the process. To achieve continuous improvement in a process, steps should be taken to clarify or limit human inputs, to control the variability. Each step of the process should be critically examined by the team members by asking the question "what happens if this step is eliminated?" If nothing happens, then that particular step in the process should be removed from the process.

Step 6: Defining Sources of Variability

Having defined the process under study with the aid of a flow chart, the continuous improvement process moves on to defining areas in which variability can creep into the process. Reducing the variability is another concept of TQM, because anything done to reduce variability will result in improved quality. ***Problem solving, systems failure analysis, statistical process control (SPC), Taguchi method and supplier teeming,*** all serve to reduce variability. Three of the most common approaches to identify variability are *(i)* brainstorming among the team members, *(ii)* cause and effect diagram (also known Ishikawa diagram) and *(iii)* taking a hard look at the process flow chart to identify where variability can enter the process. Two sources of variability are chance causes (causing normal variability which is due to the randomness associated with the process) and assignable causes (causing special variability which is induced by something not controlled in the process).

The concept of process improvement through variability reduction is key to successful TQM implementation.

The normal variability caused by chance causes which are inherent in the process is not so high that the process will produce a product that exceeds its specification limits. Variability reduction focusses on assuring that assignable causes of special variability are eliminated from the process.

This concept of ***process improvement*** through variability reduction is key to successful TQM implementation. According to Dr. Deming, 85 percent of an organisation's quality problems are due to the variability induced by problems in the process and not workmanship. Eliminating process deficiencies and minimising process variability will prevent future defects.

Once the sources of variability have been identified, potential improvements can then be developed. Teams are found to be more effective than individuals working in isolation.

Step 7: Implementing Change: Managing the Risk

Thorough evaluation of any process improvements prior to implementation is mandatory for good risk management. This involves:

(i) designing tests or experiments to evaluate the feasibility of any process modification. These tests will show whether the process modification will work and will show any required modification prior to implementation.

(ii) incorporating the process upgrades as a pilot program in a small area prior to implementation, whenever possible. The pilot program will identify the risks associated with proposed process modifications. Where problems emerge, they can be corrected prior to full implementation. *For example,* in a manufacturing organisation, if the continuous improvement team recommends modifying the method of issue of material to the shop floor, it is wise to try this new method in a small area of the plant prior to full-scale implementation throughout the organisation.

(iii) Monitoring the pilot program process upgrades using the same measurement criteria that initially targeted the process for improvement. This will help determine whether the process improvement actually resulted in an improvement in quality.

(iv) Continuing to monitor the process with the same measurement criteria once the upgrade has been fully implemented.

Step 8:

After the process improvement have been implemented and confirmed as effective, the organisation moves on to the next project to realise additional improvement benefits. This process of continuous improvement never ends.

***Box 9.14* describes continuous improvement at the Timken company.**

Box 9.14 : Continuous Improvement at the Timken Company

Continuous improvement projects may appear small and inconsequential by themselves, yet taken collectively add upto something worthwhile. Regardless of their size, the best projects are those that emanate from the employees themselves. Such a case at Timken Company, the world's leading manufacturer of precision bearings and alloy steels is discussed in the following paragraphs.

The Small Industrial Bearings Division of Timken Company produces more than 1000 different parts and assembles, several thousand combinations which are shipped to customers all over the world. A particular department responsible for three assembly lines was experiencing problems regarding scheduling, high scrap rates and low output rates. The employees decided to make improvements and formed a team consisting of assembly operators, job setters, maintenance crew, a tool engineer and a shop floor supervisor.

The activity in the department consisted of four basic operations in each assembly line, with each line requiring at least four operators. Flexibility has been introduced to the lines by adding pieces of equipments but each line had grown to an unwieldy length of 18 equipments. The operator could operate only one machine at a time, leaving most of the machines idle most of the time and hence in reality there was no flexibility. In addition, the work-in-process inventory investment was high because many partially completed products had to wait to be processed. This large work-in-process inventory also led to high inspection costs.

The team came to a conclusion that the key to the majority of the problems was the high work-in-process inventories and the team members conducted brain storming sessions to generate ideas for improvement. The team decided to solve the problem of high work-in-process inventories by changing the arrangement of the equipment. The long lines of 18 equipment were converted to short 'C' shaped lines and the equipments were positioned closer together which enabled the operators to run more than one piece of equipment at a time, thereby reducing the need of high levels of inventory between each operation. The following improvements were achieved within 10 weeks of the team's new arrangement for the workplace:

- increased output by 25 percent
- reduced floor space for the assembly operations by 13,000 square feet
- increased flexibility in production
- doubled equipment utilisation and
- increased labour utilisation by 45 percent.

9.17 THE KAIZEN APPROACH

Kaizen is a Japenese term which means gradual unending improvement by doing little things better.

'**Kaizen**' is the name given by the Japanese to the concept of continuous incremental improvement. '**kai**' means change, and **zen** means good. 'Kaizen' therefore means making changes for the better on a continual, never ending basis. The improvement aspect of kaizen refers to both **people** and **processes.**

Kaizen strategy is the single most concept in Japanese management – the key to Japanese competitive success. 'Kaizen' means 'on-going' improvement involving everyone – top management, managers and workers.

In his book "KAIZEN : **"The key to Japan's Competitive Success"**: Masaaki Imai gives an overview of the 'Kaizen' concept which his summarized below:

***(i)* Kaizen value system:** The underlying value system of Kaizen can be summarized as **"continual improvement of all things, at all levels, all the time and forever"**. All the strategies for achieving this fall under the **"Kaizen umbrella"** (which we discussed in chapter 9 – Process Management). The major elements of kaizen are : Customer focus, Team work, Just-in-time, Quality circles, Automation, Labour/ Management co-operation and Total productive maintenance.

***(ii)* Role of executive (or top) management:** Executive managers are responsible for establishing kaizen as the overriding corporate strategy and communicating this commitment to all levels of the organisation, allocating the resources necessary for kaizen to work, establishing appropriate policies, ensuring full deployment of kaizen policies and establishing systems, procedures and structures that promote kaizen.

***(iii)* Role of middle managers:** Middle managers are responsible for implementing the kaizen policies established by executive (or top) management, establishing, maintaining and improving work standards, ensuring that employees receive training necessary to understand and implement kaizen and ensuring that employees learn how to use all applicable problem solving tools.

***(iv)* Role of supervisors:** Supervisors are responsible for applying the kaizen approach in their functional roles, developing plans for carrying out the kaizen approach at the functional level, improving communication in the work place, maintaining morale, providing coaching for team – work activities, soliciting kaizen suggestions from employees and making kaizen suggestions.

***(v)* Role of employees:** employees are responsible for participating in kaizen through teamwork activities, making kaizen suggestions, engaging in continuous self-improvement activities, continually enhancing job skills through education and training and continually broadening for job skills through cross-functional training.

***(vi)* Kaizen and quality:** In a total quality setting, quality is defined by customers, Regardless of how customers define quality, it can always be improved and it should be; continually. Kaizen is a broad concept that promotes quality from the all encompassing "Big Q" perspective.

Kaizen check list: Kaizen is about continual improvement of people, processes, procedures and any other factors that can affect quality. One of the best ways to identify problems that represent opportunities for improvement is to use a checklist that focuses the attention of employees to those factors that are most likely in need of improvement. These factors include personnel, work techniques, work methods, work procedures, time, facilities, equipment, systems, software, tools, materials, plant layout, production levels, inventory and paradigms (or mind sets).

9.18 KAIZEN FIVE STEP PLAN

The five step plan to implement Kaizen by Japanese firms are:

Step 1: **Seiri** (straighten up) – This step involves separating the necessary from the unnecessary and getting rid of the unnecessary in such areas as tools, work-in-process, machinery, products, papers and documents.

Step 2: **'Seiton'** (Put things in order): This step involves putting such things as tools and materials in their proper place and keeping things in order so that employee can always find what they need to do the job without wasting time for searching tools and materials'.

Step 3: **'Seiso'** (clean up): This step involves keeping the work place clean and tidy so that work can proceed is an efficient manner, free of the problems that might crop up when the work place is messy.

Step 4: **'Seiketsu'** (Personal cleanliness): This step involves employees being neat to present an appearance that promotes professionalism in performing work tasks.

Step 5: **'Shitsuke'** (Discipline): This step involves careful adherence to standardised work procedures. This requires personal discipline.

***Box 9.15* lists 3 MUs (Muda, Muri and Mura) check list of Kaizen activities**

Box 9.15 : 3 MUs Checklist of Kaizen Activities

A number of Kaizen check points have been developed to help both workers and the management to be constantly aware of the area for quality improvement. The three check points widely used are the 3 MUs – Muda (waste), Muri (strain) and Mura (discrepancy). These three – that is waste, strain and discrepancy must be avoided to implement Kaizen (continuous improvement) in any organisation.

Elements of 3 MUs are :

Sl. No.	Muda (waste)	Sl. No.	Muri (strain)	Sl. No.	Mura (discrepancy)
1	Manpower	1	Manpower	1	Manpower
2	Technique	2	Technique	2	Technique
3	Method	3	Method	3	Method
4	Time	4	Time	4	Time
5	Facilities	5	Facilities	5	Facilities
6	Jigs and tools	6	Jigs and tools	6	Jigs and tools
7	Materials	7	Materials	7	Materials
8	Production volume	8	Production volume	8	Production volume
9	Inventory	9	Inventory	9	Inventory
10	Place	10	Place	10	Place
11	Way of thinking	11	Way of thinking	11	Way of thinking

Box 9.16 **illustrates 5 'S' Kaizen movement**

Box 9.16 : 5s Kaizen Movement (House Keeping Steps for Quality Movement)

The 5s are *(I)* Seiri, *(ii)* Seiton, *(iii)* Seiso, *(iv)* Seiketsu and *(v)* Shitsuke. These 5s words comprise a step-wise approach for quality improvement. These are also known as house-keeping steps for quality improvement.

(i) **Seiri (means to straighten-up)**

It includes : *(a)* work-in-process *(b)* unnecessary tools *(c)* unused machinery *(d)* defective products and *(e)* papers and documents.

Differentiate between the necessary and unnecessary and discard the unnecessary.

(ii) **Seiton (means putting things in order)**

Keep the things in order so that they are ready for use when required. (This will avoid waste of time due to searching for things such as tools, parts, components and the like). ***"Everything should be at its place and there should be place for everything."***

(iii) **Seiso (means to clean up)**

Every individual should clean the workplace everyday before starting the day's work and also at the time of closing the work. Japanese firms strongly believe in the slogan ***"keep the work place clean".***

(iv) **Seiketsu (means personal cleanliness)**

Every worker or manager should make it a point to give special attention to his or her ***personal cleanliness.*** Some of the Japanese beliefs are

- ***"There is a healthy mind in a healthy body."***
- ***"Cleanliness is necessary for Godliness."***
- ***"Make it a habit to be clean and tidy, starting with your own person."***

All these mean good housekeeping practices.

(v) **Shitsuke (means discipline)**

Every worker and manager has to follow procedures in the workplace and workshop with utmost sense of discipline. Japanese believe that only with discipline and sincerity in following the principles and procedures, one can contribute significantly to personal and organisational success. It is necessary to have discipline in all aspects of our work to improve quality of products and work life.

Box 9.17 **illustrates 5 Ws and one 'H' check list and** ***Box 9.18*** **illustrates 4 M's check list of Kaizen**

Box 9.17 : "Five Ws and one H" – Checklist

In an organisation, Kaizen activities should be carried out by asking the following questions under five Ws and one H. They are – ***who, what, where, when, why and how.***

Who : Who does it? Who is doing it? Who should be doing it? Who else can do it? Who else should do it? Who is doing 3 MUs?

What : What to do? What is being done? What should be done? What else should be done? What else can be done? What 3 MUs are being done?

Where : Where to do it? Where it is done? Where should it be done? Where else can it be done? Where else should it be done? Where are the 3 MUs being done?

When : When to do it? When is it done? When should it be done? When other time can it be done? When other time should it be done? When there is presence of 3 MUs?

Why : Why to do it? Why is it being done? Why else should it be done? Why else can it be done? Why do it that way? Why there are 3 MUs in the way of thinking?

How : How to do it? How is it being done? How should it be done? How this method can be used in other means? How this can be done in other ways? How are there any 3 MUs in the method?

Box 9.18 : 4 Ms check list for Kaizen

4 Ms refer to resources of management – ***men, machines, materials and methods,*** which are important for quality improvement and Kaizen. Questions to be asked related to 4 MUs to implement Kaizen activities effectively are :

(i) **Man (Operator)**

- Does he follow standards?
- Is he responsible/accountable?
- Is he assigned to the right job?
- Does he maintain good human relations?
- Is his work efficiency acceptable?
- Is he qualified?
- Is he willing to improve?
- Is he healthy?
- Is he problem conscious?
- Is he experienced?

(ii) **Machine (Facilities)**

- Does it meet production requirements?
- Is the oiling/greasing adequate?
- Is operation stopped often because of mechanical trouble?
- Does it make any unusual noise?
- Are there enough machines/facilities?
- Does it meet process capabilities?
- Is its inspection done adequately?
- Does it meet precision requirements?
- Is the layout adequate?
- Is everything in a good working order?

(iii) **Material**

- Are there any mistakes in volume?
- Are there any mistakes in the brand name?
- Is the inventory level adequate?
- Is the handling adequate?
- Is the layout adequate?
- Are there any mistakes in grade?
- Are there any impurities mixed in?
- Is there any wastage in material?
- Is the work-in-process abandoned?
- Is the quality standard adequate?

(iv) **Method (Operation)**

- Are the work standards adequate?
- Is it a safe method?
- Is it an efficient method?
- Is the set up adequate?
- Are the lighting and ventilation adequate?
- Is there adequate contact with the previous and next processes?
- Is the work standard upgraded?
- Is it a method that ensures a good product?
- Is the sequence of work adequate?
- Are the temperature and humidity adequate?

9.19 THE KAIZEN PHILOSOPHY

"Kaizen" is the Japanese term for **"continuous improvement".** It is a formal system to promote continuous improvement developed as part of just-in-time manufacturing techniques. Masaaki Imai described the elements of ***Kaizen*** in great detail in his book published in 1986, citing the system as an important basis for the success of many leading Japanese firms.

Kaizen is a philosophy that subsumes all business activities. Kaizen strategy has been called: "the single most important concept in Japanese management – the key to Japanese competitive success". Unlike the traditional view that quality improvement means simply making improvements in ***product quality,*** in the Kaizen philosophy, **improvement in all areas of business-cost, meeting delivery schedules, employee safety and skill development, suppliers relations, new product development or productivity** – all serve to enhance the ***quality of the firm.*** Thus, any activity directed towards improvement falls under the ***Kaizen umbrella.*** Activities to establish traditional quality control systems, install robotics and advanced technology, institute employee suggestion systems, maintain equipment and implement just-in-time production system – all lead to improvement.

In contrast to seeking improvement through radical technological change (*i.e.* break-through improvement), **Kaizen focusses on small, gradual and frequent improvements over the long run.** Financial investment is minimal in such improvement programs. Everyone participates in the process and many improvements result from the know–how and experience of workers. *For example,* at Nissan Motor Co, any suggestion that saves at least 0.6 seconds in a production process is seriously considered by management.

Successful kaizen program requires:
(i) Operating practices
*(ii)*total involvement and
*(iii)*training.

The first and foremost concern of the Kaizen philosophy is the ***quality of people.*** If the quality of people is improved, then the quality of products will follow. By instilling Kaizen into people and training them in basic quality improvement tools, workers can build this philosophy into their work and continually see improvement in their jobs. This process-oriented approach to improvement encourages constant communication among workers and managers.

9.19.1 Requirements for a Successful Kaizen Program

Three things that are required for a successful Kaizen program are: *(i)* **operating practices,** *(ii)* **total involvement** and *(iii)* **training.**

Operating practices expose new improvement opportunities. Practices such as just-in-time reveal waste and inefficiency as well as poor quality.

In the Kaizen approach, every employee strives for improvement. Top management views improvement as an inherent part of corporate strategy and provides support to improvement activities by allocating resources effectively and providing reward structures that are conducive to improvement.

Middle management can implement top management's improvement goals by:

(i) Establishing, upgrading and maintaining operating standards that reflect these goals.

(ii) By improving co-operation between departments.

(iii) By making employees conscious of their responsibility for improvement and

(iv) Developing their problem-solving skills through training.

Supervisors can direct more of their attention to improvement rather than "supervision" which in turn facilitates communication and offers better guidance to workers.

Workers can engage in improvement through suggestion systems and small-group activities, self development programs that teach practical problem-solving techniques and enhanced job performance skills.

All this require significant training, both in the philosophy and in tools and techniques.

9.19.2 Benefits of Kaizen

Kaizen is the simple truth behind Japan's economic miracle and the real reason the Japanese have become the masters of ***"flexible manufacturing system"*** – the ability to adapt manufacturing processes to changing customer and market requirements and to do it fast. Kaizen, which means, ***"step-by-step gradual improvement, doing things better, continuously setting and achieving ever-***

higher standards", is as important as break-through innovations. The whole of Japanese business philosophy is based on the combination of ***Kaizen and innovation.*** This has brought a reduction in costs, faster development times, prompt deliveries, customer satisfaction and enormous competitive advantage internationally.

The Kaizen philosophy has been widely adopted and is used in many firms in the US and around the world. *For example,* at ENBI Corporation in New York, Kaizen projects have resulted in a 48 percent increase in productivity, a 30 percent reduction in cycle time and a 73 percent reduction in inventory. Kaizen has been successfully applied in the Mercedes-Benz truck factory in Brazil, resulting in reduction of 30 percent in manufacturing space, 45 percent in inventory, 70 percent in lead time and 70 percent in set-up time over a three year period.

9.19.3 Kaizen and Deming

Kaizen has a lot in common with Deming's philosophy. There are many principles in Kaizen that are identical to certain of Deming's management rules; *for example,* the obsession with never-ending quality improvement, the responsibility of management, the relationships with suppliers, the process-oriented approach, total quality attainment, striving for long-term and sustained benefits rather than short-term profits, the PDCA cycle, the importance of communication, education, development and involvement of employees in quality-related activities etc.

Kaizen represents the basis of the Japanese business philosophy which was inspired by Deming's teachings in the 1950s. Since then, other concepts, systems and tools have been developed such as ***Quality Control Circles, Kanban (Just-in-time), zero defects, total quality control*** etc. which are all incorporated under the umbrella of Kaizen. But Deming's process oriented way of thinking, based on the principle of continuous quality improvement and involving people at all levels of the organisation is what the ***Kaizen*** message is all about.

Two distinct features inherent in the Kaizen philosophy are:

(i) There is an urgency about the never-ending efforts for improvement and gradual change for the better. Repetitiveness is considered as negative and as an inhibitor to progress.

(ii) There is an emphasis on the process rather than the output. The slogan is ***"build quality into the process".*** This is based on the realisation that mass inspection of the output is a non-value added activity which is not capable of improving quality.

9.19.4 Gemba Kaizen

"Gemba Kaizen" means "improvement of real place"

Masaaki Imai, chairman of Kaizen Institute in Japan, propounded the concept of **"Gemba Kaizen"**. In Japanese language **"Gemba"** means "real place" **"Kai"** means change and **"Zen"** means good. **"Gemba Kaizen"** means "improvement of real place" or improvement of the place where real activity takes place. In the manufacturing sector, 'gemba' is the factory and in the service sector, 'gemba' refers to the administrative offices.

According to Imai, the problem with most managers is that they prefer to stick to their seat in their offices and keep themselves at a distance from the events taking place in **gemba** (i e the actual work place for eg manufacturing shop floor or assembly lines). Most managers come to know about the activities taking place in gemba through daily or weekly or even monthly reports or through periodic meetings. To ensure avoidance of wastages, managers should go to the gemba (**Management by Walking Around - MBWA**) and observe the activities themselves rather than depending on reports about what happened in the 'gemba'. What the manager observes in the gemba (real work place) is the truth (primary or first – hand information) while what report they receive from gemba in their office is secondary information which may not reflect the truth.

Five Gemba Principles

1. **When a trouble, abnormality or problem occurs, go to gemba first.** Managers should go to the gemba (place of work) at once they hear about a problem that occurred (for eg an

accident) rather than waiting in their office to receive the report from the supervisors or executives in the 'gemba'.

2. **Check with gembutsu** (machines, tools, rejects, and customer complaints), **'Gembutsu'** in Japanese means tangible things on which you can put your hands. For example, if a machine breaks down, the machine is itself 'gembutsu'. If a customer complaints, he or she is 'gembutsu'. If a machine breaks down, the manager should personally go to the gemba and see the 'gembutsu' (machine) to find out the reason for the breakdown on the spot.
3. **Take temporary counter measures on the spot:** If a machine breaks down, or a customer lodges a complaint, the manager must address the problem immediately, even if the solution may be a temporary measure.
4. **Find out the root - cause:** By repeatedly asking "why" several times, the manager can find out the root cause of the problem.
5. **Standardise for prevention of recurrence:** Once the root cause is identified, the manager comes up with a counter measure and then should standardise such a countermeasure so that the same problem will not recur: **'Muda'** waste elimination is a major tool of Gemba kaizen. The various types of **Muda** (work without a product or effort wasted) are:
   i) **Muda of overproduction:** If you produce more than the customer's needs, then the surplus products will result in excess inventory requiring handling and storage.
   ii) **Muda of inventory**: This is the result of overproduction in any stage of production. If only those parts that are required in the next process are produced, muda of inventory can be eliminated.
   iii) **Muda of waiting**: This means operators are waiting for materials or tools or parts from previous operations etc. This results in production loss due to idling of workers.
   iv) **Muda of motion**: This results when operators are moving unnecessarily in search of tools or materials to be used for their work.
   v) **Muda of transportation**: This occurs when materials are being moved from place to place on materials handling equipments such as trucks, forklifts, conveyors etc.
   vi) **Muda of producing rejects**: Producing defective parts leads to rework or scrap.
   vii) **Muda of processing**: By rearranging the sequence of operations, often a particular operation can be eliminated. The concept of muda elimination is fundamental to kaizen approach.

9.20 THE UNIVERSAL "BREAKTHROUGH SEQUENCE"

It is imperative to develop the habit of making annual improvements in quality and annual reduction in quality costs, not to lose ground to those competitors who already have it. What is needed is a continuous effort to achieve a breakthrough.

Breakthrough is an organised creation of beneficial change. The main ingredients of this programme are:

- Accept the responsibility for making improvements.
- Understand the universal sequence of events for making the improvements.
- Become familiar with the key concepts and techniques by which the universal breakthrough is carried out.
- Apply the universal sequence to actual company problems.

The universal breakthrough sequence is a road map to success and it follows the following stages in a particular order:

(i) Proof of the need
(ii) Project identification
(iii) Organisation for improvement
(iv) The diagnostic journey
(v) Remedial action
(vi) Breakthrough in cultural resistance to change and
(vii) Holding the gains-control at the new level.

These stages are described briefly in the following paragraphs.

The universal breakthrough sequence is a road map to success.

(i) ***Proof of the need:*** Middle managers will be the ones to prove to the top management that quality improvement is necessary for survival. The proof of this need is easily provided by quantifying the chronic waste in the language of money wasted. A rough estimation of quality costs can indicate the area in need of improvement and can increase in awareness of opportunities of cost savings.

(ii) ***Project identification:*** General awareness of opportunities need to be converted into specific projects for action. An agreed project provides a way of achieving a breakthrough. It helps to secure the needed budgets, facilities, permission to conduct experiments, needed tools and techniques and adequate personnel. The priority projects can be decided by using "Pareto principle". The priority projects will be the ones which score highly on their monetary returns on the effort invested, the amount of potential improvement in quality and product saleability, their urgency, ease of technology involved and level of acceptance by the management and workforce.

(iii) ***Organisation for improvement:*** **Responsibilities are established for three levels of activities:**

(a) Steering or guiding the overall improvement programme.

(b) Steering or guiding each project individually.

(c) Diagnosing or analysing each project.

A broad committee or a team of top managers has to be created to guide the overall improvement programme and to commit funds, personnel and facilities.

Multiple sub-committees or task forces are needed to be set up to guide the individual projects. The choice of the subcommittee members should depend on the skill and capacity to make a useful contribution.

After the completion of the organisation for improvement, the diagnostic journey is ready to begin. This is the journey from symptoms to cause and from cause to remedy.

(iv) ***The diagnostic journey:*** The journey from symptom to cause is an essential stage in the breakthrough sequence.

Diagnostic skills are the ability to design experiments or data-sampling schemes, to collect the appropriate data without bias, to interpret the results and to test any theories or propositions on offer scientifically. The two types of defects are:

(i) Operator-controllable defects and

(ii) Management controllable defects.

Management controllable defects are 80 to 94% of the total. The operators are said to be in a state of **"self-control"** and to have all the means needed to control any resulting defect when:

(i) They know what is expected of them. *(ii)* They know what their actual performance is and
(iii) They have the means to regulate.

Diagnosis of management controllable errors requires a study of current management practices and current technology.

A successful diagnosis can take place by conducting the following:

(i) An analysis of symptoms (to measure and examine the defects).

(ii) A systematic formulation of theories for the causes of symptoms (through brain storming)

(iii) Thorough testing of the theories by analysing prior-in-house data, by studying current operation and processes and by conducting off-line experiments.

The errors are classified as:

(a) ***Inadvertent errors*** – unintentional, un-predictable errors, occurring randomly, which the operator is unaware of making.

(b) ***Technique errors*** – errors that arise from lack of knowledge of an essential new technique. They are unintentional, specific and consistent.

(c) ***Wilful errors*** – errors that the operator makes intentionally and persistently and is aware of making..

(v) Remedial action: **The remedial journey for the management controllable errors has the following phases:**

(a) Choice of alternatives: The choice among many alternative remedies can be made by quantifying for each alternative the cost impact to the company. An optimisation of company costs and customer costs is the criteria for choosing the best alternative remedy. The impact of different cost factors such as materials usage, productivity, energy consumption and market research expenditure should be considered.

(b) Preventive maintenance: Managers usually try to rectify what has gone wrong, try to make defective work good, which are wasteful and disruptive activities. Instead of fire-fighting, managers should resort to value–added activity such as preventive maintenance of machines, tools, instruments, computers and automated process equipments.

(c) Communications: Adequate, open communication and feedback between various departments are crucial. Procedures, instructions, corporate policies and objectives should be adequately and clearly documented. Incomplete communication and feed back may lead to errors.

(d) Allocation of responsibility: Clear responsibilities for quality–oriented decisions and actions are necessary and people available to make decisions and take actions should be identified.

(e) Inspection and test: Inspection is a necessary evil, which until the time comes when we can do without it, is in a disparate need of improvement. But the fact remains that mass inspection and its associated costs cannot be reduced unless the chronic defect rate is reduced by controlling the quality of production processes by utilising SPC tools and other diagnostic techniques.

(f)Separation of problems: **Pareto principle** is applied to the diagnosed problems to separate the ***vital few*** problems from the ***trivial many.*** The vital few are the minority of the problems which account for most of the defects and they should be tackled first. The ***trivial many*** problems which account for a relatively low amount of defects and costs should be tackled either individually or collectively depending on the types of problems.

(vi) Resistance to change: Beneficial application of remedies for dealing with poor quality may be inhibited by one obstacle – ***"resistance to change".*** This may take the form of delaying tactics or outright rejection of the remedy by management ranks, supervisors, labour unions and also the workers.

Resistance to technological change is due to social and cultural factors. The company's cultural pattern – a tight system of beliefs, habits, traditional practices etc. may inhibit the implementation of any change, which is seen as threat. **Certain actions to be taken to deal with cultural resistance are:**

(a) ***Provide participation:*** Participation of all those affected, both in the planning and in the execution of the changes will be helpful to overcome cultural resistance. Every participant should be treated with dignity, so that a favourable social climate if developed, can make the change more acceptable.

(b) ***Provide enough time:*** Adequate time should be allowed for the change to be accepted because it takes time to evaluate and accommodate the merits or threats of a change.

(vii) ***Holding the gains:*** This requires that the operating forces engage in control, which consists of evaluation of current performance, comparison of this performance with the desired one and corrective action when the comparison shows a large difference indicating out of control situation. **Management can assist the operations to achieve a state of self-control by providing the following:**

(a) A process capable of holding the gains (b) Established new standards
(c) Training and (d) Established system of control.

When a breakthrough into new levels of performance has been achieved and the resulting gains have been held and established as the new standard, the universal break through sequence of events is ready to start again.

9.21 THEORY OF CONSTRAINTS

Most organisations have strategies, goals, objectives and **plans to do more with less**. They usually have finite resources available, which tends to conflict with ever-increasing expectations from stakeholders. Traditional process improvement methods, for example, to reduce cycle time and to get more done with less have focused on analysis to pinpoint which process or problem area to tackle first. This results in a fragmented approach leading to improvement in target processes often at the expense of the whole organisation (suboptimisation)

Goldratt developed the "**Theory of constraints**" as an approach to managing that helps organisations improve continually, based on the concept of thinking of organisations as systems. The "Theory of constraints" is defined as follows:

"**The Theory of constraints** is an intuitive frame work for managing an organisation, implicit in the framework is a desire to continually improve performance to have a process of on going improvement. It starts, as it must, with clearly defining the goal of the organisation and establishing measurements to determine the impact of any action on the goal".

Goldratt's theory is based on the assumption that every organisation faces **constraints**. However the constraints that have the greatest negative impact on performance are policies as opposed to such physical entities as materials and resources, Goldratt defines a constraint as "anything that limits an organisation from achieving higher performance vis a vis its goal.

Goldratt's principles in the theory of constraints are:

(i) The whole organisation must be treated as a system.

(ii) Systems thinking is favoured over analytical thinking for managing change and problem solving.

(iii) The optimal system solution degenerates over a period of time as changes occur in the environment. Therefore continuous improvement is necessary to sustain the system's effectiveness.

(iv) Optimal performance of a system does not mean the aggregate of all the local optima of subsystems.

(v) Success or failure is dictated by how well the several processes within the system affect one another.

(vi) The system, much like a chair with individual links connecting the whole, is only as strong as the weakest link.

(vii) Little improvement occurs until to improvement of the weakest link is addressed.

(viii) The weakest link is the system's constraint.

(ix) A few core problems constitute the majority of the unwanted effects within a system.

(x) Linking undesirable effects by cause and effect helps surface core problems that are not apparent.

(xi) Solving individual undesirable effects and neglecting the core problems leads to short duration solutions.

(xii) Obscure underlying conflict tends to perpetuate core problems. Solution involves addressing the conflict and abolishing at least one such conflict.

(xiii) The system's current reality must be understood, and the difference between it and the goal, including the magnitude and direction.

(xiv) To improve the over all system, increase throughput, decrease inventory and operating expenses.

(xv) Continual improvement can be thwarted by inertia. Solutions appear to reflect further change.

(xvi) Carrying up with an idea is not coming up with a solution.

Steps involved in the application of theory of constraints

Step 1. Identify: In this step, any factor that tends to constrain progress toward accomplishing the goal is identified.

Step 2. Exploit: This step involves determining how the constraints can be exploited (turned into positive factors, eliminated or circumvented)

Step 3. Subordinate: Everything else is subordinated to making the decisions necessary to exploit the constraints. No other activity should have priority because the constraints are inhibiting progress toward accomplishing the organisation's goal.

Step 4. Eliminate constraints/overcome inertia:

In this step an examination is made to determine whether the constraints have been eliminated. If so, return to the first step and continue the improvement process. If not, inertia is the likely culprit. Attack this directly. An unwillingness to change should not be allowed to cause a constraint.

Because inertia is such an all-pervasive inhibitor of change, Goldratt recommended the following techniques to be taught for facilitating change:

(i) **Effect-cause-effect:** This technique involves the use of brain storming to verbalise an intuitive sense of problems and their causes.

(ii) **Evaporating clouds:** This technique involves stating a problem as a conflict and then isolating the related assumptions that can be challenged.

(iii) **Prerequisite trees:** A prerequisite is something that must occur before something else can occur. A prerequisite tree is a tool for identifying the path of least resistance from an old way of doing things to a new way.

(iv) **Socratic method:** The Socratic method is one of the oldest and most time-honoured ways of teaching. It consists of helping people find their own answers, draw their own conclusions and form their own opinions. It involves a facilitator using devil's advocate – type questions rather than expressing his or own views. The facilitator gives questions, not answers.

Constraints are categorised as physical or policy constraints. Physical contraints are easy to identify and eliminate whereas policy constraints are more difficult but their elimination usually means a higher degree of system improvement.

All resources (raw material availability, equipment capacity, work force, number of working hours per day, cash etc.) are finite or limited. Exceeding the limit causes a constraint. What drives these resources to the limit are often increased expectations of the market place, customers and management.

9.22 QUALITY IN PRACTICE

Box 9.19 : Becoming the World Champion in Meeting Customer Needs

John Aker, CEO of IBM was not happy with the company's recent growth which was half the historical levels. He planned to make IBM "the world's leader in meeting the needs of customers". IBM, with revenues of $ 60 billion and a work force of 3,87,000 at that time, was the world's largest computer company but a maturing bureaucracy. Akers vowed to shake up the company and restore the double-digit growth rates of previous years.

Aker began to discuss IBM's internal short-comings publicly, a major departure from tradition. He reorganised the domestic company into seven independent business units, among them PCs, mainframes, and software. Though IBM has a firm no-lay off policy, Aker got 6500 employees to retire. Another 20,000 were transferred from laboratory and staff jobs to the sales force. He shoved responsibility down the chain of command. *For example*, The management board previously exercised close oversight of division operations. Under Akers, executives negotiated their business plans with the board, then reported back only periodically.

US marketing head George Conrade adopted a simple slogan for sales people: "Just say yes". In general, fulfilling a promise to a customer no longer required checking with higher authority. A former staffer who had been redeployed to the sales force said that his goal is to spend 80 percent of his time with customers. Sales persons' salaries were based on number of units sold or rented. Akers changed the basis to total revenue, so the focus could be on building customer relationships, rather than the 'quick sale'. Akers promoted a new breed of executives, many of whom had technical backgrounds. Sales had formerly been the main route to the top in the managerial hierarchy. Changes were working at IBM. under the leadership of CEO, John Akers.

9.23 SUMMARY

Building an organisation that can achieve quality is a demanding task and also has an effect on the entire organisation. The set of activities involved in organising for total quality management are: *(i)* developing an organisational environment that fosters quality, *(ii)* understanding of the principles of quality and *(iii)* putting effort to engage employees in the necessary activities to implement quality. When these activities are carried out well, the organisation satisfies its customers and obtains a competitive advantage.

Historical approach for organising involved focussing on the principles of specialisation of labour, delegation of authority, span of control and unity of command; resulting in traditional pyramidal organisational structure (or chart). But today, it is necessary to build an organisation to achieve total quality. This has two prerequisites: *(i)* a quality attitude and *(ii)* an organisational structure to support the pervasive attitude.

The quality activities must be coordinated throughout the organisation (*i.e.,* companywide or organisation wide quality control). Further, organisation should be engaged in creating beneficial change as well as preventing adverse change.

Organising quality effectively and economically companywide requires a ***systems approach***. The development and operation of total quality organisation includes three considerations: *(i)* Identification and confirmation of the specific quality work and teamwork, *(ii)* Identification and confirmation of these same areas for quality control function itself and *(iii)* Leadership of company and plant management itself in establishment and ongoing maintenance of quality organisation. The systems approach views the company as an organisational system having the inputs (money, human resources, machines, materials, technology and methods), activities or conversion process (people and technical skills) and the output (objectives of customer satisfaction and profits). Synergism or synergy is a necessary attribute of a well-organised system. Also, in modern organisations, the concept of value chain is adopted to gain competitive advantage. The systems approach to organising suggests three significant changes: *(i)* the concept of inverted organisational chart, *(ii)* a system of intra-company internal quality and *(iii)* horizontal and vertical integration of functions and activities. Also, members of organisations at various levels should have a sound understanding of their roles during the transition to a TQM program. (from traditional organisation to a TQ organisation). Quality councils, work teams, cross-functional teams, quality circles and self-managed teams, are some of the forms of organising for TQM.

Continuous improvement (or Kaizen) is the philosophy of continually seeking ways to improve operations. It is an inherent part of the TQM process. The various steps involved in continuous improvement approach are: *(i)* Defining the current status, *(ii)* Defining continuing improvement objectives, *(iii)* Converting objectives into action, *(iv)* Assigning teams (people make it happen), *(v)* Defining the process, *(vi)* Defining the sources of variability, *(vii)* Implementing change (managing the risk) and *(viii)* Moving to the next improvement project.

The universal "breakthrough sequence" is an organised creation of beneficial change. It includes annual improvements in quality and annual reductions in quality costs so that the company stays in competition. What is needed is a continuous effort to achieve a "breakthrough".

"Theory of constraints' developed by Goldratt, is an approach to managing that helps organisations improve continuously based on the concept of thinking of organisations as systems. It is an intuitive framework for managing an organisation with a desire to continually improve performance to have a process of on-going improvement. This theory is based on the assumption that every organisation faces certain constraints. A constraint is defined as "anything that limits an organisation from achieving higher performance vis-a-vis its goal. The steps-involved in the application of "theory of constraints" are:

(i) Identify the constraint, *(ii)* Exploit the constraint, *(iii)* Subordinate everything else to making decisions necessary to exploit the constraints, *(iv)* Eliminate constraints/overcome inertia.

Constraints are categorised as physical constraints and policy constraints. Physical constraints can be easily identified and eliminated whereas policy constraints are more difficult but their elimination means a higher degree of system improvement.

9.24 KEY WORDS USED

Kaizen, Continuous Improvement, Generic value chain, Quality Council, Quality circles, Self – managing Teams, Self – managed Teams, Task Teams, Cross – functional Teams, Strategic Quality Management, Quality Culture, Job content, Empowerment, Change Management, Total Quality Culture, Cultural change, Work change, Kaizen Philosophy, Muda, Muri, Mura, Seiri, Seiton, Seiso, Seiketsu, Shitsuke, Gemba Kaizen, Universal Breakthrough Sequence, Theory of constraints.

9.25 OBJECTIVE QUESTIONS

(A) Match the following :

Column A	Column B
1. Synergism	1. Group of top managers
2. Quality council	2. A highly trained group of employees
3. Self managed team	3. Attribute of a well organised system
4. Kaizen	4. Continuous improvement

(B) State whether the following statements are True or False :

1. The measurement of effectiveness is fundamental to the TQM process. (T / F)
2. Quality is the sole responsiblity of the quality assurance department. (T / F)
3. No one knows the work place better than the worker. (T / F)
4. Job enrichment is also called as vertical job enlargement. (T / F)
5. Kaizen and Gemba kaizen are one and the same. (T / F)
6. Kaizen strategy has been called "The single most important concept in Japanese management". (T / F)
7. Masaaki Imai propounded the concept of both Kaizen and Gemba Kaizen. (T / F)
8. The concepts of employee involvement, empowerment and teamwork have no relevance to continuous improvement. (T / F)
9. Self control and job design are two important aspects of any job. (T / F)

(C) Multiple choice Questions : Choose the correct answer from the alternatives given under each question :

1. TQM requires
   (a) Commitment to producting quality products
   (b) Commitment to customers (c) Commitment by top managers
   (d) Commitment of the firm as a whole (e) All of the above
   (f) None of the above.
2. Top management commitment to quality is demonstrated by the following behaviour:
   (a) Signalling (b) Focus
   (c) Employee policies (d) All of the above
   (e) None of the above
3. An organisation must establish a culture based on ______ to initiate total quality management:
   (a) Customer satisfaction (b) Continuous improvement
   (c) Teamwork (d) All of the above
   (e) (a) and (b) only.
4. The core values and concepts necessary to sustain a total quality environment are:
   (a) Customer-driven quality (b) Leadership
   (c) Continuous improvement and learning
   (d) (a) and (b) only (e) (a), (b) and (c).

9.26 REVIEW QUESTIONS

1. What is meant by "organising for TQM"? Justify the need for organising for quality.
2. Discuss the requirements for organising for quality in the current business environment.
3. Explain the systems approach to organising for TQM.
4. Discuss the concept of generic value chain.
5. Discuss the factors involved in the transition from a traditional to a TQM organisation.
6. Discuss the roles of top management, middle management and the workforce in organisational transition to TQM.
7. Explain the role of teams in organising for TQM.
8. What are "quality circles"? Explain the significant characteristics of quality circles.
9. Discuss the concept and philosophy of quality circles.
10. State the potential benefits of quality circles.
11. Explain the role of management in supporting and sustaining quality circles.
12. What are self-managed teams? Describe how they work.
13. State the characteristics and benefits of self managed teams.
14. Compare the various features of a traditional organisation with that of a self managed team.
15. What are "task teams" and "cross functional teams"?
16. Describe the various steps involved in the continuous improvement approach.
17. What are the 3 MUs and their elements?
18. What are the 5 'S' in Kaizen movement?
19. What are 5 'W's and one 'H'?
20. What are the 4 Ms check list for Kaizen?
21. Discuss the concept of "Gemba Kaizen".
22. Discuss the concept of "The Universal Break-through Sequence".
23. What is meant by "Theory of constraints" Discuss the steps involved in the application of "theory of constraints".

9.27 DISCUSSION QUESTIONS

1. "TQM requires total commitment on the part of the management and workers" – Discuss
2. "No one knows the workplace better than the worker. Quality goals cannot be achieved without using the hands and heads of the work force" – Explain
3. "A change in corporate culture is an integral part of improving quality" – Comment.
4. "Recognition and rewards play an essential role in inspiring people on quality" – Do you agree or not? Justify your answer.
5. "Quality is now the responsibility of every one in the organisation and not just the quality assurance department" – Justify the statement.
6. "Quality circles pursue two types of problems: Those concerned with the personal well being of the worker and those concerned with the well being of the company" – Elaborate.

9.28 CHAPTER CASE

UNION CARBIDE'S MIC PLANTS IN THE UNITED STATES AND INDIA

One of the most famous industrial accidents in the 20th century happened on December 3, 1984, when a tragic toxic gas leak of methyl isocyanate (MIC) occurred at the Union Carbide plant in Bhopal, India, killing more than 3,400 people and leaving thousands of others sick and incapacitated. The pesticide factory simply lacked in quality anjd safety processes that exist in similar plants in the US and Germany, which include rain towers that rain down foam to neutralise leaking gases, and preventing them escaping from the premises The plant was closed and never reopened.

The Union Carbide India Limited (UCIL) was a pesticide factory operated by an all-Indian crew to produce the mildly toxic Sevin and other patented pesticides of Union Carbide Corporation (UCC), UCIL's Danbury, Connecticut parent.

In a failing market, the plant had been allowed to run down. Some of the safety equipment was in dispair, and personnel standards had been lowered substantially. Officials of the UCIL and its US parent had discussed selling the plant or dismantling it and shipping it to Brazil or Indonesia.

After the gas incident, UCC chief executive officer Warren Anderson said UCC took moral responsibility and offered medical and financial aid, but the offers were rejected by the government of India. The Indian Central Bureau of Investigation took control of the "crime scene" and began a criminal investigation. The government of India sued UCC in a New york court.

The US courts concluded the plant was built and managed by indians in India and the Indian courts were competent to hear the case. The Indian government commenced its suit in India in September 1986. The Indian government blamed UCC for faulty operating procedures and design whereas UCC continued to claim that the plant had been sabotaged by a "disgruntled employee" although it refused to name the alleged culprit. The Indian government which declared itself as the representative of all the victims, claimed damages of about $ 3.1 billion. UCC offered $ 70 million at first and $ 350 million later. The Indian government climbed down its damages claim to $ 615 million.

After more than four years of legal wrangling, The Indian Supreme Court ordered a $ 470 million settlement. UCIL paid 10 percent and UCC paid the rest.

Although its own internal inspections and reports had warned of potential problems in controlling reactions and of failures both in India and at a similar plant at Institute, West Virginia, Union Carbide took the position that potential problems had been handled and that both plants were operated in accordance with proper safety standards. It suggested sabotage as a likely but not conclusive explanation of the accident in India and sharply criticised the way Indian supervisors had loosely implemented the company's safety standards.

Subsequent investigation indicated that there had been more than 70 generally small MIC leaks at the Institute plant from 1980 to 1984. That plant was closed for a five-month period after the Bhopal disaster, but it was reopened after presumably thorough inspection by Union carbide, the state of West Virginia, and the other regulating agencies. Before reopening the plant, Union carbide put in place $ 5 million in new safety equipment, introducing new safety monitors and a new cooling system that was thought to solve the problems that had arisen in India.

A year later, on April 1, 1986, Union Carbide was fined $ 1.3 million by the US Labour Department for 221 safety violations at the Institute plant. The inspectors of regulating agencies charged that Union Carbide had intentionally underreported the number of injuries at the plant and had continued to use defective safety equipment there-by showing a careless attitude toward worker safety. However, none of these violations involved the MIC unit and no one had died. So no units were closed.

After the Bhopal incident, UCC established a corporate policy that it would take responsibility for safety "whenever we have an interest". The controversy surrounding Bhopal accident continued in 1989. In its 1989 policy statement, UCC reported it was still spending $ 7 million to $ 8 million a year on "Bhopal related litigation".

Disucssion Questions :

(i) "As environments change, the organisational cultures must adapt" - Discuss this statement with reference to the case of Union Carbide Corporation, USA.

(ii) Should a multinational company such as UCC have or assume "cradle-to-grave" and absolute responsibility for dangerous technology it exports to other countries. Justify your answer.

(iii) Was UCC responsible for the disaster? Explain.

(iv) Should the host country safety standards apply to Third World operations such as the one in Bhopal? Justify your answer.

(v) Comment on the ethical values of Union Carbide Corporation with reference to this case.

CHAPTER 10

BUILDING AND SUSTAINING TOTAL QUALITY ORGANISATION

LEARNING OBJECTIVES

After reading this chapter, you should be able to:

- Understand the terms "corporate culture" and "organisational change"
- Discuss the requirements for the design of an effective total quality structure
- Define the term "quality systems" and discuss the elements of a total quality system
- Discuss the objectives and structure of ISO 9000:2000
- Discuss the model of a process- based quality management system.
- Discuss the process of ISO 9001:2000 registration and certification
- State the benefits and limitations of ISO 9000:2000
- Discuss the steps involved in the implementation of ISO 9000:2000
- Discuss the concepts of ISO 14001
- Discuss role of employees in the implementation of total quality
- Discuss how to build a change-oriented organisation, learning organisation and fear free organisation.

10.0 INTRODUCTION

The principles of total quality focus on the customer, involvement of everyone and continuous improvement, are easy to understand and represent common sense. But still, many companies have experienced great difficulty in implementing total quality and even deciding whether to do it. Some common misconceptions which create difficulty while taking decisions – whether to implement TQM or not are:

- TQ involves lots of work like collecting data and organising teams.
- TQ applies only to large companies and the like.

A total quality strategy does, however require, significant changes in organisation design, processes and culture and many companies consider such changes as stumbling blocks for them.

The first question facing any organisation is whether to adopt the TQ philosophy or not? **Two basic reasons for companies to use TQM are:**

(i) To react to competition that poses a threat to its profitable survival and

(ii) TQ represents an opportunity to improve continuously.

Most firms in the US have moved towards total quality because of the necessity to react to competition that threatens their survival and when faced with a threat to survival, a company can effect cultural change more easily and implement TQ effectively.

Firms have used various approaches to implement quality within their organisations. Many of these approaches are one dimensional and have failed. Some such examples are:

- Firms emphasising the use of quality tools such as **statistical process control** in a particular area such as manufacturing only. This will lead to limited success.
- Firms using problem-solving approach through **quality circles** or other teams.
- Firms ignoring **customer relationship management** processes and strategic planning issues.
- Firms emphasising design, but ignoring many potential means for **continuous improvement.**

What is really required in TQM is a total change in thinking, not a new collection of quality tools. A focus on tools and techniques is easy, what is hard is understanding and achieving the changes in human attitudes and behaviour that are necessary to adopt and implement TQM successfully and in a sustained manner.

Lack of complete understanding of the TQ philosophy and TQ tools and the tendency to imitate others are dangerous. The "one best model" of TQ may not mesh with an organisation's culture and most successful companies have developed their own unique approaches to fit their own requirements. Imitation of TQ efforts made by one successful organisation may not lead to good results in another.

10.1 CORPORATE CULTURE AND ORGANISATIONAL CHANGE

While some companies make radical changes and be successful, others fail miserably. Many TQ efforts fail simply because organisations are unable to adapt to change. A prerequisite to implementing TQ is a corporate culture that will facilitate change.

Corporate culture or organisation culture refers to the collective beliefs, values, attitudes, manners, customs, behaviours and artifacts unique to an organisation.

A *corporate culture* is a company's value system and its collection of guiding principles. The value system consists of a set of values that guide the decisions of the company's staff as they work to achieve its objectives. The most often cited barriers to change are employee resistance and **"dysfunctional corporate culture"**. Example of "dysfunctional corporate culture" is a high-tech company that stresses individual rewards while innovation depends on team work.

Cultural values are often seen in the mission and vision statements of organisations. Culture has powerful influence on employee behaviour because it is shared and accepted widely among the employees in an organisation.

Culture is reflected by the management policies and actions that a company practices. Organisations that believe in the principle of total quality are more likely to implement the practices successfully. Conversely, actions set culture in motion. Behaviour leads people to think in certain ways. Thus, as total quality practices are used routinely within an organisation, its people learn to believe in the principles, and cultural changes can occur. **Developing a total quality culture depends on:** *(i)* Top management leadership, *(ii)* A relentless focus on the customer, *(iii)* Systematic improvement of all business practices, *(iv)* Decentralisation of decision making responsibility, *(v)* Breaking down of organisational barriers, *(vi)* Improvements that are linked to company objectives and *(vii)* Realignment of reward and measurement systems.

10.1.1 Designing a Total Quality Infrastructure

For a TQ culture to sustain, there is a need for a solid foundation. The organisational infrastructure is vital to successful TQ implementation. **The requirements for the design of an effective structure are:**

- understanding the best practices
- a solid, process-oriented quality assurance system and
- a process for continuous evolution towards high-performance management practices.

10.1.2 Best Practices

Managers usually are impatient and seek quick successes, often by adopting off-the-shelf quality programs and practices, by initiating Japanese approaches or by emulating large, high profile companies. But it is better for business leaders to develop approaches that maximise their own cultural strengths. **A successful quality strategy needs to fit within the existing organisation culture.** There is no magic formula, which can bring success to every organisation. The companies which won Baldrige Award had a unique **"quality engine"** that drives their quality activities. ***Table 10.1* summarises the individual strength of some of the companies that won the Baldrige Award.**

Table 10.1 : Quality Engine of Baldrige Award Winners

Company	Quality Engine	Focus
Motorola	Process control	Defect prevention, six-sigma quality
Xerox	Benchmarking	Competitive and best-in-class benchmarks
IBM Rochester	Market-driven quality	Customer needs early in the planning and design process
FedEx	Technology	Using technology to speed processes and improve customer service
Cadillac	Product development	Integrating manufacturing and design and partnering with customers and suppliers.
Zytec	Strategic planning	Involvement of cross-functional teams, customers, and suppliers in the planning process.

The quality engine customises the quality effort in the organisational culture and provides focus.

International quality study conducted by Ernst and Young and the American Quality Foundation indicated that best practices depend on a company's current level of performance. **Two measures of performance are the return on assets (after tax income divided by total assets) and value added per employee (sales less the costs of materials, supplies and work done by outside contractors).** Low performers should exert effort, which includes identifying processes that add value and then simplifying them to improve response to customers and market demands. Further, training and teamwork (particularly in resolving customer complaints) can lead to significant improvements. Other suggestions include benchmarking competitors rather than world-class companies, listening to the customer for ideas, selecting suppliers on the basis of price and reliability, buying technology that reduces costs and rewarding frontline workers for teamwork and quality.

Medium performers achieve the benefits by meticulously documenting gains and further refining practices to improve value added per employee, time to market and customer satisfaction. These companies should also emulate market leaders and selected world-class companies, use customer input, market research and internal ideas for new products, select suppliers first by quality certification and then price, find ways to use facilities more flexibly to produce a wider variety of products and services and base compensation for workers and middle managers on contributions to teamwork and quality.

High performers gain the most from using self-managed teams and cross-functional teams that concentrate on logistics and product development. Benchmarking product development, distribution and customer service against world-class firms can be highly beneficial. New products should be based on customer input, benchmarking and internal research and development. Suppliers must be chosen primarily for their technology and quality. Strategic partnership should be considered to diversify manufacturing. Senior managers should be included in compensation schemes pegged to teamwork and quality. Finally, these firms should further refine practices to improve **values added per employee (VAE),** market response and customer satisfaction.

10.1.3 Self-Assessment for Total Quality

Self- assessment helps organisations to identify their strengths and weak nesses and know where they stand.

Organisations should begin with a critical **self-assessment** of where it stands. Such an assessment helps them to identify strengths and areas of improvement (weaknesses) and determine what practices will yield maximum benefits.

Self-assessment should address the following:

- **Management involvement and leadership:** To what extent are all levels of managers involved?
- **Product and process design:** Do products meet customer needs? Are products designed for easy manufacturability?
- **Product control:** Is a strong product control system in place that concentrates on defect prevention, before the fact, rather defect removal after the product is made?
- **Customer and supplier communication:** Does everyone understand who the customer is? To what extent do customers and suppliers communicate with each other?
- **Quality improvement:** Is the quality improvement plan in place? What results have been achieved?
- **Employee participation:** Are all employees actively involved in quality improvement?
- **Education and training:** What is done to ensure that everyone understands his or her job and has necessary skills? Are employees trained in quality improvement techniques?
- **Quality information:** How is feedback on quality results collected and used?

The best way to assess the level of TQ maturity in an organisation is to evaluate its practices and results against the Malcolm Baldrige National Quality Award criteria by using trained internal or external examiners, or by actually applying for the Baldrige Award and receiving comprehensive examiner feedback.

For many companies, especially smaller firms, developing a well-documented and consistent quality assurance system will be a good start towards building a TQ organisation. The ISO 9000 standards provide a basis for doing this.

10.2 QUALITY SYSTEMS

10.2.1 What is a Quality System?

American National Standards Institute (ANSI)/American Society for Quality Control (ASQC) standard A3, defines quality system as: ***"The collective plans, activities and events that are provided to ensure that a product, process or service will satisfy given needs."***

The *systems approach* to quality integrates the various functions and responsibilities of different units and provides a mechanism to ensure that organisational goals are being met through the co-ordination of goals of the individual units. Effective quality control requires the integration of the quality actions of the people, the machines and the information into strong total quality systems. **A quality system is defined as follows: "A quality system is agreed on the companywide and plantwide operating work structure, documented in effective, integrated technical and managerial procedures, for guiding the co-ordinated actions of the people, the machines and the information of the company and plant in the best and most practical ways to assure customer quality satisfaction and economical costs of quality."**

A quality system comprises plans, activities and events that are provided to ensure that a product or service will satisfy given needs.

A clearly defined and thoroughly installed ***total quality system*** is a powerful foundation for total quality control, organisation-wide and for total quality management. Without such systematic integration in a company, ***"quality management by anticipation"*** may remain the slogan but the actual condition may be quality management by crises and reaction to complaints.

Strong quality systems provide a management and engineering basis for effective prevention oriented control which deals economically and soundly with the present levels of human, machines and informational complexity that characterise today's company and plant operations.

10.2.2 The Evolution of Quality Systems

The tools, techniques, methods and metrics (or measures) that aim at assisting in the planning, design, control and improvement of quality together comprise the *quality system.*

Quality systems evolved through several phases, the first one relying on ***inspection.***

Process control came next which also utilised inspection results, but it involved a "feedback control" of the manufacturing system based on observed deviations and certain statistical rules. Statistical Process Control (SPC) provides many tools and methods to achieve process control.

Quality improvement went further, aiming at prevention – by systematically determining the sources and causes of the errors and deviations to reduce the introduction of these factors during manufacturing. ***Worker involvement* is a key aspect of *quality improvement.***

Quality by design is the most recent phase in the evolution of quality systems. This phase aims at ***designing quality into products*** and ***the manufacturing processes,*** starting with the initial concepts of the product.

Quality by design involves systematic experimentation with prototype products/processes to uncover and compensate for problems that may hamper the satisfactory functioning of the product/process while in actual use. ***Taguchi methods*** belong to this category. High reliability is noted to be one aspect of a product's performance influenced most by its design and perhaps to a lesser degree by how it has been manufactured.

10.2.3 Elements of a Total Quality System

(i) **Policy, planning, organisation and administration:** A quality policy is essential for developing consistency in the company's goals. A proper organisation must be established to facilitate the achievement of the plan. Quality manuals are useful in this regard. Procedures for implementing the plans should be laid out in detail and the relevant costs should be identified.

(ii) **Product design assurance, specification development and control:** A product design to meet the customer's requirements is formulated. The prototype model is built and tested and the design is modified to satisfactorily meet all requirements of the customers. Tolerances on product characteristics are specified based on the manufacturing or process capabilities.

(iii) **Control of bought-out materials and component parts:** The quality of the output depends to a greatest extent on the quality of raw materials and components used. To ensure good quality raw materials and components, proper procedures must be developed to evaluate the

capability and performance of vendors. Quality costs and ability to meet due dates should be considered in choosing the vendors.

A quality system comprises plans, activities and events that are provided to ensure that a product or service will satisfy given needs.

(iv) **Production quality control:** This involves determining process specifications, selecting equipment, training personnel, designing control charts and selecting inspection points and the like.

(v) **User contact and field performance:** A system must be designed to collect information from the consumer and to determine the level of performance of the product or service. Feedback on product failure will help to decide the type of warranties to be offered.

(vi) **Corrective action:** Timely corrective action is the key to creating and maintaining a quality system. Corrective action may be required with such different entities as the incoming materials and components, the vendors, the process and equipments and the operators.

(vii) **Employee selection, training and motivation:** Every employee from the lowest to the highest level is important for the success of a total quality system. Guidelines should be established for selecting people for specific jobs. Management should demonstrate its commitment to help select, train and motivate employees to produce better quality products. Some of the motivational programs are the ***zero-defect program, quality circles*** and ***participative quality control programs.***

(viii) **Legal requirements – product liability and user safety:** The failure of products within the warranty period and the hazardous effect of malfunctions are matters of grave concern to manufacturers. Product liability is the obligation on the part of the manufacturer or seller to respond immediately to unsatisfactory quality through product service, repair or replacement. The responsibility extends through the period of the product's use and also includes coverage of environmental effects and safety aspects. Product liability, safety and environmental concerns must be integrated into the quality system.

(ix) **Sampling and statistical technique:** The total quality system is composed of analytical tools and techniques such as process control through control charts, process capability analysis, sampling plans for variables and attributes in acceptance sampling techniques, statistical methods for life testing and reliability studies, design of experiments, Taguchi method of off-line quality control etc.

10.3 ISO 9000

ISO 9000 series standards are a set of individual but related international standards and guidelines on quality management and quality assurance that develop to help companies effectively document the quality system elements to be implemented to maintain an efficient quality system

As quality became a major focus of business throughout the world, various organisations developed standards and guidelines. Terms such as quality management, quality control, quality system and quality assurance acquired different meanings in different countries, within a country and even within an industry. As the European community moved towards the European Free Trade Agreement which went into effect at the end of 1992, quality management became a key strategic objective. To standardise quality requirement of European countries within the common market and those wishing to do business with those countries, a specialised agency for standardisation, the ***International Organisation for Stardardisation (IOS)*** was founded in 1946 and composed of representatives from the national standards bodies of 91 nations. It adopted a series of written quality standards in 1987. These are called the ISO 9000 standards and were revised in 1994. and again significantly in the year 2000 (the most recent version is called the ISO 9000:2000 family of standards) The IOS adopted the ISO prefix in naming the standards.

'*ISO*' means equal (Isotherm lines of a weather map show equal temperatures). Organisations certified under the ISO 9000 standard are assured to have quality equal to their peer organisations. The standards have been adopted in the US by ANSI with the endorsement and cooperation of ASQ. The standards are recognised by over 100 countries including India and Japan. In some foreign markets, companies will not buy from non-certified suppliers. Thus, meeting ISO 9000 standards is becoming a necessity for international competitiveness. The standards are applicable to all types of manufacturing and service industries. ISO 9000 certification assures customers that a firm has designed and managed its processes to assure delivery of a quality product.

The texts of these standards released by the ISO central secretariat in Geneva are adapted as the IS 14000 series of standards by the Bureau of Indian Standards (BIS). These standards embody comprehensive quality management concepts and guidance. The control (creation, modification and deletion) of all documents related to quality management is an important requirement of ISO 9000 covering elements such as drawings, specifications, blueprints, work instructions, test procedures, inspection reports, calibration data and quality cost reports. A record retention system should be in place to facilitate the use of these documents, which are themselves organised in three tiers – *(i)* the quality manual *(ii)* the work procedures and *(iii)* the instructions and data records.

The ISO 9000 standards require that third party audits be performed leading to the suppliers becoming certified. This certification is accepted by all customers, eliminating 10 to 20 different audits by many companies interested in doing business with a supplier.

***Box 10.1* describes what is ISO 9000.**

Box 10.1 : What is ISO 9000?

A revolution occurred in 1987 in the management of quality world-wide when the International Standards Organisation (Geneva, Switzerland) bought out a set of standards pertaining ***not to the quality of products*** but rather to the ***practice of quality assurance methods*** within a company. Termed as ISO 9000 standards, these proved their value rather quickly and went global. Many countries worldwide, including India have adopted them as their own standards to benchmark quality management practices.

ISO 9000 was originally issued as a series of six internationally agreed-upon standards to guide and audit a company's quality management practices. Named as ISO 9000, ISO 9001, ISO 9002, ISO 9003, ISO 9004 and ISO 8402, each standard contains specific guidelines pertaining to a certain segment of quality-related activities. These standards are the minimum acceptable level of standards that a supplier's quality management practices should meet, in order to receive the ***"ISO 9000 accreditation or certification"***. Several additional standards have been issued subsequently by ISO, including a major revision of the original series done in 1994. and again in 2000 Today, this series covers such varied activities as design, manufacturing, software development, service activities, auditing, calibration of equipments and methods, for improving quality.

ISO 9000 is ***not a mandatory system*** nor is it a government regulation. However, it is a very important ***customer regulation.*** It provides assurance to a wide variety of customers about an organisation's quality assurance methods and quality management practices.

European Economic Community (EEC) was the first to adopt this standard formally as the requirement suppliers should meet in order to do business in Europe. ISO 9000 registration or accreditation is not a permanent certificate. An audit of the organisation's quality management system must be done by a competent agency (called the assessor) once in three or six months in order for the organisation to retain its accreditation.

The organisation's QA methods are reviewed once every three years by such an agency. ISO 9000 auditors do not audit the quality of finished product but rather the procedures and methods used in delivering quality. After accreditation, quality assurance becomes ***system driven*** and ***person-independent.***

ISO 9000 and TQM : ISO 9000 is not TQM, but is a subcomponent of TQM and a good start on the TQM path. ISO 9000 is only the ***minimum*** required quality standard that a supplier must demonstrate to receive the ISO 9000 accreditation. TQM by contrast is much more comprehensive. TQM links quality to customer satisfaction by requiring action on four essentials –

(i) a strong customer orientation (internal and external in all activities in the organisation.

(ii) top management's direct involvement in the delivery of quality.

(iii) total company-wide participation in the delivery of quality and

(iv) the systematic analysis of quality problems focussed on continuous improvement of quality performance and the prevention of quality problems.

Objectives of ISO 9000: The five objectives are:

(i) Achieve, maintain and seek to continuously improve product quality (including services) in relationship to requirements.

(ii) Improve the quality of operations to continually meet customers' and stakeholders' stated and implied needs.

(iii) Provide confidence to internal management and other employees that quality requirements are being fulfilled and that improvement is taking place.

(iv) Provide confidence to customers and other stakeholders that quality requirements are being achieved in the delivered product and

(v) Provide confidence that quality system requirements are fulfilled.

10.4 STRUCTURE OF THE ISO 9000 STANDARDS

The ISO 9000 : 2000 standards focus on developing, documenting and implementing procedures to ensure consistency of operations and performance in production and service delivery processes, with the aim of continual improvement and supported by fundamental principles of total quality.

ISO 9000 series standards consist of *(i)* ISO 9000-Fundamental and vocabulary and *(ii)* ISO 9004-Guidance for performance improvement

The standard consists of three documents:

1. ISO 9000 – Fundamentals and Vocabulary: This document provides fundamental background information and provides definition of key terms used in the standards

2. ISO 9001 – Requirements: This document provides a set of minimum requirements for a quality management system (QMS) and is intended to demonstrate compliance with recognized quality principles to customers and for third-party certification.

3. ISO 9004 – Guidance for Performance Improvement: This document provides guidelines to assist organisations in improving their quality management systems beyond the minimum requirements in ISO 9001, but does not prescribe any requirements that must be followed.

The standards are intended to apply to all types of businesses, including electronics and chemicals, and to services such as health care banking and transportation.

The ISO 9000 certification process involves the assessment of a company's stated quality policy; its conformance of quality system to the standards. This process is carried out by a three party system in which the third party or certification body checks whether the system conforms to standard or not, and if the system conforms to standards, a certification of registration will be issued to the supplier for a period of three years. The system is reviewed through surveillance audits once in six months and a complete re-assessment after 3 years because the supplier may change or their practices may change.

10.5 THE ISO 9000 : 2000 QUALITY MANAGEMENT SYSTEM

10.5.1 What is a Quality Management System (QMS)?

A QMS constitutes a formal record of an organisation's method of managing the quality of its products or services. It enables the organisation to demonstrate to itself, its customers and to an independent certification body that it has established an effective system for managing the quality of its products or services. Meeting the accreditation standards permit the organisation to claim quality certification for its products and services and advertise the fact. A QMS will also assist the organisation an attempting to formalize its operations and attain consistency of outputs.

A quality management system comprises the organisational structure, processes, procedures, and resources needed to implement, maintain, and continually improve quality management

The ISO 9000 standards are comprehensive in their coverage, ranging from product or service development to after sales-service. However, they have tended to have a clear bias towards the manufacturing sector, because the process started there and greatest use continued to be made of the standards in that sector.

The ISO 9000 : 2000 family of standards launched at the end of 2000, attempts to harmonise all the standards and remove the manufacturing bias

10.5.2 Purpose of the QMS

The purpose of the QMS is to enhance customer satisfaction through effective application of the system. The entire organisation should be customer oriented, continuously assessing the customer's stated and implied needs. The QMS also includes processes for continual improvement. QMS also results in maximisation of return on improvement along with the total employee involvement.

QMS follows a process orientation with Deming 's P–D–C–A cycle.

10.6 MAJOR ELEMENTS IN ISO 9001 : 2000

The ISO 9001 : 2000 standards are structured around four distinct processes as outlined below:

Four major elements of ISO 9000:2000 are:
1. Management responsibility
2. Resource management
3. Product realisation and
4. Measurement, analysis and improvement

1. Management responsibility: Requires top management commitment to create and maintain awareness of the importance of fulfilling customer requirements, establish the quality policy and the quality objectives and planning, establish a quality management system, perform management reviews and ensure availability of resources in time.

2. Resource management: Requires that the organisation determines and provides the needed resources to establish and maintain the quality management system.

3. Product realization: Requires an organisation to use outputs from quality planning and see that other processes are consistent to realise that required product and/or service. Their sequence and interaction must then be determined, planned and implemented.

4. Measurement, analysis and improvement: Requires an organisation to define, plan and implement measurement, monitoring and analysis of processes to ensure that the quality management system, processes and products and/or services conform to requirements and continually improve the effectiveness of quality management system.

***Box 10.2* lists the principles of ISO 9000 : 2000 QMS.**

Box 10.2 : Principles of ISO 9000 : 2000 Quality Management System

Principle 1: Customer Focused Organisation:
Organisations depend on their customers and therefore should understand current and future customer needs, should meet customer requirements and strive to exceed customer expectations.

Principle 2: Leadership
Leaders establish units of purpose and direction of the organisation. They should create and maintain the internal environment in which people can become fully involved in achieving the organisation's objectives.

Principle 3: Involvement of people
People at all levels are the essence of an organisation and their full involvement enables their abilities to be used for the benefit of the organisation.

Principle 4: Process Approach
A desired result is achieved more efficiently when activities and related resources are managed as a process

Principle 5: Systems Approach to Management
Identifying, understanding, and managing interrelated processes as a system contributes to the organisation's effectiveness and efficiency in achieving its objectives.

Principle 6: Continual Improvement
Continual improvement of the organisation's overall performance should be a permanent objective of the organisation.

Principle 7: Factual Approach to Decision Making
Effective decisions are based on the analysis of data and information.

Principle 8: Mutually Beneficial Supplier Relationships
An organisation and its suppliers are interdependent and a mutually beneficial relationship enhances the ability of both to create value.

10.6.1 Factors Leading to ISO 9000 : 2000

The original ISO 9000 : 1994 series standards consisted of 20 fundamental elements of a basic quality system that included such things as: *(i)* ***management responsibility****, (ii)* ***design control****, (iii)* ***purchasing****, (iv)* ***product identification and trace ability****, (v)* ***process control****, (vi)* ***inspection and testing****, (vii)* ***corrective and preventive action****, (viii)* ***internal quality audits****, (ix)* ***training and*** *(x)* ***statistical techniques.***

The original ISO 9000 : 1987 series of standards and the 1994 revision were controversial because the standard required only that organisations have a documented, verifiable process in place to ensure that it consistently produced what it says it will produce, A company could comply with the standard and still produce a poor quality product – as long as it does so consistently.

The deficiencies in the old ISO 9000 standards led to a joint effort in 1994 by the big three automobile manufacturers – Ford, Chrysler and General Motors and several truck manufacturers, to develop QS 9000 – an interpretation and extension of ISO 9000 for automotive suppliers. The goal was to develop fundamental quality systems that provide for continuous improvement, emphasising defect prevention and the reduction of variation and waste in the supply chain. Q S 9000 is based on ISO 9000 and includes all ISO requirements. It includes additional requirements such as continuous improvement, manufacturing capability and production part approval processes.

10.6.2 Interpretation of ISO 9000 : 2000

The features are:

(i) The 1994 version of the family of standards (ISO 9001, 9002, 9003, 9004) was consolidated into a single standard ISO 9001 : 2000 with a new ISO 9004 : 2000 providing a set of guide – lines for continuous improvement

(ii) The standard has a substantially increased customer focus.

(iii) An attempt has been made to reduce the manufacturing bias

(iv) The scope has been widened to include more management elements.

(v) All the core requirements of the 1994 version of ISO 9001 continue to be present, but the new standard restructure these under four headings: *(a)* ***Management responsibility****, (b)* ***Resource management****, (c)* ***Process management and*** *(d)* ***Measurement and analysis, and improvement.***

The aim of these changes is to encourage organisations to think about their management processes and react to the changing demands placed upon them

Management responsibility is extended to include a specific responsibility for ensuring continuous improvement and bench – marking and for management review. There is a much greater emphasis on ***supplier relationships, customer satisfaction, market and competitor analysis*** and on ***the development of improvement opportunities.***

Resource management is extended to focus very clearly on ***human resource management*** – especially the match of the skills of the individual to the requirements of the task. Issues such as health and safety, the environmental and financial management as part of the over all well being of the enterprise are also given importance.

Particular issues in this respect will be to consider the means by which the quality policy message is conveyed to employees and subcontractors and to ensure that all employees understand their contribution to quality.

Process management reflicts the managerial thinking in recent years. Within this area, There is a requirement for appropriate risk analysis, recognition of the interaction between departments and functions (the internal customer chain), capability to respond to changing customer expectations, formal and documented review of capabilities and a focus on the delivery and post delivery activity. Rather than a focus on the physical aspects of product quality, the shift is towards the customer's total experience of dealing with the organisation.

Measurement and analysis requires that an appropriate performance measurement system is in place. This captures the adherence of the product or service to the standards specified. This in – turn enables audit of the product or service delivered and monitoring of customer satisfaction and of competitor and market performance and demonstrates continuous improvement.

10.7 ISO 9000 : 2000 AND TQM

The ISO 9000 : 2000 consists of new standards with a completely new structure based on ***eight principles*** – "comprehensive and fundamental rules or beliefs for leading and operating an organisation" that reflect the basic principles of total quality and many of the core values and concepts of the M B N Q A and European Quality Award criteria. These eight principles were discussed earlier in this section with this underlying philosophy, **The ISO 9000 : 2000 revision aligns much closer to the performance excellence concept of Baldrige. For example,**

- Organisations now need a process to determine customer needs and expectation, translate them into internal requirements and measure customer satisfaction and dissatisfaction
- Managers must communicate the importance of meeting customer and regulatory requirements, integrate ISO 9000 into business plans, set measurable objectives, and conduct management reviews.
- Organisations now must view work as a process and manage a system of interrelated processes.
- Analysis now needs to be done to provide information about customer satisfaction and dissatisfaction, products and processes with the focus on improvement
- Training effectiveness must be evaluated and personnel aware of the importance of their activities in meeting quality objectives
- In the previous standards (i. e, ISO 9000 : 1987 and ISO 9000 : 1994) organisations were required to perform corrective and preventive action, whereas in the ISO 9000 : 2000 standards, the organisations must have a planned process for improvement.

10.8 DEVELOPMENT OF THE QUALITY MANAGEMENT SYSTEM (QMS)

The ISO 9000 : 2000 quality management system establishes a quality policy and quality objectives of the organisations. It then defines the products and services which are acceptable to the customer as well as are in line with the attainment of the quality objectives. The system then should have a sound quality control which means there should be an on- going measurement of the effectiveness of the processes. A documented quality management system is then established to attain the quality objectives set. After measurement, analysis and review of the effectiveness and efficiency of the processes, the Q M S finds out the, deviations and takes corrective and preventive actions for continuous improvement.

ISO 9000 : 2000 specifies requirements for a Q M S where an organisation needs to provide products that meet the customers ' requirements and aim to enhance customer satisfaction through processes for continual improvement of the system. The Q M S is based on the process approach, which believes that if the processes are correct, the product can not go wrong and has to be correct (of good quality) and consistent in performance.

10.8.1 ISO 9001 : 2000 QMS Requirements

Quality is not a chance occurrence. It has to be built up consciously and stage by stage through suitable processes, procedures, resources, responsibilities and an appropriate organisational structure that knits all these factors together. The amalgamation of all these factors which are aimed at achieving desired quality levels consistently is what is termed as **Quality Management System (QMS).**

10.8.2 ISO 9001 : 2008

ISO 9001 : 2000 which was published on 15th December 2000 was later on revised as ISO 9001:2008 which was officially released on 13the November 2008. This revised version of ISO 9001:2000 provides a set of standard requirements for a quality management system irrespective of whether the user organisation is in private or public sector, big or small and engaged in manufacturing or service.

ISO 9001:2008 does not introduce new requirements. It classifies the existing requirements of ISO 9001:2000 and introduces changes to improve consistency with ISO 14001:2004 which sets out requirements for an Environmental Management System.

When compared with the ISO 9001:2000, the ISO 9001:2008 standards contain mainly editorial changes, some classifications to existing requirements, a reemphasis on **"Process Approach"**- It also includes a few examples of increased compatibility with ISO 14001:2004. ISO 9001:2008 lays down the requirements that an organisation's quality system must meet, but does not indicate how they should be met. This provides great scope and flexibility for implementation in different business sectors and business cultures as well as in different national cultures.

The implementation of ISO 9001:2008 is done as follows:

1. The standard requires the organisation itself do self-assessment by auditing its ISO 9001:2008 quality system to verify that it is managing its processes effectively.

2. ISO 9001:2008 emphasises a **Process approach** for organisationa that are in the process of implementing or yet to implement a QMS. This includes: *(i)* Identifying the process necessary for the effective implementation of the QMS. *(ii)* Understanding the interactions between the process (iii) Documenting the process to the extent necessary to ensure their effective operation and control (iv) Analysing the processes to define the amount of documentation needed for the QMS, considering the requirements of ISO 9001:2008.

10.8.3 The Need for Quality Management System

With the gradual transition of the basic concepts of quality control from inspection to the present stage of managing quality in all activities (company wide quality control or total quality control), quality standards also changed accordingly. Customers, these days are not only concerned about the quality of purchased products but also about the manner in which quality is managed in the supplier's organisation.

Many organisation's have QMS – either informal or semiformal. But there are some areas in such systems where there is a total absence of established policies, procedures, responsibility and authority. These are known as **"system deficiencies"**. Even if procedures and policies exist, there may be ambiguity with regards to their practices.

A formal quality system helps to remove the uncertainty by formalizing the **who, why, where, what** and **how** of quality so that the processes for achieving quality are well established, whereby customer satisfaction can be achieved consistently irrespective of involvement of quality experts. A quality system standard helps to check or implement a system against standard checkpoints, there by ensuring that all aspects of managing quality have been looked into.

10.8.4 Evolution of ISO 9000 series of Quality Management Systems Standards

ISO 9000 is one of a series of quality management systems standards developed over a long period of time, beginning with quality standards in the defence industry (MIL standards and DEF – Defence standard). NATO began developing quality standard in the late 1940s after World War II, to enable a degree of harmonization between cooperating military forces. Quality system standards were first developed and widely used as a means of supplier assessment by American Defence Organisations. Such standards were later developed by UK and other European countries as well. During the post-war period, Britain refined its defence standards and formulated the BS 5750 for the civilian industry. Similarly in the US, several automobile and truck manufacturers developed QS 9000 for automobile industry. However QS 9000 : 2000 is generally accepted as the standard for quality systems practice in most countries.

International Organisation for Standards (IOS) was founded in 1946 and composed of representatives from the national standard bodies of 91 countries. It adopted a series of written quality standards in 1987 (ISO 9000 : 1987 series of standards) which were later revised in 1994 (ISO 9000 : 1994 series of Quality Assurance Standards) and again revised significantly in the year 2000 to ISO 9000 : 2000 series of Quality Management System Standards.

The ISO 9000 : 2000 standards focus on developing, documenting and implementing procedures to ensure consistency of operations and performance in production and service delivery process, with the aim of **continual improvement** and supported by fundamental principles of total quality.

ISO 9001 : 2000: This is the most comprehensive standard in the ISO 9000 : 2000 series. It specifies system requirements in purchase, design and development, production, installation and servicing. This is the only contractual standard for which organisations can be certified.

Essence of the Standard: The standard recommends that an organisation should:

(i) **Decide its Quality Policy:** Determine how the policy to be implemented and design a system accordingly.

(ii) **Implement the System:** Review the system regularly to gauge benefits from **continuous improvement of** product, process and customer satisfaction.

(ISO 9004 : 2000 standards provide guidelines to the organisation on all the above activities)

10.8.5 Importance Given to Process Approach in ISO 9000 : 2000

ISO 9000 : 2000 promotes adoption of a **process approach** when developing, implementing and improving the effectiveness of a quality management system to enhance customer satisfaction by meeting customer requirements.

For an organisation to function effectively, is has to identify and manage many linked activities. An activity using resources and managed in order to enable the conversion of inputs into outputs can be considered as a **process**. Often the output of one process directly forms the input to the next, for example, the manufactured item which is the output of manufacturing process will be the input for the assembly process for which the output is a subassembly or a major assembly (subunit of a product).

The application of a system of processes within an organisation, together with the identification and interactions of these processes and their management is referred to as the **"process approach"**. **The process approach emphasizes the importance of:**

(i) Understanding and fulfilling the requirements

(ii) The need to consider processes in terms of value added

(iii) Obtaining results of process performance and effectiveness and

(iv) Continual improvement of processes based on objective measure.

Exhibit 10.1 **shows a model of a process based quality management system.**

The ISO 9001 : 2000 standards has eight clauses:

1. Scope
2. Normative Reference
3. Terms and Definition
4. Quality Management System (QMS)
5. Management Responsibilities
6. Resource Management
7. Product and/or Service Realisation
8. Measurement, Analysis and Improvement

Exhibit 10.1 : Model of a Process-based Quality Management System

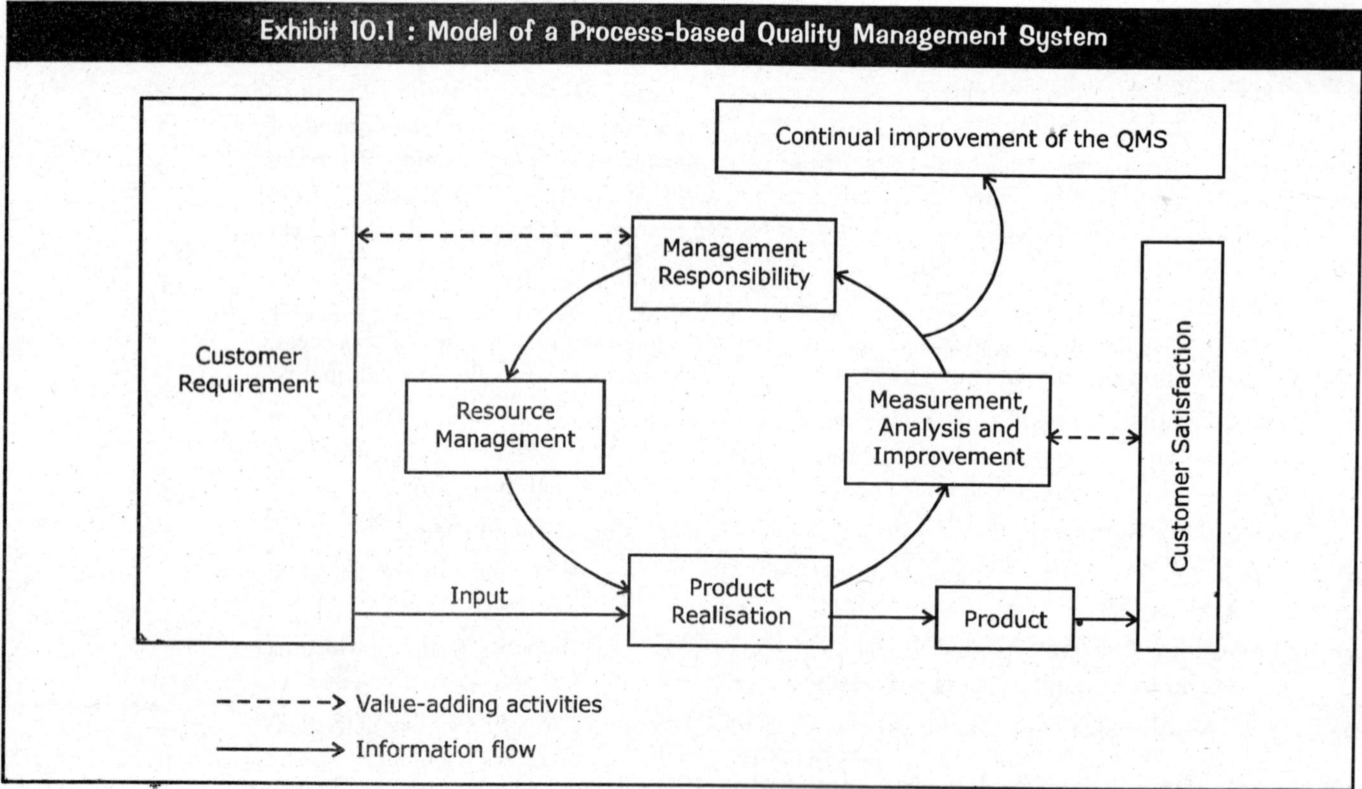

The first three clauses are for information while the last five clauses are requirements to be met by an organisation seeking certification.

The above clauses of ISO 9001 : 2000 series are briefly discussed in the following section:

1. Scope

The purpose of the standard is for the organisation to demonstrate its ability to provide a product that meets customer and regulatory requirements and achieves customer satisfaction. The purpose is accomplished by evaluating and continually improving the system. The requirements of the standard are intended to be applicable to all types of organisations.

2. Normative Reference

ISO 9000 : 2000 ***Quality Management Systems – Fundamental and vocabulary*** are a normative reference that provides applicable concepts and definitions.

3. Terms and Definitions

For the purpose of this standard, the terms and definition given in ISO 9000 : 2000 apply. In addition, the supply chain is defined as:

Supplier → Organisation → Customer

4. Quality Management System

Box 10.3 lists the major sections of ISO 9001 : 2000

4.1 General Requirements

The organisation shall establish, document, implement and maintain a quality management system and continually improve its effectiveness in accordance with the requirements of this International Standard. **The organisation shall:**

Box 10.3 List The Major Sections of ISO 9001: 2000

Section 4:	**Quality Management System**		
4.1	General Requirements	4.2	Documentation Requirements
Section 5:	**Management Responsibility**		
5.1	Management commitment	5.2	Customer Focus
5.3	Quality Policy	5.4	Planning
5.5	Responsibility, Authority and Communication	5.6	Management Review
Section 6:	**Resource Management**		
6.1	Provision of Resources	6.2	Human Resources
6.3	Infrastructure	6.4	Work Environment
Section 7:	**Product and/or Service Realisation**		
7.1	Planning of Product Realisation	7.2	Customer – Related Processes
7.3	Design and Development	7.4	Purchasing
7.5	Product and Service Provision	7.6	Control of Monitoring and Measuring Devices
Section 8:	**Measurement, Analysis, and Improvement**		
8.1	General	8.2	Monitoring and Measurement
8.3	Control of Nonconforming Product	8.4	Analysis of Data
8.5	Improvement		

(a) identify the processes needed for the quality management system and their application throughout the organisation (see 1.2).

(b) determine the sequence and interaction of these processes.

(c) determine criteria and methods needed to ensure that both the operation and control of these processes are effective.

(d) ensure the availability of resources and information necessary to support the operation and monitoring of these processes.

(e) monitor, measure and analyse these processes, and

(f) implement actions necessary to achieve planned results and continual improvement of these processes.

These processes shall be managed by the organisation in accordance with the requirements of this International Standard.

Where an organisation chooses to outsource any process that affects product conformity with requirements, the organisation shall ensure control over such processes. Control of such outsourced processes shall be identified within the quality management system.

Note: Processes needed for the quality management system referred to above should include processes for management activities, provision of resources, product realization and measurement.

4.2 Documentation Requirements

4.2.1 General

The quality management system documentation shall include

(a) documented statements of a quality policy and quality objectives,

(b) a quality manual,

(c) documented procedures required by this International Standard.

(d) documents needed by the organisation to ensure the effective planning, operation and control of its processes, and

(e) records required by this international standard (see 4.2.4)

Note 1: Where the term "documented procedure" appears within this International Standard, this means that the procedure is established, documented, implemented and maintained.

Note 2: The extent of the quality management system documentation can differ from one organisation to another due to

(a) the size of organisation and type of activities,

(b) the complexity of processes and their interactions, and

(c) the competence of personnel,

Note 3: The documentation can be in any form or type of medium

4.2.2 Quality Manual

The organisation shall establish and maintain a quality manual that includes:

(a) the scope of the quality management system, including details of and justification for any exclusion.

(b) the documented procedures established for the quality management system, or reference to them, and

(c) a description of the interaction between the processes of the quality management system.

4.2.3 Control of Documents

Documents required by the quality management system shall be controlled Records are a special type of document and shall be controlled according to the requirements given in 4.2.4

A documented procedure shall be established to define the control needed:

(a) to approve documents for adequacy prior to issue.

(b) to review and update as necessary and re-approve documents,

(c) to ensure that changes and the current revisions status of documents are identified,

(d) to ensure that relevant versions of applicable documents are available at points of use.

(e) to ensure that documents remain legible and readily identifiable,

(f) to ensure that relevant versions of applicable documents are available at points of use,

(g) to ensure that documents remain legible and readily identifiable,

(h) to ensure that documents of external origin are identified and their distribution controlled, and

(i) to prevent the unintended use of obsolete documents, and to apply suitable identification to them if they are retained for any purpose.

4.2.4 Control of Records

Records shall be established and maintained to provide evidence of conformity to requirements and of the effective operation of the quality management system. Records shall remain legible, readily identifiable and retrievable. A documented procedure shall be established to define the controls needed for the identification, storage, protection, retrieval, retention time and disposition of records.

5. Management Responsibility

5.1 Management Commitment

Top management shall provide evidence of its commitment to the development and implementation of the quality management system and continually improving its effectiveness by

(a) communicating to the organisation the importance of meeting customer as well as statutory and regulatory requirements,

(*b*) establishing the quality policy,
(*c*) ensuring that quality objectives are established,
(*d*) conducting management reviews, and
(*e*) ensuring the availability of resources.

5.2 Customer Focus

Top management shall ensure that customer requirements are determined and are met with the aim of enhancing customer satisfaction (see 7.2.1 and 8.2.1)

5.3 Quality Policy

Top management shall ensure that the quality policy

(*a*) is appropriate to the purpose of the organisation,
(*b*) includes a commitment to comply with requirements and continually improve the effectiveness of the quality management system,
(*c*) provides a framework for establishing and reviewing quality objectives,
(*d*) is communicated and understood within the organisation, and
(*e*) is reviewed for continuity, suitability

5.4 Planning

5.4.1 Quality Objectives

Top management shall ensure that quality objectives, including those needed to meet requirements for product (see 7.1 a) are established at relevant functions and levels within the organisation. The quality objectives shall be measurable and consistent with the quality policy.

5.4.2 Quality Management System Planning

Top management shall ensure that

(*a*) the planning of the quality management system is carried out in order to meet the requirements given in 4.1 as well as the quality objectives, and
(*b*) the integrity of the quality management system is maintained when changes to the quality management system are planned and implemented.

5.5 Responsibility, Authority and Communication

5.5.1 Responsibility and Authority

Top management shall ensure that responsibilities and authorities are defined and communicated within the organisation.

5.5.2 Management Representative

Top management shall appoint a member of management, who irrespective of other responsibilities, shall have responsibility and authority that includes

(*a*) ensuring that processes needed for the quality management system, are established, implemented and maintained.
(*b*) reporting to top management on the performance of the quality management system and any need for improvement, and
(*c*) ensuring the promotion of awareness of customer requirements throughout the organisation.

Note: The responsibility of a management representative can include liaison with external parties on matters relating to the quality management system.

5.5.3 Internal Communication

Top management shall ensure that appropriate communication processes are established within the organisation and that communication takes place regarding the effectiveness of the quality management system.

5.6 Management Review

5.6.1 General

Top management shall review the organisation's quality management system, at planned intervals, to ensure its continuing suitability, adequacy and effectiveness. This review shall include assessing opportunities for improvement and the need for changes to the quality management system, including the quality policy and quality objectives.

Records from management reviews shall be maintained (see 4.2.4).

5.6.2 Review Input

The input to management review shall include information on

(a) results of audits,

(b) customer feedback,

(c) process performance and product conformity,

(d) status of preventive and corrective actions,

(e) follow-up actions from previous management reviews,

(f) changes that could affect the quality management system, and

(g) recommendation for improvement

5.6.3 Review Output

The output from the management review shall include any decisions and actions related to:

(a) Improvement of the effectiveness of the quality management system and its processes, *(b)* Improvement of product related to customer requirements, and *(c)* Resource needs.

6. Resource Management

6.1 Provision of Resources

The organisation shall determine and provide the resources needed to implement and maintain the quality management system and continually improve its effectiveness, and to enhance customer satisfaction by meeting customer requirements.

6.2 Human Resources

6.2.1 General

Personnel performing work affecting product quality shall be competent on the basis of appropriate education, having, skills and experience.

6.2.2 Competence, Awareness and Training

The organisation shall

(a) determine the necessary competence for personnel performing work affecting product quality.

(b) provide training or take other actions to satisfy these needs.

(c) evaluate the effectiveness of the actions taken.

(*d*) ensure that its personnel are aware of the relevance and importance of their activities and how they contribute to the achievement of the quality objectives, and

(*e*) maintain appropriate records of education, training, skills and experience (see 4.2.4)

6.3 Infrastructure

The organisation shall determine, provide and maintain the infrastructure needed to achieve conformity to product requirements. **Infrastructure includes, as applicable**

(*a*) buildings, work space and associated utilities,

(*b*) process equipment (both hardware and software), and

(*c*) supporting services (such as transport and communication).

6.4 Work Environment

The organisation shall determine and manage the work environment needed to achieve conformity to product requirements.

7. PRODUCT REALISATION

7.1 Planning of Product Realization

The organisation shall plan and develop the processes needed for product realization. Planning of product realization shall be consistent with the requirements of the other processes of the quality management system (see 4.1).

In planning product realization, the organisation shall determine the following, as appropriate:

(*a*) quality objectives and requirements for the product;

(*b*) the need to establish processes, documents, and provide resources specific to the product;

(*c*) required verification, validation, monitoring, inspection and test activities and test activities specific to the product and the criteria for product acceptance;

(*d*) records needed to provide evidence that the realization processes and resulting product meet requirements (see 4.2.4).

The output of this planning shall be in a form suitable for the organisation's method of operations.

Note 1: A document specifying the processes of the quality management system (including the product realization processes) and the resources to be applied to a specific product, project or contract, can be referred to as a **quality plan**.

Note 2: The organisation may also apply the requirements given in 7.3 to the development of product realization processes.

7.2 Customer-related Processes

7.2.1 Determination of Requirements Related to the Product

The organisation shall determine

(*a*) requirements specified by the customer, including the requirements for delivery and post-delivery activities.

(*b*) requirements not stated by the customer but necessary for specified or intended use, where known,

(*c*) statutory and regulatory requirements related to the product, and

(*d*) any additional requirements determined by the organisation.

7.2.2 Review of Requirements Related to the Product

The organisation shall review the requirements related to the product. This review shall be conducted prior to the organisation's commitment to supply a product to the customer (e.g. submission of tenders, acceptance of the contracts or orders, acceptance of changes to contracts or orders) and shall ensure that:

(a) product requirements are defined.

(b) contract or order requirements differing from those previously expressed are resolved, and

(c) the organisation has the ability to meet the defined requirements.

Records of the results of the review and actions arising from the review shall be maintained (see 4.2.4)

(Where the customer provides no documented statement of requirement, the customer requirements, shall be confirmed by the organisation before acceptance.)

Where product requirements are changed, the organisation shall ensure that relevant documents are amended and that relevant personnel are made aware of the changed requirements.

Note: In some situations, such as internet sales, a formal review is impractical for each order. Instead the review can cover relevant product information such as catalogues or advertising material.

7.2.3 Customer Communication

The organisation shall determine and implement effective arrangements for communicating with customers in relation to:

(a) product information, *(b)* enquiries, contracts or order handling including amendments, and *(c)* customer feedback, including customer complaints.

7.3 Design and Development

7.3.1 Design and Development

The organisation shall plan and control the design and development of product.

During the design and development planning, the organisation shall determine

(a) the design and development stages,

(b) the review, verification and validation that are appropriate to each design and development stage, and

(c) the responsibilities and authorities for design and development,

The organisation shall manage the interfaces between different groups involved in design and development to ensure effective communication and clear assignment of responsibility.

Planning output shall be updated, as appropriate, as the design and development progresses.

7.3.2 Design and Development Inputs

Inputs relating to product requirements shall be determined and records maintained (see 4.2.4).

These inputs shall include

(a) functional and performance requirements,

(b) applicable statutory and regulatory requirements,

(c) where applicable, information derived from previous similar designs, and

(d) other requirements essential for design and development.

These inputs shall be reviewed for adequacy. Requirements shall be complete, unambiguous and not in conflict with each other.

7.3.3 Design and Development Outputs

The outputs of design and development shall be provided in a form that enables verification against the design and development input and shall be approved prior to release.

(a) meet the input requirements for design and development,

(b) provide appropriate information for purchasing, production and for service provision,

(c) contain or reference product acceptance criteria, and

(d) specify the characteristics of the product that are essential for its safe and proper use.

7.3.4 Design and Development Review

At suitable stages, systematic review of design and development shall be performed in accordance with planned arrangements (see 7.3.1)

(a) to evaluate the ability of the results of design and development to meet requirements, and

(b) to identify any problems and propose necessary actions.

Participants in such reviews shall include representatives of functions concerned with the design and development stage(s) being reviewed. Records of the results of the reviews and any necessary actions shall be maintained (see 4.2.4).

7.3.5 Design and Development Verification

Verification shall be performed in accordance with planned arrangement (see 7.3.1) to ensure that the design and development outputs have met the design and development input requirements. Records of the results of the verification and any necessary action shall be maintained (see 4.2.4).

7.3.6. Design and Development Validation

Design and development validation shall be performed in accordance with planned arrangements (see 7.3.1) to ensure that the resulting product is capable of meeting the requirements for the specified application or intended use, where known. Wherever practicable, validation shall be completed prior to the delivery or implementation of the product. Records of the results of validation and any necessary actions shall be maintained (see 4.2.4).

7.3.7 Control of Design and Development Changes

Design and development changes shall be identified and records maintained. The changes shall be reviewed, verified and validated, as appropriate, and approved before implementation. The review of design and development changes shall include evaluation of the effect of the changes on constituent parts and product already delivered.

Records of the results of the review of changes and any necessary action shall be maintained (see 4.2.4).

7.4 Purchasing

7.4.1 Purchasing Process

the organisation shall ensure that purchased product conforms to specified purchase requirements. The type and extent of control applied to the supplier and the purchased product shall be dependent upon the effect of the purchased product on subsequent product realization or the final product.

The organisation shall evaluate and select suppliers based on their ability to supply product in accordance with the organisation's requirements. Criteria for selection, evaluation and re-evaluation shall be established. Records of the results or evaluations and any necessary actions arising from the evaluation shall be maintained (see 4.2.4).

7.4.2 Purchasing Information

Purchasing information shall describe the product to be purchased, including where appropriate.

(a) requirements for approval of product, procedures, processes and equipment,

(b) requirements for qualification of personnel, and

(c) quality management system requirements.

The organisation shall ensure the adequacy of specified purchase requirements prior to their communication to the supplier.

7.4.3 Verification of Purchased Product

The organisation shall establish and implement the inspection or other activities necessary for ensuring that purchased product meets specified purchase requirements.

Where the organisation or its customer intends to perform verification at the supplier's premises, the organisation shall state the intended verification arrangements and method of product release in the purchasing information.

7.5 Production and Service Provision

7.5.1 Control of Production and Service Provision

The organisation shall plan and carry out production and service provision under controlled conditions. Controlled conditions shall includes, as applicable:

(a) the availability of information that describes the characteristics of the product,

(b) the availability of work instructions, as necessary,

(c) the use of suitable equipment,

(d) the availability and use of monitoring and measuring devices,

(e) the implementation of monitoring and measurement, and

(f) the implementation of release, delivery and post-delivery activities.

7.5.2. Validation of Processes for Production and Service Provision

The organisation shall validate any processes for production and service provision where the resulting output cannot be verified by subsequent monitoring or measurement. This includes any processes where deficiencies become apparent only after the product is in use or the service has been delivered.

Validation shall demonstrate the ability of these processes to achieve planned results.

The organisation shall establish arrangements for these processes including, as applicable

(a) defined criteria for review and approval of the processes,

(b) approval of equipment and qualification of personnel,

(c) use of specific methods and procedures,

(d) requirements for records (see 4.2.4) and

(e) revalidation.

7.5.3 Identification and Traceability

Where appropriate, the organisation shall identify the product by suitable means throughout product realization.

The organisation shall identify the product status with respect to monitoring and measurement requirements.

Where traceability is a requirement, the organisation shall control and record the unique identification of the product (see 4.2.4).

Note: In some industry sectors, configuration management is a means by which identification and traceability are maintained.

7.5.4 Customer Property

The organisation shall exercise care with customer property while it is under the organisation's control of being used by the organisation. The organisation shall identify, verify, protect and safeguard customer property provided for use or incorporation into the product. If any customer property is lost, damaged or otherwise found to be unsuitable for use, this shall be reported to the customer and records maintained (see 4.2.4).

Note: Customer property can include intellectual property.

7.5.5 Preservation of Product

The organisation shall preserve the conformity of product during internal processing and delivery to the intended destination. This preservation shall include identification, handling, packaging, storage and protection. Preservation shall also apply to the constituent parts of a product.

7.6 Control of Monitoring and Measuring Devices

The organisation shall determine the monitoring and measurement to be undertaken and monitoring and measuring devices needed to provide evidence of conformity of product to determined requirements (see 7.2.1).

The organisation shall establish processes to ensure that monitoring and measurement can be carried out and are carried out in a manner that is consistent with the monitoring and measurement requirements.

Where necessary to ensure valid results, measuring equipment shall

(a) be calibrated or verified at specified intervals, or prior to use, against measurement standards traceable to international or national measurement standard; where no such standards exist, the basis used for calibration or verification shall be recorded.

(b) be adjusted or re-adjusted as necessary;

(c) be identified to enable the calibration status to be determined;

(d) be safeguarded from adjustments, that would invalidate the measurement results;

(e) be protected from damage and deterioration during handling, maintenance and storage.

In addition, the organisation shall assess and record the validity of the previous measuring results when the equipments is found not to conform to requirements. The organisation shall take appropriate action on the equipment and any product affected. Records of the results of calibration and verification shall be maintained (see 4.2.4.)

When used in the monitoring and measurement of specified requirements, the ability of computer software to satisfy the intended application shall be confirmed. This shall be undertaken prior to initial use and reconfirmed as necessary.

Note: See ISO 10012-1 and ISO 10012-2 for guidance

8. Measurement, Analysis and Improvement

8.1 General

The organisation shall plan and implement the monitoring, measurement, analysis and improvement processes needed.

(*a*) to demonstrate conformity of the product,

(*b*) to ensure conformity of the quality management system, and

(*c*) to continually improve the effectiveness of the quality management system.

This shall include determination of applicable methods including statistical techniques, and the extent of their use.

8.2 Monitoring and Measurement

8.2.1 Customer Satisfaction

As one of the measurements of the performance of the quality management system, the organisation shall monitor information relating to customer perception as to whether the organisation has met customer requirements. The methods for obtaining and using this information shall be determined.

8.2.2 Internal Audit

The organisation shall conduct internal audits at planned intervals to determine whether the quality management system,

(*a*) conforms to the planned arrangements (see 7.1) to the requirements of this international Standard and to the quality management system requirements established by the organisation, and

(*b*) is effectively implemented and maintained.

An audit programme shall be planned, taking into consideration the status and importance of the processes and areas to be audited, as well as the results of the previous audits. The audit criteria, scope, frequency and methods shall be defined. Selection of auditors and conduct of audits shall ensure objectively and impartiality of the audit process. Auditors shall not audit their own work.

The responsibilities and requirements for planning and conducting audits, and for reporting results and maintaining records (see 4.2.4) shall be defined in a documented procedure.

The management responsible for the area being audited shall ensure that actions are taken without undue delay to eliminated detected non-conformities and their causes. Follow-up activities shall include the verification of the actions taken and the reporting of verification results (see 8.5.2).

Note: See ISO 10011-1, ISO 10011-2 and ISO 10011-3 for guidance.

8.2.3 Monitoring and Measurement of Processes

The organisation shall apply suitable methods for monitoring and, where applicable, measurement of the quality management system processes. These methods shall demonstrate the ability of the processes to achieve planned results. When planned results are not achieved, correction and corrective action shall be taken, as appropriate, to ensure conformity of the product.

8.2.4 Monitoring and Measurement of Product

The organisation shall monitor and measure the characteristics of the product to verify that product requirements have been met.

This shall be carried out at appropriate stages of the product realization process in accordance with the planned arrangements (see 7.1).

Evidence of conformity with the acceptance criteria shall be maintained. Records shall indicate the person(s) authorizing release of product (see 4.2.4).

Product release and service delivery shall not proceed until the planned arrangements (see 7.1) have been satisfactorily completed, unless otherwise approved by a relevant authority and, where applicable, by the customer.

8.3 Control of Nonconforming Product

The organisation shall ensure that product which does not conform to product requirements is identified and controlled to prevent its unintended use or delivery. The controls and related responsibilities and authorities for dealing with nonconforming product shall be defined in a documented procedure.

The organisation shall deal with nonconforming product by one or more of the following ways.

(a) by taking action to eliminate the detected nonconformity;

(b) by authorizing its use, release or acceptance under concession by a relevant authority and, where applicable, by the customer;

(c) by taking action to preclude its original intended use or application.

Records of the nature of non-conformities and any subsequent actions taken, including concessions obtained, shall be maintained (see 4.2.4).

When nonconforming product is correct it shall be subject to re-verification to demonstrate conformity to the requirements.

When nonconforming product is detected after delivery or use has started, the organisation shall take action appropriate to the effects, or potential effects, of the nonconformity,

8.4 Analysis of Data

The organisation shall determine, collect and analyse appropriate data to demonstrate the suitability and effectiveness of the quality management system and to evaluate where continual improvements of the effectiveness of the quality management system can be made. This shall include data generated as a result of monitoring and measurement and from other relevant sources.

The analysis of data shall provide information relating to

(a) customer satisfaction (see 8.2.1),

(b) conformity to product requirements (see 7.2.1),

(c) characteristics and trends of processes and products including opportunities for preventive actions, and

(d) Suppliers.

8.5 Improvement

8.5.1 Continual Improvement

The organisation shall continually improve the effectiveness of the quality management system through the use of the quality policy, quality objectives, audit results, analysis of data, corrective and preventive actions and management review.

8.5.2 Corrective Action

The organisation shall take action to eliminate the cause of non-conformities in order to prevent recurrence. Corrective actions shall be appropriate to the effects of the non-conformities encountered.

A documented procedure shall be established to define requirement for

(a) reviewing non-conformities (including customer complaints),

(b) determining the causes of non conformities,
(c) evaluating the need for action to ensure that non-conformities do not recur,
(d) determining and implementing action needed,
(e) records of the results of action taken (see 4.2.4), and
(f) reviewing corrective action taken.

8.5.3 Preventive action

The organisation shall determine action to eliminate the causes of potential non-conformities in order to prevent their occurrence. Preventive actions shall be appropriate to the effects of the potential problems.

A documented procedure shall be established to define requirements for

(a) reviewing of non conformities (including customer complaints).
(b) determining potential non-conformities and their causes,
(c) evaluating the need for action to prevent occurrence of the non-conformities,
(d) determining and implementing action needed,
(e) records of results of action taken (see 4.2.4), and
(f) reviewing preventive action taken.

10.9 REGISTRATION OF ISO 9001 : 2000

The registration process includes document review by the registrar of the quality systems or quality manual, pre-assessment, which identifies potential noncompliance in the quality system or in the documentation, assessment by a team of two or three auditors of the quality system and its documentation, and surveillance, or periodic audits to verify conformity with the practices and systems registered.

During the assessment, auditors might ask the following questions:

(i) Does a documented policy on quality exist?
(ii) Have management objectives for quality been defined?
(iii) Have the policy and objectives been transmitted and explained to all levels of the organisation?
(iv) Have job description for people who manage or perform work effecting quality been documented?
(v) Are descriptions of functions that affect quality available?
(vi) Has management designated a person or group with authority to prevent non-conformities in products, identify and record quality problems and recommend solutions?
(vii) What means are used to verify the solutions?

Three steps involved in the registration process are:

ISO 9001:2000 registration involves three steps: *(i)* Choosing a registrar *(ii)* Submitting an application for registration and *(iii)* Conducting the registrar's system audit

1. Choosing a registrar: The third party auditors like the "Bureau Varitas Quality International (BVQI), 'TUV', 'DNV', 'BIS' etc. are called for conducting the external certification audit. Consideration include cost, lead time, past experience with the registrar, registrar's accreditation and familiarity with the industry.

2. Submitting an application for registration: The application for registration should also include supplying the registrar with the policy and procedure manuals for their review.

3. Conducting the registrar's system audit: A registrar's audit may take time which will vary depending on the size and complexity of the organisation and the number of auditor's involved. A registrar's audit may usually take on to three days and will consist of an opening meeting to describe the process the auditors will follow, the audit itself and a closing meeting to discuss the findings of the audit. Rectification is required once in ever three years. Individual sites – not entire organisation – must achieve registration individually. All costs are borne by the applicant, so that the process can be quite expensive. (from 5 lakhs to 20 lakhs).

Some pitfall to successful implementation are:

(i) using a **generic** documentation program or documentation program of another organisation,

(ii) over documentation or complex documentation,

(iii) using external consultants without internal ownership and involvement,

(iv) limiting documentation to text rather then other types of media,

(v) neglecting to obtain involvement of top management,

(vi) developing a system that does not represent what actually occurs.

Documentation: Quality system is used to ensure that the quality level of a product or service is maintained. **The system documentation can be viewed as a hierarchy containing four tiers as shown in *Exhibit 10.2.* All documentation moves from one level to the next in a descending order.**

Exhibit 10.2 : The Documentation Pyramid

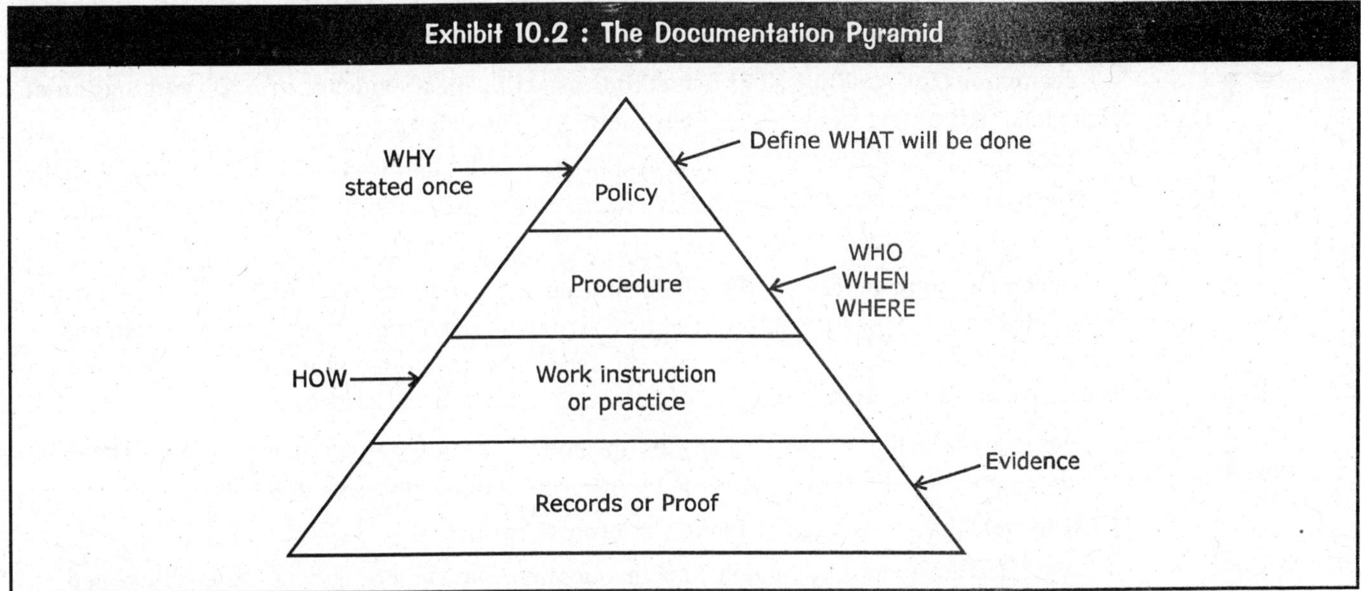

Policy: Policy manual is a document that defines what will be done and why. A quality manual should be written so that it is clear, precise, practical and easy to understand.

Procedure: The quality procedures describe the method that will be used to implement and perform the stated policies. The procedures define who should perform specific tasks, when the task should be done and where documentation will be made showing that the task was performed.

Work Instructions: Work instructions are usually department, machine, task or product oriented and spill out how a job should be done. These instructions are the most detailed of the documentation hierarchy. A work instruction may be in the form of a detailed drawing, routing sheet, specific job function etc. The writing of a work instruction is best carried out by the employee who performs the task.

Records: Records are a way of documenting that the policies, procedures and work instructions have been followed. Records may be forms that are filled out, a stamp of approval on a product, or a signature and date on some type of document, such as a routing sheet. Records are used to provide traceability of action taken on a specific product or batch of products. They provide data for corrective action and a way of recalling production, if necessary.

Internal Audit : After the policies, procedures and work instructions have been developed and implemented, checks must be made to ensure that the system is being followed and the expected results are being obtained. This activity is accomplished through the internal audit which is one of the key elements of the ISO 9000 standard. All elements should be audited at least once per year or more frequently depending on need.

The five objectives of internal audit are:

(i) Determine that actual performance conforms to the documented QMS.

(ii) Initiate corrective action activities in response to deficiencies.

(iii) Follow up on non-compliance items from previous audits.

(iv) Provide continual improvement in the system through feedback management.

(v) Cause the auditee to think about the prices, thereby encouraging possible improvements.

Auditor: Auditors should be qualified individuals who have received training in auditing principles and procedures. Training should include classroom information as well as practical demonstration by the trainer and an audit by the trainee. The auditor should be objective, honest and impartial. He should have the knowledge about the standards.

Techniques for Auditing: Three methods used to collect evidence are: *(i)* examination of documents, *(ii)* observation of activities and *(iii)* interviews.

To examine documents, the auditor should start with quality manual to determine that the policies cover the QMS standards and they are controlled and assessable. Next, the documents are examined systematically.

Document control ensures that *(i)* documents are identified with a title, revision date and responsible owner, *(ii)* documents are readily available to users, *(iii)* a master list by department or function for procedures, work instructions and records is appropriately located, *(iv)* there are no obsolete documents at work stations and *(v)* changes follow a prescribed procedure.

Observation of activities is also an easy method that requires an aptitude for detail. The most difficult method of collecting evidence is by interviewing the employee or auditee.

However, there are ways to make the process easier:

(i) Place the auditee in a nonthreatening environment by starting with introductions and an explanation of the purpose of audit.

(ii) Spend as much time listening and as little time as possible talking. Encourage the employees to talk about the process.

(iii) If and when deficiencies are found in processes and systems, separate the significant from the trivial. Reserve the major issues for your report and all minor ones for the auditee. Focus should be on the system and not on the auditee.

(iv) Discuss the major issues informally with the auditee first. The auditor's job is to identify problems and allow the organisation to find solutions to those problems.

(v) Use the appropriate type of questions. The questions could be open questions, closed questions, clarifying questions, leading questions and aggressive questions.

The auditor should primarily use open questions with an occasional closed and clarifying question, as the interview may necessitate. For effective communication, there must be mutual trust between auditor and auditee.

***Box 10.4* illustrates the stages involved in the ISO 9000 Registration Cycle.**

Box 10.4 : ISO 9000 Registration cycle

Stage 1:

(i) Decide to implement ISO 9000
(ii) Form management committee
(iii) Develop strategic plan
(iv) Begin ISO 9000 training
(v) Educate work force
(vi) Do cost assessment
(vii) Do self-assessment

Stage 2:

(i) Establish steering committee
(ii) Communicate intentions to entire corporation
(iii) Select and train audit teams
(iv) Continue ISO 9000 training
(v) Continue education
(vi) Begin implementing standards

Stage 3:

(i) Conduct internal audits
(ii) Organise quality system
(iii) Select registrar
(iv) Continue to train audit teams
(v) Continue ISO 9000 training
(vi) Continue education
(vii) Define areas for improvement

Stage 4:

(i) Continue internal audits
(ii) Begin documentation
(iii) Analyse processes
(iv) Write procedures
(v) Continue to train audit teams
(vi) Continue ISO 9000 training
(vii) Continue education
(viii) Create quality manual
(ix) Implement new procedures

Stage 5:

(i) Implement and document procedures
(ii) Initial visit made

Stage 6:

(i) Revise, improve, update, review, take corrective action based on initial visit
(ii) Revise quality manual
(iii) Conduct management review

Stage 7:

(i) Begin preassessment procedures
(ii) Correct deficiencies
(iii) Document and implement practices

Stage 8:

(i) Conduct registration assessment

Stage 9:

(i) Complete registration
(ii) Strive for continuous improvement
(iii) Conduct serveilance audits
(iv) Continue management reviews

10.10 ISO 9001 : 2000 CERTIFICATION

ISO 9000:2000 certification has both benefits and limitations

An ISO 9000 system has to be certified and regularly audited by an anthorised certifying body. Some anthorised certification bodies in india are:

(i) Burean Veritas Quality International (BVQI)
(ii) KPMG Quality Registrar India
(iii) Lloyd's Register Quality Assurance
(iv) ABS Group Inc.
(v) Banner Pharma Caps India Pvt Ltd. and
(vi) International Certification Services (Asia) Pvt Ltd (ICS)

A certificate is only valid for three years. Regular audits, both internal (one or two peryear) and external (twice a year) are needed in order to maintain the certificate. Therefore, a firm intending to maintain its certification should have a quality manager in - house who is responsible for establishing the quality management policy, procedures, implementation, monitoring and documentation. For external audits, the firm has to hire quality management consultants.

10.10.1 Steps involved in ISO 9001:2000 Certification

The general guidelines for firms desiring to implement ISO 9001:2000 QMS and obtain certification from Accredited Certification Agency are listed below:

1. Ensure management commitment
2. Form a core group
3. Establish quality policy
4. Appoint management representative
5. Train management representative
6. Conduct awareness program for all employees
7. Set quality objectives for the firm and for all functional areas
8. Prepare a list of documentation and procedure
9. Form implementation team and delegate the work of writing documentation
10. Map the existing processes/ exit procedure/ work methods/ instructions/ check lists
11. Compare with applicable ISO 9001 Standards and identify gaps
12. Write additional Procedures/ Work instructions to fill gaps.
13. Apex quality manual
14. Compile linkages among procedure
15. Conduct regular review of progress
16. Check adequacy for certification with respect to the standard
17. Identify certification agency
18. Request for certification, submit quality manual for review/ fees
19. Conduct training programme for internal quality audits
20. Conduct first internal audit including adequacy audit
21. Conduct first management review meeting
22. Take planned corrective and preventive actions
23. Conduct second internal quality audit
24. Conduct second management review meeting
25. Conduct follow up or compliance audit to check completion of corrective actions effectively
26. Conduct preliminary assessment (by Accredited certification Agency)
27. Conduct final assessment for certification (by Accredited Certification Agency)

10.10.2 Benefits of ISO 9000 : 2000 Certification

(i) ISO 9000 provides a set of good basi2c practices for initiating a quality system and can be an excellent starting point for companies having no formal quality assurance program.

(ii) ISO 9000 : provides detailed guidance on process and product control.

(iii) For companies in the early stage of developing a quality program, the standards enforce the discipline of control which is necessary before pursuing continuous improvement.

(iv) The requirements of periodic audits reinforce the stated quality system until it becomes in grained in the company.

(v) Using ISO 9000 as a basis for a quality system can improve productivity, decrease cost and increase customer satisfaction.

10.10.3 Limitations of ISO 9000 : 2000

The limitations are:

(i) Not-withstanding, the process orientation, it continues to reflect a 'static' interpretation of organisation. It deals with 'what' not 'how'.

(ii) It does not explicitly address the issue of business or organizational benefit.

(iii) The process orientation is to be welcomed, but not enough emphasis has been placed on developing the 'special processes'. The focus on people as the heart of the quality is still significantly underplayed.

(iv) It retains the potential limitations of bureaucracy disuse and disrepute associated with the previous standard.

10.11 IMPLEMENTATION OF ISO 9001 : 2000

Everyone in the organisations has to be involved in the implementation of quality management system. The responsibility will be defined for every individual in the organisation including top management. **The steps to be followed to implement Q M S in any organisations are given below:**

Step 1: Top Management Commitment

First, top management must have the willingness to implement a quality system which will either meet or exceed the ISO 9000 : 2000 standards. The top management commitment is very important because it is their responsibility to provide the necessary resources in time to achieve the ISO 9000 : 2000 certification.

Step 2: Appointment of Management Representative

The management representative may be selected preferably from top management to facilitate effective implementation and maintenance of quality standard. The management representative is responsible for coordinating all activities involved in implementation, documentation and maintenance of quality standard.

Step 3: Training Program on Awareness of ISO 9000

All employees of the organisation should undergo training on awareness of ISO 9000 standards as well as the quality policy of the organisation and the individuals role in the organisation towards the fulfilment of the organisational objectives. (i.e.,quality goods) The training program helps everyone to understand the quality system and how it affects day-to-day work and potential benefits.

Step 4: Appointment of a Task Force/core Team for Implementation

After conducting the awareness program, a task force or implementation team is formal considering of members from all departments/functions at all levels. Then the team has to identify the processes, input and output, sequence and interaction.

Step 5: Writing of the Procedure, Work Instruction and the Quality Manual

The working of the organisation is written down in terms of work instructions and the work procedures. The ***quality manual*** must be written as per the requirement of ISO 9000 : 2000 standards. It should clearly specify the quality records to be maintained as conformance to the adherence of the work instructions and the work procedures.

Step 6: Adequacy Audit of the Quality Manual

The quality manual must be evaluated by a third party expert, mainly the certifying auditor, to evaluate whether it is written as per the ISO 9000 : 2000 quality management system. The standard specifies certain guidance for writing the quality manual which has to be adhered to. ISO 9000 : 2000

QMS specifies minimum six work procedures to be written for the following: ***(i) Control of documents, (ii) Control of records, (iii) Internal audit, (iv) Control or non-conforming product, (v) Corrective action and (vi) Preventive action.***

Step 7: Training on the Implementation of Quality Manual

After the quality manual is written and adequacy audit and related corrections are carried out, The ISO 9000 : 2000 QMS with reference to the quality manual is explained to every one in the organisation with focus on the individuals work area and his/her duties and responsibilities in the implementation of the standard and its working.

Step 8: Training of Internal Auditors

The ISO 9000 : 2000 QMS requires that periodically the entire organisation must be audited for the compliance of the quality manual in practical working conditions. The internal auditor has to be trained by a certified lead auditor on the ISO 9000 : 2000 quality management system. as well as on the internal audit.

Step 9: Implementation of the Quality Manual

The ISO 9000 : 2000 Q M S can be implemented by adhering to the written down work instructions and work procedures. The quality records must be properly maintained. The organisation has to ensure its working as per the written down manual and look for opportunities for modifying the work instructions and procedures to accomplish continuous improvement.

Step 10: Periodic Internal Audit for Implementation

As per ISO 9000 : 2000, periodic internal audit is a mandatory activity for implementation of QMS, The internal audit ensures the compliance to the ISO 9000 : 2000 QMS. It identifies the conformance or non conformance of working with the quality manual. If any deviations are observed, "***non-conformity report***" is raised and suitable corrective and preventive actions must be taken within a specified period. The internal audit reports are submitted to the ***quality council*** and reviewed in the management review meeting for continual improvement.

Step 11: Certification Audit

After the ISO 9000 : 2000 Q M S is fully implemented and some sounds of internal audit completed, all the "non conformity reports" are closed by taking suitable corrective and preventive actions. Then, any of the Third – party auditors like the ***Bureau Veritas Quality Internation (BVQI)***, TUV, DNV, BIS etc are called for conducting the exernal certification audit. If everything is found to be conforming as per the quality manual and the ISO 9000 : 2000 Q M S. standard, and all the "non – conformity reports" are closed, then the third – party auditor recommends the certification to be awarded to an internal certifying agency such as 'UKAS' in the UK or ANSI in the US.

Step 12: Awarding the Certificate

After the third – party auditor recommends. The certification to be awarded, the certifying agency releases the certificate valid for 3 years with a condition that the periodic audit will be carried out (once in 3 months) to ensure continued compliance of the ISO 9000 : 2000 Q M S.

Step 13: Efforts for Continual Improvement

The organisation that has received the ISO 9000 : 2000 QMS certificate has to provide evidence of continual improvement and should have well defined ***vision, mission*** **and** ***quality objectives*** ensuring that the Q M S has an in – built system for achieving ***continuous improvement.*** Activities such as "Quality circles", Kaizen Gemba" and "Juran's Quality Improvement Project" (JQIP) etc should be implemented as evidence of continuous improvement. **The Deming's "P–D–C–A cycle"** oriented towards continuous improvement should be implemented with a ***process approach.***

Step 14: Surveiliance Audit

The surveiliance audit is a periodic third party audit once in 6 months or a year to ensure that the ISO 9000 : 2000. QMS is being adhered to by the organisation. This audit should also ensure that the evidence are available for the continuous improvement of the ISO 9000 : 2000 Q M S. The ***recertification audit*** is carried out after three years of certification.

Box 10.5 **describes Kanji and Ashler's thirteen steps for the development of an effective quality management system (QMS)**

Box 10.5 : Kanji and Ashler's 13 Steps to a Quality Management System

Step 1: Obtain management understanding of, and commitment to, the quality management approach: This commitment to fundamental to any aspect of achieving quality. Managers must be committed to quality, which implies commitment to the Q M S. Which assists the drive for quality, An effective Q M S can be erected only within the context of a fully supported quality program.

Step 2: Define the scope of the activities to be included in the QMS: If an organisation is to be effective in its quality drive, then every part of it must fall within the Q M S. However, There will certainly be a need to assess priorities for inclusion in the Q M S. for example, production before personnel and the canteen but the ultimate aim should be an all inclusive system.

Step 3: Define the organisational structure and responsibilities of those within the scope of the QMS: Which it is vital that the appropriate organisation structure is in use and that responsibilities are clearly defined, it is essential to realise that the correct organisational form is a rapidly changing element because of the dynamism and fluidity of the organisational environment.

Step 4: Audit the existing systems and procedures against the requirements of the standard

Step 5: Develop a plan to write the necessary procedures

Step 6: Train sufficient personnel to write their own procedures

Step 7: Draft and edit the procedures and gain agreement to them: The fourth, fifth, sixth and seventh steps, audit of current systems and procedures and development of new procedures, are fundamental to the achievement of QMS.

Step 8: Complete a draft quality manual

Step 9: Implement the system on a trial basis: The proposed system must be tested in action and validated or modified against empirical data.

Step 10: Train internal auditors to carryout audits of the system and its operation: Training of internal auditors is vital and should draw on the experience and knowledge of those who actually carry out the operations of the organisation.

Step 11: Revise the operation of the system in the light of the results of audits and other information

Step 12: Apply for registration from an a credited body

Step 13: Maintain the system by internal audit, using it as an opportunity to improve: This step reflects the demand for continuous improvement, not only in the core activities of the organisation but in everything that it does.

10.12 ENVIRONMENTAL MANAGEMENT SYSTEM

Iso 14000 series standards provide guidelines on the elements that an environmental management system should have and on the supporting technologies

The Quality Management system (ISO 9000) was completed in 1987 by the International organisation for standards (ISO). Later, ISO, decided to develop environmental management standards. In 1991, ISO formed the strategic Advisory Group on the environment (SAGE) which led to the formation of Technical Committee (TC 207) in 1992.

The mission of TC 207 was to develop standards for an environmental management system (EMS) which was identified as ISO 14000. Like ISO 9000, ISO 14000 standards addressed the process rather than the end goal. Thus they are process standards their performance standards.

TC 207 established six sub committees: *(i)* environmental management systems, *(ii)* environmental auditing, *(iii)* environmental performance evaluation, *(iv)* environmental aspects in product standards, *(v)* environmental labeling and *(vii)* life cycle assessment.

Experience with ISO 9000 made it easier to develop ISO 14000. A subsequent revision of ISO 9000 capitalised on many of the improvements made in ISO 14000. The environmental management system (EMS) is a part of a comprehensive management system that addresses how the over all business activities, including its products and services have an impact on the environment. The

EMS maximum company participation in environment performance for the present and in the future.

10.12.1 ISO 14000 Series Standards

Two specific areas of the ISO 14000 series standards are: *(i)* The organisational evaluation standards and *(ii)* The product evaluation standards. In addition ISO 14050 covers terms and definitions that are common to both areas.

Organisational Evaluation Standards

Exhibit 10.3 **illustrate the organisational evaluation standards which consist of three categories:** *(i)* environmental management system (EMS), *(ii)* environmental auditing, *(iii)* environmental performance evaluation (EPE).

Exhibit 10.3 : Organisational Evaluation Standards

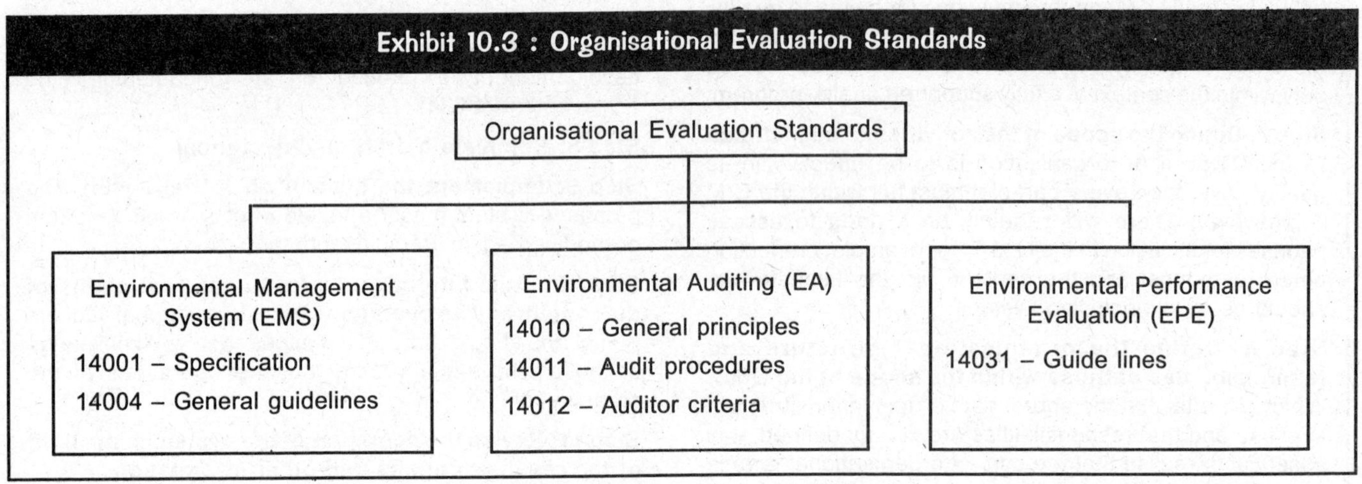

ISO 14001, entitled "environmental management systems" – specifications with guidance for use" gives the elements that organisations are required to conform to if they such registration.

ISO 14004, entitled "environmental management systems – guidelines on principles, systems and supporting techniques" provides supplementary material for information only.

ISO 14010, entitled "guidelines for environmental auditing – general principles on environmental auditing" provides information for internal or external auditing.

ISO 14011, entitled "guidelines for environmental auditing – Audit procedures – Auditing of environmental Management systems" provides information on has to plan and conduct an audit. This standard includes some topics such as audit team, audit plan implementation and report.

ISO 14012, entitled "Qualification criteria for environmental Auditors performing environmental Management system Audits" covers information an auditor qualifications, training and personal attributes and skills.

ISO 14031, entitled "Guidelines on environmental performance evaluation" presents information on recording information to track performance. It helps the organisation meet the requirements of ISO 14001, section 4.5.1; Monitoring and Measuring.

Product Evaluation Standards

Exhibit 10.4 **illustrates product evaluation standards which consist of three categories:** *(i)* Environmental aspects in product standards (EAPS) *(ii)* Environmental labeling (EL) *(iii)* Life-cycle assessment (LCA).

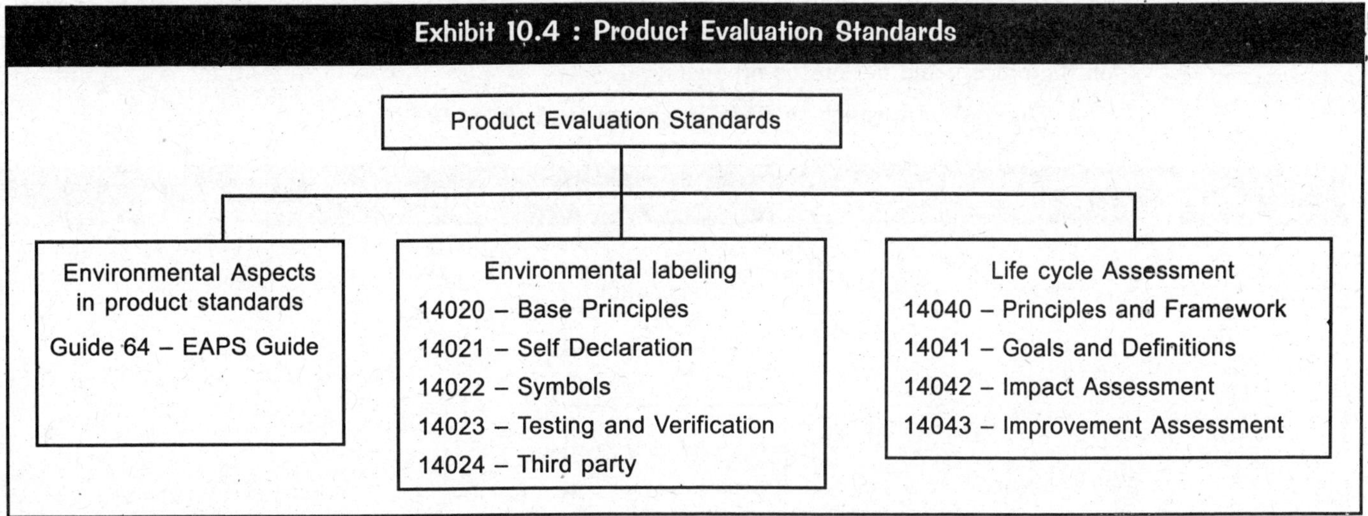

Guide 64, entitled "environmental aspects in Product Standards" is designed to help writers develop product standards.

ISO 14020, entitled "environmental labeling – Basic principles for all environmental labeling" provides guidance on goals and principles that should be used in all labeling programs.

ISO 14021, entitled "environmental labeling – Self-Declaration of environmental claims, Terms and Definitions". Applies to organisations that are declaring that their product has an environmental attribute such as being recyclable or energy efficient.

ISO 14022, entitled "environmental labeling – symbols" provides a standard set of symbols for use by organisations.

ISO 14023, entitled "environmental labeling – Testing and Verification Methodologies" provides information on the appropriate methods to use to confirm the genuineness of the product as stated by the environmental label.

ISO 14024, entitled "environmental labeling – Practioner Programs: Guiding Principles, Practices and certification procedures for Multiple Criteria Programs" establishes criteria for third party labeling or seal programs. These programs determine which products have overall environmental superiority as compared to other products.

ISO 14040, entitled "Life cycle Assessment – Principles and Framework, "provides an overview of the practice, applications and limitations of Life Cycle Assessment (LCA). Life Cycle Assessment attempts to determine the long – range environmental effect of a product.

ISO 14041, entitled, "Life cycle Assessment – Goals and Definition/Scope and Inventory Analysis" is intended to provide guidelines for the preparation, conduct, and critical review of the life - cycle inventory analysis. This analysis involves the compilation and quantification of relevant inputs of a product system.

ISO 14042, entitled "Life cycle Assessment – Impact Assessment" is intended to use the results of the inventory analysis to evaluate the significance of potential environmental impacts.

ISO 14043, entitled "Life cycle Assessment – Improvement Assessment" is intended to provide information to improve the total environmental performance of a product system.

The organisational evaluation standards are operational and affective because; like ISO 9000, the focus way on the process rather than the product.

10.12.2 Concepts of ISO 14001

ISO 14001 provides organisations with the elements for an "Environmental Management System (EMS)", which can be integrated into other management systems to help achieve environmental and economic goals. It describes the requirements of registration and/or self – declaration of the organisations "Environmental Management System". The requirements are based on the process and not on the product.

The basic approach to EMS in shown in *Exhibit 10.5.*

Exhibit 10.5 : Environmental Management System Model

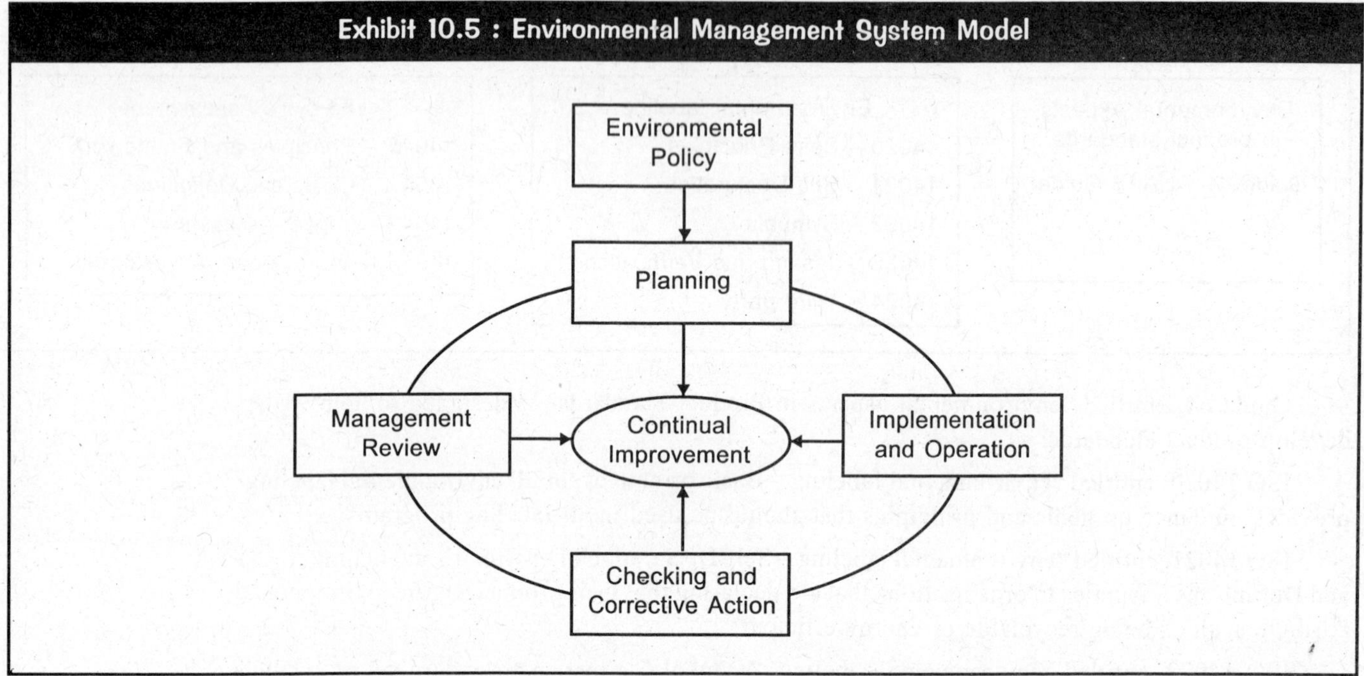

It begins with the environmental policy, followed by planning, implementation and operation, checking and corrective action and management review. The approach follows the PDSA cycle with a logical sequence of events to achieve continual improvement.

The overall aim is to support environmental protection and prevention of pollution in balance with socioeconomic needs.

The intention of the standard is not to create non tariff barriers or to change the legal obligations of organisations, Further, it does not include aspects of occupational health and safety management. However, an organisation may include these aspects in the documentation.

To understand the requirements of ISO 14001 better, we need to know the definitions of certain terms used. These definitions are listed in *Box 10.6.*

Box 10.6 : Definitions of terms used in ISO 14001

(i) **Environment:** The global surroundings in which an organisation operates. This includes air, water, land, natural resources, flora, fauna, human beings and their interaction.

(ii) **Environmental aspects:** An element of an organisation's activities, products, or services that can interact with the environment ; for example, waste water discharge, air emissions and energy usage.

(iii) **Environmental impact:** Any change, whether beneficial or adverse, wholly or partially resulting from the activities of an organisation, products or services, for example, impact on habitat, water supply and soil erosion.

(iv) **Environmental objective:** An overall environmental goal that arises from the policy statement set by an organisation for itself and which is quantified when practical. They define how the policy will be achieved. For example, an objective could be to control the temperature of wastewater efficient from industrial plants.

(v) **Environmental target:** A detailed performance requirement which should be quantified when practical. It needs to be met in order to achieve the objective. For example the wastewater temperature should be controlled between 15°C and 20°C.

10.13 REQUIREMENTS OF ISO 14001 : 1996 ENVIRONMENTAL MANAGEMENT SYSTEM (EMS)

The standard is divided into six parts or clauses and has a total of 18 requirements. The numbering system used is identical to the ISO 9000:2000 Quality Management system (QMS)

Clause 1.0: Scope: The environmental management system should enable an organisation to formulate the policy and objectives taking into account legislative requirements and information about significant environmental impact which the organisation can control and over which it has an influence. The EMS standard is applicable to any organisation concerned with the environmental management system.

Clause 2.0 – Normative References: NIL

Clause 3.0 – Definitions: All the definitions are taken from the standard ISO 1400 : 1996. **Major definitions are listed in *Box 10.6*. Some other definitions are given below:**

(i) **Environmental management audit:** A systematic and documented verification process of objectively obtaining and evaluating evidence to determine whether an organisation's environmental management system conforms to the environmental management system audit criteria set by the organisation and for communication of the results of their process management.

(ii) **Environmental performance:** Measurable result of the environment management system related to an organisation's control of its environmental policy, objectives and targets.

(iii) **Interested party:** Individual or the group concerned with or affected by the environmental performance of the organisation.

(iv) **Prevention of pollution:** use of processes, practices, materials or products that avoid, reduce or control pollution. Which may include recycling, treatment, process changes, control mechanisms, efficient use of resources and material substitution.

Clause 4.0 – Environmental Management System: The environmental management system includes organisational structure, planning activities, responsibilities, practices, procedures, processes and resources for developing, implementing, achieving, reviewing and maintaining the environmental policy. ***Box 10.7* lists the major clauses of ISO 14000, Section 4.**

Box 10.7 : ISO 14000 Section 4: Environmental Management Systems Requirements

4.1 General Requirements
4.2 Environmental Policy
4.3 Planning
- 4.3.1 Environmental Aspects
- 4.3.2 Legal and Other Requirements
- 4.3.3 Objectives and Targets
- 4.3.4 Environmental Management Program (s)

4.4 Implementation and Operation
- 4.4.1 Structure and Responsibility
- 4.4.2 Training, Awareness, and Competence
- 4.4.3 Communication
- 4.4.4 Environmental Management System Documentation
- 4.4.5 Document Control
- 4.4.6 Operational Control
- 4.4.7 Emergency Preparedness and Response

4.5 Checking and Corrective Action
- 4.5.1 Monitoring and Measurement
- 4.5.2 Nonconformance and Corrective and Preventive Action
- 4.5.3 Records
- 4.5.4 Environmental Management System Audit

4.6 Management Review.

Clause 4.1 – General Requirements: The general requirements of the organisations is to establish and maintain an environmental management system that includes policy, planning, implementation and operation, checking and corrective action, and management review.

Clause 4.2 – Environmental Policy: The organisation's policy statement should be based on its mission and values. It should reflect management's commitment, leadership and direction for the environmental activities. The organisation should declare its environmental policy and the management should ensure that the policy is implemented and carried out the policy must be relevant to the organisation's nature, sale and environmental impact of its activities, products and services. The policy must ensure that management is committed to continual improvement and prevention of pollution. The policy provides a frame work for setting and reviewing environmental objectives and targets. Their setting should aim to comply with legislative and regulatory requirements.

The policy must be documented, implemented and maintained. It also must be communicated to all employees. The policy must also be available to the public.

Clause 4.3 – Planning: This area contains four elements: *(i)* environmental aspects, *(ii)* legal and other requirements, *(iii)* objectives and targets and *(iv)* environmental management program(s).

Clause 4.3.1 – Environmental aspects: The organisation shall establish and maintain procedures to identify the environmental aspects of its activities, products and services and control them. The organisation has to ensure that the aspects related to these significant impacts are part of its environmental objectives ISO 14004 lists nine issues that can be considered in an organisation's procedures for the identification of aspects and their impacts.

Clause 4.3.2 – Legal and other requirements: The standard requires the organisation to have a procedure to identify and have access to all legal and other requirements to which it subscribes. In general, legal environmental requirements are those attributed to governmental legislative and regulatory action.

Clause 4.3.3 – Objectives and targets: The organisation should establish and maintain documented environmental objectives and targets at each relevant function and level within the organisation. They shall be consistent with the policy statements, especially in regard to the prevention of pollution. ISO 14004 lists different forms of objectives.

When establishing and reviewing its objectives, an organisation shall consider the legal and other requirements and its significant environmental aspects, its technological options and its financial, operational and business requirements and the view of the interested parties.

Clause 4.3.4 – Environmental management program(s): The organisation shall establish and maintain a program or programs for achieving the objectives and targets. It shall include designation of the responsible function, team, or individual and a time frame for achievement.

Clause 4.4 – Implementation and operation: This area contains seven elements: *(i)* Structure and responsibility, *(ii)* training, awareness and competency, *(iii)* communication, *(iv)* environmental management system documentation, *(v)* document control, *(vi)* operation control and *(vii)* emergency preparedness and response.

Clause 4.4.1 – Structure and responsibility: Roles, responsibilities and authorities shall be defined, documented and communicated to all personnel affecting the EMS in order to facilitate effective environmental management. Senior management must provide the resources in terms of people, technology and money to implement and maintain and effective system that achieves its objectives.

Clause 4.4.2 – Training, awareness and competency: The organisation shall identify and evaluate the training needs regularly (usually annually) to ensure their effectiveness. Two types of training are: *(i)* general awareness and *(ii)* job competency.

General awareness includes the importance of conformance to the EMS, the relationship of significant environmental impacts to the employee's work activities, employee role and responsibilities and potential consequences of failure to follow specific operating procedures, the personnel performing tasks that can cause significant environmental impacts shall be competent based on education, training and experience. This training should include: *(a)* record of training needs assessments, *(b)* task competency requirements, *(c)* training procedures, *(d)* training plans and *(e)* records of training delivered to specific employees.

Clause 4.4.3 – Communication: The standard requires that procedures shall be established and maintained for internal communication among all employees. Effective communication between the various levels and functions of the organisation (up, down and laterally) should be ensured. In addition, procedures shall be established for receiving, documentary and responding to relevant external communication from interested parties.

Clause 4.4.4 – Environmental system documentation: The organisation shall establish and maintain information, in written (paper) or electronic form, to describe the core elements of the system and their interaction and provide direction to related documentation.

Clause 4.4.5 – Document control: The organisations should have a written procedure for the document control. All the documents should be approved, reviewed, updated, easily available and readily identifiable, i.e all documents should be adequately legible and controlled. All the absolute documents must be removed and only the documents with revision status should be available.

Clause 4.4.6 – Operational control: The organisation should align its operations and activities with the identified significant environmental aspects, environmental policy and environmental objectives and targets. A written procedure should exist for this.

Clause 4.4.7 – Emergency preparedness and response: The organisation should establish procedures required to identify and respond to potential accidents and emergency situations. The organisation should review periodically and revise if necessary, the procedures for its response and emergency preparedness for the accidents and emergency situations and for preventing and mitigating their impact on the environment.

Clause 4.5 – checking and corrective action: This area contains four elements: *(i)* monitoring and measuring, *(ii)* non-conformance and corrective and preventive action, *(iii)* records and *(iv)* environmental management system audit.

Clause 4.5.1 – Monitoring and measuring: The organisation is required to monitor and measure the key characteristics of its objectives and activities in order to assess its performance in meeting environmental operations and targets. There should be established and documented procedures to control, regularly celibrate, maintain and record all measuring equipments. In addition the procedures are required to periodically evaluate compliance to relevant regulations.

Clause 4.5.2 – Non conformance and corrective and preventive action: The organisation should establish, maintain, review periodically and revise, if necessary, the procedure for defining authority and responsibility for handling and investigating non – conformance, taking actions to mitigate any impacts and for initiating corrective and preventive actions.

Clause 4.5.3 – Records: Procedures should be established for the identification, maintenance and disposition of environmental records such as training, audits, equipment calibration and reviews. The records should be legible, identifiable, and traceable to the activity, product or service. They should be readily retrievable, protected against damage, deterioration and loss and provided with retention times.

Clause 4.5.4 – Environmental management system audit: The organisation should conduct periodic environmental management system audits at planned intervals to ensure that the EMS conforms to plan and is being properly implemented and maintained. The audit criteria, scope, frequency, methods shall be defined along with responsibilities. The audit results should be recorded. Follow up action should be taken to eliminate the non – conformities detected during the audits. The written procedure for internal audit must be documented.

Clause 4.6 – Management Review: Management review and revision if applicable, is required to ensure the continuing suitability, adequacy and effectiveness of the EMS. The top management must be involved in the EMS continuous improvement process management must evaluate the feed back data and make improvements to the system. Reviews will mostly likely occur on a monthly basis and cover some of the elements at each review. A fixed schedule of reviews is required to cover al the elements.

10.13.1 Benefits of EMS

Two categories of benefits are: *(i)* Global and *(ii)* Organisational.

Global benefits include: *(i)* facilitating trade and removing trade barriers, *(ii)* Improving environmental performance of planet earth and *(iii)* building consensus that there is a need for environmental management and a common terminology for **EMS organisational benefits are:**

(i) Assuring customers of a commitment to environmental management.
(ii) Meeting customer requirements.
(iii) Maintaining a good public image.
(iv) Obtaining insurance at reasonable cost.
(v) Increasing market share.
(vi) Reducing incidents that result in liability issues.

10.14 OTHER QUALITY SYSTEMS

The ISO 9000 system is designed as a simple system that can be used by any industry. Other systems have been developed that are specific to a particular industry such as automotive or aerospace. These systems use the ISO 9000 as the basic framework and modify it to their needs. **There are three other quality systems: QS-9000, TE 9000 and AS 9000 which are discussed in the following paragraphs.**

Qs 9000 is an interpretation and extension of ISO 9000 for automotive suppliers

QS 9000: This standard was developed in September 1994 by the three big US automobile manufacturers – Ford, Chrysler and General Motors to define their fundamental quality expectations for suppliers of production and service parts and materials. QS 9000 is an interpretation and extension of ISO 9000 for automotive suppliers. The goal of the automobile manufacturers was to develop fundamental quality systems that provide for continuous improvement, emphasising defect prevention and the reduction of variation and waste in the supply chain.

QS 9000 is based on ISO 9000 and includes all ISO 9000 requirements. It goes well beyond ISO 9000 standards by including additional requirements such as continuous improvement, manufacturing capability, and production part approval processes. QS 9000 not only states ***what*** must be done, but often ***how*** to do it? Many of the concepts in the Malcolm Baldrige National Quality Award Criteria are reflected in QS 9000.

There are three sections in QS 9000:

((i) Common requirements, which include the exact test of ISO 9001 and the addition of automotive/heavy trucking requirements.
(ii) Additional requirements covering production part approval process, continuous improvement and manufacturing capabilities.
((iii) Customer specific requirements that are unique to Ford, Chrysler and General Motors.

Registration under QS 9000 standards will also achieve ISO 9000 registration, but ISO certified companies must meet the additional QS 9000 requirements to achieve QS certification.

TE 9000 is the tooling and equipment supplement to QS 9000

Exhibit 10.6 **shows the relationships among the Baldrige Award Criteria, ISO 9000 and QS 9000.**

TE 9000: The Tooling and Equipment Supplement (TE 9000) to QS 9000 released in 1996 was prepared by representatives of Chrysler, Ford and General Motors with the following objectives:

(i) To provide an interpretation of QS 9000 requirements as they apply to tooling and equipment suppliers.

Exhibit 10.6 : Relationships among the Baldrige Criteria, QS 9000 and ISO 9000

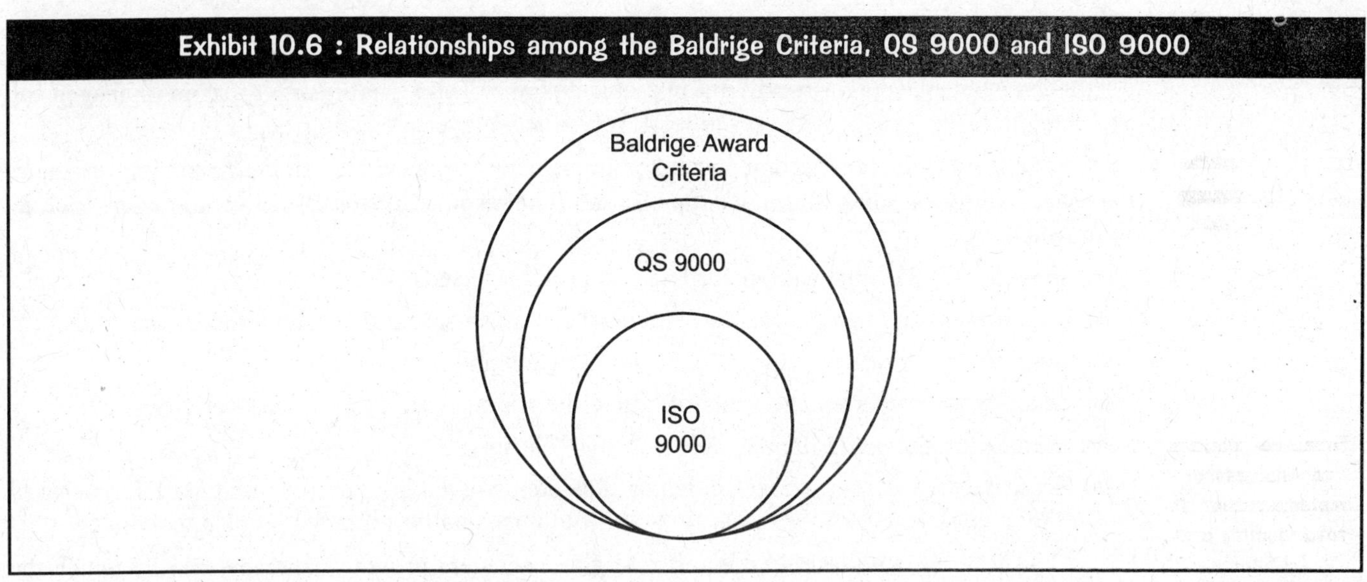

(ii) To commonise quality system requirements from Chrysler, Ford and General Motors and

(iii) To promote the effective use of reliability and maintainability.

As 9000 is similar to ISO 9000, and addresses the needs of aerospace industry.

AS 9000: The aerospace industry quality system was officially released by the Society of Automotive Engineers in May 1997. This document is identical to ISO 9000 in most respects. AS 9000 builds on ISO 9000, adding insight and addressing the distinctive needs of the aerospace industry.

10.15 IMPLEMENTING A TOTAL QUALITY STRATEGY

The journey to quality and performance excellence is quite long and time consuming. *For example,* at Armstrong Building Products Operations, US, the evolution of quality has occurred in several phases since 1983:

Phase 1 : (1981-1985)

- Commitment to try
- Philips Crosby system and
- Quality improvement teams.

Phase 2 : (1985-1990)

- Process improvement
- Quality plans added to business plans and
- Supplier quality management.

Phase 3 : (1989-1990)

- Vision clearly defined
- Empowered employees, flatter organisation and
- Use of Baldrige criteria for self-assessment.

Phase 4 : (1991-1994)

- Product and service leadership
- Baldrige Award applications (1995 winner) and
- Business results.

Phase 5 : (1994 onwards)

- High performance change process
- "Non-negotiable" business strategies and
- Achieving value for employees, customers and shareholders.

10.16 THE ROLE OF EMPLOYEES

Three key players for successful implementation of Total Quality are: *(i)* senior management, *(ii)* middle management and *(iii)* the workforce. Each player plays a critical role.

The Role of Senior Management: Senior managers must ensure that their plans and strategies are successfully executed within the organisation. **The responsibilities of senior managers include the following:**

(i) Ensure that the organisation focusses on customer needs.

(ii) Cascade the mission, vision and values of the organisation throughout the organisation.

(iii) Identify the critical processes that need attention and improvement.

(iv) Identify the resources and trade-offs that must be made to fund the TQ activity.

(v) Review progress and remove any identified barriers.

(vi) Improve the macro-processes in which they are involved both to improve the performance of the process and to demonstrate their ability to use quality tools for problem solving.

Three key players for successful implementation to total quality are: *(i)* Senior management *(ii)* middle management and *(iii)* the workforce

The Role of Middle Management: Middle managers provide the leadership by which the vision of senior management is translated into the operations of the organisation. Middle manager's role in creating and sustaining a TQ culture is critical. They improve the operational processes that are the foundation of customer satisfaction. They can make or break cooperation and teamwork and they are the principal means by which the remaining workforce prepare for change.

Middle managers must also exhibit behaviours that are supportive of total quality such as listening to employees as customers, creating a positive work environment, implementing quality improvements enthusiastically, challenging people to develop new ideas and reach their potential, setting challenging goals and providing positive feedback.

The Role of the Workforce: The workforce delivers quality and for TQ to succeed, must feel not only **empowerment,** but also **ownership. If total quality doesn't occur at the work-force level, it will not occur at all.** The work-force implements quality policies. This task requires ownership which goes beyond empowerment. It gives the employees the right to have a voice in deciding what needs to be done and how to do it.

Increased ownership requires increased sharing of information with the work-force and a commitment to the work-force at all times by the management in the form of job security for a reasonably long period and training and development of employees which makes them highly employable and marketable. With such commitments, a company can more easily develop the loyalty and commitment needed within the work-force as they jointly strive to apply the principles of total quality.

Role of Union-Management Relationships: Traditional adverse relationship between unions and the management can be a major stumbling block in implementing TQ. The management must share the responsibility in working with unions as equal partners. Both union and the management have important roles in TQ.

Labour unions must recognise the need for changing their relationship with management and then educate their members as to how to co-operate with the management. This information includes what their members can expect and how working conditions and job security might change. Labour union leaders must have a positive attitude and they must separate TQ initiatives from collective bargaining.

Management must understand that the skills and knowledge of all employees are needed to improve quality and meet competitive challenges. Management must be willing to develop closer working relationship with the labour and be ready to address union concerns and cultivate trust.

10.17 SUSTAINING THE QUALITY ORGANISATION

Getting started often seems easy by comparison with sustaining a quality focus. Numerous organisational barriers and challenges get in the way. New efforts usually begin with much enthusiasm, in part because of the sheer novelty of the effort. After some time, reality sets in and doubts surface. Real problems develop as early supporters begin to question the process. At this point, the organisation can redesign itself to inevitable failure or persist and seek to overcome the obstacles. Sustaining total quality requires both an understanding of why quality efforts fail in some organisations and the ability to develop into a ***"learning organisation."***

Barriers for Implementation: Organisations face numerous barriers to successfully implementing total quality. The fundamental structure of US business was derived from management principles of Taylor's era and these principles are no longer sufficient in the present modern era. Japan, by contrast, built its management system on the teachings of Deming, Juran and Drucker, whose focus relied on fundamental TQ principles.

One reason for failure of TQ is the lack of **'constancy of purpose'** which is the first version of Deming's 14 points. The people who implement quality initiative often have conflicting goals and priorities.

Some of the common mistakes in implementing TQM are:

(i) TQ is regarded as a "program" despite the rhetoric that may state the contrary.

(ii) Absence of short-term results may cause disappointment to the management and make the management to lose interest. Often management believes that measurable benefits lie only in the distant future.

(iii) The process is not driven by a focus on customer.

(iv) Structural elements in the organisation block change - such as compensation systems, promotion systems, accounting systems, rigid policies and procedures, specialisation and functionalisation and status symbols such as offices and perks.

(v) Goals are set too low. Management does not use outside benchmarks as targets.

(vi) The organisational culture remains one of "command and control" and is driven by fear or game-playing, budgets, schedules or bureaucracy.

(vii) Training is not properly addressed. Training may be inadequate. Training must be matched to strategy and business needs.

(viii) The focus is mainly on products rather than processes.

(ix) Empowerment given is not sufficient and is not supported in actions.

(x) The organisation is too successful and complacent. It is not receptive to change and learning.

(xi) The organisation fails to address three fundamental questions – *(i)* Is this another program? *(ii)* What is in it for me? and *(iii)* How can I do this on top of everything else?

(xii) Senior management is not personally and visibly committed and actively participating.

(xiii) An over emphasis on teams for cross-functional problems, which leads to the neglect of individual efforts for local improvements.

(xiv) Employees operate under the belief that more data are always desirable, regardless of relevance – "paralysis by analysis."

(xv) Management fails to recognise that quality improvement is a personal responsibility at all levels of the organisation.

(xvi) The organisation does not see itself as a collection of inter-related processes making up an overall system.

TQ requires a new set of skills and learning, including interpersonal awareness and competence, team building, encouraging openness and trust, listening, giving and getting feedback, group participation, problem solving, clarifying goals, resolving conflicts, delegating and coaching, empowerment and continuous improvement as a way of life.

The process must begin by creating a set of feelings and attitudes that lead to lasting value and organisational commitment. It must develop by developing a long-term TQ strategy. It must be realised through training, continuous feedback and open communications and empowerment.

Perhaps the most significant failure encountered in most organisations is a lack of alignment between expectations that arise from TQ change processes and reward systems.

TQ efforts should lead to the achievement of outstanding business results. However, a successful quality initiative does not guarantee financial success. Many companies fail to pay enough to the financial returns on quality related investments.

A prescription for implementing quality within an organisation with a focus on – return on quality (ROQ) is as below:

(i) Start with an effective quality approach (*i.e.* process and inventory controls).

(ii) Calculate the cost of current quality initiatives (*i.e.* cost of warranties, problem presentation and monitoring activities all count).

(iii) Determine what key factors retain customers and what drives them away.

(iv) Focus on quality efforts most likely to improve customer satisfaction at a reasonable cost.

(v) Roll out successful approaches after pilot-testing the most promising efforts and cutting the ones that don't have a big impact and

(vi) Improve quality efforts continually.

10.18 BUILDING A CHANGE-ORIENTED ORGANISATION

The best way to deal with change is to predict it and prepare a response

The importance of this activity changes with variations in the turbulence of a firm's business environment. A business with few competitive threats and a stable work-force may not need to focus acutely on building systems that can respond to change. Any business with respectable sales growth and profit margins will attract competition, however, and unforeseen threats often blind-side those who make the smug assumption that everything will remain constant.

A healthy sense of vulnerability can help a firm to combat smugness. In nature, constant wariness of potential danger helps animals to survive. The leader of a successful firm can also benefit from a keen sense of wariness.

The best way to deal with change is to predict it and prepare a response. This requires close relationships with customers, suppliers, employees and relevant technologies. It is necessary for a firm to track what its customers want along with the needs and preferences of competitors' customers. The firm must also try to anticipate technical and social changes that will affect its operations.

A change accepting culture stimulates and reinforces this awareness of new developments by encouraging experimentation without recrimination. An organisational culture should support individuals when they constructively challenge conventional wisdom and protect them from jeopardising their positions within the organisation.

Box 10.8 : Learning from Baldrige Winners

Scott McNealy, CEO of Sun Micro Systems invited three CEOs of Baldrige Winners (FedEx, Motorola and Xerox) to visit his company to discuss their quality processes. The key lessons that Sun learnt were:

- Quality must be elevated to the level of a "core management process".
- Quality must be the first agenda item of every executive management and board meeting.
- Quality can be managed only if it is measured.
- Quality starts with the employee.
- Achievement in quality must be a factor in compensation.

Box 10.9 : Stages of learning which individuals go through

- **Unconscious incompetence :** You don't know that you don't know.
- **Conscious incompetence :** You realise that you don't know.
- **Conscious competence :** You learn to do, but with conscious effort.
- **Unconscious competence :** Performance comes effortlessly.

Box 10.10 : Definitions of Learning Organisation

"An organisation that is continually expanding its capacity to create its future. For such an organisation, it is not enough merely to survive. "Survival learning" or what is more often termed "adaptive learning" is important – indeed it is necessary. But for a learning organisation, "adaptive learning" must be joined by "generative learning", learning that enhances our capacity to create.

– Peter Senge
Professor, M.I.T. (USA)

"An organisation that is skilled at creating, acquiring and transferring knowledge and at modifying its behaviour to reflect new knowledge and insights."

– Garvin

10.19 BUILDING OF A LEARNING ORGANISATION

A learning organisation is an organisation that has a policy to continue to learn and improve its products, services, processes and outcomes. It is an organisation that is continually expanding its capacity to create its future.

Seeing the need for adaptability is easy, but in creating an organisation design that helps both individuals and the firm as a whole to adapt to change, the managers face an arduous task. Even though some managers dismiss this goal as impossible, more committed firms have succeeded. According to Peter Senge of MIT, organisations like individuals can and often suffer from learning disorders. According to him, "learning disabilities are tragic, because of them, few corporations live even half as long as a person – most die before the age of forty."

Unfortunately, most organisations confuse learning with experience. Senge's concept of the learning organisation provides a conceptual framework for understanding why some organisations seem unable to adopt team-oriented, change-accepting management styles. In his book, ***"The Fifth Discipline"***, Senge points out that "the team that became great didn't start out great – it learnt how to produce extra-ordinary results." A firm that learns faster than its competitors can gain an important competitive advantage. Learning thrives most when it pervades an organisation. **According to Senge, the *five* so called *disciplines* that create an organisation that can "truly learn" are:**

(i) **System thinking:** A learning organisation needs a conceptual system, a body of knowledge and carefully developed analytical tools to fully understand patterns of events. The organisation needs a normal process for seeing the big picture beyond the clutter of details.

(ii) **Personal mastery:** The learning organisation's spiritual foundation enables it to continually clarify and disperse its vision of its realm, to focus its energies on areas that matter, to develop the ability to see reality objectively and to cultivate the patience needed for timely decision making.

(iii) **Mental models:** Mental models are paradigms which are deeply ingrained assumptions, generalisations or even pictures or images that influence how we understand the world and how we take action. Mental models form many barriers within people's minds. People in learning organisations need open disciplined minds to look inward at their own assumptions, to objectively evaluate external conditions and then to judiciously probe the underlying assumptions that support their mental models. "Learning-oriented conversations" occur when people expose their own thinking effectively and make that thinking open to the influence of others.

(iv) **Building shared vision:** This practice involves developing common "pictures of the future that foster genuine commitment and enrollment rather than compliance". Leaders of learning organisations must accept that even a sincerely benevolent attempt to dictate a vision is counter productive.

(v) **Team learning:** Senge's fifth discipline starts with a dialogue in which members of a team can suspend assumptions and enter into a genuine ***"think together"*** which may be called as ***"open conversation".*** The word "dialogue" has its origin in the Greek word "dia-logos" which referred to a free flow of meaning through a group, allowing the group to discover insights that individuals alone could not. The word "discussion" has its roots with percussion and concussion, literally a heaving of ideas back and forth in a "winner – takes-all" competition.

If Senge's **"learning organisation"** were a machine, he might have called these building blocks ***"necessary technologies".*** Since the learning organisation involves human beings, he calls them ***"disciplines".*** Senge observed that a great team doesn't simply emerge but rather it learns to accomplish things that it could not accomplish before.

Senge describes how to approach common organisational problems through disciplined system thinking. *Box 10.11* lists the 11 laws of his fifth discipline.

Box 10.11 : Laws of Fifth Discipline

- Today's problems come from yesterday's solutions.
- When you push harder, the system pushes back harder.
- Behaviour grows better before it grows worse, this suggests a possible time lag between short-term benefit and long-term problem.
- The easy way out usually leads back in.
- The cure can be worse than the disease.
- Faster is slower, all natural systems from ecosystems to animals in organisations, have intrinsically optimal rate of growth far below the fastest possible growth rate.
- Cause and effect are not closely related in time and space.
- Small changes can produce big results, but the areas of highest leverage are often the least obvious.
- You can have your cake and eat it, but not at the same time.
- Dividing an elephant in half does not produce two small elephants.
- There is no blame.

The last law is the most important because fear of blame is the root cause of organisational intransigence.

Senge's book explains the difficulty of quickly changing an existing firm's product design and development process to a cross-functional, team-driven system. His five disciplines discussed earlier make sense, but getting an existing organisation to practice them requires the people to ***"unlearn" beliefs, habits*** **and *values*** that have helped them to survive.

***Box 10.12* lists five main activities of learning organisations.**

Box 10.12 : 5 Main Activities of Learning Organisations (according to Garvin)

- systematic problem solving
- experimentation with new approaches
- learning from their own experiences and history
- learning from the experiences and best practices of others.
- transferring knowledge quickly and efficiently throughout the organisation.

10.20 BUILDING A FEAR-FREE ORGANISATION

One of Deming's 14 points for management urges an organisation to drive out fear as much as possible. When employees feel free to tell the truth about problems in the work-place without repercussions, then their ideas concerning innovation, quality and productivity will flourish. However, it is not easy for an existing organisation to instantly blossom into a fear-free, empowered environment.

Box 10.13 **lists results of a field study which asked employees how fear affected their feelings, relationships, quality of work and productivity.** The consequences of these negative feelings include increases in unproductive political and self-protective behaviour.

Box 10.13 : Impact of Fear at Work

Issue	Responses (%ge)
Negative feelings about the organisation	29%
Negative impact on quality or productivity	27%
Negative feelings about oneself	19%
Negative emotions	12%
Other negative effects	11%
Positive effects	2%

Fear in an organisation signals bad management. Fear can drive people towards short-term results.

The field survey conducted revealed the following qualities of an organisation that would create a fear-free environment:

- Mutual helpfulness and trust.
- Members helping one another to remain objective.
- Members sharing feedback on both strengths and opportunities for improvement.
- Members influencing one another's ideas and decisions.
- Humour and member's enjoyment of one another's company.
- Creative, synergistic problem solving with results greater than the sum of the inputs.
- Respect for differences in backgrounds and talents, reliance on one another's expertise.
- Willingness and ability to work through conflicts and disagreement.
- Commitment to common goals and one another's success.
- Intimate rapport and honesty between members and
- Straightforward communication.

Fear in an organisation signals bad management. Fear can drive people towards short-term results, but it fails to unify workers in pursuit of common goals or to sustain vigorous motivation and commitment. Fear of outside threats shared by the entire organisation can be useful if it prevents complacency. However, too many managers create ***unproductive fear*** or fear that causes waste by limiting the effectiveness of the group in working to achieve the goals of the organisation. Unproductive fear makes employees ***risk-aversive*** and promotes political infighting designed to protect individuals and their chances of survival.

A change-driven organisation encourages discovery without unproductive fear. Such an organisation needs leaders who can direct, coordinate and inspire members to accept and strive to achieve its shared goals.

Box 10.14 **shows Texas Instruments' Business Excellence standard and** ***Exhibit 10.7*** **illustrates its approach to quality**

The four steps of TI-BEST are :

Box 10.14 : Texas Instrument's Business Excellence Standard (TI-BEST)

1. Define business excellence for your business
2. Assess your progress
3. Identify improvement opportunities
4. Establish and deploy an action plan.

This process provides a *systematic approach to learning* and improvement and *benefits* the organisation by :

- Providing a framework that ties efforts together
- Providing a vehicle for identifying best practices
- Providing a structure for sharing knowledge and learning methods and techniques others have used to make improvements
- Allowing employees to speak the same language of quality, thereby increasing communication and organisational alignment towards common goals.
- Fostering teamwork across the company.
- Improving the ability to measure improvements by documenting processes and results.
- Providing a process to accelerate improvement across the organisation and
- Involving every employee in continuous improvement towards world-class benchmarks.

Exhibit 10.7 : Texas Instrument's Approach to Quality (Baldrige Award Winner)

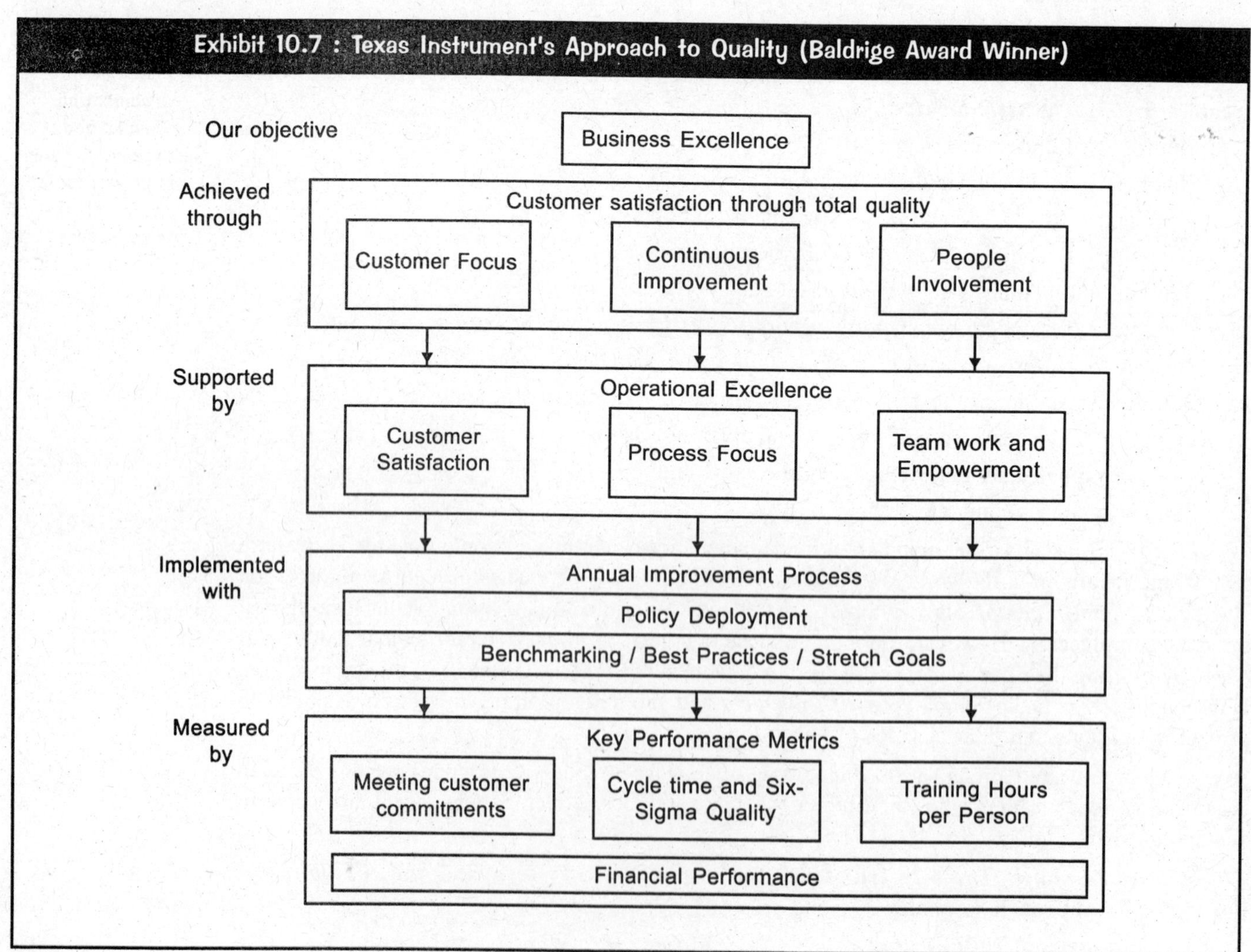

10.21 CASE ILLUSTRATION

"The Eastman Way" (Learning Organisation)

Eastman Chemical Company recognises that **people create quality.** This is embodied in a philosophy known as **"The Eastman Way"**, which describes a culture based on key beliefs and principles of respect, cooperation, fairness, trust and teamwork. Developing such a culture depends not only on learning how to recognise and reward behaviour, but also understanding the processes and procedures that work against achieving corporate goals. **"The Eastman Way" philosophy is described below. (Refer *Box 10.15*)**

Box 10.15 : "The Eastman Way"

Eastman people are the key to success. Eastman people recognise the importance of treating each other fairly and with respect. They enhance these beliefs by building upon the following values and principles :

Honesty and integrity : Honesty is exhibited through relationships with co-workers, customers, suppliers and neighbours. Their goal is truth in all relationships.

Fairness : Treat each other as one is expected to be treated.

Trust : Respect and rely on each other. Fair treatment, honesty in relationships and confidence in each other create trust.

Team-work : People are empowered to manage their areas of responsibility. They work together to achieve common goals for business success.

Diversity : People value different points of view of divergent work-force. They create an environment that enables all employees to reach their full potential in pursuit of company objectives.

Employee well being : Employees are provided with a safe, healthy and desirable work-place. Stability of employment is given high priority. Growth in employee skill is essential. Recognition for contributions and full utilisation of employee's capabilities promote job satisfaction.

Citizenship : Employees are valued by their community for their contributions as individuals and as a company.

Winning attitude : Employees' "can-do" attitude and desire for excellence drive continual improvement, making them winners in everything they do.

Milestones in the "Quality Journey" of Eastman

- **1970** : Eastman got a wake-up-call when a key customer told the company that its product was not as good as its competitors and indicated that if things didn't change, Eastman would lose business. Eastman realised that customer feed-back was essential for survival.
- **1983** : Eastman developed a ***quality policy*** and began training its employees in statistical process control, flow charting and other basic quality control tools.
- **1985** : Eatman started a **"quality management process"**, that focussed on internal and external customers and suppliers and the application of Deming (PDSA) Cycle.
- **1986** : Senior managers implemented their **own quality management process,** focussing on understanding customer needs and satisfaction measurements.
- **1987** : Eastman focussed on ***"employee empowerment"*** and discovered that a company cannot empower employees who don't care, don't have authority and don't have appropriate skills. Efforts to overcome these obstacles were addressed.
- **1988** : Eastman applied for Baldrige Award.
- **1989** : Quality systems were registered to **ISO 9000** and Eastman implemented a process, evaluation, control and improvement system.
- **1990** : Eastman assessed all its divisions using the Baldrige criteria, **changed its employee appraisal system, moving from ranking to development.**
- **1991** : Eastman developed its **vision: to be the world's preferred chemical suppliers.** Accomplishing this vision required measuring performance in areas such as customer satisfaction, employee morale, supplier co-operation and local community support.

- **1992** : Eastman implemented a **supplier recognition program** and began helping suppliers in their own quality efforts.
- **1993** : **Eastman received the Baldrige Award.**

Road Blocks Identified by Eastman During its Quality Journey

- **Focus of losing the job:** The company promised never to lay anyone off because of quality improvement.
- **The performance appraisal system:** Although those rated near the top complained, it was a clear disincentive to the majority of the workforce.
- **The employee suggestion system:** The original system rewarded individual with money which interfered with suggestions for improvement by teams.

Seven steps used by Eastman for Accelerated Continuous Improvement

1. **Focus and pinpoint:** Getting everyone to have the same goal and specifying in measurable terms what is expected of them.
2. **Communicate:** Company wide communication by publicising key result areas, the vision and mission statement.
3. **Translate and link:** Teams translate the company wide objectives into their own language and environment.
4. **Create a management action plan:** Management creates a plan with specific actions to reach a goal including metrics to measure success.
5. **Improve processes:** Teams use a six-step process similar to Juran's improvement process discussed in chapter 10.
6. **Measure progress and provide feedback:** Eastman's rule include:
   - Feedback should be visual, frequent, simple and specific.
   - The baseline performance should be shown for comparison.
   - The past, current period and future goals should be posted.
   - The best-ever score should be posted.
   - A chart should be immediately understandable.
   - A good score-card allows comments and annotations.
7. **Reinforce behaviours and celebrates results:** Eastman reinforces the learning that leads to positive results by encouraging teams at celebrations to answer the questions ; What did you do? Why did it work? Why is it important for the customer, the company and the team? How did a team accomplish its achievement?

10.22 QUALITY IN PRACTICE

Box 10.16 : Sustaining Leadership through Quality Strategy – Xerox 2000

As Xerox Corporation transformed its company vision to **"The Document Company"** in the early 1990s, it made some radical changes in its organisation and leadership system. In addition to changing the organisational structures, Xerox formed the basis for its successful turnaround.

The strategy for Xerox-2000 (termed as **reaffirmation strategy**) emphasised the company's commitment to basic **"Leadership Through Quality"** plan but broadened the scope to one that better integrates TQ into all aspects of daily business operations.

Xerox identified two critical objectives:

- Profitable revenue growth and • World-class productivity.

Elements of Xerox-2000 were:

- Team-based quality improvements
- Quantum improvements instead of gradual improvements

- Use of specific process improvement initiatives, employee involvement programs and quality tools
- Use of a range of business policies and programs and
- Use of quality intensification efforts and benchmarking.

Xerox created the Xerox Management Model as a tool box for all Xerox employees. It has been described as a ***Holistic Management Model*** because it addresses every aspect of work – planning, creating, leading, managing, changing, organising, communicating and rewarding. (Refer *Exhibit 10.8*)

Exhibit 10.8 : Xerox Management Model

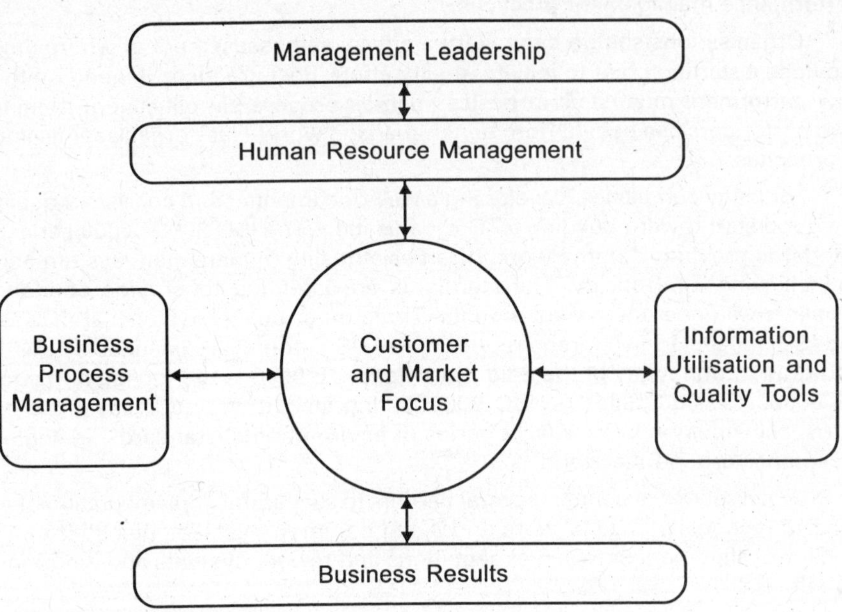

A description of the six categories follows:

1. **Management Leadership:** Xerox Management displays a customer focus, exhibits role model behaviour, establishes clear long-term goals and annual objectives, establishes strategic boundaries and provides an empowered environment to achieve world-class productivity.
2. **Human Resource Management:** Xerox Management leads, motivates, develops and empowers people to realise their full potential. All employees are personally responsible for continuously learning and acquiring competencies required to achieve business objectives and to continuously improve productivity for customers and Xerox.
3. **Business Process Management:** Business processes are redesigned to be customer driven, cross-functional and value based. They create knowledge, eliminate waste and abandon unproductive work, yielding world-class productivity and higher perceived – service levels for customers.
4. **Information Utilisation and Quality Tools:** Fact - based management is led by the line management. It is achieved through accurate and timely information and by the disciplined application and widespread use of quality tools.
5. **Customer and Market Focus:** Current, past and potential customers define the business. Xerox recognises and creates markets by identifying patterns of customer requirements. By anticipating and fully satisfying those requirements through the creation of customer value, Xerox achieves its business results.
6. **Business Results:** Business results are determined by how well Xerox performs in the first five categories.

Xerox employees use the model to define the processes, individual roles and responsibilities at regular operations reviews, for coaching and training employees, in management meetings, for identifying internal benchmarks and best practices; and as the foundation for business assessments and certification. By using the new strategy as its guide, Xerox is preparing its people to grow the company's business results, productivity and quality performance.

10.23 SUMMARY

Companies adopt total quality to react to competitive threats or take advantage of perceived opportunities. In most cases, companies act to overcome threats and change the company's culture. Successful adoption of TQ requires : *(i)* readiness for change, *(ii)* sound practices and implementation strategies and *(iii)* an effective organisation.

Implementation of TQ requires changing the corporate culture. Change is easier when management has a clear vision, a focus on customers and continuous improvement, strong measurement, cross functional orientation and high employee morale.

Designing an effective organisational infrastructure requires understanding of best practices, a process-oriented quality assurance system and a process for continuous evolution toward high-performance management practices.

Organisations should begin with a critical self-assessment of where it stands. Self assessment provides a starting point to initiate quality effort. Best practices depend on the level of performance. Low performers must stick to basics such as process simplification, training and teamwork while high performers can benefit from bench-marking world-class organisations and using more advanced approaches.

For many companies, developing a well-documented and consistent quality management system is a good start toward building a TQ organisation. The ISO 9000 : 2000 series of international quality standards provides a frame work for a basic quality management system and a good starting point for achieving total quality. The standards are intended to provide confidence to customers that suppliers will meet their requirements. Three other quality systems are QS 9000, TE 9000, AS 9000 and ISO 14000. QS 9000, required by major US automakers includes all ISO 9000 requirements but also draws upon many of the Baldrige criteria. TE 9000 is the tooling and equipment supplement to QS 9000. AS 9000 builds on ISO 9000 adding insight and addressing the distinctive needs of the aerospace industry. ISO 14000, a series of environmental standards, is beginning to gain increased acceptance around the world.

Organisations encounter several barriers to successful implementation of total quality. Companies need to recognise these barriers and avoid common mistakes that shift quality efforts, particularly the lack of alignment between expectations and reward systems and ignoring the financial impact of TQ efforts.

Sustaining total quality requires both an understanding of why quality efforts fail in some organisations and the ability to develop into a "learning organisation". Organisation must continue to learn and adapt to changing environments. Learning is a key aspect of the Baldrige criteria, thus, it is not surprising that Baldrige winners have demonstrated continual improvement and the ability to change successfully.

10.24 KEY WORDS USED

Corporate Culture, Quality System, ISO 9000:2000 Standards, Process Approach, Management Responsibility Resource Management, Process Management, Certification Audit, Surveiliance Audit, Recertification Audit, Environmental Management System, ISO 14000 standards, QS 9000 standards, TE 9000 standards, ASO 9000 standards, Environmental Management Audit, Learning Organisation, Team Learning,

10.25 OBJECTIVE QUESTIONS

(A) Match the following :

Column A	Column B
1. Quality improvement	1. Revised version of ISO 9001:2000
2. ISO 9001:2008	2. Environmental Management Systems
3. AS 9000	3. Worker involvement
4. ISO 14001	4. Peter Senge
5. Laws of Fifth Discipline	5. Aerospace industry quality system

(B) State whether following statements are True or False :

1. What is really required in TQM is a total change in thinking, not a new collection of quality tools (T / F)
2. Process control is the first phase in the evolution of quality system (T / F)
3. QMS follows a process orientation with Deming's 'P-D-C-A' Cycle (T / F)
4. If total quality does not occur at the workforce level, it will not occur at all (T / F)
5. Senge's "Laws of Fifth Discipline" has no relevance with a learning organisation.

(C) Multiple choice Questions : Choose the correct answer from the alternatives given under each question :

1. Self assessment for total quality should address the following :
   (a) Management involvement and leadership
   (b) Product and process design (c) Product control and quality improvement
   (d) employee participation, education and training
   (e) Customer and supplier communication and quality information
   (f) All of these (g) None of these
2. The levels in the documentation pyramid of a quality system include:
   (a) Policy (b) Procedures
   (c) Work instruction or practice (d) Records of proof
   (e) All of these (f) None of these
3. ISO 14011 is a part of:
   (a) Environmental Management System (b) Environmental Auditing
   (c) Environmental Performance Evaluation
   (d) All of these (e) None of these
4. __________ is an interpretation and extension of ISO 9000 for automotive suppliers
   (a) AS 9000 (b) TE 9000
   (c) QS 9000 (d) ISO 14001
   (e) None of these.
5. Systems thinking is a part of ________
   (a) Malcolm Baldrige National Quality Award
   (b) Senge's Laws of Fifth Discipline (c) Demings 14 Points for management
   (d) Crosby's philosophy (e) None of these.

10.26 REVIEW QUESTIONS

1. Explain the terms "Corporate culture" and "Organisational change".
2. How can an organisation develop a TQ supportive corporate culture?
3. Discuss the "quality engines" of Baldrige winners. Why do they differ?
4. "Organisations should begin with a critical self-assessment of where it stands" – Explain.
5. State the purpose of ISO 9000 aeries standards.
6. What are the objectives of ISO 9000 : 2000
7. Explain the structure of ISO 9000 : 2000
8. State the benefits of ISO 9000 certification.
9. What is the purpose and scope of ISO 14000 standards?
10. Explain what is meant by Total Quality Environmental Management (TQEM).
11. Discuss the barriers to successful TQ implementation.

12. What is a "learning organisation"? Why is the concept important to total quality?
13. Explain what is meant by building a fear-free organisation.
14. Discuss the role of senior management middle management and employees in the implementation of total quality strategy.
15. Discuss the role of senior management, middle management and employers in the implementation of total quality strategy.

10.27 DISCUSSION QUESTIONS

1. "What is required in TQM is a total change in thinking, not a new collection of quality tools" –Explain.
2. "Culture reflected by the management policies and action that a company practices" – Discuss the statement
3. "A successful quality strategy needs to fit within the existing organisation culture" – Comment
4. Discuss the principles of ISO 9000:2000 Quality Management System.
5. "The best way to deal with change is to product it and prepare a response" – Elaborate.

10.28 ASSIGNMENTS

1. Find an organisation - manufacturing or service oriented, which has implemented ISO 9000 or Six-Sigma. Prepare a report on the implementation issues and challenges that the organisation faced. Find out how did they address those issues and challenges and what was the result of their efforts.
2. List some key factors that differentiate quality implementation among small and large companies. Find out what things would smaller companies do better than large companies?

10.29 CHAPTER CASE

ADVANCED LASER TECHNOLOGY INC.

Preeti and her husband have a small, highly successful firm that serves a narrow niche of medical applications of laser technologies. The firm has only four customers, but each is a leading player in the emerging medical-electronics technology markets. Each firm has told Preeti that it is pleased with her product, service and ability to provide leading edge technology.

Preeti's problem begins in the form of a memo from one of her major customers who has just decided to seek ISO 9000 certification to effectively compete in international markets. Preeti understands this logic of her customer. As part of the ISO 9000 certification process, the customer expects each of his key suppliers to become ISO 9000 certified. What little Preeti knows about ISO 9000 certification is that this new requirement would pose enormous problems for Advanced Laser Technology which has only five employees including Preeti and her engineer husband. How will Advance Laser Technology Inc., be able to document all that it did. It seems to be a catch 22 situation. If Preeti and her husband divert their attention to document all the 20 aspects of section 4 of ISO 9000, then the firm risks losing its competitive edge in this fast changing technological field. If ALT hires a consultant to help with this certification process, it risks diverting both management attention and critical cash resources to the certification process. As she reflects on this dilemma, Preeti wonders "How does this add value to ALT?"

Discussion Question :

1. What would you recommend to Preeti?

CHAPTER 11

PROCESS MANAGEMENT

LEARNING OBJECTIVES

After reading this chapter, you should be able to:

- Understand the meaning and scope of process management.
- Discuss the approaches to product design processes.
- Discuss the various design concepts and techniques.
- Discuss the various phases in product design process.
- Understand the terms: "quality engineering", "system design" and "parameter design".
- Describe how the product development process is streamlined.
- Discuss the need for process improvement.
- Discuss the various process improvement methods.
- Discuss the concept of benchmarking, types of benchmarking and benefits of benchmarking.

11.0 INTROUDCTION

Processes such as product design, manufacturing and distribution are the building blocks of work. Deming and Juran observed that while majority of the quality problems are associated with processes, few are caused by workers themselves. No purpose is served by blaming individual workers for some thing over which they do not have any control. It is the management who should share the responsibility with the workforce – to continuously improve the processes with which individuals work.

Process management involves planning and administering the activities necessary to achieve a high level of performance in a process and identifying opportunities for improving quality and operational performance and ultimately customer satisfaction. It involves the design, control and improvement of key business processes. Design focusses on the prevention of poor quality by ensuring that products meet customer requirements and that production/delivery processes are capable of achieving high levels of performance. Any process performance measure naturally fluctuates around some average level. Abnormal conditions cause an unusual deviation from this pattern. Removal of the causes of such abnormal conditions and maintaining level performance is the essence of control. Improvement involves changing the performance to a new level which is better than the existing level of performance. Process management activities help to prevent defects and errors, eliminate waste and redundancy and thereby lead to better quality and improved company performance through shorter cycle times, improved flexibility and faster customer responsiveness. **The methodology for process management is based on the following principles:**

Process Management activities help to
(i) prevent defects and errors
(ii) eliminate waste and redundancy
(iii) improve quality and company performance.
(iv) reduce cycle times.
(v) improve flexibility and
(vi) speed up customer responsiveness.

- Process quality improvement focusses on the end-to-end process.
- The mind-set of quality is one of prevention of defects and continuous improvement.
- Every one manages a process at some level and is simultaneously a customer and a supplier.
- Customer needs to drive process quality improvement.
- Corrective action focusses on removing the root cause of the problem rather than on treating its symptoms.
- Process simplification reduces opportunities for errors and rework.
- Process quality improvement results from a disciplined and structured application of the quality management principles.

11.1 THE SCOPE OF PROCESS MANAGEMENT

A process is a sequence of activities that is intended to achieve some result, typically to create added value for customers.

A process is a unique combination of elements, conditions or causes that collectively produces a given outcome or set of results.

The components of a process may be classified as 7 'Ms' – Materials (raw materials and components), **Manpower** (people-power), **Methods** (product design, process design and operating procedures), **Machines** (tools and equipments used in the process), **Measurement** (techniques and tools used to gather process performance data), **Maintenance** (the system for providing care for process components, including training of people), and **Management** (policy, work rules and environment).

Process components change over time, one worker replaces another, materials come from a different supplier, a machine and its cutting tools are changed, a different maintenance schedule is started and so on. This can result in constant process restabilisation, with quality losses and costs each time.

Process performance (output, intended or incidental) depends on how the process has been designed, built or installed, operated and maintained. ***Box 11.1*** **describes what is meant by the term "process".**

Box 11.1 : What is a Process?

We define a process as "a systematic series of actions directed to the achievement of a goal".

A process should be :

- **Goal oriented :** To plan for quality, we must first establish the quality goals and standards we are trying to reach.
- **Systematic :** The 'actions' that make up a process are all interconnected and interdependent. They are also progressive, they follow a designated sequence.
- **Capable :** The proper end results of the planning is a process capable of meeting the goals under operating conditions.
- **Legitimate :** The process is evolved through authorised channels.

Varieties of processes

- Launching new products
- Filling customer's orders
- Producing goods
- Performing various tasks and operations
- Recruiting new employees
- Providing manufacturing facilities
- Providing customer service
- Maintaining control during operations.

Common business processes include acquiring customer and market knowledge, fulfilling customer orders, purchasing, new product or service development, strategic planning, production or service delivery, distribution, research and development, information management, performance measurement and training and the like. The important business processes that affect customer satisfaction fall into four categories: *(i)* Design processes, *(ii)* Production/delivery processes, *(iii)* Support processes, and *(iv)* Supplier processes.

Process Management encompasses all important business processes throughout the value chain - value creation processes (core processes) and support processes.

Design processes: Design processes include both the design of the product as well as the production/delivery processes that create or deliver the product. Poor product design will kill the market potential, no matter how well a manufactured product is made or service is delivered. Product design involves all activities that are performed to incorporate customer requirements into the product's functional specifications and thus defines its fitness for use. Careful attention to the design of production/service processes ensures that the product will conform to design specifications and be produced economically and efficiently. Design has a great influence on the efficiency of the manufacture as well as on the flexibility of service strategies and therefore must be coordinated with production/delivery process. The ultimate value of the product, and hence, the perceived quality to the consumer, depends on these design processes.

Design and production/delivery processes that drive the creation of products and services, are critical to customer satisfaction, have a major impact on the strategic goals of an organisation and are generally known as ***core processes***. On the other hand, processes that are critical to the operation of a business, but generally do not add value directly to a product or service are known as ***support processes***. Core processes are essential to adding values to products and services and hence require a higher level of attention than do support processes. In general, core processes are driven by ***external* customer** needs while support processes are driven by ***internal*** customer needs.

Process management is viewed according to the three levels of quality *viz.* ***organisational level, process level*** and the ***performer level***. At the ***organisational level***, quality concerns centre on meeting external customer requirements. The organisation must seek customer input on a regular basis. Customer-driven performance standards should be used as bases for goal setting, problem solving, performance appraisal, incentive compensation, non-financial rewards and resource allocation.

Process management is viewed according to the three levels of quality: *(i)* Organisational level, *(ii)* Process level and *(iii)* Performer level.

At the ***process level***, organisational units are classified as functions or departments, such as marketing, design, product development, operations, finance, purchasing and so on.

At the ***performer level*** (sometimes called the job level or task-design level), standards for output must be based on quality and customer-service requirements that originate at the organisational and process levels. These standards include requirements for such things as accuracy, completeness, innovation, timeliness and cost.

Major core and support processes are generally defined at the organisational level and these require attention by senior managers. Each major process consists of many sub-processes that are managed by functional managers or cross-functional teams. Each sub-process consists of many specific work steps performed by individuals at the performer level.

To apply the techniques of process management, process must be *(i)* Repeatable and *(ii)* Measurable. ***Repeatability*** means that the process must recur over time. The cycle may be long or short. Repeatability ensures that enough data can be collected to reveal useful information which is obtained through measurement. Information obtained through measurement reveals patterns about the process performance. In turn, the ability to predict performance facilitates the detection of out-of-control conditions and the search for improvements.

Process management practices: Process management requires a disciplined effort involving all managers and workers in an organisation. **Some of the practices shared by world leaders in quality are listed below:**

Process management requires a disciplined effort involving all managers and workers in an organisation. It consists of three key activities: design, control, and improvement

(i) They translate customer requirements into product and service design requirements, early in the design process, taking into account linkages between product design requirements and manufacturing process requirements, supplier capabilities and legal and environmental issues.

(ii) They ensure that quality is built into products and services and use appropriate engineering and statistical tools and approaches during the development process.

(iii) They manage the product development process to enhance cross-functional communication, reduce product development time and ensure trouble-free introduction of products and services.

(iv) They define and document important production/delivery and support processes and manage them as important business activities.

(v) They define performance requirements for suppliers, ensure that requirements are met and develop partnering relationships with key suppliers.

(vi) They control the quality and operational performance of key processes and use systematic methods to identify significant variations in operational performance and output quality, determine root causes, make corrections and verify results and

(vii) They continuously improve processes to achieve better quality, cycle time and overall operational performance. ***Exhibit 11.1*** **illustrates the structured product development process.**

Exhibit 11.1 : Structured Product Development Process

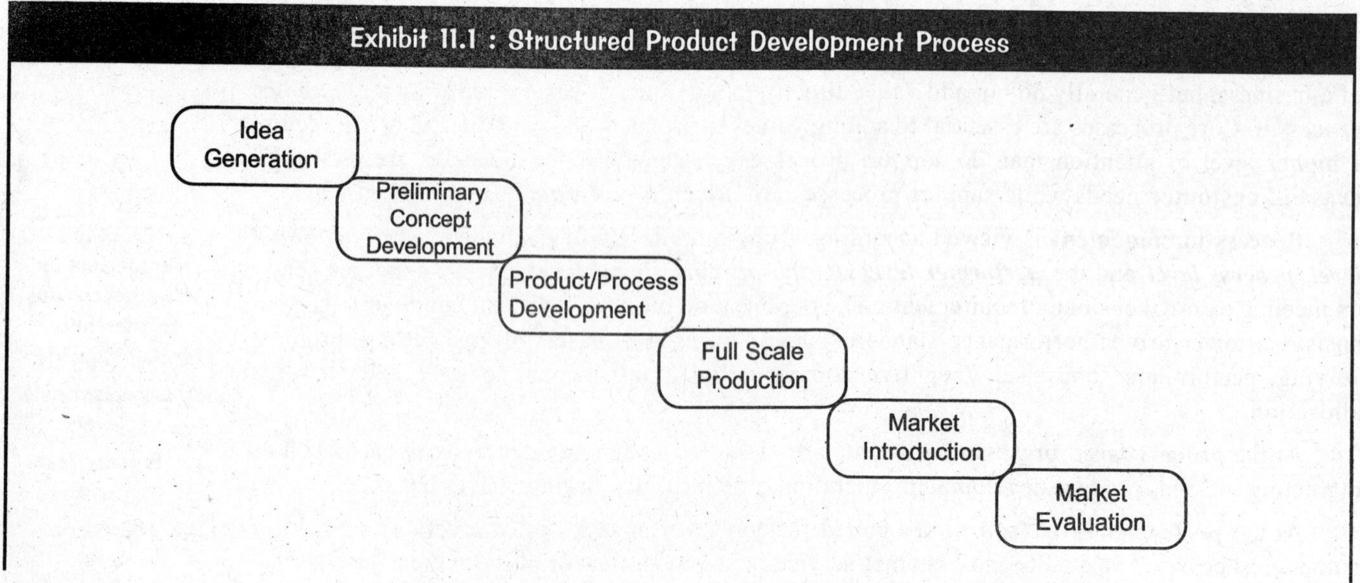

Companies today face incredible pressures to continually improve the quality of their products, while simultaneously reducing costs, to meet ever increasing legal and environmental requirements and to shorten life-cycles to meet changing consumer needs and remain competitive.

Product Development Processes

Six phases of a typical structured product development process are:

(i) **Idea Generation:** New or redesigned product ideas should incorporate customer needs and expectations.

(ii) **Preliminary Concept Development:** New ideas are studied for feasibility, addressing such questions as: *(i)* Will the product meet customers' requirements? *(ii)* Can it be manufactured economically with high quality? One tool for assisting in this step is **"Quality Function Deployment" (QFD).**

(iii) **Product/Process Development:** If an idea survives the concept stage, then the actual design process begins by determining engineering specifications for all materials, components and parts. This phase usually includes prototype testing, in which a model (real or simulated) is constructed to test the product's physical attributes or use under actual operating conditions, as well as customer's reactions to the prototypes.

(iv) **Full Scale Production:** If prototypes are acceptable to customers, the product design is released for scale production.

(v) **Market Introduction:** The product is distributed to the customers.

(vi) **Market Evaluation:** An ongoing product development process should rely on market evaluation and customer feedback to initiate continuous improvements.

"Old way" of product design (Traditional way)	New way of product design (TQM way)
• Design the product	• Design the product (With appropriate tests)
• Make the product	• Make it and test it in the laboratory and in the production.
• Try to sell it	• Put it in the market
	• Test it in service through market research, find out what the user thinks of it and why the non-user has not bought it.
	• Redesign the product, in light of common reactions to quality and price.

11.2 PRODUCT DESIGN PROCESSES

Product design refers to either a physical manufactured product or a service. A fast response organisation constantly looks for new product concepts that meet market needs and exploit the full potential of its resources. To survive the intense competition among products, a firm must provide what the customers want. Product designers face a hard challenge because changes in technology, consumer preferences and competitive conditions force them to aim at target customers. New product development is a crucial part of business. New products serve to provide growth opportunities and a competitive advantage for the firm. Increasingly, companies face a challenge to introduce new products more quickly without sacrificing quality.

Product design can significantly affect the cost of manufacturing redesign, warranty, and field repair, the efficiency by which product can be manufactured, and the quality of the out put.

New product design greatly affects operations by specifying the products that will be made, it is a prerequisite for production to occur. At the same time, existing processes and products can constrain the technology available for new products. Thus, new products must be designed with not only the market in mind, but also the production process that will be used to make the product.

Managing Customer Expectations: To effectively manage customer expectations, a firm must not only know what the customers want but also how they are likely to behave. This requires the marketing function to provide a thorough understanding of the customer's latest demands. The product innovation process must identify the set of trade-offs that will permit the firm to create and deliver a product that exceeds the expectations of target customers, while it meets the expectations of the corporate management for profitability.

Designing Products that Meets Customer's Needs

The new product development is often a sequential *(over the wall)* process in which information flows predominantly downstream and the production area is on the receiving end of the new product design. ***Exhibit 11.2* illustrates the sequential approach to product design.**

Exhibit 11.2 : The Sequential Approach To Product Design

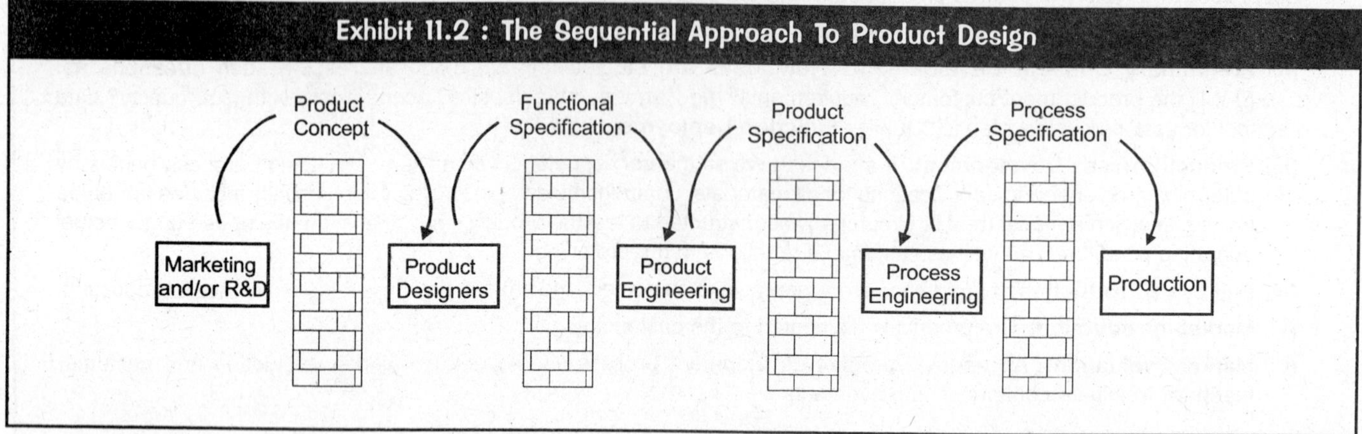

Two approaches to product design are: *(i)* "over the wall" approach and *(ii)* concurrent or simultaneous engineering approach.

Marketing or Research and Development (R & D) is frequently a source of a new product concept. Product designers convert the new product concept into a set of functional specifications. Functional specifications outline how the product should work, the features that should be included, its costs and other details. Functional specifications reflect market, legal and internal product requirements. Functional specifications are translated into product specifications which detail how the product will work. This set of specifications includes a detailed drawing of the product and a description of the parts and materials used. Manufacturing or process engineers then develop process specifications which indicate how the product should be manufactured.

The development costs associated with the ***"over the wall"* approach** is high and also the recurring costs of manufacturing the product tend to be high as well. Studies have shown that although the design of a product accounts for only about 5 percent of the total cost, its impact on costs (quality, manufacturing and equipment modification and technology acquisition) is so great that it influences at least 70 percent of the product's total costs.

An alternative to this approach has been very successful in today's competitive environment. This approach is called ***concurrent* or *simultaneous engineering* or *concurrent design.***

***Box 11.2* describes the two approaches to product design.**

Box 11.2 : Approaches to Product Design

Over-the-wall design	Concurrent (Team) Design
• Becomes common practice as organisation grows and splits into functional departments	• Tends to be common practice in very small organisations and where product redesign occur often.
• Common, especially, in businesses, with long product lines (little urgency to develop new proudcts)	• Elevated competition has made it common in consumer electronics, cars, consumer credit, mortgage loans and so on.
• Tends to be slow	• Is fast and avoids problems (design rework) stemming from poor co-ordination and lack of shared information.
• Tends to require several costly rounds of debugging.	

Concurrent Engineering: Concurrent engineering brings together representatives from various functional areas to simultaneously design a product and the process by which it should be made.

Concurrent engineering is an organisational tool that facilitates integration. It breaks down the traditional barriers – organisational walls, time and geography, separating product and process design. **Instead functional, product and process specifications are developed concurrently. This is illustrated in *Exhibit 11.3* shown below.**

Exhibit 11.3 : Concurrent Engineering

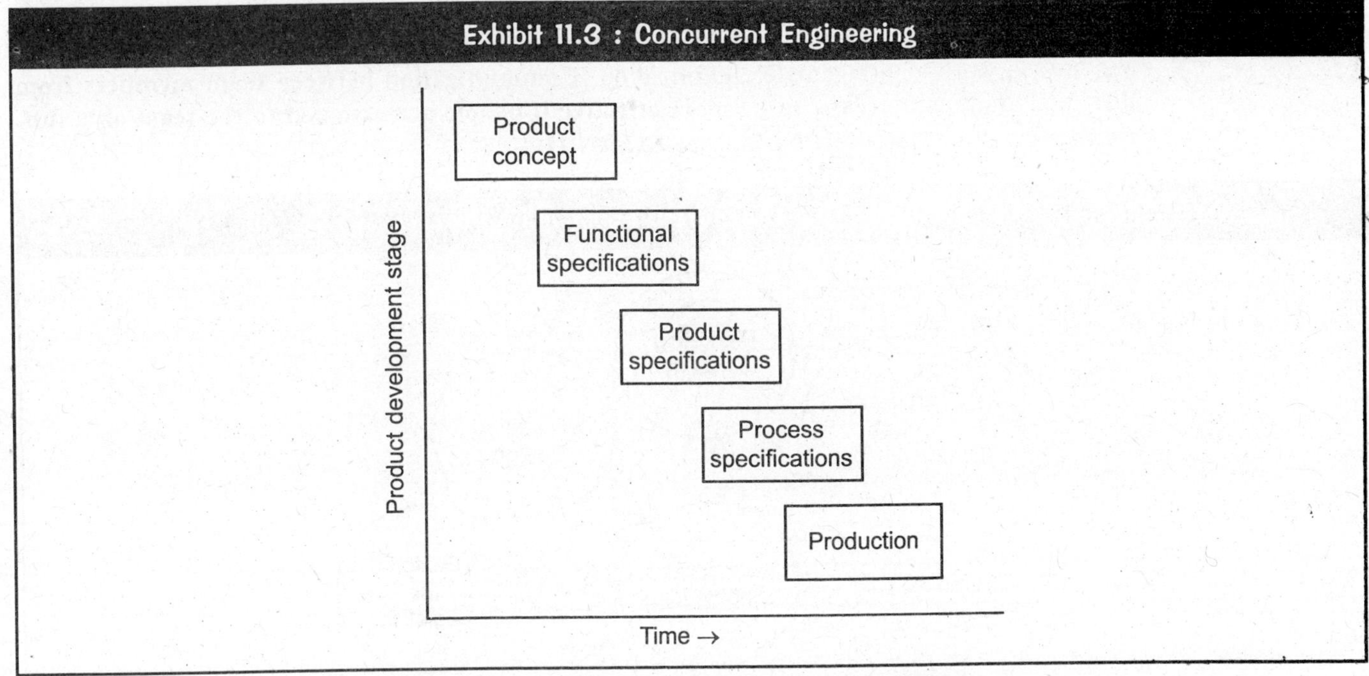

Ideally, concurrent engineering involves a firm's customers and suppliers, along with representatives from a broad range of functional areas within the firm. Including customer's representatives on the design team helps ensure that a product that really meets their needs will be developed the first time.

Concurrent engineering is a process in which all major functions involved with bringing a product to market are continuously involved with product development from conception through sales.

Since suppliers frequently have a great impact on product cost and quality, involving them from the day one of the design process makes sense. Representatives from marketing and production are also included on concurrent engineering teams. Marketing can supply valuable information on the intended customer market, production can provide feedback on the possible manufacture of product design and the feasibility of process designs. Purchasing, finance, R & D and other functional areas also can contribute valuable information and may be represented on the design team.

The speed with which products can be designed and introduced into the market is perhaps the greatest contribution of concurrent engineering. Receiving input from the various functional areas early saves a significant amount of time. Time is also saved because work on functional, product and process specifications is not performed in a strictly sequential manner, each area overlaps with adjacent activities. And because product quality is much higher, the firm's ***break-even time*** (measured from the day work begins on the product's functional specifications until the day cumulative profits for the product equal the total development investment) is much shorter.

Concurrent engineering enables the manufacturers to cut product development time considerably for new products. But the question to be answered is – "How can a firm move from an ***"over the wall"*** approach to a ***concurrent engineering*** **approach** to product and process design?" The transition involves much more than creating ***cross-functional*** teams. Major changes in the way functional areas operate and communicate are essential. **The traditional areas of responsibility, lines of authority and reward systems have to be reformulated as stated below:**

- Functional managers must delegate decision-making authority to their representative on the team so that they can review, modify and approve designs quickly. Lines of authority and reporting relationships must be reviewed and realigned.

- Any adversarial relationships that exist between functional areas must be overcome, and the status of each area must be equalised.
- Changes in the reward structure are made to encourage teamwork rather than individual efforts and also to minimise the possibility of inconsistent functional goals.

Functional specialists have to learn how to communicate effectively with specialists from other areas. They also have to learn how to share their work before it is finished, how to criticise and how to work with incomplete information. **Communication between team members from different functional areas can be more effective if people are assigned to the team on a full-time rather than part-time basis.** ***(See Exhibit 11.4).***

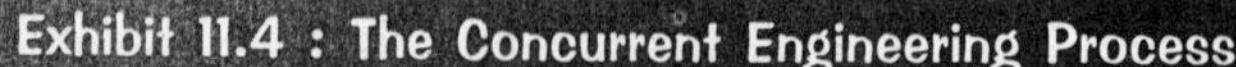

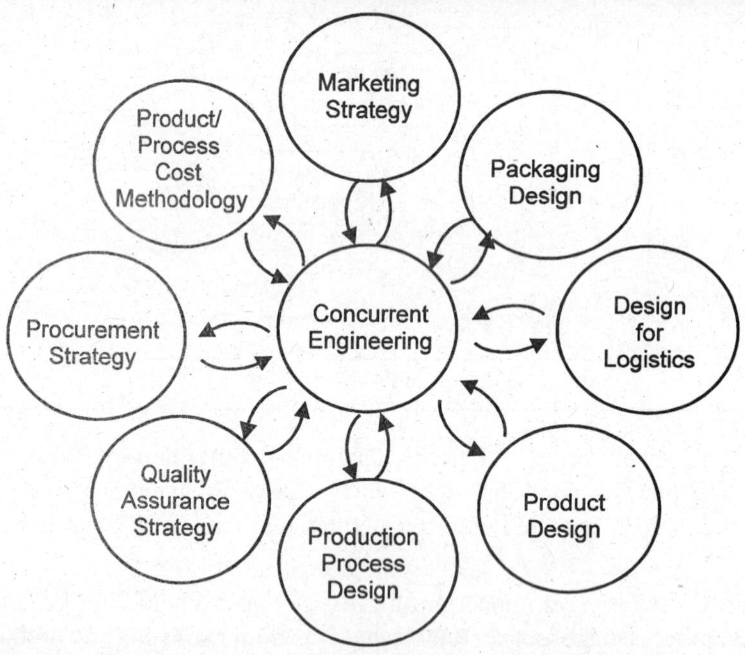

Concurrent Engineering

Concurrent engineering, also called **simultaneous engineering,** is a TQM design tool that brings together representatives from all of the functions involved in designing, producing, delivering and selling a product to contribute to its initial design. This forms a team with members from marketing, operations management, purchasing, logistics, human resource management and finance.

The ***critical objectives*** of concurrent engineering are:

(i) ***To spot a variety of potential problems*** in the product design on paper or within the computer aided design (CAD) systems by the cross-functional team. Changes made at this stage cost less and take less time than changes made later in the product introduction process.

(ii) **To improve the** ***overall quality*** **of the product** as it reduces the production cost. The design team identifies and eliminates potential problems at the design stage. This reduces the time required to solve those problems at a later stage, reduces errors and burden of reworking rejects, reduces inventory needs and reduces the cost.

(iii) To reduce the total cycle time from design to full-scale production. This speeds overall time to market as part of a ***fast to market*** competitive strategy.

Three types of teams are common in concurrent engineering approach:

- a program ***management*** team
- a ***technical*** team and
- numerous ***design-build*** teams.

Depending on the complexity of the project, an ***integration*** team may be needed to consolidate the efforts of various design-build teams. Task forces may be formed to address specific problems, such as investigating an emerging technology.

Benefits of the concurrent engineering approach are mainly from the reduced time to complete a project because of parallel completion of project phases – *for example,* simultaneously developing market concepts, product design, manufacturing process and product support structure.

Design-The First Step to Quality: Design is one of the basic management functions. A chronic weakness among many companies is under-management of design and development. Problems in design, in turn, ripple into operations. Quality suffers, processing delays and costs increase. Customers may look for competitor's products and services.

Design is the first step to quality. The quality of goods and services and the processes that provide them – begin during the initial design activities. ***Exhibit 11.5* shows how an interactive action cycle of design, discovery and improvement provides quality.**

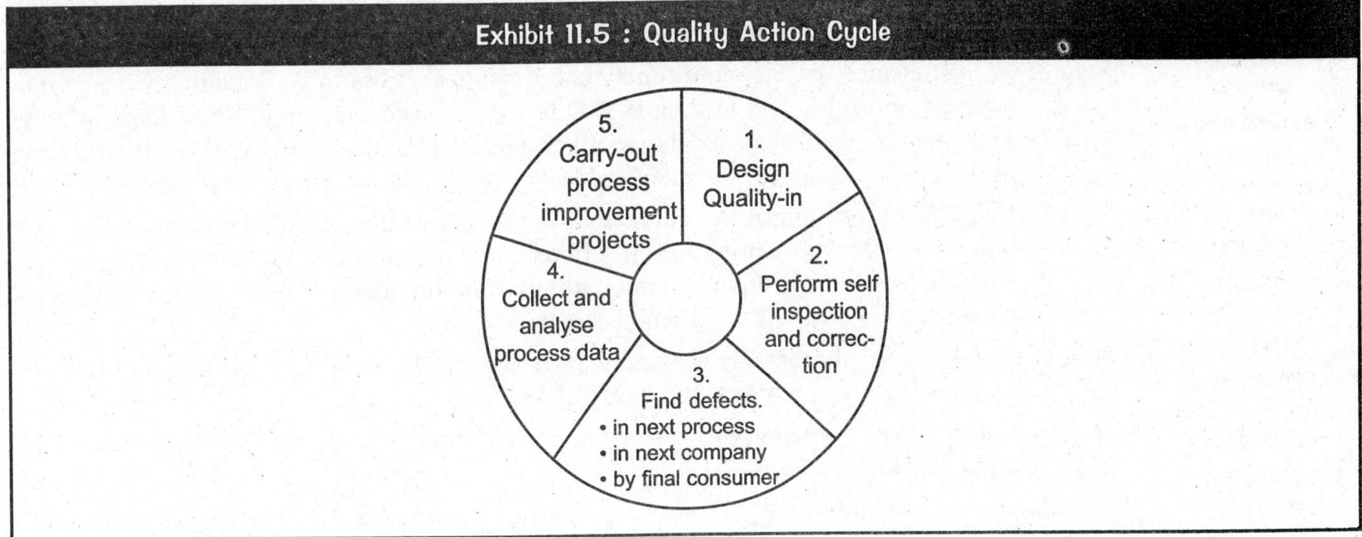

Since new features stem from market feedback or reflect advances in technology, designs that incorporate those features are likely to advance quality in the eyes of customers. Thus a strong design program, including the one that wins prestigious design awards, is itself one mark of organisational quality. The ideal way to attain quality is to have perfectly designed outputs that are created without defect or variation by perfectly functioning processes.

Comprehensive Design Program

***Exhibit 11.6* presents a model for a comprehensive design program which contains six integrated and overlapping parts.**

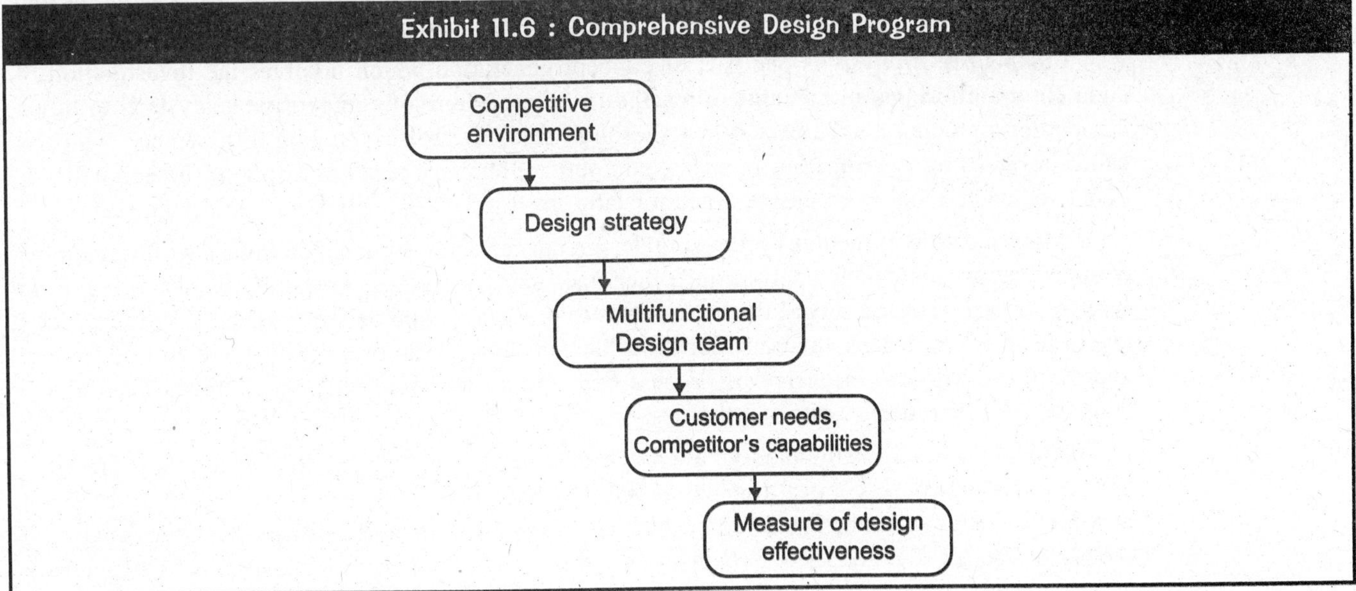

The various steps involved are:

Step 1: Senior managers decide which business to pursue and then select products and services to offer within the chosen industries. This determines the overall ***competitive environment*** in which the firm will operate.

Step 2: The firm's ***design strategy*** must be positioned and implemented within that competitive environment. This requires continuous ***environmental scanning* and *analysis*** with specific focus on customer's changing needs and wants and competitor's shifting abilities and weaknesses. Environmental changes often revoke modifications in business strategy which in turn may result in the reformulation of design strategy.

The various steps involved in a comprehensive design program are:
(i) Determining competitive environment in which to operate
(ii) Formulating the design strategy
(iii) Organising a multi functional design team
(iv) Collecting customer and competitor data (QFD approach)
(v) Deciding the design objectives and
(iv) Measuring effectiveness of design program.

Step 3: With strategies set, the multi-functional design team goes to work putting strategy into action. Companies with leading R & D programs make use of multi-functional or cross functional team concepts to address all of the historical design weaknesses. When teams also include customers and suppliers, design efforts become fully sensitised.

Step 4: Collection of customer and competitor data has an effect on design strategy and also plays a tactical role during design efforts. *For example*, information about customers and competitors is incorporated into **"quality function deployment"** – one of the design team's tools which will be discussed in next chapter.

Step 5: Effective design programs need guidelines and targets in the form of **design objectives** to overcome the traditional weakness of lack of focus.

Step 6: Teams must have relevant measures of design program effectiveness. Feedback sparks improvement.

Concept development: At the heart of any design program lies the notion of ***concept development.* A *design concept* is defined as "a combination of verbal and/or prototype form that tells what is going to be changed and how the customer stands to gain (and lose)".**

Three essential parts that must exist for an idea or plan to be elevated to the status of concept are:

- **Form:** This is the physical shape, size, material content and the like of a product (tangible good). In the case of service, ***form*** is described by the steps needed to provide the service.
- **Technology:** The principles, techniques, equipment, machines, processes and so forth to be employed in creating the goods or service collectively constitutes technology.
- **Benefit:** Benefit is the value the customer plans to derive from the goods or service.

Concept generation is the beginning of the design concept development. It is a procedure which transforms a set of customer needs and target specifications into a set of possible design concepts from which the design team will select the most promising alternative.

Competitive analysis is one part of concept generation which involves the investigation of competitor's offerings. In manufacturing, the usual procedure of competitive analysis is to buy a competitor's product and subject it to a thorough study, perhaps including disassembly, which is called ***reverse engineering***. For services, competitive analysis requires going to the competitors, being served and taking extensive notes for later use by the company's service design teams.

After selection of the most promising design concept, development continues with refinement of specifications, economic analysis and other fine-tuning activities. As the design nears final form (known as ***design freeze*** stage), the focus shifts to production and delivery systems. With effective use of team-based design, the transition from design stage to the production stage will be smooth and for those who are in charge of process design and operation will have already been active contributors to the design effort at the design stage.

"Benchmarking" is the modern approach in competitive analysis. It seeks out best practices and products anywhere, not just from competitors. A ***'benchmark'*** is a standard or point of reference by which something can be measured or judged. ***"Competitive bench marking"*** involves analysing the performance and practices of best-in-class companies. Their performance becomes a benchmark to which a firm can compare its own performance and their practices are used to improve that firm's practices. More about ***"BenchMarking"*** as a practice will be discussed in a later chapter.

11.3 PRODUCT DESIGN CONCEPTS AND TECHNIQUES

Earlier in this chapter we stressed the need for product and process designers to work together (also known as concurrent design or concurrent engineering or simultaneous engineering). **We discuss various approaches to design in the following paragraphs.**

Design for Manufacture (DFM)

Design for Manufacture (DFM) is both a process by which a product can be designed and a set of tools that help designers follow the DFM approach and meet its objectives. The "design for manufacture" process provides a framework to work together as they develop product and process designs concurrently.

Various approaches to product design are:

(i) Design for manufacture

(ii) Design For Assembly

(iii) Design For Operation

(iv) Design for Post-Sale Service

(v) Design for Recycling

(vi) Design for Reliability and Serviceability

(vii) Design for Automation

(viii) Design for Ergonomics and

(ix) Design for Environment Protection.

"Design for manufacture" methodologies and guidelines embody product design approaches, techniques and heuristics that have been developed over time. At Cadillac, DFM is a formal written strategy that is an integral part of the business plan. Engineers, suppliers and assemblers work together to reduce the ***'time to market'*** while improving quality and cutting costs. Many US companies have also found that DFM can drastically reduce the length of the design cycle, improve product quality and save considerable amount of money.

Definition: *"Design for Manufacture (DFM)* is a product innovation tool that integrates the activities of product designers with those of the designers of manufacturing or service delivery processes that make the product". American industry has produced some **simple guidelines which are given below:**

- Minimise the number of parts, including fasteners.
- Minimise the number of fabrication and/or assembly operations.
- Match the design to the customer's functional requirement.
- Determine process capabilities and design products to match them.
- Specify standard components with proven quality level whenever possible.
- Design multi-functional modules and combine them.
- Create designs that simplify fabrication, assembly and servicing.
- Avoid special-purpose fasteners or those that require special tools.
- Make parts strong enough to withstand inevitable mishandling and
- Anticipate potential misuse by the dumbest possible customer and create a design that prevents it.

Some of the guidelines for DFM listed above are explained in the following paragraphs:

- **Design for a minimum number of parts:** Reducing the number of parts reduces the cost of assembling a product. This also means fewer parts to make or buy, fewer parts to monitor and control, and fewer parts to store, handle and inspect. *For example*, by cutting the number of parts required for the rear bumper to half, Cadillac reduced assembly time by 57 percent and saved over $450,000 in annual labour costs.
- **Develop modular design:** By developing components that can be assembled in a variety of ways, a firm can offer a relatively wide range of products and while keeping the number of parts, it has to buy or produce to a minimum.

  For example, modular design at Hewlett-Packard (HP) has enabled that firm to release a steady stream of improved printers that cost less, do more and perform better than anything else in the market. Modular design also allows HP to offer up-grade packages for its personal computers. These packages can be used to add many of the new features to the older models.

- **Minimise part variations (Commonisation):** Keeping the number of part variations (*e.g.,* type of fasteners or electronic components such as resistors or capacitors) to a minimum saves time and money. Using standardised components keeps inventory levels, purchasing costs and purchasing lead times down. Standardisation of parts and components also makes products easier to repair and replacements easier to find. *For example*, sixty percent of the parts used in Honda's new 'Domani' are also used in the company's other models.
- **Design parts for ease of fabrication:** The most suitable fabrication process should be chosen for each part and the part should be designed for the selected fabrication process. The materials used to make the part should result in the lowest overall production cost.

DFM tools include relatively new methodologies such as Taguchi methods which are discussed in the later chapters.

Design For Assembly (DFA)

Design for Assembly enables a designer to evaluate the possible manufacture of a product design quantitatively and helps ensure that the DFM guidelines are correctly applied. The most widely used DFA method was developed by G. Boothroyd and P. Dewhurst. The intent of this DFA method is to minimise the cost of assembly while observing the constraints imposed by other design requirements. Designers can use this methodology to determine the minimum number of parts for an assembled unit and estimate the relative ease or difficulty with which their designs can be assembled.

At the Ford Motor Co., more than 7000 engineers have been trained to use the Boothroyd-Dewhurst DFA method and the resultant savings have been close to $1 billion.

Taguchi Methods: The intent of '*Taguchi methods*' is to design a robust product of high quality despite fluctuations in materials, manufacturing and environmental factors. Taguchi's approach to product and process design also leads to low production costs and relatively short design cycles.

Failure Mode Effect and Criticality Analysis (FMECA)

This system provides designers with a systematic way of improving the design of a product. ***"Failure mode effects and criticality analysis"* is a procedure in which the causes of potential failures are identified, their effects are assessed and corrective measures are recommended.** FMECA and Taguchi methods are discussed in detail in later chapters.

Value Engineering (or Value Analysis)

During Value Engineering (VE) or Value Analysis (VA), the product's attributes are assessed, the costs of providing the specific attributes are calculated and lower-cost alternatives are identified.

Suppliers and customers may be involved in value engineering along with representatives from engineering, manufacturing, R & D, marketing and the accounting department. The goal is to reduce costs while maintaining a product's quality and functionality, (*i.e.*, **"equivalent performance at reduced cost**). *For example*, a high-cost material may be replaced by a lower-cost material, a component unique to the product may be substituted by a standard component that is used in other products, or the products' design may be simplified. The weight of a product may be reduced or the way it is packaged may be changed.

Design For Operation (DFO)

Although design for manufacture and design for assembly were aimed at manufacturing of tangible goods, they have proven to be applicable to services as well. This has led to the use of the more general term, ***"Design for operations (DFO)"* in place of the term *"design for manufacture and assembly (DFMA)"*.**

Design for Post-Sale Service

Design for post-sale service is a product innovation tool that incorporates features to help owners and repair technicians to maintain products with ease. Designers should serve the repair technicians as customers and help solve their problems by such designs.

Design for Recycling

Design for recycling focusses on designing products so that raw materials such as plastics can be retrieved once the product has finished its useful life.

Design for Reliability and Serviceability

Reliability is the probability that an item will function as planned over a given time period. It may be calculated as follows:

$$R = e^{-\lambda t}$$

Where R = Reliability (a value from 0 to 1.0)

e = the base of natural logarithm (≈ 2.718)

λ = a constant, failure rate

t = specified point in time.

Serviceability: Serviceability is the degree to which an item may be maintained, either kept in service through preventive maintenance or restored to service after a break down. Measures related to serviceability are:

(i) ***Failure rate (λ)***: Failure rate is the average number of times an item is expected to fail within a given time period. It is a critical determinant of reliability.

(ii) ***Meantime between failure (MTBF)*** is the average time between failures of a repairable item or the average time to the first failure of a non-repairable item. MTBF is usually denoted by the Greek letter μ (mu). It is the reciprocal of failure rate: *i.e.*, $\mu = 1/\lambda$.

(iii) ***Mean time to repair (MTTR)*** is the average time required to repair (or replace), assuming that appropriate parts and sufficient expertise are available.

(iv) ***Availability*** is the proportion of time that a resource is ready for use.

$$\text{Availability} = \frac{\text{MTBF}}{\text{MTBF} + \text{MTTR}}$$

Design for Automation

In design for automation, three broad issues, affecting output and process design efforts come into play:

(i) Wasteful or unnecessary processes should not be automated. Avoid wasteful processes and eliminate the unnecessary processes before considering automation.

(ii) Simplify the design before automation. The simpler the task, the easier will it be to design equipment to do it. Development will be faster and cheaper.

(iii) When design teams strive for an easy-to-automate design, they sometimes get an unexpected dividend. The process might be simplified to such an extent that the firm can avoid the time and expense needed to acquire and install the automation.

Designing for Ergonomics (Human Factors Engineering)

Comfort, safety and ease of use are becoming important dimensions of product quality for many consumers, especially in buying products for the workplace. Poorly designed products may cause work-related accidents resulting in injuries to the users.

Although people are capable of a wide range of tasks and motions, certain consistently repeated activities are less tiring than others. Human factors engineering attempts to increase the safety and comfort of a product as well as the effectiveness of the person using that product.

Human factors engineering or ergonomics applies knowledge of human capabilities and limitations to the design of products and processes.

Decreasing the weight, and vibration of handheld tools, decreasing the force needed to push buttons, placing displays at eye level and making work stations height adjustable are examples of how products can be made safer and easier to use. The way in which the product will be used and the frequency with which it will be used are also important design considerations.

Designing for Environment Protection

This includes designing products that are environmental friendly (or green designs). Process design has concern for environment and anti-pollution laws, recycling and recovery of materials out of scrap. Sometimes, reaction to a social or environmental concern opens up a set of promising new design options. *For example*, in attempting to design products easily operable by disabled persons, designers have unearthed an attractive new approach called ***universal design***.

Phases in Product Design Process

The complexity of today's products makes design a difficult activity. Improved designs not only reduce costs but increase quality. Companies today place incredible pressure to continually improve the quality of their products while simultaneously reducing costs to meet ever increasing legal and environmental requirements, and to shorten product life cycles to meet changing customer needs and remain competitive. Most companies have some type of structured product development process applicable for both tangible goods and intangible services as well.

The typical product development process shown in *Exhibit 11.7* consists of six phases.

Exhibit 11.7 : Phases in Structured Product Development Process

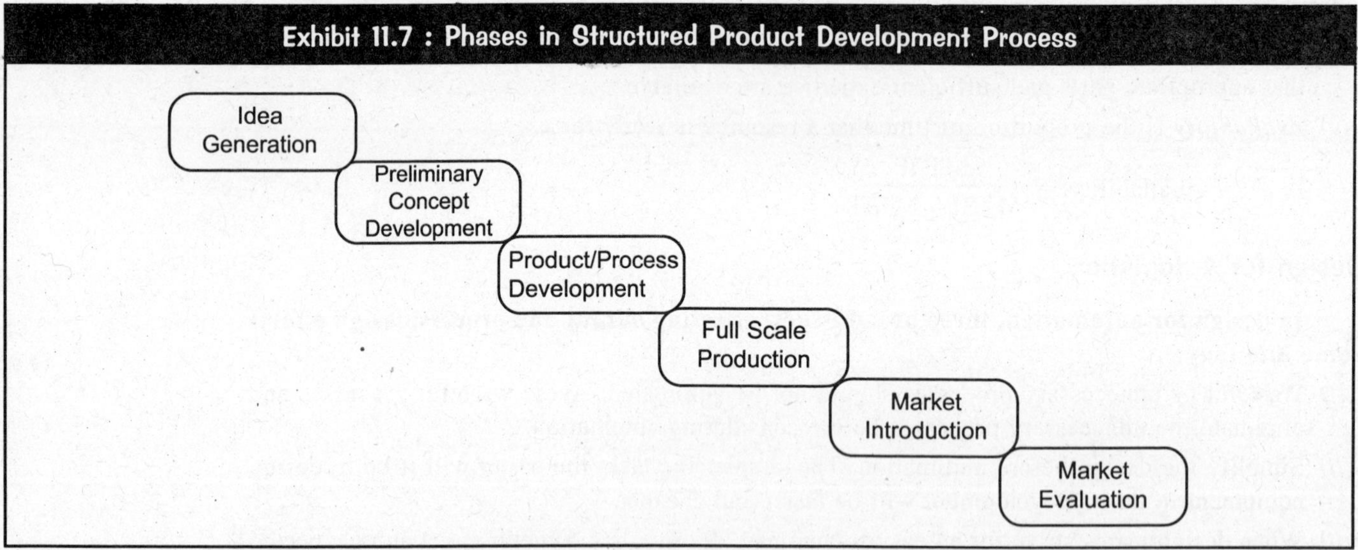

Phase 1: **Idea Generation:** New or redesigned product ideas should incorporate customer needs and expectations. However, true innovations often transcend customers' expressed desires, simply because customers may not know what they like until they have it.

Phase 2: **Preliminary Concept Development:** In this phase, new ideas are studied for feasibility, addressing such questions as:

- Will the product meet customers' requirements?
- Can it be manufactured economically with high quality? Objective criteria are required for measuring and testing the attributes associated with these questions. One tool for assisting in

this and subsequent steps is **"Quality Function Deployment" (QFD)** which will be described in the next chapter.

Phase 3: **Product/Process Development:** If a product idea survives the concept stage, the actual design process begins by determining engineering specifications for all materials, components and parts. This phase usually includes prototype testing, in which a model (real or simulated) is constructed to test the product's physical attributes or use under actual operating conditions, as well as customer's reactions to the prototypes. In addition to product development, companies develop and test the processes used in manufacturing which includes selecting the appropriate technology, tooling and suppliers and performing pilot runs.

Structured product development process has the following phases:
(i) Idea generation
(ii) Preliminary concept development
(iii) Product/ process development
(iv) Full scale production
(v) Market introduction and
(vi) Market evaluation.

Phase 4: **Full Scale Production:** If no serious problems are encountered during the product/ process development phase, the company launches the product through the manufacturing or service delivery teams.

Phase 5: **Market Introduction:** In this phase, the product is distributed to the customers through appropriate channels of distribution.

Phase 6: **Market Evaluation:** An ongoing product development process should rely on market evaluation and customer feedback to initiate continuous improvements. Deming's introductory lecture to Japanese managers in 1950 contrasted the "old way" of product design-'design it, make it and try to sell it'-with a **"new way"**:

- Design the product (with appropriate tests).
- Make it and test it in the production line and in the laboratory.
- Put in the market.
- Test it in service through market research, find out what the user thinks of it and why the non-user has not bought it.
- Redesign the product in the light of consumer reactions to quality and price.

This philosophy is one of the key ingredients in a successful TQ culture.

Many companies view customers as significant patterns in product development, thus integrating market evaluation throughout the process. **Companies that maintain close communication with the customers follow a five step process:**

(i) Initiating a new product through a series of meetings with customers and sales/marketing or technical services group.

(ii) Preparing a ***product brief,*** listing all technical, material and operational requirements and forwarding the brief to internal departments such as engineering, quality and manufacturing.

(iii) Selecting the materials, processes and procedures and then submitting the same to the customer, and making the prototype upon the customer's approval.

(iv) Delivering the prototype to the customer, who evaluates and tests and subsequently report results to the company. The company carries out the requested modification and returns the prototype for further testing by the customer. This process continues until the customer is fully satisfied.

(v) Then the company takes up a limited production run. Data collected during the pilot production run are analysed and shared with the customer. Upon approval, full scale production commences.

Design approaches often differ depending on the nature of products or services. Approaches to designing entirely new products differ from those that address minor changes or improvements pertaining to existing products. Design approach might consider factors such as ***functional performance, cost, manufacturability*** **(or *producibility*),** ***safety*** **and *environmental impacts*** (such as pollution, wastage, disposal problems etc.)

Quality Engineering

Quality engineering is concerned with establishing the functional performance of the product to meet customer requirements and to be produced economically and efficiently with high quality - through system design, parameter design and tolerance design.

Product design requires some basic engineering to establish the functional performance of the product to meet customer requirements and to be produced economically and efficiently with high quality. This is the role of ***quality engineering.*** **Genichi Taguchi views quality engineering as composed of three elements: *system design, parameter design* and *tolerance design*.** These elements are applicable to both manufactured goods and services and processes.

System Design: System design is the process of applying scientific and engineering knowledge to produce a basic ***functional design*** that meets both customers' needs and manufacturers' requirements. The designer must address the question, "what is the product intended to do?" A products' function must be driven by customer requirements. *For example*, in developing a new camera, Japanese engineers studied pictures developed at photo labs and talked to customers to determine the major causes of poor pictures. The three biggest problems they identified were under exposure, out-of-focus and out-of-film (attempting to take pictures past the end of the roll). They developed the first camera that included a built-in-flash to prevent under exposure, an autofocus lens and an automatic rewind feature. Other design considerations include the product's weight, size, appearance, safety, life, serviceability and maintainability. When decisions about these factors are dominated by engineering considerations rather than by customer requirements, poor designs that fail in the market are often the result.

Developing a basic functional design involves translating customer requirements into measurable technical requirements and subsequently into ***design specifications.*** Technical features or design characteristics translate the voice of the customer into technical language, specifically into engineering measures of product performance. Technical requirements are actionable, they lead to design specifications. Developing design specification is the task of parameter design and tolerance design.

Parameter Design: Parameter design establishes specifications which represent the transition from a ***designer's concept*** **to a *producible design*.** Manufacturing specifications consist of nominal dimensions and tolerances. ***Nominal*** refers to the ideal dimensions or the target value that manufacturing seeks to meet, ***tolerance*** is the permissible variation, recognising the difficulty of meeting a target value consistently. Specifications apply to services as well.

Tolerances are necessary because not all parts can be produced exactly to nominal specifications due to natural variations (common causes) in production processes. This is due to the "5 Ms" – men, materials, machine, methods and measurement. Common – cause variations cannot be reduced unless the production technology is improved or changed to a better one. If a process is incapable of producing within design specifications, the cost of acquiring new technology must be weighed against the consequences and related cost of allowing non-conformities in production. (includes cost of 100 percent inspection and possible loss of present and future customers due to non-conformance with specifications).

To design tolerances effectively, engineers must understand the trade-off necessary between narrow (tight) tolerances and wide tolerances. Narrow tolerances tend to not only raise manufacturing costs but also tend to increase ***interchangeability*** **of parts**, product performance, durability and appearance. Wide tolerances, on the other hand, increase material utilisation, machine through-put and labour productivity, but have a negative impact on product characteristics (*e.g.* interchangeability, accuracy, performance etc.).

Traditionally, tolerances are set by using the tolerances specified in the previous designs or basing a design on judgements from past experience. All too often, tolerance settings fail to account for the impact of variation on product functionality, manufacturability or economic consequences. A more scientific approach to tolerance design uses Taguchi loss function, discussed in later chapters.

Cost and Manufacturability

The costs affected by product design are the costs of manufacturing which include direct and indirect labour, materials and overhead costs, the cost of warranty, field repair and the amount of redesign activities. With products in which parts alone represent 65 to 80 percent of the manufacturing cost, design may account for 90 percent or more of the total manufacturing cost. *For example*, for Rolls Royce, design determines 80 percent of the total production costs.

Poor product design adversly affect manufacturability, quality and cost of the product.

Cost reduction can be achieved considerably by simplifying the design. By reducing the number of parts, material costs generally go down, inventory levels fall, the number of suppliers reduces and the production cycle time can be shortened.

Many aspects of product design can adversely affect manufacturability and hence quality. Following are some of these aspects:

- Some parts designed with features difficult to fabricate repeatedly or with unnecessarily tight tolerances.
- Some parts lacking details for self-alignment or features for correct insertion.
- Some parts so fragile or so susceptible for corrosion or contamination may be damaged in shipping or internal handling.
- Sometimes, a design has more parts than are needed to perform the desired functions, which increases the chance of assembly errors.

These problems of poor design may show up as error, poor yield, damage or functional failure in fabrication, assembly, test, transport and end use.

Design For Manufacturability (DFM) is the process of designing a product for efficient production at the highest level of quality. DFM is intended to prevent product design that simplify assembly operations but require more complex and expensive components, designs that simplify component manufacture while complicating the assembly process and designs that are simple and inexpensive to produce but difficult or expensive to service or support.

11.4 LEGAL AND ENVIRONMENTAL ISSUES

Safety in consumer products represents a major issue in design. All parties responsible for design, manufacture, sales and service of a defective product are liable for damages. According to the ***theory of strict liability***, any one who sells a product that is defective or unreasonably dangerous is subject to liability for any physical harm caused to the user, the consumer or the property of either. The principal issue is whether a defect, direct or indirect, exists. If the existence of a defect can be established, the manufacturer usually will be held liable. A plaintiff need prove only that *(i)* the product was defective, *(ii)* the defect was present when the product changed ownership and *(iii)* the defect resulted in injury.

With the doctrine of strict liability, the manufacturer is required to prove innocence. That is, the manufacturer must prove that it would be highly unlikely that a product would be shipped in defective condition (that is a design defect, poor design implementation, inadequate warnings, improper instructions, failure to anticipate misuse, improper materials, assembly errors, inadequate testing or failure to take corrective action).

Attention to design quality can greatly reduce the possibility of product liability claims. Liability makes documentation of quality assurance a necessity. Records that show that the designer has established test and monitoring procedures of critical product characteristics and feedback on test and inspection results along with corrective action taken must be maintained.

Environmental Issues: Today, in addition to legal issues, environmental concerns have a great impact on product and process designs. Because of pressures from environmental groups demanding for **"socially responsive"** designs and consumers who want the most for their money, designers have to look carefully at the concept of **"design for disassembly"**. Design for disassembly consists of two components – ***recyclability*** and ***repairability***. *For example*, firms manufacturing products using plastics, use only thermoplastics which can be remelted and recast into other shapes and products, thus making them recyclable. Recylability of products are helpful in decreasing the problems of waste disposal.

Repairable products have lost favour in the "throw away society" of U.S. where products are discarded simply because the cost of repair is too high when compared with the cost of a new item. Now design for disassembly promises to bring back easy, affordable product repair, making repair less costly than buying a new product.

11.5 STREAMLINING THE PRODUCT DEVELOPMENT PROCESS

To succeed in highly competitive markets, the speed in product development is highly emphasised. *For example*, automobile manufacturers who once took 4 to 6 years to develop new models, are now striving to do the same within 24 months or even within 18 months. The product design manufacturing cycle time can be shortened by using various advanced technologies such as computer-aided design (CAD), computer aided manufacture (CAM), flexible manufacturing (FMS) and computer integrated manufacturing (CIM). Such automation reduces opportunities for human error, thus improving the product quality.

Successful product development demands the involvement and cooperation of many different functional groups to identify and solve design problems and try to reduce product development and introduction times. Various departments such as design, manufacturing, finance, purchase, sales and packaging and distribution, though having different departmental objectives, should work together to achieve the overall objective of the business organisation.

Product development cycle time can be considerably reduced by having concurrent or simultaneous engineering approach instead of sequential approach.

Unfortunately, the product development process is often performed in a serial fashion which has the following disadvantages:

(i) Product development time is long.

(ii) Upto 90 percent of manufacturing costs may be committed before manufacturing engineers have any input to the design.

(iii) The final product may not be the best one for market conditions at the time of introduction.

The problems or advantages of sequential approach to product design and development process can be overcome by an approach called ***concurrent engineering, concurrent design or simultaneous engineering***. In this process ,all major functions involved with bringing a product to the market are continuously involved with product development from conception through sales. Such an approach results in improved quality, lower costs and shorter product development cycle time. Concurrent design or engineering was discussed in detail earlier in this chapter.

Design review: 'Design review' is an approach often used to facilitate product development. The purpose is to stimulate discussion, raise questions and generate new ideas and solutions to help designers anticipate problems before they occur. Three stages of design review are: preliminary, intermediate and final. The preliminary design review establishes early communication between marketing, engineering, manufacturing and purchasing personnel and provide better coordination of their activities. It concentrates on strategic issues in design that relate to customer requirements and the ultimate quality of the product.

After the design is well established, an intermediate review takes place to study the design in greater detail to identify potential problems and suggest corrective action. Finally, just before the release to production, a final review is held where the material lists, drawings and other detailed design information are studied to prevent costly changes after production set up.

Production/Delivery and Support Processes

Process design can be more important than product design. Japanese manufacturers spend about two-thirds of their research and development funds on process design and improvements of manufacturing processes.

The goal of process design is to develop an efficient procedure to satisfy both internal and external customer requirements. The actual process design is the specification of how the process works. The first phase is to list in detail the sequence of steps-value adding activities and specific tasks-involved in producing a product or delivering a service, usually depicted as a ***flowchart***. Flowcharts enable the management to study and analyse processes prior to implementation in order to improve quality and operational performance,

Process design can be more important than product design.

Services Process Design: Services process design has several fundamental differences from manufacturing process design. They are:

(i) Output of service processes are not as well defined as manufactured products.

(ii) Most service processes involve a greater interaction with the customer.

(iii) Customer cannot define their needs for services until after they have some point of reference or comparison.

Service process designers must concentrate on doing things right the first time, minimising process complexities and making the process free from human errors, particularly during customer interactions. Services processes often involve both internal and external activities, a factor that complicates quality design.

Internal activities are concerned with efficiency (quality of conformance) while external activities require attention to effectiveness (quality of design). The success of the process depends on both workers involved in internal as well as external activities – undestanding that they hold value to and for the customer.

Services have three basic components: *(i)* physical facilities, processes and procedures, *(ii)* employees' behaviour and *(iii)* employees' professional judgement. Designing a service essentially involves determining an effective balance of these components. The goal is to provide a service whose elements are internally consistent and directed at meeting the needs of a specific target market segment.

Service process design differs from manufacturing process design

A useful approach to designing effective services is first to recognise that services differ in the **degree of *customer contact and interaction,* the degree of *labour intensity* and the degree of *customisation*.**

For example, a rail road is low in all three dimensions. An interior design service would be high in all three dimensions. A fast-food restaurant would be high in customer contact and labour intensity, but low in customisation.

Services low in all three dimensions of this classification are more similar to manufacturing organisations. The emphasis on quality should be focussed on the physical facilities and procedures; behaviour and professional judgement are relatively unimportant. As contact and interaction between the customer and the service system increases, two factors must be taken into account: *(i)* in services low in labour intensity, the customer's impression of physical facilities, processes and procedures is important. Service organisation must exercise special care in choosing and maintaining reliable and easy to use equipments, *(ii)* with higher levels of contact and interaction, appropriate staff behaviour becomes increasingly important.

As labour intensity increases, variations between individuals become more important. However, the elements of personal behaviour and professional judgement will remain relatively unimportant as long as the degrees of customisation, contact and interaction remain low. As customisation increases, professional judgement becomes a bigger factor in the customer's perception of service quality. In services that are high in all three dimensions, facilities, behaviour and professional judgement must be equally balanced.

In total quality organisations, suppliers are treated as partners in the business. Both manufacturers and their suppliers work together to build strategic relationships.

Supplier and Partnering Processes: In todays' business, operations are often highly decentralised and dispersed around the world. Consequently, managing a complex network of suppliers becomes a critical inter-organisational issue. Suppliers play a vital role throughout the product development process from design through distribution. They can provide technology or production processes not internally available, early design advice and increased capacity which can result in lower costs, faster time-to-market and improved quality for their customers.

Increasingly, suppliers are viewed as ***partners*** with customers, because they are usually having a co-dependent relationship with manufacturers. Successful suppliers have a culture when employees and managers share customers' goals, commitments and risks to promote long term relationships.

Strong customer/supplier relationships are based on three guiding principles:

(i) Recognising the strategic importance of suppliers in accomplishing business objectives, particularly minimising the total cost of ownership.

(ii) Developing win-win relationships through partnerships and

(iii) Establishing trust through openness and honesty, then leading to mutual advantages.

In many firms, suppliers are treated as if they were actually a part of the organisation. To ensure that suppliers can provide high quality and reduce costs associated with incoming inspection or testing, many companies provide various types of assistance to their suppliers in developing quality assurance programs or solving quality problems. Joint conferences, training, incentives, recognition and long-term agreements help to improve supplier's abilities to meet key quality requirements. Joint customer-supplier teams are formed to communicate and improve performance. A supplier- management task force of top managers directs current and strategic approaches to improving supplier management practices.

Measurement plays an important role in supplier management. Supplier's quality performance is measured by parameters such as parts per million defectives (6 sigma quality), percentage of on-time deliveries and cost of ownership.

Supplier certification programs allow consistent supplier performance to be reflected in operating practices for handling received materials and awarding future business.

Supplier certification systems are used by many firms as the focal point of their supplier management system. Formal programs are established to rate and certify suppliers who provide quality materials in a cost-effective and timely manner. A ***certified supplier*** is defined as one that after extensive investigation is found to supply material of such quality that routine testing on each lot received is not necessary. Certification recognises the suppliers as high-quality suppliers, which motivates them to improve continuously.

A three-tier vendor certification program of Florida Power and Light (FPL) classifies the suppliers as a "Quality vendor", "Certified vendor" and "Excellent vendor" based on the following criteria:

- **Quality vendor:** A supplier's products or services must meet basic requirements of quality, cost, delivery and safety. Also, a supplier must have a quality improvement process in use, and be able to demonstrate that this has achieved significant improvements.

  It must also have an audit system to certify the process and the results.

- **Certified vendors:** The supplier must have demonstrated the use of statistical process control and prove that its process can meet FPL's specification requirements. It must also be able to document capability and have a plan for continuous quality improvement.

- **Excellent vendors:** Suppliers must demonstrate the ability of exceeding FPL's specification requirements, employ reliability assurance techniques and show that quality improvement is a central part of their management system.

The supplier certification processes vary from company to company and such programs are time-consuming and expensive to administer. Nevertheless, they are important means of controlling quality of incoming material in a "just-in-time" environment. Through the establishments of clear objectives and performance requirements and the measurement and review of supplier performances, companies can continuously improve and deliver maximum value to the end customers.

11.6 PROCESS IMPROVEMENT

Prior to total quality movement, most US managers maintained products and processes until new technology could replace them. But Japanese managers focussed on continually improving product and processes. Improvement should be a proactive task of management, not simply a reaction to problems and competitive threats. Organisations need to strive not only to meet or exceed customer expectations or improve internal performance measures, but also to outperform all direct competitors and be recognised as world-class leaders.

Process improvement is an important business strategy in competitive markets.

Opportunities for improvement include the following:

(i) Reducing manufacturing defects and cycle times.

(ii) Improving employee morale, satisfaction and co-operation.

(iii) Improving managerial practices.

(iv) Improving design of products with features that better meet customer's needs and that can achieve higher performance, higher reliability and other market-driven dimensions of quality.

(v) Improving the efficiency of manufacturing systems by reducing worker's idle time and wasteful motions in their work.

(vi) By eliminating unnecessary inventory (overstocking), unnecessary transportation and material handling and

(vii) By eliminating scrap and rework.

***Box 11.3* describes the seven steps involved in scientific methods for process improvement and *Box 11.4* describes the 5W 2H approach for process improvement.**

Box 11.3 : Scientific Methods for Process Improvement

Seven steps involved are:

(i) Identify and define the problem.

(ii) Study the existing situation: collect necessary data.

(iii) Generate possible solution alternatives.

(iv) Evaluate alternatives and choose the preferred one.

(v) Implement the improvement and measure results

(vi) Evaluate and revise if required

(vii) Otherwise, return to step one and start again with a new problem.

Box 11.4 : The 5W 2H approach for Process Improvement

A method of asking questions about a process that includes what, why, where, when, who, how and how much.

Category	5W 2H	Typical Questions	Goal
Subject	What?	What is being done?	Identify the focus of analysis.
Purpose	Why?	Why is this necessary?	Eliminate unnecessary tasks
Location	Where?	Where is it being done?	Improve the location Why is it done there? Would it be better to do it somewhere else?
Sequence	When?	When is it done?	Improve the sequence Would it be better to do it at another time?
People	Who?	Who is doing it?	Improve the sequence or output Could someone else do it better?
Method	How?	How is it being done?	Simplify tasks, improve output Is there a better way?
Cost	How much?	How much does it cost now?	Select an improved method What would the cost be?

11.7 PROCESS IMPROVEMENT METHODS

Process improvement methods include (i) Work simplification (ii) Planned methods change (iii) Continuous improvement (Kaizen) and (iv) Break - through improvement.

Earlier attempts to achieve continuous improvement by managers included improvement in working conditions (such as better lighting, ventilation, new safety devices etc), educating workers to improve their skills and knowledge, instituting suggestion schemes and awards for good suggestions for improvement, incentives to workers to promote continuous improvement and increased productivity and the like.

11.7.1 Work Simplification

Work simplification was developed as a productivity improvement program. This technique is based on the philosophy ***"workers know their jobs better than any one else"***. If workers are trained to analyse and challenge the work they are doing, they are more likely to be able to make improvements.

Another approach to process improvement is ***"planned methods change"***. This approach seeks not only to improve work methods but also to replace or eliminate unnecessary operations. Teams of employees are formed to study operations, establish specific goals as to how much of the cost would be reduced through planned change. Positive recognition for success is provided as a means of motivating the employees.

Traditional improvement programs focussed almost exclusively on productivity and cost whereas recent improvement programs focus on quality improvement. Japanese have been highly successful in implementing methods, improvement related ideas, which they learnt from US managers. Toyota pioneered just-in-time (JIT) which showed that companies could make products with virtually zero defects, thereby achieving substantial cost reduction. **Further, JIT established a philosophy of continuous improvement known as *"Kaizen"* in Japanese. *Exhibit 11.8* describes the triple role of every processor team and *Box 11.5* discusses the application of the triple role concept.**

Exhibit 11.8 : The Triple Role of Every Processor Team

Every processor team conducts a process and produces a product. To do so, the processor team carries out three quality - related roles. They are:

(i) **A processor:** The processor team carries out various managerial and technological activities in order to produce its products.

(ii) **A supplier:** The processor team supplies its products to its customers.

(iii) **A customer:** The processor team acquires various kinds of inputs which are used in carrying the process. The processor team is a customer of those who provide the inputs.

THE TRIPROL (TRIPLE ROLE) DIAGRAM

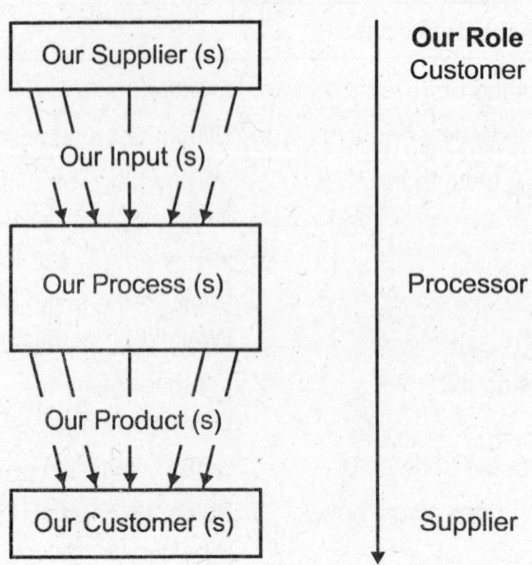

Box 11.5 : Applying the Triple Role Concept

The triple role concept provides any of the processor team with a logical basis for analysing its approach to quality planning. That analysis must provide answers to such key questions as::

- Who are our customers?
- Do our products meet customer's needs?
- Is our process capable of meeting customer needs?
- Do our products provide value commensurate with cost?
- Where are the opportunities for improvement?
- What are their quality needs?
- Are our products competitive?
- Are our process controls adequate?
- Do our products serve a useful purpose?

11.7.2 Kaizen

Kaizen is a philosophy that subsumes all business activity. **It is a key to Japanese competitive strategy**. In the West, quality improvement is viewed simply as making improvements in product quality. In the Kaizen philosophy, improvement in all areas of business – cost, meeting delivery schedules, employee safety and skill development, supplier relations, new product development or productivity., serve to enhance the ***quality of the firm***. Any activity directed towards improvement falls under the Kaizen umbrella. *For example*, statistical process control, robotics and advanced technology, employee's suggestion scheme, total productive maintenance, just-in-time production systems all lead to improvement and fall under the Kaizen umbrella. (Refer *Box 11.6*)

Box 11.6 : Kaizen Umbrella

1. Customer orientation
2. Total Quality Control
3. Robotics
4. Quality Circles
5. Suggestion System
6. Automation
7. Discipline in Workforce
8. Total Productive Maintenance
9. Kanban
10. Quality Improvement
11. Just-in-time
12. Zero-Defect
13. Small-Group Activities
14. Co-operative Labour Management Relations
15. New Product Development and
16. Productivity Improvement

Kaizen focusses on small, gradual and frequent improvements over the long term with minimum financial investment. It begins with the notion that an organisation can assure its long term survival and success only when every one in the organisation participates in the improvement process, actively pursue opportunities to identify and implement improvements every day. Kaizen sets no condition for the size of improvements. It often favours small, incremental improvements over large innovations. Pursuit of small improvements keeps people thinking about the process and its current operation. They identify potential improvements by understanding the function of the current system and its weaknesses or relative inefficiencies. Kaizen is better described by an old saying, "Every day and in every way, we are getting better and better".

"Kaizen" is a Japanese word meaning incremental and orderly continuous improvement of quality.

***Kaizen* refines its emphasis on daily, incremental improvement to develop three guiding principles:**

- **Process view of the system:** The basic unit of analysis in ***Kaizen*** is a process. This analysis affects a process for making a product or a process for designing a product, among other processes.
- **Success comes from people:** Any successful ***Kaizen*** program relies heavily on people's knowledge about their firm's processes and their insight and intuition to conceive improvements. Success requires discipline, employee participation, skill development and effective communication. If quality of people improves, then quality of products will follow.

- **Constant sense of urgency:** A successful ***Kaizen*** program depends on unceasing awareness of the need for change. Everyone must feel that they can improve performance and never accept a current process, however good as sufficient. Complacency and overconfidence drain energy from ***Kaizen.***

Three requirements for a successful Kaizen program are: *(i)* ***operating practices,*** *(ii)* ***total involvement,*** **and** *(iii)* ***training.*** Operating practices expose new improvement opportunities. Practices such as just-in-time reveal waste and inefficiency as well as poor quality. In Kaizen, every employee strives for improvement, right from the top management level to the lowest level of employees. Top management provides support to improvement activities by allocating resources effectively and providing reward structures that are conducive to improvement. Middle management improves co-operation between departments, makes employees conscious of their responsibility for improvement and develops problem solving skills of employees through training. Supervisors direct more of their attention to improvement rather than "supervision." Workers engage in improvement through suggestion systems and small group activities (quality circles) self-development programs and enhanced job skills. All this requires significant training, both in the Kaizen philosophy and in tools and techniques.

11.7.3 Stretch Goals and Breakthrough Improvement

Stretch goals force an organisation to think in a radically different way and to encourage major improvements as well as incremental ones. Stretch goals are also referred to as "break - through" objectives.

Motorola uses defects per unit as quality measure throughout the company. A defect is any failure to meet customer requirements. **A concept known as "six-sigma" quality, developed by Motorola, refers to allowing a maximum of 3.4 defects per million units produced.**

The goals set by Motorola in 1987 were:

- Improve product and service quality ten times by 1989.
- Improve product and service quality at least one hundred times by 1991.
- Spread dedication to quality in every facet of the corporation.
- Achieve a culture of continuous improvement to assure total customer satisfaction and
- Achieve the ultimate goal of 'zero defects' in everything done.

Motorola continued to set challenging goals throughout the 1990s in all areas of operation *viz.,* order entry, sales, purchasing, manufacturing and design. This is known as ***"stretch goals or break-through objectives"*** in modern terminology.

'Stretch goals' force an organisation to think in a radically different way and to encourage incremental as well as major improvements. To be successful, stretch goals should be derived unambiguously from corporate strategy. Organisations must not set goals that result in unreasonable stress to employees or punish them for their failure. In addition, employees must be provided with appropriate help and tools to accomplish the task.

Many companies have set 'stretch goals' in ***"cycle time".*** Cycle time refers to the time taken to accomplish one cycle of a process. *For example,* the time interval between receiving a customer order for a product to the time payment is received after delivery of the product to the customer. Two purposes served by reduction in cycle times are:

(i). Speeding up work processes so that customer response is improved. This may be the time to introduce a new product or the time to deliver a product to a customer and

(ii) Reducing the cycle time by streamlining processes to eliminate non-value added steps such as rework. This forces improvements in quality as well as reducing costs.

Two approaches that help companies achieve stretch goals are ***"benchmarking"*** and ***"reengineering".***

11.7.4 Benchmarking

Benchmarking is defined as ***"measuring your performance against that of best-in-class companies, determining how the best-in-class achieve those performance levels and using the***

information as a basis for your own company's targets, strategies and implementation". In short, benchmarking means "the search of industry best practices that lead to superior performance". The term 'best practices' refers to approaches that produce exceptional results, are usually innovative in terms of the use of technology or human resources and are recognised by customers or industry experts.

Benchmarking is a process of identifying, comprehending, and adapting knowledge of exemplary practices and processes from organisations world - wide to assist an organisation in improving its process or product performance.

Benchmarking helps a company to discover its strengths and weaknesses and those of other industry leaders and to learn how to incorporate the best practices into its own operations. It can provide motivation to achieve ***"stretch goals"*** by helping employees to see what others can accomplish. Benchmarking was initiated by Xerox- an eventual winner of the Malcolm Baldrige National Quality Award and has since becomes a common practice among leading firms.

Three major types of benchmarking that have emerged in business are:

(i) ***Performance benchmarking*** which involves pricing, technical quality, features and other quality or performance characteristics of products and services. It is usually done by direct comparisons or ***"reverse engineering"*** in which competitor's products are taken apart and analysed. This practice called "competitive comparison" involves studying products and processes of competitors in the same industry.

(ii) ***Process benchmarking*** which centres on work processes such as billing, order entry or employee training. This type of benchmarking identifies the most effective practices in companies that perform similar functions, no matter in what industry. Companies should not aim benchmarking solely at direct competitors within its own industry. If benchmarks are adopted from outside the industry, a company may learn ideas or processes as well as new applications that allow it to surpass the best within its own industry and to achieve distinctive superiority.

(iii) ***Strategic benchmarking*** which examines how firms compete and seek winning strategies that have led to competitive advantage and market success.

AT & T has used the benchmarking process described below:

Step 1: Project Conception: Identify the need and decide to benchmark.

Step 2: Planning: Determine the scope and objectives and develop a benchmarking plan.

Step 3: Preliminary data collection: Collect data on industry companies and similar processes as well as detailed data on your own processes.

Step 4: Best-in-class selection: Select companies with best-in-class process.

Step 5: Best-in class collection: Collect detailed data from companies with best-in-class process.

Step 6: Assessment: Compare your own and best-in-class processes and develop recommendations.

Step 7: Implementation planning: Develop operational improvement plans to attain superior performance.

Step 8: Implementation: Enact operational plans and monitor process improvements.

Step 9: Recalibration: Update benchmark findings and assess improvements in processes.

Benefits of Benchmarking

(i) The best practices from any industry may be creatively incorporated into a company's operation.

(ii) It is a motivating activity.

(iii) It provides targets that have been achieved by others.

(iv) May reduce resistance to change when ideas for improvement come from other industries.

(v) Technical breakthroughs from other industries that may be useful can be identified early on.

(vi) Broadens people's experience base and increases knowledge and

(vii) It is a tool for continuous improvement.

11.7.5 Reengineering

Reengineering is defined as "the fundamental ***rethinking*** and ***radical redesign*** of business processes to achieve dramatic improvements in critical, contemporary measures of performance such as cost, quality, service and speed". **Reengineering involves asking basic questions about business processes such as:**

Reengineering involves asking questions about business processes to achieve dramatic improvements through the fundamental rethinking and radical redesign of these existing business processes.

(i) Why do we do it? *(ii)* Why is it done this way?

The purpose of such questions is to uncover obsolete, erroneous or inappropriate assumptions. Radical redesign involves abandoning existing procedures and reinventing the process, not just incrementally improving it. **The goal is to achieve quantum leaps in performance.**

Successful reengineering requires the following:

(i) fundamental understanding of processes
(ii) creative thinking to break away from old traditions and assumptions and
(iii) effective use of information technology.

For example, Pepsi Cola has embarked on a program to reengineer all its key business processes such as selling and delivery, equipment services and repair, procurement and financial reporting.

Benchmarking can greatly assist reengineering efforts. Whereas reengineering without benchmarking probably will produce 5 to 10 percent improvements, benchmarking can increase this percentage to 50 or 75 percent. By benchmarking (that is, by studying outside best practices), a company can identify and import new technology, structure, training and capabilities.

Reengineering is not entirely different from total quality principles. Incremental and breakthrough improvement are complementary approaches that fall under that total quality umbrella and both are necessary to be competitive. The total quality philosophy encourages participation and systematic study measurement and verification of results that support reengineering efforts.

Kaizen, Stretech Goals and Breakthrough Improvement, Benchmarking and Business Process Reengineering are discussed in detail in the later chapters.

11.8 QUALITY IN PRACTICE

Box 11.7 Fast New Product Introduction for Contact Lenses

The speed at which fast products are brought to the market place often distinguishes a barely surviving company from one that thrives. As Diwakar, director of project management and intellectual properties for "PBH Eye Care" a Karnataka based contact lense and solutions company states. "If you can reduce the time between the idea and getting it to the market, you will achieve your strategic goals more quickly. It is important for the strategic alignment of the organisation to look at where to go in the future versus where you are today - and how you will get there via new product development".

Surprisingly, many companies do not have a formalised new-product development process. Projects are often chosen randomly, with minimal thought as to manufacturing feasibility or customer need. There are may be problems with developing, prototyping, testing or manufacturing. Unfortunately many companies have no goals and no procedures for accountability so new product development crawls along, haphazardly at best.

"Cross-functional process mapping" also known as **"concurrent engineering"** or **"simultaneous engineering"** is such an incredibly powerful tool, for delivery of new products, increasing gross margins and market share, reducing market risk and increasing profits, that you can't avoid using it if you want to be the one of the market leaders". said Rakesh chopra, former executive vice president of research and development for country-wide operations at PBH Eyecare.

Cross-functional process mapping involves creating teams whose members are selected from every department involved in the new-product development cycle- from marketing to manufacturing to research and development and every other department involved in the process. The next step involves mapping each step within the process from start to finish. The cross-functional teams are the key to this process.

Any company can achieve dramatic results by using cross-functional process mapping to reduce time. It can really change the mind-set of the company and ultimately result in the company embracing this process in other areas" said Rakesh chopra "Imbedding the process into your business is a lot handier than cutting your process maps. You can't just document a great process-you have to follow through and be committed to making change" he added.

11.9 SUMMARY

Process management involves design, control and improvement of business processes (that is sequence of activities intended to achieve the desired results). Process management techniques can be applied to repeatable and measurable processes only.

Processes can be categorised as ***core processes*** and ***support processes.*** Core processes drive the creation of goods and services and are critical to customer satisfaction and have an impact on strategic goals of the organisation. Support processes are critical to the operation of the business but do not add value directly to the product or service.

Leading process management practices include translating customer requirements into product and service design requirements, (this ensures that quality is built into products) effective management of product development processes, managing supplier and partnering relationships, controlling quality and operational performance of all key business processes, continuously improving processes using systematic problem-solving approaches, setting stretch goals, and employing benchmarking and business process reengineering to achieve break-through performance.

The various steps involved in the product development process are: *(i)* idea generation, *(ii)* preliminary concept development, *(iii)* product/process development, *(iv)* full-scale production, *(v)* product introduction and *(vi)* market evaluation. To remain competitive, companies are forced to reduce time-to-market, which can be achieved by eliminating design changes and improving manufacturability of products.

Designs are simplified in order to reduce cost and improve quality. Design for manufacturability (DFM) is the process of designing a product so that it can be produced efficiently at the highest levels of quality.

Quality in design reduces product liability which is a serious threat to competitiveness. Design for dis-assembly permits easy removal of components for recycling or repair, taking environmental concerns into considerations.

Concurrent engineering or ***simultaneous engineering*** is an effective approach for managing the product development process by using multi-functional teams to help remove organisational barriers between departments and there-by reduce product development time. Other approaches to product design are: *(i)* Design for assembly, *(ii)* Design for recycling, *(iii)* Design for reliability and serviceability, *(iv)* Design for automation, *(v)* Designing for ergonomics and *(vi)* Designing for environment protection.

Quality engineering aims to establish the functional performance of the product to meet customer requirements and to be produced economically and efficiently with high quality. It is composed of ***system design, parameter design*** and ***tolerance design.***

Process design can be more important than product design. The goal of process design is to develop an efficient procedure to satisfy both internal and external customer requirements. The actual process design is the specification of how the process works. Flow charts enable management to study and analyse process prior to implementation in order to improve quality and operational performance. A basic approach to process design involves identifying the product or service, customers, suppliers and process steps, fail-proofing the process and controlling and improving the process using measurements.

In designing services, the factors considered are: *(i)* physical facilities, *(ii)* processes and procedures, *(iii)* behaviour and *(iv)* professional judgement. A useful approach to designing effective services is first to recognise that services differ in the degree of ***customer contact*** and ***interaction;*** the degree of ***labour intensity*** and the degree of ***customisation.***

Controlling production/delivery and support processes is a principal responsibility of the process owners to ensure that process outputs meet operational and customer requirements. The need for control arises because of the inherent variation in any system or process. Three components of the control system are: *(i)* a standard or goal, *(ii)* a means of measuring accomplishment and *(iii)* comparison of actual results with the standard, along with feedback to form the basis for corrective action.

In process management, supplier and partnering processes are important because suppliers play a vital role throughout the product development process, from design through distribution. Strong customer/supplier relationships are based on recognising the strategic importance of suppliers in accomplishing business objectives, developing win-win relationships through partnerships and establishing trust through openness and honesty. Supplier certification systems are often used to manage supplier relationships.

Process improvement should be a pro-active task of management and not simply a reaction to problems and competitive threats. Approaches to process improvement includes work-simplification, planned methods change and Kaizen (or continuous improvement). Stretch goals force an organisation to think in a radically different way and to encourage break-through improvements in defect and cycle time reduction. Benchmarking and reengineering often help to achieve stretch goals. Reengineering complements continuous improvement efforts in a TQ culture.

11.10 KEY WORDS USED

Process management, Design processes, Core processes, Support processes, Product design processes, New product design, Concurrent engineering, Simultaneous engineering, Concurrent design, Concept generation, Competitive analysis, Reverse engineering, Design for manufacture (DFM), Design for assembly, Failure mode effect and critically analysis (FMECA), Value engineering, Design for operation, Serviceability, Failure rate, Mean time between failure (MTBF), Mean time to repair (MTTR), Design for automation, Quality engineering, System design, Parameter design, Design review, Process improvement, Work simplification, Kaizen, Stretch goals and break through improvement, Benchmarking, Reengineering.

11.11 OBJECTIVE QUESTIONS

(A) Match the following :

Column A	Column B
1. Concurrent engineering	1. G. Boothroyd and P. Dewhurst.
2. Design for manufacture	2. Equivalent performance at reduced cost.
3. Design for assembly	3. Simultaneous or parallel engineering.
4. Ergonomics	4. Reduces the length of the design cycle.
5. Value analysis/value engineering	5. Human factor engineering.

(B) State whether the following statements are True or False :

1. Process management is viewed according to two levels of quality viz performer level and process level. (T / F)
2. Product design refers to either a physical manufactured product or a service. (T / F)
3. The development costs associated with the "concurrent engineering" approach is higher than that of "over-the-wall" approach. (T / F)
4. Design is the first step to quality. (T / F)
5. "Design for disassembly" consists of two components - recyclability and repairability. (T / F)

(C) Multiple choice Questions : Choose the correct answer from the alternatives given under each question :

1. Process management is viewed according to these levels of quality :
   (a) Organisational level and process level.
   (b) Process level and performer level.
   (c) Organisational level only.
   (d) Organisational level, process level and performer level.
   (e) Process level only.
2. This system provides designers with a systematic way of improving the design of a product:
   (a) Taguchi method (b) Concurrent engineering
   (c) Failure mode effect and criticality analysis
   (d) Value engineering (e) Design for reliability and serviceability.

3. Genichi Taguchi views quality engineering as composed of these elements :
   (a) System design (b) Parameter design
   (c) Tolerance design (d) (a) and (b) only
   (e) (a), (b) and (c).
4. A vendor classification program classifies vendors as :
   (a) Certified vendor (b) Qualified vendor
   (c) Excellent vendor (d) (a) and (b)
   (e) (a), (b) and (c).
5. Reverse engineering is involved in :
   (a) Process bench marking (b) Strategic bench marking
   (c) Performance bench marking (d) Reengineering
   (e) Competitive bench marking.

11.12 REVIEW QUESTIONS

1. Define *"process management".* What are its three key components? State its importance.
2. Discuss the principles on which the methodology for process management is based.
3. Describe the scope of process management.
4. What is a *process?* List the four major categories of business processes. Explain the difference between core and support processes.
5. Summarise the leading practices in process management.
6. Describe the product design and development processes.
7. Differentiate between the *sequential approach* and *concurrent engineering* approach to product design.
8. What is "comprehensive design program"?
9. Explain the following approaches to product design.
   (i) Design for manufacture *(ii)* Design for assembly
   (iii) Design for operations *(iv)* Design for reliability and serviceability
   (v) Design for automation *(vi)* Design for ergonomics
   (vii) Design for environmental protection.
10. Describe the various steps involved in structured product development process.
11. What is "quality engineering"? Explain the three elements in Taguchi's view of quality engineering.
12. Discuss the various legal and environmental issues relating to product design facing business today.
13. What is *process improvement?* Why is it needed? Discuss the various process improvement methods.
14. Discuss the importance and impediments to reducing time for product development.
15. Explain the differences between "Kaizen" and "Break through improvement" approaches to quality improvement.

11.13 DISCUSSION QUESTIONS

1. "Many aspects of product design can adversely affect manufacturability and hence quality" – Explain.
2. "Safety in consumer products represents a major issue in design" – Discuss.
3. "Process design can be more important than product design" – Do you agree or disagree? Justify your answer.
4. "Stretch goals force an organisation to think in a radically different way and to encourage incremental as well as major improvements" – Elaborate.
5. "Benchmarking can greatly assist reengineering efforts" – Explain how.

11.14 ASSIGNMENTS

1. Design a process for the following activities :
   (a) Preparing for an examination
   (b) Preparing for a presentation
   (c) Planning a vacation.
2. Visit a nearby plant and interview the plant manager to determine his or her approach for process management. Identify the techniques they use in managing their processes.

11.15 CHAPTER CASE

EASTMAN CHEMICAL COMPANY

Eastman Chemical Company (ECC) had been a major division of Eastman Kodak Company. It was started in 1920 to provide chemicals to the parent company in the photographic business. Over the years Eastman grew into a major chemical company, with 1993 world-wide assets of about $4 billion. On January 1, 1994, it was spun off from the parent firm and became an independent company.

Eastman, head quartered in Kingsport, Tennesse, had plants in several states in the U.S. and in several other countries. Eastman had a product range of more than 400 products, including plastics for soft-drink bottles, acetate filters for cigarettes, polymer pellets for steering wheels and the other hard-moulded plastic products.

Chemical industry is a highly competitive industry and requires heavy investment in plant and equipments. Many chemical companies run around the clock as continuous production units which makes the flow of materials and the processes especially important.

Eastman also recognised that the chemical industry was a globally competitive business. Eastman decided to focus on quality by trying process improvement to customer requirements. In describing its quality journey, Eastman focussed on the role of customer requirements, continuous process improvement and statistical process control. "In 1980 Eastman established a goal to be First in Quality. This led to the implementation of improvement breakthrough as processes were brought into line to meet fitness-for-use requirements".

To implement this quality emphasis, Eastman formulated and widely disseminated its Quality Policy which had emphasis on processes through out the Quality Policy. Processes were tied to continuous improvement through statistical methods to satisfy customers.

The Eastman way deals with Eastman's approach to human resources. Its approach to diversity builds on a set of *people values* as part of a process, rather than trying to correct demographic data after the fact.

Top management leadership and training figured importantly in Eastman's focus on quality. Its chief executive officer used to conduct a *quality meeting* with his senior management team every week. Also, each employee was trained in TQM methods for a substantial amount of time.

Eastman's long quality journey has paid off well for the firm by generating above-average sales from new products, high customer satisfaction and a strong safety record.

In 1993, Eastman won Malcolm Baldrige National Quality Award after its long quality journey over a decade. The CEO of Eastman attributed this success to plain hard work at finding out what their customers wanted and then putting the processes into place that satisfied their needs. This was not a simple job for a company having over 7000 customers world wide.

Discussion Questions :

1. On the basis of the Eastman case, discuss the importance of tying process improvement to customer requirements.
2. Why is a reputation for quality so important for a company just establishing itself as an independent organisation?

CHAPTER 12

STATISTICAL CONCEPTS IN QUALITY MANAGEMENT

LEARNING OBJECTIVES

After reading this chapter, you should be able to:

- Define the term "Quality Assurance" and discuss the concepts and objectives of quality assurance.
- Describe the elements of a quality assurance system.
- Discuss the statistical methods in quality assurance.
- Define "Process Capability" and "Process Capability Index".
- Define "Acceptance Sampling" and discuss the various types of Acceptance Sampling Plans.
- Define the term "Statistical Process Control" (SPC) and discuss the "SPC Methodology".
- Describe the steps involved in-constructing the control chart for variable data and attribute data.
- Discuss the issues to be considered while designing control charts.

12.0 INTRODUCTION

Quality is viewed by all business and industrial organisations as being the most critical for their long-range survival. Nowadays quality control function is referred to as total quality management whcih emphasises the strategic importance of quality to the whole organisation and not just the manufacturing function carried out on the factory floor. TQM involves a never ending process of continuous improvement with the objective of achieving perfection. Two main approaches to quality control are :

1. Acceptance sampling and
2. Statistical process control (SPC)

12.1 QUALITY ASSURANCE

"Quality assurance" refers to any action directed toward providing consumers with products/services of appropriate quality

Quality Assurance defined: Quality assurance is the activity of providing the evidence needed to establish confidence, among all concerned, that the quality-related activities are being performed effectively. ISO 8402- 1986 defines quality assurance as related to a product or service as: "All those planned or systematic actions necessary to provide adequate confidence that a product or service will satisfy given requirement for quality." The activities of quality assurance department includes many quality related activities such as ***quality planning, quality control, quality improvement, quality audit and reliability.*** It also includes activities such as quality advice and expertise, training of personnel in quality, provision of appraisal methods for supplies, processes and finished products/services, analysis of customer complaints, warranty claims and product/service liability cases.

12.2 CONCEPTS OF QUALITY ASSURANCE

Many quality assurance activities provide protection against quality problems through early warnings of trouble ahead. The assurance comes from evidence – a set of facts. For simple products, the evidence is usually some form of inspection or testing of the product. For complex products, the evidence is not only inspection and test data, but also reviews of plans and audits of the execution of plans.

The concept of **quality audit** is similar to the concepts of financial audit which provides assurance of financial integrity. **Three forms of company wide quality assurance are: quality audits, quality surveys and product audit.**

12.3 OBJECTIVES OF QUALITY ASSURANCE

The main objective of quality assurance activity is to build quality into the product and/ or service during the upstream design and planning processes

Quality is not just the responsibility of one person in the organisation. Everyone involved directly or indirectly in the production of an item or in the performance of a service is responsible to ensure the quality in the item produced or service offered. **The role and purpose of quality assurance function is to provide a *system that ensures that all procedures that have been designed and planned are followed.***

The objective of the quality assurance function is to have in place a formal system that continually surveys the effectiveness of the quality philosophy of the company. The quality control team audits the function of various departments and assists them in meeting their responsibility for producing a quality product. The objective of quality assurance function is to ensure product quality and service quality by all those planned and systematic actions necessary to provide adequate confidence that a product or service will satisfy given requirements for quality. To be effective, quality assurance usually requires a continuing evaluation of the factors that affect the adequacy of the design or specification for intended applications as well as verification and audits of production, installation and inspection activities. Within an organisation, quality assurance serves as a management tool. In contractual situations, quality assurance also serves to provide confidence in the supplier/ manufacturer.

***Exhibit 12.1* illustrates the approaches to quality assurance**

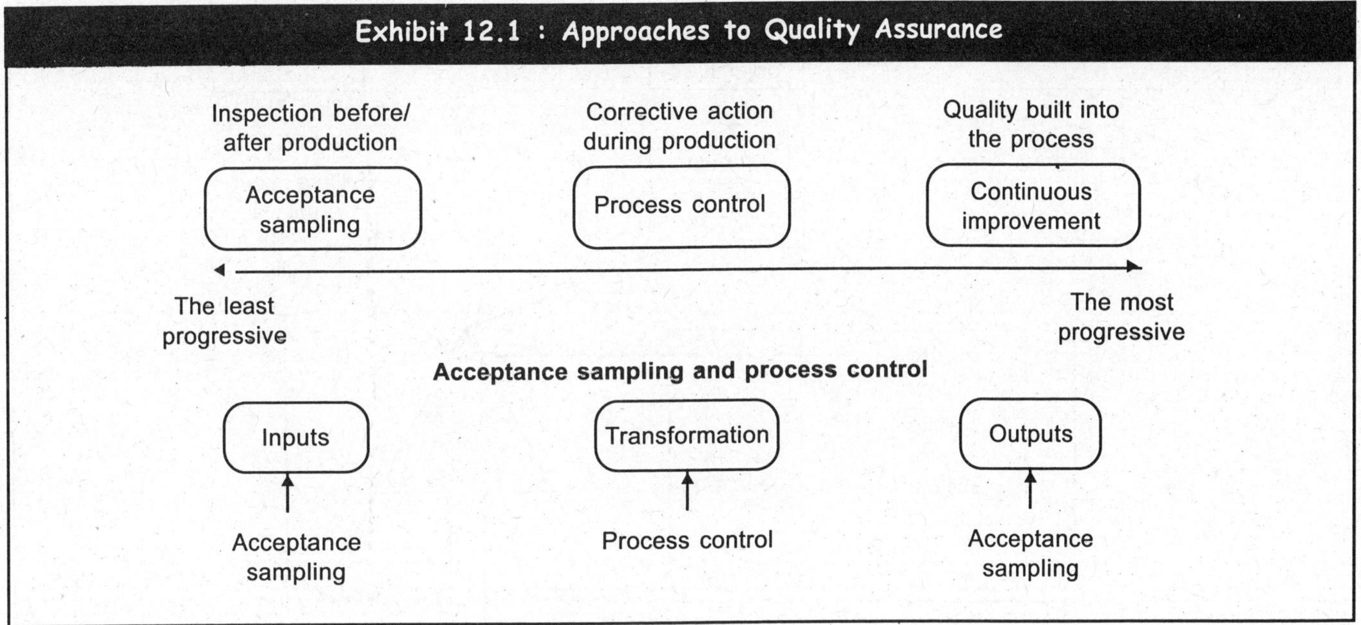

12.4 QUALITY ASSURANCE SYSTEM

A quality assurance system is an assembly of elements such as organisational structure, responsibilities, procedures, processes and resources for managing quality

Organisations ensure the quality of their products through quality assurance activities. **Quality assurance is the system of policies, procedures and guidelines that establishes and maintains specified standards of product quality.** It encompasses both external and internal elements that significantly affect quality.

Every organisation should have a quality assurance system focussed on achieving defect-free products and services that consistently meet specifications. A basic quality assurance system includes well-designed and documented procedures for product and process control, inspection and testing, control of measuring and test equipment (calibration) and appropriate statistical techniques. ISO 9000 standards provide a basis framework for such a system. ***Exhibit 12.2* describes some key elements of a quality assurance system.** It begins with the formulation of quality management objectives which reflect both customer priorities and the firm's own organisational capabilities or capacity. Product quality specifications are then formulated as part of the overall product specifications. These standards can pertain to goods or services or both.

The product specifications constitute standards against which the goods and services are measured (frequently by statistical methods). The standards for goods are used to control the quality of incoming materials from suppliers, the production process itself and the output or goods destined for customers. With services, the standards typically apply to the process whenever employees interact with customers.

Exhibit 12.2 : Elements of a Quality Assurance System

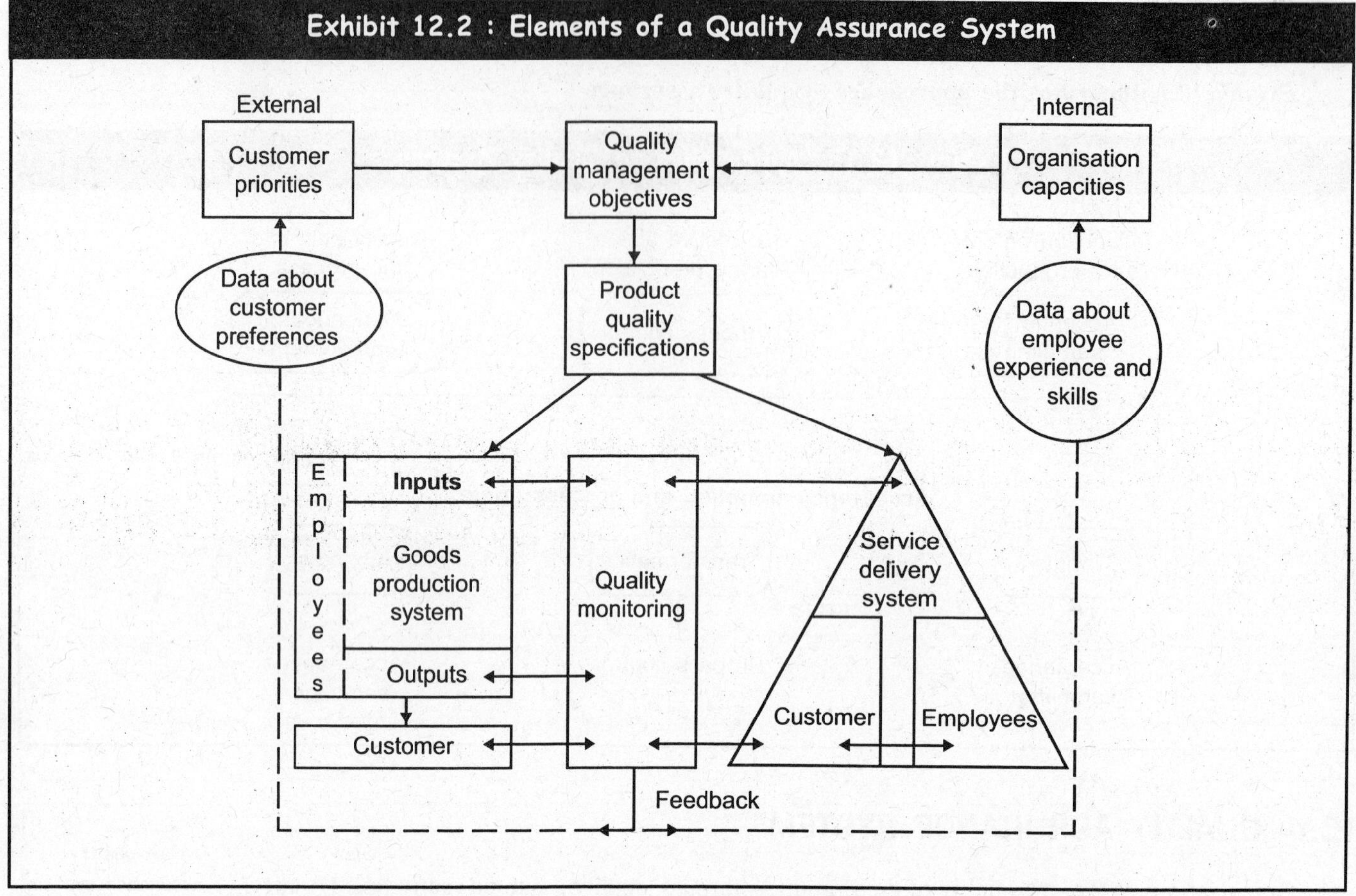

12.5 PROCESS CONTROL, INSPECTION AND TESTING

Process control is an important function of process management

Controlling processes is an important function of process management. Quality assurance systems include documented procedures for production, installation, and service activities, the appropriate equipment and working environment, methods for monitoring and controlling critical quality characteristics, approval processes for equipments, criteria for workmanship such as written standards, samples or illustration and maintenance activities. **Process control also includes monitoring the accuracy and variability of equipment, operator's knowledge and skills, the accuracy of measurement results and data used and environmental factors such as time and temperature.**

Data for process control are obtained from some type of measurement or inspection. Inspection and/or testing generally is performed at three major points in the production process: at the receipt of incoming materials, during the manufacturing process and upon completion of production (finished goods stage).

Receiving Inspection: The purpose of receiving inspection is to ensure performance to requirements of incoming materials before value-adding operations begin. The inspection of incoming material, known as ***acceptance inspection*** falls into three types – ***spot check procedures, one hundred percent inspection*** **and** ***acceptance sampling.***

Spot-check procedures select a fixed percentage of a lot for inspection, say 10 percent of the lot. This method gives different levels of risks for different lot sizes because of inspection of a fixed percentage of the lot. Spot-checking method is more useful as a quality-verification tool to reconcile billing invoices than as a decision tool for quality verification.

One-hundred percent inspection theoretically eliminates all non-conforming items from a lot. However, it is usually costly and impractical for large lot sizes or when destructive tests are used. In some situations which include inspection of products with critical safety requirements or those with high costs associated with failure, hundred percent inspection is necessary.

Various types of inspection are
(i) Receiving inspection
(ii) Hundred percent inspection
(iii) Sampling inspection
(iv) In-process inspection
and
(v) Final inspection

In *acceptance sampling,* inspectors take a statistically determined **random sample** and use a **decision rule** to determine whether to accept or reject a lot based on the observed number of non-conforming (defective) items in the sample inspected. ***Exhibit 12.3*** **illustrates the acceptance sampling procedure.**

A lot is received from the supplier, items from the lot are inspected on sample basis and the results are compared with the **acceptance criteria.** If these criteria are satisfied, the lot is accepted, otherwise the lot is rejected.

Acceptance sampling is based on statistical principles and therefore provides an assessment of risk in the decision. The other advantages are: it takes less time than hundred percent inspection, reduces inspector fatigue, affords flexibility and the like.

Exhibit 12.3 : Acceptance Sampling Procedure

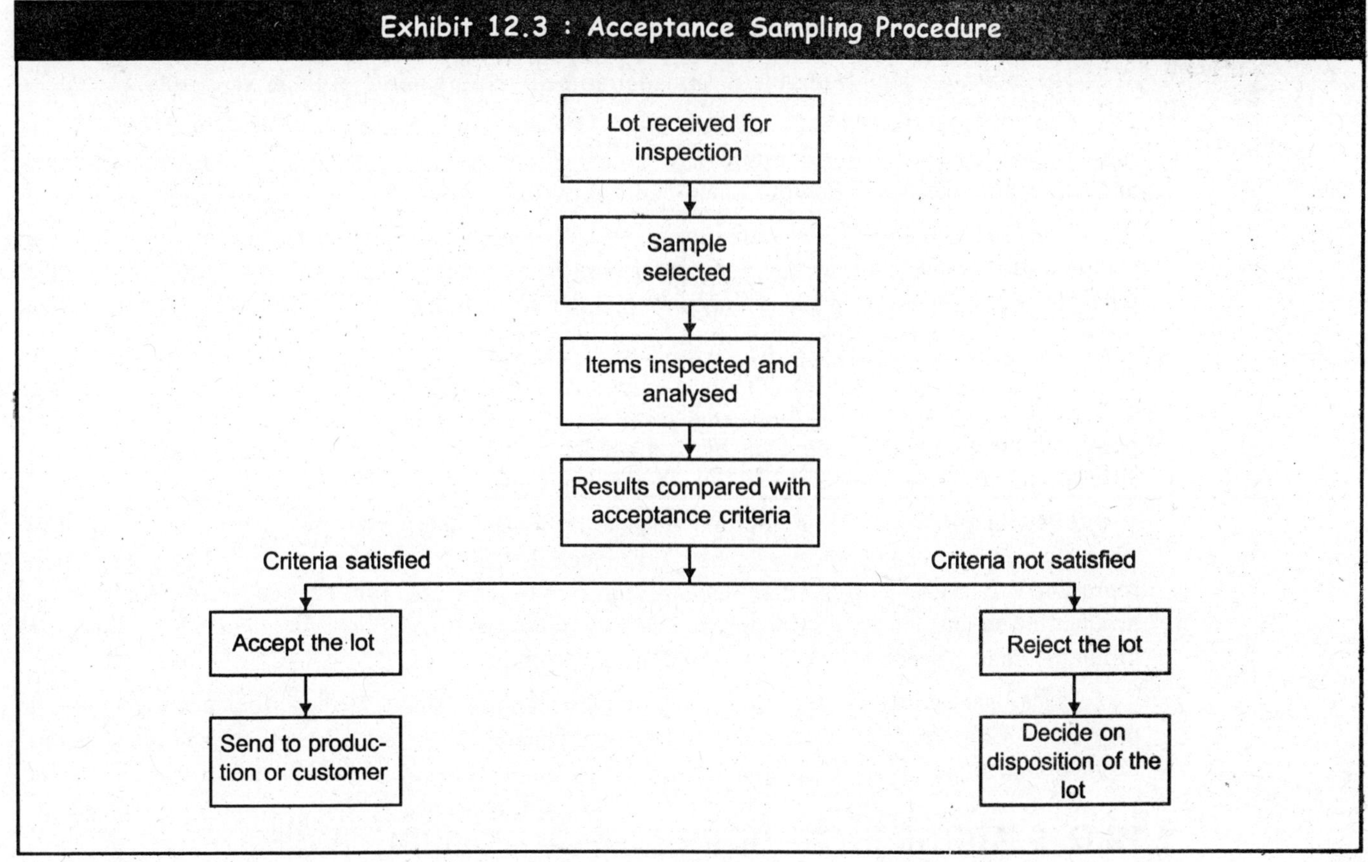

Acceptance sampling can only detect poor quality, not prevent it. Also, it has a risk of accepting bad lots as good lots or rejecting a good lot as a bad lot based on the quality of the samples inspected.

In a TQ environment, however, customers should not have to rely on heavy inspection of purchased items. The burden of supplying high quality product should rest with the suppliers themselves. Occasional inspection might be used to audit compliance. If suppliers provide documentation and statistical evidence that they are meeting required specifications, incoming inspection can be completely eliminated.

In-Process Inspection: Undesirable variation in quality characteristics can arise during production, *for example,* machines going out of adjustment, carelessness of workers or variation in

Three aspects of in process inspection are: *(i)*What to inspect *(ii)*Where to inspect and *(iii)* How much to inspect.

environmental conditions (say, temperature) and the like. Hence, there is need for **in-process inspection** throughout the production process. When the production operator assumes the role of inspector, the occurrence of special or assignable causes of variation can quickly be recognised and immediate adjustments to stabilise the process can be carried out. If done properly, this can eliminate the need for independent inspection.

The key questions to be considered in designing in-process inspection are: *(a)* **what to inspect,** *(b)* **where to inspect** and *(c)* **how much to inspect.** The in-process inspection known as **Statistical Process Control (SPC)** has the objective to control all process factors which cause variations in product features. The critical task is to ***control the processes*** that create the products, not the products that result from the processes. The quality control tools discussed in *Chapter 1* are useful to improve understanding of a process and the factors that may cause variation in the output.

Some guidelines for selection of the quality characteristics to be inspected in in-process inspection are:

- The indicator should be closely related to cost or quality.
- The indicator should be easy to measure economically.
- The indicator should show measurable variation.
- The indicator should provide information to help the organisation improve quality.

The decision of ***where*** to perform in-process inspection is basically an economic one. An organisation must consider trade-offs between the explicit costs of detection, repair or replacement and the implicit costs of allowing a non-conformity to continue through the production process.

The final question is how much to inspect, that is, whether to inspect all outputs or just a sample. If the result of allowing a non-conforming item to continue through production or on to the consumer might be a safety hazard, costly repairs or correction or some intolerable condition, then the decision would be to use 100 percent inspection.

Unless a product requires destructive testing or faces critical safety concerns (in which case 100 percent inspection is warranted), the choice among the three options – no inspection, 100 percent inspection and sampling inspection can be addressed on economic grounds. In fact, on a strict economic basis, the choice is to have either no inspection or 100 percent inspection.

Final inspection: Although final inspection should not be the primary means of quality assurance, it is still an important part of the overall quality assurance system. Final inspection represents the last stage in the manufacturing process at which the producer can verify whether the product meets customer requirements or not and avoid external failure costs. For many consumer products, final inspection consists of ***functional testing.***

Visual inspections for aesthetic characteristics such as cosmetic defects often accompany final inspection. Considerable training is required for inspectors for doing visual inspection to avoid inspection errors.

12.6 STATISTICAL METHODS IN QUALITY ASSURANCE

Three levels of quality are: *(i)* Organisational level *(ii)* Process level and *(iii)* Performer level

Statistics is a science concerned with "the collection, organisation, interpretation and presentation of data". The data provided by measurement processes are raw data which do not directly provide the information necessary for quality control or problem solving. Hence, these data must be organised, analysed and interpreted for the purpose of quality control or problem-solving. Statistics provide an efficient and effective way of obtaining meaningful information from data, allowing managers and workers to control and improve processes.

Variation exists in all processes and understanding and reducing this variation lead to improved quality. ***Statistical thinking*** is a philosophy of learning and action based on these ideas. Statistical thinking is useful at each of the ***three levels of quality.*** At the ***organisational level,*** it helps executives to understand the business system and its core processes, use data from the entire organisation to assess performance, develop useful measurement systems and encourage employees to experiment to improve their work.

At the ***process level,*** it can motivate managers to develop and assess standardised project management systems, set realistic goals, keep employees better informed and focus on the process without blaming the employees for variation.

At the ***performer level,*** statistical thinking can help employees to be knowledgeable about variation, to analyse work data better and to identify important measures and improvement opportunities.

Statistical methods have applications in many areas of quality assurance including market analysis, product design, process capability studies, sampling and inspection, analysis of non-conformities, process improvement and risk analysis. ***Dr. W.E. Deming has stood firm in his conviction that statistics is the heart of quality control.*** All managers, supervisors and production and clerical workers must have some knowledge of the technical aspects of statistical methods.

Statistical Methodology

The ***first*** major component of statistical methodology is the efficient collection, organisation and description of data, commonly referred to as ***descriptive statistics. Frequency distributions*** **and** ***histograms*** are used to organise and present data. Measures **of** ***central tendency*** (mean, median and proportion) and ***measures of dispersion*** (range, standard deviation and variance) provide important quantitative information about the nature of the data.

Exhibit 12.4 : Statistical Methodology in Quality Assurance

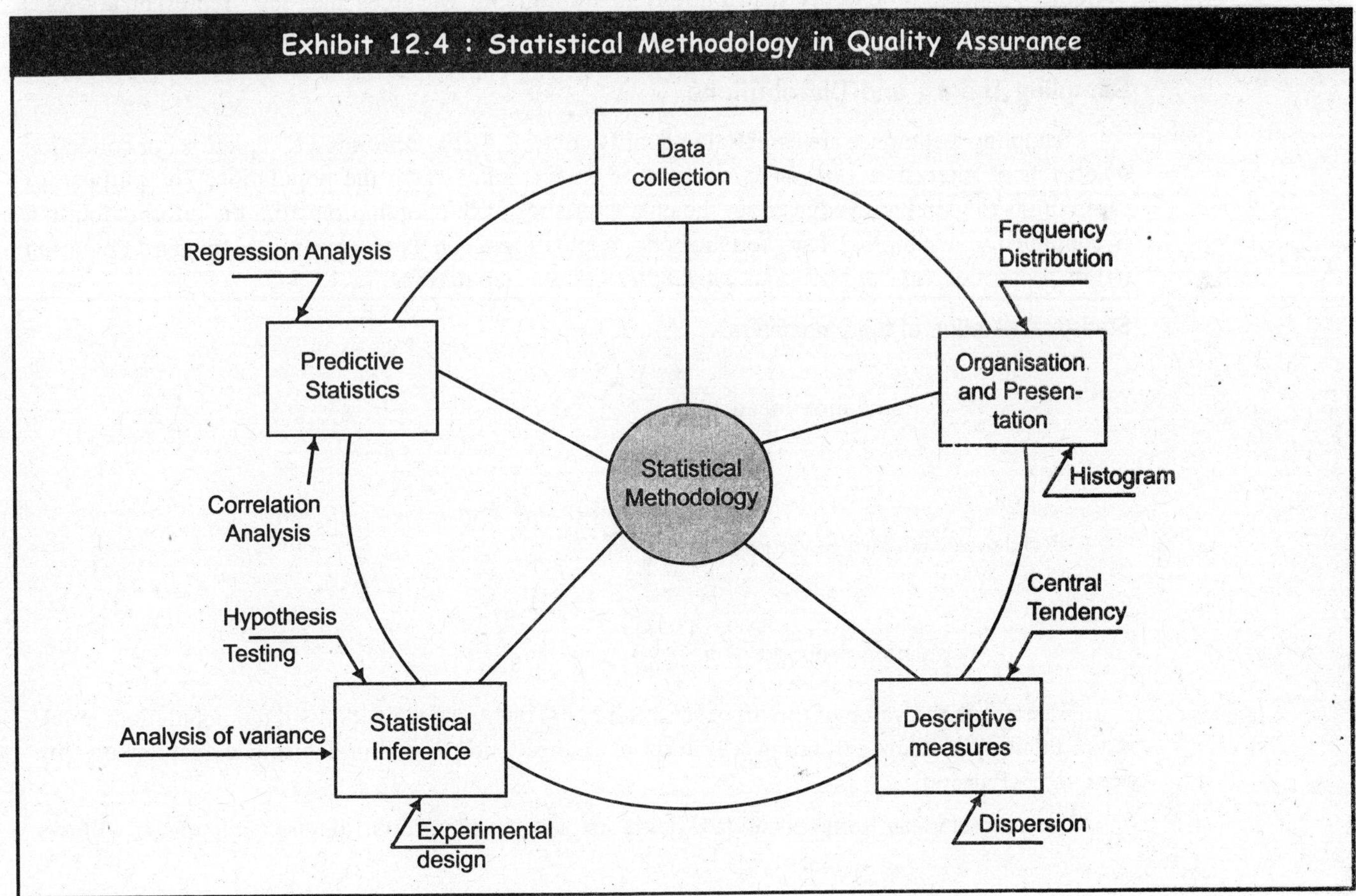

The ***second*** component of statistical problem solving is ***statistical inference*** which is the process of drawing conclusions about unknown characteristics of population from which data were taken. Techniques used in this stage are ***confidence intervals***, ***hypothesis testing*** and ***experimental design.***

The ***third*** component in statistical methodology is ***predictive statistics,*** the purpose of which is to develop predictions of future values based on historical data. ***Correlation analysis*** and ***regression analysis*** are two useful techniques. These techniques can clarify the characteristics of a process as well as predict future results.

Exhibit 12.4 **summarises statistical processes and methods commonly used in quality assurance.**

12.7 RANDOM VARIABLES AND PROBABILITY DISTRIBUTIONS

The collectively exhaustive set of outcomes from an experiment make up a ***sample space.*** A mathematical function that assigns numerical values to every possible outcome in a sample space is called a ***random variable*** which can be either ***discrete*** *or* ***continuous*** depending on the specific numerical values it may assume.

A discrete random variable can take on only finite values (*for example,* the number of defects observed in a sample). A continuous random variable can take any real values over a period of a specified interval of real numbers (*for example,* diameters of bearings being manufactured in a factory). Random variables are the key components used in the development of probability distributions.

A ***probability distribution*** represents a theoretical model of the relative frequency of a random variable. Relating probability distributions to the random variables that they represent allows a classification of the distribution as either discrete or continuous.

Sampling Theory and Distributions

Sampling techniques are essential in quality control. A ***population*** is a complete set or collection of objects of interest, **a** ***sample*** is a subset of objects taken from the population. The purpose of sampling is to gain knowledge about the characteristics of the population from the information that is contained in a sample. Characteristics of a population, such as the mean (μ), standard deviation (σ) or proportion (π) are known as ***parameters*** of the population.

Statistical notation of the parameters

$$\text{Population mean, } \mu = \frac{1}{N}\sum_{i=1}^{N} x_i$$

$$\text{Population standard deviation, } \sigma = \sqrt{\frac{\sum_{i=1}^{N}(x_i - \mu)^2}{N}}$$

$$\text{Population proportion, } \pi = \frac{Q}{N}$$

Where x_i is the value of the ith observation, N is the number of items in the population, and Q is the number of items exhibiting a criteria of interest such as manufacturing defects or on-time departure of aircraft.

The sample mean, sample standard deviation and sample proportion are computed as follows.

$$\text{Sample mean, } \bar{x} = \frac{1}{n}\sum_{i=1}^{n} x_i$$

$$\text{Sample standard deviation, } s = \sqrt{\frac{\sum_{i=1}^{n}(x_i - \bar{x})^2}{n-1}}$$

$$\text{Sample proportion, } p = \frac{q}{n}$$

Where n is the number of items in a sample and q is the number of items in a sample exhibiting a criteria of interest.

Statistical theory is devoted to exploring the relationship between such sample statistics ($\bar{x}$, s and p) and their corresponding population parameters (μ, σ and π).

Sampling Distributions: Different samples will produce different estimates of the population parameters. Therefore, sample statistics such as $\bar{x}$, s and p are random variables that have their own probability distribution, mean and variance. These probability distributions are called ***sampling distributions.*** Knowledge of these sampling distributions will help in making probability statements about the relationship between sample statistics and population parameters. In quality control, the sampling distributions of $\bar{x}$ and p are of the most interest.

When using simple random sampling, the expected value of $\bar{x}$ is the population mean μ or

$$E(\bar{x}) = \mu$$

The standard deviation of $\bar{x}$ (often called the standard error of mean) is given by the formula

$$\sigma_{\bar{x}} = \frac{\sigma}{\sqrt{n}}$$ (for finite populations or sampling with replacement from an infinite population)

$$\sigma_{\bar{x}} = \left(\sqrt{\frac{N-n}{N-1}}\right)\left(\frac{\sigma}{\sqrt{n}}\right)$$ (for finite population)

where $\frac{n}{N} \le 0.05$, $\sigma_{\bar{x}} = \frac{\sigma}{\sqrt{n}}$ provides a good approximation for finite populations.

The last step is to develop the form of the probability distribution of $\bar{x}$. If the true proportion is unknown, the ***central limit theorem*** can provide some useful insights.

The central limit theorem is stated as follows:

"If simple random samples of size 'n' are taken from any population having a mean'μ' and a standard deviation of 'σ ', the probability distribution of the sample mean approaches a normal distribution with mean μ and standard deviation (standard error) $\sigma_{\bar{x}} = \frac{\sigma}{\sqrt{n}}$ as n becomes very large.

In more mathematical terms: As $n \rightarrow \infty$, the distribution of the random variable $Z = \frac{\bar{x} - \mu}{\frac{\sigma}{\sqrt{n}}}$ approaches that of a standard normal distribution".

Next, consider the sampling distribution of p, in which the expected value of p, $E(p) = \pi$. Here π is used as the population parameter and is not related to the number $\pi = 3.14159$.

The standard deviation of p is

$$S_p = \sqrt{\frac{\pi(1-\pi)}{n}}$$ for infinite populations

For finite populations or where $\frac{n}{N} > 0.05$, modify s_p by $s_p = \sqrt{\frac{N-1}{n-1}}\sqrt{\frac{\pi(1-\pi)}{n}}$.

In applying central limit theorem to p, the sampling distribution of p can be approximated by a normal distribution for large sample sizes.

12.8 PROCESS CAPABILITY

Process capability refers to a statistical measure of the inherent process variability for a given characteristic

The determination of process capability begins only after the process has been brought to a state of statistical control. A process is said to be in statistical control when the only sources of variation in the system are common or chance causes. Identifying special or assignable causes and taking corrective action to eliminate the special or assignable causes leads to a process in statistical control.

Process capability* refers to the ability of the process to meet the design specifications for a product or service.** Design specifications often are expressed as a ***nominal value* or target** and **a *tolerance or allowance above or below the nominal value. *For example,* design specifications for the useful life of a light bulb might have a nominal value of 1000 hours and a tolerance of ± 200 hours. This tolerance gives an upper specification of 1200 hours and a lower specification of 800 hours.

The process producing the bulbs must be capable of doing so within these design specifications, otherwise it will produce a certain proportion of defective bulbs.

Process capability* is the range over which the natural variation of a process occurs as determined by the system of common or chance causes, that is what the process can achieve under stable conditions.** Process capability only makes sense if all the special or assignable causes of variation have been eliminated and the process is in a ***state of statistical control. The capability of a process is usually compared to design specifications and measured by a proportion of the output that can be produced within the specifications.

Process capability is important to both product designers and manufacturing engineers. Knowing process capabilities allows one to predict quantitatively how well a process will meet specifications and to specify equipment requirements and the level of control necessary.

Process capability has three important components: *(i)* the design specifications, *(ii)* the centering of the natural variation and *(iii)* the range or spread of variation.

***Exhibit 12.5* illustrates four possible outcomes that can arise when natural process variability is compared with design specifications.**

In *figure (a)* in ***Exhibit 12.5,*** the specifications are looser than the natural variation and we can expect that the process will always produce conforming products as long as it remains in control.

In *figure (b),* the natural variation and specifications are the same. A small percentage of non-conforming products might be produced, thus the process should be closely monitored.

In *figure (c),* the range of natural variability is larger than the specification, thus the current process could not meet specifications even when it is under control.

In *figure (d),* the capability is the same as in *(b)* but the process average is off-centre. If no corrective action is taken, a substantial portion of output will fall outside the specification limit even though the process has the inherent capability to meet specifications.

Exhibit 12.5 : Process Capability

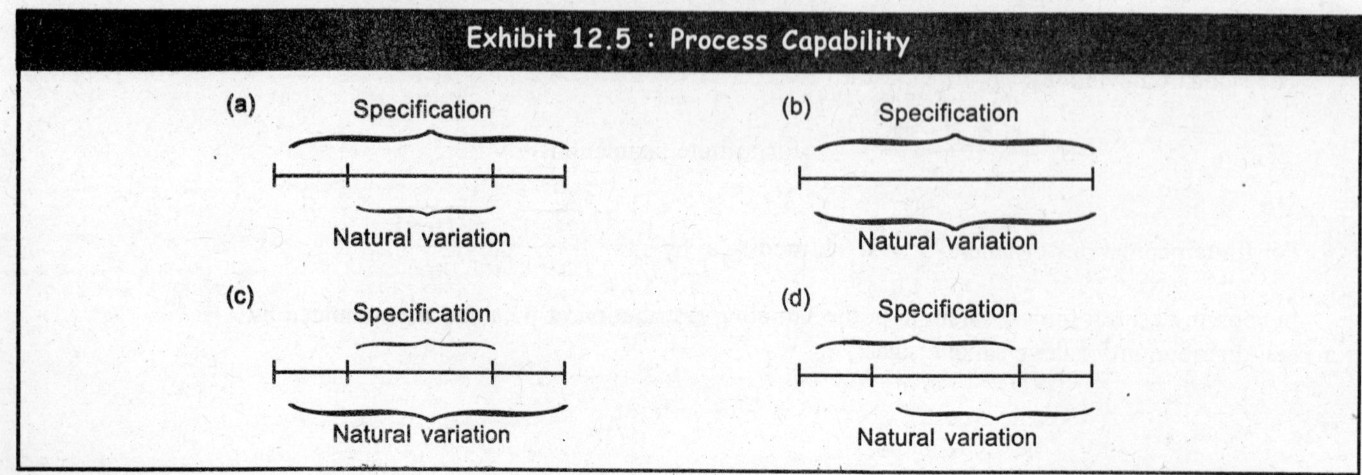

Process Capability Studies

A process capability study is a carefully planned study designed to yield specific information about the performance of a process under specified operating conditions. Typical questions that are asked in a process capability study are:

- Where is the process centred?
- How much variability exists in the process?
- Is the performance relative to specifications acceptable?
- What proportion of output will be expected to meet specifications?
- What factors contribute to variability?

Reasons for conducting a process capability study

1. Manufacturing may wish to determine a performance base line for a process.
2. To prioritise projects for quality improvement.
3. To provide statistical evidence of quality for customers.
4. To evaluate a new equipment by the purchasing department.
5. To compare different suppliers by the purchasing department.
6. To determine the adequacy of R&D pilot facilities; and
7. To evaluate new processes.

Three types of studies conducted are:

1. ***A peak performance study*** which determines how a process performs under ideal conditions.
2. ***A process characterisation study*** which is designed to determine how a process performs under actual operating conditions.
3. ***A component variability study*** which assesses the relative contribution of different sources of total variation.

Six steps in a process capability study **are:**

1. Choose a representative machine or segment of the process.
2. Define the process conditions.
3. Select a representative operator.
4. Provide materials that are of standard grade with sufficient materials for uninterrupted study.
5. Specify the gauging or measurement method to be used.
6. Provide for a method of recording measurements and conditions, in order, on the units produced.

To obtain useful information, the sample size should be fairly large, generally at least 100. **Two statistical techniques are commonly used to evaluate process capability. One is the frequency distribution and histogram, the other is the control chart.**

Process Capability Ratio: A process is capable if it has a process distribution whose extreme values fall within the upper and lower specification for a product or service. As a general rule, most values of a process distribution fall within plus or minus three standard deviations (± 3σ) of the means. This means, the range of values of the quality measures generated by the process is approximately six standard deviation. Hence, if a process is capable, the difference between the upper and lower specifications called the *tolerance width* must be greater than six standard deviations (process variability).

$$\text{The process capability ratio, } C_p = \frac{\text{Upper specification - Lower specification}}{6\sigma}$$

Where σ is the standard deviation of the process distribution.

If $C_p > 1.0$, the tolerance range is greater than the range of actual process outputs. If $C_p < 1.0$, the process will produce products or services outside their allowable tolerance.

Process capability index refers to the values of the tolerance specified for the characteristic divided by the process capability. Two widely used process capability indices are Cp and Cpk.

Process Capability Indices: The relationship between the natural variation of a process and the design specifications is often quantified by a measure known as the ***process capability index*** (sometimes called the ***process potential index***). **The process capability index is defined as the ratio of the specification width to the natural tolerance of the process.**

The ***C_p index*** is a common measure for describing the potential of a process to meet specifications. It relates the natural variation of the process with the design specification in a single, quantitative measure.

This is given by $$C_p = \frac{USL - LSL}{6\sigma},$$

where USL and LSL represents the upper and lower specification limits and σ represents the process standard deviation.

Upper and Lower Capability Indices

Suppose only a single specification limit is given. Indices can be derived that measure shifts in the process mean μ relative to the process spread. For a given upper specification limit,

Upper capability index CPU or $C_{pu} = \dfrac{USL - \mu}{3\sigma}$

If only lower specification limit is given,

the lower capability index LPU or $C_{pl} = \dfrac{\mu - LSL}{3\sigma}$

It is desirable to have both C_{pu} and $C_{pl} \geq 1$.

The C_{pk} index: The C_{pk} index takes into consideration the location of the process mean which is not so in the case of C_p index.

$$C_{pk} = \text{minimum of} \left\{ \frac{USL - \mu}{3\sigma}, \frac{\mu - LSL}{3\sigma} \right\}$$

$$= \text{minimum of } (C_{pu} \text{ and } C_{pl})$$

Desirable value of $C_{pk} \geq 1$.

whereas the C_p index represents the process potential, the C_{pk} value represents the actual capability of the process. With the existing parameter values, it measures process performance *capability ratio.*

Some controversy exists over C_p and C_{pk} as measures of process capability, particularly with respect to the economic loss function philosophy of Taguchi. *For example,* a process may have a high C_{pk} even when its mean is off target and close to the specification limits as long as the process spread is small. Several alternative measures have been proposed. One is to adjust C_p by a factor (1 – k) as follows:

$$C_{pk} = C_p (1 - k)$$

where $$k = \frac{2|\text{mean} - \text{target}|}{\text{tolerance}}$$

When the sample mean is equal to the target, k = 0 and $C_{pk} = C_p$. As the sample mean deviates from the target, the absolute difference between them increases and k increases. Specification limits are used only to determine the tolerance, thus the focus of this measure is on the target value rather than on acceptable specification limits.

Another index that has been proposed is

$$C_{pk} = \frac{C_p}{\sqrt{1 + (\text{mean} - \text{target})^2 / \sigma^2}}$$

This measure also accounts for deviations from the target value in a quadratic loss fashion based on the Taguchi loss function which was discussed earlier in *Chapter 10.*

Process capability indices depend on the assumption that the distribution of output is normally distributed. When this is not the case such as when the output is affected by tool wear and exhibits a highly skewed distribution, process capability indices can be below 1 even though all measurements are within specification limits.

12.9 SIX-SIGMA QUALITY

'Six-sigma quality is a term used generally to indicate that a process is well controlled, that is, within process limits $\pm 3\sigma$ from the central line in a control chart and tolerance limits of $\pm 6\sigma$ from the central line

Motorola created the concept of "Six-sigma" in the mid 1980s to improve the performance of key processes, productivity and quality and at the same time reduce costs. The goal of "Six-sigma" is value creation through quality improvement. The process by which this is attained would involve training of employees in tools and techniques as well as a problem solving protocol.

What does "Six-sigma" Mean?

A 'sigma' is a statistical indication of variation in terms of standard deviations of the characteristic under consideration. It indicates the spread of each unit around the target value, and therefore it is essentially and indication of how good a product or service is. In essence sigma measures the capability of a process to produce defect free work and is a means of calibrating process performance to meet the requirements of customers

Two meanings of 'six-sigma' are:

(i) In statistical sense, it describes a process, product or service with an extremely high capability (99.9997%) accuracy or 3.4 defects per million opportunities)

(ii) Six-sigma is a program designed to reduce defects to help lower costs, save time, and improve customer satisfaction. Six-sigma is a comprehensive system – a strategy, a discipline, and a set of tools- for achieving and sustaining business success

More about "six-sigma" quality will be discussed in a later chapter.

12.10 STATISTICAL QUALITY CONTROL

The purpose of quality control is to assure that processes are performing in an acceptable manner. This is accomplished by monitoring the process output using statistical techniques. If the results are acceptable, no further action is required. If not, corrective action is called for.

Acceptance sampling plan is a specific plan that indicates the sampling sizes and the associated acceptance or non acceptance criteria to be used.

The best companies emphasise designing quality into the process, thereby greatly reducing the need for inspection or control efforts. The ultimate goal of a firm is to totally avoid inspection activities and process control activities by achieving an inherent level of quality that is sufficiently high.

Quality assurance that relies primarily on inspection after production is referred to as ***acceptance sampling.*** Quality control efforts that occur during the production are referred to as **statistical process control (SPC).**

Acceptance plans : To ensure perfect quality, it is necessary to develop inspection and testing methods that are quick and effective so that all products are subjected to ***100 percent inspection and testing.*** This means that every product shipped to customer is inspected and tested to determine whether it meets customer specifications (*i.e.,* design specification). But there are situations where it is either impossible or uneconomical to inspect and test each and every product, when destructive tests are called for or the quantity to be inspected or tested is quite large where 100 percent inspection or testing are uneconomical, impractical or impossible. In such situations, sampling inspection based on acceptance plans is the only sensible basis for inspecting and testing.

An ***acceptance plan*** is the overall scheme for either accepting or rejecting a lot based on information gained from samples, regarding the quality of the samples inspected. The acceptance plan identifies both the size and type of samples and the criteria to be used to either accept or reject this lot.

Acceptance sampling is a form of inspection that is applied to lots or batches of items either before or after a process instead of during the process. The lot may represent incoming purchased items or raw materials, or semi-finished items (items that have completed certain manufacturing operations) or final products awaiting shipment to warehouses or customers. The purpose of acceptance sampling is to decide whether a lot satisfies predetermined quality standards or not. **Based on the quality of the samples drawn from the lot, the lot is accepted or rejected.** Rejected lots may be subjected to 100 percent inspection to segregate the defective items from the good ones. **Acceptance sampling procedures are most useful when :**

Three types of sampling plans used are: *(i)* Single sampling plan *(ii)* Double – sampling plan and *(iii)* Sequential sampling plan

(i) A large number of items must be processed in a short time.

(ii) Destructive testing is required and

(iii) Fatigue or boredom caused by inspecting large numbers of items leads to inspection errors.

Acceptance sampling procedures can be applied to inspection of both attribute and quality characteristics.

Sampling plans : A variety of sampling plans (acceptance plans) can be used. They are: *(i)* **Single sampling plan,** *(ii)* **Double sampling plan** and *(iii)* **Sequential sampling plan.**

Single sampling plan : In a single sampling plan, one random sample is drawn from each lot and every item in the sample is inspected or tested and classified as either "good" or "deflective". If any sample contains more than a specified members of defectives 'C' (also referred to as **acceptance number**) that lot is rejected.

Exhibit 12.6 **illustrates how single – sampling plans operate.**

Exhibit 12.6 : Single-sampling Plans

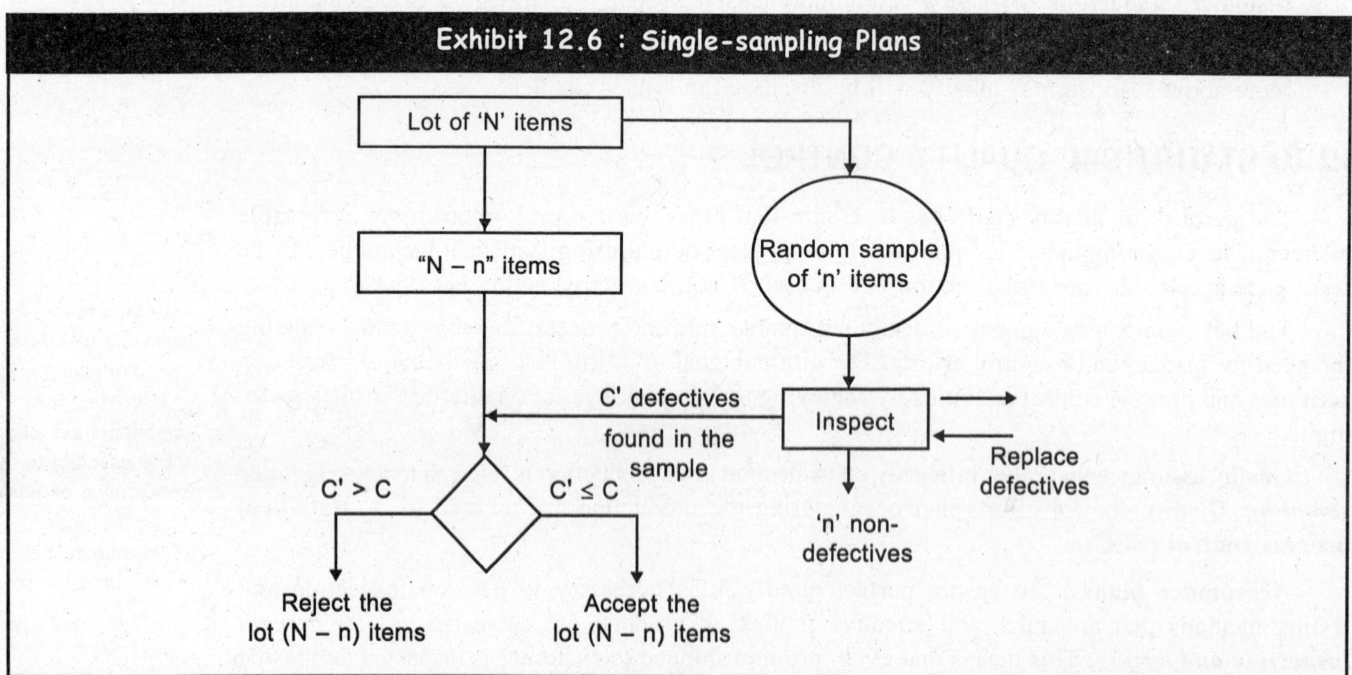

Double Sampling Plan

A double sampling plan allows for the opportunity to take a second sample if the results of the initial sample are inconclusive. *For example,* if the number of defectives (C') is less than the acceptance number 'C', the lot is accepted, otherwise the lot is rejected and subjected to 100 percent inspection.

In order to reduce such 100 percent inspection, double sampling plans allow to draw a second sample from the rejected lot and subject the sample to inspection to take the decision to accept or reject the lot.

With double-sampling plan, two values are specified for the number of defective items (acceptance numbers), a lower level C_1 and the upper level C_2. If the number of defective items in the first sample is less than or equal to the lower values (*i.e.* C_1) the lot is accepted and the sampling is terminated. If the number of defectives exceeds the upper value (*i.e.* C_2) the lot is rejected. If the number of defective falls in between C_1 and C_2, a second sample is taken and the number of defectives in both samples is compared with C_2 and lot is accepted if the total number of defects in the two samples is less than or equal to C_2, otherwise the lot is rejected.

***Exhibit 12.7* illustrates how a double-sampling plan for attributes operates.**

Exhibit 12.7 : Double Sampling Plans

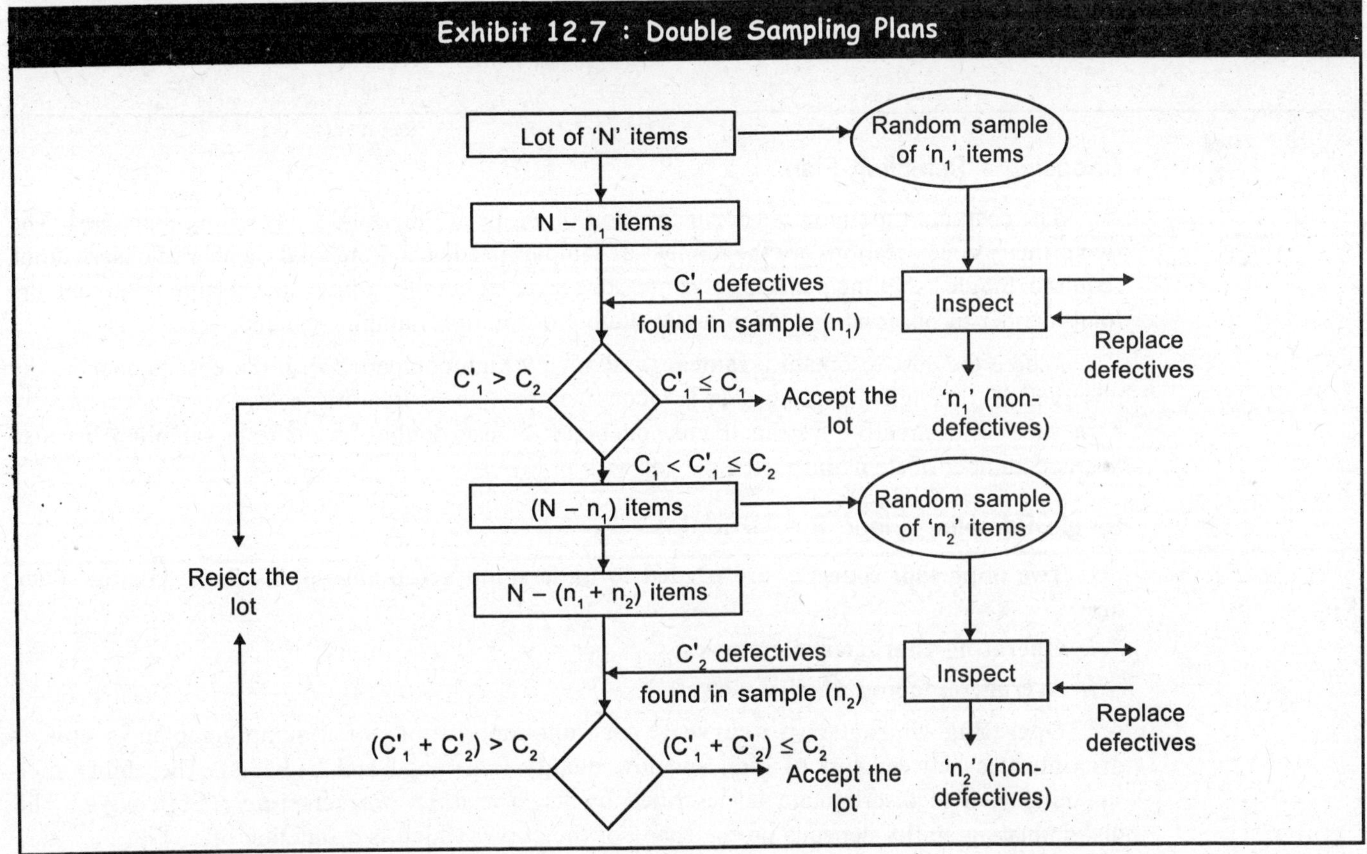

Sequential Sampling Plans (or Multisampling Plan)

In a sequential sampling plan, units (samples) are randomly selected from the lot and tested one by one. After each one has been tested, a reject, accept or continue, sampling decision is made. This process continues until the lot is accepted or rejected. ***Exhibit 12.8* Illustrates how such plans operate with attributes.**

In the exhibit above, the first defective is the 15th unit, putting us in the continue sampling zone and we continue to sample units from the lot. The second defective is the 25th unit and we continue sampling the fourth defective is the 40th unit and thus puts us in the reject zone, therefore the lot is rejected.

Exhibit 12.8 : Sequential Sampling Plans

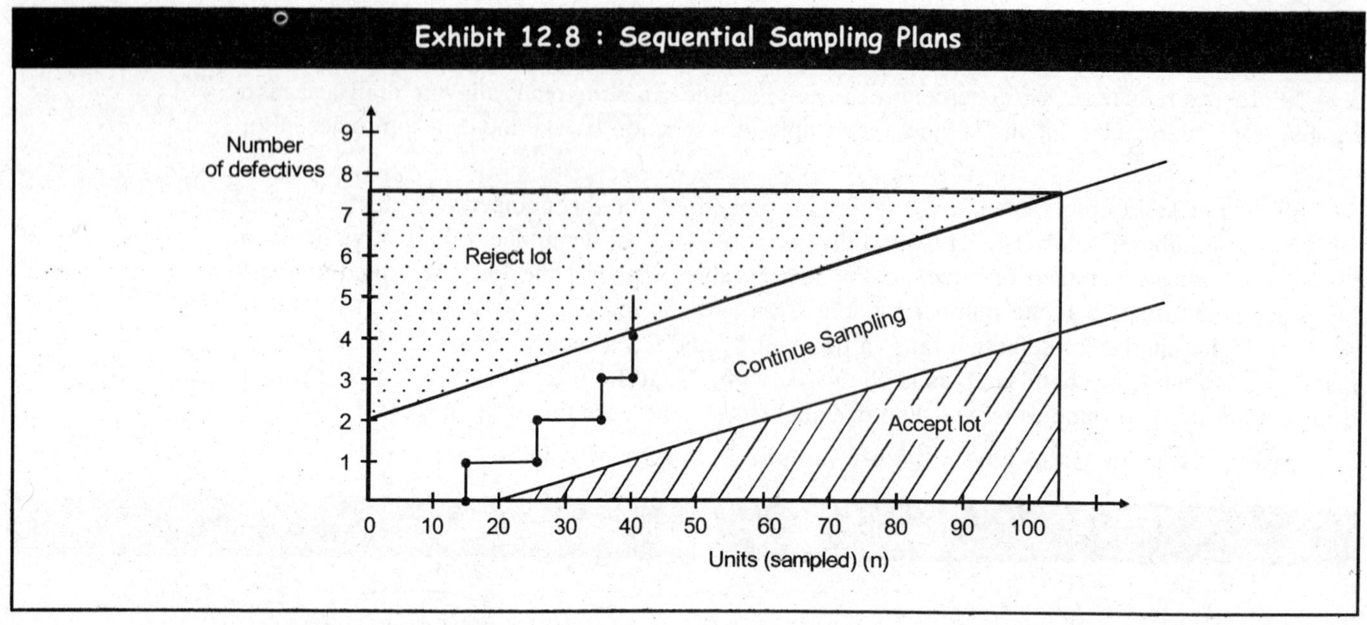

Choosing a Sampling Plan

The cost and time required for inspection often dictate the kind of sampling plan used. The two primary considerations are the number of samples needed and the total number of observations required. Single sampling plans involve only one sample, but the sample size is large relative to the total number of observations taken under double or multiple sampling plans.

Where the cost to obtain a sample is relatively high compared with the cost to analyse the observations, a single-sampling plan is recommended. Where item inspection costs are relatively high such as destructive testing it may be better to use double or multiple sampling because average number of items inspected per lot will be lower.

Single Sampling Plans for Attributes

Two important concepts are needed to understand acceptance plans for attributes. They are:

(i) **Operating characteristic curves**

(ii) **Average outgoing quality curves.**

Operating characteristic curve : An important feature of a sampling plan is how it discriminates between lots of high and low quality (*i.e.,* good and bad lots). The ability of a sampling plan to discriminate is described by its ***operating characteristic (O.C.) curve.*** The discriminating ability depends on the shape of the curve, which is a function of :

(i) the sample size "n" withdrawn from the lot.

(ii) the acceptance level or acceptance number of allowable defective units found in the sample.

A typical O.C. curve for a single sampling plan is shown in *Exhibit 12.9.*

The O.C. curve shows the probability that use of the sampling plan will result in lots with various fraction defectives being accepted. *For example,* the graph shows that a lot with 3 percent defectives would have a probability of 0.90 (*i.e.,* 90 percent) of being accepted and a probability of 0.10 (*i.e.* 10 percent) of being rejected. It may be noted from the shape of the curve that as lot quality decreases (*i.e.,* fraction defective increases), the probability of acceptance of the lot decreases, although the relationship is not linear.

A sampling plan does not provide perfect discrimination between good and bad lots. There are four possible outcomes:

- Desirables (i) A good lot can be accepted
  (ii) A bad lot can be rejected
- Undesirable (i) A good lot may be rejected
  (ii) A bad lot may be accepted.

It can be seen from the graph that a lot having more than 20 percent defectives (a bad lot) still has some probability of acceptance (say 5%) whereas a lot with a high quality (low percent defective, say 3%) has some chance of getting rejected (say probability of 0.1 or 10%).

Exhibit 12.9 : A Typical Operating Characteristic Curve

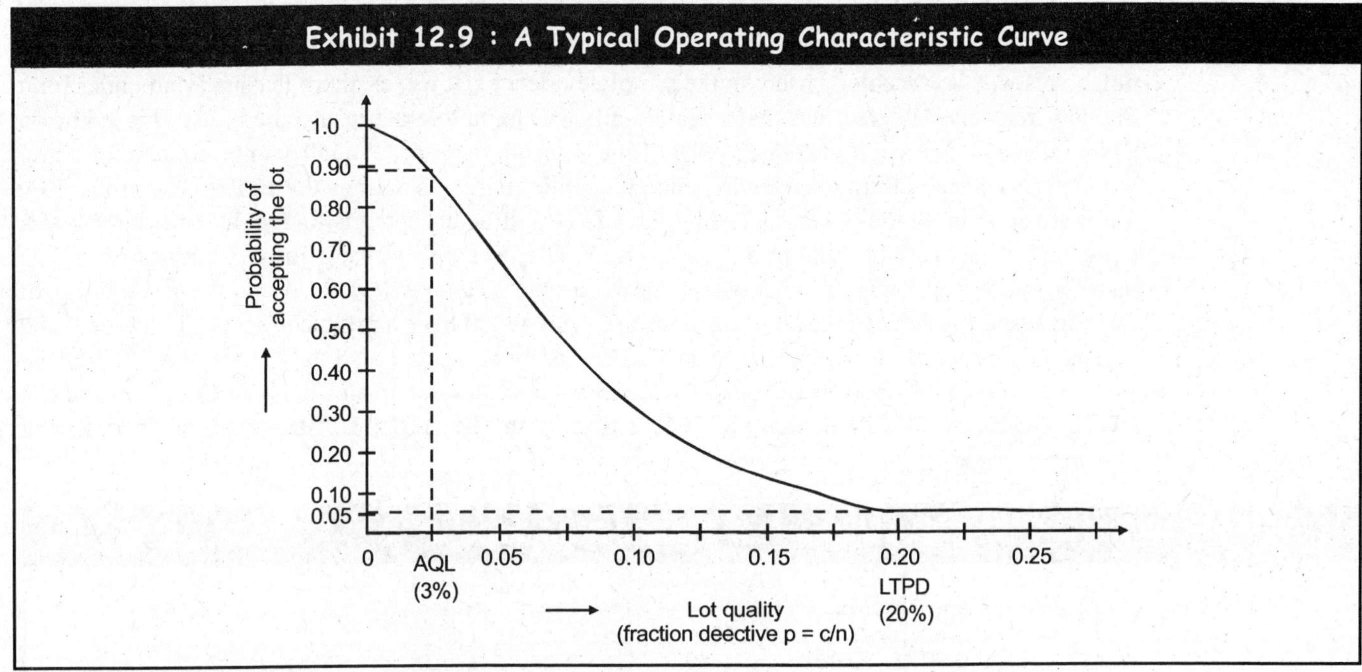

The degree to which a sampling plan discriminates between good and bad lots is a function of the steepness of the graph's O.C. curve, the steeper the curve, the more discriminating the sampling plan. *Exhibit 12.10* illustrates this.

Exhibit 12.10 : OC Curve for Discriminating between Good and Bad Lots

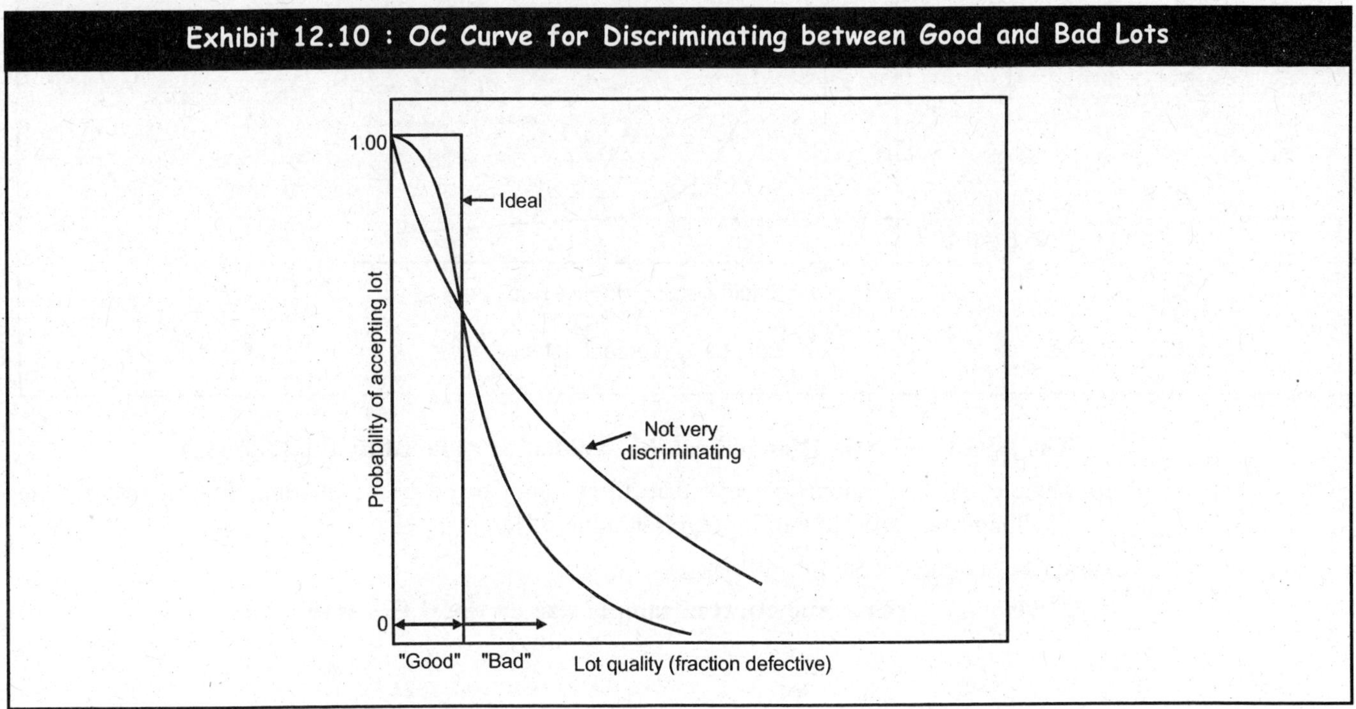

The curve for an ideal plan (*i.e.* ideal O.C. curve) can perfectly discriminate between good and bad lots. To achieve this degree of discrimination, 100 percent inspection of each lot is necessary. Because of the cost and time needed for 100 percent inspection, it is often ruled out, leaving acceptance sampling as the only viable alternative.

For these reasons, buyers (consumers) are generally willing to accept lots that contain small percentage of defective items as "good" lots especially if the cost related to a few defectives is low. Often this percentage is between 1 and 2 percent defective. This figure (fraction defective) is known as **acceptance quality level (AQL) or acceptable quality level.**

Because of the inability of random sampling to clearly identify lots that contain more than specified percentage of defectives, consumers recognise that some lots that actually contain more defectives will be accepted based on the sample evidence. However, there is usually an upper limit on the percentage of defectives that a customer is willing to tolerate in accepted lots. This is known as ***lot tolerance percent defective*** (LTPD). Thus, consumers want lot quality to be equal to or better than AQL and are willing to live with some lots with quality as poor as the LTPD. The probability that a lot containing defective exceeding the LTPD will be accepted is known as ***consumer's risk*** (β) or the probability of making a ***type II error.*** The probability that a lot containing acceptable quality level (AQL) will be rejected is known as the ***producer's risk*** (α) or the probability of making a ***type I error.*** Many sampling plans are designed to have a producer's risk of 5 percent and a consumer's risk of 10 percent, although other combinations are also used. It is possible by trial and error to design a plan that will provide selected values for α and β given the AQL and the LTPD. ***Exhibit 12.11* illustrates an O.C. curve with the AQL, LTPD, producer's risk and consumers risk.**

Exhibit 12.11 : Typical O.C. Curve

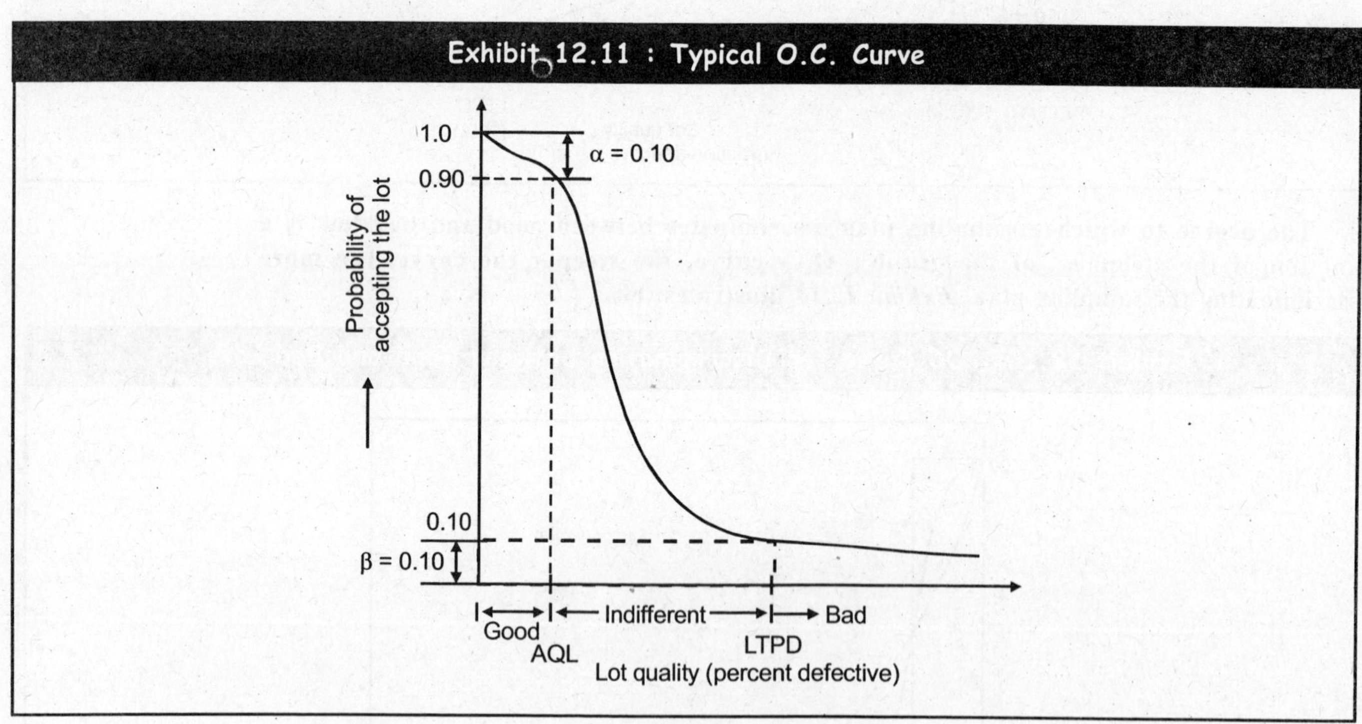

The type I and type II errors can be avoided or reduced by the following :

(i) Sample must be taken in ways that allow them to be truly random, thus improving the likelihood that sample will be representative of lots,

(ii) By increasing the sample size (n).

***Exhibit 12.12* shows the effect of sample size on the O.C. curve.**

Exhibit 12.12 : O.C. Curves for Different Sample Sizes and Acceptance Numbers (*i.e.,* n and c)

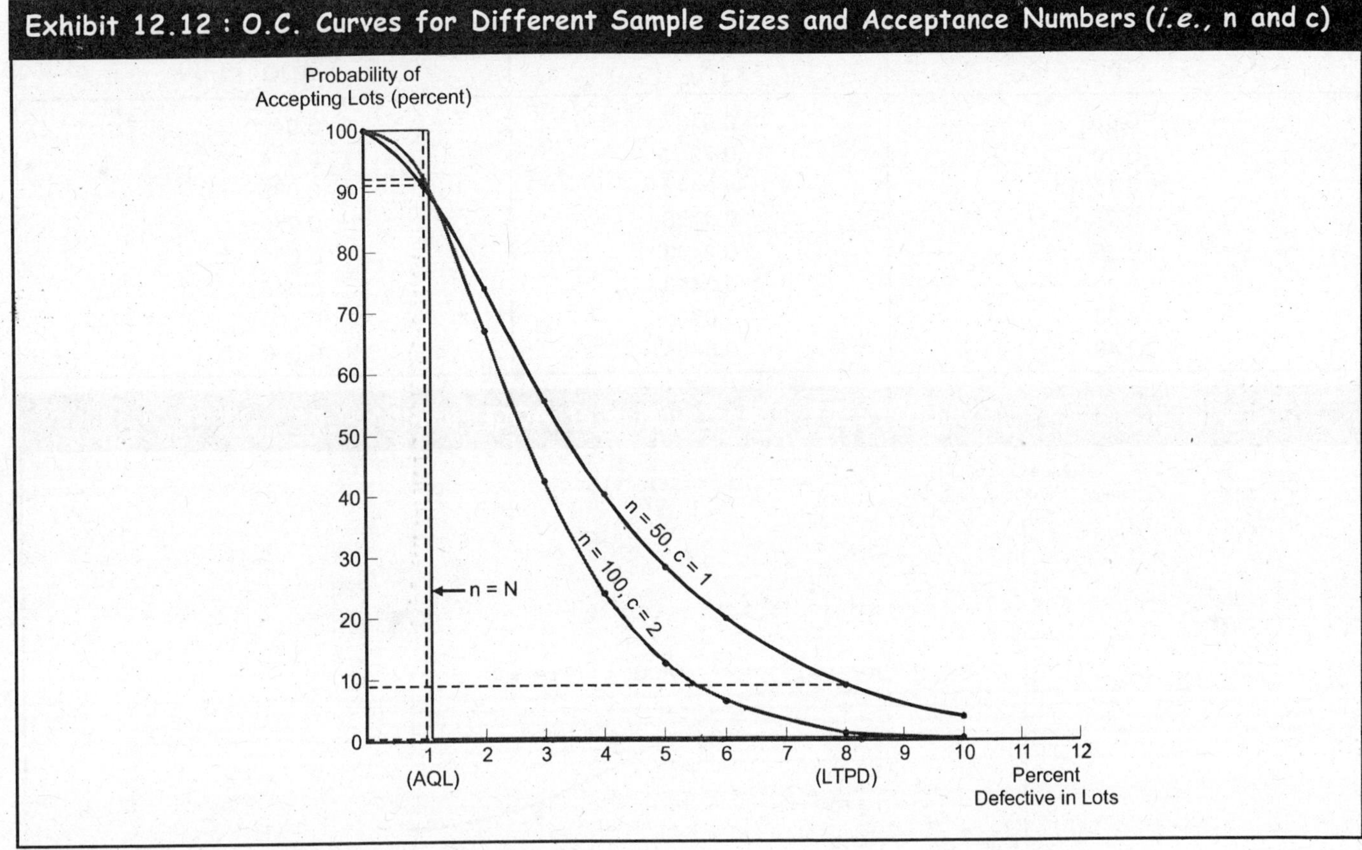

Average Outgoing Quality of Inspected Lots

An interesting feature of acceptance sampling is that the level of inspection automatically adjusts to the quality of lots being inspected, assuming rejected lots are subjected to 100 percent inspection. The O.C. curve reveals that the greater the percentage of defectives in a lot, the less likely the lot is to be accepted. Good lots have a high probability and bad lots have a low probability of being accepted. If the lots inspected are mostly good, few will end up going through 100 percent inspection. The poorer the quality of the lots, the greater the number of lots that will come under close scrutiny. This tends to improve overall quality of lots by weeding out defectives. In this way, the level of inspection is affected by lot quality.

If all lots have some given fraction defective 'p' the ***average outgoing quality*** **(AOQ)** of the lots can be computed using the following formula, assuming defectives are replaced with good items.

$$AOQ = P_{ac} \times p\left(\frac{N-n}{N}\right)$$

Where, P_{ac} = Probability of accepting the lot; p = Fraction defective

N = Lot size; n = Sample size

In practice, the last term is often omitted since it is usually close to 1.0 and therefore has little effect on the resulting values. The formula then becomes,

$$AOQ = P_{ac} \times p.$$

Illustration of construction of AOQ curve

N = 500, n = 10, c = 1

Let value of p vary from 0.05 to 0.40 in steps of 0.05. The probabilities of acceptance P_{ac} from the table of Cumulative Binomial probabilities given below. (Refer *Table 12.1*)

$$AOQ = P_{ac} \times p$$

Table 12.1 : Cumulative Binomial Properties

p	P_{ac}	AOQ
0.05	0.9137	0.046
0.10	0.7361	0.074
0.15	0.5443	0.082
0.20	0.3758	0.075
0.25	0.2440	0.061
0.30	0.1493	0.045
0.35	0.0860	0.030
0.40	0.0464	0.019

Exhibit 12.13 : Construction of AOQ curve

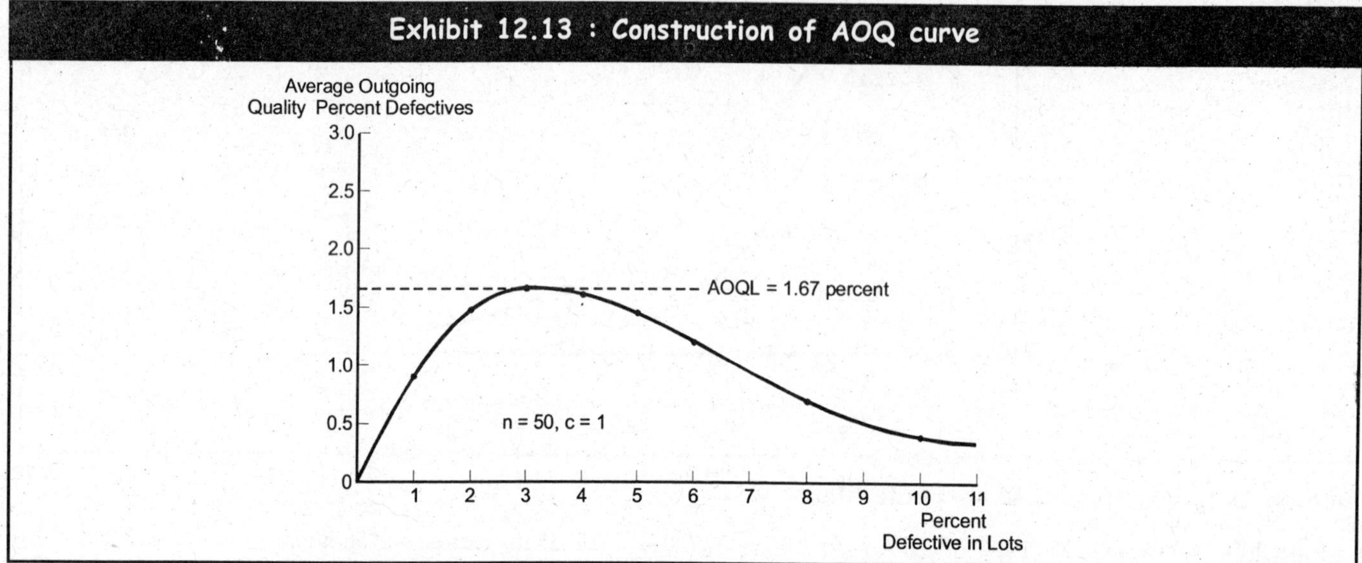

The AOQ curve illustrates the point that if lots are very good or very bad, the average outgoing quality will be high. The maximum point on the curve becomes apparent in the process of calculating values for the curve.

The several implications of the graph are :

1. A manager can determine the worst possible outgoing quality.
2. The manager can determine the amount of inspection that will be needed by obtaining an estimate of the incoming quality. The manager can use this information to establish the relationship between inspection cost and incoming fraction defective, thereby underscoring the benefits by implementing the process improvements to reduce the incoming fraction defective rather than trying to weed out bad items through inspection.

12.11 STATISTICAL PROCESS CONTROL

Statistical process control (SPC) means control of the process through the use of statistical methods.

***Statistical Process Control (SPC)* is the application of statistical techniques to determine whether the output of a process conforms to the product or service design.** In SPC, control charts are used primarily to detect production of defective products or services or to indicate that the production process has changed and that products or services will deviate from their design specifications unless something is done to correct the situation.

Source of variation : All processes are subject to a certain degree of variability. No two products or services are exactly alike because the processes used to produce them contain many sources of variation, even if the processes are working as intended. Nothing can be done to eliminate variation in process output completely, but management can investigate the causes of variation to minimise it.

Natural variations : Natural variations affect almost every production process and are to be expected as inherent in the process. Natural variations are due to ***common*** or ***chance*** causes which are purely random, unidentifiable sources of variation. These causes are unavoidable with the current process which is in statistical control. Natural variations behave like a constant system of chance causes. Although individual values are all different, as a group, they form a pattern that can be described as a ***distribution***. **When these distributions are *normal*, they are characterised by two parameters:**

(i) **mean** μ (the measure of central tendency in this case, the average value).

$$\mu = \frac{\sum_{i=1}^{n} x_i}{n}$$

where, x_i = observation of a quality characteristic ; n = total number of observations

μ = mean or average value

(ii) **Standard deviation** σ (the measure of dispersion about the mean known as spread). Another measure of the dispersion is the *range* which is the difference between the largest observation and the smallest in a sample.

$$\text{Range 'R'} = X_{max} - X_{min}$$

$$\text{Standard deviation, } \sigma = \sqrt{\frac{\sum_{i=1}^{n}(x_i - \mu)^2}{n-1}}$$

As long as the distribution (output measurements) remains within specified limits, the process is said to be **"in control"** and natural variations are tolerated.

Assignable Variations: Assignable variation in a process can be traced to a specific reason known as ***assignable cause of variation***. Factors such as machine or tool wear, misadjusted equipment, fatigued or untrained worker or new batches of raw materials are all potential sources of assignable variations.

Natural and assignable variations distinguish two tasks for the operations managers: *(i)* to ensure that the process is capable of operating under control with only natural variation and *(ii)* to identify and eliminate assignable variation so that the processes will remain under control.

Walter Shewhart of Bell Laboratories made the distinction between the common and special causes of variation which are also referred to as **natural (or chance) and assignable causes of variation.** Walter Shewhart developed a simple but powerful tool to separate the two – the ***control chart***.

Statistical Process Control (SPC) is used to measure the performance of a process. A process is said to be operating in *statistical control* when the only source of variation is chance or common or natural causes. The process is said to be out of control when assignable causes of variation enter the process. The process must to brought into statistical control by detecting and eliminating special or assignable causes of variation. Then only the performance of the process is predictable and its ability to meet customer expectations can be assessed.

SPC is used to measure the performance of a process. The objective of a SPC system is to provide a statistical signal when assignable causes of variation are present.

The objective of a SPC system is to provide a statistical signal when assignable causes of variation are present. Such signals can facilitate quick and appropriate action to eliminate assignable causes. SPC is a proven technique for improving quality and productivity. Many customers require their suppliers to provide evidence of statistical process control. Thus SPC provides a means by which a firm may demonstrate its quality capability, an activity necessary for survival in today's highly competitive markets. Because SPC requires process to show measurable variation within 3 sigma, it is ineffective for quality levels approaching six sigma. However, SPC is quite effective for companies in the early stages of quality efforts.

The Inspection Process : Many firms use quality inspection merely trying, often unsuccessfully to weed out the defectives before they reach the customers. This approach is doomed to failure because of internal and external failure costs. In contrast, world class companies combine early inspection with SPC to monitor quality and detect and correct abnormalities. Important decisions in implementing such a program include how to measure quality characteristics, what size of sample to collect and at which stage in the process to conduct inspection.

Quality Measurements : To detect abnormal variations in output, inspectors must be able to measure quality characteristics. Quality can be evaluated in two ways – *(i)* to measure ***variables*** – that is product or service characteristic such as weight, length, volume, area etc that can be measured. The advantage of measuring a quality characteristic is that if a product or service misses its quality specifications, the inspector knows by how much. But such measurements involve special equipments, employee skills, exacting procedures and time and effort.

Another way to evaluate quality is to measure ***attributes*** (quality characteristics) that is, product or service characteristics that can be quickly counted for acceptable quality. This method allows inspectors to make a simple yes-no decision about whether a product or service meets specifications. Examples of attributes are a number of bad light bulbs in a given lot or number of letters or data entry records typed with errors or number of flights arriving within 15 minutes of scheduled time.

Sampling : Because of natural and assignable variation, SPC uses averages of small samples (say 5 numbers) as opposed to data on individual parts. A sampling plan specifies a sample size, which is a quantity of randomly selected observations of process outputs, the time between successive samples and decision rules that determine when action should be taken.

SPC Methodology : Control charts, like the other basic tools for quality improvement, are relatively simple to use. **Control charts have three basic applications: *(i)* to establish a state of statistical control *(ii)* to monitor a process and signal when the process goes out of control and *(iii)* to determine process capability.**

The summary of the steps required to develop and use control charts are given below: Step 1 to 4 focus on establishing a state of statistical control. In step 5, the charts are used for ongoing monitoring and finally in step 6, the data are used for process capability analysis.

Step 1. Preparation

(a) Choose the variable or attribute (quality characteristic) to be measured.

(b) Determine the basis, size and frequency of sampling.

(c) Set up the control chart.

Step 2. Data collection

(a) Record the data.

(b) Calculate relevant statistics; averages, ranges, proportion and so on.

(c) Plot the statistics on the chart.

Step 3. Determination of trial control limits

(a) Draw the central line (process average) on the chart.

(b) Compute the upper and lower control limits.

Step 4. Analysis and interpretation

(a) Investigate the client for lack of control.

(b) Eliminate out-of-control points.

(c) Recompute control limits if necessary.

Step 5. Use as a problem-solving tool

(a) Consider data collection and plotting.

(b) Identify out-of-control situations and take corrective action.

Step 6. Use the control chart data to determine process capability if desired.

Control Charts for Variable Data

Variable data are those that are measured along a continuous scale. Examples of variable data are length, weight, speed etc. The charts most commonly used for variables are the $\overline{X}$ chart ("X bar" chart or mean chart) and the R-chart (range chart). The $\overline{X}$ chart is used to monitor the variation in the process. The range is used as a measure of variation simply for convenience, for calculations by workers on the shop floor while constructing the control charts. For large samples and when data are analysed by computer programs, the standard deviation (σ) is a better measure of variability.

Variable data are those that are measured along a continuous scale. $\overline{X}$ chart and 'R' chart are used for variable data

The $\overline{X}$ chart and R chart go hand in hand when monitoring variables, because they measure two critical parameters: ***central tendency*** and ***dispersion.***

Central limit theorem: ***Central limit theorem*** is the theoretical foundation of $\overline{X}$ charts. This theorem is stated as ***"sampling distributions can be assumed to be normally distributed even though the population distributions are not normal".*** The only exception to this theorem occurs when sample sizes are extremely small. It is found from studies that even if the sample size is fairly small (4 to 5), however, their sampling distributions are very close to normal distribution. The theorem also states that: *(i)* the mean of the distribution of the $\overline{X}$s (called $\overline{\overline{X}}$) will equal to the mean of the overall population (called μ) and *(ii)* the standard deviation of the ***sampling distribution*** $\sigma_{\overline{x}}$ will be the ***population*** standard deviation σ divided by the square root of the sample size n.

In other words, $\overline{\overline{X}} = \mu$,

$$\sigma_{\overline{x}} = \frac{\sigma}{\sqrt{n}}$$

Exhibit 12.14 **shows three possible population distributions, each with its own mean μ and standard deviation σ.**

Exhibit 12.14 : The Relationship between Population and Sampling Distribution

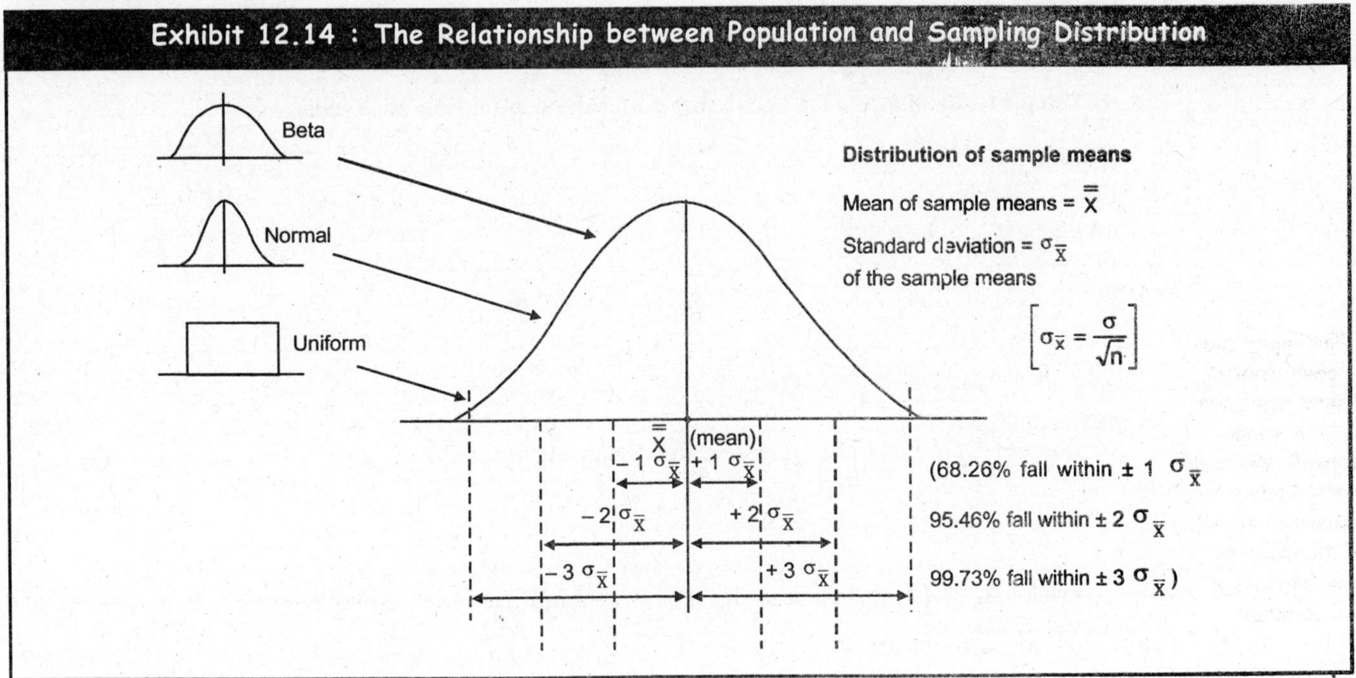

The power of the central limit theorem in quality control lies in its ability to allow use of the normal distribution to easily set limits for control charts and acceptance plans for both attributes and variables.

Constructing $\overline{X}$ and R Charts and Establishing Statistical Control

The following steps are involved:

Step 1: Collect data on the variable quality measurement and organise the data by sample number. Preferably, atleast 20 samples should be taken for use in constructing the control charts. The sample size varies between 3 and 10, generally and sample size of 5 is most common.

In general, the sample size which is constant for all samples is denoted by 'n' and the number of samples is denoted by K. (also known as sub-groups)

Step 2: Compute the range 'R' for each sample and the average range $\overline{R}$ for the set of K samples.

Range $R = X_{max} - X_{min}$ for each of the K samples.

$$\text{Average range } \overline{R} = \frac{\sum R}{K} = \frac{R_1 + R_2 + ... + R_K}{K}$$

Step 3: Determine the upper and lower control limits of the 'R' chart as below:

$$\text{Central line} = \overline{R} = \frac{\sum R}{K} = \frac{R_1 + R_2 + ... + R_K}{K}$$

Upper control limit for range = $UCL_R = D_4\overline{R}$

Lower control limit for range = $LCL_R = D_3\overline{R}$

Where D_4 and D_3 are constants that depend on sample size (n) (Refer Appendix F for values of D_3 and D_4).

Step 4: Test for homogeneity: Compare all the individual values of range R (*i.e.,* $R_1, R_2, ...R_K$) with the values of upper and lower control limits for range (R) (*i.e.,* UCL_R & LCL_R). If all range values fall between the values of UCL_R and LCL_R, the range values are treated as homogeneous. If any value of R falls outside these two limits, discard the corresponding sample values and recompute range values, UCR_R and LCL_R for remaining samples. Repeat test for homogeneity and other steps till homogeneity is reached.

Step 5: Calculate $\overline{X}$ for each sample and the central line of $\overline{X}$-chart, $\overline{\overline{X}}$

$$\overline{X} = \frac{\sum X}{n} = \frac{X_1 + X_2 + ... + Xn}{n}$$

$$\overline{\overline{X}} = \frac{\sum \overline{X}}{K} = \frac{\overline{X}_1 + \overline{X}_2 + ... + \overline{X}_K}{K}$$

The upper and lower control limits represent the range between which all plotted points are expected to fall if the process is in "statistical control"

$$\text{Central line for } \overline{X} \text{ chart} = \overline{\overline{X}} = \frac{\sum \overline{X}}{K}$$

Step 6: Determine the upper and lower control limits for $\overline{X}$. *i.e.,*

$$UCL_{\overline{X}} = \overline{\overline{X}} + A_2\overline{R}$$

$$LCL_{\overline{X}} = \overline{\overline{X}} - A_2\overline{R}$$

where A_2 is a constant that depends on sample size (n). (Refer Appendix F for values of constant A_2).

Step 7: Test for homogeneity: Compare all individual values of $\overline{X}$ with the values of $UCL_{\overline{X}}$ and $LCL_{\overline{X}}$. If any of the values of $\overline{X}$ falls outside these values, discard that sample and compute central line, UCL_R and LCL_R for the remaining samples. Repeat test for homogeneity and other steps till homogeneity is reached.

Step 8: Construct the $\overline{X}$ (mean) chart and the 'R' (range) chart and plot the $\overline{X}$ values and 'R' values in the respective charts.

The control limits represent the range between which all points are expected to fall if the process is in *"statistical control"*. If any points fall outside the control limits or if any unusual patterns are observed, then some special (or assignable) cause has probably affected the process. Then the process should be studied to determine the cause. If no assignable causes are found, the variations are due to common (chance) causes.

Using Mean and Range Charts

In determining whether a process is in statistical control, the R-chart is always analysed first. Since the control limits on $\overline{X}$ chart depend on the average range ($\overline{R}$), special (or assignable) causes in the R-chart may produce unusual pattern in the $\overline{X}$ chart even when the centering of the process is in control. Once the statistical control is established in the R-chart, attention may turn to the $\overline{X}$-chart. **The $\overline{X}$-chart is sensitive to shifts in the process mean whereas the R-chart is sensitive to shifts in the process standard deviation. Consequently, by using both charts simultaneously, we can track changes in the process distribution.**

Interpreting patterns in control charts : When a process is in statistical control, the points on a control chart fluctuate randomly between the control limits with no recognizable pattern. **The following checklist provides a set of general rules for examining a process to determine whether it is in control:**

1. No points are outside control limits.
2. The number of points above and below the central line is about the same.
3. The points seem to fall randomly above and below the central line and
4. Most points, but not all, are near the central line, and only a few are close to the control limits.

The upper and lower control limits are computed to be three standard deviations from the over-all mean.

The underlying assumption behind these rules is that the distribution of sample means is normal. This assumption follows from the central limit theorem of statistics, which states that the distribution of sample means approaches a normal distribution as the sample size increases regardless of the original distribution. Of course, for small sample sizes (4 or 5), the distribution of the original data must be reasonably normal for this assumption to hold. **The upper and lower control limits are computed to be three standard deviations from the overall mean.** Thus, the probability that any sample mean falls outside the control limits is very small.

Since the normal distribution is symmetric, about the same number of points fall above as below the central line. Also, since the mean of the normal distribution is the median, about half the points fall on either side of the central line. Finally, about 68 percent of a normal distribution falls within one standard deviation of the mean, thus, most-but not all - points should be close to the central line. These characteristics will hold provided that the mean and variance of the original data have not changed during the time the data were collected, that is, the process is stable.

Process Monitoring and Control : After a process is determined to be in control, the charts should be used on a daily basis to monitor production, identify any special causes that might arise and make corrections as necessary. ***The chart tells when to leave the process alone!*** Unnecessary adjustments to a process result in a non-productive labour, reduced production and increased variability of output.

It is more productive, if operators themselves take the samples and chart the data. In this way, they can react quickly to changes in the process and immediately make adjustments. Operators must be trained to do this effectively.

Improvements in conformance typically follow the introduction of control charts on the shop floor, particularly when the process is labour intensive. Apparently, management involvement in the operator's work often produce positive behavioural modifications. Under such circumstances and as good practice, management and operators should revise the control limits periodically and determine a new process capability as improvements take place.

Control charts are designed to be used by production operations rather than by inspectors or quality control personnel.

Control charts are designed to be used by production operators rather than by inspectors or quality control personnel. Under the philosophy of statistical process control, the burden of quality rests with the operators themselves. The use of control charts allows operators to react quickly to special causes of variation. The range is used in place of the standard deviation for the very reason that it allows shop-floor personnel to easily make the necessary computations to plot points on a control chart using only simple calculations.

Estimating process capability : After a process has been brought to a state of statistical control by eliminating special causes of variation, the data may be used to estimate process capability. This approach is not very accurate, because it uses the average range rather than the estimated standard deviation of the original data. Nevertheless, it is a quick and useful method, provided that the distribution of the original data is reasonably normal.

Under the assumption of normality, the standard deviation of the original data can be estimated as follows:

$$\sigma = \frac{\overline{R}}{d_2}$$

where d_2 is the constant that depends on the sample size and is also given in Appendix B.

Process capability is given by 6 σ. The natural variation of individual measurements is given by $\overline{\overline{X}} \pm 3\,\sigma$.

Illustration of Construction and Analysis of Control Charts

Control charts for Silicon Wafer Production

The thickness of silicon wafers used in the production of semiconductors must be closely controlled. The tolerance of one such product is specified as ± 0.005 inches. In one production facility, three wafers were selected each hour and thickness measured carefully within one ten-thousandth of an inch. ***Exhibit 12.15* shows the results obtained for 25 samples.** *For example,* the mean of the first sample is

$$\frac{41+70+22}{3} = \frac{113}{3} \approx 44.$$

The range of sample 1 is 70 – 22 = 48.

The calculations of the average range, overall mean and control limits are shown below.

$$\overline{R} = \frac{\sum R}{K} = \frac{676}{25} = 27 \quad ; \quad \overline{\overline{X}} = \frac{\sum \overline{X}}{K} = \frac{1221}{25} = 48.8$$

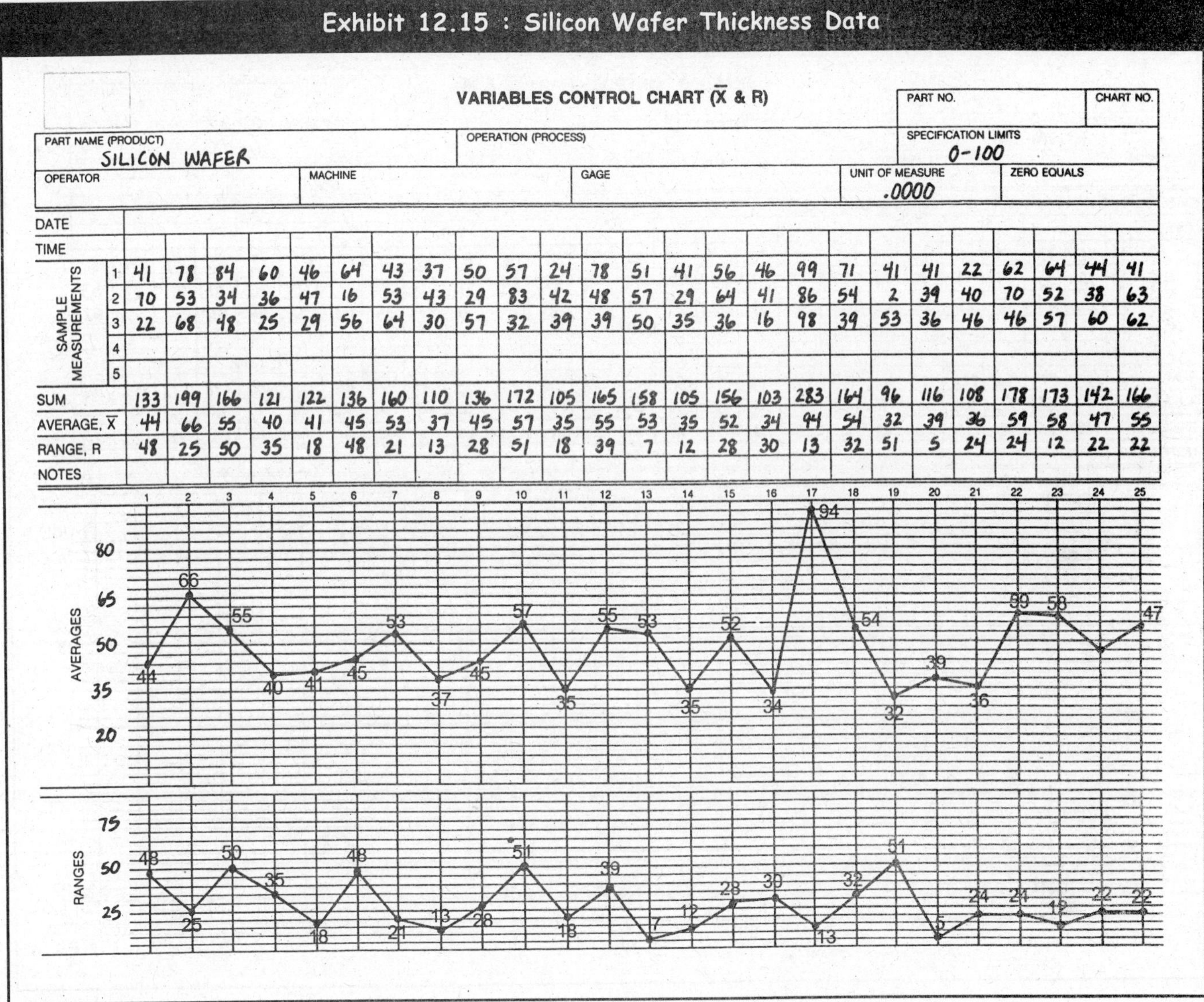
Exhibit 12.15 : Silicon Wafer Thickness Data

VARIABLES CONTROL CHART ($\bar{X}$ & R)

PART NAME (PRODUCT)	OPERATION (PROCESS)	PART NO.	CHART NO.
SILICON WAFER		SPECIFICATION LIMITS 0-100	

OPERATOR	MACHINE	GAGE	UNIT OF MEASURE	ZERO EQUALS
			.0000	

	1	2	3	4	5	6	7	8	9	10	11	12	13
DATE													
TIME													
SAMPLE MEASUREMENTS 1	41	78	84	60	46	64	43	37	50	57	24	78	51
2	70	53	34	36	47	16	53	43	29	83	42	48	57
3	22	68	48	25	29	56	64	30	57	32	39	39	50
4													
5													
SUM	133	199	166	121	122	136	160	110	136	172	105	165	158
AVERAGE, $\bar{X}$	44	66	55	40	41	45	53	37	45	57	35	55	53
RANGE, R	48	25	50	35	18	48	21	13	28	51	18	39	7
NOTES													

	14	15	16	17	18	19	20	21	22	23	24	25
DATE												
TIME												
SAMPLE MEASUREMENTS 1	41	56	46	99	71	41	41	22	62	64	44	41
2	29	64	41	86	54	2	39	40	70	52	38	63
3	35	36	16	98	39	53	36	46	46	57	60	62
4												
5												
SUM	105	156	103	283	164	96	116	108	178	173	142	166
AVERAGE, $\bar{X}$	35	52	34	94	54	32	39	36	59	58	47	55
RANGE, R	12	28	30	13	32	51	5	24	24	12	22	22
NOTES												

For sample size n = 3, A_2 = 1.023, D_3 = 0 and D_4 = 2.574. (Refer Appendix F)

$A_2\bar{R}$ = 1.023 × 27 = 27.6.

$$UCL_{\bar{X}} = \bar{\bar{X}} + A_2\bar{R} = 48.8 + 27.6 = 76.4$$

$$LCL_{\bar{X}} = \bar{\bar{X}} - A_2\bar{R} = 48.8 - 27.6 = 21.2$$

$$UCL_R = D_4\bar{R} = 2.574 \times 27 = 69.5$$

$$LCL_R = D_3\bar{R} = \text{NIL as } D_3 = 0.$$

The central line, upper and lower control limits for $\bar{X}$ chart and 'R' chart are drawn in ***Exhibit 12.16.***

Test for homogeneity: Examining the range chart first, it appears that the process is in control since all range values for 25 samples fall within the control limits for range (*i.e.* between 0 and 69.5). In the $\bar{X}$ chart, however, sample 17 lies above the upper control limit (*i.e.* $\bar{X}$ value for sample 17 which is 94 is more than the upper control limit for $\bar{X}$ = 76.4). Hence the data regarding sample 17 should be eliminated from the control chart calculations. The calculation for modified values of central line, upper and lower control limits are shown below after eliminating sample number 17, thereby reducing the samples to 24 (*i.e.* K = 24).

Exhibit 12.16 : Initial Control Chart

VARIABLES CONTROL CHART ($\overline{X}$ & R)

PART NO.	CHART NO.

PART NAME (PRODUCT)	OPERATION (PROCESS)	SPECIFICATION LIMITS
SILICON WAFER		0-100

OPERATOR	MACHINE	GAGE	UNIT OF MEASURE	ZERO EQUALS
			.0000	

DATE													
TIME													
Sample measurements 1	41	78	84	60	46	64	43	37	50	57	24	78	51
2	70	53	34	36	47	16	53	43	29	83	42	48	57
3	22	68	48	25	29	56	64	30	57	32	39	39	50
4													
5													
SUM	133	199	166	121	122	136	160	110	136	172	105	165	158
AVERAGE, $\overline{X}$	44	66	55	40	41	45	53	37	45	57	35	55	53
RANGE, R	48	25	50	35	18	48	21	13	28	51	18	39	7
NOTES													
	1	2	3	4	5	6	7	8	9	10	11	12	13

DATE												
TIME												
Sample measurements 1	41	56	46	99	71	41	41	22	62	64	44	41
2	29	64	41	86	54	2	39	40	70	52	38	63
3	35	36	16	98	39	53	36	46	46	57	60	62
4												
5												
SUM	105	156	103	283	164	96	116	108	178	173	142	166
AVERAGE, $\overline{X}$	35	52	34	94	54	32	39	36	59	58	47	55
RANGE, R	12	28	30	13	32	51	5	24	24	12	22	22
NOTES												
	14	15	16	17	18	19	20	21	22	23	24	25

AVERAGES: $UCL_{\overline{x}}$ 76.4; $CL_{\overline{x}}$ 48.8; $LCL_{\overline{x}}$ 21.2

RANGES: UCL_R 69.5; CL_R 27; LCL_R = 0

$$\overline{R} = \frac{\sum R}{K} = \frac{663}{24} = 27.6$$

$$\overline{\overline{X}} = \frac{\sum \overline{X}}{K} = \frac{1127}{24} = 47.0$$

Central line for $\overline{X}$ chart = $\overline{\overline{X}}$ = 47.0.

Upper control limit $UCL_{\overline{X}} = \overline{\overline{X}} + A_2\overline{R} = 47.0 + (1.073 \times 27.6) = 75.2$

$LCL_{\overline{X}} = \overline{\overline{X}} - A_2\overline{R} = 47.0 - (1.073 \times 27.6) = 18.8$

Central line for 'R' chart = $\overline{R}$ = 27.6.

Upper control limit $UCL_R = D_4\overline{R} = 2.574 \times 27.6 = 71.0$

Lower control limit $LCL_R = D_3\overline{R} = 0 \times 27.6 = 0.$

Test for homogeneity : All range values for 24 samples lie between zero and 71.0 which are the control limits for range. All $\overline{X}$ values for 24 samples lie between 18.8 and 75.2 which are the control limits for mean ($\overline{X}$). Hence the test for homogeneity is satisfied and the resulting charts appear to be in control.

Exhibit 12.17 **shows the revised control chart after testing for homogeneity.**

Exhibit 12.17 : Revised Control Chart

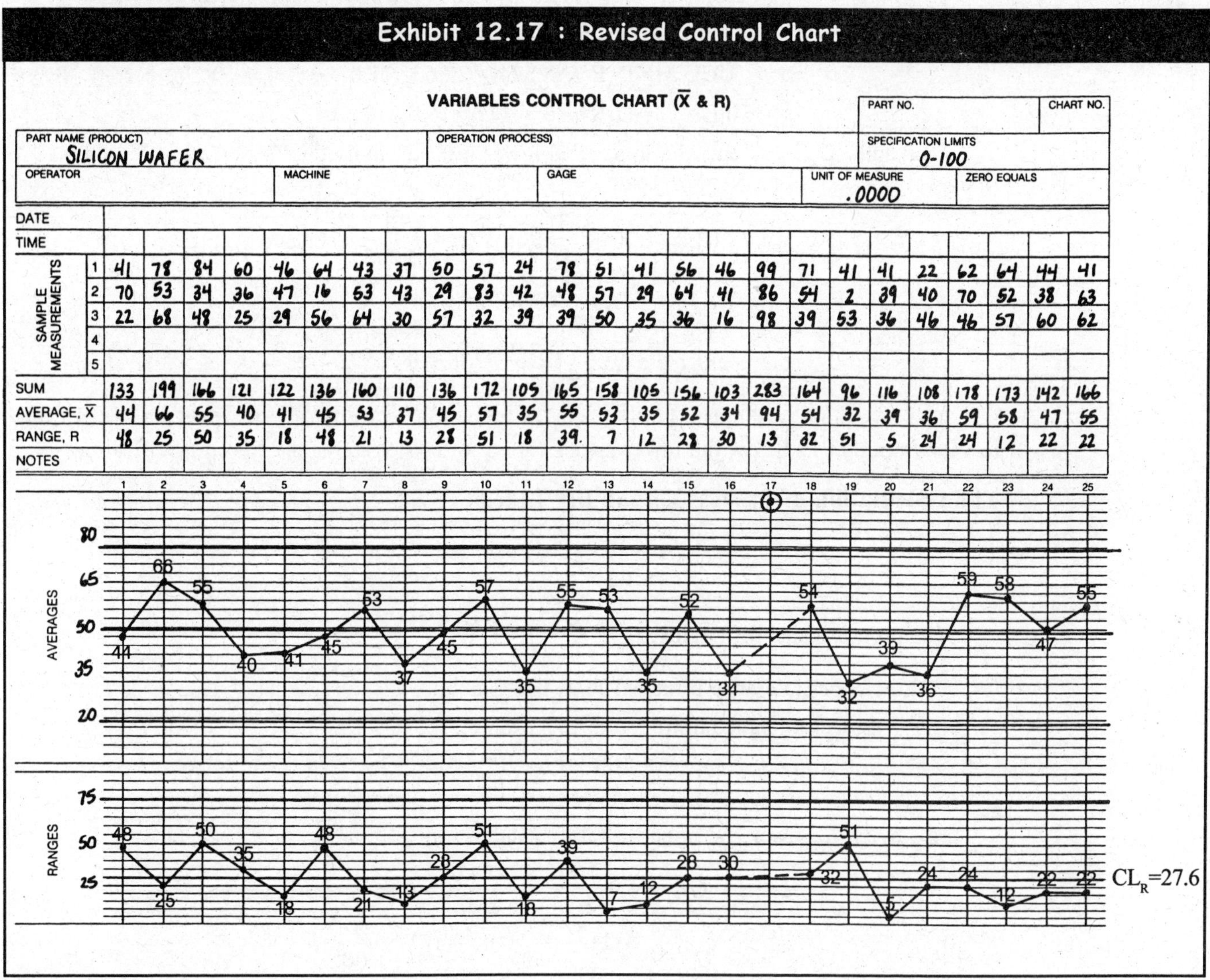
VARIABLES CONTROL CHART ($\overline{X}$ & R)

PART NO. | CHART NO.

PART NAME (PRODUCT): SILICON WAFER | OPERATION (PROCESS) | SPECIFICATION LIMITS: 0-100

OPERATOR | MACHINE | GAGE | UNIT OF MEASURE: .0000 | ZERO EQUALS

	1	2	3	4	5	6	7	8	9	10	11	12	13	14	15	16	17	18	19	20	21	22	23	24	25
DATE																									
TIME																									
SAMPLE MEASUREMENTS 1	41	78	84	60	46	64	43	37	50	57	24	78	51	41	56	46	99	71	41	41	22	62	64	44	41
2	70	53	34	36	47	16	53	43	29	83	42	48	57	29	64	41	86	54	2	39	40	70	52	38	63
3	22	68	48	25	29	56	64	30	57	32	39	39	50	35	36	16	98	39	53	36	46	46	57	60	62
4																									
5																									
SUM	133	199	166	121	122	136	160	110	136	172	105	165	158	105	156	103	283	164	96	116	108	178	173	142	166
AVERAGE, $\overline{X}$	44	66	55	40	41	45	53	37	45	57	35	55	53	35	52	34	94	54	32	39	36	59	58	47	55
RANGE, R	48	25	50	35	18	48	21	13	28	51	18	39.	7	12	28	30	13	32	51	5	24	24	12	22	22
NOTES																									

Estimating Process Capability : After a process has been brought to a state of statistical control by eliminating special causes of variation, the data may be used to estimate process capability. Under the normality assumption, the standard deviation of the original data can be estimated as follows: $\sigma = \overline{R}/d_2$ where d_2 is a constant that depends on the sample size and is given in Appendix B. Process capability is given by 6σ. The natural variation of individual measurements is given by $\overline{\overline{X}} \pm 3\sigma$.

Estimating the process capability for the Silicon Wafer Thickness Example

For the sample of size 3, d_2 = 1.693 from Appendix F. The calculations for 24 samples are:

$$\overline{R} = \frac{\sum R}{K} = \frac{663}{24} = 27.6$$

$$\overline{\overline{X}} = \frac{\sum \overline{X}}{K} = \frac{1127}{24} = 47.0$$

$A_2\overline{R}$ = 1.023 × 27.6 = 28.2.

$$UCL_{\overline{X}} = \overline{\overline{X}} + A_2\overline{R} = 47.0 + (1.073 \times 27.6) = 75.2$$
$$LCL_{\overline{X}} = \overline{\overline{X}} - A_2\overline{R} = 47.0 - (1.073 \times 27.6) = 18.8$$
$$UCL_R = D_4\overline{R} = 2.574 \times 27.6 = 71.0$$
$$LCL_R = D_3\overline{R} = 0 \times 27.6 = \text{NIL.}$$

UL_X and LL_X represents the upper and lower limit on individual observations based on 3 σ limits.

$$UL_X = \overline{\overline{X}} + \frac{3}{d_2}\overline{R} = 47.0 + \frac{3}{1.693} \times 27.6$$
$$= 47.0 + 48.9 = 95.9$$
$$LL_X = \overline{\overline{X}} - \frac{3}{d_2}\overline{R} = 47.0 - 48.9 = -1.9$$

The zero point of the data is the lower specification, meaning that the thickness is expected to vary from 0.0019 below the lower specification to 0.0959 above the lower specification.

The Calculation of Process Capability Index

$$6\,\sigma = \frac{6}{d_2}\overline{R} = 97.8$$

The process capability index, $C_p = \dfrac{UTL - LTL}{6\sigma}$

UTL = Upper tolerance limit = 100 in this example.

LTL = Lower tolerance limit = 0 in this example.

$$C_p = \frac{100 - 0}{97.8} = 1.02$$

However, the lower and upper capability indicis are

$$C_{pl} = \frac{\mu - LTL}{3\sigma} = \frac{47 - 0}{48.9} = 0.96$$

$$C_{pu} = \frac{UTL - \mu}{3\sigma} = \frac{100 - 47}{48.9} = 1.08$$

This analysis suggests that both the centering and the variation must be improved.

If the individual observations are normally distributed, then the probability of being out of specification can be computed. The data is assumed to be normal. The mean is 47 and the standard deviation $\sigma = \dfrac{97.8}{6} = 16.3$. ***Exhibit 12.18*** **shows the calculation for specification limits of 0 and 100.**

Exhibit 12.18 : Process Capability Probability Computation

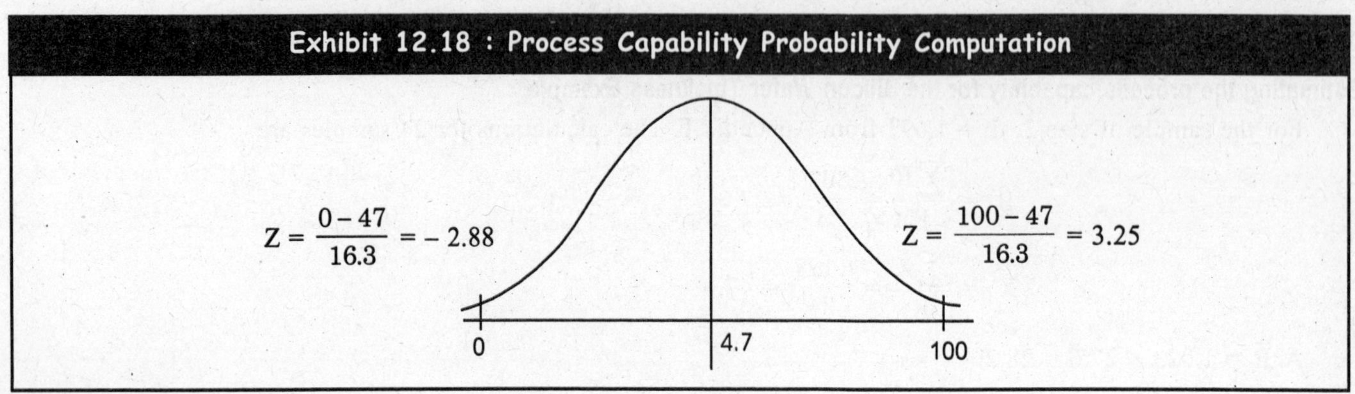

In Appendix E, the area between 0 and the mean (47) is 0.4980 (corresponding to the value of Z = 2.88), which means 0.2 percent of the output would be expected to fall below lower specification. The area to the right of 100 is approximately zero. Therefore, all the outputs can be expected to meet the upper specification.

Control limits are often confused with specification limits. Specification dimensions are usually stated in terms of individual parts for "hard" goods such as automotive hardware. However, in other applications such as chemical processes, specifications are stated in terms of average characteristics. Thus, control charts might mislead one into thinking that if all sample averages fall within the control limits, all output will be conforming. This assumption is not true. Control limits relate to ***average***, while specification limits relate to individual measurements. A sample average may fall within the upper and lower control limits even though some of the individual observations are out of specification. Since $\sigma_{\overline{X}} = \frac{\sigma}{\sqrt{n}}$, control limits are narrower than the natural variation in the process and do not represent process capability.

12.12 SPECIAL CONTROL CHARTS FOR VARIABLES DATA ('$\overline{X}$' AND 'S' CHARTS)

An alternative to using the R-chart along with $\overline{X}$ chart is to compute and plot the standard deviation 's' of each sample. Although the range has traditionally been used, (since it involves less computational effort and is easier for shop-floor personnel to understand), using 's' rather than 'R' has its advantages. The sample standard deviation is a more sensitive and better indicator of process variability, especially for larger sample sizes. Thus, when tight control of variability is required, 's' should be used.

The sample standard deviation is computed as

$$s = \sqrt{\frac{\sum_{i=1}^{n}(x_i - \overline{x})^2}{n-1}}$$

To construct an 's' chart, compute the standard deviation for each sample. Next, compute the average standard deviation $\overline{s}$ by averaging the sample standard deviations over all samples. Control limits for the 's' chart are given by

$$UCL_S = B_4\overline{s}$$

$$LCL_S = B_3\overline{s}$$

where B_3 and B_4 are constants found in Appendix B. For the associative $\overline{X}$ chart, the control limits derived from the overall standard deviation are:

$$UCL_{\overline{X}} = \overline{\overline{X}} + A_3\overline{s}$$

$$LCL_{\overline{X}} = \overline{\overline{X}} - A_3\overline{s}$$

where A_3 is a constant found in Appendix B.

Charts for Individuals (Sample size of one number)

Because of the development of automated inspection for many processes, every item produced can be now easily inspected and quality characteristics measured on every item produced. Hence, the sample size for process control is n = 1 and a control chart for ***individual measurements*** also called X chart – can be used.

With individual measurements, the process standard deviation can be estimated and three sigma control limits used. $\overline{R}/d_2$ provides an estimate of the ***process standard deviation.*** Thus, an 'x-chart' for individual measurements would have three sigma control limits defined by,

$$UCL_X = \overline{\overline{x}} + \frac{3\overline{R}}{d_2}$$

$$LCL_X = \overline{\overline{x}} - \frac{3\overline{R}}{d_2}$$

Sample of size 1, however, does not furnish enough information for process variability measurements. However, process variability can be determined by using a moving average of ranges or a ***moving range*** of n successive observations. *For example,* a moving range for n = 2 is computed by finding the absolute difference between two successive observations. The number of observations used in the moving range determines the constant d_2, hence for n = 2, from Appendix B, d_2 = 1.128. The moving range chart has control limits defined by,

$$UCL_R = D_4\overline{R}$$

$$LCL_R = D_3\overline{R}$$

which is comparable to the ordinary range chart.

Illustration of 'x' Chart with Moving Range

Consider a set of observations measuring the percentage of cobalt in a chemical process as given below:

Observation	Value	Observation	Value
1	3.75	13	3.5
2	3.8	14	3.0
3	3.7	15	3.8
4	3.2	16	3.4
5	3.5	17	3.6
6	3.05	18	3.1
7	3.5	19	3.55
8	3.25	20	3.65
9	3.6	21	3.45
10	3.1	22	3.30
11	4.0	23	3.75
12	4.0	24	3.5
		25	3.4

The moving average is computed as shown by taking absolute values of successive range and using the constants in Appendix B. *For example,* the first moving range is the absolute difference between the first two observations.

i.e. $|3.75 - 3.80| = 0.05$

The second moving range is computed as

$$|3.80 - 3.70| = 0.10$$

From these data, we find that $LCL_R = 0$

$$UCL_R = (3.267)\,(0.352) = 1.15$$

The moving averages are calculated as below:

Observation	Moving Range	Observation	Moving Range
1		14	0.50
2	0.05	15	0.80
3	0.10	16	0.40
4	0.50	17	0.20
5	0.30	18	0.50
6	0.45	19	0.45
7	0.45	20	0.10
8	0.25	21	0.20
9	0.35	22	0.15
10	0.50	23	0.45
11	0.90	24	0.25
12	0.00	25	0.10
13	0.50		

The moving range chart indicates that the process is in control since all the moving range values are found to be in between the control limits of moving averages (*i.e.* between zero and 1.15).

Next, the 'x' chart is constructed for the individual measurements.

$$UCL_x = \bar{x} + \frac{3\bar{R}}{d_2} = 3.498 + \frac{3(0.352)}{1.128} = 4.43$$

$$LCL_x = \bar{x} - \frac{3\bar{R}}{d_2} = 3.498 - \frac{3(0.352)}{1.128} = 2.56$$

Since all individual values of x for 25 samples lie between the control limit values of x (*i.e.* between 2.56 and 4.43), the process appears to be in control.

***Exhibit 12.19* shows the 'x' chart and Moving Range Chart.**

Some caution is necessary when interpreting patterns on the moving range chart. Points beyond control limits are signs of assignable causes. Successive ranges are correlated and they may cause patterns or trends in the chart that are not indicative of out-of-control situations. On the 'x' chart, individual observations are assumed to be uncorrelated, hence patterns and trends should be investigated.

Control charts for individuals have the advantage that specifications can be drawn on the chart and compared directly with the control limits. Some disadvantages also exist. Individuals' chart are less sensitive to many of the conditions that can be detected by $\bar{X}$ and 'R' - charts, *for example,* a process must vary a lot before a shift in the mean is detected. Also, short cycles and trends may appear on an individual's chart and not on $\bar{x}$ and 'R' chart. Finally, the assumption of normality of observations is more critical than for $\bar{X}$ and R-charts. When the normality assumption does not hold, greater chance for error is present.

Attributes can not be measured, but can be observed and counted Attribute data assume only two values: good or bad, defective or non-defective.

12.13 CONTROL CHARTS FOR ATTRIBUTES

Attributes data assume only two values – ***good or bad, defective or non-defective, acceptable or not acceptable, pass or fail*** and so on. Attributes usually cannot be measured, but they can be observed and counted and are useful in many practical situations. *For example,* in printing packages

Exhibit 12.19 : The 'x' Chart and Moving Range Chart

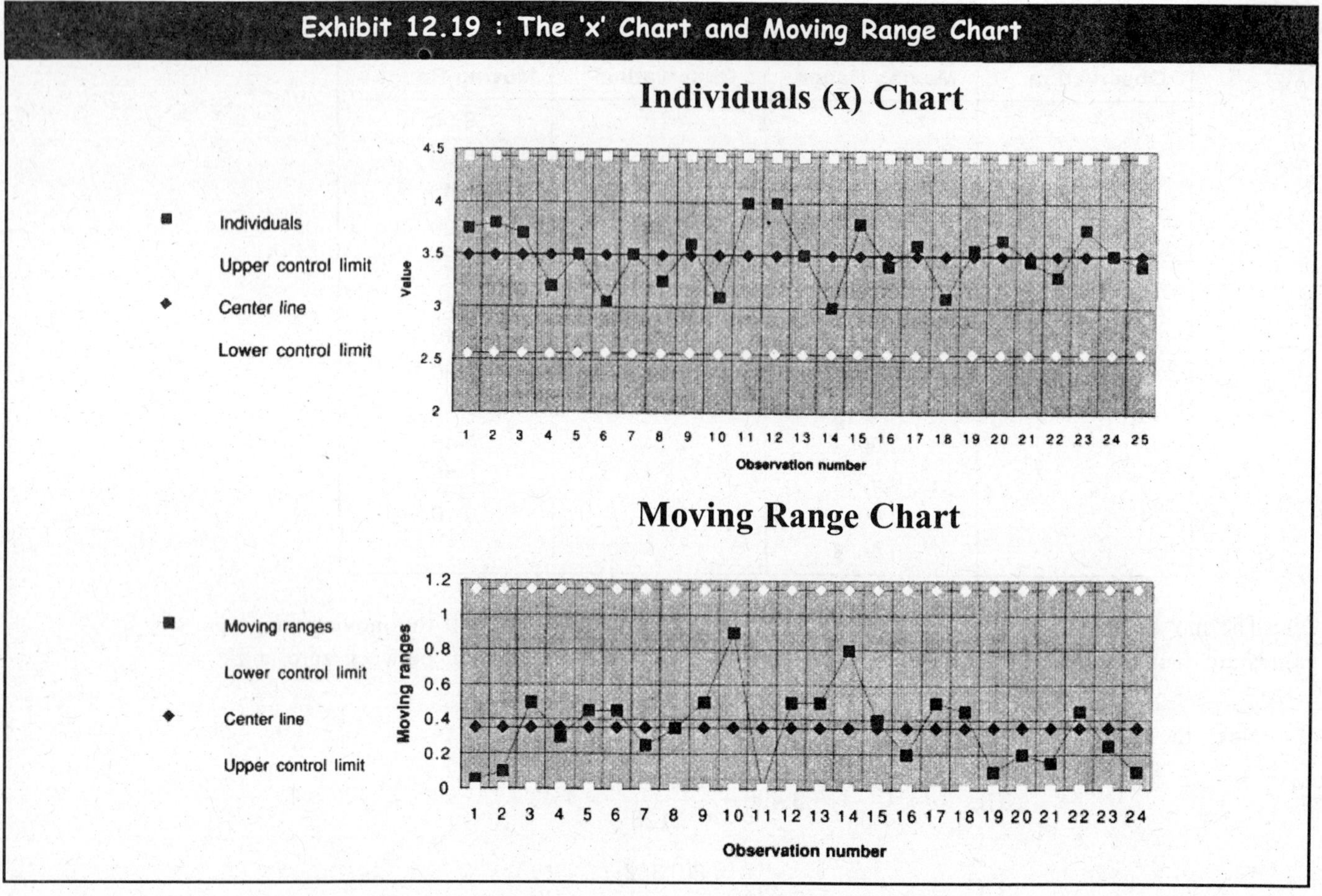

for consumer products, colour quality can be rated as acceptable or not acceptable, or a sheet of cardboard either is damaged or not, a polished or painted surface of a job may be good or bad. Usually, attributes data are easy to collect, often by visual inspection. **However, one drawback in using attributes data is that large samples are necessary to obtain valid statistical results.**

Several different types of control charts are used for attributes data. **The two major categories of attributes charts are *(i)* those that measure the percent defectives in a sample – known as *"number of defectives"* charts and *(ii)* those that count the number of defects – called *"number of defects charts"*.** We must know the difference between the terms **"defectives"** and **"defects"**. A ***defect*** is a single non-conforming quality characteristic of an item. An item may have several defects. The term ***"defectives"*** refers to items having one or more defects.

"Number of defectives" charts are of two types:

(i) **Fraction defectives chart or fraction – non-conforming chart also known as p-chart for varying sample size or constant sample size.**

(ii) **'np' chart also known as chart for the number - non-conforming, for constant sample size only.**

The control charts based on attribute data are of two types: *(i)* "Number of defective" chart and *(ii)* "Number of defects" chart

'p' Charts (Fraction Defectives Chart)

A 'p' chart monitors the proportion of non-conforming items produced in a lot. The 'p' chart is constructed by first gathering 25 to 30 samples of the attributes being measured. The size of the sample should be large enough to have several non-conforming items. If the probability of finding a non-conforming item is small, a large sample size is usually necessary. Samples are chosen over time periods so that any special causes that are identified can be investigated.

Let us suppose that k samples, each of size 'n are selected. If 'c' represents the number of non-conforming or defectives in a particular sample, the proportion non-conforming or fraction defective is $\frac{c}{n}$. Let p_i be the fraction defective in the 'i'th sample, then the average fraction defective for the group of k sample is

$$\bar{p} = \frac{p_1 + p_2 + \ldots + p_k}{k} \text{ or } \frac{\sum_{i=1}^{k} p_i}{k}$$

This statistic reflects the average performance of the process. One would expect a high percentage of samples to have a fraction defective within three standard deviations of $\bar{p}$. An estimate of the standard deviation is given by,

$$\sigma_{\bar{p}} = \sqrt{\frac{\bar{p}(1-\bar{p})}{n}}$$

The central line is given by $\bar{p}$ and the upper and lower control limits are computed as:

Fraction defective charts can be drawn both for constant sample size and variable sample size.

$$UCL_p = \bar{p} + 3\,\sigma_{\bar{p}} = \bar{p} + 3\sqrt{\frac{\bar{p}(1-\bar{p})}{n}}$$

$$LCL_p = \bar{p} - 3\,\sigma_{\bar{p}} = \bar{p} - 3\sqrt{\frac{\bar{p}(1-\bar{p})}{n}}$$

If LCL_p is less than zero (*i.e.,* negative value), a value of zero is used.

Analysis of 'p' chart: Points outside the control limits signify an out-of-control situation. Patterns and trends should also be sought to identify special or assignable causes. However, a point on a p-chart below the lower control limit or the development of a trend below the centre line indicates that the process might have improved since the ideal is zero defective.

'P' Chart For Variable Sample Size

Often 100 percent inspection is performed on process output during fixed sampling periods. However, the number of units produced in each sampling period may vary. In this case, the p-chart woud have a variable sample size. One way of handling this is to compute a standard deviation for each individual sample. Thus, if the sample size for k samples is $n_1, n_2, \ldots n_k$, then central line = $\bar{p}$.

$$\text{Upper control limit} = \bar{p} + 3\sqrt{\frac{\bar{p}(1-\bar{p})}{\text{sample size}}}$$

$$\text{Lower control limit} = \bar{p} - 3\sqrt{\frac{\bar{p}(1-\bar{p})}{\text{sample size}}}$$

where $\bar{p} = \frac{p_1 + p_2 + \ldots + p_k}{k}$ and $p_1 = \frac{c_1}{n_1}$, $p_2 = \frac{c_2}{n_2}$ ...... $p_k = \frac{c_k}{n_k}$.

where $c_1, c_2, \ldots c_k$ are the number of defectives in samples 1 to k respectively.

An alternative approach is to use the average sample size $\bar{n}$, to compute approximate control limits. Using the average sample size, the control limits are computed as

$$UCL_p = \bar{p} + 3\sqrt{\frac{\bar{p}(1-\bar{p})}{\bar{n}}}$$

$$LCL_p = \bar{p} - 3\sqrt{\frac{\bar{p}(1-\bar{p})}{\bar{n}}}$$

where $$\bar{n} = \frac{n_1 + n_2 + \ldots + n_K}{K} \text{ or } \frac{\sum_{i=1}^{K} n_i}{K}$$

The disadvantages of this approach are:

1. Since the control limits are only approximate, points that are actually out of control may not appear to be so on this chart.
2. Runs or non-random patterns are difficult to interpret because the standard deviation differs between samples as a result of the variable simple sizes.

As a general guideline, the average sample method is used when the sample sizes fall within 25 percent of the average.

12.14 NP CHARTS FOR NUMBER NON-CONFORMING FOR CONSTANT SAMPLE SIZE

In the 'p' chart, the fraction non-conforming or defective of the ith sample is given by $p_i = \frac{c_i}{n}$ where c_i is the number found non-conforming (or defective and 'n' is the sample size. This relationship can be rewritten as $c_i = n\,p_i$. That is the number of non-conforming is equal to the sample size times the proportion non-conforming (or fraction defective).

Instead of using a chart for the fraction non-conforming, an equivalent alternative – a chart for the ***number*** **of non-conforming items** (instead of proportion non-conforming or fraction defective) is useful. Such a control chart is called as ***np chart.***

The 'np' chart is a control chart for the number of non-conforming items in a sample. To use np chart, the size of the sample must be constant. Equal sample sizes are not required for p-charts.

The 'np' chart is a useful alternative to the 'p' chart because it is often easier to understand for production personnel that the ***number*** **of non-conforming items** is more meaningful than a fraction. Also the computations are simpler.

The control limits for the np chart, like those for the 'p' chart are based on the binomial probability distribution. The centre line is the average number of non-conforming items per sample as denoted by $n\bar{p}$ which is calculated as,

$$n\bar{p} = \frac{\sum_{i=1}^{K} c_i}{K}$$

or $$n\bar{p} = \frac{c_1 + c_2 + \ldots + c_K}{K}$$

An estimate of the standard deviation is

$$S_{np} = \sqrt{n\bar{p}\,(1-\bar{p})}$$

where $$\bar{p} = \frac{n\bar{p}}{n} = \frac{\sum_{i=1}^{k} c_i}{n \times K}$$

Using three-sigma limits, the control limits are specified:

$$UCL_{np} = n\bar{p} + 3\sqrt{n\bar{p}(1-\bar{p})}$$

$$LCL_{np} = n\bar{p} - 3\sqrt{n\bar{p}(1-\bar{p})}$$

Example: *Construct a fraction defective (p-chart) chart for the following data. The sample size is n = 100 for each sample of the 20 samples.*

Sample Number	Number of defectives	Sample Number	Number of defectives
1	6	11	6
2	5	12	1
3	0	13	8
4	1	14	7
5	4	15	5
6	2	16	4
7	5	17	11
8	3	18	3
9	3	19	0
10	2	20	4

Solution:

Calculation of fraction defective is shown below:

Sample Number	Fraction defective	Sample Number	Fraction defective
1	6/100 = 0.06	11	0.06
2	5/100 = 0.05	12	0.01
3	0.00	13	0.08
4	0.01	14	0.07
5	0.04	15	0.05
6	0.02	16	0.04
7	0.05	17	0.11
8	0.03	18	0.03
9	0.03	19	0.00
10	0.02	20	0.04

$$\text{Central line } \bar{p} = \frac{\sum_{i=1}^{K} p_i}{K} = \frac{\sum_{i=1}^{K} \frac{c_i}{n}}{K} = \frac{\sum_{i=1}^{K} c_i}{n \times K}$$

$$\bar{p} = \frac{80}{100 \times 20} = 0.04$$

$$\sigma_p = \sqrt{\frac{\bar{p}(1-\bar{p})}{n}} = \sqrt{\frac{0.04(1-0.04)}{100}} = 0.02$$

$$UCL_{\bar{p}} = \bar{p} + 3\,\sigma_p = 0.04 + 3\,(0.02) = 0.10$$

$$LCL_{\bar{p}} = \bar{p} - 3\,\sigma_p = 0.04 - 3\,(0.02) = -\,ve = 0$$

Illustration of Construction of 'p' Chart for Varying Sample Size

The number of non-conforming or defectives for 20 samples of varying sample sizes are given below. Construct a 'p' chart.

Sample Number	Number non-conforming	Sample size	Sample Number	Number non-conforming	Sample size
1	18	137	11	8	140
2	20	158	12	13	179
3	14	92	13	5	196
4	6	122	14	15	163
5	11	86	15	25	140
6	22	187	16	12	135
7	6	156	17	16	186
8	9	117	18	12	93
9	14	142	19	15	181
10	12	140	20	18	160

The fraction non-conforming or fraction defective is calculated for each sample as

$$p = \frac{\text{Number non-conforming}}{\text{Sample size}}$$

The fraction non-conforming is as below:

Sample	Fraction non-conforming	Sample	Fraction non-conforming
1	18/137 = 0.1314	11	0.0571
2	20/158 = 0.1266	12	0.0726
3	0.1522	13	0.0255
4	0.0492	14	0.0920
5	0.1279	15	0.1786
6	0.1176	16	0.0889
7	0.0385	17	0.0860
8	0.0769	18	0.0622
9	0.1273	19	0.0829
10	0.0845	20	0.1125

Calculation of standard deviation, central line (CL), upper control limit (UCL_p) and lower control limit (LCL_p) is given by:

$$\text{Standard deviation } s_{\bar{p}} = \sqrt{\frac{\bar{p}(1-\bar{p})}{n}}$$

$$CL = \bar{p} = \frac{\sum_{i=1}^{K} p_i}{K} = 0.0909$$

$$UCL_p = \bar{p} + 3s_{\bar{p}}$$

$$LCL_p = \bar{p} - 3s_{\bar{p}}$$

The calculated values are listed as follows:

Sample	$s_{\bar{p}}$	CL	$UCL_{\bar{p}}$	$LCL_{\bar{p}}$
1	0.02045	0.0909	0.1646	0.0172
2	0.0228	0.0909	0.1596	0.0223
3	0.02997	0.0909	0.1806	0.0010
4	0.0260	0.0909	0.1690	0.0128
5	0.0310	0.0909	0.1840	0.0000
6	0.0210	0.0909	0.1540	0.0279
7	0.0230	0.0909	0.1600	0.0219
8	0.0265	0.0909	0.1707	0.0112
9	0.0274	0.0909	0.1732	0.0087
10	0.0241	0.0909	0.1633	0.0186
11	0.0243	0.0909	0.1638	0.0180
12	0.0214	0.0909	0.1554	0.0265
13	0.0205	0.0909	0.1526	0.0293
14	0.0225	0.0909	0.1585	0.0234
15	0.0243	0.0909	0.1638	0.0180
16	0.0247	0.0909	0.1652	0.0167
17	0.0210	0.0909	0.1542	0.0277
18	0.0206	0.0909	0.1530	0.0289
19	0.0213	0.0909	0.1551	0.0268
20	0.0227	0.0909	0.1591	0.0227

For the same data given in this problem, an alternative approach for calculation of CL, UCL_p and LCL_p is given below:

$$CLp = \bar{p} = \frac{\sum \text{non-conforming}}{\sum \text{sample size}} = \frac{c_1 + c_2 + \ldots.. + c_K}{n_1 + n_2 + \ldots.. + n_K}$$

$$= \frac{18 + 20 + \ldots.. + 18}{137 + 158 + \ldots.. + 160} = \frac{271}{2980} = 0.0909$$

$$\text{Upper control limit } UCL_p = \bar{p} + 3\sqrt{\frac{\bar{p}(1-\bar{p})}{\bar{n}}}$$

$$\text{Lower control limit } LCL_p = \bar{p} - 3\sqrt{\frac{\bar{p}(1-\bar{p})}{\bar{n}}}$$

$$\text{where } \bar{n} = \text{average sample size} = \frac{n_1 + n_2 + \ldots.. + n_K}{K} = \frac{2980}{20} = 149$$

$$UCLp = 0.0909 + 3\sqrt{\frac{0.0909(1-0.0909)}{149}} = 0.1616$$

$$LCLp = 0.0909 - 3\sqrt{\frac{0.0909(1-0.0909)}{149}} = 0.0202$$

Illustration of Calculation for 'np' Chart

Construct the 'np' chart for the following data. (Sample size = 100)

Sample	Number non-conforming	Sample	Number non-conforming
1	3	13	1
2	1	14	3
3	0	15	4
4	0	16	1
5	2	17	1
6	5	18	2
7	3	19	5
8	6	20	2
9	1	21	3
10	4	22	4
11	0	23	1
12	2	24	0
		25	1

$$n\bar{p} = \frac{\sum \text{non - conforming}}{\text{Total number of samples}} = \frac{\sum c}{K}$$

$$= \frac{3+1+0......+0+1}{25} = 2.2$$

$$\bar{p} = \frac{\sum c}{nK} = \frac{3+1+0......+0+1}{100 \times 25} = \frac{2.2}{100} = 0.022$$

Standard deviation $s_{np} = \sqrt{n\bar{p}\,(1-\bar{p})}$

$$= \sqrt{2.2(1-0.022)}$$

$$= \sqrt{2.2(0.978)} = \sqrt{2.1510} = 1.4668$$

The control limits are computed as

$$UCL_{np} = n\bar{p} + 3\sqrt{n\bar{p}\,(1-\bar{p})} = n\bar{p} + 3\, s_{np}$$

$$= 2.2 + 3\,(0.14668) = 6.6$$

$$LCL_{np} = n\bar{p} - 3\sqrt{n\bar{p}\,(1-\bar{p})}$$

$$= 2.2 - 3\,(0.14668) = -\,2.20 = \text{Zero.}$$

Charts for Defects

A ***defect*** is a single non-conforming characteristic of an item, while a defective is an item that has one or more defects. In some situations, quality assurance personnel may be interested not only in whether an item is defective but also in how many defects it has. **Two charts can be applied in such situations:**

(i) The ***'c' chart*** which is used to control the total number of defects per unit when sub-group size is constant.

(ii) The ***'u' chart*** which is used to control the average number of defects per unit, when the sub-group sizes are variable.

The ***'c' chart*** is based on the ***Poisson probability distribution.*** To construct a 'c' chart, first estimate the average number of defects per unit '$\bar{c}$' by taking at least 25 (K) samples of equal size (n), counting the number of defects per sample (c) and finding the average ($\bar{c}$).

The standard deviation of the Poisson distribution is the square root of the mean.

The computations are as below:

The number of sub-groups = K

Sample size per sub-group = n

Number of defects in sub-groups = $c_1, c_2, \ldots\ldots, c_K$.

$$\text{Average number of defects } \bar{c} = \frac{\sum_{i=1}^{K} c_i}{K}$$

$$= \frac{c_1 + c_2 + \ldots\ldots + c_K}{K}$$

Standard deviation Sc = $\sqrt{\bar{c}}$

Central line (CL) = $\bar{c}$.

Upper control limit $UCL_c = \bar{c} + 3\sqrt{\bar{c}}$

Lower control limit $LCL_c = c - 3\sqrt{\bar{c}}$

Illustration: Construct the number of defects chart ('c' chart) for the data given below.

Subgroup	Number of defects	Subgroup	Number of defects
1	2	13	0
2	3	14	2
3	0	15	4
4	1	16	1
5	3	17	2
6	5	18	0
7	3	19	3
8	1	20	2
9	2	21	1
10	2	22	4
11	0	23	0
12	1	24	0
		25	3

Calculation of central line, upper and lower central limits is given below:

$$\text{Central line } (CL_C) = \bar{c} = \frac{\sum c}{K} = \frac{2 + 3 + \ldots + 0 + 3}{25}$$

$$\bar{c} = \frac{45}{25} = 1.8$$

$$\text{Upper control limit } UCL_C = \bar{c} + 3\sqrt{\bar{c}}$$

$$= 1.8 + 3\sqrt{1.8} = 5.82$$

$$\text{Lower control limit } LCL_C = \bar{c} - 3\sqrt{\bar{c}}$$

$$= 1.8 - 3\sqrt{1.8} = -2.2 \text{ or zero.}$$

As long as the sub-group size is constant, a *'c' chart* is appropriate. In many cases, however, the sub-group size is not constant or the nature of the production process does not yield discrete, measurable units. In such cases, a standard unit of measurement is used such as ***defects per unit.*** The control chart used in such situations is called **a *u-chart*.**

The variable 'u' represents the average number of defects per unit of measurement, that is u = c/n where 'n' is the size of the sub-group. **The computations of central line, upper and lower control limits are as below:**

$$\text{Central line } (CL_C) = \bar{u} = \frac{\sum u}{K} = \frac{u_1 + u_2 + \ldots\ldots + u_K}{K}$$

$$\text{where } u_1 = \frac{c_1}{n_1},\ u_2 = \frac{c_2}{n_2}, \ldots\ldots,\ u_K = \frac{c_K}{n_K}.$$

Alternately,
$$\bar{u} = \frac{c_1 + c_2 + \ldots + c_K}{n_1 + n_2 + \ldots + n_K}$$

The standard deviation of the ith sample is given by

$$s_u = \sqrt{\frac{\bar{u}}{n_i}} \text{ or } s_u = \sqrt{\frac{\bar{u}}{\text{sample size}}}$$

$$\text{Upper control limit } UCL_u = \bar{u} + 3\sqrt{\frac{\bar{u}}{\text{sample size}}}$$

$$\text{Lower control limit } LCL_u = \bar{u} - 3\sqrt{\frac{\bar{u}}{\text{sample size}}}$$

For the ith sample,

$$UCL_u = \bar{u} + 3\sqrt{\frac{\bar{u}}{n_i}}$$

$$LCL_u = \bar{u} - 3\sqrt{\frac{\bar{u}}{n_i}}$$

Note that if the size of the sub-group varies, the control limits also will vary.

Illustration: Construct the 'u' chart for the following data.

Subgroup	Number of defects	Sample size	Subgroup	Number of defects	Sample size
1	8	92	11	7	136
2	15	69	12	4	80
3	6	86	13	2	70
4	13	85	14	11	73
5	5	123	15	13	89
6	5	87	16	6	129
7	3	74	17	6	78
8	8	83	18	3	88
9	4	103	19	8	76
10	6	60	20	9	101

Calculation of Defects Per Unit (u)

$$\text{Defects per unit (u)} = \frac{\text{Number of defects}}{\text{Sample size}} = \frac{c}{n}$$

Subgroup	Defects per unit (u)	Subgroup	Defects per unit (u)
1	8/92= 0.0870	11	0.0515
2	15/69 = 0.2174	12	0.0500
3	0.0698	13	0.0286
4	0.1529	14	0.1507
5	0.0407	15	0.1461
6	0.0575	16	0.0465
7	0.0405	17	0.0769
8	0.0964	18	0.0341
9	0.0388	19	0.1053
10	0.0100	20	0.0891

$$\text{Central line } \bar{u} = \frac{\sum u}{K} = \frac{1.5898}{20} = 0.0794$$

Alternately $$\bar{u} = \frac{u_1 + u_2 + \ldots\ldots + u_K}{n_1 + n_2 + \ldots\ldots + n_K} = \frac{142}{1782} = 0.0796$$

Calculation of upper and lower limits:

The standard deviation

$$s_u = \sqrt{\frac{\bar{u}}{\text{sample size}}}$$

Upper control limit for subgroup 1

$$= \bar{u} + 3\sqrt{\frac{\bar{u}}{\text{sample size}}}$$

$$= 0.079 + 3\sqrt{\frac{0.079}{92}}$$

$$= 0.079 + 3\ (0.029)$$

$$= 0.079 + 0.087 = 0.166$$

Lower control limit for sub-group 1

$$= \bar{u} - 3\sqrt{\frac{\bar{u}}{\text{sample size}}}$$

$$= 0.079 - 0.087 = -\text{ve} = 0.$$

The calculation of upper and lower control limits are given below.

Subgroup	LCL_u	UCL_u
1	0	0.166
2	0	0.176
3	0	0.165
4	0	0.166
5	0.0016	0.151

6	0	0.175
7	0	0.172
8	0	0.167
9	0	0.158
10	0	0.183
11	0.0053	0.147
12	0	0.169
13	0	0.175
14	0	0.173
15	0	0.164
16	0.0034	0.149
17	0	0.170
18	0	0.164
19	0	0.171
20	0	0.158

Application of 'c' Charts and 'u' Charts

One application of 'c' charts and 'u' charts is in a quality rating system for rating vendors (suppliers). When some defects are considered to be more serious than others, the defects can be rated or categorised into different classes. For instance,

A – very serious defect

B – serious defect

C – moderately serious defect and

D – not serious defect.

Each category can be weighted using a point scale, such as 100 for A, 50 for B, 10 for C, and 1 for D. These points or demerits can be used as the basis for a 'c' chart or a 'u' chart that would measure total demerits or demerits per unit respectively. Such charts are often used for internal quality control and as a means of rating suppliers.

Choosing between 'c' chart and 'u' chart

Choosing 'c' chart and 'u' chart applies to situations in which the quality characteristics inspected do not necessarily come from discrete units. The key issue to consider is ***whether the sampling unit is constant.*** *For example,* suppose that an electronics manufacturer produces printed circuit boards. The boards may contain various defects such as faulty components and missing connections. Because the sampling unit – the printed circuit board is constant (assuming that all boards are the same), a 'c' chart is appropriate. If the process produces printed circuit boards of varying sizes with different numbers of components and connections, then the 'u' chart would be the choice.

Summary of Control Chart Construction

Box 12.1 **summarises the formulae used for constructing the different types of control charts discussed in this chapter.** ***Exhibit 12.20*** **provides a summary of guidelines for chart selection.**

Box 12.1 : Summary of Control Chart Formule

Type of chart	LCL	CL	UCL
$\overline{X}$ (with R)	$\overline{\overline{X}} - A_2\overline{R}$	$\overline{\overline{X}}$	$\overline{\overline{X}} + A_2\overline{R}$
R	$D_3\overline{R}$	$\overline{R}$	$D_4\overline{R}$
p	$\overline{p} - 3\sqrt{\frac{\overline{p}(1-\overline{p})}{n}}$	$\overline{p}$	$\overline{p} + 3\sqrt{\frac{\overline{p}(1-\overline{p})}{n}}$
$\overline{X}$ (with s)	$\overline{\overline{X}} - A_3\overline{s}$	$\overline{\overline{X}}$	$\overline{\overline{X}} + A_2\overline{s}$
s	$B_3\overline{s}$	$\overline{s}$	$B_4\overline{s}$
X	$\overline{X} - \frac{3\overline{R}}{d_2}$	$\overline{X}$	$\overline{X} + \frac{3\overline{R}}{d_2}$
np	$n\overline{p} - 3\sqrt{n\overline{p}\left(1-\overline{p}\right)}$	$n\overline{p}$	$n\overline{p} + 3\sqrt{n\overline{p}\left(1-\overline{p}\right)}$
c	$\overline{c} - 3\sqrt{\overline{c}}$	$\overline{c}$	$\overline{c} + 3\sqrt{\overline{c}}$
u	$\overline{u} - 3\sqrt{\frac{\overline{u}}{n}}$	$\overline{u}$	$\overline{u} + 3\sqrt{\frac{\overline{u}}{n}}$

Exhibit 12.20 : Control Chart Selection

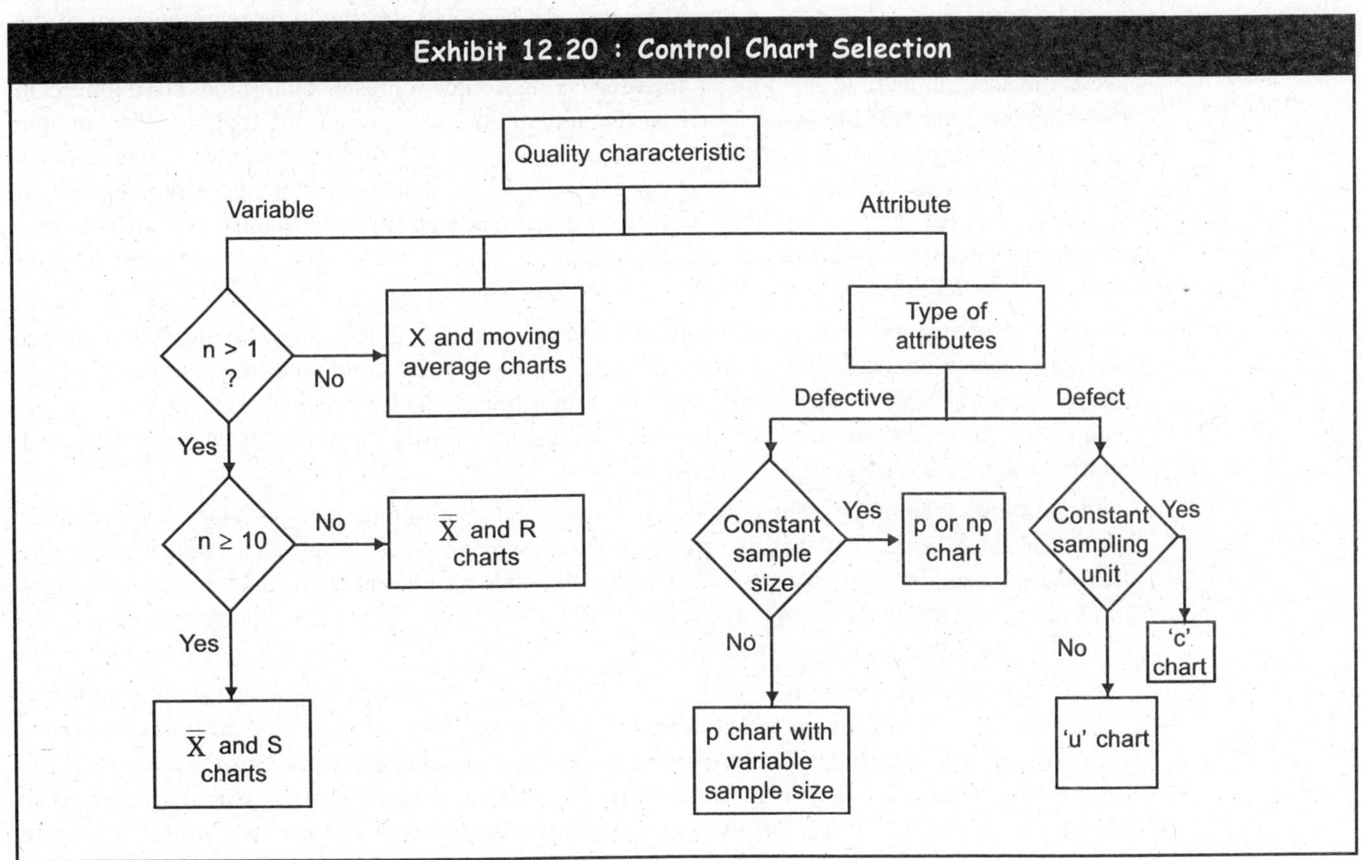

Designing Control Charts

Designing control charts requires the following considerations:
(i) The basis for sampling
(ii) The sample size
(iii) The frequency of sampling and
(iv) The location of the control limits

The four issues to be considered while designing control charts are:

1. the basis for sampling
2. the sample size
3. the frequency of sampling and
4. the location of the control limits.

Basis for sampling : The purpose of a control chart is to identify the variation in a system that may change over time. In determining the method of sampling, samples should be chosen to be as ***homogeneous*** as possible so that each sample reflects the system of common (or chance) causes or assignable causes that may be present at that point of time. If assignable causes are present, the chance of observing differences between samples should be high while the chances of observing differences within a sample should be low. Samples which satisfy these criteria are called ***rational sub-groups.***

Rational sub-groups can be constructed by using consecutive measurements over a short period of time. Consecutive measurements minimise the chance of variability within the sample while allowing variation between samples to be detected. This approach is useful when control charts are used to detect shifts in process level. Also, care should be taken not to overlap production shifts, different batches of materials and so on, when selecting the basis for sampling. The sample should be selected carefully so as not to bias the results.

Sample size : Sample size is a second critical design issue. A small sample size is desirable to ensure that the opportunity for within-sample variation due to assignable (or special) causes would be minimum. This issue is important because each sample should be representative of the state of control at one point in time. Also, the cost of sampling should be kept low. (In a strict accounting sense, the time spent by an operator taking sample represents non-productive time). On the other hand, control limits are based on the assumption of a normal distribution of the sample means. If the process is not normal, this assumption is valid only for large samples. Large samples also allow smaller changes in process characterises to be detected with higher probability. **In practice, samples of about five have been found to work well in detecting process shifts of two standard deviations or larger. To detect smaller shifts in the process mean, larger sample sizes of 15 to 25 must be used.**

For attributes data, too small a sample size can make a 'p' chart meaningless. The proper sample size should be determined statistically, (even though some guidelines suggest use of atleast 100 observations) particularly when the true proportion of non-conformance is small. If 'p' is small, 'n' should be large enough to have a high probability of detecting at least one non-conformance.

Sampling frequency : The third design issue is the sampling frequency. Taking large samples on a frequent basis is desirable but clearly not economical. No hard and fast rules exist for the frequency of sampling. Samples should be close enough to provide an opportunity to detect changes in process characteristics as soon as possible and reduce the chances of producing a large amount of non-conforming output.

Location of control limits : This issue in the design of control charts is closely related to the risk involved in making an incorrect assessment about the state of control. **Two types of errors would occur-one called *type I error* when an incorrect conclusion is reached that *a special (or assignable) cause is present when infact one does not exist* and the other called *type II error* which occurs when *special* (or *assignable*) *causes are present but are not signalled in the control chart* because the plotted points fall within the control limits by chance.** Since non-conforming products have a greater chance to be produced, a cost will eventually be incurred as a result. The size of a type I error depends only on the control limits that are used, the wider the limits, the less chance of a point falling outside the limits and consequently, the smaller is the chance of making a type I error. On the other hand, a type II error depends on the width of the control limits, the degree of which the process is out of control and the sample size. For a fixed sample size, wider control limits increase the risk of making a type II error.

The traditional approach of using three-sigma limits implicitly assumes that the cost of a Type I error is large relative to that of a Type II error. Certain costs are associated with making both Type I and Type II errors. A Type I error results in unnecessary investigation for an assignable cause, including costs of lost production time and special testing. A type II error can be more significant. If an out-of-control process is not recognised, defectives that are produced may result in higher costs of scrap and rework in later stages of production and after the finished goods reach the customer.

The costs associated with Type I and Type II errors conflict as control limits change. The tighter the control limits, the higher the cost of a Type I error and lower the cost of. Type II error. The costs associated with sampling and testing may include lost productive time when the operator takes sample measurements, performs calculations and plots the points on the control charts. If the testing is destructive, the value of lost products would also be included. Thus, larger sample sizes and more frequent sampling results in higher costs.

The sample size and frequency also affect the cost of Type I and Type II errors. As the sample size or frequency is increased, both Type I and Type II errors are reduced since better information is provided for decision making. ***Table 12.1* lists the economic decisions for control chart construction.**

Table 12.1 : Economic Decisions for Control Chart Construction

Source cost	Sample size	Sampling frequency	Control limits
Type I error	large	high	wide
Type II error	large	high	narrow
Sampling and testing	Small	low	—

In the economic design of control charts, the costs of Type I error and Type II error must be considered simultaneously. Most models for such decisions can become quite complex. As a practical matter, one often uses judgement about the nature of operations and the costs involved in making these decisions. **Raymond Mayer suggests the following guidelines:**

1. If the cost of investigating an operation to identify the cause of an apparent out-of-control condition is high, a Type I error becomes important and wider control limits should be adopted. Conversely if that is low, narrower limits should be selected.
2. If the cost of the defective output generated by an operation is substantial, a Type II error is serious, and narrower control limits should be used. Otherwise, wider limits should be selected.
3. If the cost of a Type I error and the cost of a Type II error for a given activity are both significant, wide control limits should be chosen and consideration should be given to reducing the risk of a Type II error by increasing the sample size. Also, more frequent samples should be taken to reduce the duration of any out-of-control condition that might occur.
4. If past experience with an operation indicates that an out-of-control condition arises quite frequently, narrower control limits should be favoured because of the large number of opportunities for making a Type II error. In the event that the probability of an out of control condition is small, wider limits are preferred.

(v) **Study process performance:** Using control charts to monitor performance and identifying special causes lead to identification of various sources of variation and eventually to their elimination.

(vi) **Implement process control:** Ensure employee participation in previous steps to have real time control of the processing.

12.15 QUALITY IN PRACTICE

Box 12.2 : Assessing the Process Capability of the Intensive Care Unit Laboratory

The intensive care unit laboratory process has an average turnaround time of 26.2 minutes and a standard deviation of 1.35 minutes. The nominal value for this service is 25 minutes with an upper specification limit of 30 minutes and a lower specification limit of 20 minutes. The administrator of the laboratory wants to have four-sigma performance for his laboratory. Is the laboratory process capable of this level of performance?

Solution: The administrator began by taking a quick check to see whether the process is capable by computing the process capability index.

$$\frac{\bar{\bar{X}} - \text{Lower specification}}{3\sigma} = \frac{26.2 - 20}{3\,(1.35)} = 1.53$$

$$\frac{\text{Upper specification} - \bar{\bar{X}}}{3\sigma} = \frac{30 - 26.2}{3\,(1.35)} = 0.94$$

$$C_{pk} = \text{Minimum of } (1.53, 0.94) = 0.94$$

Since the target value for-sigma performance is C_{pu} = 1.33, the finding is that the process index of 0.94 was not capable of four- sigma performance.

However, the administrator did not know whether the problem is the variability of the process, the centering of the process, or both. The option available to improve the process depended on what is wrong with the process

Next, the process variability is cheeked by computing the process capability ratio C_p

$$C_p = \frac{(\text{Upper specification}) - (\text{Lower specification})}{6\sigma}$$

$$= \frac{30 - 20}{6\,(1.35)}\ \mathbf{1.23}$$

The process variability also did not meet the four-sigma target of 1.33. Consequently the administrator initiated a study to see where variability was introduced to the process. Two activities, report preparation and specimen slide preparation, were identified as having inconsistent procedures. These procedures were then modified to provide consistent performance, New data were collected and the average turn- around was found to be 26.1 minutes with a standard deviation of 1.20 minutes.

The process variability is newly calculated as

$$C_p = \frac{30 - 20}{6\,(1.2)} = 1.39 \text{ which is more then the target value of 1.33}$$

However, the process capability index Cpk indicated that there were still some problems to resolve

$$C_{pk} = \text{Minimum of} \left\{ \frac{(26.1 - 20)}{3(1.20)}, \frac{(30 - 26.1)}{3(1.20)} \right\} = 1.08$$

The conclusion is that the laboratory process was still not at the level of four- sigma performance on turn - around time. The laboratory administrator searched for the causes of the off- center turn - around time distribution. He discovered that there were periodic backlogs at a key piece of testing equipment. Acquiring a second machine provided the capacity to reduce the turn around times to four-sigma capability.

Box 12.3 : ABC computer systems' costly experiment in Healthcare service

ABC computer systems expanded its operations into the computerized health care service business by bagging a contract of rupees one crore to serve "Karnataka State Employee Health Insurance services". Its job was to handle the two lakh Karnataka state government employees' claims processing – a seemingly simple and lucrative growth area for an old line computer services company like ABC computer systems.

But one year later, the contract was terminated and ABC computer systems was fined Rs 50 lakhs for not meeting quality standards. Here are two of the measures of quality, both attributes (that is either 'defective' or 'not defective') on which the firm was out of control.

(i) **Percent of claims processed with errors:** An audit over a 3 month period by an external auditor showed that ABC computer systems made errors in 8. 5% of the claims processed against the industry standard of 3.5% defectives.

(ii) **Percent of claims processed within 30 days :** For this attribute measure, a 'defect' is a processing time longer than the contract's time allowance. In one month's sample, 13% of the claims exceeded the 30 day limit, far above the 5% allowed by the client.

The CEO of ABC camputer Systems hired the services of a quality expert in 'Statistical Process Control' (SPC) in order to avoid repetition of such failures in the company's operations in any future contracts undertaken for insurance claims processing.

12.16 SUMMARY

Quality assurance is the activity of providing the evidence needed to establish confidence among all concerned that the quality related activities such as quality planning, quality control, quality improvement, quality audit and reliability are being performed effectively. Objective of quality assurance function is to ensure product and service quality and to provide confidence in the supplier/ manufacturer.

An effective ***quality assurance system*** includes well-designed and documented procedures for product and process control, inspection and testing, control of measuring and test equipments, corrective and preventive action and the use of appropriate statistical techniques. A ***quality policy*** identifies key objectives of products and services such as fitness for use, performance, safety and dependability. A firm may have a quality policy regarding ***customer satisfaction, conformance to requirements*** and ***continuous improvement. A quality manual*** is a document, which includes the organisation structure, responsibilities, procedures, process and resources for implementing quality policies.

Traditional inspection practices involve stringent inspection of incoming materials and final products with a focus on separating the good from the bad. Since inspection practices are inefficient and ineffective, they should be used as an auditing tool to control processes and identify opportunities for improvement. Three stages of inspection are receiving inspection, in process inspection and final inspection. The optimal level of inspection is determined by trade off between cost of vigilance (inspection) versus cost of error, that keeps the total cost minimum. While this is the traditional viewpoint, modern viewpoint advocates attempts to drive defects to zero, depending on increase in market share and customer acceptance to affect the cost of "excess" quality assurance beyond the optimum level.

Statistics is concerned with the collection, organisation, analysis, interpretation and presentation of data and has extensive applications in quality assurance. Statistical methods are used in many areas of quality assurance such as ***statistical process control and acceptance sampling.***

Process capability is the range over which the natural variation of a process occurs as determined by the system of common causes (chance causes). It is determined through statistical analysis of variation in a production process and measured relative to specification by process capability indices.

If we assume that the process output is represented by a normal distribution, about 99.73 percent of the output is contained within ± 3 standard deviation (3 sigma limits) from the mean. This means 0.27% of the items fall beyond the tolerance limits which means a deviation of ± 0.135% beyond ± 3 sigma limits. This means the proportion of non-conforming product is 2700 parts per million. This level of quality was not acceptable for Motorola who coined the word **six-sigma** to designate a quality level with only 3.4 defects per million parts or opportunities.

Statistical Process Control (SPC) is a methodology for monitoring a process to identify special causes of variation and signal the need to take corrective action when appropriate.

Variation in quality characteristics (variable or attribute) in any process could be due to ***chance causes*** or ***assignable* causes.** Control charts developed by Walter Shewhart enable operations managers: *(i)* to ensure that the process is operating under statistical control with only natural variation due to chance causes and *(ii)* to identify and eliminate assignable variation so that the processes will remain under control.

Operations managers would like a process to have both ***high capability*** and be ***in control*** even though both are independent concepts. If a process is not in control it should be brought into control before attempting to evaluate ***process capability***.

Control charts have three basic applications: *(i)* establishing a state of statistical control, *(ii)* monitoring a process to identify assignable causes and *(iii)* determining the process capability.

Control charts are classified as *(i)* Charts for variables and *(ii)* Charts for attributes depending on whether the quality characteristics can be measured (variable) or described as good or bad (attributes). Control charts for ***variable*** data include: *(i)* '$\overline{X}$' and R charts (*i.e.,* Mean-Range Charts) and *(ii)* '$\overline{X}$-s' charts (*i.e.,* Mean-Standard deviation charts) and individual and moving range charts. '$\overline{X}$ – R' charts are used for sample sizes ≤ 10 whereas '$\overline{X}$- S' charts are used for larger sample sizes. The sample standard deviation provides a better indication of process variability than the range. Individual charts are useful when every item can be inspected and when a long lead time exists for producing an item. Moving ranges are used to measure the variability of individual charts.

Charts for ***attributes*** include 'p' chart, 'np' chart, 'c' chart and 'u' chart. The first two charts (*viz.,* 'p' and 'np' charts) are called control charts for number of defectives whereas the other two charts (*viz.,* 'c' chart and 'u' chart) are called control charts for number of defects.

The 'p' chart is a fraction defective chart for constant or variable sample size whereas the 'np' chart is number of defectives chart for constant sample size. The 'c' chart is the number of defects chart for constant sample size whereas the 'u' chart is the number of defects per unit" chart for varying sample size.

The various steps required to develop and use control charts are: *(i)* Preparation, *(ii)* Data collection, *(iii)* Determination of trial control limits, *(iv)* Analysis and interpretation and *(v)* Using as a problem-solving tool.

A process is said to be in control if no points when plotted on the chart fall outside control limits (upper and lower control limits) and the number of points above and below the centre (central line) is about the same. The points seem to fall randomly above and below the central line and most points are near the central line, with only a few close to the control limits.

Typical out of control conditions are represented by sudden shift in the mean value, cycles, trends, hugging of the central line, hugging of the control limits and instability.

The four issues to be considered while designing control charts are: *(i)* The basis of sampling, *(ii)* The sample size *(iii)* The frequency of sampling and *(iv)* The location of the control limits.

The six steps used for implementing SPC are: *(i)* Define the process, *(ii)* Identify characteristics to study, *(iii)* Determine the ability to measure the characteristic, *(iv)* Perform capability studies, *(v)* Study process performance and *(vi)* Implement process control.

12.17 KEY WORDS USED

Quality Assurance, Quality Assurance System, Process Control, Inspection, Statistical Methodology, Process Capability, Acceptance Sampling, Acceptance Quality Level, Lot Tolerance Percent Defective, Producer's Risk, Consumer's Risk, Statistical Process Control (SPC), Standard

Deviation, Control chart, Mean, Median, Variables, Attributes, Sampling, Central Limit Theorem, Range, Test for Homogeneity, Process capability, Central Line, Upper Control Limit, Lower Control Limit, Fraction Defectives Chart, Poison Probability Distribution, Sample size, Sampling Frequency.

12.18 OBJECTIVE QUESTIONS

(A) Match the following:

Column A	Column B
1. Statistical Process control	1. p chart
2. Control for variable data	2. np chart
3. Number of defects chart	3. used to measure the performance
4. Control chart for attribute data	4. $\overline{X}-R$ chart
5. Fraction defective chart	5. 'c' Chart

(B) State whether the following statements are True or False.

1. The objective of a SPC system is to provide a statistical signal when assignable causes of variation are present. (T / F)
2. Variable data are those that are measured along a continuous scale. (T / F)
3. The upper and lower control limits are computed to be six standard deviations from the overall mean. (T / F)
4. Control charts are designed to be used by inspectors or quality control personnel rather than production operators (T / F)
5. There is no difference between the term "defectives" and "defects" (T / F)
6. Inspection does not add to the value or quality of a product. (T / F)
7. Acceptance sampling can neither detect poor quality nor prevent it. (T / F)
8. Process capability indices C_p and C_{pk} are one and the same. (T / F)
9. Statistical thinking is a philosophy of learning and action based on the ideas that variation exits in all processes and understanding and reducing this variation will lead to improved quality (T / F)

(C) Multiple choice Questions: Choose the correct answer from the alternatives given under each question:

1. The control chart for the number of non-conforming items in a sample the size of which must be constant is known as:
   - (a) 'p' chart
   - (b) 'c' chart
   - (c) 'np' chart
   - (d) $\overline{x}-R$ chart
   - (e) 'u' chart
   - (f) None of the above.
2. ____________ inspection is also known as statistical process control (SPC):
   - (a) Receiving inspection
   - (b) Sampling inspection
   - (c) In-process inspection
   - (d) 100 percent inspection
   - (e) None of the above
3. Statistical thinking is useful in the following level of quality:
   - (a) Organisation level
   - (b) Process level
   - (c) Performer level
   - (d) All of these
   - (e) None of these.

4. Process capability index (Cp) is calculated using the formula

(a) $\frac{USL - \mu}{3\sigma}$ (b) $\frac{\mu - LSL}{3\sigma}$

(c) $\frac{USL - LSL}{3\sigma}$ (d) $\frac{USL - LSL}{6\sigma}$

(e) None of these

5. The probability that a lot containing defectives exceeding the LTPD will be accepted is known as:

(a) Producer's risk (b) Consumer's risk

(c) acceptance quality level (d) Type I error

(e) None of the above.

6. Central limit theorem is the theoretical foundation of:

(a) $\bar{x} - R$ chart (b) $\bar{x}$ chart

(c) np chart (d) 'p' chart

(e) None of the above

7. The formula for computing upper control limit in chart is:

(a) $\bar{\bar{X}} + A_2\bar{R}$ (b) $\bar{\bar{X}} - A_2\bar{R}$

(c) $D_3\bar{X}$ (d) $D_4\bar{X}$

(e) None of the above.

8. The following are two types of 'number of defectives' chart:

(a) $\bar{x}$ chart and 'R' chart (b) 'p' chart and 'np' chart

(c) 'c' chart and 'u' chart (d) $\bar{x}$ chart and 's' chart

(e) None of the these.

9. The issues to be considered while designing control charts are:

(a) the basis for sampling (b) the sample size

(c) the location of control limits (d) the frequency of sampling

(e) all of these (f) none of these

12.19 REVIEW QUESTIONS

1. Define the term "quality assurance" and state its objectives.
2. Describe the components of a basic quality assurance system.
3. Discuss the role of inspection in quality assurance. What are the three major areas of inspection in a manufacturing firm?
4. Discuss the difference between the three major components of statistical methodology. Why these differences are significant in quality assurance?
5. Define a ***population*** and a ***sample.*** What are their major characteristics?
6. What is meant by sampling distribution?
7. Explain the term ***"process capability".*** Mention the reasons for conducting a process capability study.
8. Explain the term ***"process capability ratio"*** and ***"process capability indices"***. Explain how the process capability indexes may be used to establish or improve quality policies in operating areas or with suppliers.
9. Explain the concept of "six-sigma" quality.
10. Discuss the various types of sampling plans.
11. Discuss the concepts of (a) Operating characteristic curve. (b) Average out-going quality.
12. Write short notes on; (a) Producer's risk (b) Consumer's risk (c) AQL (d) LTPD.
13. Distinguish between "chance causes" and "assignable causes" of variation giving suitable examples.

14. Define the term "statistical process control" and discuss its advantages.
15. Discuss the three primary applications of control charts.
16. Briefly describe the methodology of constructing and using the control charts.
17. State the "central limit theorem". What is its relevance to control charts?
18. Distinguish between variable and attribute data. What types of control charts are used for each?
19. How do you interpret control charts? Explain the possible causes of different out-of-control indicators.
20. What is meant by 'testing for homogeneity'? Why is it necessary?
21. What are modified control limits? Why they should be used?
22. How are variable control charts used to determine process capability?
23. Differentiate between *control limits* and *specification limits.*
24. State the reasons for using 'S' chart in place of 'R' chart.
25. Distinguish between *'defect'* and *'defectives'* giving examples.
26. Briefly describe the process of constructing a 'p' chart.
27. Discuss the differences between a 'p' chart and an 'np' chart. Why would an 'np' chart be used?
28. Explain the difference between a 'c' chart and a 'u' chart.
29. Describe the rules for determining the appropriate control chart to use in any given situations.
30. Discuss the various issues to be considered while designing control charts.

12.20 DISCUSSION QUESTIONS

1. "Organisations ensure the quality of their products through quality assurance activities" – Explain
2. "Controlling processes is an important function of process management" – Explain
3. "Acceptance sampling can only detect poor quality, not prevent it" –Comment on the statement
4. "Process capability is important to both product designers and manufacturing engineers" – Discuss.
5. "Control charts are designed to be used by production operators rather than by inspectors or quality control personnel". Do you agree or not? Justify your answer.
6. Discuss the implication of control limit location in terms of Type I and Type II errors.
7. Discuss the trade – offs involved in selecting the sample size for a control chart.
8. Discuss the five key elements required for successful implementation of statistical process control (SPC).
9. "Control limits are often confused with specification limits" – Comment on the statement

12.21 EXERCISES

1. A manufacturer of precision machine parts produces round shafts for use in the construction of a drilling machine. The average diameter of a shaft in 56 mm. Inspection samples contain 6 shafts each. The average range of these samples is 0.6 mm Determine the upper and lower control chart limits for the mean chart.
2. The table below gives the variable data for 8 samples.

Sample	Sample range	Sample average
1	4.1	40.0
2	5.5	41.6
3	4.4	39.9
4	4.8	40.0
5	5.6	41.7
6	6.2	39.3
7	5.4	39.8
8	4.4	40.1

Is the machine properly adjusted and in control?

3. Twenty samples of n=200 were taken by an operator at a work station in a production process. The number of defective items in each sample were given in the table below.

Sample	Number of defectives	p	Sample	Number defectives	p
1	12	0.060	11	16	0.080
2	18	0.090	12	14	0.070
3	10	0.050	13	12	0.060
4	14	0.070	14	16	0.080
5	16	0.080	15	18	0.090
6	19	0.095	16	20	0.100
7	17	0.085	17	18	0.090
8	12	0.060	18	20	0.100
9	11	0.055	19	21	0.105
10	14	0.070	20	22	0.110

Management wants to develop a 'p' chart using 3 sigma limits. Draw the 'p' chart and plot the observation to determine whether the process was out of control at any point.

4. An automobile manufacturing firm produces auto pistons in a forging press and the diameter (155mm) is a critical factor that must be controlled. From sample sizes of 10 pistons produced each day, the mean and the range of this diameter have been as given bellows:

Day	Mean	Range
1	156.9	4.2
2	153.2	4.6
3	153.6	4.1
4	155.5	5.0
5	156.6	4.5

Construct the 3 sigma $\bar{x}$ - chart and the 3 sigma 'R' chart for this data.

5. The results of inspection of samples taken over the past 10 days are given below. The sample size in 100

Day	1	2	3	4	5	6	7	8	9	10
Defection	7	6	6	9	5	6	0	8	9	1

(a) construct a 3- sigma 'p' chart

(b) If the number of defectives on the next three days are 12, 5 and 13, is the process in control?

6. Telephone inquiries of 100 customers are monitored daily at random. Incidents of incorrect information or other non conformities are recorded. The data for last week follows:

Day	Number of nonconformities
1	5
2	10
3	23
4	20
5	15

Construct a 3 standard deviation 'C' chart of nonconformities. What does the control chart indicate about the telephone operators?

7. XYZ company is monitoring a filling process that has an overall average of 705cc The average range is 6cc if you use a sample size of 10, what are the upper and lower control limits for the mean and range?

8. The XYZ company packages potato chips in bags. The net weight of the chips in each bag is designed to be 100 grams with a tolerance of ± 5 grams. The packaging process results in

bags with an average weight of 88 gram and a standard deviation of 12 grams. The company wants to determine whether the process is capable of meeting the design specification.

9. The difference between the upper specification and the lower specification for a process is 0.6 mm. The standard deviation is 0.1 mm. What is the process capability ratio C_p?
10. The manager of a food processing plant desires a quality specification with a mean of 16 grams. an upper specification of 16-5 grams and a lower specification limit of 15-5 gram. The process has a standard deviation of one gram. Determine the C_{pk} of the process.
11. An acceptance sampling plan has lots of 500 pieces and a sample of 60. The number of defects in the sample may not exceed 2. This plan, based on an OC curve, has a probability of 0.57 of accepting lots when the incoming lots have a defective rate of 4%, which is the historical average of this process. What do you tell your customer the average outgoing quality is?
12. Given mean $\overline{X}$ = 8-01 gram, standard deviation $\sigma = 0.03$ and the specifications are μ = 8.0 and σ = 0. 04, determine the C_{pk} performance.
13. For a sampling plan N = 1000, n = 60, and C = 1, determine the probability of acceptance of the following lots:
    (a) 0.5 percent defective (b) 1.0 percent defective (c) 2.0 percent defective
    (d) 5.0 percent defective (e) 10.0 percent defective
    Draw an O.C curve
14. ABC company is attempting to determine whether an existing machine is capable of machining an engine part that has a key specification of 5 ± 0. 05 mm. After a trial run on this machine, the company has determined that the machine has a sample mean of 5.01 mm. With a standard deviation of 0.02 mm (a) Calculate the C_{pk} for this machine. (b) Should the company use this machine to produce this part?

12.22ASSIGNMENTS

1. Visit any industrial unit in your vicinity and interview the manager in charge of quality management to find out the kind of acceptance sampling plans used by them for incoming materials and outgoing products.
2. Visit any service organisation for which you have access and study the sampling techniques used to obtain responses from respondents in a survey to determine the quality of service offered by the organisation.

12.23 CHAPTER CASES

1. TINY TOYS HAVE A QUALITY PROBLEM

Tiny Toys is a 20 year old company engaged in the manufacture and sale of toys. The company has built a reputation on quality and innovation. Al though the company is one of the leaders in its field, the sales have leveled off in recent years. For the most recent six-month period sales actually declined compared with the same period last year. The production manager Eshwar Murthy attributed the lack of sales growth to "the economy." He was prompted to undertake a number of economy measures that included cuts in production costs and lay- offs in the design and product development departments. Although profits are still flat, he believes that within the next six months, the results of his decision will be reflected in increased profits.

The general manger of sales, Janardhan has been concerned with customer complaints about the company's "Realistic" line of working – models The moving parts on certain models have become disengaged and fail to operate or operate erratically, His manager Keshavamurthy has proposed a "trade-in" program by which customers could replace mal-functioning models with new ones. Keshavamurthy believes that this will demonstrate good-will and appease dissatisfied customers. He also proposes rebuilding the trade – ins and selling them at discounted prices in the companies retail outlets. He doesn't think that this will take away from sales of new models. Under his program, no new staff would be needed. Regular worker would perform needed repairs during period of seasonal slow- down, thus keeping production level.

When Balaji, a production executive, heard Keshava murthy's proposal, he said that a better option would be to increase inspection of finished models before they were shipped to prevent defective models reaching the customers. According to Balaji, 100 percent inspection would weed out any defective models and avoid the problem entirely.

Discussion Questions :

1. What exactly is the problem faced by Tiny Toys?
2. Assuming the role of a consultant who has been called in for advice by the company CEO, what would you recommend?

2. HOW VELCRO GOT HOOKED ON QUALITY

One morning in August 1985, the CEO of Velcro received a phone call from his Detroit sales manager informing that General Motors was dropping Velcro from its highest supplier quality rating to the next to lowest level, four (on a one to five scale). GM allowed Velcro 90 days .time period to set up and start a program of total quality control or else face the loss of not only an important customer (General Motors) but also Velcro's most promising growth market.

At this time, Velcro had 23 quality control people in their plant. To the machine operators, quality was the responsibility of quality control people. The quality control people were stationed at certain points and they would inspect on a sample basis and say whether the particular run was good or bad. What was bad was scrapped. Nobody changed the process and there was no pressure on anybody to make a change to improve quality and reduce wastages.

It is wrong to assume that the production employees were causing the waste and to blame them for it without giving them the tools to deal with the problem would have been a bigger mistake. Under such conditions, production employees were afraid to report defects in products produced and the scrap was being disposed off to scrap yard during the third shift (night shift). The management felt that it was necessary to train the operators in quality control and more attention to be given to operators, machine repair and redesign and to measurement and reporting techniques that tracked results, focussed on responsibilities and established up-and-down communications.

The pressure on production employees to reduce wastages was lacking due to the attitudes of supervisors who took the wastages due to bad quality very lightly. The supervisors infact were a big barrier to making the operators responsible for quality.

Velcro installed the "Statistical Process Control" (SPC) system, which went a long way toward pin-pointing where the production process went wrong and needed improvement. The charting mechanism (control charts) of SPC put pressure on the line operators who had difficulty with the idea that quality and quantity are not mutually exclusive expectations. The production employees were reluctant to speed up production for the fear of making more mistakes and thereby increase wastages or scrap. Gradually, the quality control people will pull out of stations early in the process and then out of points later in the process entrusting the production employees the job of maintaining quality in their work. The number of mistakes declined as a result.

Discussion Questions :

1. Unless threatened with losing a major customer (General Motors in this case) why should an organisation work to improve its quality.
2. Discuss the role of managers, workers`and quality control inspectors in quality improvement.

CHAPTER 13

SIX-SIGMA QUALITY

LEARNING OBJECTIVES

After reading this chapter, you should be able to:

- Understand what is "Six-Sigma Quality" and its concept
- Discuss "Six-Sigma" process capability
- Discuss the principles and core elements of "Six-Sigma"
- Discuss the structured problem solving approaches used in "Six-Sigma" projects
- Discuss the "Six-Sigma" approach to TQM
- Understand "the Do's" and "the Dont's" of "Six-Sigma"
- Discuss the role and responsibilities of people responsible for implementing "Six-Sigma" projects
- Give an overview of "Six-Sigma" tools
- Understand what is meant by "Design for Six-Sigma" (DFSS)
- Describe the steps involved in 'DFSS' procedure
- Describe the "IDOV" approach

13.0 INTRODUCTION

Sigma (σ) is a term used in statistics to represent "**standard deviation**" which indicates the degree of variation in a set of measurements or a process. Sigma indicates the spread of each unit around a target value, and therefore it is essentially an indication of how good a product or service is. Traditionally designers used the three sigma (3σ) rule to evaluate whether or not a part would meet the design specification. When a part's specifications are consistent with a spread of six standard deviations of process variation, *i.e.*, (3σ) to either side of the mean or target value, around 99.73 percent of the parts for a process which is centred would be expected to conform to design specification. The higher the sigma value, the lower the number of defects associated with the process. In other words, sigma measures the capability of a process to produce defect free work and is a means of calibrating process performance to meet the customer requirements. For example, a process which is at a quality level of 3σ means 66,807 defects per million opportunities (DPMO) while 6σ means 3.4 defects per million opportunities (DPMO) (these values assume a normal distribution with a process shift of 1.5 sigma). ***Table 13.1*** **presents various levels of sigma and their corresponding number of defects per million opportunities.**

Table 13.1 : Sigma Value and Corresponding Defects per Million Opportunities (DPMO)

Sigma Value	DPMO
1σ	6,91,462.5
2σ	3,08,537.0
3σ	66,807.0
4σ	6,210.0
5σ	233.0
6σ	3.4

Most organisations in developed and developing countries are operating at 3σ to 4σ quality levels. This means these organisations could be losing up to 25 present of their total revenue due to processes that deliver too many defects (ie cost of poor quality) 'Since sigma levels indicate the capability of the process to improve the overall sigma level, the whole process needs to be understood in considerable detail and changed (redesigned) so that defect levels are reduced permanently. The central idea of Six-Sigma Quality management is that we can measure the defects in a process and can simultaneously figure- out ways to eliminate them and improve the quality level progressively (say from 3σ to 6σ) and ultimately approach a **quality level of zero defects.**

So, in short, Six-Sigma means:

(i) a statistical basis of measurements: 3.4 defects per million opportunities (DPMO).

(ii) a philosophy and a goal: as perfect as practically possible.

(iii) a methodology and

(iv) a symbol of quality.

13.1 SIX-SIGMA QUALITY

One might think that having the natural tolerance equal to the design tolerance would mean good quality. If we assume that the process output is represented by a normal distribution, about 99.73% of the output is contained within bounds that are 3 standard deviations (3σ) from the mean. As shown in ***Exhibit 13.1,*** **these are represented as the lower and upper tolerance limits (LTL & UTL).**

Exhibit 13.1 : Process Output Represented by a Normal Distribution

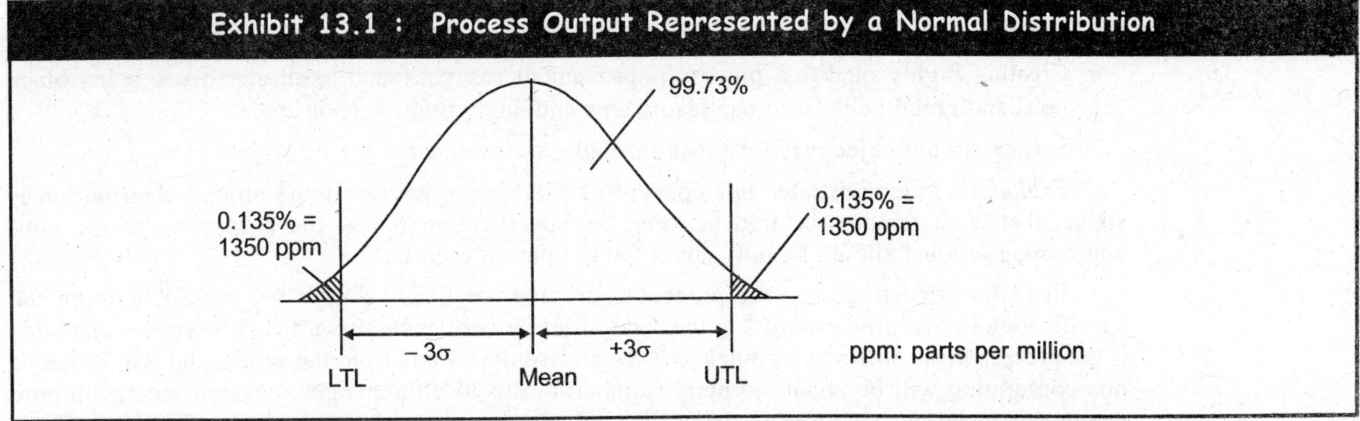

The **normal distribution** is characterised by two parameters : the **mean** and the **standard deviation**. The mean is a measure of the location of the process. If the product specification limits are 3 standard deviation from the mean, the proportion of the non-conforming product is about 0.27% (or 2700 ppm). On the surface, it appears to be a good process, but appearance can be deceiving. Consider what such a level of quality really means:

- at least 20,000 wrong drug prescriptions each year
- more than 15,000 babies accidentally dropped each year by nurses and obstetricians
- no electricity and water for about nine hours each year.
- 2000 lost pieces of mail each hour.
- 500 incorrect surgical operations each week.

Are we satisfied with such quality?

For a product to be built virtually defect free, it must be designed to tolerance limits that are significantly more than ± 3σ from the mean. In other words, the process spread is measured by ± 3σ has to be significantly less than the spread between the upper and lower specification limits (USL & LSL). Motorola's answer to this problem is **Six-Sigma quality** that is, process variability must be so small that the specification limits are 6 standard deviations from the mean.

13.2 CONCEPT OF SIX-SIGMA QUALITY

In recent years, a new interest in basic quality principles emerged in many corporate board rooms under the concept of **Six sigma**; which is a customer-focused and result oriented approach to business improvement. Six sigma integrates many tested and validated quality tools and techniques, with a bottom-line orientation.

Six sigma can be described as a business improvement approach that seeks to find and eliminate causes of defects and errors in manufacturing and service processes by focussing on outputs that are critical to customers and a clear financial return for the organisation.

Some key concepts on which the core philosophy of Six-Sigma is based are:

1. Thinking in terms of key business processes and customer requirements with a clear focus on overall strategic objectives of the organisation.
2. Focussing on corporate sponsors, support team activities, helping to overcome resistance to change and obtaining resources.
3. Emphasising quantifiable measures such as defects per million opportunities (ppm) that can be applied to all parts of an organisation: manufacturing, engineering, administration, software etc.
4. Ensuring that appropriate metrics are identified early in the process and also ensuring that these metrics focus on business results, thereby providing incentives and accountability.

5. Providing extensive training and deploying a project team to improve profitability, reduce non-value added activities and achieve reduction of cycle time.
6. Creating highly qualified process improvement experts (such as master black belts, black belts and green belts) who can lead teams and apply improvement tools.
7. Setting stretch objectives for break-through improvement.

Exhibit 13.2 demonstrates this concept of Six-Sigma quality. If the process distribution is stable, that is, it remains centred between the specification limits, the proportion of the non-conforming product should be only about 0.001 ppm on each tail.

In real world situations, the process distribution will not always be centred between the specification limits, process shifts to the right or left are not uncommon. It can be shown that even if the process mean shifts by as much as 1.5 standard deviations from the centre, the proportion of non-conforming will be about 3.4 ppm. Comparing this to a three-sigma capability of 2700 ppm demonstrates the improvement in the expected level of quality from the process. If we consider a product containing 1000 parts and we design it for Six-Sigma capability, then an average of 0.0034 defect per product unit (3.4 ppm) is expected, instead of the 2.7 defects expected with three-sigma capability.

Exhibit 13.2 : Six-Sigma Capability

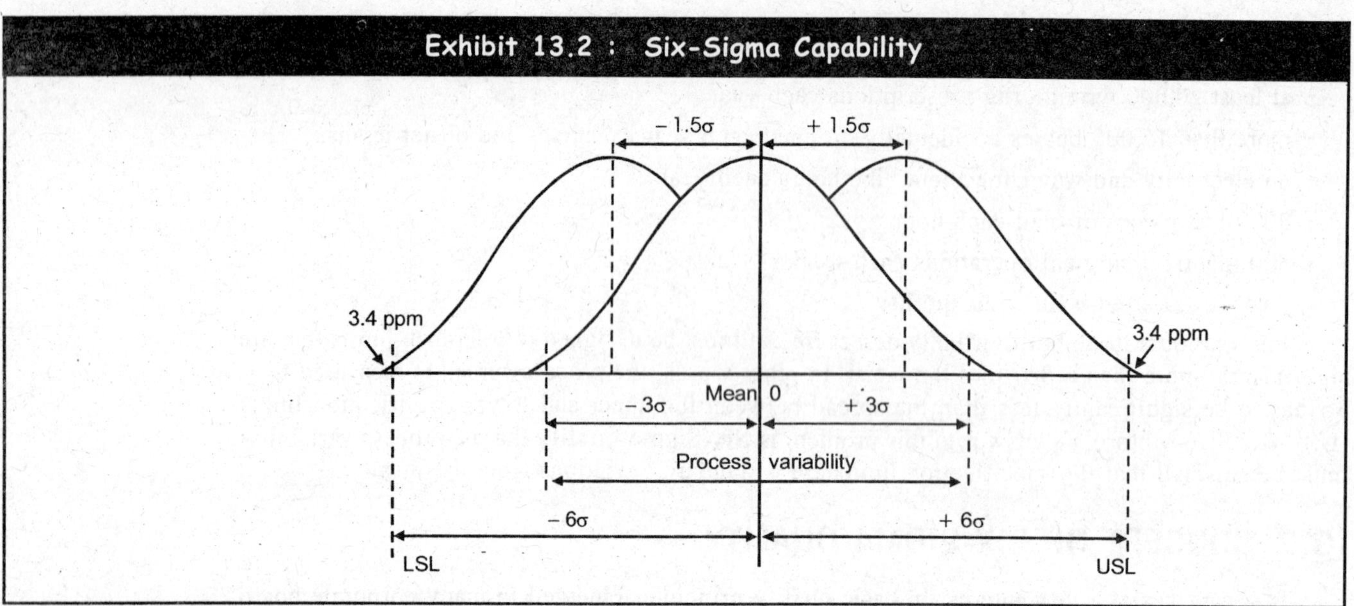

Box 13.1 **describes six sigma quality and** ***Box 13.2*** **describes the six sigma quality in Motorola.**

Box 13.1 : Six Sigma Quality

Six sigma quality is related to the normal distribution with sigma (σ) denoting the standard deviation of the process. Motorola assumed that the process mean would experience a 1.5 σ shift before a 3 σ change. Thus, six sigma corresponds to a ± 4.5 σ deviation on either side of the mean resulting in 3.4 ppm defects. (This can be verified by referring to the normal probability tables at ± 4.5 σ).

The six sigma criterion is equivalent to a process capability of C_{pk} = 1.5. This can be seen by referring to the formula for C_{pk} with USL – μ = 4.5 σ. As a result, the six sigma criterion will ensure processes that are not just barely capable of producing the specifications but will provide somewhat better process capability.

Establishing a goal of three sigma capability is acceptable at a starting point, however because it allows the organisation to set a base line for improvement. As management becomes more process oriented, higher goals such as ***"Six-Sigma capability"*** become possible. Such goals may require fundamental changes in the management philosophy and the organisational culture.

Box 13.2 : Six Sigma Quality - What TQM did for Motorola

Once you get good at something, such as TQM, there is no turning back. Consider what happened when Motorola gained statistical control of its processes but still was not satisfied. Using TQM tools, they achieved plus or minus three sigma (3σ) quality levels. Motorola then developed a new system to achieve higher levels of quality of at least six sigma (6σ).

Why a six sigma level of quality? At this level, 99.99966 percent of all products will be "good". Furthermore, for every extra 9 after the decimal point, there is a corresponding 10 fold reduction in non-conformities as shown below:

Quality Confidence	Quality Risk	Total defects (parts per million)	PPM change factor
0.9	0.1	1,00,000	29,411.0
0.99	0.01	10,000	2,941.0
0.999	0.001	1000	294.0
0.9999	0.0001	100	29.0
0.99999	0.00001	10	3.0
0.999999	0.000001	1	0.3

Motorola's six sigma program improves quality by changing the processes used in the design and delivery of products. In this respect, the six sigma program is like the process capability tools of C_p and C_{pk}.

However, like these tools, six sigma improves the various processes by actively involving all the design and delivery functions. It also draws on a wide range of tools, including:

- Design for manufacturability
- Statistical process control (SPC)
- Supplier SPC (the application of SPC at the supplier's site)
- Participative management practices
- Part standardisation and supplier certification and
- Computer simulation.

These tools identify and attack all the forms of variance that can affect quality and customers who want quality products will perceive higher levels of value.

One might wonder why a process shift of 1.5 σ would be allowed. Since many common statistical process control plans are based on sample sizes that only allow detection of shifts of about 2 σ, it would not be unusual for a process to drift this much and not be noticed.

A quality level of 3.4 defects per million can be achieved in several ways, for instance:

- With 0.5-sigma off-centering and 5 sigma quality
- With 1.0-sigma off-centering and 5.5 sigma quality
- With 1.5-sigma off-centering and 6 sigma quality.

13.3 SIX-SIGMA PROCESS CAPABILITY

Six-Sigma is a total quality management (TQM) process which uses process capability analysis as a means of measuring progress. Sigma (σ) is the Greek symbol used to represent the statistical measurement of dispersion called ***"standard deviation"***. It is the best measurement for process variability. The smaller the value of deviation, the lesser the variability in the process.

Statistically speaking, sigma is a term that indicates the extent a process varies from perfection. The number of defects divided by the quantity of units processed and then multiplied by one million results in defects per million. Adding a 1.5 sigma shift in the mean results in the following defects per million.

1 sigma = 690,000 defects per million
2 sigma = 308,000 defects per million
3 sigma = 66,800 defects per million
4 sigma = 6,210 defects per million
5 sigma = 230 defects per million
6 sigma = 3.4 defects per million

Exhibit 13.3 shows a process that is normally distributed and centred with the upper and lower specification limits (USL and LSL) established at ± 6σ. For this situation, 99.9999998% of the product or service will be between specifications. This means the defect or non-conformance rate is 0.002 parts per million (ppm) or 2.0 per billion. This represents a process capability index (C_p) of 2.0.

***Table 13.2* shows the non-conformance rate and process capability for different specification limits, when the process is centred.**

Exhibit 13.3 : Non-conformance rate when the process is centred

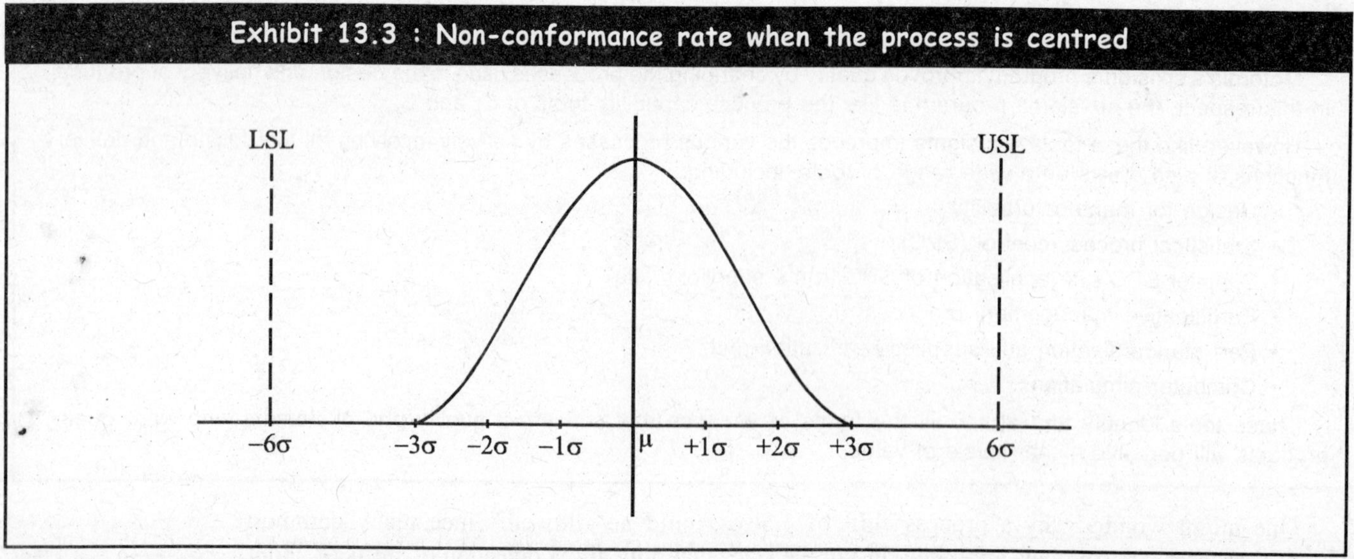

Table 13.2 : Non-conformance Rate and Process Capability when the Process is Centred

Specification limit	Percent conformance	Non-conformance rate (ppm)	Process capability (C_p)
± 1σ	68.7	3,17,300.0	0.33
± 2σ	95.45	48,500.0	0.67
± 3σ	99.73	2700.0	1.00
± 4σ	99.9937	63.0	1.33
± 5σ	99.999943	0.57	1.67
± 6σ	99.9999998	0.002	2.00

In reality, processes rarely remain centred. The centre tends to shift above or below the target (*i.e.*, mean 'μ'). ***Exhibit 13.4* shows a process that is normally distributed but the mean has shifted within a range of 1.5σ above and 1.5σ below the target.**

For the above situation where the process mean has shifted by ± 1.5σ, 99.9996600% of the product or service will be between specifications and the nonconformance rate will be 3.4 parts per million (ppm). This situation gives a process capability index C_{pk} of 1.5.

Exhibit 13.4 : Non-conformance Rate When the Process is Off-centre by ± 1.5σ

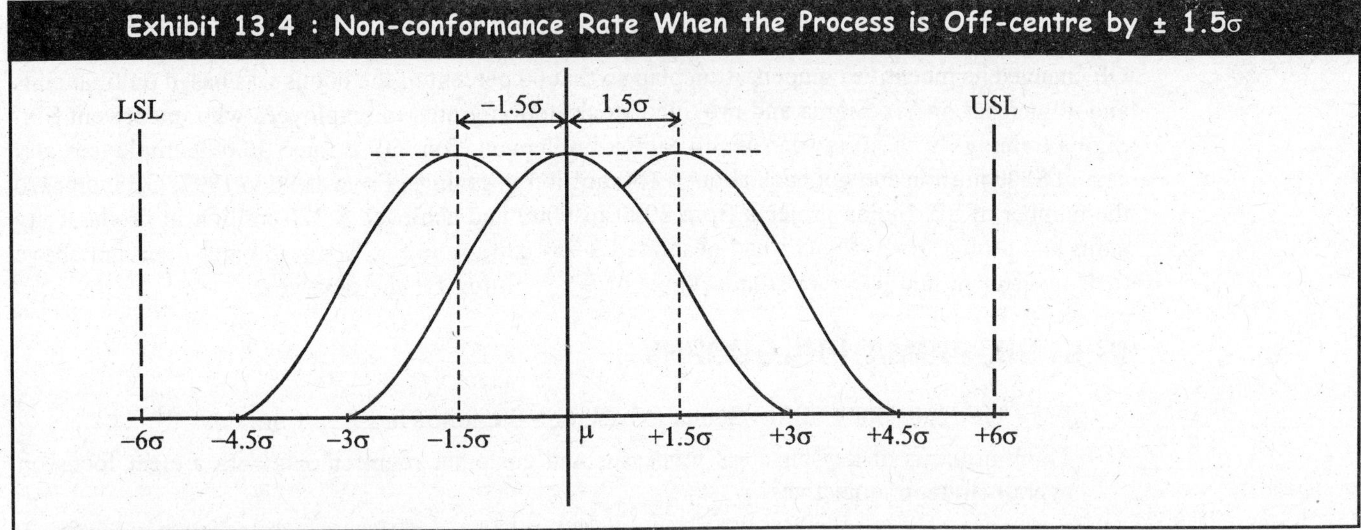

Table 13.3 **shows the non-conformance rate and process capability when the process is off-centre by ± 1.5σ.**

From the above, we can infer that the statistical aspects of Six-Sigma tell us that we should reduce the process variability, σ and try to keep the process centred on the target mean (μ).

Six-Sigma methodology was first initiated by Motorola in the 1980s followed by General Electric in 1995.

Six-Sigma constitutes an evolving set of principles, fundamental practices and tools - a breakthrough strategy.

Table 13.3 : Non-conformance Rate and Process Capability when the Process is Off-centred by ± 1.5σ

Specification limit	Percent conformance	Non-conformance rate (ppm)	Process capability (C_{pk})
± 1σ	30.23	697700.0	−0.167
± 2σ	69.13	308700.0	0.167
± 3σ	93.32	66810.0	0.500
± 4σ	99.3790	6210.0	0.834
± 5σ	99.97670	2330.0	1.167
± 6σ	99.9996600	3.4	1.50

13.4 EVOLUTION OF SIX-SIGMA APPROACH

Motorola Pioneered the concept of Six-Sigma as an approach to measuring product and service quality. **Bill Smith** , a reliability engineer was credited with originating the concept during the mid-1980s and selling it to Motorola's CEO, **Robert Galvin**. Robert Galvin was convinced of the importance of Six- Sigma approach to achieve very high levels of consistent quality in all the processes undertaken at Motorola and set the following goals for Motorola in 1987.

(i) Improve product and service quality 10 times by 1989 and at least 100 times by 1991.

(ii) Achieve Six-Sigma Capability by 1992.

(iii) With a deep sense of urgency, spread dedication to quality to every facet of the corporation, and achieve a culture of continual improvement to assure total customer satisfaction. The ultimate goal is to achieve zero defects in everything done.

After Motorola, in 1995, General Electric's CEO, Jack Welch directed the implementation of Six-Sigma in his corporation and GE became a recognised bench-mark for Six-Sigma implementation. GE changed its incentive compensation plan so that 60 percent of the bonus was based on financials and 40 percent on Six-Sigma and provided stock option grants to employees who underwent Six-Sigma training. In the first year of Sig-Sigma implementation, GE trained 30,000 employees at a cost of $200 million and got back about $ 150 million in savings. From 1996 to 1997, GE increased the number of Six-Sigma projects from 3000 to 6000 and achieved $ 320 million in productivity gains and profits. By 1998, GE had generated $ 750 million in Six-Sigma savings over and above their investment and had estimated savings of $ 1.5 billion for the next year.

13.5 SIX-SIGMA PHILOSOPHY

The Core Philosophy of Six-Sigma is based on the following Key Concepts:

(i) Think in terms of key business processes and customer requirements with a clear focus on overall strategic objectives.

(ii) Focus on corporate sponsors responsible for championing improvement projects, support team activities, help to overcome resistance to change and obtain resources.

(iii) Emphasise quantifiable measures such as defects per million opportunities.

(iv) Ensure that appropriate metrics are identified early in the process and that they focus on business results.

(v) Provide extensive training followed by project team deployment to improve profitability, reduce non- value-added activities and achieve cycle reduction.

(vi) Create highly qualified process improvement experts (green belts, black belts and master block belts) who can apply improvement tools and lead teams.

(vii) Set stretch objective for improvement.

13.6 TEN PRINCIPLES OF SIX SIGMA

1. Committed and strong leadership is absolutely necessary. This means a major cultural change in the organisation.
2. Existing initiatives, strategies, measures and practices must be integrated with Six-Sigma activities.
3. Data-based management having quantitative analysis and statistical thinking as key concepts.
4. Application of consistent effort to learning everything possible about customers and the market place.
5. Six-Sigma approach must produce a significant pay-off in a reasonable time period.
6. Highly trained individuals (referred to as Master Black Belts, Black Belts and Green Belts in that order of hierarchy) are necessary to lead at all levels of the organisation.
7. Systems that track, measure and report performance are needed to monitor progress, allow for needed course corrections and link the Six-Sigma approach to the goals, objectives and strategic plans of the organisation.
8. The organisation must have suitable reward and recognition systems that support continuous reinforcement of the people at all levels who significantly contribute to the viability and success of Six-Sigma approach. Compensation systems need to be reengineered in order to motivate employees.
9. Successes achieved due to Six-Sigma approach should be celebrated internally and frequently in the organisation.
10. Successful organisation should give wide publicity to its Six-Sigma achievements.

    This would further enhance the organisation's image and self-esteem of its employees.

13.7 PRE REQUISITES OF SIX-SIGMA APPROACH

Six-Sigma, like any other major organisational change programme, is not easy to implement successfully. Success will depend on at least four major factors discussed in the following paragraphs.

***(i)* High levels of commitment and involvement of management:** Six-Sigma is based on an understanding of statistics which is not a popular area for most managers. Also, it is necessary that high-performing managers are released to be trained and after training that they commit a significant amount of their time to the implementation of Six-Sigma approach.

***(ii)* Six-Sigma is not just another quality program or stand-alone activity:** Six-Sigma is not just theory or a mere training program, It is an active, involved effort that puts practical tools to work to root defects at all levels of the organisation. It defines analyses, improves and controls the vital few processes that matter most, to tie quality improvement directly to bottom line results. Like TQM, Six-Sigma requires adherence to a whole philosophy rather than usage of a few tools and techniques. Six-Sigma is a business strategy that fosters a cultural shift at all levels. It changes the outlook and practices of everyone in the organisation.

***(iii)* Six-Sigma is about reducing defects and improving quality:** Improvement depends on how opportunities for defects or failures are defined and measured. What matters in a Six-Sigma approach, as in any other quality approach, is what the customer wants or needs. The most critical effects or failures are those that cause maximum concern to the customer. Increasing complexity of systems and products used by consumers created higher-than-desired system failures. Therefore, to increase system reliability and reduce failure rates, the components utilised on complex systems and products must have individual failure rates approaching zero, for example Six-Sigma approach to be used in an airline where the measure of failure needs to be defined.

***(iv)* Six-Sigma involves a problem - solving approach:** Six-Sigma needs to be concentrated on those elements of a business which will result in customers perceiving that they would rather deal with them than with one of its competitors. Therefore, Six-Sigma, like any other performance improvement drive, should start from a strategy which is essentially a highly focused system of problem solving. Six-Sigma is essentially about results- enhancing profitability through improved quality and efficiency resulting in high levels of customer satisfaction. Improvement projects are chosen based on their ability to contribute to the bottom-line on a company's income statement by being connected to the strategic objectives and goals of the corporation.

13.8 CORE ELEMENTS OF SIX-SIGMA

Six-Sigma builds on a range of improvement methods that have proven to be effective. The core elements of Six-Sigma approach are.

***(i) Focus on the Customer*:** Since Six-Sigma, measures start with customer satisfaction, the emphasis is on understanding customer expectations and requirements.

***(ii) Date-and-fact driven management*:** Specking with data, management decisions based on fact and developing as in-depth understanding of internal processes are basic to Six-Sigma approach.

***(iii) Specific Training*:** Six-Sigma implementation requires trained people-both managers and workers- a defined and formal infrastructure consisting of champions, master Black Belts, black belts and green belts that head and influence Six-Sigma projects. **Master black belts** are the technical experts who provide training and support for other belts and also lead major cross-functional Six-Sigma projects. The **Black Belts** undertake full-time work on Six-Sigma projects and lead the project team. The **Green Belts** are part-time process-owners and usually undertake work on a small scale, in contrast to the Black Belts.

***(iv) Structured approach*:** Six-Sigma is based on a structured problem-solving approach. For existing processes, an approach known as 'DMAIC' approach consisting of steps "Define, Measure, Analyse, Improve and Control" is used and for new processes the steps include-Define , Measure, Analyse, Design and Verify-(called "DMADV" approach)

***(v) Quality Engineering*?** Six-Sigma was a full range of tools and techniques. Specific tools and techniques are used in each stage of the 'DMAIC' and 'DMADV' problem solving approaches.

***(vi) Process Focus, Control and Improvement*:** The key aspect is understanding the process in order to control its input and there by facilitate its improvement. It is important to examine potential defects, root causes and potential corrective and long-term actions. Also it is important to understand the relationship between inputs and outputs, with respect to issues such as which inputs have the biggest positive effect on which output.

***(vii) Proactive management*:** An understanding of key principle of Six-Sigma is vital at all levels of management. Managers must be proactive in challenging why' things' are done in a certain way, defining root causes of problems, setting and maintaining aggressive improvement targets and devoting a large amount of their time for improvement projects.

***(viii) "Boundary less" Collaboration*:** Since many Six-Sigma projects involve cross-functional teams, team work is essential and it is important to have a range of skills with in the team.

***(ix) Drive for perfection*:** In the drive to eliminate defects, often things will go wrong and some projects will not achieve their goals. But it is important to understand the reasons for failure, to learn from experiments and take counter measures to prevent defects occurring in the future.

***(x) Cost savings of each project*:** A sense of urgency is created with Six-Sigma, through the financial targets linked to each project. Therefore, each project should lead to verifiable bottom-line results.

***(xi) Short-term improvement projects*:** It is necessary to fix a time-scale for each specific project's completion. The duration of each project is relatively short- say between three and six months.

13.9 STRUCTURED PROBLEM-SOLVING APPROACHES USED IN SIX-SIGMA PROJECTS

Six-Sigma improvement projects adhere to strict problem-solving approaches which vary depending on the organisational processes to which they are applied.

For existing processes, the approach is known as 'DMAIC' approach or model, whereas for new processes the approach is known as "DMADV" approach.

Implementation of Six-Sigma involves three aspects of process development:

1. Process improvement.
2. Process design/redesign and
3. Process management.

These are briefly discussed in the following paragraphs:

1. Process Improvement

This primarily concerns the elimination of the root causes of process problems and is clearly associated with continuous improvement of activities or processes which are existing already. Process improvements projects involve the identification of the vital few inputs which influence the results or outputs.

The DMAIC approach is a structured problem solving approach which is employed in making improvement s to existing processes and products. It is related to other problem-solving approaches, including Deming's PDCA cycle.

Steps involved in the DMAIC approaches are:

***(i)* Define the customer and organisational requirements:** The specific problem to be solved and the process to be improved should be defined in clear terms. The problem should be the one where it is critical to succeed and /or the one that will give the quickest and greatest returns. In addition, the project scope and boundary conditions, must be defined, appropriate performance metrics must be selected. This phase also involves agreeing the goals of the selected projects, its financial impact and the identification of the project champion, process owner and team members.

(ii) **Measure the factors which are critical to quality (i.e. input factors):** This step involves the selection of process inputs that must be improved, development of a data collection plan, gathering data to evaluate correct performance and an assessment of the performance measurement system and their capability.

(iii) **Analyse the relationship between the cost of defects and key process variables:** The purpose of this step is to determine the root cause of variation and defects and to develop a base line (process capability). This involves pinpointing opportunities and setting objectives.

(iv) **Improve the process:** This involves using experimentation, pilot studies and simulation techniques to address the root causes of the problems identified in the analysis phase. It also involves various improvement loops, with appropriate confirmation studies related to each phase of process improvement.

(v) **Control the system through established process:** This involves controlling the process outputs to ensure the long-term gains and improved performance of the process. It also involves verifying the benefits and savings, fully integrating the changes into procedures and communicating the findings as appropriate.

Tools and Techniques DMAIC Approach

The applicable tools used in various steps are:

Step (i) Define:

(a) **Data collection tools:** Check sheets, brainstorming and flow charts.

(b) **Data analysis tools:** Cause and effect diagrams, affinity diagrams, tree diagrams, root-causes analysis.

(c) **Customer data collection and analysis:** Quality function deployment, and Surveys

Step (ii) Measure:

(a) **Process control tools:** control charts

(b) **Process improvement tools:** Process mapping. Pareto charts, Process benchmarking, Theory of constraints (TOC), Risk assessment, Design of experiments (DOE) and Lean thinking techniques.

Step (iii) Analyse:

(a) Root-cause analysis and

(b) SWOT analysis.

Step (iv) Improve:

(a) Project planning and measurement techniques and

(b) Training.

Step (v) Control:

(a) Cost-benefit analysis and

(b) Evaluation of process performance.

2. Process Design/Redesign

This is the next step after process improvement. Here, the emphasis is on the existing ones. This is similar to Business Process Reengineering. The method used is the "DMADV" approach which is also known as the design for Six-Sigma (DFSS).

The steps used in the "DMADV" approach are:

(i) **Define** the goals of the project and customer (internal and external) deliverables.

(ii) **Measure** and determine customer needs and specifications.

(iii) **Analyse** the process options to meet customer needs.

(iv) **Design** the process to meet the customer needs.

(v) **Verify** the design performance and ability to meet customer needs.

3. Process Management

This is the third type of problem-solving approach. It reflects a change of emphasis from the oversight and direction of functions to understanding the process facilitation. The key activities include:

(a) managing the processes end to end.

(b) identifying clearly the customer requirements.

(c) having meaningful measures of input

(d) developing process activities and

(e) developing outputs.

A Six-Sigma approach to process management can be considered to have the following five stages:

Stage 1: ***Identify the need***: Gather data, analyses data, define cost of poor quality and consider the voice of the customer.

Stage 2: ***Clarify the vision***: Define the project brief, set goals / target objectives, establish realistic time-scales.

Stage 3: ***Develop the Plan***: Establish the project initiative, identify the project champion, select the team, and understand the present system of documentation, review the current process, understand the performance of the current process, consider training requirements and define the available resources.

Stage 4: ***Implement the Plan***: Provide clear ownership of the process, optimise the process, record progress results and display using appropriate visual management methods evaluate improvement and process management, review cost savings and establish continuous improvement mechanisms.

Stage 5: ***Sustain improvement***: Document the initiative, maintain team responsibility, apply knowledge gained across the board, communicate and recognise success and identify the next project.

13.10 SIX-SIGMA AS A QUALITY FRAMEWORK

Six-Sigma provides a blue print for implementing total quality system. In many ways, Six-Sigma is a way for realising many fundamental concepts of "total quality management", mainly the integration of human and process elements of improvement. Human issues include managing leadership, a sense of urgency; focus on results, and customers, team-work, and culture change. Process issues include the use of process management techniques, analysis of variation and application of statistical methods, a disciplined problem-solving approach and management by fact.

However Six-Sigma has some features in contrast to total quality (TQ). These are:

(i) TQ is based largely on worker involvement and team-work whereas Six-Sigma is owned by business leader champions supported by Master Black-Belts, Black Belts and Green Belts.

(ii) TQ activities usually occur within a function, process or individual workplace or department whereas Six-Sigma projects are cross-functional in nature.

(iii) TQ Training is generally limited to simple improvement tools (7 QC tools) and concepts whereas Six-Sigma focuses on a more rigorous and advanced set of satisfied methods and a problem-solving methodology such as "DMAIC" *(iv)* TQ is focused on improvement with little accountability for financial results whereas Six-Sigma requires a verifiable return-on-investment and focus on the bottom line.

13.11 APPLICATION OF SIX-SIGMA IN SERVICE ORGANISATIONS

All Six-Sigma projects have three major characteristics: (1) A problem to be solved, (2) A process having a problem and (3) One or more measures that quantify the gap to close and can be used to monitor progress.

The above characteristics are present in all business processes either manufacturing or service. Six-Sigma can be applied to a wide variety of transactional, administrative and other service areas. Generally speaking, 50 present or more of the total saving opportunity in an organisation lies outside of manufacturing. However, services have some unique characteristics as compared to manufacturing processes. The service employees usually do not think in terms of processes, measurements and data. The service processes are often invisible, complex and not well defined and documented. Also the service requires considerable human intervention, such as customers' interaction, underwriting (guarantees, warranties) or approval decisions, or manual report generation. Because of these differences, it becomes difficult to identify opportunities and define service projects. In addition it is quite common that similar service activities are often performed in different ways because of differences in service providers and customer expectations.

Because service processes are largely people-driven, measurements are often non-existent or difficult to define. Therefore for applying Six-Sigma approach, it is necessary that measurement systems are created before data collection.

To apply Six-Sigma to service, four key measures of performance must be examined:

1. ***Accuracy*** – as measured by correct financial results, completeness of information or freedom from data errors.
2. ***Cycle time*** – which is a measure of the time taken to complete a service activity such as bills payment.
3. ***Cost*** – the internal cost of process activities.
4. ***Customer satisfaction*** – which is typically the primary measure of success in service performance.

The ***"DMAIC' approach*** used in the application of Six-Sigma in manufacturing can be used for service operations also. For example in the ***'Define'*** stage, a key question would be to define what a defect represents. A flow chart may be used for the service process specifying what activities are performed. A defect in service may be a source of customer dissatisfaction and critical to service quality.

In the ***"Measure"*** stage, it is necessary to collect data on the frequency of defects and information about products and tools to be used by the employees. The ***"Analyse"*** stage might include evaluating differences among employees to determine why some can be better at performing the service process than others. In the ***"Improve"*** stage, standard operating procedure might be developed. In the ***"Control"*** stage, employees are taught the correct technique to perform the service satisfactorily and the improvement is measured from time to time.

Some examples of application of Six-Sigma in financial services include the following:

(i) Reducing the average and variation of days out-standing of accounts receivables.
(ii) Improving the accuracy and speed of the audit process.
(iii) Reducing variation in cash flow.
(iv) Improving the accuracy of journal entries.
(v) Improving the accuracy and cycle time of standard financial reports.

13.12 SIX-SIGMA MANAGEMENT

'Six-Sigma' management is the relentless and rigorous pursuit of the reduction of variation in all critical processes to achieve continuous and break through improvements that impact the bottom line of the organisation and increase customer satisfaction. It is an organisational initiative designed to create manufacturing, service and administrative processes that produce approximately 3.4 defects per million opportunities (DPMO). Most of the manufacturing organisations have strategies in place that produce a maximum of 6210 defects per million opportunities (i.e. 4 sigma processes).

Six-Sigma management promotes the idea that the distribution of output for a process (the voice of the process) should take up no more than half of the tolerance allowed by the specification limits (the voice of the customer), assuring measurement data from a stable and normal distribution of output whose means can shift by as much as 1.5 standard deviations overtime. A shift of 1.5 standard deviations in a process's mean over time has been accepted as a common phenomenon early in an organisation's Six-Sigma process.

Six-Sigma Approach to TQM

Six-Sigma is believed to be the most powerful break-through management tool ever devised for TQM. ***What is Six-Sigma?*** It is a **business process** that allows companies to drastically improve their bottom line by **designing** and **monitoring everyday business activities** in ways that **minimise waste** and **resources** while **increasing customer satisfaction.**

Six-Sigma guides companies into making fewer mistakes in everything they do eliminating lapses in quality at the earliest possible occurrence.

Quality control programs have focused on **detecting** and correcting defects whereas Six-Sigma encompasses something broader. **It provides specific methods to re-create the process so that defects and errors never arise in the first place.**

Six-Sigma represent **extraordinary sense,** not ordinary or common sense, common sense by itself rarely produces extraordinary results. Six Sigma approach has proved that many well-accepted past management practices and quality-control methods are less than optimal or even wrong. Some well known companies e.g. General electric, Sony, Honda, Texas Instruments, Canon, Hitachi, have adopted Six-Sigma.

Six-Sigma produces superior financial results, using business strategies that not only revive companies but help them leaf-frog ahead of their competition in term of market share and profitability, by decreasing costs. By reaching for the seemingly impossible (zero defect) companies achieve the impossible.

Six-Sigma helped many executives who have undergone training in Six-Sigma principles at Six Sigma Academy in scottdale, Arizona, USA to transform their companies into world–class organisations.

Six-Sigma can achieve faster working capital turns, lower capital spending, more productive R&D spending, faster new product development and greeter customer satisfaction.

Six-Sigma Breakthrough Strategy should be of paramount interest to any forward thinking (i.e. progressive) executive or manager who wants to make his organisation more competitive and profitable and enhance its ability to drive change.

Six-Sigma principles applies to business of any size, not to just industrial processes, but also to engineering product design and any commercial process such as processing mortgage applications, credit card transactions, customer service call centers etc.

By attacking "variation" during the design of products and services it is possible for any organisation to achieve unprecedented profitability.

3.13 HOW DOES SIX-SIGMA WORK?

The first step in the break- through strategy is to ask a new set of questions, questions that take the managers out of their comfort zone and ultimately provide them with a new direction. Six Sigma forces business to let go of bad habits. Bureaucracy becomes delayered. Those employees who are closest to the actual work and to the customer become motivated to meet or exceed consumer requirements. By questioning the speed with which products are produced and services are rendered, people begin to think about new systems that can be put into place to produce a higher-quality product or service in a shorter amount of time. People who are close to the work discover more effective and profitable ways of working, and are able to inform top management about what changes need to be made and as a result, push those higher in the organisation to reexamine the ways in which they do business.

Six-Sigma is about asking tougher and tougher questions until we receive quantifiable answers that **change behavior.** Through Six Sigma, companies relentlessly question every process, and every step along the way to creating a final product. Managers, employees and customers ask different kinds of questions of each other than they have asked before. As Six-Sigma takes hold across an organisation it creates an internal infrastructure that includes executives, managers, engineers and operations and service personnel. When 50 percent or more of an organisation's staff embrace Six-Sigma, those individuals are able to mobilise massive changes in the way business is done, dramatically increasing profitability.

The methodology behind Six-Sigma is designed to pave way to find the right answers for the company. When an organisation starts to question **what it does** and **why it does it,** it can begin to lay a road that will lead to its own long-term goals.

The fact is, organisations need ways of measuring what they claim to value. Measurements or "metrics" carry relevance to every member, for every activity of an organisation. **"You can't change what you can't measure"**. The foundation of Six-Sigma uses metrics to calculate the success of everything an organisation does. Exhortations won't change things for the better, only measuring the things a company values can produce quantum changes. Without measuring a company's process. - and its changes to these processes, - it is impossible to know where you are or where you are going – Six-Sigma tells us:

- We don't know what we don't know
- We can't do what we don't know
- We don't know until we measure
- We don't measure what we don't value
- We don't value, what we don't measure.

So in a general way, Six-Sigma is a process of asking questions that lead to tangible, quantifiable answers that ultimately produce profitable results.

To date, every company that has followed Six-Sigma methodology has achieved breakthrough profitability.

Why Six-Sigma?

Why companies are embracing Sig-Sigma? What drives companies to implement Six-Sigma? **The goal of sig-sigma is not to achieve Six-Sigma levels of quality. Six-Sigma is about improving profitability** although improved quality and efficiency are immediate by – products of Six-Sigma. Companies that implement Six-Sigma do so with the goal of improving their margins. Prior to Six-Sigma, improvements brought about by quality programs usually had no visible impact on a company's net income. Organisation that cannot track the effect of quality improvements on profitability don't know what changes need to be made to improve their profit margins.

Every company that has implemented Six-Sigma has seen profit margin grow 20 percent per year after year for each sigma shift (up to 4.8 to 5 sigma). Some companies suffered from stagnating or shrinking project margin despite improvements they made in quality. These companies could no longer afford to reduce prices to increase market share and market competition would not allow them to raise prices to improve profit margins. When they offered products and services with new features at no extra charges to the consumer, market share might increase but profit margins would shrink.

What Sigma-Six can do for a Company?

While Six-Sigma is a long term, forward thinking initiative designed to fundamentally change the way corporations do business, it is first and fore-most designed to generate immediate improvements to profit margins. It focuses on achieving financial targets in 12 month increments.

A company operating at a 3 sigma level that marshal all its resources around Six-Sigma can expect to make one sigma shift improvement each year.

These companies will experience.

- a 20% margin improvement.
- a 12 to 18% increase in capacity.
- a 12% reduction in the number of employees.
- a 10 to 30% capital reduction.

Companies can expect to make one sigma shift improvement per year up to 4.7 sigma.. This means a 3 sigma company that focuses all its resources on Six-Sigma can expect to move to four sigma during the first year of implementation and then from 4 sigma to 4.7 sigma during the second year of implementation. It can expect to move from 4.7 sigma to 5 sigma in the third year and will progress from 5 to 5.1 sigma in the fourth year. The closer companies come to achieving Six-Sigma, the more demanding the improvements become. At 4.8 sigma companies hit a **"wall"** that requires a redesigning of processes known as **"Design for Six-Sigma"**.

However the profit margin increases between 3 sigma level and 4.8 sigma level are so dramatic. The companies achieving this level can become much more profitable than their competitors and they can selectively pick what plant, product, operation on process they need to improve to attain 5 sigma or higher. The company can achieve significant savings by Six-Sigma application irrespective of their size of revenue (sales turnover). But after the company reaches 4.7 Sigma, the cost savings are not so dramatic. However improved profit margins allow companies to create products and services with added features and functions that result in greater market share. So while Six-Sigma improves the quality of a company's products and services it also improves the firm's competitive position by increasing its profit margins.

How Six-Sigma helps Improving Profitability?

Companies measure what they value. A corporation's value can be understood by finding out what it measures, records, analyses and takes action on. A company which values growth measures growth by tracking and analysing market share data and sharing that information throughout the company.

Almost all organisations claim to be customer focused but there should be a system of measurements in place to gauge customer satisfaction for proving this focus. A company's business 'metrics' can show whether it values profitability over customer satisfaction. Organisations that do not measure what they profess to value, don't know much about what they value. Companies cannot control out-comes of the things they value if they do not measure what they value (say customer satisfaction or profitability). Companies cannot improve what they don't measure.

Six-Sigma Starts with metrics - measuring the things that matter (for example profitability, quality etc.

Six-Sigma at General Electric :

To Jack Welch, CEO of G.E, GE is not about numbers, it is about values. The values include **employee satisfaction, customer satisfaction** and **cash flow.** GE believes that employee satisfaction translates into productivity, that high customer satisfaction means strong market share and cash flow means that employees have maintained the company's customer-focused vision, its passion for excellence and its desire to push forward with energy and enthusiasm. GE backs up its values with performance-based metrics, complete with goals linked to executive incentive pay. G.E's values clearly show its determination to maintain a reality based, customer focused company.

New Definitions of Quality

Quality is most commonly defined as **"conformance to standards"** and companies strived to create products and services that fill within certain specification limits. Such definitions of quality assured that if companies produced quality products and services, their performance standards were correct regardless of how those standards were met, (performance standards would have been met after considerable rework of a specific item or service).

"The Six-Sigma Break through Strategy" broadens the definition of quality to include **economic value** and **practical utility** to both the company and the consumer. **Quality may be defined as a state in which value element is realised for the customer and provider in every aspect of the business relationship.**

This new definition of quality focuses on achieving" **Value entitlement" "Value"** represents economic worth, practical utility and availability for both the consumer and the company that creates the product or service .

The Sigma concept of measuring defects was created in the early 1980s as a way to develop a universal quality metric that applied regardless of product complexity or dissimilarities between different products. Higher sigma values indicate better products and lower sigma values represent less desirable products, regardless of what the product is. Higher the sigma level, the fewer the number of defects per unit of product or service. The lower the sigma level, the greater the number of defects per unit. Products produced at a Six-Sigma level of quality operates visually defect free with only 3.4 defects per million opportunities. As such Six-Sigma has become recognised as the standard for product and service excellence. Four sigma means 6210 defects per million opportunities. Six-Sigma standards are about 1800 times $\left(\text{i.e., } \frac{6210}{3.4}\right)$ demanding than the old standard of 4 sigma level.

Benefit of Six-Sigma Quality

When the opportunities for non-conformance – defects – are brought to Six-Sigma levels– whether in manufacturing, engineering, administration, sales or service , companies can then take valuable resources spent on anticipating, detecting and fixing defects to perform activities that add value for customers and ultimately to the company. Every time a defect is produced in a process, time, labor, equipment, overhead and material have to be used to detect, analyse and fix that defect, The cycle of detection, analysis and correction ties directly back to the three elements of customer satisfaction – delivering the **highest quality product** (defect free products and services), **On time** (reduced cycle time) and at a **right price** (which impacts manufacturing costs) . When the probability of defect becomes so low that a company rarely encounters one, maintaining systems to detect, analye and fix defects are virtually unnecessary. Expenses drop dramatically. This is the ultimate goal of Six-Sigma.

The Origin of Six-Sigma

The quest to achieve Six-Sigma had its birth at Motorola in 1979 to overcome its quality problems. Motorola realised that done right, improving quality would actually reduce costs. They believed that high quality products should cost less not more. The highest quality producer should be the lowest-cost producer. At that time Motorola was spending 5 to 10% of its annual revenues in correcting poor quality.

At Motorola executives began looking for ways to cut waste. In 1985 am engineer at Motorola's communication sector studied the correlation between a product's field life and how often that product had been repaired during the manufacturing process. He concluded that if a product was found defective and corrected during the production process, other defects were bound to be missed and found later by the customer during early use of the product. However when the product was manufactured error-free, it rarely failed during early use by the consumer.

As a result, people at Motorola started debating the question – "Was the effort to achieve quality really dependent on detecting and fixing defects? Or could quality be achieved by preventing defects in the first place through manufacturing controls and product design? It was observed that a connected effort at directing and fixing defects would lead Motorola only to 4 Sigma whereas foreign competitors (Japanese) were making products that required no repair or rework during the manufacturing process. As result, Motorola began its quest to improve quality and simultaneously reduce production time and costs by focusing on **how the product was designed and manufactured.**

It was this link between higher quality and lower cost that led to the development of sigma-an initiative that at first focused on improving quality through the use of exact measurements to anticipate problem areas, not just to react to them. **Six–Sigma allows a business leader to be proactive** rather than **reactive** to quality issues.

The **difference** between previous TQ approaches and the Six-Sigma concept was a **matter of focus.** TQM programs focus on improvements in individual operations with unrelated processes. This is time consuming because a process has a number of operations. The Six Sigma architects at Motorola focused on making improvements in **all operations within a process, producing results** far more rapidly and effectively

Motorola first applied Six-Sigma to the development of its Bondit pager. It could be produced within 72 minutes from the time an order was placed by the customer. Superior design and manufacturing process resulted in an overage life expecting for its pager of 150 years. The pagers were so reliable that product testing was ultimately eliminated and it was cost-effective to replace a pager in the unlikely event that it failed than to spend time and money for taking the product that was virtually defect free.

Motorola started reaping financial reward from the Six-Sigma concept because of reduction in defects and manufacturing ncycle time. Therefore the company could produce higher-quality products and could have happier customers at a cheaper cost within four years, Six-Sigma had saved Motorola $2.2 billion. By 1993, Motorola was operating at nearly Six-Sigma in many of its operations

Six-Sigma applies to products and services and not to the companies who create them. A company with Six-Sigma products can still be in financial disarray. Six-Sigma products and processes are different from Six-Sigma companies. The **"Six-Sigma break-through strategy"** creates specific improvement goals for every process within an organisation, allowing organisations to understand and incorporate technological advances. Six-Sigma forces organisations to re-examine the way on which work gets done, rather than tweaking existing systems. **It simplifies systems and processes, improves capability and ultimately finds a way to control systems and processes permanently.**

Six–Sigma is a Performance Target

It is important to understand that Six-Sigma is a performance target that applies to a single **"Critical-to-Quality" (CTQ)** characteristic, not to the total product. When an automobile is described as "Six-Sigma" product, this does not mean that only 3-4 automobiles out of one million will be defective. Six-Sigma means that within a single automobile, the average opportunity for a defect of a CTQ is only 3-4 defects per million opportunities

What exactly does Six-Sigma 3.4 defects per million opportunities-mean? – What is the difference in practical terms, between, say 3σ and 6σ. For example, if a wall to wall carpet in a 1500 square foot home were cleaned to 3σ level (the average company operates at about, 3.4σ to 4σ level), about four square feet of carpet would still be soiled This means, a three sigma level would lead to a good number of unsatisfied customers

Design limit	Defective parts	% of defective
+1σ	317 per thousand.	31.73%
±2σ	45 per thousand	4.55%
±3σ	27 per thousand (99.73% good Quality)	0.27% (2700ppm)
±4σ	63 per million(6300 per billion)	63 ppm
±5σ	574 per billion	5.74 ppm
±6σ	2 per billion	0.02 ppm

(Six-Sigma with a shift of the process mean by 1.5σ gives 3.4 defects per million. If the mean is exactly in the center, then 2 defects per billion is expected)

± 7σ	0.3 per billion	0.003 ppm
± 8σ	0.001 per billion	0.00001 ppm.

If the same carpet work cleaned to the Six-Sigma level, the soiled area would be size of a pi-head, virtually invisible. The higher the Six-Sigma level, the less likely process will produce defects. Each sigma increase creates an exponential reduction in defects. As Sigma level increases product quality improves, the need for testing and inspection diminishes, costs go down, cycle time decreases and customer satisfaction goes up.

For example air line's record of getting passengers safely from one city to other exceeds 6 sigma, with less than 0.5 failure per million. However air line's baggage operations are in the 6000 to 23000 defects per million range (or 3.5to 4 sigma) which is typical for manufacturing and service operations. When products and service are produced at ***"Sis-Sigma"*** quality, companies can be 99.99966% certain that each opportunity contained with in the product will be created and delivered to the customer's expectation

Effect on Cost of Quality

Companies below 3σ don't survive usually. At 3σ the cost of quality is roughly **25 to 40 percent** of sales revenue. At 6σ level cost of quality declines to less the 1percent of sales revenue.

Sigma Level	Defects per million opportunities	Cost of quality
2	308,537	— NA —
3	66,807	25-40% of sales
4	6210 (Industry average in US	15-25% of sales
5	233	5-15% of sales
6	3.4 (world class)	less then 1% of sales.

Six-Sigma Break-Through Strategy

Six-Sigma and Break-through Strategy are two different elements. Six-Sigma is the philosophy and a goal - 3.4 defects per million opportunities.

The Break through Strategy provides the means to achieve that goal through a highly focused system of problem solving. Although defects decrease as the process improves, Six-Sigma focuses on the process that creates or eliminates the defects rather than the defects themselves.

The "Six-Sigma Break-through Strategy" is a disciplined method of using extremely rigorous data gathering and statistical analysis to pinpoint sources of errors and ways of eliminating them.

The methodology uses specific tools to reduce operating costs, improve capacity, improve margins, shorten the length of time it takes to bring a new product to market, reduce inventory and process transactions in shorter time period with fewer errors. It has a short-term strategy of defect removal and a long-term strategy of refining the system.

13.14 SUCCESS OF SIX-SIGMA

Even though Six-Sigma has been known about for quite some time and many firms have gained substantial benefits through implementation of Six-Sigma approach to quality management, still some people have negative views about Six-Sigma and are waiting for a new trend. Some of the current criticisms for 'Six-Sigma' are:

(i) It hinders innovation processes.

(ii) it is best applied to strictly defined projects only.

(iii) it has no relevance for day-to-day operations.

(iv) it is often used as a stand-only methodology, which does not involve the entire organisation.

(v) it only leads to short-term success because it offers quick gains but limited long-term success.

However an international survey comprising respondents who are knowledgeable and experienced with 'Sig-Sigma' and quality management revealed that the respondents perceived Six-Sigma to be useful in relation to innovation and long-term developments.

Considering the long-term success of Six-Sigma, top management should take into account the fact that the actual process of any improvement approach adopted by an organisation may be predictable over the first year or so, but will then tend to lose its predictability because of the following reasons:

(i) Organisations will soon begin to change in different ways, as internal opposition to change, as external competitors react and the actions of customers, supplies and corporate office will vary.

(ii) Organisations themselves differ in how they handle these reactions.

A related issue is the extent to which Six-Sigma improvement projects are capable of reaching their stated initial goals/ objectives. All organisation – wide change programmes are expensive in terms of time and money and therefore the consultants or internal activities who initiate such projects need to sell their ideas aggressively to the top management. But the unpredictability of operating in a competitive environment means that both internal and competitive reactions are difficult to predict and counter. Therefor it is very difficult to demonstrate the effectiveness of the Six-Sigma programmes to justify their adoption. While some improvement projects are influenced by factors within the control of operators and management, some change goals suffer from lack of any clear relationship between improvement actions and improvements results. For example improving customer satisfaction or increasing profitability by a certain; amount within a certain specified time may be specific measurable goals, but they can be influenced by many factors that are beyond the ability of employees to influence – from competitive reactions to changes in global economy.

13.15 IMPLEMENTING SIX-SIGMA

The Do's

1) Do keep the focus on results
2) Do embrace customers
3) Do plan for success
4) Do communicate the commitment companywide.
5) Do demonstrate the commitment of company leaders.
6) Do empower your key human resources
7) Do provide on – site monitoring for black belts
8) Do choose an implementation partner (an outside expert) who will actively assist in serving and selecting Six-Sigma projects
9) Do be patient at the inception of your Six-Sigma initiative
10) Do claim and advertise early "wins)
11) Do bench – mark
12) Do establish project baselines and goals
13) Do get advance buy in from your controller.

Don'ts

1) Don't make Six-Sigma a massive 'training' exercise
2) Don't take 'Big-Bang' approach to Six-Sigma
3) Don't focus resources on reworking training material
4) Don't let the controller waffle about your saving calculations.
5) Don't skip steps.
6) Don't be afraid to learn and use statistical tools.

The **"do's"** and **"don'ts"** listed above are briefly discussed in following paragraphs:

The 'Do's'

1. Do keep the focus on results: It is important to have a clear vision of where a firms is and where it wants to be in terms of decreasing costs and increasing bottom – line profits. Usually, a qualified implementation partner (a consultant) may be helpful in using a project tracking system to monitor results. The firm needs to focus on a vital few factors rather than the trivial many.

2. Do embrace customers: Achieving phenomenal business growth depends on how well the firm understands and meets those "critical-to-quality" expectation of its customers. The firm must constantly keep in touch with its customers and know what they want in terms of price, quality and delivery.

3. Do plan for success: Proper planning is necessary to ensure that the firm will meet its goals. Planning provides the milestones and progress reports that indicate how well and fast the firm is reaching its goals.

4. Do communicate the commitment company-wide: It is important that the firm communicates with every employee and lets them know what the firm is doing and intending to accomplish. From the CEO to the worker in the production line-every employee should have a sense of ownership of the Six-Sigma projects undertaken and there should be time commitment and enthusiasm at every level.

5. Do demonstrate the commitment of company leaders: The leaders of the firm (top management) should actively show their own commitment to the success of Six-Sigma implementation. The leaders shows their commitment by serving as mentors and champions allocating the needed company resources and breaking down barriers to support Six-Sigma projects

6. Do empower key human resources: Right people must be selected to lead the Six-Sigma project teams. These key persons must be empowered. The black belts and team members should be provided with the essential quality tools for the implementation of Six-Sigma projects throug the phases-Define, Measure, Analyse, Improve and Control (DMAIC)

7. Do provide on-site mentoring for black belts: The top management must assure the black belts total support for their projects. The black belts must have access to information or dat –both from within the firm and form outside, and their interpretation of it must be unrestricted

8. Do choose an implementation partner who will actively assist in screening and selecting Six-Sigma projects: A qualified outside expert (consultant) who is engaged in introducing, training and supporting the firm's Six-Sigma projects is of vital value in helping the management select not only the right project, but also the right people to run it.

9. Do be patient at the inception of your Six-Sigma initiative: The Six-Sigma projects require the front-end commitment of training, time and resources to achieve the end results. The management and employees have to learn how to select the projects, develop appropriate metrics and assign key roles. These require proper planning.

10. Do claim and advertise easy "wins": Even though patience is essential, it is also important to communicate and celebrate each milestone of success in Six-Sigma projects. This is necessary to keep the team's enthusiasm high and to demonstrate how Six-Sigma is working. The top management, employees, customers and vendors – all need to know the value of the efforts put in by Six-Sigma project teams.

11. Do bench mark: A bench mark plan that looks at both internal and external performance standards would be helpful to conduct the right gap analysis to know where the firm is and where it should be

12. Do establish project base lines and goals: The firm should know its current defect levels, its defect – reduction targets and the savings it wants to achieve. This enables the firm to have the right baselines and goals to measure the progress of its Six-Sigma projects.

13. Do get advance buy – in from your controller: The leader of the Six Sigma project and the financial controller of the firm must agree on how the real savings are calculated. If they work together, the results can be verified by the controller which further validates the work of Six-Sigma project.

"The Don't"

1. Don't make Six-Sigma a massive training exercise: As Six-Sigma focuses on real, tangible financial results (exact, quantifiable cost savings, such as reduced hours, reduced inventory levels etc.), It is important that the leader and the members of Six-Sigma project teams learn how to implement the project and get started. They don't need extensive training to develop their Six-Sigma skills. They need to know what they are doing, but once they are trained as black belts, they will know exactly how and what they need to do to achieve their goals.

2. Don't take a "Big-Bang "approach to Six-Sigma: It means, all employees need not be trained at once to be Six-Sigma practitioners. Most organisations can't manage a lot of changes simultaneously or support hordes of black belts or projects.. Therefore, it is vital to have right people to work on right projects, and to train selected people to keep the projects going and capture gains case by case.

3. Don't focus resources on reworking training material: Even though training is an important part of Six-Sigma, it is not advisable to spend excessive time in "tweaking" training materials to fit the firm's exact business model. The training materials should be related to the business focus; recognising the overall and adaptable nature of Six-Sigma.

4. Don't let the controller waffle about your savings calculations" Financial controllers play an important role in the implementation of Six Sigma projects and therefore they must be included right from the beginning of Six-Sigma initiative. They need to know that the company's executive leadership expects them to cooperate and support the efforts of Six-Sigma project teams. The controller and the Six-Sigma project leader must be in agreement on how the project leader defines and assigns savings to the project.

5. Don't skip steps: Skipping necessary steps in Six-Sigma projects to speed up won't yield the needed information to correct and eliminate the problem in question. Data is vital because Six-Sigma needs quantifiable facts and does not deal with assumptions. Statistical measurements and metrics are applied to analyse the issues so that the project team can prove with data and not by opinion, why and how lasting changes can be made.

6. Don't be afraid to learn and use statistical tools: Statistics and statistical tools are essential to Six-Sigma. However, it is not necessary to spend exorbitant amounts of time reviewing statistical data. With the systems and software available, technology and training work together to yield results.

13.16 READYING THE ORGANISATION

Once the firm clearly knows what to do and what not to do, the next step is to prepare the organisation for the Six-Sigma journey.

Since communication is key to success of Six-Sigma projects, the importance of Six-Sigma must be to communicate to all employees and executives involved in such projects. All communications tools available such as Internet, newsletter or other communication channels must be used to communicate information on what, how and when to kick off the Six-Sigma project and also publicise the roles and responsibilities of every person involved in the process. The goals / objectives, outcomes expected and the expected benefits for the company must be clearly stated and communicated to all those concerned with the project.

Another key element to initiate Six-Sigma is to endorse support of senior management through corporate newsletters, e-mails and also company leaders directly addressing employees. Also videos and company meetings may be used to give wide publicity and support to Six-Sigma projects.

The next step is to survey the company's knowledge base. Every organisation differs in terms of the preparedness of its employers to use Six-Sigma tools. Since there are some basic requirements and training aspects for the process management tools used in Six-Sigma, it is necessary to accurately survey and assess the knowledgebase of the company, to identify the gaps or misconceptions and determine how best to provide training in the methodology to ensure correct implementation.

The statistical tools which are essential components for implementing Six-Sigma are *(i)* Check sheets, *(ii)* Histograms, *(iii)* Brainstorming, *(iv)* Process mapping, *(v)* Pareto chart, *(vi)* Run chart and *(vii)* Cause-and-effect (fishbone) diagram.

Assessing readiness for Six-Sigma

For Six Sigma to succeed, it is important to have the required data. The company must have basic measurements in place and also collect reliable data in a structured manner. Accuracy and credibility of information is critical to Six-Sigma. The company should be able to define success for every step in every process so as to determine what constitutes a defect or an error. A check list may be helpful for quickly assessing the company's readiness for Six-Sigma.

13.17 PLANNING FOR SIX-SIGMA

After getting ready for Six-Sigma, the company needs to know how to plan for it. There are certain phases in Six-Sigma planning which serve as the foundation for any implementation and each phase consists of certain steps that build separately to launch the Six-Sigma project.

1. Communication and Education

One of the best ways to build awareness about Six-Sigma is through a company-wide communication from the CEO or president of the company. Once this has been done, Six-Sigma is further introduced in key sessions to managers and executives to reinforce their understanding and support. All senior managers need to undergo ***"Champion training"*** and "managers at all levels need to undergo ***"Executive training"***. ***"Executive training"*** should include an overview of Six-Sigma review of ease studies, related product and service demonstrations, strategies for deployment of Six-Sigma and exploration of tools and methods, statistical analysis, improvement, measurements and management controls.

"Champion training" provides the managerial and technical knowledge necessary to plan and implement Six-Sigma and ***mentor black belts*** This training covers principles, tools and applications of Six-Sigma including deployment tactics and strategies for establishing metrics., selecting black belts and projects and implementing Six-Sigma. The next steps in this planning phase are to order training materials, select black belt candidates and schedule training programmes.

2. Identification of Projects

The planning phase also involves selection of Six-Sigma projects using appropriate process to identify the chromic issues that the Six-Sigma project teams should investigate and improve. If needed, support of outside consultant may be sought to select the projects that have high impact on quality and customer satisfaction and will deliver bottom-line savings. Further to identifying the projects, the departments and people needed for supporting these projects should be identified.

3. Infrastructure

"Job descriptions" for the new roles of the black belts must be developed and these black belts must be posted to the selected Six-Sigma project teams. Human measures department must also benchmark compensation plans that reward black belts and their teams upon successful completion of Six-Sigma projects. Once the black belts are selected, their compensation plans are decided, the training phase will begin based on what the project will entail. The objective of training black belts is to create technical leaders, advanced users and teachers for Six-Sigma. The black belts should learn Six-Sigma philosophy, application tactics (including statistics, benchmarking, process control techniques, diagnostic methods and experimental design) and group dynamics. After undergoing training, the black belts are assigned to the selected projects.

The support of an experienced master black belt (usually provided by an outside consultant) is crucial to the success of black belts. A "master black belt" will guide and coach the "black belt" candidates and work with 'champions" to help overcoming barriers and obstacles.

Periodie review meetings involving top management, other champions, senior leaders, and outside consultant are held to discuss the progress of Six-Sigma initiative and to ensure that the teams are meeting the objectives.

4. Implementation Partner

Each Six-Sigma deployment follows the same success model for implementation. The specifics of a particular situation, the projects selected and the champions and black belts will determine how a plan is created and all activities are scheduled. An outside consultant directs, trains and executes the critical elements of the planning process. The consultant acts as ***implementation partner*** and helps to orchestrate all responsibilities, roles and schedules to make a smooth transition from planning phase to implementation phase. The outside consultant or implementation partner should be focused on knowledge transfer, on sharing how to solve problems through the most effective methods and fix process defects with the right tools.

13.18 ROLES AND RESPONSIBILITIES OF PEOPLE RESPONSIBLE FOR SIX-SIGMA IMPLEMENTATION

The success of Six-Sigma relies on the people who are responsible for implementing it. Six-Sigma provides some powerful techniques and tools, but success depends on the people who play the primary roles and assume the central responsibilities for using those techniques and tools to work for their organisation.

Six-Sigma invariably disturbs the status-quo. It creates a major interruption as job descriptions are redefined and activities are radically changed in order to bring real, permanent changes. Everyone is a player in the implementation of Six-Sigma, regardless of individual organisational positions.

However, not every one is slated for full Six-Sigma **responsibilities**. People should be chosen to run the projects, participate on teams and to pursue the objective using Six-Sigma tools like metrics and other statistical measurements. The right mix of right talents is needed to refocus on Six-Sigma projects.

Key Players: Basically there are five categories of key players. They are:

(i) **Executive Leaders:** who commit to Six-Sigma and promote it throughout the organisation.

(ii) **Champions:** who fight for the cause of black-belts and remove the barriers if any

(iii) **Master Black Belts:** who serve as trainers, mentors, and guides.

(iv) **Black Belts:** who work full time on Six-Sigma projects.

(v) **Green Belts:** who assist black belts on part-time basis.

(vi) **Process Owners:** individual who have the ultimate authority to change a process.

The roles and responsibilities of these Key Players are briefly discussed in the following paragraphs.

1. Executive Leaders: The key role of executive leaders is to decide to do Six-Sigma and to endorse it publicly, throughout the organisation. They kick-off and reinforce the comprehensive scope of Six-Sigma to ensure participation and support of everyone in the organisation. Six-Sigma being a company-wide initiative involving major permanent changes, requires visible leadership to signal its importance to the organisation.

Executive leadership can be built on some essential aspects such as ***determination, confidence, integrity*** and ***patience.*** Executive leaders need to show ***determination*** in their actions. They need to be resolute in believing that Six-Sigma will succeed. They should be determined to get the training, understand the savings, perpetuate the use of metrics and show-case achievements of black belts, mark key milestones and keep the overall initiative on track. For example, Jack Welch, The CEO of General Electric in the US could be considered the ideal executive leaders for Six-Sigma. From the top down and throughout all points in the organisation, executive leaders can inspire and promote a' Six-Sigma culture that continually produce results.

Executive Leaders need to actively display ***confidence***-not only in the Six-Sigma method, but also in the people charged with making it work. The leaders show confidence with rewards and incentives and inspire sustained commitment and effort on the part of employees. This confidence exhibited by executive leaders acts as a powerful motivator. Executive leaders can validate their confidence in champions, black belt or project team by pointing out specific outcomes that emerge from project metrics.

Executive leaders must also need to show integrity in their actions. ***"They need to do what they say they are going to do".*** This inspires ever-increasing confidence among project teams in the words of their executive leaders. Executive leaders demonstrate a high standard of ethical leadership of following through on commitments. Integrity stimulates loyalty and respect which are essential catalysts for employee motivation across the organisation.

Executive leaders must practice patience and be models to others even though this is difficult to practice in a business environment that demands quick results and solutions to problems. As Six-Sigma projects are time consuming exercises, skipping steps or rushing the process can prove disastrous.

By demonstrating their determination, confidence, integrity and patience, company executive can develop good relationship with their employees commanding respect and loyalty.

2. Champions: The success or failure of a Six-Sigma project critically depends on the champions. A champion is an advocate who fights for the cause of black belts and to remove functional, financial or personal barriers so as to enable black belts to do their work efficiently.

Champions know the process very well and can be considered as the **'owners'** of the process in every respect. The champions are drawn from the ranks of managers and executives depending on the size of the organisation. They are responsible for the daily oversight and management of each critical element. They are responsible for reporting to top management about progress of the project and also for supporting their teams. They must ensure that the projects they select align with the executive strategy and can be easily understood and embraced by project teams.

Champions also have the responsibility of selecting black belt candidates, identifying project areas and establishing clear and measurable goals for the selected projects. They are also responsible for keeping the projects on schedule.

Champions must be fully involved in process. They identify and remove obstacles to enable Black belts to focus on their projects and achieve the bottom-line outcomes. The champion plays the role of an advocate and defender, a mentor and a coach; He is ultimately responsible for the success of the Six Sigma project. While the black belts and project teams hunt for defects and waste, the champion selects the project and monitors its performance. Therefore the champions must have thorough knowledge of the strategy and discipline of Six-Sigma and also be able to educate others about its tools and implementation.

3. Master Black Belt: Often, a member of the implementation partner's (consultant's) team may fulfill the role of Master Black Belt in the initial stages. He / She serves as the trainer, mentor and guide for the firm's project team. The master black belt is responsible for selecting the right people and assisting in screening and selecting projects that will best achieve the firm's objectives.

Once the firm has firmly established Six-Sigma activities in place and designated and trained people in their roles, started projects and achieved some desired results, the members of the project teams can be elevated to the rank of master black belts.

The master black belt has expertise in Six-Sigma tools and tactics and is a valuable resource in terms of technical and historical expertise. He plays the role of a teacher, mentor and lead agent of change and ensures that the required infrastructure is in place and black belts are trained. The focus of master black belt is entirely on process improvement.

A key aspect of the role of master black belt is the capacity to skill-fully facilitate problem solving without actually taking over a project. A master black belt is an important asset at the initial stage of a Six-Sigma initiative because of his/ her role in co-coordinating and collaborating with the champion, top management, advising and coaching black belts. He or she enables the champion to keep focused on what is important in selecting projects and implementing Six-Sigma.

4. Black Belts: Black belts have multiple roles and responsibilities. They work full-time on selected projects. Black belts are not masters of the process under study but masters of the change process. They act as full-time change agents. They supervise the green belts working on a Six-Sigma project. Black belts are trained to dig into the chronic and high impact issues and fix them with Six-Sigma techniques and practices.

Other roles and responsibilities of a black belt are:

(i) Preparing a draft project charter for the Six-Sigma projects under his\her supervision.

(ii) Working closely with a project team to keep it functioning and progressing toward speedy and effective conclusion to the Six-Sigma project.

(iii) Communication with the individual responsible for the financial and political well-being of the team (called a champion)

(iv) Serving as the team leader for Six-Sigma projects because of his / her expertise in Six-Sigma theory, tools and method.

(v) Helping team members analyse data and design experiments.

(vi) Providing training to the team members in Six-Sigma theory, tools and methods.

(vii) Helping team members prepare for management reviews.

(viii) Recommending Six-Sigma teams for Six-Sigma projects

(ix) Leading and coaching green belts dealing simpler Six-Sigma projects

In summary, black belts are selected to solve problems within Six-Sigma frame work and are trained to be technical leaders in using Sig-Sigma tools and methods to improve quality.

5. Green Belts: Most green belts serve as team member on Six-Sigma projects. They assist black belts in their functional areas. They apply Six-Sigma tools to examine and solve chronic problems on projects within their regular jobs. They also help black belts in collecting or analysing data, running experiments or conducting other important tasks in a project. However, if a green belt acts as a team leader for simpler projects, then he or she has the following responsibilities;

(i) Preparing a draft charter for the Six-Sigma project

(ii) Selecting team members for Six-Sigma projects

(iii) Communicating with the champion, black belt and process owners concerning the status of the project.

(iv) Facilitating the Six-Sigma project team members and

(v) Providing training to team members in basic Six-Sigma tools and methods.

A green belt spends one-quarter of his / her work time as a team member on one or more Six-Sigma projects.

Green belts are the "work horses" or "work bees' driving bottom-line results.

A green belt must pass a certification examination and participate in at least one successful Six-Sigma project

6. Process Owners: A process owner is the individual who has the ultimate authority to change a process. The process owner should be identified for every project or task that is entered on to an organisation's metric tracking system. The roles and responsibilities of a process owner are:

(i) Monitoring the performance of his / her process through key indicators

(ii) Empowering the people who work in his / her process

(iii) Working with all Six-Sigma project teams in his / her area to enable them to successfully complete their projects.

(iv) Managing the process after completion of the Six-Sigma project to sustain the gains made by the Six-Sigma project team and

(v) Continuing to improve and / or innovate, his / her process through the application PDCA Cycle. A process owner should pass the champion certification examination because he

/ she should have Six-Sigma knowledge to be effective. A process owner must understand the PDSA cycle to accept a project from control phase of the DMAIC model.

Difference Between Black Belt and Green Belt Six-Sigma Projects

Green belt Six-Sigma projects tend to be less involved [e.g. they have one "Critical to Quality (CTQ) characteristic and up – steam variable *(x)*], do not deal with political issues, do not require many organisational resources, do not require significant capital investment to realise the gains identified during the project, and utilise only basic statistical methods.

On the other hand, black belt projects tend to deal with more complex situations that may involve two or more CTQs and many 'x's, may involve substantial political issues or be cross-functional in nature, require substantial organisational resources, may need substantial capital investment to realise the gains made during the project and utilise sophisticated statistical methods.

Selection of Black Belts

Black belts are central to Six-Sigma projects with important responsibilities as technical experts, team leaders and project heads. Being a black belt is a full time discipline that combines leadership ability, technical skills and some statistical knowledge, the ability to communicate clearly and motivated curiosity.

Black belts are the technical leaders and change agents, the key players who implement the Six-Sigma principles, techniques and tools. Successful black belts share the following traits:

(i) Ability to work well on their own and also in groups / teams.

(ii) Remaining calm under external pressure

(iii) Anticipating problems and acting on them immediately

(iv) Respecting their fellow workers and commanding respect by them.

(v) Inspiring others (team members)

(vi) Ability to delegate tasks to other team members and co-ordinate their efforts

(vii) Understanding and recognising the abilities and limitations of their fellow workers

(viii) Showing genuine concern for others, for what they need or want

(ix) Accepting criticisms well

(x) Having concern about the current processes and results and improving the systems

(xi) Having the intelligence and interest to learn how to apply Six-Sigma tools.

13.19 OVER VIEW OF SIX-SIGMA TOOLS

The overall Six-Sigma methodology is implemented by using a specific set of statistical tools throughout each phase of the DMAIC model discussed earlier in this chapter.

Taking the Six-Sigma journey requires a map which is made up of a set of specific analytical tools that direct the course of all the efforts and point to the path to be followed to improve the processes.

Warm-up Tools: These are the first tools to be used in Six-Sigma approach at the beginning of the project to conduct initial investigations into a specific process. The key types of tools are basic statistics, graphical analysis and simple correlation studies. These warming tools help us begin to understand and represent the data obtained from measuring a process.

Basic statistics involve the understanding and use of measures such as **'mean'**, **'mode'** and **'median'**. Graphical analysis uses a key warm up tool – **the histogram** to represent data graphically. Histogram shows the distribution of elements in the process.

When we calculate the mean, the mode, and the median we are measuring the **central tendency** of the data. To measure the **dispersion** of data, we need to calculate **"range" "variance"** and **"standard deviation".**

The 'standard deviation' is the most commonly used measure of spread or dispersion. Another means of discovering patterns in a graphic form is the "**run chart**" – Run Charts are used to analyses processes according to time or order and reveal patterns that occur over time.

Simple correlation study is also classified under warm-up tools. **Correlation** as a statistical concept is the degree to which variables are related. For factors to correlate there must be a cause and effect relationship, not just a coincidence. The input must affect the output. Correlation also describes direction as well as linkage. However it must be remembered that correlation does not necessarily mean **causation.** A correlation study is used to quantify the relationship if any between two sets of data points. An example of graph used in correlation study is a '**scatter plot**' or scatter diagram which provides a good visual display between two sets of data points.

The warm up tools are used to find out fundamental information about a process, including the average and spread of data and then understanding cause and effect relationships. These steps serve as the building blocks for all the rest of the Six-Sigma actions. The key tools used to track down defects and quantify them are discussed in the following paragraphs.

Key Tool No 1: Process Mapping: This tool is used during the ***"Measure" phase*** of DMAIC. Process mapping is an integrally important tool that helps us to understand every aspect of every input and output. It helps to document the process in order to maintain control and reduce variation due to changes over time, process mapping is done through a **flow chart** which shows operations, decision point, delays, movements, rework loops and controls or inspections. By breaking down the process into steps, the flowchart simplifies analysis of the process.

Key tool No 2: The XY Matrix: It is also called as the ***"House of Quality"*** which is another tool used in the ***"Measure" phase.*** XY matrix is used to link the customer's "critical to-quality" (CTQ) requirements to the process inputs, to ensure that we have the **right set of priorities** in the process improvement activities.

Two techniques used in XY matrix are: *(i)* Brain-storming and *(ii)* Cause-and-effect diagram.

Brainstorming is a method for generating ideas. Participants in the brainstorming session focus on a problem or an opportunity and come up with as many ideas as possible and push the ideas as far as possible. Participants can build on each other's ideas. Then after brainstorming, the team can analyse the results and explore the best ideas. Brainstorming is a valuable tool for probing during the "Analyse" phase and for generating ideas during ***"Improve" phase.***

Cause-and - Effect Diagram is a graphical tool which can be used to identify the relationship between a problem and possible causes of the problem.

The purpose of using the XY matrix is to study and understand the relationship between what we are putting into a process and what our customer is getting out of it. The XY matrix allows the team to identify gaps and areas for improvement.

Key Tool No 3: Measurement Systems Analysis (MSA): This tool helps to ensure that the measurement system is statistically confident – that it is both accurate and precise whenever it is used. Undertaken during the ***"Measure" phase,*** this tool determines whether or not we can make a certain measurement and repeat or reproduce it among different people who take the same measurement.

Within the MSA tool there is another specific tool – the gauge repeatability and reproducibility study, which compares our measurement devices against others.

Key Tool No 4: Process Capability Tool: Process capability is the measure of process being able to meet required specification and fulfill CTQ needs on a long-term basis. Process capability analysis uses a series of steps to establish short and long term deviation patterns and baseline performance for each process. The tools determine whether or not the process is performing within the specifications, show how to decrease variation and help to chart the direction necessary to reach optimum capability.

Pareto Chart: gives graphical representation of the relative **importance of process causes or** defects based on **Pareto Principle 80-20 rule**. Pareto Chart is used to identify factors in a process that the greatest cumulative effect so that we can focus on a few important factors (vital few) rather than the trivial many (80 percent of problems result for 20 percent of causes)

Key Tool No 5: Multivariate Study: This is an analysis which offers a way to reduce possible causes of variation in a process to a family of related causes, by graphing the interrelationship of multiple variables. The multivariate studies look at sources of variation within a piece or batch, variation from piece to piece and variation related to time (temporal) to discuss which one contributes the most to that variation. Multivariate studies compare how the same functions, performed by different people or in different shifts, perform over time. This tool is used in the beginning of the ***"Analyse" phase.***

Key Tool No 6: Hypothesis Testing: This tool is used in the ***"Analyse" phase.*** This involves procedures for making rational decisions about possible causes of a given effect. Hypothesis testing involves a logical sequence of steps defining the problem, statistically testing whither or not the probability of defect caused by random chance or has a more tangible cause hidden in the process. One of the ways to test hypotheses is through **simulations.**

Key Tool No 7: Failure Mode Effect Analysis (FMEA): Failure mode effect analysis takes place during the ***"Analyse" phase.*** It is the manner in which a part or process can fail to meet a specification, creating a defect or non-conformance, and the impact on the customer if that failure mode is not prevented or corrected. It is a method for designing in reliability while minimising causes of failure. Preventing failure modes prevents defects. FMEA charts the type of effect, severity of defect, probability of occurrence and whether or not systems are in place to properly detect it.

Key tool No 8: Design of Experiments (DOE): This tool is used in the ***"Improve" phase***. It helps to identify and quantity the effect of the X's on the 'Y's. It helps to determine which inputs are significant in affecting the output of a process. It also helps to quantify the values of the input variables to meet the output requirements.

DOE is a way of determining and measuring the importance of two or more factors on the outcome of a process, by experimenting with many factors and variables simultaneously.

Key tool No 9: Control Plan: This tool is used in the ***'control' phase*** which is the concluding phase of DMAIC. It improves quality by doing a thorough evaluation of process characteristics and variation sources. It helps to increase customer satisfaction by focusing resources on process and product characteristics that are important to customers. **Control Chart** are used to indicate the range of variability that is built into a process known as common cause variation). It helps to determine whether or not a process is operating consistently or if a special cause has occurred to change the process mean or variance. Control Chart is a fundamental tool of statistical process control.

13.20 SELECTING SIX-SIGMA PROJECTS

Deciding how to select projects that will be most successful and that will return the maximum result is a big question. There are certain criteria that must come into play when choosing a Six-Sigma project.

Project Criteria: Two important criteria for a successful project are: *(i)* **effort required** and *(ii)* **the probability of success.**

A good understanding of the duration of the project in relation to the return on investment is necessary. It is also important to consider the probability of success for a project. The time, effort and implementation factors must be examined to figure out whether the project is desirable. The scope of the project should be manageable but not so narrow that solution is already visible. Keeping the project focused keeps the objectives clear and makes best use of Six-Sigma resources. Priority must be given to projects that address one or more factors that are critical to the customer's expectations of quality, cost and delivery. Addressing all these three elements helps maximise the leverage of the project in delivering the CTQ standard demanded by the customers.

Defeating the defects means defeating the cost of poor quality (COPQ) – Basically COPQ is the criterion by which the potential projects are judged. Projects must have defined cost savings attached to them.

Project selection should reflect the major issues confronting the business. Projects are designed to attack and reduce or even eliminate costs in the areas viz sales, marketing, manufacturing or other areas.

First the suspected sources of issues affecting the critical – to – quality (CTQ) metrics must be identified and prioritised. Then, the 'owners' of the suspected sources are identified, who then become the project champions for those issues. Next, the Six-Sigma methods of improvement to be deployed on a particular project are identified. Then two questions are answered: *(i)* Has the project been undertaken before? and *(ii)* If not, then will its business benefit outweigh the cost and effort required?. Next, a timeline boundary for the project is set-usually not more than 6 months.

Project Problem Statement: Creating a good project statement is one of the hardest things to do in Six-Sigma. The problem statement must be quantifiable and specific. Two purposes of having a problem statement are:

(i) To focus the team on the process deficiency or the actual defect

(ii) To communicate the project's purpose to "significant others" (company's leaders, executive teams)

Project Objective Statement: Further to stating what the problem is , we need to indicate how it is going to be solved. This is done by following up the problem statement with a strong objective statement which does the following:

(i) It quantifies the expected performance

(ii) It indicates the improvement target for the performance

(iii) It identifies the expected time frame for both expected performance and the improvement target for that performance.

The project objective statement must include the following: *(i)* Where we are, *(ii)* What we need to do to change the process, *(iii)* How long it will take and *(iv)* How much money we will save.

Characteristics of Successful Projects

Selecting the right project ultimately comes down to understanding how it will fulfill our customers' expectations of quality, cost and delivery and will also drive savings to our bottom line .Key project characteristics are:

(i) Project will increase sales, either by unit volume or net price

(ii) Project will reduce accounts receivable and net inventory or increase accounts payable

(iii) Project will reduce actual spending

(iv) Project will avoid costs not currently incurred

(v) Project will reduce cycle time on critical path steps in a bottle- neck operation

(vi) Project will improve quality and service levels, as measured by the customer

(vii) Project will help achieve the objectives.

13.21 SUSTAINING SIX-SIGMA

Successful implementation of Six-Sigma helps companies to improve performance to meet or exceed the customer 's', expectations for quality, delivery and cost. However, investments in Six-Sigma are not made to train people, to select projects and to drive down the costs of poor quality for one time only. Six-Sigma is an ongoing project. It is a constant, 'living" methodology that needs to continue as long as the company's business does.

Naturally, individual Six-Sigma projects that fix specific problems have start and finish times but as existing projects are completed, we need to initiate new projects, improve quality levels and maintain the momentum of our initiative. We need to sustain the gain in order to achieve the best return on our investment and keep our customers competitive and contented. .

Sustaining Six-Sigma is not easy. But it is essential. No matter how difficult it may be, we must strive to keep Sig-Sigma alive.

There are a few key indicators and guidelines that we must put in place to keep the energy level high and keep Six-Sigma moving in the right direction.

Basic Infrastructure Requirements

The basic infrastructure requirements for successful Six-Sigma can be broken down over a period of two years. In the first year the foundation is laid for achieving success and in the second year, follow up on the successful start is done and the infrastructure is built on the foundation.

In the first year, the following needs to be done:

(i) Setting up a database for the lessons learnt.

(ii) Developing the on-going project list which registers both projected and actual savings.

(iii) Establishing the on-going communication plan, both externally and internally.

(iv) Growing the number of black belt and green personnel.

(v) Creating compensation plans and progression plan for a period of two years.

(vi) Developing a common metric and reporting/ reviewing system to evaluate and update the status of all projects monthly.

In the second year, the following needs to be done:

(i) Engaging key suppliers in the Six-Sigma methodology.

(ii) Building Six-Sigma goals into company -wide strategic plans

(iii) Hosting quarterly review meeting with top management.

(iv) Hosting certification events which reward and recognise achievements of black belts.

(v) Developing compensation/incentive plans which include black belt, team members and top management to ensure continued support.

(vi) Getting each black belt to work on four to six projects a year.

(vii) Creating a "pull" system for the Fix-sigma initiative.

(viii) Determining the next year's goals in the number of black belts, green belts, master black belts, project selection and savings projections.

Since major elements listed above will be discussed in the following paragraphs:

***(i)* Lessons Learnt:** The first thing to be **done is to** build and maintain a data base of **"lessons learnt"** that means documenting what has been learnt and achieved with projects to date and then relying on and sharing that information. Eliminating defects and keeping it to ourselves is of no value unless the knowledge transfer happens continually, both inside and outside of the on-going project.

***(ii)* Communication Plan:** A communication plan is necessary for sharing lessons learnt and for sustaining the success of Six-Sigma. The communication media used include press releases, monthly newsletters, company instant updates, video presentations or quarterly company meetings. The message should reach people both inside and outside the organisation on a regular basis. The progress of Six- Sigma projects, actual rupee savings to date, key tools used etc., must be communicated to all concerned. All levels of personnel should be familiar with the basics of Six-Sigma mission, including terminology, roles and metrics.

***(iii)* Training for Six-Sigma:** To start with, the focus should be on training black belts since they are the tactical leaders for each and every Six-Sigma project. In the first year, the number of Green Belts will be three times that of black belts. In the second year, green belts generally increase to about 10% of the company's population.

As black belts and green belts become more proficient, they reach out to train others. At least 70% of black belts must be certified in the first year of Six-Sigma initiative. Black belts also undergo a tool assessment to investigate whether they are using the tools correctly or not.

Further, it is important that the black belts are retained in the organisation. At least 75% of black belts must be focused and working on Six-Sigma projects. The drop-out rate among black belts must be maintained within 5 percent.

***(iv)* Black belt certification event:** As the black belts meet or exceed their individual objectives, their success must be celebrated, along with the company's overall results.

Certification events signal that black belts and their events are highly valued.

***(v)* Company Culture:** Linking all recognition of Six-Sigma contributors to the structure of the compensation plans provides a powerful motivator at the employee level to sustain the gain .All master black belts, black belts and green belts must be rewarded for their efforts. The "brain drain" or attritions level can be minimised by clearly communicating and committing to a specially structured, incentive based compensation plan for those involved in Six-Sigma at any level.

***(vi)* Signs of success:** There are certain characteristics to each year's efforts that indicate how well the Six-Sigma methodology is sustained. What is required in the first year includes.

(i) Training the best of the best for black belt projects.

(ii) Drop-out rate under 5 percent.

(iii) Break-even within 8 months after initial training.

(iv) Starting the back-log projects and actively managing the reviews.

(v) Establishing process metrics and setting baseline data into strategic plans for the second year.

(vi) Setting up the data base which captures savings and lessons learnt

(vii) Discovering two or four master black belts upon the completion of training

(viii) Getting green belt training underway

As Six-Sigma progresses into its second year, the signs of success will be:

(i) Internal master black belts training black belts

(ii) Monetary savings increase by 300 percent over the first year's targets

(iii) Green belts represent 10 percent of the company population

(iv) All training has transitioned from an outside consultant to the company's own resources

(v) Communication is on-going, both internally and externally

(vi) The project backlog represents not more than 3 to 5 percent of company revenue.

(vii) **Company Cycles:** Companies implementing Six-Sigma should make their suppliers to be part of their initiative. The suppliers must be trained to speed up with Six-Sigma so that they can fix and eliminate defects in their firms. The suppliers should conform to the Six-Sigma standards of the buying organisation.

Partnership with suppliers in Six-Sigma initiatives is an excellent source of improvement and savings, by equally sharing in the techniques, tools and rupee savings, for both parties.

(viii) **Reinforcement and Control:** The executive management must regularly review and oversee the entire Six-Sigma initiative. This is necessary in order to reinforce the depth of the Six-Sigma commitment and to keep senior leaders involved and engaged in the process. Senior executives should know and understand the progress of all current projects, the financial results achieved and the projects ahead at least on a quarterly basis.

Six-Sigma plan must be built into the business plan and should be considered as integral part of any strategic planning. Six-Sigma must become part of the "generic code" of the business by inspiring and promoting a Six-Sigma culture throughout the organisation. The financial impact on the bottom line provides a proof that Six-Sigma works. Sustaining Six-Sigma takes commitment and leadership.

13.22 DESIGN FOR SIX-SIGMA

"Design for Six-Sigma" is an approach to designing or redesigning products and/or services to meet or exceed customer requirements and expectations.

In the field of product/service design and development, it has been observed that only about 60 percent of new products launched are actually a success and for every seven new product ideas, only four make it to development stage-and out of these four products developed and launched to market only one succeeds. The interpretation of this phenomenon is that the new product cycle is definitely not operating at a Six-Sigma level. In fact it is clear to the average four sigma quality level at which many firms operate now a days. Even though manufacturing problems are fixed and solved by deploying Six-Sigma methods, newly developed products often are the sources of new problems. Therefore, an organisation practicing Six-Sigma methodology in various functional areas and attaining Six-Sigma status may well be far below that level in developing new products or services.

Therefore, it is important for firms to carryout improvement in the development and design of new products / services deploying Six-Sigma methods.

Design for Six-Sigma (DFSS) is based on the notion that when Six-Sigma quality is designed right at the outset of new product development, it is probable that customers accept that product. By incorporating DFSS, there is assurance that the product or service launched will perform dependably in the market place.

Design for Six-Sigma (DFSS) uses a disciplined set of tools to bring high quality to product or service launches. To start with, a ***gap analysis*** is conducted for the entire product development system. A gap analysis finds the gaps in the processes which are negatively affecting new product performance. It also addresses the ***"Voice of the customer"*** **(VOC)** which is a highly significant factor in new product design and development. Every new product decision must be driven by the voice of the customer (VOC). This means, the voice of the customer must respond to it at the design stage itself. This approach will enable the firm to deliver a new product or service that customers actually want.

Once the gap analysis is done and the voice of the customer is identified, DFSS is implemented with its own version of the DMAIC (define, measure, analyse, improve and control) of Six-Sigma. This is known as PIDOV. This has the following steps.

(i) **Plan:** Enable the team to succeed with the project by making all important steps

(ii) **Identify:** Listen to the voice of the customers to select the best product / service concept

(iii) **Design:** Build a thorough knowledge base about the product and its processes.

(iv) **Optimise**: Achieve a balance of quality, cost and time to market.

(v) **Validate:** Demonstrate with data that the voice of the customer has been heard and that customer expectations have been satisfied.

The success of DFSS using PIDOV approach requires the active participation of management. The top management must monitor its progress to keep it on track.

Ultimately DFSS is not much different from the Six-Sigma work the firm has already undertaken. Infact it is a natural progression to continually and relentlessly root out defects and route hidden rupees to the bottom line.

Because of the similarities between Six-Sigma and DFSS, people recognise DFSS as the logical extension of Six-Sigma at the manufacturing and service level, (DMAIC).

However, there are some basic differences between the six sigma DMAIC and DFSS they are:

(i) DMAIC is more focused on reacting, on detecting and resolving problems, a means for preventing problems.

(ii) DMAIC is for products or services that are currently offered by the organisation, DFSS is for the design of new products or services or processes.

(iii) DMAIC is based on manufacturing or transactional processes and DFSS is focused on marketing, research and development and design.

(iv) Monetary benefits obtained from DMAIC can be quantified rather quickly, while the benefits from DFSS are more difficult to quantify and tend to be much more long-term.

(v) DFSS involves greater cultural change than DMAIC because for many organisations DFSS represents a huge change in roles. The DFSS team is cross- functional, it is key for the entire team to be involved in all aspects of the design process, from market research to new product launch.

Design for Six-Sigma (DFSS) Defined and Explained

DFSS is a business process which is focused on improving profitability, if properly applied, it generates ***the right product or service at the right time at the right cost.***

DFSS enhances the firm's new product development process and does not replace it. The new product development process provides the road map to success. DFSS provides tools and teamwork to get the products design and development job done efficiently and effectively. Rigorous application of the tools of DFSS assures predictable product quality

DFSS has its roots in ***systems engineering***. In the systems engineering approach, management of requirement (such as those aspects of the end product that must meet customer expectations) guides and drives the entire process.

Requirements at the top management level or 'point-of-use' level can evolve through use of a variety of techniques under the heading of ***"requirements flow down"***

"Requirements flow down" is the process by which all high-level requirements are allocated to the various elements of a system, to ensure that some part of the process is meeting every requirement and non-requirement is overlooked.

DFSS provides a systematic integration of tools, methods, processes and team members throughout product and process design. Though DFSS initiatives vary from company to company, a typical initiative starts with a charter linked to the company's strategic plan, an assessment of customer's needs, a functional analysis, and an identification of critical-to-quality (CTQ) characteristics, concept selection, a detailed design of products and processes and control plans.

To start with, the customer wants and needs are discovered using tools such as ***"Concept Engineering"*** and ***"Quality Function Development" (QFD).*** Understanding the needs of the customer for a particular market segment is critical to success. Focus groups and interviews can provide valuable information about the customer. It is important for the design team to understand the latent underlying need of the customer and then allow the technical arm of the design team to determine the best technical solution.

Myths and Misconceptions about DFSS

(i) Myth: DFSS is a replacement for the current new product development process.

Truth: DFSS could be used to guide the development process but it typically provides the tools, teamwork and data to supplement the new product development process which already exists in organisations

(ii) **Myth:** DFSS is just Six-Sigma in design.

Truth: DFSS is a complex methodology of systems engineering analysis that uses statistical methods.

(iii) **Myth:** DFSS is just "Design for Manufacturability and Assembly (DFMA) and/or Design of Experiment (DOE) and Robust Design concept in engineering.

Truth: Actually DFSS is a comprehensive process that involves DFMA issues and applies DOE and Robust Design among many methods

(iv) **Myth:** DFSS demands extensive statistical analysis and modeling of all requirements.

Truth: DFSS calls for dealing with each engineering requirement optimally, consequently some requirements are analysed statistically but some requirements are handled with traditional engineering methods.

(v) **Myth:** DFSS allows too much design margin, so that costs are higher, and/or increases development cycle times, so that market opportunities are missed.

Truth: DFSS balances cost, cycle times and schedule and quality.

(vi) **Myth:** DFSS is simply a collection of tools.

Truth: Although DFSS uses some powerful tools, those tools alone will not ensure success, not unless those using them know how to apply them to specific engineering design opportunities .

(vii) **Myth:** DFSS involves just the core product design team and has no impact on marketing research and manufacturing.

Truth: The most effective product development teams are cross-functional, with strong project management leadership and management support. Marketing, research, design and advanced manufacturing are typical representatives in a DFSS wave. The team works together to determine the scope of customer requirements, select design concepts, detail the product and process design, select suppliers and ensure that suppliers capability meet or exceeds customer driven engineering needs.

(viii)**Myth:** DFSS may apply to many engineering disciplines but not to all

Truth: Since DFSS is not specific to any discipline, it applies to all. The analysis will differ according to the discipline, but most of the DFSS principles will apply.

(ix) **Myth:** All management needs to do is "Sign the cheque" and DFSS will happen overnight.

Truth: It is not that easy. Management must play an important role in leading the change effort.

(x) **Myth:** DFSS tools can be learnt through class-room training.

Truth: Training in tools with no implementation plan does not result in cultural change. Class-room training that is not integral to implementation does not work. Just-in-time training is a useful approach. Team members learn about a tool as they need it, initial facilitation support is provided as they learn how to apply the tool and simultaneously work on the new product.

13.23 WHY DO DESIGN FOR SIGMA?

It is estimated that only about 60 percent of new products launched in all industries succeed in the market and about 45 percent of resources allocated to develop and commercialise new products that fail to provide adequate financial return:

The reasons for failure of new products are:

(i) Inadequate market analysis (24%)

(ii) Product problems or defects (16%)

(iii) Lack of effective marketing effort (14%)
(iv) Higher costs than anticipated (10%)
(v) Competitive strength or reaction (9%)
(vi) Poor timings of introduction (8%)
(vii) Technical or production problems (6%)

DFSS could help companies to overcome many of the problems that cause new products to fail.

DFSS is a rigorous approach to designing products, services and processes to ensure that the products and services meet customer expectations. It also enables the organisation to reduce time, improve quality and improve profitability.

Advantages of DFSS

(i) Provide a structure for managing development projects
(ii) Add value and improve customer satisfaction
(iii) Anticipate problems and avoid them
(iv) Minimise design changes
(v) Reduce product development cycle times
(vi) Reduce life cycle cost
(vii) Reduce manufacturing cycle times and time to market
(viii) Improve product quality, reliability and durability.
(ix) Improve communication among functions, particularly sales and marketing, product development and manufacturing
(x) Reduce costs of after-sale service and support.

This advantage can be summed up in the following four terms: ***Customer satisfaction, quality, time*** and ***money.***

DFSS and the Customer: Conventional product design processes tend to rely on assumptions about product features and services that are expected to sell. But DFSS addresses the question – "What will customers buy" DFSS considers the ***"voice of the customer"*** which is an essential element of Six-Sigma concept.

DFSS identifies key customer; needs before starting a design project and then prioritises and translates these requirements into the design. These customer requirements (known as ***critical-to-customer*** or ***critical-to-satisfaction*** characteristics or ***critical-to-quality*** characteristics) are combined with cost factors (***critical-to-cost*** characteristics) and time factors (***critical - to schedule*** characteristics) and other quality factors in making design decisions. The team can then establish specific step targets for each component and for the process.

DFSS and Quality: By focusing on determining customer requirements, expectations and priorities from the beginning, DFSS improves the quality of new products and services. It also prioritises other quality factors in design decisions,. The project team follows the following basic steps:

(i) Defining requirements of customers, company and regulatory agencies
(ii) Working to find creative ways to meet those requirements
(iii) Anticipating things that could go wrong
(iv) Optimising the function of the design in terms of costs and benefits.
(v) Verifying that the product or service meets the requirements.

DFSS and Time: In business it is a well-known and proved fact that "Time is money" or "Speed is life". Companies are undergoing more and more pressure to develop and provide products and services with greater value at lower cost in less time. DFSS allows an organisation to reduce time to market – once the organisation acquires some experience in applying the principles and tools of DFSS. In today's competitive business world, time-based competition has assured great significance and an organisation that decreases its cycle time captures a higher market share and develops a competitive advantage.

DFSS and the Bottom Line

Design for Six-Sigma provides the following benefits to organisations:

1. Long-term cost reductions in the areas of *(a)* development and verification *(b)* manufacturing and/or transactional processes and *(c)* service and support after the sale.

DFSS has one primary goal of reducing life cycle costs. By establishing priorities and requirements for design and development activities, iterations and verifications are fewer, easier and therefore less costly.

DFSS to start with, focuses on achieving the optimal design for a product or service and the project team then will work on the processes that deliver the product or service to optimise their design as well.

By focusing on improving the design of products, services and processes, DFSS help to reduce the time and material costs of poor quality- scrap, rework, repair, inspection, delays, customer complaints, returns, recalls, lost sales and accounts etc. DFSS leads to better design of products, services and processes with a focus on customer CTQs, which in turn will result in lesser problems with customer service and support. The better the design, in terms of customer requirements, expectations and priorities and in terms of quality, the easier it is to provide service and support such as maintenance, repairs, troubleshooting etc.

2. The intangible benefits of DSS include the new ways of thinking and a culture of accountability that manifest when a company earnestly pursues Six-Sigma.

Employees and managers learn to think in terms of customers, statistics and cause-and-effect which will develop a culture of accountability, to customers, shareholders and also to employees. These new ways of thinking and the culture of accountability provides some intangible benefits which will add to the competitive advantage of the organisation.

DFSS Procedure

DFSS is a rigorous approach to designing products, services and/or processes to reduce delivery time, development cost, increase effectiveness and better satisfy the customers. DFSS is not an established methodology and any design activity that leads to product or services or processes performing at a Six-Sigma level should be considered as part of DFSS.

The basis of DFSS is IDOV (Identify, Design, Optimise and Verify). In terms of basic procedure, the steps include:

- Step *(i)* Capturing the customer requirements
- Step *(ii)* Analysing and prioritising the requirements
- Step *(iii)* Developing a design
- Step *(iv)* Flow of the requirements down from the system level to subsystems, components and processes
- Step *(v)* Tracking the capability of the product or service and process at each step and highlighting gaps between requirements and capabilities and making them actionable.
- Step *(vi)* Establishing a control plan.

Difference between Generic Design Process and DFSS Design Process:

Exhibit 13.5 describes the Generic Design Process and *Exhibit 13.6* describes the DSFSS design process. DFSS does not greatly differ from the generic engineering process. However, the value of DFSS lies in the details of the approach, the attitude (focus on Six-Sigma) and the tools (statistical and non-statistical)

Exhibit 13.5 : Generic Design Process

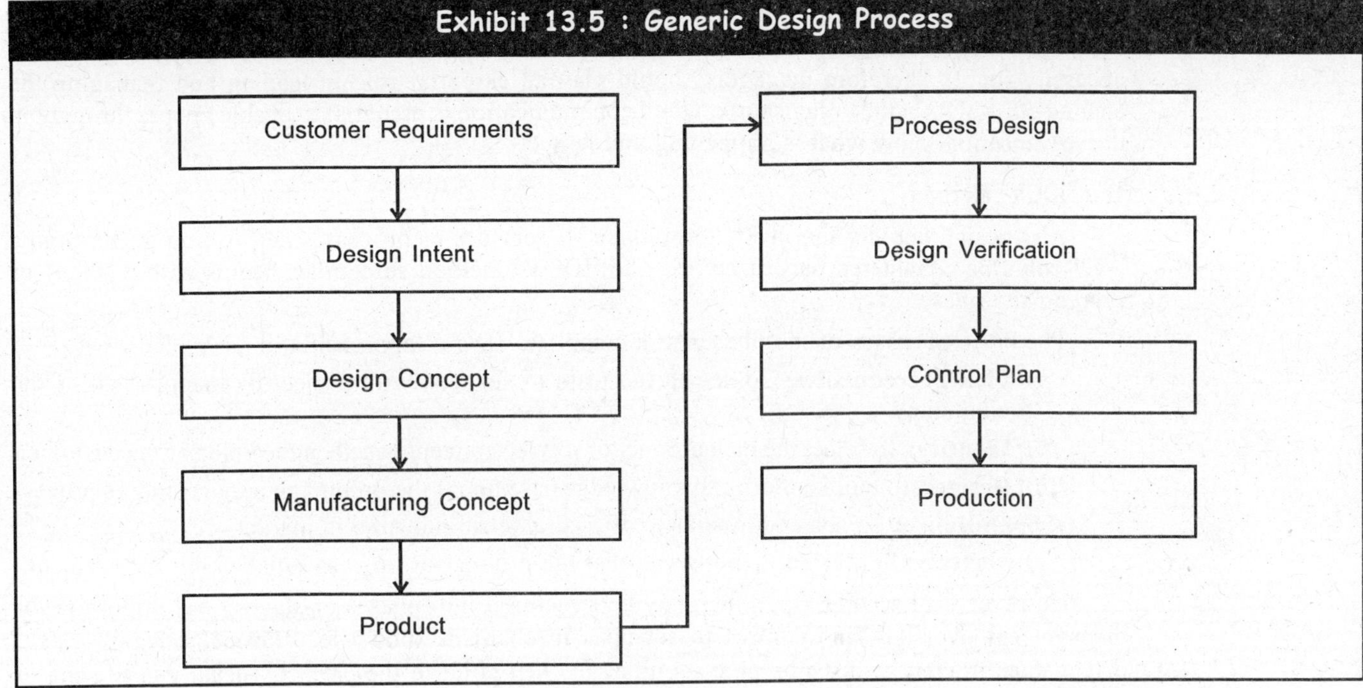

The DFSS method shown in the *Exhibit 13.6* is a **CTQ flow down**. The DFSS approach varies according to whether the design is of a product or of a process. It may also vary according to the type of product. For example ***for developing technology DFSS uses the steps: Invent and Innovate, Develop, optimise and verify (I DOV)*** and ***for designing products the steps: Concept Development, Design Development, Optimisation and Verification (CDOV)*** DFSS focuses on the design of products, services and processes, but implementing.

Exhibit 13.6 : DFSS Design Process

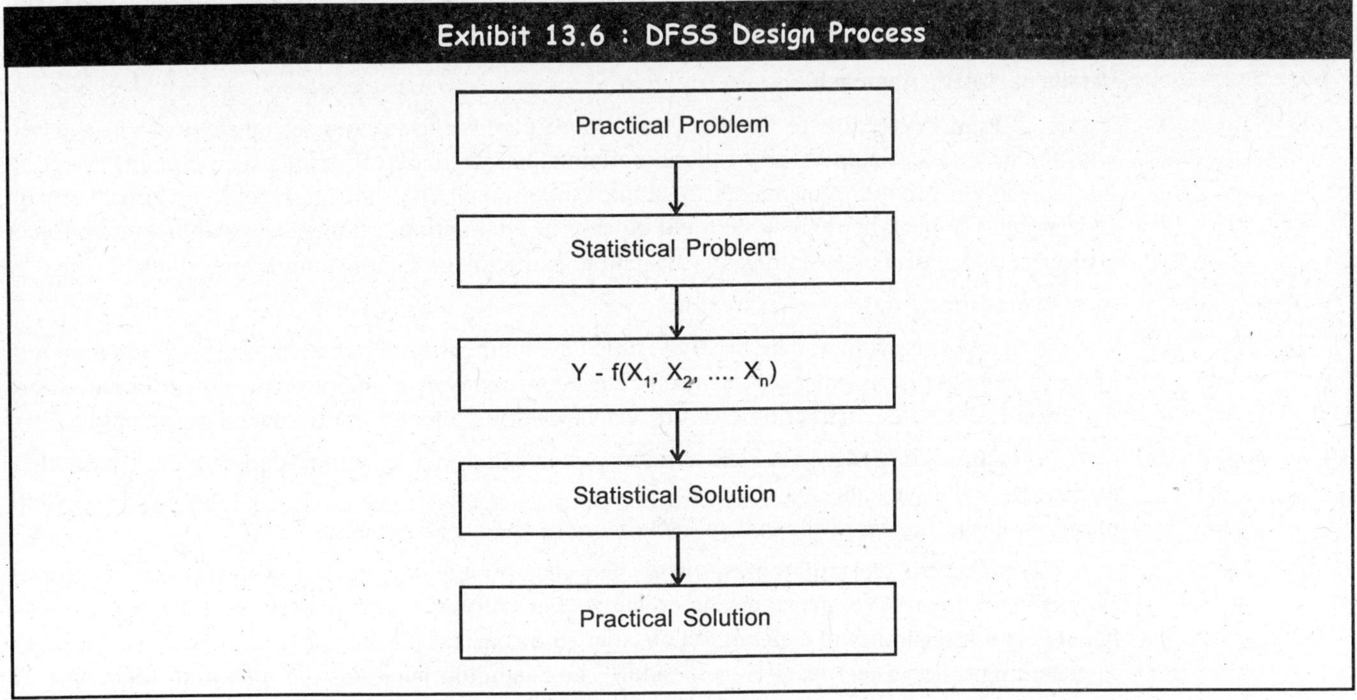

DFSS successfully involves major cultural changes across the organisation. DFSS has direct impact on people working in research and development, product design, advanced manufacturing engineering, manufacturing, marketing, distribution and sales. All people working in these areas need to make fundamental changes in their day-to-day roles in new product development.

Generally people have resistance to change. They oppose changes unless they recognise the necessity for it. Therefore managers should play an essential role in leading and managing the change effort within the organisation. Good communication is essential to enable people throughout the organisation know what is happening and why.

The "IDOV" Method

Any design activity that leads to products or services or processes performing at Six-Sigma level could be considered part of DFSS. The 'IDOV' method sometimes begins with a 'Plan" or Prerequisite phase.

The basic purposes of the phases in a complete 'IDOV' approach are:

(i) **Plan/Prerequisites:** To set up the team to succeed with project by mapping all of the vital steps.

(ii) **Identity:** To select the best product or service concept based on the voice of the customer.

(iii) **Design:** To build a thorough knowledge base about the product or service and its process

(iv) **Optimise:** To achieve a balance of quality, cost and time to market

(v) **Verify/Validate:** To demonstrate that the product or process satisfies the requirement.

However well a DFSS approach may be structured into phases or stages, it is important for management oversight and control to set up a mechanism known as ***"Project review"*** It is a management review or decision gate set up at any key point in the project – usually at the end of a stage or a phase – to allow a management team to review progress, assess the project and determine whether or not it should continue.

The ***'Project review'*** is also known as a ***"stage-gate review", a phase-gate review, "a phase review", a "Project toll –gate review"*** or a ***"Project milestone review".***

Through this mechanism, a management team reviews and assesses the project at the end of each phase according to plan set-forth in the project charter and well-defined criteria. The managers review timelines and check key progress deliverables to decide whether or not the project is successful and worth further expenditures of resources.

Details of "IDOV" Approach

1. P-Plan/Pre-requisite Phase: The purpose of this phase is to set up the team to succeed with the project by mapping all of the important steps. It involves various steps viz. (a) selecting the project, *(b)* providing managers to support the project, *(c)* choosing people to form the team consisting of a black belt, green belt and others, *(d)* conducting training, *(e)* establishing a project charter and objectives, *(f)* setting metrics and a goal and *(g)* establishing a time frame.

Procedure:

***(i)* Select the project:** The highly visible development project may be selected based on any of the following: *(a)* customer comments, *(b)* customer surveys, *(c)* input from within the organisation, e.g. from R&D, sales, marketing etc., *(d)* bench marking and *(e)* multi-generation planning.

***(ii)* Initiate the project:** A well-defined implementation plan with responsibilities, time tables, milestones and deliverables is necessary for every Six-Sigma project for a rigorous examination of progress on the project at the end of each phase of the DFSS process.

***(iii)* Select the champion or sponsor:** The champion who is critical to any Six-Sigma project should be an upper-level manager. He or she is responsible for new product development and can handle the responsibility of a champion on a part-time basis. The champion must have the authority to ensure that the project team is successful. The champion performs the following functions:

(a) Establishing project goals

(b) Choosing black belts and green belts

(c) Providing a direction to the team

(d) Allocating resources

(e) Breaking through barriers – functional, financial, personal or other to the performance of the team

(f) Holding team members accountable for the project goals

(g) Asking team-members to show results

(h) Ensuring that the project is on track

(i) Interfacing with executive managers and

(j) Doing whatever is required to make the project successful.

***(iv)* Select the black belt:** A black belt is essential to lead a DFSS Project. He or she should have a strong desire to do things in a different way and better to be a change agent. The black belt should have exceptional people skills, communication skills and facilitation skills in addition to skills in product development. The black belt has the following responsibilities:

(a) Committing full-time to the project

(b) Achieving the project goals

(c) Facilitating the use of DFSS tools

(d) Coaching and mentoring team members

(e) Breaking through barriers

(f) Translating between the team and others in the organisation

(g) Keeping the progress of the project

(h) Coordinating all project team activities.

***(v)* Select green belts and team members:** Open minded and highly skilled people must be chosen from all areas affected by the DFSS project (e.g. marketing, design, manufacturing, quality assurance and vendor development) The team should be represented by members from all key functions that contribute to developing and testing the design and then working with the product, service or process.

The team members must have functional expertise and relevant knowledge of the project. Each member is assigned specific duties and responsibilities for making the project successful.

***(vi)* Conduct "just-in-time" training:** Each member must undergo training linked to real work because of the pressure they undergo to meet deadlines. Team members should be applying the tools of DFSS as and when required.

***(vii)* Define the implementation schedule:** The implementation should have specified time schedules to start and end.

***(viii)* Define the attendance matrix:** This is the summary of the people who should attend each of the training sessions based on their area of expertise.

***(ix)* Establish the project charter:** The purpose of a project charter is to formalise the DFSS initiative, to capture the vision of the project, to convey a feeling of enthusiasm, to set direction for the project team and to define the parameters of the project.

***(x)* Establish the project objectives:**

Three parts of this step are:

(a)* *Define the metrics: which provide a measurable, quantitative scale for assessing performance.

(*b*) ***Collect base line data:*** The base line defines a starting point, based on the ***competition*****, similar products or services.**

(*c*) ***Set the improvement goal:*** The goal defines an improvement target.

(xi) **Establish the time line:** This should indicate the major milestones in the project.

(xii) **Develop a strategic Plan:** The plan established by executive management earlier is elaborated by the project team.

(xiii) **Review lessons learnt:** Team members should plan to share and document what they learn throughout the project.

(xiv) **Identify channels for process capability data:** Process capability data is necessary to allow members of the team to contrast engineering requirements with process capability.

(xv) **Conduct a measurement system analysis:** This step is key to get good process data.

(xvi) **Map the process:** Process map is necessary to show how the process flows, to list and categorise all the key process variables (KPVs) and to begin understanding how key process input variables generate key output variables.

(xvii) **Plan for communicating project information:** The plan should specify who will communicate what to whom, why, how and when.

2. I–Identiey Phase: The purpose of this phase is to select the best product or service concept based on the ***"voice of the customer"*** (VOC). The focus is on defining the requirements of the product or service. The team identifies the customer, the critical-to-quality specifications (CTQs) the technical requirements and the quality targets to be met.

Procedure involved:

(i) **Define the customer:** The SIPOC (supplier –input-process- output-customer) map for the product or service is used by the team to help identify and even prioritise the customers. Both internal as well as external customers are considered.

A prioritisation matrix may be used to distinguish among customers.

(ii) **Identify and understand customer requirements:** Gathering voice of customer is important to DFSS. Various means of capturing customer information are used to capture both expressed needs and latent or hidden needs. Voice of customers can be gathered using the following methods.

(*a*) Reviews of customer complaints

(*b*) Customer surveys (e.g. preference surveys)

(*c*) Focus groups

(*d*) One-on-one interviews

(*e*) Contextual inquiry

(*f*) Customer specifications

(*g*) Conjoint analysis

(*h*) Interactive prototyping.

The various tools used by the team include the following:

a. ***Affinity diagram*** or a ***"Voice-of-Customer" table*** for recording information about customer needs that allow the team to capture the context of those needs to better understand explicit and implicit customer requirements.

b. ***The 'Kano" model*** is used to categorise customer requirements in terms of level of customer satisfaction.

c. ***Quality Function Deployment (QFD) uses*** a "house of quality" method to identify factors which are critical to customer satisfaction and factors that are critical to quality (CTQ). The house-of-quality is used to rank the importance of features that affect meeting the performance specifications.

***(iii)* Prioritise customer requirements:** The team analyses customer feedback and marketing data to qualify and rank benefits to customers, using such tools as *(a)* rank ordering *(b)* sensitivity analysis, *(c)* trade-off analysis and *(d)* analytic hierarchy process to weigh the relative importance of each requirement. FMEA may also be used which provides an excellent basis for classifying CTQs and other critical variables. This will help the team to direct resources towards the most promising opportunities.

***(iv)* Establish other requirements:** Organisational, regulatory and environmental requirements are established.

***(v)* Identify the CTQs and technical requirements, performance targets and specification limits:** The customer and other requirements are translated into critical-to-quality (CTRQs) factures using quality function deployment (QED)

***(vi)* Prioritise the CTQS:** QFD and Failure Modes and Effect Analysis (FMEA) is used to prioritise CTQ features.

***(vii)* Document the CTQS in formal specifications:** Technical requirements, performance target, and specification limits are identified by the team which sets a target and a range of acceptability for each CTQ, using bench marking and competitive analysis. The team may also decide to establish performance base line to understand the current design well enough.

***(viii)* Establish CTQ metrics:** The team establishes ways to measure to what extent the product or service design meets the specifications.

***(ix)* Create the score cards:** Score cards are used to record design requirements, capture information, estimate performance, track results and make any gaps obvious and actionable.

***(x)* Select the design concept:** Based on the information obtained from the first phase of QFD, the team addresses potential design concepts for the various subsystems within the design. Many sub systems and components can be reused or leveraged from previous generations of the design. The concepts provided for the new product or service in the plan phase are taken and developed into a working paper design, generating concepts that address all the key requirements. The DFSS teams frequently conduct a preliminary FMEA for each design concept at this stage In case of designing a product a "design for a manufacture and assembly" (DFMA) test could be conducted on each alternative concept..

***(xi)* Move from a focus on CTQs to a focus on Critical –to-Process(CTPs) metrics:** At this stage, the team will have a set of design CTPs that will constrain the formal and technical design.

***(xii)* Analyse the influence of the CTQs on the technical requirements:** QFD (house of quality) can be used to translate customer CTQs into technical requirements (CTQs for engineering)

***(xiii)* Develop innovative alternatives to satisfy the functional requirements**: Various tools such as brain storming may be used for identifying design alternatives.

***(xiv)* Perform risk analysis:** FMEA is used to reduce the risks (possibilities that things could go wrong)

***(xv)* Consider means of error proofing:** Tools such as Design for Manufacture and Assembly (DFMA), Design for Reliability, Design for Testing, Design for Cost, Design for Serviceability etc., could be used. Poka-Yoke which is the first step in error proofing could also be used.

***(xvi)* Perform an engineering analysis and select materials:** For designing a product, the **team** can use engineering analysis such as "**simulation**" and then computer programs for selection of materials.

***(xvii)* Select equipment based on needed capability:** This step is important for products with long lead times.

(xviii) **Formulate the concept design and predict the sigma level of quality:** The design concepts are evaluated and refined and strengthened to select a best solution concept for optimising.

(xix) **Conduct the Identify Phase-gate project review:**

3. D-Design Phase: The purpose of the ***Design phase*** is to build a thorough base of knowledge about the product or services and its processes. The customer CTQs are translated into functional requirements and alternative concepts or solutions. The team uses a selection process to evaluate the alternatives and reduce the list of solutions to one, the best-fit concept.

Procedure involved:

(i) **Formulate concept design:** The design alternatives are evaluated to select or improve upon the best alternatives. Next FMEA is used to evaluate a selected design concept for potential failure modes.

(ii) **Identify part and process CTQs:** "Critical-to-Quality" design parameters are identified for each technical requirement. Also the influence of CTQs on the technical requirements are identified using analysis, Design of Experiments, simulation and/or modeling – representations of the relationships Y=f*(x)* between customer requirements (Ys)and design elements (Xs)

(iii) **Populate the DFSS Scorecard:** At this point, CTQs are recorded on the project score card. Score cards contain CTQs, specification, process capability data, process capability calculations, and flags (for any processes for which process capability may not be adequate)

(iv) **Quantify transfer functions:** The transfer functions are developed and refined through:

(a) Bench marking historical transfer functions

(b) Performing analytical simulations and

(c) Conducting design of experiments (DOE) tests

The transfer functions are applied to develop the general layout and to approximate overall performance

(v) **Establish target values and tolerances:** The team does this with parameter design and tolerance design such as ***empirical tolerance design*** and ***analytical tolerance design*** to create a robust design.

(vi) **Assess process performance:** The performance indices P_p, P_{pk} and P_r are calculated. P_p is a performance index that summarises the performance of a process in terms of meeting upper and lower specification limits. P_{pk} is a performance index that tells how well a system is meeting the specifications P_r is a performance ratio which summarises the spread of the process in comparison with the spread of the upper and lower specification limits.

(vii) **Do a gap analysis:** Any gaps in the processes that are negatively affecting the performance of the new design are found.

(viii) **Identify, assess, address and manage risks:** FMEA is used to better understand the risks and compensate for them.

(ix) **Assess design for X (design element), depending upon the product or service:** The tests could be Design for Manufacture, Design for Assembly, Design for Manufacture and Assembly (DEMA) , Design for Reliability, Design for Testability/ Testing, Design for Cost, Design for Serviceability/Service, Design for Quality, Design for Fabrication, Design for Disassembly, Design for Diagnosis, Design for Inspection, Design for International , Design for Green or for Environment, Design for Environment, Safety and Health etc.,

(x) **Update the score cards**

(xi) **Conduct the Design phase-gate project review**

4. O-Optimise Phase: The purpose of this phase is to achieve a balance of quality, cost and time to market. Advanced statistical tools and modeling are used to predict quality level, reliability, and performance. The team uses process capability information and a statistical approach to tolerance to develop detailed design elements and optimise design and performance.

Procedure involved:

***(i)* Identify potential failures:** FMEA or Anticipatory Failure Determination (AFD) are the two tools which are applied to both the design of the product and the design of the process. Reliability data is used to make predictions of field failure rates. In addition, pilot and small –scale implementations may also be used to test and evaluate performance. At this stage, testing is done to finalise the design and not to try out design ideas. Corrective actions should be taken to prevent the failure.

***(ii)* Develop a robust design:** The focus of the design process is to create a design which is robust, that can perform acceptably despite variations in design parameters, operating parameters and processes. The team ensures that the processes are capable of meeting the design requirements, especially with critical design parameters and CTQs. The team uses Design of Experiments (DOE) or Taguchi methods to optimise parameter values and reduce variation.

***(iii)* Apply response surface methodology (RSM):** RSM is usually applied following a set of designed experiments intended to screen out the unimportant factors. The primary purpose of RSM is to find the optimum settings for the factors which influence the response.

***(iv)* Apply evolutionary operations (EVOP), if appropriate:** Evolutionary operation involves a continuous improvement process of optimising the operating conditions of a process.

(v) EVOP consists of systematically making small changes in the levels of the process variables being investigated.

***(vi)* Update the CTQ selection:** Know what CTQs have emerged at the subsystem or process level

***(vii)* Update capability and measurement system analysis(MSA) data**

***(viii)* Update the score cards**

***(ix)* Conduct and optimise phase-gate project review**

5. V-Verify/Validate Phase: This phase demonstrates that the product or service satisfies the **Voice of the customer** and ensures that the design will meet the customer CTQs. It consists of testing, verifying and validating the design, assessing performance and reliability. In this phase, prototypes are tested and the design goes through interactions as necessary.

Procedure involved:

***(i)* Validate product or service and processes:** This step may include testing prototypes.

***(ii)* Demonstrate the process capability**

***(iii)* Verify tolerances**

***(iv)* Evaluate reliability**

***(v)* Conduct an MSA:** The team checks again to determine to what extent variation within the measurement process contributes to overall process variability.

***(vi)* Implement statistical process control (SPC)**

***(vii)* Define and implement the control plan:** After the design has been proved to meet the specifications of the established requirements, action taken to stabilise the design. The team sets up a control plan so that the process owners can monitor and maintain the process.

***(viii)* Update and validate the score cards.**

***(ix)* Conduct the validate / verify phase-gate project review**

In conclusion, we may say that the DFSS methods-whether the PIDOV approach outlined above or variants-extends the power and discipline of Six sigma to the beginning, where it makes the most difference is terms of time and money.

13.24 QUALITY IN PRACTICE

Box 13.3 : Applying Six-Sigma at Wipro

Wipro limited is a diversified Indian conglomerate, having business interests in IT services to FMCG manufacturing, Wipro Technologies, the Global IT service arm of Wipro Limited, is among the top 10 global players in the IT service space.

Being a global player, Wipro had to meet the global standards for quality, delivery and customer satisfaction. Wipro's search for a global methodology to improve operational efficiencies and customer focus culminated in the choice of Six-Sigma being the means of achieving sustained competitive advantage.

The Six-Sigma in Wipro's view is:

(i) Very measurable, *(ii)* A tool, a methodology to remove defects in products, processes and service, *(iii)* All encompassing (manufacturing and transactional quality), *(iv)* Focused on the customer and *(v)* Based on data and facts.

In may 1997, Chairman, Mr Premji, at a Six-Sigma launch stated that Wipro would not compromise with integrity or quality.

The challenge at Wipro was to change Six-Sigma view from manufacturing to that of accepted quality standards at all levels. In the initial years, Wipro took help from Motorola University – the pioneers of Six-Sigma journey-to launch the program and later on became self- reliant in taking the journey forward.

The Six-Sigma first mapped the processes and identified the problem areas. The process variables of concern were identified, data was collected and analysed. The identified improvements were studied for feasibility and the feasible ones were implemented.

Over the years Wipro has put in substantial effort into Six-Sigma and also reaped rich dividends proportional to the effort put. The major organisational gains Wipro has achieved through Six-Sigma are:

- Culture of team work and problem solving
- Improved quality and delivery of the software services and other businesses
- Successfully leveraged Six - Sigma to get certification like SEI – CMM level- 5, and SEI- CMMi level-5.
- Run over 2000 projects with cumulative financial benefits of over Rs 5000 million
- Over 200 black belts across the corporation. Today, Six Sigma is an umbrella initiative covering all business units and division of Wipro. It strives to make Wipro products and services globally competitive and consistently exceed customer expectations. It has succeeded in making quality and timely delivery a part of Wipro culture

13.25 SUMMARY

Six-Sigma is a well-structured approach to improvement projects with verifiable financial results. Sigma (σ-standard duration) is a measure of the capability of process to produce defect free work. For example, a process which is at a quality level of 3σ means 6,807 defects per million opportunities (DPMO) while 6σ means 3.4 defects per million opportunities (DPMO). Most organizations in developed countries are operating at 3σ to 4σ quality levels.

The central idea of Six-Sigma quality management is that we can measure the defects in a process and can simultaneously figure out ways to eliminate them and improve quality level progressively from 3σ to 6σ level and ultimately achieve a quality level of zero defects.

Motorola pioneered the concept of Six-Sigma in 1980 as an approach to measuring product and service quality. Through implementation of Six-Sigma approach, Motorola achieved very high levels of consistent quality in all the processes undertaken and ultimately won Malcolm Baldrige National Quality Award for excellence in quality.

The core philosophy of Six-Sigma is based on several key concepts such as *(i)* Thinking in terms of key business processes and customer requirements, *(ii)* Focusing on corporate sponsors responsible of improvement projects, *(iii)* Emphasizing quantifiable measures such as DPMO, *(iv)* Identifying appropriate metrics, *(v)* Providing executive training and deploying project teams for Six-Sigma implementation, *(vi)* Creating highly qualified process improvement experts (green belts, black belts, master black belts) and *(vii)* Setting stretch objectives for improvement.

A successful Six-Sigma implementation should be based on certain principles and should build upon a number of prerequisites such as existing quality culture and certain level of quality maturity. Several factors such as top management commitment, being able to show successful projects, high investment in training, high investment in management time and development of key players in the organization-all influence the sustainability of Six-Sigma in the long term.

The core elements of Six-Sigma include: *(i)* Focus on the customer, *(ii)* Data-and –fact driven management, *(iii)* Specific training, *(iv)* Structured approach, *(v)* Quality engineering, *(vi)* Process focus, control and improvement, *(vii)* Proactive management, *(viii)* Boundary-less collaboration *(ix)* Drive for perfection, *(x)* Cost savings of each project and *(xi)* Short –term improvement projects.

Six-Sigma projects use structured problem-solving approaches which vary depending on the organizational processes to which they are applied. For existing processes "DMAIC" approach or model is used and for new processes "DMADV" approach is used.

Three aspects involved in Six-Sigma implementation are: *(i)* Process improvement, *(i)* Process design / redesign and *(iii)* Process management.

The DMAIC is structured problem solving approach involving the following steps:

(i) **Define** the customer and organizational requirements.

(ii) **Measure** the factors which are critical to quality.

(iii) **Analyse** the relationship between the cost of defects and key performance variables.

(iv) **Improve** the process

(v) **Control** the system through established process.

The steps involved in "DMADV" approach are:

(i) **Define** the goals of the project and customer deliverables

(ii) **Measure** and determine customer needs / specifications.

(iii) **Analyse** the process options to meet customer needs.

(iv) **Design** the process to meet customer needs

(v) **Verify** the design performance and ability to meet customer needs.

Six-Sigma approach to process management involves the following stages:

(i) Identify the need, *(ii)* Clarify the vision, *(iii)* Develop the plan, *(iv)* Implement the plan and *(v)* Sustain improvement.

Six-Sigma provides a blue print for implementing total quality system. It is a way of realizing many TQM concepts such as interaction of human and process elements of improvement. However Six-Sigma differs from TQM in several aspects:

(i) TQ is based on worker involvement and team work, whereas Six-Sigma is owned by business leader champions supported by experts (green belt, black belts, master black belt)

(ii) TQ activities usually occur within a function whereas Six-Sigma projects are cross-functional.

(iii) TQ training is generally limited to simple improvement tools (7 QC tools) whereas Six-Sigma focuses on more advanced set of statistical methods and problem-solving methodology such as DMAIC.

Six-Sigma projects can be applied in service organization also. **To apply Six-Sigma to service, four key measures of performance must be examined:**

(i) Accuracy, *(ii)* Cycle time, *(iii)* Cost and *(iv)* Customer satisfaction.

Six-Sigma Management is the relentless and rigorous pursuit of the reduction of variation in all critical processes to achieve continuous and break through improvements that impact the bottom-line of the organization and increase customer satisfaction. It is an organisational initiative designed to achieve 3.4 defects per million opportunities by creating manufacturing, administrative and service processes.

Six-Sigma guide's organization into making fewer mistakes in everything they do-eliminating lapses in quality at the earliest possible occurrence.

Six-Sigma is a break-through strategy to improve processes, reduce variations in processes and outputs, improve quality consistently, and improve profitability. Implementing Six-Sigma requires the organizations to follow certain "Do's" and "Don'ts" to ensure the success of Six-Sigma, projects. For successful implementation of Six-Sigma, The organization should be willing to implement major changes and have an effective system of communication to communicate the importance of Six-Sigma to all employees and executives involved in such projects. Top Management commitment and support is very important for the success of Six-Sigma projects. The organisation's knowledge base must be surveyed and the members of Six-Sigma project teams must be provided adequate training in the use of statistical tools and techniques involved in Six-Sigma implementation.

Once the readiness of the organisation is assessed, the organization must plan for Six-Sigma. The various phases involved in planning for Six-Sigma are: *(i)* Communication and education, *(ii)* Identification of projects, *(iii)* Infrastructure and *(iv)* Implementation Partner.

The success of Six-Sigma relies on the people who are responsible for implementing it. The key players include is *(i)* Executive leaders, *(ii)* Champions, *(iii)* Master Black Belts, *(iv)* Black Belts, *(v)* Green Belts and *(vi)* Process Owners.

The role of Executive leaders is to decide to do Six-Sigma and to endorse it publicly throughout the organization. The role of the champion is to advocate and fight for the cause of Black Belts and to ensure that the projects they select align with the executive strategy. They select the black belts, identify project areas and establish goals for selected projects.

Master Black Belts serve as trainers, mentors and guides for the firm's project team. They have expertise in Six-Sigma tools and tactics. A Master Black Belt supervises several Black Belts and Green Belts simultaneously. Black Belts, work full-time on selected projects. They act as full-time change agents and supervise Green Belt working on a Six-Sigma project.

Green Belts serve as team members on Six-Sigma projects. They assist Black Belt in their functional area. They are the real "work horses" or "work bees" driving bottom-line results.

Process owner is the individual who has ultimate authority to change process. Process owner has multiple roles-monitoring the performance of the process, empowering people, and working with all Six-Sigma project teams, managing the process after completion of Six-Sigma project and continuing to improve/innovate the process through the application of 'PDSA' cycle.

Six-Sigma tools can be classified as :

(i) Warm-up tools and *(ii)* Key tools.

The warm-up tools are the first tools to be used in Six-Sigma approach to conduct initial investigation into a specific process. For example, histogram is a key warm-up tool. In addition, correlation study is also considered as a warm-up tool.

The various key tools include *(i)* Process mapping, *(ii)* The 'XY' matrix, *(iii)* Measurement Systems Analysis, *(iv)* Process capability tool, *(v)* Multivariate study, *(vi)* Hypothesis testing, *(vii)* Failure Mode Effect Analysis, *(viii)* Design of Experiments and *(ix)* Control Plan (control charts)

Six-Sigma projects are selected based on two important criteria: *(i)* Effort required and *(ii)* The Probability of success.

After selecting the project, two tasks to be carried out are: *(i)* Project problem statement and *(ii)* Project objective statement. Characteristics of successive Six-Sigma projects are:

(i) Increase in sales, *(ii)* Reduction in accounts receivables and net inventory, *(iii)* Reduction in actual spending, *(iv)* Avoiding costs not currently incurred, *(v)* Reduction in cycle time on critical path steps in bottle neck operations, *(vi)* Improvement in quality and service levels as measured by the customer and *(vii)* Achievement of objectives set.

Design for Six-Sigma DFSS is an approach for designing or redesigning products and / or services to meet or exceed customer requirements and expectations.

DFSS is based on the notion that when Six-Sigma quality is designed right at the outset of new product development, it is probable that customers accept that product. By incorporation of DFSS, a firm can have the assurance that the product or service launched will perform dependably in the market place. DFSS starts with a gap analysis for the entire product development system to find the gaps in the processes which are negatively affecting new product performance. It also addresses the "Voice of the customer".

DFSS is implemented with its own version of the DMAIC approach known as "PIDOV" which has the following steps: *(i)* Plan, *(ii)* Identify, *(iii)* Design, *(iv)* Optimise and *(v)* Verity.

DFSS could help companies to overcome many of the problems that cause new products to fail in the market place. DFSS has several advantages in terms of customer satisfaction, quality time and money (profitability)

The basic procedure of DFSS involves the following steps:

(i) Capturing the customer requirements

(ii) Analysing and prioritizing the requirements

(iii) Developing a design

(iv) Flow of requirements down from the system level to subsystems, components and processes

(v) Tracking the capability of the product or service and process at each step and highlighting gaps between requirements and capabilities and making them actionable.

(vi) Establishing a control plan.

13.26 KEY WORDS USED

Sigma, Standard Deviation, Defects Per Million Opportunities (DPMO), Zero Defect, Six-Sigma Quality, Six-Sigma Capability, Six-Sigma Process Capability,, Six-Sigma Philosophy, Quality Engineering, Process Improvement, "DMAIC' model, Process Design, Process Management, Six-Sigma Management, Champions, Master Black Belts, Black Belts, Green Belts, Process Mapping, The 'XY' Metric, Brain Storming, Cause-and-Effect Diagram, Measurement Systems Analysis (MSA), Process Capability Tool, Pareto Charts, Multivariate Study, Hypothesis Testing, Failure Mode Effect Analysis (FMEA), Control Plan, Control Chart, Design For Six-Sigma (DFSS), Voice Of The Customer (VOC), Systems Engineering, Requirements Flow Diagram, Concept Engineering, Quality Function Development (QFD) , Critical-To-Quality (CTQ).

13.27 OBJECTIVE QUESTIONS

(A) Match the following :

Column A	Column B
1. 6 sigma quality	1. 66810 ppm.
2. DMAIC approach	2. used in the measure "phase" of DMAIC
3. 3 sigma quality	3. 3.4 ppm.
4. Process mapping	4. 6210 ppm
5. Four sigma quality	5. Related to Deming's 'PDCA' cycle

(B) State whether the following statements are True or False :

1. Green belts undertake full-time work on Six-Sigma projects and lead the project team.(T / F)
2. The goal of Six-Sigma is not to achieve Six-Sigma levels of quality. (T / F)
3. Six-Sigma allows a business leader to be proactive rather than reactive to quality issues. (T / F)
4. Champions are the individuals who have the ultimate authority to change a process.(T/ F)
5. DFSS is just Six-Sigma in design. (T / F)

(C) Multiple choice Questions : Choose the correct answer from the alternatives given under each question :

1. A quality level of 3.4 defects per million can be achieved:
   (a) With 0.5 sigma off - centering and 5 sigma quality
   (b) With 1.0 sigma off - centering and 5.5 sigma quality
   (c) With 1.5 sigma off - centering and 6 sigma quality
   (d) All of these
   (e) None of these
2. Implementation of Six-Sigma involves the following aspect of process development:
   (a) Process improvement (b) Process design/redesign
   (c) Process management (d) All of these
   (e) None of these.

3. To apply Six-Sigma to services, the key measures of performance that must be examined are:

   (a) Accuracy (b) Cycle time
   (c) Cost (d) Customer satisfaction
   (e) All of these (f) None of these

4. The persons who serve as trainers, mentors and guides in Six-Sigma quality projects are known as:

   (a) Executive leaders (b) Champions
   (c) Master Black Belts (d) Block Belts
   (e) Green Belts.

5. _______ is the individual who has the ultimate authority to change a process

   (a) Process Owner (b) Green Belt
   (c) Black Belt (d) Master Black Belt
   (e) Champion (f) Executive leader.

13.28 REVIEW QUESTIONS

1. What is meant by "Six-Sigma Quality"?
2. Discuss the Key Concepts on which core philosophy of Six-Sigma is based?
3. What is meant by Six-Sigma Process Capability?
4. State the ten principles of Six-Sigma?
5. Discuss the fundamental Six-Sigma practices and applicable tools?.
6. Outline the evolution of Six-Sigma approach.
7. Discuss the core elements of Six-Sigma.
8. Briefly describe the structured problem-solving approaches used in Six-Sigma projects.
9. Write short notes on (a) Process improvement *(b)* Process design/Redesign *(c)* Process management.
10. Describe the DMAIC approach used in Six-Sigma project implementation.
11. Explain how Six-Sigma approach can be applied to services.
12. What is meant by 'Six-Sigma' management'?
13. How does Six-Sigma work?
14. Discuss the application of Six-Sigma approach at Motorola
15. Why Six-Sigma approach is used in organisations?
16. Discuss the benefits of Six-Sigma approach for a company.
17. How does Six-Sigma help improving profitability?
18. Discuss the Do's and Don'ts'\ of implementing Six-Sigma.
19. Explain how to prepare an organisation for the Six-Sigma journey.
20. What is meant by "Planning for Six-Sigma"?
21. Discuss the roles and responsibilities of people responsible for Six-Sigma implementation.
22. Discuss the differences between black belt and green belt Six-Sigma projects.
23. Give an overview of Six-Sigma tools.
24. Describe how Six-Sigma projects are selected.
25. What is meant by "Sustaining Six-Sigma"?
26. What is meant by "Design for Six-Sigma " (DFSS)?
27. What is meant by "Voice of the customer" (VOC)?
28. What is meant by "PIDOV" approach to DFSS
29. Discuss the "Myths" and "Truths" about DFSS.
30. Why do "Design for Six-Sigma" (DFSS)?
31. What are the advantages of DFSS?

32. Discuss the following:
    (a) DFSS and Quality (b) DFSS and Time
    (c) DFSS and the 'Bottom- line'
33. Discuss the DFSS Procedure.
34. Discuss the difference between 'Generic' design process and 'DFSS' design process.
35. Describe the 'IDOV' method used in DFSS.

13.29 DISCUSSION QUESTIONS

1. "Six-Sigma is not just another Quality Program or stand-alone activity" – Discuss the statement.
2. "Six-Sigma involves a problem-solving approach" – Explain
3. "Design for Six-Sigma (DFSS) is a business process which is focused on improving profitability" – Justify the statement.
4. "Six-Sigma provides a blue print for implementing total quality system" – Discuss.
5. Discuss the relevance of Six-Sigma approach for continuous improvement.

13.30 ASSIGNMENTS

1. Visit a company in your vicinity that has implemented a Six-Sigma programme. Prepare a report about their experiences, focusing on the challenges they faced during their implementation efforts
2. There are 200 savings account opening forms that need to be entered into the computer system in a bank. Each form has 10 fields for which data is to be entered. It was found leater that there were defects in the entries made as given below: *(i)* 5 crrors in the name field *(ii)* 9 crrors in the data of birth field and *(iii)* 11 crrors in the "mode of operation" code

   Calculate the DPMO assuming the same number of errors occurs while entering 400 savings account opening form, will the DPMO increase or decrease? Give reasons.

13.31 CHAPTER CASES

1. MOTOROLA'S SIX-SIGMA APPROACH TO TOTAL QUALITY RENEWS THE FIRM

Motorola was founded in 1928 by Paul Galvin who led the company until 1959. After his death, his son Robert Galvin was chief executive officer from 1959 until 1986. His son Christopher Galvin became president of Motorola in 1993.

The company had over 1,20,000 employees and about $17 billion in sales in 1993 out of which international sales accounted for about 52 percent. All of its products and services were in the area of electronics, including mobile radio and paging systems, cellular phones and systems, space communications and computers.

In such an industry new product development and adaptability to rapidly changing technology are critical to survival. How is a company the size of Motorola continually renewed?

In the early 1980s, Motorola stressed quality improvement with a goal of a tenfold improvement in quality levels in five years. In 1987 Motorola adopted a formal Total Quality initiative named as "Six Sigma". "Six Sigma" refers to a defect rate of no more than 3.4 per million opportunities for error. In 1988, its Total Quality process won Motorola one of the first Malcolm Baldrige National Quality Awards. The six steps in Motorola's Six-Sigma process are as follows :

(i) Identify the work you do (your "product")
(ii) Identify who your work is for (your "customer.")
(iii) What do you need to do your work, and from whom (your "supplier")
(iv) Map the process
(v) Mistake-proof the process and eliminate delays.
(vi) Establish quality and cycle-time measurement and improvement goals.

The Six-Sigma process was implemented in the context of the Motorola culture. Motorola's fundamental objective, key beliefs, goals and initiatives were printed on a small card for employee to carry and has been translated into 11 languages for Motorola's world-wide operations. The contents of the card were as follows :

Side 1 : Our fundamental objective : (Everyone's over riding responsibility)

- *"Total Customer Satisfaction"*

Side 2 : Key beliefs – how we will always act

- Constant Respect for People
- Uncompromising Integrity.

Key Goals : What we must accomplish?

- Best-in-Class
- People
- Marketing
- Technology
- Product; Software, Hardware and Systems
- Manufacturing
- Service
- Increased Global Market Share
- Superior Financial Results

Key Initiatives :

- Six-Sigma Quality
- Total Cycle Time Reduction
- Product, Manufacturing and Environmental Leadership
- Profit Improvement
- Empowerment for all, in a Participative, Cooperative and Creative Workplace.

Discussion Questions :

1. What does "empowerment for all" mean in such a large organisation with over 1,20,000 employees?
2. What is the role of teams in a process such as Six Sigma?

2. GENERAL ELECTRIC'S SIX-SIGMA QUALITY GOAL

General electric set itself a corporate goal of becoming a Six-Sigma quality company, which means one that produces virtually defect-froe products, services and transactions. Cost of quality at 3 σ to 4 σ quality is typically 10 to 15 percent of revenues. In G.E's case, with over $ 80 billion in revenues, that amounts to $ 8 to 12 billion annually, mostly in scrap, reworking of parts and rectifying mistakes in transactions. So the financial rationale for embracing on this quality journey towards Six-Sigma quality is obvious.

But beyond the pure financial benefits, there are even more important rewards that will come with dramatically improved quality. Among them is the unlimited growth from selling services and products universally recognised by customers as being, on a completely different plane of quality from those of competitors. The journey towards Six-Sigma quality was the most difficult and invigorating stretch goal that GE had ever undertaken. The magnitude of the challenge of going from 35,000 defects per million to fewer than 4 defects was huge. It would require the company to reduce defect rates 10,000 fold- about 84 percent for five consequent years. But GE wonted to makes its quality so special, so valuable to its customers, so important to their success that GE's services and products became their only real value choice.

Discussion Questions :

1. What will be the key tasks for GE to reach its goal?
2. How will this change the competitive factors in its markets and what strategic advantages will result?

CHAPTER 14

TOOLS AND TECHNIQUES FOR TOTAL QUALITY MANAGEMENT

LEARNING OBJECTIVES

After reading this chapter, you should be able to:

- Understand the various classifications of total quality tools and techniques.
- Discuss the tools for design processes.
- Briefly describe Taguchi methods, Design of experiments, Orthogonal arrays, Taguchi designs, Quality function deployment and Poka-yoke.
- Discuss the management model for quality improvement.
- Describe Deming's cycle, Juran's improvement program and Crosby program for quality improvement.
- Discuss the various tools used for process improvement.
- Discuss the various analytical tools for total quality management.
- Understand the concepts of regression analysis, resource utilisation, the "Five Whys" technique and over-all equipment effectiveness.
- Discuss the various improvement techniques such as Just-in-time systems, Continuous improvement (Kaizen), Quality circles, Force-field analysis and Japanese 5 'S' principles.
- Discuss the various control tools and techniques such as : Project scheduling techniques (PERT/CPM), Radar chart, Milestone tracker diagram, Failure mode and effect analysis, Balanced score card etc.

14.0 INTRODUCTION

In a total quality setting, new products are designed with full participation of manufacturing, materials and quality specialists throughout the design phase in a process known as **concurrent engineering**. This ensures that when the design is turned over to manufacturing, it will no longer be attended by a team of inspectors because the people doing the work will do their own inspection as the work progresses. Beyond that, and this is where the total quality tools that come in a process of **continuous improvement** will ensure that the product not only meets its customer's expectations but actually improves for as long as production is continued. For this to happen, all the people involved in the process, from design through production, must employ a few simple statistical tools.

Total Quality Tools

Total quality tools enable employees, whether engineers, technologists, production workers or office staff, to do their jobs. Virtually no one can function in an organisation that has embraced total quality without some or all of these tools. These tools are **intellectual** tools which are used for collecting and displaying information in ways to help people graph thoughts and ideas that when applied to physical processes, cause the processes to yield better results. **Quality improvement tools can be grouped according to how they are used. These groups are listed below.**

1. **Project planning and implementation tools**, which are used for managing the improvement project by the project team.
2. **Idea creation tools** are used to come up with new ideas or to organise many ideas.
3. **Process analysis tools** are used to understand a work process or some part of a process. Processes start with inputs coming from suppliers, change those inputs and end with outputs going to customers.
4. **Data collection and analysis tools** are used to collect data or analyses data, which are already collected.
5. **Cause analysis tools** are used to discover the cause of a problem or situation.
6. **Evaluation and decision-making tools** are used when it is necessary to narrow down a group of choices to the best one, or when it is required to evaluate how well an individual or group has done something. This includes evaluating project results.

Generic Tools

There are several generic kinds of quality tools that can be customised for particular purposes. *For example,* "graph" is a general name for a generic tool. There are many types of graphs – line graphs, bar charts, pie charts, box charts, histograms, control charts and so on, which have been developed over the years to respond to specific needs or uses for graphs. A list of generic tools with unique variations is given below.

1. **Check sheet and checklist :** Examples are defect concentration diagrams, project charter checklist, guidance questions, etc.
2. **Flow chart :** Examples are: deployment flow chart, macro flow chart, process mapping, top down flow chart, work flow diagram, etc.
3. **Graph :** Examples are control chart, histogram, Pareto chart, run chart, scatter diagram, etc.
4. **Matrix Diagram :** Examples are decision matrix, prioritisation matrix, house of quality, etc.
5. **Table:** Examples are contingency table, check sheet, "stakeholder analysis" table, "voice of customer" table, etc.
6. **Tree Diagrams :** Examples are: decision tree, fault tree analysis, process decision program chart, why-why diagram, etc.
7. **Two Dimensional Charts :** Examples are effective-achievable chart, Kano model, plan-results chart.

Another way of classifying total quality tools under the name – "Problem solving tools" is shown below:

1. **The Seven Classic Quality Tools** or the seven quality control tools (also referred to as 7 QC tools) which include: *(i)* Pareto charts, *(ii)* Cause-and-effect diagrams, (or Ishikaw diagram or Fish-bone diagram) *(iii)* Flow chart, *(iv)* Check sheet, *(v)* Control charts, *(vi)* Histograms and *(vii)* Scatter diagrams.

2. **The Seven Basic Management and Planning Tools** which include: *(i)* Affinity diagrams, *(ii)* Inter-relationship Diagraphs, *(iii)* Tree Diagrams, *(iv)* Matrix Data Analysis, *(v)* Process Decision Program Charts, *(vi)* Prioritisation Matrices and *(viii)* Activity Network Diagram.

3. **Process Improvement Tools** which include: *(i)* Root cause Analysis, *(ii)* Five whys, *(iii)* PDCA/PDSA Cycle, (Plan-Do-Check-Act or Plan-Do-Study-Act), *(iv)* SIPOC Analysis (Supplier-Input-Process-Output-Customer), *(v)* Six-Sigma and the DMHIC (Define-Measure-Analyse-Improve-Control) Model, *(vi)* Failure Mode and Effects Analysis (FMEA) and *(vii)* Statistical Process Control (SPC).

4. **Innovation and Creativity Tools** which include: *(i)* Brain storming, *(ii)* Mind Mapping, *(iii)* Nominal Group Technique, *(iv)* Motivating, *(v)* Lateral Thinking, *(vi)* Critical Thinking, *(vii)* Designing for manufacturing (DFMA), *(viii)* Designing for Six Sigma (DFSS), *(ix)* TRIZ (Russian acronym for the Theory of the solution of inventive problems) and *(x)* The Story board Technique.

The tools and techniques, along with management practices and the organisational infrastructure are fundamental components of total quality management. Many of these tools are associated with the practice of *process management*. While we have a number of tools for design process and process improvement, we should not view quality management only from a tool-based perspective and fail to see the management practices and infrastructures required to make use of these tools successfully. However, without some effective tools and guidance on how to use them, it is difficult to make continuous improvement in designs and processes. When used properly, these **tools and techniques** are powerful and effective in helping organisations to design their products and processes and to identify and solve quality problems that will ultimately lead to better customer value and operational performance.

14.1 TOOLS FOR DESIGN PROCESSES

In TQM design tools, managers have a set of procedures and techniques that can help them to design either a product or a process to ensure consistent quality. TQM practitioners use design tools to prevent quality problems by eliminating potential causes of variance in either product or processes and to enhance customer awareness, ensuring that product or process designs accommodate customer's needs and requirements. **They also involve other areas of the firm:**

- ***Marketing*** must identify exactly what the targeted customers want and are willing to pay for.
- ***Accounting*** contributes product costing support.
- ***Purchasing*** must identify outside resources that might enhance the product or process development activities.
- ***Engineering and R&D*** must identify what is technically possible.
- ***Organisational design*** must provide the type of learning organisation to effectively utilise TQM design tools.

The various techniques or tools for improving design process are:

(i) Statistical Experimentation or Experimental Design or **Design of Experiments (DoE)**.

(ii) Taguchi's methods/**Taguchi loss function**

(iii) **Quality Function Deployment** (QFD) and

(iv) **Poka-Yoke or Fail-safing**

Various techniques or tools for improving design process are:

(i) Design of Experiments

(ii) Taguchi's loss function

(iii) Quality function deployment and

(iv) Poka-yoke.

Statistical Experimentation

A product's performance is affected by manufacturing imperfections, environmental factors and human variations in operating the product. A high-quality product performs near its performance target consistently throughout the product's life span and under all different operating conditions. Good design identifies the settings of products or process parameters that minimise the sensitivity of design to sources of variation in the factory and in use. **Products that are insensitive to external sources of variation are called *robust*.** *For example,* a television whose picture quality (sharpness or clarity) varies with environmental conditions such as room temperature and humidity would not be regarded as robust.

A Japanese engineer, Dr. Genichi Taguchi, proposed the use of statistically planned experiments for parameter design. **Experimental design or design of experiments (DoE)** is one of the most powerful techniques for improving quality and increasing productivity. Through experiments, changes are intentionally introduced into the process or system in order to observe their effects on the performance characteristic or response of the system or process. **Any experiment that has the flexibility to make desired changes in the input variables of a process to observe the output response is known as *experimental design.*** It is a systematic manipulation of a set of variables in which the effect of these manipulations is determined, conclusions are made and results are implemented. **The primary goals of a designed experiment are to:**

(i) determine the variables and their magnitude that influences the response

(ii) determine the levels for these variables and

(iii) determine how to manipulate these variables to control the response.

According to Taguchi, it is not sufficient to control processes, inspect output, identify and remove defects and rely on customer feedback. To improve quality, one must look upstream at the design stage because that is where quality design begins. **Quality must be designed in, it cannot be inspected later**. One fact of obtaining better design is experimentation on variables that contribute to a product's performance. Taguchi's strong belief in this approach has brought ***design of experiments (DoE)*** into wider use by quality experts, designers and other members of design build teams. Taguchi also believes that the team should aim for ***robust design* – designs that can withstand the hard-to-eliminate variabilities that occur in conversion processes or later in customer use.**

Design of experiments is a numerical study that identifies the variables in a process or product that are the critical parameters or excess significant variations in the process. By using formal experimental techniques, the effect of many variables can be studied at one time. Changes in the process or product are introduced in a random fashion or by carefully planned, highly structured experiment. **Experimental design can be used to:**

(i) Improve a process by increasing its performance and eliminate troubles.

(ii) Establish statistical control of a process variable, that is identify the variable to control the process, and

(iii) Improve an existing product or develop a new product.

14.2 TAGUCHI METHODS

Taguchi, a trained textile engineer, worked in the Japanese Navy, in the Ministry of Public Health and Welfare and the Institute of Statistical Mathematics in Japan. Later he began his carrier as a consultant.

His early work in the field of quality was mainly concerned with production processes, but during the 1980s he shifted his focus to product and process design. Taguchi's contribution brought about an inspired revolution in the quality movement by eliminating the need for mass inspection through his process of building quality into the product at the design stage.

Taguchi was awarded the Deming Prize and the Deming award for literature on quality.

Taguchi's Philosophy

The two founding ideas of Taguchi's quality work are essentially qualitative. First is a ***belief in statistical methods*** to identify and eradicate quality problems. The second rests on designing products and processes ***to build quality in,*** right from the outset.

Taguchi stated that "quality is the loss a product casues to society by its intrinsic functions".

Taguchi's philosophy and methods support, and are consistent with, the Japanese quality control approach that asserts that ***"higher quality generally results in lower cost".*** Furthermore, Taguchi's philosophy and methods support the Japanese approach to move quality improvement upstream. Taguchi's methods help design engineers build quality into products and processes.

Taguchi's view of quality is viewed as a negative, ***"the cost of non-quality"***- that is ***"the loss imparted to society from the time the product is shipped".*** Taguchi's prime concern is with customer satisfaction and with the potential for ***loss of reputation and goodwill"*** associated with failure to meet customer expectations. Such a failure, would lead the customer to buy elsewhere in the future, damaging the prospects of the company, its employees and society.

Taguchi's Definition of Quality

The traditional definition of quality **states** that ***"quality is conformance to specifications" or "quality is fitness for use".*** The ASQC defined quality as "the totality of features and characteristics of a product or service that bear on its ability to satisfy given needs".

Taguchi's definition of quality stressed the losses associated with a product. Taguchi stated that ***"quality is the loss a product causes to society by its intrinsic functions".***

Taguchi asserted that losses in his definition should be restricted to two categories:

(i) loss caused by variability of functions and

(ii) loss caused to the society by harmful side effects.

According to Taguchi, "a product or service has good quality if it performs its intended functions without variability, and causes little loss through harmful side effects; including the cost of using it".

The term "society" includes both the manufacturer and the customer. Loss associated with function variability includes for example, energy and time (problem fixing) and money (replacement cost of parts) Losses associated with harmful side effects could be decline in sales and market share for the manufacturer and the physical effects such as injury and health hazard for the customer using the product or service.

Consequently, a company should provide products and services such that the possible losses to society are minimized or the purpose of quality improvement is to discover innovative ways of designing products and processes that will save society more than they cost in the long run. The concept of ***"reliability"*** is more appropriate in this context.

(1) TAGUCHI'S QUALITY LOSS FUNCTION

Is it sufficient to control process, inspect output, identify and remove defects and rely on customer feedback? Genichi Taguchi says no. To improve quality, he argues, one must look upstream at the design stage because that is where quality begins. Quality must be designed in, it cannot be inspected later. One facet of obtaining better design is experimentation on variables that contribute to a product's performance. Taguchi's strong belief in this approach has brought ***Design of Experiments*** (DoE) into wider use by quality experts, designers and other members of design-building teams.

Taguchi also believes that teams should aim for ***robust designs*** — designs that can withstand the hard-to-eliminate variabilities that occur in transformation processes or later in customer use.

Taguchi originated ***quality engineering*** which is an approach that involves combining engineering and statistical methods to reduce costs and improve quality by optimising product design and manufacturing processes. ***Taguchi methods*** help product designers estimate the true cost of quality and then cost-effectively improve quality. This is done by improving the design of the product as well as the process by which it is made.

Taguchi's quality loss function: Taguchi asserts that the quality of a product is a function of key product characteristics referred to as ***"performance characteristics"***. The ideal value (or state) of a performance characteristic is its target value. A high-quality product performs near these target values consistently throughout its life span and under all operating conditions. Taguchi's quality loss function estimates the loss to society from the failure of a product to meet its target value for a particular performance characteristic. This loss can be incurred by the consumers (*e.g.*, short product life, increased maintenance and repair costs), by the company (*e.g.*, increased scrap, rework and warranty costs, damage to the company's reputation, loss of market share) or by society in general (*e.g.* pollution, safety).

Taguchi's **quality loss function** is a statement that any deviation from the target value of a quality characteristic results in extra costs to some segment of the society. Taguchi defines quality in terms of the social loss, loss to producers and consumers from the time a product is conceived. The smaller the value of this social loss, the more desirable is the product.

Exhibit 14.1 **illustrates Taguchi's Quality Loss Function.**

Exhibit 14.1 : Taguchi's Quality Loss Function

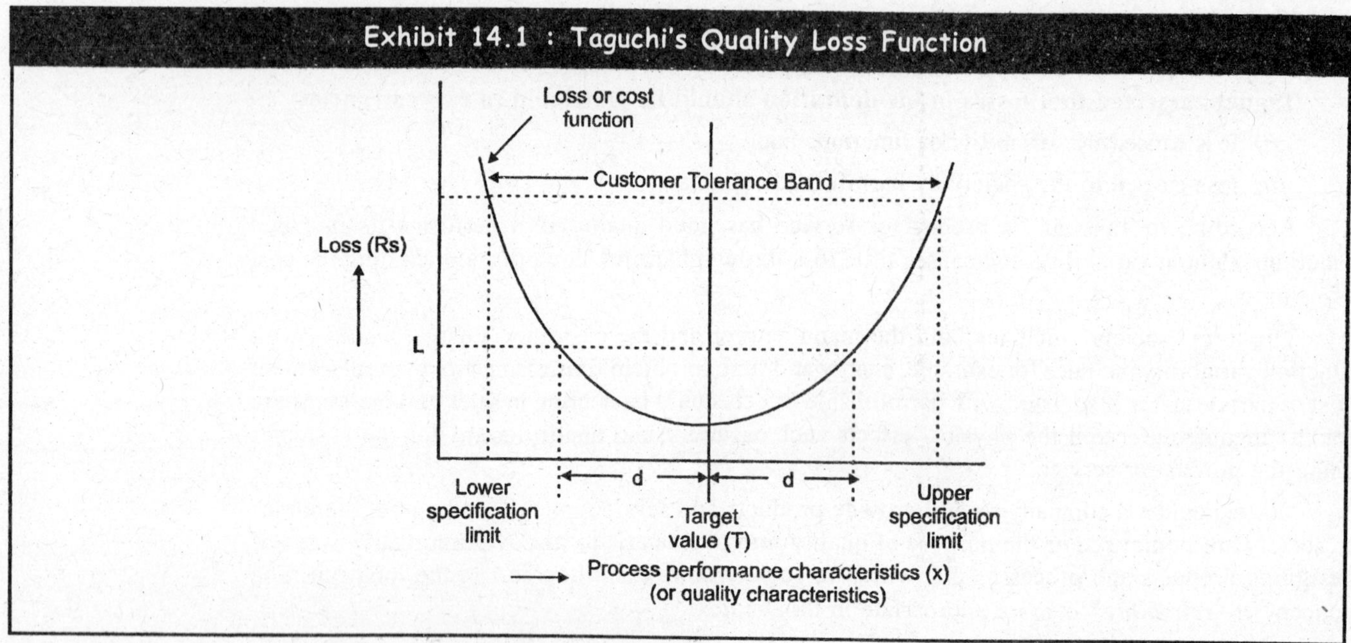

Quality loss function is expressed as:

$$L = C\,(X - T)^2$$

Where L = total loss

C = a cost constant

X = actual average value of quality characteristic and

T = target value of quality characteristic.

Taguchi holds that the unwelcome costs are associated with any deviation of process performance (or quality characteristic) from the quality characteristic's target value. The loss from performance variation (L) is directly related to the square of the deviation (d) of the performance characteristic (X) from its target value (T).

i.e.,
$$L = C\,d^2$$
$$= C\,(X - T)^2$$

Where L = Total loss
C = a cost constant
X = actual average value of quality characteristic and
T = target value of quality characteristic.

Taguchi intends that the loss function remains valid at all times during a product's life. In theory, when process output performance reaches the specification limit (upper or lower specification limit), the customer's ***economic*** interest in the item is neutral, that is, the losses will exactly offset any gain from having the item.

For Taguchi, social loss must affect quality cost management decisions, that is, investments in quality improvement should be compared with savings to society rather than to the firm alone. Ultimately, the society will reward or penalise the firm for its record of societal savings or loss respectively. Taguchi's view is meant to be sound for business.

Example: Estimating the Taguchi Loss Function

A certain quality characteristic has a specification of 1.00 ± 0.020. An analysis of company records reveals that if the value of the quality characteristic exceeds the target of 1.00 by the tolerance of 0.020 on either side (*i.e.*, ± 0.020), the product is likely to fail during the warranty period and costs Rs. 100/- for repair. Determine the total loss using Taguchi's loss function for a deviation of ± 0.010.

Solution:

$$100 = C\,(0.020)^2$$

$$C = \frac{100}{(0.020)^2}$$

$$= \frac{100}{0.0004}$$

$$= 250{,}000$$

The loss function is

$$L(X) = C\,(X - T)^2$$

$$= 2{,}50{,}000\,(X - T)^2$$

If the deviation is only ± 0.010, then the estimated loss is

$$L\,(0.010) = 250{,}000\,(0.010)^2$$

$$= \text{Rs. } 25/\text{-}$$

Strengths and Weaknesses of Taguchi's Ideas

The main strengths are:

(i) Taguchi's method pulls quality right back into the design stage rather than relying on adjustments to the process online or inspection of the final product.

(ii) The philosophy identifies quality as a societal issue and not just an organisational one.

The main weaknesses are:

(i) There are no directives about how to manage a quality-oriented organisation, particularly the people.

(ii) Taguchi has nothing to say about humans as social, cultural or political beings and therefore makes no contribution to managing employees.

Box 14.1 : Taguchi's Seven Points

Conventionally, quality control activities centre on final inspection sampling or on control charts and process control. This is known as ***"on-line quality control"***. Taguchi pushed the process upstream to focus on product and process design. This is known as ***"off-line quality control"***.

Taguchi's ***seven points*** are stated as:

(i) Product quality is measured by the total loss to society created by that product.

(ii) Continuous quality improvement and cost reduction are necessary to survive in world competition.

(iii) Quality improvement requires continual and repeated reduction of variation in the product/process performance around the standard nominal values.

(iv) Quality loss is frequently proportional to the square of the deviation of the performance from the nominal value.

(v) Product and process design can have an important impact on a product's quality and cost.

(vi) Performance variation can be reduced by suitable adjustment of the product's parameters and/or the process parameters.

(vii) The appropriate parameter settings that reduce variation can be identified with the appropriate statistically designed experiments.

(2) TAGUCHI'S ROBUST DESIGN AND THE DESIGN OF EXPERIMENTS (DOE)

Robust Design : Taguchi's methods is a generic term covering a variety of practices developed by Genichi Taguchi for statistically determining required quantitative features of a design that makes it **robust** against disturbances, variances and uncertainties, with the objective of reducing loss to society.

Robustness as defined by Taguchi, describes the state in which the performance of a product or a process is minimally sensitive to factors causing variability (either in the manufacturing or use environment) and aging at the lowest manufacturing cost.

Developing a ***robust design*** means optimizing the settings of controllable factors that will make a product or process insensitive to variation in factors that are uncontrollable or that we choose not to control.

The methods consider the "***noise factors***" –variation in manufacturing, environmental variation during use of the product and deterioration of component-and the ***cost of failure in the field*** in order to help ensure customer satisfaction. Taguchi's methods focus on ***designing efficient experiments,*** increasing ***signal-to-noise ratios*** and building in ***tolerances*** to allow for manufacturing variables known to be avoidable.

Traditional engineering focuses on testing one factor at a time or selecting test combinations based upon technical knowledge. In contrast, robust design allows design teams to perform experiments and test prototypes on multiple factors at once, so it is an efficient, cost-effective way to improve the design of products and processes.

***Robust design strategy* uses five primary tools:**

1. ***P-diagram*** for classifying the variables associated with the product into four types- ***signal*** (input), ***response*** (output) ***noise*** and ***control***
2. ***Ideal function,*** for identifying the ideal relationship between the signal and the response
3. ***Quadratic loss function*** (or quality loss function) for quantifying the loss due to deviation from target performance,
4. ***'Signal-to-noise ratio'*** for predicting field quality through laboratory experiments and
5. ***Orthogonal arrays***, for gathering dependable information about control factors (design parameters) with a small number of experiments.

The various topics associated with Taguchi's approach to robust design, namely :

(i) Design of Experiments,

(ii) Orthogonal Arrays,

(iii) Signal-to-noise Ratio and

(iv) Parameter design and Tolerance design

will be discussed in the following section.

(3) DESIGN OF EXPERIMENTS

The term'*experiment*" is defined as the systematic procedure carried out under controlled conditions in order to discover an unknown effect, to test or establish a hypothesis or to illustrate a known effect. When analyzing a process experiments are often used to evaluate which process inputs have a significant impact, on the process output, and what the target level of those inputs should be to achieve a desired result (output). Experiments can be designed in many different ways to collect this information.

Design of Experiments (DOE) is also referred to as ***"Designed Experiments"*** or ***"Experimental design"***- all of the terms have the same meaning. The design of experiments is a series of techniques which involve the identification and control for parameters which have a potential impact on the performance and reliability of a product design and/or the output of a process, with the objective of optimizing product design, process design and process operation, and limiting the influence of noise factors. The methodology is used when we need to analyse the significance of effects on system outputs of different values of design parameters. The objective is to optimize the values of these design parameters to make the performance of the system immune to variation. The concept can be applied to the design of new products and processes or to the redesign of existing products and processes. **The purpose of using "design of experiments" approach is to:**

(i) Optimise product design, process design and process operation,

(ii) Achieve minimum variation of best system performance,

(iii) Achieve reproducibility of best system performance in manufacture and use,

(iv) Improve the productivity of design engineering activity,

(v) Evaluate the statistical significance of the effect of any controlling factor in the outputs,

(vi) Reduce costs.

Design of experiments technique in particular for process improvement involves the identification and control of those parameters or variables (termed **"factors"**) which have a potential influence on the output of process, choosing two or more values (termed **"levels"**) of these variables and running the process at these levels. Each combination of factors and levels, or experimental run is known as a **"trial"**. The basic idea is to conduct a small number of experiments with different parameter values and analyse their effect on a defined output.(for example plating thickness in electroplating process) . On the basis of the analysis a prediction of system performance can be made.

Components of Experimental Design

There are three aspects of a process that are analysed by a designed experiment :

(i) **Factors** or inputs to the process. Factors can be classified as controllable or uncontrollable variables. For example in a cake baking process, the controllable factors are the ingredients for the cake and oven that cake is baked in. There could be other factors such as the mixing method or tools, the sequence of mixing or even the people involved in the cake baking process. People are generally considered as a ***"Noise Factor"***- an uncontrollable variable which causes variability under normal conditions, but we can control it during

the experiment. Potential factors can be categorized using the Fish Bone Chart (Cause and Effect Diagram)

(ii) **Levels** or settings of each factor. Examples include the oven temperature setting and the quantity of sugar, flour and eggs used to prepare the cake,

(iii) **Response** or output of the experiment. In the case of cake baking, the taste, consistency and appearance of the cake are measurable outcomes potentially influenced by the factors and their respective levels. Experiments often desire to avoid optimizing the process for one response at the expense of another. For this reason, important outcomes are measured and analysed to determine the factors and their settings that will provide the best overall outcome for the critical-to-quality (CTQ) characteristics-both measurable variables and assessable attributes.

Purpose of Designed Experiments

Designed experiments have many uses in improving processes and products including:

(i)* Comparing alternatives :** In the case of cake-baking example, we might want to compare the results from two different types of flour. If it is found that the flour from different vendors was not significant, we could select the lowest-cost vendor. If flour were significant, then we would select the best quality flour. The experiment should allow us to make an informed decision that evaluates both quality and cost. Identifying the ***significant inputs (Factors) affecting an output (Response)-separating the vital few from the trivial many.

Achieving an Optimal Process Output: (Response): "What are the necessary factors, and what are the levels of those factors, to achieve the exact taste and consistency of the cake?"

Reducing Variability: "Can the recipe be changed so it is more likely to always come out the same?"

Minimising, Maximising or Targeting an Output (Response):

"How can the cake be made as moist as possible without disintegrating?, improving process or product.

Robustness: Fitness for use under varying conditions "Can the factors and their levels (recipe) be modified so the cake will come out nearly the some no matter what type of oven is used?"

***(ii)* Balancing Trade-off :** When there are multiple "Critical to Quality Characteristics" (CTQs) that require optimization. "How do your produce the best tasting cake with the simplest recipe (least number of ingredients) and shortest baking time?"

Experimental Design Process

The flowchart below illustrates the experimental design process (Refer *Exhibit 14.2*).

Guidelines for Experimental Designs

1. The design of an experiment addresses the questions outlined above stipulating the following: *(i)* the ***factors*** to be tested , *(ii)* the ***levels*** of those factors, *(iii)* the ***structure*** and ***layout*** of experimental runs or conditions.
2. A well designed experiment is as ***simple*** as possible-obtaining the required information in the ***cost-effective*** and ***reproducible*** manner,
3. When designing an experiment, pay particular attention to four potential traps that can create experimental difficulties:

Exhibit 14.2 : Experimental Design Process

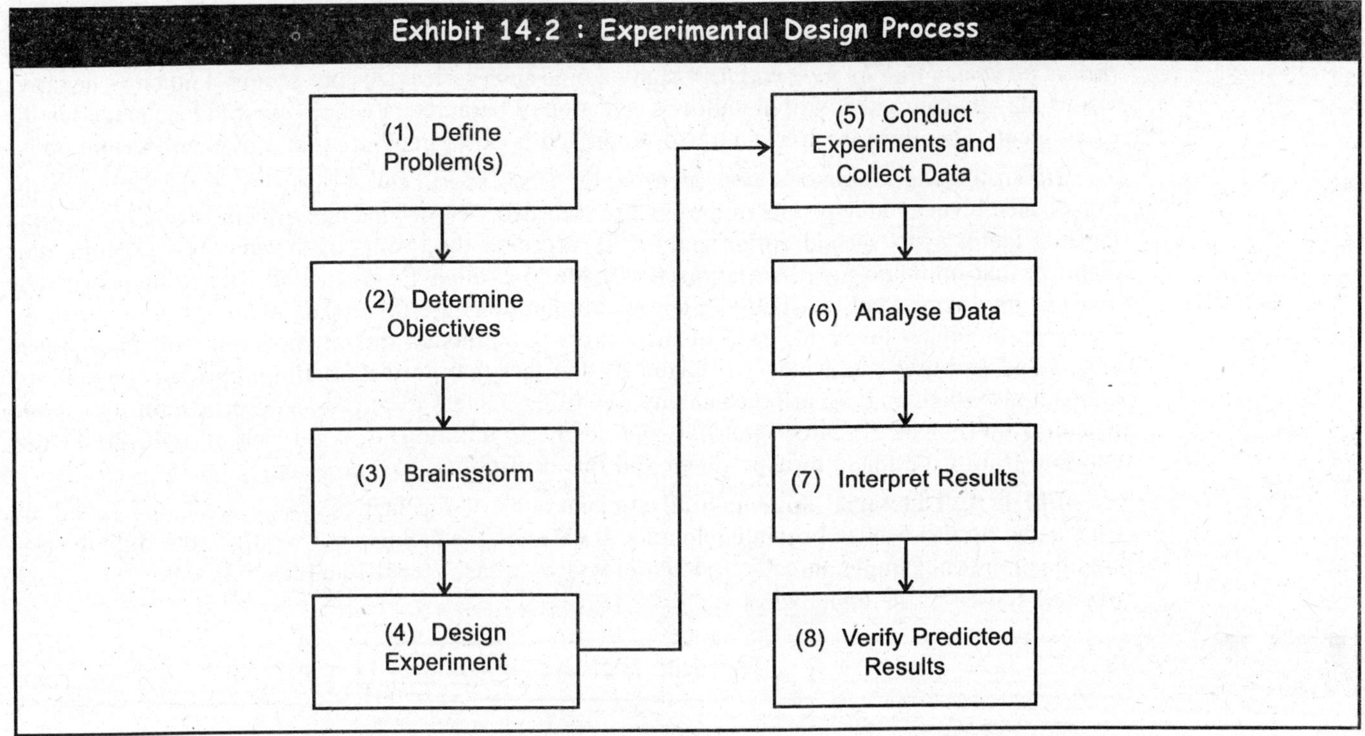

(i) In addition to measurement error, other sources of error or unexplained variation can affect results. Error is not mistake. Error refers to all unexplained variation that is either within an experiment run and associated with level settings changing. Properly designed experiments can identify and quantify the sources of error.

(ii) Uncontrollable factors that induce variations under normal operating conditions are referred to as **"Noise Factors"**. These factors, such as multiple machines, multiple shifts, raw materials, humidity etc., can be built into the experiment so that their variation does not get lumped into the unexplained or experiment error. A key strength of Designed Experiments is the ability to determine factors and settings that minimize the effects of the uncontrollable factors.

(iii) Correlation can often be confused with causation. Two factors that vary together may be highly correlated without one causing the other-they may both be caused by a third factor. Therefore, it is important to factor-in operational knowledge when designing an experiment. Brainstorming exercises and Fishbone [Cause and Effect Diagram] are both excellent techniques available to capture this operational knowledge during the design phase of the experiment. The key is to involve the people who live with the process on a daily basis.

(iv) The combined effect or interactions between factors demand careful thought prior to conducting the experiment. Factors may generate non-linear effects that are not additive; but these can only be studied with more complex experiments that involve more than two level settings. Two levels are defined as linear, three levels are defined as quadratic, four levels are defined as cubic and so on.

Methods of Experimention

There are a number of methods of experimentation : *(i)* the trial-and-error method, *(ii)* the step-by-step method of changing one factor at a time, *(iii)* the full factorial method and *(iv)* the fractional factorial method.

(i) In the **trial-and-error approach,** unsystematic changes of factor, levels using the experience of the experimenter form the guiding principle. The experimenter performs a series of experiments

each of which gives some understanding. This requires making measurements after every experiment so that analysis of observed data will allow him to decide what to do next.- ***"which parameters should be varied and by how much?"*** Many a time such series does not progress much as negative results may discourage or will not allow a selection of parameters which ought to be changed in the experiment. Therefore the trial-and-error approach is not a good approach in experimentation.

(ii) In the ***one-factor-at-a time method,*** the first experiment is run with all the factors at the first chosen level and the results of the run are recorded. The second experiment is run by changing the first factor to its second option and again recording the results of the run. Then keeping this factor at that optimum level, variations are made to another factor to find its optimum, with the other factors being kept constant and so on. Assumptions are then made about the preference for the lower or higher levels for each of the factors. Eventhough this method is simple and easy to understand and use, it is widely criticized for the fact that no information is provided about any interactions which may occur between any two of the factors tested and so reproducibility is poor. It is also inefficient, resource-intensive and costly. In addition, it is not easy to hold the factors constant from experiment to experiment and this in itself creates variation.

(iii) In **full factorial approach** all combinations of the factors which are being tested are considered. In this way all possible interactions between the factors are investigated to find the best combination for example, three factors with two levels each (level 1 and level 2) would need $2^3 = 8$ trials as shown in the table below:

Table 14.1 : The full factorial method

Trial number	Control factors.		
	A	B	C
1	→ 1	1	1
2	→ 1	1	2
3	→ 1	2	1
4	→ 1	2	2
5	→ 2	1	1
6	→ 2	1	2
7	→ 2	2	1
8	→ 2	2	2

This method may be feasible for a small number of factors and when experimentation is easy, but becomes complicated as the factors and levels increase, for example with say seven factors at two levels, the minimum number of trials would be 2^7 (ie. 128) . The time and cost associated with running such a large number of experiments are usually considered as prohibitive and unrealistic in industrial situations

(iv) The **fractional factorial method** overcomes the disadvantage of the number of trials necessary in a full factorial design. Fractional factorial designs are used where the chosen fraction of the full design gives an even and balanced spread throughout all the factors being studied. For example, typically, a quarter of the 128 experiments required for seven factors at two levels would involve just 32 experiments. This method uses **orthogonal arrays** with a limited number of runs as a subset of the full factorial layout. This method of experimentation involves changing several factors at the same time in a systematic way so as to ensure the reliable and independent study of the main factors and interaction effects.

The technique of orthogonal arrays enables the size of the experiment to be reduced to a practicable level by carrying out only a fraction of the total number of combination of factors

(4) ORTHOGONAL ARRAYS

Orthogonal Arrays (OA) **are** a simplified method of putting together an experiment. The original development of the concept was by Sir A.R.Fisher of England in the 1930s. Taguchi added three Orthogonal Arrays to the list in 1956 and the National Institute of Science and Technology of the US added three

***(i)* Fisher Orthogonal Array:** Fisher took the lead on the problem of experimental size in fractional factorial designs. His method of experimentation was to change several factors at the same time in a systematic way so as to ensure the reliable and independent study of the main factors and interaction effects. He constructed orthogonal arrays with a limited number of runs as a subset of the full factorial layout. The subsets are balanced in such a way that an even number of each level of each factor is tested during the running of the experiment (ie the array is balanced between columns rather than between trials). The technique of orthogonal arrays enables the size of the experiment to be reduced to a practicable level of carrying out a fraction of the total number of combination of factors. However., in doing this some interaction information will be sacrificed. It is therefore important to use the technical knowledge of those involved in the experiment to ensure that this loss of information is relatively insignificant. A typical Fisher Array is shown in *Table 9.2* below:

It can be observed that in the array the ***coloumns*** represent the ***independent variables or factors*** to be studied and tested at one of two levels and the ***rows*** represent the ***tests*** or ***experiments*** to be performed. In an experiment which has eight experimental runs (*i.e.*, $L_{8)}$) , the first option or level of factor A is tested four times and the second option or level of factor A is also tested four times. In addition to this, during the experimental run, the array tests all the combinations of options or levels of any two factors. Thus A1 is tested against both B1and B2 as well as A2, similarly testing B1 and B2. The other properly that orthogonal arrays have, due to their full factorial heritage and balance is the ability to study the effects of interactions between factors. The number of interactions that can be studied is dependent on the size of the array.

Table 14.2 : A typical Fisher Array

Runs (N)	Factors (P)						
	A	B	C	D	E	F	G
1	1	1	1	1	1	1	1
2	1	1	1	2	2	2	2
3	1	2	2	1	1	2	2
4	1	2	2	2	2	1	1
5	2	1	2	1	2	1	2
6	2	1	2	2	1	2	1
7	2	2	1	1	2	2	1
8	2	2	1	2	1	1	2

The simple analysis of an orthogonal array is done by averaging the responses that are applicable to the level of each factor. Therefore in the Fisher Array shown above, factor A at level 1 is given by averaging the results obtained from running experiment numbers 1 to 4 and factor A at level Z by averaging the results obtained from running experiments numbers 5 to 8. The difference between level 1 and level 2 of each factor is an indication of the significance of that factor in influencing the response measured. Generally the larger the difference the greater the significance.

Analysis of the orthogonal array enables the strength of each level of each factor to be measured, and their relative significance in influencing the designated output to be assessed. Analysis of variance is used to estimate the significance that any factor has in influencing the measured response in relation to the "error" in the experimental system.

(ii)* Taguchi's Orthogonal Array:** The arrays suggested by Taguchi (1986) gave economies of scale and time in the cost of experimentation. They are also practiced to use in a team environment where maximum use is made of technical knowledge which exists within the team for details such as: *(i)* the choice of factors, *(ii)* the setting of the levels, *(iii)* whether to study an interaction between factors and *(iv)* the choice of responses of the experimental runs. There are a small number of orthogonal arrays or experimental designs that constitute a fundamental set of arrays, sometimes referred to as the ***"cook book".

In the orthogonal array shown in *Table 14.3* the 8 in the designation OA8 represents the number of rows, which is also the number of treatment conditions (TC) and the degrees of freedom.

Across the top of the orthogonal array is the maximum number of factors that can be used, which in this case is seven. The levels are designated by 1 and 2. If more levels occur in the array, then 3, 4, and so forth are used.

The orthogonal property of the Orthogonal Array is not compromised by changing the rows or the columns. Taguchi changed the rows from a traditional design so the TC 1 was composed of all level 1s and if the team desired, could thereby represent the existing conditions. Also the columns are switched so that the least amount of change occurs in the columns on the left. This arrangement can provide the team with the capability to assign factors with long set up times to those columns.

Table 14.3 : Orthogonal Array (OA8)

TC	1	2	3	4	5	6	7
1	1	1	1	1	1	1	1
2	1	1	1	2	2	2	2
3	1	2	2	1	1	2	2
4	1	2	2	2	2	1	1
5	2	1	2	1	2	1	2
6	2	1	2	2	1	2	1
7	2	2	1	1	2	2	1
8	2	2	1	2	1	1	2

To determine the appropriate orthogonal array the following procedure is used:

Step 1: Determine the number of factors and their levels,

Step 2: Determine the degree of freedom,

Step 3: Select the orthogonal array

Step 4: Consider any interactions.

These steps are discussed below:

Step 1: The project team completes the first step.

Step 2: Degrees of freedom: The number of degrees of freedom is a very important value because it determines the minimum number of treatment conditions. It is equal to the sum of

(Number of levels – 1) for each factor. (Number of levels – 1) (number of levels – 1) for each interaction

One for the average.

Example: Given four two levels factors A,B,C,D and two suspected interactions, BC and CD determine the degrees of freedom. What is the answer if the factors are three level?

Solution:

Degrees of freedom df = 4(2 – 1) + 2(2 – 1)(2 – 1) + 1 = 7 (for 2 level factors)

Degrees of freedom df = 4(3 – 1) + 2(3 – 1)(3 – 1) + 1 = 17 (for 3 level factors)

At least seven treatment conditions are needed for the two-level and 17 conditions are needed for the three-level.

The maximum degrees of freedom is equal to

$df = l^f$ where l = number of levels

f = number of factors

For the example problem with two levels,

$df = 2^4 = 16$

Step 3: Selecting the Orthogonal Array (OA): Once the degrees of freedom are known, the next step the selection of the Orthogonal Array becomes easy. The number of treatment conditions is equal to the number of rows in the OA and must be equal to or greater than the degrees of freedom.

To define an Orthogonal Array, one must identify

(i) Number of factors to be studied ,

(ii) Level for each factor,

(iii) The specific 2-factor interactions to be estimated and

(iv) The special difficulties that would be encountered in running the experiment

There are options for creating Taguchi arrays for the design of experiments depending on how many times we choose to test each level of each parameter. For example, consider an experiment with 3 parameters and 3 levels of each parameter (P= 3 and L=3).

Two Taguchi's arrays for this case are:

(i) a 6-run array for testing each level of each parameter ***twice.***

(ii) a 9-tun array for testing each level of each parameter ***three times.***

The 9-run array is more desirable (if cost and time permit) because for each level of any one parameter, ***all three levels of other parameters are tested.*** Each array here costs less to run than a full-factorial analysis, since the number of required runs for a full factorial analysis is $N = L^P = 3^3 = 27$.

The Taguchi array is called an ***orthogonal array*** (or full orthogonal array) when ***for each level of a particular parameters all levels of each of the (P-1) other parameters are tested at least once.***

Sometimes as 'P" increases, it is necessary to test all levels of all parameters (or factors) more than once in order to meet the rules for Taguchi arrays. In such cases there should be no unnecessary repeats.

For example consider the P = 4, L = 3 case (Ref *Table 14.4* below) when parameter 'a' is at level 1, parameter 'b' is tested at level 1, 2 and 3 (all levels).

Similarly, parameters' 'c' and 'd' are tested at levels 1, 2 and 3 (all L levels). The same thing holds when parameter 'a' is at level 2 or level3. The same thing holds for all of the parameters. Hence, we observe that the definition of all full orthogonal array holds for this case-for each level of a particular parameter, all L levels of each of the (P-1) other parameters are tested at least on a-Only once in this particular case. The required number of runs is therefore 3(L = 3 levels) X 3 (each level of each parameter tested 3 times) = 9 required runs for his full orthogonal array.

Table 14.4

P → / L ↓	2				3					4						5						
	P=2, L=2				P=3, L=2					P=4, L=2						P=5 , L=2						
	Run	a	b	x	Run	a	b	c	x	Run	a	b	c	d	x	Run	a	b	c	d	e	x
2	1	1	1	x_1	1	1	1	1	x_1	1	1	1	1	1	x_1	1	1	1	1	1	1	x_1
	2	1	2	x_2	2	1	2	2	x_2	2	1	1	1	2	x_2	2	1	1	1	2	2	x_2
	3	2	1	x_3	3	2	1	2	x_3	3	1	2	2	1	x_3	3	1	2	2	1	1	x_3
	4	2	2	x_4	4	2	2	1	x_4	4	1	2	2	2	x_4	4	1	2	2	2	2	x_4
										5	2	1	2	1	x_5	5	2	1	2	1	2	x_5
										6	2	1	2	2	x_6	6	2	1	2	2	1	x_6
										7	2	2	1	1	x_7	7	2	2	1	1	2	x_7
										8	2	2	1	2	x_8	8	2	2	1	2	1	x_8

Taguchi's Robust Design

Dr. Taguchi of Japan developed a method based on "**Orthogonal Arrays**" experiment which gives much reduced "variance" for the experiment with optimum setting of control parameters. Orthogonal Arrays (OA) provide a set of well balanced (minimum) experiments and signal-to-Naise ratios (S/N) which are logarithmic functions of desired output, serve as objective functions for optimisation, help in data analysis and prediction of optimum results.

Taguchi's methods cover a variety of practise developed by Taguchi for statistically determining required quantitative features of design that make it robust against disturbances, variations and uncertainties, with the objective of reducing loss to society.

Taguchi: methods treat optimisation problems in two categories:

1. Static Problems : Generally a process has several control factors which directly decide the target or designed value of the output. The optimisation then involves determining the best control factor levels so that the output is at a target value. Such a problem is called as a ***"Static problem"***.

This is best explained using a 'P' diagram which is shown below (Refer *Exhibit 14.3*) ('P' stands for Product or Process). Noise is shown to be present in the process but should have no effect on the output. This is the primary aim of the Taguchi experiment to minimise variations in output even though noise is present in the process. The process is them said to have become ROBUST.

Exhibit 14.3 : 'P' Diagram for Static Problems

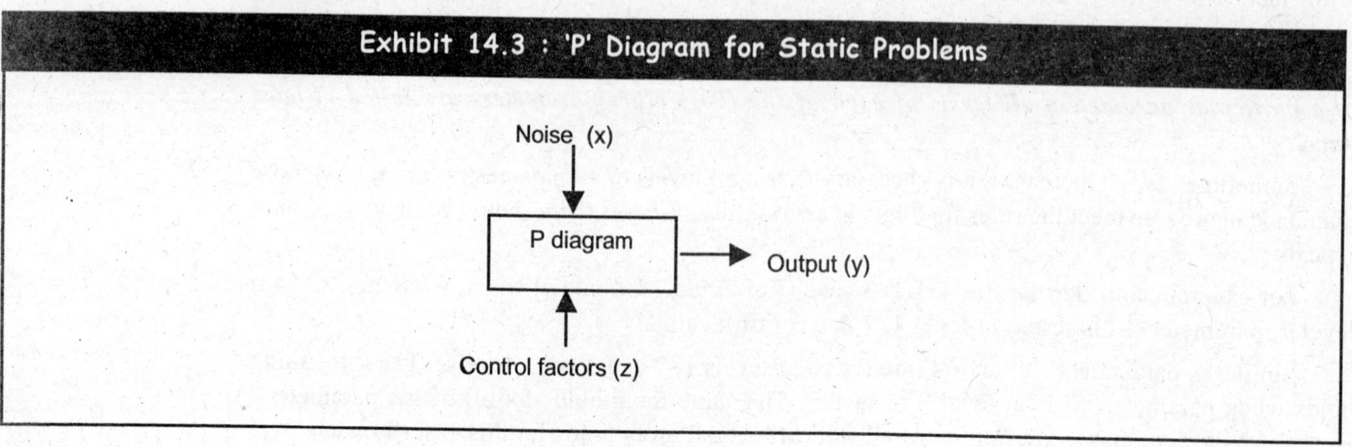

2. Dynamic Problem : If the product to be optimised has a signal input that directly decides the output, the optimisation involves determining the best control factor levels so that the "input signal / output" ratio is closest to the desired relationship. Such a problem is called as a ***"dynamic problem"***.

This is best explained by the 'P' diagram which is shown below (Ref *Exhibit 14.4*)

Again, the primary aim of the Taguchi experiments to minimise variations in output even though noise is present in the process is achieved by getting improved linearity in the input / output relationship.

Exhibit 14.4 : P-diagram for Dynamic Problems

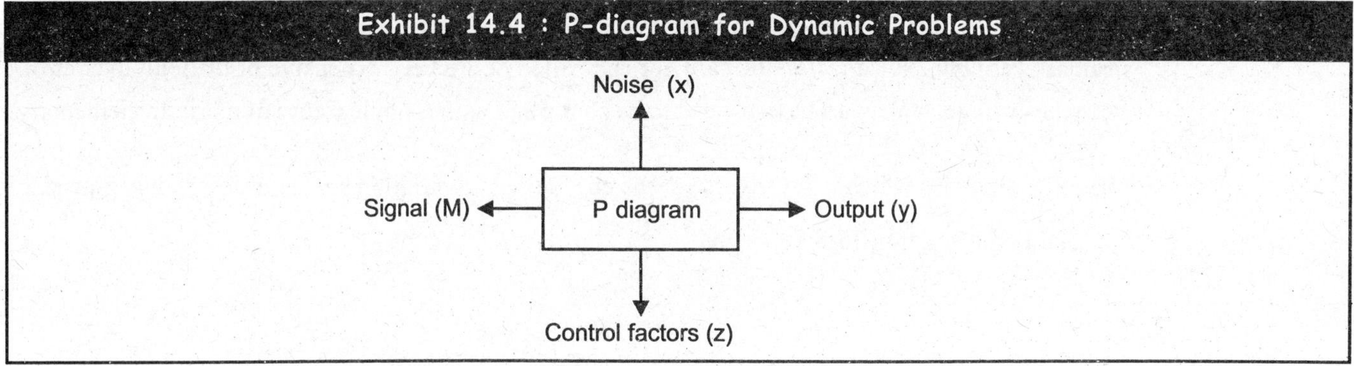

(5) SIGNAL-TO-NOISE RATIO (S/N RATIO)

Quality engineering is in essence the evaluation of functionality and the concept of a measure known as the signal-to-noise ratio (S/N ratio) is employed for this purpose. This concept is generalised by Taguchi and is commonly used for the evaluation of measurement systems as well as for the function of products and processes.

The S/N ratio can be viewed as the ratio of sensitivity to variability. The larger the SN ratio, the better the quality of a product or process. The SN ratio highlights the interactions between the signal factor, the control factor and the noise factors and when used along with orthogonal arrays enable us to avoid undesirable interactions between control factors.

Signal, Noise and Control Factors

The products of ideal quality should always respond in exactly the same manner to the signals provided by the user. For example, when we turn the key in the ignition of our car, we expect that the starter motor turns and the engine starts. In the ideal-quality car the starting process would always proceed in exactly the same manner-for example, after three turns of the starter motor the engine comes to life. If in response to the same signal (turning the ignition key) there is random variability in this process, then we have less than ideal quality. For example, due to such uncontrollable factors such as extreme cold, humidity, engine wear etc. the engine may sometimes start after tuning over 20 times and finally not start at all. We want to minimise this variability in the product's response to noise factors while maximising the variability in response to signal factors.

Noise factors are those that are not under the control of the operator of a product. In the example of car, those factors (noise) include temperature charges, different qualities of gasoline, engine wear etc.

Signal factors are those factors that are set or controlled by the operator of the product to make use of its intended functions (turning the ignition key to start the car).

Finally, the goal of our quality improvement effort is to find the best settings of factors under our control that are involved in the production process, in order to maximise S/N ratio, thus the factors in the experiment represent control factors.

Types of S/N Ratios: Quality can be quantified in terms of the respective product's response to noise factors and signal factors. The ideal product will only respond to the operators' signal and will be unaffected by random noise factors. (for example, weather, temperature, humidity etc.). Therefore the goal of our quality improvement effort can be stated as attempting to maximise the signal –to-noise (S/N) ratio for the respective product.

In general, S/N ratio is defined by the following equation:

$$\text{S/N ratio} = \frac{\text{Power of signal}}{\text{Power of noise}} = \frac{(\text{sensitivity})^2}{(\text{variability})^2}$$

Signal factors $(\bar{y})$ are set by the designer or operator to obtain the intended value of the response variable. Noise factors (s^2) are not controlled or are very expensive or difficult to control. Both the average, $\bar{y}$ and variance, s^2 need to be controlled with a single figure of merit. In elementary form S/N ratio $= \frac{\bar{y}}{s}$ which is the inverse of the coefficient of variation and a unitless value. Squaring and taking the log transformation gives:

$$S/N_N = \log_{10}\left[\frac{(\bar{y})^2}{s^2}\right]$$

There are many different S/N ratios. The basic once are:

(i) Nominal-the-Best
(ii) Target-the-Best
(iii) Smaller-the-Best
(iv) Larger-the-Best.

These ratios are discussed below:

(i) Nominal-the-Best: Here we have a fixed signal value (nominal value) and the variance around this value can be considered the result of noise factors. It is used wherever there is a nominal or target value and a variation about the value such as dimensions, voltage, weight etc. The target (T) is finite but not zero. For robust design the S/N ratio should be maximised. The nominal-the-best S/N value is a maximum when the average is large and the variance is small. The S/N ratio is given by the formula:

$$S/N_N = \log_{10}\left[\frac{(\bar{y})^2}{s^2}\right]$$

Adjusting for small sample sizes and changing from Bels to decibels by multiplying by ten, we have

$$S/N_N = 10\log_{10}\left[\frac{(\bar{y})^2}{s^2} - \frac{1}{n}\right]$$

which is the nominal-the-best S/N_N ratio [$\bar{y}$ = average, s = standard deviation, n = sample size (number of observations) and s^2 = variance]

(ii) Target-the-Best: When the average is off-target on the high side, the S/N_N value can give more favourable information. When off-target is on the low side, the value can give less favourable information; Taguchi's approach is to reduce variation and then bring the average on target. Another S/N_N ratio called the target-the-best eliminates these problems provided the target is known.

(iii) Smaller-the-Better: The S/N_N ratio for smaller-the-better is used for solutions where the target value (T) is zero, such as computer response time, automotive emissions, or corrosion.

The equation is:

$$S/N_N = -10 \log_{10}[MSD]$$

$$= -10 \log_{10}\left[\frac{(\Sigma y^2)}{n}\right]$$

The negative sign is used to ensure that the largest value gives the optimum value for the response, variable and therefore robust design. Mean standard deviation (MSD) is given to show the relationship to the loss function.

(iv) Larger-the-Better: This ratio is used where the largest value is desired such as weld strength, gasoline mileage or yield. From a mathematical view point, the target value is zero. Like the loss function, it is the reciprocal of smaller-the-better.

The equation is

$$S/N_L = -10 \log_{10}[MSD] = -10 \log_{10}\left[\Sigma\left(\frac{1}{y^2}\right)\Big/ n\right]$$

(6) TAGUCHI DESIGNS

Genichi Taguchi, a Japanese engineer proposed several approaches to experimental designs that are sometimes called "Taguchi Methods". These methods use two, three and mixed-level factorial designs.

Taguchi refers to experimental designs as ***"off-line quality control"*** because it is a method of ensuring good performance in the design stage of products or processes. Some experimental design, however, such as when used in evolutionary operation, can be used on-line while the process is running.

"Of-line quality control" means optimising production process and product parameters in such a way as to minimise item-to-item variation in the product and its performance. Clearly this focuses attention on the design process.

Taguchi promoted three distinct stages of designing in quality. These are:

1. System design : The basic configuration of the system is developed. This involves the selection of parts and materials and the use of feasibility studies and prototyping. In systems design technical knowledge and scientific skills are of significance. The systems design is aimed at applying scientific and engineering principles to the development of and engineering principles to the development of functional design. It has two elements: (a) ***product design*** and (b) ***process design***.

2. Parameter design : The aim here is to make a product or process less variable (more robust) in the face of variation over which we have little or no control. The numerical values for the system variables (product and process parameters which are called factors) are chosen so that the system performs well: no matter what disturbances or noises (i.e. uncontrollable variations) are encountered by it (i.e. it is robust). The objective is to identify optimum levels for those control factors so that the product and / or process is least sensitive to the effect of charges of noise factors. The experimentation pinpoints this combination of product/process parameter levels. The emphasis in parameter design is on using low cost materials and processes in the production of the system. It is the key stage of designing in quality.

The parameter design focuses at establishing process and machine settings that minimise performance variation. A distinction is made at this stage between controllable and uncontrollable factors (parameters and noise). The specification criterion is for optimisation and is usually expressed as monetary loss arising from variation.

3. Tolerance design: If the system is not satisfactory, tolerance design is then used to improve performance by tightening the tolerance. Tolerance design deals with the problem of how, and when to specify tightened tolerances of a product or a process so that quality and performance / productivity are enhanced. Every product or process has a large number of components. The critical components have to be targeted when tolerances have to be tightened.

It is generally believed that the quality and performance of any item can be easily improved by merely tightening up on some or all of its tolerance requirements. For example, if the old version of an item specified machining to ±1 micron, we naturally believe that we can obtain better performance by specifying machining to ±0.5 micron. This can become expensive however, and is often not a guarantee of much better performance. Tight-Tolerance level items involve high initial and maintenance costs to realise that tolerance design therefore the selection of critical tolerances and the specification of those critical tolerances is not a task to be undertaken without carful thought. In fact, it is recommended that only after extensive parameter design studies have been completed should tolerance design be performed as a last resort to improve quality and productivity. Tolerance design is aimed at minimising the total sum of product manufacturing and life time costs.

14.3 QUALITY FUNCTION DEPLOYMENT

Quality function deployment also known as the "house of quality" is a relationship matrix technique to systematically translate a customer's requirements/ wants into operational requirements.

Even when products are designed by cross-functional teams, translating customer requirements into detailed technical product specifications can be very difficult. Customer requirements are often vague and it is not unusual for some of them to conflict with each other. And since technical product specifications are expressed in a "different language" than are the needs of the customer, **"the *voice of the customer*"** is often lost. The end result is a product that does not fully meet customer needs.

The Japanese developed an approach called ***"quality function deployment"*** (QFD) to meet customer's requirements throughout the design process and also in the design of production systems. **Quality function deployment is a method by which cross-functional teams translate customer requirements into appropriate design requirements at each stage of the product development process.**

QFD is an excellent way for firms to capture the ***"voice of the customer"***. It ensures that the customer is the focus of all design activities and "dictates" all design trade-offs. QFD is a customer-driven planning process to guide the design, manufacturing and marketing of goods. It tries to eliminate the gap between what customers want in a new product and what the product must deliver.

Quality function deployment refers to both determining what will satisfy the customer and secondly, translating those customer desires into the target design. QFD is used early in the production process to determine ***what*** will satisfy the customer and also ***where*** to deploy quality efforts.

QFD originated as a formal concept at Kobe Shipyards of Mitsubishi Heavy Industries in 1972 and quickly spread to other Japanese industries, particularly the automobile industry. Companies that use QFD claim that design cycle time can be cut in half, engineering changes can be reduced by two-thirds and customer demands can be met better than ever before.

At the ***strategic level,*** QFD represents a challenge and the opportunity for the top management to break out of its traditional narrow focus on results which can only be measured after the fact, and to view the broader process of how results are obtained. At the ***tactical*** and ***operation levels,*** QFD departs from the traditional product planning in which product concepts are originated by design teams or research and development groups, tested and refined, produced and marketed. A considerable amount of wasted effort and time is spent redesigning products and production systems until customer needs are met. If customer needs can be identified properly in the first place, then such wasteful effort is eliminated. This is the principal focus of QFD. ***Exhibit 14.5*** **gives an overview of QFD.**

Exhibit 14.5 : QFD Overview

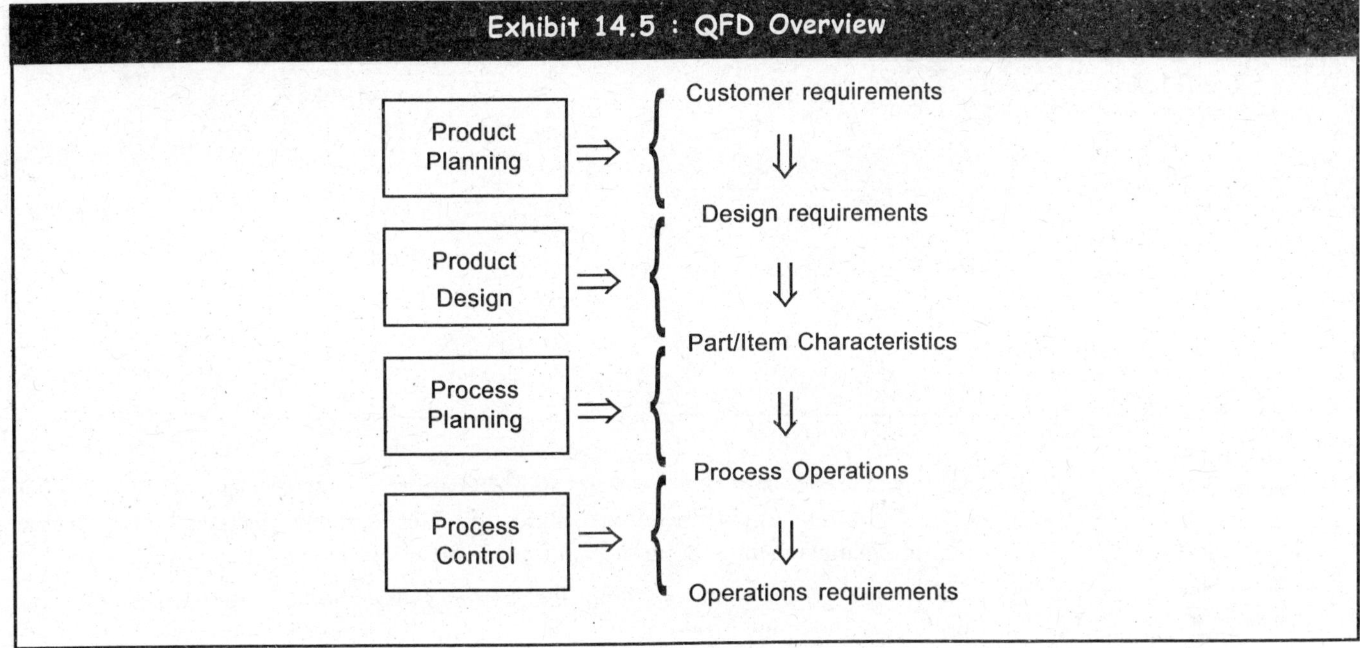

Benefits Attributed to QFD

(i) QFD process provides a structure to help managers to identify both ***expected quality*** and ***exciting quality*** and to focus process design and implementation specifically to meet these needs. ***Expected quality*** refers to statement of product traits that customers expect to find in a product. These traits usually represent order qualifiers or order losers. Customers may not appreciate them explicitly, but failure to meet these specifications cause customer dissatisfaction. In contrast, ***exciting quality*** refers to traits that customers do not expect. They do not notice lack of such traits, but special characteristics can excite them and induce them to choose one product over another. In general, excited quality enhances the ***value*** of a product, while expected quality maintains value.

(ii) QFD benefits companies through improved communication and teamwork between all constituencies in the production process, such as between marketing and design, between design and manufacturing and between purchasing and suppliers. Product objectives are better understood and interpreted during the production process.

(iii) Use of QFD determines the cause of customer dissatisfaction, making it a useful tool for competitive analysis of product quality by the top management.

(iv) It improves quality and productivity, reduces the lead time for product development, lower product costs and reduces changes after the design stage.

(v) It allows companies to simulate the effects of new design ideas and concepts.

(vi) QFD process helps to integrate a firm's TQM effort by unifying four major functional strategies: *(i)* marketing *(ii)* sales *(iii)* product design and *(iv)* operations management process.

The Quality Function Deployment Process

In its simplest form, QFD can be stated as four linked matrices. In many cases, these four matrices represent an important subset. **The four-step process of QFD generates four matrices which are shown in *Exhibit 14.6.***

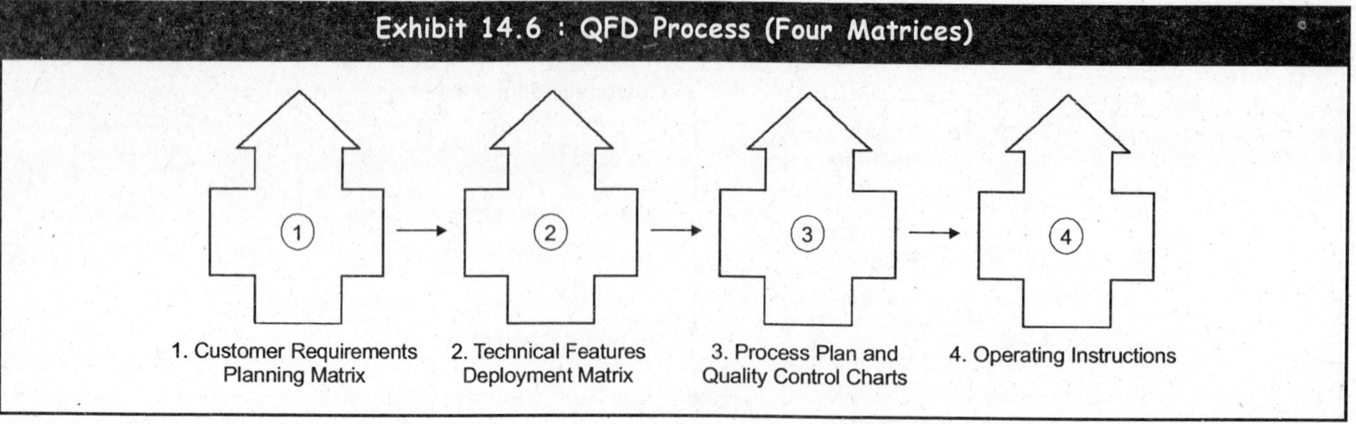

The four steps or matrices in QFD are:
(i) Customer requirements planning matrix
(ii) Technical features deployment matrix
(iii) Process plan and quality control charts and
(iv) Operating instructions.

In the first stage, the ***customer requirements planning matrix*** identifies customer requirements and translates these requirements into a set of technical product features. This stage joins together marketing, operation management and engineering to identify both expected and exciting quality.

In the second stage, QFD generates a ***technical features deployment matrix*** which translates the technical product features identified in the columns of the customer requirements matrix into design requirements for critical product components.

In the third stage, QFD translates the columns of the technical features deployment matrix into critical process and product parameters and appropriate process control limits through ***process plan and quality control charts.***

In the fourth and final stage, QFD generates matrices of operating instructions, that translate critical process and product parameters into specifications for operations to be performed by plant personnel. This step ensures that the activities of shop floor personnel contribute to the firm's efforts to meet the requirements set down in the process and product parameters. At each step in the process, QFD generates requirements (listed in the rows of the matrices) and translate these requirements into supporting actions to meet those requirements (listed in the columns of the matrices).

Because of its structure, QFD users often call the customer requirements planning matrix the ***House of quality (HoQ)***, a term coined by Mr. Sawada of Toyota Auto Body. Most firms view it as the most important of the four QFD matrices.

House of quality consists of a set of maxtrixes used to relate the voice of the customer to a product's echnical requirements, component requirements, process control plans and manufacturing operations.

House of Quality: The House of Quality relates customer-defined product traits to the technical product and process requirements needed to support and generate these features. Building the House of Quality consists of six basic steps:

(i) Identify customer requirements.
(ii) Identify supporting technical characteristics.
(iii) Relate the customer requirements to the supporting technical characteristics.
(iv) Conducting and evaluation of competing products.
(v) Evaluate technical requirements and develop targets and
(vi) Determine which technical requirements to deploy in the remainder of the production process.

Exhibit 14.7* illustrates the *"House of Quality".

The six steps mentioned earlier are described in detail in the following paragraphs.

Step 1: Identify customer requirements: The voice of the customer is the primary input to the QFD process. The most difficult step of the process is to capture the essence of the customer's comments. The customer's own words are vitally important in preventing misrepresentation by designers and engineers. Listening to customers can open the door to creative opportunities.

Exhibit 14.7 : The House of Quality

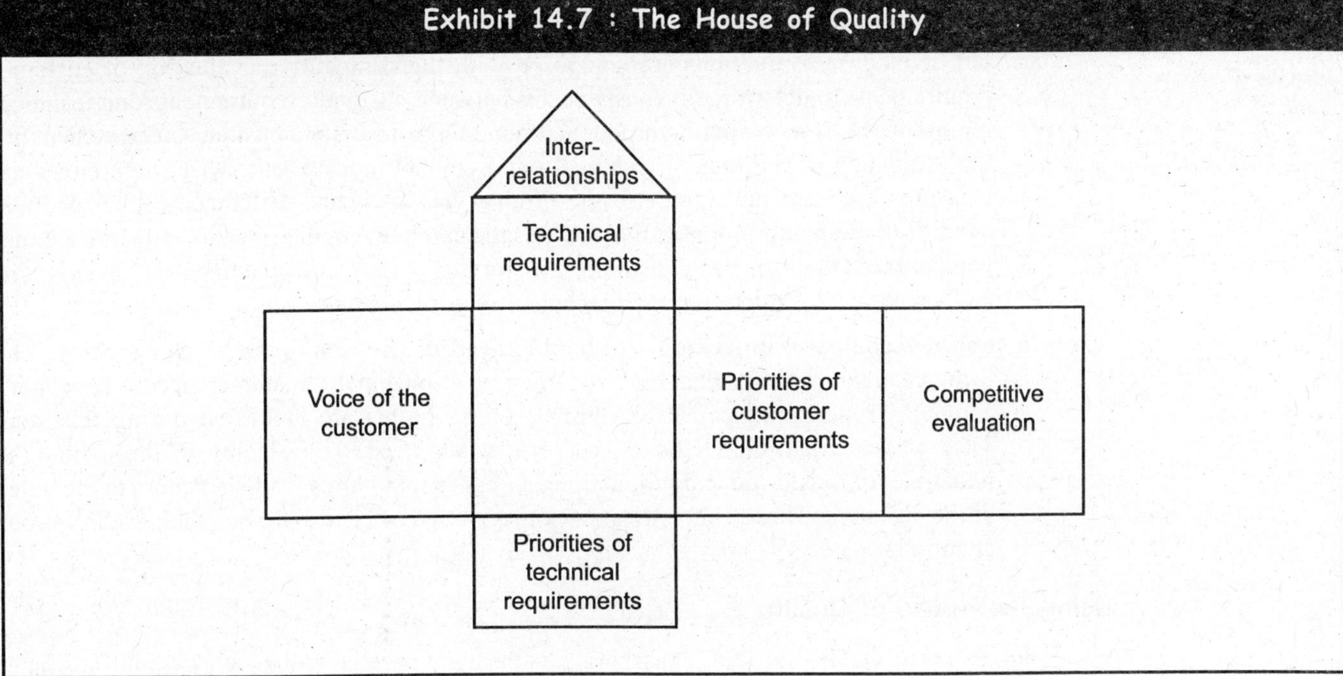

Step 2: Identify product requirements (technical) necessary to meet the customer's requirements: Product requirements are design characteristics that describe their requirements as expressed in the language of the designer and engineer. They must be measurable, since the output is controlled and compared to objective targets. Eventually, technical requirements are the ***"hows"*** by which the company will respond to the ***"whats"*** – customer requirements. The roof of the House of Quality shows the inter-relationships between any pair of technical requirements. Various symbols denote these relationships. *For example,* the symbol denote a very strong relationship, for a strong relationship and to denote a weak relationship. These relationships indicate answers to questions such as "How does one change of product attributes affect others?" and assessment of trade-offs between attributes.

Step 3: Develop a relationship matrix between the customer requirements and the technical requirements: Customer requirements are listed down left column, technical requirements are written across the top. In the matrix itself, symbols indicate the degree of relationship in a manner similar to that used in the roof of the House of Quality. The purpose of the relationship matrix is to show whether the final technical requirements (receives a low evaluation on all competitior's) adequately address customer requirements. This assessment is usually based on expert experience, customer responses or controlled experiments.

Step 4: Add market evaluation and key selling points: This step identifies importance ratings for each customer requirement and evaluates existing products for each of them. Customer importance ratings represent the areas of greatest interest and highest expectations as expressed by the customer. **Competitive evaluation** highlights the absolute strengths and weaknesses in competing products. By using this step, designers can discover opportunities for improvement. It also links QFD to a company's strategic vision and indicates priorities for the design process. *For example,* if a customer requirement receives a low evaluation on all competitor's products, then by focussing on this need a company can gain a competitive advantage. Such requirements become **key selling points** and the basis for formulating promotion strategies.

Step 5: Evaluate technical requirements of competitive products and develop targets: This step is usually accomplished through inhouse testing and then translated into measurable terms. Inhouse evaluations are composed with the competitive evaluation of customer requirements to determine inconsistencies between customer requirements and technical requirements. If a competing product is found to best satisfy a customer requirement but the evaluation of the related technical requirements indicate otherwise, then either the measures used are faulty or else the product has an image difference (either positive towards the competitor or negative towards the company product), which affects customer perceptions. On the basis of customer's importance ratings and existing product strengths and weaknesses, targets for each technical requirements are set.

Step 6: Select technical requirements to be deployed in the remainder of the process: The technical requirements that have a strong relationship to customer needs, have poor competitive performance, or are strong selling points are identified during this step. These characteristics have the highest priority and need to be "deployed" throughout the remainder of the design and production process to maintain a responsiveness to the voice of the customer. Those characteristics not identified as critical do not need such rigorous attention.

Using the House of Quality

The House of Quality provides marketing with an important tool to understand customer needs and gives top management strategic direction. However, it is only the first step in the QFD process. The voice of the customer must be carried throughout the production processes. **Three other houses of quality are used to deploy the voice of the customer to component part characteristics, process planning and production planning. *Exhibit 14.8* illustrates the four houses of quality.**

Exhibit 14.8 : The Four Houses of Quality

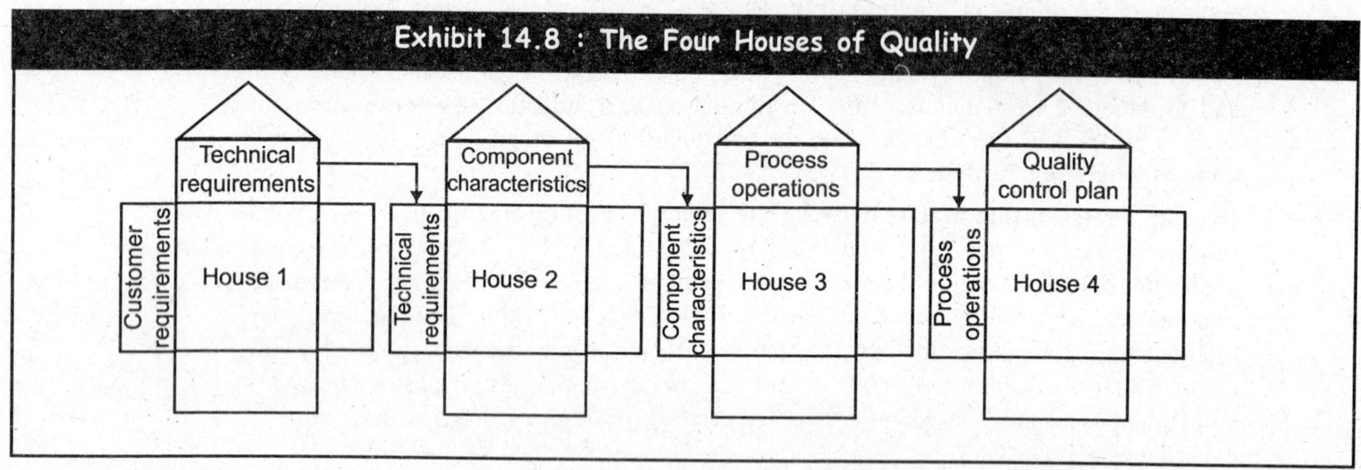

The four houses of quality in QFD are:
(i) Technical requirements
(ii) Component characteristics
(iii) Process operations and
(iv) Quality control plan.

The second house is similar to the first house but applies to subsystems and components. The technical requirements from the first house are related to detailed requirements of subsystems and components. At this stage, target values representing the best values for fit, function and appearances are determined.

Most of the QFD activities represented by the first two houses of quality are performed by product development and engineering functions. At the next stage (third house), the planning activities involve supervisors and production line operators. In the third house, the process plan relates the component characteristics to key process operations, the transition from planning to execution. If a product component parameter is critical and is created or affected during process, it becomes a control point. A **control point** indicates what needs to be monitored and inspected. It forms the basis for a quality control plan, delivering those critical characteristics that are crucial to achieving customer satisfaction.

Finally, the last house (fourth house) relates the control points to specific requirements for quality control. Most of the QFD literature and effort is devoted to meeting customer requirements with design characteristics and its importance is not to be underestimated. However, the sequence of houses is a very effective way of identifying, communicating and allocating resources throughout the system. The series of houses helps operation managers determine when to deploy quality resources. In this way, we meet customer requirements, produce quality products and win customer orders.

Illustration of how to construct a house of quality

Great Cameras Inc. first determined, through extensive market research, what the customer *wants*. **Those *wants* are shown on the left of the house of quality in *Exhibit 14.9*.** They are light weight, easy to use, reliable, easy to hold, steady and no double exposures.

Exhibit 14.9 : Phases of Use of QFD

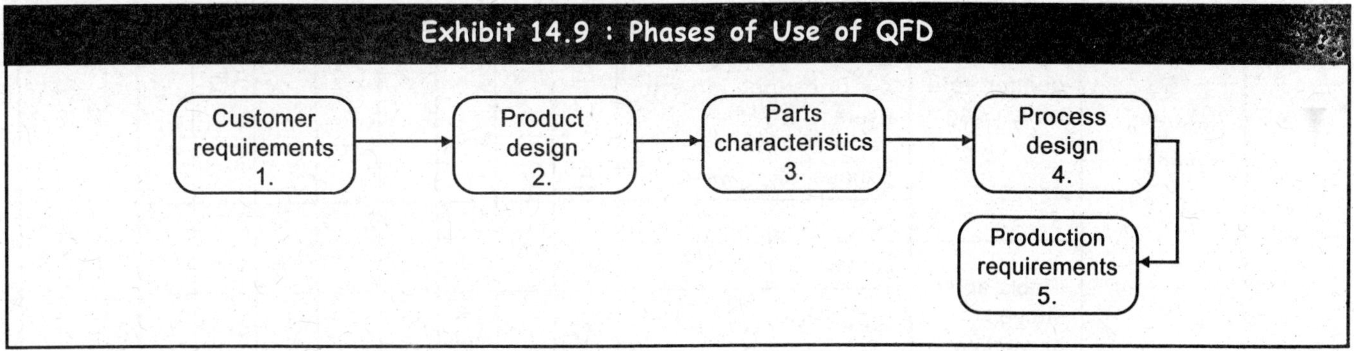

Second, the product development team determined ***how*** the organisation is going to translate those customer ***wants*** into product design and process attribute targets. These ***hows*** are entered across the top portion of the house of quality. These characteristics are low electricity requirements, aluminium components, auto focus, auto exposure, auto film advance and ergonomic design.

Third, the product team evaluated each of the customer ***wants*** against the ***hows***. In the relationship matrix of the house, the team evaluated how well its design will meet customer needs.

Fourth, in the **'roof' of the house**, the product development team developed the relationship between the attributes.

Fifth, the team developed importance ratings for its design attributes on the bottom row of the table. This was done by assigning values (5 for very strong relationship, 3 for strong/medium relationship and 1 for weak relationship) to each entry in the relationship matrix and then multiplying each of these values by customer importance ratings. These values in "our importance ratings" row provide a ranking of how to proceed with product and process design, with the highest values being the most critical to a successful product.

Sixth, the house of quality is used for the evaluation of competitors. How well do competitors satisfy and meet customer demands? The two columns on the right indicate how market research thinks competitors satisfy customer wants (good, fair or poor). So company A does a good job on "light weight", "easy to use" and "easy to hold steady", a fair job on "reliability" and a poor job on "no double exposures". Company B does a good job with "reliability" but poor on other attributes. ***Exhibit 14.9* illustrates the various phases of QFD and *Exhibit 14.10* describes the QFD table for a vacuum cleaner to be designed. *Exhibit 14.11* describes house of quality for a camera.**

Exhibit 14.10 : Quality Function Deployment Table for a Vacuum Cleaner to be Designed

Quality Function Deployment (QFD) is a technique, with highest pay-offs of ensuring that the ***voice of the customer*** (his needs and desires) is clearly heard and followed in developing and offering him a product or service. QFD enables the producer to respond not only more precisely to customer needs but also to do it faster than by traditional, informal customers. QFD begins with a statement of the customer's ***need, want, expectation*** **and** ***concern*** and then expresses these as quality characteristics of a "product" to meet these requirements.

Exhibit below shows a QFD table for a Vacuum Cleaner to be designed.

Customer's requirements \ Quality Characteristics			Motor		Load		Body			
1st level	2nd level	3rd level	Power	Location	Torque	Angle of the fans	Material	Strength	Thicknes	Density
Cleaning is easy	Feel comfortable while using	Less noisy	⊙		○		Δ		Δ	
		Less Vibration, exhaust air does not blow to users.	Δ				○		⊙	
		Exhaust air is weak	Δ							
	Stable and strong absorption	Exhaust air does not contain dust								
		Absorb all dust	⊙		○	○				
		Keep strong absorption even when dust bag is full	Δ							

Legend: ⊙ Strong relationship ○ Medium Relationship Δ Weak Relationship

14.4 POKA-YOKE(FAIL SAFING/FAIL PROOFING)

(***Poka-Yoke*** from ***Poka*** meaning inadvertent errors and ***Yokeru*** meaning to prevent). Defects in production may be due to omitted processing (or operations), processing errors, equipment set-up errors, missing parts/components, wrong parts/components and adjustment errors. A good process design prevents defects from occurring at all. This is called by **Japanese as zero defect program or Zero Quality Control (ZQC)** which means **zero defect quality control. ZQC consists of the following:**

(i) **Source inspection:** Checking for factors that cause errors, not the resulting defect.

(ii) **100 percent inspection:** The operator inspects his or her own work 100 percent, or inexpensive ***Poka-Yoke*** (mistake-proofing) devices inspect automatically for errors or defective operating conditions and

(iii) **Immediate action:** Stopping operations instantly when a mistake is made and not resuming operations until the error is rectified. Feedback is provided through successive checks, in which the next person in the process immediately feeds back information to the supplying operator to stop production and fix the error.

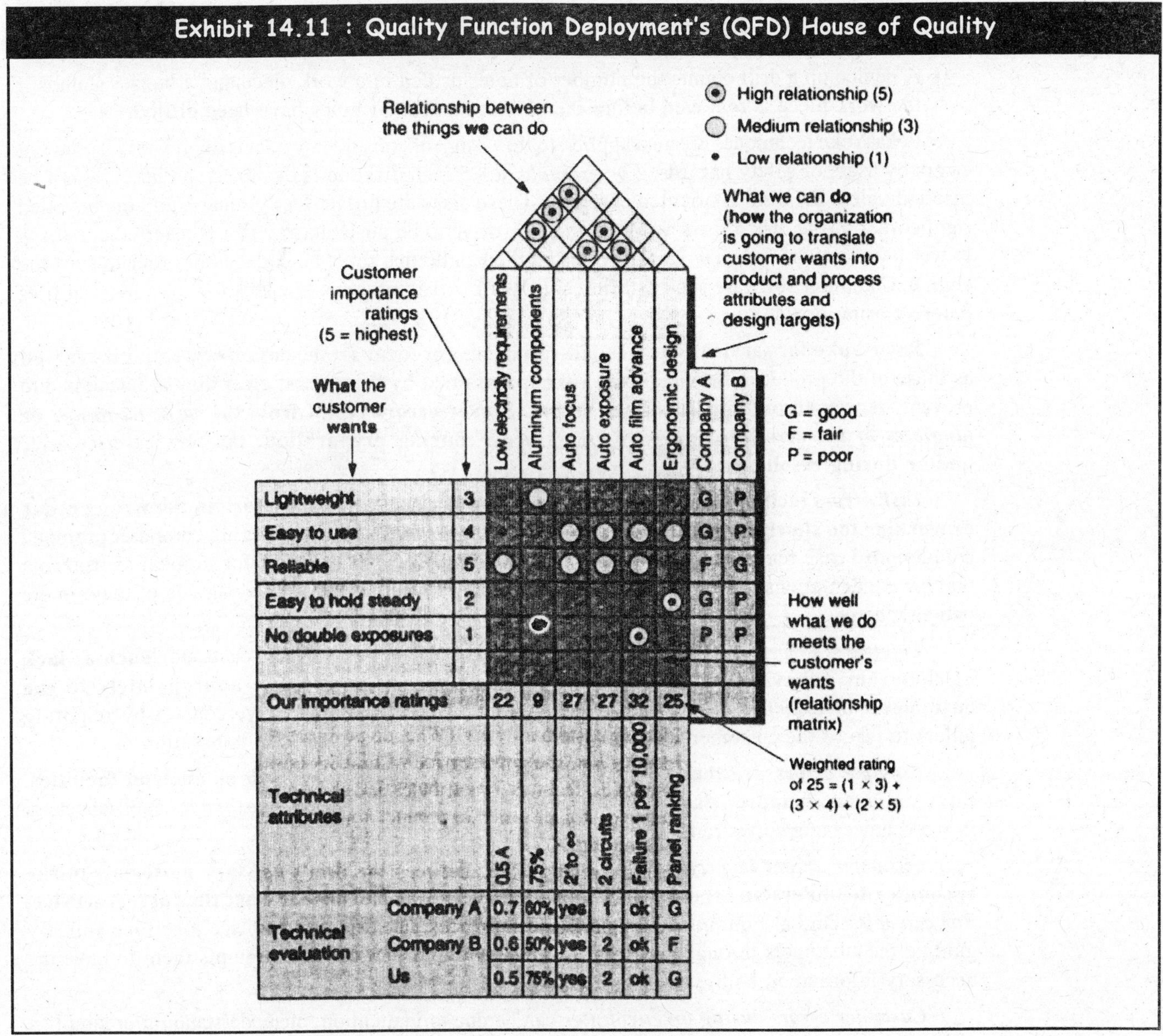

ZQC is based on the fact that human beings tend to make mistakes unknowingly or inadvertently. Mistakes can result from forgetfulness, misunderstanding, errors in identification, lack of skills, absentmindedness, lack of standards or equipment malfunctions. Blaming workers for errors not only discourages them and lowers morale, but does not solve the problem.

Poka-yoke or "mistake proofing" is a technique which is used to prevent errors being converted into defects.

Two main steps in Poka-yoke are:

(i) Preventing the occurrence of a defect

and

(ii) Detecting the defect.

Poka-Yoke **is an approach for fail safing or mistake-proofing processes using automatic devices or methods to avoid simple human error**. The Poka-Yoke concept was developed and refined by the late ***Shigeo Shingo***, a Japanese manufacturing engineer who developed the ***"Toyota Production System"***. The idea is to avoid repetitive tasks or actions that depend on vigilance or memory in order to free worker's time and minds to pursue more creative and value-adding activities.

Two aspects focussed by Poka-Yoke are:

(i) ***Prediction***, or recognising that a defect is about to occur and providing a warning.

(ii) ***Detection***, or recognising that a defect has occurred and stopping the process.

Many applications of *Poka-Yoke* are simple, yet creative and inexpensive to implement. Examples are:

- Many machines have **limit switches** connected to **warning lights** that tell the operator when parts are positioned improperly on the machine.
- A device on a drill counts the number of holes drilled in a work piece and a buzzer sounds if the work piece is removed before the correct number of holes have been drilled.

Poka-Yoke techniques are also applied to the design of consumer products to prevent inadvertent errors by users or safety hazards. *For example,* a 3.5 inch diskette is designed so that it cannot be inserted unless the disk is oriented correctly. These disks are not perfectly square, and the bevelled right corner of the disk allows a stop in the disk drive to be pushed away if it is inserted correctly. Power lawn-movers now have a safety bar on the handle that must be engaged in order to start the engine. Computer software such as Microsoft Word will automatically check for any unsaved files before closing down.

Poka-Yoke for services: Service fail-safing must account for the customer's activities as well as those of the producer. Service Poka-Yoke is classified by the type of error they are designed to prevent: **server errors and customer errors. Server errors result from the *task, treatment or tangibles of the services. Customer errors occur* during preparation, the service encounter and/or during resolution.**

***Task errors* include doing work incorrectly, work not requested, work in the wrong order or working too slowly.** Some examples of Poka-Yoke devices for task errors are computer prompts, colour coded cash register keys and signalling devices. Hospitals use trays for surgical instruments that have indentations for each instrument, preventing the surgeon from leaving one of them in the patient's body.

***Treatment errors* arise in the contact between the server and the customer such as lack of courteous behaviour and failure to acknowledge, listen or react appropriately to the customer.** *For example,* to avoid treatment errors, a bank encourages eye contact by requiring tellers to record the customer's eye colour on a checklist as they start the transaction.

***Tangible errors* are those in physical elements of the service such as unclean facilities, dirty uniforms, inappropriate temperature and document errors.** *For example,* spell-checkers in word processing software eliminate document mis-spellings.

***Customer errors in preparation* include the failure to bring necessary materials to the encounter, to understand their role in the service transaction and to engage the correct service.** *For example,* Digital Equipment provides a flowchart to specify how to place a service call. By guiding the customers through three yes-or-no questions, the flowchart prompts them to have the necessary information before calling.

Customer errors during an encounter can be due to inattention, misunderstanding or simply a memory lapse and include failure to remember steps in the process or to follow instructions. Poka-Yoke examples include beepers that signal customers to remove cards from ATM machines and locks on airplane lavatory doors that must be closed to turn on the lights.

Customer errors at the resolution stage of a service encounter include failure to signal service inadequacies, to learn from experience, to adjust expectations and to execute appropriate post-encounter actions. Poka-Yoke examples are: Hotels might enclose a small gift certificate to encourage guests to provide feedback.

Fail-safing as a service process requires identifying when and where failures generally occur. Once a failure is identified, the source must be found. The final step is to prevent the mistake from occurring through ***source inspection, self-inspection or sequential checks***.

Applications of Fool-proof Mechanisms or Poka-Yoke

Poka-Yoke tries to change either the process or its resources to eliminate the need to rely on human experience and accumulated knowledge. Examples of Poka-Yoke applications are:

(i) **Colour code** similar parts to help workers distinguish them as left and right. (*e.g.* right is red, left is green).

(ii) Place **template** over an assembled component to show operators the differences between the parts and how to insert them.

(iii) Modifying a machine so that it will operate only if parts are inserted correctly.

(iv) A combination of **optical scanners** and **bar codes** at the supermarket to eliminate cash register keying errors.

(v) Including self-addressed, stamped envelopes with customer invoices to reduce the chance of customers incorrectly addressing envelopes or forgetting to affix a stamp on the envelope.

(vi) McDonald's French fry scoop and standard size bag used to measure the correct quality.

(vii) The diameter of the petrol filter hole in a vehicle that uses unleaded petrol is smaller than normal so that a leaded petrol filter pistol cannot be inserted.

(viii) To avoid erroneous assembly, guide notches are installed that match in only one sense on components that are to be assembled together. *For example,* guide notch is provided on automobile headlights, so that they cannot be installed upside down.

(ix) Different types of plug fittings to avoid 110 volts appliances being connected to a 230 volt outlet.

(x) Round and not square covers are made for containers and manholes. Square covers of containers can fall through the opening since the length of the side of a square is less than the diagonal. Square manhole covers could fall through the hole into the sewer.

Examples of Poka-yoke include:
(i) colour code
*(ii)*template
(iii) optical scanners
(iv) bar codes.

Poka-Yoke and Human Discretion

Poka-Yoke may seem likely to make a work setting boring for employees. It may be criticised as a system of work that leaves no opportunity to think about operations. Infact, however, employees want to use some skills more than others. People in general do not perform especially well in tasks that involve monitoring, data recording and checking. These are the tasks that Poka-Yoke tries to eliminate by replacing them with fool-proof mechanisms. In contrast, people excel at recognising patterns and differences and at problem solving. By eliminating the need for people to monitor data and check operations, Poka-Yoke tries to free employees to focus on more complex problems.

Jidoka or Autonomation: Jidoka, (Japanese name for ***autonomation***), the idea pioneered by Taiichi Ohno, a Japanese quality specialist, **describes technological features of equipment and processes that detect problems while the systems run and flag these problems to operators.** In this system, an automatic mechanism stops the entire production system whenever a defective part is found along the process line. Appropriate adjustments then take place so that major problems are prevented from arising in the future. This concept, apart from adhering to the **principle of prevention rather than cure**, can substantially save on work allocation times, since the worker only needs to attend to the machine when it stops because of a problem, not at any other time.

Autonomation involves two mechanisms: one that detects abnormalities or defects and the other that automatically stops the machine or process when a defect or abnormality is detected. Machines can be designed to recognise abnormalities or defects and stop automatically when one is found. As a result, machines can run unattended and workers can perform other duties. *For example,* photocopiers are designed in a manner that will stop automatically and tell the user what the problem is and how to correct it.

14.5 MANAGEMENT MODEL FOR QUALITY IMPROVEMENT

Problem Solving

Successful quality improvement depends on the ability to identify and solve problems. A ***problem*** is a deviation between what should be happening and what actually is happening and that is important enough to make someone think the deviation ought to be corrected. ***Problem solving* is the activity associated with changing the state of what is actually happening to what should be happening.**

Problem solving is the activity associated with changing the state of what is actually happening to what should be happening.

Most managers first recognise problems by noticing ***symptoms***. Symptoms indicate that something is wrong, but they do not tell the reasons for the trouble. Managers often talk about symptoms when they use words as ***too much, too little*** and ***not enough***.

Examples of symptom statements are:

- We have ***too much*** inventory in stock.
- Our product return rate is ***too high***.
- Output per worker is ***too low***.
- Our scrap rate is ***too high***.
- We do not have ***enough*** items in stock.
- Absenteeism rate among workers is ***too high***.

Managers can never attack symptoms or resolve them directly. To eliminate symptoms, managers must identify and attack causes of symptoms.

Managers spend much time identifying, stating and solving problems. **"A problem well stated is a problem half solved". *Problem* is defined in several ways:**

- Felt difficulty
- Gap or obstacle to be circumvented.
- Dissatisfaction with a purposeful state.
- Something that fails to bring about a desired effect or result.
- Perceived variance or gap between present conditions and some desired state of affairs.
- Undesirable situation.

A problem is something that people see or perceive as undesirable. It is a perceived gap between a present situation and some desired situation. Because people's perceptions may differ, problem solving requires a clear understanding of the general agreement on a problem statement.

Classification of Problems

Problems can be classified as: *(i)* structured *(ii)* semi-structured or *(iii)* ill-structured problems.

Problems can be categorised in one of the three ways: **structured, semi-structured** or **ill-structured**. This classification is determined by the amount of information available about the problem. For structured problem, complete information about the problem – what is happening, what should be happening and how to get there – is available. Ill-structured problems are characterised by high degree of vagueness. Semi-structured problems fall somewhere in between.

Structured problems generally can be solved using routine, programmed decision making techniques. Ill-structured and semi-structured problems require more corrective solutions and hence a systematic process to find these solutions.

Managers' response to a problem: Solve, resolve and dissolve

A solution can affect an identified problem in one of three ways: it can **solve** the problem, it can **resolve** the problem, or it can **dissolve** the problem. To solve a problem, managers try to identify the optimum solution for a given set of conditions. To resolve the problem, they look for a solution that is both acceptable to everyone and sufficiently effective rather than the best possible solution. Finally, an effort to dissolve a problem tries to eliminate the conditions that erected the problem in the first place.

Problem Solving Process: As a problem solver, every manager must evaluate gaps between current and desired future situations, develop several courses of action designed to close this gap and select one to implement. This approach is complicated in practice due to changing situations which the managers must confront. The five step problem solving process provides a useful structure for dealing with any problem, from the most poorly structured to the most routine, well structured problem.

Exhibit 14.12 **shows the steps in the problem solving process.**

Step 1: Size-up/Description: This is the step in the problem solving process at which managers gather information to **accurately characterise a problem**. *First,* the problem may not be clearly defined. Managers may perceive a gap between the current and desired future situations, but still lack a clearly defined notion of the current situation, leaving the problems ill-structured.

Exhibit 14.12 : Steps in the Problem Solving Process

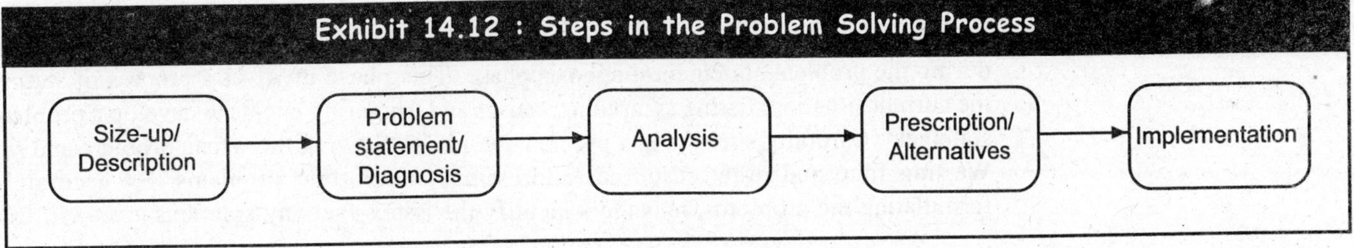

The level of problem definition is illustrated in *Exhibit 14.13*.

Exhibit 14.13 : Level of Problem Definition

Present state \ Desired state	Unknown	Known
Unknown	Ill-structured problem	Semi-structured problem
Known	Semi-structured problem	Well-structured problem

The second reason for size-up/description is to confirm that managers have identified the **right problem**. They may confuse symptoms with problems.

As a third reason for size-up/description, it can help managers to avoid wasting time working on problems that they think they can solve rather than those that they really should solve.

Finally, size-up/description may reveal **new problems** that others in the organisation have overlooked. Such problems often persist because people see the same situation every day, so they accept a problem as part of the normal operations. Some structured information gathering during size-up/description forces a fresh look.

Tools for size-up/description : Managers can rely on a number of tools and techniques to complete this process. The most important of these are:

- **Observation:** Observation offers one way to learn about a system, provided the observer spends enough time to become familiar enough to understand completely everything that is taking place.
- **Participation:** Actually working in a system offers a second way to learn about the system.
- **Questionnaires:** Surveys of system participants can provide valuable information.
- **Interviews:** An analyst may speak to participants in person, by fax, by telephone or even by e-mail over the Internet.
- **Written documents:** Annual reports, office memoranda, product records and so on can shed light on an investigation.
- **Process mapping:** This tool involves documenting the actual activities of a process using a set of standard symbols.
- **Check sheets:** This technique helps the analyst to collect information such as types of defects and errors and their locations.
- **Bench marking:** Benchmarking offers a set of tools and techniques by which the analyst can compare a system against the best practices either in the industry or overall.

Step 2: Problem Statement/Diagnostics: Having become familiar with a system during size-up/description, managers can begin to identify the problem or problems that need attention during the problem statement/diagnosis phase. This phase involves a process of stating the current situation, listing symptoms, causes and triggering events to develop a problem statement. Carefully specifying a problem avoids: *(i)* Solving the wrong problem and *(ii)* Wasting time and other resources addressing unimportant problems. By accurately formulating the problems, managers identify the issues that any solutions must address.

Characteristics of a good problem statement

(i) It should show the relationship between identified symptoms and the problem it describes.

(ii) It should distinguish between controllable variables and uncontrollable variables.

(iii) It should identify constraints in the situation, that is, limitations or requirements imposed on possible outcomes or alternative solutions.

(iv) It should also identify desired outcomes and the values of those outcomes.

In the problem statement/diagnostics stage, the problem-solving process builds critical agreement over the problem to address, which must precede any solution. A problem statement must clearly and unambiguously tell people what the proposal asks them to do.

Step 3: Analysis: This step often overlaps with problem statement/diagnostics. As a major task, analysis explains the development of the current situation. It details the relationships between features of that situation and outlines its problems, causes and symptoms. By laying out causal relationships, analysis directs attention to changes needed to solve the problems described in the problem statement/diagnostics step. This forms a foundation on which to construct strategy alternatives in the next step (*i.e.* prescription/alternative step).

Step 4: Prescription/Alternatives: In this step, the problem-solving process focusses attention on developing a solution to the problem evaluated during size-up/description, formally stated in problem-statement/diagnostics and explained in analysis. Based on the results of analysis, managers identify problem features that they must attack or change to close the gap between the current and the desired future situations. They also establish criteria for an acceptable solution, specifying time limits, cost limits and strategic emphasis.

This step should not try to present a single solution, but rather a number of different solutions. Managers should present each alternative in a brief statement about what changes it proposes, why and how those changes should improve operations and the strengths and weaknesses of the alternative.

Step 5: Implementation: In the final step, *i.e.* implementation, the problem-solving process formulates a single solution and puts it into practice. The previous four steps have carefully explored the current and desired future situation and developed a solution that will effectively close the gap between them. Implementation involves choosing one of the alternatives identified in the previous step or some combination of these alternatives when one cannot solve the problem by itself.

After selecting a solution alternative, managers must develop an implementation plan that describes how they intend to put it in practice. This plan lays out the changes that managers intend to make and the order in which they intend to introduce those changes for both short-term and long-term actions. The plan should describe short-term action to improve the effects of the problem and long-term action to eliminate or control the causes.

An effective response requires actual changes in company operations to successfully implement the chosen alternative. Much of the success depends on how completely people affected by the solution accept its changes. A solution that makes sense to managers may not gain acceptance by the people on the shop floor especially if that solution will eliminate their jobs.

Four principles that govern user acceptance of problem solutions are:

- **Survival:** Employees will usually accept a solution when they recognise that other alternatives will eliminate jobs. (*For example,* automation, computerisation etc.). In case of solution alternatives that would reduce the number of jobs, managers should be able to convince the employees that it would be beneficial to the employees and the company in the long run to implement a solution alternative that may temporarily cut down jobs.
- **Lack of surprises:** Employees tend to accept solutions that eliminate nasty surprises that a current system causes.
- **Simplicity:** Employees tend to accept a solution that makes their jobs and their lives simpler.
- **Pride:** Employees accept solutions that help them to do their job better. They want to take pride in their work and will often welcome changes that improve it.

GENERAL OBSERVATION REGARDING PROBLEM SOLVING PROCESS

Effective problem solving requires careful attention to do each of the five steps in this process in order. The sequence of steps is important, first because it forms the process into a sort of checklist that helps managers to avoid ignoring or overlooking valuable information. Inexperienced problem solvers often try to move straight to problem statement in an attempt to quickly frame a decisive solution. This haste risks spending too little time on the critical size-up/description stage or even skipping it entirely. Time invested in sizing up a problem often pays returns in improved problem statements and more thorough understanding of a problem's background, which can help to smooth the implementation step. The five step problem-solving process imposes some order on a potentially chaotic situation by providing a structure for understanding and responding to that situation.

Approaches to Creative Problem Solving

Many problems require a systematic process to develop and implement solutions. A structured process provides all employees with a common language and a set of tools to communicate with each other, particularly as members of cross-functional teams. "Speaking the same language" builds confidence and assumes that solutions are developed objectively, rather than by intuition. Leaders in the quality revolution – Deming, Juran and Crosby – have proposed specific methodologies for quality improvement. Most leading companies have adopted one of these or have developed their own version. **The following paragraphs review their approaches and then introduce a generic process for problem solving based on principles of creative thinking.**

The Deming Cycle: The Deming Cycle is a methodology for improvement. It was originally called the **Shewhart Cycle** after its founder, Walter Shewhart, but was renamed **Deming Cycle** by the Japanese in 1950. **The Deming Cycle consists of four stages –** ***plan, do, check*** (or study) **and** ***act*,** **as shown in** ***Exhibit 14.14.***

Exhibit 14.14 : Deming Cycle (P-D-C-A cycle or P-D-S-A Cycle)

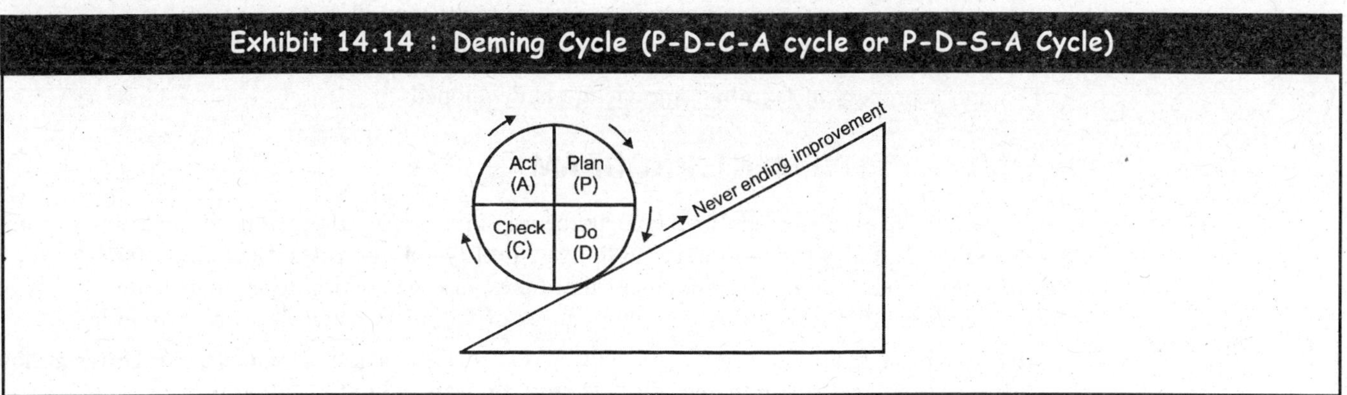

Deming cycle focuses on both short-term continuous improvement and long-term organisational learning.

Much of the focus of the Deming Cycle is on implementation. **The four steps are described below:**

- **Plan:** Managers identify a problem by studying the current situation to detect a gap between it and the desired future situation. A large gap can create significant opportunities for improvement. During this stage, managers also identify acts to improve the situation (*i.e.* close the gap). This step ends in formulation of a plan for closing the recognised gap. The activities involved in this stage are: defining the process, its inputs, outputs, customers and suppliers, understanding customer expectations, identifying problems, testing theories of causes and developing solutions.
- **Do:** Having formulated the plan, managers proceed to implement the plan in this step. Frequently, the plan is implemented on a trial basis (*for example,* a pilot project or a pilot production process or with a limited group of customers). This limited implementation is an experiment to evaluate a proposed solution and provide objective data to assess the large-scale feasibility of the plan.
- **Check:** This step is also known as "study" step. The primary activities in this step involve monitoring and inspecting results. It determines whether the trial plan is working correctly and if any further problems or opportunities are found often, a proposed solution must be modified or scrapped. New solutions are proposed and evaluated by returning to the *"Do"* stage.

  Two critical questions to be answered in this stage are:
- Whether the anticipated relationship between the manipulated variable and performance is occurring and
- Whether the implementation is creating any downstream problems or improvements.

The manager compares the actual results and studies reasons for any gap between them. ***Performance measurement*** becomes critical in this step because data must accurately reflect real events.

- **Act:** In this final stage, managers review information in the **'*check*'** step and take appropriate corrective action. The final plan is implemented and the improvement becomes standardised and practiced continuously. This process then leads back to the ***"plan"*** stage for further diagnosis and improvements.

The Deming Cycle is never ending, *i.e.* it is focussed on **continuous improvement**. The improved process is only a springboard for further improvements.

The Deming Cycle is based on the premise that improvement comes from the applications of knowledge. This knowledge may be knowledge of engineering, management or how a process operates that can make a job easier, more accurate, faster, less costly, safer or better meet customer needs. **The fundamental questions to consider are:**

(i) What are we trying to accomplish?
(ii) What changes can we make that will result in improvement? and
(iii) How will we know that a change is an improvement?

Through a process of learning, knowledge is developed.

JURAN'S IMPROVEMENT PROGRAM

Joseph Juran emphasised the importance of developing the habit of making **annual improvements in quality** and **annual reductions** in **quality-related costs**. He defined ***breakthrough*** as the accomplishment of any improvement that takes an organisation to unprecedented levels of performance. Breakthrough attacks common causes of variation which lead to chronic losses.

All breakthroughs follow a sequence of **discovery, organisation, diagnosis, corrective action** and **control. This breakthrough sequence is summarised below:**

(i) **Proof of the need:** Top managers need to be convinced that quality improvements reduce costs. Through data collection efforts, information on poor quality, low productivity or poor service can be translated into costs to justify a request for resources to implement a quality improvement program.

(ii) **Project identification:** All breakthroughs are identified project by project. By taking this approach, management provides a forum for constructive action in place of an atmosphere of defensiveness or blame. Participation in a project increases the likelihood that the participants will act on the results.

(iii) **Organisation for breakthrough:** Organisation for improvement requires a clear responsibility for guiding a project. This could be in the form of a small group of workers, or in the form of committee structures encompassing the entire division. These groups provide the definition and agreement as to the specific aims of the project, the authority to conduct experiments and implementation strategies. The path from problem to solution consists of two journeys: one from symptom to cause (the diagnostic journey) and the other from cause to remedy (the remedial journey) which must be performed by different individuals with the appropriate skills.

(iv) **Diagnostic journey:** People skilled in data collection, statistics and other problem – solving tools are needed at this stage. Some projects will require full-time specialised experts while others can be performed by the workforce. Problems controllable by managers and controllable by operators require different methods of diagnosis and remedy.

(v) **Remedial journey:** The remedial journey consists of the following phases: choosing an alternative that optimises total cost, implementing remedial action and dealing with resistance to change.

(vi) **Holding the gains:** This final step involves establishing new standards and procedures, training the workforce and instituting controls to ensure that the breakthrough does not die over time.

THE CROSBY PROGRAM

Philip Crosby proposed a 14 step program for quality improvement which are briefly discussed below:

Philip Crosby proposed a 14 step program for quality improvement.

(i) **Management commitment:** The quality improvement program begins with obtaining commitment from the top management with an emphasis on the need for defect prevention. The personal commitment of the top management raises the visibility of a quality improvement program and encourages everyone's cooperation.

(ii) **Quality improvement team:** This team is formed with representatives from each department. The team is oriented to the content and purpose of the quality improvement program.

(iii) **Quality measurement:** Quality measurement for each activity must either be reviewed or established to show where improvement is possible, where corrective action is necessary and to document actual improvement later.

(iv) **Cost of quality:** Data on cost of quality indicate where corrective action will be profitable. This step provides company-wide measurement of quality management performance.

(v) **Quality awareness:** Supervisors and employees must develop the habit of sharing the measurements of what quality is lacking and also develop the habit of talking positively about quality and changing existing attitudes.

(vi) **Corrective action:** As people are encouraged to talk about their problems, opportunities for corrections come to light from the workers themselves. These problems must be brought to the attention of managers and resolved. This will encourage employees to develop the habit of identifying further problems.

(vii) **Establish an adhoc committee for the zero defect program:** Three or four members of the team are selected to investigate the **"zero-defect"** concept and the ways to implement the program of doing it right the first time.

(viii) **Supervisor training:** Training helps supervisors to understand the program and realise its values for themselves.

(ix) **Zero-defects day:** The establishment of zero-defects as the performance standard of the company should be done in one day so that everyone understands it the same way.

(x) **Goal setting:** Each supervisor should establish specific and measurable goals.

(xi) **Error cause removal:** Individuals are asked to describe any problem that keeps them from performing error free work on a simple one page form. The appropriate functional group develops the answer. Problems should be acknowledged quickly by the management to develop trust in management.

(xii) **Recognition:** Establish award programs to recognise those who meet their goals or perform outstanding tasks. The awards should not be financial but should be in the form of recognition for performance.

(xiii) **Quality councils:** The quality professionals and team leaders meet regularly to discuss and decide about actions that are necessary to upgrade and improve the quality program.

(xiv) **Do it over again:** A typical program may take one year to 18 months – changes in the organisation require new organisation efforts. Quality must be ingrained in the organisation and appreciated by its work-force.

14.6 TOOLS FOR PROCESS IMPROVEMENT

Problem solving being a highly creative effort, has four components:

(i) Redefining and analysing the problem. *(ii)* Generating ideas.
(iii) Evaluating and selecting ideas and *(iv)* Implementing ideas.

In ***redefining and analysing a problem,*** problem solvers collect and organise information, analyse data and underlying assumptions and re-examine the problem for new perspectives. The goal of the problem solver is to collect facts and achieve a workable problem definition.

The purpose of ***generating ideas*** is to develop potential solutions. Two most important considerations in this step are to defer all judgements about the ideas and to use many different techniques to generate them.

After the ideas have been generated, the problem solvers ***evaluate*** them to identify and select the best ones. When problem solving is done in a group, conflicts can easily develop if the problem is an ill-structured one. A good leader and facilitator is critical for reaching consensus within the group. Finally, ***implementing*** ideas involves putting the solution to work, which requires a great deal of psychology in selling ideas and solutions and in gaining acceptance. ***Box 14.2*** **lists the various tools used for process improvement.**

Box 14.2 : Tools for Process Improvement

General Tools	Coarse-Grained Tools	Fine-Grained Tools
1. Team-building and group-interaction tools	3. Process flow-chart 4. Check sheets and Histograms	7. Fail Safing 8. Design of Experiments (DoE)
2. Specific process/ technology tools	5. Pareto Analysis 6. Fishbone Charts	9. Run Diagram 10. Process Control Chart

Creative Problem – Solving Method

An effective problem – solving method for quality improvement is adapted from creative – problem solving concepts advocated by Osborn and by Parnes. **This strategy consists of the following steps:**

(i) Understanding the "mess" (ii) Finding facts
(iii) Identifying specific problems (iv) Generating ideas
(v) Developing solutions and (vi) Implementation.

This problem solving methodology is supported by:

(a) ***Seven simple tools* known as seven Q.C. tools** – flowcharts, check sheets, histograms, pareto diagrams, cause-and-effect diagrams, scatter diagrams and control charts.

(b) ***Seven Management and Planning Tools*** – Affinity diagrams, Inter-relationship Digraphs, Tree diagrams, Matrix Data analysis, Process decision program charts and Arrow diagrams.

***Box 14.3* shows the primary application of each tool in the problem solving process.**

Box 14.3 : Creative Problem - Solving and Quality Improvement Tools

Problem Solving Step	Principal Tools
1. Understanding the "mess"	Flowcharts, Run charts and Control charts
2. Finding facts	Check sheets
3. Identifying problems	Pareto diagrams and Histograms
4. Generating ideas	Cause and effect diagrams
5. Developing solutions	Scatter diagrams
6. Implementing the plan	The Seven management and planning tools.

How the methodology and tools can be applied to improve quality is examined in the following sections:

1. Understanding the Mess or Mess Finding

A ***"mess"* is defined as a "system of external conditions that produces dissatisfaction".** Problems are different from messes. Managers generally deal with messes and identify and extract problems from the mess.

A "mess" is defined as a system of external conditions that produces dissatisfaction.

The mess in quality assurance is often a **poor state of quality** within an organisation. Significant indicators of mess are high quality costs, high defect costs and low customer satisfaction. **Sources from which messes arise are:**

- A lack of knowledge about how a process works resulting in inconsistency and increased variation in outputs.
- A lack of knowledge about how a process should work (customer expectations and the goals of the process)
- Errors in performing the steps involved in a process (inadvertent errors).
- Waste and complexity (unnecessary steps for a process, excess inventories).
- Excess variation.

Contributors to poor quality (often faults of the production system itself) include the following:

- hasty design and production of parts and assemblies
- poor design specifications
- inadequate testing of incoming materials
- inadequate testing of prototypes
- failure to understand the capability of a process to meet specifications
- failure to provide workers with statistical signals of control.
- inadequate training

- lack of calibration of instruments
- false reporting of test results and
- poor environmental conditions such as light, temperature and noise.

In service organisations, **customer complaints** provide a starting point for identifying quality-related problems. Focus groups can be used effectively to learn about customer's experiences with a particular service.

Tools used:

A flowchart is a map of the sequence of steps and decision points in a process.

(i) **Flow Charts:** To understand messes, one must first determine how a process works and what it is supposed to do. By clearly defining a process, all involved reach a common understanding and do not waste collecting irrelevant data. Understanding how a process works also enables one to pinpoint obvious problems, error-proof the process and streamline it by eliminating non-value added steps. Developing a flow chart of the process usually aids in understanding a mess. Flow charts are best developed by having the people involved in the process – employees, supervisors, managers and customers – construct the flow chart. A facilitator provides objectivity in resolving conflicts. A facilitator can guide the discussions through questions such as "What happens next?", "Who makes the decision at that point? and "What operation performed at this point?"

Flow charts help the people who are involved in the process understand it much better and more objectively. Employees realise how they set into the process and who are their suppliers and customers which will lead to improved communications among all concerned.

Once the flow chart is constructed, it can be used to identify quality problems as well as areas of productivity improvement. ***Exhibit 14.15* shows a simple flow chart for processing incoming orders.**

A run chart is a line graph in which data are plotted over time.

(ii) **Run Charts or Trend Charts:** Control of a process is a continuous activity, requiring that measurements be made periodically over time. By using a visual picture, participants can determine at what point a process goes out of control.

A ***run chart*** is a line graph in which data are plotted over time. The vertical axis ('Y' axis) represents the measurement, the horizontal axis ('X' axis) represents the time scale. Run charts show the performance and the variation of a process or some quality or productivity indicator over time. They can be used to track such things as production volume, costs and customer satisfaction indices.

Run charts summarise data in a graphical fashion that is easy to understand and interpret, identify process changes and trends over time and show the effects of corrective actions. They provide some idea of the general trend and degree of variability present in the process or data collected.

***Table 14.5* provides the data for construction of a 'run chart'. *Exhibit 14.16* illustrates the construction of a 'run' chart.**

Steps involved in the construction of run charts are:

Step 1: Collect the data.

Step 2: Examine the range of data.

Step 3: Plot the points on the chart and connect them.

Step 4: Compute the average of all plotted points and draw it as a horizontal line through the data. (This line is called the centre line of the chart).

A control chart is a basic tool that consists of a chart with upper and lower control limits on which values of some statistical measure for a series of samples or subgroups are plotted.

(iii) **Control Chart: A control chart is simply a run chart to which two horizontal lines called control limits are added, the *upper control unit* and *lower control limit* as illustrated in *Exhibit 14.17.***

Control charts were first proposed by Walter Shewhart at Bell Laboratories in the 1920s and were strongly advocated by Deming. Control limits are chosen statistically so that there is a high probability (generally greater than 0.99) that points will fall between these limits if the process is in control. Control limits make it easier to interpret patterns in a run chart and draw conclusions about the state of control.

Exhibit 14.15 : Flow Chart for incoming Order Processing

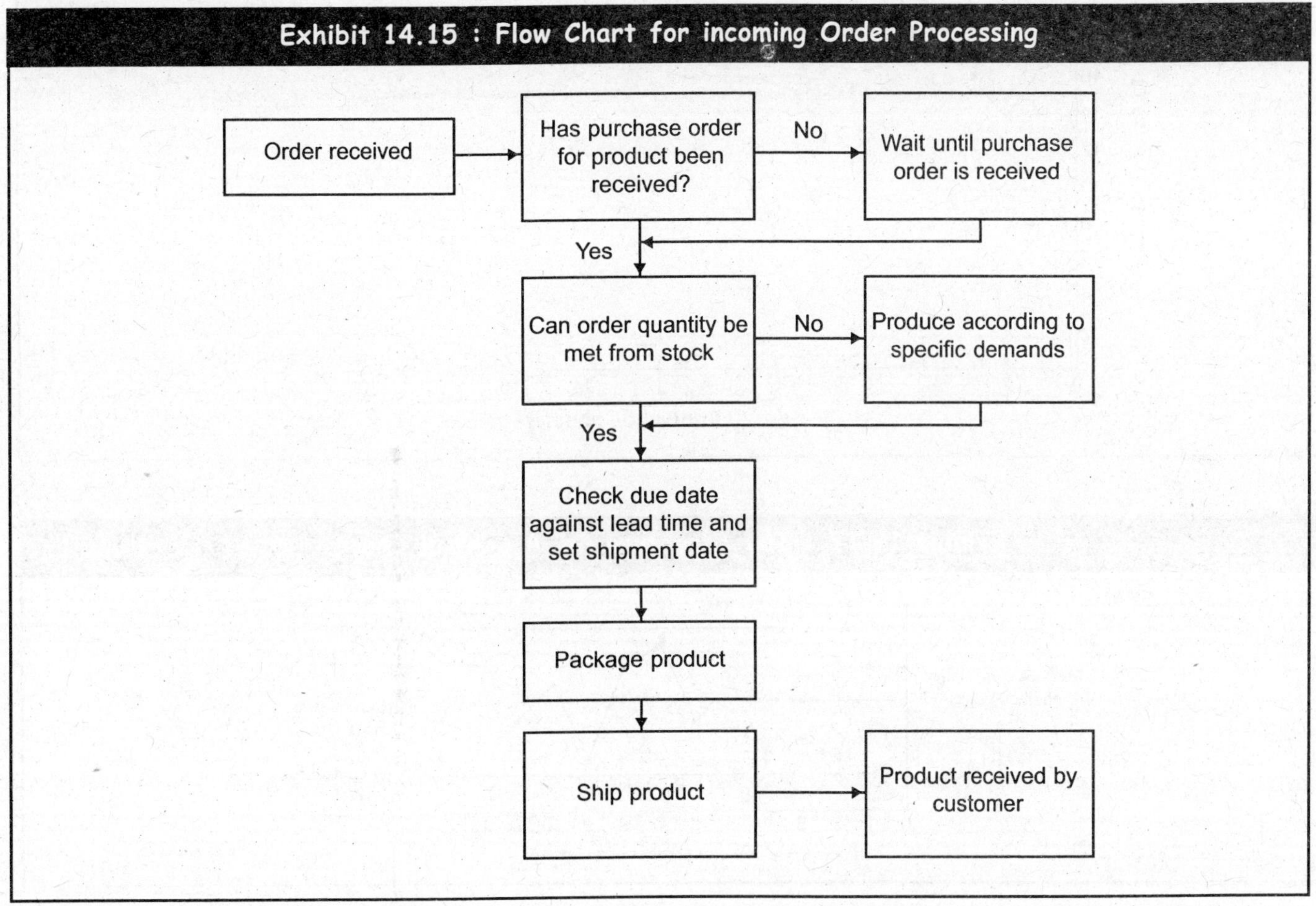

Table 14.5 : Run Chart for Acidity

p^H values of Dye compound are given below in the table.

Observation	*p^H value*	*Observation*	*p^H value*
1	16.5	11	15.8
2	13.8	12	16.7
3	15.9	13	16.6
4	15.5	14	16.8
5	17.3	15	17.0
6	16.1	16	16.6
7	16.5	17	15.5
8	15.2	18	15.2
9	15.8	19	15.2
10	16.0	20	14.8

Exhibit 14.16 : Run Chart For Acidity

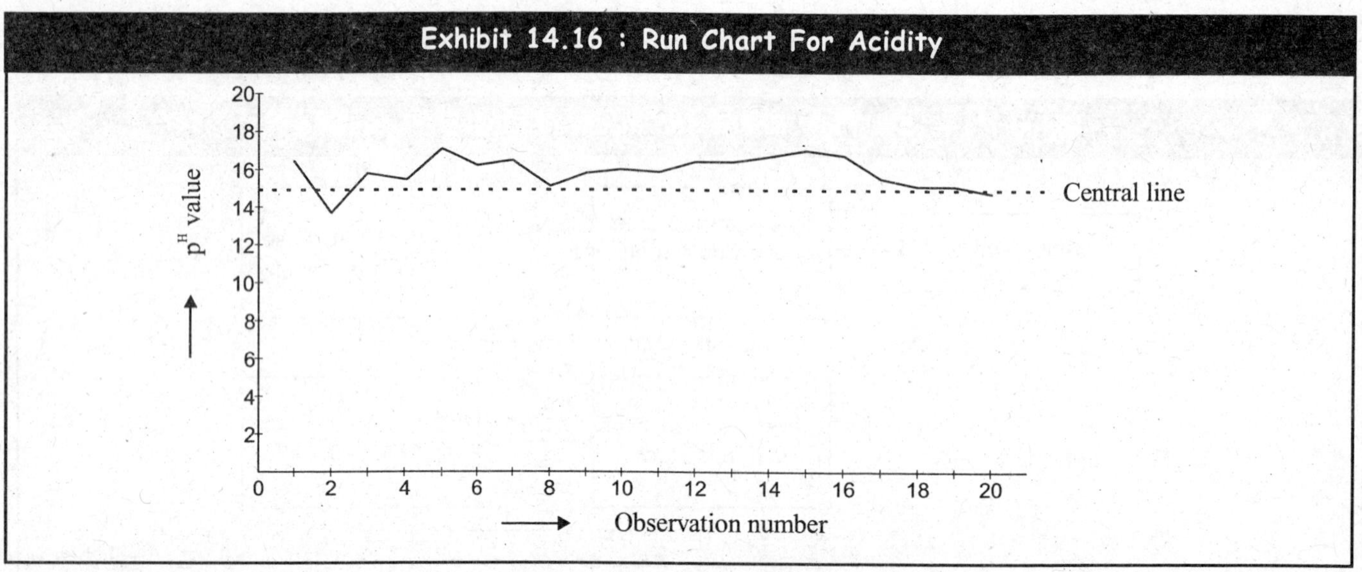

Exhibit 14.17 : The Structure Of A Control Chart

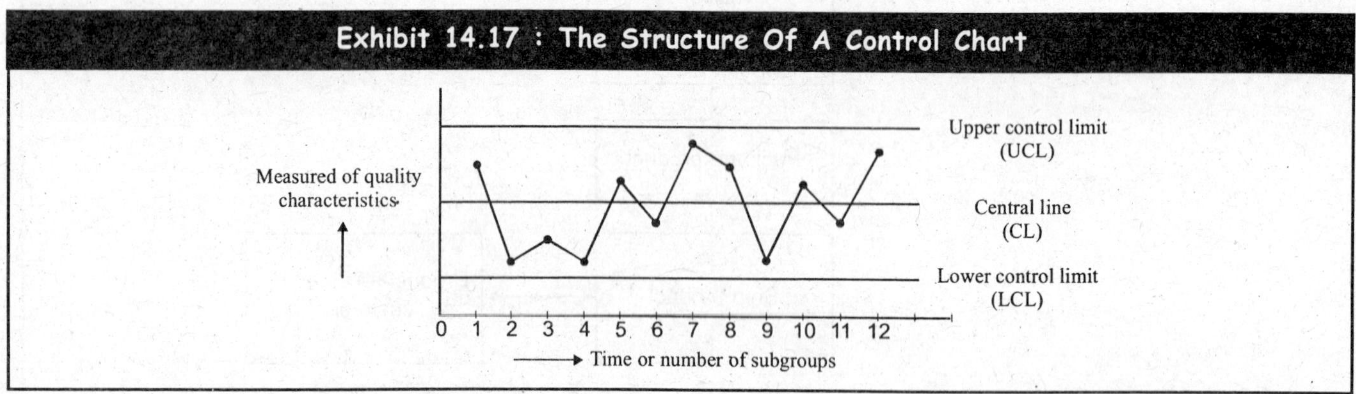

If sample values fall outside the control limits or if non-random patterns occur in the chart, then assignable causes may be affecting the process and the process is not stable. The process should be examined and corrective action taken as appropriate. If evaluation and correction are done in real time, then the chance of producing non-conforming products is minimised. Thus, as problem-solving tools, control charts allow operators to identify quality problems in processes as they occur. Control charts only give the signal when the process tends to go out of control and cannot determine the source of the problem. Operators, supervisors and engineers may have to resort to other problem solving tools to seek the root cause.

2. Fact Finding

Fact finding means understanding the true state of quality. It depends on data collection, observation and careful listening. Past and current data are collected and analysed to establish a base of information for problem identification and idea generation. Many aspects of the quality information system – including control charts, process capability studies, analysis of customer complaints and warranty claims – contribute to understanding of the state of quality within an organisation. Inspection of current production processes and practices often provides important information. The other sources of information are opinions of supervisors and workers, feedback from customers and field service employees. Such opinions must be based on facts and not on emotion. Proper design of the quality information system and the organisational structure is a pre-requisite for effective problem solving for quality improvement.

Tools used:

(i) **Check sheets:** Check sheets provide a systematic means of collecting and analysing data. Check sheets are special types of data collection forms in which the results may be interpreted on the form directly without additional processing. Check sheets facilitate systematic record keeping or data collection. Observations are recorded as they happen, which reveals patterns or trends.

***Table 14.6* shows a check sheet for an organisation's computer related problems.** A tally was kept of each problem type on a weekly basis.

Table 14.6 : Check Sheet For Computer Related Problems

Problems	*Week*				*Total*
	1	*2*	*3*	*4*	
Software access	1111	1	11	1	8
Network problems	111	11	~~1111~~	111	13
Insufficient memory	11	11	111	11	9
E-mail	1111	~~1111~~ 1	~~1111~~ ~~1111~~ 11	~~1111~~ 1111	31
Server problems	1		11	1	4

3. Identifying Problems

Problem Finding: "A problem clearly stated is half solved". ***The purpose of problem finding is to understand what the true problem is, that is to identify the problem from the mess.*** A major flaw in traditional problem – solving approaches is a lack of emphasis of problem finding.

The creative thinking literature emphasises a redefinition of the problem, which is done by first asking, "In what way might I ....." followed by "why?" to redefine the problem.

For example, consider the following simplified scenarios for redefining, "In what ways might I reduce the cost of final inspection?"

Question : Why do I want to reduce the cost of final inspection?

Answer : To reduce total quality costs.

Redefine : In what ways might I reduce total quality costs?

Question : Why do I want to reduce total quality costs?

Answer : To improve profitability.

Redefine : In what ways might I improve profitability?

As problems are restated in this fashion, new perspectives emerge. One must then converge to select the problem definition that best captures the real problem.

Tools used:

(i) **Histograms: Histograms display large amounts of data that are difficult to interpret in their raw form.** By providing a visual summary of the data, histograms reveal whether the process is centred around a target value, the degree of variation in the data and whether the data meet specifications. Thus, histograms could help in identifying process capability relative to customer requirements.

A histogram analyses and graphically displays quantitative data rather than qualitative data. TQM practitioners use histograms to display information about process and activity performance. Histograms are most effective when they display information with some natural order, such as number of defects found.

A histogram is a basic statistical tool that graphically shows the frequency or number of observations of a particular value or within a specified group.

Histograms help managers to achieve deeper insight into the characteristics of data distributions associated with activities. Practitioners of TQM use histograms to summarise data and display patterns. They know that any set of observations must display some variation. Histograms present graphic pictures that quickly summarise this variation. ***Exhibit 14.18* shows an example of histogram. Pattern of histograms capture three critical traits of distribution:**

Exhibit 14.18 : Histogram: Effluent Analysis - p^H

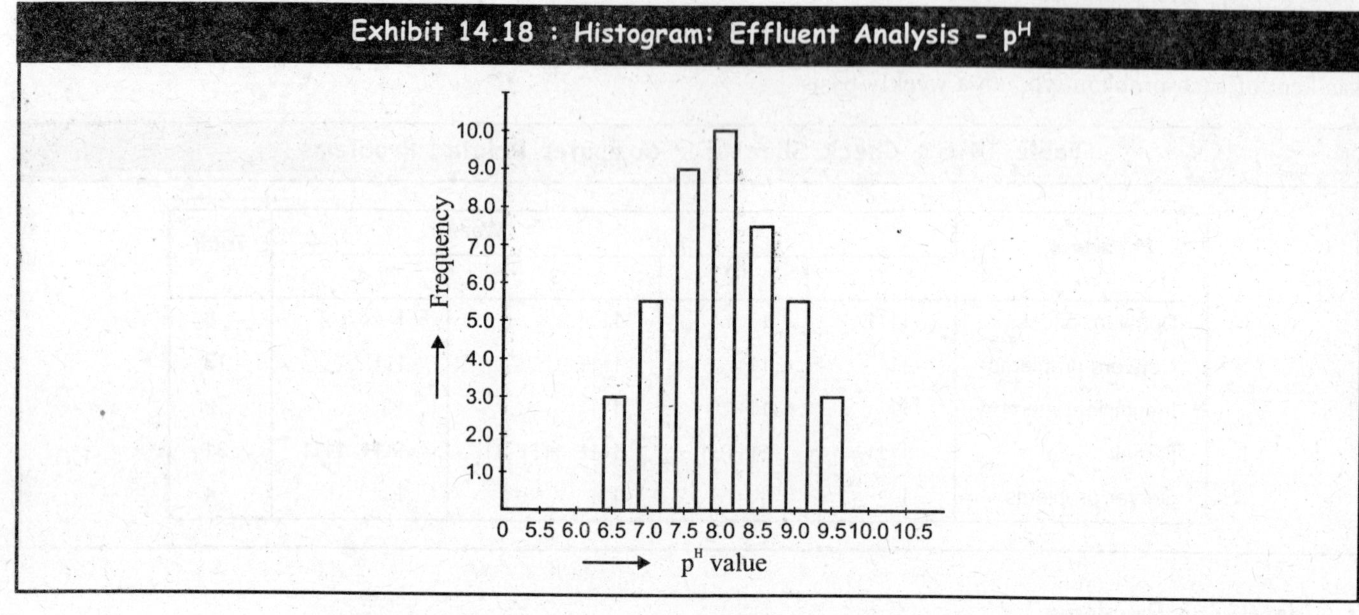

- **Centre of the distribution:** This point usually coincides with the mean of the overall distribution. The theoretical mean should fall at the centre of the histogram's graphic picture of the distribution.
- **Width of the distribution:** In statistics, the difference between the highest and lowest value in a distribution is its *range*. A histogram graphically shows the range as the width of the distribution, which often indicates how predictably the activity that generated the distribution operates. A wider distribution represents a less predictable activity, a narrower distribution indicates a more predictable activity.
- **Sample of the distribution:** The overall shape of the distribution often indicates different problems in the data or influences on the overall distribution.

Types of histograms: The histograms in *Exhibit 14.19* show five different types of distributions and each indicate a very different type of behaviour. The various types of distributions are:

(i) Bell shaped distribution *(ii)* Double – peaked distribution *(iii)* Plateau distribution
(iv) Comb distribution and *(v)* Skewed distribution.

Histograms are easy to construct but more difficult to interpret. To get meaningful data, one must select the category sizes carefully. Too many categories spread data too thinly across the histogram, breaking down potential patterns into scattered points, too few categories lump together conflicting data, observing patterns that might otherwise emerge.

***Table 14.7* gives some general guidelines for choosing the numbers of categories.**

A pareto diagram is a histogram of the data from the largest frequency to the smallest.

(ii) **Pareto Analysis or Pareto Diagrams (or Pareto Charts):** Pareto analysis is a technique based on the **Pareto principle** of ***"the vital few and the trivial many"***. The Pareto principle is also called the **80 – 20 rule**, *i.e.* approximately 20 percent of a group of items, people, inventory, causes and the like accounts for approximately 80 percent of the work, effort, problems and the like.

Exhibit 14.19 : Common Shapes of Distribution

(i) **Bell-shaped distribution**

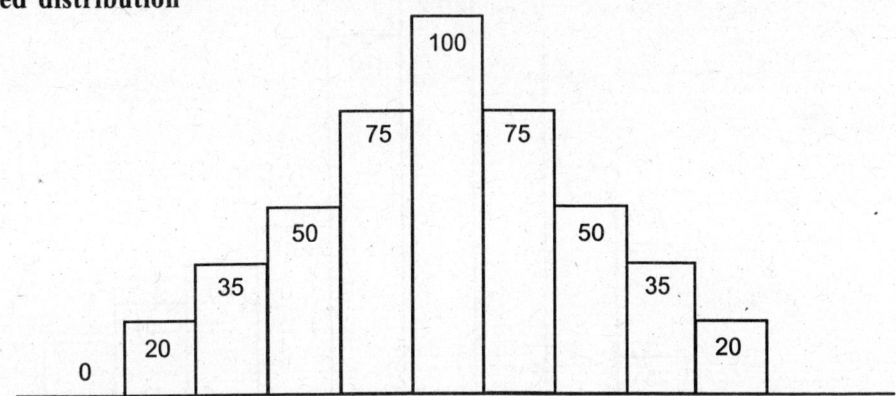

***(ii)* Double – peaked distribution**

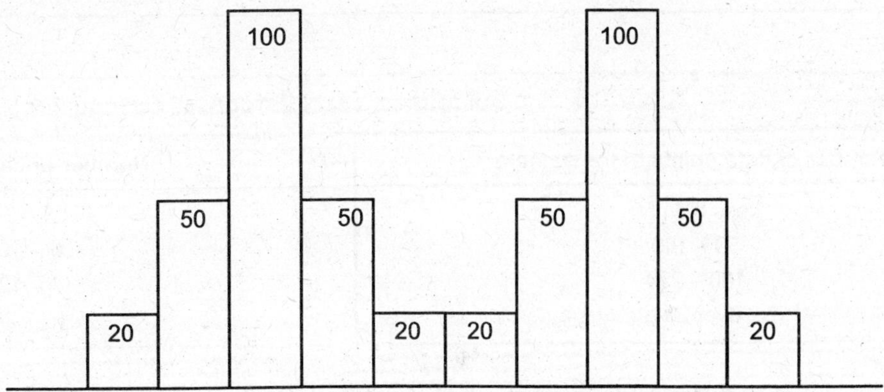

***(iii)* Plateau distribution**

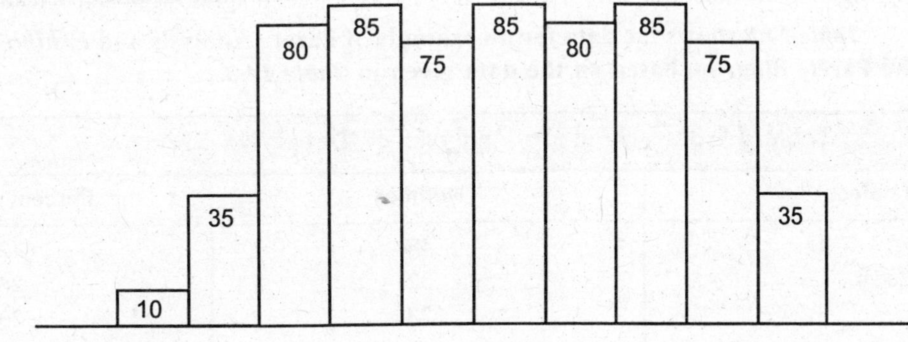

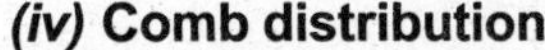

***(iv)* Comb distribution**

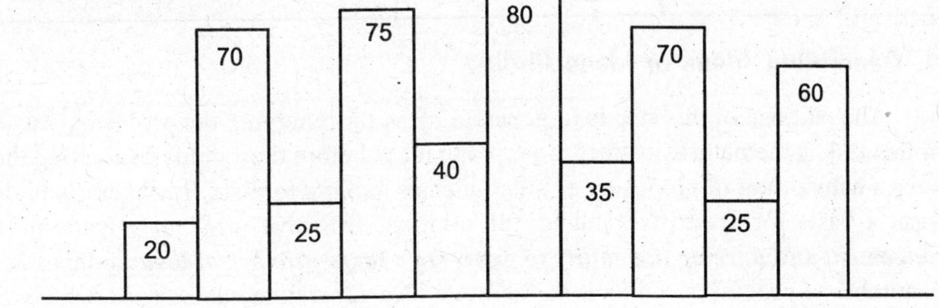

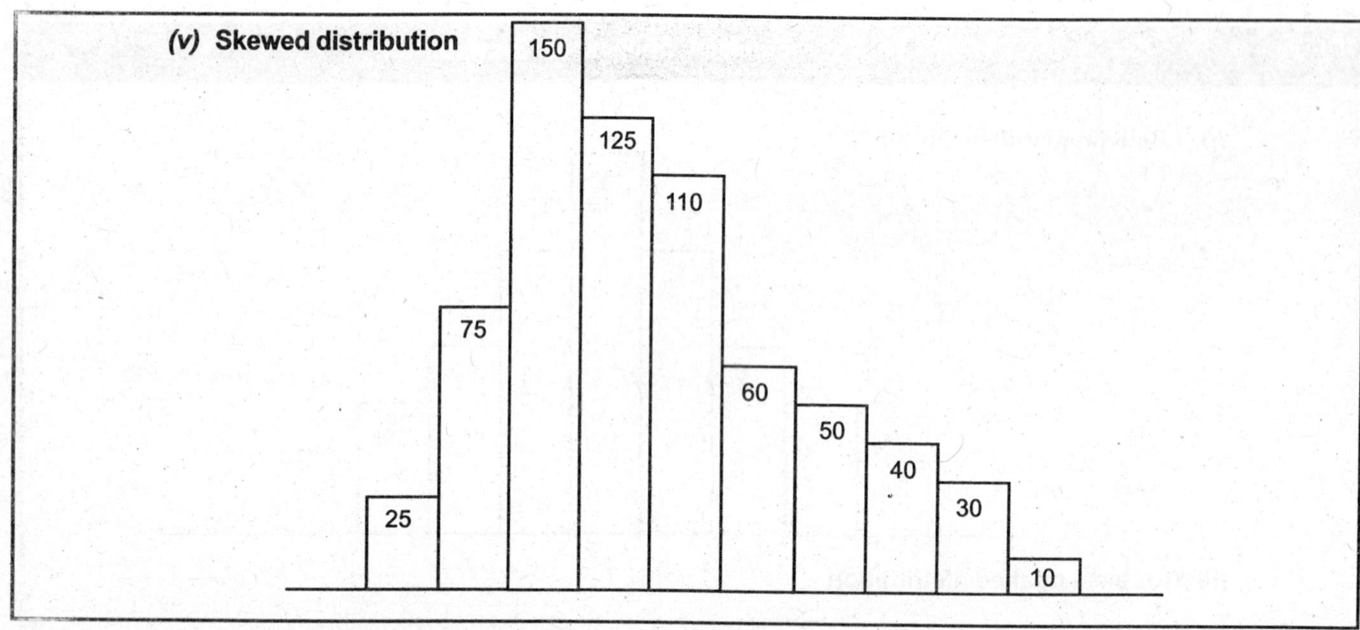

Table 14.7 : Guidelines for Histogram Categories

Number of data points in the sample	Number of categories
Less than 50	5 – 7
50 – 100	6 – 10
100 – 250	7 – 12
over 250	10 – 20

A Pareto diagram is a bar chart that illustrates the frequency of recurrence or the cost of a set of items. The items are shown in the descending order of importance from left to right. By highlighting the most frequent or most costly items, Pareto diagrams can help a team focus its efforts.

Table 14.8 **shows the data for an example of Pareto Analysis and** ***Exhibit 14.20*** **illustrates the Pareto diagram based on the data given in** ***Table 14.8.***

Table 14.8 : *(i)* Pareto Analysis of Defective Items

Type of defect	Number	Percent of total
Incomplete	48	42
Surface Scars	32	28
Cracks	23	20
Others	8	7
Misshapen	4	3

Brainstorming is a problem solving tool that teams use to generate as many idea as possible related to a particular subject.

4. Generating Ideas or ideas finding

The purpose of this step is to generate ideas for removing the problem. One of the difficulties in this task is the natural instinct to prejudge ideas before thoroughly evaluating them. Most people have a natural fear of proposing a "silly" idea or looking foolish. However, such ideas may actually form a basis for a creative and useful solution. Effective problem solvers must learn to ***defer judgement*** and ***develop the ability to generate a large number of ideas*** at this stage of the process. A number of processes and tools to facilitate idea generation can be used. One of the most popular among *these* is ***brainstorming.***

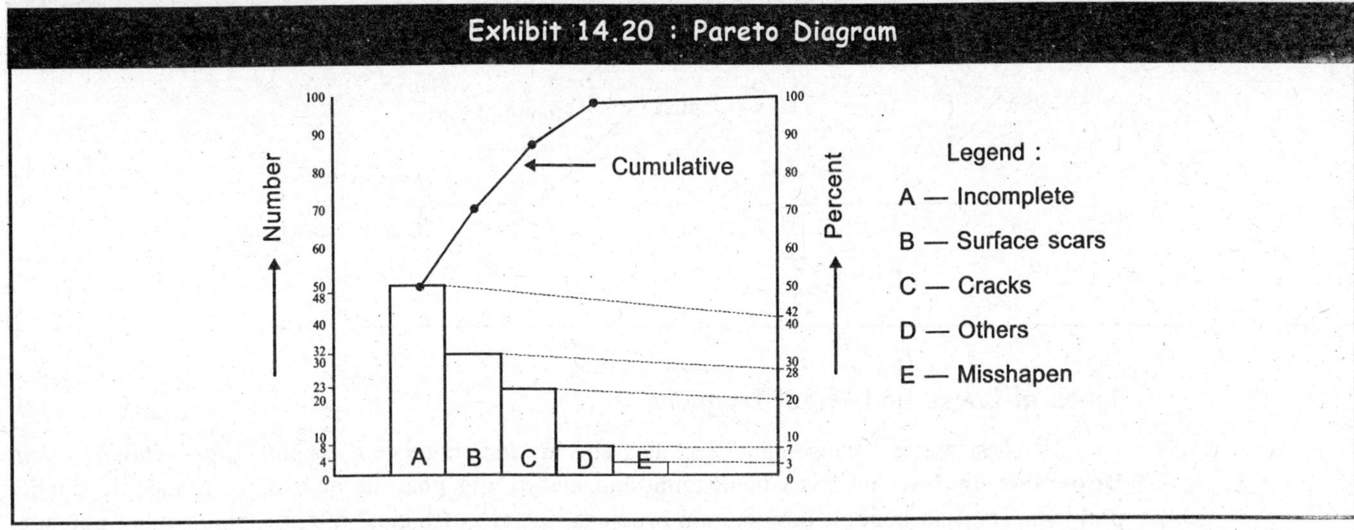

Exhibit 14.20 : Pareto Diagram

Tools used:

(i) **Brainstorming:** Brainstorming helps people **uncover hidden quality issues** and generally facilitates creativity within the total quality management process. It encourages people to envision and suggest any potential cause of relationships, reserving judgement about their accuracy for later analysis. This non-judgemental massing of information and ideas has become a critical element in the entire TQM problem solving process.

With brainstorming, **no criticism is permitted** and people are encouraged to generate a large number of ideas through combination and enhancement of existing ideas. Wild ideas are encouraged and frequently trigger other good ideas from somewhere else.

Brainstorming process often works in the following manner: Each individual in the group suggests an idea relating to the problem at hand, working in a **round-robin fashion**. If a person cannot think of anything he or she passes, a facilitator writes down all ideas on the blackboard so that everyone can see them. Only one idea is presented at a time by each individual. The process is repeated until no further ideas can be generated. By writing down the ideas in plain view of the group, new ideas are usually built from old ones by combining or extending previous suggestions.

Cause-and-effect-diagram: This is a diagram which gives the relationship between quality characteristic and its factors. It is a pictorial presentation in which all possible causes and their effects (problems) are displayed. A problem can be due to a variety of reasons or causes. The solution to the problem becomes simpler and easier if only true causes for the problem can be identified.

A cause-and-effect diagram is a simple graphical method for presenting a chain of causes and effects and for sorting out causes and organising relationships between variables.

Variation in process output and other quality problems can occur for a variety of reasons such as materials, machines, method, people and measurement. The goal of problem-solving is to identify the causes of problems in order to correct them. The cause-and-effect diagram is an important tool in this task, as it assists the generation of ideas for problem causes and in turn, serves as a basis for solution finding.

The ***cause-and-effect diagram*** was introduced by **Kaoru Ishikawa** of Japan. It is a simple, graphical method for presenting a chain of causes and effects and for sorting out causes and organising relationships between variables. Because of its structure, it is often called ***fish-bone diagram***. Because it was introduced by Kaoru Ishikawa, it is also known as ***Ishikawa diagram***.

The general structure of the cause-and-effect diagram is shown in *Exhibit 14.21*.

At the end of the horizontal line, a problem is listed. Each branch pointing into the main stem represents a possible cause. Branches pointing to the causes are contributors to those causes. The diagram identifies the most likely cause of a problem so that further data collection and analysis can be carried out.

Exhibit 14.21 : General Structure of Cause-and-Effect Diagram

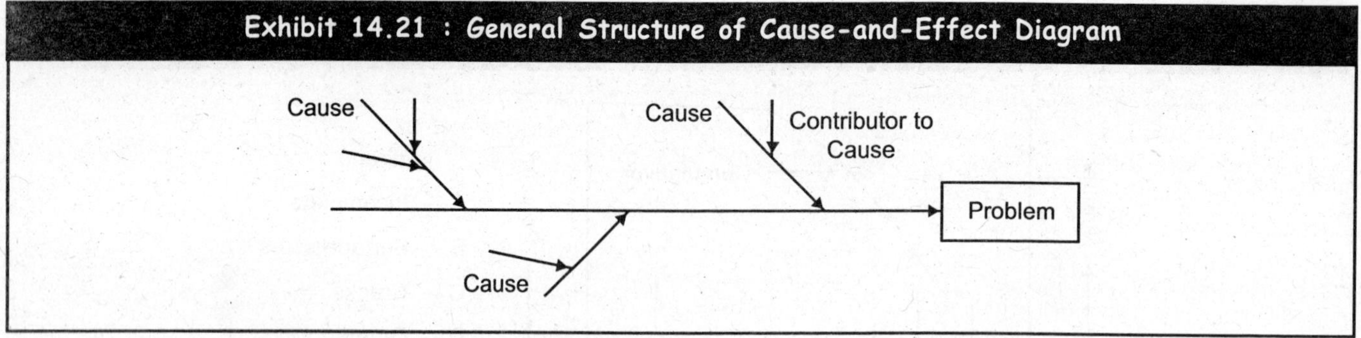

Types of Cause-and Effect Diagrams

Two basic types of cause-and-effect diagrams are ***dispersion analysis*** and ***process classification***. **Dispersion analysis** involves identifying and classifying possible causes for a specific quality problem. The fish bone in the diagram provides a chain of logical relationships among potential causes. ***Exhibit 14.22*** **shows the cause-and-effect diagram for the problem of excess scrap.**

Exhibit 14.22 : Potential Causes of Excess Scrap

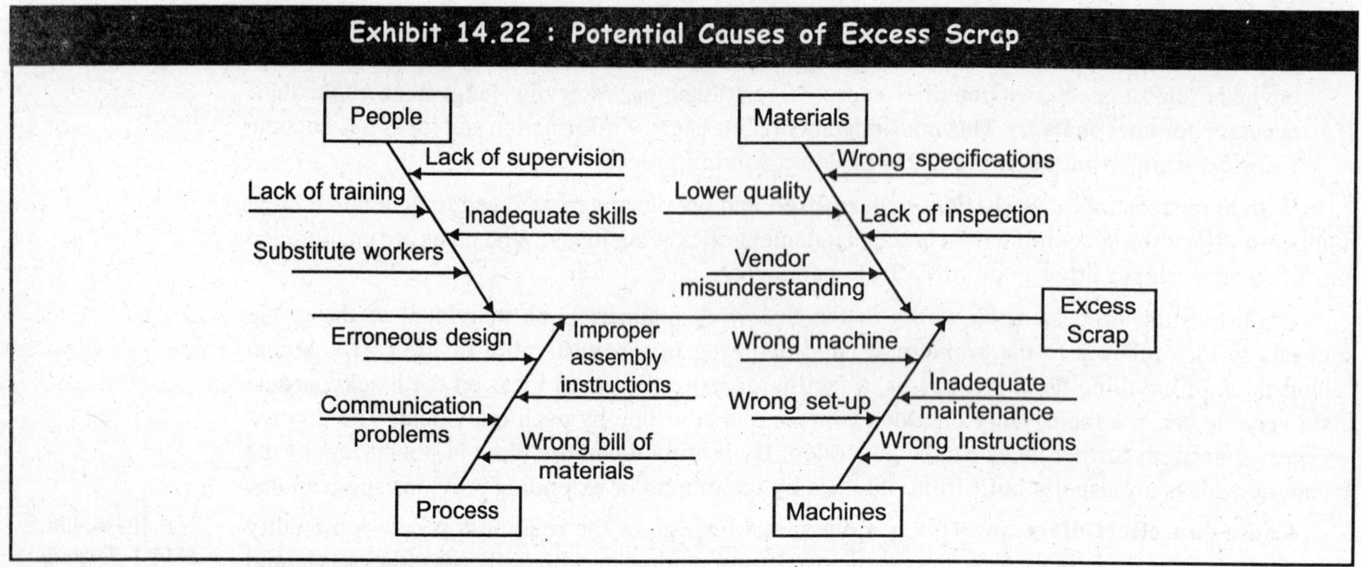

A process classification cause-and-effect diagram is based on a flowchart of the process. The key factors that influence quality at each step are drawn on the flowchart.

Construction of cause-and-effect diagram

Cause-and-effect diagrams are constructed in a brainstorming type of atmosphere. Everyone can get involved and feel they are an important part of the problem-solving process. Usually small groups drawn from manufacturing or management work with a trained and experienced facilitator. As a group technique, the cause-and-effect method requires significant interaction between group members. The facilitator who listens carefully to the participants can capture the important ideas.

Steps for constructing cause-and-effect diagram

(i) Decide on the quality characteristic (effect).

(ii) Draw the backbone from left to right, terminating at the head and write the quality characteristic (effect).

(iii) Draw the big bone and write the primary cause.

(iv) Draw the medium size bone and write the secondary cause (sub-cause)

(v) Draw the small bone and write the tertiary cause (cause which is secondary to the sub cause).

(vi) Ensure that all causes (factors) which influence the effect (quality characteristic) are displayed in the diagram.

***Exhibit 14.23* shows the construction of a cause-and-effect diagram which was described above.**

Exhibit 14.23 : Construction of Cause-And-Effect Diagram

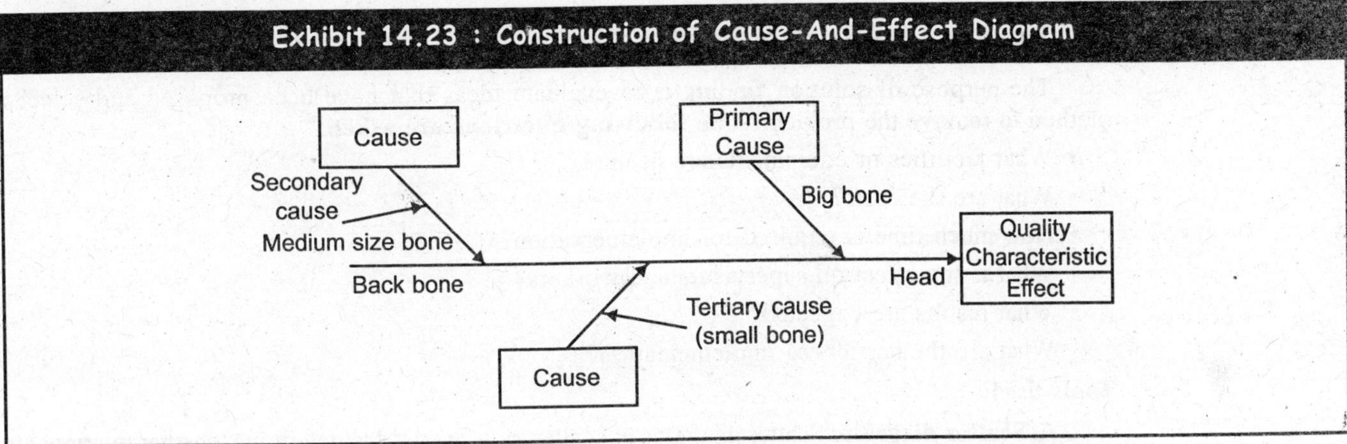

The main quality characteristic chosen is **"quality of machined parts"**. First, the major causes are listed like the machines, the tools, quality control training, process, the design of the parts, inspection instruments and the operator. Under each of the major causes, the sub-causes are listed. This could be done exhaustively by brainstorming amongst the members of the Q.C. circle. Then each cause is analysed thoroughly to find the most influential cause resulting in poor-quality of machined parts. This will vary from place to place. Under each environment, it could be analysed. The most influential cause chosen among other causes is questioned through using five 'W's and one 'H' *i.e.* ***What, Where, When, Why, Who and How.***

***Exhibit 14.24* illustrates an example of cause and effect diagram.**

Exhibit 14.24 : Cause And Effect Diagram

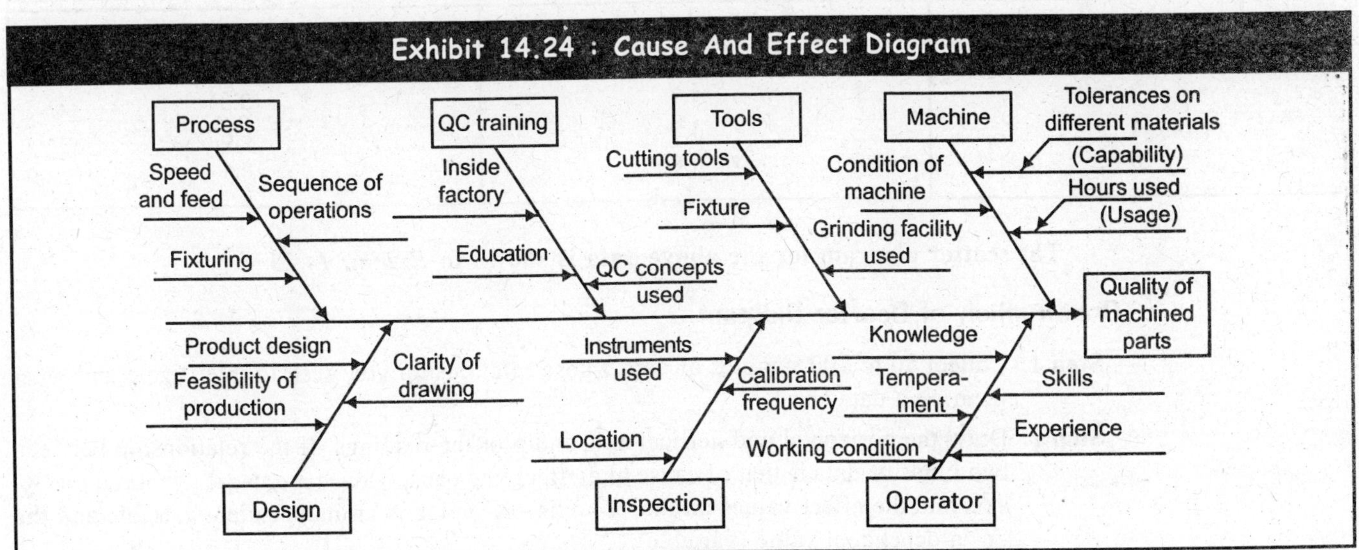

Advantages of cause and effect diagrams

(i) By constructing cause and effect diagram, the potential causes of a problem become readily apparent. Each of these can be evaluated one by one in order to find the true cause of the problem.

(ii) Cause and effect diagrams are frequently constructed by the use of ***brainstorming*** that enables to develop a wide variety of possible causes for a problem.

(iii) By using cause and effect diagrams, it is possible to reduce defects and thus improve quality.

(iv) Through cause and effect diagram, a clear picture of the process is seen visually. It educates people to improve their skills and helps in understanding the process better.

(v) It is an effective tool for the diagnosis of the various causes of the problem and helping to solve the problem.

5. Developing Solutions or Solution Finding

The purpose of solution finding is to evaluate ideas that have been proposed and select a method to remove the problem. **The following questions are asked:**

- What facilities or equipments are needed?
- What are the costs?
- How much time is required for implementation?
- What is the effect on supervisors and workers?
- What results are expected?
- What are the barriers to implementation?

Tools used:

***(i)* Scatter diagram:** Scatter diagrams or scatter plots are used to determine whether relationship really exists between two process characteristics and the direction of the relationship.

A scatter diagram graphically illustrates the relationship between variables, typically based on quantitative data. They reveal bi-variate relationships, that is relationships between pairs of variables, such as number of defects per batch against changes in the speed of production line, or production time per unit against hours of training. ***Table 14.9* shows the data for a scatter diagram.**

Table 14.9 : Data for Scatter Diagram of Relationship between Moisture Content and Elongation of Thread

Sample No.	Moisture content (X) (%)	Elongation (Y) (%)
1	1.5	8.5
2	1.3	8.1
3	1.9	8.3
4	1.9	8.6
5	1.6	8.1

The scatter diagram for the above data is shown in *Exhibit 14.25.*

Construction of Scatter Diagram

Step 1: Collect 50 to 100 samples of data whose relationship you wish to investigate and enter them on a data sheet.

Step 2: Draw the horizontal and vertical axis and plot the readings. If the relationship between two kinds of data is that of cause and effect, the cause values are usually marked on 'X' axis and the effect values on the 'Y' axis. 'X' value is an independent variable and the 'Y' a dependent value (variable).

Step 3: If data values are repeated and fall on the same point, mark concentric circles as needed.

Scatter diagrams are the graphical component of regression analysis. They point out important relationships between variables, such as the percentage of an ingredient in an alloy and hardness of the alloy. Typically, the variables in question represent possible causes and effects obtained from Ishikawa diagrams. Statistical correlation analysis is used to interpret scatter diagrams. ***Exhibit 14.26*** **shows three types of correlation.**

Exhibit 14.25 : Scatter Diagram for Moisture Content (%ge) Vs Elongation (%ge)

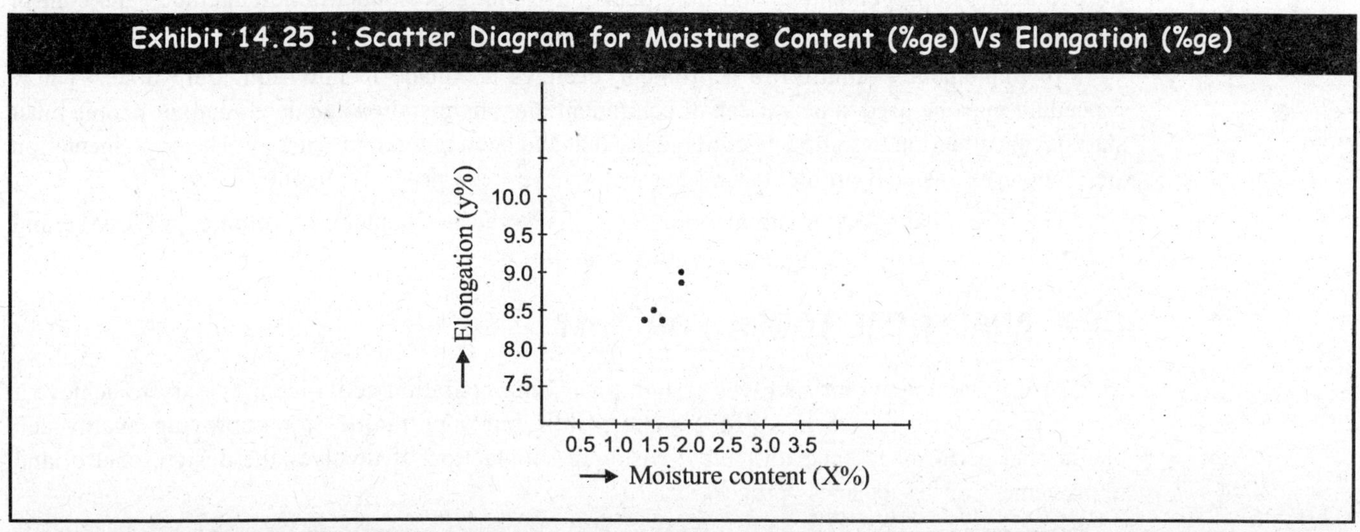

Exhibit 14.26 : Three Types Of Correlation

Y

X

Positive correlation

Y

X

Negative correlation

Y

X

No correlation

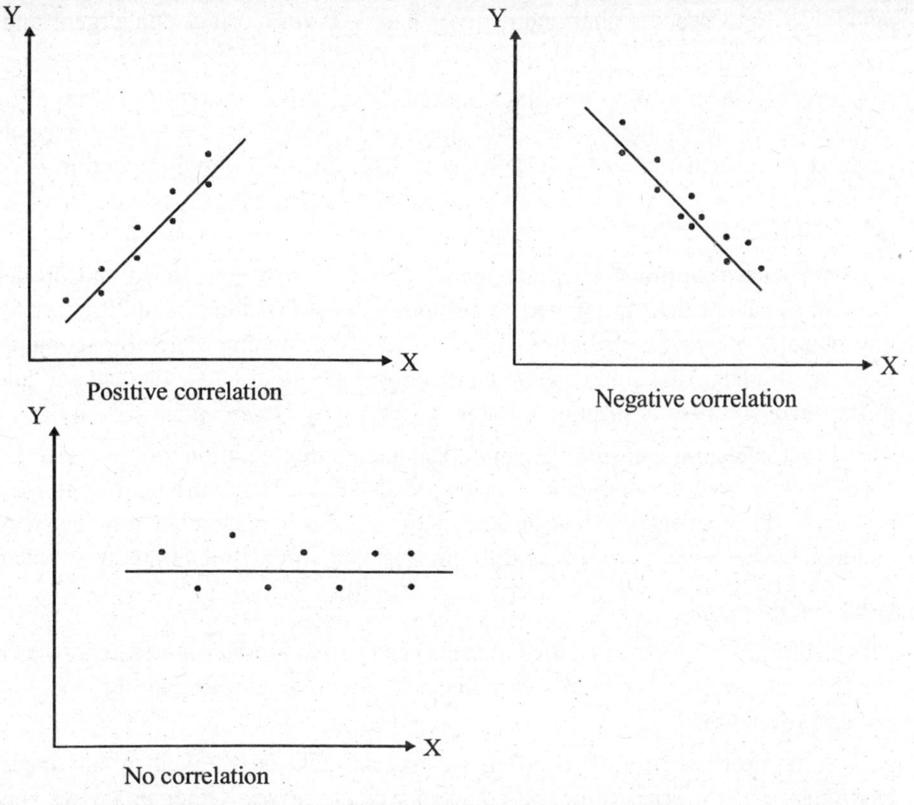

If the correlation is positive, an increase in variable x is related to an increase in variable y, if the correlative is negative, an increase in x is related to a decrease in y and if the correlation is close to zero, the variables have no linear relationship.

Implementation: To implement a solution, responsibility must be assigned to a person or a group who will follow through on what must be done, where it will be done, when it will be done and how it will be done. The potential consequences of each action should also be evaluated. The implementation phase of problem solving is often governed by considerations of personnel planning, budget issues, facilities, scheduling and methods. It is necessary to establish goals and milestones for evaluating improvement. In addition, plans for training personnel in new methods and control mechanisms for monitoring the process are essential.

To implement a solution to a problem, changes are made in how things are done. A new procedure must be used, a new piece of equipment must be installed and debugged, or people must start paying attention to some aspect of quality that had been ignored previously. The implementation step would be easier if problem - solving teams have been properly organised.

The seven management and planning tools discussed in Chapter 6 of volume 1 of TQM Hand Book are indispensable for implementation planning.

14.7 ANALYTICAL TOOLS FOR TQM

Process management involves planning and administration activities necessary to achieve a high level of performance in a process and identifying opportunities for improving quality and operational performance and ultimately customer satisfaction. It involves the design, control and improvement of key business processes.

Process analysis is defined as the mapping, analysis and critical examination processes because it is vital to appreciate whole processes, not just functional parts. The techniques used to critically examine the existing processes in order to improve the processes involve process charting or process mapping (using process charts and flow charts), brain storing, convergent and divergent thinking etc.

Process analysis is a technique for helping quality improvement team to understand a process so that the existing process may be improved or a new process is designed and developed. **The various analytical tools of TQM are discussed in the following section.**

(1) PROCESS MAPPING

"Process mapping" is a management tool initially developed and implemented by General Electric as part of their integrated "Work-out", "Best Practices" and "Process Mapping" strategy to improve significantly their bottom-line business performance. The process mapping concept is used to describe every vital step in the business processes in order to analyse and understand them so as to improve, simplify or eliminate them.

Process mapping is a proven analytical and communication tool intended to help improving the existing processes or to implement a new process-driven structure in order to reengineer the business processes. Process mapping is an excellent process management tool that can be used to better understand the current process and to eliminate or simplify those requiring change.

What is a Process?

A business process is a series of steps designed to produce a product or service. Some processes may be contained wholly within a function (for example-a programming process) and most processes are cross-functional.

Some processes result in product or service that is received by an **organisation's external customer**. Such processes are called ***customer processes***. Other processes such as **management processes** and ***administration processes*** are not visible to the external customer.

A process can be seen as a value chain. By its contribution to the creation or delivery of a product or service, each step in a process should add value to the preceding step. ***Box 14.4*** **lists examples of business processes.**

Box 14.4 : Examples of Business Processes

1. **Generic Customer Processes:**
   - *(a)* Marketing and sales
   - *(b)* Product development
   - *(c)* Manufacturing
   - *(d)* Distribution
   - *(e)* Billing
   - *(f)* Order processing
   - *(g)* Customer Service
2. Industry-specific Customer Processes:
   - *(a)* Loan processing (Banking)
   - *(b)* Claim processing (Insurance)
   - *(c)* Food preparation (Restaurant)
   - *(d)* Baggage handling (Airlines)
   - *(e)* Reservation handling (Hotel / Airlines)
3. Generic Administrative Processes:
   - *(a)* Formal Strategic and tactical planning
   - *(b)* Budgeting
   - *(c)* Training
   - *(d)* Purchasing
   - *(e)* Facilities management

Some of the ways of improving business processes are:

(i) Eliminating duplicating activities.
(ii) Combining related activities.
(iii) Eliminating inspections.
(iv) Simplifying processes.
(v) Reducing batch sizes.
(vi) Processing in parallel.
(vii) Eliminating movement of work.
(viii) Organising multifunctional teams.
(ix) Designing cellular work places.
(x) Centralising / Decentralising.

Why should you look at your Processes?

The business enterprise is only as effective as its processes. Business goals / objectives can be achieved only through development of logical business processes. People can influence the effectiveness and efficiency of the processes to which they contribute. However, individual and team problem- solving seldom focuses properly on the total system process improvement. Neither strong people nor process improvement teams can compensate for a weak systemic process.

The ***process level*** is important because process effectiveness efficiency should drive a multitude of business decisions.

Process mapping provides a process tool with which to understand and change the processes to help improve the bottom-line and competitive position.

The pivotal link between the business enterprise performance and individual performance can be established through the three process-based variables: ***1. Process goals/objectives, 2. Process design*** and ***3. Process management.*** which are discussed in the following paragraphs:

1. Process Goals/Objectives

Every Business process, whether customer process or administrative process exists to make a contribution to one or more business enterprise goals / objectives. Therefore each process should also be measured against process goals / objectives that reflect the contribution that the process is expected to make to one or more business enterprise goals / objectives.

Performance measurement is most effective if it is done in relation to strategic or tactical business enterprise targets or goals. Process goals are derived from three sources: *(a)* Business enterprise goals, *(b)* Customer requirements and *(c)* Benchmarking information.

Process benchmarking-comparing a process to the same process in an exemplary organisation is very useful. Often the business enterprise that is best in its class for a given process is not a competitor and is therefore easy to study.

Process goals are linked both to business enterprise goals and to customer's requirements.

2. Process Design

After goals are established for critical processes, managers need to ensure that the processes are designed to achieve theses goals efficiently. To determine whether each process and sub process is appropriately structured across functions, teams should be created to build a **process map** that shows input-output relationships among process-dependant operations and departments, and that documents in a step-by-step process sequence the activities that are required to convert inputs to outputs for the specific process.

Exhibit 14.27 illustrates an ***"As-Is"*** (current state) **Process map** of an order-filling process, as developed by a **process mapping team** representing all factions that contribute to the process. The process mapping team traces the process of converting the input (orders) through all the intervening steps until the final requested output (payment) is produced. This process mapping structure allows the team to identify all the critical interfaces, overlay the time to complete various sub processes on the map, start to define the opportunities for process simulation, apply activity-based costing methods and identify "disconnects" (illogical, missing or extraneous steps) in the processes.

Exhibit 14.27 : Current Process "As-Is" Process Map

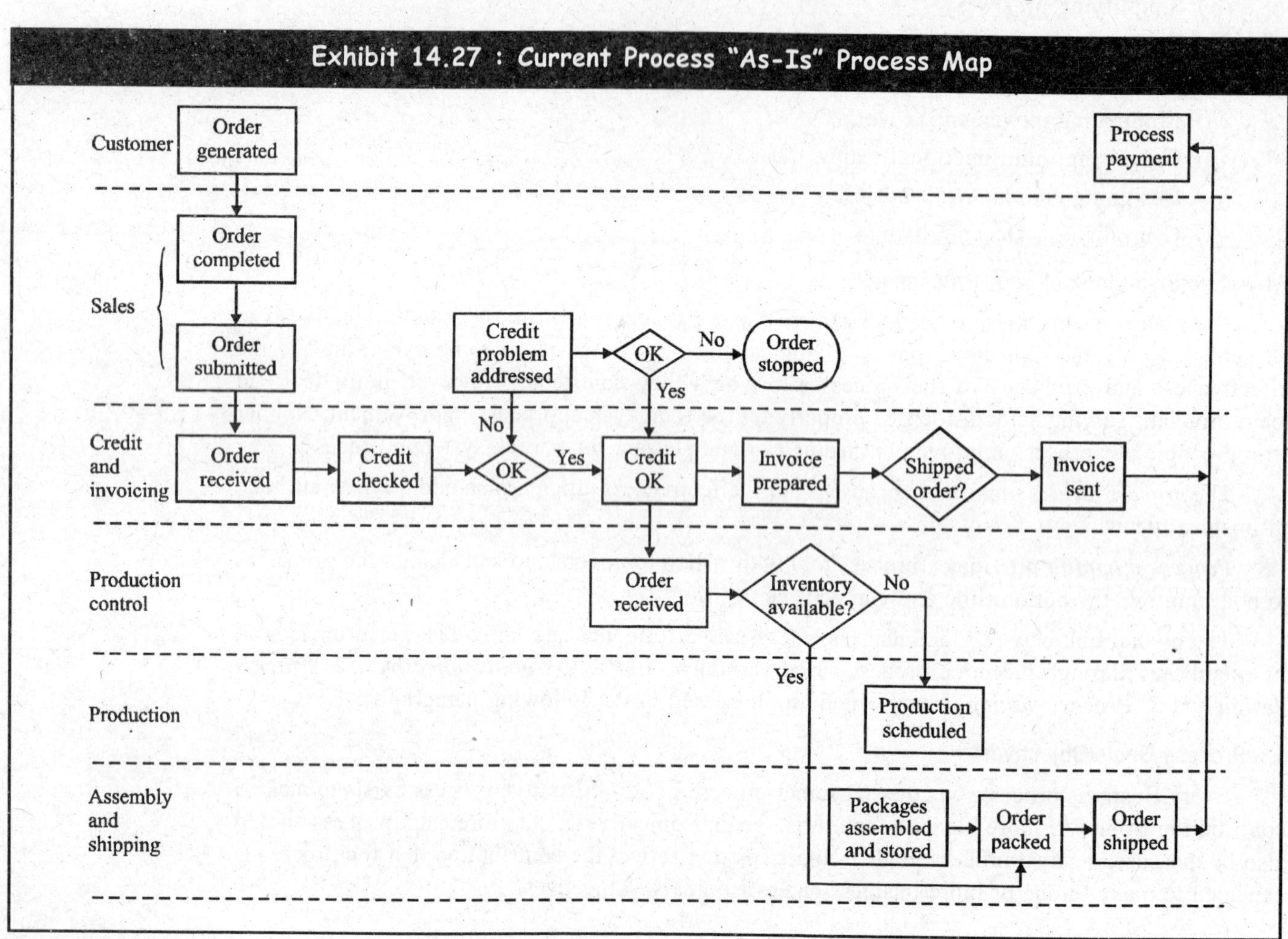

As the process mapping team documents and analyses current ***"As-Is" process*** for filling an order, the following ***"disconnects"*** may be identified.

(i) Sales representatives take too long to submit orders.

(ii) There are too many process steps.

(iii) Sales administration slows down the process by batch-processing orders.

(iv) Credit-checking is done for both old and new customers.

(v) Credit checking delays the process because it is done before order picking.

The team then creates a ***"To-Be" Process Map,*** which reflects a disconnect-free order-filling process.

The ***"To-Be" Process Map*** is shown in ***Exhibit 14.28.***

Exhibit 14.28 : Reengineered "To-Be" Process Map

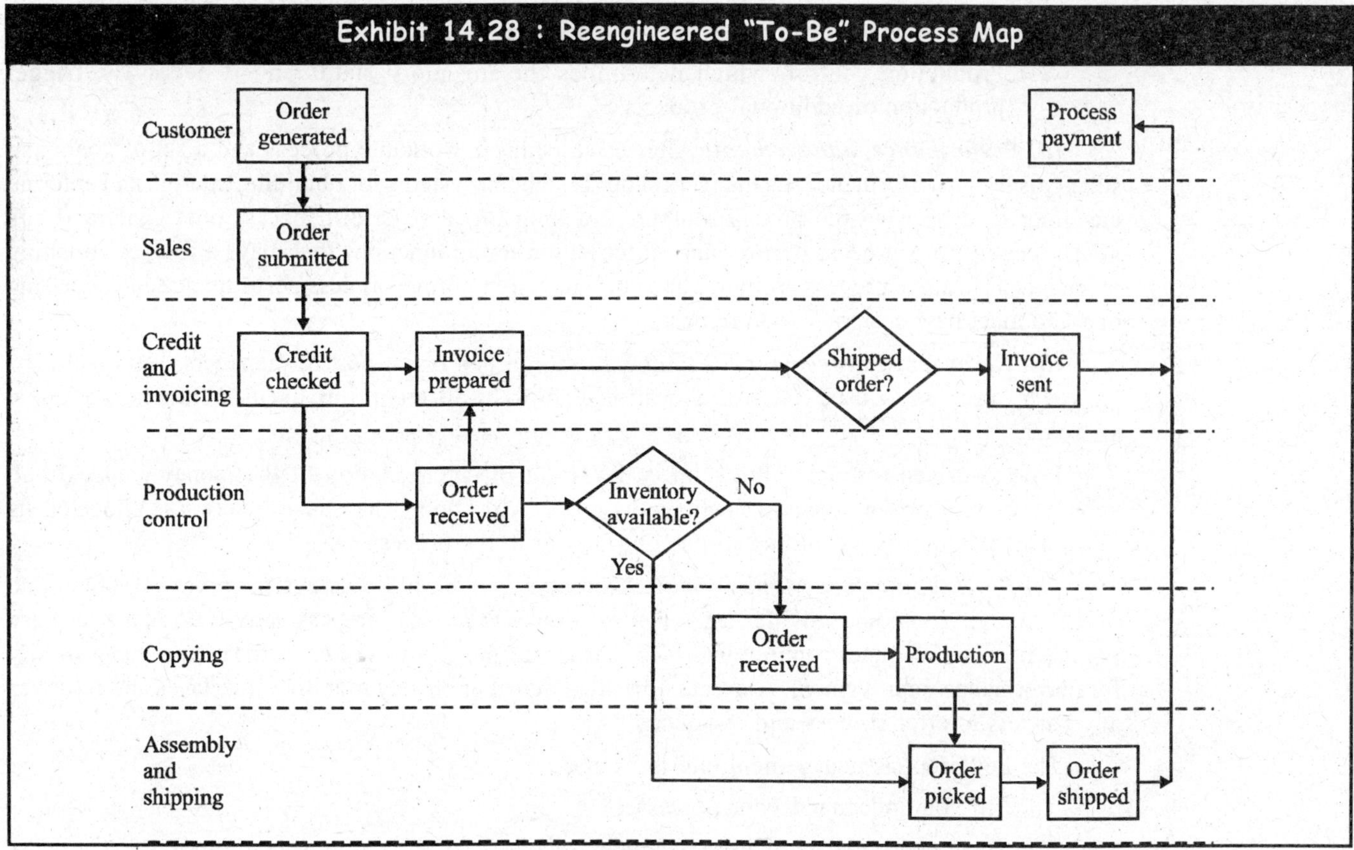

As shown in *Exhibit 4.2*, the major changes in the *"To-Be" process* are:

(i) Direct order entry by sales, eliminating sales administration.

(ii) Parallel order processing and credit checking.

(iii) Elimination of multiple order entry and order logging steps.

"As-Is" and "To-Be" process mapping are the central steps in process improvement projects. The objective is to aggressively eliminate, simplify or improve the "To-Be" processes.

A successful process improvement effort results in a positive answer to the key process design or improvement question:

"Is this the most efficient and effective process for accomplishing the process goals?"

3. Process Management

Four Components of effective process management are:

***(i)* Process Goal Management:** The overall process-goals should serve as the basis for the establishment of sub goals throughout the process. We need to establish process sub goals on the ultimate customer-driven process goals.

Once process sub goals have been established, functional goals can be developed. Any functional activity goals established at the business enterprise level should be modified, if necessary to reflect maximum functional contributions to the process goals and sub goals.

The first step should be identifying each activity function's contribution to the process. Three specific activity functions contributing to the process of "order entry" are:

(a) Sales, which enters the order via telephone.

(b) Finance which determines the customer's credit status.

(c) Production control, which determines the inventory status and if necessary, trigger production of additional products.

(ii) Performance management: After establishing a workable process and a set of goals and sub goals for its performance, its mangers should establish systems for obtaining internal and external customer feed back on the process outputs, tracking process performance against goals and sub goals, feeding back process performance information to the functions that plays a role, establishing mechanisms to solve process problems and continuously improve process performance and adjusting goals to meet new customer requirements.

(iii) Resource Management: Resource allocation is a major part of managers' responsibility. However, "process-focused resource allocation tends to be different from the usual function-oriented approach.

Process-driven resource allocation is the result of determination of the money (rupees) and people required for the process to achieve its goals. After doing that, each function is allocated its share of the resources, according to its contribution to the process.

(iv) Process Interface Management: A process map clearly displays the points at which one process activity function provides a product or service to another process activity. At each of these points, there is a customer-supplier interface. These interfaces often represent the greatest opportunity for performance improvement. A process-oriented manager closely monitors interfaces and removes any barriers to effectiveness and efficiency.

The key process management questions are:

(a) Do you understand your processes?

(b) Have appropriate process goals been set?

(c) Is process performance managed?

(d) Are sufficient resources allocated to each process?

(e) Are the interfaces between process steps being managed?

ORIGINS OF PROCESS MAPPING

Process mapping has its roots in a variety of areas:

(i) Work study in manufacturing plants in which industrial engineers seek, using scientific methods of observation, data collection and analysis, to make work more productive.

(ii) Organisation and Method (O&M) studies in which office operations are analysed to achieve even loading and efficient utilisation of clerical time.

(iii) Process control, in which the dynamic characteristics of production facilities are analysed as a basis for gathering information and then using this data to control outputs by adjusting inputs to the process.

(iv) Process simulation, in which complex processes such as nuclear reactors, chemical plants or highly automated facilities in the engineering industry are modeled on computers or by other means to test their response to a wide variety of operating conditions.

(v) Business modeling in which, as an aid to corporate planning, business results are predicted in a simulation using mathematical and statistical modeling techniques in order to gain an understanding of major influences such as price, volume, capacity and input costs.

(vi) Systems engineering and analysis, in which flow diagrams are used to define the operation of procedures for which the intention is to utilize computers and telecommunications equipment to affect some or all of the process.

The origin of most of the above techniques can be attributed to F.W.Taylor who is known as ***"father of scientific management".*** Taylor's contribution was related to the study of the ways people work-rather than machines so as to improve the productivity. This focus exits even today in business process reengineering programs. Even though the emphasis in reengineering is to start with the boundaries of a process, and look at how all elements-people, machines, organisation and supporting infrastructure-need to be reconfigured to achieve higher levels of performance.

Work study is defined as a tool or technique of management involving the analytical study of job or operation for the following purposes:

(i) The determination of what exactly has to be done, the optimum conditions-methods, layout, batch size and equipment and what causes of ineffective work can be removed.

(ii) The measurement of the work content of the job for use in planning, costing, incentive wage payment and control.

Work study aims to establish the most efficient way of doing the work, standardise on these methods, establish the time required and then install the work method as standard practices.

The techniques evolved from work study include: *(i)* Flow diagram, *(ii)* String diagram, *(iii)* Travel chart, *(iv)* Multiple activity charts, and *(v)* Process charts.

THE PROCESS MAPPING CONCEPT

The fundamental concepts of process mapping are based on the idea of *structural analysis.* The benefits of process mapping include reductions in product and service development costs, fewer system integration failures, uniformly better process understanding and improvement in overall business enterprise operations and performance. The following key points summarise the basic process mapping concepts:

1. Understand a process or system by creating a **"process map"** that graphically shows things (objects or information) and activities (performed by people or machines). The process map is designed to properly relate both things and activities.
2. Distinguish what functions a system should perform from how the system is built to accomplish those factions. The distinction must be clearly evident in the process map.
3. Structure the process map as a hierarchy with major functions at the top and successive process map levels revealing well bounded details. Each process map should be internally consistent.
4. Establish an informed ***"process map review cycle"*** to "proof read" the developing map and record all decisions in writing. This ensures that the process map reflects the best efforts of a committed team.

For new or reengineered systems, projects or processes, process mapping may be used to specify the needs, requirements and functions and then may be used to improve the process that meets the customer's requirements and performs the required functions.

A process map consists of graphical hierarchical diagrams, supporting text and a glossary of common terms and process definitions, all cross-referenced to one another. The major output of the process map is a ***work flow diagram*** drafted on either conventional paper drawing or created by computer graphic process mapping techniques.

A process map considers activities, information and interface constraints simultaneously. Process mapping usually starts with a functional process representation of **"WHAT"** the process problem is, carefully separated from the design of **"HOW"** the process problem will be solved or implemented. The process map shows HOW and WHAT is to be realised.

PROCESS-DRIVEN REENGINEERING

The increasing competitive pressure to minimize the "time taken to service customers, increase profits, and develop new products" promises a broad range of applications for process-driven business process reengineering.

All service processes and processes that support production (*e.g.,* order management, integrated product design and development, engineering changes, purchasing, marketing support and pay roll) can be considered as business processes and thus subject to improvement or reengineering.

Some examples of business process reengineering opportunities are:

(i) Order Management Processes: Purchasing, contracts, receiving, shipping, storage and management.

(ii) Financial Management Processes: Payroll, ledger control, taxes, accounts receivables and accounts payable.

(iii) Information Management Processes: Database management, net working and client-server application.

(iv) Product Development Processes: Product design, testing, configuration and documentation processes.

(v) Human Resource Processes: Hiring, placement, personal services and training.

PROCESS MAPPING TOOLS

If a business enterprise has to be rebuilt or reengineered from ground zero, it is necessary to carryout process mapping. Through a flow diagram or process map simulation, the processes should be defined. The processes may take inputs such as raw materials or potential customers and turn them into outputs such as products or services

Over the past years, several new software tools have been developed specifically for mapping business processes and work flows .

Three categories of the process mapping tools are: ***1. Flow Diagramming Tools,*** ***2. CASE Tools*** and ***3. Simulation Tools***

These are briefly discussed below:

1. Flow Diagramming Tools: These are the basic level tools that help define processes and workflows by linking text descriptions of processes to symbols. Typically, ***flow chart models*** provide limited analysis capability.

2. CASE Tools: These tools provide a conceptual framework for modeling hierarchies and process definitions. They are typically built on relational data bases and include functions that provide linear, static and deterministic analysis capability.

3. Simulation Tools: Simulation tools provide continuous or discrete-event, dynamic and more sophisticated analysis capability. Simulation tools typically provide animation capabilities that allow the process designer to see how customers and/or work objects flow through the system.

SIMULATION FOR PROCESS MAPPING

A ***process map simulation*** is an analysis that focuses on changes that occur over time. Generally process map simulation addresses the dynamic properties that are often of greatest interest to process improvement. Process map simulation provides a relatively low-cost means to examine process improvements before substantial funds are invested in a new product or process improvement effort.

Three specific reasons for why process simulation is important are:

1. Process map simulation also provides a means of measuring overall changes in the value (output) of an organisation or system caused by the specific changes you make to the processes.
2. Process map simulation's graphic capabilities help decision makers understand complex operations through a simple graphic representation
3. Process map simulation identifies utilisation rates of activities, (money, time, people) revealing bottlenecks or under-utilised activities. Bottlenecks tell you where to apply resources or suggest a redesign of your systems, Underutilised activities tell you where waste exists and identify resources for reallocation and activities that can be discontinued for a cost savings without degrading overall productivity.

NEED FOR A PROCESS ROAD MAP

Most people do not understand how their business enterprise really works. It is process driven, they do not really know the processes that drive their operations. Process mapping helps people to understand and improve their processes and their bottom line performances Therefore, there is a strong need for a **process road map.**

Work gets done in business enterprises through their customer and administrative processes. To understand the way processes really work, to apply a proven methodology to improve the way work gets done, and to manage the way work gets done, process mapping should be the focus of attention and actions of employees in their organisations..

Who needs to apply Process Mapping?

1. Executives, who can use the process perspective and tools to link business enterprise goals to individual performance, measure what is really going on in the business, benchmark performance against other companies, establish competitive advantages, assess the impact of mergers and acquisitions, and evaluate alternative organisational structures.

2. Managers, who can use the process perspective and process mapping tools to identify and close quality, cost and cycle time gaps, manage the interfaces with other departments, implement change and effectively allocate resources.

3. Analysts, who can use the process perspective and process mapping tools to diagnose business needs and recommend improvements that will have a significant impact on business enterprise performance, to evaluate actions they are asked to take and to facilitate improvement teams.

Process mapping can provide a disciplined way of describing the detailed structure of the processes and how they relate. Since understanding the process is critical to understanding and changing process-driven systems, process mapping and process map simulation are particularly useful. Process mapping provides a proven methodology that can be used in business enterprise for effective simulation, cost and schedule analysis and significant process improvement.

PROCESS MAPPING APPROACH

The ten key process mapping steps are:

Step 1: Determine whether you need a process map

Step 2: Assess your need to improve or reengineer your business processes

Step 3: Define the role of process mapping in your reengineering strategy.

Step 4: Determine whether you really understand your business processes.

Step 5: Understand the value of process mapping through success stories from a broad variety of process map users.

Step 6: Learn how to apply process mapping methodology in your own businesses.

Step 7: Create your own process mapping team.

Step 8: Find the right process mapping tools and make a comparative assessment. Know how to select the best process mapping tools

Step 9: Collect process map information and process details via focused interviews.

Step 10: Follow the specific steps for implementation of process mapping.

The above steps are briefly discussed in the following paragraphs:

Step 1: Determine whether you need a process map:

In an organisation driven by the process, process mapping helps to understand and improve the processes and the bottom-line performance. If the organisation is implementing process reengineering (BPR) to improve its processes and become more competitive and customer focused, process mapping is very much useful in this approach. Executives, managers and analysts who can use the process perspective and tools to link business enterprise goals to individual performance need to apply process mapping.

Step 2: Assess your need to improve or reengineer your business processes

In order to satisfy its customers, an organisation must develop new products cheaper, better and faster than it did in the previous year. The firm should examine the possibility of reengineering its processes to assure that its competition, by significantly changing the way they do business, won't surprise the firm in the competitive game of global survival. Businesses do not reengineer their processes just to cut costs. Reengineering is a state-of-the-practice management approach that applies the "best practices"' process understanding, process simplification principles, computer aided analytical tools and management techniques to help assure survival in this very competitive global market place.

Step 3: Define the role of process mapping in your reengineering strategy

In order to improve its business process, an organisation needs to understand and adopt a ***process management approach.*** Reengineering of a business is fundamentally driven by the simplification, elimination, or improvement of the business processes for which the organisation must adopt a process management approach. Successful businesses that have implemented process management have formulated their own unique approach by defining critical process management needs, applying the appropriate level of process mapping tools and techniques to meet their needs and prioritising the process improvement needs that directly drive organisation - wide business performance improvement.

After defining their core business processes, businesses embark upon multiple process mapping stages. Initially, businesses do high-level process mapping to further define and understand key business processes and examine how they work together. High-level process mapping provides a manageable overall picture of the key processes showing the complete chain of related activities within the business.

Defining processes at a high level can help create enterprise-focused process maps. These process maps can reflect processes across the entire business enterprise. It is important to look at the whole business process so business leaders can see the interconnections when they want to make hard decisions on reengineering priorities.

Step 4: Determine whether you really understand your business processes:

Most business managers and process leaders believe they understand their business processes until a problem occurs in their operations or they begin to examine how they can eliminate, simplify or improve their business processes, to provide better, cheaper or faster products or services to their customers. The process improvement model shown in ***Exhibit 14.29*** (often referred to as the Plan-

Do-Check-Act cycle for process improvement) is a four step cycle that begins with the activities needed to create an environment conducive to process understanding by anticipating and planning for change, implementing change, checking performance improvements and continuing to improve process activities.

Exhibit 14.29 : The Plan-Do-Check-Act (PDCA) Improvement Model

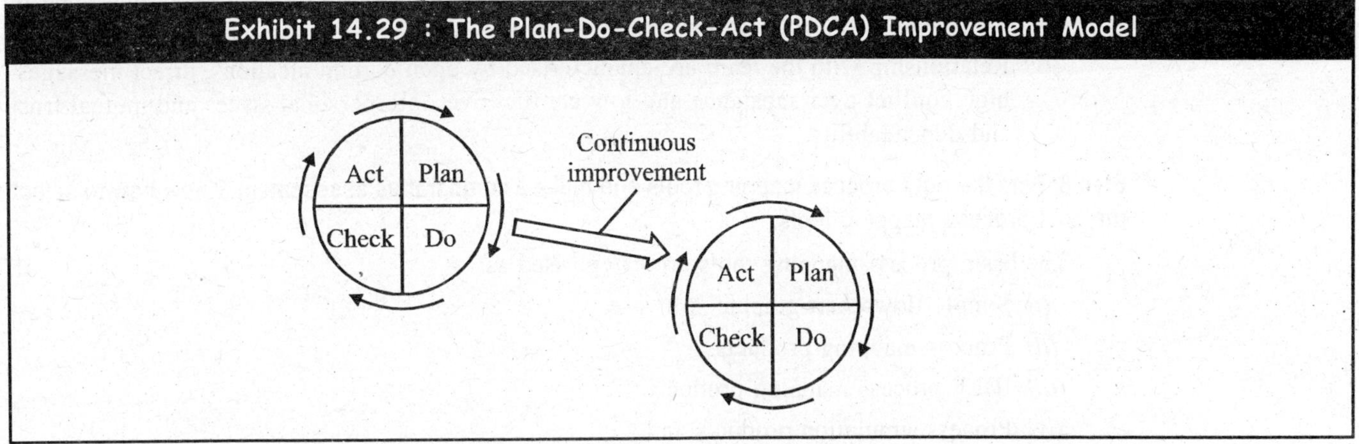

Step 5: Understand the Value of Process Mapping through success stories from a broad variety of Process Map users

The concept behind process mapping and reengineering business processes is to remove the non-value added process activities, thereby lowering the process costs. In order to achieve this it is necessary to identify where non-value added process elements are located.

Process mapping is tool that has proved to be helpful in the process of decomposing the overall top-level process into lower layers of sub processes, Once the basic "As-Is" process map attributes are defined, simulation software tools can be applied to facilitate "what-if" and "To-Be" scenarios. An organisation embarking on process mapping for reengineering can understand the value of process mapping by analysing the success stories of other organisation's use of process mapping and the lessons learnt.

Step 6: Learn how to apply process mapping methodology in your own business

The process map can be used to describe what a process does, what controls it, what things it works on, what means it uses to perform its functions and what it produces. IDEF (Integration Definition for Function Modeling) is a process mapping technique based on combining graphics and text that are then presented in an organised and systematic graphic presentation to gain understanding, support analysis, provide logic for potential changes, specify requirements or support system-level design and integration activities, benefits analysis, cost trade-off, requirements definition, functional analysis, system design, maintenance and base line documentation for business process reengineering.

Step 7: Create your own process mapping team

The success of each process improvement effort depends on the ability of the team members to work together, thus, team satisfaction with the change process and the resulting process definition is important. Having all members satisfied with the change process ensures ownership and responsibility among team members.

Much of the success of a team is determined by the choice of the process mapping team members. Achieving the required level of team work requires a structured process and competent people with specific expertise and understanding of the customer needs, product or process requirements, technology base, information, material, production capabilities and administrative support capabilities. Effective process mapping teams share certain characteristics listed below.

(i) Team members have a clear commitment to the team's goals and find that their individual goals are highly compatible with the team's goals.

(ii) Team members' notes and responsibilities are clear.

(iii) The established procedures for functioning are clear, appropriate, efficient and open to modification as needs arise.

(iv) Relationship with the team are characterised by open communications, direct messages, high conflict over substance and low conflict over interpersonal issues and mutual trust and dependability.

Step 8: Find the right process mapping tools and make a comparative assessment. Know how to select the best process mapping tools.

The basic process mapping tools are categorised as:

(i) Simple flow-chart graphic software.

(ii) Process mapping products.

(iii) IDEF process mapping products.

(iv) Process simulation products and

(v) Process-mapping-related Activity-Based-Costing (ABC) products.

These categories of process mapping tools are briefly discussed below:

(i) Simple Flow-Chart Graphic Tools and Software: Several inexpensive and very-easy-to-use software products can be used to document the processes. With their aid a computer process map can be developed.

One Basic software tool in this category is Micrograph's ***ABC Snap Graphics 2.0,*** which is cheap and easy to use and can be used to describe and document the basic process map. VISIO 2.0 for windows is the next-higher level flow-chart graphic software product-VISIO is the state-of-the-practice "Best Buy" product for this type of process mapping software tool.

(ii) Process Mapping Software Products: These are non IDEF-type process planning tools. Very effective new process mapping software products have been developed to meet the needs of commercial product and service reengineering business community. One example is Logic Works Inc., which has brought to market their powerful windows-based product ***BP Win. BP Win*** is an excellent example of an integrated software approach that provides process mapping and simulation and also provides an easy link to ABC software products.

(iii) IDEF Process mapping Software Products: The fundamental concepts of IDEF (Integrated computer - aided DEFinition) process mapping are based on the ideas of structured analysis that have produced significant pay offs in diverse business applications. Such benefits include reductions in development costs, fewer system integration failures and uniformly better communication.

IDEF software tools provide a disciplined way of graphically describing the detailed structure of the processes and how they relate to another. IDEF process mapping software provides a tool that can effectively be used to link process simulation, process analysis and process improvement efforts.

(iv) Process Simulation Software Products: Generally, process simulation software tools are used to address the dynamic properties such as "What-If" and "To-Be" process mapping analysis steps that often provide the greatest benefit to the process improvement initiatives. These tools provide an effective means to examine potential process improvements before substantial funds are invested in a new product or process improvement effort. They also provide an early warning if disconnects or implementation conflicts can be identified without actually making the planned change in the process.

The various simulation software techniques available include petrinets, ITHINK-type systems dynamics, **SIMSCRIPT simulation software** *etc.* Detailed description of these simulation software tools are beyond the scope of this book.

(v) Activity-Based-Costing Software Products: Activity-Based-Costing (ABC) segregates and manages products and process costs differently and better than the traditional cost accounting approach. ABC is a proven methodology that measures the cost and performance of activities, resources and cost objects. A very good example of ABC software for business process reengineering is ***Easy ABC plus*** by AB Technologies Inc. It is a state-of-the-art-practice tool and is one of the "Best-Buy" software products.

Step 9: Collect Process Map Information and Process Details Via Focused Interviews

To create the process map several phases of author / interviewer activities need to be completed including: *(i)* Data gathering phase, *(ii)* Process map structuring phase, *(iii)* Map documentation phase and *(iv)* Feedback interaction phase.

There are five stages to a successful data-gathering interview: *(i)* Preparing for the interview, *(ii)* Opening the interview, *(iii)* Conducting the interview *(iv)* Terminating the interview and *(v)* Completion of the interview.

The purpose of the interview in to gather information from an individual who possesses an expertise considered important to the process mapping assessment.

In Stage 1- "Preparing for the interview"- the activities involved are:

(i) Selecting the interviewee (process expert).
(ii) Making an appointment with the interviewee.
(iii) Establishing tentative agenda for the interview.
(iv) Reviewing available background information.
(v) Reviewing appropriate terminology and
(vi) Ensuring co-ordination with other interviewers.

In Stage 2- "Opening the interview" the following activates are involved:

(i) Providing the process expert with tangible means of introduction.
(ii) Describing in some detail the purpose of the interview.
(iii) Confirming that note-taking is acceptable.
(iv) Establishing quickly the process expert / author relationship.
(v) Starting with broad, general questions that will get the expert talking.
(vi) Assuring the expert's ability to provide pertinent information.
(vii) Beginning to formulate specific questions that complement the agenda.

In Stage 3- "Conducting the interview"- it is recommended to follow a set of guide-lines dealing with qualifying the information being obtained and another set of guidelines relating to stimulating the information flow from the expert

In Stage 4- "Terminating the interview"- the reasons for termination and depending on the cause of termination what topics should be considered during the termination of the interview are to be noted.

In Stage 5- "Completion of the interview"-The activities included are:

(i) Identifying additional sources of information.
(ii) Summarising the essential elements of information.
(iii) Identifying new terms for the project glossary.
(iv) Listing follow-up questions and areas of concern either postponed or not covered during the interview.
(v) Completing activity and data lists.
(vi) Preparing rough process map sketches and diagrams that reflect the information obtained.

Step 10: Follow the Specific Steps for Implementation of Process-Mapping:

The basic steps involved in creating the process map are:

(i) Selecting a context, view point and purpose.

(ii) Creating the context diagram.

(iii) Creating the topmost process activity diagram.

(iv) Creating subsequent diagrams.

(v) Writing text.

(vi) Selecting a box to decompose.

A detailed discussion of these steps in beyond the scope of this book.

(2) REGRESSION ANALYSIS

Regression analysis is a statistical tool used to find a model for relationship between pairs of numerical data. The model is a straight line (linear regression) or a curve (non-linear regression) that fits the data best. The results of a regression analysis are an equation for that line or curve, a value called r^2 that indicates how good the fit is and other statistical measures that tell how well the data match the model.

The ***Linear regression*** identifies the best straight line through a scatter diagram of the data. The type of regression is the most straight forward analytical tool used in statistical analysis. ***Non linear regression*** looks for a curve that best fits the data. ***Multiple regression*** is used when several independent variables affect one dependent variable. Non-linear and multiple regressions are more complicated then linear regression.

Application of regression analysis: Regression analysis is generally used:

(a) When we have paired numerical data.

(b) After drawing a scatter diagram of the data.

(c) When we want to know how a change in the independent variable affects the dependent variable.

(d) When we want to be able to predict the dependent variable if we know the independent variable.

(e) When we want a statistical measure of how well a line or curve fits the data.

In linear regression, one dependent variable (say demand) is related to one or more independent variables by a linear equation. The dependent variable is demand for a product (say TV or refrigerator) and the independent variable such as advertising expenditure or new housing are assumed to affect the dependent variable and thereby cause the results observed in the past.

***Exhibit 14.30* shows how a linear equation relates to the data.**

In a simple linear regression model, the dependent variable (Y) is a function of only one independent variable (X) and the theoretical relationship is linear or a straight line.

i.e., $y = a + bx$

where
y = dependent variable
x = independent variable
a = y-intercept of the line (a constant value)
b = slope of the line (a constant value)

The objective of **linear regression analysis** is to determine the values of a and b that minimises the sum of the squared deviations of the actual data points from the graphed straight line. Two measures commonly used are the **sample correlation coefficient** and the **sample coefficient of determination**.

Exhibit 14.30 : Simple Linear Regression Analysis

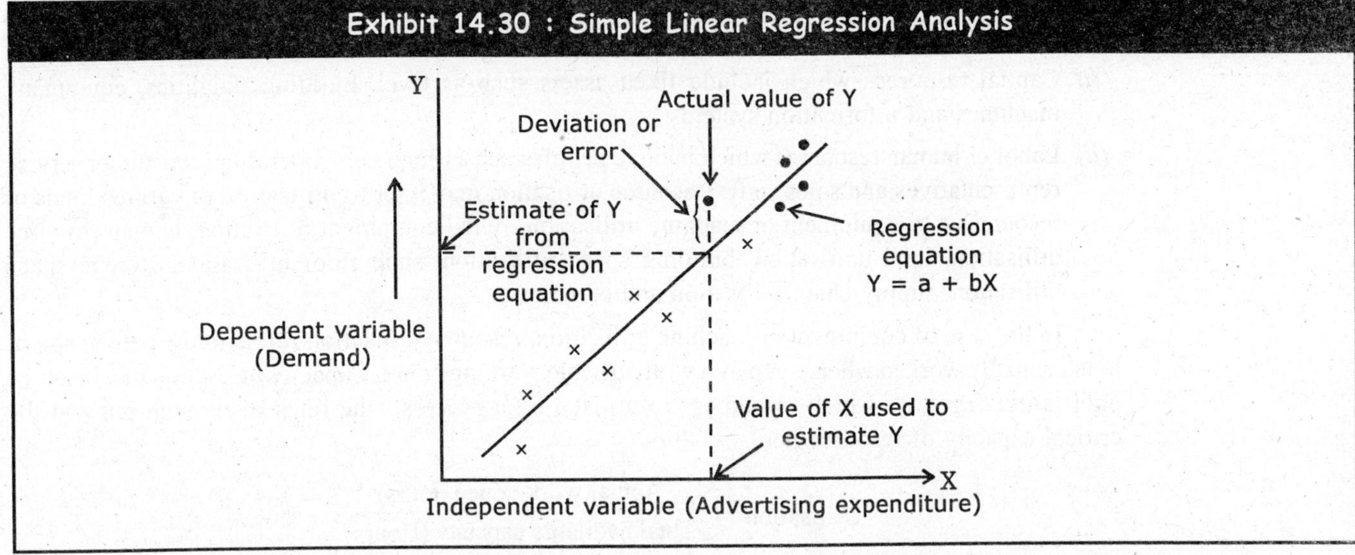

The sample coefficient of correlation γ measures the direction and strength of the relationship between the independent variable and the dependent variable. The value of γ varies from –1 to +1.

The sample coefficient of determination measures the amount of variation in the dependent variable about its mean and is explained by the regression line. It is the square of the coefficient of correlation (*i.e.*, γ^2), and its value varies from 0 to 1.

The formulae used to calculate 'a' and 'b' which are coefficients of the regression equation Y = a + bx, are

$$b = \frac{n(\Sigma xy) - (\Sigma x)(\Sigma y)}{n(\Sigma x)^2 - (\Sigma x)^2}$$

$$a = \frac{\Sigma y - b\,\Sigma x}{n}$$

where n = number of paired observations

$$\text{The coefficient of correlation } \gamma = \frac{n(\Sigma xy) - (\Sigma x)(\Sigma y)}{\sqrt{n(\Sigma x^2) - (\Sigma x)^2}\,\sqrt{n(\Sigma y^2) - (\Sigma y)^2}}$$

The coefficient of correlation $= \gamma^2$.

Multiple Regression Analysis : It is a practical extension of the simple regression model. It allows us to build a model with several independent variables instead of just one variable (in the case of simple linear regression)

For example, $\hat{y} = a + b_1 x_1 + b_2 x_2 + \ldots b_n x_n$

where, $\hat{y}$ = dependent variable

$x_1, x_2 \ldots x_n$ are values of independent variables

a = constant

$b_1, b_2 \ldots b_n$ are coefficients for independent variables

(3) RESOURCE UTILISATION

"Resources management" is focused on the effective use and maintenance of the organisation's physical assets (buildings, finance, information, technology, suppliers and materials) ***"Utilisation"*** can be thought of as the percentage that a resource (e.g. machine, server, cashier, inspector etc.) is used.

"Resources" refer to tangible assets that help transform inputs into outputs in a process. Two categories of resources are:

(i) Capital resources which include fixed assets such as level, building, facilities, equipment, machines and information systems.

(ii) Labor or human resources which include people such as engineers, operations, customer service representatives and sales staff. Resource utilisation may refer to utilisation of various kinds of resources e.g. equipment or machine utilisation, rental equipment utilisation, human resource utilisation, land unitisation, building space utilisation, shop floor utilisation, storage space utilisation, supply chain utilisation and so on.

In the case of equipment or machine utilisation, resource utilisation refers to the percentage of hours actually worked when compared with possible working hours. Capacity utilisation of a resource pool is the degree to which resources are utilised by a process, the rates of through-put and the critical capacity of resource pool.

$$\text{Utilisation} = \frac{\text{Actual work done (Hours)}}{\text{Total available capacity (Hours)}}$$

In production, an increase of the utilisation of equipment or a machine will require more preventive maintenance and more wear and tear on the machine. The objective of operations management is to increase the utilisation of production resources by reducing the idle time and down time of the productive assets to the extent possible.

(4) CUSTOMER SERVICE ANALYSIS

Customer service can be defined as a process which takes place between the buyer, seller and third party. The process results in a value addition to the product or service exchanged. The value added might be short-term as in a single transaction or long-term as in a contractual relationship. The benefits of value addition are shared by each of the partners to the transaction or contract and they are better off after the completion of the transaction. Thus, in a process view, customer service is a process of providing significant value added benefits to the supply chain in a cost effective way. Customer service can be thought of as something a firm or service provider provides to those who purchases its products or services. Customer service frequently affects every area of the firm by attempting to ensure customer satisfaction through the provision of service to the customer.

Customer service analysis investigates customer interactions with an organisation including point-of-sale, service delivery and follow-on-support, to ensure customers are being serviced well. Executives and marketers monitor service and satisfaction levels over time to measure business effectiveness in retaining and attracting customers.

(5) THE "FIVE WHYS" TECHNIQUES (WHY-WHY DIAGRAM)

For every effect there is cause. But the results chain between the two is fairly long and becomes finer as one move from the inputs to activities, outputs, outcome and impact. In results based management, the degree of control one enjoys decreases higher up the chain and the challenge of monitoring and evaluating correspondingly increases.

When looking to solve a problem, it helps to begin at the end result, reflect upon what caused that and **question the answer five times.** This elementary and often effective approach to problem solving promotes deep thinking through questioning, and can be adopted quickly and applied to most problems. Most obviously and directly, the five whys technique relates to the principle of systematic problem solving. Without the intent of the principle, the technique can only be a shell of the process. Hence there are three key elements to effective use of the "Five Whys" techniques: *(i)* accurate and complete statement of problems, *(ii)* complete honesty in answering the question and *(iii)* the determination to get to the bottom of problems and resolve them. The technique was developed by Sakichi Toyoda for the Toyota Industries Corporation.

The "Five Whys" technique or "Why-Why diagram" helps to identify the root causes of a problem. The method helps the problem-solving team to reorganise the broad network of problem causes and the relationship among these causes. It can indicate the best areas to address for short and long-term solutions.

When to use: *(i)* When the team needs to probe for the root cause of a problem, *(ii)* When the team's analysis of a problem is too superficial, *(iii)* When the many contributing cause to a problem are confusing and *(iv)* As a graphic communication tool, to explain to others the many causes of a problem.

Procedure:

1. Develop a statement of the specific problem for which the causes are to be found. Write it on a note pad or flip chart or white board.
2. Ask "Why?" this problem does or could occur. List all these causes on notes and place them in a column immediately to the right of the problem.
3. Each of the cause statements becomes a new problem statement. Again ask "Why?"-Why does this situation cause the problem? Create another column of cause statements. Show the relationships to the first column of causes with arrows.
4. Continue to turn each cause into a problem and ask "Why?". Do not stop until you reach an answer that is fundamental (company policy or procedures, systems, training needs and so forth).

***Exhibit 14.31* shows ''Five Whys" work sheet.**

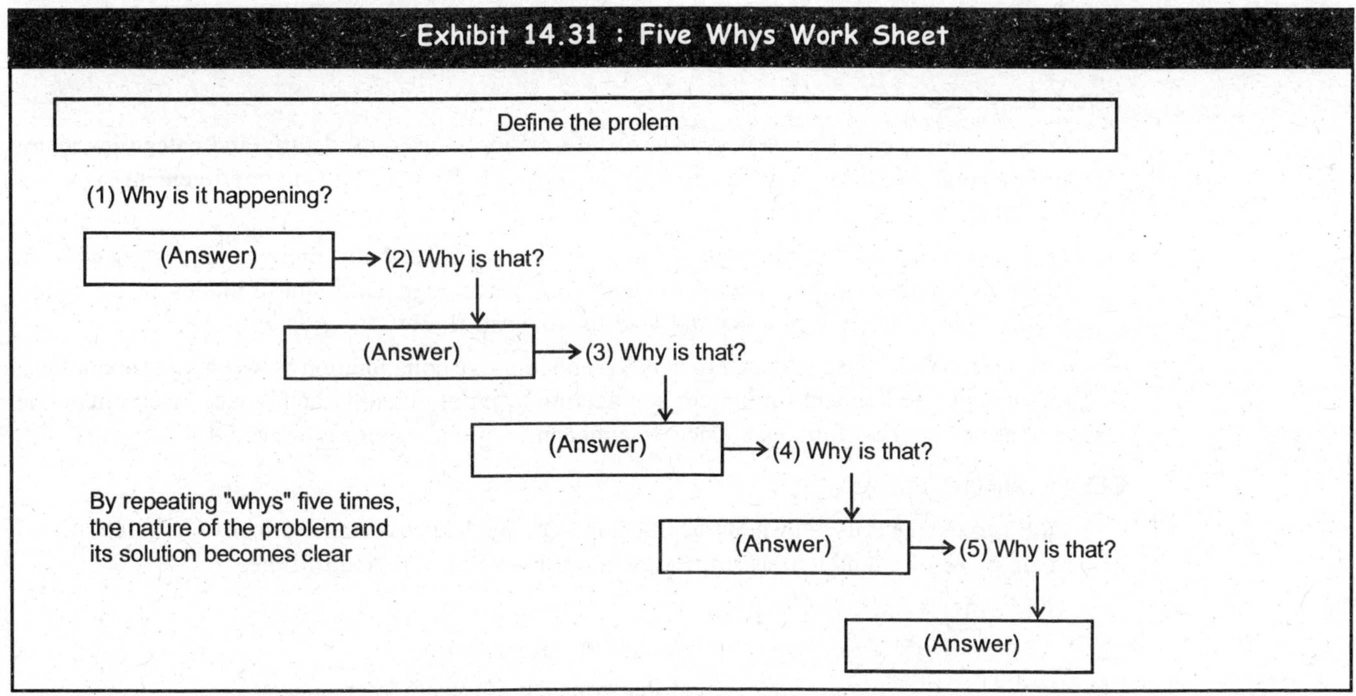

Example: There was an accident that occurred in a manufacturing plant. A worker had damaged his finger. The five whys technique was used to find the cause of the accident as below:

Question (1): **Why did the worker damage his thumb?**

Answer: Because his thumb got caught in the conveyor.

Question (2): Why did his thumb get caught in the conveyor?

Answer: Because he was chasing his lunch box which was on the running conveyor.

Question (3): Why did he chase the lunch box?

Answer: Because he had placed his lunch box on the conveyor, which had then started unexpectedly.

Question (4): Why he has placed his lunch box on the conveyor?

Answer: Because he was using the conveyor as his dining table.

Question (5): Why the conveyor started unexpectedly?

Answer: Because the conveyor operator stated it before the siren indicating end of the lunch break.

The root cause of the accident is that the worker simply needed a table for taking his lunch.

The solution: The plant manager must provide a place for workers to have their lunch other than their place of work. Also the workers should undergo safety training.

(6) OVERALL EQUIPMENT EFFECTIVENESS (OEE)

Overall equipment effectiveness (OEE) is a measure of total (complete, inclusive, whole) equipment performance- the degree to which the asset in doing what it is supposed to do. OEE is a "best practice" way to monitor and improve the effectiveness of the manufacturing processes (*i.e.* machines, manufacturing cells, assembly lines etc.)

OEE takes into consideration the most common and important sources of manufacturing productivity loss, places them into three primary categories and distills them into metrics that provide an excellent gauge for measuring where we are and how we can improve.

OEE is frequently used as a key metric in total productivity maintenance (TPM) and Lean manufacturing programs.

Objectives of OEE

Overall equipment effectiveness data or information is used to identify and categories major losses or reasons for poor performance. OEE provides the basis for setting improvement priorities and beginning root cause analysis.

OEE expressed as a percentage is used to track and trend the improvement or decline in equipment effectiveness over a period of time. OEE percentage can point to hidden or unutilised capacity in a manufacturing process and lead to balanced flow.

The use of OEE is also intended to develop and improve collaboration between asset operations, maintenance, purchasing and equipment engineering to jointly identify and reduce or eliminate the major causes of poor performance since "maintenance" alone cannot improve OEE.

OEE Percentage Formula

OEE percentage is useful when tracking and trending the performance effectiveness (reliability) of a single piece of equipment or single-stream process over a period of time.

The formulas are given below.

$$\text{OEE (percentage)} = \text{Availability (percentage)} \times \text{Performance efficiency (percentage)} \times \text{Quality rate (Percentage)}.$$

$$\text{Availability (\%)} = \frac{\text{Actual operating time}}{\text{Gross available time}}$$

$$\text{Performance efficiency (\%)} = \frac{\text{Actual production rate}}{\text{Designed production rate}} \times 100$$

$$\text{Quality rate (\%)} = \frac{\text{(Total unit produced)} - \text{(Defective units produced)}}{\text{Total units produced}} \times 100$$

OEE Factors

1. OEE analysis starts with **plant operation time** which is the time the facility is open and available for equipment operation.
2. From plant operating time, the **"planned shutdown"** time is subtracted to obtain **"planned production time"**. It is shown below in the form of a horizontal bar chart.

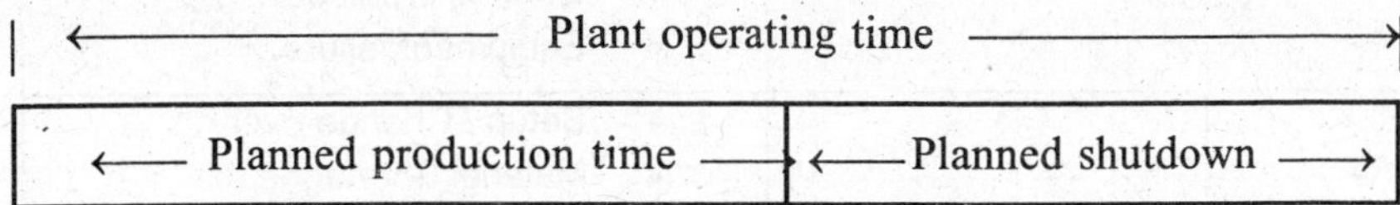

The planned shutdown includes all events that should be excluded from efficiency analysis because there was no intention of running production (e.g. lunch and coffee breaks, scheduled maintenance, or periods where there is nothing to produce).

OEE begins with **planned production time** and scrutinises efficiency and productivity losses that occur, with the goal of reducing or eliminating these losses. There are three general categories of loss to consider: *(i)* Down time loss, *(ii)* Speed loss and *(iii)* Quality loss.

3. **Availability:** Availability takes into account **"down time loss"** which includes any **events** that stop planned production for an appreciable length of time. Examples include equipment failure, material shortages, and change over times (which is a form of equipment downtime). While it may not be possible to eliminate change over time, in many cases it can be reduced (for e.g. using single minute exchange of dies-SMED). The **operating time** is obtained by subtracting down time loss from planned production time.

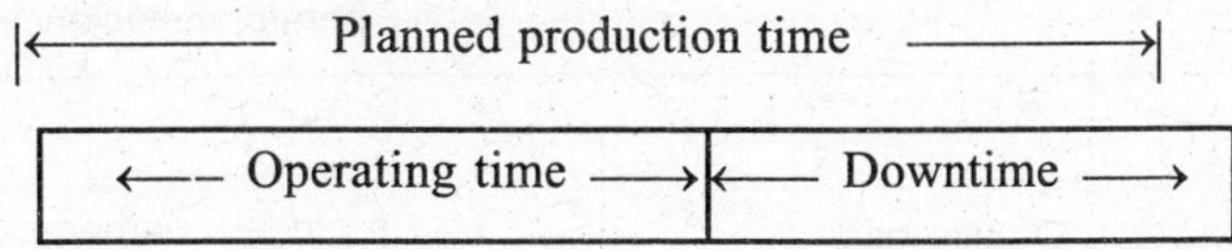

4. **Performance:** Performance takes into account **"speed loss"** which includes any factors that cause the process to operate at less than the maximum possible speed, when running, Examples include machine wear, substandard materials, misfeeds, and operator efficiency. The remaining available time is called **"net operating time"**

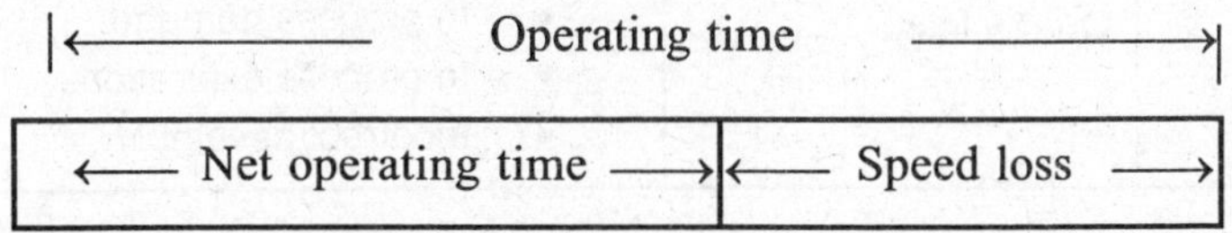

5. **Quality:** Quality takes into account **"quality loss"** which accounts for produced pieces that do not met quality standards, including pieces that require rework. The remaining time is called **"fully production time"**

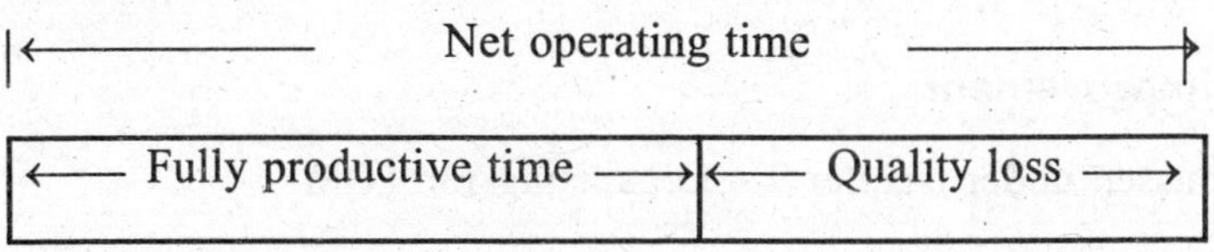

Six big loss: One of the major goal of TPM and OEE program is to reduce and / or eliminate what are called **"Six big losses"**, the most common cause of efficiency loss in manufacturing . The six big losses are shown in *Table 14.10* below.

Table 14.10

Six Big Loss Categories.	OEE Loss Category	Event Examples
1. Break downs	Down time loss	• Tooling failures. • Unplanned maintains. • General break downs. • Equipment failure.
2. Set up and adjustments	Downtime loss	• Setup / Change over. • Material Shortages. • Operator Shortages. • Major adjustments. • Warm up time.
3. Small stops	Speed loss	• Obstructed product flow • Component jams. • Misfeeds. • Sensor blocked. • Delivery blocked. • Cleaning / checking.
4. Reduced Speed	Speed loss	• Rough running. • Under name plate capacity. • Under design capacity. • Equipment wear. • Operator inefficiency.
5. Startup rejects	Quality loss	• Scrap. • Rework. • In process damage. • In process expiration. • Incorrect assembly.
6. Production rejects	Quality loss.	• Scrap. • Rework. • In process damage. • In process expiration. • Incorrect assembly.

14.8 IMPROVEMENT TOOLS AND TECHNIQUES

(A) Continous Improvement

Already discussed under chapter 9 – Organising for TQM.

(B) Just-in-Time Sustems (JIT)

Just-in-time (or JIT) is defined as "a philosophy of manufacturing based on planned elimination of all wastes and continuous improvement of productivity".

JIT is an approach that seeks to eliminate all sources of waste in production activities by providing the **right part** at the **right place** at the **right time.**

JIT encompasses the successful execution of all manufacturing activities required to produce a final product, from design to delivery and including all stages of conversion from raw materials onward. The primary elements of JIT are to have only the required inventory when needed, to improve quality to zero defects, to reduce lead times by reducing set-up times, que-lengths and lot sizes, to incrementally revise the operations themselves and to accomplish these things at minimum cost.

In short, JIT means :

(i) Producing the **quantity** of units **that is needed**, no more or no less.

(ii) Producing them **on the date** and at the **time required**, not before, not after.

Objectives of JIT Manufacturing

The ultimate goal or objective of JIT system is a balanced system, that is one that achieves a smooth, rapid flow of materials through the system. The idea is to reduce the process time to as low as possible by making best of the resources. The specific goal or objective is to provide the **right quality level at the right place**. JIT tries to build only what internal (employees) and external customers want and when they want it. **The supporting goals or objectives of JIT are :**

(i) Produce only the products that customers want.

(ii) Produce products only as quickly as customers want to use them.

(iii) Produce products with perfect quality.

(iv) Produce products with features that customers want.

(v) Produce with no waste of labour, materials or equipment and with zero inventory.

The major focus in JIT is on reduction of wastes. Wastes includes : *(a)* Overproduction, *(b)* waiting time or delays, *(c)* unnecessary handling or transportation, *(d)* unnecessary inventory, *(e)* processing waste (scrap), *(f)* inefficient work methods (waste of labour effort), *(g)* defective products.

Building Blocks of JIT

The design and operation of a JIT system provides the foundation to achieve the goals or objectives of JIT system. **The four building blocks of this foundation are :** *(i)* Product design, *(ii)* Process design, *(iii)* Personnel and organisational elements and *(iv)* Manufacturing planning and control.

Three elements of product design that are key to JIT systems are : *(i)* standard parts, *(ii)* modular design and *(iii)* quality.

Seven aspects of process design that are particularly important for JIT systems are : *(i)* small lot sizes, *(ii)* set-up time reduction, *(iii)* cellular manufacturing, *(iv)* limited work-in-process inventory, *(v)* quality improvement, *(vi)* production flexibility and *(vii)* minimum inventory.

The five elements of personnel and organisation are : *(i)* workers as assets, *(ii)* cross-trained (multi-skilled) workers, *(iii)* continuous improvement, *(iv)* cost accounting and *(v)* leadership.

Five elements of manufacturing planning and control are : *(i)* level loading, *(ii)* pull systems, *(iii)* visual systems **(kanban)**, *(iv)* close vendor relationships, and *(v)* reduced transaction processing.

Characteristics of JIT System

The salient characteristics are :

(i) pull method of material flow, *(ii)* constantly high quality, *(iii)* small lot sizes, *(iv)* uniform workstation loads, *(v)* standardised components and work methods, *(vi)* close supplier ties, *(vii)* flexible workforce, *(viii)* line flow strategy, *(ix)* automated production and *(x)* total preventive maintenance.

JIT Purchasing : JIT purchasing has the same pull type approach used in JIT manufacturing, applied to purchasing shipments of parts from suppliers. The essentials of JIT purchasing are :

(i) Supplier–development and supplier relationship.

(ii) Long-term relationships with few supplier (referred to as JIT suppliers).

(iii) Suppliers are rated not based on price, but on product quality, delivery schedules, reliability of

supply and flexibility.

(iv) Suppliers are located near the buying firm.

(v) Shipments are delivered directly to the customer's production line.

(vi) Parts are delivered in small size containers.

(vii) Delivered material is of near-perfect quality.

Benefits of JIT System

(i) Inventory levels are drastically reduced and high inventory turnovers (50 to 100 times per year) have been achieved.

(ii) Reduced production cycle time or product throughput time.

(iii) Improved product quality and minimum scrap.

(iv) Root-cause elimination approach to solve production problems.

(v) Multiskilled and flexible work-force reduces worker idle time, overheads, fewer lay-offs etc.

(vi) Elimination of unpleasant suppliers.

(vii) Reduced customer-related problems.

(viii) Near zero defects.

(ix) Improved communications.

(x) Lesser work-in-process and finished goods inventory.

(xi) Shorter procurement lead times.

(xii) Improved employee morale due to high employee involvement and employee empowerment.

(xiii) Reduced amount of inspection.

Kanban System or Pull Scheduling

To build only what customers demand when they demand, JIT manufacturing needs a scheduling system that can immediately and clearly communicate the demands of the customer to the delivery system. The Kanban or pull scheduling system does this. ***'Kanban'*** is a Japanese word meaning ***"card"*** and these cards are the means of communicating within, to and from a work centre. Kanbans are the heart of the JIT system. They effectively replace all written work orders, move tickets and routing sheets. No parts can be moved, produced or used without an appropriate Kanban. Parts and components are transferred from one work area to another in rigid plastic containers. These containers are just large enough to hold a small and fixed quantity of units of the same component reference. Different parts are not put into the same container. There are two kinds of Kanbans – production Kanban and withdrawal Kanban (or conveyance Kanban). The information written on Kanban includes reference number, storage areas and associated work centres.

The purpose of the Kanban system is to signal the need for more parts and to ensure that those parts are produced in time to support subsequent fabrication or assembly. This is done by pulling parts through from the final assembly line. Only the final assembly line receives a schedule from the dispatching office and this schedule is nearly the same from day to day. All other machine operators and suppliers receive production orders (Kanban cards) from the subsequent (using) work centres. If production should stop for a time in the using work centres, the supplying work centres will also soon stop, since they will no longer receive Kanban orders for more materials.

The Kanban system is a physical control system consisting of cards and containers. To control movement of the containers, the Kanban cards (production cards and withdrawal or move cards) are used. These cards are used to authorise production and to identify parts in any container. The Kanban cards may be made of paper, metal or plastic and they generally contain the information shown in ***Exhibit 14.32.***

Kanban cards take the place of shop paperwork used in traditional repetitive manufacturing.

Exhibit 14.32 : Kanban Cards

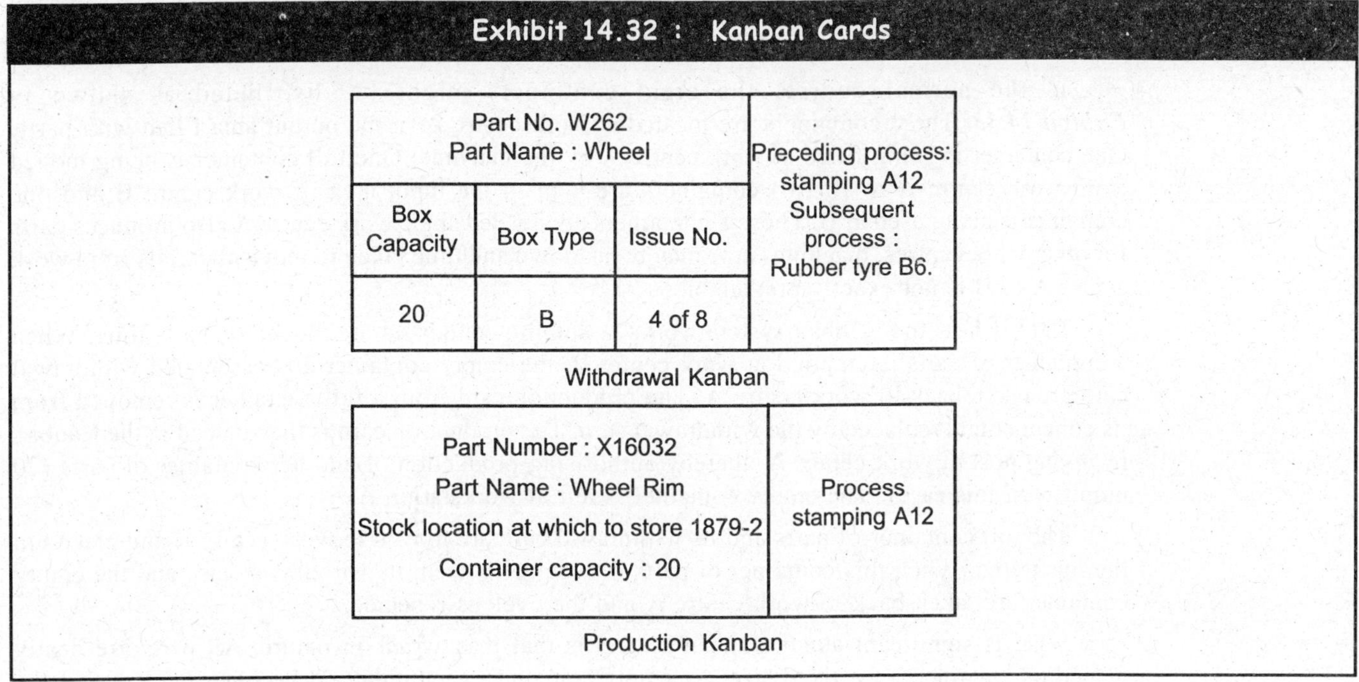

Working of the Kanban System

Exhibit 14.33 illustrates the working of the Kanban system.

Exhibit 14.33 : Kanban System

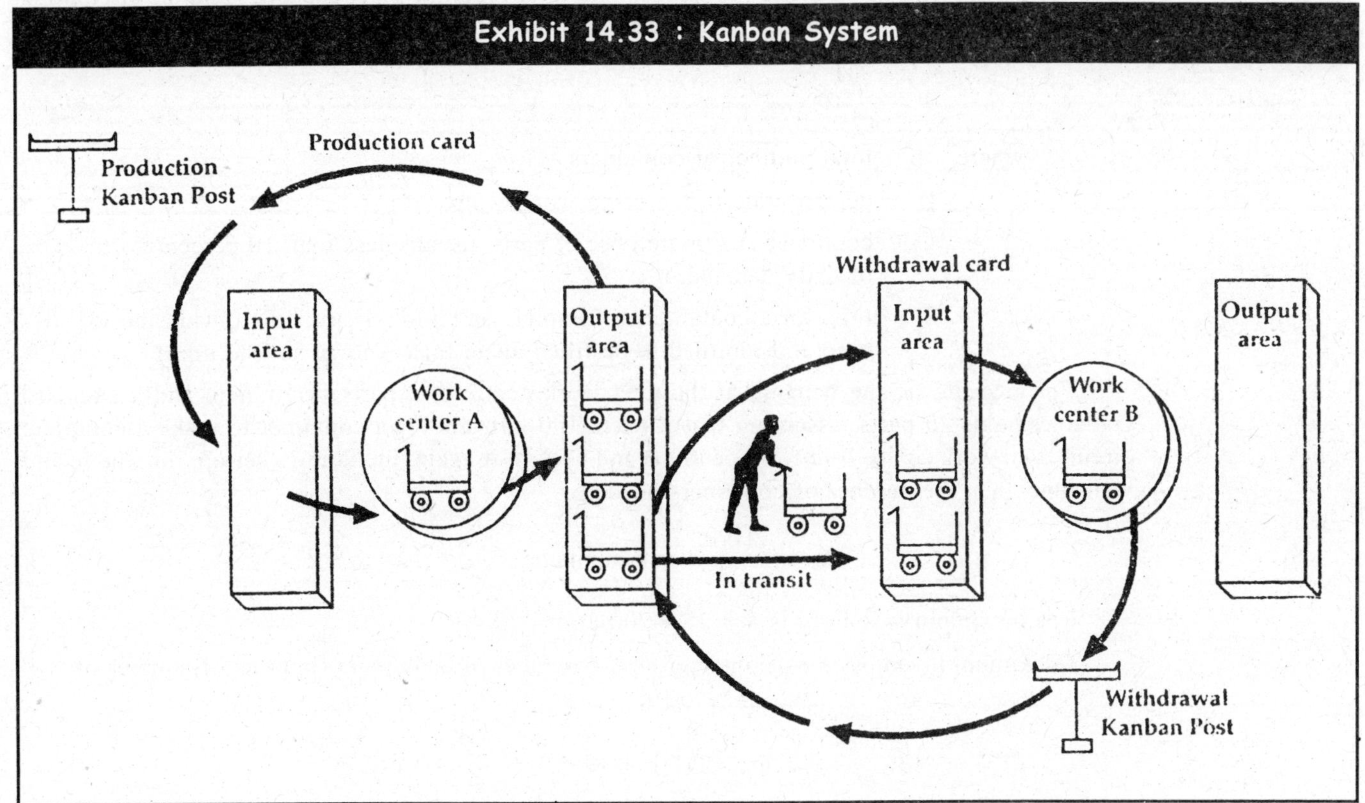

Assume that eight containers are used between work centre A and B (A supplies B) and each container holds exactly 20 parts. The maximum inventory that can exist between these two work centres is then 160 units (*i.e.,* 8 × 20) since production work at work centre A will stop when all containers are filled.

In the normal course, the eight containers might be distributed as shown in ***Exhibit 14.33***. Three containers are located at work centre A in the output area filled with parts. One container is being filled at work centre A by the machine. One full container is being moved from work centre A to B, two containers are kept in the input area of work centre B and one container is being used at B. These 8 containers are needed since work centre A also produces parts for other work centres, machines at A may break down and time taken to move materials from work centre A to B is not exactly predictable.

Here is how the Kanban system works, assuming containers are moved one at a time. When a container of parts is emptied at work centre B, the empty container and associated withdrawal card are taken back to work centre A. The production card from a full container is removed from its container and replaced by the withdrawal card. The production card is then placed in the Kanban receiving post at work centre A, thereby authorising production of another container of parts (20 numbers in this case). The empty container is left at workstation A.

The full container of parts and its withdrawal card are moved to work centre B and placed in the input area. When this container of parts is eventually used, its withdrawal card and the empty container are taken back to work centre A and the cycle is repeated.

What is significant about Kanban system is that it is *visual* in nature. All parts are neatly placed in containers of a fixed size. As empty containers accumulate, it becomes evident that the producing work centre is lagging behind. On the other hand, when all containers are full, production is stopped. The production lot size is exactly equal to one container of parts.

Calculation of the number of containers needed: The number of containers needed to operate a work centre is a function of the deamnd rate, container size (capacity) and the circulating time for a container. The number of containers required for an item is calculated as :

$$n = \frac{DT}{C}$$

where n = total number of containers

D = demand rate of the using work centre

C = container size in number of parts, usually less than 10 percent of daily demand.

T = time for a container to complete an entire circuit; filled, wait, moved, used and returned to be filled again (also known as lead time)

For example, if the demand at the next work centre is 2 parts per minute and a standard container holds 25 parts, assuming that it takes 100 minutes for a container to make a complete circuit from work centre A to work centre B and back to A again, including a set-up, run, move and wait time, then the number of containers needed is

$$n = \frac{2(100)}{25} = 8 \text{ numbers}$$

The maximum inventory is 8 × 25 = 200 units.

(Maximum inventory = container size × number of containers (interms of number of times to fill)

$$= Cn = DT \left(\text{because } n = \frac{DT}{C}\right)$$

Inventory can be reduced by reducing the size of the containers or the number of containers used. This is done by reducing the time required to circulate a container, including its machine set-up time, run time, wait time and move times. When any of these times has been reduced, certain numbers of Kanban cards can be removed from the system along with an equal number of containers. Hence, reducing lead time is the key to JIT production.

Exhibit 14.34 illustrates a complete Kanban system which links all work centres in a production facility and the suppliers. All material is pulled through by the final assembly schedule, based on a highly visible shop floor and supplier control system.

Exhibit 14.34 : Complete Kanban System

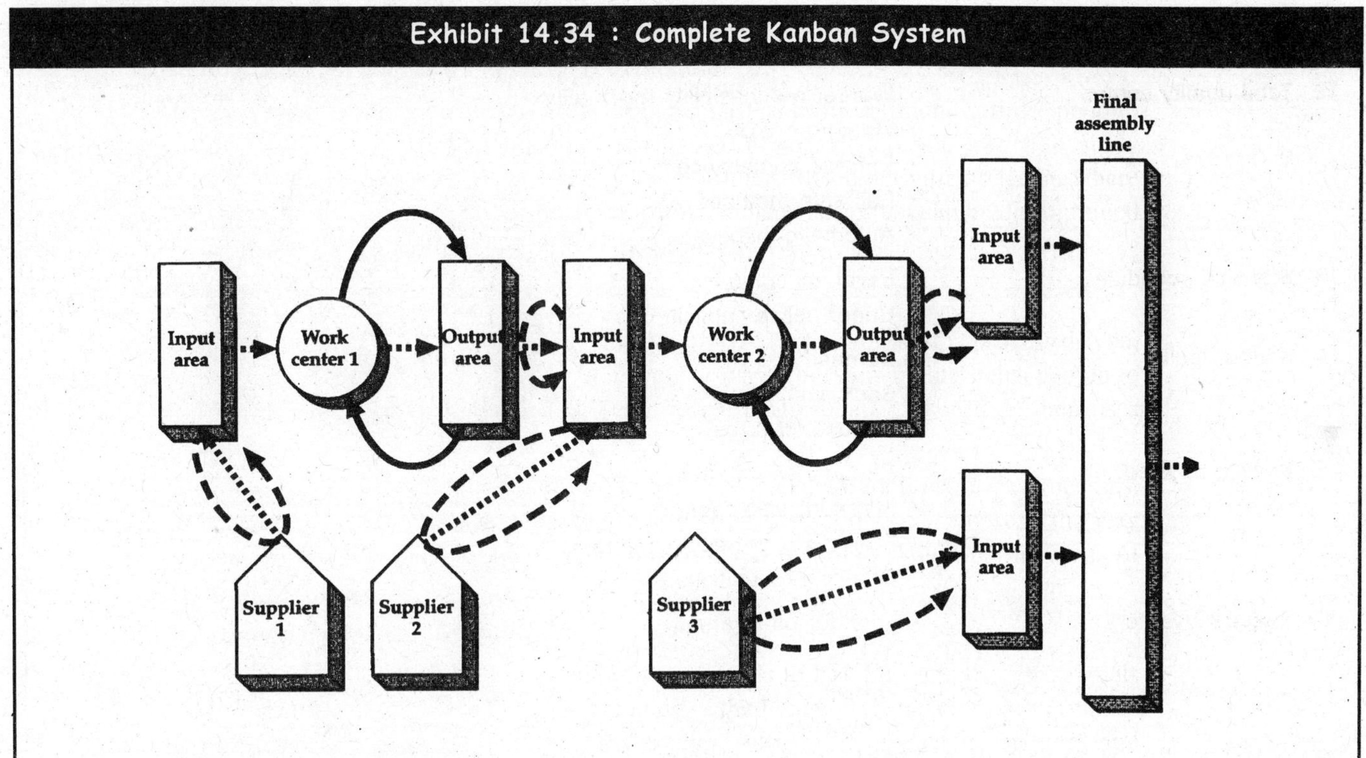

Benefits of Kanban

Kanban systems have resulted in significant benefits :

(i) Reduced inventory level
(ii) Less confusion over sequence of activities
(iii) Less obsolescence of inventories while in storage
(iv) Smaller floor space requirements for storing inventory
(v) Reduced lead times
(vi) Improved quality
(vii) Higher employee productivity and
(viii) Greater system flexibility.

Box 14.5 lists JIT implementation requirements.

(C) Quality Circles

Already discussed under chapter 3.

Box 14.5 : JIT Implementation Requirements

1. Design flow process :	• Link operations • Balance workstation capacities • Re-lay-out for flow • Emphasise preventive maintenance • Reduce lot sizes • Reduce set-up, change over times
2. Total quality control :	• Worker responsibility for quality • Measure : SQC • Enforce compliance • Fail safe methods • Automatic inspection
3. Stabilise schedule :	• Level schedule • Under utilise capacity
4. Kanban pull :	• Demand pull • Back flush • Reduce lot sizes
5. Work with vendor :	• Reduce lead times • Frequent deliveries • Project usage requirements • Quality expectations
6. Reduce inventory :	• Look for other areas • Stores • Transit • Carousels • Conveyors
7. Improve product design :	• Standard product configuration • Standardise and reduce number of parts • Process design with product design • Quality expectations
The above activities lead to	
(i) Solving problems concurrently :	• Root cause • Solve permanently • Team approach • Line and specialist responsibility • Continual education
(ii) Measuring performance :	• Emphasise improvement • Track trends

(D) Force Field Analysis

A Force field Analysis is a problem-solving tool used to analyse the driving forces and restraining forces that impact a proposed change or decision. Force field Analysis is useful in deciding if, when or how to initiate a change.

A Force Field Analysis is a very useful tool to use when considering any form of change where people are involved. It is very useful when making a decision about introducing a new product or a new service.

The aim is to highlight the valid reasons or driving forces, for the change and to be aware of possible resistance or restraining forces. ***Exhibit 14.35* illustrates this:**

Exhibit 14.35 : Illustration of Force Field Analysis

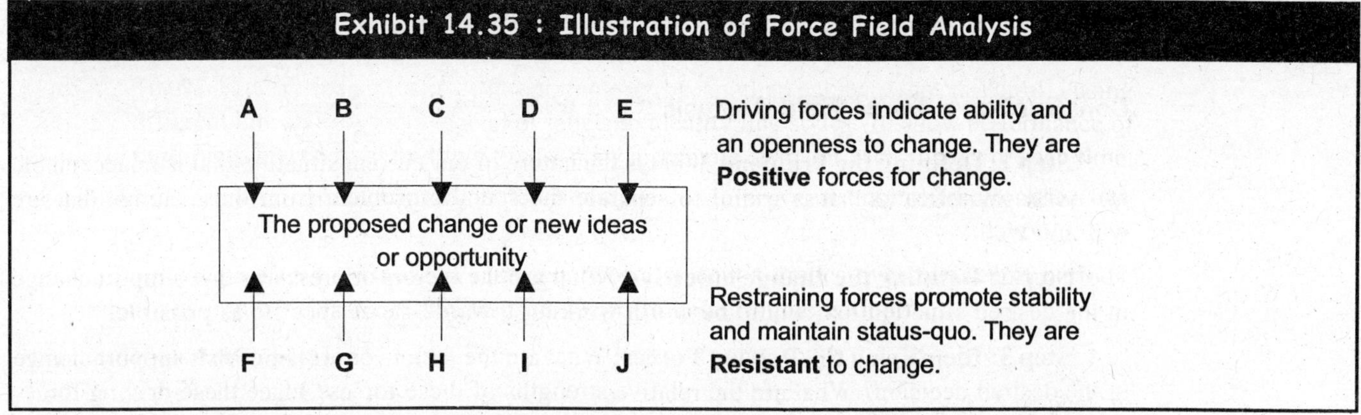

Force Field Analysis is used to identify the forces and factors that may influence the problem or goal. It helps an organisation to better understand promoting or deriving and restraining or inhibiting forces so that the positives can be reinforced and the negatives reduced or eliminated. The procedure is to define the objective, determine criteria for evaluating the effectiveness of the improvement action, brainstorm the forces that promote and inhibit achieving the goal, prioritise the forces from greatest to least, and take action to strengthen the promoting forces and weaken the inhibiting forces.

An example given below will illustrate this tool:

Objective: Stop Smoking.

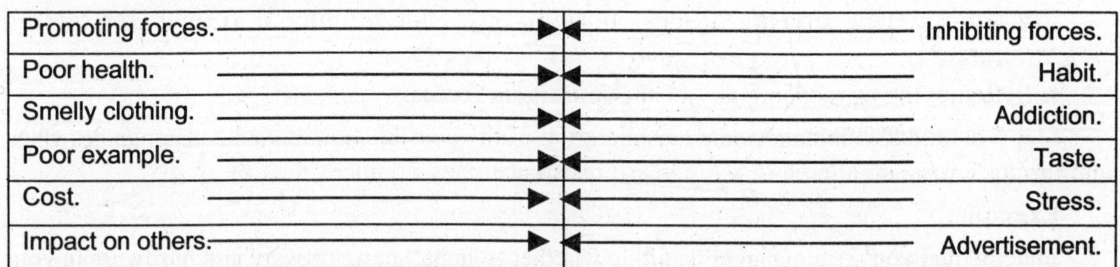

Promoting forces.	Inhibiting forces.
Poor health.	Habit.
Smelly clothing.	Addiction.
Poor example.	Taste.
Cost.	Stress.
Impact on others.	Advertisement.

The benefits are the determination of the positives and negatives of a situation, encouraging people to agree and prioritise the competing forces and identify the root causes.

Force Field analyses clarifies opposing aspects of a desired change: *(a)* Driving or positive forces that support an action or situation. *(b)* Restraining or negative forces that hinder it.

When opposing forces are equal, no change can occur. For a change to happen, the driving forces must be stronger than the restraining forces. When all the forces have been considered, plans can be made that will encourage the desired change.

Force Field Analysis is used:

(i) When the team is planning a change, such as implementation of a solution or .

(ii) When the team is identifying causes of a problem.

Essentials of Force field Analysis

(i) The team must have sufficient knowledge of the context surrounding the proposed change.

(ii) A method of brainstorming must be decided on prior to using the tool.

Advantages:

(i) Can support a team in realistically predicting the potential success of a change initiative.

(ii) Can support a team in identifying and lessening the restraining forces that may slow down or stop a proposed change.

Construction a Force Field Analysis

Step 1: Defining the Problem: What is the nature of our current situation that is unacceptable and needs modification? It is useful to separate the specific problem from those things that are working well.

Step 2: Defining the change objective: What are the factors or pressures that support change in the desired situation that would be worth working toward? Be as specific as possible.

Step 3: Identifying the Driving Forces: What are the factors or pressures that support change in the desired decision? What are the relative strengths of these forces? Place these driving forces on the chart on the Force Field Analysis diagram as labelled arrows with the length of the arrow reflecting the relative strength of each force. What are the inter-relationship among the driving forces.

Step 4: Identifying the Restraining Forces: What are the factors or pressures that resist the proposed change and maintain the status-quo? Represent these forces on the diagram as you did those for the driving forces. What are the inter-relationships among the restraining forces?

Step 5: Developing the Comprehensive Change Strategy: The diagram created in steps three and four reflect what could be called a state of quasi-stationery equilibrium. Although this is a relatively stable state, movement can be achieved altering the factors currently contributing to this equilibrium. Change can occur as a result of any combination of the following:

(i) Strengthening any of the driving forces.

(ii) Adding new driving forces (possibly by transforming a former restraining force)

(iii) Removing or reducing any of the restraining forces.

Step 5 should also include some consideration of the possible unintended consequences when equilibrium forces are altered (*e.g.,* increase resistance, new alliances, fear etc.)

Example:

Imagine that you are a manager deciding whether to install new software and hardware in your office. You might draw up a force field analysis as shown below:

You can now decide whether your plan is viable. You might initially question whether it is worth going ahead with the plan. However if you decide to go ahead, your force field analysis can help you to work out how to improve its probability of success.

You have two main choices:

(i) Reduce the strength of the forces opposing your plan or.

(ii) Increase the forces pushing your plan.

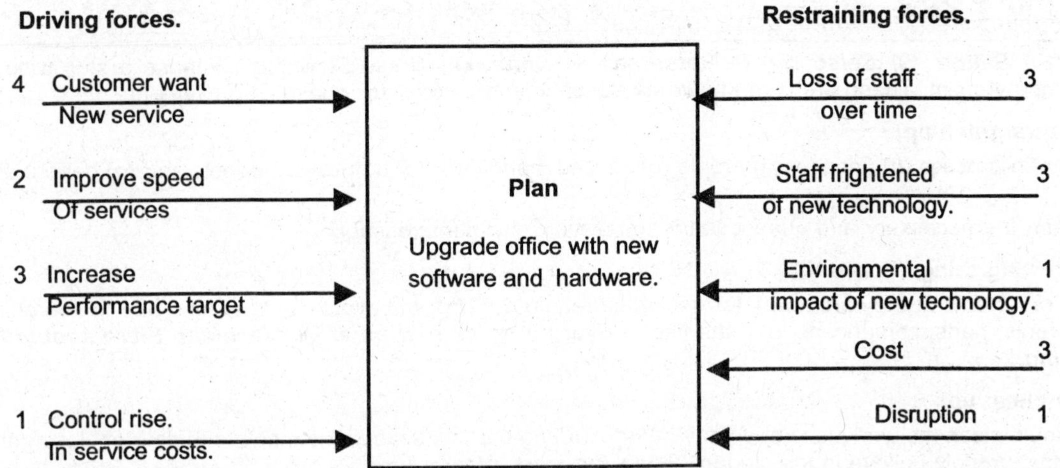

Often the most elegant solution is the first because just trying to force change through may cause its own problem. People can be non-cooperative if change is forced on them. The analysis might suggest a number of changes in the initial plan:

(i) By training staff (increase cost by 1) you could eliminate the fear of technology (reduce staff freighted by new technology by 2)

(ii) It would be useful to show staff that change is necessary for business servile.(add a new force in favour +2)

(iii) Staff could be shown that new equipment would introduce variety and interest to their jobs, (add a new force in favour, +1)

(iv) You could raise wages to reflect new productivity (increase cost by 1 but reduce loss of staff by 2)

(v) Slightly different machines that were more modern and greener could be installed (environmental impact of new technology reduced by 1)

These charges would swing the balance of the Force field analysis from 11:10 against the plan to 8:13 in favour of the plan.

(E) Japanese 5 'S' Principles

***Box 14.6* describes the 5 'S' Kaizen movement and *Box 14.7* describes 5W 1H check list for Kaizen activities.**

14.9 CONTROL TOOLS AND TECHNIQUES

(A) PROJECT SCHEDULING TECHNIQUES

Scheduling Chart (Gantt chart or Horizontal bar chart)

This chart is the most frequently used tool to manage small projects. The chart indicates - ***what must be done and when it must be done.*** As the project progresses, the chart is updated to indicate the amount of accomplishment toward the plan. In this way the project managers can compare actual project work accomplishment with planned project progress. This chart time-phases activities. Every activity should have a start date and finish date. ***Exhibit 14.36* shows a typical Gantt chart or Horizontal bar chart for a building construction project.**

The chart is prepared in advance of the project to plan and schedule the activities of the project. After the bar chart is initially prepared, managers can be assured that all the activities of

Box 14.6 : 5 'S' Kaizen Movement (House Keeping Steps for Quality Movement)

The 5s are *(i)* ***Seiri***, *(ii)* ***Seiton***, *(iii)* ***Seiso***, *(iv)* ***Seiketsu*** and *(v)* ***Shitsuke***. These 5s words comprise a step-wise approach for quality improvement. These are also known as house-keeping steps for quality improvement.

(i) **Seiri (means to straighten-up)**

It includes : *(a)* work-in-process *(b)* unnecessary tools *(c)* unused machinery *(d)* defective products and *(e)* papers and documents.

Differentiate between the necessary and unnecessary and discard the unnecessary.

(ii) **Seiton (means putting things in order)**

Keep the things in order so that they are ready for use when required. (This will avoid waste of time due to searching for things such as tools, parts, components and the like). ***"Everything should be at its place and there should be place for everything."***

(iii) **Seiso (means to clean up)**

Every individual should clean the workplace everyday before starting the day's work and also at the time of closing the work. Japanese firms strongly believe in the slogan ***"keep the work place clean"***.

(iv) **Seiketsu (means personal cleanliness)**

Every worker or manager should make it a point to give special attention to his or her ***personal cleanliness***. Some of the Japanese beliefs are

- ***"There is a healthy mind in a healthy body."***
- ***"Cleanliness is necessary for Godliness."***
- ***"Make it a habit to be clean and tidy, starting with your own person."***

All these mean good housekeeping practices.

(v) **Shitsuke (means discipline)**

Every worker and manager has to follow procedures in the workplace and workshop with utmost sense of discipline. Japanese believe that only with discipline and sincerity in following the principles and procedures, one can contribute significantly to personal and organisational success. It is necessary to have discipline in all aspects of our work to improve quality of products and work life.

Box 14.7 : "Five Ws and one H" - Checklist

In an organisation, Kaizen activities should be carried out by asking the following questions under five Ws and one H. They are – ***who, what, where, when, why and how.***

Who : Who does it? Who is doing it? Who should be doing it? Who else can do it? Who else should do it? Who is doing 3 MUs?

What : What to do? What is being done? What should be done? What else should be done? What else can be done? What 3 MUs are being done?

Where : Where to do it? Where it is done? Where should it be done? Where else can it be done? Where else should it be done? Where are the 3 MUs being done?

When : When to do it? When is it done? When should it be done? When other time can it be done? When other time should it be done? When there is presence of 3 MUs?

Why : Why to do it? Why is it being done? Why else should it be done? Why else can it be done? Why do it that way? Why there are 3 MUs in the way of thinking?

How : How to do it? How is it being done? How should it be done? How this method can be used in other means? How this can be done in other ways? How are there any 3 MUs in the method?

the project are planned for, the order in which the activities must be performed is taken into account, the time estimates for completing each activity are included and finally the overall estimated time for completing the project is developed. The horizontal bar chart becomes the overall plan for the project.

As the project progresses and the activities are completed, actual progress is recorded by shading in the horizontal bars.

Exhibit 14.36 : Gantt Chart for Construction of a House

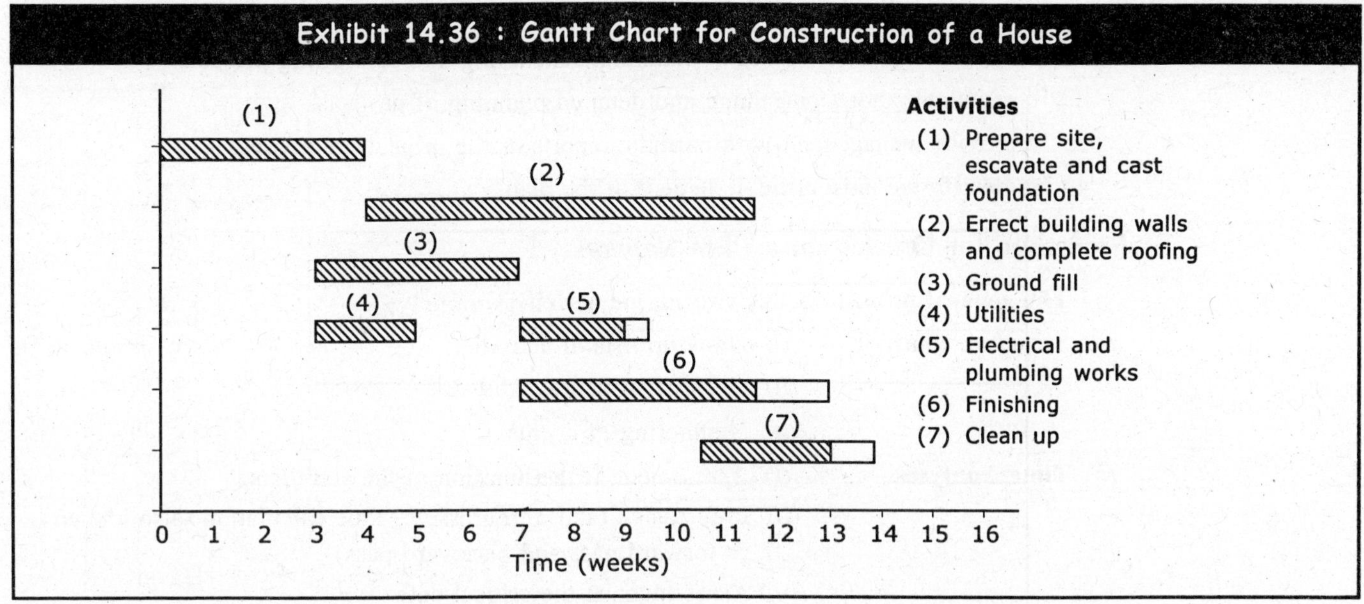

These charts are easy to understand, and to modify. They are of low cost. The draw back is that these charts do not adequately indicate the degree of interrelationships among the project's activities.

Programme Evaluation & Review Technique (PERT) and Critical Path Method (CPM)

PERT is the name given to a networking approach to planning, monitoring, controlling and evaluation of complex projects. It consists of a **network diagram** which is a two-dimensional schematic of the relationships between tasks in a project. PERT is used for non-repetitive projects that have been done before and will not be done again in precisely the same manner. PERT technique has been used for projects such as developing missiles, nuclear powered submarines and for the programme that landed the first man on the moon. It is a planning tool which enables the project manager to estimate the time required to complete a proposed project. It also provides a time schedule for various project activities and for checking of the scheduled time against the actual time taken for an activity. PERT helps to design a management control system for activities that are subject to a considerable degree of uncertainity in performance time. It is based on a statistical treatment of activity performance time.

PERT also minimises delays in various parts of the overall job and helps in expediting the completion of the project. It is a method of budgeting resources to predetermine the job on schedule. Above all PERT is an outstanding approach for the timely completion of projects.

With PERT, projects can be better planned and controlled for cost when they are broken-down into their components. PERT tells how to set up network, how to calculate completion time and how to monitor and control work.

Critical Path Method (CPM)

CPM refers to a quantitative technique which when applied to network planning, is helpful in calculating the minimum time and the sequence of tasks needed to complete a project. This technique is mostly used for construction projects such as bridges, building, dams, canals etc., where engineers and contractors try to complete the job at the earliest to avoid rising costs. In CPM technique, the precedence, the relationships between activities and their mutual dependence are suggested, leading to the final objective of reducing the cost and completion time of the project.

Purpose of CPM :

1. To ensure logical discipline in planning, scheduling and controlling projects.
2. To encourage more long range and detailed planning of projects.
3. To provide management with periodic reports as the project progresses.
4. To identify the most critical element of the plan.

Procedure for Drawing up a CPM Network

The general procedure has two major activities namely:

(a) **Structure analysis** — (i) Draw up lists of activities
(ii) Draft of structure / Network
(iii) Numbering of events

(b) **Time Analysis** — (i) Assessment of the duration of the activities
(ii) Progressive (and retrogressive) time calculation (also known as forward pass and backward pass)
(iii) Assessment of the critical path
(iv) Assessment of the float or slack

(a) CPM - Structure Analysis

(i) **Preparing the list of activities :** The list of activities is a catalogue of all activities and processes in the project for example, ***Table 14.11*** **shows the list of activities relating to a project.**

Table 14.11 : List of Activities Relating to the Project

i	j	Task areas	Description of activity	Duration (days)
1	2	Design department	Design parts for sub-assembly A & B	25
2	3	Purchase department	Procure materials for sub-assembly 'A'	30
2	4	Purchase department	Procure materials for sub-assembly 'B'	10
3	5	Fabrication shop	Fabricate parts for sub-assembly 'A'	20
4	6	Fabrication shop	Fabricate parts for sub-assembly 'B'	40
5	7	Assembly line	Sub-assembly A	40
6	7	Assembly line	Sub-assembly B	5
7	8	Assembly line	Final assembly	6

(ii) **The drafting of the network :** While drafting the network, the insertion of every activity is to be carried out systematically by means of a technique to pose suitable questions. To obtain the correct sequences, the following questions should be answered for each activity.

(a) Which activities must be ended directly before the new one begins?
(b) Which activities can only begin directly afterwards?
(c) Which activities can take place autonomously and simultaneously?
(d) Can this activity be subdivided into others?

In the structure analysis no time factors are considered but only the sequence and interrelation of the activities.

(iii) **Numbering of events :** Every activity in the network is defined by its start and end events. Events must be numbered by positive integers (say 1, 2, 3 etc.). The numbering must be done in the ascending order.

Exhibit 14.37 **gives an example of numbering of events in a CPM network.**

Exhibit 14.37 : Numbering of Events

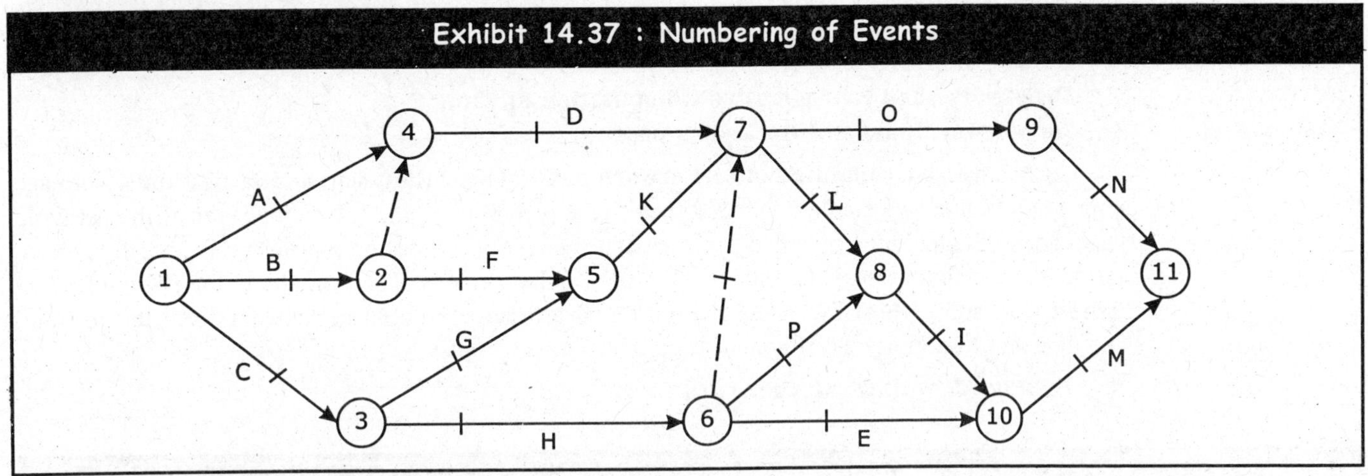

The procedure is as follows:

The initial "start" event of the project is numbered by 1 and all arrows beginning in this event are crossed. Put the next higher numbers for particular events where only crossed arrows end. All arrows beginning at the newly numbered event are then crossed. This procedure is repeated in the same way until all the events are numbered.

CPM - Time Analysis

The symbols used are :

D = Duration of activity (hours or days or weeks or months)
ESA = Earliest (possible) starting time of the activity
LSA = Latest (permitted) starting time of the activity
EEA = Earliest (possible) ending time of activity
LEA = Latest (permitted) ending time of the activity
EE = Earliest (possible) time of the event
LE = Latest (permissible) time of the event
TF = Total float of the activity
FF = Free float of the activity
IF = Independent float of the activity

Mode of representation : ***Exhibit 14.38*** **shows how to represent the events and activities.**

Exhibit 14.38 : Representation of Events and Activities

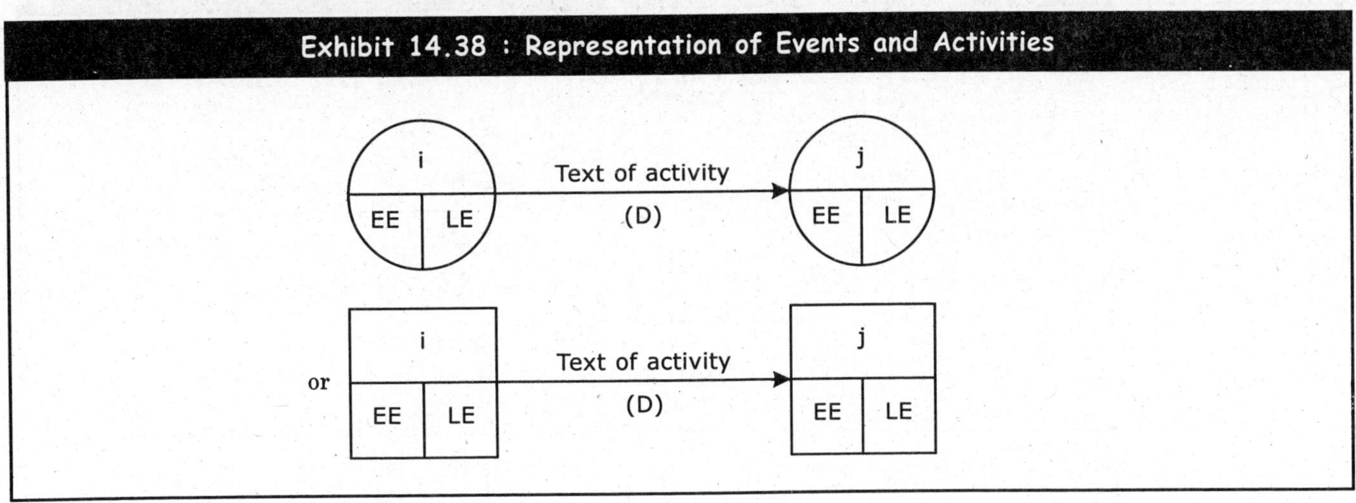

(i) Determination of the Activity's Duration `D'

For each activity of the project, the duration must be indicated by means of a determinate unit of time and the same is entered in the list of activities.

(ii) Progressive and Retrogressive Computation of Time (or Forward pass and Backward pass)

(a) **Progressive computation or Forward pass :** The earliest start and earliest finish for each activity are found by calculations performed in sequence from the left to the right of the network. This series of calculation is called the **forward pass.** We first assign a project day, usually zero to the start of the first activity, to represent the ES for that activity. Then we obtain the ES and EF *i.e.,* earliest start and earliest finish by making a forward pass through the network form left to right. The duration of activity 'D' is added to its ES to obtain its EF.

Exhibit 14.39 **illustrates forward pass.**

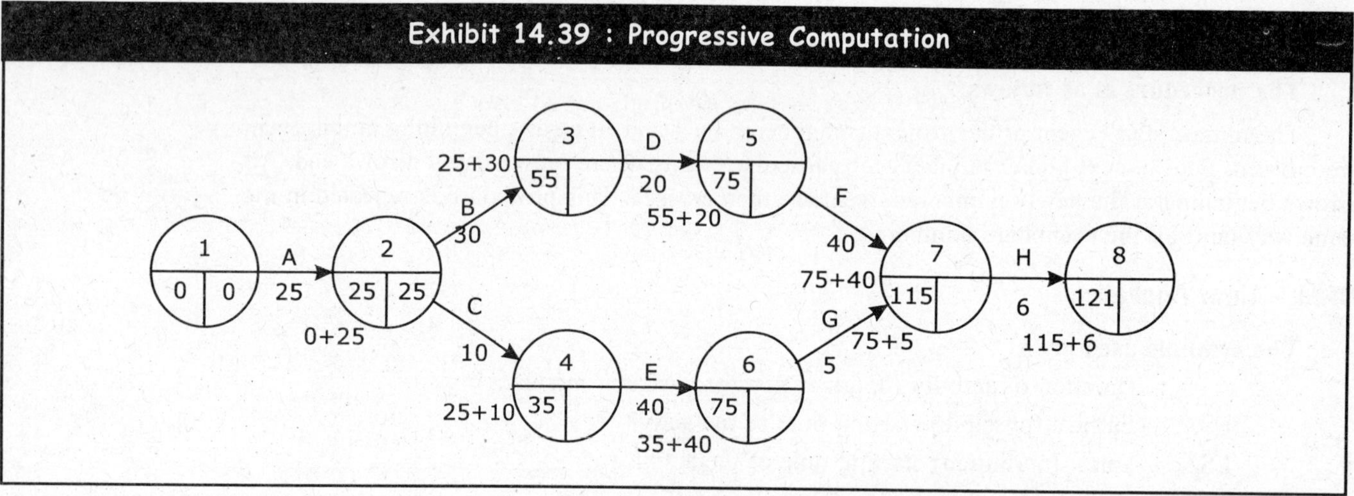

Exhibit 14.39 : Progressive Computation

Note : Where several arrows converge, enter the biggest from EE.

(b) **Retrogressive computation or Backward pass :** The Latest finish and latest start dates are calculated by means of a backward pass. The LF is usually set equal to the EF of the project. Starting with the last activity, subtract the activity duration from the LF to obtain L.S. ***Exhibit 14.40*** **illustrates the backward pass.**

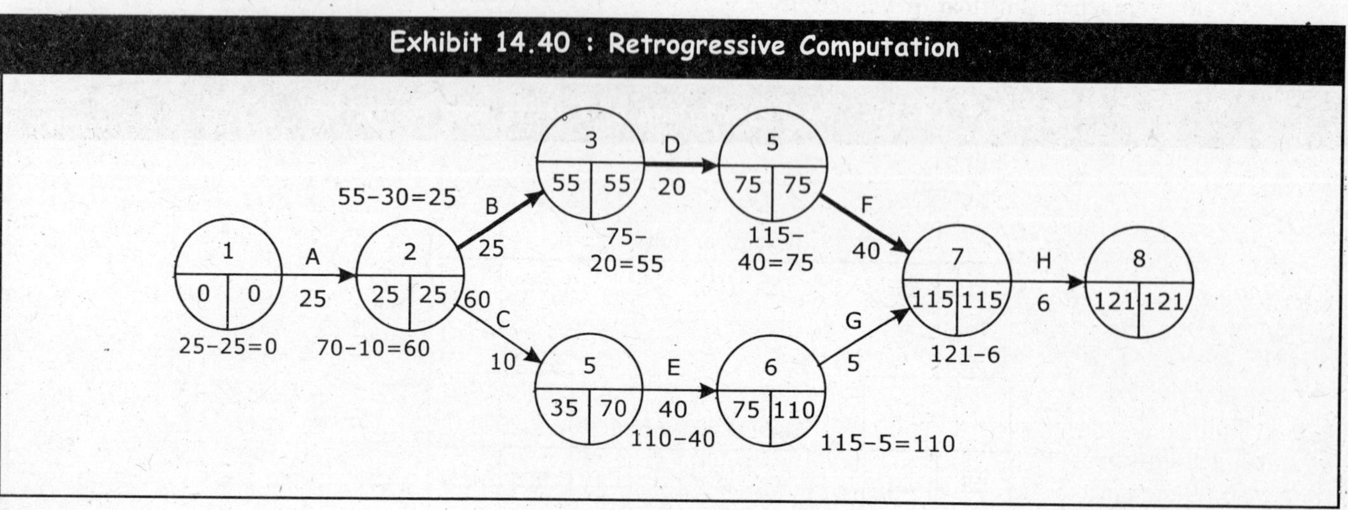

Exhibit 14.40 : Retrogressive Computation

Note : Where arrows branch off, insert the smallest sum as LE

(c) **Calculation of Earliest Ending time of Activity (EEA) and Latest Starting time of Activity (LSA)** *:* The earliest ending time is arrived at by adding the activity's duration D to the earliest starting time of the activity (ESA).

i.e., EEA = ESA + D or EEA = EE + D

The latest starting time (LSA) is arrived at by substracting the activity's duration D from the latest ending time of the activity (LEA).

LSA = LEA – D or LSA = LE – D

For example, considering the process 5 - 6 from the network diagram given at ***Exhibit 14.40***, we can calculate ESA, EEA, LSA & LEA as shown in ***Exhibit 14.41***.

ESA = Earliest starting time of the activity (5-6) *i.e.,* 35th day

EEA = Earliest ending time of the activity (5-6) *i.e.,* 75th day

EE = Earliest time of the event (5) *i.e.,* 35th day

LSA = Latest starting time of activity (5-6) *i.e.,* 70th day

LEA = Latest ending time of activity (5-6) *i.e.,* 110th day

LE = Latest time of the event (6) *i.e.,* 110th day

Exhibit 14.41 : Determination of EEA & LSA

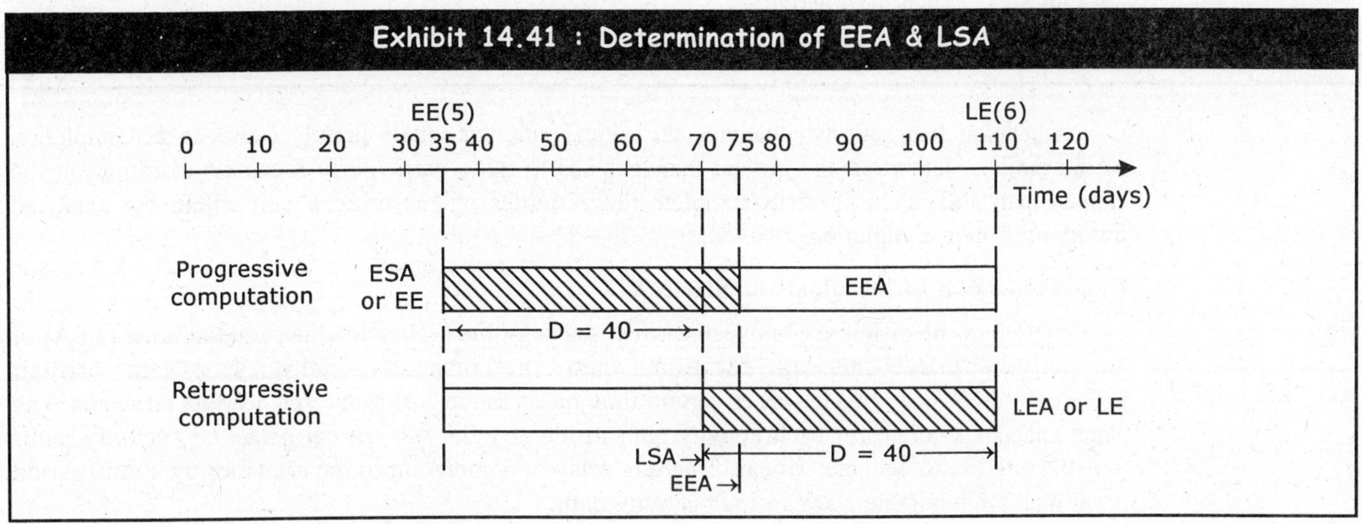

(iii) Assessment of the Critical Path

If, in respect of any activity, the earliest and latest times of occurrence are identical both at the start and the finish of the activity, then the activity lies on the critical path. In other words, if for two events say event 'i' and event 'j' the earliest event time and the latest event time (*i.e.,* EE & LE) are the same, the activity (i – j) connecting these two events is said to be on the critical path. In the figure 6.5, it is observed that the events 1,2,3,4,7 and 8 have identical earliest event time and latest event time *i.e.,*

For event	1,	EE = 0	LE = 0
– do –	2	EE = 25	LE = 25
– do –	3	EE = 55	LE = 55
– do –	4	EE = 75	LE = 75
– do –	7	EE = 115	LE = 115
– do –	8	EE = 121	LE = 121

Hence the activities connecting events 1,2,3,4,7 and 8 are on critical path. In otherwards, all these activities do not possess any slack or time reserves and hence designated as critical.

Every network (where EE = LE) contains one or several such uninterrupted chains of critical activities leading from the start event to the end event. This chain is designated as **critical path.**

Exhibit 14.42 **shows the critical path depicted by dark or heavier lines.**

Exhibit 14.42 : Determination of Critical Path

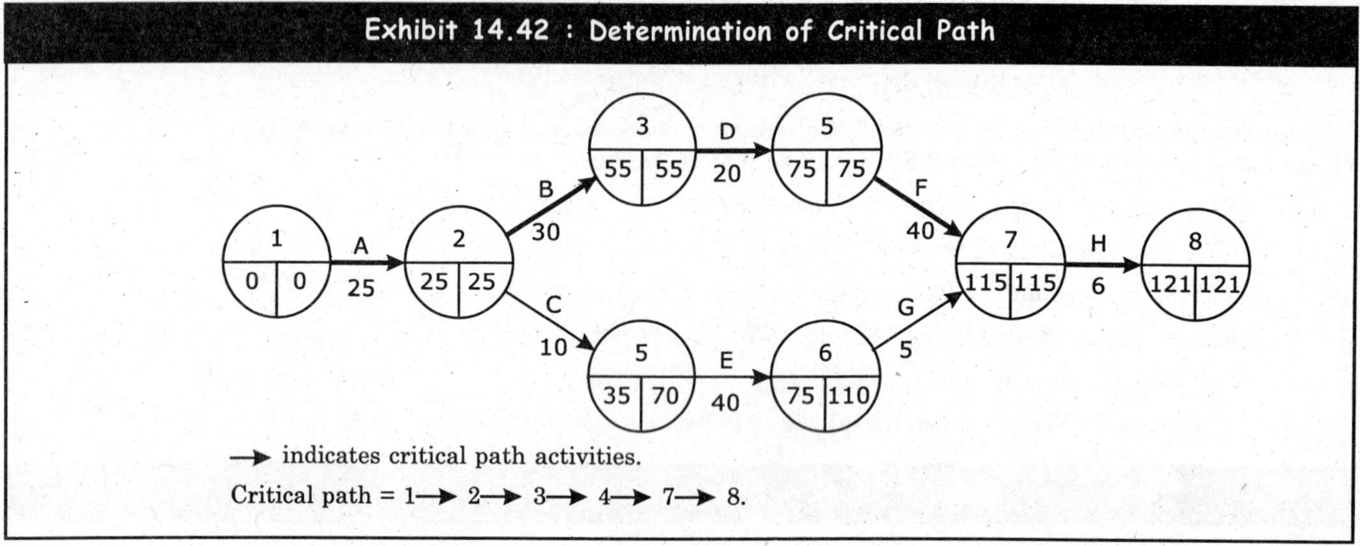

→ indicates critical path activities.

Critical path = 1→ 2→ 3→ 4→ 7→ 8.

Any delay in an activity situated on the critical path thus entails directly a delay in the completion of the project. Therefore the project manager has to quite particularly focus his attention on the critical path and do his best to complete the activities on the critical path within the expected duration of their completion.

(iv) Assessment of the Floats or Slacks

In case of the difference between earliest starting time (ESA) and latest ending time (LEA) of an activity exceeding its duration, then the respective activity is not critical *i.e.,* LEA – ESA > D. In such cases certain time reserves are ensuring termed **floats** or **slacks.** The slack analysis is done for each activity path to identify the sub-critical paths *i.e.,* activity paths which are likely to become critical if there is delay in completion of the activities by a time period more than the available slack in each activity path.

Slack analysis can be made from the stand point of the events or activities in the network. Two type of slacks identified are

(a) Event slack *(b)* Activity slack

$$\text{Event slack} = \text{Latest event time} - \text{Earliest event time}$$
$$= \text{LE} - \text{EE}$$

All events having zero slack represent critical events *i.e.,* events on the critical path. Any schedule slippage of these events will cause delay in completion of the project.

Activity slack analysis provides with the information on the margin of allowance available for the commencement and completion of various activities. Activities with zero slack value represent activities on the critical path.

Three types of activity slacks or floats are identified:

(i) Total float or Slack

(ii) Free float or Slack

(iii) Independent float or Slack

(i) **Total float :** Total float usually referred to as simply float or slack is the amount of time an activity can be delayed beyond its earliest possible starting time without delaying the project completion, if other activities take their estimated duration. Total float gives some indication of the criticality of an activity. An activity with little float stands a good chance of delaying the project and should be carefully monitored

Total float for activity (i – j) = LE (j) – EE (i) – D

(ii) **Free float :** Free float is the amount of time an activity can be delayed without delaying the early start of a successor activity. To find free float, we subtract the early finish of an activity from the early start times of its succeeding activities.

Free float for activity (i – j) = EE (j) – EE (i) – D

(iii) **Independent Float :** This indicates the time span by which the activity (i – j) can be expanded or shifted if, for the event (i) the latest and for the event (j) the earliest times of occurrence shall be maintained. A shifting of the activity in this area has no influence on the further progress of the project. Independent float can be negative also. Since a negative float has no meaning, independent float is taken as zero if negative.

***Exhibit 14.43* illustrates the relationship between the three type of floats and their calculations for an activity (i – j).**

Exhibit 14.43 : Relationship Between 3 Types of Floats

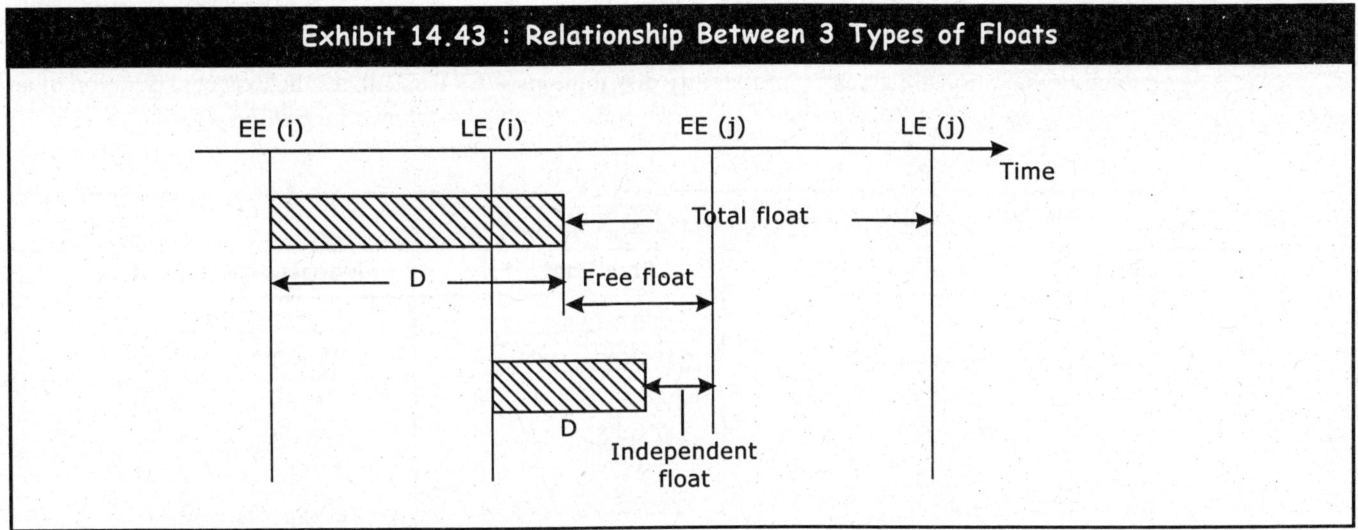

EE (i) = Earliest event time for event (i)

LE (i) = Latest event time for event (i)

EE (j) = Earliest event time for event (j)

LE (j) = Latest event for event (j)

D = Duration of activity i – j

Total float TF = LE (j) – EE (i) – D

Free float FF = EE (j) – EE (i) – D

Independent float IF = EE (j) – LE (i) – D

If D > [EE (j) – LE (i)], IF will be negative (assumed to be zero).

Illustration : For the net work diagram shown at *Exhibit 6.7*, the activities, earliest event time (EE) and latest event time (LE) and the duration of the activity (D) are listed in the ***Table 14.12***.

Table 14.13 **lists the total float, free float and independent float for the activities listed in** ***Table 14.11.***

Table 14.12 : Activity Completion Time and Duration

Activity	EE (i)	LE (i)	EE (j)	LF (j)	D
1-2	0	0	25	25	25
2-3	25	25	55	55	30
2-5	25	25	35	70	10
3-4	55	55	75	75	20
5-6	35	70	75	110	40
4-7	75	75	115	115	40
6-7	75	110	115	115	5
7-8	115	115	121	121	6

Programme Evaluation and Review Technique (PERT)

So far we have discussed the procedure for determining the project completion time, the earliest and latest times for the start and completion of activities and the occurrence of events. In C.P.M. Analysis, activity durations are assumed to be known whereas in PERT, the activity duration are given by probability distributions. PERT calculates the expected duration of an activity as a weighted average of the three time estimates as shown in ***Exhibit 14.44***.

Table 14.13 : Calculation of Three Types of Floats

Activity	Total float (TF)	Free float (FF)	Independent float (IF)
1 - 2	(25 – 0) – 25 = 0	(25 – 0) – 25 = 0	(25 – 0) – 25 = 0
2 - 3	(55 – 25) – 30 = 0	(55 – 25) – 30 = 0	(55 – 25) – 30 = 0
2 - 5	(70 – 25) – 10 = 35	(35 – 25) – 10 = 0	(35 – 25) – 10 = 0
3 - 4	(75 – 55) – 20 = 0	(75 – 55) – 20 = 0	(75 – 55) – 20 = 0
5 - 6	(110 – 35) – 40 = 35	(75 – 35) – 40 = 0	(75 – 70) – 40 = 35 or nil
4 - 7	(115 – 75) – 40 = 0	(115 – 75) – 40 = 0	(115 – 75) – 40 = 0
6 - 7	(115 – 75) – 5 = 35	(115 – 75) – 5 = 35	(115 – 110) – 5 = 0
7 - 8	(121 – 115) – 6 = 0	(121 – 115) – 6 = 0	(121 – 115) – 6 = 0

The average or expected time is, $t_e = \dfrac{t_o + 4t_m + t_p}{6}$

Where t_e = Expected activity time t_o = Optimistic time

t_p = Pessimistic time t_m = Most likely time.

These are defined in the following lines.

(a) **The optimistic time (to)** is the particular time estimate that has a very small probability of being reached *i.e.,* a **probability of 1 in 100.** This particular time estimate represents the time in which an activity could be completed if every thing went along properly with no problem. This would be most unusual, but it could happen with a probability of 1 in 100.

Exhibit 14.44

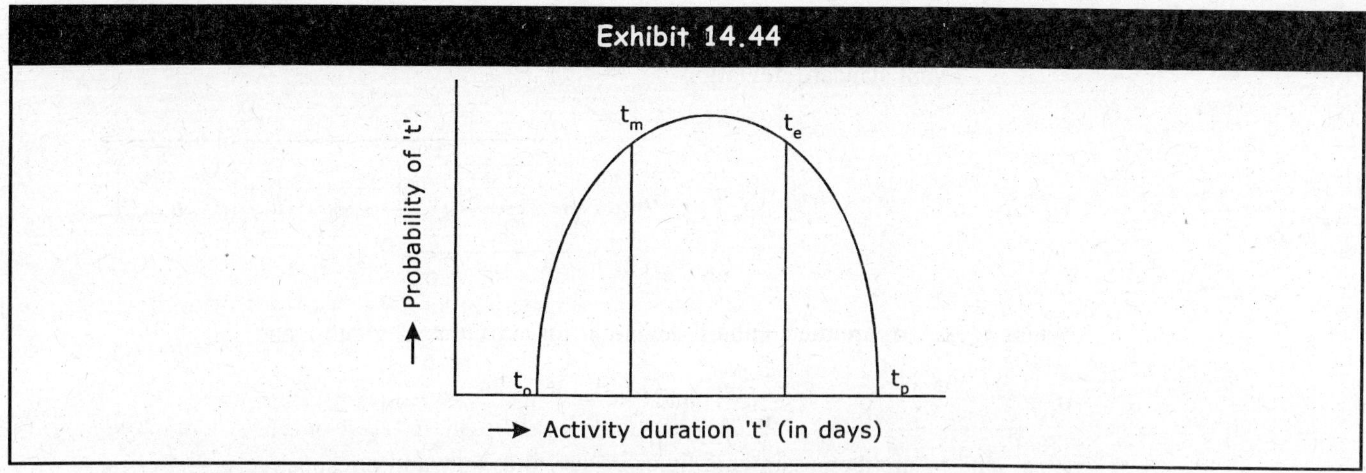

(b) **The pessimistic time (tp)** is another particular time estimate that has a very small probability of being realized, once again with a **probability of 1 in 100**. This time estimate represents the time in which an activity could be completed even if everything went wrong. This also would be most unusual, but could happen with a probability of 1 in 100.

(c) **The most likely time (tm)** is a particular time that in the mind of the estimator, the time the activity would most often require if the work were done again and again under identical conditions. This has a **probability of 50 in 100.**

The PERT network provides a measure of the probability of completing the project by the **scheduled date** The probability concept is only associated with PERT and not CPM because the activity time estimates in CPM are deterministic (*i.e.,* known) and not probabilistic.

In PERT, the assessment of uncertainty for the entire network *i.e.,* the probability of occurrences of the end event of the project is related to the degree of uncertainty - associated with the three time estimates t_o, t_m and t_p. PERT is almost identical to CPM in regard to its function, network diagram, calculations etc., except that the method of estimating activity times are different *i.e.,* in CPM, an activity duration is based on a single time estimate whereas there are three time estimates made for each activity in PERT which is converted into one time estimate (*i.e.,* expected time t_e) using the formula $t_e = \dfrac{t_o + 4t_m + t_p}{6}$.

Activity standard deviation : The measure of error associated with the expected time of an activity is known as activity standard deviation.

For example, if the expected time of an activity is 8 days and its standard deviation is 2 days, it means that the probability of completing the activity between 8 – 2 = 6 days and 8 + 2 = 10 days in calculated as $\dfrac{10-6}{6} = \dfrac{4}{6} = 0.66$.

i.e., if an activity's optimistic time is t_o and its pessimistic time is t_p, then the standard deviation

$$\sigma = \frac{t_p - t_o}{6}.$$

Event standard deviation : The measure of error associated with the cumulative expected time of an event is called the event standard deviation. The cumulative expected time (T_E) of an event represents the sum of the expected times of all the activities leading to the event along the longest path.

If the activities leading to an event are x, y and z, then

$$\text{Event standard deviation } \sigma_{TE} = \sqrt{\sum_{i-j}^{n} \sigma_{i-j}^2}$$

$$\text{or} \quad \sigma_{TE} = \sqrt{\left(\frac{t_{px} - t_{ox}}{6}\right)^2 + \left(\frac{t_{py} - t_{oy}}{6}\right)^2 + \left(\frac{t_{pz} - t_{oz}}{6}\right)^2}$$

$$\text{or} \quad \sigma_{TE} = \sqrt{\sigma_x^2 + \sigma_y^2 + \sigma_z^2}$$

Where σ_x, σ_y, σ_z are the standard deviation for activities x, y and z and

$$\sigma_z = \frac{t_{px} - t_{ox}}{6}, \quad \sigma_y = \frac{t_{py} - t_{oy}}{6} \quad \text{and} \quad \sigma_z = \frac{t_{pz} - t_{oz}}{6}$$

t_{px}, t_{py} and t_{pz} are the pessimistic times of activities x, y and z respectively.

t_{ox}, t_{oy} and t_{oz} are the optimistic times of activities x, y and z respectively.

Determining Probability of Meeting Scheduled Date in PERT Analysis

Cumulative expected time of an event T_E represents a 50-50 chance. If a scheduled date T_S is given for an event and if it indicates a value higher than T_E value, then the probability of completing the event by scheduled date is greater than 50%. If T_S is lower than T_E than the probability of completing the event by scheduled date is less than 50%.

Determination of the probability of meeting the scheduled date can be best illustrated with the help of an example given below:

***Exhibit 14.45* represents the critical path in a PERT network.**

Exhibit 14.45 : Activities Along Critical Path with Expected Times and Standard Deviations

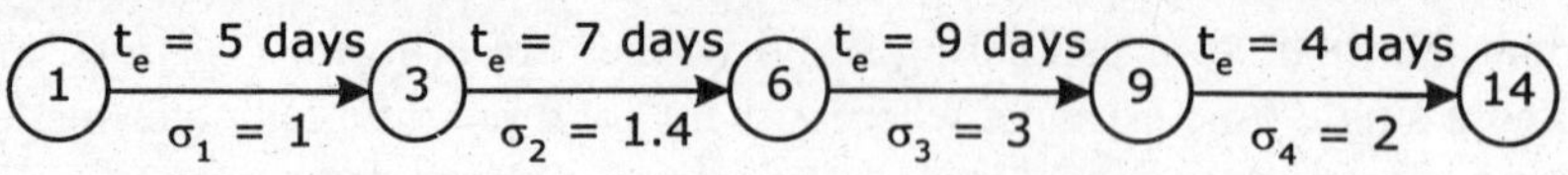

Event	Activity	Event	Activity	Event	Activity	Event	Activity	Event
1	t_e = 5 days, σ_1 = 1	3	t_e = 7 days, σ_2 = 1.4	6	t_e = 9 days, σ_3 = 3	9	t_e = 4 days, σ_4 = 2	14

The cumulative expected time T_E of event 14 is say 25 days.

(a) Determine the probability of completing the project in 28 days and 21 days.

(b) What is the expected time of completion which assures the management a 95% confidence level of completing the project.

Solution :

The distribution of completion time of the project is assumed to follow normal distribution as shown in ***Exhibit 14.46***.

Standard deviation for the end event (event number 14)

$$\text{is } \sigma_{TE} = \sqrt{\sigma_1^2 + \sigma_2^2 + \sigma_3^2 + \sigma_4^2} = \sqrt{1 + 1.96 + 9 + 4} = \sqrt{15.96} \approx 4$$

To determine the probability of completing the project by 28 days : Since this completion period of 28 days is more than the expected completion time of 25 days, the probability is greater than 0.5. But the question is by how much. To find this, the number of standard deviations (Z) has to be calculated as

$$Z_1 = \frac{T_S - T_E}{\sigma_{TE}} = \frac{28 - 25}{4} = 0.75 \text{ standard deviation}$$

Where T_S = Scheduled time

T_E = Cumulative expected time

T_E = Event standard deviation

Exhibit 14.46 : Distribution of Completion Time of the Projects

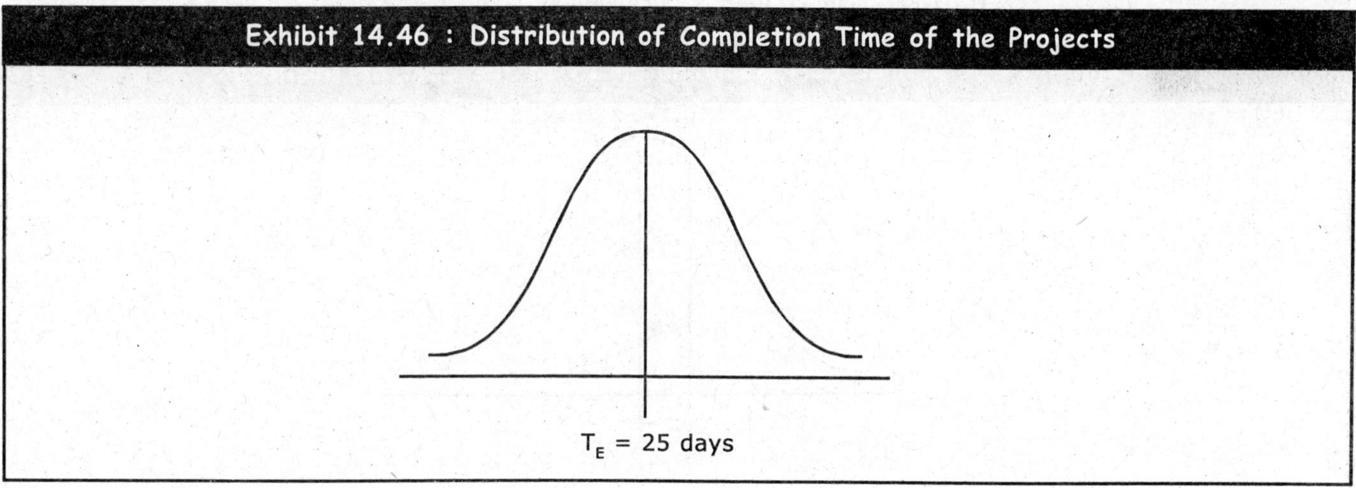

Exhibit 14.47 shows the area under the normal distribution curve which corresponds to 0.75. This can be ascertained from the table of values under a normal curve (*Appendix E*) that the area corresponding to 0.75σ is 0.27337. The probability of completing the project by 28 weeks is 0.5 + 0.27337 *i.e.,* 0.77337 or a probability of 77%.

In a similar manner the probability of completing the project by 21 weeks is determined as below:

The number of standard deviation $Z_2 = \frac{T_S - T_E}{\sigma_{TE}} = \frac{21 - 25}{4} = \frac{-4}{4} = -1\sigma$

Exhibit 14.17 : Area Corresponding to 0.75σ to to the Right of the Mean

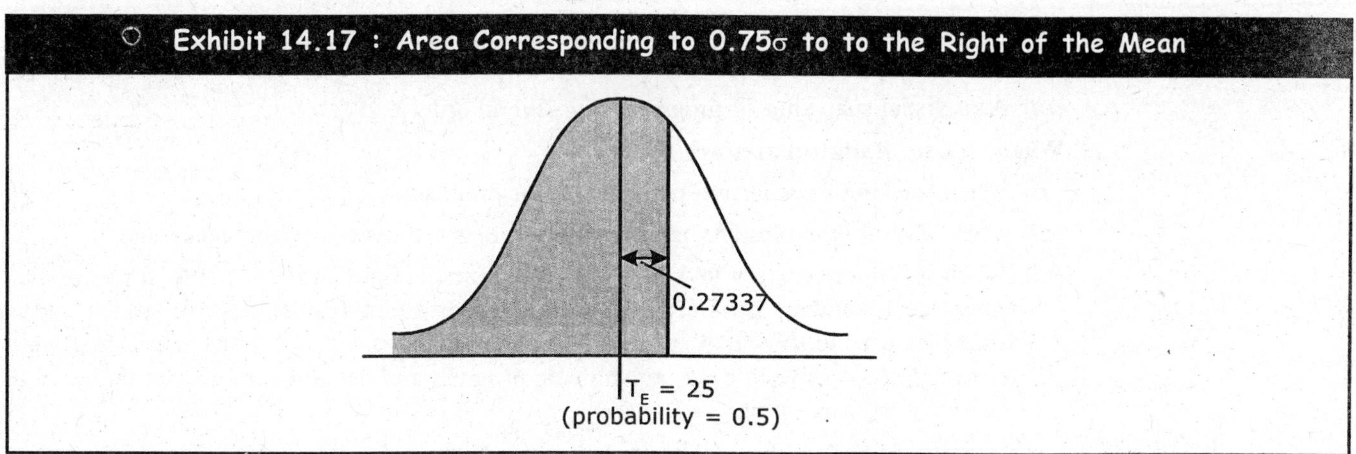

From the table of values of area under normal curve (*Appendix E*) it is found that 1σ corresponds to an area of 0.34134 (**Ref. *Exhibit 14.48***).

The probability of completion of the project in 21 days is found by subtracting the area under the curve corresponding to 1 σ *i.e.,* 0.34 from 0.5 which is equal to 0.16. This means the probability of completing the project in 21 days is 16%.

To determine the scheduled time for completing the project which assures 95% probability: The area under the curve corresponding to 0.95 is taken into consideration and from the table of values for the area under the normal curve, the number of standard deviation which corresponds to 0.95 has to be found out. This is observed from the table (*Appendix E*) as 1.65σ to the right of the mean (*i.e.*, T_E) The scheduled time is calculated as T_E + 1.64σ *i.e.*, 25 + 1.64 × 4 = 31.6 days.

Exhibit 14.48 : Area Corresponding to 1σ to the Left of the Mean

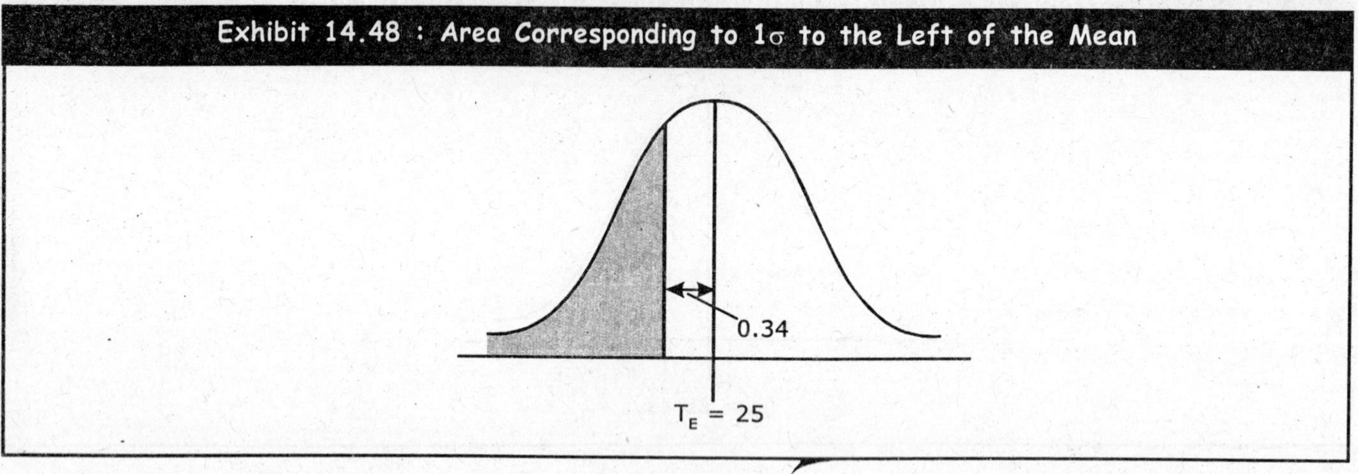

(B) RADAR CHART

Also called as **web-chart, spider chart and star chart**, the radar chart is a graph that looks like a spider web, with spokes radiating from a central point and lines connecting them.

It shows measurements, where several variables contribute to the overall picture. All variables are considered to be of equal importance on a radar chart. Radar chart is used to track or report performance or progress on multiple criteria.

Radar charts are used:

(i) To visually depict the incremental improvements over a period of time

(ii) To measure performance against benchmarks

(iii) As a visual snap shot of progress over several criteria

When to Use: Radar charts are used

(i) When tracking or reporting performance or progress

(ii) when several variables are being measured to assess overall performance and,

(iii) When it is not necessary to weight the relative importance of the variable, for example, when team members need motivation to achieve results against difficult targets, radar charts are used to show how their performance compares with the best achievable. Radar charts give a very visible way of showing progress and performance against the several targets at the same time.

Construction of radar chart: The steps involved are:

1. Identify the variables that will be measured. These may come from customer requirements, key performance indicators or organisational goals,
2. For each variable, determine the measurement scale. It is simplest for each variable to have the same measurement scale such as 1 to 5 or a percentage. However different scales can be used if necessary. Determine which end of the scale represents desirable performance, (i.e. 1 or 5)
3. To draw the chart, divide 360 degrees by the number of criteria to determine the angle between spokes. (For example, if there are four variables, then the angle between stokes is 360/4 or 90 degrees).

Draw spokes of equal lengths radiating from a central point and spaced evenly around the circle. Label each spoke with its variable. Mark the measurement scale on the spokes, with undesirable performance at the center.

4. For each variable, mark its measurement on the spoke with a large dot. Connect the dots,
5. To show performance at a different time or by another subject, repeat step 4., using different line styles. Add a legend or labels to identify line styles. To show performance of multiple subjects or at multiple times, draw a separate chart for each subject or each time,
6. Assess overall performance and determine needed improvement by observing where the 'web" lies closest to the center point.

Example: ***Exhibit 14.49*** shows a radar chart of a student's grades over two report periods. The student has improved in four subjects, but seems to have trouble with art.

Why a radar chart is used?

(i) The radar chart shows at a glance the progress being made towards targets or with respect to previous performance.

(ii) When bench marking, the radar chart can be used to show current performance, the immediate target and "the average is class" or "the overall best in class" performance.

Exhibit 14.49 : Single Radarchart for period 1 and 2

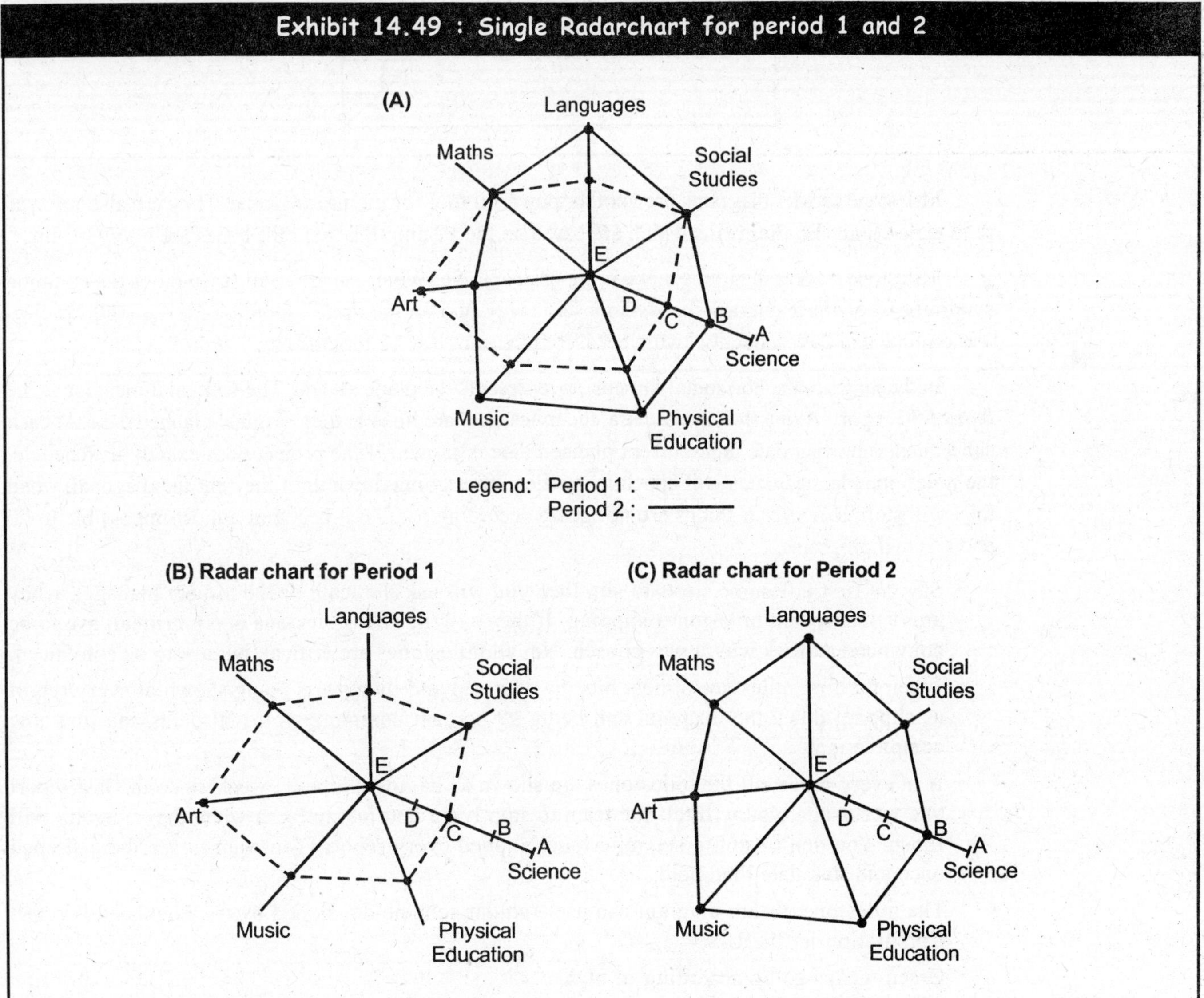

(C) MILESTONE TRACKER DIAGRAM

Exhibit 14.50 **shows a milestone trackers diagram.**

Exhibit 14.50 : Milestone Tracker Diagram

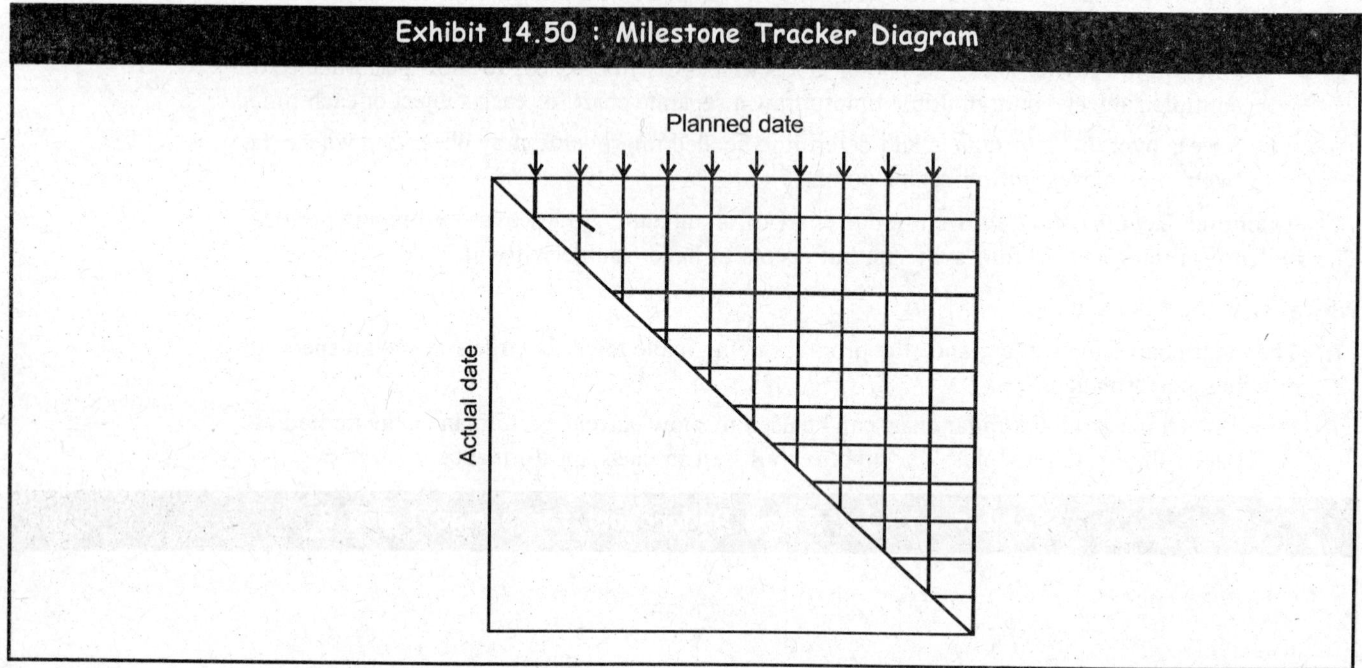

Milestone tackler diagrams are another powerful tool for monitoring time. They are also referred to as **mile-stone slip diagrams** which are based on the assumption that milestones are going to slip.

Milestone tracker diagrams make it impossible to lie. What you are trying to avoid is the common syndrome when the team track the last milestone only, and for the first 11 months of a 12 months project it is on time and then suddenly, two weeks from the end, it is 12 months late.

In the diagram the horizontal dimension represents the planned date. The vertical dimension is the date of the report. Along the top abscissa, the milestones are lined at their original planned data. At each subsequent reporting date their current planned date is shown. If the project goes exactly to schedule, the milestone planned dates will appear as vertical lines going down until they cut the diagonal, when they will stop. However if things are not going according to plan it becomes almost impossible to lie about actual programs.

- Say the first milestone starts to slip then you will ask the team or the project manager, whey aren't subsequent milestones slipping. If they say the first milestone is not critical, ask to be convinced and ask why it was chosen. Not all milestones are critical, but ask to be convinced.
- When the first milestone almost hits the diagonal and then starts being shown at every report as slipping down the diagonal and being 99 percent complete, you will be asking just how complete is it.
- If in every report all the milestones are shown as having slipped a week since the last report two weeks ago, you will tell the team to stop lying and just tell you when they actually will finish. You don't want to see milestones slipped every report. You want to see them slipped once and that date then held.

The milestone tracker diagram can use a colour scheme developed by the Lockheed Aircraft Corporation in the U.S.

- Green means going according to plan.

- Amber means not going according to plan, but containable.
- Red means not going according to plan, with serious impact on the project.

(D) FAILURE MODES AND EFFECTS ANALYSIS

Failure modes and effects analysis (FMEA) is a step-by-step approach to identify all possible failures in a design, a manufacturing or assembly process, or a finished product or a final service. **"Failure modes"** means the ways or modes, in which something may fail. **"Failures"** are errors or defects which affect the customer and can be potential or actual failures. **"Effects analysis"** refers to the study of the consequences or effects of those failures.

Failure modes and effects analysis (FMEA) is also called as **"potential failure modes and effects analysis"**, or **"failure mode, effects and critically analysis" (FMECA)**.

Definitions

(i) FMEA is one of the **tools of total quality management** which helps in finding out the possible failure modes of a design, product, process or service and setting up ways of preventing their recurrences.

(ii) It is a **methodology** to assess and reduce risk in systems, products or services. It aims to define, identify, prioritise and eliminate known or potential failures at an early stage as possible.

(iii) FMEA is a **preventive approach** for systematically mapping the causes, effects and possible actions regarding the observed problems or failures.

(iv) FMEA is a **pro-active tool** which is used to foresee the probable failures which can occur at a later stage. It involves critical analysis of each and every process with the aim of identifying problems which may emerge in the future.

The failures are prioritised according to how serious their consequences are, how frequently they occur and how easily they can be detected. FMEA helps to take actions to eliminate or reduce failures, starting with the highest priority ones. It also documents current knowledge and actions about the risks of failures, for use in continuous improvement.

FMEA is used during design stage to prevent failures, before and during on going operation of the process for controlling the process. Ideally, FMEA begins during the earliest conceptual stages of design and continues throughout the life of the product or service.

FMEA emphasises the analysis of the processes, whereby answers to the following questions are sought in advance for each process step:

(i) How can process execution fail?

(ii) What are the possible causes of this failure?

(iii) How important is the prevention of this failure?

(iv) Who is responsible for the implementation of the solution to this problem?

(v) When will this be executed?

When to use FMEA?

(i) When a product or service; a process is being designed or redesigned after QFD and before the design is finalised, or

(ii) When an existing process, product or service is being applied in a new way, or

(iii) Before developing control plans for a new or modified process, or

(iv) When improvement goals are planed for an existing process, product or service, or

(v) When analysing failures of an existing process, product or service.

(vi) And periodically throughout the life of the process, product or service.

Types of FMEA

Four types of FMEA are:

(i) **A System FMEA** which is used at the design stage to analyse overall systems including the interactions in order to minimise the effects of failure.

(ii) **A Design FMEA** which is used to minimise design faults before the defects are passed on to the manufacturing stage.

(iii) **The Process FMEA** which focuses on failures caused in the manufacturing process.

(iv) **The Service FMEA** which focuses on service failures.

Steps involved in FMEA procedure

The general procedure of FMEA is given below. Specific details may vary with the standards of the organisation or industry.

Step 1: Form a cross-functional (or multi-disciplinary) team of people with diverse knowledge about the process, product or service and customer needs. The size of the team varies usually from 5 to 8 members.

Step 2: Identify the scope of the FMEA. The questions to be answered are: *(a)* Is it for concept, system, design, process, or service?, *(b)* What are the boundaries? and *(c)* How detailed should we be? Use flow charts to identify the scope and to make sure that every team member understands it in detail.

Step 3: Fill in the identifying information at the top of the FMEA format. ***Table 14.14*** shows a typical format.

Step 4: Identify the ***functions*** of your scope by asking the question — "What is the purpose of this system, design, process or service? What do our customers expect it to do?

Step 5: For each function, identify all the ways that it could fail to happen. These are referred to as **potential failure modes.**

Step 6: For each failure mode, identify all the consequences on the system; related systems, process, related processes, product, service, customer or regulations. These are potential effects of failure. Ask the questions — *(a)* What does the customer experience because of this failure?, *(b)* What happens when this failure occurs?

Step 7: Determine how serious each effect is. This is referred to as ***severity rating*** *(S)*. Severity is usually rated on the scale from 1 to 10, where 1 is insignificant and 10 is catastrophic.

Step 8: For each failure mode, determine the potential root causes, use the ***cause analysis tools***, as well as the best knowledge and experience of the team. List all possible causes for each failure mode on the FMEA format.

Step 9: For each cause, determine the ***occurrence rating (O)***. This rating eliminates the probability of failure occurring because of that cause during the life time of your scope. Occurrence is usually rated on a scale from 1 to 10 where 1 is extremely unlikely and 10 is inevitable. List the occurrence rating for each cause on the FMEA table.

Step 10: For each cause, identify ***current process controls***. These are tasks, procedures or mechanisms that you now have in place to keep failures from reaching the customer. These controls might help to prevent the cause from happening, reduce the likelihood that it will happen or detect failure after the cause has already happened but before the customer is affected.

Step 11: For each control, determine the ***detection rating (D)***. This rating estimates how well the control can detect either the cause or its failure mode after they have happened but before the customer is affected. Detection is usually rated on a scale from 1 to 10 where 1 means the control is absolutely certain to detect the problem and 10 means the control is certain not to detect the problem or no control exists. List the detection rating for each cause on the FMEA table.

Table 14.14 : FMEA Format

Function	Potential Failure Mode	Potential Effects of Failure	S	Potential Cause of Failure	O	Current Process Controls	D	RPN	CRIT	Recommended Actions	Responsibility and Target completion date	Action Results					
												Action taken	S	O	D	RPN	CRIT

Step 12: This step is optional for most industries. Ask the question – "Is this failure mode associated with a ***critical characteristic?***" (Critical characteristics are measurements or indicators which affect safety or compliance with government regulations and need special controls). If so, a column, labelled **"classification"** receive a Y or ∇ to show that special controls may be needed. Usually critical characteristics have a severity of 9 or 10 and occurrence and detection ratings above 3.

Step 13: Calculate the ***risk priority number (RPN)*** as RPN = S × O × D. Also calculate criticality = S × O by multiplying severity by occurrence. These numbers provide guidance for ranking potential failures in the order they should be addressed.

Step 14: Identify ***recommended actions***. These actions may be design or process changes to lower severity or occurrences. They may be additional controls to improve detection. Also note who is responsible for the actions and target completion dates.

Step 15: As actions are completed, note results and the date on the FMEA format. Also note new S, O or D ratings and new RPN.

(E) STATISTICAL PROCESS CONTROL

Already discussed under chapter 12 – Statistical Concepts in Quality Management.

(F) BALANCED SCORE CARD

The balanced score card is a strategic planning and management system that is used extensively in business and industry, government and non-profit organisations world-wide to align business activities to the vision and strategy of the organisation, improve internal and external communications and monitor organisation performance against strategic goals. It was originated by Dr. Robert Kaplan and Dr. David Norton as a performance measurement framework that added strategic, non-financial performance measures to traditional financial metrics to give managers and executives a more **"balanced"** view of organisational performance. The balanced score card provides a set of measures that allow for a holistic, integrated view of business performance. The score card was originally created to supplement "traditional financial measure with criteria that measured performance from three additional perspectives-those of ***(i) customers***, ***(ii) internal business process*** and ***(iii) learning and growth.***

By 1996, the organisations that used this approach developed it as a strategic management system linking long-term strategy to short-term targets. The development of the balanced score card method occurred because many business organisations realised that focus on a one-dimensional measure of performance (such as return on investment or increased profit) was inadequate. Too often, bad strategic decisions were made in an effort to increase the bottom line at the expense of their organisational goals. The theory of balanced score card suggested that rather than the focus, financial performance is the natural outcome of balancing other important goals. These other organisational goals interact to support excellent overall organisational performance. If any individual goal is out of balance with other goals, the performance of the organisation as a whole will suffer. The balanced score card system also emphasises anticipation of strategic targets in support of goals, In addition, measurement systems are developed to provide data necessary to know when targets are being achieved or when performance is out of balance or being negatively affected.

The Kaplan and Norton "balanced score card" looks at a company from four perspectives:

(i) ***Financial:*** How do we look at shareholders?

(ii) ***Internal business processes:*** What must we execl at?

(iii) ***Innovation and bearing:*** Can we continue to improve and create value?

(iv) ***Customer:*** How do customers see us?

By viewing the company from all four perspectives, the balanced score card provides a more comprehensive understanding of current performance.

***Table 14.15* illustrates the balanced score card factors from the above perspective.**

Table 14.15 : Balanced Score Card Factors

Department	Areas
1. Finance	*(a)* Return on investment *(b)* Cash flow *(c)* Return on capital employed *(d)* Financial Results (Quality/Yearly)
2. Internal Business Processes	*(a)* Number of activities per function *(b)* Duplicate activities across functions *(c)* Process alignment (is the right process in the right department?) *(d)* Process bottlenecks *(e)* Process automation
3. Learning and Growth	*(a)* Is there the correct level of expertise for the job? *(b)* Employee turn-over. *(c)* Job satisfaction. *(d)* Training / Learning opportunities.
4. Customer.	*(a)* Delivery performance to customer. *(b)* Quality performance for customer. *(c)* Customer satisfaction rate. *(d)* Customer percentage of market. *(e)* Customer retention rate.

The balanced score card should result in : *(i)* Improved processes, *(ii)* Motivated / educated employees, *(iii)* Enhanced information systems, *(iv)* Monitored progress, *(v)* Greater customer satisfaction and *(v)* Increased financial usage.

Why Implement a Balanced Score Card?

(i) Increase focus on strategy and results.
(ii) Improve organisational performance by measuring what matters.
(iii) Align organisational strategy with the work people do on a day-to-day basis.
(iv) Focus on the drivers of future performance.
(v) Improve communication of the organisation's vision and strategy.
(vi) Prioritize.

When to use Balanced Score Card?

For senior managers:

(i) When developing the organisation's mission and strategy or
(ii) When communicating the mission and strategy throughout the organisation or
(iii) When planning programs and initiatives to achieve the organisation's goals or.
(iv) Later, when routinely reviewing the organisation's performance.

For everyone in the organisation:

(i) Only after the balanced score card has been created for the entire organisation or business unit.

(ii) When planning what areas to address for improvement or

(iii) When assessing how well current processes are meeting the needs of the customers of the organisation or

(iv) When setting improvement goals and planning how to achieve them or

(v) When planning what measures to use to monitor your improvement efforts, either during initial trial of a new solution or during standardisation.

Construction of Balanced Score Card

The construction of a balanced score card starts with the statement of the company vision. It includes the definition of "strategic business unit" (SBU), statement of the mission and the vision. The next question regarding each perspective is now:

If my vision succeeds, how will I differ? The process continues by definition of the ***"critical success factors"*** (CSFs). Finally, measures can be linked to identified CSFs….. The set of critical measure forms the company specific balanced score card.

After the introduction of the concept, balanced score card has been developed towards a strategic tool. Balanced score card lets managers introduce new management processes that, separately and in combination, contribute to linking long-term strategic objectives with short-term action. The processes are:

1. **Translating the vision** – helps mangers to build a consensus regarding the organisation's vision and strategy.
2. **Communicating and linking** – lets managers communicate the strategy up and down the organisation and link it to departmental and individual objectives.
3. **Business Planning** – enables companies to integrate their business and financial plans and coordination of various change programs towards long-term strategic objectives.
4. **Feedback and learning** – it gives companies the capacity for what can be called strategic learning. The scorecard enables, companies modify their strategies to real-time learning.

Gaining Understanding by Linking business Perspectives

Principle of the balanced score card is shown in *Exhibit 14.51.*

Exhibit 14.51 shows the essential characteristic of balanced score card (BSC) concept. The perspectives are connected to each other to demonstrate causal relationships in company operations, in addition, the company vision and strategy strongly influences the collection of measures and targets regarding each perspective.

Measurement system's ability to systematically demonstrate various causal relationships may be a questionable issue, however, Kaplan and Norton set an example concerning the creation of causal measures. This is demonstrated in ***Exhibit 14.52***.

Return on capital employed (ROCE) can be a scoreboard measure in the financial perspective, the drives of which could be repeat and expanded sales from existing customers-as a result of a high degree of loyalty among customers. Analysing customer preferences may reveal that on-time-delivery of orders is highly valued by customers. Thus both on-time-delivery and customer loyalty are selected into the customer perspective of balanced scorecard (BSC). Next question is what internal processes the company must excel to achieve excellent on-time delivery. Improved on-time-delivery (OTD) may require short cycle time of internal processes as well as the high quality of them. Both of the factors can be measures in internal perspective. Organisation can improve internal processes for instance by training and improving employee skills. That would be a quite possible objective for learning and growth perspective.

Exhibit 14.51 : The perspectives of Balanced Score Card

Financial
• Objectives
• Measures
• Targets
• Initiatives
Customer
• Objectives
• Measures
• Targets
• Initiatives
Vision and Strategy
Internal Busines Process
• Objectives
• Measures
• Targets
• Initiatives
Learning and Growth
• Objectives
• Measures
• Targets
• Initiatives

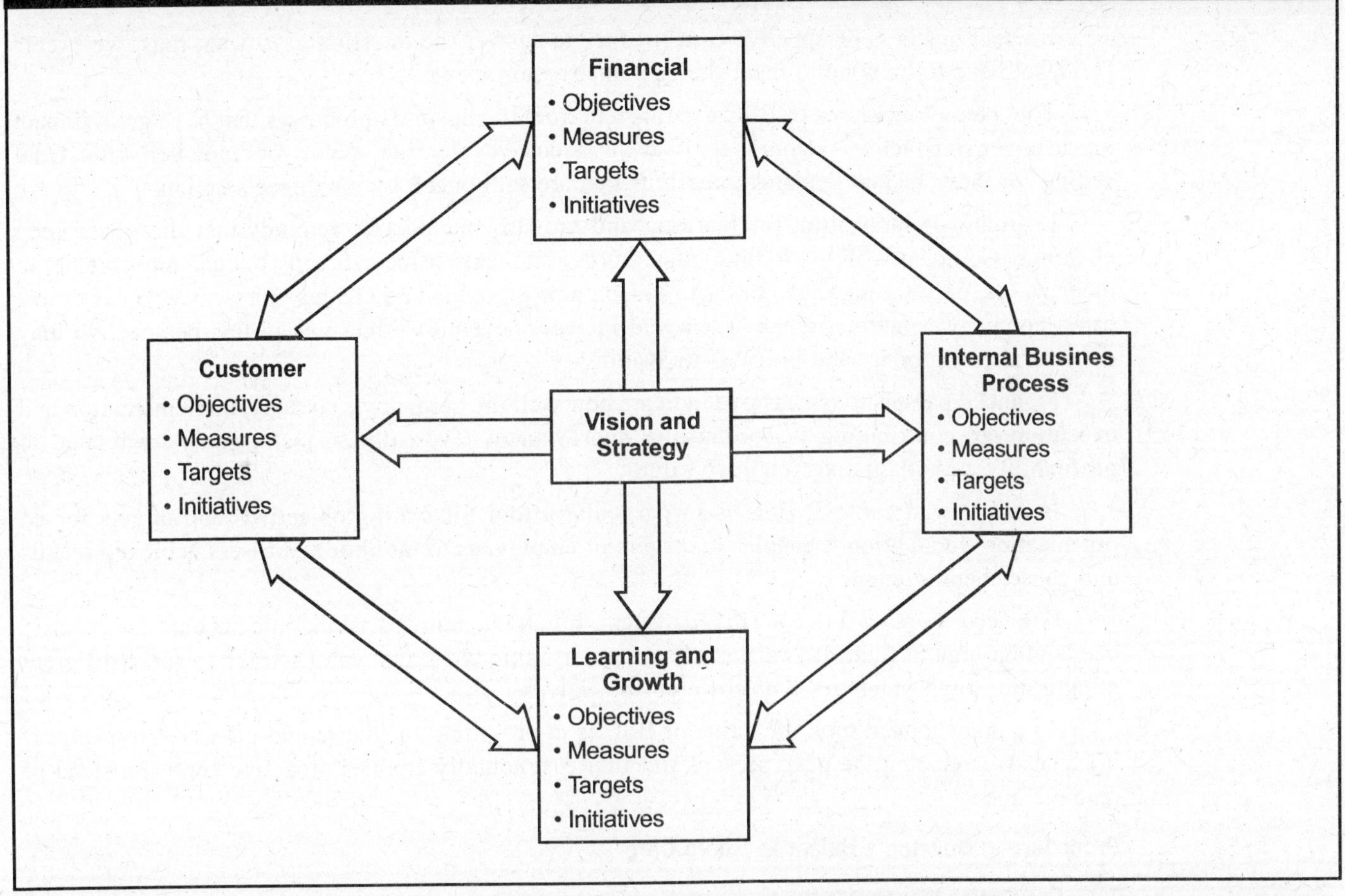

Exhibit 14.52 : The Cause and Effect Measures of Balanced Score Card Concept.

Learning and growth
Internal busines process
Customer
Financial
Employee skills
Process quality
Process cycle time
On-time delivery
Customer loyalty
ROCE

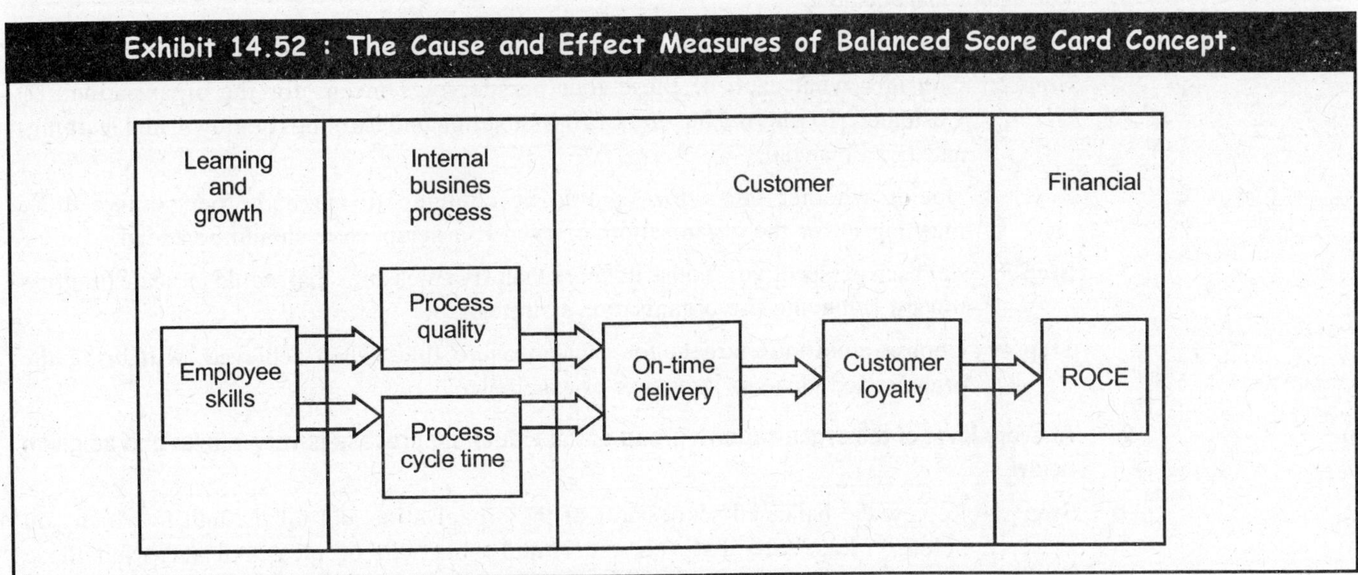

The actual construction of measurement system with clear causal relationships requires deep understanding of company operations.

Customer perspective measures are to answer the question: How do customers see us? BSC demands that managers translate their general mission statement-many times focused on customers into specific measures that reflect the factors that really matter to customers. Often customers' concerns fall into four categories *(i)* time, *(ii)* quality, *(iii)* performance and service and *(iv)* cost.

Internal business perspective measures try to answer the questions: *(a)* what must we excel? *(b)* What have to be done to meet the customer requirements?

The internal measures of BSC should stem from the business processes that have great impact on customer satisfaction-factors that affect for instance cycle time, quality or employer skills. Goal setting for these factors demands measures that are influenced by employee's actions.

Learning or innovation (or learning and growth) perspective reminds that the goals keep charging. Company's ability to innovate, improve and learn affects directly to company's value. In other words, only through the ability to launch new products and creates more value to customers can a company penetrate new markets and increase revenues. Measures in this perspective may concentrate on product and process innovations.

Financial perspective measures indicate how well the company's strategy, implementation and execution are contributing to bottom-line improvement. Typically financial goals are related to profitability, growth and shareholder value.

In managerial context, BSC is in particular a tool for stating objectives and targets for an organisation. In addition it enables managers or employees to monitor and assess achieved results and causes behind them.

Balanced score card is not a fixed system. It must be tailored taking into account the specific needs of an organisation. It is a flexible system-a frame work that can be filled to serve different organisations and industries with different objectives.

As a management tool, the value of BSC is in providing the cause-and-effect relationship. If it succeeds balancing the past, present and future, it actually enables proactive control instead of reactive one.

Procedure to Develop a Balanced Score Card

1. **For Senior Management**

Step 1: Reach a consensus on the vision and strategy of the organisation.

Step 2: Consider what each of these four perspectives means for the organisation: *(i)* Customer, *(ii)* Internal business, *(iii)* Innovation and learning (or growth and learning) and *(iv)* Financial.

Decide whether the names should be changed to make the perspective more meaningful for the organisation, or even if a perspective should be added.

Step 3: For each perspective, choose no more than five measures that would indicate progress toward achieving the organisation's strategy.

Step 4: Choose ambitious targets for each measure that, when achieved, will bring the organisation close to its vision of excellence.

2. **At every level of the organisation - group or individual the process is very similar and as given below**

Step 1: Review the balanced score cards of the organisation and for the unit to which you belong. Make sure that you understand what will be measured and what those measures say about what is important to the organisation.

Step 2: Within each of the perspective, choose no more than five measures at your level that indicate your contribution to the organisational measures.

Step 3: Choose ambitious targets for your measures. This becomes your level's balanced score card.

3. **For everyone in the organisation, the following steps are to be followed to put the balanced score card into action**

Step 1: Identify actions that will achieve the targets. For each action, identify which measures will indicate success of the actions.

Step 2: Set intermediate milestones for improvement in the measures. Include when the milestone will be reached as well as the numeric target.

Step 3: Review the scorecard, measures regularly. Adjust actions, milestones, targets or even measures or strategy when necessary.

Primary Implementation Success Factors

1. Obtaining executive sponsorship and commitment.
2. Involving a broad base of leaders, managers and employees in scorecard development.
3. Agreeing on terminology.
4. Choosing the right BSC Program champion.
5. Beginning interactive (two-way) communication first.
6. Working through mission, vision, strategic results, and strategy mapping first to avoid rushing to judgment on measures or software.
7. Viewing the score card as a long-time journey rather than a short-term project.
8. Planning for and managing change.
9. Applying a disciplined implementation frame work.
10. Getting outside help if needed.

14.10 QUALITY IN PRACTICE

Box 14.8 : Improving Service At A Restaurant

The manager of a restaurant decided to do something about the long lines (queue) that occurred every day in the place of business. After discussions with employees, several important facts came to light:

- Customers waited in line for upto 15 minutes.
- Usually tables were available.
- Many of the customers were regulars.
- People taking orders and preparing food were getting in each other's way.

To measure the improvement that might result from any changes made, the manager decided to collect data on the number of customers in line, the number of empty tables and the time until a customer received the food ordered.

In the plan stage, the manager wanted to test a few changes. He decided on three changes:

1. Provide a way for customers to fax orders in ahead of time (rent a fax machine for a month).
2. Construct a preparation table in the kitchen with ample room for fax orders.
3. Devote one of the two cash registers to handling fax orders.

Both the length of the line (queue) and the number of empty tables were measured every 15 minutes during the lunch hours by the manager. In addition when the 15 minutes line check was done, he noted the last person in line and measured the time until that person got served.

In the *"Do"* phase, the manager observed the results of the three measures for three weeks. In the *"study"* or *"check"* phase, he detected several improvements. Time in line went down from 15 minutes to an average of 5 minutes. The line length was cut to a peak average of 12 people, and the number of empty tables decreased slightly. In the *"Act"* phase, the manager held a meeting with the employees to discuss the results. He decided to purchase the fax machine, prepare phone orders in the kitchen with the fax orders and use both cash registers to handle walk-up and fax orders.

14.11 SUMMARY

The total quality tools that come in a process of continuous improvement will ensure that the product not only meets its customer's expectations but actually improves for as long as production is continued.

Quality improvement tools can be grouped as : *(i)* Project planning and implementation tools, *(ii)* Idea creation tools, *(iii)* Process analysis tools, *(iv)* Data collection and analysis tools, *(v)* Cause analysis tools and *(vi)* Evaluation and decision-making tools.

The generic kinds of quality tools that can be customised include : *(i)* Check sheet and checklist, *(ii)* Flow chart, *(iii)* Graph, *(iv)* Matrix diagram, *(v)* Table, *(vi)* Tree diagram and *(vii)* Two-dimensional charts.

Total quality tools can also be classified as problem-solving tools as : *(i)* The seven classic quality tools (also called seven Q.C tools), *(ii)* The seven basic management and planning tools, *(iii)* Process improvement tools and *(iv)* Innovation and creativity tools.

The tools and techniques along with management practices and the organisational infrastructure are the basic components of total quality management.

There are a number of tools for design process and process improvement. The various tools and techniques used for improving design process are : *(i)* Statistical experimentation or Design of experiments, *(ii)* Taguchi's methods/Taguchi's loss function, *(iii)* Quality function deployment and *(iv)* Poka-yoke or fail safing.

Design of experiments or experimental design is one of the most powerful techniques for improving quality and increasing productivity. Any experiment that has the flexibility to make desired changes in the input response is known as experimental design. It is a branch of applied statistics dealing with planning, analysing and interpreting controlled tests to evaluate the factors that control the value of a parameter or group of parameters.

Taguchi's definition of quality stressed the losses associated with a product *(i)* the loss caused by variability of functions and *(ii)* the loss caused to the society by harmful side effects.

Taguchi's loss function states that any deviation from the target value of a quality characteristic results in extra costs to some segment of the society.

Taguchi's loss function is expressed as :

$$L = C(X - T)^2$$

where, L = total loss, C = a cost constant, X = actual average value of quality characteristic and T = target value of quality characteristic.

Taguchi developed a variety of practices for statistically determining required qualitative features of a design that makes it robust against disturbances and uncertainties, with the objective of reducing loss of society.

Various topics associated with Taguchi's approach to robust design include : *(i)* Design of experiments, *(ii)* Orthogonal arrays, *(iii)* Signal-to-noise ratio and *(iv)* Parameter design and Tolerance design.

Orthogonal arrays are a simplified method of putting together an experiment. Two types of orthogonal arrays are : *(i)* Fisher orthogonal array and *(ii)* Taguchi's orthogonal array.

Signal-to-noise ratio (S/N ratio) can be viewed as the ratio of sensitivity to variability. The larger the S/N ratio, the better the quality of a product or process. Noise factors are those that are not under the control of the operator of a product. Signal factors are those factors that are set or controlled by the operator of the product to make use of its intended functions.

Taguchi designs involve three phases : *(i)* System design, *(ii)* Parameter design and *(iii)* Tolerance design.

System design involves investigating process, procedure and product factors that may cause variation in the final product. It has two elements : *(i)* product design and *(ii)* process design.

Parameter design establishes specifications which represent the transition from a designer's concept to a producible design.

Tolerance design deals with the problem of how and when to specify tightened tolerances of a product or a process so that quality and performance/productivity are enhanced.

Quality function deployment (QFD) is a process or system to solve quality problems and carefully define customer requirements before the design phase of a product. QFD involves finding out what the customer wants and then supplying it. It means listening to the 'voice' of the customer

The customer requirements planning matrix also referred to as the "house of quality" relates customer defined product traits to the technical product or process requirements needed to support and generate these features.

The four houses of quality in QFD are : *(i)* Technical requirements, *(ii)* Component characteristics, *(iii)* Process operations and *(iv)* Quality control plan.

Poka-yoke, a Japanese name for "mistake proofing" and fool proofing is a technique to help avoid human error. 'Poka' means 'error' and 'yokeru' means 'to avoid'. Poka-yoke means to mistake-proof a process by building safeguards into the system that avoid or immediately find errors. Examples of Poka-yoke are : colour coding, check lists, templates, optical scanners, bar codes etc.

Problem solving is the activity associated with changing the state of what is actually happening to what should be happening. Problems can be : *(i)* structured, *(ii)* semi-structured and *(iii)* ill-structured problems.

The steps involved in the problem-solving process are : *(i)* size up/description, *(ii)* problem statement/diagnosis, *(iii)* analysis, *(iv* prescription/alternatives and *(v)* implementation.

Approaches to creative problem solving process include : *(i)* The Deming cycle or P-D-C-A cycle or P-D-S-A cycle, *(ii)* Juran's improvement program and *(iii)* The Crosby program.

Tools used for process improvement can be classified into : *(i)* Generic tools, *(ii)* Coarse-grained tools and *(iii)* Fine-grained tools.

Generic tools are *(i)* Team-building and group-interaction tools, and *(ii)* Specific process/technology tools.

Coarse-grained tools are : *(i)* Process flow-chart, *(ii)* Check sheets and histograms, *(iii)* Pareto analysis, and *(iv)* Fishbone charts.

Fine-grained tools are : *(i)* Fail safing, *(ii)* Design of experiments, *(iii)* Run diagram and *(iv)* Process control chart.

The various quality improvement tools used in the creative-problem-solving process are :

1. Flow charts, run charts and control charts in the first step - understand the mess or mess-finding.
2. Check sheets in the second step-finding facts or fact finding.
3. Pareto diagrams and histograms in the third-step. Identifying problems or problem finding.
4. Cause and effect diagrams in the fourth step - generating ideas or ideas finding.
5. Scatter diagrams in the fifth step - developing solutions or solution finding.
6. The seven management and planning tools in the sixth step - implementing the plan or implementation.

The analytical tools for TQM are : *(i)* Process mapping, *(ii)* Regression analysis, *(iii)* Resource utilisation, *(iv)* Customer service analysis, *(v)* The "five whys" technique or "why-why diagram" and *(vi)* Overall equipment effectiveness.

Improvement tools and techniques are : (1) Continuous improvement, (2) Just-in-time systems, (3) Quality circles, (4) Force-field analysis and (5) Japanese 5 'S' principles.

Control tools and techniques involved are :

1. Project scheduling techniques viz., *(i)* Scheduling chart or Gantt chart, *(ii)* Programme evaluation and review technique (PERT) and *(iii)* Critical path method (CPM).
2. Radar chart or web chart or spider chart.
3. Milestone tracker diagram.
4. Failure modes and effects analysis.
5. Statistical process control (SPC).
6. Balanced score card.

14.12 KEY WORDS USED

Statistical Experimentation, Experimental Design, Design of Experiments, Taguchi Methods, Taguchi's Quality Loss Function, Robust Design, Orthogonal Arrays, Signal-to-Noise Ratio, System Design, Parameter Design, Tolerance Design, Quality Function Deployment (QFD), House of Quality, Poka-yoke, Fail Safing, Fail Proofing, Problem Solving, Jidoka, Autonomation, The Deming Cycle, P-D-C-A Cycle, P-D-S-A Cycle, Seven Q.C. Tools, Seven Management and Planning Tools, Mess

Finding, Flow Charts, Run Charts, Trend Charts, Control Chart, Fact Finding, Check Sheets, Problem Finding, Histograms, Ideas Finding, Pareto Diagram, Brain Storming, Cause-and-Effect Diagram, Ishikawa Diagram, Fish-bone Diagram, Solution Finding, Scatter Diagram, Process Mapping, Process Design, Process Management, Flow-diagramming Tools, CASE Tools, Process Road Map, Regression Analysis, Resource Utilisation, Customer Service Analysis, The "Five Whys" Technique, Overall Equipment Effectiveness, Continuous Improvement, Just-in-Time Systems, Kanban System, Pull Scheduling, Force-field Analysis, Project Scheduling Techniques, Scheduling Chart (Gantt Chart), Programme Evaluation and Review Technique (PERT), Critical Path Method (CPM), Radar Chart, Web Chart, Spider Chart, Star Chart, Milestone Tracker Diagram, Failure Modes and Effects Diagram, Statistical Process Control (SPC), Balanced Score Card.

14.13 OBJECTIVE QUESTIONS

(A) Match the following:

Column A	Column B
1. Taguchi	1. Orthogonal Arrays
2. A.R. Fisher	2. Poka-yoke
3. Shigeo-Shingo	3. Quality loss function
4. Deming	4. Cause and effect diagram
5. Kaoru Ishikawa	5. P-D-C-A cycle

(B) State whether the following statements are True or False.

1. Flow charts are used for fact finding in the creative problem solving process. (T / F)
2. The fundamental concepts of process mapping are based on the idea of structural analysis. (T / F)
3. In the Japanese 5 'S' Kaizen system, "Seiton" means "putting things in order". (T / F)
4. Pareto principle is also called the 80-20 rule. (T / F)
5. CPM uses probabilistic time estimates to determine the average or expected time for an activity. (T / F)

(C) Multiple choice Questions: Choose the correct answer from the alternatives given under each question:

1. The Japanese name for autonomation is :
   (a) Kanban (b) Kaizen
   (c) Jidoka (d) Andon
   (e) Seiso
2. ____________ display large amounts of data that are difficult to interpret in their raw form :
   (a) Pareto diagrams (b) Histograms
   (c) Flow charts (d) Run charts
   (e) None of the above
3. _________ is the amount of time an activity can be delayed without delaying the early start of a successor activity :
   (a) Total float (b) Free float
   (c) Independent float (d) Activity slack
   (e) Event slack
4. The cause-and-effect diagram was introduced by __________
   (a) Taguchi (b) Taichi ohno
   (c) Shigeo Shingo (d) Kaoru Ishikawa
   (e) Masaaki Imai

5. The balanced score card was originated by :
   (a) Dr. Walter Shewhart (b) Shiego Shingo
   (c) Dr. Robert Kaplan and Dr. David Norton
   (d) Genichi Taguchi (e) None of these

14.14 REVIEW QUESTIONS

1. Discuss the classification of total quality management tools.
2. Explain the four major components of problem solving. How can the seven QC tools support each step?
3. Discuss the differences between a "run chart" and a "control chart".
4. What is "idea finding". Describe the various methods used for idea finding.
5. Briefly describe the following: (i) Check sheets, (ii) Histograms, (iii) Scatter diagrams, (iv) Pareto analysis, (v) Cause and effect diagram, (vi) Brainstorming.
6. What is "Taguchi's philosophy"?
7. State Taguchi's definition of quality?
8. Discuss Taguchi's "quality loss function" concept.
9. Define the term "Quality Engineering".
10. State the strengths and weaknesses of Taguchi's ideas.
11. Define the terms:
    (a) robustness (b) robust design.
12. State the five primary tools of robust design strategy.
13. Define the terms:
    (a) Experiment (b) Design of Experiments (c) Experimental design.
14. Discuss the purpose of using "design of experiments".
15. Discuss the components of experimental design.
16. Describe the purpose of designed experiments.
17. Discuss the steps involved in the experimental design process.
18. State the guidelines for experimental designs.
19. Discuss the various methods of experimentation.
20. What are orthogonal arrays? Differentiate between Fisher orthogonal array and Taguchi orthogonal array.
21. Discuss the steps involved in the procedure to determine the appropriate orthogonal array according to Taguchi
22. What is meant by "Signal-to-Noise Ratio"?
23. Differentiate between signal factors and noise factors.
24. What are the various types of signal-to-noise factors? Discuss briefly.
25. Distinguish between "on-line quality control" and "off-line quality control".
26. Discuss the following:
    (a) Systems design (b) Parameter design (c) Tolerance design.
27. What is "Quality function deployment?"
28. What is "voice of the customer"?
29. Define the following: (a) expected quality, (b) exciting quality
30. Describe the Quality Function Deployment" process.
31. What is meant by "House of Quality". Illustrate the house of quality with a diagram.
32. Discuss the six steps involved in constructing a "house of quality".
33. Explain the use of four houses of quality in the QFD process.
34. Discuss the five phases of use of QFD.
35. Define the terms: (a) Process, (b) Process Analysis, (c) Process Management and (d) Process Mapping.

36. What are the various types of processes? Give examples for each.
37. What is meant by a business process? Mention some ways of improving business processes.
38. "The business enterprise is only as effective as its processes" – Explain
39. Discuss the three process – based variables through which the pivotal link between the business enterprise performance and individual performance can be established.
40. Discuss the following: (a) Process goals/objectives, (b) Process design
41. Distinguish between "As-Is" Process Map and "To-Be" Process Map giving example of an "order – filling" process.
42. Discuss the four components of effective process management.
43. Give the outline of the origins of process mapping.
44. Discuss the "process mapping concept".
45. What is meant by "process – driven reengineering"?
46. What are the various tools used for process mapping? How they are categorised?
47. What is a "process map simulation"?
48. Discuss the need for a process road map.
49. Discuss the ten key steps involved in process mapping.
50. What is "P–D–C–A" – improvement model?
51. What is "regression analysis"? Discuss its application in business.
52. What is meant by the terms: (a) Resources, (b) Resources management and (c) Resource utilisation.
53. Define the terms "customer service" and "customer service analysis".
54. What is meant by "Five Whys" technique or Why – Why diagram? When it is used?
55. Discuss the procedure used in the "Five – Whys" technique.
56. What is meant by "over all equipment effectiveness"? What are its objectives?
57. How do you compute overall equipment effectiveness of a single piece of equipment?
58. Discuss the various factors involved in "overall equipment effectiveness analysis".
59. Discuss the "six big losses" which are the most common causes of efficiency loss in manufacturing.
60. Why a scheduling chart or Gantt chart is used?
61. Distinguish between PERT and CPM.
62. State the purpose of CPM
63. Discuss the procedure for drawing a CPM network.
64. Discuss the following:
    (a) CPM – Structure Analysis (b) CPM – Time Analysis
    (c) Progressive computation (d) Retrogressive computation
65. Define the following terms:
    (a) Event slack (b) Activity slack (c) Total float
    (d) Free float (e) Independent float
66. Define the following:
    (a) Optimistic time (b) Pessimistic time (c) Most likely time
    (d) Expected time (e) Activity standard deviation (f) Event standard deviation.
67. Describe how the probability of meeting scheduled date can be determined in PERT analysis.
68. What is a "network diagram?" Discuss the terms used in network based scheduling techniques.
69. Distinguish between AON and AOA conventions used in network analysis.
70. What is a "radar chart?". When it is used? Why it is used?
71. Discuss the steps involved in the construction of a radar chart.
72. What is "Deming cycle?" Discuss the steps involved in Deming cycle.
73. What is a "milestone tracker diagram?" How it is used for monitoring time in projects.
74. What is "Failure mode and effects Analysis?"
75. When do you use FMEA?

76. What are the various types of FMEA?
77. Discuss the steps involved in FMEA procedure.
78. What is meant by "Balanced Scorecard" ?
79. Discuss the four perspectives of the Kaplan and Norton "Balanced Score card" and the balanced score card factors based on these perspectives.
80. Why implement a "balanced score card"?
81. When to use "balances score card"?
82. Describe the process of constructing a "balanced score card"
83. Describe the essential characteristics of balanced score card concept with a diagram.
84. Describe the "cause and effect" measures of balanced score card concept.
85. Discuss the steps involved in the procedure to develop a balanced score card:
    (a) for senior management (b) at every level of the organisation.
    (c) for every one in the organisation.
86. What is "Kanban system" or "pull scheduling"?
87. Distinguish between "Production Kanban" and "Withdrawal kanban".
88. Describe the working of the Kanban system.
89. State the requirements for JIT implementation.
90. State the benefits of kanban.

14.15 DISCUSSION QUESTIONS

1. "The tools and techniques, along with management practices and the organisational infrastructure are fundamental components of total quality management" – Discuss.
2. "Quality function deployment is a method by which cross-functional teams translate customer requirements into appropriate design requirements at each stage of the product development process" – Explain.
3. "Poka-yoke may seem likely to make a work setting boring for employees" – Do you agree or disagree? Give reasons for your answer.
4. "Problem solving is the activity associated with changing the state of what is actually happening to what should be happening" – Critically examine the statement.
5. "Process-mapping provides a process tool with which to understand and change the processes to help improve the bottom-line and competitive position" – Elaborate.
6. "The kanban system is a physical control system consisting of cards and containers" – Explain.

14.16 ASSIGNMENTS

1. Consider the everyday task of getting to work on time in the morning. Draw a fish-bone diagram showing reasons why you might arrive late in the morning to the work place.
2. Visit two or three companies and conduct a study to identify the type of problem solving approach they are in their improvement efforts.
3. Develop cause-and-effect diagrams for the following problems :
    (a) Poor performance in examinations (b) Poor job performance.
    (c) Late for school or college.

14.17 CHAPTER CASE

QUALITY CIRCLE AT LION'S EYE HOSPITAL

Lion's Eye Hospital in the city introduced quality circles in different areas of operation to solve several operational problems. A QC was formed in its pharmacy section. It consisted of 9 members with one leader and one facilitator. The facilitator was DMO of the pharmacy section. The hospital dispenses medicines to nearly 30,000 patients per month. It caters to all sections of the people in city. The role of the pharmacist is to be alert, vigilant and quick in dispensing correct medicines to patients, explain the correct dosage to them and render service smilingly, enter receipts and issue of all the medicines on a scroll sheet.

The main objectives of the QC were

(i) to improve quality of service
(ii) reduce work pressure on the pharmacists
(iii) improve the working system
(iv) to effect cost reduction
(v) to work simplification
(vi) to improve work environment and
(vii) to make work a pleasure.

Several problems were identified through brain storming among the QC members and were listed as below.

(i) Waiting time for patients was more
(ii) Too many brands of the same drug
(iii) No action on slow moving drugs
(iv) Filling in forms is time consuming
(v) Disease code numbers not being mentioned on prescriptions
(vi) Inadequate facilities for pharmacists to reduce stress and fatigue.
(vii) Manpower not commensurate with increasing load.
(viii) Inadequate attention to control costly drugs.

All these problems were clubbed into 4 broad categories

(a) Working systems
(b) Operational costs
(c) Facilities and
(d) Man power

Pareto analysis was conducted by drawing a pareto diagram. It was found that problems (a) and (b) occurred more often. A problem from category (a) was selected ie waiting time of patients for medicines is more, it was of the order of 2 to 15 minutes.

Another brain storming session, on this point, among the QC members resulted in the following solutions.

(i) *2 more dispensing windows to be opened.*
(ii) *Separate children and women from general queue to one counter.*
(iii) *Shift 1 has to be strengthened by withdrawing one employee from shift 1 to meet the increasing* demand in shift 1
(iv) Straight back chairs to be replaced by revolving chairs.
(v) Ready made packets should be provided to start with
(vi) Prepacking of drugs for common ailments to be considered
(vii) If disease codes are religiously marked, data could be collected about fast moving drugs and could be kept nearer.
(viii) It helps to plan 'Prevention health care'.
(ix) Work tables with racks should be provided for keeping drugs and dispense quickly.
(x) To draw a cause and effect diagram with major causes as dispensing windows, packing, difficulty of movement and data on fast moving drugs.

The major effect shown on the fish bone diagram was-waiting time of patients was more leading to frustration. Many number of sub cases were added to complete the cause and effect diagram. Presently one window each for males, ladies and children exists. Common queue for gynaecology cases and children at ladies counter is there. Straight back chairs is restricting the movement. Load imbalance in shifts 1 and 2. Manual packing of medicines involve time. Long straight pigeon-hole rack for medicines restrict accessibility of drugs at the farthest end. With implementation of QC suggestions additional dispensing windows were opened and were seggregated from general ladies windows. Revoling chairs were provided, load was equitably distributed which led to faster service. Ready made packets helped quicker distribution. It also facilitated collecting data and making suitable arrangements on the racks. Patients become happy, pharmacists morale was boosted as they were less strained.

Discussion Questions :

1. Draw a Pareto diagram after systematically categorising the problems.
2. Draw a fish-bone diagram giving various causes and sub-causes and probable results.
3. Draw a quality circle structure for the case, give their functions, problem solving tools, benefits in the context of Indian organisations.

CHAPTER 15

BENCHMARKING

LEARNING OBJECTIVES

After reading this chapter, you should be able to:

- ➡ Define 'benchmarking' and understand its essence.
- ➡ Discuss the advantages and limitations of benchmarking.
- ➡ Discuss the levels and types of benchmarking.
- ➡ Describe the seven-step benchmarking model.
- ➡ Understand the four phases of benchmarking process.
- ➡ Discuss the factors to be kept in mind to ensure success with benchmarking.
- ➡ Discuss the "gap analysis" in benchmarking.
- ➡ Discuss the prerequisites of benchmarking.

15.0 INTRODUCTION

The development and realisation of improvement objectives, particularly *stretch objectives,* isoften aided through a process known as *benchmarking.* Benchmarking is a systematic method by which organisations can measure themselves against the best industry practices. Benchmarking is the search for best practices that will lead to superior performance. Benchmarking helps a company learn its strengths and weaknesses and those of other industrial leaders and incorporate the best practices into its own operations. It promotes superior performance by providing an organised framework through which organisations can learn how the ***"best-in-class"*** do things, understand how these best practices differ from their own and implement changes to close the gap. **It is a tool for continuous improvement.**

Benchmarking is defined as *"measuring our performance against that of best-in-class companies, determining how the best-in-class achieve those performance levels and using the information as a basis for our own company's targets, strategies and implementation."* Or more simply, "the search of industry *best practices* that lead to superior performance". The term ***"best practices"*** refers to the approaches that produce ***exceptional results,*** are usually ***innovative*** in terms of the use of ***technology*** or ***human resources*** and are recognised by customers or industry experts.

The Essence of Benchmarking

Benchmarking is an important process in which a company measures its performance against that of best-in-class companies, determines how those companies achieved their performance levels and uses the information to improve its own performance.

The ***essence of benchmarking*** is the continuous process of comparing a company's strategy, products and processes with those of world leaders and best-in-class organisations in order to learn how they achieved excellence and then setting out to match and even surpass it. In other words, it is ***"moving from where we are to where we want to be."***

A benchmark is a point of reference against which things are measured. In business, these points of reference or standards can take many forms. They are measured by questions about the product or service (*e.g.* ***how many, how much time, how much money, how reliable or how well made is it?***). By studying other organisations and comparing the answers to these questions, we will be able to measure our performance against that of others.

As a result, we will be able to set new goals and adapt the best practices to our organisation. This, in turn, will help us to satisfy our customers with the ***best quality, cost, product and service.***

15.1 THE EVOLUTION OF BENCHMARKING

The concept of benchmarking is not new. In the early 1800s, Francis Lowell, a New England industrialist, travelled to England to study manufacturing techniques at the best British factories. Henry Ford created the assembly line after taking tour of a Chicago slaughterhouse and watching carcasses hung on hooks mounted on a monorail move from one workstation to another. Toyota's just-in-time production system was influenced by the replenishment practices of U.S. supermarkets. Modern benchmarking was initiated by Xerox (in the 1980s), an eventual winner of the Malcolm Baldrige National Quality Award. IBM, Motorola and Xerox became the pioneers in instituting the benchmarking process. **Xerox initially studied their direct competitors and discovered that:**

- their unit manufacturing cost equalled the Japanese selling price in the United States.
- the number of production suppliers was nine times that of the best companies.
- assembly line rejects were 10 times higher
- product lead times were twice as long and
- defects per hundred machines were seven times higher.

These results helped them to understand the amount of change that would be required to set realistic targets to guide their planning efforts.

The Xerox Experience: Xerox instituted the benchmarking process in the 1980s because the company's market share shrank to 35 percent in 1981 even though the company invented the photocopier in 1959 and maintained a virtual monopoly for many years thereafter (Xerox name became a generic name for all photocopiers). On introducing benchmarking process, Xerox met with resistance at first by its employees who did not believe that someone else could do it better. When faced with the facts, reaction went from denial to dismay to frustration and finally to action. Once the process began, the company benchmarked virtually every function and task for productivity, cost and quality. Comparisons were made for companies both in and outside the industry.

By the company's own admission, it would probably not be in the copier business if it were not for benchmarking. Results were dramatic:

- Suppliers were reduced from 5000 to 300.
- ***"Concurrent engineering"*** was practiced. Each product development group has input from design, manufacturing and service from the initial stages of the project.
- Commonality of parts increased from about 20 percent to 60-70 percent.
- Hierarchical organisation structure was reduced and the use of cross-functional teams were established.
- **Results included:**
  (i) Quality problems cut by two-thirds.
  (ii) Manufacturing cost cut by 50 percent.
  (iii) Development time cut by two-thirds and
  (iv) Direct labour cut by 50 percent and corporate staff cut by 35 percent.

Benchmarking is a tool to achieve business and competitive objectives.

However, it should be noted that all of these improvements were not the direct result of benchmarking. What happened in Xerox was that in adopting the process, the climate for change and continuous improvement followed as a natural result. In other words, **benchmarking can be a very good intervention technique for positive change.**

The Motorola Experience: In the early 1980s, Motorola set a goal of improving a set of basic quality attributes ***tenfold*** in five years. Based on ***internal*** benchmarking, the goal was achieved in three years. The company began to look outside, sending teams to visit competitor plants in Japan. To their chagrin, the team found that Motorola would have to improve its tenfold improvement level another two to three times just to match the competition.

Borrowing process benchmarks from companies as diverse as Walmart, Benetton and Domino's Pizza, the company now routinely fields benchmarking requests from their Japanese competitors.

Reasons for benchmarking: Benchmarking is a tool to achieve business and competitive objectives. It is a powerful and effective tool when used for the right reasons and aligned with organisation strategy. In a competitive market, organisations have to decide which markets to serve and determine the strengths they need to have to gain competitive advantage. Benchmarking helps organisations to develop those strengths and reduce weaknesses.

Traditionally, companies used to set their next year's goals based on previous year's performance. Benchmarking enables goals to be set objectively based on external information rather than internal.

15.2 ADVANTAGES AND LIMITATIONS OF BENCHMARKING

15.2.1 Advantages

(i) A primary advantage of benchmarking practice is that it promotes a thorough understanding of the company's ***own* processes** *i.e.*, the company's current profile (***strength* and *weaknesses***) is well understood.

(ii) Benchmarking process involves ***limitation*** and ***adaptation*** of the practices of superior competitors, rather than ***invention***, thereby saving ***time*** and ***money*** for the company practising benchmarking.

(iii) Intensive studies of existing practices often lead to identification of ***non-value-added activities*** and plans for process improvement.

(iv) Benchmarking enables comparison of ***performance measures*** in different dimensions, each with best practices for that particular measure. It involves comparison with several companies who are best for the chosen measure. (Some common performance measures are return on assets, cycle time, percentage of on-time delivery, proportion of defects, percentage of damaged goods and time spent on administrative functions).

(v) Benchmarking focusses on performance measures and processes and not on products. Thus, it is not restricted to the industry to which the company belongs. It extends beyond these boundaries and identifies organisations in other industries that are superior with respect to chosen measures.

(vi) Benchmarking allows organisations to set realistic, rigorous ***new performance targets*** and this process helps convince people of the credibility of these targets. This tends to overcome the ***"not invented here"*** syndrome and the ***"we are different"*** justification for the status zero. Benchmarking indicates to a company that there may be people else where who do things better than they do.

Benchmarking has certain advantages and also certain limitations and pitfalls.

(vii) Benchmarking allows organisations to define ***specific gaps in performance*** and to select the processes to improve. It enables the company to redesign its products and services to achieve outcomes that meet or exceed customer expectations.

(viii) Benchmarking provides a basis for ***training human resources***. Employees begin to see the gap between what they are doing and what best-in-class are doing. Closing the gap emphasises the need for personnel to be involved in techniques of ***problem solving*** and ***process improvement***. The synergy between organisational activities is improved through cross-functional cooperation.

15.2.2 Limitations

(i) The primary limitation or weakness of benchmarking is the fact that best-in-class performance is not a static but a moving target. New technology can create quantum leap performance improvement – *for example,* the use of electronic data interchange (EDI).

(ii) Benchmarking is ***not a panacea*** that can replace all other quality efforts or management processes that can improve the competitive advantage of a company.

(iii) Benchmarking is not an ***"instant pudding"***. It will not improve performance if the proper infrastructure of a total quality program is not in place. Unless a corporate culture of quality and the basic components of TQM such as information system, process control and human resource programmes are in place, trying to initiate the best-in-class may very well disrupt operations.

15.2.3 Pitfalls of Benchmarking

The potential pitfalls of benchmarking include the failure to do the following:

(i) Involve the employees who will ultimately use the information and improve the process. (participation can lead to enthusiasm).

(ii) Relate process improvement to strategy and competitive positioning.

(iii) Define the firm's own process before gathering data for the purpose of comparison.

(iv) Perceive benchmarking as an ongoing process and not as an one-time project with a finite start and completion dates.

(v) Expand the scope of the companies studied instead of confining to one's own area, industry or to direct competitors, which is a narrow approach in identifying excellent performances that are appropriate to one's own processes.

(vi) Perceive benchmarking as a means to process improvement, rather than an end itself.

(vii) Set goals for closing the gap between the existing performance (what is) and the benchmark (what can be).

(viii) Empower employees to achieve improvements that they identify and for which they solve problems and develop action plans.

15.3 LEVELS OF BENCHMARKING

To compare one's business practices with those of other organisations, four common approaches to benchmarking are adopted. They are:

(i) Internal benchmarking *(ii)* Competitive benchmarking

(iii) Non-competitive benchmarking and *(iv)* World-class benchmarking.

The four levels of benchmarking are:
(i) Internal benchmarking
(ii) Competitive benchmarking
(iii) Non-competitive benchmarking and
(iv) World-class benchmarking.

Internal benchmarking is done within one's organisation or perhaps in conjunction with another division or branch office. Internal benchmarking is the easiest to conduct since data and information should be readily available and confidentiality concerns are minimised.

Competitive benchmarking involves analysing the performance and practices of best-in-class companies. Their performance becomes a benchmark to which a firm can compare its own performance and their practices are used to improve that firm's practices. However benchmarking the competition could be difficult since it might be impossible to collect or learn a competitor's secrets. This type of information can often be obtained through a confidential survey of all competitors, usually conducted by a third party consulting firm.

Non-competitive benchmarking is learning something about a process a company wants to improve by benchmarking including –

- a related process in the industry with a firm, the company does not directly compete with
- a related process in a different industry
- an unrelated process in a different industry.

An advantage of this type of benchmarking is that new processes which could easily be adapted to one's organisation might be discovered.

World-class benchmarking: This approach to benchmarking is the most ambitious. It involves looking towards the recognised leader for the process being benchmarked – an organisation that does it better than any other.

15.4 TYPES OF BENCHMARKING

Three major types of benchmarking that have emerged in business are:

(i) Performance benchmarking or operational benchmarking.

(ii) Process benchmarking or functional benchmarking and

(iii) Strategic benchmarking.

The various types of benchmarking are:
(i) Performance or operational benchmarking
(ii) Process or functional benchmarking and
(iii) Strategic benchmarking

Performance benchmarking involves pricing, technical quality, features and other quality or performance characteristics of products and services. Performance benchmarking is usually performed by direct comparisons or "reverse engineering" in which competitor's products are taken apart and analysed. This process is also known as ***"operational benchmarking"*** or ***"competitive benchmarking"*** and involves studying of products and processes of competitors in the same industry.

Process benchmarking centres on work processes such as billing, order entry or employee training. This type of benchmarking identifies the most effective practices in companies that perform similar functions, no matter in what industry. *For example,* the warehousing and distribution practices of L.L. Bean were adapted by Xerox for its spare parts distribution system. Texas Instruments studied the kitting (order preparation) practices of six companies, including Mary Kay Cosmetics and designed a process that captured best practices of each of them and thereby cutting the cycle time by 50 percent. Companies should not aim benchmarking solely at direct competitors and it would be a mistake if they do so. If a company simply benchmarks within its own industry, it may be competitive and have an edge in those areas in which it is the industry leader. However, if benchmarks are adopted from outside the industry, a company may learn ideas and processes as well as new applications that allow it to surpass the best within its own industry and to achieve distinct superiority.

Strategic benchmarking examines how companies compute and seek the winning strategies that have led to competitive advantage and market success. One way to determine how well a company is prepared to compete in a segment and to help define a best-in-class competitor is to construct a ***key success factor*** **(KSF)** matrix similar to the one shown in *Exhibit 15.1*.

Exhibit 15.1 : Key Success Factor Matrix

	Compeitive Analysis - Computer Industry ... Segment				
	Performance Rating				
Key success factor	**Weight**	**Our company**	**Competitor A**	**Competitor B**	**Competitor C**
Sales force					
Distribution					
Suppliers					
R & D					
Service					
Cost structure					

Areas to benchmark: ***Specific areas to benchmark at the operating level might include the following:***

(i) customer service levels
(ii) inventory management
(iii) inventory control (extent of automation)
(iv) purchasing
(v) billing and collection
(vi) purchasing practices
(vii) quality process
(viii) warehousing and distribution and
(ix) transportation.

Guidelines to benchmarking: Companies approach benchmarking in different ways. IBM has a four step approach. **AT & T has a nine step approach and *Xerox a ten step approach*.** All these approaches have the general guidelines given below:

(i) **Do not go on a fishing expedition:** When preparing a benchmarking study, pick-up a specific area in the organisation that needs improvement. This may be quality, customer satisfaction, accounts payable or delivery time. Then do your homework, including thoroughly reviewing your own process and procedures before picking a company that excels in the particular area chosen.

(ii) **Use company people:** The people who are going to implement changes need to see and understand for themselves, so it is they who should make the visits to other firms which are benchmarked and have the discussions with the concerned people. Further the visits should be short and the working teams small.

(iii) **Exchange information:** You should be ready to exchange information and provide answers in turn to any questions you might ask another company.

(iv) **Legal concerns:** Avoid legal problems which might arise as a result of discussions that might imply price fixing, market allocation or other illegal activities. This could lead to problems. Do not expect to learn much about new products of competitors by the benchmarking process. Most benchmarking missions focus on existing products, business practices, human resources and customer satisfaction.

(v) **Confidentiality:** Respect the confidentiality of data obtained. Companies that agree to share information with you may strongly object if that information leaks out to a competitor.

FOUR PHASES OF BENCHMARKING

The four phases of benchmarking are:
(i) Planning
(ii) Analysis
(iii) Integration and
(iv) Action

The four phases of benchmarking are:

(i) **Planning:** Identify the product, service or process to be benchmarked and the firm(s) to be used for comparison, determine the measures of performance for analysis and collect the relevant data.

(ii) **Analysis:** Determine the gap between the firm's current performance and that of the firm(s) benchmarked and identify the causes of significant gaps.

(iii) **Integration:** Establish goals and obtain the support of managers who must provide the resources for accomplishing the goals.

(iv) **Action:** Develop cross-functional teams of those most affected by the changes, develop action plans and team assignments, implement the plans, monitor progress and recalibrate benchmark as improvements are made.

Benchmarking Process: Specific steps in benchmarking vary from company to company but the fundamental or basic approach is the same. One company's benchmarking may not work at another organisation because of differences in their operating concerns. Successful benchmarking reflects the culture of the organisation, works within the existing infrastructure and is harmonious with the leadership philosophy.

Motorola Inc., winner of the Malcolm Baldrige Award for 1988, uses a *five step* benchmarking process:

(i) ***decide*** what to benchmark

(ii) ***select*** companies to benchmark

(iii) ***obtain*** data and collect information

(iv) ***analyse*** data and form action plans and

(v) ***recalibrate*** and start the process again.

AT&T, which has two Baldrige winners among its operating units uses a *nine step* process:

(i) ***Project conception:*** identify the need and decide what to benchmark.

(ii) ***Planning:*** determine the scope and objectives and develop a benchmarking plan.

(iii) ***Preliminary data collection:*** collect data on industry companies and similar processes as well as detailed data on your own processes.

(iv) ***Best-in-class selection:*** select companies with best-in-class processes.

(v) ***Best-in-class collection:*** collect detailed data from companies with best-in-class processes.

(vi) ***Assessment:*** compare your own and best-in-class processes and develop recommendations.

(vii) ***Implementation planning:*** develop operational improvement plans to attain superior performance.

(viii) ***Implementation:*** enact operational plans and monitor process improvements.

*(ix) **Recommendations:*** update benchmark findings and assess improvements in processes.

Xerox divided its initial benchmarking procedure into ***ten steps*** but other experts have noted successful programs based on as few as four defined stages. What matters is not the number of steps but that all necessary actions are completed in the benchmarking process. *Exhibit 15.2* shows one common format for this process.

Exhibit 15.2 : The Benchmarking Process – Common Steps

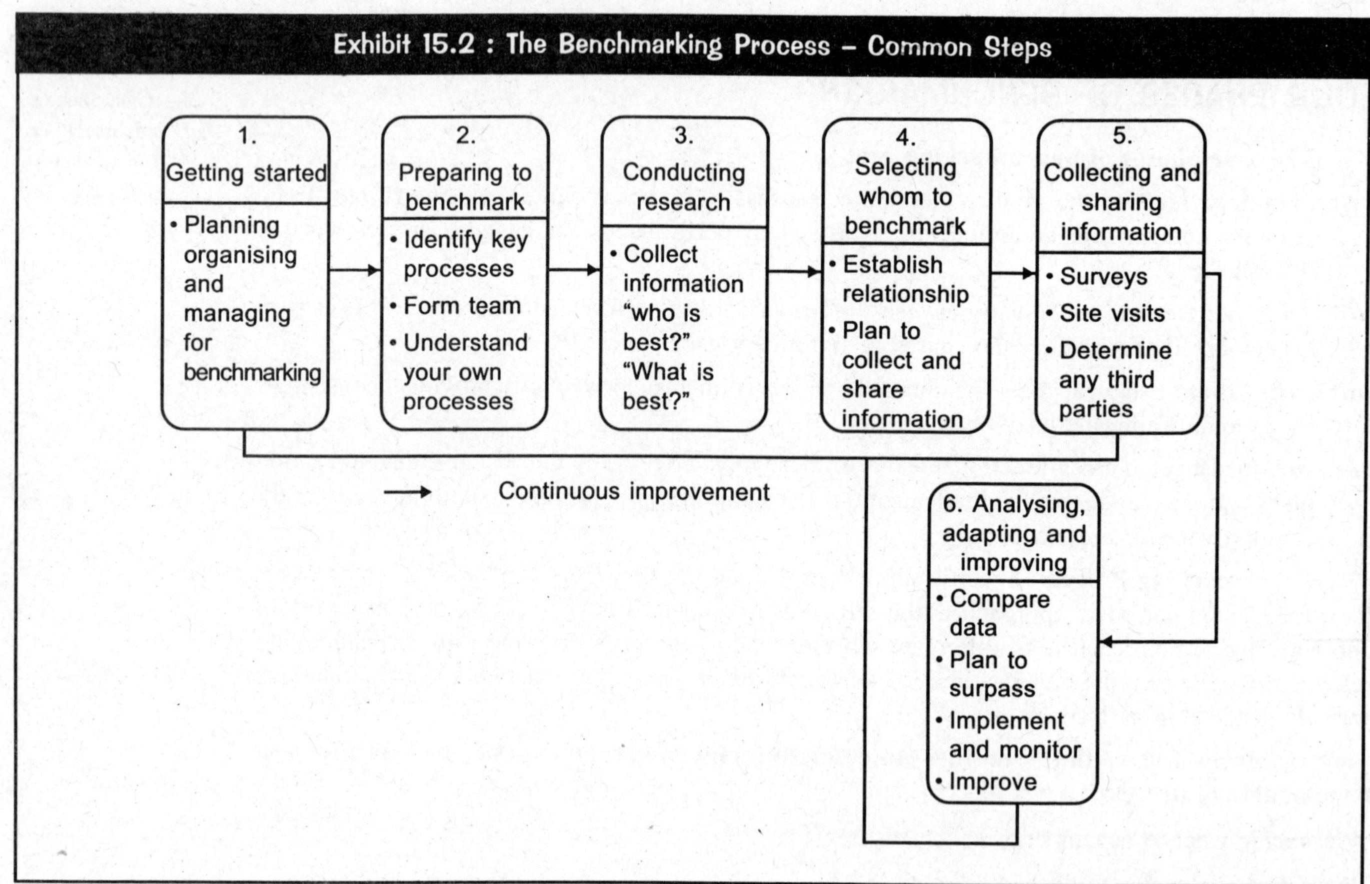

15.6 THE SEVEN STEP BENCHMARKING MODEL

Benchmarking model consist of seven steps.

Benchmarking is an ongoing process that requires data gathering, goal setting and analysis. These are accomplished by a seven step model. The seven steps are:

Step 1 : Identify what to benchmark

Step 2 : Determine what to measure

Step 3 : Identify who to benchmark

Step 4 : Collect the data

Step 5 : Analyse data and determine the gap

Step 6 : Set goals and develop action plan and

Step 7 : Monitor the process.

What each step includes is illustrated in *Box 15.1* shown below.

Box 15.1 : Seven step benchmarking

Step	Activity	What is included
1.	Identify what to benchmark	*(i)* Clarify the benchmarking objective *(ii)* Decide whom to involve *(iii)* Define the process *(iv)* Consider the scope *(v)* Set the boundaries *(vi)* Agree on what happens in the process *(vii)* Flow chart the process.
2.	Determine what to measure	*(i)* Examine the flow chart *(ii)* Establish the process measures *(iii)* Verify that measures match objectives
3.	Identify who to benchmark	*(i)* Conduct general research *(ii)* Choose level to benchmark
4.	Collect data	*(I)* Use a questionnaire *(ii)* Conduct a benchmarking site visit
5.	Analyse data and determine the gap	*(i)* Quantitative data *(ii)* Qualitative analysis
6.	Set goals and develop an "Action Plan"	*(i)* Set performance goals *(ii)* Develop an Action Plan
7.	Monitor the process	*(i)* Track the changes *(ii)* Make benchmarking a habit.

The steps listed above are discussed in the following paragraphs:

Step 1: Identify what to Benchmark?

Benchmarking can be a very powerful vehicle for driving peak process performance. But if the approach to benchmarking is not targeted, well-planned or organised, it can be a very costly investment of resources with minimal return on investment.

The first step which keeps the efforts of the company focussed involves the following sub-steps:

(i) Clarify the benchmarking objective
(ii) Decide whom to involve
(iii) Define the process
(iv) Consider the scope
(v) Set the boundaries
(vi) Agree on the process and
(vii) Flow chart the process.

These sub-steps are detailed below:

(i) **Clarify the benchmarking objective: Benchmarking decision may be driven by any one or more of the following factors:**

- *An* organisation wide strategy, setting priorities for improvement.
- The need to address a specific problem that requires immediate attention.
- A new business requirement (a new product line or a modification to the existing one).
- Not meeting goals in previous attempts to improve a process.

(ii) **Decide whom to involve:** After deciding what to benchmark, decide who will be on the team. Even though benchmarking can be done individually, best results typically come from team effort. The team members are selected on the following considerations:

- It is critical for management to be actively involved with the team.
- Include employees involved with the day-to-day flow of the process and
- Include employees who have an interest in and knowledge about what goes on just outside the boundaries of the process.

(iii) **Define the process:** The process should be clearly defined. A process is a series of interrelated tasks that are organised to produce an output. An output might include a product or a service. ***It is important to know as much about your process before you benchmark it against another organisation's process.***

(iv) **Consider the scope:** The scope should not be *too broad* or *too narrow*. If the scope of your focus is too large, you might not be able to tackle it effectively. *For example,* benchmarking the ***"human resources function"*** at another organisation might be too broad in scope. A narrower focus, such as the "recruiting and interviewing process" is more realistic.

If the scope is too narrow, your benchmarking efforts might miss important opportunities. *For example,* benchmarking the "prospective employee interview scheduling process" might miss critical information and opportunities not related to this narrow focus.

(v) **Set the boundaries:** Every system is made up of separate and distinct processes. Boundaries of each process can be defined by identifying its inputs and outputs. Boundaries exist at the point where inputs are received from internal suppliers and outputs go to internal customers. Defining the boundaries more specifically will make you more successful in improving the process. You will be better able to stay focussed, make plans and stay on track as you benchmark.

(vi) **Agree on the process:** Once your team has defined the process, you must agree on the tasks involved. It is a good idea to brainstorm the tasks first and put them in the right order later. The objective is to include all the major tasks in the process from start to finish.

Flow chart is a graphical representation of the steps in a process. Flow chart helps to better understand the processes.

(vii) **Flow chart the process:** A flow chart is a step-by-step picture of the tasks in your process. Use it as a ***"working document"*** to help define the process. Later, it can be used as the tool to continuously improve the process. The following symbols are used to draw the flow chart.

Start and end point of a process

Decision points

Step or activity

A Connector from one step to another.

Step 2: Determine what to measure

Once the process to be benchmarked has been defined, you are almost ready to look at similar processes in other organisations. Comparison of your processes with those in other organisations should be meaningful. This requires clear and accurate *measures* before looking at processes in other organisations.

There are three sub-steps included in determining the process measures. They are:

(i) Examine the flow chart

(ii) Establish the process measures and

(iii) Verify that measures match objectives.

These sub-steps are detailed below:

(i) **Examine the flow chart:** Some of the measurable items might include

- Overall time to complete the process.
- Completion time at each individual task.

- Time spent at each decision point.
- Number of repeats.
- Variation of task time.
- Number of defects showing up.
- Costs and
- Scrap.

***(ii)* Establish process measures**

***(a)* Consider measures outside the process** – When deciding which measures to address in benchmarking a process, look outside the process itself. Consider measures of your external customer's requirements and measures of internal suppliers and customer's requirements. You can determine which measures should be benchmarked by identifying who your internal customers and suppliers are and determining which measures are important to them.

***(b)* Comparing and selecting your benchmarking measures:** The effective approach to ensure that the measures you decide to benchmark are aligned with measures that are critical to your internal suppliers and customers has the following steps:

- **Determine customer "result" measures:** Interview your internal customer to create a list of measures of process output from the customer's perspective – use customer surveys and interviews to gather information.
- **Determine supplier "input" measures:** Create a list of measures to assess your supplier's inputs. These are measures that: are in use by you, should be in use by you or are in use by your supplier.
- **Brainstorm in-process measures:** Make a list of all possible measures for your process. Use the flow chart as a guide as well as reports and charts currently used in the process.
- **Link supplier and customer measures with in-process measures:** Match up the supplier and customer measures that relate directly to-process measures. Select measures to be benchmarked based on what is critical to the process and important for suppliers and customers.

***(iii)* Verify that measures match objectives:** When deciding which measures to use, refer back and examine your original objectives. If you improve each benchmarked measure, then you should achieve your overall goals.

Step 3: Identify who to Benchmark

The steps to be followed are:

***(a)* Conduct general research:** Once you have identified "what to benchmark", find organisations to research. Some sources of benchmarking information are:

(i) Trade magazines
(ii) Industry publications
(iii) Professional journals
(iv) Market research
(v) Government studies
(vi) Computer databases
(vii) Telephone or mail surveys and
(viii) Benchmarking consultants.

At this point, search for benchmarking targets such as organisations that are recognised as the ***"industry best"*** in process, similar to yours. Since benchmarking has proven to be a very effective quality improvement tool, many large organisations have separate departments or teams setup specifically for benchmarking studies.

***(b)* Choose the level to benchmark:** Out of the few organisations that have sparked your interest, narrow the list to most suitable choices for your process. Consider more than one organisation for benchmarking, keeping in mind the four levels *viz.* - internal, competitive, non-competitive and world-class.

Step 4: Collect the data

Once you have identified the levels and organisations to benchmark, gather information on the performance level of your benchmarking targets and how they manage their processes to achieve these levels. **Three main sources of data are:**

(a) **Internal:** Data from past research available within the organisation (product studies, R & D research, market surveys, customer surveys or in-house surveys) are collected before moving on to information available from external sources such as public access resources and other companies.

(b) **Public Information:** Useful information can be found in public-access resources. Specific information may be collected from each source of information.

(c) **Other Companies:** It is exciting to actually go out and discover new ideas and make careful observations. However, it should be kept in mind that issues such as confidentiality and time constraints need to be carefully considered.

The benchmarking information from other organisations may be obtained by using questionnaires or by conducting a benchmarking site visit.

Step 5: Analyse data and determine gap

(a) **Quantitative data:** Quantitative data collected can be analysed and plotted on graphs to identify the performance gap between your organisation and other organisations selected for benchmarking. Some of the performance measures that are calculated are: *(i)* average process time *(ii)* average down time per unit and *(iii)* average percent of reworks and the like.

Gap analysis is a step in benchmarking which is still growing and evolving advanced statistical techniques to get into the root of a process. However, the basic idea of benchmarking is to make comparisons between a process used in your organisation and in an organisation with a higher level of performance. This comparison or gap is measured to help you set and attain new standards for yourself.

(b) **Qualitative analysis: Some of the qualitative factors you should look for are:**

(i) ***System policies and practices – philosophy or approach used:*** employment level – level and experience of the staff.

Management – cooperative or distant, incentives used.

(ii) ***Procedural policies and practices:***

- Technology
- Task function and
- Method or process

(iii) ***Structural policies and practices***

- Budgeting
- Purchasing and inventory practices and
- Organisational structure.

Step 6: Set goals and develop an action plan:

(a) **Set performance goals:** After carefully analysing the information and clarifying both the quantitative and qualitative gaps, you will need to set goals for your process. A goal is really a ***"desired state"***. It provides direction and a focus point. The following should be kept in mind while setting the goals:

- goals should be achievable in increments
- goals should be realistic
- goals must be measureable
- goals should be finite and
- goals should be supported.

The goal should be divided into steps. *For example,* if the goal is to decrease ***"turn around time"*** by 15 hours, this goal might be best achieved by decreases of three hours each month for five months.

Realistic goals should be set considering all the resources needed and available, *for example,* consider the issues such as time needed, resources, abilities, skills and budget.

Goals must be measurable in order to be attainable, that is measure the goal before, during and after implementation of the changes.

Goals should be finite, *i.e.* should have a set starting and ending point.

Goals should be supported by both the management and the people who are directly involved with the process.

(b) **Develop an action plan:** After establishing the goals to be accomplished and determining the time periods for completing them, an ***'action plan'*** has to be developed. Two steps involved in creating an ***'action plan'*** are:

(i) Determine tasks, timeliness and responsibilities by:

- dividing the goals into separate and measurable tasks and putting them in order.
- determining who is responsible for each task and setting target dates for the start and completion of each task.

(ii) ***Develop a contingency plan:*** This step is actually a ***"What if?"*** step – a contingency plan. Contingency plan is prepared to handle any unexpected problems or occurrences.

Step 7: Monitor the Process

Once the action plan is in place and everyone is adjusting to all the new changes, it is necessary to monitor the process to keep the benchmarking effort alive. For this, it is important to:

- track the changes and
- make benchmarking a habit.

Track the changes

Tracking the changes requires that the following steps are implemented:

(i) Evaluate measures in increments.
(ii) Publish periodic benchmarking progress reports.
(iii) Hold regular progress meetings.
(iv) Monitor customers (internal and external).
(v) Monitor suppliers (internal and external) and
(vi) Implement benchmarking as an ongoing process.

Make benchmarking a habit

To understand the benefit from benchmarking, it has to be periodic and regular course in action. It should eventually become part of the total quality management system in your organisation.

To summarise, it may be stated that benchmarking is a process of discovering and adapting new and innovative practices to improve overall organisational effectiveness. It is also a ***"learning process"*** – learning and adapting new practices by establishing new goals and introducing new ideas. The seven steps discussed earlier not only guide you through the benchmarking process, but is the roadmap to your success.

Factors to be kept in mind to ensure success with benchmarking

(i) Benchmarking must have the ***full support of senior management.*** Management should also be actively involved.

(ii) ***Training*** is critical for the benchmarking team and process.

(iii) Benchmarking should be a ***team activity.*** The teams should include management, experts, consultants and especially those people directly involved in the process.

(iv) Benchmarking is an ongoing process. It must be part of ***an organisation's strategy and development.*** If well monitored, it serves as an important segment of a total quality management system.

(v) Benchmarking efforts must be ***organised, planned*** and ***carefully managed.*** It is a structured approach and requires planning and monitoring just like any other management tool.

Ultimately, benchmarking can be your best weapon against complacency. Used correctly, benchmarking can lead you to the competitive edge in today's business market place.

Box 15.2 **lists Xerox's 10 steps process in benchmarking and** ***Box 15.3*** **lists 21 steps in benchmarking process developed by IBM's Rochester, Minnesota facility.**

Box 15.2 : Xerox's 10 step process in benchmarking

1. Identify what is to be benchmarked.
2. Identify comparative organisations.
3. Determine data collection method and collect data.
4. Determine current performance gap.
5. Project future performance levels.
6. Communicate benchmark findings and gain acceptance.
7. Establish functional goals.
8. Develop action plans.
9. Implement specific actions and monitor progress.
10. Recalibrate benchmarks.

Box 15.3 : 21 Steps in Benchmarking Process Developed by IBM's Rochester, Minnesota Facility

1. Determine what to benchmark.
2. Identify key performance variables to measure.
3. Estimate the cost of benchmarking study and obtain management approval.
4. Select benchmarking team and provide training in the technique.
5. Complete a detailed analysis of the firm's own process or business practice.
6. Decide on methods such as phone surveys, mailed questionnaire, personnel visits or some combination.
7. Develop questions to ask through these methods.
8. Identify companies against which to benchmark.
9. Identify contacts within the companies.
10. Collect internal and public domain data on the appropriate companies, processes or business practices.
11. Analyse existing information to determine additional data needs.
12. Plan the specific methods for the benchmarking study.
13. Collect data by performing phone, mail or personal interviews as planned.
14. Analyse the data, projecting future performance levels of the benchmarked companies.
15. Develop recommendations from the study's conclusions.
16. Prepare an implementation plan and budgets for the recommendations.
17. Identify appropriate performance standards for supporting departments or functions in the new process.
18. Present the plan to management for approval.
19. Upon approval, communicate the plan and performance requirements to the supporting departments.
20. Implement the plan, monitor progress and conduct periodic management reviews.
21. Periodically, review market conditions to assure that goals and objectives remain valid.

15.7 SOME ISSUES RELATED TO BENCHMARKING PROCESS

1. **Focus of benchmarking:** A benchmarking exercise generally does not cover the entire range of another company's processes. ***Box 15.4*** **details some narrower focuses for typical benchmarking efforts.**

Box 15.4 : Focuses of Benchmarking

Type of Benchmark	Focus	Teams	Guidelines
Product	Dissecting products	Designers, operations managers and manufacturing engineers	Requires no site visits and provides hard, historical and short-lived design information. Any process information only implicated.
Process	Manufacturing processes	Manufacturing engineers, specialists and operation managers	Requires site visits, focusses on specific functions and requires some humility
Best practices	Management processes	Staff and middle management	Combine visits and industry observations to look beyond an industry to combine process and management practices.
Strategic	Management directions	Top management	Long term and seldom based on site visits or sharing, but on personnel information and is very uncertain and subjective to other benchmarking efforts.

Other types

Tactical – Strategic focus not particularly industry specific
Industry – Focussed on general characteristics of an industry
Generic – Focussed on general, not industry specific, business practices
Competitive – Focussed only on head-to-head competitors
Functional – Isolates specific business or management functions
Performance – Focusses on numerical characteristics of specific products or processes.

2. **Gap analysis:** Benchmarking promotes a thorough understanding of the company's own processes. Intensive studies of existing practices may lead to identification of non value added activities and plans for process improvement. Benchmarking enables comparisons of performance measures in different dimensions each with the best practices for that measure. The comparison is not with one selected company, but with several companies who are best for the chosen measure. The ***"spider chart"*** shown in *Exhibit 15.3* is used to compare multiple performance measures and gaps between the host company and industry benchmark practices.

Gap analysis is a technique that compares a company's existing state to its desired state to help determine what needs to be done to remove or minimise the gap.

Eight Performance Measures (PM) are being considered. The scales are standardised – between zero to 1, zero being the centre and 1 at the outer circumference of the circle which represents the most desired value. Best practices for each performance measure are indicated along with the companies that achieve them. The current performance of the company performing benchmarking (*i.e.* company A) is also indicated in thc Exhibit. The difference between company A's level and that of the best practice for that performance is identified as the gap. The analysis that focusses on methods and processes to reduce this gap and thereby improve the company's competitive position is known as ***gap analysis.***

3. **'Hard' and 'Soft' systems in benchmarking process:** *Exhibit 15.4* demonstrates how benchmarking brings the ***'soft'*** and ***'hard'*** systems together. Benchmarking not only identifies best practices, but also seeks to determine how such practices can be adapted to the organisation. The real value of benchmarking is accomplished only when the company has successfully integrated the identified best practices into its operations. Meshing the 'soft' and 'hard' systems

will complete this task successfully. The emerging organisational culture should empower employees to make decisions based on the new practice.

Exhibit 15.3 : Spider Chart for Gap Analysis

PM8 (Company A)
PM1 (Company C)
PM2 (Company B)
PM3 (Company A)
PM4 (Company B)
PM5 (Company A)
PM6 (Company B)
PM7 (Company B)
Legend :
Best Practices
Current level of company performance
PM : Performance measure

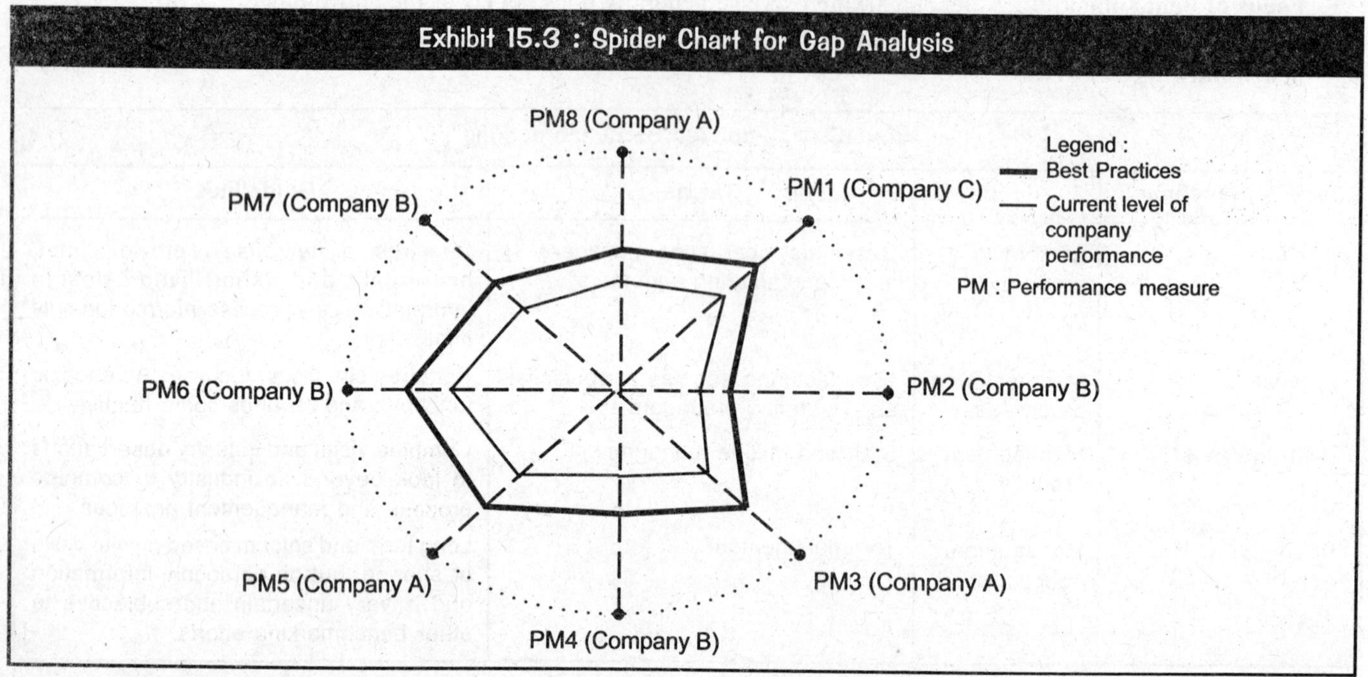

Exhibit 15.4 : Role of Benchmarking in Implementing Best Practices

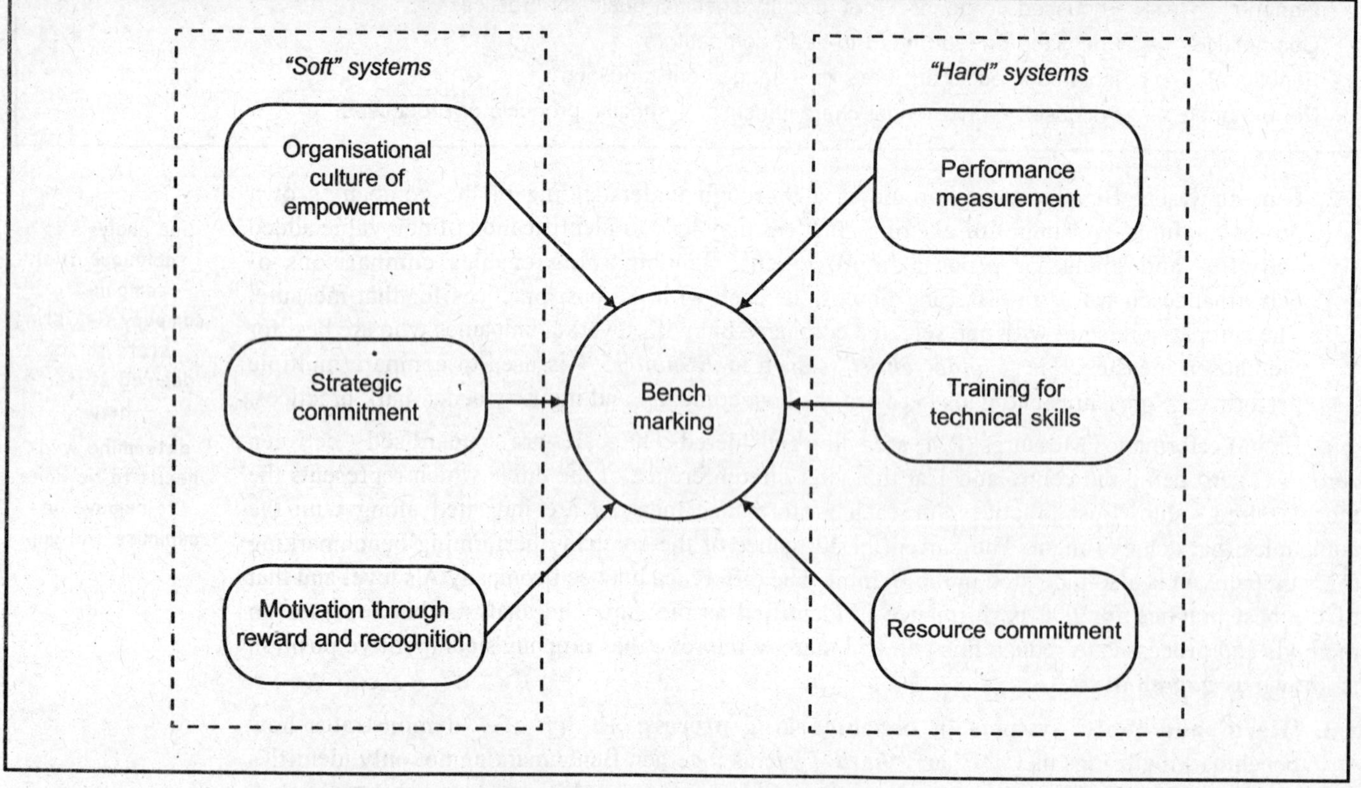

"Soft" systems
Organisational culture of empowerment
Strategic commitment
Motivation through reward and recognition
Bench marking
"Hard" systems
Performance measurement
Training for technical skills
Resource commitment

4. **Influences on benchmarking and its outcomes:** Several factors influence the adoption of benchmarking. *Exhibit 15.5* shows the influence of some of the factors on benchmarking and its outcomes.

Exhibit 15.5 : Influence on Benchmarking and its Outcomes

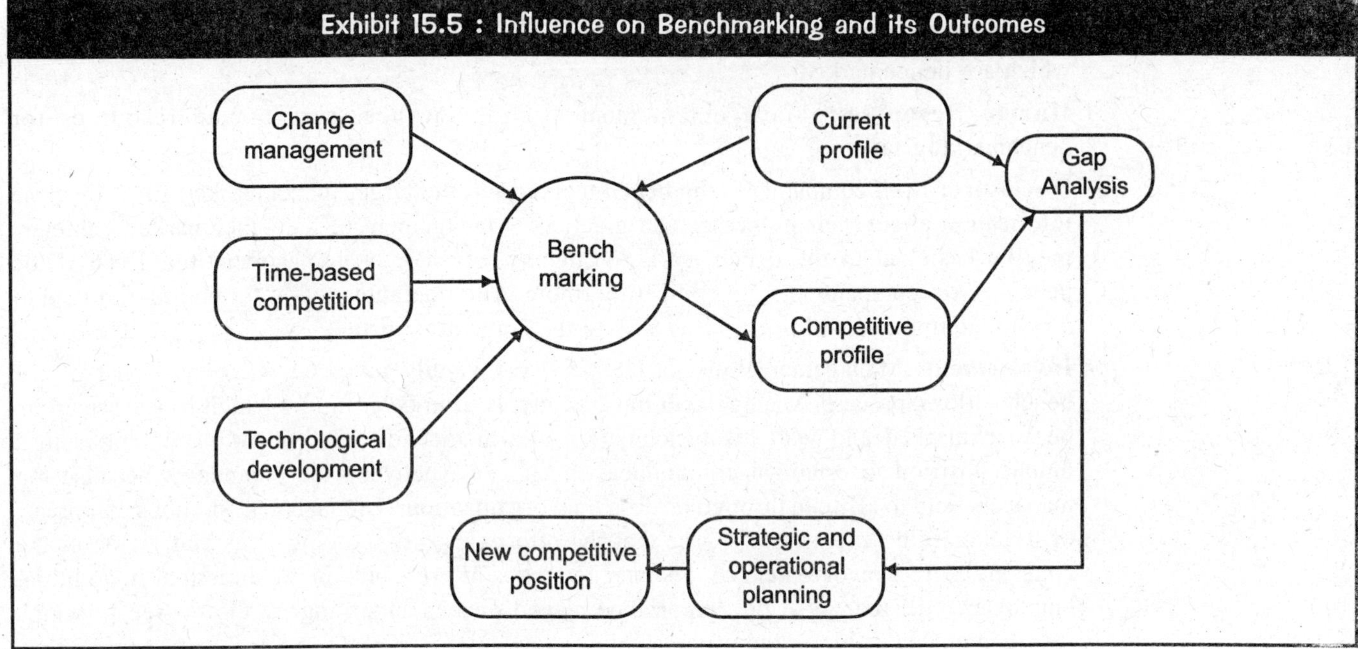

Some of these factors are detailed below:

(a) ***Change management:*** In the current environment of global competition, change is inevitable. Rather than reacting haphazardly to change, benchmarking helps in effectively managing the change. Benchmarking provides a road map for adopting best practices, a major component of change management. Benchmarking facilitates managing both process-oriented changes and cultural changes in the organisation. It helps in overcoming resistance to change by a people oriented approach. Change is not viewed as a threat but an opportunity.

(b) ***Time-based competition:*** In global competition, the ability to reduce process time and create a mode of quick response provides a distinct competitive advantage to a firm. The concept of time based competition is linked to reduction in ***cycle time*** which is the interval between the beginning and the end of a process which may involve a series of activities. From the customer's point of view, cycle time is the elasped time between placing an order by him/her and its satisfactory fulfilment by the supplier. Cycle time can be reduced by reducing decision points and inspection points, using electronic media for communication and flow of information, standardising procedures and reporting forms and consolidating purchases.

(c) ***Technological development:*** The rapid technological development nowadays leaves the progressive companies with no choice other than benchmarking the technology leaders. *For example,* the technological development in electronic and computer hardware and software industries is so rapid that falling behind the competition in these industries means going out of business. In such a situation, benchmarking is critical both for survival and growth.

5. **Role of Management in Benchmarking:** Benchmarking needs the approval of top management. Several benchmarking considerations require approval of management before the process can start: *(a)* Commitment to change, *(b)* Funding, *(c)* Personnel, *(d)* Disclosure and *(e)* Involvement. **These considerations are briefly discussed in the following paragraphs.**

(a) **Commitment to change:** Benchmarking is a serious undertaking for both benchmarking partners. Unless a firm commitment to change exists – unless the organisation fully intends to radically improve its processes to come up to best-in-class standards-benchmarking should not be considered.

(b) **Funding:** Only top management can authorise the expenditure of funds for benchmarking. These funds will support travel for teams visiting the organisation with best–in–class processes.

Teams are usually composed of five to eight people and visits may last from two days to two weeks. Travel expenses can be costly depending on the locations of the best – in – class firms which are benchmarked.

(c) **Human Resources:** Management must provide the necessary human resources for benchmarking tasks.

(d) **Disclosure:** Both companies – the bench marker and the target (benchmarked firm) disclose information about their processes and practices. Management of the benchmarked company may be hesistant to the bench marker company which may be a competitor. Even if the benchmarker company is a noncompetitor, there is no guarantee that information divulged to a non – competitor will not find its way to the competitor firm.

(e) **Involvement:** Management must be actively and visibly involved in every aspect of the benchmarking process. Management must be involved in determining which processes are to be benchmarked and who the benchmarking partner candidates are. Management is in a unique position to establish communication channels between the companies because top managers tend to affiliate through professional organisations. Management should stay abreast of benchmarking events and ensure that the effort supports the objectives and vision of the company. Direct involvement of top management is of great help in the direction. In addition, employees will recognise the importance placed on benchmarking by the degree to which management is visible in the process.

6. **Prerequisites of Benchmarking:** Prerequisites of benchmarking include:

(a) **Will and Commitment:** An organisation requires the will and commitment to benchmarking in order to proceed with benchmarking effort. Otherwise it would be a waste of time for both organisations (the bench marker and the benchmarked organisation)

(b) **Vision/ strategic objective link:** Benchmarking requires a strong focus. Before it is started, objectives must be linked to the company's vision and strategic objectives, providing specific direction and focus for the effort. Failure to do this will almost certainly result in wasted resources and frustration.

(c) **Goals to become best – not simply improved:** If organisation is not at the world class level, incremental improvement may only ensure that it remains inferior to the best-in-class forever. Benchmarking requires that the goal be to leap to the head of the field in one radical, break – through change rather than small continuous incremental improvement.

(d) **Openness to new ideas:** If a company is imbued with the ***"not-invented here"*** syndromes, it will have a problem with benchmarking. This affliction is reflected by a short-sighted mind set that is characterised by a reluctance to consider other ways of doing things. Many people are reluctant to consider ideas or approaches that are not their own. Because the essence of benchmarking is capitalising on the work and ideas of others, a company must be open to new ideas for benchmarking to provide any value. The benchmarking process may help bring about more receptivity to new ideas by demonstrating that they really work.

(e) **Understanding of existing processes, products services and customer needs:** It is mandatory that an organisation thoroughly understands its own processes, products, services, practices and the needs of its customers so that it can determine what needs to be benchmarked. In addition, it is necessary to have a solid understanding of your process in order to make meaningful measurements against that of the partner firm.

(f) **Processes documented:** It is not enough to understand the processes, they must be completely documented for three reasons:

(i) All associated with the process should have a common understanding of it, which is possible only from documentation,

(ii) A documented starting point is needed against which to measure performance improvement after benchmarking changes have been implemented.

(iii) The organisation will be dealing with the partners who are not familiar with its processes. With an understanding of where the benchmarking organisation is, the partner will be better able to help.

(g) **Process Analysis Skills:** To achieve an understanding of your own processes, products, and services and to document those processes, you must have people with the skills to characterise and document processes. Then same people will be needed to analyse the benchmarking partners' processes and to help adapt those processes to the organisation's needs. Ideally they should be employees, and it is possible to use consultants in this role.

(h) **Research, Communication and Team-building skills:** Additional skills required include research, communication, and team building. Research is required to identify the best–in–class process owners. Communication and team building are required to carryout the benchmarking both on an internal basis and with the partners.

7. Obstacles to successful Benchmarking: Some of the common obstacles to successful benchmarking are:

(a) **Internal focus**: For benchmarking to produce the desired result, you have to know that someone out there has a far better process. If a company is internally focused, it may not know to what extent its process is less efficient than the best-in-class. An internal focus limits vision.

(b) **Benchmarking objectives too broad**: An overly broad benchmarking objective such as "improve the bottom-line performance" can guarantee failure. The benchmarking team should do something more specific and oriented not to ***what*** but to the ***how.*** A team could struggle with the bottom line forever without knowing that it achieved success or failure. The team needs a narrower target like "Refine or replace the invoicing process to reduce errors by 50%.

(c) **Unrealistic time tables**: Benchmarking is an involved process that can not be completed in a few weeks. The shortest schedule for an experienced team could be 4 to 6 months and the norm is 6 to 8 months. Trying to do it in less time than that will force the team to cut corners, which can lead to failure.

(d) **Poor team composition**: When a process is benchmarked, those who own the process, the people who use it must be involved. In addition to the production line operators who are the process owners, supervisors and engineers may be included in the team. The process owners are the ones who know the most about how the process really operates and they can most readily detect the often subtle differences between their process and that of the benchmarking partner.

(e) **Settling for "OK-in-class"**: Too often organisations choose benchmarking partners who are not best–in–class for any of the following reasons:

(i) The best-in-class is not interested in participating.

(ii) Research identified the wrong partner.

(iii) The benchmarking firm may be lazy and picked a handy partner because of convenience.

Organisations should identify the best and go for it. Only if the absolute best will not participate, can taking second – best be justified.

(f) **Improper emphasis**: Benchmarking may fail if the teams get bogged down in collecting endless data and put too much emphasis on numbers. The most important issue is the process itself. Keep emphasis on the process, with data and numbers supporting that emphasis.

(g) **Insensitivity to partners**: Nothing will break up a benchmarking partnership quicker than insensitivity to the 'benchmarking partner. You are taking valuable time from the partner firm's key people and disrupting the routine of the daily business of the benchmarked firm. Therefore the bench marker should observe protocol and common courtsey in all its transactions with the benchmarking partner.

(h) **Limited top management support**: Top management support is critical to success at all stages of the benchmarking activity, unwavering support from the top management is necessary to get bench-marketing started, to carry it through the preparation phase and finally to secure the promised gains.

8. **Selection of Processes/ Functions for Benchmarking:** The strongest processes are sometimes benchmarked as a means of obtaining a report card against the best–in–class. This is a waste of time and effort because the organisation is proud of this process and has no intention of replacing it or radically modifying it. The processes that are the weakest are the ones that are most detrimental to competitiveness. Moreover the weakest offer the most scope for dramatic improvement. This is where the benchmarking effort should be focused.

Box 15.5 : "Benchmarking Quality" – in a Nutshell

Benchmarking means measuring one's performance against that of one's competitors.

Two definitions of benchmarking are:

(i) Benchmarking is the continuous process of measuring products and services against the toughest competitors or those companies recognised as industry leaders

(ii) Benchmarking is the search for industry best practices that lead to superior performance.

Competitive benchmarking is gaining importance in the light of increasing global competition. Setting one's priorities and being certain that those priorities are consistent with the needs of the market place are essential. The top five competitive priorities in Europe, Japan and the United States, in 1992 were as below:

Priority	Europe	Japan	United States
1	Conformance quality	Product reliability	Conformance quality
2	On-time delivery	On-time delivery	On-time delivery
3	Product reliability	Fast-design change	Product reliability
4	Performance quality	Conformance quality	Performance quality
5	Delivery speed	Product customisation	Price

The four types of benchmarking are: *(i)* Product benchmarking, *(ii)* Functional or Process benchmarking, *(iii)* Best practices benchmarking and *(iv)* Strategic benchmarking.

Product benchmarking refers to the practice of tearing down a competitor's product to see what can be learnt from its design and construction (also known as reverse engineering).

Functional benchmarking focusses on the process rather than on the product. Typical processes might be order entry, assembly, test, product development and shipping.

Best practice benchmarking is similar to functional benchmarking except that it focusses on management practices rather than on specific processes. Best practices might consider factors such as the work environment and salary incentives for employees in firms with exceptional performance.

Strategic benchmarking has a goal of considering the result of other benchmarking comparisons in the light of the strategic focus of the firm.

What is the purpose of benchmarking?: It is to ensure *continuous improvement* and is only one of the means of achieving this. Competitive benchmarking provides a means of learning from one's competitors.

Phases in benchmarking

(i) **Planning phase:**

(a) Identify what is to be benchmarked.

(b) Identify comparable companies

(c) Determine data collection methods

(d) Collect data.

(ii) **Analysis phase:**

(a) Determine the current performance "gap"

(b) Project future performance levels.

(iii) **Integration phase:**

(a) Communicate benchmark findings and gain acceptance.

(b) Establish functional goals

(iv) **Action phase:**

(a) Develop action plans

(b) Implement specific actions

(c) Monitor progress

(d) Recalibrate benchmarks.

Return to phase 1, step 1.

To evaluate, we may remember that ***benchmarking*** is a process of discovering and adapting new and innovative practices to improve overall organisation effectiveness. It is also a process of learning and adapting new practices by establishing new goals and introducing new ideas. It is to be kept in mind that the seven steps in the benchmarking process discussed earlier in this chapter are followed metriculously as a road map to success. This will enable a firm not only to match but to exceed competition and achieve total customer satisfaction.

15.8 QUALITY IN PRACTICE

Box 15.6 : Look Far and Wide

When you look for best-in-class process owners as possible benchmarking partners, don't restrict your search to your own industry. For example, when Southwest Airlines was looking for a faster way to off load passengers and cargo and get the planes ready for their next flights, it benchmarked Indianapolis 500 pit crews. When Xerox needed major improvements in its warehousing operations, they benchmarked LL Bean, one of the world's best catalog sales organisations. IBM studied Las Vegas casinos to find ways to reduce employee theft.

Henry Ford created the assembly line in his automobile company after taking a tour of a Chicago slaughterhouse and watching carcasses, hung on hooks mounted on a monorail, move from one workstation to another.

Toyota's just-in-time production system was influenced by replenishment practices of US supermarkets., Convex Computer Corporation sent its facilities manager to Disney World to see what they could learn about facilities management.

Motorola, one of the original Malcolm Baldrige Award winners, has found that even after achieving best-in-class, there is much to be gained through continued bench marking. Every new program, every new product and every new improvement effort at Motorola is preceded by a search for the best-in-class. In this way, Motorola ensures that every new process introduced will be world-class.

Box 15.7 : International Benchmarking At Taurus

This box illustrates how Ford pays attention to global competition by internationally benchmarking competitors for the design and production of its Taurus model

Features	Car	Features	Car
1. Lowest ignition switch effort	Ford	10. Best clock readability	Audi 100
2. Lowest air register operating	Audi 100	11. Best fuel Gauge accuracy	Toyota- Supra
3. Best accelerator pedal feel	Audi 100	12. Best oil-filter accessibility	Nissan- Maxima
4. Best accelerator pedal location	Chevrolet Celebrity	13. Best transmission control (travel/feet)	Open-Senator
5. Lowest effort to rotate sun visor	Honda - Accord	14. Least transmission gear noise	Ford-Escort, Supra
6. Lowest effort to adjust rear view mirror	Toyota- Cresside	15. Best steering wheel feel	Porsche 924
7. Best hand control ergonomics	Opel-Senator	16. Best outside mirror remote control	Mazda 626
8. Best visual ergonomics	Honda - Accord	17. Most effective sun visor (travel / feet)	Honda- Accord
9. Best night-time illumination of switches	Honda - Accord Fast-design change	18. Best trunk storage capacity	Chevrolet- Celebrity

15.9 SUMMARY

Benchmarking is a systematic method by which organisations can measure themselves against the best industry practices. It promotes superior performance by providing an organised framework through which organisation can learn how the best-in-class do things, understand how these best practices differ from their own and implement change to close the gap.

The essence of benchmarking is ***"moving from where we are to where we want to be?"*** A *benchmark* is a point of reference against which things are measured. Benchmarking helps organisations to develop their strengths and reduce their weaknesses and thereby achieve business and competitive objectives.

Benchmarking is carried out at various levels. They are: *(i)* Internal benchmarking, *(ii)* Competitive benchmarking, *(iii)* Non-competitive benchmarking and *(iv)* World-class benchmarking. Further benchmarking can be classified as: *(i)* Performance or operational benchmarking, *(ii)* Process or functional benchmarking and *(iii)* Strategic benchmarking.

Various areas that might be included for benchmarking are: *(i)* Customer service levels, *(ii)* Inventory management, *(iii)* Purchasing, *(iv)* Billing and collection, *(v)* Purchasing practices, *(vi)* Quality process, *(vii)* Warehousing and distribution and *(viii)* Transportation.

Four phase of benchmarking are: *(i)* Planning, *(ii)* Analysis, *(iii)* Integration and *(iv)* Action.

The benchmarking processes have various steps in different organisations but the most popular approach to the process is the *"Seven step benchmarking model"*. These seven steps are: *(i)* Identify what to benchmark, *(ii)* Determine what to measure, *(iii)* Identify who to benchmark, *(iv)* Collect the data, *(v)* Analyse the data and determine the gap, *(vi)* Set goals and develop action plan and *(vii)* Monitor the progress.

For the success of benchmarking process, the following are considered essential: *(i)* Full support of senior management, *(ii)* Training for the benchmarking team, *(iii)* Team activity of team including management, experts, consultants and people directly involved in the benchmarking process, *(iv)* On-going process as a part of total quality management system and *(v)* Planning and monitoring of the benchmarking efforts. Some of the important issues related to benchmarking process are: *(i)* Focus of benchmarking, *(ii)* Gap analysis, *(iii)* 'Hard' and 'soft' systems in benchmarking and *(iv)* Influence of factors such as change management, time based competition and technological development on benchmarking and its outcomes.

15.10 KEY WORDS USED

Benchmarking, Bench Mark, Concurrent Engineering, Internal Benchmarking, Competitive Benchmarking, World – class Manufacturing, Performance Benchmarking, Operational Benchmarking, Process Benchmarking, Strategic Benchmarking, Gap Analysis, Hard and Soft systems, Change Management, Time–based Competition, Technological Development.

15.11 OBJECTIVE QUESTIONS

(A) Match the following :

Column A	Column B
1. Benchmarking	1. Used in Gap Analysis
2. Spider chart	2. Also known as operational benchmarking
3. Performance benchmarking	3. A good intervention technique for positive change
4. Internal benchmarking	4. A level of benchmarking
5. Process benchmarking	5. A type of benchmarking

(B) State whether the following statements are True or False :

1. Benchmarking is a tool for continuous improvement (T / F)
2. Benchmarking is a tool to achieve business and competitive objectives (T / F)
3. Benchmarking is not a technique of problem solving or process improvement (T / F)

4. Process benchmarking is also known as internal benchmarking. (T / F)
5. A flow chart is a step-by-step picture of tasks in a process which is used as a working document to help define the process (T / F)

(C) Multiple choice Questions : Choose the correct answer from the alternatives given under each question :

1. Benchmarking process which involves analysing the performance and practice of best-in-class companies is known as:
   (a) World-class benchmarking (b) Process benchmarking
   (c) Competitive benchmarking (d) Internal benchmarking
   (e) None of these
2. Key success factor matrix is used in the following type of benchmarking:
   (a) Non-competitive benchmarking (b) Strategic benchmarking
   (c) Operational benchmarking (d) Process benchmarking
   (e) None of these
3. Cross-functional teams are developed in the following phase of benchmarking:
   (a) Planning phase (b) Analysis phase
   (c) Integration phase (d) Action phase
   (e) None of these
4. Areas to bench mark include the following:
   (a) Customer service levels (b) Inventory management
   (c) Purchasing practices (d) Quality processes
   (e) All of these (f) None of these
5. Benchmarking influences the following:
   (a) Change management (b) Time-based competition
   (c) Technological development (d) All of these
   (e) None of these

15.12 REVIEW QUESTIONS

1. What is meant by "benchmarking"?
2. What is a "benchmark"?
3. Trace the evolution of 'benchmarking' giving some examples of U.S. firms who could achieve dramatic results by implementing benchmarking process.
4. Discuss the reasons for benchmarking stating their advantages and limitations.
5. Mention some of the pitfalls of benchmarking.
6. What do you understand by "levels of benchmarking"? Explain.
7. Discuss the various types of benchmarking.
8. List out some of the guidelines to benchmarking.
9. What are the four phases of benchmarking? Discuss briefly.
10. Explain the "seven step benchmarking model".
11. Discuss some of the important issues related to benchmarking process.
12. Discuss the relevance of benchmarking to total quality management.

15.13 DISCUSSION QUESTIONS

1. Benchmarking is a tool to achieve business and competitive objectives" – Discuss the statement.
2. "Benchmarking can be a very good intervention technique for positive change" – Elaborate.
3. "Benchmarking can be a very powerful vehicle for driving peak process performance" – Do you agree or not. Justify your answer.

4. Explain the difference in objectives for continuous improvement and benchmarking.
5. Explain the importance of linking the benchmarking objectives with the organisation's strategic objectives.
6. Explain how the not invented here syndrome can be a hindrance to benchmarking effectiveness.

15.14 ASSIGNMENTS

1. Identify some of the major processes a student encounters in a college or university. Find out what type of non-educational institutions perform similar processes and might be suitable candidates for benchmarking.
2. Visit a nearby manufacturing plant of small or medium scale and discuss with the manager to find out whether they have been following the benchmarking practices. If so which other industry they have benchmarked.

15.15 CHAPTER CASE

BENCHMARKING PRACTICE AT XEROX CORPORATION

By the late 1970s, Xerox was losing significant market share to its Japanese competitors. Not only were the Japanese products excellent, but to Xerox's dismay, they were sold cheaper than Xerox could manufacture them. Xerox found that it had nine times as many suppliers as the Japanese companies and made seven times as many manufacturing defects. Lead times for new products were twice as long, and production set up times were five times as long as the competitors.

Xerox introduced benchmarking in 1980. Its processes and practices were benchmarked against the best in and out of its industry. As a result of these efforts, Xerox saved itself. Today, Xerox is a world class competitor, capable of holding its own in terms of technology, price, service and customer satisfaction against any competition. Benchmarking at Xerox has reached into every facet of the company and remains a primary feature of the corporation.

Discussion Questions :

1. Why was benchmarking inevitable for Xerox?
2. What type of benchmarking Xerox undertook to overcome its problems?
3. What benefits Xerox could obtain by implementing benchmarking practices?

CHAPTER 16

BUSINESS PROCESS REENGINEERING

LEARNING OBJECTIVES

After reading this chapter, you should be able to:

- Understand the term "Reengineering" and its principles.
- Discuss the application of Reengineering in manufacturing and service industries.
- Discuss the requirements of Reengineering process.
- Discuss the relationship between Reengineering and TQM.
- Discuss the steps involved in the Reengineering process.
- Discuss the process Reengineering tools and techniques.
- Compare Reengineering with Benchmarking.
- Know the benefits and limitations of Reengineering.
- Discuss the types of 'holonic' networks and the working of holonic network.
- Discuss the advantages of "holonic" networks.

16.0 INTRODUCTION

Customer satisfaction has increasingly become the cardinal principle governing any successful business. In some cases, marketing campaigns have been reformulated and new slogans invented to take advantage of the impact of advertising on customers. Despite the new emphasis on customer satisfaction by companies, there has been a high incidence of complaints, anger, rage and acute disappointment over products. One of the reasons for this lies in the fact that the old ways and processes have become severely inadequate and that the mere realignment of old values (old wine in a new bottle!) is no longer acceptable. In many cases, the present system can no longer be fixed and incremental improvements are not sufficient. What is needed is the reengineering of the entire system.

According to Michael Hammer of the US who coined the term "re-engineering", the definition of reengineering is as follows : **Re-engineering has been defined as *"the fundamental rethinking and radical design of business processes to achieve dramatic improvements in critical contemporary measures of performance such as cost, quality, service and speed"*. The term is also known as "Process re-engineering" or "Business process re-engineering".**

Reengineering involves radical redesign of business processes, reinventing the processes, not just incrementally improving them.

Re-engineering does not strive to revamp an existing process. It involves asking basic questions about business processes: why do we do it? Why is it done this way? Such questioning often uncovers obsolete, erroneous or inappropriate assumptions. Radical redesigning involves tossing out existing procedures and reinventing the process, not just incrementally improving it. The goal is to achieve quantum leaps in performance.

Re-engineering seeks to enhance the celerity of the delivery of a product without compromising its quality by improving the utilisation of materials, labour and equipment. According to Janson, a proponent of reengineering, by focussing on making improvements in all dimensions of the service organisation – human dimension, work process dimension and the technological dimension – re-engineering helps companies overcome systematic work barriers that interfere with efforts to achieve higher levels of customer satisfaction. According to Lawrence, another proponent of reengineering, **"reengineering involves redesigning business processes to take advantage of the enormous potential of the computer and information technology".** In order for companies to embrace the concept of reengineering, they must be able to break away from previously followed conventional rules and policies and be open to changes that would make their businesses more productive.

Hammer states that "Reengineering strives to break away from the old rules about how we organise and conduct business. It involves recognising and rejecting some of them and finding imaginative new ways to accomplish work".

***Box 16.1* describes reengineering at IBM Credit Corporation.**

Box 16.1 : Reengineering at IBM Credit Corporation

IBM Credit Corporation cut the process of financing IBM Computers, software and services from *seven days* to *four hours* by rethinking the process. Originally, the process was designed to handle difficult applications and required four highly trained specialists and a series of hand offs. The actual work took only 1 to 5 hours, the rest of the time was spent in transit or delay. By questioning the assumption that every application was unique and difficult to process, IBM Credit Corporation was able to replace the specialists by a single individual supported by a user friendly, computer system that provided access to all the data and tools that the specialists would use.

Reasons for Reengineering?

"Business Process Reengineering" or ***"process reengineering"*** (or **process redesign**) or simply ***"reengineering"*** is focussed on ***"break through"*** **improvement** to dramatically improve the quality and speed of work and to reduce its cost by fundamentally changing the processes by which work gets done.

For organisations that want to survive and grow, improvement is not an option but a compulsion. For organisations that seek to thrive, dramatic improvement is often the only key to success. Small improvements are always necessary, but sometimes quantum leaps are needed if an organisation is to forge ahead. (Ten percent improvement can be created by tinkering, but 50 percent improvements call for process redesign).

Success in reengineering requires basic understanding of processes, creative thinking and effective use of information technology.

Whether an organisation realises that the old ways of doing things needs changing or its customers are demanding a change or competitors are taking over its market share, or not, many processes in the organisation may need reengineering, not a minor tweak, but a major overhaul. **Some of the symptoms that signal that it is time to start reengineering are:**

(i) it takes too long for an organisation to move its products from conception to the market place as compared to its competitors.

(ii) the budgeting process may be too complex and

(iii) the services provided by the organisation are not compatible with its customers' needs.

Business process reengineering is a refreshing new approach to do business. There is plenty of evidence that it works well – perhaps with performance gains of 100 to 300 percent for some recognised processes.

Success in reengineering requires fundamental understanding of processes, creative thinking to break away from old tradition and assumptions and effective use of information technology. Pepsi-Cola, *for example,* had embarked on a program to reengineer all of its key business processes such as selling and delivery, equipment service and repair, procurement and financial reporting. In the selling and delivery of its product, *for example,* customer representatives typically experience stock-outs of as much as 25 percent of the products by the end of the day. Many other routes would return with overstock of other products, increasing handling costs. By redesigning the system to include hand held computers, the customer representatives could confirm and deliver that day's order and also take a future order for the next delivery to that customer.

16.1 HISTORY AND DEVELOPMENT OF BUSINESS PROCESS RE-ENGINEERING

The idea of "Business Process Reengineering" originated in 1990 by James Champy and Michael Hammer.

The concept of reengineering has been around for nearly two decades and was implemented in a piecemeal fashion in organisations. Production organisations have been in the vanguard without knowing it. They have undertaken reengineering by implementing ***concurrent engineering, lean production, cellular manufacturing, group-technology*** **and** ***pull – type production systems.*** These represent fundamental rethinking of the manufacturing process. Manufacturers generally made significant improvements in their internal operations during the 1980s. But excellence in manufacturing has not always translated to superior sustainable results in the market place. More recently, the focus appears to have shifted out of the manufacturing process to other inter-functional and inter-organisational and customer-based processes. Rapid advances in information technology and its applications have been a major enabler of business process re-engineering in services.

In 1990, two Americans, James Champy and Michael Hammer presented the idea of business process re-engineering. They coined the word **"Business Process Reengineering"**, (BPR in short form) in their famous book, ***"Re-engineering the Corporation"***, published in 1993. Their argument was that most business processes had been antiquated and needed to be completely redesigned. Hammer and Champy advocated radical redesign as compared to the more incremental approach associated with total quality management.

Box 16.2 : Reengineering in a Major Insurance Company

Consider this problem in a major insurance company: When the customer called the home office about an insurance problem, the call was taken by the incoming calls department. The problem was entered into the computer and passed electronically to one of the several departments: underwriting, policy service and accounting. The problem was waited in line, often for several days until a clerk had time to check it out. In some cases, the customer's problem had been routed to the wrong department and had to be routed to another department again taking several days in the queue. If the problem required more than one department to answer the question, the process of waiting was repeated. Finally, some one in customer service would get back to the customer after several weeks. In many cases, the original question was not completely answered or answered wrongly.

This process was reengineered by completely reorganising the entire insurance operation around customer services representatives who would attempt to handle the customer's request on the phone, if possible, using detailed computer protocols and standard scripts. If more detailed work was required, the customer service representative checked with other specialists and got back to the customer in one week or less with an answer. This greatly improved the speed and accuracy of the service while saving many millions of dollars. It also provided a single point of contact and less hassle for the customer.

***Box 16.2* describes reengineering in a major insurance company.**

16.2 PRINCIPLES OF REENGINEERING

Reengineering is about achieving a significant improvement in process so that contemporary customer requirements of quality, speed, innovations, customisation and service are met. **This entails *seven new* rules of doing work proposed by Hammer, relating to *who does the work, where and when it is done* and information gathering and integration. These seven rules are:**

Five key principles of BPR are: *(i)* Business Process Redesign *(ii)* Information technology *(iii)* Team work *(iv)* Continuous Improvement and *(v)* Change Management.

Rule 1 : Organise around outcomes, Not tasks

Several specialised tasks previously performed by different people should be combined into a single job. The new job created should involve all the steps in a process that creates a well-defined outcome. Organising around outcomes eliminates the need for hand-offs, resulting in greater speed, productivity and customer responsiveness.

Rule 2 : Have those who use the output of the process perform the process

In other words, **"work should be carried out where it is"**, makes the most sense to do it. This results in people closest to the process actually performing the work, which shifts work across traditional intra and inter-organisational boundaries. For instance, employees can make some of their purchases without going through the purchasing department. Customers can perform simple repairs themselves and suppliers can be asked to manage parts inventory.

Rule 3 : Merge information processing work into the real work that produces the information

This means that people who collect information should also be responsible for processing it which greatly reduces errors by cutting the numbers of external contact points for a process.

Rule 4 : Treat geographically dispersed resources as though they work centralised

Centralised databases and telecommunication networks allow companies to link separate units or individual field personnel, providing them with economies of scale while maintaining their individual flexibility and responsiveness to customers.

Rule 5 : Link parallel activities instead of integrating their results

The concept of only integrating the outcome of parallel activities that must eventually come together is the primary cause of rework, high costs and delays in the outcome of the overall process. Such parallel activities should be linked continuously and coordinated during the process.

Rule 6 : Put the decision point where the work is performed and build control into the process

Decision-making should be made part of the work performed. This is possible today with a more educated and knowledgeable workforce plus decision–aiding technology. Controls are now made part of the process.

Rule 7 : Capture information once – at the source

Information should be collected and captured in the company's on-line information system only once at the source where it is created. This approach avoids erroneous data entries and costly re-entries.

***Exhibit 16.1* illustrates five key principles of Business Process Reengineering**

Exhibit 16.1 : Five Key Principles of Business Process Reengineering

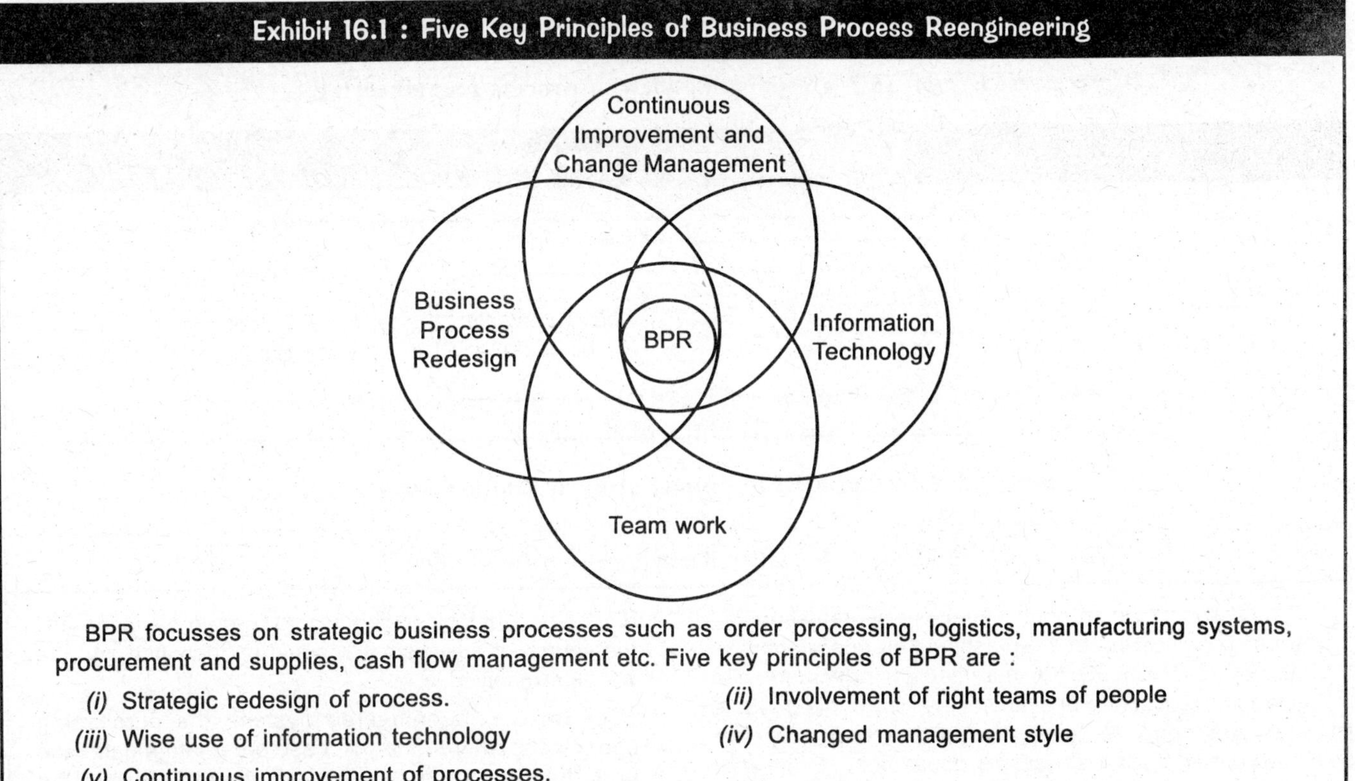

BPR focusses on strategic business processes such as order processing, logistics, manufacturing systems, procurement and supplies, cash flow management etc. Five key principles of BPR are :

(i) Strategic redesign of process.
(ii) Involvement of right teams of people
(iii) Wise use of information technology
(iv) Changed management style
(v) Continuous improvement of processes.

16.3 APPLICATION OF REENGINEERING

Reengineering can be applied to both manufacturing and service processes.

Reengineering as applied to any business process

Hammer states that business process may be defined as a set of logically related tasks to achieve a defined business outcome. A set of processes forms a business system – the way in which a business unit or a collection of units carries out its business.

Assuming that a company has decided that its processes are ineffective and inefficient, **the following are the major steps the company should embark on to redesign its process, according to Hammer :**

(i) **Develop business vision and process objectives :** This step involves prioritising objectives and setting targets for the future. A BPR vision statement describes the ideal state of a process.

(ii) **Identify processes to be redesigned :** This involves identifying critical or bottleneck processes and envisioning the steps to avert shortcomings in them.

(iii) **Understand and measure existing processes :** This involves identifying current problems and setting a base line.

(iv) **Identify information technology levels :** This involves bringing those involved in the process to a brain-storming session to identify new approaches.

(v) **Design and build a prototype of the process :** This includes implementing organisational and technical aspects.

16.4 PROCESS REENGINEERING IN A MANUFACTURING ORGANISATION

A process is a group of activities that takes an input, adds value to it and provides an output to an internal or external customer. Processes enable the organisation to focus on the customer. Viewing the material transformation process in terms of those activities tied to transforming material into something of value to the customer is a process view. Such a view examines inventory in terms of customer value, not internal economies. Such a view can be the basis of reengineering processes. ***Exhibit 16.2*** **presents one view of process reengineering.**

Exhibit 16.2 : Process Reengineering

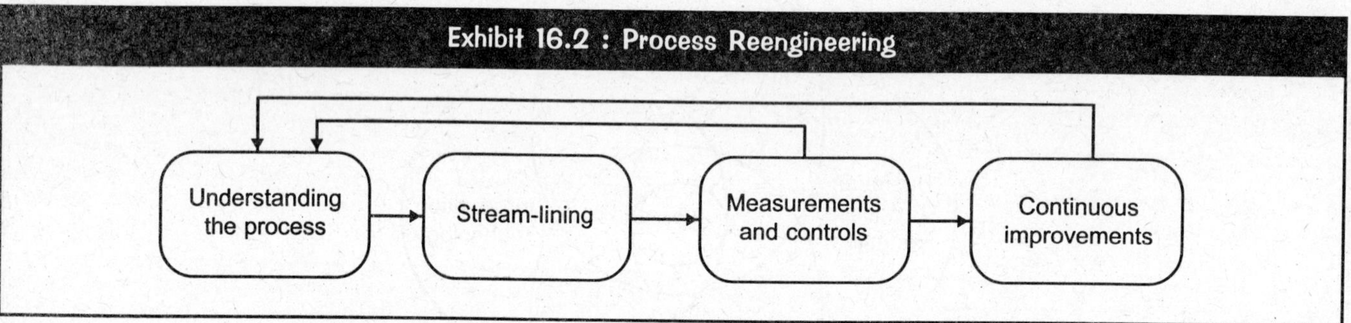

Box 16.3 **describes a BPR Project at Ford Motor Company**

Box 16.3 : BPR Project at Ford Motor Company

The accounts department of Ford employed 500 people before reengineering and represented an opportunity for major improvement. Ford had formed a joint venture with Mazda and decided to benchmark their accounts payable department only to learn that Mazda had only five employees in accounts payable department. Even after accounting for the difference in sizes of the two companies, this could only be attributed to a much different process.

The process that was being used by Ford before reengineering started with the purchasing department issuing a purchase order to the supplier with a copy to accounts payable. When the merchandise was received from the supplier, a receiving document was sent to accounts payable. Later, the supplier sent an invoice to Ford accounts payable for the merchandise. If account payable could match the three documents, they would authorise payment to the supplier. Most of the time in accounts payable, however, was spent in mismatches among documents. A clerk would hold up payment until the source of the mismatch could be identified and the problem resolved.

Under the reengineered system, the purchasing department entered the purchase order into a database and did not send a copy to anyone. When the merchandise arrived, the receiving clerk would enter the database and determine whether the shipment agreed with the electronic purchase order. If it did, payment was authorised to be made at the appropriate time. If it didn't match, the merchandise would be returned or the Ford purchasing department would be notified to give the okay nod to receive the material. Ford also instituted ***"invoiceless purchasing"*** where the supplier did not need to send an invoice to be paid. This generally simplified the process for all concerned. As a result, Ford was able to reduce the work of its accounts payable department and the headcount by 75 percent.

16.5 THE ESSENCE OF REENGINEERING

At the heart of reengineering, is the notion of discontinuous thinking of organising and breaking away from the outdated rules and fundamental assumptions that underlie operations. Unless these rules are changed, ***break-throughs*** in performance are extremely difficult. Old assumptions must be challenged and the old rules that made the business under perform must be discarded. Most contemporary businesses are run on the basis of decade old policies. These assumptions about technologies, people and organisational goals probably are outdated and no longer valid.

Reengineering seeks to challenge old assumptions and rules and seek to provide a new perspective to business operations and processes.

Quality **and** ***customer service*** are increasingly becoming the primary focus of any company. A large portion of the population is educated and capable of assuming responsibility and workers cherish their autonomy, expect to have a say in how the business is run and demand quality. Consequently, the present business process and structures are outmoded and obsolete. Work structure and processes have not kept pace with changes in technology, demographics and business objectives. Conventional process structures are fragmented, piecemeal and myopic. Consequently, employees substitute the narrow goals of their particular department for the larger goals of the process as a whole. Reengineering seeks to provide a new perspective to business operations and processes. According to Hammer and Champy, **"Reengineering requires looking at the fundamental processes of the business from a cross-functional perspective."**

One way to ensure that reengineering has a cross functional perspective is to assemble a team that represents the functional units involved in the process being reengineered and all the units that depend on it. Rather than looking for opportunities to improve the current process, the team should determine which of its processes really add value and search for new ways to achieve the end results.

In short, reengineering efforts strive for dramatic levels of improvement. They break away from conventional wisdom and the constraints of organisational boundaries and are broad and cross-functional in scope. They use information technology not to automate an existing process but to create a new one.

16.6 THE THREE 'R'S OF REENGINEERING

Janson states that every reengineering effort involves three basic phases :

"Rework", "Redesign" and "Retool" are referred to as the Three "R's of Reengineering.

1. **Rethink :** This phase requires examining the organisation's current objectives and underlying assumptions to determine how well they incorporate the renewed commitment to customer satisfaction. Another valuable exercise in this phase is to examine the critical success factors – those areas in which the organisation clearly stands apart from the competition and to check whether they contribute to the new customer satisfaction goals.
2. **Redesign :** This phase requires an analysis of the way the organisation produces the products or services it sells – how jobs are structured, who accomplishes what tasks and the results of each procedure. Then, a determination must be made as to which elements should be redesigned to make jobs more satisfying and more customer focussed.
3. **Retool :** This phase requires a thorough evaluation of the current use of advanced technologies, especially electronic data processing systems, to identify opportunities for change that can improve quality of services and customer satisfaction.

16.7 REQUIREMENT OF REENGINEERING PROCESS

A process selected for reengineering should be a core process, which has great scope for **'breakthrough' improvements rather than incremental improvement.** Reengineering is accompanied by massive change involving lay-offs and large cash outflows for investments in information technology and automation. However, reengineering processes can result in big pay-offs. Bell Atlantic, *for example,* reengineered its telephone business. After five years of sustained effort, it cut the time to connect new customers from 16 days to just few hours. The changes caused Bell Atlantic to lay off 20,000 employees, but the company has become decidedly more competitive.

Reengineering requires focussing on *critical processes,* often using cross-functional teams, information technology, leadership and process analysis. These are explained in the following paragraphs.

Requirements of Reengineering processes are: *(i)* Critical or core processes *(ii)* Strong leadership *(iii)* Cross-functional teams *(iv)* Information technology *(v)* Clean-slate philosophy and *(vi)* Process analysis

(i) **Critical processes :** The emphasis of reengineering should be on core business processes, rather than functional departments such as purchasing or marketing. By focussing on core processes, managers may spot opportunities to eliminate unnecessary work and supervisory activities. Reengineering should be reassured for essential processes, such as new product development or customer services because of the time and energy involved.

(ii) **Strong leadership :** Senior executives must provide strong leadership for reengineering to be successful. Otherwise cynicism, resistance ("we tried that before") and boundaries between functional areas can block radical changes. Managers can help overcome resistance by providing the clout necessary to ensure that the project proceeds within a strategic context. Executives should set and monitor key performance objectives for the process. Top management should also create a sense of urgency, making a case for change that is compelling and constantly refreshed.

(iii) **Cross-functional teams :** A team consisting of members from each functional area affected by the process is charged with carrying out a reengineering project. Reengineering works best at high-involvement work places, where self-managing teams and employee empowerment are the rule rather than exception. Top-down and bottom-up initiatives can be combined – the top down for performance targets and the bottom-up for deciding how to achieve the targets.

(iv) **Information technology :** Information technology is a primary enabler of process reengineering. Most reengineering projects design processes around information flows such as customer order fulfilment. The **"process owners"** who will actually be responding to events in the market place need information network and computer technology to be more effective in their jobs. The reengineering team must think through and find answers to questions : **who needs the information, when they need it and where.**

(v) **"Clean slate philosophy" :** Reengineering requires a **"clean slate philosophy"**, that is starting with the way the customer wants to deal with the company. To ensure a customer orientation, teams begin with internal and external customer objectives for the process. Teams often first establish a price target for the product or service, deduct profits desired and then find a process that provides what the customer wants at the price the customer will pay. Reengineers start from the future and work backward, unconstrained by current approaches.

(vi) **Process analysis :** Despite the clean slate philosophy, a reengineering team must understand things about the current process : **what it does, how well it performs and what factors affect it.** Such an understanding can reveal areas in which new thinking will provide the biggest pay-off. The team must work at every procedure involved in the process throughout the organisation, recording each step, questioning why it is done and then eliminating it if it isn't really necessary. Information on standing relative to competition process by process is also valuable.

16.8 REENGINEERING IN THE SERVICE INDUSTRY

In the service sector, despite speed and courtesy in addressing customers, customer's hostility persists due to the inability of the service provider to maintain consistency in delivery and service. Another frequent problem is delay due to the inability of the service employee to make pertinent and satisfying decisions when confronted by an impatient customer. Sufficient evidence of this is found in banks and fast food restaurants. Even though some companies which start anew seem to better satisfy their customers in the beginning, after some years, they become sluggish due to growth in size and becoming increasingly intense and complex. Work habits evolve into unacceptable levels of performance which further complicate their problems. To remain competitive today, service organisations need to focus on customer satisfaction and on real customer needs and expectations. They need to operate according to the standards of the customers.

According to Janson, the concept of reengineering holds a significant promise for the service sector. The following are some of the salient features :

(i) **Make the customer the starting point for change :** This means identifying what the customers really want and then creating the kinds of jobs and organisational structures that can satisfy those expectations.

(ii) **Design work processes in light of organisational goals :** Companies that design work processes according to organisational goals become more focussed towards the customer. Organisations that reengineer often make drastic changes in existing jobs by integrating work procedures or tasks and empowering workers with more authority and responsibility.

(iii) **Restructure to support front-line performance :** In a customer focussed environment, every aspect of the organisation strives to promote the highest level of service to its customers, especially those who come in direct contact with customers. Consequently, organisations that undertake reengineering build work teams to support their customer service representatives or create **"work-station professionals"** who can perform both front and back office functions.

16.8.1 The Impact of Reengineering on the Service Industry

According to Janson, reengineering represents a major advance over conventional management strategies for improvement. As an integral approach, it involves three dimensions of a service organisation :

Reengineering involves three dimensions of a service operation viz:
(i) The human dimension
(ii) The work process dimension and
(iii) The technology dimension

(i) **The human dimension :** To achieve a stronger customer focus, employees at all levels must readjust their thinking and recognise that customer satisfaction is the overriding goal. Some companies achieve this by rewriting their mission statement to reflect the primacy of the customer or by promoting a new vision to reinforce the central role that customer satisfaction now plays. Some other companies engage in training to help employees become better listeners, probe for customer concerns more effectively or satisfy customer needs more creatively. The motive in reengineering is to become more motivated to provide superior service and be skilled at doing it.

(ii) **The work process dimension :** Work systems must be designed not according to their internal logic or any external definition of efficiency, but according to how well they satisfy customer needs. This sometimes requires substantial structural changes in an organisation – changes that do more than just revamp job descriptions. It may mean setting up work teams to perform all the functions once divided among several departments or combining several individual jobs to create, one ***"multi-skilled customer service professional."*** In every case, total reevaluation of the management's role in the organisation comes into play and lower level workers typically assume far greater responsibility for service quality.

(iii) **The technology dimension :** New technologies should be introduced not only because they are more advanced, but because they truly support the organisation in its drive to achieve higher levels of customer satisfaction. Most importantly, technology should be used to automate secondary work functions, leaving service workers free to concentrate on more critical matters such as satisfying customer needs and solving problems.

16.9 QUALITY AND REENGINEERING

Reengineering is not completely different from total quality principles. The issue is not ***Kaizen*** versus ***break-through*** improvement. Infact, Juran talked about breakthrough improvement long before Hammer and Champy popularised the term ***reengineering***. **Incremental and breakthrough improvement are complementary approaches that fall under the total quality umbrella, both are necessary to remain competitive.** Infact, some suggest that reengineering requires support of total quality management in order to be successful. If reengineering alone is driven by top management without the support and understanding of the rest of the organisation, the radical innovations may end up as failures. The total quality philosophy encourages participation and systematic study, measurement and verification of results that support reengineering efforts.

16.9.1 Continuous Process Improvement versus Process Reengineering

Some organisations shy away from process reengineering because they feel it is too costly and too time consuming. The questions asked by them are : "Why scrap a process when we can try to fix it instead?" The answer is to investigate and appreciate the problem. We need to determine whether a certain process within the organisation requires minor healing **(continuous process improvement)** or major surgery **(process reengineering)**.

Both **continuous process improvement** (referred to as CPI) and **process reengineering** are necessary to drive **"break-throughs"** (significant advances) in organisational performance but they differ in a number of ways. The differences are :

Even though both business process engineering and continuous process improvement are necessary to drive "break-through" there are some differences between BPR and CPI.

(i) **Management Involvement :** CPI typically involves employees at all levels and emphasise continuous incremental improvement of work processes. Process reengineering typically involves managers in a more ***"hands-on"*** role, since it often leads to changing organisational structure and redesigning jobs.

(ii) **Intensity of Team Member Involvement :** CPI involves team members on an "as needed" part-time basis over an extended time frame. Process reengineering requires much more intensive involvement of team members, often on a regular full time basis over a condensed time frame.

(iii) **Improvement Goals :** CPI results in the achievement of successive incremental improvements over a period of time, starting from how a work process currently operates and improving upon it. Process reengineering is periodic and focusses on the achievement of dramatic improvement, radically redesigning how a process operates without being constrained by how things were previously being done.

(iv) **Implementation Approach :** CPI builds on making incremental improvements that add up to significant improvement overall for an organisation. Process reengineering focusses on outcomes and on making break-through improvement at one time instead of adding up the sum of multiple gains.

(v) **Magnitude of organisational change :** With CPI, organisational changes happen over an extended period of time, often with limited disruption of existing jobs, management systems and organisational structures. With process reengineering, radical process changes go hand in hand with changes in job design, management systems, training and retraining, organisational structure and information technology.

(vi) **Extent of focus :** CPI focusses on narrowly defined processes, which often involve frontline employees who are working to improve a sub-process which is part of a higher level process. Process reengineering focusses on broad-based, cross-functional processes that span the larger part of an organisational system.

(vii) **Dependence upon information systems :** Organisations using CPI occasionally reinvent a process whereas those using process reengineering use information technology to pave the way for radical improvements in reduction of cycle time and information access.

Both CPI and process reengineering have a place in today's organisation. While CPI is the mainstay, process reengineering is necessary at certain times in certain situations, when CPI is not adequate for the job.

16.10 THE REENGINEERING PROCESS

Process engineering is an innovative process for which a disciplined approach to the effort is essential. **It involves a six-step plan. These steps are :**

Step 1 : State a case for action.

Step 2 : Identify the process for reengineering.

Step 3 : Evaluate enablers for reengineering

Step 4 : Understand the current process.

Step 5 : Create a new process design and

Step 6 : Implement the reengineered process.

Process reengineering may be viewed as a six-step process.

These steps are explained below.

(i) **State a case for action :** The need for change should be effectively communicated to the employees of the organisation through educational and communication campaigns. Two key messages to be articulated are *(i)* **a need for action** and *(ii)* **a vision statement.**

The objectives of reengineering must be in the form of a qualitative and quantitative ***vision statement.*** These objectives include goals for cost reduction, time-to-market, quality and customer satisfaction levels and financial indicators. *For example,* the vision statement by Federal Express (a US courier company) in its infancy was "we will deliver the package by 10 30 a.m. the next morning".

Box 16.4 **lists the steps manufacturers take when reengineering.**

Box 16.4 : Steps Manufacturers Take When Reorganising

Steps	Percentage of Manufacturers
(i) Outsourcing one or more operations	31%
(ii) Eliminating a product line	34%
(iii) Reducing the number of suppliers	34%
(iv) Reducing the number of production workers	41%
(v) Flattening the layers of management	56%
(vi) Organising operations by customer or product line	60%
(vii) Investing in automated equipment	76%
(viii) Significantly improving process flows in the factory	87%

The CEO of the company is responsible for communicating the vision statement first to the senior management and then to the rest of the firm. A senior management ***steering committee*** that includes the CEO typically champions the change process, sets goals, assigns resources and expedites progress.

(ii) **Identify the process :** All the major processes in the firm should be initially identified and few processes should be selected for reengineering. The following questions define the criteria for selecting processes for reengineering:

- Which processes are currently more problematic?
- Which processes are critical to accomplishing company strategy and have the greatest impact on the company's customer?
- Which processes are most likely to be successfully redesigned?
- What is the scope of the reengineering project and what are the costs involved?
- What is the strength of the reengineering team and the commitment of process owners and sponsors?
- Can continuous improvement deliver the required improvements?
- Is the process antiquated or is the technology used outdated?

Response to these questions can be weighted in accordance with the company's need for improvement. The selected process should have a manageable reengineering project scope with well-defined process boundaries.

(iii) **Evaluate enablers :** Information technology and human/organisational issues act as enablers of the reengineering process. **Technology evaluation** has now become a core competency required of all companies. Companies should develop the ability to evaluate current and emerging information technology and identify creative application to redesign their existing processes.

The current organisational culture should also be evaluated in light of the impending change to be brought about by reengineering. Participative and customer-oriented cultures that have evolved from the quality revolution provide a suitable environment for further change. But the magnitude of change created by process redesign makes the management of change a necessity. Issues of measurement and compensation, career paths, work enrichment and new skills training should be addressed.

(iv) **Understanding the current process :** The current process must be understood by making use of **process evaluation techniques such as flow charts, fishbone diagrams and quality function deployment.** The purpose is to create a new, radically better process. The current process must be studied to understand the activities which are essential to completion. All activities can be classified into three types :

Process evaluation techniques such as flow charts, fishbone diagrams and quality function deployment are used to understand the current process.

(a) ***Value-adding work*** – work for which customer is willing to pay.

(b) ***Non-value adding work*** – work which creates no value for the customer but is required in order to get the value adding work done.

(c) ***Waste*** – work that neither adds nor enables value.

Value adding work consists of all of the activities that create the goods and services that customers want. *For example,* if a customer's order has to be executed, value adding activities include inventory allocation, picking, packing, route planning and shipping. Waste work is work whose absence would not be noticed by the customer. Waste work needs to be eliminated.

Non-value adding work is the glue that binds the value-adding work in conventional processes. It is mainly the administrative overhead – the reporting, checking, supervising, controlling, reviewing and coordinating. Michael Hammer argues that it is necessary to design non-value adding work by reorganising the value-adding tasks into a new and more efficient process.

(v) **Create a new process design :** Process redesign requires beginning with a clean slate. Reengineers should suspend current rules, procedures and values so as to create new process design. They also need to utilise the principles of reengineering.

The first emphasis in reengineering a process is to ***eliminate all waste work.*** Next, the focus is on the **elimination of non-value-adding work.** Hammer has found that less than 10 percent of the activities in a process are value-adding activities.

(vi) **Implement the reengineered process :** Leadership is critical to the implementation process as well as to the entire reengineering effort. Process engineering teams are typically responsible for implementing the new designs. However, support and buy-in from line managers are crucial to success. Training employees in additional skills needed to perform in the new environment is also essential.

16.11 PROCESS REDESIGN TOOLS AND TECHNIQUES

(i) **Inductive thinking :** This involves reengineering potential solutions and then seeking and recognising obvious or latent problems that may be solved. This approach is required in the creative application of information technology to reengineer processes. For instance, the use

of teleconferencing is not to eliminate business travel entirely but to be able to get more individuals working together.

(ii) **Flowcharting :** Flow charts or blue prints are the basic tools when initiating Business Process Reengineering. They are used to study the process currently used.

(iii) **Creative process redesign :** Creative process design uses the application **of *principles of reengineering*** discussed earlier in this chapter. This approach involves questioning the assumptions that underlie current business practices thereby leading to new methods. Many successes in process reengineering are in the areas of purchasing and procurement, which have resulted because of challenging long-held beliefs. *For example,* eliminating the view that the supplier is a business adversary and sharing operational information has improved the combined performance of both supplier and buyer. The rule that invoices are needed as a prerequisite for payment of bills has been changed. Reengineered firms now pay on receipt of goods, thus eliminating the need for invoices.

(iv) **Process benchmarking :** Benchmarking which is usually considered as a continuous improvement tool can also be used to gain information regarding a company's relative position in key business processes and core competencies. During the initial stages of process reengineering program, benchmarking is helpful to create an industry context for goals being set. Benchmarking will also provide a firm with examples of best practices in terms of new processes and the approach to their implementation. Benchmarking is not intended just to imitate another company's processes. Benchmarking is of vital importance in process reengineering because a team's imagination is stimulated when it comes across creative solutions implemented by the other companies which are being benchmarked.

(v) **Simulation :** Discrete-event computer simulation and animation can be very useful in understanding processes. Also, the simulations could be used to visualise and evaluate the redesigned processes and new processes before the pilot project stage.

(vi) **Reengineering software :** Adequate software tools and methodologies are available to help draw detailed process maps and to understand existing processes and design new processes. The availability of such software tools and methodologies aids the redesign phase of process reengineering.

Process redesign tools and techniques involve:
(i) Inductive thinking
(ii) Flow charting
(iii) creative process redesign
(iv) Process benchmarking
(v) Simulation and
(vi) Reengineering software

16.12 REENGINEERING AND TOTAL QUALITY MANAGEMENT

Some people have said that both TQM and Reengineering are the same, while others have argued that they are incompatible. Michael Hammer argues that the two concepts are compatible and actually complement each other. Both concepts have the same focus – customer satisfaction.

Basic concepts of both BPR and TQM have the same focus viz: customer satisfaction.

TQM has contributed the concept of *teamwork, worker participation and empowerment, cross-functionality, process analysis and measurement, supplier involvement and benchmarking.* Also, TQM has emphasised the need for a "total" view of the organisations in its approach to problem solving. TQM has also influenced company culture and values by exposing organisations to the need for change.

TQM has advocated continuous and incremental improvement of processes (Kaizen) whereas reengineering is about radical discontinuous change (breakthrough improvement) through ***process innovation. Exhibit 16.3* illustrates how TQM and reengineering fit together over time in the life of a process.**

First, the process is ***enhanced*** until its useful life time is over, at which point it is ***reengineered.*** Then enhancement is resumed and the entire cycle repeats again. Hammer points out that this is not a once-in-a-life time endeavour. As business circumstances change in major ways, so must process design.

Exhibit 16.3 : How TQM and Reengineering fit Together Over the Life of a Process

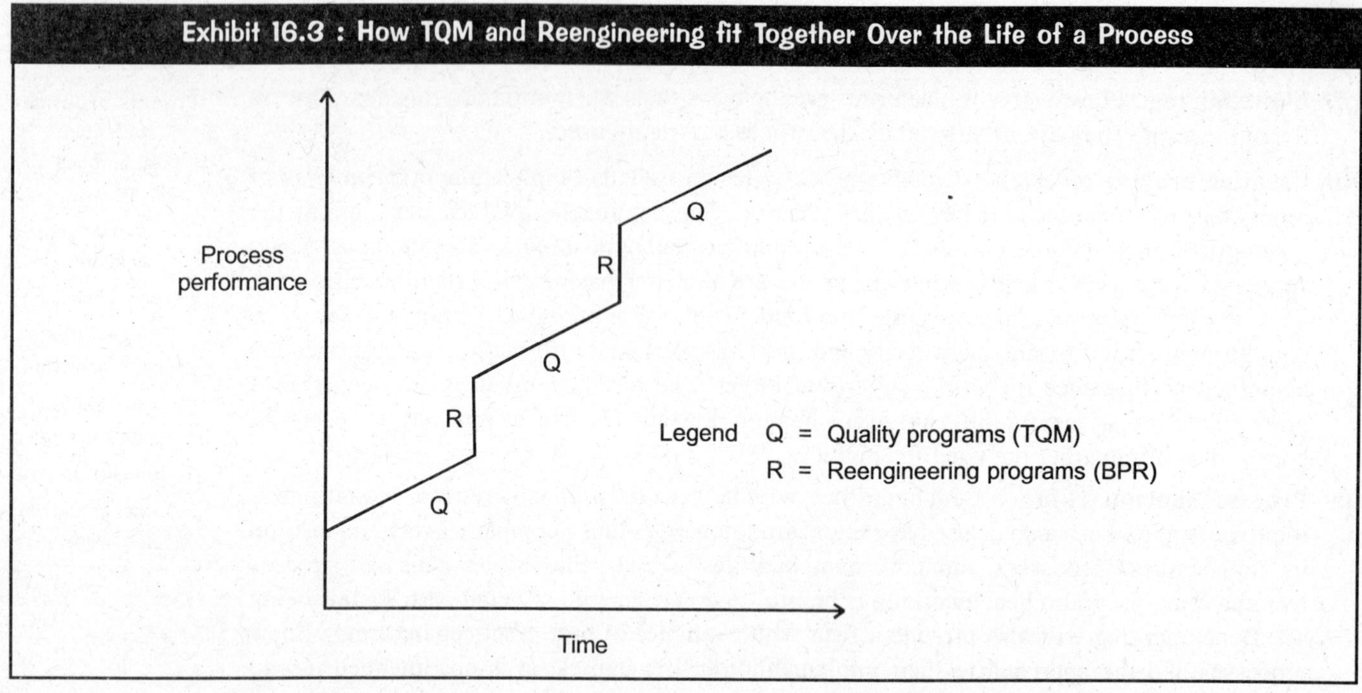

Box 16.5 **contains a list of some similarities between TQM/Continuous Improvement and Reengineering (BPR).**

Box 16.5 : Reengineering versus TQM (CPI)

Similarities	**Reengineering**	**TQM (CPI)**
Basis of analysis	Processes	Processes
Performance measurement	Rigorous	Rigorous
Organisational change	Significant	Significant
Behavioural change	Significant	Significant
Time investment	Substantial	Substantial
Differences		
Level of change	Radical	Incremental
Starting point	Clean slate	Existing process
Participation	Top-down	Bottom-up
Typical scope	Broad, cross-functional	Narrow, within functions
Risk	High	Moderate
Primary enabler	Information technology	Statistical control
Type of change	Cultural and structural	Cultural

The dissimilarities that have been identified may create an impression that reengineering is outside the realm of quality management. Hammer, the reengineering guru, together with quality gurus such as Deming and Juran, all agree that ***innovation and break-throughs*** in processes are essential parts of quality management. TQM assumes that the design of the process is sound and that all it needs is some improvement or enhancement. But if the world has changed dramatically since the process was first (or most recently) designed, the current design may be incapable of delivering the required performance. Reengineering is then necessary.

16.13 INTEGRATING REENGINEERING AND PROCESS IMPROVEMENT

Organisations must develop a framework for placing reengineering activity in the context of other change activities they may undertake. Integrating will help keep the different change initiatives, expectations, methods and results distinct from each other, thereby minimising the confusion and cynicism that usually result from undertaking an assortment of management initiatives. **Four approaches to integrating process improvement and reengineering activities in organisations are:**

Process improvement and reengineering activities can be integrated through the following approaches: *(i)* Sequencing change activities *(ii)* Creating a portfolio of process change programs *(iii)* Limiting the scope of work design and *(iv)* Undertaking improvement through innovation.

(i) **Sequencing change initiatives :** This approach suggests cycling through ***process stabilisation, process reengineering*** and ***continuous improvement.*** The drawback of this approach is that it may take at least ***five years*** to go through one cycle of change which would be longer than many ***organisational learning cycles*** **or** ***product life cycles.***

(ii) **Creating a portfolio of process change programs :** This method involves the categorisation of all processes and sub-processes in an organisation on the basis of the type of change necessary. The criteria for selecting processes for reengineering could include ***relevance to strategy, current performance levels, capability of sponsors, available investment*** **and** ***history of change.***

(iii) **Limiting the scope of work design :** In this approach, high level processes are designed by the responsible reengineering teams. But employees who perform the jobs design the detail work processes involved within the specifications decided by the reengineering team. This attempts to combine the participative nature of continuous improvement with the top down approach common to process reengineering.

(iv) **Undertaking improvement through innovation :** This approach combines short term improvement methods and long-term reengineering in the same process change effort. Improvement methods such as ***value analysis*** can be used to obtain quick benefits, which are then invested in the long-term reengineering effort. The improvement projects may also be a means to move the current process forward to a stage where radical process change is possible.

The different approaches to process change discussed above are complementary. Oganisations need to determine how and when they need to apply the appropriate methods to their different processes. While it is important to have an integrated approach to operational change, it is far more important to effect that change.

16.14 REENGINEERING VERSUS BENCHMARKING

Benchmarking involves partnering with the owner of a best-in-class process so that the benchmarking firm (bench marker) might adopt or adapt that process in its operation without having to spend the time and energy to try to design a duplicate of the superior (benchmarked) process. But in Business Process Engineering (BPR) the company requires to develop the improved process on its own. Therefore, process reengineering should only be considered when it is impossible to use benchmarking. This could happen for a number of reasons: *(a)* No known process available for benchmarking, *(b)* Best-in-class not willing to partner and, *(c)* Best-in-class is not accessible due to geography or expense.

If, for a firm, its process is not satisfactory and the firm can not benchmark for any of these reasons, then it may have to resort to BPR. However, if the process is a wrong process for the job or if it is out of statistical control, reengineering will not solve the problem. The process should be modified and brought under statistical control first. Still if the process is not capable to produce the desired result then redesigning the process through BPR is a good approach.

One disadvantage with process reengineering is that there is no guarantee of redesigning a competitive process inspite of spending the time and resources whereas it is not the case with bench marking. Bench marking helps the company to achieve a competitive process that is bench marked.

When a process is improved by continuous improvement approach, improvement typically comes out by changing or eliminating activity in the process that does not add value or consumes too much of time or resources. But as an alternative, process reengineering involves abandoning the current process and replacing it with a brand new process that provides the same functionality but better, faster or cheaper.

If an organisation could achieve the same results by either benchmarking or process reengineering, then the question of "which one stands the best chance of success in the work place" occurs. The continuous improvement route would be more readily accepted by the work force than the radical and sudden change that results from process reengineering. Many times BPR is seen as a management tool for laying off workers. Therefore, if the firm finds process reengineering to be the approach for one of its core or critical processes, it should involve the process owners (workers who currently perform the process) and their internal suppliers and customers along with other appropriate employees in its process reengineering project.

In summary, if a firm has a good process to begin with, it should use continuous improvement to make it better. On the other hand, if the process is clearly inferior to some used by other firms, bench marking would be the better approach. When the firm can not achieve the kind of improvement needed from either continuous improvement or benchmarking, then process reengineering would be the best option.

16.15 BENEFITS OF REENGINEERING

The following are the benefits of reengineering:

(i) By reengineering, an organisation can achieve **radical changes in performance** (as measured by cost, cycle time, service and quality).

(ii) It **boosts competitiveness** in the operations network through simpler, leaner and more productive processes.

Reengineering has certain benefits and limitations also.

(iii) Reengineering encourages organisations to abandon conventional approaches to problem solving and to "think big" **(revolutionary thinking).**

(iv) The slow, cautious process of incremental improvements leaves many organisations unprepared to compete in today's rapidly changing market place. Reengineering helps organisations make noticeable changes in the pace and quality of their response to customer needs (*i.e.* **break-through improvements**).

(v) Through reengineering, an organisation can be transformed from a rule driven and job centred organisation structure to a **marketing organisation structure** that focusses directly on the customer.

(vi) Reengineering often results in **radically new organisational designs** that can help companies respond better to competitive pressures, increase market share and profitability and improve cycle times, cost ratios and quality (organisational renewal).

(vii) The major accomplishment of the reengineering effort is the change that occurs in the corporate culture and the basic principles by which departments operate. Workers at all levels are encouraged to make suggestions for improvement and to believe that management will listen to what they have to say. Reengineering will eventually help the culture in the organisation to evolve from an insular one to one that accepts change and knows how to deal with it.

(viii) Reengineering has helped create more challenging and more rewarding jobs with broader responsibilities for employees (job redesign).

16.16 LIMITATIONS OF REENGINEERING

(i) Although business process reengineering is presented as a recipe for instant competitive advantage, **it is not a panacea.** Like any other management approach, how you apply it makes a difference.

(ii) It is not simple or easily done, nor is it appropriate for all processes for all organisations. Many firms can't invest the time and resources to implement a radical, clean slate approach.

(iii) Moderate gains that better fit corporate strategy and culture might give greater cumulative results than the pursuit of break-through.

(iv) Significant process improvements cannot be realised without use of information technology.

(v) It is not enough if a firm improves its cross-functional processes but also processes within each functional areas must be improved.

(vi) The best understanding of a process and how to improve it, often lies with all people who perform the work each day, not cross-functional teams or top management.

16.17 BEYOND BUSINESS PROCESS REENGINEERING

Business Process Reengineering (BPR) has become hardwired in individual companies. The core-business processes are designed to satisfy in the ***"one best way"*** a particular customer need. Many Business Process Reengineering efforts do not seem to consider what will happen if that need changes. The ***"holonic business system"* allows businesses continually to de-invent and re-invent themselves as they face increasingly ambiguous markets.**

BPR experience is now being established. **The leaders of reengineering efforts must turn their attention beyond the analysis of complex process maps and information systems towards two new challenges. They are :**

(i) How can the reengineered core business processes contribute to a strategic re-positioning of the business and

(ii) How to effectively direct and accelerate major organisational change.

The "holonic business system" extends the idea of BPR and allows business to continually de-invent and re-invent in the dynamic, ambiguous markets in which companies operate.

There are three kinds of BPR efforts and these define the scope and ambition of a company's BPR efforts. They are :

(i) **To achieve improvement** – usually through cutting costs and aims at support or management processes. It is often accompanied by such efforts as divestment, delayering and downsizing.

(ii) **To achieve a "Break-Point"** – A Break-point is a new level of process innovation – as measured by the value set of cost, quality, lead time, delivery reliability and product functionality – that provides a significant and positive market impact. Break-Point Process Reengineering is concerned therefore to go beyond traditional efforts to improve performance. It has the focus on re-inventing the industry.

The **"holonic business system"** extends this idea. For any core business process, a set of nodes within the ***holonic network*** can be found that can carry out a core business process in the most effective and efficient manner possible.

The Holonic Concept : A ***"holonic network"*** is a set of companies that acts integratedly and organically, it is constantly reconfigured to manage each business opportunity a customer presents. Each company in the network provides a different process capability and is called a ***"holon"***.

Each configuration of process capabilities within the holonic network is called a ***"virtual company"***. By combining the core competencies of many individual companies within the network, each virtual company is more powerful and flexible than the participating members alone could be. Each company in a virtual company is chosen because of its process excellence.

BPR is market and opportunity driven; and customer focussed. So is the holonic business system. The customer focusses on the holonic network. Each customer can move from being a ***consumer* to a *prosumer*.** Prosumers contribute by various degrees to the design of the product they request. They are ***proactive consumers*** that work with sellers to define the products and services they are buying. Through the design process, the consumer forces the network to configure itself to provide the optimum processes to meet his needs. In this way, holonic networks go beyond Business Process Reengineering in that they define for the first time how to sell customer specific products while realising economies of scale.

In a holonic network, continuous improvement occurs at the network level because the network is constantly improving co-ordination and communication between nodes. And at the individual node level, each node is constantly improving its core competencies. But within any one virtual company, only nodes that operate the "best practices" level participate. The only way to improve a virtual company is to remove one or more of the nodes and replace them with better nodes. This is tantamount to creating a new virtual company. This is what is meant by the network constantly configuring itself to present the best core business processes in virtual companies.

Within a holonic network, each holon is unique and is unable by itself to create a Break-Point in the market. Only the power of the virtual company formed of nodes within a holonic network can create a Break-Point.

***Exhibit 16.4* illustrates a holonic network of a Printed Circuit Board manufacturing Company.**

Exhibit 16.4 : MEGA – PC's Holonic Network

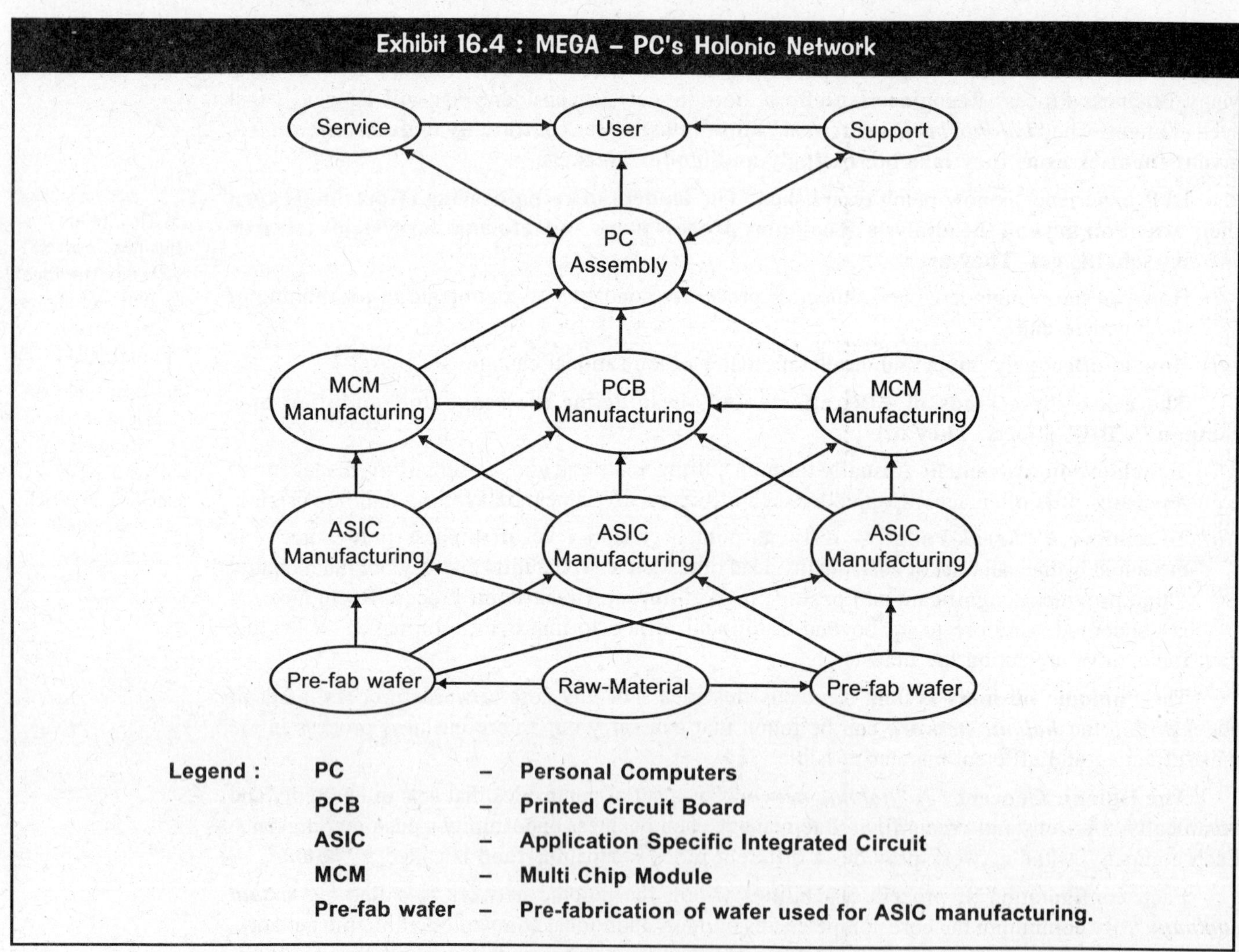

Legend :

PC	–	**Personal Computers**
PCB	–	**Printed Circuit Board**
ASIC	–	**Application Specific Integrated Circuit**
MCM	–	**Multi Chip Module**
Pre-fab wafer	–	**Pre-fabrication of wafer used for ASIC manufacturing.**

In a single company BPR model, the market place does not ***"know what it wants"***. It is only through a ***design of experiments*** that a company can decide what is most important to the market place. In this, a company asks the market "If we could provide you, *for example,* with three of the following eight characteristics, which three would you like?" In the holonic business system, by contrast, each prosumer knows what he wants and therefore the virtual company knows the Break-Point needed by its customers. Going beyond Business Process Reengineering, it is possible to see how with the holonic business system, small companies can compete with large companies. Also, large companies can become cost competitive with small businesses.

16.17.1 Working of Holonic Networks

Take *for example*, **the nine-day house built by the Japanese Company Sikisui.** The customers, a wife and husband, enter the sales office to buy a house. There they find several computer terminals, each linked to company's design office. First, the couple design the basic layout of the house, restricted only by building codes and the size of the plot on which the house will be built. Then they begin to personalise it.

They discuss options, with or without the help of the salesperson. They try out "what ifs" on the screen. Eventually they devise a plan that meets their exact specifications. The sales agent offers them tea while they wait for their quotation to be ready, including the cost of building the house. The couple agree to the quotation and come to terms on a payment schedule. The contract is signed.

Within minutes, the company has sent orders to all of its suppliers to prepare the materials for this customer-designed house. If a supplier of one item cannot fulfil its order within three days, it is responsible for finding another vendor in the network of suppliers who can.

Two days before the house is to be built on the customer's site, the components of the house are at the building company's factory. Here, they are assembled into modules.

Sikisui, with its sales staff and design centres, acts as the integrator in this holonic network that includes dozens of suppliers. Each home-designed by the prosumer – is supplied by a different group of suppliers – in effect a different virtual company for each product. Fifty percent of the parts in the typical home are ordered on a ***kanban*** system (*i.e.* they are repetitive orders) while the other 50 percent are special orders for each home.

This kind of process can only take place within a network of companies that work with real time communication tools. The user interface software enables the customer to design his or her own product.

That the holonic network is effective can be attested by the fact that annual revenues per Sikisui employee are almost $ one million each.

Holonic networks are classified as:
(i) vertical networks
(ii) Horizontal networks,
(iii) Regional networks
(iv) Out-of-necessity networks and
(v) Self-promoted networks.

16.18 TYPES OF HOLONIC NETWORKS

The various types of holonic networks are :

- Vertical networks
- Horizontal networks
- Regional networks
- Out-of-necessity networks and
- Self-promoted networks.

Vertical networks : These most closely resemble what we think of as the traditional supply chain. Usually one node adds some value to an object and passes it off to another node, which in turn adds value and so on down the value chain.

But within the virtual company, there are differences from the traditional model. Automotive Original Equipment Manufacturers (OEMs) used to be vertically integrated. *For example,* General Motors still makes almost every sub-assembly in GM shops and those it cannot make are made by suppliers quasi-dedicated to them. In this way, GM maintains control, GM's leverage over the supplier is the fear of losing GM as a customer.

Horizontal Networks : These are networks in which all nodes have the ***same core competence*** and share capacity back and forth. This type of network exists to a large extent in the textile and clothing industry. Here, large retail companies order large blocks of items – more than any supplier who receives the contract can deliver in the short period given. To meet demand, the supplier lays off parts of the order into preselected competitors, creating a system of cooperation. The relationships are usually reciprocal within a small group of companies.

Regional Networks : These networks are created by large groups of small companies, each having about 45 employees on an average. To handle orders of any size, these companies form tight partnerships with other entrepreneurs. Over time, they have come to specialise in small, discrete parts of the value chain. Such networks are common in clothing, jewellery manufacturing industries and in agriculture.

Out-of-necessity Networks : These networks consist of small companies that do not have the capital to develop a market or product. *For example,* a group of seven small cabinet making companies pooled their collective expertise to develop a computer numerical control (CNC) router that has become their core technology. Their collective goal was to produce a machine that would cost in the range of $ 30,000 to $ 70,000, bringing down the cost of the machine from $ 200,000. Not only can the seven companies manufacture finished products more effectively, but by pooling their capital they can expand into new product lines. Moreover by acting as holonic partners, they can specialise more closely in the components they are best at making and work for each other.

Self-Promoted Networks : These are usually single nodes that have core competence and seek partnerships with other nodes. In each case, the company has defined a strategic direction that sets the company's mission to be a node in as many holonic networks as possible irrespective of the ultimate consumer product being made. These companies survive on their ability to be a node.

16.19 ADVANTAGES OF HOLONIC BUSINESS SYSTEM

The "holonic business systems" have the following advantages:
(i) Leverage
(ii) speed
(iii) Flexibility
(iv) Shared risk
(v) Independence
(vi) Faster growth and increased profits
(vii) Sustainable customers
(viii) Less capital required
(ix) Quick failure recognition and
(x) Increased ability to deal with inevitable change

(i) **Leverage :** There is true synergy achieved by combining the best capabilities of many operations. Small companies can develop the competitive clout of large companies at a fraction of the cost.

(ii) **Speed :** Decision making is streamlined and hence fast. There are no "layers of management", so no need to sell ideas up the management ladder. Information moves through all forms of telecommunication (Electronic Data Interchange). Businesses as that are able to act as nodes in a virtual company have had their core competence that they alone manage. Thus, decisions are as rapid as saying "yes" or "no" to the questions. This speed shows up as ***"time to market"*** because one company does not have to "invent" an entire new product. It can call on a host of partners with their own core competencies to create a virtual company and to design the new product. It can also show up as "speed to customer" since the virtual company establishes the most effective production core business process.

(iii) **Flexibility :** Coupled with speed is the ability to change the service or product capabilities to match rapidly changing market requirements.

(iv) **Shared risk :** Because several nodes form a holonic network, there is a shared risk and reward. There is also a reduction in the fear of change, since each ***holon*** is confident in its capabilities.

(v) **Independence :** Each holon is independent, free to come and go as it pleases and to compete and cooperate as it wants, but the holonic system requires a great deal of cooperation.

(vi) **Faster growth and increased profits :** It was observed that companies that are one-third more responsive to their customers had a growth rate of three or more times their competition and were two to five times more profitable.

(vii) **Sustainable customers :** Once customers have become used to the flexibility and responsiveness of a holonic system as their supplier, it will be tough for competitors to wean them away.

(viii) **Less capital required :** A holonic system significantly requires less capital because each node only uses equipment that is specific to its core business processes. This in turn results in requirement for less working capital, lower maintenance costs, higher return on assets and considerably fewer fixed assets.

(ix) **Quick failure recognition :** Since the network operates in real time it should recognise failure quickly. A well-designed network will have an exit strategy that can be put into effect

quickly. The network should be capable of getting dismantled without damaging the reputation or image of any node.

(x) **Increased ability to deal with inevitable change :** This can be explained with an example of a joint venture of Digital Equipment Company (DEC) of US with Tandy, the low cost manufacturer of radio shank products to participate in the personal computer (PC) market in the mid 1980s. Along came Compaq which offered higher performance to the market. DEC forced to compete on the performance plans, reconfigured its alliance, adding Intel as a partner in the development of its next generation of PCs. Then came Dell into the market, which offered both low cost and good performance. DEC dropped the alliance with Tandy and began manufacturing on its own. This was a mistake as it turned out and in practice was also directly contrary to the PC industry's trend towards holonic network.

16.20 QUALITY IN PRACTICE

Box 16.6 Reengineering at Sundaram Fasteners

When Sundaram Fasteners, the Chennai based fasteners-manufacturer realised the necessity to upgrade its quality to global levels – in order to export large enough volumes to offset imports – it reengineered ruthlessly. Identifying manufacturing as its core process, the firm discovered that manufacturing was clustered more around operations – forging, heat treatment and tooling – than around products. Each worker was concentrating only on his area and the efficiency of the entire process for producing a product was not being maximised.

With the help of reengineering consultants – Lucas Engineering System, Sundaram Fasteners transformed the process from being ***task-centric*** to ***product-centric***. Machines was regrouped into two **zones of autonomous production** (ZAP): ZAP 1 to handle products between 6 mm and 16 mm diameter and ZAP 2 to handle parts upwards of 16 mm diameter.

Reengineering shifted the responsibility for meeting customer requirements from the marketing department to the manager of each of the two ZAP modules. The module manager was empowered to order components from the in-house raw material module according to requirements and even outsourcing if necessary. The module manager has become the single reference point for the customer and the owner of the process. The gains were significant 50 percent improvement in adherence to delivery schedule, increase in inventory turnover from 4 times to 20 times at its Chennai factory and a 25 percent increase in productivity.

(*Source:* Business Today: December 7–21. 1995)

16.21 SUMMARY

"Business Process Reengineering" (BPR in short) is also known as "Process Reengineering" or simply "Reengineering". According to Michael Hammer, Reengineering has been defined as ***"the fundamental rethinking and radical design of business processes to achieve dramatic or break-through improvement in critical contemporary measures of performance such as cost, quality, service and speed".***

Reengineering does not strive to ***revamp*** the existing process but it involves ***reinventing*** the process to achieve quantum leaps in performance and to achieve higher levels of customer satisfaction.

Reengineering entails the following seven rules or principles :

(i) Organise around outcomes, not tasks.

(ii) Have those who use the output of the process perform the process.

(iii) Merge information processing work into the real work that produces the information.

(iv) Treat geographically dispersed resource as though they work centralised.

(v) Link parallel activities instead of integrating their results.

(vi) Put the decision point where the work is performed and build control into the process.

(vii) Capture information once – at the source.

According to Hammer the major steps the company should embark on to redesign its process are:

(i) Develop business vision and process objectives

(ii) Identify processes to be redesigned

(iii) Understand and measure existing processes

(iv) Identify information technology levels and

(v) Design and build a prototype of the process.

Janson states that every reengineering effort involves three basic phases. They are: *(i)* Rethink, *(ii)* Redesign and *(iii)* Retool.

The reengineering process requires : *(i)* focusing on critical processes, *(ii)* strong leadership, *(iii)* cross-functional teams, *(iv)* information technology, *(v)* clean-slate philosophy and *(vi)* process analysis.

Reengineering is necessary not only in manufacturing industry, but in service industry as well. Three salient features of reengineering in the service sector are : *(i)* Make the customer the starting point for change, *(ii)* Design work-processes in light of organisational goals and *(iii)* Restructure to support front-line performance. Three dimensions of a service organisation on which reengineering has an impact are:

(i) The human dimension (focus on customers and employees)

(ii) The work process dimension (multiskilled service profession) and

(iii) The technology dimension (new technology and automation).

Reengineering is not opposed to total quality management even though the former focuses on breakthrough improvement as opposed to the continuous improvement (Kaizen) approach of the latter. Infact incremental and breakthrough improvements are complementary approaches that fall under TQM umbrella. Reengineering requires the support of TQM to be successful. The six steps involved in the reengineering process are :

(i) state a case for action

(ii) identify the process for reengineering

(iii) evaluate enablers for reengineering

(iv) understand the current process

(v) create a new process design

(vi) implement the reengineered process.

The various tools and techniques used in reengineering are : *(i)* Inductive thinking, *(ii)* Flow charting, *(iii)* Creative process redesign, *(iv)* Process benchmarking, *(v)* Simulation and *(vi)* Reengineering software.

The four approaches to integrating process improvement and reengineering activities in an organisation are : *(i)* Sequencing change initiatives, *(ii)* Creating a portfolio of process change programs, *(iii)* Limiting the scope for work design and *(iv)* Understanding improvement through innovation.

Some of the major benefits of reengineering are :

(i) Achievement of radical changes in performance measured by cost, cycle time, service and quality.

(ii) Boosting competitiveness in the operational network.

(iii) Helps to think big (revolutionary thinking)

(iv) Helps to make noticeable changes in the pace and quality of response to customers needs.

(v) Results in new organisational designs that help firms respond better to competitive pressures, increase market shares and profitability and improve cycle times, cost ratio and quality (organisational renewal).

(vi) Brings change in the corporate culture and the basic principles by which departments operate, encourages workers at all levels to make suggestions for improvements and eventually helps the culture in the organisation to evolve from an insular one to the one that accepts and knows how to deal with it.

However, reengineering has some limitations. They are :

(i) Not a panacea for all problems.

(ii) Not simple or easily done, nor is it appropriate for all processes for all organisations.

(iii) Use of information technology is a must to gain significant process improvement.

(iv) Improvement of processes require active participation of people who actually perform the work.

Business process reengineering redesigns the core processes of an organisation to satisfy in the "one best way" a particular customer need. If that customer needs changes, BPR does not have an immediate answer. In such cases one can look beyond B.P.R. to the ***"holonic business system"*** which allows businesses continually to deinvent and re-invent themselves as they face increasingly ambiguous markets.

A "holonic business system" or a "holonic network" is a set of companies that act integratedly and organically. Each company in the network is by itself a ***virtual company*** which is chosen because of its process excellence in its own field. The network is constantly reconfigured to manage each business opportunity a customer presents. This "holonic business system" is capable of achieving continuous improvement as well as breakthrough improvements.

The advantages of holonic business system includes leverage, speed, flexibility, shared risk, independence, faster growth and increased profits, sustainable customers, less capital required, quick failure recognition and increased ability to deal with inevitable change.

The various types of holonic networks are : *(i)* Vertical networks, *(ii)* Horizontal networks, *(iii)* Regional networks, *(iv)* Out-of necessity networks and *(v)* Self-promoted networks.

16.22 KEY WORDS USED

Reengineering, Process Reengineering, Business Process Reengineering (BPR), Break – through Improvement, Process Redesign, Clean-slate Philosophy, Continuous Process Improvement (CPI), Process Benchmarking, Simulation, Reengineering Software, Holonic Concept, Holonic Network, Prosumer, Virtual Company.

16.23 OBJECTIVE QUESTIONS

(A) Match the following :

Column A	Column B
1. Business process reengineering	1. Rethink, Redesign and Retool
2. Three 'R's of reengineering	2. Pioneers of reengineering
3. Hammer and Champy	3. Involves redesigning business process
4. Creative process redesign	4. Allows business continually to de-invent and re-invent themselves
5. Holonic business system	5. Uses the application of principles of reengineering

(B) State whether the following statements are True or False :

1. Reengineering requires looking at the fundamental processes of the business from across-functional perspective. (T / F)
2. For organisations that want to survive and grow, improvement is not an option but a compulsion. (T / F)
3. A process selected for reengineering should be a core process which has great scope for incremental improvements rather than break-through improvements. (T / F)
4. Reengineering is completely different from total quality principles. (T / F)
5. Both TQM and reengineering concepts have the same focus - customer satisfaction. (T / F)

(C) Multiple choice Questions : Choose the correct answer from the alternatives given under each question :

1. Business Process Reengineering is also known as:

   (a) Process reengineering (b) Process redesign
   (c) Reengineering (d) All of these
   (e) None of these

2. Every reengineering effort involves
   (a) Rethink phase (b) Redesign phase
   (c) Retool phase (d) All of these
   (e) None of these
3. Process redesign tools and techniques include:
   (a) Inductive thinking (b) Flow charting
   (c) Creative process design (d) Simulation
   (e) All of these (f) None of these
4. Benefits of reengineering include:
   (a) Radical changes in performance (b) Boosts competitiveness
   (c) Revolutionary thinking (d) Breakthrough improvement
   (e) All of these (f) None of these
5. Advantages of Holonic business system include:
   (a) Leverage and speed (b) Flexibility and shared risk
   (c) Independence and sustainable customers
   (d) Faster growth and increased profits (e) All of these (f) None of these

16.24 REVIEW QUESTIONS

1. What is meant by "Business Process Reengineering"?
2. Why an organisation needs reengineering?
3. Discuss the seven rules or principles of reengineering.
4. Describe the reengineering process in a manufacturing organisation. How does it differ from that in a service organisation?
5. What do you understand by "the three 'R's" of reengineering?
6. Explain the requirements of reengineering process.
7. Discuss the impact of reengineering on the service industry.
8. Discuss the relationship between TQM and BPR.
9. Compare and contrast continuous process improvement and process reengineering.
10. Describe the various steps involved in the reengineering process.
11. Explain the various tools and techniques used in process redesign.
12. "Some people have said that both TQM and Reengineering are the same, while others have argued that they are incompatible". Comment on this statement.
13. Explain how reengineering and process improvement are integrated.
14. State the benefits and limitations of reengineering.
15. Explain what is meant by "Beyond Business Process Reengineering".
16. What is meant by "holonic concept". Describe the working of a "holonic business system" with an illustration.
17. Discuss the advantages of "holonic business system".
18. Discuss the various types of "holonic networks".
19. Mention the similarities and differences between Reengineering and Continuous improvement.

16.25 DISCUSSION QUESTIONS

1. "For organisations that want to survive and grow, improvement is not an option but a compulsion" Critically examine the statement.
2. "Reengineering requires looking at the fundamental processes of the business from a cross – functional perspective" – Explain.
3. "A process selected for reengineering should be a core process, which has great scope for 'break–through improvement rather than incremental improvement" Do you agree or not. Justify your answer.

4. "Reengineering requires focusing on critical processes, often using cross functional teams, information technology, leadership and process analysis" – Elaborate.
5. "The concept of reengineering holds a significant promise for the service sector" – Explain.
6. "Incremental and break–through improvement are complementary approaches that fall under the total quality umbrella, both are necessary to remain competitive" – Comment on the statement.
7. "Some people have said that both TQM and Reengineering are the same; which others have argued that they are incompatible. Michael Hammer argues that the two concepts are compatible and actually complement each other" – What is your opinion? – Justify your answer.

16.26 ASSIGNMENTS

1. Identify a process in your college or workplace. Use the principles of process redesign to suggest improvements.
2. Visit the Websites of the following organisations and prepare a report on the implementation of Business Process Reengineering and the improvements achieved through BPR.
   (i) Mahindra and Mahindra
   (ii) Infosys technologies
   (iii) Wipro Infotek
   (iv) IBM credit corporation
   (v) South-West Airlines

16.27 CHAPTER CASE

THE SATURN PROJECT

In June 1982, General Motors (GM) assigned its Advanced Product and Design team a task to find answer to the question "Can GM build a world-class-quality small car in the U.S. that can compete successfully with the imports?" This effort grew into what GM called *"The Saturn Project"*. The team used a "clean-slate" approach – unbound by traditional thinking and industry practices to set up the small car project. This approach afforded the opportunity to design manufacturing process in parallel with the product and to adopt "lean production" philosophies and techniques. Saturn Project faced a challenge to eliminate the $2000 cost advantage that Japanese automakers had over US manufacturers.

To face this challenging task, GM formed another group known as "Group of 99" composed of GM managers and staff personnel from 17 GM divisions and United Auto Workers members from 140 regions with the objective of improving management labour relations at GM divisions. These two functions revealed their willingness to work together as partners of business to accomplish business objectives. In 1985 the Saturn Project merged with the "Group 99" to become the *"Saturn Cooperation"*. GM established Saturn as a wholly owned subsidiary with a $5 billion commitment. A "Gang of six" was appointed including a president and vice presidents for planning, engineering, manufacturing, sales and finance.

The newly assembled group separated into Research Teams which visited 49 GM plants and 60 benchmark companies world wide to gather ideas in preparation for setting up the new system. This new group had the opportunity of starting everything new and take some risks in high technology unlike other units of GM. GM planned to export successful processes and operations developed at Saturn to improve efficiency and competitiveness of all its manufacturing facilities.

Five years after selecting the site for Saturn at Spring Hill, Tennessee and establishing the manufacturing facility, the first Saturn rolled off the assembly line in 1990. Saturn went on to roll out its one millionth car in early summer 1995. The sales increased to 2,67,450 cars in 1994 from that of 2,28,833 in 1993. (Saturn's share of the total US new car market was more than 3%). Saturn's mission included a commitment to protect and preserve the environment.

The Spring Hill plant was a "fully integrated" auto factory which means all major parts for Saturn's various models of cars, sedans and wagons were manufactured at one facility. This facilitated better interaction between business units and perpetuation of quality mindedness and information exchange throughout the system.

Saturn manufactured roughly one car per minute (1150 cars in a day of 2 shifts of 10 hours each). In 1995, the average price of a Saturn automobile was $14,500. Approximately 8000 team members worked at Spring Hill facility. Saturn had three major "business units" – Powertrain (engine and transmission), Body Systems and Vehicle Systems (general assembly and interior systems).

Production Activities:

Powertrain – Die casting operation, lost foam casting, transmission assembly, engine machining line and final engine assembly.

Body systems – Steel body (or frame) components, body panels, body fabrication and painting.

Vehicle systems – Skillet application, cockpit operation, trim installation, toweyor operation, exterior (body) panels scissor lift, interior systems.

Quality and Teamwork : Quality is paramount to success in the small car market. Meeting and exceeding customer requirements and expectations on a consistent basis was one of the Saturn's key strategies for success. Quality at Saturn starts at the shop floor level with the teams (work units) Teams are responsible for day to day car building and product quality monitoring.

All Saturn employees are called "team members" and every one at the Saturn is associated with a team. All shop floor United AutoWorkers members are on a team. Each business unit (Powertrain, Body system and Vehicle systems) had about 217 work units (or teams). Business units were divided into modules which are subdivided into teams (or work units).

Within each team one person was responsible for gathering and analysing information on quality issues and share the information with other team members. Module quality advisors look at outgoing quality (between teams). These advisors provided a communication bridge between the teams so each team knew what its internal customer upstream and downstream in the process required to make a quality, world-class vehicle. A series of Quality Councils, composed of team members and management were holding meeting on a periodic basis to set quality goals and provide general direction in terms of quality elements.

When problems arise, causes were identified by the teams. Some times, team members sought the help of engineering and operations staff in dividing what actions to take to solve the problems. A "Total Quality Action Team" (TQAT) used to be formed to work on a specific problem. Saturn team members were empowered to decide how to perform work or solve problems. All decisions were made by consensus with the goal of promoting quality.

Quality was at focus from the very beginning of the Saturn project in ascertaining what its target customers were looking for in a vehicle. Other quality inputs obtained through warranty information and outside surveys were also taken into consideration to improve quality on a continuous basis. All customer-related information gathered were analysed and formatted to be understood by the teams. This helped team members understand what piece of the information they can affect to improve the product from the customer's perspective. Customer feedback helped to improve product quality at Saturn.

Discussion Questions :

1. Discuss the role of TQM in the Saturn Project.
2. Explain how the Saturn project in effect "reengineered" the automobile manufacture process?
3. How did and how should the Saturn teams impact TQM?
4. How was quality ensured at Saturn? Discuss the role of Quality Councils and TQAT.

CHAPTER 17

MANAGING SERVICE QUALITY

LEARNING OBJECTIVES

After reading this chapter, you should be able to:

- Understand the meaning of 'service quality' and service environment.
- Discuss the dimensions and determinants of service quality.
- Discuss the factors that influence customer perceptions of service.
- Describe the general model for service quality.
- Describe the Gronroose model and PZB model of service quality.
- Discuss the generic dimensions used by customers to evaluate service quality.
- Discuss the role of personnel in service delivery.
- Discuss the various elements of "costs of service quality" and the concept of "return on service quality".

17.0 INTRODUCTION

Today service industries dominate our economy. The service sector accounts for more than 70 percent of jobs and it is on the rise and expected to reach 85 percent in the near future. Quality management and quality improvement are mandatory for the success of the service sector of our economy. The statistical techniques discussed in earlier chapters are also applicable for service operations. But there are major differences in the quality characteristics of manufacturing and services. This makes it necessary to have different measurement processes and focus of the management. In service industries, it is not enough if the product meets the functional requirements of the customer, but the employee behaviour must also meet customer's expectations and must be of a high standard. **Then, *the service concept is a combination of both technical and human behavioural aspects.*** The human behavioural aspect is difficult to quantify, measure and control.

Quality in Services

Service is a social act which takes place in direct contact between the customer and representative of the service provider. The service concept combines both technical and behavioural aspects.

Service has been defined as *"a social act which takes place in direct contact between the customer and representatives of the service company".* A service might be as simple as handling a complaint or as complex as a home mortgage. **Many organisations are pure service businesses, their products are *intangible.*** Examples would include education, banking, insurance, defence, municipal services, welfare services, legal services, health services and so on. Other examples of services are marketing, travelling and tours, restaurants, public utilities (including electricity, gas, water and telephone services) and transportation. **Some service industries provide a tangible product and an intangible component that affects customer satisfaction.** Certain service functions are found in both the manufacturing and service sectors. For instance, customer services (after-sales service, warranty replacement, repairs under guarantee clauses etc.) purchasing, accounting, pay roll and personnel are service functions that support the manufacturing function in manufacturing organisations. Even research and development (R&D) function is considered as a service function.

Difference between Goods and Services

(i) Services are ***usually intangible*** as opposed to goods which are ***tangible.***

(ii) Services are often ***produced and consumed simultaneously.*** *For example,* the surgeon executes (or produces) a surgical operation which is "consumed" by the patient as it is produced or executed.

(iii) Services are ***often unique.*** *For example,* the mix of financial coverage, such as investments and insurance policies may vary for each customer as per his/her unique requirements. Goods may be ***standardised*** to meet most of the requirements of a large number of customers.

(iv) Services have ***high customer interaction.*** Services are often difficult to standardise, automate and make as efficient as we would like because customer interaction demands uniqueness.

(v) Services have ***inconsistent product definition.*** Product definition may be rigorous, as in the case of auto insurance policy, but inconsistent because policy holders change their cars.

(vi) Services are often-***knowledge based,*** as in the case of educational, medical and legal services.

(vii) Services are frequently ***dispersed.*** Dispersion occurs because services are frequently brought to the customer/client via a local office, a retail outlet or even a house call. ***Box 17.1* shows the differences between goods and services.**

Eventhough we can differentiate goods from services, the distinction is not clear-cut. **In reality, almost all services are a mixture of service and a tangible product.** *Similarly,* the sales of many goods includes or requires a service. For instance, many products have the service component of financing (automobile financing) and transportation (automobile sales). Many goods also require after-sales training and maintenance. (*e.g.*, photo-copiers). When a tangible product is not included in the services, the service is known as a ***pure service.*** For instance, counselling is a pure service.

Box 17.1 : Differences between Goods and services	
Attributes of Goods	**Attributes of Services**
• Tangible products	• Intangible products
• Can be inventoried	• Can not be inventoried
• Can be resold	• Reselling is unusual
• Selling is distinct from production	• Selling is often part of the service
• Product is transportable	• Provider, not product (service) is often transportable
• Location of facility is important for cost	• Location of facility is important for customer contact
• Often easy to automate	• Often difficult to automate
• Revenue is generated primarily from the tangible product.	• Revenue is generated primarily from the intangible service.

***Box 17.2* lists the differences between manufacturing and service sector**

Box 17.2 : Differences in the Manufacturing and Services Sector	
Manufacturing Sector	**Service Sector**
Product is tangible	Service consists of tangible and intangible components
Back orders or inventories are possible	Services can not be stored
Producer or company is the only party involved in the making of the product	Producer and consumer are both involved in the delivery of the service
Product can be resold	Services can not be resold
Customer usually provides formal specifications for the product	Formal specifications need not be provided by the consumer. In fact, in monopolies involving public utilities such as electricity, gas, telephone etc., federal and state laws dictate the requirements.
Customer acceptance of the product Is easily quantifiable	Customer satisfaction is difficult to quantify because a behavioural component associated with the delivery of the service is involved
Ownership of a product changes hands at a specific point in time	Rendering of a service takes place over an interval of time.

17.1 THE SERVICE ENVIRONMENT

Environmental trends that impact on service and quality issues relate to consumer's awareness and expectations, technological developments and competitive elements.

Consumers (individuals, house hold or businesses) are more aware of the alternatives on offer (products, services and provider organisations) and increasing standards of service. They have high expectations of service and quality and are increasingly critical of the quality of service they experience. Customers' expectations include what they feel a service/product should offer and what they relate to the company and its marketing mix, both the traditional elements (product, price, place and promotion) and the extended elements (physical evidence, process and people). The physical environment includes tangible clues which might be essential (for e.g., computers in a travel agency) or peripheral clues (decor, uniform) to a service being bought. The service process is also critical, if systems are poor (e.g. breakdown of computer access to customer accounts in a bank), employees get blamed and consumers perceive poor quality service. Personnel are also integral to the production of a service and even though their degree of customer contact varies, all have a contribution to make Advances in technology include: *(a)* management information system, *(b)* marketing information systems and *(c)* the development of the Internet for accessing information and for shopping These technological developments provide a major contribution to customer –

service provider interactions and increase levels of customer service. Increased mechanization and computerisation results in increases in speed, efficiency, accuracy and improved services even though depersonalisation of service also results. On the other hand, depersonalised service could lead to reduced customer loyalty. But technology can free employees' time and allow them to concentrate on the customer and enhance customer – service provider interaction. It must be noted that technology will not replace people in the provision of service whatever may be the level of automation and use of Internet in providing services to customers.

The business environment has become increasingly complex and competitive as a result of economic conditions, government regulations and deregulations, and increased customer choice and sophistication. Competing companies appreciate the importance of customer service and quality, and the possible opportunities for attaining differentiation and achieving a competitive edge by providing superior service. Consequently, service quality is viewed as a mechanism to achieve competitive edge in the market place and also an important factor in strategic planning of business firms.

Benefits of Good Service

Good service enhances customers loyalty through customer satisfaction.

Organisations having no focus on service quality will face problems such as: *(a)* complaints from both consumers and employees, *(b)* associated financial and other costs, *(c)* adverse word of mouth publicity and *(d)* employees having the organisation to join the competitors who have better quality image.

Organisations focusing on service quality programs can expect to have many benefits relating to customers, employees and corporate image. These are:

(i) Enhancing customer loyalty through customer satisfaction. Present customers who are satisfied with the service provided by the firm can help to generate repeat and increased business and may lead to the attraction of new customers from positive word of mouth communication.

(ii) Better relationships and rapport with customers will enable staff to identify customer needs and suggest relevant products and services.

(iii) Employees will have job satisfaction and morale, commitment to the company, good employer employee relationships and increased loyalty resulting in reduced employee turnover and costs of recruitment, selection and training.

(iv) Good service quality enhances corporate image and may provide insulation from price competition, some customers will pay a premium for reliable service quality.

(v) Overall, successful service quality leads to reduced costs and increased productivity and sales, market share, profitability and business performance.

Service Quality

Service quality is essentially concerned with meeting customer needs and requirements and with how well the service level delivered matches customer expectations.

Service quality includes both the quality of ***core services*** and ***facilitating*** **services,** which enhance the value of core services to the customer. Facilitating services are also provided by businesses that produce tangible goods. *For example,* in banking services, a checking account is a core service product whereas additional services provided by banks, such as automated teller services, and 24 hours telephone access to account information are facilitating services. Sometimes facilitating services may be more valuable to the customers than the core services. For instance, the fast food restaurant may produce tangible goods in the form of pizzas and french fries, which are the restaurant's core products. However, the restaurant's distinctive feature may be its ***quick service*** and ***friendliness of its service*** (which are the facilitating services).

The importance of quality in services cannot be under estimated. Nowadays many firms offering service lose their customers because of poor customer service. Studies have shown that firms can boost their profits by almost 100 percent by retaining just 5 percent more of their customers than their competitors retain. This is because the cost of acquiring new customers is much higher than the costs associated with retaining customers. Firms with loyal, long-time customers can financially outperform competitors with higher customer turnover even when their unit costs are higher and their market share is smaller.

The definitions of quality that apply to manufactured products apply equally to service products. The very nature of service implies that it must respond to the needs of the customer. The service must meet or exceed customer expectations. The production of services differs from manufacturing in many ways and these differences have important implications for quality management in services.

The eight dimensions of service quality are: *(i)* Performance *(ii)* Features *(iii)* Reliability *(iv)* Conformance *(v)* Durability *(vi)* Serviceability *(vii)* Aesthetics and *(viii)* Perceived quality

The eight dimensions of quality defined by Garvin which are applicable to services as well as manufactured goods are:

(i) ***Performance*** - a product's (good or service) operating characteristics.
(ii) ***Features:***
(iii) ***Reliability***
(iv) ***Conformance*** (to preestablished standards)
(v) ***Durability***
(vi) ***Serviceability***
(vii) ***Aesthetics***
(viii) ***Perceived quality.***

In addition to the above, services have other unique dimensions:

(i) **Time:** How long must a customer wait for the service and for completion of the service?
(ii) **Timeliness:** Will the package be delivered by 10.30 the next morning?
(iii) **Completeness:** Are all ordered items delivered?
(iv) **Courtesy:** Do front-line employees greet each customer?
(v) **Consistency:** Are services delivered in the same fashion each time for each customer?
(vi) **Acceptability and Convenience:** Is the service easy to obtain?
(vii) **Accuracy:** Is the service performed accurately the first time? and
(viii) **Responsiveness:** Can service personnel react quickly to unexpected problems?

Box 17.3 **lists ten determinants of service quality and** ***Box 17.4*** **presents four aspects of service quality that affect customer's perceptions.**

Box 17.3 : Ten Determinants of Service Quality

(i) ***Reliability*** involves consistency of performance and dependability. It means that the firm performs the service right the first time and also means that the firm honours its promises.

(ii) ***Responsiveness*** concerns the willingness or readiness of employee to provide service. It involves timeliness of service.

(iii) ***Competence*** means possession of the required skills and knowledge to perform the service.

(iv) ***Access*** involves approachability and ease of contact.

(v) ***Courtesy*** involves politeness, respect, considerations and friendliness of contact personnel (including receptionists, telephone operators etc).

(vi) ***Communication*** means keeping customers informed in language they can understand and listening to them. It may mean that the company has to adjust its language for different customers – increasing the level of sophistication with a well-educated customer and speaking simply and plainly with a novice.

(vii) ***Credibility*** involves trustworthiness, believability and honesty. It involves having the customer's best interest at heart.

(viii) ***Security*** is the freedom from danger, risks or doubt.

(ix) ***Understanding/knowing the customer*** involves making the effort to understand the customer's needs.

(x) ***Tangibles*** include the physical evidence of the service.

Box 17.4 : Four Aspects of Service Quality that Affect Customer's Perceptions

(i) **Technical Quality**: to include skills of service personnel and the design of the service system.

(ii) **Integrative Quality**: the case with which different portions of the service delivery system work together.

(iii) **Functional Quality**: to embrace all aspects of the manner in which the service is delivered to the customer, including style, environment and availability.

(iv) **Outcome Quality**: whether or not the actual service product meets both service standards or specifications and customer needs/expectations.

17.2 TOTAL QUALITY MANAGEMENT IN SERVICES

Quality of services is more difficult to measure than quality of manufactured goods.

Quality of services is more difficult to measure than quality of manufactured goods. Generally a user of services has a few features in mind as a basis for comparison among alternatives. Lack of one feature may eliminate a service firm from consideration.

Extensive in-depth interviews with consumer focus groups in USA resulted in the following conclusions:

(i) ***Consumer's perceptions of service quality result from a comparison of their before-service expectations with their actual service experience.*** In other words service quality is judged on the basis of whether it meets expectations.

(ii) ***Quality perceptions are derived from the service process as well as from the service outcome.*** From the consumer's view point, the way the service is performed can be as important as the actual service.

(iii) ***Services quality is of two types, normal and exceptional.*** This mean *(a)* there is a quality level at which the regular service is delivered. *(b)* there is a quality level at which "exceptions" or "problems" are handled.

Component of Service System Quality

Employees and Information technology are the two key components of service system quality.

The differences between manufacturing and service organisation create distinct challenges for managing quality. Many service organisations such as air lines, banks and hotels have well developed quality assurance systems but they are more product-oriented than service oriented. Standards for intangible quality characteristics are difficult to establish. Often they must be set judgmentally and then tested for satisfactory levels, because ***employee performance and behaviour* and *service transaction speed* are the strongest determinants of perceived service quality. The two key components of service system quality are *employees* and *information technology.***

Employees: Customers evaluate a service primarily by the quality of human contact. It has been found by research that when service employee's job satisfaction is high, customer satisfaction is high and that when employee job satisfaction is low, customer satisfaction is also low. Many service companies have the motto ***"If we take care of our employees, they will take care of our customers".***

Information technology: Information technology incorporates computing, communication, data processing and various other means of converting data into useful information. Information technology is essential in modern service organisations because of high volumes of information that must be processed and also because customers demand service at ever-increasing speeds. Intelligent use of information technology not only leads to improved quality and productivity, but also to competitive advantage. Every service industry is exploiting information technology to improve customer service.

***Box 17.5* lists the distinguishing characteristics of service quality.**

Box 17.5 : Distinguishing Characteristics of Service Quality

(i) Behaviour of the delivery person.
(ii) Image of the organisation (service provider)
(iii) The customer present during the service process and performing the final inspection
(iv) The measure of the output is difficult to define.
(v) Variance and acceptance ranges may not apply.
(vi) Adjusting the control system if the customer is present.

The most significant problem with the delivery of services is that it is typically measured at the customer interface – the one-on-one, face-to-face interaction between supplier and customer. If a problem exists, it is already too late to fix it.

Customer Expectations in Service

Thorough knowledge of customer expectations is critical to service marketers in delivering quality service.

Customer expectations are beliefs about service delivery that function as standards or reference points against which performance is judged. Because customers compare their perceptions of performance with these reference points when evaluating service quality, **thorough knowledge about customer expectations is critical to service marketers. Knowing what the customer expects is the first and possibly most critical step in delivering quality service.** Being wrong about what customers want can mean losing a customer's business when another company hits the target exactly.

***Exhibit 17.1* highlights the role of expectations in service.**

Exhibit 17.1 : The Role of Expectations in Service

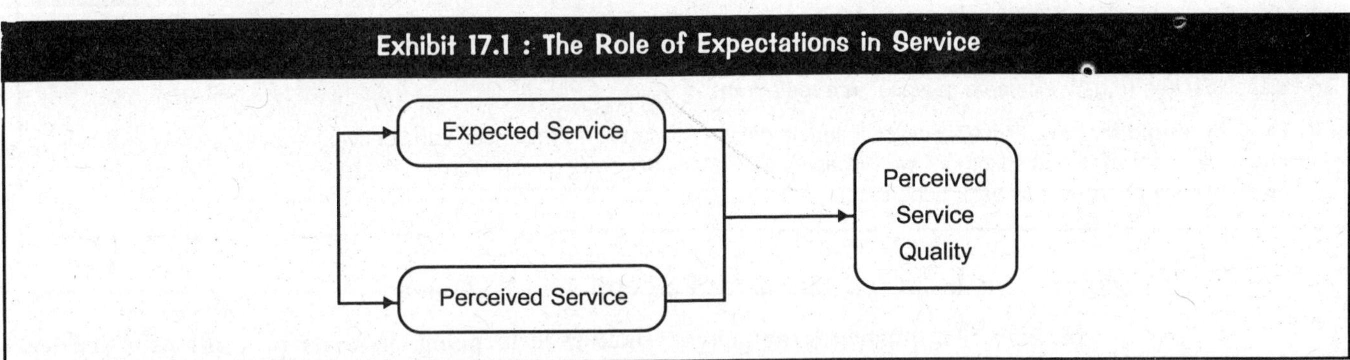

Two levels of expected service are: *(i)* desired service and *(ii)* adequate service

Expected Service: Two levels of expectations are *(i)* ***desired service*** and *(ii)* ***adequate service.*** The ***desired service*** is defined as the level of service the customer hopes to receive – the "wished for" level of performance. Desired service is a blend of what the customer believes "can be" and "should be". *For example,* a student will engage the services of his/her college's placement office when he or she is ready to graduate. The student expects the placement office to find him or her a job in the right organisation for the right salary – because that is what he or she hopes and wishes for.

The ***adequate service*** is the level of service the customer will accept. *For example,* in the case of placement service, the economy may constrain the availability of ideal job openings in companies. In this situation customers (students) hope to achieve their service desires but recognise that this is not always possible. For this reason, they hold another, lower level expectation for the threshold of acceptable service. This lower level of service is termed *adequate service.*

The "zone of tolerance" refers to the difference between what is desired and what is considered adequate.

Zones of Tolerance: Consumer's expectations with respect to dimensions of service quality are generally reasonable, for example, they expect luggage to arrive with them on an aircraft, and planes to arrive on time, most of the time. They also expect basics. For example from a hotel in terms of security, cleanliness, and being treated with respect. However customer expectations vary depending on a host of circumstances and experiences and they also vary over time. Also, experience with one service provider can influence expectations of other service providers providing the same type of service or an entirely different kind of service.

In addition, consumer's have what is referred to as ***"zones of tolerance"*** – the difference between ***what is desired*** and ***what is considered adequate***. The desired level of service is what the consumer hopes to receive, a blend of what 'can' and 'should' be, which is a function of past experience. The adequate level is what they find acceptable, it is partly based on their assessment of what the service will be, the ***'predicted'*** *service* and it depends on alternatives available. Tolerance zones vary between individuals, between service aspects and with experience, and tend to be smaller for outcome features than for process dimensions.

In addition, if options are limited or non existent, desire may not decrease but tolerance levels may be higher. Conversly, if many alternatives are available, it is easy to switch and tolerance zones are more limited. Further, expectations are higher in emergency situations and when something was not right the first time.

Customer Perceptions of Service

How customers perceive services and how they assess whether they have experienced quality service, whether they are satisfied and whether they have received good value are important in services marketing.

Box 17.6 **lists three factors of service which affect the service quality and customer satisfaction.**

Box 17.6 : Factors Affecting Service Quality and Customer Satisfaction

(i) Hygiene factors: Those that are expected by the customer, failure to deliver them will cause dissatisfaction (e.g., cleanliness in restaurants, train arrival time, lack of queues etc)

(ii) **Enhancing factors:** Those which lead to customer satisfaction, failure to deliver them will not necessarily cause dissatisfaction (e.g., welcome of a waiter in a restaurant).

(iii) **Dual threshold factors:** Those for which failure to deliver will cause dissatisfaction and delivery above a certain level will enhance customer's perceptions of service and lead to satisfaction (e.g. explanation of a mortgage service repayment level, interest charges, pay back period etc).

Factors that Influence Customer Perceptions of Service

Exhibit 17.2 **illustrates the primary factors influencing customer perceptions of service.**

Exhibit 17.2 : Factors Influencing Customer Perceptions of Service

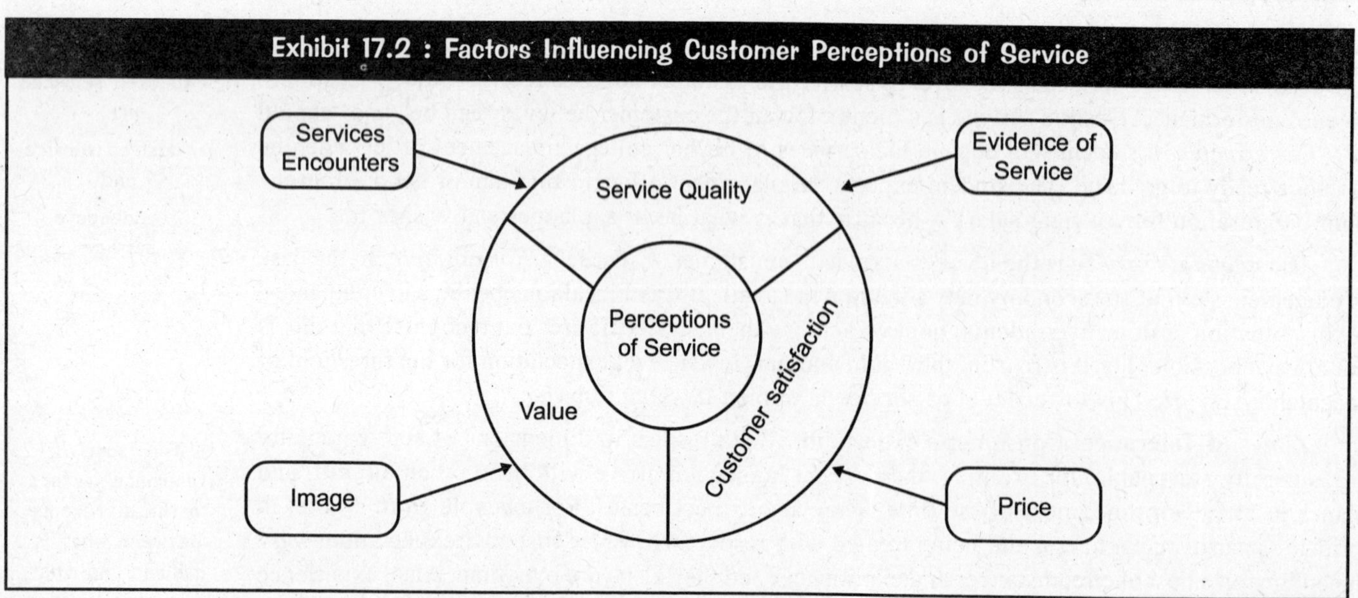

Factors influencing customer perceptions of service are:
(i) service encounters
(ii) evidence of service
(iii) Image and
(iv) Price

(i)* Service encounters:** ***Service encounters or the **"moment of truth"** occurs when the customer interacts with the service provider. *For example,* among the service encounters a hotel customer experiences are: *(i)* checking into the hotel, *(ii)* being taken to a room by a bell person, *(iii)* eating a restaurant meal *(iv)* requesting a wake-up call and *(v)* checking out.

Among the service encounters that a business-to-business customer experiences in purchase and use of a piece of equipment are: *(i)* sales contract, *(ii)* delivery, *(iii)* installation, *(iv)* billing and *(v)* servicing. It is in these encounters that customers receive a snapshot of the organisation's services quality and each encounter contributes to the customer's overall satisfaction and willingness to do a business with the organisation (service provider) again. From the organisation's point of view, each encounter thus presents an opportunity to prove its potential as a quality service provider and to increase customer loyalty. The number of service encounters may vary from service to service. *For example,* the Disney Corporation estimates that each of its amusement park customers experiences 74 service encounters and that negative experience in any of them can lead to a negative overall evaluation. Mistakes or problems that occur in the early levels of the service cascade are particularly critical, because a failure at one point results in a greater risk for dissatisfaction at each ensuing level.

***(ii)* The Evidence of Service:** Another major set of factors influencing customer perceptions of service is referred to as **"evidence of service".** Because services are intangibles, customers are searching for evidence of service in every interaction they have with an organisation (service provider).

***Exhibit 17.3* illustrates the evidence of service.**

Exhibit 17.3 : The Evidence of Service (from the customer's point of view)

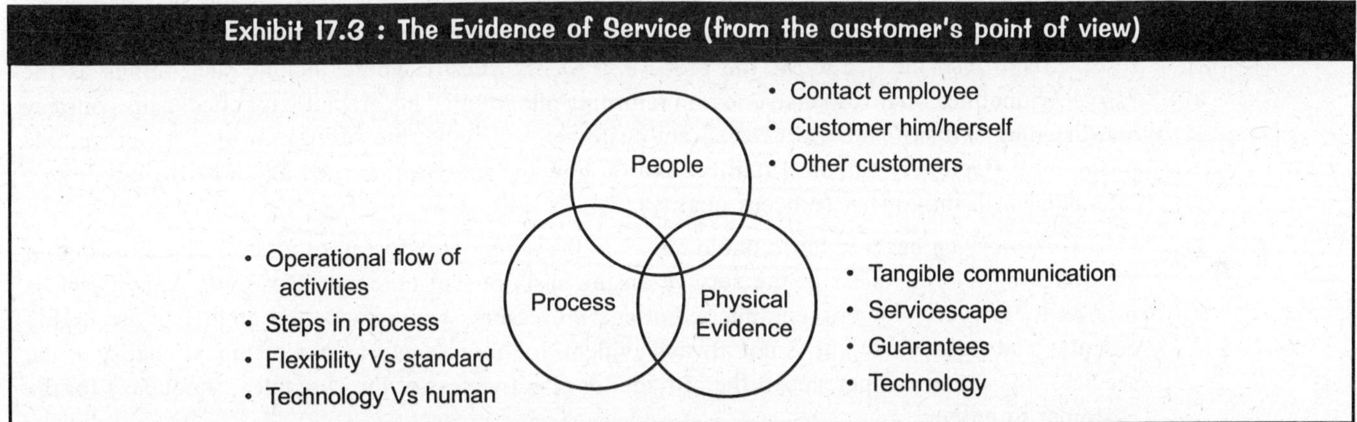

All of the above service elements or a subset of them, are present in every service encounter a customer has with a service firm and are critically important in managing service encounter quality and creating customer satisfaction. *For example,* when a patient has an appointment with a doctor in a health clinic, the first encounters of the visit is frequently with a receptionist in the reception room (a clinic waiting area). The quality of that encounter will be judged by how the appointment registration ***process*** works (Is there a line? How long is the waiting time? Is the registration system computerised and accurate?), the actions and attitude of the ***people*** (Is the receptionist courteous? Helpful, knowledgeable? Does he/she treat the patient as an individual? Does he/she handle inquiries fairly and efficiently?) and the ***physical evidence*** of the service (Is the waiting area clean and comfortable?). The three types of evidence may be differentially important depending on the type of service encounter (remote, phone, face-to-face).

(iii)* Image:** Beyond impressions from the immediate service encounters and evaluations of service evidence, customer perceptions can be influenced by the image or reputation of the organisation. ***The organisational image is defined as perceptions of an organisation reflected in the associations held in consumer memory. These associations can be very concrete such as hours of operation, number of flights per day, length of time in business, ease of access etc. Or they can be less concrete and even emotional, such as excitement, trustworthiness, tradition, ingenuity, fun and reliability. The association can relate to the service experience itself, the company or the user of the service.

Organisational image can exist on several levels. A large organisation with multiple outlets or branches has a corporate image. But it also has a local image that is closely associated with a specific location. A favourable and well-known image – corporate and/or local – is an asset for any organisation because image can impact perceptions of quality, value and satisfaction.

***(iv)* Price: The price of the service can also greatly influence perceptions of quality, satisfaction and value.** Because services are intangible and often difficult to judge before purchase, price is frequently relied on as a surrogate indicator that will influence quality expectations and perceptions. If the price is very high, customers are likely to expect high quality and their actual perceptions will be influenced by this expectation. If the price is too high, the organisation may be sending a message of unconcern for customers. On the other hand, if the price is too low, customers may doubt the organisation's ability to deliver the quality.

The price charged will also figure greatly into customer's perceptions of value, particularly following consumption of the service when customers assess whether the benefits they received were worth the cost of the service.

After knowing the factors that influence customer perceptions of service, it is important to know how customers judge service quality:

Process Vs Technical Outcome Quality: Ultimately, consumers judge the quality of services on their perceptions of the ***technical outcome*** provided and on how that outcome was delivered. *For example,* a legal service client will judge the quality of the outcome or how the court case was resolved and also the quality of the process. ***Process quality*** would include such things as the lawyer's timeliness, has responsiveness in returning phone calls, his empathy for clients, his courtesy and listening skills. *Similarly,* a restaurant customer will judge the service on his/her perceptions of the meal (technical outcome quality) and on how the meal was served and how the employees interacted with him or her (process quality).

If the service has a specific outcome, as in the winning or losing of a law suit, the customer can judge the effectiveness of the service on the basis of that outcome. However, many services offered by lawyers, doctors, engineers, college professors, accountants and architects are highly complex and a clear outcome is not always evident. In these situations, the technical quality of the service – the actual competence of the provider or effectiveness of the outcome – is not easy for the customer to judge.

Service Quality Dimensions: Research suggests that customers do not perceive quality as a unidirectional concept – that is, **customer's assessment of quality includes perceptions of multiple factors.** *For example,* the following eight dimensions of quality are applicable to all goods and services: ***performance, features, reliability, conformance, durability, serviceability, aesthetics*** **and *perceived quality.***

***Box 17.7* lists major dimensions of service quality**

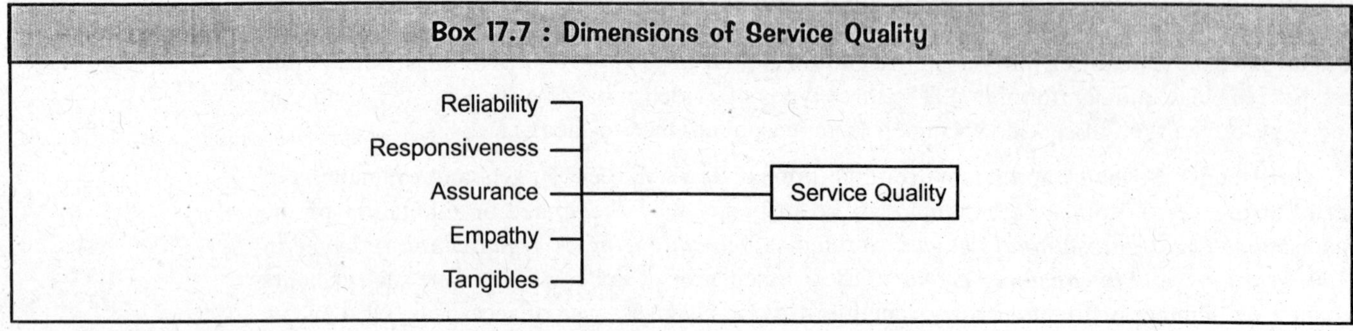

Other researchers have found that consumers consider five dimensions in their assessment of service quality as shown in *Box 17.8*.

***Exhibit 17.4* describes the five stars of service quality.**

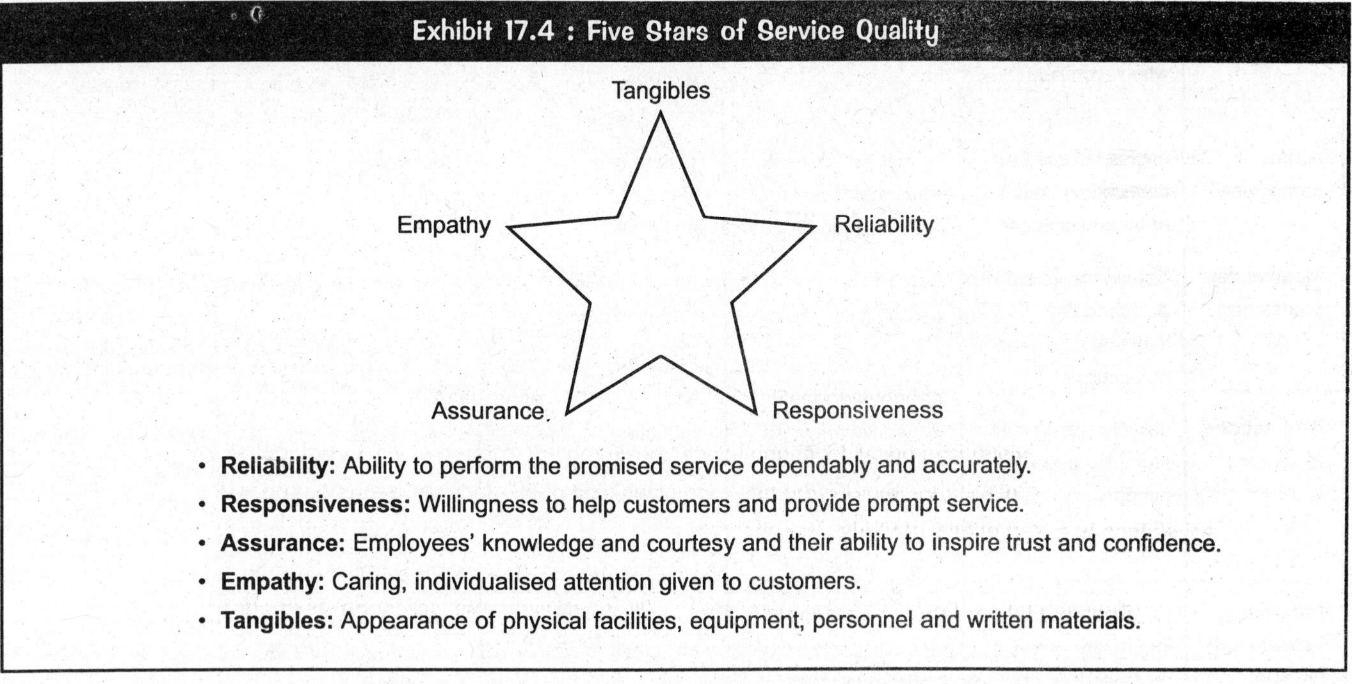

- **Reliability:** Ability to perform the promised service dependably and accurately.
- **Responsiveness:** Willingness to help customers and provide prompt service.
- **Assurance:** Employees' knowledge and courtesy and their ability to inspire trust and confidence.
- **Empathy:** Caring, individualised attention given to customers.
- **Tangibles:** Appearance of physical facilities, equipment, personnel and written materials.

These dimensions represent how consumers organise information about service quality in their minds. These five dimensions of service quality were found relevant for services such as banking, insurance, appliance repair and maintenance, securities brokerage, long distance telephone service, automobile, repair service and the like. These dimensions are also applicable to retail and business services. Some times, customers will use all the dimensions to determine service quality perception, at other times not. *For example,* in a remote encounter such as an encounter with an ATM, empathy is not likely to be a relevant dimension. And in a phone encounter such as scheduling a repair call, tangibles will not be relevant.

We will expand on each of the five dimensions of service quality and provide illustration of how customers judge each dimension. ***Box* 17.8 gives examples of each for consumer service (car repair, airline, medical care), business-to-business service (architecture) and internal service (information processing within a company).**

Reliability is the ability to perform the promised service dependably and accurately.

Reliability: (Delivering on Promises) – Of the five dimensions of service quality, reliability has been consistently shown to be the **most important determinant of perceptions of service quality among majority of customers. *Reliability is defined as the ability to perform* the promised service dependably and accurately.** In the broadest sense, reliability means that the company delivers on its promises about delivery, service provision, problem resolution and pricing (service attributes).

All firms need to be aware of customer expectations of reliability. When service failures occur, customers' tolerance zones are likely to shrink and their adequate and desired service levels are likely to rise.

Responsiveness is the willingness to help customers and to provide prompt service.

Responsiveness: (Being Willing to Help). Responsiveness is the willingness to help customers and to provide prompt service. This dimension emphasizes attentiveness and promptness in dealing with customer requests, questions and complaints and problems.

To excel on the dimension of responsiveness, a company must be certain to view the process of service delivery and the handling of requests from the customer's point of view rather than the company's point of view.

Box 17.8 : Examples of how Customers Judge the Five Dimensions of Service Quality

	Reliability	Responsiveness	Assurance	Empathy	Tangibles
Car repair (Consumer)	Problem fixed the first time and ready when promised	Accessible; no waiting; responds to requests	Knowledgeable mechanics	Acknowledges customer by name; remembers previous problems and preferences	Repair facility; waiting area; uniforms; equipment
Airline (consumer)	Flights to promised destinations depart & arrive on schedule	Prompt and speedy system for ticketing;in-flight, baggage handling	Trusted name; good safely record, competent employees	Understanding of special individual needs; anticipates customer need	Aircraft; ticketing counters; baggage area; uniforms
Medical care (consumer)	Appointments are kept on schedule; diagnoses prove to be accurate	Accessible; no waiting; willingness to listen	Knowledge, skills, credentials, reputation	Acknowledges patient as a person; remembers previous problems; good listening; patience	Waiting room; exam room; equipment; written materials
Architecture (business)	delivers plans when promised and within budget	Returns phone calls; adapts to changes	Credentials; reputation; name in the community; knowledge and skills	Understands client's industry; acknowledges and adapts to specific client needs; gets to know the client	Office area; reports; plans themselves; billing statements; dress of employees
Information processing (internal)	Provides needed information when requested	Prompt response to requests;not "bureau-cratic", deals with problems promptly	Knowledgeable staff; well-trained, credentials	Knows internal customers as individuals; understand individual and departmental needs	Internal reports; office area; dress of employees

Assurance, is employees' knowledge and courtesy.

Assurance: (Inspiring Trust and Confidence): Assurance is defined as employees' knowledge and courtesy and the ability of the firm and its employees to inspire trust and confidence. This dimension is likely to be particularly important for services that the customer perceives high risk and/or about which they feel certain about their ability to evaluate outcomes, *for example,* banking, insurance, brokerage, medical and legal service.

Trust and confidence may be embodied in the person who links the customer to the company, *for example,* securities brokers, insurance agents, lawyers and counsellors. In such service contexts the company seeks to build trust and loyalty between key contact people and individual customers.

Empathy is 'caring, individual attention" the firm provides its customers.

Empathy (Treating Customers as Individuals): Empathy is defined as the caring, individualised attention the firm provides its customers. The essence of empathy is conveying, through personalised or customised service, that customers are unique and special. Customers want to feel understood by and important to firms that provide service to them. Personnel at small service firms often know their customers by name and build relationships that reflect their personal knowledge of customer requirements and preferences. In business-to-business service, customers want supplier firms to understand their industries, issues and needs and often more customised services.

'Tangibles' refer to the physical aspects of service such as facilities, equipment, people and communication materials.

Tangibles: (Representing the Service Physically): Tangibles are defined as the appearance of physical facilities, equipment, personnel and communication materials. All of these provide physical representations or image of the service that customers, particularly new customers, will use to evaluate quality. Service industries that emphasise tangibles in their strategies include hospitality services where the customer visits the establishment to receive the service, such as restaurants and hotels, retail stores and entertainment companies.

Customer Satisfaction: Eventhough the terms **"satisfaction"** and **"quality"** are often used interchangeably, these two concepts are fundamentally different in their underlying causes and outcomes. While they have certain things in common, satisfaction is generally viewed as a broader concept than service quality assessment, which focusses specifically on dimensions of service. With this view, **perceived service quality is a component of customer satisfaction.**

***Exhibit 17.5* illustrates growing agreement on the distinctions between the two constructs.** As shown, service quality is a focussed evaluation that reflects the customer's perception of the five specific dimensions of service. Satisfaction on the other hand is more inclusive. It is influenced by perceptions of service quality, product quality and price as well as situational factors and personal factors.

Another difference between quality and satisfaction is that quality perceptions can occur in the absence of actual experience with an organisation which provides a service whereas customer satisfaction can only be assessed following an actual experience with an organisation.

Exhibit 17.5 : Customer Perceptions of Quality and Customer Satisfaction

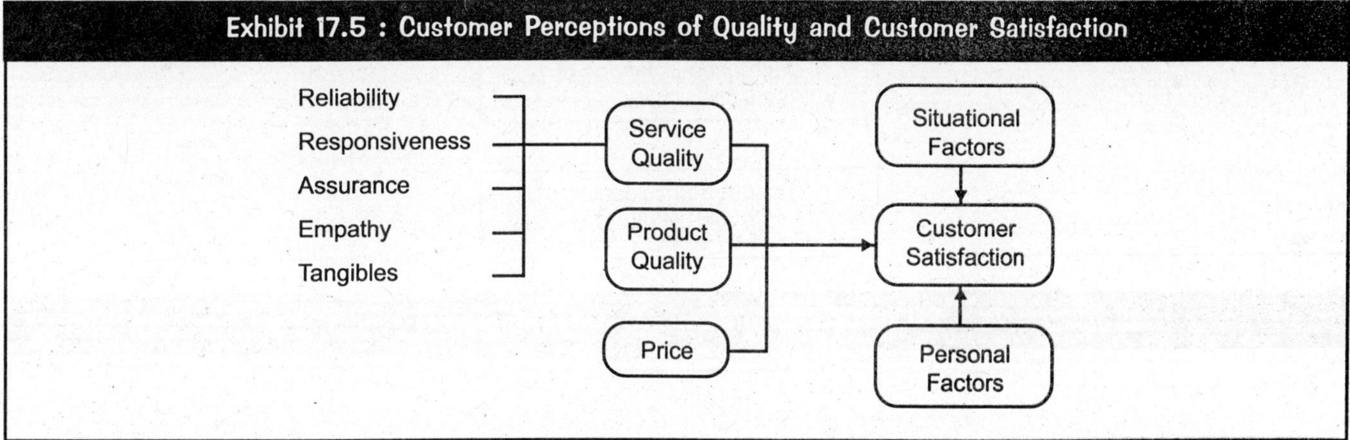

Understanding Quality Management in Services

Quality has emerged as a key competitive component of strategies of service organisations. Three reasons which may account for necessary relevance of quality management in services are:

(i) Service organisations need to find ways of creating ***differential advantage*** by having better service levels than their competitors.

(ii) Increasing level of ***consumerism*** and the greater media attention on quality have meant that service organisations have to be more responsive to quality issues.

(iii) There has been growing sophistication of consumer markets, with the non-price factors such as ***image, product positioning*** and ***service delivery processes*** becoming more important.

Approaches to Quality Management: Two approaches to quality management are: *(i)* Product attributed approach and *(ii)* Consumer oriented approach.

Product Attributed Approach: In this approach customers try to judge the products (goods and services) conformance to standardised requirements which have been set. Organisations try to control their products using an ***internal product perspective.***

***Exhibit 17.6* illustrates this approach.**

Product attributed approach focusses on the following elements: Performance, Features, Reliability, Conformance, Durability, Serviceability, Aesthetics and Perceived quality.

Consumer Oriented Approach: This approach, also known as ***user based approach,*** starts from the assumption that ***"quality lies in the eyes of the beholder".*** This approach recognises that the holistic process of service delivery has to be controlled by taking into consideration the expectations and attitudes of service clients. The major problem with this approach is its equating of quality with maximum satisfaction. **The consumer oriented approach is illustrated in *Exhibit 17.7.***

Two broad approaches to quality management are:
(i) Product attributed approach and
(ii) Consumer-oriented approach

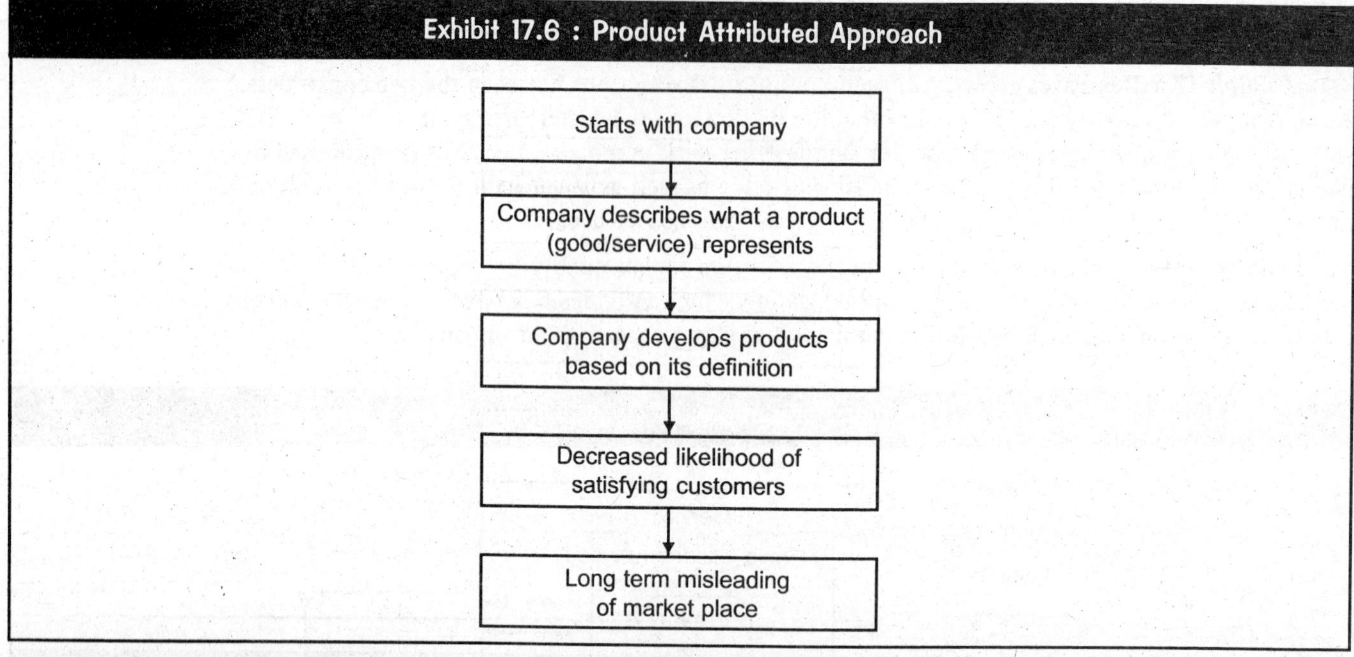

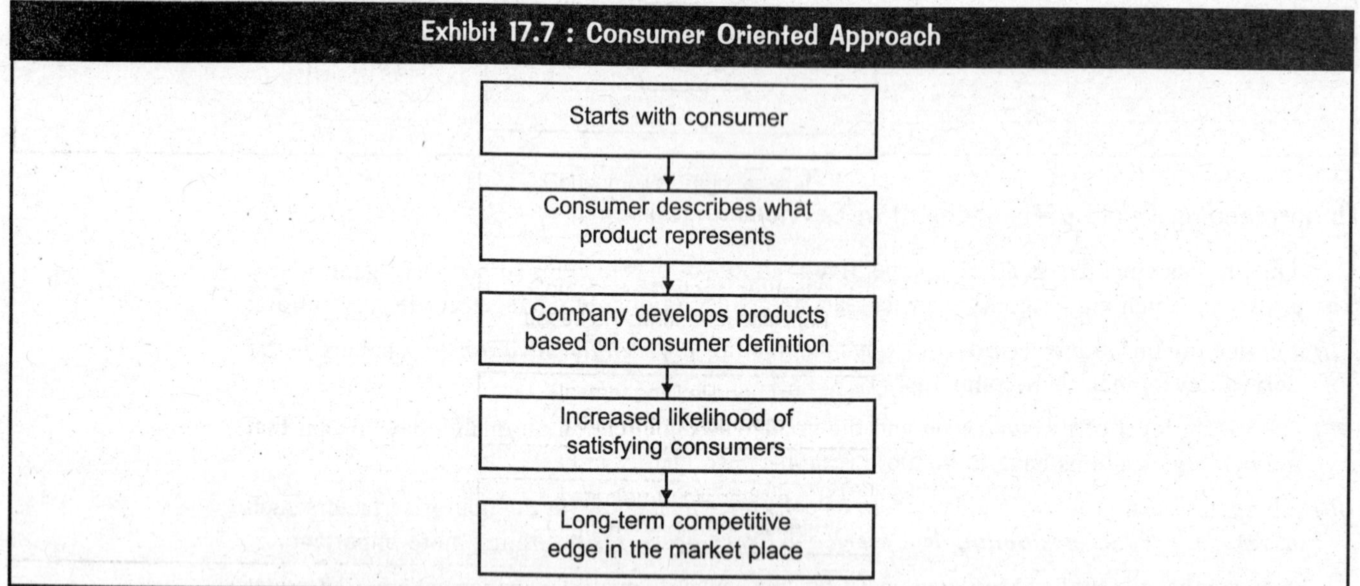

17.3 MODELS FOR SERVICE QUALITY

Service quality models are used to understand the role of management in service quality management.

Service Quality Models have been used to understand the role of management in service quality management.

Exhibit 17.8 **shows a service quality model which has the key concept stated as "customer satisfaction is a function of perceived quality of service, which is a measure of how actual quality compares to expected quality."**

Internal and external factors affect customer perceptions of quality. External factors (which are not directly under the control of service provider) include the social values and lifestyle of customers; knowledge of the services and the services offered by the competitors. The image presented by the company also influences customer perceptions. Companies use various techniques for monitoring customer perceptions. Typical methods are annual company reports and quarterly sales reports. A customer who comes to know about high sales volume of a company, perceives it as a competent company. This effort put by the company is part of its **image management.**

Exhibit 17.8 : A Model for Service Quality

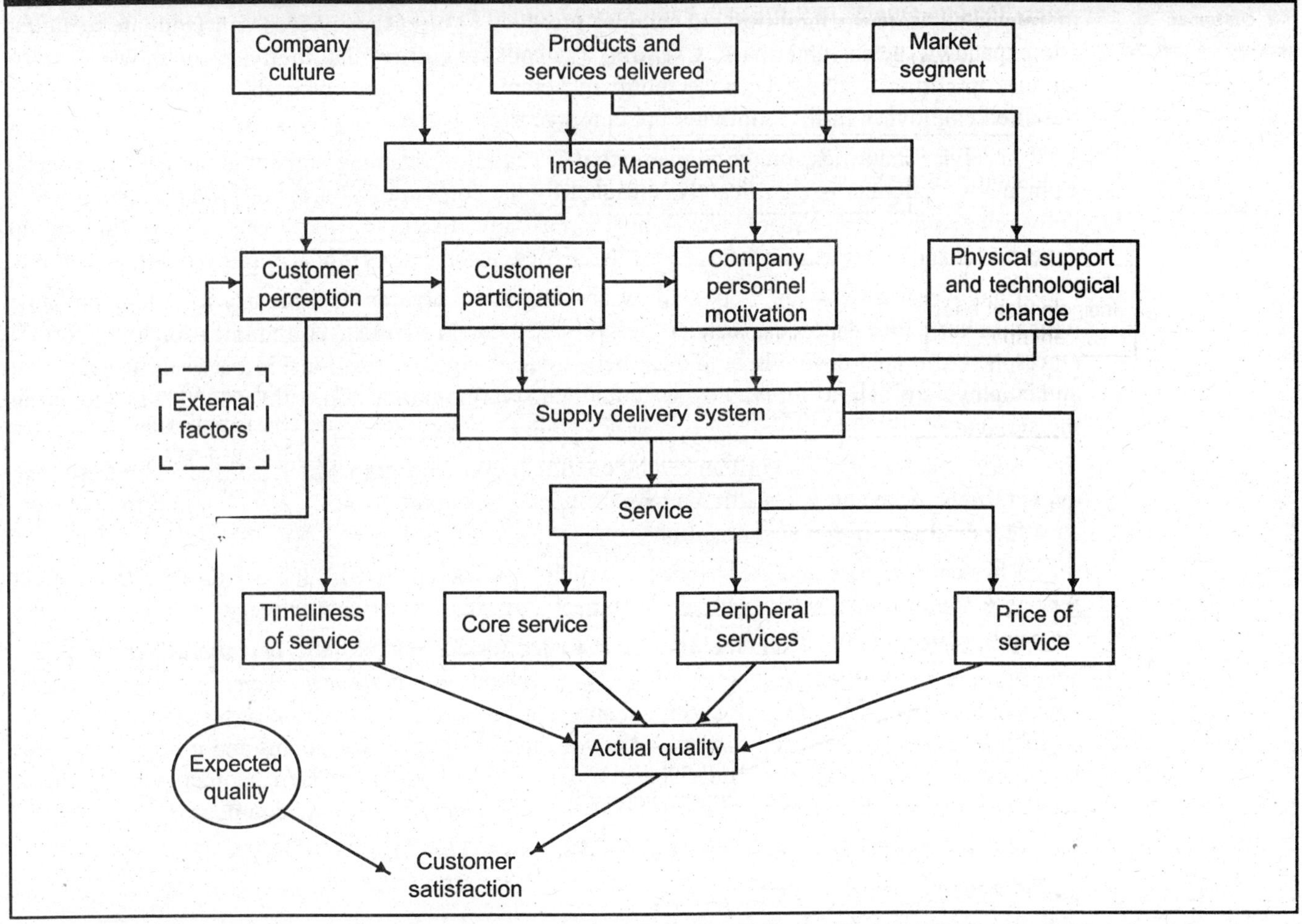

Company culture
Products and services delivered
Market segment
Image Management
Customer perception
Customer participation
Company personnel motivation
Physical support and technological change
External factors
Supply delivery system
Service
Timeliness of service
Core service
Peripheral services
Price of service
Actual quality
Expected quality
Customer satisfaction

Exhibit 17.9 **shows the internal and external factors that influence customer perception**

Exhibit 17.9 : Factors that Influence Customer Perception

Customer perception of quality
External factors
Internal factors
Social values and changes in life style
Knowledge explosion
Competitor's offering
Annual and quarterly report
Client manage-ment
Advertisement
Identify clients' needs through interviews, polls and surveys
Update facilities and services to meet client needs and expand customer base
Increase consumer participation in service delivery through motivated employees

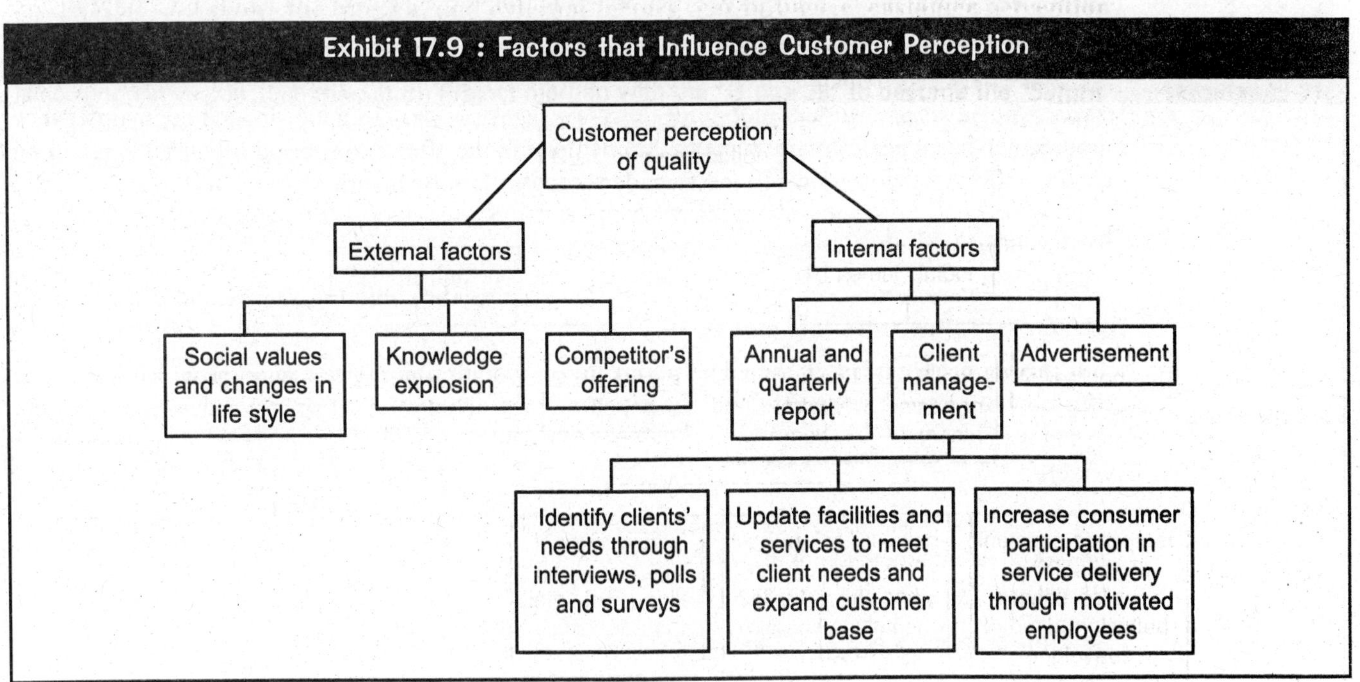

Factors that influence customer perception can be classified as:
(i) External factors and
(ii) Internal factors

Client management is important for improving the service and for meeting the changing needs of customers. Keeping abreast of customer needs through interviews, polls and surveys and making changes in the facilities and services provided to meet those needs will facilitate retaining and expanding the customer base. **Creating a corporate culture** that motivates employees is also another important concept because motivated employees create favourable customer attitudes. Satisfied employees further motivate the employees.

In service industries, **image management** is central to retaining and attracting new customers. Company's reputation is significantly impacted by the corporate culture, the products and services delivered and the market share. The company must advertise only what it can deliver. Building up expectations and failing to meet them creates dissatisfied customers and results in a decreased market share.

Employees can also be motivated by creating a **positive environment** within the company, which in turn influences the service delivery. Channels of open communication in a cordial atmosphere promote desirable employee behaviour. Congenial relationship between management and employees is helpful for employees to maintain warm relationship with customers in delivering the services.

Service delivery is also influenced by **customer participation** which is affected by **customer expectations.** An employee's attitude may influence a customer's attitude, which in turn may have an effect on the employees' motivation.

Physical facilities and the manner in which they keep pace with the customers' needs affect service functions and also the efficiency and effectiveness of service delivery.

Two components of service are: *(i)* ***the core service*** and *(ii)* **the *peripheral services.*** The benefits received by the customers are both ***tangible*** and ***intangible.*** *For example,* a tourist service company provides the core service of transporting customers from one city to another city. The peripheral services are the comfort and safety of the bus stations, rest rooms and meal services and also pick-up from and drop to various parts of the city for the customers. Sometimes peripheral services influence the customers to select one service company over its competitors.

Service quality is a function of several factors. They are:

(i) **timeliness** of the service

(ii) the **manner** in which the service is performed

(iii) the **adequacy** of the service (both core and peripheral services) and

(iv) the **price** of service.

Some service companies use a broad-based systems concept and provide several ancillary services. *For example,* an automobile dealer may also provide financing, insurance, maintenance contracts and gasoline. A commitment to the customer in the after-sales period is helpful in retaining customers. Evidence of good service spreads through word of mouth.

The Gronroos Model

The Gronroos model (developed in 1982) explains the *"missing service quality concept".* *Exhibit 17.10* illustrates this model.

According to Gronroos model, "perceived quality" is dependent on
(i) Experienced service and
(ii) Perceived service

This model focusses on the construct of image, which represents a point at which a gap can occur between expected service and perceived service. This model brings to our awareness the ways in which image is created from the aggregation of different aspects of technical and functional variables.

According to Gronroos, the range of resources and activities of marketers of services include:

- What customers are looking for?
- What customers are evaluating?
- How customers perceive the quality?
- What way service quality is influenced?

Exhibit 17.10 : Managing the Perceived Service Quality (Gronroos Model)

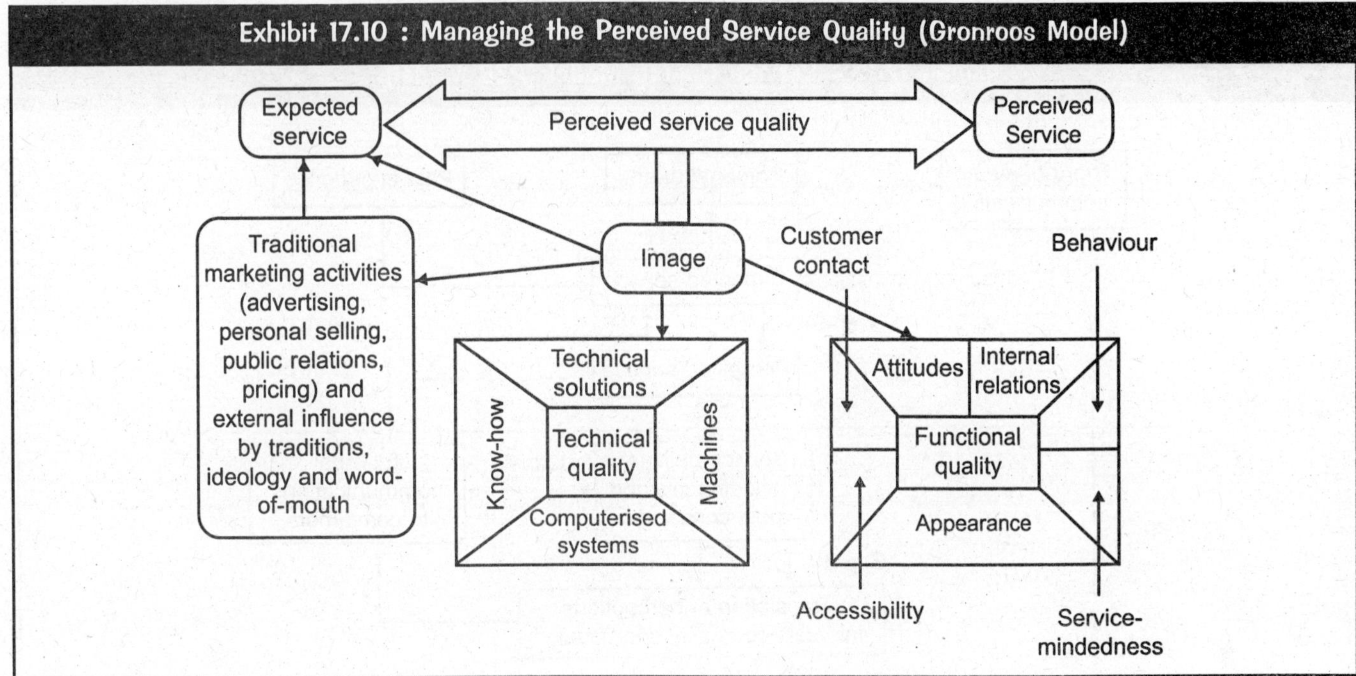

According to Gronroos the "perceived quality" of service is dependent on two variables: *(i)* **Experienced service** and *(ii)* **Perceived service.**

These two variables together provide the outcome of evaluation of service quality. Also, the analysis of Gronroos distinguishes between ***technical quality*** and ***functional quality*** as two components of service image delivery. ***Exhibit 17.11*** **shows the two service quality dimensions.**

Exhibit 17.11 : Two Service Quality Dimensions

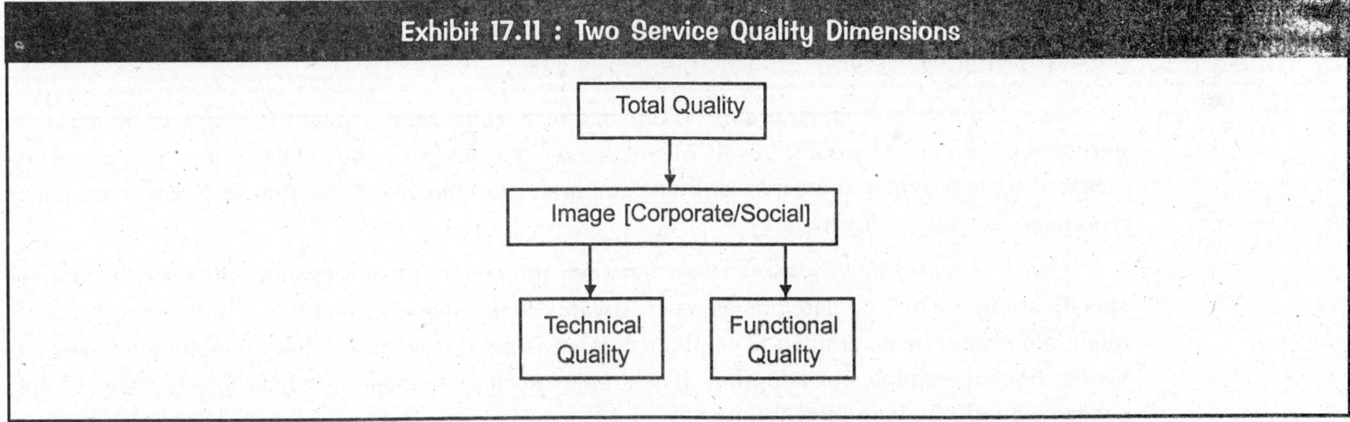

Technical quality refers to what the customer is actually receiving from the service. This can be quantified and measured objectively as in the case of tangible goods.

Functional quality refers to how the technical quality elements of the service are transferred to the customer. *For example,* a customer in a restaurant will evaluate not only the quality of the food consumed, but also the way in which it was delivered (the style, manner and appearance of the staff or the ambience of the place itself).

The Parasuram, Zeithaml and Berry Model (PZB Model)

This model developed in 1985 claims that the consumer evaluates service quality experience as the outcome of the gap between expected and perceived quality. The model emphasises on the key requirements for a service provider delivering the expected service quality.

Exhibit 17.12 illustrates the PZB service quality model.

Exhibit 17.12 : Service Quality Model (PZB Model)

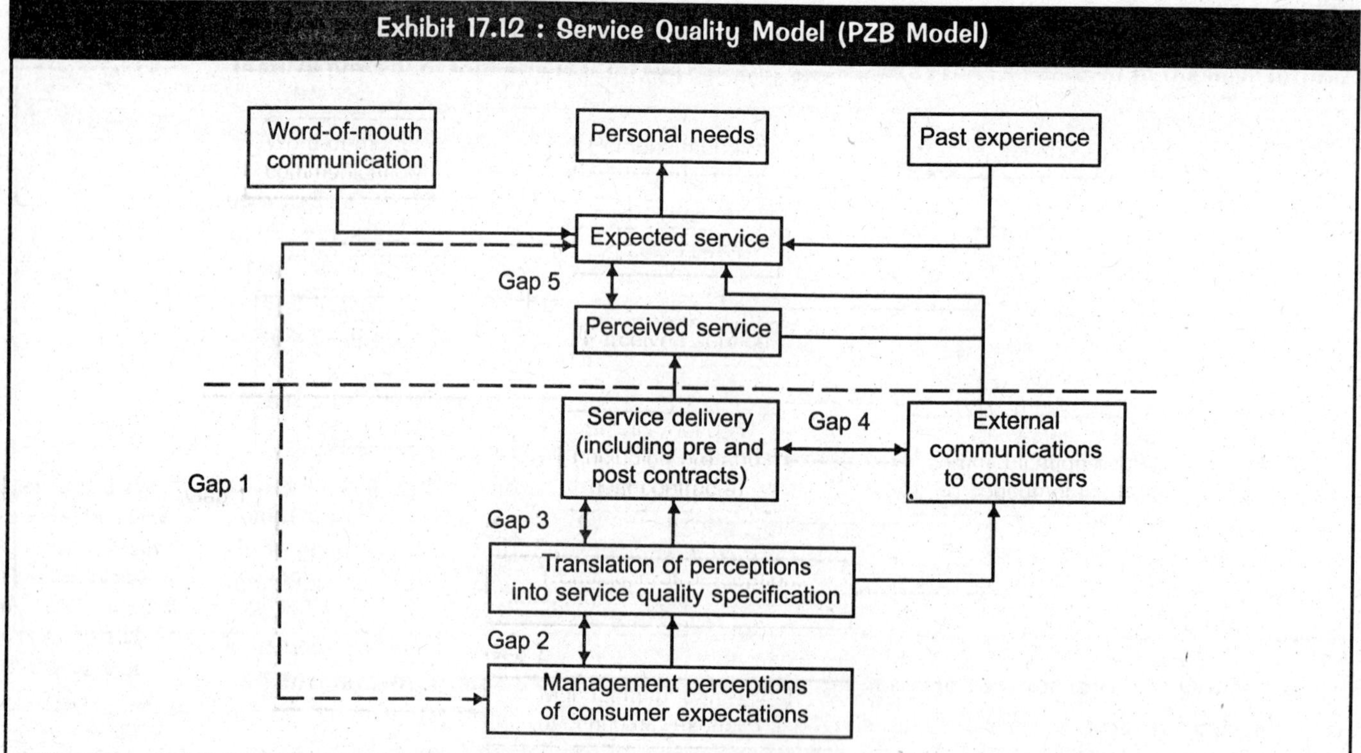

The model identifies **five gaps** that can cause unsuccessful service delivery. By learning the flow of this model, management can exercise greater control over the consumer relationships. The study of this model helps to have an improved realisation of the key issues in which the service provider can influence the satisfaction of consumers.

***Gap 1: Lack of understanding* (Gap between consumer expectation and management perception)** – This gap is the result of not knowing what consumer expects in a service. This means – what providers perceive as being important to consumers is often different from what consumers actually expect.

***Gap 2: Lack of development* (Gap between management perception and service quality specification)** – This is where managers are aware of customer expectations. But the management might not simply be committed to implement what is necessary, either through ignorance, lack of vision, limited resources or adoption of a strategy such as harvesting where management is not concerned with the long term future.

***Gap 3: Poor delivery* (Gap between service quality specifications and service delivery)** – The management understands the levels of service desired by the customer and specifies an appropriate set of standards. However, service delivery may not be of appropriate quality due to poor employee performance (perhaps because of insufficient training). Employee's role is vital in determining the quality of service.

***Gap 4: Unrealistic expectations* (Gap between service delivery and external communication)** – A gap between customer expectations and service provided exists sometimes because pre-purchase promotional materials project unrealistic levels of service which can not be delivered in reality. Marketers must pay close attention to ensure consistency between the quality image projected in promotional activity and the actual quality of services offered.

***Gap 5: Service Gap* (Gap between perceived service and delivered service)** – This gap represents the difference between expected and perceived quality in any given situation. It provides a clear indication of the degree to which service quality exists in a service organisation.

Christopher Lovelock, a leading author on services marketing expanded PZB model to include two more gaps, there-by offering seven gaps as shown in *Exhibit 17.13.*

Exhibit 17.13 : Seven Gaps that may Lead to Customer Disappointment

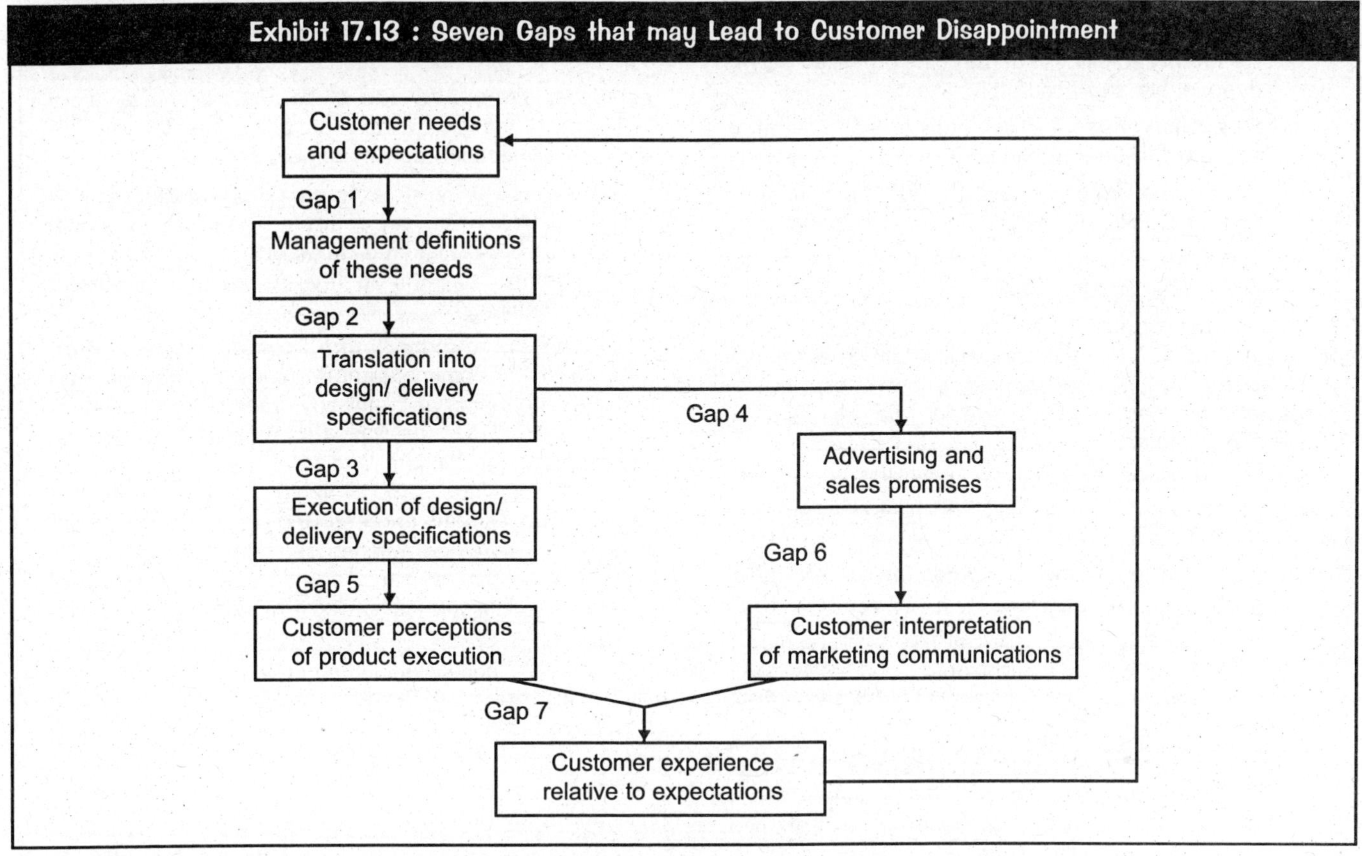

The seven gaps shown in *Exhibit 17.13* are illustrated below:

Gap 1: is not knowing what your customers need and expect. This is not desirable and hence, a market research is to be undertaken to find out the customer's needs and expectations.

Gap 2: is not using knowledge of customer needs and expectations as the basis for defining and specifying service quality standards.

Gap 3: results when execution fails to match the pre-defined standards. This is the conformance problem and often reflects poor internal communications and lack of quality controls.

Gap 4: results from a failure on the part of advertising and sales personnel to project the service accurately in their marketing communications to customers. Usually, the sales promotion personnel over-promise to their customers. Excessive claims by promotion personnel raise customer's expectations to height that can not be possibly met.

Gap 5: results when the customer wrongly perceives the quality of a service performance. A customer may simply not realise the quality of work performed, especially with an infrequently used service such as health care, consulting or specialised repair work.

Gap 6: occurs when a customer misunderstands what a sales executive says or misinterprets the nature of advertising message and expects something different from what was actually promised.

Gap 7: Occurs when the customer compares what he or she experienced with what was expected (additional expectations as modified by marketing communications).

Box 17.9 : Delivering Quality Service

What makes a service a quality service? Parasuraman, Zeithaml and Berry have identified five dimensions of service quality.

(i) ***Tangibles*** – Appearance of physical facilities, equipment, personnel and communication materials.

(ii) ***Reliability*** – Ability to perform the promised service dependably and accurately.

(iii) ***Responsiveness*** – Willingness to help customers and provide prompt service.

(iv) ***Assurance*** – Knowledge and courtesy of employees and their ability to inspire trust and confidence.

(v) ***Empathy*** – Caring, individualised attention the firm provides its customers.

Customers consistently rate reliability as most important and tangibles as least important. The message is clear: look good, be responsive, be reassuring, be empathetic, but most of all, the reliable – ***do what you say you are going to do.***

Barriers to service quality: Towards improving service quality, Parasuraman, Zeithaml and Berry have identified some significant barriers to service quality. They are:

(i) ***Customer expectation, management perception gap*** – A gap between what managers think customers expect and what customers actually expect from the service firm.

(ii) ***Management perception, service quality specification gap*** – Managers set service quality specifications on standards that fall short of customers' expectations.

(iii) ***Service quality specifications, service delivery gap*** – the service delivered falls short of the service specifications that managers set.

(iv) ***Service delivery, external communications gap*** – Customers' expectations have been media advertising, sales presentations and other communications to levels beyond the firm's capabilities.

(v) ***Customer expectation, customer perception gap*** – There is a gap between what the customer expects and what the customer perceives that is received .**This is the ultimate gap.**

Parasuraman, Zeithaml and Berry have developed an approach to continuous improvement of service quality. The quality improvement process begins with an external assessment of customer-perceived quality short falls (Gap 5), followed by an internal assessment of the underlying causes of original short falls (Gap 1 to 4).

Box 17.9 **describes the aspects of delivering quality servics.**

17.4 MEASURING SATISFACTION

Parasuraman, Zeithaml and Berry developed a survey research instrument called 'SERVQUAL' to measure customer satisfaction with different aspects of service quality. It is based on the promise that customers can evaluate a firm's service quality by comparing their perceptions of its service with their expectations. SERVQUAL is seen as a generic measurement tool that can be applied across a broad spectrum of service industries. **The SERVQUAL scale contains 21 perception items and a series of expectation items reflecting the five dimensions of service quality namely *Tangibles, Reliability, Responsiveness, Assurance* and *Empathy*. *Exhibit 17.10* (a) lists the generic dimensions used by customers to evaluate service quality and the contents of the SERVQUAL scale.**

Respondents complete a series of scales that measure their expectations of companies in a particular industry on a wide array of specific service characteristics subsequently, they are asked to record their perceptions of a specific company whose services they have used on those same characteristics. When perceived performance ratings are lower than expectations, this is a sign of poor quality, the reverse indicates good quality.

To evaluate the stability of the five underlying dimensions when applied to a variety of different service industries, Mels, Boshoff and Nel analysed data sets from banks, insurance brokers, vehicle repair shops, electrical repair shops and life insurance firms. **Their findings suggests that in reality SERVQUAL difference scores measure only two factors: *intrinsic service quality* (resembling what Gronroos termed *functional quality*) and *extrinsic service quality* (which refers to the tangible aspects of service delivery and *"resembles to some extent* what Gronroos refers to as *technical quality*).**

Box 17.10(a) : Generic Dimensions Used by Customers to Evaluate Service Quality		
Dimension	***Definition***	***Examples of Questions That Customers Might Raise***
Credibility	Trust worthiness, believability, honesty of the service provider	Does the hospital have a good reputation? Does my stock broker refrain from pressurising me to buy? Does the repair firm guarantee its work?
Security	Freedom from danger, risk, or doubt	Is it safe for me to use the bank's ATM at night? Is my credit card protected against unauthorised use? Can I be sure that my insurance policy provides complete coverage?
Access	Approachability and ease of contact	How easy is it for me to talk to a supervisor when I have a problem? Does the airline have a 24-hour toll-free phone number? Is the hotel conveniently located?
Communication	Listening to customers and keeping them informed in language they can understand	When I have a complaint, is the manager willing to listen to me? Does the electrician call when unable to keep a scheduled appointment?
Understanding the customer	Making the effort to know customers and their needs	Does someone in the hotel recognise me as a regular customer? Does my stockbroker try to determine my specific financial objectives? Is the moving company willing to accommodate my schedule?
Tangibles	Appearance of physical facilities, equipment, personnel, and commu-nication materials	Are the hotel's facilities attractive? Is my accountant dressed appropriately? Is my bank statement easy to understand?
Reliability	Ability to perform the promised service dependably and accurately	When a lawyer says she will call me back in 15 minutes, does she do so? Is my telephone bill free of errors? Is my television repaired right the first time?
Responsiveness	Willingness to help customers and provide prompt service	When there's a problem, does the firm resolve it quickly? Is my stockbroker willing to answer my questions? Is the cable TV company willing to give me a specific time when the installer will show up?
Competence	Possession of the skills and knowledge required to perform the service information I need?	Can the bank teller process my transaction without fumbling around? When I call my travel agent, is she able to obtain the Does the dentist appear to know what he is doing?
Courtesy	Politeness, respect, consideration, and friendliness of contact personnel	Does the flight attendant have a pleasant demeanor? Are the telephone operators consistently polite when answering my calls? Does the plumber take off his muddy shoes before stepping on my carpet?

Box 17.10(b) **describes the SERVQUAL scale.**

Box 17.10(b) : The SERVQUAL Scale

The SERVQUAL scale includes five dimensions: tangibles, reliability, responsiveness, assurance, and empathy. Within each dimension are several items measured on a **seven-point scale** from *strongly* ***agree to strong disagree,*** for a total of 21 items.

Servqual Questions

Note: For actual survey respondents, instructions are also included and each statement is accompanied by a seven-point scale ranging from "strongly agree = 7" to "strongly disagree = 1". Only the end point of the scale are labelled- there are no words above the numbers 2 through 6.

Tangibles

- Excellent banks [refer to cable TV companies, hospitals, or the appropriate service business throughout the questionnaire] will have modern-looking equipment.
- The physical facilities at excellent banks will be visually appealing.
- Employees at excellent banks will be neat in appearance.
- Materials associated with the service (like brochures or statements) will be visually appealing in an excellent bank.

Reliability

- When excellent banks promise to do something by a certain time, they will do so.
- When customers have a problem, excellent banks will show a sincere interest in solving it.
- Excellent banks will perform the service right the first time.
- Excellent banks will provide their services at the time they promise to do so.
- Excellent banks will insist on error-free records.

Responsiveness

- Employees of excellent banks will tell customers exactly when service will be performed.
- Employees of excellent banks will give prompt service to customers.
- Employees of excellent banks will always be willing to help customers.
- Employees of excellent banks will never be too busy to respond to customer requests.

Assurance

- The behaviour of employees of excellent banks will instill confidence in customers.
- Customers of excellent banks will feel safe in their transactions.
- Employees of excellent banks will be consistently courteous with customers.
- Employees of excellent banks will have the knowledge to answer customer questions.

Empathy

- Excellent banks will give customers individual attention.
- Excellent banks will have operating hours convenient to all their customers.
- Excellent banks will have employees who give customers personal attention.
- The employees of excellent banks will understand the specific needs of their customers.

17.5 ROLE OF PERSONNEL IN SERVICE DELIVERY

Having assessed customer needs, organisations must set standards/specifications and systems for service delivery to include the relevant dimensions of customer service *i.e.,* to avoid the gap between management perceptions of consumer expectations and service quality specifications actually set. This implies a requirement for management commitment to a service culture and service quality and the allocation of appropriate resources – in relation to products, systems, environment and people.

Further, the organisation must ensure that the service delivered meets the specifications or standards set. The delivered service quality depends on the performance of all employees, who must be able and willing to deliver the desired levels of service. Employees have a major role in meeting customer needs and influencing customer perceptions of service. The success of the organisation in the delivery of quality service depends on the development of progressive personnel policies for recruitment and selection, training, motivation and rewards for all employees – both customer contact and back-office employees.

Internal Marketing

Internal marketing concept views 'employees' as internal customers and 'jobs' as internal products.

The understanding of the concept of internal marketing is central to personnel policies. Internal marketing views employees as ***internal customers*** and jobs as internal products. An organisation needs to sell its jobs to employees before selling its service to ***external customers.*** This means satisfying the wants of internal customers which upgrades their capability to satisfy the needs of external customers.

Three objectives of internal marketing are:

(i) ***Over all objective***: To achieve motivated, customer-conscious and care-oriented personnel.

(ii) ***Strategic objective***: To create an internal environment which supports customer-consciousness and sales-mindedness among personnel and

(iii) ***Tactical objective***: To sell service campaigns and marketing efforts to employees through staff training programmes and seminars.

Organisations should carry out research among employees to identify their needs, wants, and attitudes with respect to working conditions, benefits and company policies, for instance, flexible working hours are attractive to employees and lead to increased job satisfaction, increased productivity and reduced absenteeism. Employees expect other benefits such as health insurance, pensions, paid holidays etc to be provided by their employers. **The central idea of internal marketing is that "satisfied internal customers (employees) have the motivation to develop and improve capability to satisfy the needs of external customers by providing them the expected service".**

Personnel policies: Successful personnel policies include recruitment and selection of the right people. Key characteristics for employees to perform effectively may relate to: process and technical skills, interpersonal and communication skills, flexibility and adaptability, and empathy with the customer. It is crucial to identify the training needs of new and present employees with respect to technical and interpersonal dimensions, and to consider employment conditions, *i.e.,* employees' wants and attitudes with regard to working conditions, benefits and welfare.

The success of an organisation in reducing the gap between service quality specifications and the actual service delivery depends on factors such as:

(i) ***Team work***: Evidenced by a caring management and employees who are involved in and committed to achievement of their organisation's goals.

(ii) ***Employee-job fit***: The ability of employees to perform a job

(iii) ***Technology-job fit***: Are the 'tools' appropriate for the employees to do their job?

(iv) ***Perceived control***: Do employees have flexibility in dealing with customers? (if not stress levels may increase and performance decrease).

(v) ***Supervisory control systems***: Based on behaviours rather than "output quality".

(vi) ***Avoidance of role conflict***: For employees in satisfying their expectations of the organisation and the expectations of customers.

(vii) ***Avoidance of role ambiguity***: *i.e.,* Employees should know what is expected of them and how performance will be evaluated and rewarded.

17.6 SERVICE DELIVERY

To ensure service quality, the gap between actual delivery and promised or expected delivery should be avoided or minimised.

In relation to service delivery, organisations need to avoid the gap between actual service delivery and external communications about the service. In otherwords, the organisation needs to avoid a failure to deliver the service as promised.

Once an organisation has successfully assessed customer needs, translated them into service systems and standards/specifications, and recruited and trained employees, it must be able to manage delivery of promised service. Quality systems are helpful to ensure this.

Further, the organisation needs appropriate advertising and promotion so that the service that is offered in external promotions matches the actual service the organisation is able to deliver. Advertising and promotion influence customer's expectations and perceptions of the delivered service. Therefore, it is important that the organisation does not promise more than 'what it can deliver and ensures that its marketing communications are realistic. Also, the organisation has in place systems to measure and monitor success in delivering the promised service quality to its customers.

Service failure: Customer complaints indicate service failures but it is found that only a small proportion of dissatisfied customers complain. Therefore, complaint data are not a true reflection of the extent of customer dissatisfaction. **Many dissatisfied customers may not complain and keep quiet because:**

(a) Of fear of or too much trouble to complain

(b) None is available to complain to or there is no easy channel to redress their grievances.

(c) No one cares and it won't do any good

(d) Do not know where to complain.

Management must appreciate that the additional costs of replacing customers would be more than the costs of retaining dissatisfied customers by addressing their complaints and removing the causes of dissatisfaction. Customers who complain and who then receive a satisfactory response subsequently are more likely to purchase other services or products of the organisation, engage in positive word-of-mouth communication and be loyal. Effective service recovery can have a strong positive influence on recovery satisfaction and loyalty.

Organisations should aim at zero defects in their service delivery - i.e., to get things right the first time.

Organisations should strive for zero defects in their service delivery – to get things right the first time. Even though many firms develop rigid service quality systems with sophisticated techniques and structured personnel policies to try to provide consistent high quality service, there are many situations in which they fail in their encounters with customers with respect to one or more dimensions of service quality and consequently they need to deal with customer dissatisfaction and complaints. Also service failures may occur if the service fails to live upto the customer's own expectations eventhough from the service provider's point of view the delivered service meets the service promised. The consequences of service failures include: customer dissatisfaction, decline in consumers confidence, negative word-of-mouth, and inability to retain customers. In addition, it results in increased costs of putting the services right, providing compensation and obtaining new customers to replace lost ones. Service failure may also lead to decline in employee morale and service performance.

Service recovery: The actions that a service provider takes to respond to service failures are referred to as service recovery.

Service recovery is defined as "specific actions taken to ensure that the customer receives a reasonable level of service after problems have occurred to disrupt normal service". It is a thought – out, planned, process for returning aggrieved customers to a state of satisfaction with the organisation after a service has failed to live up to expectations.

When a service failure occurs, customer's expectations for service recovery are:

(a) to receive an apology for the fact that the customer is put to inconvenience.

(b) to be offered a 'fair fix' for the problem

(c) to be treated fairly by the organisation and

(d) to be compensated for the inconvenience.

'Service recovery' refers to the actions that a service provider takes to respond to service failures or customer complaints.

Service recovery is emotional and physical repair, organisations need to fix the customer first and then fix the customer's problem.

Service recovery process requires the front line employees to be empowered. They must be given authority, responsibility and incentives to identify, care about and solve customer problems and complaints, to allow them to use their initiative and judgement to respond flexibly and to act with respect to the best solutions to satisfy consumers.

Requirements for organisations to create an effective service recovery programme are:

1. Seek out possible failure points. Focus on critical service encounters and try to anticipate problems.
2. Educate customers and encourage complaints. Make it easy to complain (eg 24 hour customer service hot lines) and offer service guarantees.
3. Monitor service process, detect and track service failures and analyse complaint data Measure service performance against company standards and use the findings to improve service quality.
4. Engage in customer research, focused on both the process and outcome of service delivery to identify when things go wrong, track how service recovery is implemented and measure again to see if the recovery has satisfied the customer.
5. Develop proactive service recovery to include, in addition to reinstatement, elements such as initiation of the recovery process, which can enhance customer's evaluation of the service provider, apologies to show that the customer's problem is being taken seriously, speedy response and recompense as appropriate.
6. Train, empower and facilitate employees to recover. Service recovery typically involves interpersonal interaction and communication skills, and knowledge skills, with implications for human resources management.
7. Show management commitment. Employees need the support of top management who are committed to achieve absolute customer satisfaction.

17.7 QUALITY ASSURANCES IN SERVICES

The most common quality characteristics in **services time** (waiting time, service time, delivery time) and **number of non-conformance**, can be measured rather easily. Insurance companies, *for example,* measure the time to complete different transactions such as new issues, claim payments and cash surrenders. Hospitals measure the percentage of nosocomial infections and the percentage of unplanned re-admissions to the emergency room, intensive care or operating room within, say 48 hours. Other quality characteristics in services are observable such the ***type of errors*** (wrong kind, wrong quantity, wrong delivery date etc.) and ***behaviour*** (courtesy, promptness, competency and so on).

Internal measurements of service quality are commonly performed with some type of data sheet or checklist. **Time is easily measured by taking two observations: starting time and finishing time.** Many observed data assume only "yes" or "no" values.

Even though human behaviour is easily observable, the task of describing and classifying the observations is far more difficult. The major obstacle is developing operational definitions of behavioural characteristics. *For example,* how does one define courteous versus discourteous or understanding versus indifferent? Defining such distinctions is best done by comparing behaviour against understandable standards. For instance, a standard for "courtesy" might be to address the customer as "Mr" or "Ms". Failure to do so is an instance of an error. "Promptness" might be defined as greeting a customer within five seconds of entering the store or answering letters within two days of receipt.

Box 17.11 **describes 1-10-100 'Rule' in quality.**

Box 17.11 : 1-10-100 "Rule" in Quality

One interesting rule-of-thumb in quality is called **"1-10-100 Rule".** If some one produces defective work and rectifies it immediately, it only costs him another equal effort to do so. If it has slipped to his ***internal customers*** and he wants to rectify it then, it will cost 10 times more effort. If unfortunately, it has passed on to the ***external customer,*** then he has to pay around 100 fold in order to get the error rectified and the adverse consequences that follow. This is particularly significant for the service industries as most of their work directly deals with external customers. They have less chance to rework internally. **So quality is compulsory for survival in service industries.**

17.8 RETURN ON SERVICE QUALITY

Managers of virtually all industries have come to recognise the importance of services to their firm's continued success. However, whereas service quality is an important element to a firm's operations, it is necessary for all firms to recognise the need to identify and track the cost of operations. Quality improvement leads to profits at least in part because of cost savings achieved through increased efficiency. Before a firm can calculate its return on investment in quality, it must determine the costs associated with poor quality and what, if any, cost reduction it can expect from its quality improvement efforts. The understanding that high levels of quality can lead to cost savings has required a shift in management thought about the cost of quality and its return. Common belief held that it could not be economical for any process to reduce defects to zero. **Managers used to believe that for any process there was a trade-off between cost and product or service quality. This means for every process there is a theoretical optimum quality level where the marginal benefit of improved quality is less than its marginal cost. This concept is illustrated in *Exhibit 17.14.***

Exhibit 17.14 : Classic Model of Optimum Quality Costs

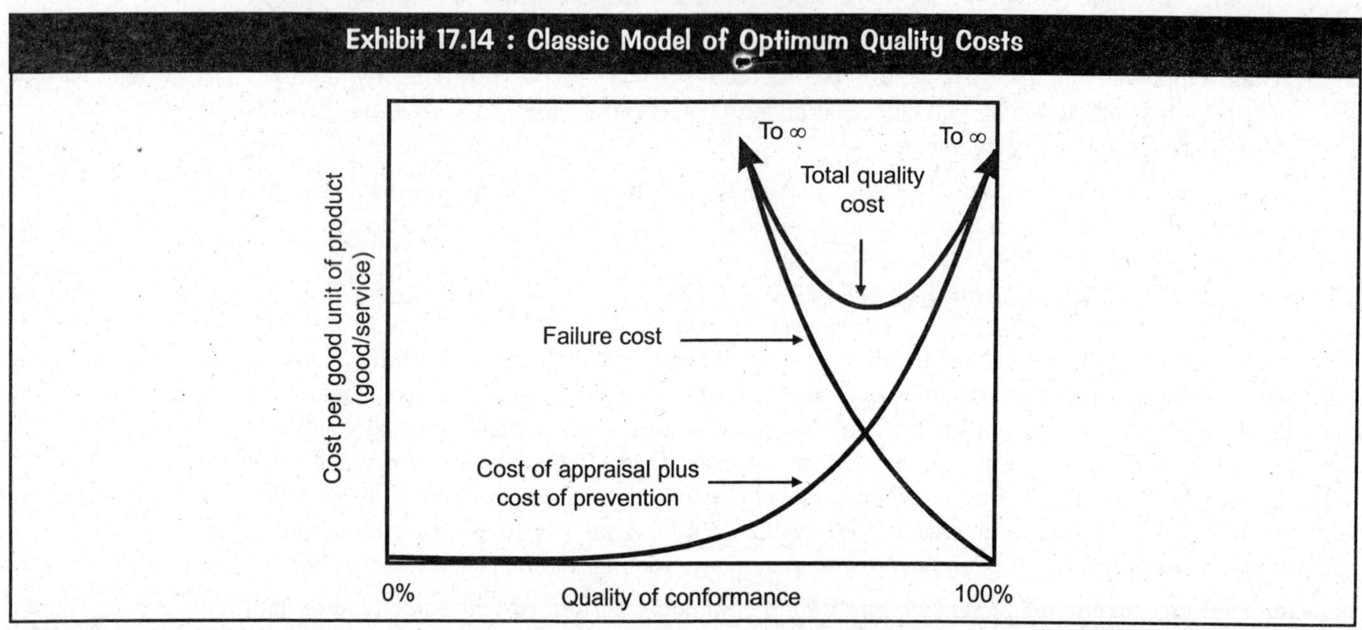

Exhibit 17.15 : New Model of Optimum Service Quality Costs

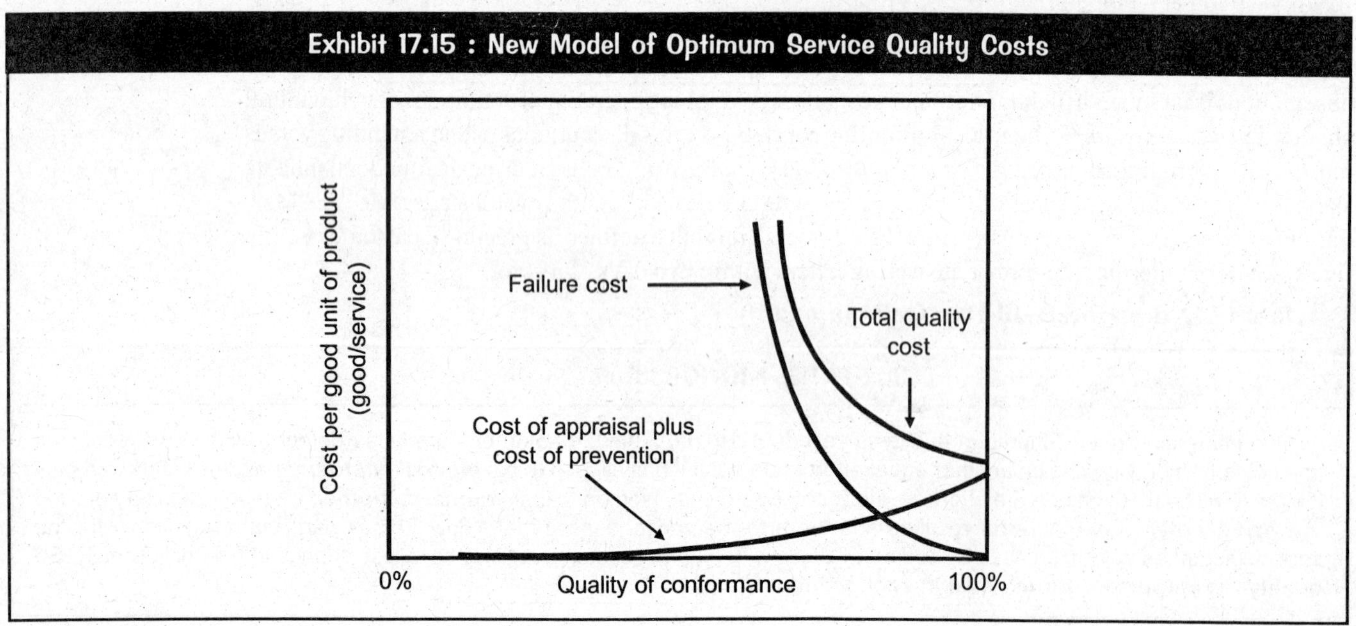

The traditional view failed to identify all the costs associated with poor quality. By some estimates these costs average 30% to 50% of sales for service companies. **Firms which have established total quality programs have found that when the full costs of poor quality are recognised, the most economical process is one where all services offered meet specifications (*i.e.,* zero defects). This concept is illustrated in *Exhibit 17.15.***

Costs of Quality: The cost of quality discussed in previous chapters with reference to product quality applies to quality of services also. The cost of quality can be divided into: *(i)* **Internal failure costs,** *(ii)* **External failure costs,** *(iii)* **Appraisal costs** and *(iv)* **Prevention costs.**

Exhibit 17.16 : Assignment of Cost Elements to Quality Cost Categories

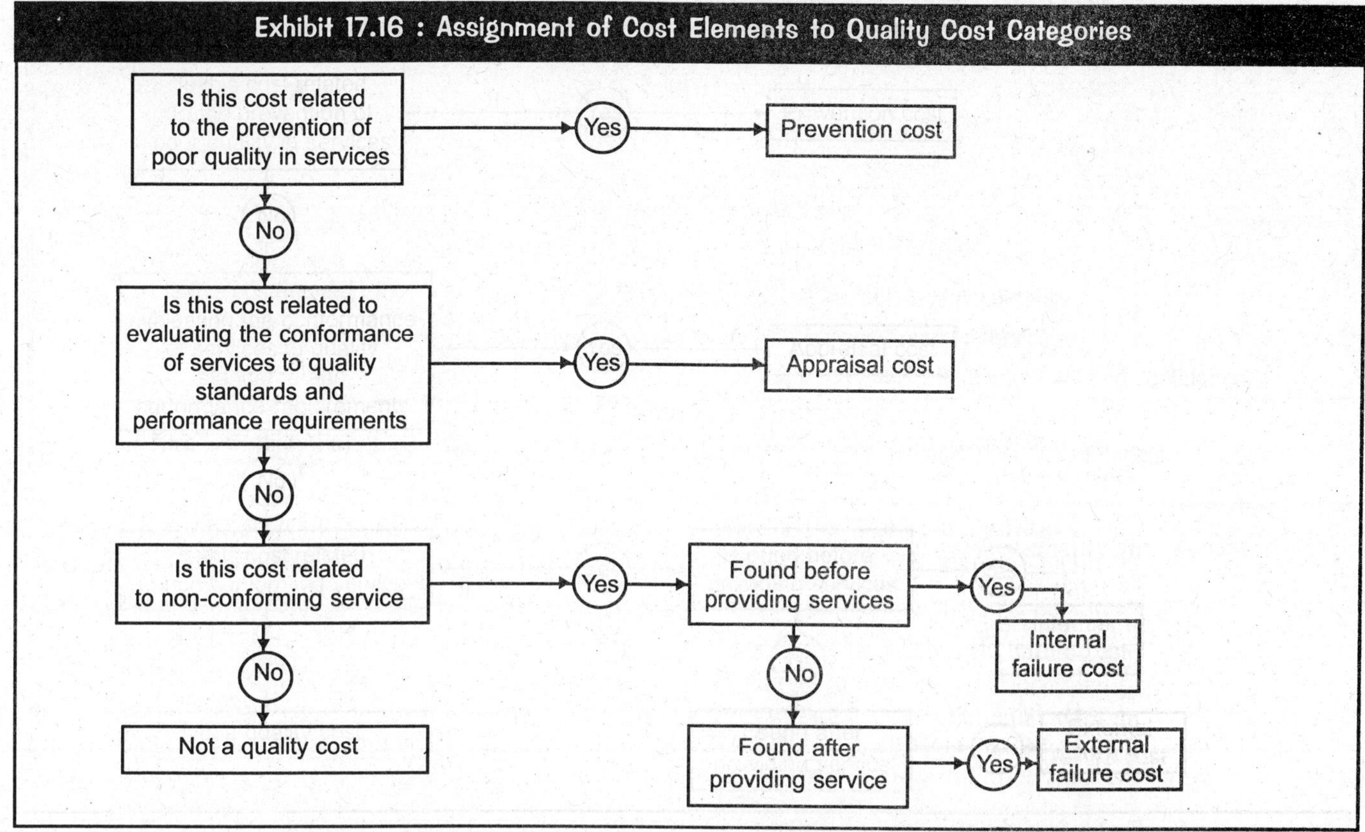

All businesses (service providers) incur costs associated with each of these four categories of the cost of quality. **Although quality expert Philip Crosby has popularised the notion that "quality is free", there is no way to reduce the cost of quality to zero.** Firms that have not embraced total quality control tend to find that most of their quality costs occur in the failure and appraisal categories. Quality conscious firms have found that it is much more cost-effective to focus on preventing errors. Focussing on prevention requires restructuring of processes. If a company is serious about eliminating quality problems, it must design processes that produce error free services. ***Exhibit 17.16* illustrates assignment of cost elements to quality cost categories.**

Further more, not every customer-planning service enhancement is equally important in building loyalty or in generating cost savings. Consequently, given limited resources to invest, spending on service improvement becomes a classic resource allocation decision.

As a result, many managers are now estimating the return on proposed service improvement efforts referred to as the ***"return on quality"*** method. This approach is based on the assumption that it is possible to measure the impact on profits through the improved retention of the firm's current customers due to improved service. There are, infact, many improvement initiatives in services such as increased variety at a restaurant, for which improved customer satisfaction and not lower cost, is the primary effect and primary source of increased profits. Because its goal is to retain current customers, it is called ***"defensive"*** **marketing** (a type of service). **The chain effects by which service improvements increase loyalty, repeat purchases and ultimately profits is shown in *Box 17.12.***

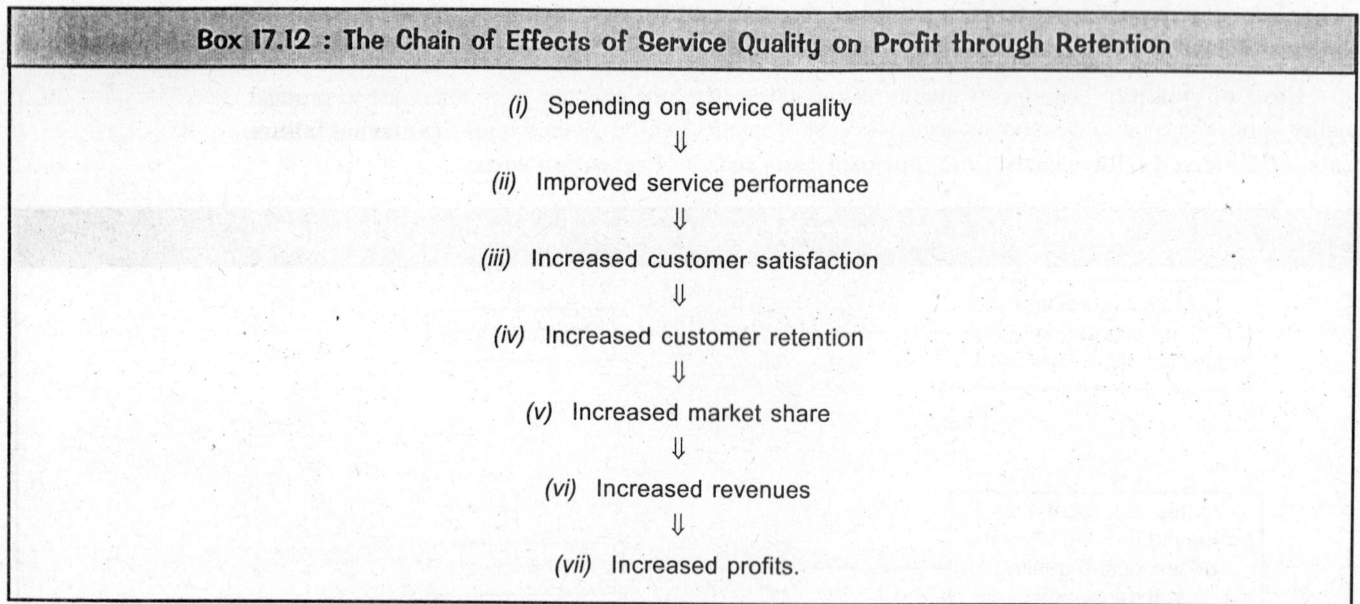

Box 17.12 : The Chain of Effects of Service Quality on Profit through Retention

How improving service will impact customer retention, market share and profits is illustrated in *Exhibit 17.17.*

Linking customer satisfaction to retention: Determining the relationship between customers' satisfaction levels and retention is especially important is choosing areas for attention. The most important areas are those that cause customers to leave or to be loyal, not necessarily those that receive the largest number of complaints on those for which satisfaction is rated the worst.

A survey of the firm's customers is required, asking them about how various aspects of the firm's services meet their expectations and their likelihood of remaining a loyal customer during the next period of time.

Linking retention to market shares (in case of marketing of services)

For a firm to determine the relationship between its customer retention rate and its market share, it must have an understanding of the dynamics of the market under the current competitive conditions. **Simply tracking revenues, profits or market share will not provide enough information to link retention to market share. Therefore, firms must track the following information:**

(i) The extent of brand/firm switching by customers in the market.

(ii) The rate of entry of new customers into the market.

(iii) The percentage of customers that are new to the market that are attracted to the firm and

(iv) The percent of customers who leave the market. Basically, a firm improves its market share by attracting new customers at a rate greater than its market share percentage and/or increasing its retention rate as a result of improving customer's satisfaction levels through improved service. However, the firm's attractiveness to new customers is assumed to be unrelated to the satisfaction of existing customers. Therefore, the only way to increase market share through customer satisfaction is by raising the firm's retention rate. **Improving customer satisfaction increases the retention rate;** which allows the firm to keep a larger percentage to its customers and thereby improve its market share.

Exhibit 17.17 : Service Customer Retention → Profitability

Customer defection is a problem and customer retention an opportunity in both manufacturing and service firms. Service quality is gaining importance due to the size and growth of service industries and the growing importance of service as a means of strategically competing in the market place.

Because so many services are intangible, the interaction between employees and customers is critical. An employee's ability to meet or exceed customer expectations when conducting a routine transaction influences the customer's satisfaction with the organisation. In fact, this interaction influences satisfaction more than the actual product or service obtained. The one-on-one or face-to-face contact between the customers and the person delivering the service is extremely important.

Service companies have quality costs which are reflected in the cost of customers who will not come back because of poor service. These are **customer defections** which have substantial impact on cost and profits. It is estimated that customer defections can have a greater impact than economies of scale, market share or unit cost of services. Despite this many companies fail to ***measure*** **defections, determine the** ***cause*** **of defections** and **improve the** ***process*** **to reduce defections.**

Customer retention leads to profitability. One way of putting a value on customer retention is to assign or estimate a ***"life time retention value",*** the additional sales that would result if the customer were retained. The system for improving customer retention and profits is illustrated in the diagram below:

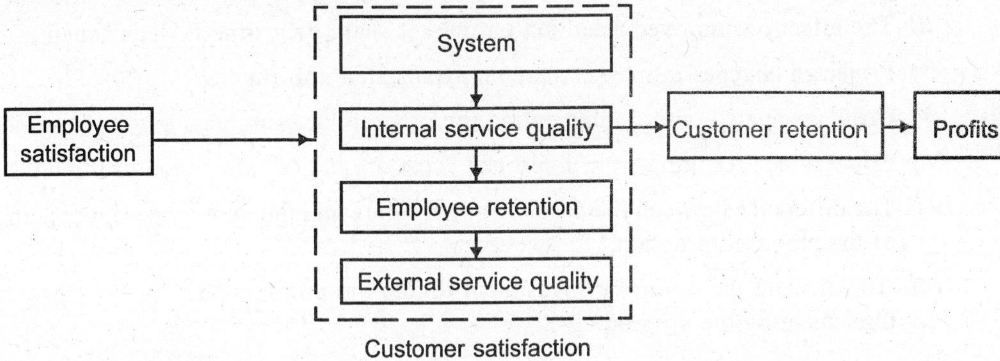

Customer satisfaction

The system components are:

(i) **Internal service quality,** which establishes and reinforces a climate and organisation culture directed toward quality.

(ii) ***Employee retention,*** which is achieved through good human resource management practices and organisation development methods such as teams, job development and empowerment. Employee retention depends on employee satisfaction, which in turn can be related to external service and customer satisfaction.

(iii) ***External service quality,*** which is delivered through the organisation's quality infrastructure.

(iv) **Customer satisfaction** and follow up, in order to reduce customer defections and improve retention.

Linking market shares to revenues: Two pieces of information *viz.,* the size of the market and the average profitability per customer of the market segment facilitate linking of market share and revenues. By multiplying the market share by the number of people in the market times the average profit per customer, it is possible to convert the market share forecasts into sales revenues in rupees.

Linking service improvement to customer satisfaction

Once the links between customer satisfaction and revenues are understood, it then becomes possible to estimate how changes in customer's satisfaction level will impact market share and revenues. What is needed is way for the manager to explore the profit impact of various proposed service improvement programs. However, these programs usually have some costs associated with their implementation. Therefore, the expected changes in the percentage of dissatisfied, satisfied or delighted customers must be linked to various levels of spending to improve service.

Changes in customer's satisfaction level will impact market shares and revenues of the service provider firm.

Managers should have some idea of what the firm currently spends on various processes and sub-processes to keep customers satisfied". (*i.e.,* reduce dissatisfied customers) and to exceed their expectation (*i.e.,* increase delighted customers). Further, the customer satisfaction surveys show how many customers are dissatisfied, satisfied or delighted with various aspects of the firm's service. Therefore, the level of customer satisfaction that corresponds to spending on service for a process or sub-process is known for the current level.

Managers must also estimate the expected impact on customer satisfaction that will result from proposed spending to improve service. The estimation can be made through management judgement or through experimenting with the program on a small scale to determine the likely effect.

With this information, the firm can estimate the profit impact of proposed service programs by linking the following steps:

(i) The impact of changes in market shares are determined for the current competitive situation in terms of rupee value.

(ii) The effect of a proposed service improvement program on customer retention is estimated based on expected changes in customer satisfaction.

(iii) The effect of improved retention on market share over time is determined.

(iv) Projected changes in market share are translated into rupees.

(v) Costs associated with implementing the program are subtracted.

(vi) Cost savings resulting from improved "cost of quality" are added to the total.

(vii) The difference between the baseline profit figure and the new rupee figure is the profit impact of the proposed program.

(viii) To calculate the return on investment divide the profit impact by the costs associated with implementing the program.

Illustration of Calculation of Return on Investment on Service Quality

An analysis of the responses to customer satisfaction survey reveals that 16% of respondents were "dissatisfied", 38% were satisfied and 46% were "delighted" with the firm's overall level of service. The retention rate for dissatisfied was 25%, satisfied was 67.37% and delighted was 95.65%.

The average retention rate for all customers is (16% × 25%) + (38% × 67.37%) + (46% × 95.65%) = 73.6%

Suppose the firm initiated a service improvement effort that would reduce the number of dissatisfied customers to 5%, then the expected retention rate resulting from this effort would be

$$(5\% \times 25\%) + (49\% \times 67.37\%) + (46\% \times 95.65\%) = 78.26\%$$

If we know the number of customers in the market and the firm's market share, we can then estimate the resulting market share impact. If the market has 8,00,000 customers and the firm has a 10% market share, then the expected gain in customers for the next time period resulting from the change in retention rates would be

$$(8,00,000 \times 0.10) \times (0.7826 - 0.7360) = 3,728 \text{ customers}$$

To determine the profit impact for the next time period, the firm need to know

(i) The average profit per customer

(ii) The expected costs associated with improvement effort

(iii) The expected costs savings (if any) associated with the improvement effort.

(iv) The firm's discount rate.

If the average annual profit for each customer is ₹ 200/- and the firm uses a 10% discount rate to determine the net present value of the investment, then the profit impact for the next time period, if there were no costs to implement the program and no cost savings resulting from the program, would be 3,728 × 200 = ₹ 7,45,600.

Therefore the present value (PV) would equal

$$PV = ₹\frac{7,45,600}{(1+0.1)} = ₹\ 6,77,818$$

If we assume that there was an up-front cost of ₹ 4,75,000 to implement the program, then the net present value (NPV) of the expected profit in ₹ 6,77,818 – ₹ 4,75,000 = ₹ 2,02,818 and the expected return on investment (ROI) is $ROI = \frac{₹2,02,818}{₹4,75,000} = 42.7\%$.

17.9 MEASURING SERVICE QUALITY

In service marketing, the single most researched area is service quality. In the service quality during the last decade the focus had been on quality, total quality management and customer satisfaction in business. Parasuram, Zeithaml and Berry have pioneered research in service quality in marketing and a measurement instrument SERVQUAL was developed for assessing it.

Originally SERVQUAL consisted of ten dimensions which were reduced to five by pooling some of the dimensions together. Refer *Box 17.13*.

Box 17.13 : Dimensions of Service Quality

Ten dimensions (Original model)	Five dimensions (Later Model)
(i) Tangibles	*(I)* Tangibles
(ii) Reliability	*(ii)* Reliability
(iii) Responsiveness	*(iii)* Responsiveness
(iv) Competence	*(iv)* Assurance
(v) Courtesy	*(v)* Empathy
(vi) Credibility	
(vii) Security	
(viii) Access	
(ix) Communication	
(x) Understanding the customer.	

Three of the ten original dimensions *viz.*, tangibles, reliability and responsiveness remained intact. New dimensions *viz.*, assurance and empathy were introduced by pooling competence, courtesy, credibility and security under ***assurance*** and access, communication and understanding the customer under ***empathy.*** The SERVQUAL has 22 items allocated into 5 quality dimensions.

Tangibles	—	4 items
Reliability	—	5 itmes
Responsiveness	—	4 items
Assurance	—	4 items
Empathy	—	5 items
Total	=	22 items

The SERVQUAL for a typical service having 22 items is given in *Box 17.14.*

Box 17.14 : SERVQUAL for a Typical Service	
Dimension	**Question**
Tangibles	1. ABC company will have modern looking equipment
	2. The physical facilities of ABC companies will be visually appealing
	3. Employees of ABC company will be well dressed and appearing neat.
	4. Materials and tools associated with the service will be visually appealing.
Reliability	5. When ABC company promise to do something by a certain time, the promise is always kept.
	6. When customers complain or have problems, ABC company will show great concern for solving them.
	7. ABC company will perform the service right the first time.
	8. ABC company will provide the services at the time agreed on.
	9. ABC company will assist on error free records.
Responsiveness	10. Employees of ABC company will inform customers exact time of service delivery.
	11. Employees of ABC company will give prompt service to customers.
	12. Employees of ABC company will always be willing to help customers.
	13. Employees of ABC company will never be busy to help customers immediately.
Assurance	14. The behaviour of employees of ABC company will impress customers with reliability of service and instil confidence.
	15. Customers will feel safe and confident when transacting with employees of ABC company.
	16. Employees of ABC company will always be friendly and courteous.
	17. Employees of ABC company possess knowledge to answer questions of customers.
Empathy	18. ABC company will pay attention to each customer individually.
	19. ABC company will have opening hours convenient to all their customers.
	20. ABC company will have employees who give personal attention to each customer.
	21. ABC company will have customer's best interest at heart.
	22. The employees of ABC company will understand the specific needs of their customers.

Application of ServQual

SERVQUAL is most valuable when it is used periodically to track quality trends. SERVQUAL can be used for variety of purposes to:

(i) Determine the average gap between customers' perceptions and expectations for each service attribute.

(ii) Assess the organisation's service quality along each of the five dimensions of SERVQUAL.

(iii) Compute organisation's overall weighted SERVQUAL score, which not only accounts for service quality gap for each dimension individually but also the relative importance of dimension (as reflected by the number of points allocated to it).

(iv) Track customer's expectations and perceptions over time.

(v) Compare organisation's SERVQUAL score against those of competitors.

(vi) Identify and examine customer segments that significantly differ in their assessment of company's service performance.

(vii) Assess internal service quality (*i.e.,* the quality of service rendered by one department or division of a company to others within the company).

17.10 BUILDING A SERVICE QUALITY INFORMATION SYSTEM

Customer defined standards and measures of service quality can be grouped into two broad categories. Soft and hard. Soft measures are those that can not easily be observed and must be collected by talking to customers, employees or others. Soft standards provide direction, guidance and feedback to employees in ways to achieve customer satisfaction and can be quantified by measuring customer perceptions and beliefs. SERVQUAL is an example of a sophisticated soft measurement system.

Hard standards and measures relate to those characteristics that can be counted, timed or measured through audits. Measures may include the following:

- How many telephone calls were abandoned while the customer was on hold?
- How many minute customers had to wait in line at a particular stage in service delivery?
- Time required to complete a specific task.
- The temperature of a particular food item.
- How many trains arrived late?
- How many bags were lost?
- How many orders were filled correctly?

The challenge for service marketers is to ensure that operational measure of service quality reflect customer input.

Organisations that are known for excellent service make use of both soft and hard measures. These organisations are good at listening to both their customer and their customer contact employee.

Companies need to establish ongoing service research processes, using multiple methods among different customer groups, that provide timely, relevant trend data that managers can use in their decision making. Some of the possible techniques are:

(i) Analyse customers' complaints

(ii) Post transaction surveys

(iii) Ongoing surveys of account holders by telephone or post, using scientific sampling procedures to determine customers' satisfaction in terms of broader relationship issues.

(iv) Customer advisory panels to offer feedback and advice on service performance.

(v) Employee surveys and panels to determine perceptions of the quality of service delivered to customers on specific dimensions, barriers to better service and suggestions for improvement.

(vi) Focus group interviews, conducted separately with both customers and customer-contact employees to study qualitative issues in depth.

(vii) Total market surveys to compare a firm's performance relative to competitors, bench mark the leaders and identify relevant trends.

(viii) Capture of service operating data, including service response time, failure rate and delivery cost.

Hard Measures of Service Quality

Where a problem is caused by controllable, internal forces, there is no excuse for allowing it to recurr. In fact, maintaining customers' good will after a service failure depends on keeping promises made to the effect that service failures will not happen again. **Some of the tools for monitoring quality (with prevention in mind) and determining the root cause of specific problems that upset customers are discussed in the following paragraphs:**

(i) **Control charts to Monitor a Single Variable:** These charts offer a simple method of displaying performance over time against specific quality standards. Trends can be easily identified because of the visual nature of control charts. ***Exhibit 17.18* shows an airlines performance on the quality standard of on-time departure.** The control chart shows the trends which suggest the needs to be addressed by management because performance is erratic and not very satisfactory.

(ii) **Service Quality Indices:** In a complex service operation, there will be multiple measures of service quality recorded at many different points in the various processes that create the outcome desired by customers. In low-contact services where the customer is not deeply involved in the service delivery process, there is a natural tendency to create many operational measures that apply only to backstage activities, which may have only a second-order effect on activities experienced by customer.

Exhibit 17.18 : Control Chart of Departure Delays of Airlines (showing percentage of flights departing within 15 minutes of schedule)

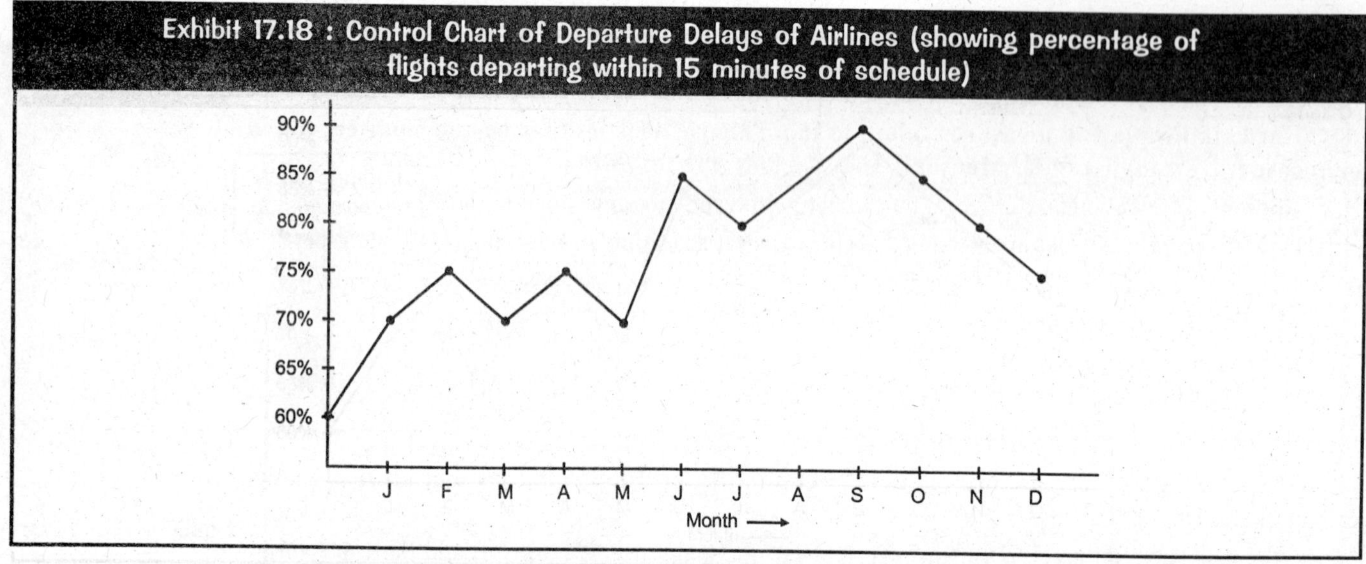

Federal Express, a courier service company in USA, was one of the first companies to understand the need for a companywide index of service quality, that embraced all the key activities that had an impact on customers.

***Box 17.15* shows the composition of Federal Express's Service Quality Index (SQI).**

(iii) **Root-Cause Analysis (The Fish-Bone Chart):** Cause-and-effect analysis is a technique, first developed by Japanese quality expert Kaoru Ishikawa. In this technique a group of managers and staff brainstorm all the possible reasons that might cause a specific problem. The resulting factors are categorised into five groupings – equipment, people, material, process and others on a cause-and-effect chart, known as fishbone chart. This technique which has been used for many years in manufacturing is used in services also recently.

In service organisations the factors of cause are grouped under eight categories namely Equipment (facilities), Front stage Personnel, Backstage Personnel, Process (or Procedures), Information, Material Supplies, Customers and Other causes.

(iv) **Pareto Analysis:** This seeks to identify the principal causes of observed outcomes. This analysis underlies 80/20 rule because it often reveals that around 80 percent of the value of one variable is accounted for by only 20 percent of the causal variable.

Box 17.15 : Composition of Federal Expresse's Service Quality Index

Failure type	Weigthing factor	×	Number of incidents	=	Daily points
Late delivery - Right day	1		......		......
Late delivery - Wrong day	5		......		......
Facing requests unanswered	1		......		......
Complaint reopened	5		......		......
Missing proof of delivery	1		......		......
Invoice adjustments	1		......		......
Missed packets	10		......		......
Lost packages	10		......		......
Damaged packages	10		......		......
Aircraft delays (minutes)	5		......		......
Total failure points (SQI)					XXXXXX

Box 17.16 describes "quality in action" in the service sector.

Quality in Action

Box 17.16 : TQM at Work in the Service Sector

Quality in U.S. service industry in the 1990s was inconsistent, costs were high, profit margins were low and competition increasing each year.

In the photo copier industry, technology in copier design had evened out product distinctions. Savin, a copier manufacturer owned by Japan's Ricoh Corp, believed that **competitive advantage** was to be found in service by stressing **customer service** rather than product specifications.

Savin could cut **service expenses** by two ways while improving services quality. They were:

(i) using statistical analysis by which Savin found that significant time on service calls was being wasted when service engineers had to go back to their trucks for spare parts. The firm assembled a "call kit" which allowed engineers to carry into customer premises all parts with highest probability of use. This has resulted in faster and less costly service calls thereby increasing the number of calls that could be made per day.

(ii) Savin used the **"Pareto principle"** to tackle the "call-back" problem (assuming that 20% of the staff causes 80% of errors). Call-back meant the job was not done right the first time and that a second visit, at Savin's expense was needed to carryout repairs. Retraining only 11% of customer engineers with the most call-backs resulted in a 19% drop in return visits.

According to Rober Williams, Vice-President of Savin, "Total Quality Management is an approach to do business that should permeate every job in the service industry."

17.11 SUMMARY

TQM in services is gaining importance nowadays because of the domination of service industries in our economy and the rising job potential in service industries.

Service quality includes both the quality of the ***core services*** and ***facilitating services.*** The importance of quality in services can not be underestimated because of the growing importance of achieving customer satisfaction and retention of customers in the service sector due to intense competition among service providers. The eight dimensions of quality applicable to services as well as manufactured goods are: *(i)* Performance, *(ii)* Features, *(iii)* Reliability, *(iv)* Conformance, *(v)* Durability, *(vi)* Serviceability, *(vii)* Aesthetics and *(viii)* Perceived quality.

In addition to the above, the unique dimensions of service quality include: *(i)* Time and Timeliness, *(ii)* Completeness, *(iii)* Courtesy, *(iv)* Consistency, *(v)* Acceptability and Convenience, *(vi)* Accuracy and *(vii)* Responsiveness.

A service quality system has the following components: *(i)* Employees, *(ii)* Information Technology, and *(iii)* Customer expectations of service.

The five dimensions of service quality are: *(i)* Reliability, *(ii)* Responsiveness, *(iii)* Assurance, *(iv)* Empathy and *(v)* Tangibles.

Quality management in services is relevant because of the following reasons:

(i) Quality is a key ***competitive component*** of strategies of service organisations.

(ii) Service organisations need to create ***differential advantage*** as compared to competitors.

(iii) Increasing levels of ***consumerism*** and greater media attention to quality have made it necessary for service organisations to be more responsive to quality issues.

(iv) Growing importance of ***service image, service positioning*** and ***service delivery processes*** in the growing consumer markets for services.

Two approaches to quality management of services are: *(i)* Product attributed approach and *(ii)* Consumer oriented approach or user based approach. Product based approach focuses on performance, features, reliability, conformance, durability, serviceability, aesthetics and perceived quality aspects of service while consumer based approach recognises the holistic process of service delivery from the point of view of expectations and attitudes of service clients.

Service Quality Models have been used to understand the role of management in service quality management. The models describe the factors that influence customer perception of quality. Some of the models of service quality are: *(i)* The Gronroos Model, *(ii)* The PZB model (Parasuraman, Zeithaml and Berry Model).

The Gronroos model explains the *"missing service quality"* concept whereas the PZB model identifies five gaps that can cause unsuccessful service delivery. By means of this model, management can exercise greater control over consumer relationships by taking necessary action to bridge or close these gaps.

Parasuraman, Zeithaml and Berry have identified five barriers to service delivery. They are:

(i) Customer expectation, management perception gap.
(ii) Management perception, service quality specification gap
(iii) Service quality specification, service delivery gap
(iv) Service delivery, external communication gap and
(v) Customer expectation, customer perception gap.

Parasuraman, Zeithaml and Berry also have developed a survey research instrument called 'SERVQUAL' to measure customer satisfaction with different aspects of service quality. The SERVQUAL scale contains 21 perception items and a series of expectation items reflecting the five dimensions of service quality namely Tangibles, Reliability, Responsiveness, Assurance and Empathy.

Quality assurance in service includes measurement of quality characteristics in services such as time (waiting time, service time and delivery time), the number of non-conformance and also the costs of service quality and return on service quality. Service quality has a chain of effects on profits through retention of customers through the following linkages:

(i) Linking employee satisfaction to customer satisfaction.
(ii) Linking customer satisfaction to customer retention
(iii) Linking customer retention to market shares
(iv) Linking market shares to revenues
(v) Linking revenues to profits
(vi) Linking profits to service improvement and
(vii) Linking service improvement to customer satisfaction.

Service quality measurement uses the SERVQUAL which has 22 items allocated for 5 quality dimensions. This instrument can be used periodically to trace quality trends through SERVQUAL scores.

A service quality information system must be built to collect relevant data regarding customer perceptions and beliefs, data regarding employees etc. which will be helpful in achieving customer satisfaction regarding service offered. Some of the techniques used to collect the data are: *(i)* Analysis of customer complaints, *(ii)* Post transaction surveys, *(iii)* Sampling surveys to determine customer – satisfaction, *(iv)* Feedback from customer advisory panel, *(v)* employee surveys, *(vi)* focus group interviews, *(vii)* Total market surveys for competitor analysis and *(viii)* Capture of service operating data such as service response time, failure rate and service delivery cost.

Hard measures of service quality relate to monitoring service quality (with prevention of service failure in mind) and determining the root cause of specific problems related to service that affects customer satisfaction. Some of the tools used are:

(i) Control charts to monitor a single variable.
(ii) Service quality indices
(iii) Root cause analysis (using fish-bone chart) and
(iv) Pareto Analysis.

17.12 KEY WORDS USED

Service Quality, Reliability, Conformance, Durability, Serviceability, Perceived Service Quality, Credibility, Responsiveness, Competence, Courtesy, Access, Creditability, Security, Tangibles, Information Technology, Expected Service, Desired Service, Adequate Service, Service Encounters, Moment of Truth, Evidence of Service, Process Quality, Technical Outcome Quality, Empathy, Customer Satisfaction, Client Management, Image Management, Experienced Service, Perceived Service, Technical Quality, Functional Quality, Service Quality Model, Service Quality Indices, Pareto Analysis, Root-cause Analysis, Fish-Bone chart, Cause-and-Effect Analysis.

17.13 OBJECTIVE QUESTIONS

(A) Match the following :

Column A	Column B
1. Service encounter	1. Identifies five gaps
2. 'Gronroos' model	2. Treating customers as individuals
3. Empathy in service	3. Also known as "Moment of truth"
4. PZB model	4. A measuring instrument for service quality
5. SERVQUAL	5. Explains missing service quality concept

(B) State whether the following statements are True or False :

1. The service concept is a combination of both technical and human behavioural aspects. (T / F)
2. Customers evaluate a service primarily by the quality of human contact. (T / F)
3. The price of the service does not have any influence on the perceptions of quality, satisfaction and value. (T / F)
4. Technical quality and functional quality are one and the same. (T / F)
5. There is no way to reduce the cost of service quality to zero. (T / F)

(C) Multiple choice Questions : Choose the correct answer from the alternatives given under each question :

1. The aspects of service quality that affects customer's perceptions is / are:
   (a) Technical quality (b) Integrative quality
   (c) Financial quality (d) Outcome quality
   (e) All of these (f) None of these
2. The major dimensions of service quality is (are):
   (a) Reliability (b) Responsiveness
   (c) Assurance (d) Tangibles
   (e) All of these (f) None of these
3. The assumption "quality lies in the eyes of the beholder" is used in the following approach to quality management:
   (a) Product attributed approach (b) Consumer oriented approach
   (c) Seller oriented approach (d) None of these
4. Service quality is a function of:
   (a) Timeliness of service (b) Manner in which service is performed
   (c) Adequacy of the service (d) Price of service
   (e) All of these (f) None of these
5. The objectives of internal marketing is (are):
   (a) Overall objective (b) Strategic Objective
   (c) Tactical objective (d) All of these
   (e) None of these

17.14 REVIEW QUESTIONS

1. State the differences between goods and services.
2. State how a manufacturing sector differs from a service sector.
3. State the eight dimensions of quality defined by Garvin which are applicable to services as well as

manufactured goods.

4. Define the term "Service quality" and state the ten determinants of service quality.
5. Describe the various components of service system quality.
6. What is meant by "Five stars of service quality"?
7. Describe the five dimensions of service quality.
8. Describe the two approaches to quality management in services.
9. What is a "service quality model"? Explain with a diagram, a model for service quality.
10. Discuss the various internal and external factors that influence customer perception.
11. Describe with a diagram, "The Gronroos Model" for managing the perceived service quality.
12. Describe the PZB service quality model with a diagram, explaining the various gaps in the model.
13. What are the barriers to service quality according to Parasuraman, Zeithaml and Berry.
14. What is "1-10-100 Rule" in quality?
15. Explain how customer satisfaction can be measured by "SERVQUAL".
16. What is meant by "return on service quality"? Explain with an illustration.
17. Discuss the linkages between
    (a) Customer satisfaction and retention
    (b) Retention and market share
    (c) Market share and revenues and
    (d) Service improvement and customer satisfaction.
18. Explain how a "service quality information system" is built?
19. Describe the various hard measures of service quality.

17.15 DISCUSSION QUESTIONS

1. "In reality all services are a mixture of service and a tangible product" – Discuss.
2. "Quality of services is more difficult to measure than quality of manufactured parts" – Comment on this statement.
3. "Employee performance and behaviour and service transaction speed are the strongest determinants of perceived service quality" – Explain.
4. "Customers evaluate a service primarily by the quality of human contact" – Critically examine this statement.
5. "Knowing what the customer expects is the first and possibly most critical step in delivering quality service" Do you agree or not? Justify your answer.
6. "The price of the service can also greatly influence perceptions of quality, satisfaction and value" – Elaborate.
7. "Quality lies in the eyes of the beholder" – Discuss the statement in view of service quality.
8. "Managers used to belive that for any process there was a trade off between cost and product or service quality" – Explain.

17.16 ASSIGNMENTS

1. Using the SERVQUAL instrument, measure the service quality of an educational institution or a hospital in your locality.
2. Visit a three star or a five star hotel in your city and find out the criteria used for rating of hotels and suggest the action to be taken by the hotel to improve its rating.

17.17 CHPATER CASES

1. F.C. GENERAL HOSPITAL (FCGH)

FC General Hospital is a privately owned 600 patient bed facility in Bangalore, Karnataka. The hospital is located in the suburban - Whitefield. All affluent, urban / suburban communities with a highly educated population composed largely of employees of the information technology companies and high-tech engineering firms surround the township of Whitefield.

The hospital has 900 employees and provides a broad range of healthcare services, including drug / alcohol abuse wards, emergency rooms, X-ray and laboratory facilities, maternity wards, intensive and cardiac care units and outpatient facilities.

With strong competition from other super specialty hospitals located in the nearby townships, FCGH has had to concentrate on offering high-quality treatment at reasonable prices. FCGH has not attempted to obtain all of the latest up-to-date diagnostic equipment (such as CAT scans, MRI facility etc.) because its board felt it would not be cost-effective to try to compete with the super-specialty hospitals in the vicinity. Even though FCGH is considered a 'medium-to-large' hospital, it has attempted to stress personal attention to each patient. Of late, the hospital began a series of ads in the local English daily newspaper highlighting its concerned doctors and nurses, its friendly support to staff and its overall philosophy that its employees care about their work and their patients.

Quality health care is a goal all hospitals profess, but few have developed comprehensive and scientific means of asking customers to judge the quality of service they receive. Much effort has been put to assess the clinical quality of hospital care, books, journals and papers on the topic abound.

The problem, however is that past efforts to measure hospital quality have largely ignored the perceptions of customers - the patients, physicians and health insurance subscribers. Instead of formally considering customer judgments of quality, the health care industry has focused almost entirely on internal quality assessments made by the health professionals who operate the system. In effect, a system for improving healthcare has been created that all but ignores the voice of the customer.

The board of FCGH believes that all hospitals need to make the transformation from the current practice of attempting to ensure quality to actually measuring and improving the quality of care from both the external and internal customer perspective and internal, provider perspective. Fueled by concerns in recent years about costs and medical practice variation and by the demand for greater social accountability, there is an emerging demand by patient and health insurance that quality healthcare be provided at best value.

As board president Dr. Ishwar recently stated at the annual FCGH meeting, " As the prices people pay in the future for given levels of service become more similar, hospitals will be distinguished largely on the basis of their quality and value as assessed by customers. We must have accurate information about how our customers, not just the health care professional, who work here, judge the quality of care in this hospital. Many hospitals have some methods for measuring patient satisfaction. A recent survey of more than 100 hospitals in Bangalore district show that two thirds routinely conduct patient satisfaction surveys. Typically, the surveys are distributed at discharge to patients who are free to respond or not. The main value of such surveys are to gain a quick knowledge of problems experienced by patients, many of whom often fill out questionnaires because they are disgruntled about some specific aspect of the care they received".

In response to Dr. Ishwar's statement, and in the light of the advertising campaign, hospital administrator Dr. Kamala called a meeting of her department heads to discuss the issue of quality. "Can we really deliver on our promises? Or are we in danger of failing to live up to the level of health care our patients expect and do we risk losing them?" Ms Kamala asked. Ms Preeti, head of nursing continued the debate:

"I argue that surveys such as the one Dr. Ishwar mentioned in his speech, are valuable. But how do we measure the quality of our health care? Some patients who leave FCGH happy may have actually received poor treatment here. If we are serious about improving the quality of care, we need more valid and reliable data on which to act. We need answers to specific, quality related questions about activities in areas that affect patient's admission, nursing, medical staff, daily care and ancillary staff."

'I have an idea' said Meenakshi, the staff director of Dr Kamala. "I just finished reading a book by Dr.Jagadish, who is the director for quality at TRW, a big manufacturing firm. He says there are 14 steps in TRW's internal quality audits. I made a philosophy of those steps. Why don't we consider his approach?" When the meeting ended, Dr. Kamala read the list of 14 steps of Dr.Jagadish again and began to think about the whole issue of quality control in the manufacturing firms. It had worked in many manufacturing firms, but could the concepts of quality control used by manufacturing firms really be used in a hospital?

Discussion Questions :

1. Why is it important to get the patient's assessment of healthcare quality? Does a patient have the expertise to judge the health care he or she receives?
2. How might a hospital measure quality?
3. How can the value of human life be included in the cost of quality control.
4. There are certain parallels between the evaluation of health care quality and educational service quality. How are the customer surveys used to evaluate the quality of teaching in your institution? How are the results used? Are any other measures available to assess educational quality? What improvements would you suggest to the current system?

2. THE CASE OF LOST BAGGAGE IN THE AIRPORT

Upon his arrival in Indira Gandhi International airport the weary traveler went to collect his suitcase. But it never appeared. After filing a lost bag report, he was told that when his bag was found, it would be delivered to his hotel. When he asked how soon that might be, he was told most bags are located and delivered within 24 hours. "That just wont do!" he exclaimed. "I just completed a training session for my client in Bangalore and I will have to make a presentation to the client's top management executive board tomorrow morning at 9.00AM. I must have my suit for that presentation.!" The claim's manager replied "If you are such a hot-shot consultant, that should it be a problem".

Discussion Questions :

1. Evaluate the above situation for how well the service provider responded.
2. What did the claim's manager do well?
3. How could the claim's manager could have improved his response?

CHAPTER 18

IMPLEMENTING TOTAL QUALITY MANAGEMENT

LEARNING OBJECTIVES

After reading this chapter, you should be able to:

- Discuss the requirements for implementation of TQM.
- Understand the implementation variation among organisations.
- Discuss the evolution of implementation approaches.
- Illustrate the 20 steps of total quality implementation process.
- Discuss the steps of TQM implementation process when top management committment is absent.
- Know the various implementation strategies.

18.0 INTRODUCTION

We have discussed in the previous chapters the importance of quality, concepts and philosophies of total quality management, planning and organizing for total quality in organisations, various tools and techniques involved in total quality management, how to build and sustain total quality organisation, and various approaches such as "Just-in-time production", "Six-Sigma quality", "Benchmarking", Business process reengineering" Supply Chain Management and World-class manufacturing" etc. used by total quality organisations to achieve excellence in their field of business.

Implementation of total quality is crucial for achieving sustainable growth and competitive advantage leading to business excellence.

However, whatever quality system is in place, whatever be the process capability for quality and the tools and technique employed, the most important thing is the implementation of total quality in any organisation for achieving sustainable growth and competitive advantage leading to excellence in business. This chapter provides the insights to help you implement total quality.

However it must be remembered that **there is no one best way that fits the needs of all organisations as far as implementing total quality in concerned.** It is true that when an organisation is facing the possibility of going out of business, there is a better chance that its management can be convinced to embrace the principles of total quality and implement the same enthusiastically. On the other hand, when an organisation is doing pretty well, and then taking on the work that is involved in becoming a total quality organisation in more difficult to sell, unless you are at the top of the organisation chart.

Change is always difficult and changing a culture that has been ingrained for many years is a herculean task. When change is seen as the last hope for survival, it becomes easier to implement change initiatives. People are more receptive to change when they realist that they will certainly lose their jobs unless change is implemented. However there is no guarantee that change will assure survival but the other side of the coin is that going out of business is virtually certain if change is not implemented. Every organisation, no matter what the type, will be under severe pressure as total quality pervades the industry. Whether one likes it or not, change is inevitable in a competitive business environment and **when the going is tough, only the tough gets going,** Therefore managers should consider whether they would prepare to go ahead of the quality grounds well or engulfed by it-out of control, fighting for survival with the odds against success much higher.

In this context, it is worth mentioning about the success story of Japan after it had been decimated by World War II and its economy was in shambles. Japan was in a state of crisis after its two cities were destroyed by the nuclear bombs dropped by US air force. This ultimately put an end to the run-away success of Japanese in the war against USA after its attack on Pearl Harbor. Japan had to struggle to rebuild its economy and put people to work. This involved more than just running the factories to meet the needs of the domestic market. Japan had to look beyond its shores for global markets. The attractive market was the US market but convincing Americans that they should buy goods from the enemy nation that attacked Pearl Harbour and overcoming the American association of Japanese goods with poor quality were the two major problems Japan was facing at that time. Before World War II, Japan had been unsuccessful in American markets because of the perception of poor quality in its goods.

Therefore the Union of Japanese Scientists and Engineers (JUSE) invited Dr. W. Edward Deming, an American statistician, in 1950 to visit Japan and deliver a series of lectures to plant manager, engineers and research workers in Japan to help them understand, apply the statistical techniques developed by Dr. Walter Shewhart of Bell Laboratories USA in a quest to improve the quality of Japanese products. Deming arranged a meeting of 500 people including the top executives or 21 Japanese companies and told them that they could compete in the world's markets within 5 years if they followed his teachings. The incredible Japanese did it in just four years. The Japanese earnestly listened to and acted on Deming's recommendations because they were at the point of **seeking a route to survival.**

18.1 RATIONALE FOR CHANGE

Why change is inevitable? What is wrong with the traditional way we do business?

***(i)* We are bound to a short-term focus:** Most of the organisations are driven by short-term objectives, it is true whether the organisations are engaged in manufacturing or services we use to judge every thing we do on the basis of a measurable pay-back (return-on-investment) in the next quarter or next year (i.e., Keynesian economics)

Change is always difficult and inevitable. Implementation of total quality brings about the beneficial change in organisations.

***(ii)* The traditional approach tends to be arrogant, rather then customer focused:** Most traditional organisations are arrogant. They think they know more about what their customers need than their customers do. Or worse yet, they don't care about their customers' needs.

***(iii)* We seriously underestimate the potential contribution of our employees, particularly those in hands-on functions:** The person who knows the most about a job and the one who is most likely to know how to solve problems-is the person who is doing the job and facing the problem day in and day out. But this truth is often overlooked by supervisors and managers who direct the workers to do their job as they are told to do by their superiors. Even though every employee would generally want to do a good job, faced with processes that are not capable and management that is not willing to listen, they end up living with the situation and do what best they can do with the existing limitations. This will result in wastage of the brain power employed in the organisation.

***(iv)* The traditional approach equates better quality with higher cost:** The perception of higher quality is usually associated with higher cost. Price is the indicator of quality to the customer. However, Phillip Crosby wrote a book titled **"Quality is Free"** in 1979. In the beginning, many traditional managers did not buy the idea that quality is free. However, organisations that have successfully changed themselves into total quality enterprises have found not only that quality is free but that it also brings unforeseen benefits. One glaring example is that of Japanese cars or consumer electronic goods which have become better in quality and cheaper in price over a period of time.

***(v)* The traditional approach in short on leadership and long on "boss-man ship":** Many traditional managers see their jobs as simply telling their subordinates what to do and when to do it. A classic example was the mass production and assembly lines evolved in Ford Automobile manufacturing plants in the early decades of 20th century. Mass production has brought in **"specialisation"**- a way to divide the labor into other areas to minimize the need for worker skills and knowledge. The moving assembly lines and interchangeable parts produced by mass production methods eliminated the need for highly skilled workers (craftsmen). However, the Japanese demonstrated a better approach where in, the manager acts like leader and not a boss thereby fostering team work and better interpersonal relationships which motivated the employees to improve their productivity.

18.2 REQUIREMENTS FOR IMPLEMENTATION OF TQM

There are some symptoms which signal the need for implementing total quality in an organisation. For instance, a particular division or a department may be concerned that the future will not be bright unless some fundamental changes are brought about. Another indicator may be dwindling market share, the company's market share is being taken by competitors. The product quality may not be good enough and there is lack of co-operation among different units or departments of the company. The company my observe that total quality approach is working for others and so it is needed for it also. However there are certain requirements for implementation of total quality for achieving the desired benefits. These requirements are discussed in the following paragraphs.

***(i)* Commitment by Top Management:** For total quality to become the **way we do business** an unwavering and unquestioned commitment is required at the top management level in any organisation. The chief executive officer (CEO), the president or the managing director, or whatever title the top executive has, must commit not only the required resources, but also a considerable amount of his / her own time for implementing total quality. Top executives should plan on a third to half their time being used in the total quality effort. Delegation of implementation of total quality to lower levels of management is not recommended because there is no success story of delegated total quality implementation. If the top executive delegates total quality, it is interpreted by others that total quality is not number one in his or her priority list. Since cross-functional coordination is the essential ingredient of total quality implementation, problems could arise unless the top management is very much involved in the implementation effort.

The requirements for implementation of total quality are: *(i)* Commitment by top management *(ii)* Commitment of resources *(iii)* Organisation wide steering committee *(iv)* Planning and publicising and *(v)* Infrastructure that supports deployment and continuous improvement

For an organisation-wide total quality effort, from the lowest level employee to the CEO, a profound change is required in the corporate culture. To make it happen every one must be willing for the change needed which is a rare thing to happen by itself. **There are many barriers to change-both personal and organisational.** People resist change as a matter-of-fact as they see danger in change, danger to their personal position, the threat of loss of power or prestige, perhaps even loss of employment. Some like status-quo in everything and see no reason for implementing any kind of change. Some will be unwilling to put in the extra work required. Some can not believe that total quality is beneficial and makes sense. If the message from the top is not clear and if the top-executive is not seen as totally committed to and involved in total quality, people below are encouraged to either go slow or totally discard total quality implementation.

Another reason for the top management to be committed to total quality is that it is a great **learning experience.** Unless the top executive is involved in day-to-day activities of total quality implementation, he or she will never know about what is happening and they will not be able to make rational decisions affecting the change. Since many of the changes affect more than one department or function, the implementation becomes difficult when the affected departments do not see eye-to-eye. Some changes may need changes in organisational structure, and may be beyond the scope of the department heads. Only the person at the top can do that.

***(ii)* Commitment of resources:** Total quality implementation need not be expensive, but everything has a cost, for example, the cost of training people in applying Q.C tools to solve their problems at work place, or the expenses involved in hiring external consultants who are experts, (say in six-sigma quality management). Therefore top management must commit the needed resources for total quality effort. But the difficulty is that it will not be easy to project a payback as so many factors will be affecting a company's performance and profitability, making it impossible to directly link benefits with expenses incurred for implementing total quality. **The commitment of money for implementing total quality should be based on reasoning, based on the following question.**

(a) Does it make sense to do this?
(b) Is the timing right?
(c) Is the money available?
(d) Can we afford it?
(e) Is it the right thing to do?

***(iii)* Organisation-wide Steering Committee:** For company-wide implementation of total quality, a top-level steering committee is necessary. This committee should be headed by the CEO and its members should be comprised of the direct subordinates of the CEO. For example, in a company, the chairman of the steering committee may be the managing director and the members comprise the functional directors. The steering committee is responsible to establish how total quality is to be implemented and then to see that it happens.

Cross-functional teams must be set up, objectives of these terms be established and results must be monitored. The steering committee operates as a team and sets the vision and goals for the company, establishes teams to pursue the goals, monitors their progress and rewards them for their achievements. It is important that the implementation of total quality needs to be managed by the top management in the form of a steering committee to channelise the energy of the human resource in the direction of achieving the company's objectives.

Further, the steering committee symbolizes teamwork and gives a strong message to the executives and employees down the line to exhibit the same kind of teamwork in their areas of operation.

(iv) **Planning and Publicising:** After securing the commitment from top management for the implementation of total quality and establishing the steering committee, the real work starts. The steering committee must now develop the vision statement and guiding principles, set the goals and objectives, put the TQ implementation plan in place and then develop an awards and recognition program and other publicity efforts.

The **vision statement** is a long-range view of what the company will be after say 5 or 10 years from now. Total quality needs a long-range vision because it is only achieved over a relatively long period. TQ involves fundamental changes in the way things are done, how people work together, involving customers and suppliers in ways never considered before. Vision must be a distant tangent to provide a consistent course into the future.

The **guiding principles** are the second element of the vision and usually accompany the vision statement in a single document. The guiding principle establish the rules of conduct for the organisation and it employees. These principles may be concerned with honesty, respect, fairness, quality, supplies, community, environment, role of management and employees.

The broad **goals and objectives** established by the steering committee must harmonise with the vision statement. They flow from the vision statement and are frequently part of the organisation's strategic plan. From these goals and objectives which are established for the total organisation, specific supporting objectives will be developed for departments, teams and even individuals. The vision points the company in the desired direction and guides employees with the principles they must use in pursuit of the vision. The broad goals and objectives represent the strategic targets along the way to achieving the vision. A lower tier of specific tactical objectives describes what must be done as the company goes about achieving the vision. At both levels, objectives should be stated relating to total quality implementation.

The **total quality implementation plan** is driven by the vision, goals and objectives. It spells out precisely the route to be taken by the implementation program. No two quality implementation will be the same. The implementation plan must provide for training, starting with training of top executives and the steering committee to function as a total quality team. After the steering committee has been trained, it will be ready to start work. Before initiating the pilot program; the people who are to be involved must be trained. In an approach called **cascading training,** first the steering committee is trained. They go off and do their planning to get ready for total quality. Then just prior to the first implementation, members of the steering committee train the total quality project leaders who in turn train the team members.

An **award and recognition program** must be in hand before the implementation starts. The award and recognition should be for team and not individuals. The reward and recognition programs usually operate on two levels: *(a)* the employee review establishes pay raises, frequently based on annual or semi-annual performance review, and *(b)* a kind of spot award for having achieved something special. Both need to be oriented toward the team-not the individual.

An **approach for publicising** total quality activities and result is important. All the employees need to know what is going on all the time. Only when employees are fully informed can they understand many decisions of management and consequently support management. When it comes to total quality implementation, every employee will be affected and it is absolutely essential that they understand what is going on and why. They should know what is planned and how they will be affected. Various means of communication include company newsletter, all-employee meetings, and special total quality bulletins, the intercom system etc.

(v) **Infrastructure That Supports Deployment and Continual Improvement.** With commitment from the top management level, a high-level steering committee, a set of plans for at

least the early phases of implementation and the means of providing the required training, what we need is the infrastructure that will support the deployment of total quality throughout the organisation and continuous improvement on a never-ending basis. The vision and its harmonised objectives, the awards and recognition program and the means of communications can be considered as part of the supporting infrastructure. Three other infrastructure features that can offer support for total quality implementation efforts are a) operating procedures b).organisational structure and c). union situation.

Virtually all organisations operate in accordance with published procedures. But many of these procedures may not support total quality and represent an opportunity for improvement. If the current procedures are not conducive to implementation of total quality, they need to be changed.

Typically, organisations have hierarchical structures which do not fit with total quality. As total quality implementation progresses, it may be necessary to alter the organisation structure and eliminate the barriers or walls which are built up around departments.

In organisations with organized labour, the union is an inherent part of the infrastructure. Usually labour unions do not easily accept the changes necessary for maximum benefit of total quality. Basically union embraces the concept of division of labour to a fault and may emphasise work rules which are incompatible with total quality. However in progressive organisations, enlightened and well informed unions have realized that the benefits of total quality outweigh the disadvantages and have come forward to help in the company's quest for total quality.

18.3 IMPLEMENTATION VARIATION AMONG ORGANISATIONS

People who have to assume leadership position for quality implementation in their organisations are likely to look to published literature or the experiences of others for choosing the recipe that will help them succeed. But there is no such magic formula, which brings success every time. Since organisations and their cultures vary and organisations employ people who are all different from each other and also their business situations are unique, the implementation plan that worked well for ABC company will never fit exactly the needs of XYZ Company. However, one can find the ideas and techniques that can be tailed to his or her organisation by going through the published literature and sharing the experiences of other organisations. The approaches to implementation that have been successfully used by other organisations cover the spectrum of possibilities. However it must be remembered that there is no **one right way.** An organisation with its special strengths and weaknesses, its peculiar business situation, its unique culture, may have identified some **wrong ways** and also more than one **right way.**

Steps involved in implementing total quality are:
(i) Training the steering committee
(ii) Identifying organisational strengths and weaknesses
(iii) Identifying the probable advocates of total quality
(iv) Identifying both external and internal customers
(v) Developing a means for determining customer satisfaction.

While the starting tasks in implementation of total quality include: *(a)* making a commitment at the top management level, *(b)* forming a steering committee of the top management executives and *(c)* defining the organisations vision and broad objectives, there are some other necessary steps. These are:

Step 1. Training the steering committee:

This training should include:

(a) Deming's Fourteen Points, The Seven Deadly Diseases and the Obstacles.

(b) The seven Q.C tools and management tools and

(c) Team building.

Step 2. Identifying organisational strengths and weakness:

This step includes

a) Statistical capability and

b) Data collection and analytical ability.

Step 3. Identifying the probable advocates of total quality:

This step includes finding

a) Which departments are most likely to be advocates of total quality? and

b) Who will resist total quality?

Step 4. Identifying customers, both external and internal:

a) Who are the real, ultimate customers of the organisation?

b) Who are the internal customers of the various departments or processes?

c) Who are the customers of the individual employees?

Step 5. Developing a means for determining customer satisfaction (external/internal)

a) establishing the current base line against which improvement will be measured.

By doing the above steps, the steering committee will be able to make rational judgments about how the implementation journey should start. For example, if a company is strong in data collection and analysis, it might first venture the establishment of one or more process teams where task will be to flowchart a key process, understand how it works, characterise it to base line its process capability and then set about improving the process. In such a situation, the steering committee should identify the key processes and establish cross-functional teams for each one. Then each of the key process teams should establish lower level process teams as required.

If an organisation has a manufacturing group, which will advocate total quality, then the organisation might start by introducing "just-in-time" production techniques on the shop floor to implement total quality. On the other hand if an organisation has some particular problem that has not been solved by the traditional methods, then cross-functional teams should be formed to apply total quality techniques to analyse and solve the problems. This kind of **"problem-solving team approach"** is probably the most common introduction to total quality.

If an organisation is strong in statistical area, it is better to start total quality by implementing the use of seven Q.C. tools.

Another approach to starting total quality is the customer satisfaction approach. From this the employees will have to identify their internal customers and determine their basis for customer satisfaction. The same approach can be extended to external customers.

18.4 EVOLUTION OF IMPLEMENTATION APPROACHES

There may be many examples of inappropriate total quality implementation. But one can not learn about most of the failures with out being directly involved. Still, lot of information is available from which one can identify the approaches that must be avoided. Also, there are volumes of information available on successful implementations from which one can learn much. However it must be remembered that merely duplicating another's success by mimicking, no organisation can implement total quality. So it is better to learn all one can and adopt approaches that seem most likely to produce good results in his / her organisation.

The following paragraphs discuss the ideas of implementation approaches that should be avoided:

***(i)* Don't train all your employees at once:** Some organisations spend lot of money to train all employees-from. the top-level to the bottom-most level in total quality, seven Q.C. tools, statistical process control etc., before implementing total quality. This many be waste of money as majority of those employees who have been trained would have no immediate use of the training they have undergone. Therefore, the right way to do is to train small groups of employees just-in-time-just as they need it.

(ii) **Don't rush into total quality by putting too many people in teams:** Many organisations are interested in keeping score by the number of teams deployed as the percentage of employees on teams (for e.g. quality circles) in order to satisfy the top management. But it is difficult to develop meaningful number of teams which would lead to increased profitability, higher customer satisfaction, reduction of waste etc. which are all attributable to total quality in the real sense and it is not the number of teams or the total number of employees in the teams that matters. What is important is that teams take on on specific problems as directed by the steering committee and solve them.

(iii) **Total quality implementation must not be delegated:** In many organisations, top management's approach has been to commit the organisation to total quality and then delegate the implementation to the quality assurance department. The top management treated total quality as just another program to be endured, without knowing the real meaning of total quality. It must be remembered that without the leadership of top management, successful implementation of total quality will not be possible. Top management involvement is necessary to remove the road blocks that will hinder the smooth implementation of total quality programs. A successful implementation of total quality requires both complete commitment and active, personal, day-in, day-out involvement by top management and staff.

(iv) **Don't start an implementation before you are prepared:** Some time, senior-level managers may not have good knowledge of total quality but they do not accept the fact. Plunging into anything as technically sociologically complex as total quality without having a grasp of the subject will guarantee failure. Just having control charts hanging on the walls of the shop floors or near the machines and conducting weekly review meetings and using slogan like " worker involvement" will not bring success in total quality implementation. Real continuous Improvement and real worker involvement are the hallmarks of total quality. Therefore, the first step should be to get educated on the subject of total quality before attempting to implement. This should include top manager and his or her immediate subordinates.

18.5 IMPLEMENTATION PHASES TO BE CONSIDERED

***Box 18.1* illustrates the 20 steps total quality implementation process.**

Box 18.1 : Total Quality Implementation Process

THE PREPARATION PHASE

The preparation phase includes steps 1 to 11 shown in the *Box 18.1* and they are done in sequence. These steps are briefly discussed below.

Step 1. Commitment to total quality: The top executive (e.g. CEO, President etc.) must make the commitment of time and resources before forming the steering committee. Without top management commitment, nothing should be done in respect of total quality implementation.

Step 2. Formation of the total quality steering committee: The top executive designate immediate staff (who report to top executive directly) to be the total quality steering committee, with the top executive being the chairman of the steering committee.

If the organisation has a recognized trade union, a senior union official should also be a member of the steering committee. The steering committee will be a permanent entity and will replace the former staff organisation established for quality assurance.

Step 3. Steering committee team building: The steering committee needs to go through a team-building exercise before it starts any total quality work. Usually, an outside consultant (total quality expert) will be helpful in this regard. This team building session usually requires 1 to 3 days, preferably conducted away from the work environment.

Step 4. Steering committee total quality training: The steering committee will require training in total quality philosophy, techniques and tools before it starts any total quality work. Usually, an outside consultant will be helpful in training the steering committee members. Two or three days of intensive training followed by self study and appropriate seminars in the long run will be necessary.

Step 5. Creation of the vision statement and guiding principles: The real total quality work effort starts with the creation of the organisation's **vision statement** and putting on paper the **guiding principles** under which the company is to operate. The top executive initiates discussion by using raw vision and principles which will be refined after discussing with the steering committee members resulting in short meaningful documents that embody the hopes and aspirations of the organisation. This requires at least one full day.

Step 6. Establishment of strategic objectives. The steering committee flows the vision statement into a set of **broad** company objectives which are **strategic** (long-term) in nature. (for e.g. a time horizon of 5 years) From these **strategic objectives,** a set of supporting **tactical objectives** that go into specifics are derived, (for e.g. these **tactical objectives** have a time horizon of 1 year to 3 years). The establishment of strategic and tactical objectives will take at least a full week or more depending on the nature of the business carried out by the organisation.

Step 7. Communication and publicity: The top executive and the steering committee should communicate information about steps 2 and 4 as they occur. It is important that everyone in the organisation knows about the vision, the guiding principles, the objectives and total quality. Every employee should know why total quality is being implemented. The employees should see the top executive as the champion of total quality, with the support of the steering committee. This activity should start at this point and should go on forever.

Step 8. Identification of organisational strengths and weaknesses: The steering committee must objectively identify the strengths and the weaknesses of the organisation. This information will be helpful to guide the steering committee to the best total quality implementation approach and to help it to correct the deficiencies of the organisation. The duration of this activity should be planned as a full day.

Step 9. Identification of advocates and resisters: The steering committee should try to identify those in key positions in the organisation who are likely to be advocates (or supporters) of total quality and those who are likely to resist (or oppose) total quality. This knowledge will be helpful in selecting the early projects and team members.

Step 10. Baseline employee satisfaction / attitudes: The steering committee should attempt to gauge the current state of employee satisfaction and attitudes with the help of the human resources department or an outside consultant. An objective judgment of employee satisfaction and attitudes help to determine whether total quality changes are working effectively or not (i.e. whether employee satisfaction and attitudes will improve or not after implementing total quality)

This exercise may take a week if done using in-house resources (i.e. human resource department) and at least a month if an outside firm is hired. The exercise should be repeated annually.

Step 11. Baseline customer satisfaction: The steering committee, by taking the help of marketing department, should attempt to obtain objective feed back from customers to determine the level of satisfaction. The sample size (member of customers surveyed randomly) depends on the size of the customer base. The survey using a printed questionnaire may take 2 months, while telephone interview may take 2 weeks. This survey should be repeated annually.

THE PLANNING PHASE

This phase includes four steps (i.e. step 12 to 15) which are briefly discussed below:

Step 12. Plan the implementation approach. Then use "Plan / Do / Check /Adjust" Cycle (PDCA cycle):

At this point, the steering committee should start planning the implementation of total quality. This step becomes continuous, because after initial projects are underway, information will be fed back to this step to accommodate course correction, adjustment and so on. In addition, this step will continue to spin out new projects and teams. This activity never ends. It repeats as long as the process exists (PDCA Cycle)

Step 13. Identification of projects: The steering committee is responsible for selecting the initial total quality projects, based on the strengths and weaknesses of the organisation, the personalities involved, the vision and objectives established and the probability of success. The initial projects must be selected to assure success to set a foundation of experience from which difficult challenges can be accepted later on. The initial project identification and selection may take a few days and this process continues forever later.

Step 14. Establishing team composition: After selecting the initial projects, the steering committee establishes the composition of the team that will execute them, Most teams will be cross-functional in nature, having representatives from multiple departments or disciplines as appropriate for the project at hand. This task goes on forever.

Step 15. Provide team training: It is important to train the new team before it can go to work. Training should cover basics of total quality and tools appropriate to the project. Training may be done by a member of the steering committee. The duration of the training may be at least one-half day; followed by facilitation. As new teams are formed, the need for training will continue until eventually all employees are trained and experienced.

THE EXECUTION PHASE

This phase includes 5 steps (steps 16 to 20), which are briefly discussed below.

Step 16. Team activation and direction (use PDCA cycle): The steering team gives each team its direction and activities. Teams work on their assigned projects using the total quality techniques learnt by them. They use the "plan-do-check-adjust" cycle as their total quality process model. Project teams, depending on the project may have life spans of weeks, months, or longer. The team's effectiveness is seen by the measurable results that continue to flow.

Step 17: Team feedback loop to the steering committee: The project team closes the loop with the steering committee by providing feed back information on progress and results achieved by the team. The feedback is usually in the form of presentations to the steering committee. In the initial stages of the project, weekly feedbacks may be necessary. As the project gets on track and stabilizes,

are fed back to the project team for implementation. Both the project team and the steering committee use the PDCA cycle. Specific projects may have finite life cycle in terms of weeks, months or longer, but this process across all projects goes on forever.

Step 18. Customer satisfaction feed back loop: Special project teams may be assigned the task of obtaining customer feedback information, covering both external and internal customers. Formal external customer surveys should be conducted annually. Other customer satisfaction data such as sales results, warranty data, customer service input, data from customer visits etc. are collected on a continuous basis. Internal customer satisfaction is baselined for key processes and monitored continuously. All of this information is fed back to the steering committee regularly (e.g. once in a quarter). Based on this information the steering committee issues direction changes to the project teams and forms new project teams.

Step 19. Employee satisfaction feed back loop: Another special project team is given the responsibility to take the pulse of employee attitude and satisfaction. Formal surveys may be conducted annually. However, in-between the annual surveys, the steering committee and other managers stay close to the employees to develop rather accurate information on attitude and satisfaction. This information is used by steering committee to evaluate progress and determine any necessary corrections. This activity continues forever.

Step 20. Modify infrastructure as necessary: Feedback to the steering committee from project teams, customers and employees will guide the steering committee to address necessary changes in the corporate infrastructure- the procedures and processes, organisation structure, awards and recognition program, union rules etc. Changes in organisation structure may have to be effected by the steering committee itself,. Project teams may be authorized to make the changes that are needed in their area of operation (i.e. the processes they are working on).

18.6 GETTING ON WITH TOTAL QUALITY

Virtually every type of enterprise can be benefitted from total quality.

Earlier we discussed the various phases and steps involved in the implementation of total quality. Whether an organisation can go through this kind of an implementation without the help of an outside consultant (quality expert) will depend on the availability of one or more experts within the organisation. If the organisation doesn't have an internal quality expert, it is better to enlist the aid of a consultant to get through the implementation and into execution of total quality. Most consultants can be hired on a part-time basis and typical 6 months implementation program would probably require one person-month or less of consulting services and the expenses for such service will not be prohibitive.

Virtually every type of enterprise can be benefitted from total quality. It will help an enterprise to be put ahead of its competition. Failure to start total quality may leave the enterprise behind competition and it will certainly be doomed to failure as the whole world embraces the principle of total quality to survive and achieve sustainable growth.

18.6.1 What to do in the absence of commitment from the top management?

No organisation can truly become a total quality organisation without complete, unwavering, participative commitment from the top management. If you have the top management commitment, your path to total quality is clear-you know what to do and how to proceed. If you are in an organisation where top management is not committed to total quality, you are in a dilemma-whether to try to push total quality from where you are, or forget it and wait for top management to come around. Much depends on where you are in the organisation and whether top management is outwardly hostile to total quality or merely lacks the knowledge of total quality. If your top management is hostile to total quality it would not be wise for you to push for total quality beyond trying to enlighten them. So in your long-term interest of your career, it may be time to consider moving on to a different employment in an organisation where total quality culture pervades.

On the other hand if your top management is simply ambivalent toward total quality and do not know much about it, you may be able to plan a mini-implementation within your department that can improve performance in many areas. For this either you must be the head of the department or must be able to influence the department head who will work with you. If your department is a stand-alone facility far removed from the head-office, your job may be easier compared to a situation where your department is one of many, proximally located where you may not have the same freedom of action, but it is still worth pursuing. You may start with all processes contained within the department even though they have extra-department suppliers and customers. You should concentrate your efforts to implement total quality within your department first. After you have gained some successes that have been noticed by top management and other departments, you can begin to push for expansion into the cross-functional processes, requiring other departments to participate in your total quality initiatives.

Even though **departmental total quality** is a contradiction in terms, implementing total quality in a single department is better than not doing it at all. If the gains are significant enough to attract the attention of other departments and the top management, your effort may provide the seeds for the larger organisation to become involved in total quality.

Getting started with total quality in a single department is not much different from the process of company-wide implementation of total quality. The number of people involved in every step may be smaller, but most of the steps are required. **The following list briefly addresses each of the 20 steps we discussed earlier for applicability in a departmental implementation of total quality:**

Step 1: Commitment to total quality by top management is not applicable in this situation.

Step 2: Unless it is a very large department, like a stand-alone plant, steering committee may not be required.

Step 3 and 4: If there is a steering committee, then its members will have to be trained as economically as possible because top management will not provide the funds to meet the training expenses.

Step 5, 6 and 7: It is good to set the vision, mission and guiding principle in your department. If these exist at the company level, yours should be derived directly from them and support them. If the company doesn't have any vision, mission, guiding principles, you should have yours approved by top management before proceeding further. Once that is done, communicate them to every employee of you department.

In the absence of commitment from top management in an organisation, the departmental manager if interested may implement total quality in his department only.

Step 8 and 9: The identification of the strengths and weaknesses of the department and the identification of those likely to advocate total quality will be helpful in selecting your initial projects.

Step 10 and 11: It is important to know the attitudes of employees within the department. In terms of base-lining customer satisfaction, you will probably be looking at internal customers in other departments.

Step 12: It is necessary to thoroughly plan the implementation approach irrespective of the scale of operation.

Step 13: You should identify your initial projects based on the strength and weaknesses of your department. Process the activaties that are contained completely within your department. Select initial projects that can yield measurable gains without much expenses.

Step 14, 15 and 16: Follow the same procedure as for the larger organisation (company – wide total quality) but it is necessary to improvise in the training step in the absence of financial support from the top management.

Step 17, 18 and 19: These steps follow the same procedure as for the larger organisation except that the customer feed back will probably be from your internal customers in other departments.

Step 20: You may be able to do some minor interdepartmental infrastructure changes; it would be advisable to obtain top management approval before doing the same.

18.6.2 Understanding the Obstacles to TQM Success

Over the last decade, a number of survey- based research studies focused on total quality management have been carried out with the objectives of:

(i) Identifying critical TQM factors, *(ii)* Examining issues in the implementation of TQM and *(iii)* Investigating the link between TQM factors and performance.

Of primary interest among researchers has been addressing the question" **What makes TQM work?"** Since most would agree that the philosophy and principles of TQM are sound, instances of failed TQM initiatives have led researchers to direct their attention to problems associated with its implementation. There have been many studies that have focused on the obstacles to TQM. Other have narrowed their view to concentrate on specific barriers to TQM such as organisational culture, management style, employee factors and ineffective project management. In order to assess whether TQM does work, some studies have emphasised the measurement of TQM outcomes.

While some may consider TQM outdated, organisations still pursue competitive advantage through improved quality and satisfied customers. The recent revision of ISO 9000- ISO 9000: 2000- represents a fundamental change in approach to quality from one that is totally compliance based (quality assurance) to one that includes the evaluation of management techniques (quality management) ISO 9000: 2000 is based on eight principles that are easily recognisable as the **key elements of quality management. They are:**

1. Customer focus, 2. Leadership, 3. Involvement of people, 4. Process approach, 5. Systems approach to management, 6. Continuous improvement, 7. Factual approach to decision making and 8. Mutually beneficial supplier relationships.

Aside from the mandate to adopt quality management practices as result of ISO 9000: 2000, it appears that many organisations have continued in their efforts to transform the way they do their business, whether it is called TQM, Reengineering or Cultural change. For some companies, the recent focus on **"business excellence"** is really quality management.

Researches used scales to measure seven core dimension of quality: 1. Top management, 2. Quality information, 3. Process management, 4. Product design, 5. Workforce management, 6. Supplier involvement and 7. Customer involvement.

It was observed that quality leadership had the strongest relationship to quality performance and employee involvement was the best differentiator amonssg, low, intermediate and high performing plants.

18.6.3 Obstacles to Quality Transformation

According to researchers, TQM failures follow one of the three patterns : 1. Conceptual weakness 2. Design flaws or 3. Ineffective implementation.

Conceptual Weakness is failures occuring because organisations make only superficial attempts at change.

Design flaws occur when TQM systems are not designed to fit the circumstances of the organisation.

Ineffective implementation results when TQM becomes so much extra work instead of a new way of doing things.

Without a change in management evaluation and reward policy, TQM can not be taken seriously. Managers will need to know that their evaluations, and subsequent pay increases and bonuses are dependent on having high levels of quality, satisfied staff and customers and successful implementation of TQM in their respective areas of responsibility.

Researchers interviewed the managing directors at 21 leading TQM organisations about organisational characteristics affecting the success of TQM. Of the seven quality -critical organisational characteristics (QCOC) considered, they found that management style and shared values were the two QCOCs having the maximum impact on the successful implementation of TQM. Process factors were reported to have the least effect. It was found that failure of management to lead was the primary obstacle to successful implementation of TQM. Among several poor management practices that contribute to failed TQM initiative, a management style that inhibits learning culture, is based on fear or intimidation and that creates barriers between departments was found to be a significant practice that leads to failure of TQM. Another researcher, in his study of MBNQ Award winners, found that difficulties in implementing TQM are rooted in three causes

1. The holistic change of corporate culture, 2. Achieving and maintaining employee buy-in and acceptance of TQM and 3. Integration with suppliers and customers. However, the only factor that 100 percent of MBNQA winners considered critical to the success of TQM was top management's commitment and involvement. Recent studies continue to show that management plays a critical role in an organisation's successful quality transformation.

Another research finding was that the major enabler of TQM implementation was communication between managers/ supervisors and staff and that poor communication between departments was a real barrier to implementing TQM. The success of TQM depends largely on managements' ability to lead the organisation's quality transformation. A key factor in achieving a successful change to a quality culture is management support. Managers much be clearly perceived to support the change through communication, resource allocation and recognition/reward.

From the review of research literatures, it has become apparent that many of the obstacles founds to hinder TQM efforts (such as poor communications, lack of employee empowerment, inadequate resources, employee resistance to change. inadequate performance evaluation and reward systems etc) are linked to how effectively the quality transformation is managed. Ultimately, it is management's responsibility to plan for, to lead and effect the organisational change required for success of TQM implementation in any organisation.

18.7 IMPLEMENTATION STRATEGIES

Some organisations may not be ready to undertake full total quality implementation at once and may want to move in that direction in a phased manner. Such organisations can use the criteria of several different award and certification programs as a starting point. Two such programs that are recommended are ISO 9000: 2000 and Business Excellence Awards relevant to the countries in which the organisations originate and operate, for example, Malcolm Baldrige Award in USA, European Quality Award in Europe, Canadian Awards for Business Excellence for Canadian enterprises, Australian Quality Award in Australia, Deming prize awarded by Japanese Union of Scientists and Engineers (JUSE) to Japanese Companies with outstanding total quality implementation, CII-Exim Bank Award for Excellence in India etc.

18.8 QUALITY IN PRACTICE

Box 18.2 : Mc Donnel Douglas Corporation

Mc Donnel Douglas is now part of the Boeing company, but that does not diminish in anyway the turnaround that took place at Mc Donnel Douglas between 1992 and 1997. The company was not doing well in the early 1990s. With the military build up a thing of past, the huge military division watched as sales plummeted. The commercial aircraft division of Mc Donnel Douglas struggled to be competitive with Boeing and Air bus because of rampant wastage and inefficiency. Mc Donnel Douglas stock sank to $ 9.00 a share in 1992 - the lowest in any one's memory. The company, once the largest defense contractor and the world's number two supplier of commercial aircraft was in serious trouble.

The senior management and staff under the leadership of John Mc Donnel, then chairman of the board, decided to implement total quality management. They got off to a very rocky start but learnt from their mistakes and by 1992 were making good progress. Starting that year, executives were measured on three items: cash flow, return on assets and TQM., with the latter being tied to improvement on a Baldrige self-assessment score. In 1992, their self-assessment score was 200 (on the 0 to 1000 scale). Over the next 3 years, the score increased by 100 points per year. This took them from being a so-so performer in the traditional ranks to a high mid level in the TQM realm.

Mc Donnel Douglas found that as their Baldrige self-assessment score improved each year, their key business performance indicators tracked in parallel fashion. By 1995, their stock valuation reached $ 70 per share, profits were several times greater than in 1992. Cash was up, debt was down - all in a vastly smaller market. TQM literally turned this giant company around to the extent that the Boeing company considered it imperative to merge in order to save Boeing. The merger took place on 1st August 1997.

18.9 SUMMARY

Implementation of total quality in any organisation is crucial for the survival and growth of any organisation in the 21st century because of the intense competition in the business environment. However, it must be remembered that there is no single best way for implementing total quality that fits the needs of all organisations. Generally, when an organisation is doing well it may not be keen on implementing total quality, rather than when it is facing the possibility of going out of business giving way for competition.

For traditional organisations implementing total quality means a paradigm change, changing the organisation structure, changing the organisational culture, changing the way of working, behavioral and attitudinal changes in the employees etc. Whether one likes it or not, change is inevitable in a competitive environment.

Japan was a devastated country at the end of World War II and its products didn't have a favourable quality image in the Western countries. Japan had to rebuild its industrial base and had to look for markets beyond its national borders in order to rebuild its economy. So the Union of Japanese Scientists and Engineers (JUSE) invited Dr. Deming-an American statistician and professor to train Japanese engineers and managers in the basic concepts and techniques of statistical quality control so as to improve the quality of Japanese products. However, the Japanese were quick to learn total quality and implement the same in their own way and achieve amazing success, and thereby flood American markets with Japanese goods, especially the automobiles threatening the big auto giants of US such as Ford, General Motors, Chrysler etc.

Changes in way of managing business is imminent because the traditional way of managing has several draw backs, for e.g., short-term business focus, lack of customer focus, underestimating the capabilities of base-line employees, equating better quality with higher cost, lack of leadership approach etc.

Implementation of total quality in organisations requires the following:

(i) Commitment by top management.

(ii) Commitment of necessary resources.

(iii) Organisation-wide steering committed.

(iv) Planning and publishing total quality implementation programs.

(v) Infrastructure the supports deployment and continual improvement.

However, implementation approach varies from one organisation to another since organisations differ in their cultures and management styles. Therefore the implementation plan that worked for 'x' company may not work for 'y' or 'z' companies. There is no one right way of implementing total quality, Organisations may be able to identify the many wrong ways and also more than one right way depending on their strengths and weaknesses, business situation and unique cultures. The initial tasks in implementing total quality involve: *(a)* making a commitment at the top management level, *(b)* forming a steering committee comprising top management executives and *(c)* defining the vision and broad objectives of the organisation.

The other steps involved are:

(i) Training the steering committee.

(ii) Identifying organisational strengths and weaknesses.

(iii) Identifying the probable advocates of total quality.

(iv) Identifying customer-both internal and external and

(v) Developing a means for determining customer satisfaction-both external and internal.

By performing the above steps, the steering committee will be able to make rational judgments about how the implementation journey should start.

Once total quality is implemented it is necessary to evaluate the approach adopted by the oragnisation to implement total quality. Even though an organisation may obtain lot of information on successful implementation of total quality by other organisations, it can achieve success by imitating others. The idea of implementation approaches that organisations must avoid are:

(i) Don't train all your employee at once

(ii) Don't rush to total quality by putting too many people in teams.

(iii) Total quality implementation must not be delegated.

(iv) Don't start an implementation before you are prepared. .

The implementation phases and steps in each phase to be considered and listed below:

Phase 1: The preparation phase

Step 1: Commitment to total quality.

Step 2: Formation of total quality steering committee.

Step 3: Steering committee team building.

Step 4: Steering Committee total quality training.

Step 5: Creation of the vision statement and guiding principles.

Step 6: Establishment of strategic objectives.

Step 7: Communication and publicity.

Step 8: Identification of organisational strengths and weaknesses.

Step 9: Identification of advocates and resisters.

Step 10: Basel .e employee satisfaction / attitudes

Step 11: Baseline customer satisfaction.

Phase 2: The planning phase

Step 12: Plan the implementation approach and use "Plan /Do / Check/ Adjust" cycle (PDCA)

Step 13: Establish team composition

Step 14: Provide team training.

Phase 3: The execution phase

Step 15: Team activation and direction (use PDCA Cycle)

Step 16: Team feedback loop to the steering committee.

Step 17: customer satisfaction feedback loop

Step 18: Employee satisfaction feedback loop

Step 19: Modify infrastructure as necessary.

An organisation can get on with implementation of total quality by performing the above twenty steps either with the help of an outside consultant (quality expert) or using the expertise of experts available from within. Every type of enterprise can be benefitted from total quality by staying ahead of competition.

If in an organisation, the top management is not committed to total quality but a department head is keen on implementing total quality, it is better to start with implementation with in the department. The success gained by the department may motivate other departments to follow suit and gradually the total quality culture may pervade through the entire organisation thereby ensuring commitment from top management.

Some organisations may not be willing or ready to take a plunge into total quality implementation on a full scale. Such organisations may use the criteria of several different award and certification programs for e.g. ISO 9000: 2000 certification, Business Excellence Awards (e.g. CII-Exim Bank Award in India, Malcolm Balding National Quality Award in USA) to start with towards implementing total quality before becoming a total quality organisation.

18.10 KEY WORDS USED

Top Management Commitment, Learning Experience, Steering Committee, Vision Statement, Guiding Principles, Cascading Training, Problem-solving Team Approach, Base-line Employee Satisfaction, Baseline Customer Satisfaction, Plan-Do-Check-Adjust (PDCA) cycle, Customer Satisfaction Feed Back Loop.

18.11 OBJECTIVE QUESTIONS

(A) Match the following :

Column A	Column B
1. Top Management	1. Establish the rules of conduct for the organistaion and its employees
2. Commitment of resources	2. Commitment to total quality
3. Company wide implementation of total quality	3. Organisation wide steering committee
4. Vision statement	4. Cost of training people in applying QC tools
5. Guiding principles	5. Long view of what the company will be after say 5 or 10 years from now.

(B) State whether the following statements are True or False :

1. There is no best way that fits the needs of all organisations as far as implementing total quality is concerned. (T / F)
2. There are many barriers to change- both personal and organisational. (T / F)
3. The total quality implementation is not driven by vision, goals and objectives. (T / F)
4. The right way to do is to train small groups of people just-in-time - just as they need training in total quality, the seven QC tools etc. (T / F)
5. Total quality implementation can be delegated from top management to lower level management. (T / F)

(C) Multiple choice Questions : Choose the correct answer from the alternatives given under each question :

1. The training of steering committee should include:
   (a) Deming's 14 points, The seven deadly diseases and the obstacles.
   (b) The seven QC tools and management tools
   (c) Team building (d) All of these
   (e) None of these
2. Identifying organisational strengths and weaknesses include:
   (a) Statistical capability (b) Data collection
   (c) Analytical ability (d) All of these
   (e) None of these
3. The following ideas are to be considered before implementing total quality.
   (a) Do not train all the employees of the organisation at once
   (b) Do not rush into total quality by putting too many people in teams.
   (c) Total quality implementation must not be delegated
   (d) Do not start an implementation before you are prepared.
   (e) All of these (f) None of these
4. In the implementation of total quality the step of establishing strategic objectives falls under:
   (a) The preparation phase (b) The planning phase
   (c) The execution phase (d) None of these
5. The team responsible for the total quality implementation project uses "P-D-C-A" cycle in the following phase.
   (a) The preparation phase (b) The planning phase
   (c) The execution phase (d) None of these

18.12 REVIEW QUESTIONS

1. Why change is inevitable for organisations in today's business environment?
2. Discuss the rationale for change.
3. Distinguish between 'leadership' and "bossmanship"
4. Explain the requirements of total quality implementation.
5. Discus the role of organisation-wide steering committee in total quality implementation
6. Why planning and publicizing are important in total quality implementation? Explain
7. Why total quality implementation vary among organisations? Elaborate
8. List and explain the ideas of implementation that should be avoided
9. Briefly discusses the various phases and the steps involved in each phase in the total quality implementation program.
10. How total quality can be implemented in the absence of commitment from top management in an organisation?

18.13 DISCUSSION QUESTIONS

1. "There is no one best way that fits the needs of all organisations as far as implementing total quality is concerned" – Discuss the statement.
2. "The traditional approach equates better quality with higher cost. However, quality guru Philip Crosby advocates that quality is free"- Explain.
3. "No organisation can truly become a total quality organisation without complete, unwavering, participative commitment from the top management" – Discuss
4. Discuss the importance of base-line employee satisfaction and base line customer satisfaction in implementing total quality.
5. "The real total quality work effort starts with the creation of the organisation's vision statement and putting in paper the guiding principles under which the company is to operate" Do you agree? Why or why not?

18.14 CHAPTER CASE

THE CASE OF A U.S. COMPANY WITH A JAPANESE TQC PROGRAM

In 1974, a division of Motorola was acquired by Matsushita Electric Industrial Company. It employed 1200 people in Franklin Park to produce colour television receivers and microwave ovens. Five years after the change over, in-process defects had dropped from 1.4 to 0.07 defects per set and productivity had jumped almost 30 percent. The labour required to produce a colour television receiver was cut in half. These gains were achieved by blending new equipment, technology, training and managerial practices to revitalise an already skilled labour force.

Equipment : Automatic equipment developed in Japan for Chassis assembly was used. Design changes reduced the number of required workers by 26 percent. Equipment and design engineers worked together to improve "producibility" making quality products easier to manufacture.

Technology : New assembly lines allowed workers to control their work flow individually. In place of a continuous, conveyour paced line, operators were given foot levers to detour work to their station and to forward finished pieces to the next work stations. Closed-circuit television systems were installed to broadcast quality information to workers on the production line.

Training : The importance of quality was continually emphasised, placing responsibility on production workers, not inspectors. End-product inspection teams were replaced by a few in-process inspectors who moved from one assembly line to another carrying out sampling inspection. New employees are trained both in the class room and on-the-job, upto 5 days of each, during which they learn about quality expectations, are judged on whether they can do the work adequately and see whether they like the work conditions.

Managerial practice : Once a week all work stops for 10 to 15 minutes while supervisors communicate with their subordinates. A supervisor typically communicates with 45 workers about quality, productivity, absenteeism, scrap and any other subjects that might come up. If the supervisors can not answer a question, they make a note of it and come prepared with an answer in the next meeting.

Every six month, manufacturing and quality control people meet to set quality goals for different areas. Bar charts are kept to signal which areas are above, near or below their targets. Special effort is concentrated on a particular production line, called the *model line,* to improve its performance. Workers on that line and support groups meet once a week to explore progress. Reasons for successes in the model line are identified and adapted to fit other lines.

A *quality emphasis month* is declared twice a year. Awareness is aroused by slogan and posters competitions, cross word puzzles with quality terms and suggestion contests. Winners are entertained at a felicitation party and given a modest reward.

The underlying purpose of all activities is to create an environment that will be conducive to cooperation and encouraging people to work together to identify problems and offer suggestions to solve them.

Discussion Questions :

1. Discuss the relative contribution to quality improvement of the engineering/technology investments with the human resource management changes made at the Motorola plant.
2. Quality control circles were not established at the plant by the Matsushita company. Suggest reasons that circles were not used, even though they enjoy great success in Japan.

CHAPTER 19

MANAGING QUALITY – MODERN IMPROVEMENT APPROACHES

LEARNING OBJECTIVES

After reading this chapter, you should be able to:

- Understand the meaning of the term "approaches" and "interconnection pyramid".
- Discuss the various modern improvement approaches to managing quality.
- Discuss "Total Productive Maintenance" and its relationship with TQM.
- Discuss the 5 's' approach to quality management.
- Discuss the role of BPR in quality management.
- Discuss "Six-Sigma" approach to quality management.
- Discuss the concept of "Lean" and its relevance to quality management.
- Analyse the five approaches to quality management namely TQM, BPR, Six-Sigma and "Lean management" and discuss their managerial implications.

19.0 INTRODUCTION

Modern quality management approaches relate in many ways to modern project management approaches overall. More and more attention is being paid to the human aspect of the processes, the team approach to quality and the concept of total quality management. The quality management process is more oriented toward permanent small incremental improvements and multiple inspection points in the process than it was in the past. In the modern approach to quality, the changed view is that quality is everybody's business and everyone in the organisation is responsible for quality. This view allows for many more inspection points and allows for corrections to be made before additional work is done and results in significant reduction in scrap and rework cost.

The continuous elimination of errors, defects and waste and their associated value-adding activities to improve the quality of products and services is essential for all organisations, irrespective of their size, product/service offerings or the sector in which they operate. During recent decades a number of approaches have been used by organisations to assist with the key corporate objective to make continuous improvements in business processes.

19.1 APPROACHES SYSTEMATICALLY DEFINED

The quality management principle is a broad and diverse area which encompasses many control and improvement activities. These activities can be structured in a hierarchical way by distinguishing four categories: *(i)* Concepts, *(ii)* Approaches, *(iii)* Systems and, *(iv)* Tools and techniques. ***Exhibit 19.1* is a diagrammatic representation of how these categories fit together.**

Exhibit 19.1 : The Interconnection Pyramid

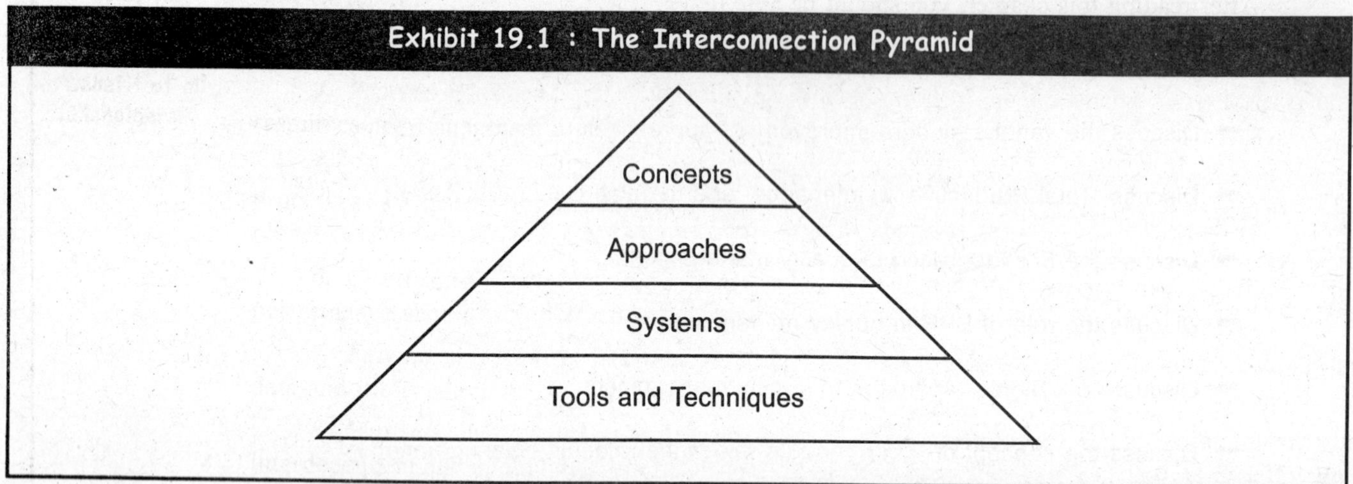

The five most popular improvement approaches used by modern organisations are:
***(i)* TQM**
***(ii)* TPM**
***(iii)* BPR**
***(iv)* Six-Sigma and**
***(v)* 'Lean' management**

Each approach that is used to make improvements in an organisation's business processes is based on a set of core concepts centred around ***customer orientation*, *process control*** and ***process improvement*.** An approach requires a certain amount of intellectual effort in term of its deployment and adoption. The application also requires a strategic decision on behalf of the senior management team. It requires resources in terms of training and hiring additional and specific personnel. It also demands the commitment of senior management, who must be prepared to learn and understand the approach and be committed to its use over the longer term. **The modern approaches to quality management include:**

1. Total quality management
2. Total productive maintenance
3. Business process reengineering
4. Six sigma and
5. Lean management (Toyota production system, lean manufacturing, theory of constraints, just-in-time etc.)

A **"system"** comprises written information in the form of instructions and procedures in order to direct and control some form of operation. Typical examples of systems involved in process improvement include advanced quality planning, quality management, visible management and performance measurement. Systems of one kind or another are used in all the approaches, for example, a quality management system is an essential element of TQM.

Tools and techniques comprise methods and skills applied to particular tasks, projects and problems to facilitate change and improvement. The two terms – 'tools' and techniques are used interchangeably. A single tool may be described as a device which has a clear role and defined application. It has a narrow focus and can be used on its own. Examples of tools are: *(i)* Cause and effect diagram, *(ii)* Pareto analysis, *(iii)* Relationship diagram, *(iv)* Control chart, *(v)* Histogram, *(vi)* Flow chart etc.

A tool is a device which has a clear role and defined application whereas techniques has a wider application than a tool.

A technique, on the other hand, has a wider application than a tool. There is also a need for more thought, skill, knowledge, understanding and training to use them effectively. A technique may even be viewed as a collection of tools. For example, Statistical Process Control employs a variety of tools such as graphs, charts, histograms and capability studies, as well as other statistical methods, all of which are necessary for the effective use of the technique.

Examples of techniques are:

(i) Statistical process control, *(ii)* Bench marking, *(iii)* Quality function deployment, *(iv)* Failure mode and effect analysis, *(v)* Design of experiments and *(vi)* Self–assessment.

The use of tools and techniques to improve quality has been around for a long time, commencing with the control chart in the late 1920s, sampling tables and design of experiments in the 1940s and the quality engineering methods proposed by Juran in the 1950s. In more recent times, starting with quality circles in the 1960s, a number of techniques such as SPC, design of experiments, failure mode and effects analysis, quality function deployment, benchmarking etc. were being used to add impetus to an organisation's improvement efforts. The use of techniques requires that a certain set of procedures is followed and a specific infrastructure is established. These are often considered the essentials of approaches; for example, problem-solving methodologies, training programs, management commitment etc.

Tools and techniques can be used on their own but are more effective as part of an integrated approach to business improvement. All the approaches require the use and application of tools and techniques with some, such as six sigma being more prescriptive than say TQM.

19.2 APPROACH 1: TOTAL QUALITY MANAGEMENT (TQM)

The history of TQM is interesting. It was first developed by W. Edwards Deming and many Japanese managers. After World War II, Deming and many other American consultants were invited to Japan to develop tools to improve quality practices of Japanese enterprises. The **"quality circle"** concept gave significant results when applied to Japanese enterprises. Deming's next step was to build mechanisms allowing this information to be most effectively communicated to the company decision makers and to make this process as a continuous practice. "Quality circles" improved productivity in Japanese companies by 10 percent. But unfortunately American companies took 20 years to rediscover the idea of TQM. The concept of **"continuous process improvement" (CPI)** was developed later and has now become the basic idea underlying most modern standards. Now TQM has become a relatively established entity with accepted components of teamwork, systems thinking and statistical tools being applied to the areas of "customer, counting and culture".

Modern quality management practices generally require the implementation of the whole new concept of personnel management and human resource development. All the modern concepts suggest that a high land of people's responsibility and involvement. This in turn develops a feeling of ownership in each and every employee within the company. The result of this type of thinking is enriched job assignments introducing elements of creativity and challenging tasks to be fulfilled.

Another important feature of modern quality management is that it considers small incremental improvements as the best approach to improving quality. The TQM approach has many formalized practices for introducing step–by–step, small change processes in the normal operation cycle of the organisation. For introducing small incremental improvements to the processes, Deming suggested **"Deming cycle"** or "P–D–C–A" cycle (i.e. Plan-Do-Check-Act cycle).

TQM can be considered as the foundation upon which other improvement approaches are based. While TPM is based on TQM, BPR and Six-Sigma are viewed as better than or replacement for TQM.

The **"Seven Tools of Quality Management"** form a basis for overall TQM methodology. In general, all the tools are based on two major approaches: statistics and team involvement. The major tools are the flow chart, the cause and effect diagram, the Pareto diagram, the check sheet, the scatter diagram, the histogram and the control chart. (called the 7 QC tools) Flow charts and Cause- and- effect diagrams are used in quality planning and quality assurance processes, and the remaining five tools are used as instruments of quality control.

TQM is based on a set of principles viz. customer focus, leadership, involvement of people, process approach, system approach to management, continual improvement, factual approach to decision making and mutually beneficial supplier partnerships.

TQM comprises a number of elements viz commitment and leadership of the chief executive officer, planning and organisation, use of tools and techniques, education and training, employee involvement and empowerment, team work, measurement and feed back and ensuring that the organisational culture is conducive to continuous improvement activity. Because of its well developed set of principles and key elements, TQM can be considered as the foundation upon which other improvement approaches are based. **The approaches which have followed on from TQM can be divided into two types:**

(i) those that have used TQM as a foundation block (e.g. Total Productive Maintenance) and

(ii) those that are seen as better than or a replacement for TQM. (e.g. six sigma and BPR)

19.3 APPROACH 2: TOTAL PRODUCTIVE MAINTENANCE (TPM)

TPM is an additional driver which is complementary to TQM.

Total productive maintenance concept was evolved by the Japanese based on preventive maintenance. TPM combines preventive maintenance with TQM, employee involvement and effective house keeping. The Japanese manufacturers consider TPM as an additional driver which is complementary to TQM. They tend to apply TPM when their TQM approach is reasonably well established and when their improvement approach needs to be accelerated. TPM focuses on the condition of manufacturing equipment and machinery and their influence on the quality of the outputs. The specific aim of TPM is the maintenance, quality and efficiency of equipment using the overall equipment effectiveness metric.

Total productive maintenance is a maintenance program which involves a newly defined concept for maintaining plants and equipments. The goal of the TPM program is to marked by increase production, while at the same time, increasing employee morale and job satisfaction. TPM resembles TQM in several aspects such as *(i)* total commitment to the program by upper level management is required, *(ii)* employees must be empowered to initiate corrective action and, *(iii)* a long range outlook must be accepted as TPM may take a year or more to implement and is an on – going process.

TPM requires a change in employee mindset towards their job responsibilities.

TPM brings maintenance into focus as a necessary and important part of the business. It is no longer regarded as a non – profit activity. Down time for maintenance is scheduled as a part of the manufacturing day and in some cases as a part of the manufacturing process. The goal is to hold emergency and unscheduled maintenance to a minimum.

19.3.1 Why Total Productive Maintenance?

TPM was introduced to achieve the following objectives:

(i) To avoid wastage in a fast changing economic environment.

(ii) To produce goods without reducing product quality.

(iii) To reduce cost.

(iv) To produce a small batch quantity at the earliest possible time.

(v) To ensure that the goods sold to customers are free from defects

19.3.2 Organisational characteristics of TPM

(i) Integration of maintenance and production departments, *(ii)* Small teams of operators/ maintenance staff, *(iii)* Training operators to feel like owners of equipments on which they work, *(iv)* Good habits are developed, *(v)* Cleaning becomes checking, *(vi)* Cleaning highlights abnormalities, *(vii)* Abnormalities are rectified, *(viii)* Continuous improvement of environment and equipment.

TPM is a scientific, company–wide approach in which every employee is concerned about the maintenance, quality and efficiency of their equipment. The objective is to reduce the whole – life cost of machinery and equipment through more efficient maintenance management and manufacturing departments. Teamwork is a key element of TPM. The TPM approach involves analysis of each piece of equipments and focus on reducing manufacturing losses and costs. The six major losses are due to: *(i)* breakdown, *(ii)* set up/adjustment, *(iii)* speed, *(iv)* idling and minor stoppages, *(v)* quality defects and, *(vi)* start up. TPM establishes a system of preventive maintenance over a machines working life. The emphasis of TPM is to improve the skills of operators in relation to machine technology and to train and educate them to clean, maintain and make adjustments to their machine. In this way machines and equipments are kept at optimal operating efficiency.

TPM starts with 5 's' - Seiri, Seiton, Seiso, Seiketsu and Shitsuke. (all Japanese words).

TPM starts with 5S (Japanese words – Seiri, Seiton, Seiso, Seiketsu and Shitsuke meaning Sort, Systematise, Sweep (or clean) Standardise and Self-discipline respectively). The "5 S" are essential activities in TPM and they also provide more visible management. The "5 S" approach to quality management will be discussed briefly in the following paragraphs:

19.3.3 The 5 's' Approach to Quality Management

Since the early 1980's Japanese industries widely practice 5 'S' as a powerful technique to improve quality and productivity: 5 'S' is the name of a work place organisation methodology that uses five Japanese words: *(i)* **Seiri**, *(ii)* **Seiton**, *(iii)* **Seiso**, *(iv)* **Seiketsu** and, *(v)* **Shitsuke**. The corresponding English words are: *(i)* Sorting out *(ii)* Systematic arrangement, (Setting in order), *(iii)* Swaping or shining or cleanliness, *(iv)* Standardising and, *(v)* sustaining discipline or self discipline.

These five words describe how to organise a workplace for efficiency and effectiveness by identifying and storing the items used, maintaining the storage area and items, and sustaining the new order. The decision making process usually comes from a dialogue about standardisation which builds a clear understanding among employees of how work should be done. It also instills ownership of the process in each employee. These five 5 's' activities are briefly described below:

'Seiri' means "Sorting"

***(i)* Seiri (sorting):** Eliminate all unnecessary tools, parts and instructions. Check all tools, materials etc, kept in the work area and the plant. Keep only the essential items and eliminate what is not required, prioritising things as per requirements and keeping them in easily accessible places. Everything else is stored in separate storage area or discarded.

"Seiton" means "Straightening" or "Setting in order"

***(ii)* Seiton (straightening or setting in order/stabilise):** There should be a place for everything and everything should be in its place. The place for each item should be clearly labeled or demarcated. Items should be arranged in a manner to promote efficient workflow, with equipment used most often being the most easily accessible. Workers should not have to bend repetitively to access materials or tools. Each tool, material, part or piece of equipment should be kept close to where it will be used. This means straightening the path of flow.

"Seiso" means "cleaning", "sweeping" or "shining"

(iii) **Seiso (sweeping or shining or systematic cleaning):** Clean the workspace and all equipments and keep them clean, tidy and organised. At the end of each shift, clean the work area and ensure that everything is restored to its place. This makes it easy to know what goes where and ensure that everything is kept where it belongs. Spills, oil leaks and other messes also then become a visual signal for equipment or process steps that need attention. Maintaining cleanliness should be part of the daily routine.

"Seiketsu" means " standardising"

(iv) **Seiketsu (standardising):** Work practices should be consistent and standardised. All workstations for a particular job should be identical. All employees doing the same job should be able to work in any workstation with the same tools that are in the same location in every station. Everyone should know exactly what his or her responsibilities are for adhering to the first three "S" s.

"shitsuke" means "sustaining discipline" or "self-discipline"

(v) **Shitsuke (sustaining the discipline or self–discipline):** Maintain and review standards. Once the previous 4 'S' s have been established, they become the new way to operate. Maintain focus on this new way and do not allow a gradual decline back to the old ways. While thinking about the new way, also think about yet better ways. When an issue arises such as a suggested improvement, a new way of working, a new tool or a new output requirement, review the first 4 'S's and make changes as appropriate.

It is important to have continuous education about maintaining standards. When there are changes that affect the 5 'S' program such as new equipment, new products or new work rules, it is essential to make changes in standards and provide training.

We have earlier discussed "Total productive maintenance" in Chapter 5 under the title "Reliability, Maintenance and Product Liability". However, we discuss the seven steps of a TPM program below:

Step 1: Initial cleaning, to identify problems with equipment that are not noticed during normal operations.

Step 2: Counter–measures at the source of problems, to minimize accumulation of and other contaminant and put in place improvements to make it easy to access parts of the equipment which need cleaning.

Step 3: Set maintenance, cleaning and lubrication standards for groups of equipment and carry out appropriate training.

Step 4: General inspection of procedures and schedules.

Step 5: Autonomous inspection procedures and schedules.

Step 6: Orderliness and tidiness

Step 7: Full autonomous maintenance.

19.4 APPROACH 3: BUSINESS PROCESS REENGINEERING (BPR)

BPR emerged as the concept which enables an organisation to make a radical and revolutionary examination of the way in which it operates and how work is performed. BPR challenges the need for a process in contrast to TQM which looks for continuous improvement to a process. BPR emphasizes structural process redesign, process reengineering and fundamental rethinking by ignoring the status-quo. Some writers believe that BPR is a successor to TQM, while some others believe that TQM and BPR are complementary and integral approaches.

The principles underlying BPR are not necessarily new. For example, many of the principles of BPR, infrastructure and project phasing have direct counterparts within TQM. The break – through type thinking is present in both BPR and TQM.

Two main approaches in BPR are:

(i) Business process redesign and

(ii) Business process reengineering

BPR comprises a central set of principles:

(i) Strategic in concept, *(ii)* Customer – focused, *(iii)* Output – rather than input focused, *(iv)* focused on key business processes, *(v)* Process responsibility and decisions are made at the point where work is performed, *(vi)* Cross functional in nature, *(vii)* Involves internal and external customer – supplier relationships, *(viii)* Requires top management commitment and involvement, *(ix)* Involves networking people and their activities, *(x)* Involves integration of people and technical aspects, *(xi)* Requires clear communication and visibility, *(xii)* Based on the mindset of radical improvement.

Some experts believe that BPR is a successor to TQM while some others believe that TQM and BPR are complementary and integral approaches.

Many factors need to be considered in the implementation of a BPR project. They are: *(i)* project champion, *(ii)* steering committee, *(iii)* process design team, *(iv)* process owner and *(v)* implementation team.

A BPR project requires four phases: *(i)* Preparation phase, *(ii)* Innovation and design phase, *(iii)* Implementation phase and, *(iv)* Assessment phase. More about BPR was already discussed in chapter 16.

19.5 APPROACH 4: SIX-SIGMA

"Six-Sigma" is an approach to improve performance of key processes. As a five phase improvement process, Six-Sigma uses the "DMAIC" approach and as an approach to process design redesign, it uses the "DMADV" approach.

We have earlier discussed "Six-Sigma" approach to quality management in chapter 16. However we will discuss some salient features of "Six-Sigma" approach in this section.

Motorola created "Six-sigma" in the mid 1980s to improve the performance of key processes. 'Six-sigma' focuses on the use of quality engineering methods within a defined problem-solving structure to identify and eliminate process defects and solve problems and improve yield, productivity, operating effectiveness, customer satisfaction etc. Interest in "Six-sigma" approach is currently high and a wide range of organisations are following the adoption of "Six-sigma"

"Six-sigma" follows a five phase improvement process – **define, measure, analyse, improve and control (DMAIC)** – and specific improvement tools and techniques are linked to each of these phases. "Six-sigma" is more specific and more structured than TQM and is the recommended approach to all improvement projects. With respect to process design/redesign rather than process improvement, the phases become: **define, measure, analyse, design and verify (DMADV).**

The time scale to complete a "Six-Sigma" project is always agreed and the intention is to complete it in as short a time frame as possible with defined bottom–line savings and improvements in the "Six-Sigma" performance metric.

A rigorous and structural training program is deployed to appropriate levels of the master black belts, black belts and green belts. **"Six-Sigma" has many objectives in common with TQM – namely**

(i) customer orientation and focus

(ii) team-based activity

(iii) problem-solving methodology etc. "Six-sigma" undoubtedly builds upon TQ.

19.6 APPROACH 5: LEAN MANUFACTURING

Lean manufacturing can be considered to be an essential element of all the main improvement approaches. During the period from 1970 s to 1990 s, Japanese organisations spearheaded by Toyota, Mazda, Nissan, Honda and Mitsubishi developed a new kind of production methodology referred to as "Lean Production Systems". These systems consist of processes that have been designed to minimize their inherent waste of time, materials and money. Lean production systems use minimal amount of resources to produce a high volume of high quality goods with some variety. Lean production systems use much lesser resources than mass production systems use – less space, less inventory, and fewer workers to produce a comparable quantity of output. These systems use a highly skilled workforce and flexible equipments.

The concept of "lean" originated in "Toyota production system" (TPS) started in Japan during the period 1970 to 1990.

Lean production systems focus on elimination of **seven types of waste ('muda'** in Japanese) viz. *(i)* **excess production,** *(ii)* **waiting time,** *(iii)* **conveyance or transportation,** *(iv)* **motion,** *(v)* **processing time,** *(vi)* **inventory** and, *(vii)* **defects.**

However, the term "lean" was coined by **Womack,** etal (1990) in their book. **"The Machines that changed the world".** "Lean" is a "specific way of thinking", consisting of a set of methods and operating principles to identify and eliminate waste in business processes.

The focus is on making processes more efficient in conjunction with a target to make specific reductions in resources used within a specified time period (e.g. the number of suppliers reduced by 20 percent by the end of 2012). It involves the use of a range of approaches and techniques such as **"Single minute exchange of die" (SMED), "Mistake–proofing" (Poka–Yoke), "Kanban" (Just-in-time), "Concurrent engineering" and "Rapid prototyping".** The lean concept can be implemented as part of the **"Toyota Production System" (TPS)** which required specific activities to be followed in some form of sequence.

The key issues of "lean" are: *(i)* value *(ii)* value stream *(iii)* Flow *(iv)* Pull and *(v)* Perfection.

The key issues of lean are:

(i) **Value:** providing the customer with the right product/service, for the right price at the right time.

(ii) **Value stream:** the set of actions from a product/service concept to realisation, order to delivery, raw material to finished goods etc.

(iii) **Flow:** seamless movement through a series of value–creating steps.

(iv) **Pull:** acting only to satisfy customer needs (both internal and external customers).

(v) **Perfection:** continuously and improving the value, value stream, flow and pull in business operations, along with the associated reduction in defects.

The key elements in "lean manufacturing" are:

(i) Visual control and management, *(ii)* Rapid change over, *(iii)* One piece flow, *(iv)* Cellular manufacturing, *(v)* Employee empowerment, *(vi)* Pull-rather-than-push, *(vii)* Work standardisation, *(viii)* Five 'S' s, *(ix)* Point–of–usage storage, *(x)* Small batch production, *(xi)* Quality at the source and *(xii)* Effective plant layout.

19.7 ANALYSIS OF THE FIVE APPROACHES

TQM and TPM emerged from Japanese experience in the 1960 s and 1970 s and later adopted by western organisations. But many organisations have had major problems in implementing some of the tools and techniques involved in TQM and TPM. Organisations needed clearer guidance regarding the change process and so more top-down, hierarchical, faster moving approaches such as BPR and "Six-sigma" were developed. These approaches gave a clear change structure of champions, steering committees and process owners and placed more emphasis on the widespread communication and celebration of any success stories.

BPR and "Six-sigma" aim at much faster results than TQM and TPM. Emphasis was on break through and radical improvements rather than small, step-by-step incremental, continuous improvements. The whole process is led from top-down and specialists either from outside the organisation, or more often specially trained from within the organisation are used to implement the projects and to realise the short-term financial goals. The commitment was more from the specially trained team members rather than the relevant line management and employees.

TQM and TPM aim at widespread involvement and commitment throughout the implementing unit (company–wide). They include tools and techniques which can enable anyone at any level to improve their daily work on a step-by-step basis. They aim to use the organisation's own employees and managers, rather than outside consultants (specialists) and trainers. Often managers and even employees were given freedom to set their own targets in order to develop a feeling of involvement. The emphasis is on long-term attitude change rather than short-term financial gain. TQM and TPM are far less restrictive in their change processes than BPR and "Six-sigma".

The change process would start at a lower level and gradually permeate upwards in Japanese approach whereas it is acceptable to work top-down in American approach. However, the descriptions rather than any specific kind of change process are the key.

TQM and TPM aim at widespread involvement and commitment (company wide) and aim at long-term results while BPR and six-sigma are project specific and aim at faster results.

The best examples of an original Japanese approach which has become a description of a desired end–state is "lean". **"Lean"** can be considered us an essential element of all the major improvement approaches. The lean management model can best be understood by comparing it with traditional mass production model. The feature of the two models are summarised below:

***(i)* Characteristic features of mass production:** Special purpose machines, long production runs, infrequent product changes, narrow product lines, mass marketing, low worker skill requirements, specialised skill jobs, central expertise and co-ordination, hierarchical planning and control, vertical internal communication, sequential product development, accent on volume, high inventories, supply management, manufacture to stock and sell, limited communication with customers, market dealings with employees and suppliers (not partnership relationships) and vertical integration.

***(ii)* Characteristic features of lean management:** Flexible machines, low set-up costs, short production runs, frequent product improvements, broad product lines, targeted markets, highly skilled, cross–trained workers, worker initiative, local information and self–regulation horizontal communication, cross–functional development teams, continuous improvement, accent on cost and quality, low inventories, demand management, make to order, extensive communication with customers, long-term, trust–based relationships, reliance on outside suppliers.

A move of anyone element from the mass production model to the lean production model is complementary with the corresponding move on each of the other variables. Therefore, it can be understood that there are clear connections between the flexibility of capital equipment, the length of production runs, the level of inventory, the breadth of the product line and the frequency of product changes. Given this, then the approach to marketing and to communicating with customers is largely driven by the need for them to fit in with the product strategy. The frequency of changes in products drives the value of speed in the product development process. The sequential approaches to product development which might work in mass production model are infeasible in the lean production model, which requires the use of cross–functional teams to get new products designed and manufactured in a much shorter time period.

The lean management approach cannot be implemented at the whim of top management but is rather the culmination of a whole series of internal strategic and organisational choices such as product variety, product innovations, workforce training and skill levels, flexibility of manufacturing equipment and delivery of services approaches.

In the lean approach, many elements fit together in a complementary way in a self–supporting and self–sustaining entity. Lean is not down to a single approach, the pieces of which can be implemented in a stand–alone fashion to yield needed improvements.

19.8 MANAGERIAL IMPLICATIONS: WHICH IMPROVEMENT APPROACH IS BEST?

All the approaches discussed earlier in this chapter will involve major changes in most organisations. Any major organisational change process is a complex dynamic phenomenon and the results can not be precisely predicted. Therefore, investment decisions in this area should be seriously examined by top management and if the organisation does not have the required resources (management time and money) it should not attempt any of these approaches.

However if the organisation is not in immediate danger of collapse or anticipating a change of ownership, then the top management might well consider what options they have. They should assess the degree to which it is predictable that any of the improvement approaches will yield major benefits for them. This will depend largely on two factors: how bad the organisation is: *(i)* in terms of key operating parameters and *(ii)* in terms of the rate of turn-over of key the personnel.

Which improvement approach to be implemented depends on the current financial performance of the company and its ability to invest on tools and techniques needed for improvement approaches.

If the organisation is not doing well in terms of key operating parameters, then all the five approaches can result in quick major cost reductions if the organisation has many improvement opportunities.

To assess how much scope for improvement it might have, the organisation needs to benchmark its key operating parameters against its major competition.

If the organisation has considerable improvement opportunities then ideally it also ought to encourage every individual to make them. So while making a choice between the different approaches, management should examine the degree to which an approach aims to help any individual employee to improve their day-to-day work. While BPR and Six-sigma lay little stress in this area, TQM and TPM are rich in this field.

Secondly, the turnover rate of key personnel need to be noted. If the organisation has high turnover of key personnel and little rapid formalisation of learning, then even an initially highly successful improvement process may result in little ever reaching storage in the organisation's memory traces. So using an approach such as TPM or TQM which aims at overall long-term involvement and attitude change might not be as sensible as using a program more oriented to the short-term, such as Six-sigma and BPR. In contrast, if the organisation can easily change internal systems and procedures and its turnover of key personnel is reasonable, then the choice of TQM and TPM becomes a real possibility.

In conclusion, we may say that all the approaches can be useful – if handled carefully. Many of the principles, tools and techniques of the approaches discussed in this chapter could be regarded as timeless. But they can be costly to implement in terms of the time and money involved. So, one should be careful while selecting the most suitable approach for his or her organisation. Suitability of an approach will depend upon the organisation's history, culture and business situation. All the five approaches can be useful if treated with caution. An organisation must develop an approach which works for that organisation.

19.9 QUALITY IN PRACTICE

Box 19.1 : The Four Rules of Toyota Production System

The tacit knowledge that underlies the Toyota Production system can be captured in four basic rules. These rules guide the design, operation and improvement of every product and service. The rules are as follows:

Rule 1: All work shall be highly specified as to content, sequence, timing and outcome.

Rule 2: Every customer - supplier connection must be direct and there must be an unambiguous yes-or-no way to send requests and receive responses.

Rule 3: The pathway for every product and service must be simple and direct.

Rule 4: Any improvement must be made in accordance with the scientific method, under the guidance of a teacher, at the lowest possible level in the organisation.

All the rules require that activities, connections and flow paths have built-in tests to signal problems automatically. It is the continual response to problems that makes the seemingly rigid system so flexible and adaptable to changing circumstances.

Box 19.2 : Toyota Production System as a Learning Organisation

The Toyota Production System (TPS) has been well documented and imitated by companies World-wide, especially in the automobile industry. And yet, only 2 per cent of companies using JIT have achieved the leanness of Toyota.

Elements of the system such as small – lot production, cellular layouts and Kaizen have been used successfully, but implementing the integrated system has proved elusive. Researchers suggest that Toyota has created a learning organisation based on the following four basic rules concerning:

1. ***How people work*** – work content, sequence, timing and outcomes must be specified and rigidly followed.
2. ***How people connect*** – every customer-supplier relationship must be direct. There must be no ambiguity in sending requests and receiving responses.
3. ***How production flows***- every pathway must be simple and direct, and
4. ***How to improve*** – improvements must follow the scientific method under the guidance of a teacher and the lowest possible level in the organisation.

Teaching and learning follows the Socratic approach. Supervisors do not tell workers about the four rules, rather they allow their workers to discover the rules as a consequence of solving problems. For example, to teach a worker about work content a supervisor might ask:

(a) How do you do this work? *(b)* How do you know you are doing this work correctly? *(c)* How do you know that the outcome in free of defects? *(d)* What do you do if you have a problem?

Answering these questions leads the worker to a better understanding of the work they do, as well as an insight into how work should be designed and improved.

19.10 SUMMARY

In the modern approach to quality, the changed view is that quality is everybody's business and everyone in the organisation is responsible for quality. Every organisation, small or big, offering product or service, has the necessity to strive for the continuous elimination of errors, defects and waste and improve the quality of their products/services.

During recent times, organisations have been using a number of approaches to assist with the key corporate objective to make continuous improvement in their business processes. Their quality improvement activities can be structured in the form of four hierarchical categories as *(i)* Concepts, *(ii)* Approaches, *(iii)* Systems and, *(iv)* Tools and Techniques.

Each approach used to make improvements is based on a set of core concepts centred around *(i)* customer orientation, *(ii)* process control and, *(iii)* process improvement.

An approach requires intellectual effort to its deployment and adoption. The application requires a strategic decision by senior management and resources in terms of training and hiring specialists in quality improvement techniques. The modern approaches to quality management include: *(i)* Total quality management (TQM), *(ii)* Total productive maintenance (TPM), *(iii)* Business Process reengineering (BPR), *(iv)* Six-Sigma and *(v)* Lean management.

A system comprises written information in the form of instructions and procedures in order to direct and control some form of operation. Quality planning, quality management, visible management and performance management are typical examples of systems involved in process improvement.

Tools and techniques comprise methods and skills applied to particular tasks, projects and problems to facilitate change and improvement. The terms 'tools' and "techniques" are used interchangeably. Examples of tools are "7 QC tools" and examples of techniques include SPC, Benchmarking, QFD and DOE etc.

The various modern approaches to quality management are briefly discussed in the following paragraphs:

1. Total Quality Management (TQM)

TQM is based on a set of principles viz customer focus, leadership, employee involvement and empowerment, process approach, systems approach to management, continuous improvement (Kaizen), factual approach to decision making and mutually beneficial supplier partnerships. TQM makes use of statistical tools and techniques, for analysing data and interpreting the same to identify the nature and causes of defects so that corrective and preventive actions can be taken by process/ product design improvements. TQM can be considered as the foundation upon which other improvement approaches are based: for example, total productive maintenances uses TQM as its foundation and Six–Sigma, and BPR are improvements beyond TQM.

2. Total Productive Maintenance: (TPM)

TPM combines preventive maintenance with TQM., employee involvement and effective house keeping. TPM is considered as complementary to TQM. TPM focuses on the condition of manufacturing equipment and machinery and their influence on the quality of outputs. It is a modern concept for maintaining plants and equipment. TPM helps to improve production and productivity along with employee morale and job satisfaction. TPM brings maintenance into focus as a necessary and important part of business. It integrates maintenance and production departments. It is a company – wide approach in which every employee is concerned about the maintenance, quality and efficiency of their equipment. The objective is to reduce the whole–life cost of machinery and equipment through more efficient maintenance management by integrating the maintenance and manufacturing departments. Teamwork is a key element in TPM.

TPM starts with 5 'S' approach of Japanese industries which aim at reducing wastages (6 major losses) in the work place. The 5 'S' are essential activities of TPM which provide more visible management. The 5 'S' are *(i)* Seiri (sorting), *(ii)* Seiton (straightening or setting in order/stabilise), *(iii)* Seiso (sweeping or systematic cleaning), *(iv)* Seiketsu (standardising) and, *(v)* Shitsuke (sustaining the discipline or self–discipline). The six major losses are due to *(i)* breakdown of machinery and equipment, *(ii)* setup/adjustment of machines/equipments, *(iii)* speed, *(iv)* idling and minor stoppages, *(v)* quality defects and, *(vi)* start–up.

3. Business Process Reengineering

BPR is a successor to TQM. Whereas TQM emphasises continuous, small, incremental improvements in the process and work activities, BPR advocates major, radical, break–through improvements through major change initiatives and innovations in the process. Two main approaches in BPR are *(i)* Business process redesign and, *(ii)* Business process reengineering.

BPR comprises a central set of principles:

(i) Strategic in concept
(ii) Customer focused
(iii) Output-rather-than-input focused,
(iv) Focused on key business processes,
(v) Cross–functional in nature,
(vi) Involves internal and external customer relationships,
(vii) Requires top management commitment and involvement,
(viii) Requires clear communication and visibility.

Four phases of a BPR project are: *(i)* Preparation phase, *(ii)* Innovation and design phase, *(iii)* Implementation phase and, *(iv)* Assessment phase.

4. Six-Sigma Quality

"Six-Sigma" is also considered as the successor to TQM. Motorola created "Six–Sigma" concept in the mid 1980 s to improve the performance of their key processes.

'Six-Sigma' follows a five–phase improvement process – define, measure, analyse, improve and control (referred to as DMAIC approach). Specific improvement tools and techniques are linked to each of these phases. 'Six-Sigma' is more specific and more structured than TQM and is recommended as the approach to all improvement projects. With respect to process design/redesign rather than process improvement, the phases become: define, measure, analyse, design and verify (DMADV). Implementation of 'Six-Sigma' projects are time bound with well defined bottom–line savings and improvement. This requires deployment of training programs to appropriate levels as master black–belts, black–belts and green belts who have specific responsibilities and duties.

5. Lean Manufacturing

It is considered as an essential element of all the major improvement approaches. Toyota Motor Company in Japan developed a new kind of production methodology (Toyota Production Systems) which is now referred to as "Lean Production Systems". These systems consist of processes designed to minimise their inherent waste of time, material and money. They utilise minimal amount of resources to produce a high volume of high quality goods with some variety.

Lean production systems focus on elimination of seven types of waste ('muda' in Japanese) viz *(i)* excess production, *(ii)* waiting time, *(iii)* conveyance or transportation, *(iv)* motion, *(v)* processing time, *(vi)* inventory and *(vii)* defects.

"Lean manufacturing" or "Lean production" involves a range of approaches and techniques such as "Single – minute exchange of die" (SMED), Mistake proofing (Poka-Yoke), Kanban, (Just-in-time), Concurrent engineering and Rapid prototyping.

The key issues of lean are: *(i)* Value, *(ii)* Value stream, *(iii)* Flow, *(iv)* Pull, and *(v)* Perfection.

The key elements in "lean manufacturing" are *(i)* visual control and management, *(ii)* rapid change over, *(iii)* one–piece flow, *(iv)* pull-rather-than push, *(v)* cellular manufacturing, *(vi)* employee empowerment, *(vii)* work standardisation, *(viii)* five 'S' s, *(ix)* point-of-usage storage, *(x)* small batch production, *(xi)* quality at the source and, *(xii)* effective plant layout.

An analysis of the five approaches revealed that BPR and 'Six-sigma' approaches aim at much faster results than TQM and TPM with emphasis on break–through and radical improvements rather than small, step-by-step, incremental, continuous improvements. TQM and TPM aim at the widespread involvement and commitment through–out the implementing unit. While BPR and 'Six-sigma' projects may require outside experts, TQM and TPM can be implemented using the expertise of organisation's own employees and managers. "Lean" can be considered as an essential element of all the major improvement approaches.

All the approaches discussed will involve major changes in most organisations and require heavy investments for change initiatives to be implemented. Therefore, investment decisions need to be carefully examined by top management.

19.11 OBJECTIVE QUESTIONS

(A) Match the following :

Column A	Column B
1. Seiri	1. Systematic change
2. Seiton	2. Sorting
3. Seiso	3. Self-discipline
4. Seiketsu	4. Setting in order, stabilise
5. Shitsuke	5. Standardising

(B) State whether the following statements are True or False :

1. A technique has a wider application than a tool. (T / F)
2. TPM requires a change in employee mind-set towards their job responsibilities. (T / F)
3. The concepts of "Lean Production system" and " The Toyota Production system" are entirely different. (T / F)
4. BPR and 'Six-Sigma' aim at much faster results than TQM and TPM. (T / F)
5. Lean Production Systems do not focus on elimination of seven types of wastes. (T / F)

(C) Multiple choice Questions : Choose the correct answer from the alternatives given under each question :

1. The modern approaches to quality management includes:
   (a) Total quality management (b) Total productive maintenance
   (c) Business Process Reengineering (d) Six-Sigma approach
   (e) Lean Management (f) All of these
   (g) None of these
2. TQM is based on a set of principles consisting of the following:
   (a) Customer focus (b) Continuous improvement
   (c) Leadership (d) Involvement of people
   (e) Process approach (f) All of these

(g) None of these

3. "There should be a place for everything and everything should be in its place". This Japanese house keeping principle is known as:
   (a) Seiri (b) Seiton
   (c) Seiso (d) Seiketsu
   (e) Shitsuke
4. BPR comprises a central set of principles including the following:
   (a) Focus on customer and supplier relationships
   (b) Process responsibility and focus on key business processes.
   (c) Top management commitment and involvement
   (d) Cross-functional in nature (e) All of these
   (f) None of these
5. Six-Sigma and TQM have the following common objectives:
   (a) Customer orientation and focus (b) Team-based activity
   (c) Problem-solving methodology (d) All of these
   (e) None of these

19.12 REVIEW QUESTIONS

1. Define the term "approach".
2. What is meant by "The interconnection pyramid".
3. Discuss briefly the five modern approaches to quality management.
4. Distinguish between 'tools' and 'techniques' giving examples.
5. What is "total productive maintenance"?
6. In what way "total productive maintenance" (TPM) resembles TQM?
7. Why total productive maintenance is important to quality management?
8. Discuss the organisational characteristics of TPM.
9. Discuss the 5 'S' approach to quality management.
10. Discuss the seven steps of a TPM program.
11. Discuss the application of "Business Process Reengineering" in quality management.
12. Discuss the principles involved in BPR.
13. What is 'Six-Sigma' approach?
14. Discuss the 'D M A I C' and "D M A D V' cycles used in "Six-Sigma.
15. What is meant by "lean management"?
16. Discuss the salient features of lean production systems.
17. Discuss the key issues of lean.
18. State the key elements of lean manufacturing.
19. Compare the characteristic features of mass production with that of "lean production".
20. Discuss the managerial implications of the five approaches to modern quality management.

19.13 DISCUSSION QUESTIONS

1. "Now TQM has become a relatively established entity with accepted components of team work, systems thinking and statistical tools being applied to the areas of "customer, counting and culture" – Explain.
2. "TPM resembles TQM in several aspects" – Discuss.
3. "TPM starts with 5 'S' – Elaborate.
4. "Some writers believe that BPR is a successor to TQM, while some others believe that TQM and BPR are complimentary and integral approaches". What is your opinion in this regard. Justify your answer.

5. "Lean" is a "specific way of thinking" consisting of a set of methods, and operating principles to identify and eliminate waste in business processes" – Explain.
6. "BPR and 'Six-Sigma' aim at much faster results than TQM and TPM". Do you agree or not? Substantiate your answer.

19.14 CHAPTER CASE

LEAN BANKING: IT IS NOT ALWAYS JUST SINGLE-PIECE FLOW

"Let the process flow." "Let the customer pull." This is what is written in manufacturing books about making processes Lean. But it is hot always that simple.

Consider this banking example. A customer arrives at a bank branch: He is welcomed by an employee and offered a cup of coffee. He explains his interest in obtaining a loan and a salesperson asks the right questions to identify his exact needs. They enter a lot of data into the bank's computer systems. The data is evaluated at a central clearing point where a decision is made to approve the loan, and the customer gets the loan.

On the surface, this seems like a Lean process. There is flow in the process, no batching and the customer pulls (nobody gives him advice, or a loan, unless he comes into the bank or otherwise expresses his interest). But is the process Lean?

Actually, in most cases it is far from Lean given these factors:

a) The double entry into different systems that were not linked

b) Many data points that were not really needed

c) A lot of waste because decision making had to be taken to the central underwriters

There are many projects where Lean is not about flow and pull, but about straightforward waste reduction. Most of the waste is relatively easy to find but hard to eliminate from an information technology-driven process, The key is to make Lean thinking (and usability) a key building block of the design and the review of IT applications.

Lean Approach Should Differ by Industry

A successful Lean approach needs to be designed for the industry in which it is supposed to deliver results. It is not enough to adapt the manufacturing experience. And it is certainly not enough to use a reduced manufacturing toolkit. Lean banking includes elements that Lean manufacturing gurus have never thought of.

One of the challenges in banking and financial services is that processes often are not easily seen because they are hidden in workflow systems, phone calls and emails. There is no production line to follow with a "walk the process" as a first step in trying to find waste. Sometimes people up and down the process have never even talked to each other before.

At another bank, the back office was carrying a significant backlog and the decision was made to use Lean to improve the situation. Of course, it was useful to do 5-S (an approach to ensure having "a place for everything and everything in its place") and to eliminate some non-value-added steps. When loans are sourced over the phone, there is no batching either and a transaction is only initiated once the customer says go. No job for the introduction of flow and pull. However, while the front office was selling extremely well, it too was overloaded at times. The answer was level loading, or smoothing the demand curve to avoid extreme peaks and deep valleys leading to a better capacity management. Generally, idle time for staff is an important area for waste in services and transactions.

Customers are regularly required to fill out insurance claim forms, loan applications or other documents. Unfortunately these documents too often are incomplete or incorrectly filled out. This can be a big problem and a challenge for Lean. That also is true of customers who move without providing their new address. A great deal of waste is generated and sales volumes are reduced when applications are not completed, and extra resources must be expended to fill the missing gaps or correct the errors.

Mistake proofing (designing errors out of the process using simple solutions) is the most promising Lean answer to these problems, and it can be implemented relatively easily in electronic application processes. In many situations, simplifying requirements is the key to success. The less asked of the customer, the less the chance the customer will make an error or forget something, or be frustrated by their own mistake. But sometimes mistake proofing is not required; the bank need only explain why it needs the information in question.

Flow also is difficult to implement if the bank must wait for the customer to react. Take a collections process for example. The agent calls, the customer pays (or does not pay), the agent calls again, the customers pays, and often stops paying again. In this case, the bank was able to improve the performance without even thinking about flow. The solution was to standardize the process, the decisions and their consequences. Giving call agents clear guidelines and simplifying a process for them and the customers, can make collecting the outstanding money more effective while keeping customers away from the hassle and costs of legal actions.

Of course, flow makes great sense for longer banking processes, such as" mortgage applications. There are many successful examples of this. However, for shorter processes or ones that do not need attention to flow and pull, Lean can still be successfully applied.

Next Challenge: 'Deliberate Simplification'

"Deliberate simplification" is banking's next big challenge after Lean. Most people have had the experience of shopping for a product such as a mobile phone, and finding that the salespeople were unable to explain all of the phone service's many options. Even if many product engineers and marketing people admire complexity (they call it "sophistication"), most customers love and want simple, hassle-free services.

Discussion Questions :

1. What are the various kinds of waste that happened/could happen as mentioned throughout the business case in banking services?
2. There could be different challenges in the implementation of Lean approach in the banking sector. What are the challenges highlighted in the business case and suggest possible alternative solutions?
3. Can you identify some of the areas from your work environment where lean approach could be implemented? Substantiate.

CHAPTER 20

MANAGING QUALITY – ISSUES AND NEW CHALLENGES

LEARNING OBJECTIVES

After reading this chapter, you should be able to:

- Discuss the "quality management principles" and key elements of TQM.
- Discuss the critical issues in effective implementation of TQM
- Discuss the TQM issues which need to be considered in the future.
- Discuss the new challenges faced by quality management.

20.0 INTRODUCTION

TQM involves the application of quality management principles to all aspects of the organisation including customers and suppliers, and their integration with the key business processes.

TQM requires that the principles of quality management should be applied in every branch and at every level of the organisation with an emphasis on integration into business practices and a balance between ***technical, managerial*** and ***people issues.*** It is a company–wide approach to quality, with improvements undertaken on a continuous basis by every one in the organisation. The spread of the TQM philosophy would also be expected to be accomplished by greater sophistication in the application of tools and techniques, increased emphasis on people, process management, improved training and personnel development and greater efforts to eliminate wastage and non – value–adding activities. The process will also extend beyond the organisation to include partnerships with suppliers and customers and all shareholders of the business. Activities will be reoriention to focus on the customers; internal and external, with the aim to build partnerships and go beyond satisfying the customer to delighting them. The need to self–assess progress towards business excellence is also a key issue.

TQM is both a philosophy and a set of guiding principles for managing an organisation to the benefit of all stakeholders. The eight quality management principles are:

TQM is both a philosophy and a set of guiding principles for managing an organisation to the benefit of all stakeholders.

1. Customer focus: Understanding current and future customer needs, meeting customer requirements and striving to exceed customer expectations.

2. Leadership: Leaders establish unity of purpose and direction of the organisation.

3. Involvement of people: People at all levels are the essence of an organisation and their full involvement enables their abilities to be used for the organisation's benefit.

4. Process approach: A desired result in achieved more efficiently when activities and related resources are managed as a process.

5. System approach to management: Identifying, understanding, and managing inter–related processes as a system contributes to the organisation's effectiveness and efficiency in achieving its objectives.

6. Continuous improvement: Continual improvement of the organisation's over all performance should be a permanent objective of the organisation.

7. Factual approach to decision:making: Effective decisions are based on the analysis of data and information.

8. Mutually beneficial supplier relationships: An organisation and its suppliers are interdependent and a mutually beneficial relationship enhances the ability of both to create value.

20.1 THE KEY ELEMENTS OF TQM

1. Commitment and leadership of the Chief Executive Officer (CEO)

Without the total demonstrated commitment of the CEO and his or her immediate top management executives and other senior managers, nothing much can happen towards implementing total quality. They have to take charge personally, lead the process, provide direction and exercise powerful leadership.

2. Planning and Organisation

Planning and organistation feature many facts of the improvement process including:

(i) Developing a clear long–term strategy for TQM which is integrated with other strategies such as production/operations, human resources, information technology and also with the business plans of the organisation.

(ii) Deployment of the policies through all stages of the organisational hierarchy.

(iii) Building product/service quality into designs and processes.

(iv) Developing prevention–based activities.

(v) Putting quality assurance procedures into place.

(vi) Planning the approach to be taken to the effective use of quality systems, procedures and tools and techniques.

(vii) Developing the organisation and infrastructure to support the improvement activities.

(viii) Pursuing standardisation, systematization and simplification of work instructions, procedures and systems.

The key elements of TQM are:
(i) Commitment and leadership of CEO
(ii) Planning and organisation
(iii) Using tools and techniques
(iv) Education and training
(v) Involvement
(vi) Team work
(vii) Measurement and feed back
(vii) Ensuring a culture that is conducive to continuous improvement

3. Using Tools and Techniques

To support and develop a process of continuous improvement an organisation will need to use a selection of tools and techniques within a problem–solving approach. The tools and techniques should be used to facilitate improvement and be integrated into the routine operation of the business. The use of tools and techniques as the means will help to get the process of improvement started, employees use them, feel involved and that they are making a contribution, quality awareness is enhanced, behaviour and attitude change starts to happen and projects are completed satisfactorily.

4. Education and Training

All employees (from top to bottom) of an organisation should be provided with the right level and standard of education and training to ensure that their general awareness and understanding of quality management concepts, skills, competencies, and attitudes are appropriate and suited to the continuous improvement philosophy and also provides a common language through-out the business. **Without training it is difficult to solve problems and without education, behaviour and attitude change will not take place.**

5. Involvement

There must be a commitment and structure to the development of employees with recognition that they are an asset which appreciates over time. All available means, from suggestion schemes to various forms of team work must be considered for achieving broad employee interest, participation and contribution in the improvement process. Management must be prepared to share information and some of their powers and responsibilities with the employees to create a sense of employee involvement in the implementation of total quality approach. Participation also involves seeking and listening carefully to the views of employees and acting upon their suggestions. Management must ensure that everyone has a clear understanding of what is required of them, how their processes relate to the business as a whole and how their internal customers are dependent upon them. People must be encouraged to control, manage and improve the processes which are within their sphere of responsibility.

6. Teamwork

Management should consider the operating characteristics of the teams employed, how they fit into the organisational structure and the roles of members, team leader, sponsor and facilitator. Teamwork is one of the key features of involvement. Without teamwork, it will be difficult to achieve commitment and participation of people through–out the organisation. Teamwork also helps in maximizing the output and value of individuals.

Recognition for positive performance achievement and celebration and reward for success are also key to success of TQM. Also if TQM is to be successful, it is essential that communication must be effective and widespread.

7. Measurement and Feed Back

Measurement, from a base line, needs to be made against a series of key results indicators – internal and external – in order to provide encouragement that things are getting better. External indicators are the most important as they relate to customer perceptions of product and/or service improvement. The indicators should be developed from existing business measures, external, competitive and functional, generic and internal bench marking, as well as customer surveys and other means of external input. This enables progress and feed back to be clearly assessed against a roadmap or check points. From these measurements, action plans must be developed to meet objectives and bridge gaps.

8. Ensuring that the Culture is Conducive to Continuous Improvement Activity

An organisation culture which is conducive to continuous improvement and in which everyone can participate is necessary, Quality assurance also needs to be integrated into all of an organisation's processes and functions. This requires change in people's behaviour and working practices in many ways:

(i) Everyone in the organisation must recognise that whatever they do can be improved. They must be involved in improving the processes under their control on a continuous basis.

(ii) Employees must be encouraged to identify wastage in all its various forms to take out cost and get more value into a product/service.

(iii) Employees must be empowered to stop a process without seeking permission from management, if they consider it to be faulty.

(iv) Employees must be inspecting their own work.

(v) Defects must not be passed to the next process in whatever form. The internal customer – supplier relationship must be recognized.

(vi) Each person must be commiited to satisfying their customers – both internal and external.

(vii) External suppliers and customers must be integrated into the improvement process.

(viii) Mistakes must be viewed as opportunities for improvement,

(ix) Honesty, sincerity and care must be an integral part of daily business life.

One of the most difficult tasks facing management is – changing people's behaviour and attitudes. It requires considerable powers and motivational skills and persuasion. Considerable thought needs be given to facilitate and manage cultural change. Changing people's attitude and getting them committed to continuous improvement presents the greatest challenge to management.

20.2 CRITICAL ISSUES IN EFFECTIVE IMPLEMENTATION OF TQM

Quality improvement efforts in the 1980's and continuing into 1990's throughout the world has been fueled by a host of good ideas to make quality integral to the business decision making process.

While on the technical front, SPC, JIT, DOE, Taguchi methods, QFD and TPM philosophies and methodologies have been attempted, on the system front, ISO 9000 has been interpreted as a must. On the human front, **"total employee involvement"**, **participative management,** and **quality circles** have attracted the attention of many companies. On the motivational front, many awards for quality improvement and business excellence have been instituted – both nationally and internationally.

Inspite of the widespread interest and massive investment, there are reports of only isolated success. By and large, quality is not yet integral to all businesses or all activities in any given business.

The TQM concept has the potential to integrate all the improvement philosophies proposed in this book. However TQM can end up being diffused if the TQM concept is not executed well.

It is difficult to execute the improvement philosophies of TQM because it is a soft science. The elements of TQM are rather straight forward, but the execution is quite difficult. It is wrong to believe that TQM is simply a matter of common sense.

Even though the principles of TQM are straight forward, it is difficult to execute the improvement philosophies of TQM because it is a soft science. TQM should not be viewed as a mere "common sense". There are many critical issues and superior choices in TQM

Critical Issues and Superior Choices

Issue 1: Listening to a single versus many quality experts

Any one quality improvement expert does not have answers to all problems. Each offers one unique idea to advance the soft technology of looking at quality related problems. To solve real – life problems, one has to be able to select, sequence and synthesise the messages from many different experts to come to a useful conclusion.

Issue 2: Method focus versus problem focus

In the 1980's, many different improvement concepts have been presented; for eg SPC, JIT, and QFD. As soon as a new quality concept or a newly packaged old quality concept has been introduced, it becomes a focus of the company. The company becomes focused to the new quality concept and performs all activities required for its implementation. These activities continue until another quality concept is introduced that seems to have more potential than the previous and the whole set of activities repeats again. Rather than having a problem focus, companies try to fit their current problems into the newly learnt method. The focus on method rather than the real problem. Can drain the vital resources of the company into non strategic activities.

Issue 3: Focusing on productivity versus focusing on quality improvement

Generally, management focus is directed toward productivity improvement with quality improvement as a by – product. But the truth is most focus on quality results in productivity improvement as a by product which fact is overlooked by management. For TQM practice to be effective, the focus must be on quality with productivity as a by–product and not vice–versa.

Issue 4: Focus on Japanese strengths versus on internal strengths

The focus on quality is attributed to Japanese success in numerous markets and the trend is to copy what they have done. The path chosen to accomplish quality is the copying of the so called Japanese quality methods throughout the world. Actually there is no such thing as Japanese quality methods. Any real improvement is based on sound scientific principles. The reason for some companies not succeeding in improving their quality is a lack of understanding and/or poor execution of these principles. Direct duplication of Japanese practices is not an appropriate way to duplicate Japanese successes. The better approach is to focus on a company's internal strengths in a given cultural setting and seek the duplication of results achieved by Japanese companies.

Issue 5: Administration–based versus technology-based supplier quality model

There are numerous customer–designed supplier quality improvement models which can consfuse many suppliers. A strategic quality improvement model has to be consistent with the product/process technology. Therefore, a supplier who is most knowledgeable about the technology, is in a better position to design the quality improvement model. If suppliers are to be true partners, then their improvement models must be consistent with their technology.

Issue 6: Automating human tasks versus automating human tendencies

Automation has a high potential of delivering a quality product. For example, replaces human effort. Programmable controls automate the maintenance of process variable ranges. SPC automates the closed–loop signals and corresponding corrective actions on the output signal measurements. However, no single form of automation for improving quality is a strategic choice. SPC guided automation decisions are recommended.

Issue 7: Focus on the system versus focus on quality

The need for quality system such as ISO 9000 is universally recognised, The question is not whether or not to have a quality system, but what is the best way to formulate one. Since the elements in quality systems are industry environment dependent, it is necessary that the company's problems must be recognised first to determine the priority of these system elements. The development of the system elements is directly dependent on the company's needs. Eventually, as solutions continue to develop, system elements continue to emerge.

Issue 8: Use of SPC as an on-line control versus use of SPC for process improvement

Using SPC as an on-line control measure is a form of a process control or process capability maintenance solution. The process is periodically monitored for potential variations and instantaneous action is taken when such variations occur. SPC simply provides a timely signal for actions.

On the other hand, the use of SPC as a process improvement tool is a better choice to consider. The use of SPC as an on-line control is only an option in selecting the process maintenance tool.

Issue 9: Horizontal thinking versus vertical thinking

Horizontal thinking creates the perfection of the sub –step. In this approach, decisions are made to perfect one of the steps in the quality improvement process rather than all the steps. For example, gages for all operations in the plant with the objective of perfecting the measurement system would require a big investment. Instead, it is better to upgrade a few selected gages rather than investing in upgrading the gages in the whole plant.

Vertical thinking, on the other hand requires the completion of a closed loop. Vertical thinking require that all the steps needed in making improvement happen be thought out and applied to a few selected cases.

Issue 10: Process teaching versus content teaching

Companies must consider two most popular options in making a choice regarding how to go about training company employees.

The first preference of teaching general ideas and leaving specific applications to be developed by individuals is stronger in the academic community which is referred to as ***process teaching***. But people in the working environment prefer to learn what is immediately applicable to their own problems before being able to generalize the use of quality methodology, which is referred to as ***content teaching***. Teaching quality is most likely to be effective if it starts from a content teaching and develops into a process teaching.

Issue 11: Management lip service versus management commitment

The commitment to quality through speeches delivered by the CEO and supported by budgetary measures to carryon quality activities cannot create a TQM environment.

The CEO should get personally committed on many TQM fronts – *(i)* Self-education in quality concepts before speaking about them to others, *(ii)* Understanding the company restructuring process by participating in some problem solving activities, *(iii)* Navigation by top leadership is necessary to identify and formulate the most significant problems, *(iv)* Aligning the financial rewards for quality work with the introduction of TQM in the organisation.

Issue 12: Soft progress versus hard progress

Quality progress is often described in soft terms (immediate results) instead of hard terms (end results). For example, some companies will describe their progress in terms of how many employees are trained rather than how many problems have been resolved. Other companies will describe how many Q. C circles have been formed rather than how many Q. C circles have resolved inherent problems. The better choice is to require progress reports in hard terms rather than in soft terms.

Issue 13: Improvement of manufacturing systems alone versus all other systems that relate to manufacturing

Quality improvement efforts are usually talked about in the manufacturing sense; rather than in the sense of business systems. Most of the problems associated with business processes are handled as incidents rather than considered as candidates for permanent solution. To derive the full benefits, quality improvement ideas should be extended to business processes and not confined to manufacturing activities alone.

Issue 14: Mathematical models versus reality

Mathematical models help us to visualise difficult physical concepts. Mathematical methods conceptualise the most efficient approach to investigative problems. For example, a point outside the plus or minus three sigma limits in SPC is a practical definition of instability of the process.

However, according to the mathematical model there is a 0.27 % chance that points may fall outside the three-sigma limits due to common causes or natural reasons. Thus the question is when an occasional point falls outside the control limits, should it be investigated as instability or ignored as a chance event. The recommended choice is to consider it as instability and investigate the underlying assignable cause.

Issue 15: Mathematical efficiency of experiments versus execution difficulty of experiments

Recently emphasis has been given to a family of fractional factorial experiments (Design of experiments – Taguchi Methods) which claim mathematical efficiency. Based on certain assumption, Taguchi applies fractional factorial ideas and seeks robustness against uncontrollable (noise) factors. What is important in this approach is that it is difficult in execution. It is extremely difficult to arrange fractional factorial experiments for a large number of factors because it is very expensive to seek out the needed extremities of factors. Also such experiments may be prohibitively expensive. When such methods are tried in the actual production environment, there is no budget set aside to bear the initial expense of these type of investigations. Therefore, the solution of an improvement methodology is not solely dependent on mathematical efficiency but has to be balanced with execution considerations.

20.3 TQM ISSUES WHICH NEED TO BE CONSIDERED IN THE FUTURE

There are some issues which need to be given more attention by organisations which aim at achieving a "World-class" quality status in the future

The issues which organisations will need to give more attention in order to achieve world – class quality status are:

1. Quantitative tools and techniques employed by an increasing number of organisations as important aids in facilitating and measuring continuous improvement include:
   (i) Statistical Process Control (SPC)
   (ii) Failure mode and effects analysis (FMEA)
   (iii) Quality function deployment (QFD)
   (iv) Mistake proofing (Poka–Yoke)
   (v) Bench marking.
   (vi) Seven management tools. (7 QC tools)

The less–used tools and techniques such as policy deployment, quality function deployment and the seven management tools need more attention. Business process reengineering will continue to be useful with respect to its role in business improvement and in connection with TQM. The EFQM and MBNQA business excellence models will increasingly be recognised by business as general management models as a starting point which individual business units then need to develop to fit their own situations.

Since there is considerable scope for improving the use of tools and techniques, organsiations need to consider a number of issues, including a route map for their use and application, identifying which tools and techniques should be used together to make their best use.

In the near future, quality will gain more importance in e-commerce. One of the challenges will be to explore and adapt the quality tools and techniques to the e-commerce environment. For example, **QFD** can be used to capture the **"voice of the customer"** and the data used to build a website that the customer wants. **SPC** can be used to monitor the **"voice of the process"**, to check whether the processes are in control and provide guidance for improvement. Design of experiments (DOE) can be used to find the optimum interaction of technical features in a site with marketing requirements.

2. Activity–based costing and throughput accounting will become more important in relation to the collection and use of quality costs. **Also other issues which need to be evaluated include:**
   (i) The different approaches and strategies that can be employed in identifying and collecting quality costs.
   (ii) The development of quality cost models.
   (iii) The justification of investment in prevention–type activities,
   (iv) The development of cost performance indicators,
   (v) The best means of identifying and reporting "bottom–line" and intangible benefits to demonstrate the effectiveness of TQM.
3. A large number of organisations world-wide have based their quality systems on the ISO 9000 series of quality standards because without an ISO 9001 certificate of registration, organisations will find it very difficult to do business in the global market place. The development of environmental management systems to meet the requirements of ISO 14001 will help to make quality management systems which are based on the ISO 9000 series more improvement – oriented.
4. There will be a development in the direction of integrating quality into the normal management procedures and operations of a business. This will be supported by the development of integrated management systems dealing with quality management, environment, occupational health and safety and data protection.
5. Attention needs to be given to the development of problem-solving skills, competencies and talents of all employees in the organisation.
6. Continuous improvement initiatives must reach every part of an organisation and every employee and every function needs to be involved if TQM is to become total in the real sense. Quality needs to be seen and treated as an integral part of each departments activities.
7. There will be a greater focus on process streams linked directly to customer groups and suppliers, replacing the traditional function-oriented structure.
8. Many organisations are currently facing the task of revitalising TQM after a period of stagnation.
9. Organisations should have measures of performance based on hard measures of customer satisfaction.
10. Teamwork in all its forms should be encouraged and different types of team activity need to be integrated to get the best influence of synergy.
11. Winning the 'hearts and minds' of all employees and cultivating motivation and commitment amongst the work force is and will remain a key issue.
12. Timely and accurate data are a prerequisite of effective, quality related decision making. Quality information systems and quality databases need to be developed in order to facilitate this, feed back of data internally and externally being a key issue.
13. As a high proportion of quality problems are caused by poor communications, organisations to develop effective method and channels which encourage open and honest communication

in terms everyone can understand between employees at all levels and between themselves, their suppliers and their customers.

14. "How to develop effective working relationships with their supply base and jointly pursue improvement initiatives" – is a key concern of major organisations.
15. Education and training are basic for any quality initiative. Therefore organisations must invest to train employees at all levels in improvement skills in order to facilitate changes in behaviour and attitude.
16. It is vital that members of the senior management team continue to develop their understanding of TQM. Management's attention must be kept focused on TQM and they must devote sufficient time to improvement activities and initiatives.

20.4 NEW CHALLENGES FACED BY QUALITY MANAGEMENT

There are two kinds of quality management:

(i) "Old" or "classical" quality management of the 20th century (1980s and 1990s) and

(ii) "New" quality management of the 21st century.

The aim of classical quality management was to analyse errors and eliminate their causes and the associated variation by improved product and process design. In recent years, a number of major changes have taken place. These changes are being driven by developments in production operations, competitive pressure, the need for improved results from the financial market and shrinkage of buying points. As a result, pressure on prices, performance and innovation, has increased. Also there is a need for flexibility and economies of scale, with a focus on core competencies within the business. This situation demands a "new" form of quality management.

In recent times, major changes have taken place, for example *(i)* companies have started offering a wide range of product variants to their customers and these product variants are updated frequently to maintain high sales levels, *(ii)* Manufacturing industries have shifted from individual part assembly to modular assembly, *(iii)* Pressure to produce increased profit means that companies in the supply chain are continuously experimenting with cheaper, more effective materials, suppliers and technologies etc. which has increased the likelihood of defects, *(iv)* In many industries, the pressure is now on innovation with a shift to technological break–through (i.e., cutting–edge technologies) which can result in disruption, *(v)* There are fewer buying points with more power in the hands of a small number of suppliers/distributors with less flexibility in terms of delivery, timing and quality.

Changing conditions such as developments in production operations, increasing competition, increasing levels of technological innovation, pressure for results from the money markets and shrinkage of buying points in many markets, coupled with the way in which businesses are now organising their manufacturing and service delivery systems and processes are giving rise to major problems in quality management because they demand new measures which have not been developed so far. The new measurement problems are concerned with four major areas: *(i)* the shift from a focus on initial quality to durability, *(ii)* the increased importance of non–technical, softer influences on customer satisfaction, *(iii)* the growing importance of software within products and, *(iv)* the need for closer co-operation both internally between functions and externally between partners in the supply chain. These four major areas are briefly discussed in the following paragraphs:

***(i)* Durability as a measure of quality:** Now a days, the customer is no longer solely interested in satisfaction with the product or service on delivery, but rather over its life time. It is vague and complicated to measure customer satisfaction in the future. What influences satisfaction in the future? What influence do after–sales–support, training costs, cost of upgrades, speed of maintenance, cost of maintenance contracts and experience with all these possible factors have on customer expectations of future satisfaction?

Durability is highly dependent on the way the customer uses a product, which is something the manufacturer has little influence on. Therefore, judgement about quality are not only subjective but may also shift in response to recent events rather than being based on considered experience over a longer period.

The new challenges faced by quality management are in the following areas:
(i) Durability as a measure of quality
(ii) The impact of softer influences on customer satisfaction
(iii) The growing importance of software.
(iv) The need for closer co-operation both internally between functions and externally between partners in the supply chain.

***(ii)* The impact of softer influences on customer satisfaction:** Now a days, the increasing importance of the softer kinds of customers, for example their emotional reactions to products or services has become a problem area to many businesses. Customers expect something more beyond the product or service that meets specifications and does what it was intended to do. This is often complicated as a result of the brand image which the organisation is trying to develop. Products that have a favourable brand image should have differentiating features as compared to competitior's products. With the increase in globalisation in recent years, the impact of emotional quality issues on organisations has increased. Manufacturers targeting global markets have tried to reduce costs by standardising their product offerings in all parts of the world. But the disadvantage of this approach is that the product even though technically good, may not be able to satisfy customers in all markets over the world. Brand image adds value to a product but it is difficult to measure that value contributed by brand image. The perceived quality of a product which varies from customer to customer is difficult to measure as it is associated with the behavioural characteristics of individual customers.

***(iii)* The growing importance of software:** Another growing area that is very difficult to measure is the increase in the amount of software in many products. For example in the automotive industry the electronics and software in a car are expected to represent to about 30% of the total value of the car.

Manufacturers are having problems with integrating different electronic components in one product because they were developed on the basis of differing technologies and software standards. Combining different modules into a final product regularly leads to unanticipated problems because of incompatibility between two or more modules. It is difficult to apply the classical "root–cause analysis" in these situations because the cause is not in one individual module, but in a complicated interplay between different modules.

***(iv)* The need for closer cooperation both internally between functions and externally between partners in the supply chain.**

In todays competitive business environment, "speed to market" or "time to market" is significantly important in both manufacturing systems and the process of delivery of services. For achieving this competitive advantage, the following are vital:

***(i) The innovation process needs to speed up*:** Delay in launching innovative products or services to the market can mean missing a key window of opportunity, thus reducing the chance of financial success.

***(ii) Poor quality has to be prevented*:** Because of wide spread competition, with the power of the reduced number of purchasing points, the brand image is becoming more and more important. No producer or service provider can afford to have poor quality image, or either his brand image or reputation of his company will suffer in the market place. Nowadays, many products are so complex and the production process spread over many suppliers, that once faults occur, any causes are likely to be multiple and difficult to trace.

(iii) While it is inevitable that some mistakes will always happen, it is essential that they be cured fast. The whole supply chain upto and including the customer operates on a just-in-time basis and so is susceptible to disruptions. It is not enough if products are able to meet customer's expectations. Time and price are also important for the customers.

Disruptions and delays due to inadequate quality (product returns and replacements) are therefore major operational risks.

The three areas of weakness (viz, speed of innovation, poor product/service quality, disruption of the entire supply chain due to quality problems) demand major changes in internal and external relationships. For increasing the speed and accuracy of innovation, more decision making power and autonomy has to be delegated downward and more cooperation is required horizontally between functions within the organisation.

Continuous improvement means that all functions will be involved, but only if there is trust between them will improvement be realised. Externally, because of the growth of outsourcing, closer cooperation both with outside suppliers and between them is essential to avoid production and marketing problems. Continuous performance improvement, if it is to be successfully implemented involves close cooperative relationships between the many functions involved. If the quality of relationships is so important to achieving high levels of performance improvement and quality, then we clearly need reliable ways to measure this. How can relationship quality be managed if it cannot be measured? This is a challenge facing quality management today.

20.5 QUALITY IN PRACTICE

Box 20.1 : Baldrige Pays off for Texas Instruments

Texas Instruments (TI) Defense Systems and Electronics Group faced a critical issue that many businesses struggle with: Is the pay-off of greater competitive advantage worth the effort of achieving total quality, specifically competing for the Baldrige Award? The answer is a definite "yes"

TI understands first-hand that the real benefit by applying for the Baldrige Award lies in adopting its quality criteria. The application itself is the singe most powerful catalyst for the kinds of organisational and cultural changes that companies must make to compete.

TI's commitment to quality and productivity improvements dates back to 1950s. But, most of its efforts were aimed at improving manufacturing and product quality. In the early 1980s, a total quality initiative was formalised across the entire corporation. Some business units made good progress, the semiconductor operation of TI in Japan won the Deming Prize in 1985

When the Baldrige Award criteria appeared, TI used them to provide focus and coherence to the activities across the corporation. Using the criteria, they ware able to tackle a part of total quality that previously had been unreachable: implementing quality efforts in staff, support, and nomenclaturing areas. In 1989, TI asked every business unit to prepare a mock award application as a way of measuring its progress. This task represented a radical change for some operations because, until that time, most staff functions were not required to measure their processes or their results.

The Defense Systems and Electronics Group's self-assessment revealed that they were long way from applying for winning the Baldrige Award. But the group aggressively adopted the criteria as a blueprint for improving its business.

TI discovered that all companies irrespective of whether big or small, defense contractors or not, have one thing in common: customers. Focusing on customers to make the company more competitive gives meaning to the award.

The Baldrige Award application process changed almost everything within the Defense Systems Electronics Group. Before applying, the group had no way of systematically measuring how well it understood its customers concerns, captured customers' feed back, or made improvements in interacting with customers. Mountains of data were being collected, but most of the data measured internal criteria, not customer satisfaction. The structured, hierarchical management environment made it difficult to adopt ideas from outside sources

The Baldrige Award process provided a way to make the customer the center place of daily activities. it led to much better communication with customers and employees and accelerated progress toward less hierarchical, more functional work teams, It changed the management process from an individual activity to a team effort, leading to better decisions. Finally, it introduced two radical new ideas: bench marking and stretch goals. Changing the culture was not easy and did not happen quickly. It took teamwork, consensus building and buy-in. At Texas Instruments, it took about five years of dedicated pulling in the same direction to begin seeing measurable results.

20.6 SUMMARY

In TQM approach to quality management, the principles of quality management are applied in every branch and at every level of the organisation with the emphasis on integration into business practices and a balance between technical, managerial and people issues. TQM is both a philosophy and a set of guiding principles for managing an organisation to the benefit of all stakeholders. The eight quality management principles are: *(i)* customer focus, *(ii)* leadership, *(iii)* involvement of people, *(iv)* process approach, *(v)* systems approach to management, *(vi)* continuous improvement, *(vii)* factual approach to decision making and, *(viii)* mutually beneficial supplier relationships:

The key characteristics of TQM are:

(i) Commitment and leadership of the chief executive officer.
(ii) Planning and organisation.
(iii) Using tools and techniques.
(iv) Education and training.
(v) Involvement of employees.
(vi) Teamwork
(vii) Measurement and feedback.
(viii) Ensuring that the culture is conducive to continuous improvement.

There are some critical issues in effective implementation of TQM. They are:

(i) Listening to a single versus many quality experts.
(ii) Method focus versus problem focus.
(iii) Focusing on productivity versus focusing on quality improvement.
(iv) Focus on Japanese strengths versus on internal strengths.
(v) Administration–based versus technology–based supplier quality model.
(vi) Automating human tasks versus automating human tendencies.
(vii) Focus on the system versus focus on quality.
(viii) Use of SPC as an on–line control versus use of SPC for process improvement.
(ix) Horizontal thinking versus vertical thinking.
(x) Process teaching versus content teaching.
(xi) Management lip service versus management commitment.
(xii) Soft progress versus hard progress.
(xiii) Improvement of manufacturing systems alone versus all other systems that relate to manufacturing.
(xiv) Mathematical model versus reality.
(xv) Mathematical efficiency of experiments versus execution difficulty of experiments.

There are some issues which need to be considered in the future. These are the issues which organisations will need to give more attention in order to achieve world-class quality status. They are:

(i) Quantitative tools and techniques used in facilitating and measuring continuous improvement, for example, SPC, FMEA, QFD, Poka–Yoke, Bench marking and seven Q.C. tools.
(ii) Activity–based costing and throughput accounting.
(iii) ISO 9000:2000 series standards, ISO 9001: 2000 registration and certification, ISO 14001 environmental management systems – registration and certification.
(iv) Integrating quality into the normal management procedures and operations of a business.
(v) Development of problem-solving skills, competencies and talents of all employees.
(vi) Continuous improvement initiatives to reach every part of the organisation and every employee.
(vii) Greater focus on process streams linked directly to customer groups and suppliers.
(viii) Revitalsing TQM after a period of stagnation in many organisations, for examples, renewal of quality circles.

(ix) Measuring performance based on hard measures of customer satisfaction.

(x) Encouraging teamwork in all its forms.

(xi) Winning the 'hearts and minds' of all employees and cultivating motivation and commitment amongst the workforce.

(xii) Obtaining timely and accurate data for effective quality related decision making.

(xiii) Developing effective methods and channels of communication.

(xiv) Developing effective working relationships with the supply base.

(xv) Education and training for employees at all levels.

(xvi) Top management focus on TQM.

Quality management today faces many new challenges. There are two kinds of quality management. *(i)* 'Old' or 'classical' quality management and, *(ii)* New "quality management of the 21st century.

In recent times, major changes have taken, for example, *(i)* companies have started offering a wide range of product variants to their customers which need to be updated frequently to ascertain high sales levels, *(ii)* Manufacturing industries have shifted from individual part assembly to modular assembly, *(iii)* Pressure to produce increased profits, *(iv)* Pressure on innovation with a shift to technological break–throughs, *(v)* Fewer buying points with more power in the hands of smaller number of suppliers/distributors.

These changes give rise to major problems in quality management because they demand new measures which have not been developed so far. The new measurement problems are concerned with four major areas:

(i) Shift from a focus on initial quality to durability.

(ii) Increased importance of non–technical, softer influences on customer satisfaction.

(iii) Growing importance of software within products and

(iv) Need for closer cooperation internally between functions and externally between partners in the supply chain.

20.7 OBJECTIVE QUESTIONS

(A) Match the following :

Column A	Column B
1. Process approach	1. One of the key elements of TQM
2. Team work	2. One of the eight quality management principles
3. Focusing on productivity versus focusing on quality improvement	3. A necessary TQM tool on the human front.
4. Quality circles	4. One of the several TQM issues to be considere in the future
5. Benchmarking	5. One of the key issues in effective implementation of TQM.

(B) State whether the following statements are True or False :

1. TQM is both a philosophy and a set of guiding principles for managing an organisation to the benefit of all stake - holders (T / F)
2. Recognition for positive performance achievement and celebration and reward for success are also keys to success of TQM (T / F)
3. It is easy to execute the improvement philosophies of TQM because it is a soft science. (T / F)
4. QFD can be used to capture the "Voice of the customer" and SPC can be used to monitor the "Voice of the process" (T / F)
5. The quality management of the 20th century (1980s to 1990s) is refered to as "new" quality management (T / F)

(C) Multiple choice Questions : Choose the correct answer from the alternatives given under each question :

1. TQM requires that the principles of quality management should be applied in every branch at every level of the organisation with an emphasis on integration into business practices and a balance between the following:
   (a) technical issues (b) managerial issues
   (c) people issues (d) All of these
2. Quality improvement efforts have used the following ideas to make quality integral to the business decision making process:
   (a) Statistical Process control (b) Total employee involvement
   (c) Participative management (d) Quality circles
   (e) All of these (f) None of these
3. Quantitative tools and techniques employed by an increasing number of organisations as important aids in facilitating and measuring continuous improvement include the following:
   (a) Quality Function Deployment (b) Failure mode and effects analysis
   (c) Statistical process control (d) Seven Q.C tools
   (e) All of these (f) None of these
4. To achieve the competitive advantage of achieving "speed to market", the following are vital
   (a) The innovation process needs to speed up
   (b) Poor quality has to be prevented
   (c) Disruptions in the entire supply chain must be reduced to meet customers' expectations
   (d) All of these (e) None of these
5. On the human front, the following ideas have attracted the attention of many firms in their quality improvement efforts
   (a) Quality function deployment (b) Total employee involvement
   (c) Participative management (d) Quality circles
   (e) (b), (c) and (d) only (f) None of these

20.8 REVIEW QUESTIONS

1. Discuss the eight quality management principles.
2. Briefly describe the key elements of TQM.
3. Discuss the critical issues in effective implementation of TQM.
4. Discuss the issues in TQM which need to be considered in the future.
5. Discuss the new challenges faced by quality management.
6. Distinguish between 'old' or "classical" quality management and "New quality management".
7. Discuss the four major areas with which the new measurement problems are concerned.

20.9 DISCUSSION QUESTIONS

1. "TQM is both a philosophy and a set of guiding principles for managing an organisation to the benefit of all stakeholders" – Explain.
2. "Planning and organisation feature many facts of the improvement process" – Elaborate.
3. "Team work is one of the key features of involvement" – Do you agree or not. Justify your answer.
4. "Generally management focus is directed toward productivity improvement with quality improvement as a by–product" – Discuss.
5. "In the near future, quality will gain more importance in e–commerce" – Explain.

20.10 ASSIGNMENTS

1. Visit a manufacturing firm for which you have access and study the continuous improvement program implemented by the firm and submit a report.
2. Visit a large transportation service company and study the implementation of TQM in the firm and the problems faced by the firm in the implementation of TQM.

20.11 CHAPTER CASE

INTEGRATING DESIGN AND PRODUCTION AT SUNDSTRAND

"If it isn't broken, fix it any way, Improve the process. We look everything as a process" said Richard Baker, manager of continuous improvement systems at Sundstrand Data Control Inc, manufacturers of instruments and avionics for the defence industry. Sundstrand had prime defence contractors such as General Dynamics, McDonnell Douglas and Honeywell Space Systems.

The company claims remarkable production, cost and quality improvement. Rework on some production lines is down by 66 percent, scrap cost cut by 60 percent, quality up by 50 percent and cycle time down by 90 percent. Despite these advances, Baker was of the view that fully integrating the Total Quality Philosophy with company culture, could take another five years and that the ongoing effort will never be complete.

Production workers were especially proud of a magnet assembly, a delicate small device loaded with integrated circuits. It is used in inertial navigation systems. Sundstrand planned to knock out the Japanese out of this market.

Manufacture of the magnet assembly is a complicated process, progressing through six work stations (each in one room). The workers in each work station make up a work team. The process is called *"Kanban"* and relies on simple visual cues from the previous step in the process to inform the work team when parts are needed (using a pull system of production). With this information, the team can distribute the workload, since each team member is cross-trained to do all the tasks necessary to move the item to the next step in the process.

Another simplification is a *"traffic light"* like the one seen at a street intersection, which hangs in the hallway where every one in the work teams of a particular production line can see it. If the production process is flowing smoothly, the light turns green. If a problem occurs, the light turns yellow and then red. This is the one for workers to scramble and find a solution for the problem causing red light.

Sundstrand's TQM program also contains *"concurrent engineering"* which integrates the manufacturing engineers with design personnel. This approach is vital because 80 percent of the cost of Sundstrand's products is in the design process. To make them cheaper, one has got to design a part better.

The "traffic light system" at Sundstrand is a method pioneered by Shigeo Shingo and frequently called *"Shingo Method"*. This method in justified by giving two basic reasons for the use of traffic signals :

1. They are a great visual communicator to all employees, telling them the status of their production lines.

2. They lend an air of urgency, reminding the employees all of the key thing that counts : on-time shipments of quality products to their customers! By indicating the problem and who is directly responsible for solving it, there is little left to the chance in order to drive to get the line going again.

A *green light* indicates a production line is running smoothly. There are no material, people, machine or process problem at this time. Finished products are being produced on schedule.

A *yellow light* indicates a problem exists or is about to surface that is either impending the scheduled flow of material or is about to. Yellow lights indicate things such as faulty machines requiring attention, missing personnel, parts requiring modification on the line or potential missing parts that may cause the line shutdown in the near future (two to three days).

A *red light* indicates a line is shutdown, that is, no finished products are able to flow off this line. Typical causes of red lights are missing material, broken down equipment, missing key personnel, irregular parts requiring excessive modifications to work properly and missing or dysfunctional tools.

In all cases at Sundstrand, it is the responsibility of the line manager and his or her personnel to operate the traffic light to indicate that a production problem exists. According to Shingo "It is a poor supervisor who never shuts down his line, for he is not exposing quality and productivity problems. His product is not getting better. Likewise it is a poor supervisor who continuously shuts down his line for the same reason. For he is continuously exposing the same problem over and over with no permanent solution."

Discussion Questions :

1. What are the implications of the statement "If it isn't broken, fix it anyway"?
2. To what extent, can the remarkable improvement at Sundstrand be attributed to the *Shingo* method.
3. How would you go about integrating design and production?

CHAPTER 21

ACHIEVING BUSINESS EXCELLENCE

LEARNING OBJECTIVES

After reading this chapter, you should be able to:

- Understand the meaning of the term "Business Excellence" and the dimensions of performance for excellence
- Discuss the topics- "Quality Certification," "Lead Assessment" and "Self-Assessment for Business Excellence"
- Discuss the various "Business Process Maturity Models"
- Describe the five levels of "Capability Maturity Model"
- Describe the structure of people CMM
- Describe the levels of Business Process Maturity Model

21.0 INTRODUCTION

Today's organisations are under pressure to enhance their productivity and gain competitive edge in global market. They are called up to strengthen financial viability, discharge environmental and social responsibilities and to be accountable to customers, employees, regulatory bodies and the public for their decisions and actions.

For any business organisation, global market access depends on compliances with international standards in performances, products and services. For example, for many companies, registration to ISO 9001:2000 is a key to securing and maintaining global business.

21.1 BUSINESS EXCELLENCE

Business Excellence, like beauty, is in the eyes of the beholder and there are many 'beholders' of business excellence. Every company has a set of stakeholders and each has its own criteria for excellence. Outside stakeholders (such as investors and share holders), suppliers, employees and customers-all judge the performance of the company from their own parameters, which vary from one stakeholder to the other.

However different the expectations of different stakeholder groups, it is universally accepted that an excellent company is the one that performs well from the viewpoint of all stakeholders. Many world-class companies, which are dedicated to the continuous improvement philosophy, have excellence as a fundamental goal. However, improvements whether continuous or break-through do not necessarily lead to world-class excellence. Many companies begin their quest for improvement by focusing on their own processes and practices and eventually look outward to improve their suppliers' behaviour and even their own behaviour as customers of suppliers. Highly successful companies are those that have succeeded in maximising customer satisfaction at the lowest possible cost., thereby maximising the firm's value.

Business excellence requires balanced performance, that is a genuine improvement in at least one dimension of performance without slipping on other dimensions

Excellence requires balanced performance, that is genuine improvement in at least one dimension of performance without slipping on other dimensions (for e.g. improving quality without increasing costs) Some of the dimensions of performance for excellence include: *(i)* External quality *(ii)* Internal quality *(iii)* Dependability *(iv)* Resource use *(v)* Human resource improvement *(vii)* Innovation *(viii)* Environmental soundness and *(ix)* Financial results.

Each of these dimensions is important to the world-class or excellent companies.

21.1.1 The Business Excellence Model

Revised in the year 2000, the "Business Excellence Model" (BEM) is sponsored by the European Foundation for Quality Management (EFQM). This model is developed from the belief that contented customers, satisfied employers and positive societal impact can be achieved only through effective leadership. Leadership in turn steers both **organisation policy and strategy** in relation to **organisational processes** and **human resources actions**. Taken together, this integrated approach in considered to drive the organisation towards excellence in business. The European Quality Award and CII/Exim Bank Award for Business Excellence- both based on the Business Excellence Model were discussed in detail in an earlier chapter.

21.2 QUALITY MANAGEMENT AWARDS AND FRAME-WORKS

The philosophies of Deming, Juran, Crosby and others provide much guidance and wisdom in the form of "best practices" to managers around the world, leading to the development of many awards and certifications for recognizing effective application of total quality principles. Although awards recognize only a select few, the award or certification criteria provide frameworks for managing from which every organisation can benefit. The two frameworks that have had the most impact on quality management practices worldwide are US Malcolm Baldrige National Quality Award and the international ISO 9000 certification process. Recently the concept of Six-Sigma has evolved into a unique framework for managing quality. All these topics were discussed in detail in the earlier chapters.

The Malcolm Baldrige National Quality Award, The Canadian Award for Business Excellence Australian Business Excellence Award and the national award in India such as the CII-Exim Bank Award, Rajiv Gandhi National Quality Award and IMC-Ramakrishna Bajaj National Quality Award- all have set their own criteria for performance excellence, based on which, the applicant firm for these awards are evaluated and selected for the award every year.

21.3 QUALITY CERTIFICATION

In today's global market, many organisations are utilizing ISO 9001:2000 as a platform to build their quality management systems. For many companies, registration to ISO 9001:2000 is a key to securing and maintaining global business. An ISO 9000 system has to be certified and regularly audited by an authorised certifying body such as Bureau Veritieas Quality International (BVQI), Lloyd's and SGS. A certificate issued by any of the authorised certifying agency is valid for three years only. Consequently, in order to maintain the certificate, regular audits, both internal (self-assessment) and external (lead assessment) are necessary. Therefore, the company should have a quality manager in-house who is responsible for the quality management policy, procedures, implementation, monitoring and documentation thereof and the quality management consultants need to be hired for external audits.

The Indian Quality Certification Institutes are:

(i) Quality Assurance Institute (India) ltd
(ii) Central Power Research Institute
(iii) Standardisation, Testing and Quality Certification (STRC)
(iv) URS India Quality Certification
(v) Quality Council of India
(vi) Bureau of Indian Standards (BIS)
(vii) Integrated Quality Certification Pvt Ltd.
(viii) DQS Certification India Pvt Ltd.

21.4 LEAD ASSESSMENT

If an organisation has not yet committed to total quality but is in a business that could benefit from ISO 9000 registration, then it must go through the preparation steps which will provide a start into total quality. Any TQM organisation should apply the kinds of procedures, checks and management involvement required by ISO 9000 which is a subset of total quality management.

ISO 9000 registration requires a lot of work starting with having written procedures, well documented processes and establishing a quality system or quality manual. Preparing for ISO 9000 registration can get an organisation started on a total quality implementation.

In countries where ogranisations compete for the Malcolm Baldrige National Quality Award (MBNQA), the competing organisations go through lot of preparation work to meet the Baldrige criteria for performance excellence. The self-assessment criteria derived from the Baldrige criteria can be used by organisations to assess themselves against world class standards without going through actual competition.

Conducting such self-assessments or assessment through third party (external experts) organisations (known as lead assessors) will provide a score card for comparison against the best in the world. More than that, such assessments will clearly identify the areas that most need improvement, thus providing the needed impetus for implementing total quality and putting all the resources needed to work on the area of need.

In our country, organisations compete for CII-Exim Bank award for excellence. This excellence model is based on universally accepted standards and practices that are found in the European

Quality Award, Japan Quality Award, the US Malcolm Baldrige National Quality Award and Australian Quality Award. This award for excellence administrated by the Confederation of Indian Industries (CII) encourages organisations to strengthen their management systems, practices and capabilities to enhance and sustain their competitiveness to become world class organisations.

Excellence model is a frame work that reflects the world's best-validated management principles and practices. Regardless of sector, size, structure or maturity, to be successful, organisations need to establish appropriate management frame work with clear purpose, mission and objectives or goals. Excellence model is a practical and holistic tool to achieve this.

Excellence model is used by firms in a number of ways:

(i) As a tool for self-assessment by measuring where they are on the path to excellence, thereby helping them to understand the gaps and then stimulating solutions to bridge the gaps.

(ii) As the basis for a common way of thinking about the organisation. This thinking is shared across all functions.

(iii) As a frame-work for positioning existing initiatives and identifying gaps.

(iv) As a structure for the organisation's management system.

The various parameters or metrics used in the excellence model are: *(a)* Result orientation, *(b)* Customer focus, *(c)* Leadership and constancy of purpose, *(d)* Management by processes and facts, *(e)* People development and involvement, *(f)* Continuous learning and improvement *(g)* Partnership development and *(h)* Corporate social responsibility.

21.4.1 How the Organisation is Assessed

A team of assessors (referred to as lead assessors), all of whom have undergone training to ensure a high level of consistency in scoring, will examine the application document of the organisation seeking CII-Exim Bank Award for Excellence. Assessors are drawn from the ranks of experienced practicing managers from Indian organisations.

Exhibit 21.1 **illustrates the above criteria used for assessment.**

Exhibit 21.1 : Criteria for Assessment for CII-Exim Award for Excellence

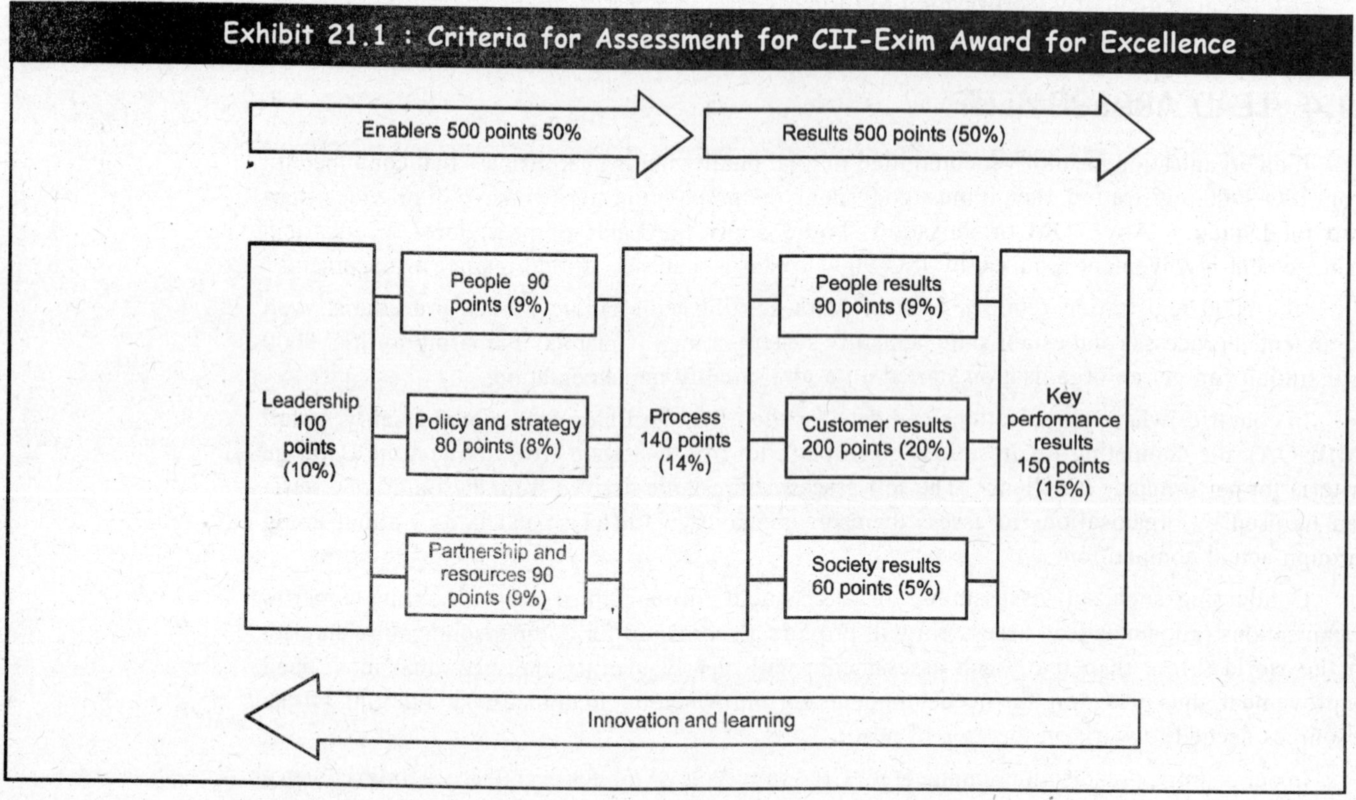

The application document is assessed and scored on a scale of 0-1000 points using the excellence model, based on the EFQM excellence model.

The model conveys that excellent results with respect to performance, customers, people and society are achieved through leadership, driving policy and strategy, people, partnerships and resources and processes.

500 points are awarded for enablers criteria and 500 points for results criteria.

The results criteria are concerned with what the organisation has achieved and is achieving. The enablers criteria are concerned with how results are being achieved.

21.4.2 Award Assessment Process

1. **Companies obtain application brochure :** Potential applicants check the eligibility criteria for entry and requirements of the Award secretariat.
2. **Selection of assessors :** Senior mangers from the industry are selected as assessors. They undergo 4 day's training program on understanding the award criteria and assessment process.
3. **Applicant submits documents :** Applicants send application document to CII.
4. **Assessment and consensus scoring :** Assessor team is appointed for each applicant organisation. Assessors individually list strengths and opportunities for improvement and score. Team meets to reach consensus scores.
5. **Screening for site visits :** On the basis of consensus reports, the applicants are short listed for site visits.
6. **Site visits :** Assessor teams are appointed to make site visits. Assessors meet and plan for site visits of 4 to 6 days duration to check the validity of application and clarify issues.

   Applications are recorded after site visits and reports are finalised.
7. **Jury meeting :** Distinguished persons from business and academics are appointed as jurors. They are trained on the Award model and the process. Jurors examine the reports from site-visit teams and decide on the winners of the Award, Prizes and Commendation Certificates.
8. **Award presentation :** The CII - Exim Bank Award for Excellence, Prizes and Commendation Certificates are presented to the winning applicants.
9. **Feedback report :** Senior assessors (leaders of the assessment team) send feedback reports to all applicants identifying the strengths/opportunities for improvement. Score-ranges are given for each criterion. On request by the organisation, senior assessor visits applicant organisation to discuss feedback report.

21.4.3 Lead Assessment Activities

Under the Australian Quality Training Framework, leadership of assessment activities is critical in three particular areas:

(i) Confirming assessment-only pathways.

(ii) Establishing roles, responsibilities and relevant accountabilities for assessors and

(iii) Ensuring that the assessor is appropriately competent and qualified to assess.

***Exhibit 21.2* illustrates lead assessment activities.**

Exhibit 21.2 : Lead Assessment Activities

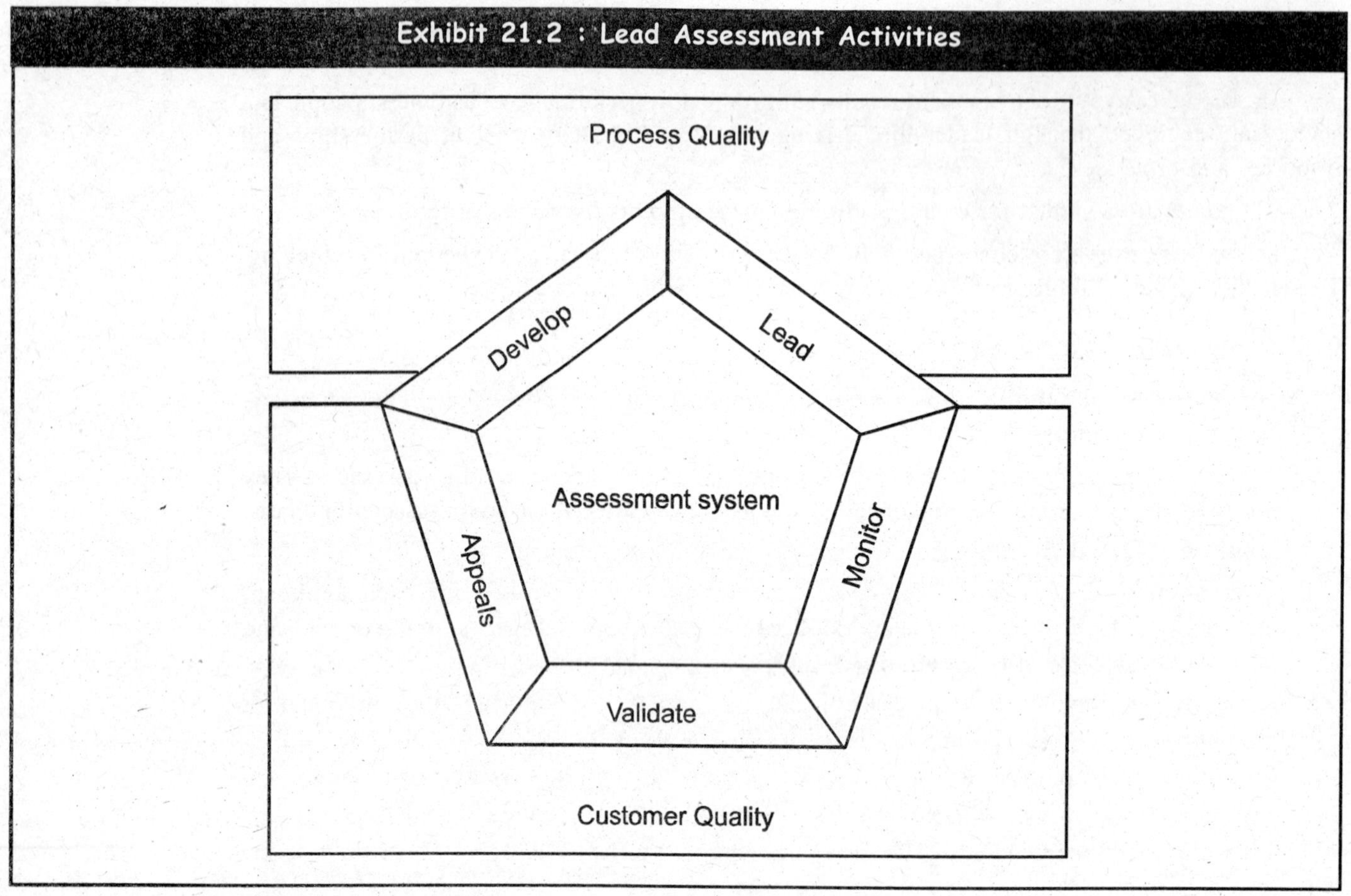

21.4.3 Characteristics of Assessment Teams

Effective assessment teams seem to always have a clear purpose and members who understand the goals that the team has to achieve.

Self - assessment is basically about continuous improvement of the organisation.

Value-adding assessment teams:

(i) Are goal driven.
(ii) Are committed to the organisation's goals and purposes.
(iii) Integrate team plan with strategic goals and objectives.
(iv) Have individual performance plans tied to strategic objectives.
(v) Are capable and competent.
(vi) Are competent to assess in known areas.
(vii) Know the process.
(viii) Understand financial and resource limitations.
(ix) Secure and use resources effectively.
(x) Are continuously improving.
(xi) Respond to immediate customer needs.
(xii) Anticipate and eliminate problems.
(xiii) Link assessment to competency and workplace performance standards and
(xiv) Continually improve assessment tools and processes.

Independent Assessment and Certification by a lead assessor, for example, Bureau Veritas Quality International (BVQI) is illustrated in the following paragraphs:

"More and more purchasers are looking for proof of their supplier's commitment to quality in the form of independent assessment and certification. In recent years BVQI has assisted over 2000. Major companies worldwide to achieve certification of ISO 9000, EN 29000 and other equivalent national or international standards for Quality Management System.

BVQI is a wholly owned subsidiary of Bureau Veritas, a large multinational organisation founded in 1828. Bureau Veritas has offices in 125 countries with a total staff of over 5000, all offering classification, survey and inspection services for ships, aircrafts, material and equipments, vehicles, machines, engineers and all kinds of structures and systems including building and civil engineering works. Bureau Veritas is also concerned with product certification.

BVQI is an independent international service for the assessment and certification of Quality Management Systems.

Once the supplier's Quality Management System has been assessed and certified, the supplier will receive a **"Certificate of approval".** This will be valid for 3 years, subject to the satisfactory maintenance of the systems.

The basic procedure of certification involves the following steps:

1. Contact your local BV/BVQI office who will ask you for details of your organisation. Any information supplied will be treated with strict confidence.
2. On the basis of this initial data, BVQI will submit a quotation for the cost of the initial and subsequent **Routine Survelliance.**
3. Approximately four works prior to the **Assessment visit,** BVQI staff will review your **Quality Manual** or equivalent system documentation. This is to establish that your **Quality System** covers all the requirements of ISO 9000. A report on this manual will be sent to you, allowing time to implement any changes necessary before the **Initial Assessment.**
4. The **Initial Assessment** will include a detailed examination of your Quality System. Any non-conformities will be noted and corrective action discussed. For major non-conformities, corrective action must be completed prior to certification.
5. When the Initial Assessment has been successfully completed, BVQI will issue your **Certificate of Approval,** which in valid for three years.
6. To maintain approval, BVQI monitors your conformance with ISO 9000 by carrying out **Routine survelliance visits** at approximately six-monthly intervals.
7. At the end of the three year certification period, a complete re-assessment will be made by BVQI if you wish to continue your certification. This is normally much shorter than the Initial Assessment.

The BVQI assessment and certification process often leads to enhanced quality performance and a boost to morale. An excellent quality management brings with it economies in design, production and administration – improved all-round performance that will be reflected in better sales, more customer satisfaction in a wide variety of ways. Independent third-party certification gives your customer what they are looking for-complete quality assurance.

21.5 SELF-ASSESSMENT FOR BUSINESS EXCELLENCE

Even if an organisation is successful today, it will always have to develop and get better. To improve or not improve performance will in the long-term be the difference between success and failure for an organisation. Organisations that manage to improve continuously will be more flexible and competitive than the ones, which get stuck in the past.

A carefully performed self-assessment will give management the possibility to base decisions on facts rather than perceptions

In all organisations, goal setting and strategic planning activities should be aimed at answering three basic questions:

(i) Where are we? *(ii)* Where do we want to go?

(iii) How do we get there?

When trying to answer these questions, the organisation must create a picture of its strength and areas where improvements can be made. The process of doing this is often called **self-assessment.** A carefully performed self-assessment will give management the possibility to base decisions on facts rather than perceptions.

If a process of continuous improvement is to be sustained and its pace increased, it is essential that organisations monitor on a regular basis what activities are going well, which have stagnated, what needs to be improved and what is lacking. Self-assessment provides the framework for generating this type of feed-back about an organisation's approach to continuous improvement. Self-assessment against the criteria of a quality award/excellence model (eg-MBNQ Award, EFQM Award, and CII-Exim Bank Award) on which evaluation and diagnostics can be based is now being given a considerable amount of attention by organisations worldwide.

"Self-assessment is a comprehensive, systematic and regular review of an organisation's activities and results referenced against the EFQM excellence model. The self-assessment process allows the organisation to discern clearly its strengths and areas in which improvements can made and culminates in planned improvement actions that are then monitored to achieve progress."

The models on which the awards are based and the guidelines for application are helpful in defining TQM in a way that the management of all types of organisations-small or large, public or private, manufacturing or service-can easily understand. A large number of companies follow the guidelines and award criteria of the chosen model and are using them to help them diagnose the state of health of their improvement process and provide indications of how to achieve business excellence.

Self - assessment has become an important management technique to continuously improve the overall business performance of an organisation

Self-assessment has become an important management technique to continuously improve the overall business performance of an organisation. It is a **quality management initiative**, routed in a process management view on business and often referred to as a **catalyst for driving business improvement.**

Even though, the European Foundation for Quality Management established "The EFQM Excellence Model" in 1991 as the basis for the European Quality Award, many organisations started using the model as a way of defining areas for improvement and to direct the improvement process internally.

Today, hundreds of organisations from various disciplines all around the world use the EFQM model as a tool for conducting self-assessment.

Process of Self-assessment: The whole cycle of self-assessment is viewed as **"five-component cycle of self-assessment". These five components are:**

1. **Plan and implement** the self-assessment cycle in the organisation.
2. **Assess:** Conduct self-assessment and **prioritise** actions to be taken into further action planning.
3. **Improve performance:** Plan, handle and implement actions for improvement.
4. **Share knowledge and experiences** with others, both within and outside the organisation.
5. **Develop and improve** the work procedures cautiously.

The five-component cycle of self-assessment can be viewed as a system with five gear wheels, in a gear train, each gear driving the other gear it meshes with, in the same direction. All the components have to be in place and well greased to make the machinery to work smoothly.

21.5.1 The Concepts of Self-Assessment

There are basically two different types of self-assessment that are in use in organisations. The first one is the type of self-assessment **asked for in the** ISO standard. These ***quality assurance*** self-assessments or audits will confirm that the requirements in the standards **are being met.** The second type is a ***quality management*** self-assessment based on an excellence model that has its origin in the TQM philosophy. These models work as a basis for quality awards like the MBNQ Award, the European Quality Award (EQA) or the CII-Exim Bank Award or any other national quality award (for example, the Deming Prize in Japan). We refer to the second type of self-assessment which is used as a way of improving business performance (i.e. business excellence).

21.5.2 Benefits of using Self-Assessment

The main benefits of self-assessment highlighted by EFQM are that it gives: *(i)* A rigorous and structured approach to organisational improvement *(ii)* An assessment based on facts and not perceptions and *(iii)* A means to achieve consistency of direction and consensus on what needs to be done.

Self-assessment improves awareness and generates ownership for TQM among senior managers and encourages training in TQM among employees. It will enable measurement of progress to be made, help to pin-point improvement opportunities, facilitate benchmarking and organisational learning.

The benefits of self-assessment falls into four categories: (i) Results (ii) Culture (iii) Process management and **(iv) Benchmarking** First, self-assessment according to the EFQM model, links ***business results*** to the ***enablers***.

Second, it gives an important cultural benefit since it encourages an **ethos of continuous improvement,** promotes the holistic perspective and allows people to gain a broad understanding of the business.

Third, using the EFQM model for self-assessment enforces a process management perspective since the model places a heavy emphasis on business processes, both implicitly and explicitly.

21.5.3 Self-assessment and TQM

The concept of TQM used by an increasing number of organisations, is considered by many to be the management paradigm capable of facilitating the attainment of organisation-wide quality awareness and continuous improvement. Since the 1980s, it has developed into an established concept for improving business performance at all levels. Self-assessment is said to a driver for TQM and in turn for business performance.

Self - assessment is basically about continuous improvement of the organisation

Continuous Improvement Through Self-Assessment: Self-assessment is basically about continuous improvement of the organisation. Continuous improvement has been defined as "A company-wide process of focused and continuous incremental innovation or improvement".

Two main themes of continuous improvement are: *(i)* encouraging involvement and *(ii)* encouraging creativity.

Continuous improvement is one of the core values in the TQM philosophy. The objective is the improvement of the efficiency and flexibility of the entire business. It enables the organisation as a whole to become more dynamic, responsive and competitive.

21.5.4 Self-assessment and Business Excellence

The aim of using TQM in organisations is to establish a culture based on the **core values,** this means to "increase external and internal customer satisfaction with a reduced amount of resources". The overall objective of TQM is to achieve balanced stakeholder satisfaction, often referred to as "business excellence" The European Foundation for Quality Management defines business excellence as "The way of working which enables an organisation to achieve balanced stakeholder satisfaction, so increasing the probability of long-term success."

21.6 BUSINESS PROCESS MATURITY MODELS

Business Process Management consolidates objectives, frameworks, methodologies and tools which have been proposed in a number of approaches including Business Process Reengineering., Business Process Innovation, Business Process Modeling and Business Process Automation. Work flow Management / Process-Aware Information Systems.

The popularity of Business Process Management leads to the question of how advanced different organisations are in their BPM development. The notion of "maturity" has been proposed for other management approaches as a way to evaluate the "state of being complete, perfect or ready" and the "fullness or perfection of growth or development"

"Maturity" as a measure to evaluate the capabilities of an organisation in regards to a certain discipline has become popular since the Capability Maturity Model (CMM) has been proposed by the Software Engineering Institute of Carnegie Mellon University., Pittsburg USA. Whilst the original CMM has a specific focus on the evaluation of software development processes, this model has been varied and extended in a number of approaches and is now applied for the evaluation of IT Infrastructure Management, Enterprise Architecture Management and Knowledge Management.

Today management has no standards by which to assess the merits of their business processes. As a result they have no method to assess the risk immature processes pose the enterprise IT projects or to identify the causes of weaknesses in their process workflows that if addressed, could reduce cost and increase operating efficiency.

To provide a needed standard for evaluating the capability and maturity of business processes, the Business Process Maturity Model (BPMM) has been developed. This model provides an open-standard road map for assessing process maturity and guiding business process improvement.

21.6.1 Introduction to BPMM

The BPMM describes an evolutionary improvement path that guides organisations as they move from immature, inconsistent business activities to mature, disciplined processes. The BPMM orders these stages so that improvements at each stage provides a foundation on which to build improvements undertaken at the next stage. Thus an improvement strategy drawn from the BPMM provides a road map for continuous process improvement. It helps identify process deficiencies in an organisation and guides the improvements in logical incremental steps.

21.6.2 Business Process Management Maturity Models

Recently a number of models to measure the maturity of Business Process Management have been proposed. The common bases for the majority of these models have been the Capability Maturity Model (CMM). Improved maturity results in an increase in the performance of process of an organisation. CMM introduced the concept of five maturity levels defined by cumulative requirements. Harmon (2004) developed a Business Process Management Maturity (BPM) model based on the Capability Maturity Model.

21.6.3 Capability Maturity Model (CMM)

The Capability Maturity Model (CMM) is a service mark registered with the US Patent and Trademark Office by Carnegie Mellon University (CMU). It refers to a development model that was created after study of data collected from organisations that contracted with the US Department of Defense, who funded the research. This became the foundation from which CMU created the Software Engineering Institute (SEI). Like any model, it is an abstraction of existing system.

When CMM is applied to an existing organisation's software development processes, it allows an effective approach toward improving them. Eventually it became clear that the model could be applied to other processes. This gave rise to more general concept that is applied to business processes and to developing people (People CMM).

21.7 OVERVIEW OF CMM

The CMM was originally developed as a tool for objectively assessing the ability of government contractor's ***processes*** to perform a contracted software project. The CMM is based on the process maturity framework first described in the 1989 book – "***Managing the Software Process***" by Watts Humphrey.

Though the CMM comes from the field of software development, it is used as a general model to aid improving organisational business processes in diverse areas, for example, in software engineering, systems engineering, project management, software maintenance, risk management, system acquisition, information technology (IT) services, business processes and human capital management. The CMM has been used extensively world-wide in government offices, commerce, industry and software development organisations'.

21.7.1 Capability Maturity Model Integration (CMMI)

The CMM model proved useful to many optimisations, but its application in software development has sometimes been problematic. Applying multiple models that are not integrated within and across an organisation would be costly in training, appraisals, and improvement activities. The Capability Maturity Model Integration (CMMI) project was formed to sort out the problem of using multiple CMMs.

For software development processes, the CMM has been superseded by CMMI, though the CMM continues to be a general theoretical process capability model used in the public.

21.7.2 Model Topics

The CMM was originally intended as a tool to evaluate the ability of government contractors to perform a contracted software project. Though it comes from the area of software development, it can be, has been and continues to be widely applied as a general model of the ***maturity of process*** (*e.g.*, IT service management processes) in IS/IT and other organisations.

1. Maturity Model: A maturity model can be viewed as a set of structured levels that describe how the behaviours, practices and processes of an organisation can reliably and sustainably produce required outcomes.

A maturity model may provide, for example: *(a)* a place to start, *(b)* the benefit for a community's prior experiences, *(c)* a common language and a shared vision, *(d)* a way to define what improvement means for your organisation.

A maturity model can be used as a bench mark for comparison and as an aid to understanding, for example, for there is something in common that can be used as a basis for comparison. In the case of CMM, for example the basis for comparison would be the software development processes of the organisation.

2. Structure of CMM: The Capability Maturity Model involves the following aspects:

The structure of CMM includes.
(i) Maturity levels
(ii) Key process areas
(iii) Goals
(iv) Common features and
(v) Key practices

(i) ***Maturity Levels:*** A 5 level process maturity continuum-where the uppermost (5th) level is a notional ideal state where processes would be systematically managed by a combination of process optimisation and continuous process improvement.

(ii) ***Key process Areas:*** A Key Process Area (KPA) identifies a cluster of related activities that, when performed together, achieve a set of goals which are considered important to the company.

(iii) ***Goals:*** The goals of a key process area summarise the stakes that must exist for that key process area to have been implemented in an effective and lasting way. The extent to which the goals have been accomplished is an indicator of how much capability the organisation has established at that maturity level. The goals signify the scope, boundaries, and intent of each key process area.

(iv) ***Common Features:*** Common features include practices that implement and institutionalise a key process area. There are five types of common features *(a)* commitment to perform. *(b)* ability to perform, *(c)* activities performed, *(d)* measurement and analysis and *(e)* verifying implementation.

(v) ***Key Practices:*** The key practices describe the elements of infrastructure and practice that contribute most effectively to the implementation and institutionalisation of the key performance areas (KPA).

3. Levels: There are five levels defined along the continuum of the CMM and according to the SEI, predictability, effectiveness and control of an organisation's software processes are believed to improve as the organisation moves up these five levels. **These five levels of CMM are:**

(i) ***Initial :*** (chaotic, adhoc, individual heroics) – the starting point for use of a new process

(ii) ***Repeatable:*** – the process is managed in accordance with agreed metrics

(iii) ***Defined:*** – the process is defined / confirmed as a standard process

(iv) **Managed:** – quantitatively managed, and

(v) **Optimising:** – process management includes deliberate process optimisation

Within each of these maturity levels are Key Process Areas (KPA) which characterise that level and for each KPA there are five definitions identified: *(i)* Goals, *(ii)* Commitment, *(iii)* Ability, *(iv)* Measurement and *(v)* Verification.

The five maturity levels of CMM are
(i) Initial
(ii) Repeatable
(iii) Defined
(iv) Managed
and
(v) Optimising

The KPAs, are not necessarily unique to CMM, representing as they do the stages that organisations go through on the way to becoming mature.

The CMM provides a theoretical continuum along which process maturity can be developed incrementally from one level to the next. Skipping levels is not allowed/ feasible.

The five levels of CMM are briefly discussed below:

- **Leve l:** ***Initial (chaotic):*** It is the characteristic of processes at this level that they are typically undocumented and in a state of dynamic change; tending to be driven in an adhoc, uncontrolled and reactive manner by users or events. This provides a chaotic or unstable environment for the processes.
- **Level 2:** ***Repeatable:*** It is the characteristic of processes at this level that some processes are repeatable, possibly with consistent results. Process discipline is unlikely to be rigorous, but where it exists it may help to ensure that existing processes are maintained during times of stress.
- **Level 3:** ***Defined***: It is the characteristse of processes at this level that, there are sets of defined and documented standard processes established and subject to some degree of improvement over time. These standard processes are in place (*i.e.,* they are the "As-Is processes) and used to establish consistency of process performance across the organisation.
- **Level 4:** ***Managed:*** It is the characteristic of processes at this level that, using process metrics, management can effectively control the "As-Is" process (*e.g.,* for software development). Particularly management can identity ways to adjust and adopt the process to particular projects without measurable losses of quality or deviation from specifications. Process capability is established from this level.
- **Level 5:** ***Optimising :*** It is a characteristic of processes at this level that the focus is on continually improving process performance through both incremental and innovative technological changes/improvements

At maturity level 5, processes are concerned with addressing statistical ***common causes*** of process variation and changing the process (for example, to shift the mean of the process performance) to improve process performance. This would be done at the same time as maintaining the likelyhood of achieving the established quantitative process improvement objectives.

Exhibit 21.3 **illustrates the Capability Maturity Model.**

Exhibit 21.3 : Capability Maturity Model

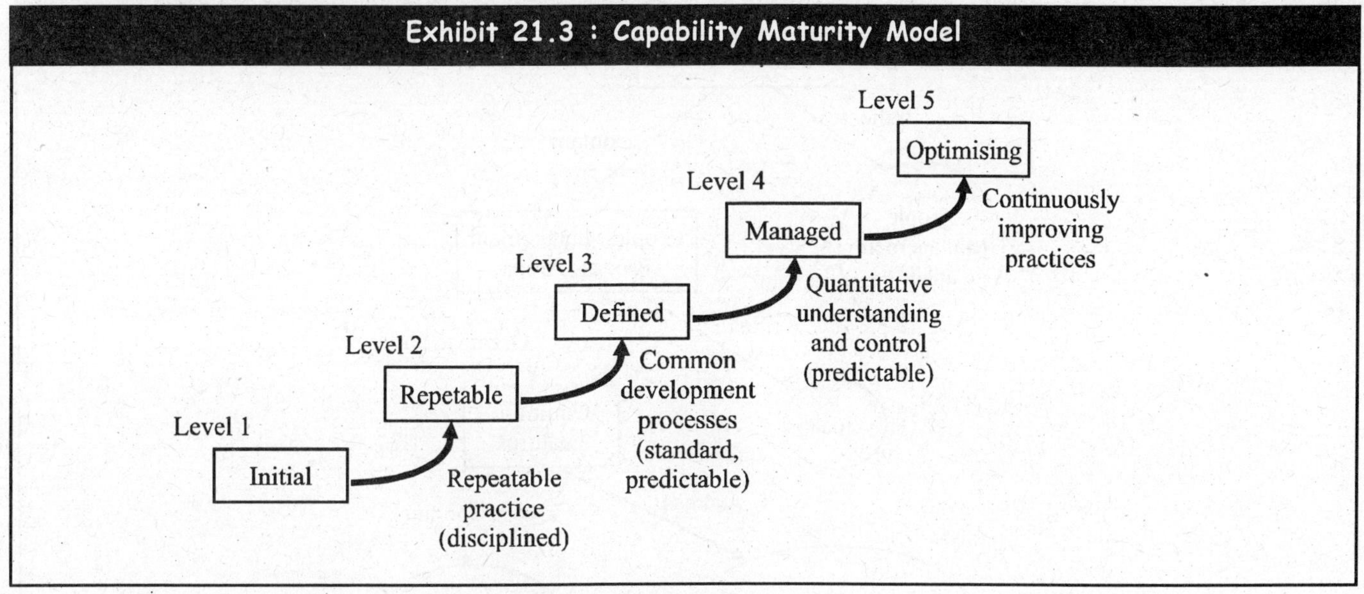

21.8 PEOPLE CAPABILITY MATURITY MODEL

People Capability Maturity Model (People CMM, PCMM or P–CMM) is a maturity framework that focuses on continuously improving the management and development of the human assets of an organisation. It describes an evolutionary improvement path from adhoc, inconsistently performed practices, to a mature disciplined and continuously improving development of the knowledge skill, and motivation of the workforce that enhances strategic business performance. The people CMM is a framework that helps organisations successfully address their critical people issues. Based on the best current practices in the fields such as human resources, knowledge management and organisational development, the people CMM guides organisations in improving their processes for managing and developing their workforces. The people CMM helps organisations characterise the maturity of their workforce practices, establish a program of continuous development of workforce, set priorities of improvement actions, integrate workforce development and establish a culture of excellence.

People CMM focuses on continuously improving the management and development of the human assets of an organisation

The salient features of people Capability Maturity Model are:

(i) Characterise the maturity of the workforce practices of the organisation

(ii) Set priorities for immediate action

(iii) Integrate workforce development with process improvement and

(iv) Become an employer of choice.

21.8.1 Structure of People CMM

Exhibit 21.4 **illustrates People Capability Maturity Model**

The people CMM document describes the People CMM, the practices that constitute each of its maturity levels and information on how to apply it in guiding organisational improvements. It describes an organisation's capability for developing its workforce at each maturity level. It describes how the people CMM can be applied as a standard for assessing workforce practices and as a guide in planning and implementing improvement activities.

Exhibit 21.4 : People Capability Maturity Model

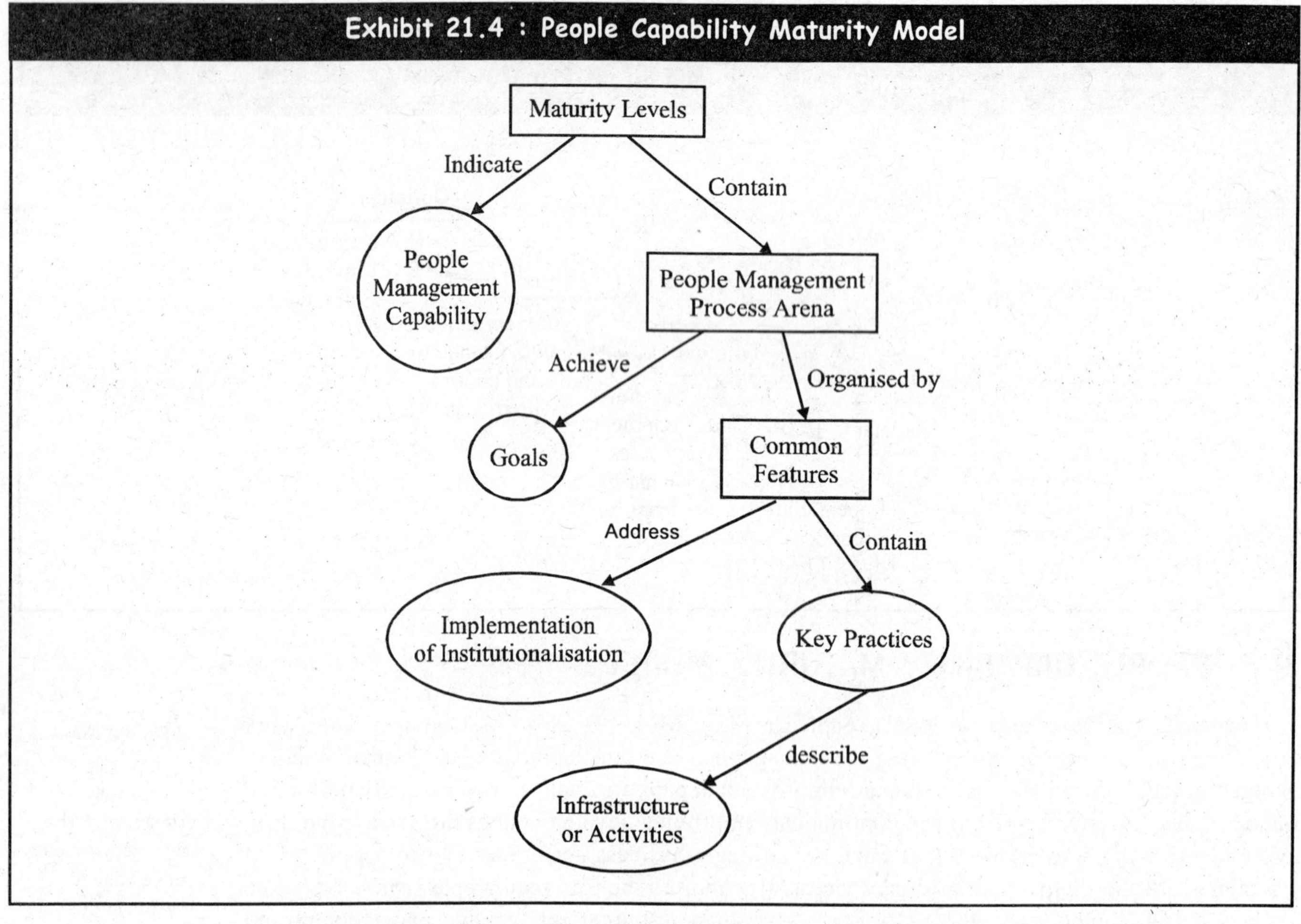

21.8.2 Capability Maturity Model Integration (CMMI)

CMMI is a process improvement approach that helps organisations to improve their performance

CMMI is a process improvement approach that helps organisations improve their performance. It can be used to guide process improvement across a project, a division, or an entire organisation.

CMMI in software engineering and organisational development is a process improvement approach that provides organisations with the essential elements for effective process improvement.

According to the Software Engineering Institute, CMMI helps "integrate traditionally separate organisational functions, set process improvement goals and priorities, provide guidance for quality processes and provide a point of reference for appraising current processes.

21.8.3 Business Process Maturity Model (BPMM)

Understand your business process maturity: In many companies, business processes are often carried out manually, via mail, phone, fax, meetings etc. Information can be lost during these processes and if changes are involved, it could be time consuming, resulting in inefficiency. Therefore it is vital for companies to document, communicate and assign accountability for their processes. A business process management (BPM) solution can manage the full scale process life cycle without being restricted by departmental boundaries.

Business Process Management can help an organisation to clarify and document processes, automate processes, monitor process performance, identify opportunities for improvement and deploy them successfully.

The Business Process Maturity Model (BPMM) was developed by the Object Management Group (OMG), a not for profit international industry consortium. The model describes an evolutionary improvement path that guides organisations in moving from immature, inconsistent processes to mature, disciplined processes. In following the BPMM path, organisational behaviour and culture will change allowing the organisation to produce continually improving business results. ***Exhibit 21.5* illustrates the Business Process Maturity Model.**

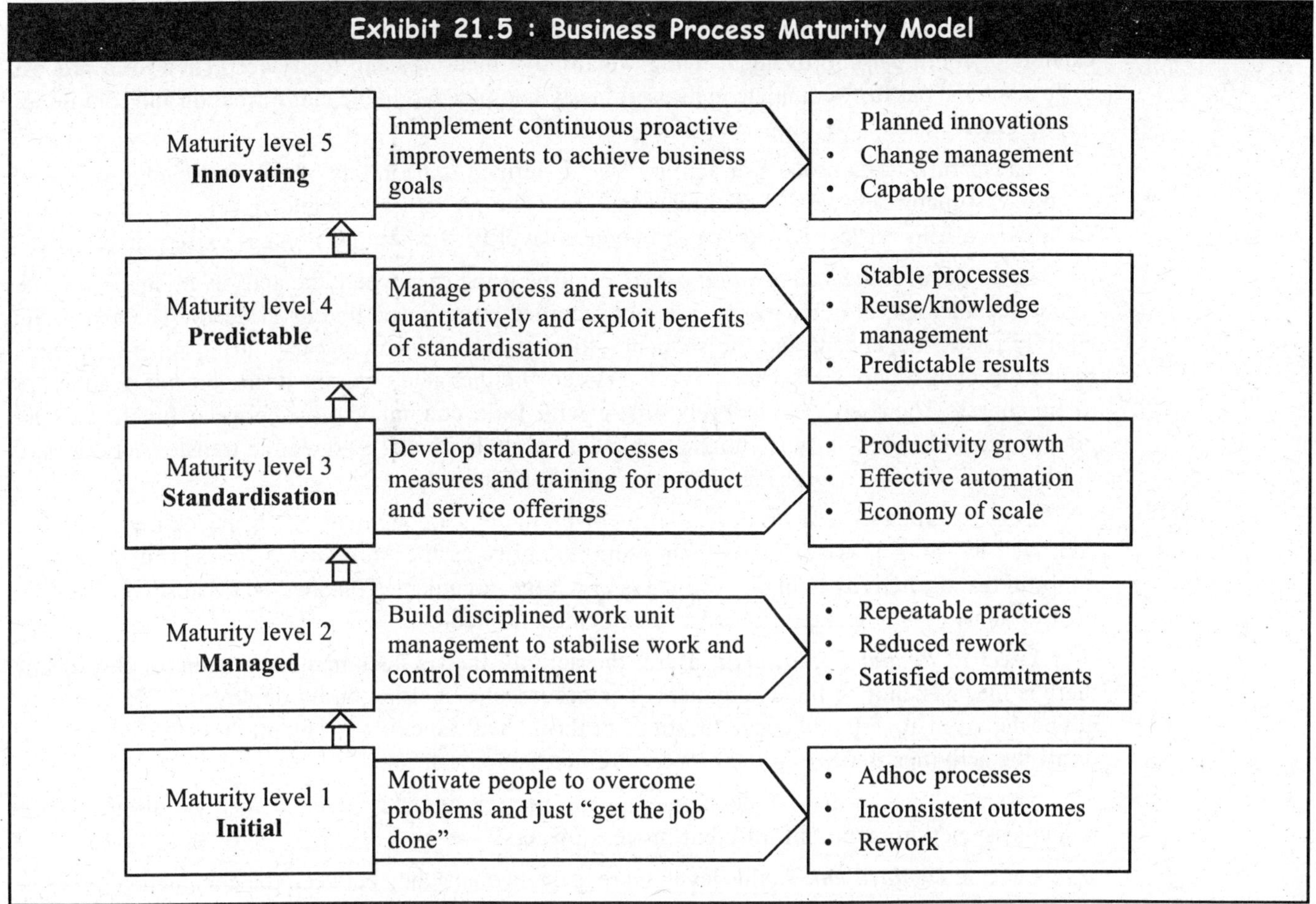

The five maturity levels shown in *Exhibit 21.5* can be briefly described in terms of their management focus and primary objective.

1. **Initial: *"Fire-fighting management"*** – There are no specific objectives. Success in these organisations depends on the competence and heroics of the people in the organisation and not on the use of proven processes
2. **Managed: *"Work-unit management"*** – The objective is to create a management foundation within each work unit or project.
3. **Standardised : *"Process Management"*** – The objective is to establish and use a common organisational process infrastructure and associated process assets to achieve consistency in how work is performed to provide the organisation's products and services
4. **Predictable: *"Capacity management"*** – The objective is to manage and exploit the capability of the organised process infrastructure and associated process assets to achieve predictable results with controlled variation
5. ***Innovating: "Change Management"*** – The objective is to continuously improve the organisation's processes and the resulting products and services through defect and problem prevention, continuous capability and planned innovative improvements.

The five maturity levels of BPMM are:
(i) Initial
(ii) Managed
(iii) Standardised
(iv) Predictable
and
(v) Innovating

The maturity of an organisation provides a way to predict the future performance of the organisation for a given domain or set of domains. Theses five maturity levels reflect the fact that BPMM is a model for improving the capability of organisations.

21.8.4 Description of Process Maturity

Process maturity is an indication of how close a developing process is to being complete and capable of continual improvement though qualitative measures and feed back. Thus for a process to be mature, it has to be complete in its usefulness, automated, reliable in information and continuous improvement.

The maturity of a process or activity can be defined to be at one of the five levels from level 1, (the least mature) to level 5 (the most mature). The processes at higher levels also address the features of the lower levels. The ground level is level zero where no process exists for activity.

Level Zero: ***Person-dependent practices:*** This is the case where the activity being performed in not documented, in other words, it is not recorded either in outline or in detail. The activity is entirely person-dependent and the sequence, timing and result may vary during repetition. This requires a lot of supervision. There is no guarantee of either achieving the desired result or adhering to timeliness. The activity is entirely adhoc with little communication between functions. The effectiveness of the activity is entirely dependent on individuals. Knowledge transfer may or may not happen if there is any change in the owner of the activity.

Level 1: ***Documented Process:*** At this level, there is a document that has been reviewed and approved by the supervisor or the approving authority as the ***standard process.*** But it may be doubtful that the activity being performed is as per the document. This may be because of a process drift or some drastic change since the document is drafted.

Level 2: ***Partial Deployment:*** Here, the activity that is documented is being deployed but there is inconsistency in the deployment. The process may not be totally deployed. That is it may not be deployed at all the intended locations or through all functions, or by all the intended owners, or all the activities defined in the process are not being performed.

This would mean that the document has not been designed to cater to such variations. There is inconsistency in results of different process owners

Level 3: ***Deployment:*** At this level, there is no inconsistency between the documented process and the deployed process. The process documented and deployed caters to all the intended locations, owners and all the activities that need to be performed. The process also shows seamless linkage between functions and other processes wherever there needs to be any interaction. This means that the process shows grater consistency of actions and better communication between functions.

Level 4: ***Measured and Automated:*** The process has set it-self goals such as adherence to timelines, customer satisfaction, cost *etc.* The process also is being measured against its goals. The process is system-driven by enablers such as using enterprise resource planning (ERP) or customer resource management or any other customer-made software.

Level 5: ***Continuously Improving:*** The goals set for the process are being analysed for achievements and improved regularity. The timeliness, cost targets, satisfaction levels are being achieved regularly and targets are also being tightened by using continuous quality improvement techniques such as Six-Sigma, Kaizen *etc.* The enabling system also is being improved and being made error free by strategies such as Poka-Yoke (mistake proofing).

From the inception of an organisation through its growth, the maturity of its processes usually improves. But this may still be at the lower levels. This shows that the organisation has not had an all-round maturity of its processes. There also are instances where the maturity level may drop if not monitored or if the documents are not revised according to changes the business undergoes. Thus a fully established business can contain processes at different levels of maturity.

21.8.5 Improving Business Process Maturity

To have an all-round improvement of business processes the Six-Sigma DMAIC methodology can be used. The phases involved are:

1. Define: It is important to align the applicability of the maturity levels to the organisation. Design a questionnaire to map the maturity level of each business process. Applying the questionnaire to each process will obtain the maturity level for that process.

2. Measure: A cross-functional team should be assigned to utilise the questionnaire and audit processes to arrive at each one's maturity levels. All the activities and processes performed by the business should be audited by the team based on the questionnaire. It must be noted that if a process is at a higher level but does not meet some lower-level maturity criteria, it will still deemed to be at the lower level.

3. Analyse: The measurement of the processes will indicate the current overall level that processes are at and the gaps that exist. This needs to be addressed. Analysis must be conducted and a plan of action must be made on how to bridge the gap and raise the maturity level of specific processes, thus improving the overall level.

4. Improve: This is the most important phase in the methodology. The plan of action designed must be put into effect. This could include redefining or redesigning processes, identification of owners, automation etc.

5. Control: If processes are not monitored at defined intervals, maturity levels may drop. Thus a control plan must be generated and based on the plan, subsequent audits of maturity levels of process must be performed and the processes improved accordingly.

The phases involved in Six-Sigma DMAIC methodology are:

(i) Define

(ii) Measure

(iii) Analyse

(iv) Improve and

(v) Control

21.9 QUALITY IN PRACTICE

Box 21.1 : Infosys awarded CII-Exim Bank Award for Business Excellence-2002

On 14th November 2002 Infosys Technologies was declared the winner of the CII-EXIM Bank Award for Business Excellence –2002, becoming the first software services company to win this prestigious award. The award acknowledges Infosys' excellence in Total Quality Management in the following areas: leadership, policy and strategy, people, customer-driven processes, partnerships, corporate citizenship and performance in creating value for all its stakeholders (customers, shareholders, employees, partners and society at large).

The Confederation of Indian Industry and the Export Import Bank of India, jointly, instituted the CII-EXIM Bank Award for Business Excellence, in the year 1994. It is today recognized as one of the most prestigious awards in India for business excellence. The rigorous process of assessment, lasting six months, follows The Business Excellence Model based on the European model for Total Quality Management, a global benchmark.

Announcing the award, Mr. Narayana Murthy, Chairman and chief Mentor, Infosys Technologies said, "The 13,000 strong family of Infoscions and the Infosys Foundation are very honoured to have been conferred this award. I am very thankful to CII and the EXIM Bank for having partnered with is in our journey to excellence.

"This award is a great honour for Infosys and recognises our passion for excellence. At Infosys, it is our mission to continuously strive to set higher standards, The CII assessment takes a holistic view of excellence, fosters integration and promotes a uniform understanding of improvement strategies and opportunities.

The review and feedback process has been a great learning experience and we look forward to sharing our journey with other corporations." Remarked by Mr.K. Dinesh, Member of the Board and Director-Quality, HR and IS., Infosys Technologies, while presenting the Infosys journey at the Quality, summit.

Leading the software service industry, Infosys in placed with previous eminent winners from the manufacturing sector in India such as Hewlett Packard, Maruti Udyog and Tata Steel. Reputed global corporations in Europe who have received awards based on this mode include Rank Xerox, Ericsson, IBM, Texas Instruments, British Telecom and TNT.

About Infosys Technologies: Infosys, a world leader in consulting and information technology services, partners with Global 2000 companies to provide business consulting, systems integration, application development and product engineering services. Through these services, Infosys enables its clients to fully exploit technology for business transformation. Clients leverage Infosys' Global Delivery Model to achieve higher quality, rapid time-to-market and cost-effective solutions. Infosys had over 13,000 employees in over 30 offices worldwide as on Novermber 2002

21.10 SUMMARY

In today's competitive business environment, organisations are compelled to improve their productivity in order to gain competitive edge in the global market. At the same time, the organisations should achieve maximum stakeholder satisfaction at minimum costs. This makes it necessary to organisations achieving compliance with international standards in the performance of their business.

Achieving business excellence has become a crucial issue for business organisations for their survival and growth. Many world-class companies are dedicated to the continuous improvement philosophy and have excellence as a fundamental goal. Excellence requires balanced performance and the dimensions of performance for excellence include: *(i)* External quality *(ii)* Internal quality *(iii)* Dependability *(iv)* Resource use the dimensions of performance *(v)* Flexibility *(vi)* Human resource improvement *(vii)* Innovation *(viii)* Environmental soundness and *(ix)* Financial results.

The European Foundation for Quality Management (EFQM) has developed the Business Excellence Model in the year 2000 which provides the necessary framework for organisations to perform self-assessment and understand their strengths and areas which need improvement.

Various quality management awards, both national and international provide much guidance and wisdom in the form of "best practices" to managers around the world. Malcolm Baldrige National Quality Award and the ISO 9000 certification process have impacted quality management worldwide along with the concept of Six-Sigma quality. Quality Certification helps companies to establish quality management systems and implement the same – ISO 900:2000 certification involves both internal quality audit (self-assessment) and external third party quality audit (lead assessment) There are various national and international Quality Certification Institutes which perform the lead assessment and facilitate quality certificational for organisations which implement quality management systems in their operations. Self-assessment for business excellence is different from self-assessment asked for in the ISO standard which are quality assurance self-assessments. Self-assessment for achieving business excellence are "quality management" self-assessments This involves self-assessment against the criteria of a quality award/excellence model (e.g. EFQM Award or CII-Exim Bank Award) on which evaluation and diagnostics can be based. Self-assessment has become an important management technique to continuously improve the overall performance of the organisation. It is a catalyst for driving business improvement. The process of self-assessment involves a "five –component cycle of self-assessment" Self-assessment provides certain benefits which are categorised as *(i)* Results *(ii)* Culture *(iii)* Process management and *(iv)* Benchmarking, Self-assessment links business result to the enablers. It gives an important cultural benefit by encouraging an ethos of continuous improvement. By using the EFQM model, self-assessment enforces a process management perspective and finally it provides organisations with a benchmarking tool.

Self-assessment is said to drive TQM and in-turn business performance and business excellence. Self-assessment is basically about continuous improvement of the organisation. Continuous improvement is a company-wide process of focused and continuous incremental innovation or improvement.

TQM aims to increase external and internal customer satisfaction with a reduced amount of resources. The overall objective of TQM is to achieve balanced stakeholder satisfaction which is often referred to as "business excellences"

"Maturity" as a measure to evaluate the capabilities of an organisation in regards to a certain discipline is represented by the "Capability Maturity Model" proposed by the Software Engineering Institute of Carnegie Mellon University; Pittsburg; USA.

This model is now applied for the evaluation of IT Infrastructure Management, Enterprise Architecture Management and Knowledge Management. The "Business Process Maturity Model" has been developed for evaluating the capability and maturity of business processes employed in organisations which have the objective of achieving business excellence. The Capability Maturity Model (CMM) provides the common bases for the majority of the maturity models used to measure the maturity of business processes. Improved maturity results in an increase in the performance of the process of an organisation.

A maturity model can be viewed as a set of structured levels that describe how the behaviour, and practices will, and the processes of an organisation can reliably and sustainbly produce required outcomes.

The CMM involves the following aspects:

(i) ***Maturity levels:*** A five level process maturity continuum where the fifth level is a notional ideal state where processes would be systematically managed by a combination of process optimisation and continuous process improvement.

(ii) ***Key process areas*** which identify a cluster of related activities, that when performed together, achieve a set of goals.

(iii) ***Goals*** summarize the stakes that must exist for the key process area.

(iv) ***Common features*** include practices that implement and institutionalise a key process area.

(v) ***Key practices*** which describe the elements of infrastructure and practices that contribute most effectively to the implementation of the key process areas.

There are five levels along the continuum of the CMM, predictability, effectiveness and control of an organisation's software processes are believed to improve as the organisation moves up these five levels.

These five levels of CMM are:

(i) ***Initial:*** The starting point of a new process.

(ii) ***Repeatable:*** The process is managed in accordance with agreed metrics.

(iii) ***Defined:*** The process is defined/confirmed as a standard process.

(iv) ***Managed:*** quantitatively managed and

(v) ***Optimizing:*** process management includes deliberate process optimisation.

Within each of these maturity levels are Key Process Areas (KPAs), there are five definitions identified: *(i)* Goals *(ii)* Commitment *(iii)* Ability *(iv)* Measurement and *(v)* Verification.

People Capability Maturity Model (PCMM) is a maturity framework that focuses on continuously improving the management and development of the human assets of an organisation.

Capability Maturity Model Integration (CMMI) is a process improvement approach that helps organisations improve their performance. CMMI helps integrate traditionally separate organisational functions, set process improvement goals and priorities, provide guidance for quality processes and provide a point of reference for appraising current processes.

The Business Process Maturity Model (BPMM) describes an evolutionary improvement path that guides organisations in moving from immature, inconsistent processes to mature, disciplined processes. The five maturity levels are:

1. ***Initial*** – Fire-fighting management
2. ***Managed*** – Work-unit management
3. ***Standardised*** – Process management
4. ***Predictable*** – Capacity management
5. ***Innovating*** – Change management

21.11 OBJECTIVE QUESTIONS

(A) Match the following :

Column A	Column B
1. Business excellences	1. Quality certification agency
2. Business excellence model	2. Balanced performance
3. B V Q I	3. Provides feed back to an organisation about its performance.
4. Self assessment	4. Sponsored by EFQM
5. CMM	5. The general model of the maturity of processes.

(B) State whether the following statements are True or False :

1. A Capability Maturity model has 6 levels. (T / F)
2. Both CMM and PCMM are one and the same. (T / F)
3. BVQI is an agency or lead assessor for independent assessment and quality certification (T / F)

4. Self-assessment is often referred to as a catalyst for driving business improvement (T / F)
5. Two types of self-assessment are *(a)* quality assurance self-assessment and *(b)* quality management self assessment (T / F)

(C) Multiple Choice Questions : Choose the correct answer from the alternatives given under each question :

1. Some dimensions of performance for excellence include:
   (a) External quality (b) Internal quality
   (c) Dependability (d) Resource use
   (e) All of these (f) None of these
2. Self-assessment for business excellences is
   (a) A quality management initiative (b) A catalyst for driving business improvement
   (c) A driver of total quality management (d) Concerned with continuous improvement
   (e) All of these (f) None of these
3. The following are the categories of the benefits of self-assessment
   (a) Result (b) Culture
   (c) Process management (d) Benchmarking
   (e) All of these (f) None of these
4. The Capability Maturity Model (CMM) involves the following aspects:
   (a) Maturity levels (b) Key Process Areas
   (c) Goals (d) All of these
   (e) None of these
5. CMM involves the following levels:
   (a) Initial (b) Repeatable
   (c) Defined (d) Managed
   (e) Optimising (f) All of these

21.12 REVIEW QUESTIONS

1. What is meant by "business excellence"?
2. What is a "business excellence model"?
3. What is meant by "quality certification"? Why it is necessary for organisation?
4. What is "lead assessment"?
5. How an organisation is assessed against the requirements of a business excellence model?
6. List the various lead assessment activities.
7. Discuss the "Award Assessment Process" for the CII-Exim Bank Award for excellence.
8. Discuss the characteristics of assessment team.
9. Discuss the steps involved in the basic procedure of quality certification by an independent external lead assessor or certifying agency.
10. Discuss the concept of "five component cycle of self-assessment".
11. Discuss the benefits of using self-assessment.
12. Discuss the relationship between self-assessment, continuous improvement, total quality management and business excellence.
13. Define the term: *a.* Capability Maturity Model *b.* Business Process Maturity Model *c.* People Capability Maturity Model *d.* Capability Maturity Model Integration (CMMI.)
14. Give an overview of "Capability Maturity Model" (CMMI.)
15. Describe the structure of CMM.
16. Discuss the five levels of CMM.
17. Describe the structure of People CMM.
18. Describe the various levels of process maturity.

21.13 DISCUSSION QUESTIONS

1. "Business excellence, like beauty, is in the eyes of the beholder and there are many beholders of business excellence" - Discuss.
2. "Excellence requires balanced performance" - Elaborate.
3. "Excellence model is framework that reflects that world's best-validated management principles and practices" - Do you agree or disagree? Justify your answer.
4. "Self-assessment is often referred to as a catalyst for driving business improvement" - Explain.
5. "The people CMM is a framework that helps organisations successfully address their critical people issues" - Examine this statement.

21.14 ASSIGNMENTS

1. Visit the website www.baldrige.org and prepare a report using the information available on the website.
2. Visit the website of Infosys technologies and study how the company achieved business excellence.

21.15 CHAPTER CASE

SUNDARAM CLAYTON – WINNING THE DEMING PRIZE

The case examines the quality initiatives taken up by leading Indian air-brakes manufacturer, Sundaram Clayton Ltd (SCL) to win the world's highest award for quality, -"The Deming Prize".

"The Deming Prize" is not just recognition of product quality. It is the recognition of the organisation itself. Clearly, Sundaram Clayton meets the requirements of a World-class company.

This case illustrates three things:

1. Total quality is not a prerogative of only Japanese companies.
2. Indian workers and managers are capable of international standards and
3. Neither size nor location matters in achieving world-class standards.

Background of the company: The leading manufacturer of air braking systems in India, Sundaram Clayton Limited (SCL) is the flagship company of the US $ 1.6 billion TVS group, Named after its founder, T.V. Sundaram Iyengar, the TVS Group began its journey with a small transport business in Chennai in 1911,

Over the years, the group diversified into two wheelers, automotive parts, computer peripherals and financial services. In 2001, the TVS group had 29 globally recognised companies and an employee base of over 30,000.

SCL was established in 1962, in collaboration with UK based Clayton Dewandre Holdings Plc (renamed WABCO Automotive), a division of American Standards INC. for manufacturing air-assisted and air-brake systems for commercial vehicles in India.

Over the next few decades, SCL went on to become the principal supplier of airbrake systems to the heavy and light commercial vehicle segments of the Indian automobile sector.

SCL was the original equipment manufacturer (OEM) for Ashok Leyland and Tata Engineering and Locomotive Company (Telco). Other major clients of SCL included Hindustan Motors, Maruti Udyog and Bharath Earth Movers.

OEM sales contributed 60% of the company's total sales while the replacement market accounted for an estimated 25%.

SCL used 65% of the castings produced by its foundry division and supplied the remaining 35% to the group companies or other companies. The company's vast network of over 205 wholesale dealer outlets, situated across the country enabled it to become the leader in the automotive air-brake systems market in India and garner a 70% market share.

SCL -Winning the Deming Prize: SCL has a full-fledged Research and Development (R&D) centre that enables design, development, simulation and testing processes of products. By focusing on R&D, the company was able to substitute its imports by its indigenously developed components.

SCL was also to indigenously manufacture some components for the export markets. These initiatives were expected to help the company achieve its goal of becoming the leader in the automotive air-braking business in Asia.

Inspite of the slump in the automobile sector in the late 1990s, SCL registered improved revenues year after year between 1998 and 2000. Industry analysts largely attributed the company's success to its focus on quality.

According to TVS sources, the group as a whole had always aimed at competitiveness without compromising on quality. This belief was proved when the company adopted Total Quality Management (TQM) in all its manufacturing plants, including SCL.

SCL followed the core principles of the TVS group- "Quality, Reliability and Service". Quality measures at SCL were not only applicable to the product but also to systems, operations and processes at all levels of manufacturing.

As a result of its company-wide quality control (CWQC) over the years, the company won the Deming Prize for CWQC in 1998. SCL was the first Indian company and the forever non-Japanese Company to receive the Deming Prize in the 50year history of the award.

About the Deming Prize: One of the three highly recognized and coveted quality award in the world, the Deming Prize was established in Japan in 1951, by the Union of Japanese Scientists and Engineers (JUSE).

SCL's Deming Prize Journey: SCL had decided to apply for the Deming Prize in the early 1990s itself.

This decision was the result of management's belief in the total quality control efforts that had started in 1979, after Venu Srinivasan became the CEO in 1977. A SWOT analysis conducted by Srinivasan in 1977 revealed that though the company had a 90% share of the air brake systems market in India, it was not competent enough to deliver world-class quality products. This analysis prompted the company to seek excellence through total quality control/management. As a part of this initiative, SCL managers were introduced to the concept of Total Quality Control (TQC) and exposed to the quality control practices of world's leading companies.

The managers were also trained in modern manufacturing techniques. By the mid 1980s, the TQC culture was well established at SCL. Famous Japan's quality control expert like Yoshio Kondo and Washio trained managers and employees extensively in TQC. The company also introduced the concept of "quality circles." To remain focused on quality control and to keep the employees interested in quality control practices, external targets such as winning national quality awards were set, following which the company won the Quality circle Award of the confederation of Indian Industry (CII) in 1989 and The Quality Circle Federation of India awards successively for the next few years.

After Winning the Deming Prize: The defect rate in the manufacturing process at SCL decreased substantially and customer returns came down as a result of these quality control initiatives. New product development time was reduced from 24 to 30 months to 12 to14 months. The turnover per employee increased by an estimated 18% annually while the gross value addition by every employee increased by 12% per annum. The quality practices in the company also reflected in its financial performance. Between 1992 and 1997, sales grew at an annual rate of 35% while its net profits grew at an annual rate of 83%.

Disucssion Questions :

1. Did winning a quality award like "Deming Prize" improved the competitiveness of Sundaram Clayton in its market?
2. Give an account of the efforts put by SCL while preparing for challenging the Deming Prize.
3. In what way, performance of SCL improved after winning the Deming Prize?
4. Discuss the effect of quality circles on the performance of companies in India.

APPENDICES

APPENDIX A

CASE ANALYSIS

The case study method of teaching and learning has fulfilled a major role in senior level management education for a number of years. The case study approach was pioneered by Harvard Business School in the USA and by Cranfield School of Management in the U.K. It continues to play a major role in business schools.

What is a case study?

A case study offers often in great detail, **a real-life situation** that has been or is currently confronting a senior manager. In this way, a case study is a living scenario within which you are invited to display and demonstrate your **ability to apply the theoretical knowledge** that you have acquired in the subject to which the case study is linked.

Cases will vary in their layout, style, format, data and background. The case material can comprise one or two pages (about 500 words) or even ten to twelve pages of text with a number of appendices, charts etc. However, in this book only short cases (within 500 words) are discussed taking into consideration the limitation on the length of case study from the examination point of view.

Data in the case will also vary greatly from the copious to the meager. The amount and quality of data presented depends on the data available and considered relevant. **The reader must decide what is important and what is not among the given data.**

Guide lines for preparing case analysis

1. **The need for practicality :** There is no such thing as a **complete case** and **no case gives you all the information you need** to conduct analysis and make recommendations. In the business world, managers never have all the information they need to take decisions. All information may not be available, too costly to obtain or may take too much time to obtain. So, in analysing cases, make reasonable assumptions if necessary, state assumptions clearly, perform analysis and make decisions. Be practical. Avoid saying **"I don't have enough information".**
2. **The need for justification :** The most important part of analysing cases is not what strategies you recommend, but rather how you propose that they be implemented. ***There is no single best solution or one right answer to a question asked in the case.*** So, **give ample justification to your recommendations.**
3. **The need for realism : Avoid recommending a course of action beyond the organisation's means. Be realistic.** Make sure your recommendations are **feasible.** Present the major advantages and disadvantages of several feasible alternatives. Try not to exaggerate, stereotype, prejudge or over dramatise.
4. **The need for specificity : Do not make broad generalisations while suggesting some strategies. Be specific in telling *what, why, when, how, where and who.***
5. **The need for originality :** Do not necessarily recommend the course of action that the firm plans to take or actually undertook, if those actions resulted in improved revenues and earnings. The aim of the case analysis is for you **to consider all the facts and information relevant to the organisation at the time, generate feasible alternate strategies, choose among the alternatives and defend your recommendations.**

Case Analysis Techniques

The checklist to enable the reader to develop a quick approach for case analysis is given below:

1. Quickly glance through the material.
2. Try to get the general ideas by reading the case as a whole.
3. Comprehend the perspective of the case.

4. Make mental notes or marginal notes of important facts and ideas.
5. Arrive at some preliminary information of the problem.
6. Grasp the relevant facts and firm up logically and orderly relationships between them.

One must remember that one is not aiming at perfection in analysing a case, but is developing analytical capability for problem solving. The following practical guide-lines will assist in the case analysis.

1. Suggestions offered for analysis of facts are :
   (a) List of facts should be prepared in a logical manner.
   (b) If any assumption has been made, the same should be stated clearly.
   (c) Quantitative analysis should be done with the help of statements, charts and graphs.
2. Main questions to be answered should be identified and questions which need to be answered to tackle the main questions should be stated.
3. Criteria for the decision should be based on the objectives.
4. Implementation plans should be determined by examining the following aspects.
   (a) Programme orientation – What is to be done?
   (b) Responsibility identification – Who has to do it?
   (c) Schedule of events – When exactly is the job to be done?
   (d) Budget perspective – How much will it cost?
5. Contingency plans – Contingency plans may be kept ready in case of need.

Case Analysis Process

The steps involved in case analysis process are :

1. **Analysis of facts**
   - Prepare list of facts in a logical order.
   - Develop quantitative analysis through statements, charts and graphs.
   - Identify statements of attitudes or opinions in the case.
2. **Identify questions to be answered**
   - Determine main questions to be answered.
   - State questions which need answering to tackle the main questions.
3. **Ascertain objectives and criteria for decision**
   - Comprehend the objectives.
   - Determine the criteria for decisions.
4. **Suggest alternate solutions**
   - State advantages and disadvantages of each alternative.
   - Give your suggested solutions stating evidence supporting you position.
5. **Information plan**
   - Programs – Details of actual action to be taken to be developed.
   - Responsibility – Personnel responsibility to be identified.
   - Schedule – Implementation strategy in terms of time should be reviewed.
   - Budget – Financial implications should be examined.
6. **Contingency plan** – Due to uncertainties, contingency plan may be needed.

APPENDIX B

CASE ILLUSTRATIONS

1. SPEEDY PIZZA EMBRACES TOTAL QUALITY MANAGEMENT

(A) Speedy Pizza guarantees delivery in thirty minutes or less. Pizza delivery boys are given detailed instructions for reaching every neighborhood in the service area. However, based on experience, drivers modify their routes to suit the current traffic situation. Even faster delivery resulted.

Question : How speedy Pizza has been able to maintain quality service?

Answer : Speedy Pizza has two products: Pizza (a good) and fast delivery (a service). Thirty minute delivery is a performance specification. Quality of service was increased by giving the producer (delivery boy) autonomy to change production methods (routes). It is a clear example of employee empowerment which is one of the basic principles of total quality management.

(B) Speedy Pizza is a vertically integrated corporation. Pizza dough and topping are manufactured centrally and delivered to the pizzerias in refrigerated trucks. Pizza is assembled and baked at the pizzeria and delivered in oven- equipped trucks.

Question : (i) For each stage of this system, who are the suppliers and who are the immediate customers?

(ii) How can quality problems of one stage affect quality and cost at the other stages?

Answer to question (i) : The factory's suppliers are vendors who sell flour, eggs, salt and other ingredients. The factory's customers are the refrigerated trucks (The factory's job is to get the right materials to the truck at the appropriate time, with packaging desired to maintain quality).

In turn, these trucks have the pizzerias as customers. The pizzerias have two customers: delivery trucks and consumers who come to the restaurant. The customers of the delivery trucks are the pizza eaters. Viewed in this way, it is the responsibility of each stage to neither accept nor pass on defective product. This places a great responsibility on the truck drivers.

Answer to question (ii) : Raw material quality problems can result in bad pizza dough (cost for the factory) or delayed deliveries that cause pizzerias to run out of dough.

Poor quality pizza preparation makes customers unhappy. This affects the whole company regardless of whether it occurs at the factory or at the pizzeria. For example, if a pizza is improperly prepared, the customer may demand a replacement. Dealing with this situation wastes time and ingredients. This affects the factory as well as the pizzeria because wasted ingredients consume factory resources.

Excessive waste of material is a process-quality problem that increases cost. In addition, the random nature of this kind of error imposes more variable demands on the delivery of ingredients, which makes the control of inventory more difficult and expensive.

2. ANALYSING COST OF QUALITY AND COMPUTING QUALITY - COST INDICES

Consider a printing company that produces a variety of books, brochures, reports and other printed materials for business customers. The printing manager has tracked quality related costs over the past year. Sales were ₹ 16.2 million last year. What do the following data suggest?

Cost element	Amount (₹)
Proof reading	7,10,000
Quality planning	10,000
Press down time	4,05,000
Bindery waste paper	75,000
Checking and inspection	60,000
Customer complaints and job redo	40,000
Printing plate revisions	40,000
Quality improvement projects	20,000
Other wastes	55,000
Correction of typographic errors	3,00,000
Total quality related costs	**₹ 1,715,000**

Answer : The first step in the cost-of-quality analysis is to assign each quality-cost to the appropriate category viz. prevention cost, appraisal cost, internal failure cost and external failure cost.

The classification of quality-costs is shown below:

(i) Prevention Costs

Quality planning	₹ 10,000
Quality improvement projects	20,000
Total	**₹ 30,000**

(ii) Appraisal cost

Proof-reading	₹ 7,10,000
Checking and inspection	60,000
Total	**₹ 7,70,000**

(iii) Internal failure cost

Press down time	₹ 4,05,000
Bindery waste paper	75,000
Printing plate revisions	40,000
Other wastes	55,000
Correction of typographical errors	3,00,000
Total	**₹ 8,75,000**

(iv) External failure cost

Customer complaints and rework **₹ 40,000**

Quality costs expressed as percentage of total quality related costs.:

(i) Internal failure cost $= \frac{8,75,000}{1,715,000} \times 100 = 51\ \%$

(ii) External failure cost $= \frac{40,000}{1,715,000} \times 100 = 2.3\ \%$

(iii) Prevention cost $= \frac{30,000}{1,715,000} \times 100 = 1.8\ \%$

(iv) Appraisal cost $= \frac{7,70,000}{1,715,000} \times 100 = 44.9\ \%$

Interpretation

Although the company is spending lot of money in appraisal (detection) activities, it still has a significant amount of internal failure. Apparently much more effort needs to be expended on quality improvement initiatives, particularly to reduce press down time and typographical errors and better practices and training for proof reading.

The company is in the early stages of continuous improvement with 95.9 percent (i.e. 51+44.9) of its quality costs in appraisal and internal failure costs put together. External-failure costs are relatively low (2.3 percent) meaning that the company catches and corrects most errors prior to delivering the goods to customer or it doesn't do a good job of measuring customer retention and repeat business rates. More over quality costs are 10.6 percent of sales, a dismal performance statistic. It is not unusual for quality costs to be as high as 20 percent or more of sales in manufacturing companies and over 30 percent of operating costs in service companies. Top performing companies have quality costs as a percentage of sales in the 1 percent to 5 percent range.

Computing Quality Cost Indices

A company collects quality costs by cost category and product for each time period say 1 month, as shown in the Table 1 given below.

Table 1 : Computing Quality-Cost data

A Cost category	January		February	
	Product- A	Product - B	Product - A	Product - B
Prevention	₹ 2,000 /-	₹ 4,000 /-	₹ 2,000 /-	₹ 4,000 /-
Appraisal	₹ 10,000 /-	₹ 20,000 /-	₹ 13,000 /-	₹ 21,000 /-
Internal failure	₹ 19,000 /-	₹ 106,000 /-	₹ 16,000 /-	₹ 107,000 /-
External failure	₹ 54,000 /-	₹ 1,46,000 /-	₹ 52,000 /-	₹ 1,56,000 /-
Total	**₹ 85000 /-**	**₹ 2,76,000 /-**	**₹ 83,000 /-**	**₹ 2,88,000 /-**
Standard direct labour costs	₹ 35,000 /-	₹ 90,000 /-	₹ 28,000 /-	₹ 86,000 /-

The company might compute a total quality - cost index as

$$\text{Quality-cost index} = \frac{\text{Total quality costs}}{\text{Direct labour costs}}.$$

Alternately it might compute individual indexes by category; product, and time period, as summarised in Table below.

Table 2 : Computing Quality-Cost index

Cost category	January		February	
	Product- A	Product - B	Product - A	Product - B
Prevention	$\frac{2000}{35,000} = 0.057$	0.044	0.071	0.047
Appraisal	0.286	0.222	0.464	0.244
Internal failure	0.543	1.178	0.571	1.244
External failure	1.543	1.622	1.857	1.814
Total	**2.429**	**3.067**	**2.964**	**3.349**

Such information can be used to identify areas that require improvement of course, it is upto managers and engineers to discover the precise nature of the improvement needed. For example, a steady rise in internal-failure costs and decline in appraisal costs might indicate a problem in assembly, maintenance of testing equipment, or control of purchased parts.

Quality costs in service organisations differ from those in manufacturing organisations. In manufacturing, they are primarily product oriented, in services, they are process and service provider dependent and usually more difficult to identify and quantify.

Since quality in service organisations depends on service-provider and customer interaction, appraisal costs tend to account for a higher percentage of total quality costs than they do in manufacturing.

Internal failure costs tend to be lower for high-contact service organisations.

External failure costs can become extremely significant out-of-pocket expenses to consumers of services.

3. THE RESERVATION NIGHTMARE

Mr. Harish, a noted business consultant related the following story in "Quality International" magazine. His story goes as below:

"I called to make a flight reservation just yesterday. The telephone rang five times before a recorded voice answered. "Thank you for calling XYZ Travel Services" it said, "To ensure the highest level of customer service, this call may be recorded for future analysis" Next I was asked to select from one of the following three choices. "If the trip is related to company, business, press 1, personal business, press 2, group travel, press 3". I pressed 1.

I was asked to select from the following four choices: "If this is a trip within India, press 1., international, press 2, scheduled training, press 3, related to conference, press 4". Because I was going to Singapore, I pressed 2.

Now two minutes into my telephone call, I was instructed to be sure that I had my customer identification card available. A few seconds passed and a very sweet voice come on, saying "All international operators are busy, but please hold because you are a very important customer". The voice was then replaced by music. About two minutes later, another recorded message said, "Our operators are still busy, but please hold and the first available operator will take care of you." More music. Then yet another message "Our operators are still busy, but please hold. Your business is important to us" More bad music. Finally the sweet voice returned, stating "to speed up your service, enter your 19-digit customer service number." I frantically searched for their card, hoping that I could find it before I was cut off. I was lucky. I found it and entered the number in time. The same sweet voice came back to me saying "To confirm your customer service number, enter the last four digits of your PAN card". I pushed the four numbers on the key pad.

The voice said "Thank you. An operator will be with you shortly. If your call is an emergency, you can call 1-800-CAL-HELP or push all of the buttons on the telephone at the same time. Otherwise, please hold, as you are a very important customer". This time, in place of music, I heard a commercial about the service that the company provides."

At last, a real person answered the telephone and asked "Can I help you?" I replied "Yes certainly". He answered "Please give me your 19 digit customer- service number, followed by the last four digits of your PAN card so that I can verity who you are. (I thought I gave these numbers in the first place to speed up service. Why do I have to rattle them off again?)

I was now convinced that he would call me by the 19 digit number. But to my suspires, he said "Mr. Harish, where do you want go and when?". I explained that I wanted to go to Singapore the next Monday morning. He replied "I only handle domestic reservation. Our international desk has a new telephone number 1-800 - IWE - GOTU. I will transfer your call". A few clicks later a message came on saying "All our international operators are busy. Plesde hold and your call will be answered in the order it was received. Do not hang up or redial, as it will only delay our response to your call. Please continue to hold, as your business is important to us".

Discussion Questions

1. Summarie the service failures associated with this experience.
2. What might the travel agency have done to guarantee a better service experience for Mr. Harish? How do your suggestion relate to the TQ principles?

Answer to Question No 1:

The service failures have occurred in several stages of the reservation process.

(i) When Harish pressed 2 to indicate that his choice was international travel, his call should have been diverted to the international desk instead of making him to go through all the later stages and finally told by the person at the domestic reservation desk, that he will transfer Harish to the international desk

(ii) At every stage, Harish had to wait because all operators at reservation desk are busy and Harish was asked to hang on, listening to the music whether he likes it or not.

(iii) In any service, customer focus is the most important aspect and the service provider should anticipate the customer's problem and provide him the services sought with maximum possible speed. (reducing the waiting time and stages of waiting involved in the whole reservation process)

(iv) Instead of asking to key in the 19 digit customer service card number and the last 4 digits of the PAN card, the customer might be asked to key in a simplified customer code number or identity card number having lesser number of digits.. (e.g., three or four digits.)

Answer to Question No 2:

(i) The travel agency might have kept the entire reservation process software updated, so that Mr. Harish need not have gone through a wrong process of contacting the domestic reservation clerk instead of the clerk at international reservation desk.

(ii) The travel agency might have provided more reservation clerks at the reservation desks to answer the phone calls instead of making the customer wait for too long a time. At the maximum, the call waiting time should not exceed one minute at any stage.

(iii) The travel agency should not expect the customer to bring his customer service card or PAN card to identify himself when calling the reservation desk clerk.

It should simplify the process by asking any other simpler form of identification from the customer who calls for reservation of air tickets.

(iv) The travel agency's concern for service quality should be reflected in meeting the expectations of the customer as speedily as possible and making the reservation process simple and a pleasant experience for the customer. Satisfying the customer, if possible delighting the customer and retaining the customer for repeat services should be the motto of the travel agency if it is serious about implementing total quality management in its operations.

These suggestions are related to total quality management principles such as customer focus, customer satisfaction, customer retention, systems approach, process quality, cycle time reduction, responsiveness, speed of service, empathy in service, and reliability of service.

4. A CASE STUDY ON "PENDING PAPERS" BY QUALITY CIRCLE – 1 (STAFF) OF M/S TECHTRONICS PVT. LTD., HYDERABAD

Profile : "Meets on every Saturday"

Date of starting : October 3rd 2001

No. of meetings held = 10

Leader : Sri K. Ravikumar

Deputy Leader : Sri S. Shivakumar

Facilitator : Sri K. Babu Rao

Deputy facilitator : Sri K. Subba Rao

Members : 10 members

Problem Identified : After discussing various problems among members of the QC Circle, it was unanimously decided to take up the problem of "pending papers" for analysis and finding solution.

Problem defined : To reduce the time gap between receipt of letters or communication and the disposal or action taken.

Data Collected : From various sources, data collected revealed that on an average 4 to 7 days are taken to dispose a paper or letter of communication.

Brainstorming : Brainstorming session conducted revealed the following reasons for delay to dispose papers or letters received or for taking action on communication received through letters. *(i)* Disturbance, *(ii)* Tension, *(iii)* Postponement, *(iv)* Insufficient time, *(v)* No proper assistance, *(vi)* No clear instruction, *(vii)* Lack of concentration, *(viii)* Lack of proper planning, *(ix)* Lack of efficnecy, *(x)* Insufficient staff, *(xi)* For want of information, *(xii)* Lack of memory power, *(xiii)* No self help, *(xiv)* Improper allocation of work, *(xv)* No clear job specification, *(xvi)* Improper codification of files, *(xvii)* Wasting of time on unwanted matters, *(xviii)* Ineffective communication, *(xix)* Lack of initiative, *(xx)* Lack of interest, *(xxi)* Lack of coordination, *(xxii)* Everything is not in place, *(xxiii)* Non-availability of stationery in time, *(xxiv)* Not seeing pending papers daily, *(xxv)* House-keeping is not proper, *(xxvi)* Not creative in job., *(xxvii)* Not planning for next day's work on previous day itself., *(xxviii)* Not handling one task at a time, *(xxix)* Not knowing what is important.

After discusions it was identified that the major causes for the delay are as below :

(i) Lack of planning – about 40%

(ii) The presence of tension – about 20%

(iii) The attitude to post pone – about 15% (Habit of procrastination)

(iv) Lack of allocation of work – about 10%

(v) Other reasons – about 15%

These major causes are illustrated in *Case Exhibit C.1* in the form of a "Pareto chart".

Case Exhibit C.1 : Pareto Chart

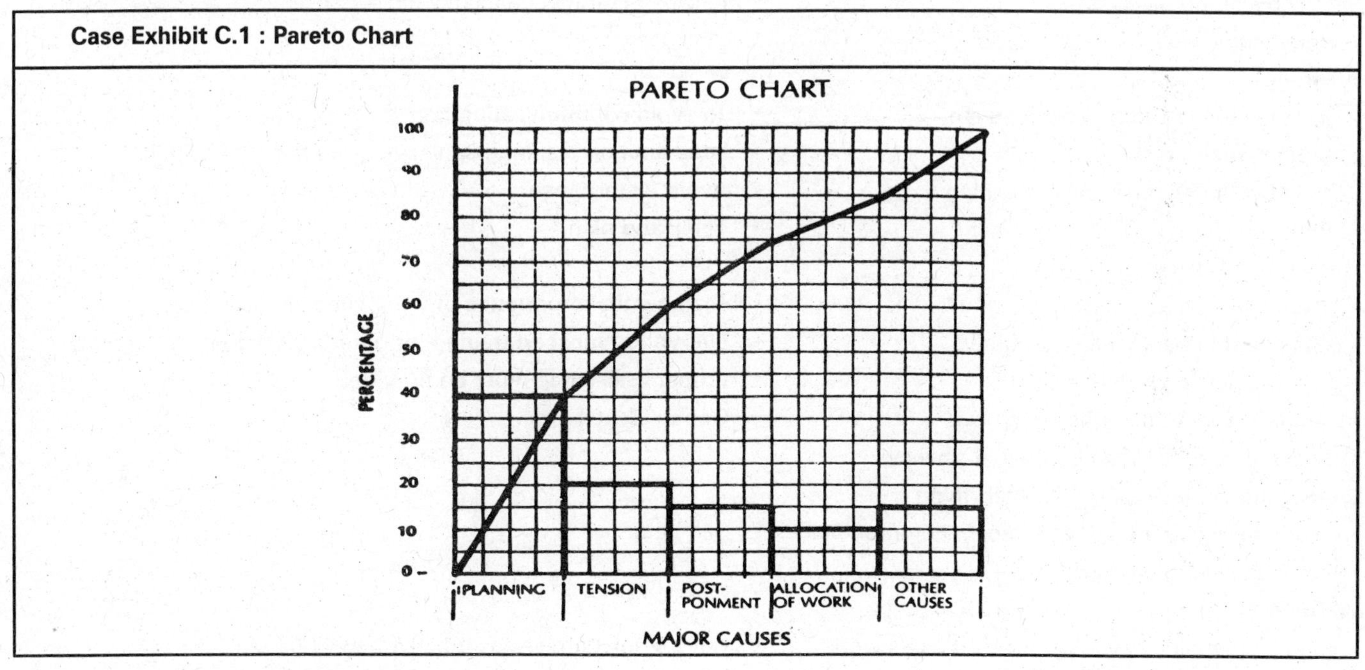

Case Exhibit C.2 illustrates cause and effect diagram.

Case Exhibit C.2 : Cause and effect diagram

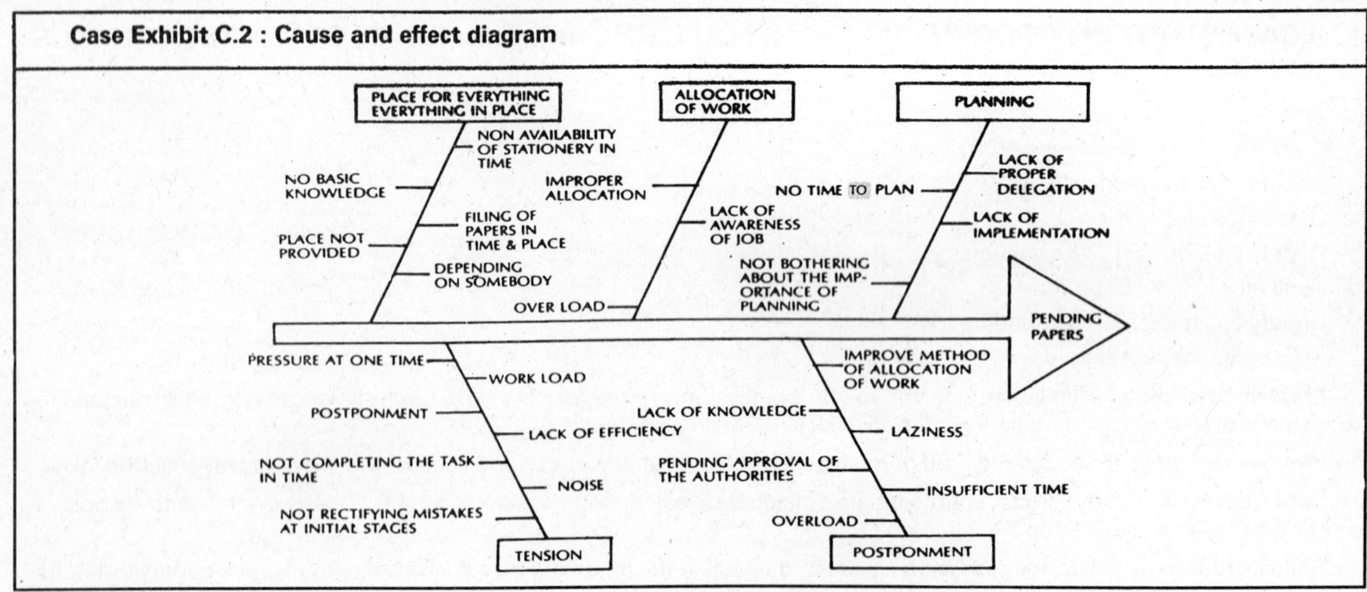

Solutions and Recommendations

1. Tension

- To rectify the mistakes at the initial stage itself
- Complete the task in time
- Improve knowledge
- Over work-load may be reduced.
- Avoid noise
- Improve efficiency and concentration
- Avoid postponement

2. Postponement

- Increase efficiency
- Reallocation of work
- To contact proper authorities and try to clear papers
- May be kept busy all times
- Read magazines.
- Share work load
- Additional man power
- Can do some physical exercise to avoid laziness
- Improve attitude, efficiency etc.

3. Planning

- To know the capacity, work load etc.
- Create time to plan
- To know the importance of planning
- Prioritise
- To avoid communication gap
- Little time on planning can save more time of wasting
- Avoid disturbance
- Think and plan.

4. Allocation of work

- Proper allocation of work
- Work load to be equally distributed.
- Communication must be clear.
- To think what to do, when and how.
- Silent atmosphere can improve efficiency
- To know the importance of work, time factor.
- Everybody must be trained for other's work to meet urgency.
- Proper assistance must be provided.
- One work at a time.

5. Everything in place, place for everything

- Files, stationery etc. may be kept in common place.
- Basic knowledge of filing
- Self help.

Final Solution

- Plan previous day evening, for next day's work.
- Do things right at the first time.
- Do one job at a time.
- Have a quiet time – say 10.00 am to 11.00 am.
- Fixed time for executives to discuss (*i.e.,* 9.00 am)
- Never postpone, if necessary, sit late and work.
- Be clear, specific in communication. If something is not understood properly, never proceed until it is under stood.

- Prioritise your work and plan your time.
- Never disturb others.
- Think about the work as what to do, how to do and when to do.
- Maintain silence in the office.
- "Everything in a place and a place for everything" must be strictly followed.

Conclusion : The average time that was taken to dispose off the papers previously was 4 to 7 days. After implementation and a detailed study of this case in the quality circle, the papers are disposed off within 48 hours.

5. SHORTENING CUSTOMER'S TELEPHONE WAITING TIME

This case illustrates how a bank applied some of the basic seven QC tools to improve customer service. It is the case of a quality circle program implemented in the main office of a large bank. An average of 500 customers call this office everyday. Surveys indicated that callers tended to get irritated if the phone rang more than five times before it was answered and often would not call again. A prompt answer after just two rings reassured the customers and made them feel more comfortable doing busines by phone.

Selection of a theme : Telephone reception was chosen as a QC theme for the following reasons : *(i)* Telephone reception is the first impression a customer receives from the company, *(ii)* This theme coincided with the company's telephone reception slogan "Don't make customers wait and avoid needless switching from extension to extension" and *(iii)* it also coincided with a companywide campaign being promoted at that time that advocated being friendly to everyone met. First, the staff dicussed why the present method of answering calls made callers wait.

Case Exhibit C.3 : Why customer had to wait

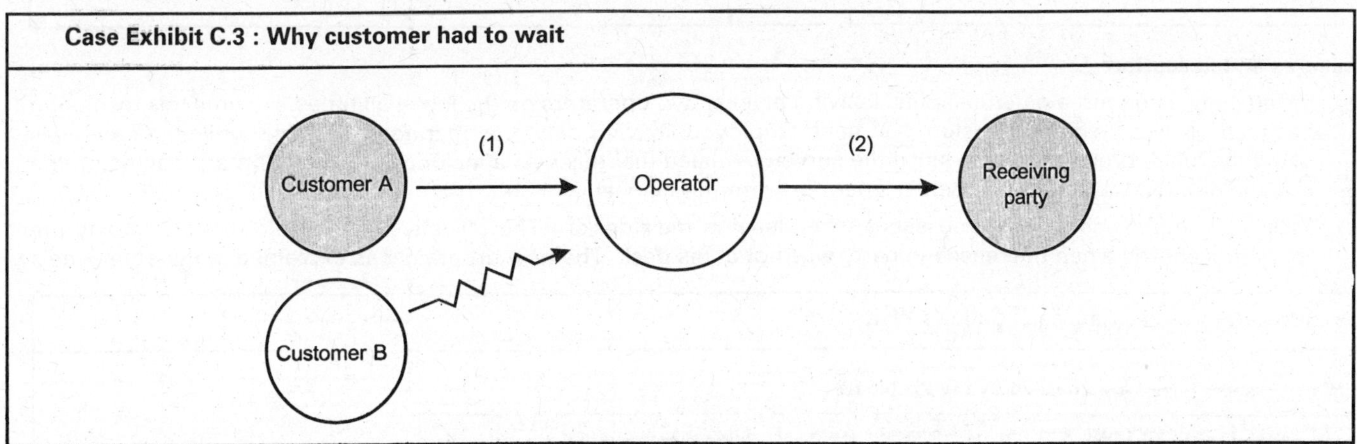

Case exhibit C.3 illustrates a frequent situation, where a call from Customer B comes in while the operator is talking with Customer A. Let us see why the customer has to wait.

At 1. in the *Case Exhibit C.3,* the operator receives a call from the customer, but does not know where to connect the call. At 2. the receiving party can not answer the phone quickly, perhaps because he or she is not available in the seat and no one else can take the call. The result is that the operator must transfer the call to another extension while apologising for the delay.

Cause-and-effect diagram and Situation Analysis :

To fully understand the situation, the quality circle members decided to conduct a survey regarding callers who waited for more than five rings. Circle members itemised the factors at a brainstorming session and arranged them in a cause-and-effect diagram. (*See Case Exhibit C.4*). Operators then kept check sheets on several points to tally the results spanning 12 days (*See Case Exhibit C.5A*).

Results of the check sheet situation analysis

The data recorded on the check sheets unexpectedly revealed that "one operator" topped the list by a big margin, occurring a total of 172 times. In this case, the operator on duty had to deal with large numbers of calls when the phones were busy. Customers who had to wait a long time averaged 29.2 daily, which accounted for 6 percent of the calls received every day. (*See exhibit C.5B and C.5C*)

Setting the Target

After an intense but productive discussion, the staff decided to set a QC program goal of reducing the numbers of waiting callers to zero. That is to say that all incoming calls would be handled promptly without inconveniencing the customer.

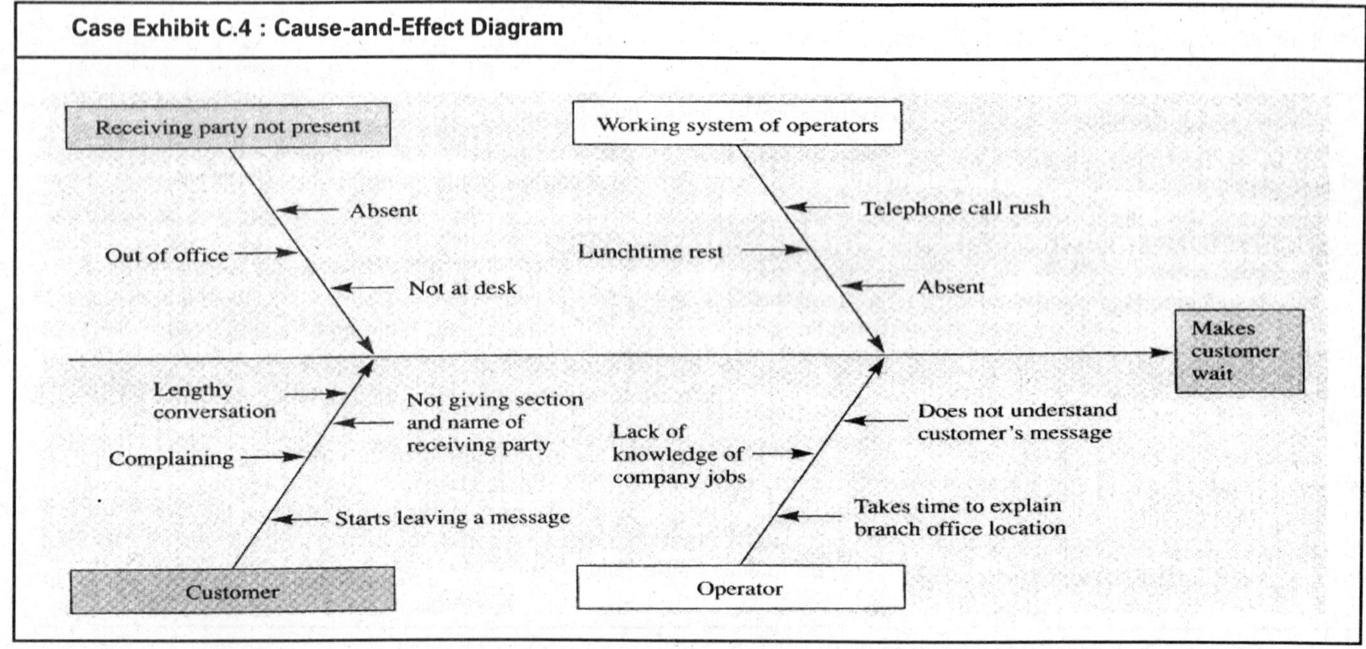

Measures and Execution

(a) Taking lunches on three different shifts. Leaving at least two operators on the job at all times. Up until this resolution was made, a two-shift lunch system had been employed, leaving only one operator on the job while the other was taking the lunch break. However, since the survey revealed that this was a major cause of customers waiting on the line, the company brought in a helper operator from the clerical section.

(b) Asking all employees to leave messages when leaving their desks : The objective of this rule was to simplify the operator's chores when the receiving party was not at his desk. The new program was explained at the employee's

Case Exhibit C.5 : Causes of Caller's Waits

A. Checksheet—Designed to Identify the Problems

Reason / Date	No one present in the section receiving the call	Receiving party not present	Only one operator (partner out of the office)	Total
June 4	||||	卌 |	卌 卌 |	24
June 5	卌	卌 |||	卌 卌 ||||	32
June 6	卌 |	||||	卌 卌 ||	28
June 15	卌	卌	卌 |||	25

B. Reasons Why Callers Had to Wait

		Daily average	Total number
A	One operator (partner out of the office)	14.3	172
B	Receiving party not present	6.1	73
C	No one present in the section receiving the call	5.1	61
D	Section and name of receiving party not given	1.6	19
E	Inquiry about branch office locations	1.3	16
F	Other reasons	0.8	10
	Total	29.2	351

Period: 12 days from June 4 to 16, 1980

C. Reasons Why Callers Had to Wait (Pareto Diagram)

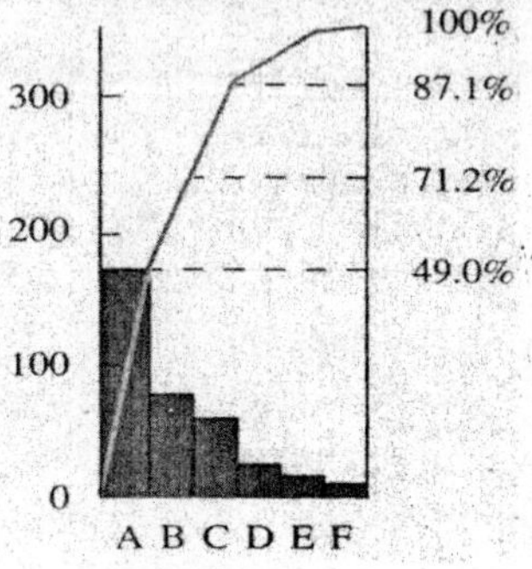

300
200
100
0
100%
87.1%
71.2%
49.0%
A B C D E F

regular morning meetings, and companywide support was requested. To help implement this practice, posters were placed around the office to publicize the new measures.

(c) Compiling a directory listing the personnel and their espective jobs : The notebook was specially designed to aid the operators, who could not be expected to know the details of every employee's job. The notebook would help properly route calls.

Confirming the Results

Although the waiting calls could not be reduced to zero, all items presented showed a marked improvement as shown in *Case Exhibits C.6A and C.6B*. The major cause of delays, "one operator (partner out of the office)" plummeted from 172 incidents during the control period to 15 in the follw-up survey.

Case Exhibit C.6 : Effects of QC

A. Effects of QC (Comparison of before and after QC)

	Reasons why called had no wait	Total Number Before	Total Number After	Daily Average Before	Daily Average After
A	One operator (partner out of the office)	172	15	14.5	1.2
B	Receiving party not present	73	17	6.1	1.4
C	No one present in the section receiving the call	61	20	5.1	1.7
D	Section and name of receiving party not given	19	4	1.6	0.3
E	Inquiry about branch office locations	16	3	1.3	0.2
F	Others	10	0	0.8	0
	Total	351	59	29.2	4.8

Period: 12 days from Agu. 17 to 30

Problems are classified according to cause and presented in order of the amount of time consumed. They are illustrated in a bar graph. 100% indicates the total number of time-consuming

B. Effects of QC (Pareto Diagram)

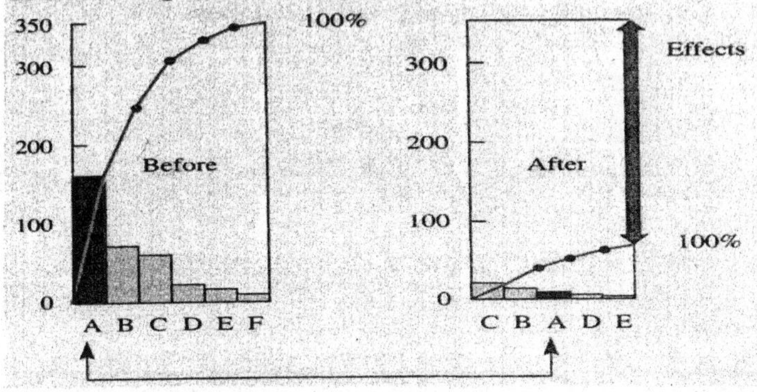

350 300 200 100 0 — 100% — Before — A B C D E F

300 200 100 0 — After — Effects — 100% — C B A D E

6. COLGATE RETHINKS A SUPPLY CHAIN

When it comes to tooth paste in China, Colgate is the market leader, according to a recent AC Nielsen Media International survey on China's emerging consumer society. But in the shampoo category, a Colgate-Palmolive rival tops the list.

Driving sales through brand building and smart marketing is as necessary for fast-moving consumer products companies in China and the rest of Asia as it is in the mature markets of North America and Europe. But in Asia, with its fickle tastes, falling prices and unpredictable competitors, the pressure to keep ahead of the pack and make a proper return on investment is relentless.

The trick is to control tightly what can be controlled. The one area a consumer products company can be firmly in charge of is its own internal business processes. Eliminating waste and wringing out costs can have a dramatic effect, especially with products like shampoo, toothpaste and soap, where volumes are large but margins are thin and tight.

In the past two years Colgate-Palmolive has rolled out an ambitions program to do just that in the Asia Pacific region. The company's entire supply chain was reengineered, and new back-office systems were put in place with stunning speed-all the more remarkable considering that the undertaking involved 57 sites across 11 different markets including China. As a result, these far-flung operations were transformed into a single, closely integrated organisation.

Colgate-Palmolive's entire business-process reengineering effort-code named "Project Dragon" - was accomplished without missing a single self-imposed deadline. All the while the company had to battle in a furiously competitive market place - that was being rocked by regional economic turmoil.

Well Positioned

Today Colgate-Palmolive is following a new model. Subsidiaries throughout Asia use the same automated systems, whether they are handling orders or managing credit. Sourcing has become more economical, with selected countries being the primary suppliers of products for the region. Supporting each market is a shared service organisation providing region-wide information technology and financial functions.

The upshot is that one of the global leaders in consumer products is strongly positioned to win profitable market share as Asia's economies shake off the malaise of the past three years.

Project Dragon was conceived and driven by both wider corporate goals and specific Asian issues. The former included Colgate Palmolive's strategy to allocate 60 percent of capital expenditures to cost savings programs. Among the latter was the realisation that there was no guarantee that the company could sustain its double-digit growth rates of the past few years, which, in past, had been due to the region's rising prosperity.

Many operational anomalies had also arisen in Asia over the years, with Colgate-Palmolive units in various countries conducting businesses in different ways. The result was a series of separate systems and procedures often unique to individual markets. This made it more difficult to obtain a more complete picture of the company's global finances - a crucial task, given the fact that 70 percent of Colgate-Palmolive's revenues come from outside the U.S, a figure that is expected to grow.

To Simpson (the general manager of Asia Pacific Information Technology for Colgate-Palmolive) who led a similar reengineering effort in the US, the goal was to streamline the production and distribution cycles. "To do this meant matching information flows" he explains "so that the right products were made at the right time and unwanted inventory did not sit on the shelf".

This goal translated into three specifics: *(i)* Reengineer the entire supply chain, *(ii)* Standardise business processes and *(iii)* Build regional hubs for information technology and finance

The first step was to decide where to base "project dragon". Given the region's cultural diversity and operational quirks, the question was crucial. Australia was too far away. Hongkong and Singapore were convenient, but their markets were too small.

Malaysia was finally chosen because Colgate-Palmolive produced all categories of goods there and the market was large enough to provide a valid test bed. The Malaysian government was also actively seeking IT investments in that country.

The strategy was to develop the overall plan from Kaula Lampur and then roll out in Malaysia-Simpson assembled a core team in Asia to run the project. The company brought together Colgate-Palmolive people from Philippines, Thailand, India and Malaysia and teamed with a multinational Accenture team from Australia and Asia. They quickly embarked on an intense five-month design phase.

From the beginning the idea was to avoid the notion of imposing a solution from "on high" and instead to encourage involvement from the subsidiaries. Simpson brought people from local subsidiaries to Kaule Lampur for training and to be involved in the Malaysian roll out. Having enthusiastic staff from one market support their colleagues in another became a feature of the entire program.

According to Brian Strange, the Accenture client partner on the project, it was necessary to have a "quick win" to boost the project's credibility within Colgate-Palmolive's Asia Pacific operations. A decision was made up front to standardise the processes. Because of time pressures, specific features were added later.

The Malaysian roll out started in early 1997. A flurry of new finance, procurement, sales and distribution systems was introduced. Staff members-including warehouse men, production managers, shift supervisors, accounts clerks and sales teams - had to understand the new processes. The final weeks before the "big bang" implementation, set for July 1977 were characterised by workshops, coaching sessions with practice databases and a final full **"day in the life"** simulation.

Firm Dead lines

As soon as Malaysia was up and running, attention moved to other markets. The unfolding regional economic crisis in mid 1997 encouraged Colgate-Palmolive to drive the project faster, instead of doing one market after another, markets were rolled out simultaneously.

To Simpson, the key to successful implementation is **"to copy, copy, copy"** rather than **reinvent**. He estimates that 85 percent of Colgate experiences in the US and Europe fit Asia. But he advocated accepting the **"80 percent rule"**. It was better to achieve 80 percent of the design requirement now than to wait for 100 percent and miss dead lines.

And dead lines were set in store. "As part of the change-management process, we set up clear communications with country managers" says Simpson. "They were told what was expected of them and were given a set of dates two years out".

The roll out was aggressive. The final two markets, China and Hongkong, went live in May 1999.

Each market offered its own challenges, although many had been identified in advance in Kaula Lumpur during visits by staff from the local markets. And in every market, systems had to be adapted to take account of local taxes and other official requirements.

Capturing orders, credit management and accounts receivables are among a host of functions that have improved. More crucially, better information flows make it easier to predict demand and therefore create better manufacturing schedules and working back down the supply chain, the source materials more effectively.

In the wider picture, project dragon will allow Colgate-Palmolive to take advantage of the revival of Asia's economies. The economist poll of forecasters has predicted that GDP growth in 2000 for the likes of India, Singapores, Taiwan and Malaysia should top rates achieved in 1999. With confidence returning, the battle for consumers' wallets will intensity. Colgate-Palmolive will be ready.

7. "REBUILDING MAHINDRA"

It is remaking itself. Exactly half of a century after it was born, the Rs. 1700 crore Mahindra and Mahindra (M & M) - the Bombay based producer of automobiles and tractors, which was incorporated on October 2, 1945 - is trying to manufacture a future for itself.

In what is the biggest exercise in the history of manufacturing in India - not in terms of **men, materials** or **machines,** but in terms of **methods** - MM is going back to the basics : **manufacturing.** And for the first time, an Indian engineering giant seems to be implicating Peter Drucker's rule for managing manufacturing: "Production is not the application of tools to materials, but the application of logic to work".

By rapidly revamping the production systems at its factories in Bombay, Nashik and Igatpuri - which together employ over 15,000 workers - M & M is trying to instil sense into its systems. On the drawing boards, therefore, is a blue print that could well create a **"factory of the future"**. Keshub Mahindra, M & M's 73 year old chairman declares "We are working towards a new goal. We have to be the leaders in the automotive business".

Over the past 50 years. M & M had constantly regeared itself for growth, forging **alliances** with global automobile giants on three continents: with Willys and Chrysler of the US for utility vehicles, with Automobile Peugeot of France for engines and now with Ford Motor company of the US to produce its Fiesta and Escort cars in India.

With a 26 percent share of the Rs. 2500 crore tractors market and a 70 percent share of the Rs. 1600-crore utility vehicles market, M & M has not only secured market leadership, but has also succeeded in consolidating its bottom line over the years.

M & M is not trying to fix anything that isn't broke. It is merely cementing the cracks in its shop floor that could become the chasms into which it could tumble tomorrow. Despite its prime position, the M & M - mobile is actually a bureaucratic, flabby and inefficient manufacturer that guzzles costs and throttles margins. But until the early 1990s, M & M didn't care because **it didn't know what competition was.**

Raw materials costs at M & M have risen from 45 percent of its operating costs in 1993-94 to 57 percent in 1994-95. Labour costs account for almost 12 percent of the total, and at **eight vehicles per worker per annum.**" M & M has one of the lowest productivity ratios in the automobile industry in the world" according to its managing director R.K. Pitamber who is 63. In contrast to M & M, Maruti Udyog's productivity was 60 vehicles per employee per year.

The low labour productivity is dangerous to M & M because of competition from their archrival Telco (the Sierra, the Estate and the Sumo) and Bajaj (Tempo Trax) who are muscling into the utility vehicles market. And M & M's market share has actually fallen from 76 percent in 1992-93 to 70 percent in 1994-95.

Anand Mahindra, deputy managing director admits "we were aware that there was growing vulnerability within M & M, especially in manufacturing". According to K.J. Devasia (president and executive director of tractors division) of M & M "we are following expensive and inefficient ways of production. We figured that to stop or we wouldn't be able to survive".

Suspecting the need for outside help to solve its problem, M & M went scouting for a consultant. By late 1993, M & M had found the driver and the vehicle for change: the UK based Lucas Engineering and Systems was brought in to implement what is code named as **"Mahindra Top Gear Programme"**, with the aim to boost productivity by 50 percent in a year.

For starters, M & M's twin-factory complex at Kandivli, a suburb of Bombay, is being **retooled** while its other factories at Nashik and Igatpuri in Maharastra will soon follow. The first thing of course, has been **retraining,** in India and abroad, starting with Pitamber and going down to every worker. "I feel that our people are most enthusiastic about what we are going through" says Keshub Mahindra.

Change has slowly started sweeping across M & M's shop floors, where the writing is literally on the wall. Placards and signs loudly hector the virtues of M & M's new manufacturing systems every where and the employee morale is high. Alan Durante, 55, president and executive director (automotive division) M & M says "This is only the beginning, we have a long way to go".

There are several lessons that corporate India can learn from M & M today as it tries to rebuild its factories. Especially since M & M's new production systems are a synthesis of the best practices on three continents.

What, then, are the **six principles of manufacturing management** that can be learnt from the shop floors - and the board rooms - of M & M?

These are:

(i) Build Product Units
(ii) Create Cellular Systems
(iii) Deploy Flexible Processes
(iv) Try to Cut Cycle Times
(v) Customerise Your Shop Floors
(vi) Let Your Workers Own the Factory.

These six principles are briefly presented in the following sections:

(i) Build product units

Take a walk between the yellow lines on your shop floor and ask yourself the following three questions:

(i) Does the factory flow **linearly** or do your men, materials and methods keep doubling up?
(ii) Does the structure encourage or hamper work flows?
(iii) Do you see cohesion, confusion or chaos around you?

If the answer to even one of these is not clear, your shop floor is a doodle. This was exactly the situation at M & M.

When the top management team at M & M looked down at the bays of M & M's tractors and automotives factory at Kandivli, it realised that even they were actually laid out with all the subtlety of a snarled piece of knitting, over the decades the various segments had been scattered over 40 acres of land with **little rationality in the linkages**. For instance, the transmissions machining unit and the engine machining unit had been clubbed together while the transmissions gear assembly and subassemblies were on the other side of a field. And every bit of spare space was being haphazardly used as a dump for tractors, tyres and components. "It was a classic **functional layout**, which had itself gone awry" says Ashok Pai, 35, module manager (engine product unit) M & M.

The situation was no better in the automobiles plant as well. The machine shop where automobile components were manufactured and the assembly shop where these components were assembled into subunits were separated by a 20 feet wide road. According to HB Deasi, 50, general manager (reengineering) M & M. "The lack of a structural design had led to long lead times, poor material flows, inefficient space utilisation and low productivity." "The quality was poor. Since similar operations were clubbed together, there was little focus on the products that each shop floor produced" says Vijay Dhongde, 41, manager (manufacturing systems design) M & M.

So M & M decided to evolve a **new layout** for its production units, based on the **product unit structure**: each facility would be relaid in a fashion that allowed it to manufacture a single, homogeneous group of components that went straight into the final assembly line.

The fresh blue print for the tractors factory streamlined its operations into three product units: *(i)* **the transmissions,** *(ii)* **engine** and *(iii)* **final assembly**.

Likewise at the automotives plant, M & M has broken its operations into six product units: *(i)* **chassis,** *(ii)* **axle,** *(iii)* **engine,** *(iv)* **transmission,** *(v)* **body** and *(vi)* **final product**.

Desai explains "If we classify our main components as products, there is bound to be a focus on the quality".

Within each unit, production modules have been created for sequential work patterns. Two or more cells form a module and within each module, cells are grouped in such a way that they are aligned with the logical work process sequence. *For example,* the transmission case cell, the transmission case cover cell, and the gear lever forks and shafts cell form one module. And three or four such modules constitute a product unit.

One immediate benefit is that the movement of materials is far more disciplined. Vinay Devrath, 41, a senior consultant at process engineering, the Pune-based manufacturing consultancy, says "once you focus on products and not parts or components - your production system will immediately spring to life". At M & M, production is expected to increase by 60 percent per annum over the next five years because of the new structure.

(ii) Create Cellular Systems

If any component used in the manufacture of a product is being pulled round and round the shop floor, and gathering dust several times a day, then the manufacturing systems are not cellular.

M & M's A-team found that at all its four factories, every component visited the same shop several times, travelled upto 1-5 km and frequently came to dead halt. According to the team, M & M was losing about 1000 man-hours a year per worker because of the time wasted in the transportation of components. This amounts to three hours a day. This would lower M & M's employee productivity.

M & M decided to discontinue function-based manufacturing under which factories were broken up into a number of shops, each of which specialised in a particular task. *For example,* in function-based manufacturing, a crank shaft would be going through a cumbersome machining process: from the central stores the raw component would travel to the cutting shop, to the lathe, to the milling, drilling and grinding shops and finally to the polishing and honing shops before being stored in an intermediate store prior to the final assembly.

In the cellular manufacturing system introduced by M & M, the plant has been broken into a number of cells. A cell is defined as the smallest building block of a factory. It consists of a natural group of machines and people to complete a task.

The steps in the process of completing the task need not be sequential but follow a natural order. The cellular manufacturing system was invented by Toyota and is the key to the success of the Japanese automobile companies.

Since the parts processed by a cellular manufacturing system flow continuously from one operation to another in each cell - either one or a few at a time - the amount of time that elapses between the start of the first and last operations is approximately the same as the processing plus handling time for one piece. This is the reason for reduction of production time by 50 percent in cellular than in functionally organised factory.

So shop floors at M & M's Kandivili plant are being divided into 80 cells with each cell being responsible for completing one process. *For example*, the new jeep axles product unit is divided into 10 cells, which undertake all the functions needed to make them. At one end, the raw component enters and finished axles come out of the other end of the product unit.

Cell manufacturing promotes team work and thereby the workers are becoming more motivated. By March 1996, in the first year of its implementation, the company plans to reduce idle man-hours by half, reduce its inventory costs by Rs. 50 crores and boost employee productivity by 60 percent.

(iii) Deploy Flexible Processes

At M & M, it was found that production units were as rigid as rigormortis and that didn't come as a surprise. For, it manufactures seven basic models of utility vehicles which are classified by engine and transmission, at four different locations. While the Kandivli plant produces MDI 2500A, the direct injection diesel engines and the Peugeot XDP 4.90 four speed engines are produced at Igatipure plant, the commander 650 vehicle which uses the former engine and the Armada which needs the latter engine, are both assembled at Nashik.

While the commander-650 is also produced at Kandivli, so is the CL-340 short-chassis jeep. This interlocking grid of dependence also meant that if one factory ran into a glitter, the M & M machine would grind to a dead halt all across the country. Also the productivity levels at any one plant can not be pushed up unless the backward linkages were cranked up too.

The key to the future is a **flexible manufacturing system (FMS)**. Flexible manufacturing would allow M & M to use all their factories as complete production units. FMS allows M & M switch between manufacturing different products, or event different product lines without losing anytime while doing so.

FMS not only optimises resources but also boosts production. "The concept of sticking to the manufacture of only one kind of product is going out. Each manufacturing facility will have to start producing diverse and rich mix of products". In otherwords, cells at all the M & M's plants will learn to cope with all the vehicle configurations. The 'U' shaped shop layout in which each cell is laid out lends itself to easy switching between product lines since there is only a single-piece flow.

Critically, workers are being taught to tool, or put together subassemblies for various vehicles without loss of time (multiskilled workers). As a result, the axles unit at the Kandivli factory will soon roll out complete assemblies for the commander 650s and Armada with the same ease as the Nashik plant.

Flexible manufacturing will enable M & M to respond well to customers' requirements. Since the shop floor is broken into the smallest processes and each is managed by a team and the same team could start interacting with suppliers and customers to buy and produce what is required.

(iv) Try to Cut Cyle Times

Once, the time each component took to get processed and assembled - WIP infact - dragged on, at M & Ms factories averaging 20 to 24 days. In the process, costly component-like the shifter fork that is used in the transmission assembly lay idle for almost 65 percent of the time.

Similarly, a drive shaft languished in M & M's store for almost 20 percent of the time it was present in a plant compared to the 15 percent of the total time that was needed to perform operations on it. Hence it is necessary to tackle this is order to cut down time-consuming activities that do not add value and increase product cycle times.

To do this M & M set itself a **stretch target:** bring the high WIP time down to a maximum of four days once the rationalisation was fully under way. Going cellular is critical to the process of paring down WIP. For starters, M & M is abolishing the institution of intermediate stores. That instantly cuts some of the slack as time-wasting cartages from one shop floor to the other are eliminated.

All product units will also ensure that they only clear finished components which will then be shipped to the final assembly line. Cutting cycle times by almost a sixth, will result in huge profits - M & M estimates that it will save upto Rs. 2 crores a years by whipping WIP into shape. Even if there will be an increase in capital expenditure, it will be offset by increase in production and quick switches between products.

(v) Customerise your Shopfloors

If a customer brings a manufacturing defect to the company's notice, and if no part of the production process will be ready to accept the responsibility for it, the problem bounces from one function to another and finally if the customer's grievance is put in the complaints file (the dust bin), then the company would lose the customer and soon the company wouldn't have any customer.

Whenever there was a problem with an M & M tractor or jeep, the system would uncoil slowly. The field services engineer would inform the service manager in the administrative office located near the shop floor. He would in turn, get in touch with the controller of operations who would then intimate the deputy general manager of production.

The latter would notify the department head, who would pass it on to the floor supervisor. The floor supervisor then shout at the machine operator who would reluctantly rectify the production fault. This process would take anything upto 2 weeks. By this, not only would the customers be unhappy, the same thing would happen with the suppliers too.

Recognising that the manufacturing can not remain insulated from the people who actually use its products, customer care is getting a new priority at M & M. Ever since the company has gone cellular, cross-functional teams on each shop floor are now responsible for interacting with customers. These teams are attached to each product unit and supply customer feed back every day.

Increasingly each product unit will also interact with suppliers and customers to get a first-hand feel of the market place that will not only help improve the quality of M & M's suppliers, but also it will make the company more responsive to customer demand. "The supply module and the customer interaction functions are going to play important roles in keeping the company's reaction - mechanism in place" says Anand Mahindra.

(vi) Let your Workers own the factory

Until recently, M & M's workforce consisted of 10,000 workers who didn't care how the wheel moved. There was no team spirit, no motivation, no quality consciousness and certainly no customer focus. Wage settlements were battle grounds between labour unions and management. If the management asked for a 10 percent increase in production, it had to be matched by a 10 percent increase in wages. M & M's management go into all these agreements without looking at what the existing machines and workmen would actually produce.

From the moment M & M began overhauling its systems, it tried to win the workers over. When the company directors and senior general managers went to England for an orientation course on manufacturing management and reengineering at various automobile and auto-component plants, they took with them union leaders like Devram Bosle, 53, the president of M & M's tractor division union and vice president of the Bhartiya Kamgar Sena, the Shiva sena's trade union wing.

Devram Bhosle returned a changed man. For him, the orientation was an eye-opener. He saw factories abroad actually practicing what was being told to him and his workers and producing effectively. The union leaders and the workers who participated in the orientation gave their peers presentation on effective manufacturing.

One concept that is lubricating operations on M & M's shop floors is **ownership**. Each worker understands that he owns the machine he operates and is responsible for its maintenance. (essence of the concept of total productive maintenance approach in total quality management). Moreover, hierarchy on the shop floor is crumbling, which is motivating. The cells function as teams, with the cell-leader at the top and the rest as co-workers.

Every cell which could have as many as 20 workers or as few as three, sets its own targets and reports to the module chief who, in turn will report to the product unit manager. This will reduce the number of hierarchical levels at the factory from the present eight to three in about a year's time: the product unit manager, supervisors and workers in the cells and modules. Soon, each cell will have its own office, which will consist of lockers for the workers, a conference table and an IBM. AS/400 terminal which will be a node to M & M's national network. Devasia says "If there is a problem in one machine, it affects everybody because the productivity of each worker and work station must be high. That is why ownership and employment are important".

To be sure, it is going to be a long and bumpy ride before M & M's new manufacturing systems drive home. Mahindra has set the company an ambitious mission: to become one of the largest global producers of tractors and a leader in the automotive business. "If M & M is successful in addressing technology upgradation and finance too, it could stand a chance of staking a claim in the global market place" says Raj Nair, 40, director, Business Consulting Group.

Like all revolution, this one too is beginning on the shop floor. For, only by involving its manufacturing into top gear today can M & M hope to emerge as a mean machine that will survive tomorrow.

8. THE STORY OF REINVENTION OF TATA STEEL

"The story of Tata Steel example is a model for corporate reinvention for Indian companies. While India has made significant strides in the software industry, on a global scale, the ascent of an 'old world' manufacturing company, Tata Steel, into a global leadership position through corporate entrepreneurship provides significant lessons for struggling large Indian Companies."

- By Dr. D.V. Sheshadri and Dr. Arabinda Tripathy

It is interesting to note that rather than becoming complacent with the success already achieved through a decade of reinvention, the company has acquired increasing appetite for scaling even greater heights over the next several years. This is truly the case of success breeding desire for more success, and appears to be the most appropriate response of the company in the era of hyper-competition that companies of the world find themselves in today. The mechanism the company has chosen to retain its leadership position is through unleashing the innovation potential of its human resources across the entire organization.

Wakeup call

During the mid-eighties, Dr. Irani told Mr. J.R.D. Tata, the company's then chairman, that if we do not modernize the plant, we might soon turn it into a steel industry museum and stand at the gates selling tickets, and saying, 'Come and see the steel museum.' In fact, according to Dr. Irani, the company knew as early as the mid-eighties, that the old ways of doing things would no longer be relevant. It was apparent that one day the company would have to face international competition. He was part of a high-level delegation to Japan in 1988, to learn what the Japanese had achieved through TQM. One glimpse, and he was convinced that his company had a long way to go and that there was no time to waste. In this sense the trip to Japan was a defining moment for the company and came as a wake-up call. The company was uncompetitive, burdened with an old plant, huge workforce and many costs that were totally unacceptable.

Launch of business excellence: focus on quality and the customer

Despite the spectacular on-going implementation of modernization and resulting success, the management did not rest. While modernization was in progress, the company embarked on a series of steps, during the mid-nineties, to better manage its resources, expenses, and assets; streamline the company's cost structure; and aspire to become among the top steel producers in the world. A core team, comprising fifteen carefully selected people from different parts of the plant, was formed to drive the quality initiative in the company, with the chief executive in the driver's seat. This group reports directly to the chief executive, and its office is located in close proximity to the managing director's (MD's) office. The team was trained in Japan, and these engineers became trainers within the company, to drive the process. They were then let loose in the company and given full authority. This group is now called the 'Business Excellence' (BE) group. Tata Steel now has one of the best BE groups among steel-makers in the world.

Demonstrating personal commitment by the top management

More than the use of tools and techniques, Tata Steel's journey to international competitiveness had much to do with the personal commitment and change oriented leadership of its top management, through focus on the 3Cs: Change ("mutate and improve furiously"), Costs ("Cut wasteful expenditure ruthlessly") and Customers ("strive relentlessly to build relationships and influence consumption"). There was also a clear strategy in place, and strong mechanisms to foster accountability at every level in the company. The mechanism to achieve strategy focus, translate strategy into action and have a strong tie-in at every level, from the grass-root level all the way up to the company's vision, was achieved through the extensive deployment of the Balanced Scorecard.

Dr. Irani's checklist for driving change

1. Lead the change process and take personal ownership; the responsibility cannot be delegated.
2. Play role model and be the first to change; personal involvement and investment of time by the chief executive is the key to success.
3. Create endless opportunities for two-way communication within the company
4. Create a sense of urgency, but do not panic
5. Embrace change even when it does not appear necessary.
6. Set up a small hand-picked group to drive change in the organization; train and empower them.
7. Set key result areas (KRAs) carefully; include themselves (the top management) in it (in TISCO this is done through the MD's Balanced Scorecard). This means that the managing director puts himself/herself on the credibility test by including himself/herself in the accountability process.

Cultural transformation

An important part of these initiatives was getting the labor unions to buy-in

Since these initiatives potentially touch the working of every employee, it was important to carry every one. This mental transformation has come about from a sense of urgency and the willingness of the top management to subject itself to discipline and scrutiny. TISCO relies heavily on the balanced scorecard, the performance management and strategy deployment method, developed by Harvard Professor Robert Kaplan and Consultant David Norton to break down strategy to its component elements and track performance from top to bottom, including the performance of the managing director.

What is refreshingly unique about TISCO's implementation of this concept is the willingness of the top management to create total transparency of the whole process. The MD's balanced scorecard is on prominent display in the form of huge billboards at various important locations in the company. A similar culture prevails at other levels, such as at EIC (Executive-in-charge) and at Department levels. The balanced scorecards of these executive, which is derived from the MD's balanced scorecard, is displayed prominently in the respective divisions/departments. EIC is a top management designation in the company, after the MD and Deputy MDs.

Business excellence model

Having put the company on the course of being the best in class in technology and hardware in the early nineties, through a very ambitious facilities modernization program, it was imperative for Tata Steel to simultaneously address itself to the creation and expansion of a new kind of an asset base – the intellectual asset. As a first measure, the company created a strong quality movement across the organization. Most of the divisions attained either an ISO certification or an equivalent internal certification.

The most significant event in the quest for business excellence was the adoption of the JRDQV as a barometer for achieving business excellence. The JRDQV has also synonymously been refereed to as the Tata Business Excellence Model. This is an award for excellence of the organization as a whole, through the JRDQV process administered by the Tata group. It leads to JRD Tata Quality Value Total Quality Award. The JRDQV is a tribute to the visionary chairman of the group, Mr. JRD Tata, who passed away in 1993.

The JRDQV was fashioned on the lines of the prestigious Malcolm Baldrigde model of USA. Any company that follows and obtains a score of over 600 points on the Baldridge model is sure to be one of the world's topmost companies in its field. The model assesses a company on seven criteria – leadership, strategic planning, customer and market focus, information and analysis, human resource focus, process management and business results. The progress of TISCO can be seen from the JRDQV scores of 587,616 and 643 during 1999,2000 and 2001 respectively. In 2000, TISCO was the only Tata group company to qualify for the JRDQV award, achieving 616 points, and continues to be the only company of the group to cross 600 points.

Tata Steel has successfully made the transition from operating in a totally sellers' market prior to liberalization, to a highly customer friendly attitude, supported by extensive usage of IT tools. "It is an issue of leadership and motivating people," is what Mr. B. Muthuraman, Managing Director since 2002, has to say of the spectacular turnaround of the company, from its gloomy days of the early 1990's and late 1980's.

Results

Based on all these efforts, by January 2002, the company has achieved a preeminent position, moving into the top slot among world steel manufacturers. The company had successfully completed an ambitious modernization program, implemented the Cold Rolling Mill project in world record time and cost, right-sized its headcount from about 80,000 employees in 1990 to about 40,000 at present. The company made record profits last year (2000-2001), and this will be even bettered the current year (2002-2003).

Efforts to improve operating yields, efficiencies and costs; quality initiatives; improvement efforts; etc.; have continued with unabated intensity. The continuing sense of urgency in the minds of the employees has been strongly inculcated. The result is that the company has become much better prepared to face the future with renewed confidence. There have been major cultural shifts during the last fifteen years. There is more willingness to share knowledge. The knowledge Management community has significantly evolved. There is a vibrant knowledge management site in the company. Tata Steel's knowledge Management initiative is among the best being practiced by Indian companies.

We have examined the vital role played by corporate entrepreneurship, in the reinvention of Tata Steel, from a precarious strategic inflection point that the company found itself in during the early 1990's, to emerge over the last few years, on the top of the list of world steel makers. The journey that the company has made over the last decade has been long and arduous. It was possible only by the single-minded focus of the top management to develop a clear strategy, whose major ingredient was corporate entrepreneurship, and relentlessly drive the process with clarity, sense of purpose and discipline. The Tata Steel story of reinvention is a corroboration of the book by Gerstner, Jr. that indeed Elephants can Dance! Indeed it is not therefore surprising that the period of return to their past glories for both IBM and Tata Steel (early 1990's to 2002) is identical.

Dr. D.V. Seshadri and Dr. Arabinda Tripathy are faculties at IIM Bangalore & IIM Ahmadabad respectively. The article is an abstract of the paper presented at the 3rd International Conference on Entrepreneurial Innovation, March 2003.

(Source: "Management Next"- Jan.2004 Issue)

APPENDIX C

CASELETS

Caselet 1: Excellence Program at Milliken and Company

Millken & Company – This textile manufacturer headquartered in Spartanburg, South Carolina, produces over 48,000 textile and chemical products. In 1981, Milliken initiated its pursuit of Excellence Program to create an overall commitment to customer satisfaction at all levels of the organization. As part of the program. Milliken reduced the number of management levels and dispersed authority throughout the company. Some 14,300 associates (employees) were reorganized into self-managed teams. The teams were formed to address business challenges and to respond to customer needs. Milliken's investment in training is substantial: approximately $1300 per associate in 1988. The company believes that the investment was worthwhile. The percentage of on time deliveries increased from 75 percent in 1984 to an industry- leading 99 percent in 1988. The price of nonconformance has been reduced by 60 percent. Because of these improvements, Milliken has made significant inroads into the Japanese and Korean auto- manufacturing markets.

Questions

1. Discuss the role of self-managed teams in the pursuit of "Excellence Program" at Milliken & Co.
2. List the benefits achieved by Milliken by implementing the "Excellence Program"

Caselet 2: Quality Improvement Program at Motorola

This electronics manufacturer, headquartered in Schaumburg, Illinois, initiated its quality improvement program because of fierce competition from the Japanese. In 1981, Motorola set a goal to improve the quality of its products and services tenfold within five years. In 1987, after having achieved its initial goal, Motorola set two additional goals. One was to improve its quality tenfold within two years: the second was to improve quality one-hundredfold within four years. To each Motorola invested $170 million in training between 1983 and 1987. Data from employees, customer surveys, complaint hotlines, and other sources are used in quality improvement and product development efforts. The price of nonconformance has been reduced from 13 percent to 8 percent of annual revenues over the last three years, a savings of approximately $480 million. Motorola has also made significant inroads into foreign markets. In some markets, Motorola products enjoy a major share.

Questions

1. What goals did Motorola set as a part of its quality improvement program?
2. How did Motorola achieve these goals?
3. What benefits did Motorola achieve?

Caselet 3: Quality Improvement Program at Globe Metallurgical Inc

This metal- alloys manufacturer, headquartered in Ohio, initiated its quality improvement program in 1985. Faced with increasing amounts of lower-cost imports, Globe developed its program with one goal in mind: to become the standard of excellence in the metals industry. The quality program was based on three factors: quality, efficiency, and cost. Using computer-controlled systems and statistical process control, Global monitors every aspect of the manufacturing process. In addition, quality committees were formed at every level of the organization to improve inter level communication, determine source of uncontrollable lapses in quality, review corrective actions, evaluate suggestions from quality circles, and address other quality-related issues. The results of these efforts are impressive: worker productivity has increased, over 50 percent in some areas. Furnace productivity has also increased, reducing energy consumptions. Customers complaints have decreased significantly as well.

Questions

1. What goal did Globe Metallurgical Inc set in its quality improvement program?
2. How did Globe Metallurgical Inc achieve its goal?
3. What were the results of its quality improvement program?

Caselet 4: Values and Quality in Japan

"We have focused on individuals, yet there are some dramatic examples of changes for entire nations that have come from conscious application of values. "As a young Japanese business man visiting the West in the 1950 s, Akio Morita was deeply humiliated to learn that "Made in Japan" was an international synonym for shoddiness, a phrase that produced jokes. Morita retuned to Japan determined to change that, and as chief executive of Sony, he is one of the business leaders who have made that determination a reality. Over the past thirty years, Morita says "We have been striving to be the Picassos and Beethovens of electronics. Is this as good as the ones made in Japan?"

Questions

1. In your opinion, how did Japan become the world's leading producer of consumer electronics products?
2. What will the United States have to do to regain its leadership in this critical market?

Caselet 5: "A Supplier-Buyer Partnership That Works"

F.W. Precision Machining supplies aluminium consoles for various types of electronic measuring devices used in hospitals and clinics. The devices are manufactured by Health care Electronics Inc. During the awareness stage of the development of their supplier-buyer partnership, both companies agreed to allow teams to visit their production facilities to identify cost-cutting strategies. A team of managers and employees from F.W. Precision Machining spent a week in the production facility of Health Care Electronics observing how their consoles were used and talking to production personnel. At the same time, a team from Health Care Electronics visited F.W.Precision Machining.

F.W. Precision Machining personnel discovered that two simple design changes in its consoles would allow Health Care Electronics Personnel to eliminate two whole steps in their assembly process. Correspondingly, Health Care Electronics Personnel found that F.W. Precision Machining was spending an inordinate amount of time achieving a surface finish on a part of its consoles that did not require such a finish. In all the two teams were able to identify ways to cut costs by 15%.

Questions

1. Have you ever thought "I wish they would have asked me" about some design features in an automobile or a piece of electronic equipment?
2. Do you see any advantage to be gained by asking for customer input before manufacturing a product?

Caselet 6: What The CEO of Lego Should do?

The CEO of Lego, a toy manufacturing company is worried that the annual toy fair is right round the corner and news papers and magazines around the world are publishing their lists of the most successful toys of last year and their predictions of what will be hot next year. The CEO very well knows that none of his company's products will be on any of them. Founded nearly 70 years ago by the CEO's grand father, Lego has a long history in the toy industry, but it can't seem to keep up with today's kids' thirst for so called interactive toys.

Technically, Legos are interactive, but nowadays that means battery-operated, software-driven, and "done-for-you" rather than "do-it-yourself". Today's children grew up in an entertainment saturated environment, and open-ended, self-guided play is fading into a nostalgic memory.

The Lego name was created in 1934 by a Danish toy maker who introduced the first plastic Lego brick in 1949. His son then designed an entire system of play around the bricks in the mid 1950's. Since these revolutionary moments, the only real innovation at Lego has been the introduction of themed sets, like towns, farms and space stations, which didn't start until 1970's. Not even the formula for making the plastic bricks has changed since then!

The only thing brighter and more enduring than Lego's vividly coloured blocks is the company's core value of inspiring and nurturing creativity and play. An extension of this is Lego's refusal to produce any toy that resembles a modern day weapon. These admirable values however don't seem to be helping the company succeed. Lego hasn't had a toy on the list of the top 20 US sellers in the last seven years and this year doesn't look to be any different.

Lego is the seventh most powerful worldwide brand among families, behind giants such as Coca-Cola, and Disney; but Lego hasn't changed the way kids play; let alone the way they learn, for a long time.

Questions

1. Can Lego be that kind of leader again and if so how?
2. Will the CEO have to change his company values and management or just his products?
3. What are the risks of not changing?

Caselet 7: Excellence in Product Quality at Commercial Nuclear Fuel Division of Westing house

The CNFD of Westing house realized early on that future business success depended on excellence in product quality. That is why the division set a goal to become the world's most efficient supplier of nuclear fuel. To reach its goal, the division adopted the total quality approach, based on four key imperatives: management leadership, product and process leadership, human resource excellence, and customer satisfaction. Employees monitor over 60 performance areas using statistical techniques. This information is used to set future goals. In the past three years, approximately 90 percent of the CNFD employees have received training. These efforts at improving quality have paid off for Westing house. The CNFD's on-time delivery rate now stands at 100 percent, and the fuel reliability performance rate at 99.995 percent. Quality improvements have enabled the CNFD to achieve a 40 percent U.S. and 20 percent worldwide market share. It is interesting to note that not one of these award-winning companies provided precise figures for either the costs or benefits of their quality programs. This is true for other winners, such as Cadillac and Xerox, as well, underscoring the difficulty that even the very best American manufacturers experience when trying to quantify the effect that improved quality has on financial performance.

Questions

1. What goal did the Commercial Nuclear Fuel Division (CNFD) of Westinghouse set to achieve excellence in product quality?
2. How did CNFD achieve its goal?
3. What benefits did CNFD achieve through its quality improvement program?

Caselet 8: "The Ritz Means Quality"

The Atlanta-based Ritz-Carlton Hotel Corporation operates 23 luxury hotels in the United States and two in Australia. The hotel chain, which employs 11,500 people, claims distinctive facilities and an unusual environment, highly personalized services, and exceptional food and beverages. With average room rates higher than $150 per night, Ritz-Carlton realized it must do more than just please its customers in order to succeed. The hotel, known simply as "The Ritz, "did what many experts thought no hotel chain could accomplish: In 1992, the Ritz became the first hotel to win the coveted Malcolm Baldrige National Quality Award.

While the name "Ritz" has been synonymous with quality for years, the luxury hotel chain did not actively begin its quest for total quality management until 1989. It was then that Horst Schulze, Ritz President and CEO, told senior managers that he was not satisfied with hotel quality. He believed that the only reason the chain was considered the leading luxury hotel in the industry was that everyone else was even more unsatisfactory. Schulze therefore introduced a total quality initiative grounded in participatory executive leadership, thorough information gathering, and coordinated planning and execution. A trained, empowered, and committed workforce was another essential element. All employees learn the company's "Gold Standards" -the Ritz's minimum set of standards or premium service.

Schulze and a team of the chain's 14 top executives form the senior management quality team, which meets weekly to review performance and set standards. "They spend a lot of time working on ways to improve our product by talking to as many guests and employees as possible, "reported corporate director of quality Patrick Mene."

Ritz-Carlton carefully selects and trains its employees to be quality engineers capable of spotting defects and immediately correcting them. Employees receive 126 hours of annual training on quality issues. Ritz management believes that high-quality personnel reduce costs because they do the job right the first time. The company reinforces its employee improvement program by recognizing superior individual performance. Annual raises are tied to the individual's level of performance, and work teams share in bonus pools when solutions they recommend for quality issues are successfully implemented.

Management empowers employees to "move heaven and earth" to satisfy customer needs without waiting for management direction. The Ritz gathers quality data on all aspects of a guest's stay to determine if the customer's expectations are being met. The chain surveys more than 25,000 guests each year to determine where improvements are necessary. Ritz computers maintain data on the likes and dislikes of more than 240,000 repeat customers.

Ritz-Carlton won 121 quality-related awards in 1991, and earned the industry – best ranking by all. A customer enjoys the peace and beauty of a Ritz – Carlton lobby. The 1992 Baldrige Award told Ritz customers and employees what they already knew-the Ritz means quality.

Questions

1. Why the CEO of Ritz Carlton hotel was not satisfied with the quality of his hotel?
2. Discuss the features of the total quality initiative introduced by the CEO.
3. Discuss the approach adopted by the 'Ritz' to do more than just please its customers in order to succeed.
4. How did "Ritz-Carlton" justify its image. "Ritz means quality".

Caselet 9: Business Process Reengineering at Escorts

Escorts Construction Equipment Limited (ECEL) set up at Faridabad has around 500 employees of which 300 are members of labour unions of the company. ECEL belongs to Escorts group which has 12 plants employing around 15,000 people. Escorts Tractor Plant which employs around 200 employees is located in the same premises along with ECEL.

ECEL had a need to acquire and adopt new technologies which necessitated ECEL to take up business process and performance reengineering. Reengineering was defined as a process need for a quantum improvement in the level, methods and quality of the operations at ECEL. ECEL hired the services of a UK based consulting firm for reengineering its manufacturing processes. ECEL realised that changing the attitudes, work practices and making the employees accept change in role-set were the most difficult part of the entire process of BPRE. This difficulty was augmented by the fact that ECEL belongs to a big group with various plants located in the same locality and sharing almost same values, ethos, work culture and work practices.

The environment of ECEL consists of technology, customer base, government, information technology, media association - all in a state of flux and demanding changes. Hence there was a need for transition from a functional organisation to a process-oriented organisation. For this, the employees have to accept multi-skill mode of function including some menial jobs such as carrying materials, tools, filling oil, water etc.

Since the workers were not developed and business information was not being shared with them by managers, the workers had developed attitudes against the management, with perceptions that management has interests which are detrimental to interest of employees and workers must fight against the management for their rights. This kind of situation was discouraging for BPRE because worker's involvement is very crucial for its success. Hence this management had to deal with issues like trust, commitment, skill, attitude and values concerning employees. To do this, the following actions were taken.

(i) Introduction of extensive communication exercises. This included extensive sharing of ideas, information and facilities between management and employees.

(ii) Focusing on a set of commonly shared values through communication sessions and at individual levels.

(iii) Transparency in all the processes of implementation.

(iv) Mindset change programmes carried out for every employee.

(v) Multi skill approach training was provided for 8 to 45 days' durations.

(vi) Skill inventory analysis was carried out and training was provided to develop additional skills.

These processes motivated workmen to such an extent that they started demanding for multi skill training to be imparted to them.

Questions

1. Give reasons for ECEL to take up BPRE.
2. Discuss the issues that ECEL identified as those needed attention.
3. Describe the planning done by ECEL for introducing BPRE. What results did it achieve?

Caselet 10: Quick Response Apparel

Imagine walking into store and ordering clothing manufactured to your size and specifications. This phenomenon called "apparel on demand" is an extension of JIT linking retailers and manufacturers for a just-in-time responsiveness. With this response, retailers can send their point-of-sale information directly to the factory floor to minimize lead-time. Clothing is delivered to the purchaser through normal retail channels. "Custom Clothing Corporation" (CCC) is making reasonably priced jeans for women. This "apparel-on-demand" concept could result in 30% production savings. It also reduces the need for inventory and discount sales of slow moving items. CCC was launched by S.K. Jain who feels women will pay Rs.500 price for a pair of jeans guaranteed to fit. Women are electronically measured and select their jeans' style in stores contracting with CCC's JIT service. The jeans are shipped to the customer in less than two weeks. The current market for women's jeans is Rs.2 crores; so S.K. Jain feels this is a great market to test JIT jeans.

Questions

1. If you were a traditional retailer, selling jeans, would you think this new trend will succeed? Do you think customers will be willing to wait two weeks for product delivery?
2. How can CCC compete with other ready-made garment retailers selling jeans off-she-shelf?

APPENDIX D

CASE EXERCISES

Case 1: Toyota's Kaizen Experiences

Abstract: The case looks at how Kaizen was adopted by Toyota Motor Corporation to improve productivity and efficiency in its production systems. The case examines in detail the labour crisis faced by Toyota in the early 1990s and how the company used Kaizen to modify its assembly line and wage systems in order to make them human friendly. The case also details the concept of Kaizen and the prerequisites for its successful implementation in the organisation.

Background: Toyota's history goes back to 1897, when Sakichi Toyoda diversified into the hand loom machinery business from his family traditional business of carpentry. He founded Toyota Automatic Loom Works (TALW) in 1926 for manufacturing automatic looms. Sakichi invented a loom that stopped automatically when any of the threads snapped.

This concept of designing equipment to stop so that defects could be fixed immediately formed the basis of the Toyota Production System (TPS) that went on to become a major factor in the company's success.

In 1933, Sakichi established an automobile department within TALW and the first passenger car prototype was developed in 1935.

Sakichi's son Kiichiro Toyoda convinced him to enter the automobile business. After this the production of Model AA began and Toyota Motor Corporation was established in 1937. Kiichiro visited the Ford Motor Company in Detroit, USA to study the US automotive industry.

He observed that an average US worker's production was nine times that of a Japanese Worker. He realised that the productivity of the Japanese automobile industry had to be increased if it were to compete globally.

Back in Japan, Kiichiro customised the Ford production system to suit Japanese market. He also devised a system wherein each process in the assembly line of production would produce only the number of parts needed at the next step on the production line, which made logistics management easier as material was procured according to consumption. This system was referred to as "Just-In-Time" (JIT) within the Toyota Group.

The JIT production was defined as "Producing only required units in a required quantity at a required time resulting in decreased excess inventories and excess workforces, thereby increasing productivity"

Kiichiro realized that by relying solely on the central planning approach, it would by very difficult to implement JIT in all the processes for automobile manufacture.

Hence, TPS followed the production flow conversely. People working in one process went to the preceding one to withdraw required units in the required quantities at the required time. This resulted in the preceding process producing only quantities of units to replace those that had been withdrawn.

When Kaizen is applied to the workplace, it means continuous improvement for managers and workers. Thus Kaizen involves everyone in an organisation to make improvements without large capital investments. It can be seen as a culture of continuous sustained improvement focusing on eliminating waste in all systems and processes. The Kaizen strategy begins and ends with people. With Kaizen, an involved leadership guides people continuously to improve their abilities to meet high quality expectations, low cost and on-time delivery, which in-turn helps the organisation gain a competition edge.

The Modification: The modification began with the management deciding to allow plants to set their own annual production efficiency targets. The production divisions council, which checked the plant's objectives occasionally modifying them, taking into account the company's profit targets, replaced the production allowance councils. After approval, these objectives became the Kaizen norm of each plant in terms of production efficiency. The method of determining the production efficiency was altered to make it less constrained as the standard time was fixed by measuring the time really acquired for worker's operations whereas earlier standard time was fixed on the basis of the best time marked in the past.

Salient Features of TPS:

Two key concepts used in Toyota Production System (TPS) were: 1. 'Just-in-time' and 2. Autonomation.

'Just-in-time' has the objective of producing the necessary units in the quantities needed at the time they were needed. Autonomation is a word coined by Toyota that means 'autonomous defects control' i.e. "worker-controlled quality control".

The principles involved in TPs are:

(i) Reduced set up times *(ii)* Small-lot production *(iii)* Employee involvement and empowerment *(iv)* Quality at the source *(v)* Equipment maintenance *(vi)* Pull production *(vii)* Supplier involvement *(viii)* Flexible resources *(ix)* Cellular layouts and *(x)* Uniform production levels.

Questions:

1. Discuss the concept of Kaizen and the prerequisites for its implementation in an organisation.
2. Explain how Toyota Motor Company implemented Kaizen and achieved competitive edge in the automobile industry.
3. Briefly discuss how the ten principles mentioned in the case can improve productivity of an organisation.

Case 2: General Motors Suffers from International Competition and Demanding Customers

Few companies have responded as slowly to global competition and paid such a steep price, as General Motors. Perhaps the world's largest industrial organisation had grown too big and too inwardly focused for it to be responsive to a changed world.

In the early 1980s both Ford and Chrysler suffered huge losses and restructured themselves to become more responsive to customers. Their increased customer responsiveness yielded increased profitability.

Despite intense Japanese competition and in roads in the North American car market, GM delayed its restructuring until it had realized some staggering losses. GM lost $ 2 billion in 1990, over $ 4 billion in 1991 and $ 23.5 billion in 1992. The loss in 1992 was the largest loss ever reported by a Fortune 500 company. The losses at GM were so severe that ratings on its financial debt were downgraded by the debt-rating agencies.

In terms both profitability and growth in sales, GM trailed competitors in the 1987-1991 period. After considering inflation, GM's sales growth was flat in the five-year period.

GM's miserable profitability and sales growth performance were reflected in customer satisfaction and market share data in the 1992 J.D Power Customer Satisfaction survey, only one GM car, the 'Saturn', placed in the top five. Of the top-selling cars for the first half of 1992, the top selling GM car was in the fifth position, behind the higher sales of Honda Accord, Ford Taurus, Toyota Camry, and Ford Escort.

Not only were Ford, Honda and Toyota beating GM in terms of the most popular individual models, but GM's North American market share had been in a persistent slide for over a decade. GM's market share slid from 44.5 percent in 1982 to near 35 percent in 1993.

Associated with GM's poor market share and profitability data are the successes of the Japanese automakers. In the 1960s and early 1970s, a "Made in Japan" automobile was synonymous with poor quality. By continuously improving their production processes, quality and products, the Japanese automakers slowly but steadily improved their popularity with US customers who found GM's products lacking. Additionally, some German cars such as the Mercedes and BMW, were selling as high-priced, well-engineered cars.

For a long time GM seemed to ignore the Japanese automakers and continued to pay inadequate attention to customer demands for quality and improved value. Instead, GM focused on its profits and shareholders' demands. GM may have ignored customers too long. When Chryslers and Fords were the only competitors, GM was able to get away with its less than responsive attitude to customers' demands. But the Japanese willingness to meet customers' need for quality and value translated into increased market share and the competitive scene changed dramatically.

Partly because GM thought it "owned" the domestic market, its managers let the firm's costs get out of control. In the early 1990s GM had the dubious honour of being the highest cost producer among the World's major automobile companies. GM paid the highest hourly wages and benefits to its workers while its competitors paid only half of these rates. In trying to control its bloated pay-roll, GM planned to reduce its hourly workforces by nearly 1,50,000 from 1985 to 1995. This has resulted in labour unrest and strikes in late 1992.

In this new era GM faced conflicting demands among its constituencies. Customers demanded high quality cars at reasonable prices which Japanese companies were willing and able to offer in their intense bid for more of the world's car market. The workers of GM affiliated to the United Auto Workers Union demanded job security and above-market wages and benefits. And finally shareholders demanded profits. The world's largest corporation reconciled such conflicting demands by focusing on profits. The short-term financial focus prevented GM from launching the minivan developed in the 1970s and the four-door versions of the GM-10 cars and the Blazer sport utility vehicle.

However, GM began to produce high-quality cars in some of its divisions. 'Saturn' had been started partly to learn how to build small cars that would be responsive to customers' demands for affordable quality.

Cadillac won a Baldrige Quality Award in 1992. the Buick Park Avenue was in the top ten of the J.D Power customer satisfaction survey for quality in 1993.

But the successes were not consistent throughout G.M. In the early 1990s Old-mobile's sales had fallen by 80% from their early 1980s levels. GM still had high costs, inconsistent quality, shrunken market share and a combative union. Ford and Chrysler took automobile market share from the Japanese in 1993.

Many called for the break-up of GM into separate companies – It was maintained that the separate companies would have a better chance of getting close to their customers, providing affordable quality and winning the war with international competitors.

In the early 1990s GM seemed to be caught in a downward spiral. By not consistently concentrating on its customers and thereby defeating the global competitors. GM was risking its future.

Questions:

1. In the era of intense international competition, how important is it for a company to provide affordable quality to customers?
2. What are the roles of management and unions in delivering affordable quality?
3. Discuss the managerial actions that need to be taken at GM for it to regain its former health.
4. Should GM try to sell its car based on a patriotic appeal of "American cars"?

Case 3: The "Toyota Touch" Philosophy

At Toyota, quality is about catering to customers. The business plan is called The Toyota Touch, because it calls for a long-term philosophy placing the customer first. In achieving quality, Toyota pays close attention to the people it brings into the fold. At Toyota Motor Manufacturing Canada, applicants had to demonstrate communication skills, departmental flexibility, and the ability to work in teams and the initiative to seek out weaknesses and improve them. "We wanted people who wanted to do things differently", recalled Bill Taylor, Toyota's vice-president of manufacturing. Experience in the auto industry was not a prerequisite. In fact, Taylor was among the few employees who could claim any such experience.

The plant in Canada is responsible for part of Toyota's success there. It is equipped with up-to-date machinery and is clean and well lit. Local competitors, such as Honda Canada Inc., Hyundai, and Cami Automotive Inc. (a joint venture between GM and Suzuki Motor Co.) do not enjoy the same benefits.

Most important, however, is The Toyota Touch philosophy, which is interwoven into all operations, Decorating the wall are signs such as, "Customer satisfaction starts at the process" and "Customer satisfaction: the heart of our business." "These may be corny values, "remarked Taylor, "but if you believe in them, they pay big dividends."

At Toyota, though, "customer" is a word defined very generally. Managers do not expect initial line workers or be thinking about the end-user all the way down the line. "My customer is the person in front of me", noted line worker Victoria Schumacher. "And I'm the customer of the person before me." This focus on internal customers gives workers a real person to cater to in their own performance.

Respect for co-workers accompanies the attention to the customer. For example, when an error occurs, the line stops and the workers together attempt to fix it. There is no blame -throwing or sulking. "What is significant is what the team does with the problem after the line is stopped," explained Taylor. "No one points a finger at the worker responsible for the problem. Instead the team focuses its energy on the problem. You have to give people room to solve problems themselves. Otherwise you stymie their initiative.

At the same time, Toyota uses errors to the company's benefit through the Japanese process of kaizen, or continuous improvement. "When a team sees a problem, they kaizen [used as a verb by the Canadians] it and come up with a better way to do the job", noted Adriaan Korstanje, manager of public affairs.

Evidence of Kaizen is scattered throughout the Toyota plant. For example, the air-driven tracks from which power tools hang-within workers' comfortable reach – resulted from a worker's suggestion. And it was the company's maintenance team that built the tracks. Workers also came up with the idea for the set of rollers that batteries slide down, making the job easier for the workers who install batteries in cars.

Kaizen has also come in the form of challenges to employees. Unlike other North American auto manufactures, Toyota does not employ a single industrial engineer. Instead, Toyota relies on Toyota employees. In 1990, when the company wanted to increase productivity from 50,000 to 65,000 cars a year, management challenged employees to make it happen. Through kaizen, employees were able to improve processes and reduce total production time by 30 seconds a car, a significant reduction.

The philosophy of Kaizen extends also to the administrative officers. A sense of community exists among the 200 administrative employees, most of whom work in a single open room approximately the six of a gymnasium. "It took some adjustment," commented Bill Easdale, senior vice-president of administration and former vice-president of personnel and industrial relations at de Havilland Aircraft of Canada Ltd. "I came from an organization where the executive offices were big and leather-lined, and had their own washrooms. We had secretaries who watched over or fixed up appointments, here, if people have a question, they just walk up to your desk. It gets a little noisy at times, but I welcome the change.

The biggest difference is that my own productivity has dropped, but the productivity of the people who work with me has gone way up. And that's the way it should be.

At Toyota, quality is not about superficial glamour inside the plant. Rather, it is about the way managers treat employees, co-workers treat one another, and the company treats its customers. It is a way of life.

Questions:

1. What is meant by "The Toyota Touch Philosophy" that was in existence in Toyota's plant in Canada?
2. How was the philosophy of Kaizen implemented at Toyota's Canada plant?
3. "At Toyota, quality is a way of life" Discuss.

Case 4: The New Yorker

The New Yorker has been read by middle to upper-middle class people all over the world and has been relied upon since 1925 to provide a weekly listing of current happenings- concerts, musicals, theatrical events, and guest appearances. It has been renowned for its satirical wit, thoughtful editorials, and cunning cartoons. By the late 1980s, though, the beloved magazine found itself in need of a face-lift. "The New Yorker lost their edge. Asserted Jann Winner, founding editor of Rolling Stone and Men's Journal. "Even the cartoons lost their edge. Dubbed the "old man's magazine" by publishers of competitor magazines, The New Yorker has an aging audience. Readership and subscriptions had slipped, and the number of ad pages had fallen dangerously low: This once-proud prince of upper-scale publications was on the verge of becoming a pauper.

Then came Tina Brown, who stepped in to resuscitate the dying artifact of days gone by. As editor-in-chief of Vanity Fair, Brown was the one responsible for displaying a nude and pregnant Demi Moore on its 1991 cover. When she took the helm at The New Yorker, fear of excessive change and innovation rocked the publishing industry, there was skepticism and concern about the sort of creative marks Brown would leave.

It is true that Brown has earned a reputation for being powerful, ambitious, controlling, and even outrageous. "She is dominating," a former subordinate reported." We were running scared of her. This is not a loveable person. She is acerbic, outspoken and stops at nothing to get her way." But she is also credited with being a shrewd editor with notable flair who does not yield to criticism. Prior to joining The New Yorker, she was recognized for turning around two other magazines: The Tatler, whose circulation she quadrupled, and Vanity Fair, which she transformed into a "hot" magazine. Several years ago when Steven T. Florio, president of The New Yorker, was asked who was the best editor in America, his answer was unequivocal: Tina Brown, then editor of Vanity Fairway? "Because she can put her ear to the tracks and hear the rumble long before the train appears," he remarked.

What rumbles she's heard since coming on board nobody knows: but results seen. Among Brown's more controversial measures was the disappearance of the magazine's enduring symbol, the refined, aristocratic Eustace Tilley, from the February 1994 cover of the annual anniversary issue, which he had previously graced each year. On the cover in his absence-for the first 1925 – what appears to be a barely – recognizable Tilley descendent in a reversed baseball cup and t-shirt. "He's just taking a vacation in his 69th year," explained Brown. "For the 70th anniversary, he'll be back in all his glory."

Overall, Brown's editorial changes constitute what she calls "a pattern of reimaging and recreating The New Yorker while keeping the most important constitute what she calls "a pattern of reimaging and recreating The New Yorker while keeping the most important things intact." Her alterations have encompassed a wide range of areas. For example, she immediately added color and photography to enhance the magazines' visual, aesthetic appeal. In addition, she has contracted with Richard Avedon for provocative portraits of people such as Audrey Hepburn, Rudolf Nureyev, Alger Hiss, and Edward Gorey. Bylines now appear at the start of stories instead of at the end, and departments have been moved, removed, and created. The magazine is now printed on heavier paper, and the print is larger and easier to read. Moreover, Brown has added a new "Letters to The New Yorker" column. "It was the one area I thought was untenable in the magazine's tradition." Brown remarked. "In today's world, a place here people can respond to, can complain to, and take issue with the magazine is very, very important. If readers feel they haven't got that, they become angry and feel that we're arrogant."

According to Brown, the challenge lay in bringing change to the magazine, without losing the qualities that made it "The New Yorker." "The challenge was to modernize", said Brown. "While keeping the franchise and not losing the flavor and value of what made it a great magazine." In addition, it was important to bring the magazine up to date. "[It] had gone from being detached to being aloof, which is different," Brown explained. "In the 80's, The New Yorker didn't do Milken, didn't do Boesky; it kind of ignored the incredible world of the 80's that was there to be written about and where it could have done something to help puncture some of those balloons. Writers were pursuing their own arcane interest to the point where it was really kind of arrogant."

Brown has walked a fine line between making changes that carry on the spirit of the magazine and making changes that threaten to do more than give it a face-lift. According to Brown, though, she has remained within the confines of the The New Yorker tradition. "The New Yorker has always been an evolving, changing magazine," she noted. "I'm using the same writers-Updike, Jane Malcolm- and I've added some new ones. I've tried to make the wonderful articles that were always there accessible. And she is convinced that the audience will stay with her. "The quality is still going to be there: many of the writers they recognize," she said. "They're going to come along with us. All the changes we've made are very much in the spirit [of The New Yorker] and don't violate anything. She claims that she is not concerned about the portion of the audience the magazine appears to have lost. "The people who criticize me are not reading the magazine. They say, oh, I so miss The New Yorker the way it was: the 100,000 words on zinc or the thousand words about the apple vendor. I tell you, those people didn't read it then and they don't read it now." Brown asserted.

Publisher Si Newhouse, Owner of the magazine and the person responsible for bringing Brown on board has placed his complete faith in her. "I think every magazine has to evolve," he commented. "Readers change, times change, interests change. There's no such thing as a static magazine. As for how it should evolve, it's going to be up to Tina. I have no specific agenda as to how to define that evolution."

Change at such a venerable institution as The New Yorker has posed a potential threat to everything-staff, readership, advertising, during the first six months of Brown's reign. However, circulation climbed 20.8% to 758,976 and news-stand sales, always the most important barometer of success more than doubled, from 20,006 to 40,427. In addition, ad pages have jumped 16.7 %. And the number of people who read a single copy has risen by 13 percent to more than 2.8 million. "It's wonderful", related a pleased Florio. "I'm enjoying every minute of it."

A central goal has been to change demographics, to hit a more enduring audience, and that is exactly what Brown is achieving, the average of the magazine's reader has already dropped from 47.7 years in 1992 to 46.1 in 1993, and median household income has risen 13 percent to $61,515.

Behind the scenes, The New Yorker has, for the most part, remained intact. Although the production department now uses Macintosh desktop publishing equipment to do its layout, the offices still reflect the traditional New Yorker culture. Brass portraits of Tilley still adorn the main doors, and office numbers are still stenciled on the white walls in the classic New Yorker "Rea Irvin" typeface. Most staffers have stayed on, with the exception of about 16, including Washington correspondent Elizabeth Drew, pop critic Elizabeth Wurtzel, and writers Stan Sesser and Ray Bonner.

According to Brown, the transition has gone smoothly. But it has not been without conflict. "I left because I love The New Yorker and because she is the wrong person to edit it," asserted Garrison Keillor. "I didn't want to be on the premises to watch it suffer under her hand."

Today, Brown's New Yorker is in many ways more relaxed. Standards have been loosened to enable the magazine to reach new heights. According to Eleanor Gould, the 78-year-old grammarian and copy editor and long-time New Yorker staff member, the most obvious change has been in language. Before Brown, obscenity and even slang were extremely rare on The New Yorker pages.

One change Brown is not going to make is the addition of a masthead to credit the approximately 140 people who comprise the magazine's staff. "That is one tradition I am happy to be without, "she asserted." This magazine is sort of a mare's – nest of strong hierarchies, yet it's non-hierarchical. Once you do a masthead you put one over another who never saw himself as over or under another. It would only encourage the management to halve the staff, so I prefer not to do it.

The overall effect of Brown's changes appears to have been positive for The New Yorker. According to Eric Utne, a writer for Columbia Journalism Review, "she has given it a face lift without changing it beyond recognition." She has revitalized the staff and reinvigorated readers. "What's interesting is that some of the earlier writers who seemed burned out have come back to life, "Gould remarked. Part of her success perhaps has resulted from the free reign she's been given by Florio." She's far and away the best editor I've ever worked with," he praised. "A big part of my job is to encourage her and then stand back and watch her test the envelope."

Though Brown may aim for perfection, it is not what she expects. "Any new administration is going to make mistakes," she admitted. "The alternative is not be alive. The alternative is to just be safe, to treat the magazine like a stuffed owl of which I'm the curator. But that is not Brown's style. "I don't intend to be a curator", she stated. "I intend to be an editor."

Questions:

1. What kind of changes did the new editor Tina Brown implement to resusciate "The New Yorker" magazine?
2. According to Brown, the challenge lay in bringing change to the magazine without losing the qualities that made it "The New Yorker"- Explain
3. "The overall effect of Brown's changes appears to have been positive for "The New Yorker" Do you agree or not? Justify your answer.

Case 5: The United Airlines Chooses Employee Ownership

The early 1990s witnessed a startling new trend among businesses: mass layoffs. Numerous headlines told of once great companies such as IBM that were having to institute tremendous labor cuts to become more competitive. More and more companies decided to downsize. Widespread layoffs, however, resulted in decreased worker productivity and poorer job performance. Fear of job loss caused employees to take less initiative and offer fewer suggests. In the meantime, employee-ownership emerged as an alternative to massive corporate downsizing. It enables companies to reduce costs and increase productivity without having to resort to layoffs. Between 1979 and 1994, the number of employee-owned companies skyrocketed from less than 1,000 to more than 11,000.

United Airlines was one company that chose employee ownership. In December 1993, United Airlines chairman Stephen M. Wolf struck a deal with union leaders to sell control of the $14 billion airline to its employees in exchange for more than $5 billion in wage and benefit reductions and work concessions. According to the agreement, almost all of United's 80,000 employees would experience a wage reduction and would accept longer work hours and an unpaid lunch break. In return, employees were to receive job security and stock worth between $40,000 and $72,434 (depending upon United's fate in the stock market) per member. Most importantly, however, the employees would collectively own 53 percent of United's common stock. In effect, they would control the company. Assuming the details could be worked out, United would become the largest and most complex employee-owned company.

A variety of factors led to this agreement between 1991 and 1993, United lost $1.3 billion, even though the airline was carrying more people to more places than ever before. United's market share was climbing and the number of empty seats was falling, but the company's profitability was nevertheless suffering. United's future seemed bleak if it could not find a way to reduce costs drastically. "We slashed and burned and did everything we could, "said J.C. Pope, president of United." It wasn't enough."

Actually, United was suffering from the same problems that almost all major carriers had been dealing with since the 1978 deregulation of the airline industry, which permitted competition between the large, established carries and the low-cost, budget airlines. "There is a secular change in our society." Wolf commented. "The American consumer wants safe, reliable transportation, but they want low fare. There is certain prudence in the American consumer, whether you are wealthy or not so wealthy. That is, I just want to go somewhere. Why do I want to spend a lot of money just getting from here to there?" In fact, in the 15 years following deregulation, no airline had been able to reduce labor costs without resorting to threats of downsizing or bankruptcy protection. In some cases the costs did not go down until the threats turned into reality. Wolf did not want that to happen at United.

In addition, severe labor-management relation problems had been dogging the airline. During the mid-1980s, United's pilots instituted a massive strike that ultimately resulted in Richard Ferris being ousted as chairman of UAL, Corp., United's parent company. In December 1993, immediately prior to the agreement to transfer company ownership to United's employees, mechanics at the San Francisco airport carried a coffin with Wolf's name on it across the tarmac. In fact, the union had decided that Wolf was going to have go. "The principal reason I feel Mr. Wolf should not be CEO is that in talking to him I just don't think his mind-set fits into employee ownership". Explained Roger Hall, head of the united pilots union. "Wolf is someone who is in control and wants to direct. He doesn't seem so interested in input from the employees."

In light of this, Wolf made a decision. The only way to gain union support of his cost reduction plan was to offer employee ownership to United's workers, and the only way to achieve employee ownership was for him to leave. He realized that the changes necessary for United's survival would not come about if he remained as CEO. He thus left the company in order to save it. "Would like to sit here and ride that stagecoach?" Wolf mused. "Of course. But that's just not in the cards." The only way for Wolf to succeed as a manager was to leave. He had the insight, but it was up to others to carry out his plans.

Wolf placed great confidence in the idea of employee ownership and the concept of empowerment. When employees have a vested interest in the company, they work harder, smarter, and enjoy work more. "The associated benefits [of employee ownership] are truly significant, "Wolf remarked. "It takes away labor animus. You are now owners of the company. You understand the reality of stock going up and what it means for yourself."

Questions:

1. Discuss the concept of "employee ownership" and how it was implemented in United Airlines.
2. Discuss the circumstances in United Airlines that brought about drastic changes in its management structure.
3. "Stephen M Wolf, the CEO of United Airlines left the company in order to save it" – Do you agree or disagree? Justify your answer.

Case 6: Reading Between The Lines

Reader's Digest is a very popular, the world's number - one general interest magazine, translated into 19 languages for over 100 million readers world wide. The Reader's Digest Association, Inc. publishes Reader's Digest in addition to books, music, videos, TV movies, and special interest magazines. The company's products are marketed through well-targeted direct mailings and an extensive consumer data-base that is considered one of the world's best. The company had struggled through difficult times. In the mid 1990s, revenues and profits in key businesses were falling. Even Reader's Digest magazine had declining circulation and readership. Thomas O. Ryder, CEO had some serious changes to make.

The Reader's Digest Association was founded in 1922 by Lila and Dewitt Wallace. The company is committed to informing, enriching, entertaining and inspiring people of all ages and cultures. Over the years, the company established itself as a solid publisher, growing by moving into different areas both geographically and in terms of products. But along with growth in size, Reader's Digest Association developed a slow-moving, entrenched bureaucracy with a culture described as "like molasses". Its employees grew accustomed to a gentle way of doing business and enjoyed a work lifestyle that was paternalistic and cultured. For instance a $ 100 million art collection graced company headquarters at Pleasant ville, Newyork. Founder Dewitt Wallace was known to give rides on the corporate jet to employees who had never flown before. And at 4.30 PM, sharp bells rang to signal the work day's end. It was a company clinging to the trappings of a bygone era.

As the company's performance continued to deteriorate, strategic and management changes were attempted. The company's board of directors changed four CEOs in as many years. These individuals tried and failed to reshape the company. Then Thomas O. Ryder was hired in 1998.

Coming from American Express Company, Ryder had a much more relaxed management style than the typical Reader's Digest Executive. He was open, accessible and sociable. However, he knew that the company had to make some serious changes and that these changes weren't going to be easy. A $ 350 million cost-cutting program led to 1000 people being laid off, the sale of the corporate jet and the elimination of senior executive perks such as country club memberships. Then the company sold its art collection. Many long time employees were up set by the sale, but Ryder believed that the art collection was an amenity that the company could no longer afford if it was going to be a nimble, web-savy publisher and direct marketer. Then Ryder tackled the company's way of working. Upon discovering, it took almost a year to develop mailing campaigns, he hired out-side firms to do some of the work. Some employees resisted tinkering with decades of standard procedure. According to Ryder, the cost-cutting strategies were signals that "everyone would have to change the way they worked".

To further instill a sense of moving forward, Ryder entered into several strategic alliances to expand the company's strong brand, including life insurance and credit cards.

Eventhough the changes seem to have made a difference in the company's financial performance, some long time employees say that Ryder's attempts to create a sense of energy and drive are no different from other previous failed efforts. They don't think the enthusiasm shown at top levels has filtered down to the lower levels. As Ryder's pedecessor said "when you have a company as successful as the digest was, the processes become embedded, and trying to change them is hard" Ryder counters by saying that his changes are different because he respects the Reader Digest's brand and the talents of its workforce which he says simply "lost its way".

Questions

1. Explain what external and internal forces created the need for Reader's Digest Association to change.
2. What conditions for facilitating cultural change existed in this company?
3. What problems did Ryder encounter in trying to change the company's culture?
4. Why did employees seem to be resisting change?

Case 7: Customer Focus at British Airways

As the world changes so the service requirements of customers change. For British Airways (B.A) the need to match and anticipate such changes has increased in recent years as the general over capacity within the passenger airline industry has led to the growing competition on many of its prime routes. Foremost of these are transatlantic flights that carry corporate and business executives to and from Europe and North America. By the late 1990s BA found itself losing first class and business class passengers to rival airlines that were transferring capacity from Asia to transatlantic routes while reducing focus to increase sales and grow market share.

Earlier, in the late 1990s, BA had severe problems such as the three-day cabin crew strike in 1997 and the problems associated with its decision to subcontract its in-flight catering facilities and provision. Because of all these, BA's profits had fallen sharply and its share price halved.

However, meeting the competition head-on is not new to BA. It had earlier turned around from an airline not well regarded and making losses into one of the most profitable airlines in the world. Its sound business management focused on orienting its staff and systems to customers and their needs partly built on the "Putting People First" initiative launched in the mid 1980's.

To keep ahead, British Airways continued to consult passengers to help identify improvements to the service it offered. In the mid 1990's it unveiled a new and very different approach to in-flight service. Cabins were redesigned, and the passenger service offering was also redesigned. The emphasis was on customised, personalised service that attempted to cater to each passenger's individual needs.

At the heart of change was the concept of customer focus. In its business class, BA's change process began with a customer consultation exercise, by which, it identified that customers perceived the service as being acceptable. But BA chose to see the result as a sign that change was needed.

The first task was to redesign the environment, as far as possible for greater passenger comfort by introducing features such as ergonomically designed seats, lounge in the sky, greater in-flight entertainment, improved dining, business amenities (such as in-seat lap-top power points and telephones), two-piece hand buggage allowance, departure lounges and arrival loungers.

Along with physical design, there was a change in the manner and mode of service delivery. Instead of a predictable service, the cabin crew wanted to be able to offer a more 'spontaneous' service to passengers. The business class passengers can now design their own service. Break-fast was not served to all at a standard time and passengers wake up at their own time and were served coffee and breakfast at their convenience.

Lunch and dinner have always been flexible, with passengers able to opt just one or two of the three courses, but now another dimension has been added, passengers who feel hungry between means can order chocolate, biscuits and cheese on short flight, while on longer flights, pies, sandwiches and other snacks are ready for passengers who wish to help themselves.

Similar design and service were extended to first class passengers also. The seats were redesigned to be more comfortable and a small visitor's seat attached to the foot. This facilitates passengers to sit together and have a drink or chat before going back to their original seats. The visitor's seat can than be converted into an extension to the main seat and whole ensemble can be converted easily into a horizontal bed.

The same flexibility is extended to food service in first class. Set meal times abolished, an extensive menu is provided and passengers order and eat when they wish, like in a restaurant.

But in markets with overcapacity, the need to stay competitive and continue to anticipate or meet the needs of customers in on going. As a result BA is continuously trying to keep one step ahead of its rivals. To this end, BA made whole series of changes starting in 1999 to reinforce its position and differentiate itself from its rivals on dimensions other than prices.

Questions:

1. How does BA compete in the highly competitive airlines market?
2. How well the service delivery system fit the needs of these market?
3. How does the concept of customer focus help BA to meet the competition?

Case 8: "Six-Sigma" at General Electric Company

Abstract: The case examines at the initiatives taken by General Electric (GE), one of the world's largest diversified companies to implement the Six-Sigma quality tool in the 1990s. The case discusses in detail the concept of Six-Sigma, its implementation procedure and its benefits. It also explores the implementation procedure at GE and the benefits reaped by the company on account of adopting Six-Sigma.

Background: By 2001, with revenues of $125.91 billion and net earnings of $ 13.68 billion, the US-based General Electric Company was easily the largest diversified company in the world. Out of the company's 24 different businesses, some were so large that could Independently feature in the Fortune 500 list of Companies.

GE operated in more than 100 companies and had over 250 manufacturing plants in 26 countries. The company was one of the largest employers in the world with strength of around 2,75,000 employees. GE remained the only company listed in the Dow Jones Industrial Index that had been included in the original index in 1896.

GE's products ranged from plastic for small compact discs to powerful locomotives.

The company was the world leader in light bulbs and power generation equipment. Its diagnostic medical imaging equipment were well known all over the world. In addition, GE had a strong presence in the financial services, consumer durable goods and entertainment businesses. In the late 1990s, GE initiated various measures to transform itself into a services and solutions-oriented company.

GE was well known for its strong focus on R & D and quality since its inception. The GE Research and Development Centre was one of the world's largest and most diversified industrial laboratories- It employed 1,600 people that included around 1,100 scientists, engineers and technicians. The centre provided GE's businesses and strategic partners with cost effective technical innovations for various products, processes and services. During the 1990s, quality became a major issue of concern to the company.

This made GE's CEO Jack Welch to consider the benefits being derived due to a quality initiative called Six-Sigma by companies such as Motorola. Though Welch felt that quality programs were only theoretical and did not show any substantial results, he was impressed by the Six-Sigma concept and decided to implement it at GE in 1995.

About Six-Sigma: Six-Sigma is a well-structured, data-driven methodology for eliminating defects, waste or quality control problems in all kinds of business activities. It is based on a combination of well-established statistical quality control techniques, simple and advanced data analysis methods and the systematic training of all personnel at every level in the organisation involved in the targeted activity or process.

Theoretically, any process would have a natural spread of 3 sigma (standard deviation) from the normal distribution mean on either side of the centre. This spread contains 99.9999998% of the process output. Thus only 0.002 parts per million are out of the design specifications. However in practice, it is difficult to control the processes and any typical physical process would deviate from the natural centre by up to 1.5 standard deviation. Thus, Six-Sigma in real life denotes a defect rate of 3.4 parts per million.

Six-Sigma is a sophisticated quality program that is designed to reduce defects to 3.4 per million opportunities. This concept was pioneered by Motorola in the early 1980s. Six-Sigma enabled Motorola to achieve defect-free performance in its performance in its manufacturing, designing, engineering and business processes. Six-Sigma was originally developed to be used for physical processes-those performed in manufacturing and easy to observe, record, analyse and measure.

However its application was extended to processes other than physical processes such as bid and proposal, procurement and contract management areas. While Six-Sigma comprised strict measurements for physical processes, it involved identifying waste in the form of delays for other processes. The primary objective of Six-Sigma was to increase customer satisfaction through continuous improvement in quality.

GE's Six-Sigma Experience:

Before implementing Six-Sigma, studies revealed that GE's operations were carried out between 3 to 4 sigma, i.e. about 35,000 defects per million opportunities (DPMO). According to company estimates, avoidable expenditure of $ 7 to 10 billion was being incurred in the form of scrap, reworking of parts, correction of transactional, errors inefficiencies and lost productivity.

The ground work for the implementation of Six-Sigma at GE had began in 1988 in the form of an initiative known as the **"Work Out" program.** The company realized that employees were an important source of intellectual power for new and creative ideas.

The "Work Out" program gave each employee an opportunity to influence and improve GE's operations. The program had set some major goals that later helped to lay the ground-work for Six-Sigma.

The goals were as follows:

1. **Build Trust:** Employees were encouraged to criticize GE and the way they performed their jobs without negative consequences to their careers.
2. **Empower employees:** As employees who performed a particular task knew how to do it perfectly, GE granted them more power to encourage them to take more responsibility for their jobs and improve the way of doing their jobs.

Reaping the Benefits: Implementation of Six-Sigma at GE enabled the CEO, Jack Welch to transform an old-economy industrial giant into a competitive and growing company. No other Corporation seemed to have integrated Six-Sigma to its operations as widely as GE. Within five years of its implementation, Six-Sigma at GE produced annual benefits of more than $2.5 billion for GE worldwide. Six-Sigma was a indisputable success at GE whether in terms of customer satisfaction, improvement in internal performance or in the improvement of shareholder value.

Questions:

1. Discuss the Six-Sigma concept and its relevance to a company such as General Electric in improving its performance.
2. Explore the benefits reaped by GE from Six-Sigma initiative and its contribution to the company's sustained superior financial performance and competitive advantage.

Case 9: Amazon.com: An Internet Giant Fine-Tunes its Strategy

Amazon.com made Internet history as one of the first large-scale retail companies to sell over the Web: in 2004 it hit $4 billion in on-line revenues and by 2006 its sales guidance estimated $ 10 billion in revenue. It has grown to become one of the largest Internet retailers on earth. But the real significance of Amazon.com is its continuous innovation in business strategy and information systems. In fact, the two are closely connected at Amazon.com: Its business innovations are all driven by huge investments in information systems.

In 1995, former investment banker Jeff. Bezos took advantage of new business opportunities created by the Internet by setting up a Website to sell books directly to the customer online. There were three million titles in print and any one physical book-store could only stock a fraction of them. A "virtual" bookstore offers a much larger selection of titles. Bezos believed consumers did not need to actually "touch and feel" a book before buying it, and Amazon.com provided online synopses, table of contents and reviews to help selection.

Amazon was able to charge lower prices than physical bookstores because it maintained very little of its own inventory (relying instead on distributors) and did not have to pay for maintaining physical stores or a large retail sales staff. Amazen tried to provide superior customer service through e-mail and telephone customer support, automated order confirmation, on-line tracking and shipping information and the ability to pay for purchases with a single click of the mouse using credit card and personal information customer had provided during a previous purchase. This was called "1-click" express shopping and it made the shopping experience even more convenient.

In 1998, Amazon started selling music, CDs, Videos and DVDs, revising its business strategy-"to become the best place to buy, find and discover product or service available online"-the online Wal-Mart. Its offerings grew to include electronic, toys, home improvement products, video games, apparel, gourmet food, travel services, personal care and jewellary. It also introduced Amazon.com auctions (similar to those offered by e Bay) and e shops (online storefronts for small retailers). To service these new product lines Amazon significantly expanded its warehouse and distribution capabilities and hired large number of employees. These moves strained its ability to adhere to its original vision of being a "virtual retailer" with lean inventories, low head count and significant cost savings over traditional book stores.

In 2001 and 2002, Amazon tried to increase revenue by cutting prices, offering free shipping and leveraging its technology infrastructure to proved e-commerce services to other businesses. "Amazon's Merchants" and "Amazon Market-place", allow other businesses to fully integrate their Websites into Amazon's site to sell their branded goods using Amazon's fulfillment and payment terms. Nordstrom, The Gap, and Target stores use "Amazon Market place" program, individuals are encouraged to sell their used and new goods on Amazon's Website even when they compete directly with Amazon's sales of the same goods. Sales by third parties now represent 25% of Amazon's revenues. Amazon refined its business model further to focus more on efficient operations while maintaining a steady commitment to keeping its 49 million customers satisfied. In early 2001, Amazon closed two of its eight warehouses, laid off 15% of its workforce, and considered orders from around the country prior to shipping to reduce shipping costs. Amazon used "Six-Sigma Quality" measures to reduce errors in fulfillment. These measures reduced fulfillment costs from 15% of the revenue in 2000 to 10% by 2003, Amazon finally became profitable in 2003 and remains an online retailing powerhouse growing at over 60% a year. It continues to innovate with IT-enabled services: free unlimited two-day shipping for $79 a year (Amazon Prime). Amazon entered the dry goods grocery business in 2006. These innovations increased its costs and reduced its profits, much to the disappointment of the stock market, which has depressed Amazon's stock (share) from a high of $1000 in 2000 down to the mid $ 20 range in 2006. But Amazon foces powerful online retail competitors such as e-Bay and Yahoo! who also are very adept at using information systems to develop new products and services. Google is emerging as a competitor because so many consumers use its search engine-six billion searches are performed each month at Google-and in the process are exposed to search engine ads, Google is expanding into other shopping services: "Google Base" offers free classified listings of goods for sale and "Google Checkout" provides an online service that stores users' financial information to facilitate purchase from participating Internet Vendors. Amazon is countering with new offerings, such as digital mapping service with street-level photographs, a grocery store for non-perishable items sold in bulk, and selling short stories online for 49 cents a piece, along with additional expenditures to improve customer convenience and shopping experience.

Recently, the company's profits have started to drop. The question is whether Amazon can turn its leadership in e-commerce into genuine long-term success. Can Amazon keep adopting its strategy to remain profitable and powerful?

Questions:

1. Analyse Amazon.com using the competitive forces and value-chain models. How has it responded to pressures from its competitive environment? How does it provide value to its customers?
2. Why did the company change its strategy? Do you think Amazon can continue to be successful? Explain your answer.

Case 10: Involvement Through Team Work at Qualchem

Qualchem is a large American owned multinational, having outlets throughout the world. It sells high quality specialty chemicals for use in both the domestic and the commercial markets. It is a leader in its market and the major market change over the last decade has been the major challenge of Japanese companies and products. Infact, in recent years, one of the major influences on corporate strategy as well as on employment policy, has been the perceived threat of Japanese import penetration into the U.S and the more competitive markets in the world.

Over one lakh people are employed by Qualchem worldwide, of which nearly 8000 work in the U.K across a number of sites in different parts of the country. The bulk of these are employed at the head office and at the principal production site, which includes a sizable research and development division and a distribution department. Two other sites employ small numbers of staff, who are engaged in production of rare materials and products for use in the main factory. In all cases, products are sold in both British and European markets. The smallest of the company's units in Britain have just over 200 staff, but the policies that it implements are broadly in line with those adopted at the other sites. This site is slightly ahead in teamwork because of its size and the nature of the technology employed at the site.

The parent company, Qualchem-like many others in the chemical industry- publishes a set of corporate principles that is distributed to all employees. This booklet is an expression of the way in which the company is managed, taking into account the external influences which are crucial to the business interests of the company. The chairman of UK operations of Qualchem asks his employees to help make these statements a living commitment, by developing the belief into plans for continuous improvement. Qualchem's mission comprises five goals of which two are particularly relevant for the UK establishment: (1) recognize that the firm's people are its most important asset and (2) adopt quality as a way of life.

The 'people' policies and practices, which are fairly typical of this kind of progressive organisation, include commitments to the best health and safety standards, equity of treatment, effective channels of communication, a superior employment package, stability of employment and high performance standards for the staff.

The "quality" policies refer to visible and reinforced managerial commitment to quality, an emphasis on customer (both external and internal to the organisation) quality as a measure of performance, and clarity of employee goals and objectives (which has a relevance for employee involvement). The quality policies state that the management will create an environment that encourages quality by ensuring that the contribution of all employees to the quality process is maximized by training, team building, leadership and ensuring that individuals are responsible for their own processes.

Team working is one part of Qualchem's World-Class Manufacturing strategy, the other two parts being performance management and Statistical Process Control (SPC). SPC is a key part of the quality improvement program and this aims to provide the teams with a mechanism for assessing the quality of production as well as a methodology that will help them to overcome problems. Ultimately, all operators will be trained in the use and meaning of statistical technique that are relevant to their part of the operation.

Performance measurement is a system designed to seek and achieve continuous improvement in the key aspects of each individual's or team's work and it operates according to "reinforcements of good behaviour". These reinforcements can be either tangible or social which are meant to reinforce actions that management defines as good for the business.

The third strand of World-Class Manufacturing is the team-working concept, and this is being extended across the whole company. This concept has developed well at the smallest size particularly with process operators in the chemical plants who are now covered by a single grade.

The move towards World-Class Manufacturing has been bolstered by two further employee relations practices:

(i) The company aims to devote 5 percent of each employee's time (on average each year) to training and development, and this includes not only technical - skills training but also team-building exercises as well. The training package includes training in how to interpret controls in the plant, their meaning and significance and their relevance for quality.

(ii) A revamped pay package that drastically reduces the number of grades on the shop floor. Under the new system there are four principal grades: ancillary work/labourer, process operator, craft worker, and team leader.

Each grade has a 'start' and 'established' rate, although variations are possible due to shift allowances and other fringe benefits. Pay levels for a process operator on shifts are high, not only for the industry but also compared with average wages for many white-collar and managerial staff in other sectors.

Questions:

1. What are the goals comprised in the mission of Qualchem that are relevant to the achievement of continuous improvement?
2. Discuss the 'people' policies and 'quality' policies of Qualchem.
3. Briefly discuss the major elements of Qualchem's Wold-Class Manufacturing Strategy.

APPENDIX E

AREAS FOR THE STANDARD NORMAL DISTRIBUTION

Entries in the table give the area under the curve between the mean and z standard deviations above the mean. *For example,* z = 1.25, the area under the curve between the mean and z is 0.3944.

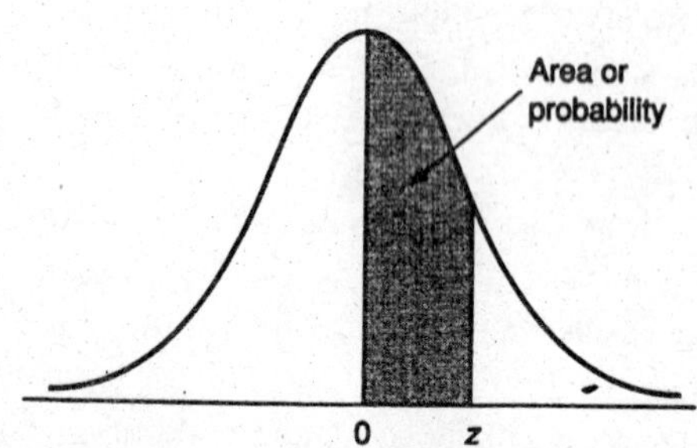

z	0.00	0.01	0.02	0.03	0.04	0.05	0.06	0.07	0.08	0.09
0.0	0.0000	0.0040	0.0080	0.0120	0.0160	0.0199	0.0239	0.0279	0.0319	0.0359
0.1	0.0398	0.0438	0.0478	0.0517	0.0557	0.0596	0.0636	0.0675	0.0714	0.0753
0.2	0.0793	0.0832	0.0871	0.0910	0.0948	0.0987	0.1026	0.1064	0.1103	0.1141
0.3	0.1179	0.1217	0.1255	0.1293	0.1331	0.1368	0.1406	0.1443	0.1480	0.1517
0.4	0.1554	0.1591	0.1628	0.1664	0.1700	0.1736	0.1772	0.1808	0.1844	0.1879
0.5	0.1915	0.1950	0.1985	0.2019	0.2054	0.2088	0.2123	0.2157	0.2190	0.2224
0.6	0.2257	0.2291	0.2324	0.2357	0.2389	0.2422	0.2454	0.2486	0.2518	0.2549
0.7	0.2580	0.2612	0.2642	0.2673	0.2704	0.2734	0.2764	0.2794	0.2823	0.2852
0.8	0.2881	0.2910	0.2939	0.2967	0.2995	0.3023	0.3051	0.3078	0.3106	0.3133
0.9	0.3159	0.3186	0.3212	0.3238	0.3264	0.3289	0.3315	0.3340	0.3365	0.3389
1.0	0.3413	0.3438	0.3461	0.3485	0.3508	0.3531	0.3554	0.3577	0.3599	0.3621
1.1	0.3643	0.3665	0.3686	0.3708	0.3729	0.3749	0.3770	0.3790	0.3810	0.3830
1.2	0.3849	0.3869	0.3888	0.3907	0.3925	0.3944	0.3962	0.3980	0.3997	0.4015
1.3	0.4032	0.4049	0.4066	0.4082	0.4099	0.4115	0.4131	0.4147	0.4162	0.4177
1.4	0.4192	0.4207	0.4222	0.4236	0.4251	0.4265	0.4279	0.4292	0.4306	0.4319
1.5	0.4332	0.4345	0.4357	0.4370	0.4382	0.4394	0.4406	0.4418	0.4429	0.4441
1.6	0.4452	0.4463	0.4474	0.4484	0.4495	0.4505	0.4515	0.4525	0.4535	0.4545
1.7	0.4554	0.4564	0.4573	0.4582	0.4591	0.4599	0.4608	0.4616	0.4625	0.4633
1.8	0.4641	0.4649	0.4656	0.4664	0.4671	0.4678	0.4686	0.4693	0.4699	0.4706
1.9	0.4713	0.4719	0.4726	0.4732	0.4738	0.4744	0.4750	0.4756	0.4761	0.4767
2.0	0.4772	0.4778	0.4783	0.4788	0.4793	0.4798	0.4803	0.4808	0.4812	0.4817
2.1	0.4821	0.4826	0.4830	0.4834	0.4838	0.4842	0.4846	0.4850	0.4854	0.4857
2.2	0.4861	0.4864	0.4868	0.4871	0.4875	0.4878	0.4881	0.4884	0.4887	0.4890
2.3	0.4893	0.4896	0.4898	0.4901	0.4904	0.4906	0.4909	0.4911	0.4913	0.4916
2.4	0.4918	0.4920	0.4922	0.4925	0.4927	0.4929	0.4931	0.4932	0.4934	0.4936
2.5	0.4938	0.4940	0.4941	0.4943	0.4945	0.4946	0.4948	0.4949	0.4951	0.4952
2.6	0.4953	0.4955	0.4956	0.4957	0.4959	0.4960	0.4961	0.4962	0.4963	0.4964
2.7	0.4965	0.4966	0.4967	0.4968	0.4969	0.4970	0.4971	0.4972	0.4973	0.4974
2.8	0.4974	0.4975	0.4976	0.4977	0.4977	0.4978	0.4979	0.4979	0.4980	0.4981
2.9	0.4981	0.4982	0.4982	0.4983	0.4984	0.4984	0.4985	0.4985	0.4986	0.4986
3.0	0.4986	0.4987	0.4987	0.4988	0.4988	0.4989	0.4989	0.4989	0.4990	0.4990

APPENDIX F

FACTORS FOR CONTROL CHARTS

	x-charts				s-Charts				R-charts					
n	A	A_2	A_3	c_4	B_3	B_4	B_5	B_6	d_2	d_3	D_1	D_2	D_3	D_4
2	2.121	1.880	2.659	0.7979	0	3.267	0	2.606	1.128	0.853	0	3.686	0	3.267
3	1.732	1.023	1.954	0.8862	0	2.568	0	2.276	1.693	0.888	0	4.358	0	2.574
4	1.500	0.729	1.628	0.9213	0	2.266	0	2.088	2.059	0.880	0	4.698	0	2.282
5	1.342	0.577	1.427	0.9400	0	2.089	0	1.964	2.326	0.864	0	4.918	0	2.114
6	1.225	0.483	1.287	0.9515	0.030	1.970	0.029	1.874	2.534	0.848	0	5.078	0	2.004
7	1.134	0.419	1.182	0.9594	0.118	1.882	0.113	1.806	2.704	0.833	0.204	5.204	0.076	1.924
8	1.061	0.373	1.099	0.9650	0.185	1.815	0.179	1.751	2.847	0.820	0.388	5.306	0.136	1.864
9	1.000	0.337	1.032	0.969	0.239	1.761	0.232	1.707	2.970	0.808	0.547	5.393	0.184	1.816
10	0.949	0.308	0.975	0.9727	0.284	1.716	0.276	1.669	3.078	0.797	0.687	5.469	0.223	1.777
11	0.905	0.285	0.927	0.9754	0.321	1.679	0.313	1.637	3.173	0.787	0.811	5.535	0.256	1.744
12	0.866	0.266	0.886	0.9776	0.354	1.646	0.346	1.610	3.258	0.778	0.922	5.594	0.283	1.717
13	0.832	0.249	0.850	0.9794	0.382	1.618	0.374	1.585	3.336	0.770	1.025	5.647	0.307	1.693
14	0.802	0.235	0.817	0.9810	0.406	1.594	0.399	1.563	3.407	0.763	1.118	5.696	0.328	1.672
15	0.775	0.223	0.789	0.9823	0.428	1.572	0.421	1.544	3.472	0.756	1.203	5.741	0.347	1.653
16	0.750	0.212	0.763	0.9835	0.448	1.552	0.440	1.526	3.532	0.750	1.282	5.782	0.363	1.637
17	0.728	0.203	0.739	0.9845	0.466	1.534	0.458	1.511	3.588	0.744	1.356	5.820	0.378	1.622
18	0.707	0.194	0.718	0.9854	0.482	1.518	0.475	1.496	3.640	0.739	1.424	5.856	0.391	1.608
19	0.688	0.187	0.698	0.9862	0.497	1.503	0.490	1.483	3.689	0.734	1.487	5.891	0.403	1.597
20	0.671	0.180	0.680	0.9869	0.510	1.490	0.504	1.470	3.735	0.729	1.549	5.921	0.415	1.585
21	0.655	0.173	0.663	0.9876	0.523	1.477	0.516	1.459	3.778	0.724	1.605	5.951	0.425	1.575
22	0.640	0.167	0.647	0.9882	0.534	1.466	0.528	1.448	3.819	0.720	1.659	5.979	0.434	1.566
23	0.626	0.162	0.633	0.9887	0.545	1.455	0.539	1.438	3.858	0.716	1.710	6.006	0.443	1.557
24	0.612	0.157	0.619	0.9892	0.555	1.445	0.549	1.429	3.895	0.712	1.759	6.031	0.451	1.548
25	0.600	0.153	0.606	0.9896	0.565	1.435	0.559	1.420	3.931	0.708	1.806	6.056	0.459	1.541

APPENDIX G

ANSWER KEY TO OBJECTIVE QUESTIONS

Chapter- 1

A. A. 1 – B. 4 A. 2 – B. 3 A. 3 – B. 7 A. 4 – B. 5 A. 5 – B. 6 A. 6 – B. 1 A. 7 – B. 2

B. 1. – True 2. – False 3. – False 4. – True 5. – False

C. 1. – (c) 2. – (b) 3. – (c) 4. – (b) 5. – (c)

Chapter- 2

A. A. 1 – B. 5 A. 2 – B. 3 A. 3 – B. 1 A. 4 – B. 2 A. 5 – B. 4

B. 1. – True 2. – False 3. – True 4. – True 5. – True

C. 1. – (b) 2. – (d) 3. – (e) 4. – (e)

Chapter- 3

A. A. 1 – B. 3 A. 2 – B. 4 A. 3 – B. 2 A. 4 – B. 1 A. 5 – B. 7 A. 6 – B. 8 A. 7 – B. 5
A. 8 – B. 6 A. 9 – B. 9

B. 1. – True 2. – False 3. – False 4. – False 5. – True
6. – False 7. – True 8. – True 9. – True 10. – True

C. 1. – (c) 2. – (b) 3. – (d) 4. – (c) 5. – (c)

Chapter- 4

A. A. 1 – B. 3 A. 2 – B. 5 A. 3 – B. 4 A. 4 – B. 2 A. 5 – B. 1

B. 1. – Zaire Model, 2. – Bill Smith, 3. – Japanese 5 'S' Practice,
4. – Golden Peacock Awards Secretariate 5. – European Quality Award

C. 1. – (c) 2. – (c) 3. – (b) 4. – (e)

Chapter- 5

A. A. 1 – B. 4 A. 2 – B. 5 A. 3 – B. 1 A. 4 – B. 2 A. 5 – B. 3

B. 1. – Consumer benefit package 2. – Needs, wants 3. – Expected 4. – Defection, retention
5. – Customer satisfaction survey

C. 1. – (e) 2. – (e) 3. – (d) 4. – (e) 5. – (c)

Chapter- 6

A. A. 1 – B. 4 A. 2 – B. 5 A. 3 – B. 1 A. 4 – B. 3 A. 5 – B. 2

B. 1. – True 2. – False 3. – True 4. – False 5. – True

C. 1. – (e) 2. – (e) 3. – (d) 4. – (f) 5. – (e)

Chapter- 7

A. A. 1 – B. 4 A. 2 – B. 2 A. 3 – B. 5 A. 4 – B. 1 A. 5 – B. 3

B. 1. – True 2. – False 3. – False 4. – True 5. – True

C. 1. – (d) 2. – (e) 3. – (e) 4. – (c) 5. – (d)

Chapter- 8

A. A. 1 – B. 1 A. 2 – B. 3 A. 3 – B. 2 A. 4 – B. 5 A. 5 – B. 4

B. 1. – True 2. – False 3. – False 4. – True 5. – True

C. 1. – (b) 2. – (d) 3. – (d) 4. – (e) 5. – (e)

Chapter- 9

A. A. 1 – B. 3 A. 2 – B. 1 A. 3 – B. 2 A. 4 – B. 5 A. 5 – B. 4

B. 1. – True 2. – False 3. – True 4. – False 5. – False
6. – True 7. – True 8. – False 9. – True

C. 1. – (e) 2. – (e) 3. – (b) 4. – (c)

Chapter- 10

A. A. 1 – B. 3 A. 2 – B. 1 A. 3 – B. 5 A. 4 – B. 2 A. 5 – B. 4

B. 1. – True 2. – False 3. – True 4. – True 5. – False

C. 1. – (f) 2. – (e) 3. – (b) 4. – (c) 5. – (b)

Chapter- 11

A. A. 1 – B. 2	A. 2 – B. 4	A. 3 – B. 1	A. 4 – B. 5	A. 5 – B. 3	
B. 1. – False	2. – True	3. – False	4. – True	5. – False	
C. 1. – (d)	2. – (c)	3. – (e)	4. – (e)	5. – (c)	

Chapter- 12

A. A. 1 – B. 3	A. 2 – B. 4	A. 3 – B. 5	A. 4 – B. 2	A. 5 – B. 1	
B. 1. – True	2. – True	3. – False	4. – False	5. – False	
6. – True	7. – False	8. – False	9. – True		
C. 1. – (c)	2. – (c)	3. – (d)	4. – (d)	5. – (b)	6. – (b)
7. – (a)	8. – (b)	8. – (e)			

Chapter- 13

A. A. 1 – B. 3	A. 2 – B. 5	A. 3 – B. 1	A. 4 – B. 2	A. 5 – B. 4
B. 1. – False	2. – True	3. – True	4. – False	5. – False
C. 1. – (d)	2. – (d)	3. – (e)	4. – (c)	5. – (a)

Chapter- 14

A. A. 1 – B. 3	A. 2 – B. 1	A. 3 – B. 2	A. 4 – B. 5	A. 5 – B. 4
B. 1. – False	2. – True	3. – True	4. – True	5. – False
C. 1. – (e)	2. – (b)	3. – (b)	4. – (d)	5. – (e)

Chapter- 15

A. A. 1 – B. 3	A. 2 – B. 1	A. 3 – B. 2	A. 4 – B. 5	A. 5 – B. 4
B. 1. – True	2. – True	3. – False	4. – False	5. – True
C. 1. – (c)	2. – (b)	3. – (d)	4. – (e)	5. – (d)

Chapter- 16

A. A. 1 – B. 3	A. 2 – B. 1	A. 3 – B. 2	A. 4 – B. 5	A. 5 – B. 4
B. 1. – True	2. – True	3. – False	4. – False	5. – True
C. 1. – (d)	2. – (d)	3. – (e)	4. – (e)	5. – (e)

Chapter- 17

A. A. 1 – B. 3	A. 2 – B. 5	A. 3 – B. 2	A. 4 – B. 1	A. 5 – B. 4
B. 1. – True	2. – True	3. – False	4. – False	5. – True
C. 1. – (e)	2. – (e)	3. – (b)	4. – (e)	5. – (d)

Chapter- 18

A. A. 1 – B. 2	A. 2 – B. 4	A. 3 – B. 3	A. 4 – B. 5	A. 5 – B. 1
B. 1. – True	2. – True	3. – False	4. – True	5. – False
C. 1. – (d)	2. – (d)	3. – (e)	4. – (a)	5. – (c)

Chapter- 19

A. A. 1 – B. 2	A. 2 – B. 4	A. 3 – B. 1	A. 4 – B. 5	A. 5 – B. 3
B. 1. – True	2. – True	3. – False	4. – True	5. – False
C. 1. – (f)	2. – (f)	3. – (b)	4. – (e)	5. – (d)

Chapter- 20

A. A. 1 – B. 2	A. 2 – B. 1	A. 3 – B. 5	A. 4 – B. 3	A. 5 – B. 4
B. 1. – True	2. – True	3. – False	4. – True	5. – False
C. 1. – (d)	2. – (e)	3. – (e)	4. – (d)	5. – (e)

Chapter- 21

A. A. 1 – B. 2	A. 2 – B. 4	A. 3 – B. 1	A. 4 – B. 3	A. 5 – B. 5
B. 1. – False	2. – False	3. – True	4. – True	5. – True
C. 1. – (e)	2. – (e)	3. – (e)	4. – (d)	5. – (f)

References

1. K. Shridhara Bhat, *"Total Quality Management"*, Text and Cases, 1. e, 2002, Himalaya Publishing House, Mumbai.
2. K. Shridhara Bhat, *"Quality Management"*, 1. e, 2007, Himalaya Publishing House, Mumbai.
3. K. Shridhara Bhat, *"Total Quality Management"*, 1. e, 2010, Himalaya Publishing House, Mumbai.
4. K. Shridhara Bhat, *"Total Quality Management"*, 1. e, 2011, Himalaya Publishing House, Mumbai.
5. David L. Goetsch, Stanley B.Davis, *"Introduction to Total Quality"*, 3. e, 2000, Prentice Hall Inc. USA.
6. Barrie G. Dale, Ton Vander Wiele, Jos Van Iwanrden, *"Managing Quality"*, 5. e, 2007, Black Well Publishing, Wiley India, New Delhi.
7. Russel T. Westcott, *"The Certified Manager of Quality / Organisational Excellence"*, Hand Book, 3. e, 2006, Pearson Education, New Delhi.
8. John Beckford, *"Quality"*, 2. e, 2002, Routledge, New York, USA.
9. Stephen George Arnold Weimers Kirch, *"Total Quality Management"*, 2. e, 1998, John Wiley & Sons Inc. USA.
10. Nancy R. Tague, *"The Quality Tool Box"*, 2. e, 2005, Pearson Education (Singapore), New Delhi.
11. Michael J. Stahl, *"Management Total Quality in a Global Environment"* 1. e, 1995, Blackwell Publishers, USA.
12. Terry L. Richard, *"Total Quality Management"*, 1. e, 1997, Delmar Publishers, USA.
13. Donna C.S. Summers, *"Quality Management"*, First Indian Reprint, 2005, Pearson Education (Singapore) Pte, New Delhi.
14. Dale H. Bester field, Carol Bester field – Michna, Glen H. Bester field, Marie Bester field – sacre, *"Total Quality Management"*, Third Indian Reprint, 2004, Pearson Education (Singapore) Pte, New Delhi.
15. James R. Evans, William M.Lindsay, *"The Management and Control of Quality"*, 6. e, 2005, Thomson- South Western Publishers, USA.
16. Paul James, *"Total Quality Management"*, 1. e, 1996, Prentice Hall, USA.
17. James R. Evans, *"Total Quality"*, First Indian Reprint, 2007, Thomson- South Western, USA
18. John S. Oakland, *"Total Quality Management"*, 1. e, Reprinted 1992, Nicholas Publishing Company, USA.
19. John L. Hradesky, *"Total Quality Management Hand Book"*, 1. e, 1995, McGraw-Hill Inc, USA.
20. Greg Brue, *"Six Sigma for Managers"*, Tata McGraw-Hill Edition, 2002, Tata McGraw-Hill Publishing Company, New Delhi.
21. Greg Brue, *"Design for Six Sigma"*, Tata McGraw-Hill Edition 2003, Tata McGraw-Hill Publishing Company, New Delhi.
22. Mike George, Dave Rowlands & Bill Kastle, *"What is Lean Six Sigma?"*, 1. e, 2004, McGraw-Hill Inc, USA.
23. Robert F. Brewer, *"Design of Experiments for Process Improvement and Quality Assurance"*, First Reprint, 1998, Narosa Publishing House, New Delhi.
24. Joseph N. Kelada, *"Integrating Reengineering With Total Quality"*, 1. e, 1996, Quality Press, USA.
25. Bill Creech, *"The Five Pillars of TQM"*, 1. e, 1995, Truman Talley Books / Plume, New York, USA.

Index